"This stimulating compendium of thoughtful discussions of American literary journalism from its colonial beginnings to the contemporary digital moment will be the go-to volume on the subject for a long time. Richly inclusive—and filled with surprising juxtapositions, fresh insights, and unexpected excursions into the past and present—*The Routledge Companion to American Literary Journalism* is a pleasure to read."

Shelley Fisher Fishkin, Joseph S. Atha Professor of Humanities; Professor of English, and Director of American Studies, Stanford University, and author of *From Fact to Fiction: Journalism and Imaginative Writing in America*

"Roberta Maguire and William Dow's *Routledge Companion to American Literary Journalism* clearly illuminates virtually every aspect of the discipline, and the volume will serve as a foundational text for scholars and students of the field for many years to come. Notably, its masterful structure—insightful scholarly essays addressing historical, then thematic, theoretical and future-study issues—is truly a *tour de force*."

David Abrahamson, Professor of Journalism, Charles Deering McCormick Professor of Teaching Excellence, Northwestern University, The Medill School

"This may be the most complete volume on literary journalism yet. Three dozen of the best thinkers on the topic write about its history, relationship to 'real life,' and the New Journalism, including the late John Pauly on the *New Yorker* magazine. Just as importantly, these scholars take new approaches, examine different writers, and create new critical directions for future study."

Norman Sims, Professor Emeritus, University of Massachusetts Amherst, and author of *True Stories: A Century of Literary Journalism*

THE ROUTLEDGE COMPANION TO AMERICAN LITERARY JOURNALISM

Taking a thematic approach, this new companion provides an interdisciplinary, cross-cultural, and international study of American literary journalism.

From the work of Frederick Douglass and Walt Whitman to that of Joan Didion and Dorothy Parker, literary journalism is a genre that both reveals and shapes American history and identity. This volume not only calls attention to literary journalism as a distinctive genre but also provides a critical foundation for future scholarship. It brings together cutting-edge research from literary journalism scholars, examining historical perspectives; themes, venues, and genres across time; theoretical approaches and disciplinary intersections; and new directions for scholarly inquiry.

Provoking reconsideration and inquiry, while providing new historical interpretations, this companion recognizes, interacts with, and honors the tradition and legacies of American literary journalism scholarship. Engaging the work of disciplines such as sociology, anthropology, African American studies, gender studies, visual studies, media studies, and American studies, in addition to journalism and literary studies, this book is perfect for students and scholars of those disciplines.

William E. Dow is Professor of American Literature at the Université Paris-Est (UPEM) and Professor of English at The American University of Paris. He is the author of the book *Narrating Class in American Fiction* (2009) and coeditor of *Richard Wright: New Readings in the 21st Century* (2011), *Richard Wright in a Post-Racial Imaginary* (2014), and *Of Latitudes Unknown: James Baldwin's Radical Imagination* (2019). He is also Associate Editor of *Literary Journalism Studies* (Northwestern University Press).

Roberta S. Maguire is the Oshkosh Northwestern Professor of English at the University of Wisconsin Oshkosh. She has published extensively on Albert Murray, including *Conversations with Albert Murray* (1998), as well as essays on Alice Childress, Anna Julia Cooper, Zora Neale Hurston, Lewis Nordan, and Walker Percy. An Associate Editor of *Literary Journalism Studies*, she served as the guest editor for the Fall 2013 special issue devoted to African American literary journalism.

Yoko Nakamura is a graduate student in Interdisciplinary Islamic and Middle Eastern Studies at the University of Iowa. She holds a BA in International Economics and International Politics from the American University of Paris.

THE ROUTLEDGE COMPANION TO AMERICAN LITERARY JOURNALISM

Edited by William E. Dow and Roberta S. Maguire

ASSOCIATE EDITOR
YOKO NAKAMURA

First published 2020
by Routledge
52 Vanderbilt Avenue, New York, NY 10017

and by Routledge
2 Park Square, Milton Park, Abingdon, Oxon, OX14 4RN

Routledge is an imprint of the Taylor & Francis Group, an informa business

© 2020 Taylor & Francis

The right of William E. Dow and Roberta S. Maguire to be identified as the authors of the editorial material, and of the authors for their individual chapters, has been asserted in accordance with sections 77 and 78 of the Copyright, Designs and Patents Act 1988.

All rights reserved. No part of this book may be reprinted or utilized in any form or by any electronic, mechanical, or other means, now known or hereafter invented, including photocopying and recording, or in any information storage or retrieval system, without permission in writing from the publishers.

Trademark notice: Product or corporate names may be trademarks or registered trademarks, and are used only for identification and explanation without intent to infringe.

Library of Congress Cataloging-in-Publication Data
Names: Dow, William (William E.), editor. | Maguire, Roberta S., editor. |
Nakamura, Yoko, editor.
Title: The Routledge companion to American literary journalism / editors:
William E. Dow and Roberta S. Maguire ; associate editor: Yoko Nakamura.
Description: London ; New York : Routledge, [2020] |
Series: Routledge
media and cultural studies companions | Includes bibliographical
references and index.
Identifiers: LCCN 2019028109 | ISBN 9781138695832 (hardback) |
ISBN 9781315526010 (ebook)
Subjects: LCSH: Reportage literature, American–History and criticism. |
Journalism–United States–History.
Classification: LCC PS366.R44 R68 2020 | DDC 071/.3–dc23
LC record available at https://lccn.loc.gov/2019028109

ISBN: 978-1-138-69583-2 (hbk)
ISBN: 978-1-315-52601-0 (ebk)

Typeset in Bembo
by Swales & Willis, Exeter, Devon, UK

IN MEMORIAM
JOHN J. PAULY
(1949–2018)

CONTENTS

Contributors   *xiii*
Foreword by Robert S. Boynton   *xix*
Acknowledgments   *xxii*

Introduction   1
Roberta S. Maguire and William E. Dow

PART I
Historical Perspectives   15

1. From the *Boston News-Letter* to the "Couranteers": Epistolarity, Reportage, and Entertaining Literature in Colonial American Newspapers   17
   Colin T. Ramsey

2. The Antebellum Origins of American Literary Journalism: Five Pioneers   28
   Carolyn L. Karcher

3. Literary Journalism in Transition: The Early Memoirs of William Grimes, Mattie Jackson, and Nicholas Said   44
   Jessie Lafrance Dunbar and Barbara McCaskill

4. American Realism and the Stirrings of Literary Journalism   57
   Thomas Connery

5. Literary Journalism and America's Naturalistic Writers   67
   Roark Mulligan

6. Journalistic Literature: Female Reporters and Newspaper Fiction, 1880–1930   81
   Karen Roggenkamp

7   Two Gilded Ages: Literary Muckrakers 1900s/2000s   91
    Cecelia Tichi

8   "Feel the Fact": The 1930s Reportage of Joseph North, John L. Spivak,
    and Meridel Le Sueur   110
    Don Dingledine

9   Performative Criticism and the Problem of Modernist Chic:
    Gertrude Stein, Janet Flanner, and Dorothy Parker   130
    Nancy Bombaci

10 The New Journalism, 1960–80   149
    John J. Pauly

11 Eternal Present Tense: The New Journalism Moved beyond Basic
    Needs to Tell Deeper Narratives about Chicago '68   163
    Bill Reynolds

12 Literary Journalism and Alternative Media   183
    Susan Keith

13 From Magazines to Newsprint: How Literary Journalism Went "Mainstream"   199
    Jim Collins

14 Literary Journalism at the Center: A Process of Maturation   213
    Miles Maguire

15 Coming of Age as a Writer in the Sixties: Realizations about Voice   225
    Mark Kramer

PART II
Themes, Venues, and Genres across Time   233

16 Of Troops and Tropes: US Literary War Journalism from the Civil
    War to the War on Terror   235
    John S. Bak

17 Literary Journalism and Social Activism   256
    Nancy L. Roberts

18 Literary Journalism and American Magazines   269
    Doug Underwood

19 Literary Journalism's Historical Lineage: In Defense of Mencken   288
    Stacy Spaulding

20	A Short, Comprehensive History of Literary Sports Journalism *Ted Geltner and Ted Spiker*	300

PART III
Theorizing American Literary Journalism: Disciplinary Intersections — 313

21	American Literary Journalism and Book History: Crossing the Divide *Kathy Roberts Forde*	315
22	Exploring the Referentiality of Narrative Literary Journalism *John C. Hartsock*	325
23	Immersion Journalism and the Second-Order Narrative *Christopher P. Wilson*	345
24	Conceptualizing an Ecological Approach to Ethical Literary Journalism *Lindsay Morton*	360
25	The Ethnographic Impulse *Bruce Gillespie*	373
26	From Major to Minor: Literary Journalism and the First Person *Lisa A. Phillips*	385

PART IV
New Directions for Scholarly Inquiry — 397

27	The "Black Difference" in African American Literary Journalism *Roberta S. Maguire*	399
28	Metabolizing Genres: American Poetry and Literary Journalism *William E. Dow*	416
29	The Revivifying Flames of Rock and Roll Journalism *Todd Schack*	434
30	Literary Journalism and the Pedagogy of Liberal Education *Jeffrey C. Neely and Mitzi Lewis*	449
31	From Magic Lantern Slides to Virtual Reality: Tracing the Visual in and around American Literary Journalism *Jacqueline Marino and Susan Jacobson*	465
32	Literary Journalism and Ecocriticism *Robert Alexander*	482

33 The Disclosure of Difference: Literary Journalism and the Postmodern   498
    Pascal Sigg

34 Beyond Comparison: American Literary Journalism in a Global Context   509
    Isabelle Meuret

35 Literary Journalism in the Digital Age   529
    David O. Dowling

    Index   543

CONTRIBUTORS

Robert Alexander is Associate Professor of English at Brock University, Ontario. With Christine Isager (University of Copenhagen), he is the editor of *Fear and Loathing Worldwide: Gonzo Journalism beyond Hunter S. Thompson* (Bloomsbury, 2018). He is also the current director of the Writing, Rhetoric, and Discourse Studies program at Brock. He can be reached at ralexander@brocku.ca.

John S. Bak is Professor at the Université de Lorraine in France and founding president of the IALJS. He holds degrees from the universities of Illinois, Ball State, and the Sorbonne. In addition to articles on literary journalism, he coedited (with Bill Reynolds) *Literary Journalism across the Globe* (2011) and (with Monica Martinez) "Literary Journalism as a Discipline" (*Brazilian Journalism Research*, 2018). He heads the research project ReportAGES on literary journalism and war and was recently awarded a three-year research grant to study the influences of the French press on the Chilean *crónica*.

Nancy Bombaci is Associate Professor of Writing and Literature at Mitchell College in New London, Connecticut. Her scholarly interests include disability studies, narrative representations of autism, and late modernist literature. She has just completed a novel.

Robert S. Boynton is the author of *The Invitation-Only Zone: The True Story of North Korea's Abduction Project* (FSG, 2016) and *The New New Journalism: Conversations with America's Best Nonfiction Writers on Their Craft* (Vintage, 2005). He directs the Literary Reportage program at NYU's Arthur L. Carter Journalism Institute. His work has appeared in the *New York Times Magazine*, the *New Yorker*, the *Atlantic*, the *Nation*, and elsewhere.

Jim Collins has been a professional writer and editor for 35 years. Under his watch, *Yankee* was nominated for a National Magazine Award in in the category of reporting. He is the author of one book, *The Last Best League*. He was a frequent speaker at the Nieman Foundation's annual conference on narrative nonfiction. He lives in New Hampshire and Seattle with his wife and two children.

Thomas Connery is a retired Emeritus Professor from the University of St. Thomas, Minnesota, where he created and taught a literary journalism course once a year for 30 years. He edited *A Sourcebook of American Literary Journalism* (1992), wrote *Journalism and Realism: Rendering American Life* (Northwestern University Press, 2011), and coauthored a textbook, *Writing Across the Media* (Bedford-St. Martin's, 1999).

Don Dingledine is Professor of English at the University of Wisconsin Oshkosh. His research and teaching interests center on nineteenth- and twentieth-century American literature and culture, with emphasis on the Reconstruction era. He received his PhD in American literature from Temple University and has published on Stephen Crane, Rebecca Harding Davis, John William De Forest, Herman Melville, and Ann Petry; honors education; and the rock musical *Hedwig and the Angry Inch*.

William E. Dow is Professor of American Literature at the Université Paris-Est (UPEM) and Professor of English at The American University of Paris. He is the author of the book *Narrating Class in American Fiction* (2009) and coeditor of *Richard Wright: New Readings in the 21st Century* (2011), *Richard Wright in a Post-Racial Imaginary* (2014), and *Of Latitudes Unknown: James Baldwin's Radical Imagination* (2019). He is also Associate Editor of *Literary Journalism Studies* (Northwestern University Press).

David O. Dowling, PhD, Associate Professor in the School of Journalism and Mass Communication at the University of Iowa, is the author of eight books, the most recent of which are *A Delicate Aggression: Savagery and Survival in the Iowa Writers' Workshop* (Yale) and *Immersive Longform Storytelling: Media, Technology, Audience* (Routledge). His research on digital media, publishing industries, and cultural production has appeared in journals such as *Digital Journalism*, *Literary Journalism Studies*, *Convergence*, *Genre*, and *Journalism & Communication Monographs*.

Jessie Lafrance Dunbar is Assistant Professor of African American and African Diasporic Studies at the University of Alabama at Birmingham. Dunbar specializes in nineteenth- and twentieth-century African American and African Diasporic literatures; she has secondary interests in Russian and AfroCuban history, literature, and cultures.

Kathy Roberts Forde is Associate Professor in the Journalism Department at the University of Massachusetts Amherst. She is a US journalism historian with expertise in the First Amendment, literary journalism, the history of the book and print culture, and the relationship of the press to the African American freedom struggle. Her book *Literary Journalism on Trial: Masson v. New Yorker and the First Amendment* won the Frank Luther Mott-KTA Book Award and the AEJMC History Division Book Award. Her journal articles have twice been awarded the AEJMC Covert Award as well as the James W. Carey Media Research Award.

Ted Geltner teaches journalism at Valdosta State University in Georgia. Prior to that, he was a reporter and editor at newspapers in Pennsylvania, California, and Florida. His book *Last King of the Sports Page: The Life and Career of Jim Murray* was published by the University of Missouri Press. He lives in Gainesville, Florida.

Bruce Gillespie is Associate Professor in the Digital Media and Journalism program at Wilfrid Laurier University in Brantford, Ontario, Canada. He is the author of *News Writing and Reporting: An Introduction to Skills and Theory* (Oxford University Press), and his research has been published in a number of scholarly collections and in *Literary Journalism Studies*.

John C. Hartsock is author of *A History of American Literary Journalism* and *Literary Journalism and the Aesthetics of Experience*. He was the founding editor of *Literary Journalism Studies*. His work has appeared in numerous journals, collections, and translations. He is also the author of *Seasons of a Finger Lakes Winery*. He was a newspaper reporter and covered Congress for UPI, as well as the collapse of the Soviet Union for several publications. He is a professor emeritus of SUNY Cortland.

Susan Jacobson, PhD, is Assistant Professor of Journalism at Florida International University in Miami. Her research is concerned with the expressive qualities of digital multimedia in journalism, with an emphasis in using digital media to communicate health and environmental stories to the general public. She also works in the area of social media communication, including political communication, health communication, and misinformation.

Carolyn L. Karcher is Professor Emerita of English, American Studies, and Women's Studies at Temple University, where she received the Great Teacher Award and the Lindback Award for Distinguished Teaching in 2002. She is the author of *Shadow over the Promised Land: Slavery, Race, and Violence in Melville's America*, *The First Woman in the Republic: A Cultural Biography of Lydia Maria Child*, and *A Refugee from His Race: Albion W. Tourgée and His Fight against White Supremacy*.

Susan Keith is Associate Professor and Chair of the Department of Journalism and Media Studies in the School of Communication and Information at Rutgers University in New Brunswick, New Jersey. A former journalist, Keith studies journalism reviews and alternative media of the 1960s and 1970s, as well as journalistic work and journalistic content, especially visual journalism and war journalism.

Mark Kramer was writer-in-residence for a decade each at Smith College and Boston University, founded the Nieman Program on Narrative Journalism at Harvard, and the Nieman Conference on Narrative Journalism (now the Power of Narrative conference at BU). His books include *Three Farms*, *Invasive Procedures*, and *Travels with a Hungry Bear*, and he coedited *The Literary Journalists* and *Telling True Stories: A Nonfiction Writers' Guide from the Nieman Foundation at Harvard University*. Reach him through tellingtruestories.com.

Mitzi Lewis is Associate Professor of Mass Communication in the Fain Fine Arts College at MSU-Texas. She serves as Secretary/Membership of the IALJS and is co-founding editor of *Teaching Journalism and Mass Communication*. Her teaching has been recognized at MSU-Texas, where she received the Faculty Award, and when she was named the AEJMC Small Programs Interest Group Ginger Rudeseal Carter Miller Teacher of the Year. Her research interests include literary journalism pedagogy.

Miles Maguire is Professor of Journalism at the University of Wisconsin Oshkosh, where he teaches writing, editing, reporting, media law, and film. He is the author of *Advanced Reporting: Essential Skills for 21st Century Journalism* (Routledge, 2015). Maguire was the founding editor of the Oshkosh Community News Network, a nonprofit online news organization whose work was cited as a notable innovation in journalism in the Knight-Batten Awards. He is an Associate Editor of *Literary Journalism Studies*.

Roberta S. Maguire is the Oshkosh Northwestern Professor of English at the University of Wisconsin Oshkosh. She has published extensively on Albert Murray, including *Conversations with Albert Murray* (1998), as well as essays on Alice Childress, Anna Julia Cooper, Zora Neale Hurston, Lewis Nordan, and Walker Percy. An Associate Editor of *Literary Journalism Studies*, she served as the guest editor for the Fall 2013 special issue devoted to African American literary journalism.

Jacqueline Marino is Professor of Journalism at Kent State University. She researches the digital evolution of storytelling. As a Donald W. Reynolds Journalism Institute Research Scholar in 2015–16, she studied how millennials interact with longform journalism on mobile devices. She is the author of *White Coats: Three Journeys Through an American Medical School* (Kent State University Press) and the coeditor of *Car Bombs to Cookie Tables: The Youngstown Anthology* (Belt Publishing).

Barbara McCaskill is Professor of English at the University of Georgia and Associate Academic Director of the Willson Center for Humanities and Arts. She has written or coedited five books on nineteenth- and early twentieth-century African American Literature. Her most recent book is *The Magnificent Lives and Writings of Rev. Peter Thomas Stanford, Transatlantic Reformer and Race Man*, coedited by Sidonia Serafini with Rev. Paul Walker, Birmingham, UK (UGA Press, 2020).

Isabelle Meuret is Associate Professor at the Université libre de Bruxelles, Belgium. Her research interests are comparative literature, narrative and medicine, and literary journalism. She is the author of *L'anorexie créatrice* (2006) and *Writing Size Zero* (2007) and was the guest editor of a special issue of *Literary Journalism Studies* devoted to the French-speaking world (Fall 2016).

Lindsay Morton lectures in literary studies and communication at Avondale College of Higher Education in New South Wales, Australia. Her primary research interests include the intersection of epistemology and ethics in narrative literary journalism, the role of affect in reader responses to narrative nonfiction, and contemporary longform Australian literary journalism.

Roark Mulligan is Professor of English at Christopher Newport University in Newport News, Virginia, where he teaches literature and writing. He has authored essays that have appeared in *American Literary Realism*, *Dreiser Studies*, *English Education*, and *Studies in American Naturalism*. In addition, he published the Dreiser Edition of *The Financier* (University of Illinois Press) and a scholarly edition of *The Titan* (Winchester University Press), the second volume in Theodore Dreiser's *Trilogy of Desire*.

Jeffrey C. Neely is Associate Professor and a freelance writer at The University of Tampa, where he teaches journalism in the Department of Communication. In addition to his interests in literary journalism and pedagogy, his research in the genre has examined the power of narrative in shaping everything from environmental ethics to collective perceptions of shared national identity in times of war.

John J. Pauly (1949–2018) was Professor Emeritus of Marquette University, where he served in several administrative roles, including University Provost. A founder of the discipline of literary journalism studies, he was the keynote speaker at the 2011 meeting of the International Association for Literary Journalism Studies. Pauly published articles and book chapters on communication studies and public journalism as well as literary journalism and had also served as editor of the periodical *American Journalism*. In the last months of his life, in addition to completing a chapter for this volume, he was working on a book-length manuscript about the origins and legacy of the New Journalism.

Lisa A. Phillips is Associate Professor and Chair of the Department of Digital Media and Journalism at the State University of New York at New Paltz. She is the author of *Unrequited: Women and Romantic Obsession* (HarperCollins) and *Public Radio: Behind the Voices* (Perseus). A former public radio reporter, she focuses her journalism and nonfiction writing on issues related to love, heartbreak, and mental health, with bylines in the *New York Times*, the *Washington Post*, *Psychology Today*, *Cosmopolitan*, and *Salon*, among other outlets. Her scholarly research interests include first-person journalism and media ethics.

Colin T. Ramsey is Associate Professor of English and American literature at Appalachian State University. He has written widely on early American literature and culture, and his current research focuses on the complex relations between the manuscript and print cultures of the eighteenth century. His most recent publication is "Disney's *National Treasure*, the Declaration of Independence, and the Erasure of Print from the American Revolution" in *The Cinematic Eighteenth Century: History, Culture, and Adaptation*, published in 2018 by Routledge.

Bill Reynolds is Associate Chair/Professor of Journalism at Ryerson University, Toronto, where he teaches feature writing. He is editor of the scholarly periodical *Literary Journalism Studies* and one of the cofounders of the International Association for Literary Journalism Studies. He and John S. Bak, Université de Lorraine, coedited *Literary Journalism Across the Globe* (University of Massachusetts Press, 2011). His current research interests include mapping phenomenology onto literary journalism and reassessing the New Journalism.

Nancy L. Roberts directs the Journalism Program, Communication Department, University at Albany, State University of New York. Her research focuses on the history of advocacy and literary journalism. Her books include *Dorothy Day and the Catholic Worker*, *American Peace Writers, Editors, and Periodicals: A Dictionary* and *The Press and America: An Interpretive History of the Mass Media*, with M. and E. Emery, 8th & 9th eds. She has taught journalism/communication history and literary journalism at all levels during the past 35 years, including at the University of Minnesota–Twin Cities.

Karen Roggenkamp is Professor of English at Texas A&M University–Commerce. She is the author of *Sympathy, Madness, and Crime: How Four Nineteenth-Century Journalists Made the Newspaper Women's Business* (Kent State University Press, 2016) and *Narrating the News: New Journalism and Literary Genre in Late Nineteenth-Century American Newspapers and Fiction* (Kent State University Press, 2005), as well as several articles that explore the intersections between journalism and literature.

Todd Schack, PhD, is Associate Professor of Media Studies and Journalism at Ithaca College, New York. In addition to music journalism, his scholarship and teaching focus on literary journalism, history and theory of media studies, graphic nonfiction, war reporting, and issues surrounding what he calls the "dark side of neoliberalism." He can be reached at tschack@ithaca.edu.

Pascal Sigg is a PhD student in the English Department of the University of Zurich. He holds a BA degree in Journalism and Communication, a BA in English and German, and an MA in English and Comparative Literature. In his PhD project on the reportage of writers such as David Foster Wallace, George Saunders, John Jeremiah Sullivan, Mac McClelland and Rachel Kaadzi Ghansah, he analyzes the author-narrators' self-awareness as media.

Stacy Spaulding lives in Baltimore, MD, and is Associate Professor of Journalism at Towson University. She is an advisory board member of the Society to Preserve H. L. Mencken's Legacy, which is working to reopen the H. L. Mencken House museum.

Ted Spiker is Professor and Chair of the Department of Journalism at the University of Florida. Among other classes, he has taught Sports Media and Society, as well as Journalism as Literature. He is a book author and magazine writer, and he has written scholarly publications on magazine covers. He was named the 2016–17 Teacher of the Year for the entire University of Florida.

Cecelia Tichi's published work includes *Exposés and Excess: Muckraking in America 1900/2000*; *Civic Passions: Seven Who Launched Progressive America*; and *Jack London: A Writer's Fight for a Better America*. She is the Gertrude Conaway Vanderbilt Professor of English and Professor of American Studies at Vanderbilt University and a past president of the American Studies Association.

Doug Underwood is Professor of Communication at the University of Washington who teaches in the areas of journalism and literature, media and religion, journalism and trauma, and media ethics and management. He is the author of six books, including *Journalism and the Novel: Truth and Fiction, 1700–2000* (2008); *The Undeclared War between Journalism and Fiction: Journalists* as *Genre Benders in Literary History* (2013); and *Literary Journalism in British and American Prose: An Historical Overview* (2019).

Christopher P. Wilson is Professor of English at Boston College. He is the author of four books on American literature and culture, and has published essays on literary journalism in *Raritan*, *Twentieth-Century Literature*, *College Literature*, and other journals. He currently serves on the advisory board of *Literary Journalism Studies* and received the Susan L. Greenberg research award from the International Association of Literary Journalism Studies in 2014. Most recently, he has created *Reading Narrative Journalism*, an introductory classroom text in the field, available at https://mediakron.bc.edu/readingnarrativejournalism.

FOREWORD

Robert S. Boynton

American academia and journalism have long had an awkward relationship. An offspring of Europe's ancient educational institutions, the American university didn't include professional schools of any kind until the nineteenth century. Columbia University didn't have a law school until 1858, or a business school until 1916. The nation's first journalism school, at the University of Missouri, was founded in 1908.

So it was unsurprising that in 1892, when newspaper baron Joseph Pulitzer offered Columbia $2 million ($55 million, adjusted for inflation) for a journalism school, the university's president swiftly rejected it. It took two more decades, and a new, more entrepreneurial president, for the university to accept the offer. The Columbia Journalism School opened in 1912, a year after its benefactor's death.

These questions linger: Is journalism an art form or a profession? Is it an object of scholarship or a craft suitable for instruction? Does it belong among the faculties of arts and sciences, as at my university, or should it be taught in a free-standing school, like law, medicine, and business? Such institutional considerations might be dismissed as inside baseball, but a discipline's academic pedigree both influences and reflects how the world perceives its value.

Given journalism's uneasy place, *literary* journalism is *twice*-cursed: At odds with or ignored by academia and neglected, sometimes denounced, by mainstream journalism, it has no natural home, institutional redoubt, or reliable constituency.[1] It ran afoul of academic and journalistic sensibilities for different reasons. With the exception of nineteenth-century polymaths like Stephen Crane and Walt Whitman, academics judged American nonfiction writers too recent, and journalism too insubstantial, to warrant study. To be fair, they felt the same way about American fiction, which English departments ignored until well after World War II. In the 1920s, mainstream journalism, under sway of Walter Lippmann, rejected literary journalism as lacking sufficient objectivity. As Miles Maguire notes in Chapter 14 of this volume, the Pulitzer Prize competition didn't acknowledge anything akin to literary journalism until 1979, when it created an award for "feature writing." Neither codified by scholars nor assimilated by mainstream journalism, this dual neglect is one of the factors behind literary journalism's enduring vitality, both across genres and across the globe. An air of raffish independence is part of its allure. The day

The Electric Kool-Aid Acid Test shows up on an Intro to Western Civilization syllabus, and it's all over. Journalism will be just another course of study.

The editors of this volume are wise enough not to try to "resolve" the above conflicts and have instead commissioned thirty-five fascinating essays that alternate between "teaching the controversy," "interrogating the assumptions," and suggesting ways that studying American literary journalism of the past might help us navigate its future. Like the best criticism, these essays are in dialogue with a living, breathing tradition, analyzing it in intellectual terms and encouraging its practitioners to be more ambitious and creative.

Like jazz—another improvisational, outsider pursuit—American literary journalism was born with a global soul, and the explosion of interest from Latin America, Europe, and beyond is one of its most exciting developments. "Making the case for literary journalism as an American household name does not deprive nor bar the rest of the world from active participation in the construction of international scholarship," argues Isabelle Meuret in Chapter 34 of this volume, titled "American Literary Journalism in a Global Context." Although the genre retains aspects of America's cultural ideals (pragmatic dataphiles, Americans have always been wary of traditional authority), it is steadfastly open and democratic. Defining its essence is a fool's errand. "Literary journalism" is one of those "essentially contested" concepts that everyone understands but few agree upon. I prefer a functional definition: Acts of literary journalism occur when one explores the factual world in an imaginative manner, the goal being to redescribe and comment on it in story form. And as with all functional definitions, the elements are weighted differently depending on the cultural moment, whether responding to, or reacting against, the impulses of the age. Between falsified memoirs and accusations of "fake news," the reading public has had its faith in literary journalism's accuracy shaken. Literary journalism must maintain a tenacious attachment to the facts generated by reporting and research. To borrow the jargon of software, I'd argue that literary journalism is an "open source" pursuit, providing a toolbox that can be employed by anyone in any context, limited only by the user's dedication, imagination, and ingenuity. The artisan manipulates the tools competently, while the artist uses them in new and unexpected ways. The tools contained therein are fairly simple, best summarized by Tom Wolfe in his 1973 New Journalism manifesto. Literary journalism has a strong visual element that often lends itself to scenes, favors dialogue over deracinated quotes, pays attention to the nuances of social status, and always presumes that journalists write with a point of view, though not necessarily their own.

The last element, subjectivity, is the bright red thread running through the tapestry of American literary journalism, separating it from the "news from nowhere," faux objectivity one often reads in newspapers. As technology became capable of delivering faster and more accurate news, the need for journalists who could limn its meaning increased. The more astonishing the spectacle, the greater the need for a reporter who could wield literary concepts (simile, satire, symbolism, metaphor, narrative, allegory, allusion, foreshadowing) with which to craft a meaningful story.

As John S. Bak explains in "Of Troops and Tropes" (Chapter 16, this volume), war played a central role in the development of literary journalism as modern man's genius for orchestrating violence resulted in ever more horrible results. Faced with the unfathomable carnage of the Civil War's 600,000 dead or World War I's 20 million, literary journalism documented "the human side of war, not just the victory marches celebrated or the trenches taken and retaken, but also the mundane and the sundry," Bak writes. Whether in the hands of Martha Gellhorn, John Hersey, or Ryszard Kapuscinski, literary journalists deploy subjectivity to convey the "feel" of wars most civilians know only through statistics, headlines, radio reports, and, later, television. "Conventional journalism could no more reveal this war than conventional firepower could win it," Michael Herr observed of his attempt to capture the truth of the Vietnam War. The twin children of nineteenth-century invention, photography and literary journalism, which coalesced in the figure of Jacob Riis, gave people access to the stories of how the "other half" lives and dies.[2]

Similar arguments have been made for the relevance of literary journalism on the home front, not only when the New Journalism chronicled the upheaval in the 1960s, but also during the bewildering US politics, circa 2019. "It is hard to deny that we are in the midst of a crisis and a ferment," Lee Siegel writes in the *Columbia Journalism Review* at the beginning of the Trump presidency. "Perhaps it is only with the license of literary journalism that one can hope to grasp our astounding new circumstances." In times of epistemological crisis, when the facts of the matter are in dispute, we require the literary journalist's subjective, imaginative view.

The leitmotif running through the essays in this volume is that literary journalism is a protean, fluid genre, allowing for the kind of experimentation traditionally associated with film or fiction. But might I make a bolder suggestion? Nearly half a century after Tom Wolfe declared that New Journalism had supplanted "the novel as literature's main event," perhaps it's time to retire the clichéd observation that an article or book "reads like fiction." Let's banish the genre of "nonfiction" to the literary scrapheap. How about merely "true stories, well told," in the words of creative nonfiction guru Lee Gutkind?

Today podcasts are the most exciting place to experience the intersection of story and innovation. Some have suggested we are enjoying the "second golden age of radio," and I'd argue that the best literary journalism today is created for the listener as much as the reader. Audio has woven the red thread of subjectivity into a nifty new pair of headphones. If intimate literary journalism whispers in the reader's ear, audio sets up shop in our auditory canal. Were Joseph Mitchell embarking on a journalism career in 2019, he'd share Joe Gould's secrets in episodes of *This American Life*, *Radio Diaries*, or *Serial*. The *New Yorker* might exist as a weekly radio show and travelling festival, punctuated by a quarterly magazine. Most podcasts don't live up to these standards in the same way that most books and articles fall flat. But those that do, combining rigorous reporting and research with imaginative storytelling and sound design, provide an experience as sublime as anything found in the history of literary journalism. The technology has changed, but the renegade spirit continues to thrive. And the essays in this volume document that spirit—in the past and present as they point to the future.

Notes

1. The situation improved slightly with the founding of the International Association for Literary Journalism Studies, and its journal, *Literary Journalism Studies*, in 2006.
2. The title of Riis's original magic lantern presentation was "The Other Half: How It Lives and Dies in New York. Illustrated with 100 Photographic Views."

ACKNOWLEDGMENTS

The editors of this volume would like to thank Routledge for its support of this project. In particular, we wish to extend our gratitude to Erica Wetter, Emma Sheriff, and Sarah Pickles for their trust and encouragement, and especially for recognizing the importance of literary journalism and literary journalism studies. Thanks also to Yoko Nakamura, our associate editor, for her meticulous editing skills, to Robert Boynton for his encouragement and incisive foreword, to Trevor Koenigs for his stunning cover image, and to Anne-Marie and Miles for their enthusiasm and insight at every stage of our work. We are grateful as well to the research group at Paris-Est (UPEM), LISAA (Littératures Savoirs et Arts), for their funding of the cover. Most of all, we would like to thank the contributors to this volume, not only for their patience and perseverance, but most importantly for their superb contributions to the field of American literary journalism studies.

INTRODUCTION

Roberta S. Maguire and William E. Dow

There is a definite need at present to clearly define and position the genre of American literary journalism in relation to the fields of literary studies, literary theory, cultural history, literary history, journalism history, and journalism practice. There is an equally urgent need to document the historical existence of a narrative form that exhibits a constant tension between factual evidence and the writer's imagination that conjures such evidence into a story. In addition to being a method or technique, the literary journalism of American writers such as Walt Whitman, Fanny Fern, Frederick Douglass, Meridel Le Sueur, James Agee, Dorothy Parker, James Baldwin, and Joan Didion, while representing a certain narrative epistemology, demonstrates a tension between "fact" and "art," uniquely well suited to express and represent American culture.

A central concern of this volume: What does the specificity of literary journalism—as the work of a genre, rhetoric, and narrative—have to offer in understanding American culture and, indeed, the larger world? Literary journalism can certainly offer knowledge, but perhaps more legitimately can be credited with fostering modes of public reflection crucial to civil society and social justice. And much more as well. The genre can provide verifiable facts and polemical astuteness but should also be characterized by its capacity to procure wisdom; to enhance attunement to certain registers of human experience; to show a sharp awareness of the capacities of language as a medium; and to provide intense, transformative experiences in ways and in forms that other narrative genres cannot.

The Routledge Companion to American Literary Journalism provides an interdisciplinary, cross-cultural, and international study of American literary journalism, engaging with such disciplines as sociology, anthropology, African American studies, gender studies, visual studies, media studies, and American studies, in addition to journalism and literary studies. The volume not only calls attention to literary journalism as a distinctive genre, the modern form of which has been evolving in the US for over 150 years, but also provides a much-needed critical foundation for future scholarship. Although the international presence of literary journalism is of vital importance, the value of the form in our time demands more than a grasp of an enlarged global circuitry.[1] Literary journalism demands a close engagement with the mutable and shape-shifting canon of nonfictional and fictional narrative forms; it requires the study of narrative expressions beyond the classic genres of objective journalism, the novel, poetry, and documentary fiction; and it calls for multimedial conceptions beyond print.

In this spirit, the collection offers a contemporary, interpretive historical survey of American literary journalism from its beginnings to the present moment. But there is an inherent challenge in doing so. Most literary and cultural critics today often have only a sketchy or emerging knowledge of journalism history and even less of literary journalism studies or of the practices of literary journalism. Similarly, most journalists and journalism historians are often unfamiliar with literary theory and literary criticism in general and their relevance to the works of literary journalism. One goal of *The Routledge Companion to American Literary Journalism* is to bring these historically separate fields together in a theoretically and culturally informed conversation that reflects the contributions of literary journalism to American history, culture, and letters. In this regard, a full range of interpretive skills, theories, and practices, found in this present volume, is needed to confront a narrative form that speaks to its times—to the immediacy of its contexts— and to the most meaningful moments of historical experience.

Another objective of *The Routledge Companion to American Literary Journalism* is to present cutting-edge scholarship that provokes reconsideration and inquiry while providing new historical interpretations. The articles selected for this volume largely focus on untreated areas as well as unexamined themes and connections in the story of American literary journalism: the antebellum beginnings of American literary journalism; the 1930s reportage of Joseph North, John L. Spivak, and Meridel Le Sueur; the historical process of how literary journalism entered the mainstream of American media; immersion journalism and "second-order narratives"; and literary journalism and the first person. From a reexamination of Colonial American newspapers to a reinterpretation of the early memoirs of William Grimes, Mattie Jackson, and Nicholas Said; from a reevaluation of female reporters in the 1880–1930 period to an incisive assessment of literary muckrakers in the twentieth century; and from an alternative approach to literary war journalism to innovative interpretations of book history, this volume breaks new ground and offers its discoveries.

Indeed, a major intention of *The Routledge Companion to American Literary Journalism* is to promote literary journalism scholarship—especially among scholars, students, and a reading public with at best a cursory knowledge of the field. In effect, as the atomized histories of American literature, American journalism, and American literary journalism illustrate, the interdisciplinary nature of literary journalism means that scholars of journalism and scholars of literature have a tendency to be equally uncertain about what to do with the genre as an academic topic. This collection addresses this uncertainty by arguing that literary journalism is a necessary category in both literary and journalistic historiography. At the same time, *The Routledge Companion to American Literary Journalism* confirms that in practice and stature literary journalism, as an academic field, *is* beginning to position itself as a collective enterprise and institution.[2]

A further goal of the volume is to bring writers who are not normally recognized as literary journalists but who indeed wrote or are writing literary journalism (Frederick Douglass, Lydia Maria Child, Margaret Fuller, Fanny Fern, James Baldwin, Ted Poston, Charlayne Hunter-Gault, C. D. Wright, H. L. Mencken, Richard Wright, George Packer, Claudia Rankine, Edwidge Danticat) into the literary journalism canon and to make them part of a literary journalism history. As this volume suggests, the fluidity of genres in literary-journalistic texts articulates that same fluidity found in much of American fiction[3] demonstrated, for instance, in the writings of John Dos Passos, Henry Miller, Richard Brautigan, Kathy Acker, Marge Piercy, and Joanna Russ —all narrative experimentalists impatient with the generic classification of the novel. In alignment with the intentions of literary-journalistic texts, their experimentations (e.g., modernistic sectionalized narratives, free-flowing monologue narratives, narratives that reappropriate documentary material) are calculated to disorient the reader from a routine generic response. Such an objective lies at the heart of a literary-journalistic aesthetic and accompanies its epistemological directions.

Relatedly, a subtext of many chapters in this volume is the role of the reader in a work of literary journalism.[4] Recognizing the reader's co-creation of a literary journalistic text might lead to the necessity of knowing more about such a text by ascertaining who has read it. As Suzanne Keen has recently remarked, "Since each reader plays a crucial role in completing the narrative transaction, … the tastes, practices, and motivations of real readers matter." She asks, "what do we discover about a reader by learning not only what he or she has read but also by how he or she has responded to it?"[5] Literary journalists generally bind themselves to their "real" and implied readers by warranting true statements that can be factually verified (e.g., Michael Herr, John Hersey, Lillian Ross); by often insisting, in first-person forms, on a verifiable autobiographical self (e.g., Agnes Smedley, James Agee, James Baldwin, Ann Petry, Adrian Nicole LeBlanc); and by simultaneously employing a literary expressiveness that is as effective as the discourse of a literary text (e.g., Jack London's *People of the Abyss* [1903]; John Hersey's *Hiroshima* [1946]; Truman Capote's *In Cold Blood* [1965]; Joan Didion's *Slouching Towards Bethlehem* [1968]; Barbara Ehrenreich's *Nickel and Dimed* [2001]). Considered in this way, literary journalism is as much a mode of reading as it is a genre of writing. Indeed, the essential role of the reader—as interpreted through, say, forms of reception theory, reader-response criticism, and rhetorical narratology—must be included in any formalist theory of literary journalism.[6] More broadly, reading literary journalism is a particular ontological and practical activity that has crucial consequences for our times: As Matthew Garrett has argued, "we need a narrative *theory* because we really cannot help but *live* in narrative."[7]

An additional goal of this volume is to more fully conjoin narrative theory with literary journalism studies. For the most part, narrative theory remains fastened to literary texts.[8] While conceiving of narrative theory as a varied set of techniques best served for dialectically approaching the relationship between literary journalistic texts and their social and historical ground, and as "a critical practice of writing that cuts across—and therefore also unites—a number of different fields,"[9] this volume takes important steps in developing a new formalism (and poetics) specific to literary journalism. Its aim is to offer ways in which the study of literary journalism can contribute to narrative theory and narrative histories. Congruently, it demonstrates that literary-journalistic narratives are unique in their potential for crafting a self-enclosed universe ruled by formal patterns that are unavailable in all other orders of discourse.[10]

An abiding concern of *The Routledge Companion to American Literary Journalism* is to recognize, interact with, and honor the tradition and legacies of American literary journalism scholarship. In the past twenty years, scholars have produced a number of excellent studies on American literary journalism and its histories. The volume is immensely indebted to Norman Sims, John Hartsock, Tom Connery, David Abrahamson, Shelley Fisher Fishkin, Phyllis Frus, Karen Roggenkamp, Doug Underwood, Ben Yagoda, Jan Whitt, John Pauly, Robert Boynton, Mark Kramer, and others. And there have been useful social histories on American newspapers that include, for example, discussions of literary realism and new journalism, such as Michael Schudson's *The Sociology of News* (2003) and *The Rise of the Right to Know* (2015); Cecelia Tichi's cultural history on muckraking in America, *Exposés and Excess* (2004); or Jeff Allred's study of 1930s documentary forms, *American Modernism and Depression Documentary* (2009). Attending to print culture, women literary journalists, public literary journalistic culture, in addition to single-author studies, these histories have challenged and expanded our understanding of literary journalism's cultural and historical importance.[11] As it acknowledges the vast accomplishments of this scholarship, this collection is intended to substantially advance American literary journalism studies by offering a range of ideas about how the *pairing* or *fusion* of literature and journalism can be formative or transformative; by offering rehistoricized readings of literary-journalistic stories and themes; by showing how literary journalism, as a compositional form but also as an area of study, can and does serve the public-oriented dimensions of both literature and journalism; and by demonstrating how literary-journalistic ideas have real-world effects.

The Literary-Journalistic Turn

Much work still needs to be done in defining "literary journalism" as a multifarious, multigeneric, and multimedia field. As Richard Keeble has pointed out, "'Literary journalism' is a highly contested term, its essential elements being a constant source of debate."[12] Indeed, it is a narrative mode that provokes contention—but perhaps no more so than "journalism," or "modernism," or "fiction," or "naturalism." Instead of obsessing with genre issues or scrambling for more taxonomic features, this volume implies that it can be more helpful to see how the modes of literature and journalism fuse and function in individual works produced at specific historical moments and from particular contexts. In broad terms, literary journalism is foremost a pairing of literature and journalism—a combination perhaps more intimately related than any other two narrative genres because it is a way of posing problems and pursuing solutions in ways that no other paired or interfused genre can. Accordingly, the chapters that follow offer a pluralistic account of the scope, impact, and critical possibilities of the literary-journalistic turn. Encompassing a large variety of interpretive methods and historical interpretations, the collection's essays signal the dynamism of the field, providing critical tools for understanding not only literary journalism scholarship and history but also the "contested term" itself.

Part I: Historical Perspectives

Part I, "Historical Perspectives," traces the trajectory of American literary journalism through selected texts of the American Revolution, the antebellum era, and the literary movements of American Realism and Naturalism, as well as the journalistic move to objectivity in the twentieth century, while illustrating the connections and conflations between newspaper reporting and literary fiction. This "fact-fiction" dialectic is examined through such perspectives as literary journalism and the mass circulation newspapers of the 1890s–1920s, women literary journalists of the 1920s–40s, sensationalism and muckraking, the American "modernist chic," the New Journalism (1960–80), alternative media and literary journalism, and the mainstreaming of narrative journalism. This section also includes a practitioner's personal account of discovering and entering into a literary-journalistic writing culture. The overall intention of Part I is to make a case for American literary journalism as an imperative category for literary and journalistic historiography.

Initiating that effort is Colin T. Ramsey's "From the *Boston News-Letter* to the 'Couranteers': Epistolarity, Reportage, and Entertaining Literature in Colonial American Newspapers" (Chapter 1), which chronicles the Colonial origins of American literary journalism. Ramsey contends that the eighteenth century was a particularly formative period for the emergence of American literary journalism and uses the *Boston News-Letter* and the essays in James Franklin's *New-England Courant*, both of which were "significantly enabled by the modalities of epistolary writing," to show this point. Carolyn L. Karcher's Chapter 2 enriches Ramsey's discussion of literary journalism's starting points by analyzing five nineteenth-century pioneers of the form: Walt Whitman, Lydia Maria Child, Margaret Fuller, Frederick Douglass, and Fanny Fern. She posits that many of the now recognizable features of American literary journalism—"free association," "imaginary dialogues," "polemic rhetoric embellished by parataxis and antithesis"—originated not during the Civil War, as some cultural historians assert, but in the antebellum period. Her essay furnishes a vital correlation between American literary journalism and social issues, a fusion that continues to thrive in our present day.

Introduction

Continuing the historiographical emphasis, Jessie Lafrance Dunbar and Barbara McCaskill's Chapter 3 focuses on "the emergence of African Americans' literary journalism ... in commercial and literary productions published primarily about and for white readers and audiences in the nineteenth-century United States." They argue how the antebellum memoirs of William Grimes, Mattie Jackson, and Nicholas Said, by "interven[ing] in the climate of the mainstream press," dialogically intersect with reportage to further advance the nascent forms of an African American literary journalism.

While proposing that literary journalism is a necessary category for literary and journalistic histories, the two following chapters, Tom Connery's "American Realism and the Stirrings of Literary Journalism" (Chapter 4) and Roark Mulligan's "Literary Journalism and America's Naturalistic Writers" (Chapter 5) provide accounts of the influence of literary realism and naturalism on literary-journalistic writers and texts. Connery addresses the topic of literary journalism's roots in relation to American urban journalism from the 1840s to the turn of the twentieth century. He focuses on the urban writings of George Foster (e.g., *New York in Slices* [1849]; *New York by Gas-Light* [1850]) while positioning journalism at the center of realism's fictional/nonfictional emergence. Moving on to the historical influence of naturalism on literary journalism, Mulligan charts how "the first generation of American naturalists [including Rebecca Harding Davis, Stephen Crane, Frank Norris, Jack London, and Willa Cather] developed literary journalism as a genre, embracing their roles as reporters dedicated to social causes." Karen Roggenkamp provides an enlightening contrast to Connery's and Mulligan's points by assessing the role of female reporters and "newspaper fiction" in her chapter, "Journalistic Literature: Female Reporters and Newspaper Fiction, 1880–1930" (Chapter 6). In arguing that this particular brand of literary journalism offers "insight into the profession and practice of journalism as experienced by women during a period in which they encountered shifting roles and challenging expectations within narrative-driven newsrooms," Roggenkamp shows how female journalists were (self-)perceived and fictionalized for a mass readership.

In their historiographical accounts, the next two chapters pursue the interplay between literary-journalistic narratives and social upheavals and concerns. Cecelia Tichi's "Two Gilded Ages: Literary Muckrakers 1900s/2000s" (Chapter 7) demonstrates how "literary muckraking is continuous from its origins in the late 1800s and early 1900s through the twentieth century and the opening decades of the twenty-first century." Placing the legacy of Ida Tarbell at the center of her overview, Tichi highlights the literary muckrakers "who have been responsive to two distinct Golden Ages that are separated by a full century and aligned in their thematic concerns." She offers several ideas that serve as points of departure for subsequent chapters. In "'Feel the Fact': The 1930s Reportage of Joseph North, John L. Spivak, and Meridel Le Sueur" (Chapter 8), Don Dingledine argues for the significance of that decade's reportage for American literary journalism and restoring it "to its rightful place in our cultural memory." His chapter is an incisive inquiry into the attitudes that characterized the various reportage impulses of the 1930s.

The remaining chapters in Part I take us from hybridic moments of American modernism and narrative journalism (1920s–40s) to the mainstreaming of American literary journalism in the twenty-first century. Nancy Bombaci's "Performative Criticism and the Problem of Modernist Chic: Gertrude Stein, Janet Flanner, and Dorothy Parker" (Chapter 9) bends received notions of literary modernism by showing how Stein, Flanner, and Parker, through their modes of what Bombaci calls "modernist chic," "criticized the pretensions of high modernism as they made modernist literary ideas accessible to a culturally ambitious middlebrow audience." She argues that these three writers, in their distinctive fusions of reportage and satire, created new renditions of literary journalism.

Offering a reassessment of American literary journalism in the mid- to late twentieth century, John Pauly (Chapter 10) challenges the idea of "New Journalism" as a "canon of exceptional works that shared a literary style." Instead, he argues in his chapter, the label functions "as a shorthand commonly used to describe far-ranging changes in the mass media and American culture." Focusing on such "New Journalists" as Norman Mailer, Joan Didion, Gay Talese, Tom Wolfe, Jimmy Breslin, Truman Capote, Hunter Thompson, and Gail Sheehy, he finds that their writing "usefully complicated the aesthetic criteria that readers and critics had applied to literary works" while they "adop[ted] the ethnographic methods of sociologists and anthropologists." In doing so, Pauly suggests, they focused on the significance of culture as the most potent source of experimental reporting.

Bill Reynolds's Chapter 11 illuminates many of Pauly's cultural points. Using Tom Wolfe's precepts, Reynolds reexamines various New Journalist responses to the 1968 Democratic National Convention. He argues that a number of writers who covered the convention—such as Norman Mailer, Terry Southern, David Lewis Stein, John Schultz, Nora Sayre, and Elizabeth Hardwick—"mov[ed] beyond daily news reporting to achieve something more lasting and permanent, something etched in the eternal present." Related to both Reynolds's and Pauly's chapters (in cultural, political, and formal senses), Susan Keith's essay on American literary journalism and alternative media (Chapter 12) examines the ways in which counter-culture newspapers and local journalism reviews deployed literary-journalistic devices. Historiographically arguing how American literary journalism was shaped by its material infrastructures, Keith shows its characteristic social practices and venues as well as its institutional supports.

The concluding chapters in Part I explore the integration of literary journalism into mainstream American media and culture. In "From Magazines to Newsprint" (Chapter 13), Jim Collins chronicles the influence of Tom Wolfe and E. W. Johnson's anthology *The New Journalism* (1973) as "a watershed moment in the history of literary journalism." As Collins contends, "Wolfe suggested that this new form was poised to sweep into the mainstream of American journalism," but it was the diverse forces of publications (e.g., *Esquire, New York* magazine, *Rolling Stone, Harper's*, the *New Yorker*), editors (e.g., Harold Hayes, Clay Felker, Jann Wenner, Willie Morris, Vivian Castleberry, Dorothy Jurney), and teachers (e.g., Mark Kramer, Melvin Mencher, Wilmott Ragsdale, Jessica Mitford) that provided the outlets and savvy for launching this process. In his detailed survey that traces "the streams of influence ... from the New Journalists of the 1960s to the newspaper reporters of the 1970s and 1980s," Collins argues for the current place of literary journalism in relation to the dramatic changes in American media culture.

Congruent with Part I's objective to provoke reconsideration and inquiry into literary journalism by way of new historical interpretations, Miles Maguire (Chapter 14) discusses other facets of this integration. In his chapter, he examines how US literary journalism, in the twenty-first century, has become "safely ensconced within the mainstream": Literary-journalistic works and their writers, for example, are increasingly the "recipients of major prizes, from the MacArthur Foundation 'genius grants' to ... the Pulitzer Prizes." The form has also gained traction through the Supreme Court case *Mason v. New Yorker* and via the rising presence of literary journalism studies in US institutions and universities. For Maguire, although these can be seen as positive developments, "such newfound acceptance and respectability may also come at a price of diminished impact and reduced levels of innovation for a genre that boasts a long history of social critique and advocacy." As he argues, a perceptual history of literary journalism is in the making, orchestrated by print culture studies and the history of a public literary-journalistic culture.

Part I ends with Mark Kramer's personal account of finding his narrative "voice" as a writer "coming of age" in the 1960s (Chapter 15). In a fascinating self-profile, Kramer details his various realizations and discoveries about the "minimal human voice," which is "unlike the voice of daily journalism or academic papers, or business memos, or partisan essays [and] in particular not the voice of someone official." Encompassing both his personal trajectory as a writer and the current state of literary journalism in the US, he astutely concludes that "this human-voiced, candid, and humane subgenre [narrative journalism] builds on the writer's individual authority, candor, companionship, and compassionate focus on people in ordinary but revealing situations." As a result, "it has become a vital sector of journalism, especially suited for witnessing specific situations nested in their social contexts."

Part II: Themes, Venues, and Genres across Time

"Themes, Venues, and Genres across Time" explores some of the problems, methods, and narrative-epistemological issues that arise when analyzing literary-journalistic texts. This section covers diverse subjects ranging from American literary journalism and war to sports literary journalism. Engaging various analytical approaches, the authors explore the porous borders between literature and journalism, artist and reporter, high culture and low, while historically considering the complex nature of "narrative truth" in fact-fiction discourses. These efforts serve to expand the literary journalism canon of writers by attending to the fluidity of the genre—and so broadening out what literary journalism is beyond previous studies.

Part II begins with John S. Bak's "Of Troops and Tropes: US Literary War Journalism from the Civil War to the War on Terror" (Chapter 16), which highlights these war journalism features: "the irony through which a war is rendered, the understatement by which it is judged, and the sensationalism in which it is captured." Chronicling the literary war journalism of Stephen Crane, Ernest Hemingway, Martha Gellhorn, Langston Hughes, and others, Bak demonstrates the ways such writers understood and represented the various "aesthetics of the war experience." In Chapter 17, "Literary Journalism and Social Activism," Nancy L. Roberts shifts the focus from literary war activism to social commitments. Concentrating on Jacob Riis and Barbara Ehrenreich, she analyzes the marshalling of literary-journalistic expression for political intent and political economy. Her analysis of their writings and also the work of Henry David Thoreau and John Reed shows how "some of our most passionate social and political activists have turned to literary journalism as a way to persuade others to adopt and to act upon their heartfelt convictions." And these writers, she argues, should be brought into the literary journalism canon.

While also expanding the canon of literary-journalistic writers, Doug Underwood's "Literary Journalism and American Magazines" (Chapter 18) shows how magazines and periodicals have been a key to the development of American literary journalism. Analyzing the ways "periodicals have launched, nourished, and promoted the careers of literary journalists," he finds "that magazines are so intertwined with the emergence and evolution of literary journalism that they exist in a near symbiotic relationship with the creative nonfiction forms that they have helped to spawn." Underwood's chapter also points to the crucial importance of literary-journalistic critical reviews, published in the book review pages of general circulation magazines (as well as in major newspapers) from the mid-to-late nineteenth and throughout the twentieth and twenty-first centuries. For Underwood, this is yet another example of the "concept of the magazine as literary journalism's vessel and catalyst."

In Chapter 19, "Literary Journalism's Historical Lineage: In Defense of Mencken," Stacy Spaulding insightfully examines the commercial influences on literary journalism at the turn of the nineteenth century. She argues that "tracing [literary journalism's] commercial trail through the marketplace" is crucial for understanding the "link between the modern emergence of the form and literary journalism today." In doing so, Spaulding emphasizes "two areas deserving of further investigation: the content strategies deployed by evening newspapers during the turn-of-the-century newspaper boom and the editorial influence of H. L. Mencken." As part of "an alternate lineage," Mencken was "one of the most prominent innovators of the human-interest story" and "one of literary journalism's most important editors."

Part II closes with Ted Geltner and Ted Spiker's Chapter 20, "A Short, Comprehensive History of Literary Sports Journalism," which charts the influence of sports writing on American literary journalism from the late nineteenth century to our present time. Geltner and Spiker provocatively suggest that

> the rules that existed in the news pages were relaxed for the no-consequence, just-for-entertainment realm of sports coverage, [which] has allowed creativity to flourish to an immense degree and produced some of the finest craftsmen in the grand tradition of American literary journalism.

Covering the contributions of such "literary-minded" sportswriters as Grantland Rice, Ring Lardner, Damon Runyon, Red Smith, Jim Murray, and others, Geltner and Spiker demonstrate how "the creation of art through sports reporting has flourished, leaving a deep record of innovation in its wake." As Geltner and Spiker assert, writing sports journalism was a critical stage in the development of certain literary-journalistic writers. Their work adds to the most vital tasks of this second section: to raise new questions about familiar texts, to suggest the importance of an expanded literary journalism canon—especially in relation to the genre's social functions—and to map changes in how literary journalism studies is constructed and used.

Part III: Theorizing American Literary Journalism: Disciplinary Intersections

Part III focuses on theoretical approaches and disciplinary assessments most conducive to analyzing hybridic narrative forms. While accounting for what writers are doing with such forms, this section looks at the connections between American literary journalism and other fields, such as book history, aesthetics, narratology, and anthropology, as well as the current critical debates surrounding literary journalism studies. The overall purpose of Part III is to outline a theoretical framework that can lead to a more nuanced understanding of the trajectory of and innovations in American literary journalism than is currently available.

In Chapter 21, "American Literary Journalism and Book History: Crossing the Divide," Kathy Roberts Forde charts the connections between book history and literary journalism studies. Through a pluri-disciplinary theoretical lens, Forde perceptively assesses "the emergence and development of both literary journalism studies and book history as distinct fields of study in the US context." Attending to the fields' intersections and divergences, she argues that literary journalism can be seen as "a particular form of public communication central to civic life" and as a vector that can "infor[m] public discussion and understanding of important social and political issues and even public policy." Forde highlights such dimensions in connection with book history to suggest "what literary journalism means to the public is what matters most for literary journalism studies."

Following Forde, John C. Hartsock (Chapter 22) discusses other forms of referentiality and intersections of disciplines. "Exploring the Referentiality of Narrative Literary Journalism" proposes a theory of "the aesthetics of everyday experience," which leads to "a phenomenal experience that prompts a sensory response." As a critical practice, Hartsock proposes, this response can result in an imaginative reconsideration of a literary-journalistic text. To capture "the ethical dimensions" of "a narrative literary journalism, or narra-descriptive journalism," he argues further, we need "the aesthetics of everyday experience as a chain of uninterrupted if imperfectly collected evidence." While suggesting how literary-journalistic texts can deautomatize perception by stimulating unexpected forms of knowing, both Forde's and Hartsock's chapters challenge some of the traditional theoretical and cultural constructions of literary journalism studies.

In a similarly disrupting vein, Christopher P. Wilson's "Immersion Journalism and the Second-Order Narrative" (Chapter 23) questions how scholars and news trade writers have employed the term "immersion" when referring to literary journalists who depend on immersion techniques in their investigative work. To explain what often accompanies such acts of conventional immersion, Wilson proposes calling this "a *second-order* narrative—that is, a coexisting literary story about how the account we're reading ostensibly came to be researched and written in the first place." Such a narrative, as Wilson demonstrates, often proves problematic for classical notions of ethnographic practice. Examining "the Victorian roots of immersion practices" and "the second-order narratives" of three contemporary practitioners, Ted Conover, Barbara Ehrenreich, and William Finnegan, he suggests several innovative ways "to interpret newer, postethnographic instances of immersion journalism."

Following Wilson, Lindsay Morton in "Conceptualizing an Ecological Approach to Ethical Literary Journalism" (Chapter 24) proposes a theory of "ecological thinking" based on "an ethical imperative that asks inquirers to re-vision what knowledge is, critique the structures that perpetuate oppression, and address inequities perpetuated by rationalist-empiricist ways of knowing." Morton's thesis disturbs commonly accepted notions of "traditional" media ethics, particularly in relation to literary journalistic practice. "Conceptualizing literary journalists as ecological subjects," she argues, "places the practitioner at the locus of moral responsibility for ethical behavior and representation." In effect, through a "situation-sensitive inquiry," the ecological approach provides a way to render ethically balanced accounts of the world.

In a related chapter, "The Ethnographic Impulse" (Chapter 25), Bruce Gillespie suggests another theoretical and institutional frame for positioning literary journalism studies. Analyzing "the shared journalistic roots of American literary journalism and autoethnography" and "comparing some of the common critiques of both fields," Gillespie shows how the corresponding discipline of ethnography "presents a valuable opportunity for literary journalism scholars to learn from how autoethnographers have engaged with their critics to help expand their field and achieve complete academicization." His chapter argues that literary journalism and autoethnography are significant locations for grasping the way narrative forms can connect with and potentially rework institutional forms.

Lisa A. Phillips's Chapter 26, "From Major to Minor: Literary Journalism and the First Person," which concludes Part III, provides an engaging overview of the opportunities and challenges regarding the use of the first person in literary journalism. Through Tracy Kidder and Richard Todd's construct of "first-person minor" and "first-person major," Phillips examines the function of the first person in such works as J. Hector St. John de Crèvecoeur's *Letters from an American Farmer* (1782), Nelly Bly's *Around the World in Seventy-Two Days* (1890), Lillian Ross's "How Do You Like It Now, Gentlemen?" (1950), and Rachel Kaadzi Ghansah's "A Most American Terrorist" (2017). In doing so, she shows how this form, "like the disembodied omniscient third person of conventional journalism, is a construct with a marked impact on the journalistic imperative to 'seek truth and report it.'" In using a range of theoretical approaches to the formal as well as contextual attributes of US literary journalism, the chapters in Part III register new interpretations in the field.

Part IV: New Directions for Scholarly Inquiry

The final section, "New Directions for Scholarly Inquiry," considers the innovative directions of literary journalism studies. Focusing on such topics as the African American tradition in literary journalism, poetry as literary journalism, literary journalism about music, literary journalism and pedagogy, the visual rhetoric of literary journalism, literary journalism and ecocriticism, and literary journalism and the postmodern, our contributors explore new scholarly formations while mapping the shifting geographies of the field. The subjects of the last two essays of the volume, American literary journalism in a global context and literary journalism in the digital age, position American literary journalism in relation to the crucial issues of the forms, themes, productions, and circulations of this genre in the twenty-first century.

Roberta S. Maguire's "The 'Black Difference' in African American Literary Journalism" (Chapter 27) begins Part IV by delineating how the different histories of mainstream and African American journalism have given rise to correspondingly different values, especially in terms of subjectivity versus objectivity. These values, in turn, she argues, have major implications for how each tradition's literary journalism should be theorized. Looking to Henry Louis Gates Jr.'s arguments regarding the role the "black difference" plays in explicating African American literature, Maguire focuses on that difference in her reading of examples of Civil Rights-era literary journalism by two African American writers, Ted Poston and Charlayne Hunter-Gault, which appeared in the *New York Post* and the *New Yorker*, respectively. Her analysis of the distinctive "double-voicedness" apparent in their work highlights a "black difference" that "exists apart from the subject/object division" so often described as "central to mainstream American literary journalism" and that has significant implications for how we understand the function and aesthetics of African American literary journalism.

In "Metabolizing Genres: American Poetry and Literary Journalism," William E. Dow (Chapter 28) traces the tradition of American poets who employ literary-journalistic and documentary devices in their poetry and/or integrate distinctly poetic forms into their journalism. Focusing on Charles Reznikoff, Muriel Rukeyser, Mark Nowak, C. D. Wright, and Claudia Rankine, Dow shows how these five poets deserve their "place in debates on genres within literary-journalistic texts and on notions of representations and stylistic innovations in journalism." The reinventions of these poets, Dow contends, at once mobilize previously excluded versions of the social past and authorize new modes of narrative experience in the present.

Todd Schack's "The Revivifying Flames of Rock and Roll Journalism" (Chapter 29) explores further dimensions of literary journalism's multiple sources and innovations and offers an evaluative criteria for music writing that in style and function should be recognized as literary journalism. While assessing the music journalism that "provides a context for, and as such a historical understanding of, what music means to us in a sociopolitical sense," Schack considers the work of such writers as Lester Bangs, Greil Marcus, Nick Tosches, and Richard Meltzer. These writers, influenced by "jazz writers, critics, and journalists such as [Ralph] Ellison, [Ralph] Gleason, and [Amiri] Baraka," began "the legacy of *literary journalism* within the genre of music writing (and further, the subgenre of rock and roll journalism)." For Schack, when "literary music journalism" works best, "it does so with an importance and an immediacy that situates music as a cultural endeavor that matters vitally."

Chapter 30, Jeffrey C. Neely and Mitzi Lewis's "Literary Journalism and the Pedagogy of Liberal Education," shifts the discussion of literary journalism to matters of pedagogy. Within the framework of the Liberal Education and America's Promise (LEAP) essential learning outcomes, Lewis and Neely convincingly argue that "the potential for literary journalism" should "be understood as answering the charge of a liberal education." They show as well that "literary journalism's support of a liberal education may offer a pathway to helping departments that teach literary journalism in the US to secure and even grow their places on campus." In the process, through their statistical analyses and surveys, they document literary journalism's innovative relevance to students and teachers.

The next two chapters explore other new developments in literary journalism studies. In "From Magic Lantern Slides to Virtual Reality: Tracing the Visual in and around American Literary Journalism" (Chapter 31), Jacqueline Marino and Susan Jacobson recount "some of the ways in which the craft of visual journalism … has evolved" and incorporated techniques from other genres, including film and virtual reality. Their analyses go from Jacob Riis's *How the Other Half Lives* (1890) and Walker Evans and James Agee's *Let Us Now Praise Famous Men* (1941) to the *New York Times*'s "Under a Cracked Sky" (2017) in order to show that "visualization tools" have been part of "journalistic missions" since the mid-nineteenth century. The authors also examine how literary journalism is likely to be affected by such immersive technologies as virtual reality and video loops.

Robert Alexander's "Literary Journalism and Ecocriticism" (Chapter 32) examines "the way some of literary journalism's most distinctive features allow it to articulate the two terms of the ecocritical relationship—literature and the physical environment—in a manner unique among genres." Alexander's argument vivifies and expands the relevance of literary journalism to other domains, a primary concern of Part IV. Showing that "the slow immersion reporting techniques of literary journalism are well suited to the incremental pace of environmental changes," he suggests how "the genre's preoccupation with everyday subjects of modest scale" make it conducive to an ecocritical agenda.

The final group of essays considers literary journalism as deeply attentive to the issues of truth discourse, suspicious of objectivity, and invested in spreading new representational trends in contemporary US culture and beyond. Pascal Sigg's "The Disclosure of Difference: Literary Journalism and the Postmodern" (Chapter 33) illustrates how "writers of literary journalism have experimented with modes of realist representation that question the limits of the subjectivity/objectivity dichotomy and show influences of postmodern ideas of knowledge and communication." The postmodern works he focuses on—David Foster Wallace's "A Supposedly Fun Thing I'll Never Do Again" (1997), John Jeremiah Sullivan's "Getting Down to What Is Really Real" (2012), Mac McClelland's "Can the Ivory-Billed Woodpecker Be Found in Cuba?" (2016), and George Saunders's "Buddha Boy" (2007)—do not "claim ... to represent reality itself." Rather, these works "convey generative senses of what cannot be represented and thus reflect postmodern ideas of knowledge and language in a specific mode of experimental realist representation." Ultimately they suggest reality is a "communal act" of representation that "makes visible possible connections between both reader and subject." Wallace, Sullivan, McClelland, and Saunders, Sigg shows, are postmodern writers who exploit convergences between literature and journalism and whose work can represent reality in more "authentic" ways than either fiction or news stories can.

Also concerned with expanding boundaries, Isabelle Meuret's "Beyond Comparison: American Literary Journalism in a Global Context" (Chapter 34) explores the international coordinates of, and the challenges for, American literary journalism. In "identify[ing] the stakes for American literary journalism in a globalized world," Meuret's chapter "reflects upon the state of international literary journalism by looking beyond the collation and constellation of its occurrences to its most urgent challenges in terms of research, development, and education." In the context of an international "renaissance of the genre," transnational theoretical and aesthetic interpretations can lead to more complex and textured accounts of American literary journalism than we currently have. As Meuret suggests, such accounts would position American literary journalism studies in relation to ethnic, postcolonial, hemispheric, and global studies while necessitating a rethinking of the reading process.

Offering a final new direction in literary journalism studies, David O. Dowling's "Literary Journalism in the Digital Age" (Chapter 35) examines cultural ramifications of a deterritorialization (and dematerialization) of American literary journalism. In contextualizing our present historical moment as the "golden age of digital literary journalism," Dowling demonstrates "how the latest developments in digital longform now offer a reading experience calibrated to reduce reader distraction and encourage focus on narrative." He argues that visual tools and traditional print media have merged with digital storytelling to create the capacity "to transport the reader to a specific time and place." In this connection, the increasingly innovative forms of digital media are demanding that literary journalism, as a narrative genre, be radically redefined in terms of reader experience (e.g., reader reception, immersion, sensory stimulus). But literary journalism scholars must also more closely consider the "author ramifications" of digital literary journalism as this form "combin[es] narrative powers of documentary cinema with the feature magazine" and becomes "more mobile, sharable, and open to discussion." Given the increasingly collaborative state of literary journalism online, these factors might eliminate, in a Barthian sense, the idea of the author as "a single isolated figure."

Dowling's conclusions dovetail with those that John Pauly, whose chapter on the New Journalism is included in this volume, was working on in an essay about the *New Yorker* he was unable to complete before his too-soon passing on August 11, 2018. Pauly was developing a history of literary journalism in the *New Yorker*, which included an analysis of how editors, readers, myriad staff, and particular cultural moments together shaped the form and content of the magazine, from its "Talk of the Town" feature to its lengthy pieces of narrative journalism. Observing the profound interventions of all of these individuals and forces combined, Pauly had concluded that the "single genius" approach to literary journalism was keeping us from fully understanding how the writing is produced and, finally, how it works. To John Pauly, whose insight Dowling's chapter affirms, we dedicate this volume.

Conclusion

The Routledge Companion to American Literary Journalism is designed both to examine and advance the field. Much of its critical energy is devoted to the ways American literary journalism studies is changing. At the same time, its chapters assess both the benefits and challenges of expanding contexts, shifting perspectives, and implementing new approaches. In effect, the volume calls us to read and think about literary journalism not as part of one narrative system and aesthetic and not as a self-sufficient autonomous expression of a national tradition, but rather as a plurality to be interpreted comparatively—through its interconnections, interdependencies, and indebtedness to other forms, epistemologies, histories, and continents.

While the genre of literary journalism is especially conducive to grasping and representing American culture, this form transcends the limits of the US, a fact to which many of this volume's chapters attest. Thus, although this collection incisively reexamines key moments and texts in an American literary journalism history, it is not an encomium to the accretions of this history. Instead, while offering a perspective on lasting and recent developments in literary journalism and its crucial importance as a narrative form, *The Routledge Companion to American Literary Journalism* is foremost intended to represent a future history of the field, to make a significant formal and textual contribution to our knowledge of American literary journalism, and to provide an index for new directions of growth.

Notes

1 This is not to deny the importance of an American literary journalism and an American literary journalism studies based on transnational coordinates and connections. The chapters in this volume generally share the idea that the nation is no longer a sufficient container for understanding American literary journalism. The global turn of literary journalism studies has led to a shift in interpretive attention from an explanation of how the form functions in relation to national culture into analyses that move beyond the nation and national categories. See, for example, Bak and Reynolds, *Literary Journalism*; Keeble, "Literary Journalism," 11–12; and the international journal *Literary Journalism Studies* (Northwestern University Press), which began in 2006 and is presently flourishing with international contributions at http://ialjs.org/publications/.

Introduction

2   For institutional evidence, see the increasing number of courses and programs devoted to literary journalism and creative nonfiction in US universities—for example, the Literary Journalism Major program at UC Irvine (www.humanities.uci.edu/undergrad/academics/major_guides/Literary%20Journalism%202018.pdf); the Introduction to Literary Journalism course at UCLA (www.uclaextension.edu/writing-journalism/creative-writing/course/introduction-literary-journalism-writing-x-42418e); the MFA in Nonfiction Writing at the University of Iowa (https://english.uiowa.edu/graduate-programs/mfa-nonfiction-writing); and the Literary Reportage program at NYU (https://journalism.nyu.edu/graduate/programs/literary-reportage/).
3   This fluidity and hybridity is especially relevant to African American literature. See Tang, "Breaks, Borders, Utopia," 154–55; Gates, *Signifying Monkey*, xix.
4   On this subject, see Christopher Wilson's groundbreaking electronic student text, *Reading Narrative Journalism*.
5   Keen, "Novels and Readers," 140.
6   As Keen has noted, "the role of the reader has not invariably been included in formalist theories of the novel or narrative" ("Novels and Readers," 146).
7   Garrett, introduction to *Cambridge Companion*, 1.
8   Exceptions include Gerald Prince, *Narratology: The Form and Functioning of Narrative*, and Mieke Bal, *Narratology: Introduction to the Theory of Narrative*. For a more recent study that qualifies as an exception, see Marie-Laure Ryan and Jan-Noël Thon, eds., *Storyworlds across Media: Toward a Media-Conscious Narratology*. See also Cecilia Aare, "A Narratological Approach to Literary Journalism: How an Interplay between Voice and Point of View May Create Empathy with the Other."
9   Garrett, introduction to *Cambridge Companion*, 1. See also Bal, *Narrative Theory*; Herman et al., *Narrative Theory*.
10 See, for example, Siegel, "In a Time," and Chapters 2, 10, 15, 17, and 28 of this volume.
11 See, for example, Sims, *Literary Journalism*, *Literary Journalists*, *True Stories*, and "Evolutionary Future"; Edelstein, *Between the Novel*; Hartsock, *History* and *Literary Journalism*; Lutes, *Front-Page Girls*; Connery, *Journalism and Realism* and *Sourcebook*; Fishkin, *From Fact to Fiction*; Abrahamson and Prior-Miller, *Routledge Handbook*; Frus, *Politics and Poetics*; Bak and Reynolds, *Literary Journalism*; Forde, *Literary Journalism on Trial* and "'To End the Racial Nightmare'"; Keeble and Tulloch, *Global Literary Journalism*; Maguire, "African American Literary Journalism"; Meuret, "Francophone Literary Journalism" and "Documentary Tradition"; Boucharenc, *Roman et reportage*; Campbell, *Journalism, Literature, and Modernity*; Joseph and Keeble, *Profile Pieces*; Löffelholz, Weaver, and Schwarz, *Global Journalism Research*; Kerrane and Yagoda, *Art of Fact*; Whitt, *Settling the Borderland*; Zelizer, *What Journalism Could Be*. The present volume is deeply indebted to these foundational studies.
12 Keeble, "Literary Journalism," 1.

Bibliography

Aare, Cecilia. "A Narratological Approach to Literary Journalism: How an Interplay between Voice and Point of View May Create Empathy with the Other." *Literary Journalism Studies* 8, no. 1 (Spring 2016): 106–39.

Abrahamson, David, and Marcia R. Prior-Miller, eds. *The Routledge Handbook of Magazine Research: The Future of the Magazine Form*. New York: Routledge, 2015.

Bak, John S., and Bill Reynolds, eds. *Literary Journalism across the Globe: Journalistic Traditions and Transnational Influences*. Amherst, MA: University of Massachusetts Press, 2011.

Bal, Mieke, ed. *Narrative Theory: Critical Concepts in Literary and Cultural Studies*. Vol. 4, *Interdisciplinarity*. New York: Routledge, 2004.

———. *Narratology: Introduction to the Theory of Narrative*. Toronto: University of Toronto Press, 1985.

Boucharenc, Myriam, ed. *Roman et reportage: Rencontres croisées*. Limoges, France: Presses Universitaires de Limoges, 2015.

Campbell, Kate, ed. *Journalism, Literature and Modernity: From Hazlitt to Modernism*. Edinburgh: Edinburgh University Press, 2000.

Connery, Thomas B. *Journalism and Realism: Rendering American Life*. Evanston, IL: Northwestern University Press, 2011.

———, ed. *A Sourcebook of American Literary Journalism: Representative Writers in an Emerging Genre*. New York: Greenwood Press, 1992.

Edelstein, Sari. *Between the Novel and the News: The Emergence of American Women's Writing*. Charlottesville, VA: University of Virginia Press, 2014.

Fishkin, Shelley Fisher. *From Fact to Fiction: Journalism and Imaginative Writing in America*. Baltimore, MD: Johns Hopkins University Press, 1985.

Forde, Kathy Roberts. *Literary Journalism on Trial: "Masson v. New Yorker" and the First Amendment*. Amherst, MA: University of Massachusetts Press, 2008.

———. "'To End the Racial Nightmare, and Achieve Our Country': James Baldwin and the US Civil Rights Movement." In *Of Latitudes Unknown: James Baldwin's Radical Imagination*, edited by Alice Mikal Craven and William E. Dow, 71–87. New York: Bloomsbury, 2019.

Frus, Phyllis. *The Politics and Poetics of Journalistic Narrative: The Timely and the Timeless*. New York: Cambridge University Press, 1994.

Garrett, Matthew. Introduction to *The Cambridge Companion to Narrative Theory*, edited by Matthew Garrett, 1–9. Cambridge: Cambridge University Press, 2018. https://doi.org/10.1017/9781108639149.002.

Gates, Henry Louis, Jr. *The Signifying Monkey: A Theory of African-American Literary Criticism*. New York: Oxford University Press, 1988.

Hartsock, John C. *A History of American Literary Journalism: The Emergence of a Modern Narrative Form*. Amherst, MA: University of Massachusetts Press, 2000.

———. *Literary Journalism and the Aesthetics of Experience*. Amherst, MA: University of Massachusetts Press, 2016.

Herman, David, James Phelan, Peter J. Rabinowitz, Brian Richardson, and Robyn Warhol. *Narrative Theory: Core Concepts and Critical Debates*. Columbus, OH: Ohio State University Press, 2012.

Joseph, Sue, and Richard Lance Keeble, eds. *Profile Pieces: Journalism and the 'Human Interest' Bias*. New York: Routledge, 2016.

Keeble, Richard Lance. "Literary Journalism." In *Oxford Research Encyclopedia of Communication*. July 2018. https://doi.org/10.1093/acrefore/9780190228613.013.836.

Keeble, Richard Lance, and John Tulloch, eds. *Global Literary Journalism: Exploring the Journalistic Imagination*. 2 vols. New York: Peter Lang, 2012–14.

Keen, Suzanne. "Novels and Readers." In *The Cambridge Companion to the Novel*, edited by Eric Bulson, 138–51. Cambridge: Cambridge University Press, 2018. https://doi.org/10.1017/9781316659694.010.

Kerrane, Kevin, and Ben Yagoda, eds. *The Art of Fact: A Historical Anthology of Literary Journalism*. New York: Scribner, 1997.

Löffelholz, Martin, and David Weaver, with Andreas Schwarz, eds. *Global Journalism Research: Theories, Methods, Findings, Future*. Malden, MA: Blackwell Publishing, 2008.

Lutes, Jean Marie. *Front-Page Girls: Women Journalists in American Culture and Fiction, 1880–1930*. Ithaca, NY: Cornell University Press, 2006.

Maguire, Roberta S. "African American Literary Journalism: Extensions and Elaborations." Special issue, *Literary Journalism Studies* 5, no. 2 (Fall 2013): 8–14.

Meuret, Isabelle. "The Documentary Tradition in James Baldwin's *Écriture Vérité*." In *Of Latitudes Unknown: James Baldwin's Radical Imagination*, edited by Alice Mikal Craven and William E. Dow, 89–112. New York: Bloomsbury, 2019.

———, ed. "Francophone Literary Journalism." Special issue, *Literary Journalism Studies* 8, no. 2 (Fall 2016): 9–13.

Prince, Gerald. *Narratology: The Form and Functioning of Narrative*. Berlin: Walter de Gruyter, 1982.

Roggenkamp, Karen. *Narrating the News: New Journalism and Literary Genre in Late Nineteenth-Century American Newspapers and Fiction*. Kent, OH: Kent State University Press, 2005.

Ryan, Marie-Laure, and Jan-Noël Thon, eds. *Storyworlds across Media: Toward a Media-Conscious Narratology*. Lincoln, NE: University of Nebraska Press, 2014.

Siegel, Lee. "In a Time of Many Questions, Literary Journalism Provides an Answer: Media in the Age of Donald Trump." *Columbia Journalism Review*, December 5, 2016. www.cjr.org/special_report/literary_jour nalism_trump_president.php/.

Sims, Norman. "The Evolutionary Future of American and International Literary Journalism." In Bak and Reynolds, *Literary Journalism*, 85–94.

———, ed. *Literary Journalism in the Twentieth Century*. New York: Oxford University Press, 1990.

———. *The Literary Journalists*. New York: Ballantine Books, 1984.

———. *True Stories: A Century of Literary Journalism*. Evanston, IL: Northwestern University Press, 2007.

Tang, Amy C. "Breaks, Borders, Utopia: Race and Critical Narrative Poetics." In *The Cambridge Companion to Narrative Theory*, edited by Matthew Garrett, 153–68. Cambridge: Cambridge University Press, 2018. https://doi.org/10.1017/9781108639149.012.

Whitt, Jan. *Settling the Borderland: Other Voices in Literary Journalism*. Lanham, MD: University Press of America, 2008.

Wilson, Christopher. *Reading Narrative Journalism*. https://mediakron.bc.edu/readingnarrativejournalism.

Zelizer, Barbie. *What Journalism Could Be*. Cambridge: Polity Press, 2017.

PART I
Historical Perspectives

1

FROM THE *BOSTON NEWS-LETTER* TO THE "COURANTEERS"

Epistolarity, Reportage, and Entertaining Literature in Colonial American Newspapers

Colin T. Ramsey

While the generic boundaries of literary journalism continue to be a subject of scholarly debate, one current, broadly applicable description of the genre describes it as "journalistically-based narratives empowered by literary technique and aesthetic sensibility."[1] Eighteenth-century readers, however, would likely have found this definition somewhat confusing, and thus to understand the colonial origins of American literary journalism, we must also examine how the terms at issue in the contemporary debates about the genre's boundaries have themselves shifted over time, with the long eighteenth century—circa 1688–1815—being a particularly important period of change. Consider, for example, Samuel Johnson's famous eighteenth-century *Dictionary of the English Language*: Johnson provides no dedicated entry at all for the word "journalism," and "journalist" Johnson defines as "a writer of journals," that is, a diarist.[2] In Johnson's day, the printed newspaper was itself rather new, and thus it is not surprising that journalism, as we understand the term, was all but unknown to Johnson.[3]

Johnson's *Dictionary* also has no dedicated entry for "newspaper," and it describes "news" as existing across a variety of communicative media, both written and spoken, defining it simply as "a fresh account of anything." Johnson, somewhat perfunctorily, follows this with what he clearly sees as a less important secondary definition: "papers which give an account of the transactions of the present times."[4] In all the above we can see the world of Anglophone textual culture shifting right under Johnson's lexicographical feet.

Johnson was correct to sense things were changing: while movable type printing had been in use since Gutenberg in the mid-fifteenth century, the eighteenth century witnessed such an explosion of print as to fundamentally alter the way people read. This shift has been described as a "reading revolution," a historical moment when reading habits radically shifted from longstanding forms of "intensive" reading of a very small number of texts, over and over (principally scripture), to a more "extensive reading" style in which readers consumed multitudes of often ephemeral texts, such as periodicals and novels, and, generally, read them only once.[5] If we bear in mind these fundamental changes in readers' habits and preferences during the eighteenth century, we can more clearly see how the generic features that define a given piece of writing as literary journalism, rather than, say, as a piece of traditional reportage journalism, are themselves derived from the development of what were still relatively new forms of media in the eighteenth century.

In this chapter, I will thus explore two moments of special significance to the colonial origins of American literary journalism. I will begin with a discussion of the first "newspaper" *qua* newspaper in British North America, the *Boston News-Letter,* and examine its close relationship with a then more common form of news-reportage periodical, the manuscript newsletter. Second, I will analyze some of the first examples of more demonstrably "literary" writing in a colonial American newspaper, the satiric and entertaining essays of "Couranteers" in James Franklin's *New-England Courant.*

A number of scholars have noted that the rise of "realism" in both fictional and nonfictional writing in the US during the post-Civil War period was a signal moment in the development of modern narrative literary journalism. Thomas Connery, for example, describes the period as marking a "shift [to] ... a new cultural paradigm, a *paradigm of actuality.*"[6] The essays of the Couranteers, though they precede the arrival of that "paradigm of actuality" by more than a century, nonetheless deployed a fictional frame that, significantly, refracted an *actual* practice: The essays were presented as printed versions of letters to the editor in order to mark them off from the more traditional forms of eighteenth-century news reportage that appeared in the *Courant*'s pages. These "letters" by the Couranteers were comically satirical, often narrative, and always designed to entertain readers, and in these ways, they were demonstrably "literary," especially as compared to the very brief and context-free reports of news that were typical to the manuscript newsletters and early printed newspapers. That is, the development of newspapers from the earlier manuscript newsletters and then the arrival of the witty and imaginative literary essays in such newspapers inaugurated by the Couranteers were both significantly enabled by the modalities of epistolary writing.

As Katrina Quinn persuasively argues, a kind of "epistolary journalism" that was popular in nineteenth-century America—a form that was discursively narrative and alternated between the subjective voice of personal correspondence and the more impersonal "journalistic" voice—constituted a variety of literary journalism a century older than the New Journalism of the twentieth century. Along similar lines, this essay pushes what Quinn calls the historical "pedigree" of American literary journalism back even further in time, to the early eighteenth century, and it highlights the importance of epistolary modes of writing and the mail service to the rise of both the printed newspaper and some of the earliest examples of literary journalism in colonial America.[7]

John Campbell's *Boston News-Letter*: Manuscript "News" and the First Printed American Newspaper

It is generally accepted that the first successful American newspaper—that is, a printed newspaper in colonial British North America that ran longer than a few isolated issues—was John Campbell's *Boston News-Letter,* which first appeared in print on April 24, 1704.[8] Campbell had succeeded his father Duncan as Boston's postmaster in 1702, and, also like his father, he had for some time been sending manuscript "newsletters" he periodically compiled to a number of regular subscribers: government officials, ministers, and other well-placed readers around Boston and other parts of New England. Postmasters occupied especially significant nodes in the information networks of the British Atlantic: They were usually the first to see manuscript newsletters coming in through the mails as well as the newer, printed news broadsheets and "newspapers" that were increasingly popular in London and were beginning to be received by readers in the colonies.[9] Postmasters also routinely participated in verbal exchanges of news with postriders and other individuals who frequently came through the post offices to send and pick up mail.[10] As Boston's postmaster, Campbell thus had ready access to large volumes of just the sort of information readers of his own manuscript newsletters wanted and needed.

As was the case in the London metropole, Campbell's colonial readers called the information they read in his newsletter "intelligence," a term that had been applied to the written news provided in manuscript newsletters all around the British Atlantic during much of the preceding century. The patron-readers of these "intelligences" expected the information relayed to be the most accurate and up to date available; they required as much for their professional activities in government, business, and, especially in New England, the church. Indeed, demand for accurate written "intelligence" had become so strong in London by the late seventeenth century that a class of professional scribes had developed who specialized in writing just such newsletters. These early journalists-in-manuscript were themselves called "intelligencers," and their individual reputations (and, correspondingly, their respective numbers of paid subscribers) depended upon the timeliness and accuracy of the "intelligences" they provided.

Another factor in the steady popularity of manuscript newsletters was continual improvement in mail service across Britain (and across much of Europe), a phenomenon that also contributed to the rise of the printed newspaper. As Andrew Pettegree argues, "The wholesale transformation of the international postal service … made possible the invention of the newspaper,"[11] because it made the communication of information that much more timely and affordable, and, over the years, this increased demand for written sources of news. Thus print became an increasingly attractive medium for news "intelligences," as print could meet this growing demand for written news more cheaply and quickly than manuscript. Campbell's decision to move his manuscript newsletter into print in early eighteenth-century Boston, then, reflected a broader, if still somewhat gradual, transformation that had been taking place all around the British Atlantic for some decades.[12]

In any case, for both manuscript newsletters and their subsequent printed "newspaper" counterparts, the news was always conveyed within a narrow set of stylistic parameters. Whether the "intelligence" reported was "court gossip, a judicial action, or a military or diplomatic report from abroad," the style was always the same: "a terse one- or two-sentence paragraph devoid of explanation or background, since the recipient was assumed to be in need of neither."[13] This was the style Campbell used for his manuscript newsletters, and he largely carried it forward into his printed *Boston News-Letter*. Indeed, the close relationship between Campbell's manuscript "intelligences" and his subsequent printed newspaper was visible on the latter's front page; "*News-Letter*" in the title makes explicit that Campbell expected his readers would understand his printed newspaper to be a continuation of his earlier manuscript newsletters, although he also copied the phrase "Published by Authority" from a leading early newspaper being printed back in London, the *London Gazette*, and he placed it directly below his title line, despite the fact there was no equivalent legal authority in Boston to grant him such "Authority" at the time.

As the above makes clear, while the manuscript newsletters arrived to their readers through the mails, they were quite distinct from the "familiar letter," the genre of personal correspondence we now think of as nearly equivalent with letters as a form; moreover, as will be discussed in greater detail below, the eighteenth-century expansion of the genre of the "familiar letter" also has historical relevance to the colonial origins of American literary journalism. In any event, newsletters like Campbell's, despite existing only in manuscript, were still "published" texts in meaningful ways: They dealt in matters we would today describe as of public interest, they were sent to multiple subscribers on periodical schedules, and they were often read by large numbers of individuals even beyond their original subscribers.[14] Indeed, copies of individual numbers of given newsletters were sometimes produced, when demand seemed especially strong, for public sale beyond the copies produced for subscribers. Also underscoring the public nature of the manuscript newsletters, Campbell's choice to switch to print did not fundamentally change the subjects he covered or the style of his reportage, and, while he appears to have generally produced more copies of the *Boston News-Letter* than of his manuscript newsletter, the change did not result in a wildly increased circulation. If printing the *News-Letter* allowed for relatively quicker production, circulation remained quite small by modern standards: a typical run for a given number of the *News-Letter* was only about 250 copies.[15]

The *Boston News-Letter* continued to report the news in the style that had long been used. The "intelligences" were written in truncated, context-free paragraphs, and the accuracy of the information communicated was of paramount importance. It would take nearly another twenty years for writing that was more clearly literary—that is, writing that was stylistically discursive, often imaginatively based, and always written to entertain readers—to appear in a colonial American newspaper.[16]

Epistolarity and Entertaining Literature in the Colonial American Newspaper: The Case of the *New-England Courant*

If the public nature of the manuscript newsletters challenges our contemporary understanding of epistolary writing as fundamentally private and "unpublished," the eighteenth-century expansion of a particular type of letter, one we might at least superficially consider as belonging to a more putatively private sphere—the "familiar" letter—was also an important vehicle through which more demonstrably literary writing came to appear in early American printed newspapers. The letter, as a form, dates to antiquity. It is nearly as old as writing itself, but, for most of that history, writing and sending letters was a practice generally limited to elites. In addition to the fact that literacy was far from universal,[17] even for those individuals of relatively modest means who were able to write, mail delivery was often prohibitively expensive. Moreover, individuals who were not in positions of rank or authority felt little need to write and send letters, particularly given that face-to-face interaction remained the most trusted source for the exchange of "news," even into the eighteenth century.[18]

But eighteenth-century improvements in literacy rates and continued reductions in the price of mail ultimately began to allow less elite individuals to engage in epistolary culture, and, as they did so, they expanded upon the subjects deemed generally appropriate for letters. Rather than mostly covering business, politics, and related matters, these newer letter writers often conveyed personal and emotional concerns, and this was especially true in cases where correspondence was exchanged only with family and friends. Thus, the familiar letter, a less common variety of correspondence for much of the history of letter writing, considerably expanded during the eighteenth century,[19] and writers of familiar letters increasingly sought to convey their innermost emotional experiences. They wrote about "the familiar and familial" and emphasized their subjective, emotional experiences of such matters.[20] This increase in the popularity of familiar letters helped also to develop some standardized conventions for the form, and those conventions—indeed, complete versions of fictionalized familiar letters—were quickly incorporated by another new genre in eighteenth-century Anglophone writing, the novel.[21] Many of the most popular early English novels were written in the form of exchanges of familiar letters, and such letters' expected focus on the inner life of their writers made them a particularly good genre for novelists to convey a kind of emotional realism, a quality many have argued is one of the essential characteristics that distinguishes novels from other forms of prose fiction.[22] Moreover, this realistic depiction of subjective, emotional experience seems to have contributed to the epistolary novels' great popularity. Indeed, such novels had become so popular by the mid-eighteenth century that their conventions could themselves be satirized: Samuel Richardson's hugely popular epistolary novel of 1740, *Pamela*, for instance, immediately spawned a series of satiric reply-novels that were also written in epistolary form, including Henry Fielding's *Shamela* and Eliza Haywood's *Anti-Pamela: or, Feign'd Innocence Detected*, both of which were published within two years of *Pamela*'s first appearance in print.

The close connection between the expanding genre of the familiar letter and the early English novel is similarly demonstrated in another work by Richardson. As is widely known, in the late 1730s Richardson was solicited by friends to create a writing manual for writers of familiar letters, and in the process of doing so, he invented his letter-writing character "Pamela." As he worked on the manual, he became so engaged with his Pamela that he continued to write letters in her voice and from her point of view, ultimately shaping them into his first novel.[23] Nevertheless, Richardson was a successful printer both before and after he became a novelist, and he seems to have recognized that there was still profit to be made in the earlier requested letter manual. He quickly completed the work after he finished *Pamela* and printed the guide in 1741. It included a variety of familiar letter templates—examples readers were to copy and adapt to their own circumstances—and its title was explicit about the genre it addressed: *Letters Written to and for Particular Friends, on the Most Important Occasions*.[24]

Moreover, the overlapping relationship between familiar letters and early English novels also hints at a crucial way the expansion of eighteenth-century epistolary culture additionally provided a mechanism through which literary writing began to appear in colonial American printed newspapers. As newer, less elite writers of letters became more comfortable writing in the familiar mode, they expanded their recipients beyond immediate family and close friends: They began, for instance, to send letters to the editors of the printed newspapers they were also increasingly reading. In such correspondence, readers addressed themselves personally to printers and editors in familiar fashion, typically offering their subjective reactions to material they had read. They also sometimes made requests for other sorts of writing to be published in future issues. Pettegree notes that by the mid-eighteenth century, newspaper editors were regularly bombarded with letters from readers offering all manner of personal comments, and some readers even asked that their own writing be printed in upcoming issues. When newspaper editors began to accept such requests, they apparently did so with the expectation that printing reader compositions might further expand their circulations and that, in any case, doing so would at least likely keep existing readers engaged and subscribing.

Much of this reader-submitted writing mimicked the essay-based narrative satires that were popular back in London, but colonial America's early newspaper correspondents also supplied writing in other literary genres, including poetry. Revealingly, however, even when a paper printed a literary production that had not actually been sent to the paper in a letter from a reader, such writing often took the form of fictional letters from readers. Such epistolary frameworks functioned to distinguish imaginative and entertaining writing from the more traditional and concise "intelligences"[25] that were the usual form of content, both in the manuscript newsletters and in their later newspaper counterparts. Thus, letters to the editor served as both an actual mechanism and also a fictional device through which literary writing was included in colonial American newspapers, and the developing conventions and personal, subjective writing styles used by the new writers of familiar letters were particularly significant to this phenomenon. That is, the familiar letter's discursive emphasis on emotional experience made that particular form of letter an especially useful tool for writing the sort of imaginative and entertaining essays that inaugurated American literary journalism in the eighteenth century and that set such writing off from the more traditional reportage-based "intelligences" that otherwise filled colonial newspapers.

James Franklin's printed newspaper, the *New-England Courant*, provides an especially useful example of the processes described above. After only a few numbers, Franklin chose to expand his paper's content beyond strictly news-based "intelligences," and he began to include more satirical and stylistically discursive writing. Franklin had some prior experience with newspapers. The *Courant*, which first appeared in Boston in August 1721, was actually his second attempt at printing a newspaper. Back in September 1719, the deputy postmaster general of the British North American colonies, John Hamilton, had become unhappy with Campbell's work as Boston's postmaster, and he decided to replace him with William Brooker. Brooker no doubt assumed Campbell would stop production of his *News-Letter*, since he would be losing access to the crucial flow of information available to postmasters, but Campbell defied expectations and continued producing it. In response, Brooker forbade his postriders from carrying the *News-Letter*, and he hired Franklin to print a competing paper that Brooker wrote himself, the *Boston Gazette*.

Franklin seems to have been glad to get the contract: It offered him the sort of regular work he needed just as he was getting started in the printing business. Unfortunately for Franklin, however, the contract was short lived: He printed the *Gazette* only for about seven months. Back in London, the Postmaster General of all Britain had appointed Philip Musgrave to the position of Boston postmaster in June 1718, but the news had not reached Hamilton when he'd appointed Brooker to the post the following September. However, when Musgrave did finally arrive in Boston, in 1720, he immediately took control of the postmaster's office, and he ended Franklin's contract for printing the *Gazette*. The last issue Franklin produced was August 1, 1720.[26]

Nevertheless, Franklin recognized the business potential in printed newspapers, and he had also noticed that some London periodicals that featured entertaining writing in addition to, or even in lieu of, the more typical "intelligences" were also growing popular with Boston readers. He thus saw a dual opportunity. The content of the *Boston Gazette* was generally limited to the simple reporting of "intelligences," and, on top of that, its coverage of what was at the time the greatest controversy in Boston, the successes and failures of smallpox inoculation, was limited to pro-inoculation stories, a position that closely adhered to the view of Boston's ministers such as Increase and Cotton Mather. Franklin decided the *Courant* would take a more neutral position, reporting on inoculation whether or not the information supported or challenged the practice, and, at the same time, Franklin also began to actively solicit literary writing for his paper from within his own circle of friends, and he distinguished his paper from the *Gazette* on the basis of this new form of content.

Indeed, the inoculation controversy soon merged with Franklin's practice of including literary content in his paper, as imaginative essays that lampooned the Mathers were particular favorites of his stable of writers. Franklin also printed some poetry in the *Courant*, but with all the literary material he printed, the goal was to entertain his readers as much or even more than it was to inform them. Indeed, Franklin's choice to include literary writing in the *Courant* was distinctive enough that Boston readers began to refer to the paper's contributors as the "Couranteers," and the explicit connection of the paper's name with its literary content demonstrates that readers saw such writing as a marked departure from the terse and largely context-free "intelligences" that had up to that time defined colonial American newsletters and newspapers. The writing of the Couranteers was much more freewheeling and lively than any "intelligence." It was, in Leo Lemay's simple description, "fun."[27]

The first writing of this sort in the *Courant* was, predictably, set off from the paper's more traditional content in the form of a fictional letter to the paper. It was printed on the front page of the *Courant* for the week beginning August 28, 1721, and it was signed pseudonymously (this was already a common practice in the periodical literary writing being produced in London) by one "Zerubbabel Tindal, chair-man of the Clan." In this "letter," Tindal comically complains about the paper's coverage of the inoculation controversy, though not because it was unfair to either side; rather, Tindal complains that the coverage had simply been dull. He then offers to improve the *Courant*'s quality by providing his own services as a literary writer, suggesting he could supply the paper with more entertaining writing on a regular basis: "How long do you intend to dwell upon *Inoculation*? It is a very *insipid Theme* to *us* … and not Superabundantly entertaining to your *Common Readers*." Tindal then wonders aloud if the "problem is because you *want Matter*?" and suggests, "Give *Us* but the Hint, & *We* will furnish you with a *Charmingly Various*, as well as *Copious* Supply!" of much more entertaining material, since "some of us are *Bachellors*, and well vers'd In the Theory of Love," while others "are Excellent *Poets*."[28]

Immediately below Tindal's comically chiding critique of the *Courant*'s "insipid" coverage of inoculation is a reply from the paper. It is addressed to the authorial collective Tindal claims to represent: "To the most generous Clan of Honest Wags," from "*The most noble and superabundantly DULL Author of the* New England Courant, [who] *sendeth Greeting*." The *Courant*'s "DULL *Author*" then suggests, with mocking helpfulness, that Tindal and his Clan should "tarry a while longer" so that they "may better understand *what* [they] *would be at*" in writing literary works for the *Courant*. This exchange of comic insults is immediately followed, in the paper's very next column, with another fictitious letter critical of the *Courant*'s dullness, this one signed "Timothy Turnstone," and closing out the front page is yet another fictional letter offering literary criticism of the paper, this one including an embedded poem in what it calls the "Grub-Street" ballad style.[29] Then, at the top of page 2, the *Courant* promises that letters from "*William Tapman and Farnaby Littlelove* … will be inserted in our next," and then, finally, the paper's more traditional and brief reportage of "intelligence" begins under headings such as "Foreign Affairs" and "Outward Bound."[30]

As the punning pseudonyms cited above suggest, these literary letters to the *Courant* were fictional rather than actual, but their epistolary framing—letters from readers that criticized a paper's content and offered writing for inclusion in upcoming issues—refracted the actual practice of readers who sent letters to the papers they read. The relation of the fictional epistolary frame to this frequent actual practice draws attention to the comic intent of the epistolary essays: the very silliness of the pseudonyms offers a self-referential mockery. Indeed, the Couranteers became particularly well known for such imaginative and comic pseudonyms, adopting authorial persona such as "Tabitha Talkative," "Harry Meanwell," "Fanny Mournful," "Will Coatless," and "John Harmony," among others. And although Franklin relied on a number of writers to supply the *Courant*'s literary content, two of the most frequent contributors were Nathaniel Gardner and Franklin himself. For instance, the two collaborated on the very exchange of "letters" between Tindal and the *Courant*'s "author" cited above: Gardner wrote as "Zerubbabel Tindal" and Franklin, of course, wrote as the paper's "DULL *Author*." Franklin also wrote under several other comic pseudonyms, such as "Betty Frugal."

It is worth noting here that Franklin and the Couranteers did not invent the style of the entertaining literary essay they were writing for the *Courant*. They had been heavily influenced by a style of periodical essay that was already popular in London, a form of writing that saw perhaps its highest expression in the work of Joseph Addison and Richard Steele in the periodicals the *Tatler* and the *Spectator*. The essays of Addison and Steele frequently addressed the current habits and manners of Londoners; in their attention to contemporary mores, the *Tatler* and *Spectator* essays were similar to the news reportage of "intelligencers" insofar as both forms of writing depended upon currency of topic (Steele had edited the early newspaper the *London Gazette* before starting the *Tatler*), but other than in the timeliness of the subjects discussed, there were few similarities. The *Tatler* and *Spectator* essays were imaginative and stylistically discursive, and they too sought to entertain readers, even if they sometimes offered gentle instruction for those readers about rules of behavior. In sum, they were much more demonstrably "literary" texts, by design and in execution, than "intelligences" that reported "news" in brief, context-free paragraphs.

The influence of the *Spectator* essays on the Couranteers was especially significant, and this is nowhere more visible than in the writing by the figure now the most famous of all James Franklin's stable of contributors, his younger brother Benjamin. The story of the younger Franklin's first submission to the *Courant* is now all but legendary, in no small part because Franklin describes the process so vividly in his *Autobiography*. In that work, Franklin notes that at the time he wrote his first essay for the paper, he was certain James would automatically reject it "if he knew it to be mine," and so Franklin "disguised [his] hand" and "put [the essay] in at Night under the Door of the Printing House," where it "was found in the Morning and communicated to his Writing Friends when they calle'd in as Usual." Franklin then describes, with happily remembered pride, that "they read it ... and I had the exquisite Pleasure of finding it met with their Approbation."[31] The pseudonymous persona Franklin adopted in this essay and in the related essays that followed was "Silence Dogood."

Lemay argues that the very name Silence Dogood was, at least for the paper's Boston readers, an obvious lampooning of Cotton Mather, who had been quite vocal in his condemnation of the earlier essays of the Couranteers, but much like the authorial persona of the *Spectator* essays, Mrs. Dogood provides a richly detailed fictional autobiography. She describes herself in "Silence Dogood Number 1" as being the daughter of a widowed mother and as a woman who "took more than ordinary delight in reading ingenious books" and who had "for years liv'd a chearful Country Life." Mrs. Dogood concludes, in mock apology for promising to submit additional literary essays to the paper in the future, that she was "not insensible of the Impossibility of pleasing all, but [she] would not willingly displease any."[32] Franklin's subsequent Dogood essays ranged across a wide variety of subjects, many of them specific to Boston and New England, but all of the essays are narrative in structure and highly imaginative. For instance, in "Silence Dogood Number 4," Franklin uses Mrs. Dogood to satirize the pretensions of Boston's elite sons at Harvard. The satire is cast as an allegory in the form of "A DREAM" that features a unique array of characters, such as "Riches" and "Poverty," "Idleness" and "Ignorance," and a particularly dastardly character, "Plagius," whom Mrs. Dogood witnesses in her dream "diligently transcribing some eloquent Paragraphs out of Tillotson's *Works*, &c., to embellish his own."[33]

The Silence Dogood "letters" are typical examples of the satirical and entertaining style of writing favored by all the Couranteers. They also demonstrate, in the very obviousness of their basis in the authorial imagination, how this early form of literary journalism was distinct from the more emotionally realistic (if, of course, still fictional) narratives of the epistolary novels of the same period. That is, the writing of the Couranteers, however imaginative and entertaining it was, did not display what Catherine Gallagher has famously described as the special "fictionality" of many early English novels. Gallagher's distinction between the imagined characters and events that distinguish the "fictionality" of the novel from the more obviously imaginative content found in other forms of eighteenth-century prose fiction, like the essays of the Couranteers, is subtle but important. Consider, for example, Tabitha Talkative and Will Coatless: Both are entirely obvious inventions of an authorial imagination, just as is Silence Dogood's allegorical dream-satire of Harvard, but the very obviousness of this imaginative basis preempts any claim to mimesis with the actual world. If readers of the *Courant* were entertained by the writing of the Couranteers, they also did not expect to run into an actual Silence Dogood in the streets of Boston because they knew she did not exist. Readers understood that real human writers created personae like Tabitha Talkative, but the comic referentiality of such pseudonyms made plain that such "authors" were literary characters, not simple stand-ins for the actual authors of the essays. The playful nature of such pseudonyms, like the humorously silly events in Silence Dogood's fictional biography, highlights their basis in imagination. Indeed, this is part of what makes the writing of the Couranteers "literary." Novels, by contrast, Gallagher argues, exchanged this type of "honest" fancy for a different kind of imaginative content. Unlike the fanciful Tabitha Talkative, the characters and events in many early English novels appeared entirely *plausible* to readers. Novels seemed as if they could be describing real persons and actual events, even if they did not, in fact, do so. Imaginatively based prose that is not novelistic, Gallagher argues, was understood as "honest," if not "true," because it was "manifestly improbable." By contrast, the narratives and characters of the early English novels created the modern conceptualization of "fiction" insofar as their imaginatively based content seemed to "lie": It carried an air of probability but was, nevertheless, not real.[34]

Gallagher's description of this "fictionality" in early English novels has special relevance to the terms by which modern critics continue to debate the parameters of literary journalism. The writing of the Couranteers was clearly based in authorial imagination and was designed to entertain readers, and, thus, it is some of the earliest writing that can be broadly understood as literary to be published in a printed, news-based, "journalistic" periodical in colonial America. But the writing of the Couranteers did not display the sort of "fictionality" that characterized many early English novels. This distinguishes the literary journalism of the Couranteers from more recent examples of the form, such as the twentieth-century "New Journalism." That is, the classic works of the New Journalism read much like novels, stylistically speaking, but they are also "true" in the sense suggested in the phrase "journalistically based." By contrast, the essays of the Couranteers used the "real" form of the familiar letter to give shape to their narratives, but they also highlighted their basis in the imagination, and thus they did not display a novelistic "fictionality." They used a different model—the familiar letter—to give shape to their narratives but then lampooned that very form by making it comically obvious they were not actual letters from readers.

Nevertheless, the essays of the Couranteers were the first major departure in content to appear in an American news periodical from the standard "intelligences" through which readers had long been getting their "news." In their departure from that long-dominant form of journalistic writing—a style in which brevity and accuracy, the "truth value," of the information relayed was of central importance—the essays of the Couranteers are among the very first examples of literary journalism in the American literary tradition.

Notes

1 "Mission Statement," 178.
2 Johnson, *Dictionary*, vol. 1: I (& J).
3 Underwood, *Journalism and the Novel*, 19. Underwood notes Johnson's understanding of "journalist" as describing writers of diaries continued well into the nineteenth century.
4 Johnson, *Dictionary*, vol. 2: N.
5 Darnton, "First Steps," 165–67; Hall, "Politics," 167–68. While Rolf Engelsing is widely credited with the phrase "reading revolution," his own work is narrowly focused on eighteenth-century German states. More applicable to Anglophone history is the work of Robert Darnton, who has substantially evaluated and expanded the concept to characterize shifts in reading in France and in Britain during the same period, as has David D. Hall in relation to the eighteenth-century British North American colonies.
6 Connery, *Journalism and Realism*, 14.
7 Quinn, "Exploring," 49.
8 Clark, "Early American Journalism."
9 McIntyre, "'I Heare It,'" 603–06.
10 John, *Spreading the News*, 25–64.
11 Pettegree, *Invention of News*, 167.
12 King, "Manuscript Newsletter." King points out the significance of mail service to the expansion of both manuscript newsletters and the later printed newspapers, noting that many titles made explicit a dependence on postal delivery (e.g., the *Post Man*, the *Post Boy*, and the *Flying Post*). She also argues that the regularity of mail delivery was central to why such texts came to be defined as "periodicals," per se.

13 Clark, "Early American Journalism," 348.
14 McIntyre, "'I Heare It,'" 614. McIntyre argues that the complexities of personal letter exchange and mail carrying were such that even putatively private correspondence often contained a public dimension: "Getting a letter from sender to receiver involved messengers who could, if they chose, read, share, broadcast, and even update the letter's content." This was so common that "many correspondents even suggested that readers ask the letter's carrier for more information" (614).
15 Clark, "Early American Journalism," 354.
16 Hartsock, *History*, 22–25. There are significant differences between the colonial American and essay-based literary journalism I discuss here and later definitions of "narrative literary journalism." For example, Hartsock offers a "preliminary definition of literary journalism" to mean "those true-life stories that read like a novel or a short story" (22). Hartsock here is relying largely on contemporary understandings of those fictional genres, though he points out that some eighteenth-century writers mused over applying what they understood as novelistic techniques to their writing about actual events and people. He cites Samuel Johnson's comment on James Boswell's writing of biography as "making a novel of his life" as a particularly important example (24).
17 Monaghan, *Learning*, 11–80.
18 Brown, *Knowledge Is Power*, 16–82.
19 Goodman, "*Secrétaire*," 183–85. The invention of the "familiar" letter had a profound impact across much of the West: Goodman notes that *secrétaire*, like the English word "secretary," began to be applied not only to individuals who served scribal functions but to an item of furniture, the "writing desk." Such desks served both as sites of intellectual composition and the manual work of writing, two tasks newly unified in single individuals. With the mediating presence of a human secretary removed, letter writers increasingly understand their *secrétaire* desks as specifically dedicated to the written expression of their most intimate emotional experiences.
20 Pettegree, *Invention of News*, 321.
21 Hartsock, *History*, 22.
22 Doody, *True Story*; Hunter, *Before Novels*. The particular qualities that define the English novel, and novels more generally, are also continual subjects of debate, but their relative degree of emotional realism remains a central concern in those debates. The works by Doody and Hunter cited here provide fulsome discussions of the genre, albeit with substantially differing points of view.
23 Curran, *Samuel Richardson*, 19–50. See Curran for a detailed analysis of the relations between Richardson's own letter writing practices and his writing of fiction.
24 Dierks, *In My Power*. Dierks argues that the expansion of letter writing to both women and members of classes beyond the uppermost strata of British-American society was crucial to the development of a new understanding of a "middle class," a conceptualization that nonetheless privileged a classically liberal image of personal agency that excluded Native Americans and Africans.
25 Pettegree, *Invention of News*, 322–23.
26 Lemay, *Journalist*, 66–67.
27 Lemay, *Journalist*, 89.
28 *New-England Courant*, 1.
29 *New-England Courant*, 1.
30 *New-England Courant*, 2.
31 Franklin, *Autobiography*, 15.
32 Franklin, *Papers*, 9–11.
33 Franklin, *Papers*, 14–18.
34 Gallagher, "Rise of Fictionality," 336–63. Gallagher argues, with special significance for the pseudonyms used by the Couranteers, that one of the most important qualities that defined the special "fictionality" of the early English novels was their use of common proper names. That is, "Pamela Andrews," the central character of the novel *Pamela*, is an entirely believable name—it is "unmarked"—whereas "Tabitha Talkative" is just the opposite, even as both are fictional products of authorial imagination.

Bibliography

Brown, Richard D. *Knowledge Is Power: The Diffusion of Information in Early America, 1700–1865*. New York: Oxford University Press, 1989.
Clark, Charles E. "Early American Journalism: News and Opinion in the Popular Press." In *The Colonial Book in the Atlantic World*, edited by Hugh Amory and David D. Hall, 347–65. Vol. 1 of *A History of the Book in America*. Cambridge: Cambridge University Press, 2000.

Connery, Thomas B. *Journalism and Realism: Rendering American Life*. Evanston, IL: Northwestern University Press, 2011.

Curran, Louise. *Samuel Richardson and the Art of Letter-Writing*. Cambridge: Cambridge University Press, 2016.

Darnton, Robert. "First Steps Toward a History of Reading." In *The Kiss of Lamourette: Reflections in Cultural History*, 154–87. New York: W. W. Norton, 1990.

Dierks, Konstantin. *In My Power: Letter Writing and Communications in Early America*. Philadelphia, PA: University of Pennsylvania Press, 2009.

Doody, Margaret Anne. *The True Story of the Novel*. New Brunswick, NJ: Rutgers University Press, 1996.

Franklin, Benjamin. *Benjamin Franklin's Autobiography*. Edited by J. A. Leo Lemay and P. M. Zall. New York: W. W. Norton, 1986.

———. *Papers of Benjamin Franklin*. Vol. 1, *January 6, 1706, through December 31, 1734*, edited by Leonard W. Labaree. New Haven, CT: Yale University Press, 1960.

Gallagher, Catherine. "The Rise of Fictionality." In *History, Geography, and Culture*, edited by Franco Moretti, 336–63. Vol. 1 of *The Novel*. Princeton, NJ: Princeton University Press, 2006.

Goodman, Dena. "The *Secrétaire* and the Integration of the Eighteenth-Century Self." In *Furnishing the Eighteenth Century: What Furniture Can Tell Us about the European and American Past*, edited by Dena Goodman and Kathryn Norberg, 183–204. New York: Routledge, 2007.

Hall, David D. "The Politics of Writing and Reading in Eighteenth-Century America." In *Cultures of Print: Essays in the History of the Book*, 151–68. Amherst, MA: University of Massachusetts Press, 1996.

Hartsock, John C. *A History of American Literary Journalism: The Emergence of a Modern Narrative Form*. Amherst, MA: University of Massachusetts Press, 2000.

Hunter, J. Paul. *Before Novels: The Cultural Contexts of Eighteenth-Century English Fiction*. New York: W. W. Norton, 1990.

John, Richard R. *Spreading the News: The American Postal System from Franklin to Morse*. Cambridge, MA: Harvard University Press, 1995.

Johnson, Samuel. *A Dictionary of the English Language* [...]. 1st ed. 2 vols. London, 1755. Facsimile reprint, New York: AMS Press, 1967.

King, Rachael Scarborough. "The Manuscript Newsletter and the Rise of the Newspaper, 1665–1715." *Huntington Library Quarterly* 79 no. 3 (2016): 411–37. https://doi.org/10.1353/hlq.2016.0022.

Lemay, J. A. Leo. *Journalist, 1706–1730*. Vol. 1 of *The Life of Benjamin Franklin*. Philadelphia, PA: University of Pennsylvania Press, 2006.

McIntyre, Sheila. "'I Heare It So Variously Reported': News-Letters, Newspapers, and the Ministerial Network in New England, 1670–1730." *New England Quarterly* 71, no. 4 (1998): 593–614. https://doi.org/10.2307/366604.

"Mission Statement." *Literary Journalism Studies* 8, no. 2 (Fall 2016): 178.

Monaghan, E. Jennifer. *Learning to Read and Write in Colonial America*. Amherst, MA: University of Massachusetts Press, 2005.

New-England Courant. August 28, 1721.

Pettegree, Andrew. *The Invention of News: How the World Came to Know about Itself*. New Haven, CT: Yale University Press, 2014.

Quinn, Katrina J. "Exploring an Early Version of Literary Journalism: Nineteenth-Century Epistolary Journalism." *Literary Journalism Studies* 3, no. 1 (Spring 2011): 32–51.

Underwood, Doug. *Journalism and the Novel: Truth and Fiction, 1700–2000*. Cambridge: Cambridge University Press, 2008.

2
THE ANTEBELLUM ORIGINS OF AMERICAN LITERARY JOURNALISM
Five Pioneers

Carolyn L. Karcher

Historians of American literary journalism are increasingly recognizing that the genre originated not during or after the Civil War, as common wisdom has long supposed, but in the antebellum period.[1] Five pioneers played major roles in shaping antebellum literary journalism: Walt Whitman (1819–92), Lydia Maria Child (1802–80), Margaret Fuller (1810–50), Frederick Douglass (1818–95), and Fanny Fern (1811–72). The affiliations of Child and Douglass with the abolitionist movement, of Child, Fuller, and Whitman with Transcendentalism, and of Child, Fuller, Douglass, and Fern with women's rights point toward a correlation between American literary journalism and social reform in these writers' conceptions of the genre. Extending the correlation, critiques of New York's penal institutions occupy a prominent place in the journalism of all except Douglass, who resided in Rochester, rather than in New York.

These writers introduced striking innovations into literary journalism. Among them, Child experimented with free association, Whitman invented imaginary dialogues between speakers articulating opposing views, Fern enlivened "sharp staccato prose"[2] with slang, Fuller perfected novelistic and theatrical techniques of representing events, and Douglass specialized in a rhetoric of persuasion embellished by parataxis and antithesis. While some of their other innovations overlap, each writer developed a distinctive style. For example, Child, Whitman, and Fern all cultivated an intimate relationship with their readers, yet each adopted a characteristic persona and voice that could never be mistaken for anyone else's. Similarly, Child and Whitman posed as *flaneurs* in their rambles around New York, sometimes describing the same spots, yet gender marked their poses in recognizable ways. Again, Fuller and Douglass both brought leading historical figures to life in gripping accounts of political struggles—Fuller in Italy, and Douglass in the United States—yet Fuller opted for dramatic narrative as her preferred mode, and Douglass for oratory as his, though he, too, sometimes resorted to dramatic narrative.

Of the five, Child and Whitman began their journalistic careers earliest. Child served her apprenticeship on her husband David Lee Child's newspaper, the *Massachusetts Journal*, between 1828 and 1831; Whitman served his on various Long Island newspapers, among them the *Long Island Patriot* (1831), the *Universalist Union* (1839), and the *Hempstead Inquirer* (1840–41).[3] Both made their most significant contributions to literary journalism as editors of New York-based newspapers, Child of the *National Anti-Slavery Standard* from 1841 to 1843, and Whitman of the *New York Aurora* in 1842. The two may well have met at least briefly in literary circles, since both wrote obituary articles about the "mad poet" McDonald Clarke, and Child referred in hers to reminiscences of Clarke by the "editor of the Aurora."[4] Whether or not they read each other's columns, Child and Whitman both sought to increase the circulation of their respective newspapers by offering readers metaphorical tours of New York that included such local attractions and curiosities as Barnum's American Museum, Greenwood Cemetery, the Battery and its ocean view, a Jewish synagogue, a reform school, and the city's markets and vendors.[5]

According to Douglas A. Noverr and Jason Stacy, Whitman "imagined an audience of readers with whom he could personally connect and whom he could influence for the better" through his journalism. Indeed, they argue, newspaper editors hired Whitman precisely because they valued his ability to create a "sense of intimacy" with a reader who stood "at the writer's elbow in a shared experience of observation and sensation"—a talent they hoped would expand their organs' subscription lists.[6] Whitman's editorial "Life in New York" (March 14, 1842) perfectly illustrates the intimate relationship he establishes with readers as he takes them on a day-long stroll down Broadway, captured in what Noverr and Stacy call an "ambulatory style."[7] "At a little before sunrise, if you are an early riser, you may behold a slight human stream, beginning to set down Broadway,"[8] Whitman tells readers, addressing them directly in the second person from the start. He catalogs the types of fellow pedestrians readers will encounter: "workmen, going to their daily toil, and most of them carrying little tin kettles containing their dinner; newsmen, also, with bundles of damp morning papers strapped to their sides; people now and then, of a more fashionable appearance" (187). Reverting to direct address, Whitman adds: "Frequently, too, you may meet a sleepy looking boy," whom he identifies as "an under clerk in some store, and on his way to open the establishment" (187). "Be careful, as you pass," Whitman admonishes readers, "lest you get a sousing from some of those Irish servant women, scrubbing the marble stoops, and dashing pails of water upon the flagging of the side walks" (187). He goes on to describe the changing character of Broadway's pedestrians as the day advances, with "beautiful women and good looking men" of the upper classes replacing working people (187). "If you have travelled over the world, you will hardly remember a livelier or more brilliant and dashy scene" than Broadway presents in midafternoon, Whitman assures readers (188). He ends the stroll at sunset, when the human tide is reversed, swallowing up the "homeward bound working men" in a huge crowd (188).

Besides expressing Whitman's democratic ethos and identification with the laboring classes, "Life in New York" deploys the literary techniques he would later transfer from his journalism to his poetry, as Shelley Fisher Fishkin, Herbert Bergman, Stacy, and Noverr have noted.[9] In particular, the piece anticipates Whitman's use of catalogs as well as his fashioning of a persona who can "weave" a panoply of representative Americans into a "song of myself."[10]

If the desire to "influence [readers] for the better" is implicit in "Life in New York," it is explicit in "A Dialogue by Walter Whitman," a protest against capital punishment published in the *United States Magazine and Democratic Review* (November 1845). To convince readers that condemning criminals to death cannot end crime—that capital punishment amounts to "cutting off the wicked, and taking no heed of the causes of wickedness"—Whitman stages an imaginary "conversation" between a personified "society" and "a pallid, shivering convict."[11] The arguments by "society" justifying capital punishment come off as mean-spirited and vengeful in comparison to those of the miserable convict begging for compassion. When the convict asks, "Is there no plan by which I can benefit my fellow-creatures, even at the risk of my own life" so as to become "fit to die[?]" society answers, "None …; you must be strangled—choked to death" because "your passions are so ungovernable that people are in danger from them …; your crime deserves it" (66–67). When the convict retorts, "Have you, then, committed no crimes?" society admits that its members have committed many: driving a mother into her grave through ill-treatment and intemperance, causing the "deaths of two little children" by evicting their "sick family" for nonpayment of rent, seducing a "young girl" whose "ruin" has culminated in suicide. Yet society refuses to concede that its own faults should prompt mercy. On the one hand, claims society, the "law" cannot "touch" the crimes of the powerful; on the other hand, "the clergy, who hate the wicked, say that God's own voice ... demands [the murderer's] blood" (67). The convict proceeds to refute the notion that capital punishment serves as a deterrent (68). He then turns the tables by suggesting that if executions are not morally repugnant, society should be willing to hold them in public rather than in private, and on a mass scale rather than singly (68–70). Finally, Whitman drops the format of the imaginary dialogue and confronts the reader in person to plead against "the blasphemy which prostitutes God's law" into casting its mantle over capital punishment. "O, Bible! ... What follies and monstrous barbarities are defended in *thy* name!" he concludes (71). In sum, this thoroughly literary piece of journalism draws on the arts of fictional portraiture and dramatic performance to arouse readers' sympathies for the condemned criminal and to discredit the advocates of capital punishment as heartless bigots and hypocrites.

Whitman likewise encourages "a wider charity and a deeper sympathy with the short-comings and frailties of our common humanity" in his article for the *Brooklyn Daily Times*, "Scenes in a Police Justice's Court Room" (September 9, 1857).[12] Here he imports into journalism the alternating "wit and pathos" of Charles Dickens, who, as Whitman reminds readers, "first became known as an author by his graphic delineations of life in the police-courts," where "life's drama is played ... on a miniature scale" (94). Amid comic sketches of hardened "rowdies," "scratching and hair-pulling" women, "flashy" counterfeiters, and habitual thieves, Whitman inserts a sentimental vignette that invites readers to suspend judgment: "two little boys whose ragged shoes ... do not touch the floor ... fair specimens of the thousands who run about the streets, destitute, uncared for, and who are training for the State Prison and the gallows" (95). Although Whitman does not spell out the message, he implies that an uncaring society bears responsibility for turning the children of the poor into criminals.

As perhaps indicated by Whitman's avoidance of overt moralizing in the above sketch, literary journalism in the cause of progressive social reform nonetheless constituted a relatively small proportion of his newspaper writing, the bulk of which took the form of political editorials for Democratic party organs. In these editorials, he not only upholds the party's stands favoring war with Mexico and opposing emancipation for slaves or rights for free African Americans but voices "surprisingly conventional" views.[13] "Is not America for the Whites? And is it not better so?" Whitman demands in an editorial for the *Brooklyn Daily Times* endorsing the "Prohibition of Colored Persons" from Oregon.[14] An editorial for the same paper also approvingly cites a new California law for the "exclusion of the Chinese."[15] Likewise, Whitman's editorials for the *Aurora* frequently inveigh against "the insults and absolute trampling upon American citizenship, by the Catholics and the ignorant Irish."[16]

In all these respects, Whitman's journalism differs strikingly from that of his contemporary Lydia Maria Child. As editor of the *National Anti-Slavery Standard*, Child made literary journalism her primary mode and honed it into a fine art serving to wean readers from their prejudices—be they against enslaved or free African Americans, impoverished Irish or Italian immigrants, beggars, street walkers, drunks, prisoners, or victims of capital punishment—whose causes she presented as interlinked. Child's greatest achievement in the genre is her column Letters from New-York, which she launched on August 19, 1841, three months after assuming the editorship of the *Standard*. Through it, Child aimed to attract readers who might not otherwise subscribe to an abolitionist newspaper but who, once induced to do so for the sake of the Letters from New-York column, might be drawn to turn from it to the adjacent editorial, couched in an almost equally literary style, and from that to more overtly political articles on the slavery question.[17]

The column's epistolary form as "letters" establishes a personal relationship between author and reader from the outset, typified by the word that opens the inaugural number: "You." The ubiquitous "you" in Letters from New-York—far more pervasive than in Whitman's journalism—charmed readers with the sense that Child was speaking personally to each of them. "I could fancy many of your letters from New York addressed to myself," wrote one fan, "so strong was the impulse on reading them to carry on the discussions as if you were present." Confirmed a reviewer of *Letters from New-York* (1843), the volume in which Child reprinted the series, its enormous popularity lay in giving every reader the impression that the letters "had been addressed to himself personally."[18] Reinforcing this impression, Child's "you" constantly expands outward. Sometimes "you" metamorphoses from an intimate friend, with privileged access to Child's innermost thoughts, into a fan who has learned to know her almost as intimately through her writings: "You know that religion has always come to me in stillness. ... You are likewise aware of my tendency to ... look at truth as *universal* ...; to observe human nature as a *whole*, and not in fragments."[19] At other times, Child promotes the illusion that readers are eavesdropping on whispered revelations to a chosen confidante: "I feel that these are thoughts that should be spoken into your private ear, not published to the world."[20] Occasionally, she invites readers to share their private thoughts with her, as she shares hers with them: "Is your memory a daguerreotype machine, taking instantaneous likenesses of whatsoever the light of imagination happens to rest upon? I wish mine were not."[21]

In addition to manipulating the epistolary form to seduce "you" the reader into an intimate relationship with Child the author, Letters from New-York features a highly metaphorical style that often slides into free association. Describing it, Child writes: "I can never pen a letter without making myself liable to the Vagrant Act. ... My pen ... paces or whirls, bounds or waltzes, steps in the slow minuet, or capers in the fantastic fandango, according to the music within."[22] This "vagrant" free association, attuned to the "music within," works to connect the progressive causes Child espouses in the column—abolitionism, racial justice, the elimination of poverty, prison reform, the protection of children, women's rights—in the process broadening readers' sympathies.

Letter 1, for example, conveys the extremes of wealth and poverty in New York through metaphors that link slavery with capitalism, suggesting that both rest on a legal system punitive toward the poor and indulgent to the rich:

> Wealth dozes on French couches, thrice piled, and canopied with damask, while Poverty camps on the dirty pavement, or sleeps off its wretchedness in the watch-house. There, amid the splendour of Broadway, sits the blind negro beggar, with horny hand and tattered garments, while opposite to him stands the stately mansion of the slave trader, still plying his bloody trade, and laughing to scorn the cobweb laws, through which the strong can break so easily.[23]

The luxury of the rich depends on the exploitation of the poor, Child suggests, the French couches of the haves on the pavements and jails to which the have-nots are relegated, the "stately mansion of the slave trader" on the homelessness of the "blind negro beggar," who may well be a slave turned out to fend for himself after losing his sight. The symbolic connections Child draws grow out of the consciousness she acquired upon becoming a social reformer, she explains: "I have lost the power of looking merely on the surface. ... Do I see crowds of men hastening to extinguish a fire? ... [S]traightway my mind is filled with thoughts about mutual helpfulness, human sympathy, the common bond of brotherhood, and the mysteriously deep foundations on which society rests; or rather," Child immediately corrects herself, "on which it now reels and totters" because the haves refuse to recognize their "common bond of brotherhood" with the have-nots.[24]

To entice readers who do not share her passion for social justice, Child frames Letters from New-York as a sightseer's guide to the city, structuring many of her columns around excursions: to Hoboken and Weehawken in Letter 4, to Ravenswood in Letter 9, to Staten Island in Letter 21, to Rockland Lake in Letter 25, to the Croton Aqueduct in Letter 30. She initiates this practice in Letter 1 by leading the reader on a "ramble" from the Battery along the Bowery to Bloomingdale. Child's "rambles" frequently thwart the tourist impulse to which she ostensibly caters, however. "It is sad walking in the city," she complains in Letter 14. "The streets shut out the sky, even as commerce comes between the soul and heaven. The busy throng, passing and repassing, fetter freedom, while they offer no sympathy."[25] Unlike Whitman, Child does not revel in a sense of comradeship with laborers heading to work but recoils from "beseeching looks, begging the comfort and the hope I have no power to give. Hungry eyes, that look as if they had pleaded long for sympathy, and at last gone mute in still despair" (59–60). "I wish I could walk abroad without having misery forced on my notice, which I have no power to relieve," she reiterates in Letter 28. The persona Child projects in these letters is as feminine as Whitman's in "Life in New York" is masculine. Letter 14, for example, recalls an evening's walk during which Child encounters a "little ragged urchin" selling newspapers (60), a "ragged, emaciated woman" whose two sons are "fighting furiously for some coppers," "two ragged little boys, asleep in each other's arms" (61), and a drunken woman lying in the street "with garments all draggled in New-York gutters" (62). Repeated three times in two pages, the word "ragged" graphically evokes the urban poverty that prevents Child from enjoying the role of *flaneur* as Whitman does.

Like Whitman, Child realizes that poverty all too often begets crime. Following the logic of that perception, she visits the prison complex of Blackwell's Island on one of her rambles, described in Letter 29, where she writes: "If we can abolish *poverty*, we shall have taken the greatest step towards the abolition of *crime*."[26] Society itself drives human beings to crime through its "unequal distribution, its perverted education, its manifold injustice, its cold neglect, its biting mockery," Child charges (125), and prisons "*increase* crime" by hardening their inmates (127). Instead of looking down on criminals, she emphasizes, readers should recognize that they, too, could have landed in prison had they been subject to the same conditions.

How much political influence Child exerted through Letters from New-York is impossible to measure, but we can measure both the popularity of the work and its literary influence. As a newspaper column, Letters from New-York doubled the circulation of the *Standard* from 2,500 to 5,000 subscribers, and as a book, it went through eleven printings in seven years.[27] According to one contemporary critic, Thomas Wentworth Higginson, moreover, Letters from New-York inaugurated a new genre:

> that modern school of newspaper correspondence in which women have so large a share, and which has something of the charm of women's private letters,—a style of writing where description preponderates over argument and statistics make way for fancy and enthusiasm.[28]

As we shall see, Fanny Fern later became the genre's most celebrated practitioner. Yet Child herself moved away from literary journalism shortly after stepping down from her editorship of the *Standard* in 1843, although she continued to advocate for multiple causes through other genres until her death in 1880.

Child's friend and successor in the field of newspaper journalism, Margaret Fuller, assumed the position of literary editor and book reviewer for Horace Greeley's *New-York Daily Tribune* in

1845. With one exception, however, the articles Fuller published during her New York phase did not match the creativity of either Child's or Whitman's. (The exception is her antiracist allegory of March 31, 1846, "What Fits a Man to Be a Voter? Is It to Be White Within, or White Without?," which puts into the mouths of a dark-skinned Mary and Jesus arguments for lifting New York's restrictions on black suffrage.[29]) Only when she began reporting from Europe on the revolutions of 1848 did Fuller truly find her voice as a literary journalist.[30] Her artistry reached its apogee in her dispatches for the *Tribune* on the Italian revolution, which carried dramatic narrative and character analysis to new heights. Fluent in Italian, passionately committed to the revolutionary cause, along with her lover Giovanni Ossoli, and personally acquainted with many of its leaders, including Giuseppe Mazzini, Fuller offered American readers an inside view of events as they unfolded.

A prime example, Fuller's extended dispatch dated April 19 and May 7 and 13 poignantly captures the "stupefaction," "indignation," and "settled grief" with which the Italian people reacted when their beloved pope, Pius IX, betrayed them by condemning the war they embraced as a holy cause.[31] The pope's actions have shown that "when there was conflict between the priest and the man, he always meant to be the priest, and that he preferred the wisdom of the Past to that of the Future," opines Fuller (226). In the same dispatch, Fuller paints a vivid portrait of Mazzini, who had just returned from seventeen years of exile, and rounds it out with an incisive analysis of his character: "There was no hour, night or day, that the thought of Italy was banished from his heart—no possible effort that he did not make to achieve the emancipation of his people. … Mazzini has a mind far in advance of his times. … And yet Mazzini sees not all: he aims at political emancipation; but he sees not, perhaps would deny" the need for social emancipation, presaged in "the cry of Communism, the systems of [the utopian socialist Charles] Fourier" (224–25). Fuller ends the dispatch by telling her American readers why she has decided to remain in Italy rather than go home to the US. The revolutionary spirit she once cherished in the US is now "more alive" in Italy, contends Fuller: "My country is at present spoiled by prosperity, stupid with the lust of gain, soiled by crime in its willing perpetuation of Slavery, shamed by an unjust war" against Mexico. In contrast, for Italy 1850 promises to be "a year of true jubilee … founded … on Truth and Justice." Fuller adds: "Should my hopes be dashed to the ground, it will not change my faith. … I hear earnest words of pure faith and love. I see deeds of brotherhood. … Here things are before my eyes worth recording, and, if I cannot help this work, I would gladly be its historian" (230).

Fuller's subsequent dispatches record not the progress toward jubilee but a desperate struggle against formidable odds, climaxed by tragic defeat. Continuing her character study of Pius IX, Fuller chronicles his devolution:

> The Pope—shut up more and more in his palace, the crowd of selfish and insidious advisers darkening round, enslaved by a confessor—he who might have been the liberator of suffering Europe, permitted the most infamous treacheries to be practiced in his name. … Again and again the people went to the Pope for satisfaction. They got only—benediction.[32]

In a later scene of almost theatrical intensity, Fuller describes the assassination of one of the pope's advisers, the hated minister Pellegrino Rossi, an agent of the French, who would soon invade Rome:

> The Chamber was awaiting the entrance of Rossi. Had he lived to enter, he would have found the Assembly, without a single exception, ranged upon the Opposition benches. His carriage approached, attended by a howling, hissing multitude. He smiled, affected unconcern, but must have felt relieved when his horses entered the courtyard

> gate of the *Cancelleria*. He did not know he was entering the place of his execution. The horses stopped; he alighted in the midst of a crowd; it jostled him as if for the purpose of insult; he turned abruptly and received as he did so the fatal blow. It was dealt by a resolute, perhaps experienced, hand; he fell and spoke no word more.[33]

So powerful is the sense of immediacy Fuller's account conjures that one would never guess she did not actually witness the murder.

Fuller did, however, witness the siege and bombardment of Rome at first hand. Her coverage of the atrocities perpetrated by the invaders sounds eerily contemporary. The French, "who pretend to be the advanced guard of civilization," are heedlessly destroying both irreplaceable monuments of the past and "hospitals for the wounded, marked to their view by the black banner," writes Fuller.[34] "Meanwhile many poor people are driven from their homes, and provisions are growing very dear" (299). Having accepted a position as director of a hospital, Fuller also reports on the conditions within, where she "saw the terrible agonies of those dying or who needed amputation, felt their mental pains," and empathized with their yearning for distant loved ones (280).

Fuller's final dispatch, ironically written at the dawn of the year she had expected to celebrate a "jubilee," 1850, laments the crushing of the revolution but attempts to discern a triumphant future rising out of its ashes:

> At this moment all the worst men are in power, and the best betrayed and exiled. All the falsities, the abuses of the old political forms, the old social compact, seem confirmed. Yet it is not so: the struggle that is now to begin will be fearful, but even from the first hours not doubtful.[35]

Fuller did not live to see the consummation she prophesied. Instead, she, Ossoli, and their child drowned off the coast of Fire Island in July 1850, when her increasingly precarious situation in Italy forced her to return home.

While Fuller was covering the Italian revolution for the *Tribune*, Frederick Douglass was launching his own newspaper, the *North Star*, in Rochester, New York, with funds collected by his British admirers. Though the two journalists' paths apparently never crossed, both were in fact traveling through England and Scotland in 1846, Fuller meeting with literary notables and investigating labor conditions, and Douglass lecturing on slavery and forging ties with British and Irish abolitionists.[36] Both were also acting as correspondents for their respective newspapers, Greeley's *Tribune* and William Lloyd Garrison's *Liberator*.

In his inaugural editorial for the *North Star* (December 3, 1847), Douglass recalled:

> Nine years ago, … we were held as a slave, shrouded in the midnight ignorance of that infernal system—sunken in the depths of servility and degradation—registered with four footed beasts and creeping things—regarded as property—compelled to toil without wages—with a heart swollen with bitter anguish—and a spirit crushed and broken.[37]

Nearly all the signature elements of Douglass's contributions to literary journalism are on display here: the mastery of parataxis demonstrated by perfectly balanced parallel clauses and phrases piled in succession, the striking adjectives and metaphors ("shrouded in the midnight ignorance"), the emotional power ("a heart swollen with bitter anguish—and a spirit crushed and broken"). These are also the signature features of Douglass's speeches, as exemplified by the definition that his December 1, 1850, "Lecture on Slavery, No. 1" provides of the master-slave relationship:

> He [the slave] toils that another may reap the fruit; he is industrious that another may live in idleness; ... he labors in chains at home, under a burning sun and a biting lash, that another may ride in ease and splendor abroad.[38]

The predominantly oratorical style of Douglass's journalism reflects the long apprenticeship he served as a prized speaker on the antislavery circuit—and possibly earlier in clandestine prayer meetings and in the Sabbath school he held for his fellow slaves—before turning to the medium of the printed word, first in his 1845 *Narrative of the Life of Frederick Douglass, an American Slave, Written by Himself*, then in his editorials for the *North Star* and its successor, *Frederick Douglass' Paper*. Douglass's oratorical style also reflects the influence exerted on him by the textbook he acquired while still a slave teaching himself to read: Caleb Bingham's *The Columbian Orator* (1797).[39] As Shelley Fisher Fishkin and Carla L. Peterson have shown, "Douglass's antebellum journalism owes much to his reading of *The Columbian Orator*." In particular, they specify, Bingham's textbook taught Douglass techniques of "forcing his opponents to enter into dialogue with him" and of "reversing the power relations between them and himself."[40]

These techniques shape his editorial of November 17, 1848, "The Blood of the Slave on the Skirts of the Northern People," which comments on the defeat of the Free Soil presidential candidate Martin Van Buren, who "represented the Anti-Slavery idea of the North," by the Whig slaveholder Zachary Taylor.[41] Douglass opens by assailing his opponents—in this case the white Northerners who voted for Taylor—from a position of seeming weakness that he transforms into a strength: "A victim of your power and oppression humbly craves your attention to a few words, (in behalf of himself and three millions of his brethren, whom you hold in chains and slavery,) with respect to the election just completed" (1:343). The enslavement he has endured, Douglass asserts, has given him the authority to "speak harshly" to his oppressors, whom he accuses of having forged his "fetters":

> If I should seem severe, remember that the iron of slavery has pierced and rankled in my heart, and that I not only smart under the recollection of a long and cruel enslavement, but am even now passing my life in a country, and among a people, whose prejudices against myself and people subjects me to a thousand poisonous stings.
>
> (1:344)

Mocking his compatriots' pretensions to "a larger love of liberty, and a broader philanthropy, than any other nation on the globe," Douglass points out that the election has revealed Americans' true values: "The issue of freedom or slavery has been clearly submitted to you, and you have deliberately chosen slavery" (1:344). Yet he predicts that the fight will continue until "slavery be abolished ... or the sun of this guilty nation must go down in blood" (1:347).

Like Fuller's, Douglass's journalism reveals another literary characteristic as well: a gift for bringing historical figures to life and plumbing their souls. Douglass's March 15 "Weekly Review of Congress" on the debates over the Compromise of 1850 analyzes the speeches of South Carolina senator John C. Calhoun and Massachusetts senator Daniel Webster. Of the two, Douglass pronounces Calhoun's superior because "it is plain, straightforward and consistent, and it shows that the object aimed at, infernal though it be, is devoutly wished for by its author."[42] Nevertheless, Douglass identifies the weakness at the speech's core—Calhoun's inability to propose a remedy for the conflict over slavery that he recognizes as imperiling the Union. "The master-spirit of the South, the great champion of human bondage" has shrunk "into a pale, feeble and deathly skeleton. ... [T]he great object of his life has been attacked by an overwhelming force; and he has no arm to defend it," exults Douglass (2:110). As for Webster, Douglass judges that "a man, how largely soever endowed with intellect, may yet be wholly devoid of that higher quality, moral integrity" (2:112). Consequently, Webster's discussion of slavery "presents us with a specimen of his skill, in the art of substituting darkness for light, and bitter for sweet, and of the manner in which he can confound ignorant bigotry with uncompromising and intelligent fidelity to principle" (2:112).

Occasionally, Douglass also demonstrates the penchant for dramatic narrative that we have seen in Fuller's journalism. His editorial "Freedom's Battle at Christiana" (*Frederick Douglass' Paper*, September 25, 1851) furnishes a memorable example. It features a scene in which slave catchers force their way into the home of a "sober, well-behaved, and religious man of color" named William Parker, who is harboring a fugitive slave,[43] and it stages a lively dialogue between Parker and the slave-catchers, culminating in a "general shooting," in which one slave catcher is killed and another "dangerously wounded" (5:207).

Both more and less fortunate than Fuller, Douglass outlived the triumph he had predicted of the abolitionist cause but spent his last years fighting a hopeless battle against the forces of reaction that swept away the progress toward racial equality achieved after the Civil War and that restored white supremacy in all but name. Douglass shared this fate with his fellow abolitionists Child and Garrison, yet he continued his métier as a journalist and editor long after Garrison terminated the *Liberator* in 1865 and Child ceased to publish articles in the surviving abolitionist newspapers of the late 1860s.

Unlike Douglass, Fuller, and Child, Fanny Fern, the wildly popular columnist who entered the field of literary journalism in 1851, did not emerge from a social reform milieu. Nor did she write for either abolitionist organs like the *Standard* and the *North Star* or mainstream political newspapers like the *Tribune*. Rather, the weeklies that published Fern's column—chiefly the *Olive Branch* (1851–53), the *True Flag* (1852–53), and the *New York Ledger* (1856–72)—can best be categorized as family papers because they contained material suitable for mothers and children as well as fathers.[44] Aimed at a broad public, these family papers eschewed the controversial topic of slavery—a taboo to which Fern conformed. Like Whitman, however, whose 1856 *Leaves of Grass* she enthusiastically reviewed in the *Ledger*, Fern sympathized deeply with the social pariahs who landed in New York's prisons—sympathies that also aligned her with Child and Fuller.[45] Hence, she, too, visited the penal institutions on Blackwell's Island that Child and Fuller had reported on for the *Standard* and the *Tribune*.[46] In a series of articles focusing on male and female inmates (*New York Ledger*, August 14, 2021, and 28, 1858), Fern pleads for each in accents that recall not only those of Child's Letter 29 but also those of Whitman's dialogue between "society" and a convict sentenced to death. In the first article, Fern confronts a conservative reader she calls "Sir Cynic" and asks: "Are *you* less guilty" than the male prisoners on Blackwell's Island because "you have been politic enough to commit only those [crimes] that a short-sighted, unequal human law sanctions?" Before she condemns "these poor wrecks of humanity," Fern pursues, "I must know … what evil influences have encircled their cradles. How many times, when their stomachs have been empty, some full-fed, whining disciple, has presented them with a Bible or a Tract, saying, 'Be ye warmed and filled.'"[47] Here Fern pointedly thumbs her nose at the hypocritical religion she grew up with as the daughter of a strait-laced Congregationalist deacon. Similarly, in the third article, which defends the prostitutes imprisoned on Blackwell's Island, Fern chastises "Mrs. Grundy," the personification of conventional morality, for applying a double standard to the sexual sins of men and women, granting male seducers "perfect absolution" while consigning their female victims to hell.[48]

Fern pushes respectable discourse to its limits in these articles but never forfeits her readers' approval. Oscillating between sentiment and humor, between emotional appeal and harangue, she puts herself on her readers' level by speaking in a slangy, conversational voice:

> But you say to me, "Oh, ... men are differently constituted from women; woman's sphere is home." That don't suspend the laws of her being. ... Fudge. I believe in no difference that makes this distinction. Women lead, most of them, lives of unbroken monotony, and have much more need of exhilarating influences than men, whose life is out of doors in the breathing, active world.[49]

As she does in so many of her articles, however, Fern pulls back to safety after almost crossing the line. "Let both [sexes] be equally pure. ... Then this vexed question would be settled," she urges at the end of her plea for fallen women.[50]

Fern uses many of the same techniques of oscillation between contrasting tones and poses in articles that playfully flirt with challenging gender roles. For example, "Family Jars" (*True Flag*, January 10, 1852) shows what happens when a wife punctures her husband's claim that "women had little or nothing to do" compared to the "responsibilities of a man of business."[51] Proposing that they exchange jobs for one day, the wife expertly tends the shop while her husband scorches the toast, boils over the coffee, and struggles in vain to keep the children out of mischief as they squall for their breakfast (222). By noon, the husband is "ready to acknowledge his mistake," but the wife holds him to their "bargain" for a full day's trial. As a result, he retreats to a bar and, unable to face his wife's wrath, simply absconds, leaving her to "the glorious independence of a '*California widow*'" (223). The sketch's sobering ending reveals the conservative message lurking behind the fun Fern allows women readers to enjoy at men's expense. Yes, the job of housewife and mother is much harder than men think—and yes, women are more capable of doing men's work than men are of doing women's—Fern agrees, yet she also implies that the roles of wife and mother are rooted in nature and that women violate them at their peril.

A pair of articles titled "A Law More Nice than Just" (*New York Ledger*, July 10 and 17, 1858) further illustrates Fern's skillful balancing act as she simultaneously rebels against and bows to rules restricting women's freedom. The law in question, "nice" in the sense of "punctilious," forbids women to wear men's apparel on pain of arrest. Pondering the law's rationale in the first article, Fern suggests that it serves to confine women to the home—since they must not walk abroad without male escorts—and to trap them in garments that impede their movements.[52] Fern decides to challenge the law by dressing in her husband's clothes to go out for a walk in the rain with him. Despite her husband's guffaws at her efforts to fit a stout female body into trousers in which "everything seems to be narrow where it ought to be broad," Fern revels in the "delicious freedom of that walk" (301). She specifies: "No skirts to hold up, or to draggle their wet folds against my ankles; no stifling vail flapping in my face, and blinding my eyes" (301), no fears "lest, in an unguarded moment, her calves should become visible to some one of those rainy-day philanthropists who are interested in the public study of female anatomy" (300). Yet Fern never reports acting on the determination she announces at the end of the first article: to order "a nicely-fitting suit of my own to wear rainy evenings" (301).

Instead, she opens the second installment with the assertion: "After all, having tried it, I affirm, that nothing reconciles a woman quicker to her femininity, than an experiment in male apparel."[53] Throughout this sequel, Fern vacillates between contrary positions—on the one hand that a woman "should not be forbidden by law to adopt" male attire (a position she immediately qualifies with the words "when necessity requires"), on the other hand that women should embrace, not transgress, their femininity (302). Male apparel would enable her "to pick up contraband bits of science in a Medical Museum, forbidden to crinoline," Fern concedes, hinting that such institutions ought to be opened to women regardless, and to "hold conversations with intelligent men, who supposing you to be a man, consequently talk sense to you" (303). Male apparel would also enable her "to climb and wade, and tramp about, without giving a thought to [her] clothes" (303). Still,

Fern rejects whatever makes her look unfeminine. "I hate a Bloomer [the dress reform invented by women's rights advocates] ... words are weak to say how much; I hate myself as much in a man's dress" (303). Tellingly, Fern conjures up a female rather than a male adversary to blame for her predicament: the "cross old termagant" Miss Nancy (a spinster version of Mrs. Grundy), whose "uplifted forefinger and ... pursed-up mouth" cow her into conformity (304). Once again, she caters to her readers' rebellious fantasies but stops well short of endorsing them.

Thanks to both her tightrope dance on the edge of propriety and her pungent wit, Fern dwarfed her more radical contemporaries in popularity. Her column in the *Ledger*, which she continued to write even on her deathbed in 1872, enjoyed a readership of 400,000 by the end of her life, and the books into which she collected her articles—among them two series of *Fern Leaves from Fanny's Portfolio* (1853, 1854)—sold as many as 70,000 copies each, far outstripping *Letters from New-York*.[54]

Much as they contributed to shaping American literary journalism in the antebellum era, Whitman, Child, Fuller, Douglass, and Fern disappeared from the genre's history. Whitman attained canonical status as a poet, but his journalism lay forgotten for most of the twentieth century. African American and Communist scholars kept Douglass's writings alive, but the rediscovery and canonization of his corpus by the (white) literary establishment did not occur until well into the 1980s. Fuller remained a ghostly—and caricatured—presence in the fiction of Nathaniel Hawthorne and Henry James and the reminiscences of Ralph Waldo Emerson, but her writings underwent a long eclipse, from which they only began to emerge in the mid-1970s.[55] Child and Fern suffered an even more complete erasure until reintroduced to the public in the mid-1980s, during the reconstruction of the American literary canon that also resurrected Douglass and Fuller.

Nevertheless, once we recognize these five writers as pioneers of a literary journalism oriented toward enlisting readers in the fight for social justice, we can discern continuities between them and later journalists who carried forward similar struggles, even if the pared-down style of the twentieth century differs from the ornamental mode of the nineteenth. Writing in the abolitionist tradition of Douglass and Child, for example, but moving back and forth between poetry and journalism, as did Whitman; using a vernacular spiced with humor, as did Fern; and conjuring up theatrical scenes, as did Fuller, Langston Hughes mercilessly exposed the contradictions between America's democratic pretensions and its white supremacist practices.[56] At the same time, Hughes, like Douglass and Child, and like the Whitman of "Song of Myself," articulated an all-encompassing vision of American democracy more relevant than ever today. We can perceive an analogous link between Fuller's dispatches on the Italian revolution of 1848 and the war correspondence of Agnes Smedley, who covered the Chinese Communist revolution of the 1930s and 1940s with the same passionate engagement, the same conviction that she was witnessing the dawn of a new era.[57] Like Whitman, Child, Fuller, and Fern, moreover, Smedley sympathetically portrayed the victims of America's unjust prison system, though from the perspective of a cellmate rather than of an outsider.[58] Finally, we can see affinities between Child's vignettes of homeless paupers in *Letters from New-York* and Meridel Le Sueur's 1930s sketches of starving women in breadlines and employment offices.[59] Equally committed to putting human faces on the poor, situating themselves among their subjects, and inducing their readers to place themselves in the shoes of society's outcasts, Child and, later, Le Sueur developed types of reportage comparably suited to achieving these aims. In sum, rescuing antebellum literary journalism from oblivion and setting it in its historical context enables us to recover and trace the roots of its neglected successors in a subgenre of literary journalism that serves to champion progressive causes.

Notes

1. The inclusion of a chapter on antebellum literary journalism in the present volume indicates a departure from the earlier view, represented by John C. Hartsock in *A History of American Literary Journalism: The Emergence of a Modern Narrative Form* (2, 16). Hartsock's subtitle also reflects a narrower definition of literary journalism than what I will be offering in this essay, which considers many more literary techniques than narrative form. Mark Canada, in *Literature and Journalism in Antebellum America: Thoreau, Stowe and Their Contemporaries Respond to the Rise of the Commercial Press*, distinguishes between literature and journalism, rather than discussing literary journalism, but provides brief treatments of Fuller, Fern, Douglass, and Whitman.
2. This apt phrase is Joyce W. Warren's, from her introduction to *"Ruth Hall" and Other Writings* (xxvii).
3. For an account of Child's journalistic apprenticeship, see Karcher, *First Woman*, 117–20. For studies and collections of Whitman's journalism, see Bergman, introduction to *The Journalism*; Noverr and Stacy, "Walt Whitman's Journalism Career."
4. Child, *Letters from New-York*, 63–69 (Letter 15). Child mentions the "editor of the Aurora" on 68, and Bruce Mills identifies him as Whitman on 226n13.
5. See Child, *Letters from New-York*, Letters 1, 6, 7, 29, and 36 for Child's descriptions of New York's vendors, the Battery, a Jewish synagogue, Greenwood Cemetery, the reform-school-like orphanage of Long Island Farms, and Barnum's American Museum. See the articles "Greenwood Cemetery" (165–68), "Life in a New York Market" (189–92), "A Peep at the Israelites" (196–98), and "A Visit to Greenwood Cemetery" (212–14) in *Walt Whitman's Selected Journalism*. Whitman's "An Hour in a Balcony" mentions Barnum's American Museum (193).
6. Noverr and Stacy, "Walt Whitman's Journalism Career," xxxi, xxxiii.
7. Noverr and Stacy, xvi.
8. Whitman, "Life in New York," 187. Page references in the paragraph are to this source.
9. Fishkin, *From Fact to Fiction*, 13–51, especially 17 and 33; Bergman, introduction to *The Journalism*, lxx; Stacy, *Walt Whitman's Multitudes*, 56–59; Noverr and Stacy, "Walt Whitman's Journalism Career," xii, xvi, xxiv, xxix, xxxi, xxxiii.
10. See the long catalog in stanza 15 of "Song of Myself" that ends "And of these one and all I weave the song of myself."
11. Whitman, "Dialogue," 66. Page references in the paragraph are to this source.
12. Whitman, "Scenes," 96. Page references in the paragraph are to this source.
13. Noverr and Stacy, "Walt Whitman's Journalism Career," xi. See also Fishkin, *From Fact to Fiction*, 23: "The nineteen or so highly distinctive pieces [Whitman] wrote for the *Aurora* were outnumbered three to one by some sixty-five conventional ones."
14. Whitman, "Prohibition of Colored Persons," 52.
15. Whitman, "About China."
16. Whitman, *Journalism*, 115, quoted in Noverr and Stacy, "Walt Whitman's Journalism Career," xv.
17. For an analysis of the literary techniques Child used in her editorials, see Karcher, *First Woman*, 274–75. For fine analyses of Letters from New-York, see Mills, introduction to *Letters from New-York*; Roberts, "'Public Heart'"; Foster, "Grotesque Sympathy"; Greiman, "'Hangman's Accomplice.'" For an especially original analysis of *Letters from New-York* as a genre of epistolary journalism indebted to George Sand's *Lettres d'un voyageur*, see Avallone, "'My Twin Sister.'"
18. For a more extensive discussion and the sources of the quotations from Child's contemporaries, see Karcher, *First Woman*, 300–301, 687nn21–22.
19. Child, *Letters from New-York*, 50 (Letter 11).
20. Child, 114 (Letter 26).
21. Child, 56 (Letter 13).
22. "Letter from the Editor," November 2, 1841, written from Northampton, MA, and published in the *National Anti-Slavery Standard* on November 11. Child later incorporated this paragraph, slightly reworded, into Letter 28 of *Letters from New York, Second Series* (257).
23. Child, *Letters from New-York*, 9.
24. Child, 10.
25. Child, 59–60. Page references in the paragraph are to this source.
26. Child, 127. Page references in the paragraph are to this source.
27. Karcher, *First Woman*, 273, 306, 309, 681n27.
28. Higginson, "Lydia Maria Child," 127–28.
29. For the most complete edition of Fuller's articles in the *Tribune* during her New York phase, see Bean and Myerson, *Margaret Fuller*. "What Fits a Man to Be a Voter?" is on 386–89. For a more positive evaluation of Fuller's New York journalism, see Steele, *Transfiguring America*.

30 Magdalena Nerio similarly argues that Fuller's journalism from Europe deserves more attention, but she examines it under the rubric of travel writing rather than literary journalism ("Transcendentalist Abroad"). Leslie E. Eckel uses the term "conversational journalism" instead ("Margaret Fuller's Conversational Journalism"). Many other scholars agree that Fuller's dispatches from Europe constitute her best writing, though they apply different terms to this body of work. See, for example, the introduction by Larry J. Reynolds and Susan Belasco Smith to their superb edition of Margaret Fuller's *"These Sad but Glorious Days"* (2) and the essays collected in Charles Capper and Cristina Giorcelli's *Margaret Fuller*. See also Bailey, "Margaret Fuller's *New-York Tribune* Dispatches."

31 Fuller, *"These Sad but Glorious Days,"* 228. Page references in the paragraph are to this source.

32 Fuller, 232.

33 Fuller, 240.

34 Fuller, 298. Page references in the paragraph are to this source.

35 Fuller, 322.

36 Fuller's travels in England and Scotland are briefly described in Reynolds and Smith's introduction to *"These Sad but Glorious Days."* Readers can also consult any of the numerous recent biographies of Fuller. For Douglass's 1846 travels, see McFeely, *Frederick Douglass*, chaps. 11 and 12.

37 Douglass, "Our Paper," 1:281–82. Douglass's editorials for the *North Star* are available both through Accessible Archives (www.accessible.com), although the transcriptions are not always accurate, and in *The Life and Writings of Frederick Douglass*.

38 Douglass, "Lecture on Slavery," 2:135.

39 See chapter 7 of Douglass's 1845 *Narrative* for his account of finding and studying *The Columbian Orator* and chapter 10 on the Sabbath school he held at St. Michael's for his fellow slaves. Douglass told the story of his life in his speeches long before committing it to print in the *Narrative*; thus, the *Narrative*, too, is written in an oratorical style and contains many examples of parataxis and antithesis.

40 Fishkin and Peterson, "'We Hold These Truths,'" 191–92. This excellent article remains the only rhetorical or stylistic analysis of Douglass's journalism.

41 Douglass, "Blood of the Slave," 1:344. Page references in the paragraph are to this source.

42 Douglass, "Weekly Review of Congress," 2:110. Page references in the paragraph are to this source.

43 Douglass, *Life and Writings*, 5:206. The additional page reference in the paragraph is to this source.

44 Joyce W. Warren's *"Ruth Hall" and Other Writings* reprints a large selection of Fern's articles in these papers. All the articles quoted below are from Warren's edition.

45 For Fern's review of *Leaves of Grass* in the *New York Ledger*, May 10, 1856, see Fern, *"Ruth Hall" and Other Writings*, 274–77. On Fern's relationship with Whitman, which soured after he failed to repay a debt, see Warren, *Fanny Fern*, 160–78.

46 Fuller's report, titled "Our City Charities," is reprinted in Bean and Myerson, *Margaret Fuller*, 98–104.

47 Fern, "Blackwell's Island," 304–05.

48 Fern, "Blackwell's Island No. 3," 306–07.

49 Fern, 308.

50 Fern, 309. For other analyses of Fern's rhetoric that focus on the techniques Fern used to position herself on controversial questions so as to appeal to a broad audience without forfeiting her popularity, see Wright, "'Joking Isn't Safe'"; Brewster, "Trading on the Exploited."

51 Fern, "Family Jars," 221. Page references in the paragraph are to this source.

52 Fern, "Law More Nice than Just," 300. Page references in the paragraph are to this source.

53 Fern, "Law More Nice than Just, Number II," 302. Page references in the paragraph are to this source.

54 Warren, *Fanny Fern*, 109, 147.

55 Bell Gale Chevigny initiated the recovery of Fuller's writings. Chevigny helpfully includes the comments of "Contemporaries on Fuller" at every stage of her career, including comments by Hawthorne, Emerson, and James. Zenobia in Hawthorne's *The Blithedale Romance* (1852) has long been recognized as a portrayal of Fuller. For an extensive study of the ways Hawthorne's fiction reflects his relationship with Fuller, see Mitchell, *Hawthorne's Fuller Mystery*. Fuller's specter hovers more distantly over James's *The Bostonians* (1886) and *The Princess Casamassima* (1886), and as Chevigny writes, "It is tempting to see Margaret Fuller lightly veiled in any number of Henry James's characters" (*Woman and the Myth*, 420). For more recent discussions of Fuller and James, see Rowe, "Swept Away"; Giorcelli, "Humbug."

56 See De Santis, *Langston Hughes*. I thank Roberta Maguire for directing my attention to this excellent collection of Hughes's literary journalism.

57 Agnes Smedley is best known for her autobiographical novel *Daughter of Earth* (1929), which became a staple of women's studies courses after its reissue by Feminist Press in 1973. Smedley's war correspondence from China is collected in her *China Correspondent*, originally titled *Battle Hymn of China* (1943), and

in *Portraits of Chinese Women in Revolution*. For the most complete account of Smedley's activities in China, see Price, *Lives of Agnes Smedley*, chaps. 8–15.
58 Smedley's first foray into journalism was a series of articles in 1920 for the *New York Call* titled "Cell-Mates."
59 On Meridel Le Sueur's literary journalism, see Don Dingledine's Chapter 8 of this volume. The best collection of it is in Le Sueur, *Ripening*.

Bibliography

Avallone, Charlene. "'My Twin Sister': George Sand, Lydia Maria Child, and the Epistolary Journalistic Essay." *George Sand Studies* 31 (2012): 31–50.

Bailey, Brigitte. "Margaret Fuller's *New-York Tribune* Dispatches from Great Britain: Modern Geography and the Print Culture of Reform." In *Transatlantic Women: Nineteenth-Century Women Writers and Great Britain*, edited by Beth L. Lueck, Brigitte Bailey, and Lucinda L. Damon-Bach, 49–70. Durham, NH: University of New Hampshire Press, 2012.

Bean, Judith Mattson, and Joel Myerson, eds. *Margaret Fuller, Critic: Writings from the "New-York Tribune," 1844–1846*. New York: Columbia University Press, 2000.

Bergman, Herbert. Introduction to *The Journalism*, by Walt Whitman, xli–lxx. Vol. 1, *1834–1846*, edited by Herbert Bergman, Douglas A. Noverr, and Edward J. Recchia. The Collected Writings of Walt Whitman. New York: Peter Lang, 1998.

Brewster, Cori. "Trading on the Exploited: Fanny Fern and the Marketplace Rhetoric of Social Justice." In *Popular Nineteenth-Century American Women Writers and the Literary Marketplace*, edited by Earl Yarington and Mary De Jong, 236–49. Newcastle, UK: Cambridge Scholars Publishing, 2007.

Canada, Mark. *Literature and Journalism in Antebellum America: Thoreau, Stowe, and Their Contemporaries Respond to the Rise of the Commercial Press*. New York: Palgrave Macmillan, 2011.

Capper, Charles, and Cristina Giorcelli, eds. *Margaret Fuller: Transatlantic Crossings in a Revolutionary Age*. Madison, WI: University of Wisconsin Press, 2007.

Chevigny, Bell Gale. *The Woman and the Myth: Margaret Fuller's Life and Writings*. Rev. and expanded ed. Boston, MA: Northeastern University Press, 1994. First published 1976 by Feminist Press (Old Westbury, NY).

Child, Lydia Maria. *Letters from New-York*. 1843. Edited by Bruce Mills. Athens, GA: University of Georgia Press, 1998.

———. *Letters from New-York, Second Series*. New York: C. S. Francis, 1845.

De Santis, Christopher C., ed. *Langston Hughes and the "Chicago Defender": Essays on Race, Politics, and Culture, 1942–62*. Urbana, IL: University of Illinois Press, 1995.

Douglass, Frederick. "The Blood of the Slave on the Skirts of the Northern People." In Douglass, *Life and Writings*, 1:343–47. Originally published in *North Star*, November 17, 1848.

———. "Freedom's Battle at Christiana." In Douglass, *Life and Writings*, 2:204–08. Originally published in *Frederick Douglass' Paper*, September 25, 1851.

———. "Lecture on Slavery, No. 1." In Douglass, *Life and Writings*, 2:132–39. Originally delivered in Corinthian Hall, Rochester, NY, on December 1, 1850, and published in *North Star*, December 5, 1850.

———. *The Life and Writings of Frederick Douglass*. Edited by Philip S. Foner. Vols. 1, 2, and 5. New York: International Publishers, 1950.

———. *Narrative of the Life of Frederick Douglass, an American Slave, Written by Himself*. 1845. In *The Oxford Frederick Douglass Reader*, edited by William L. Andrews, 21–97. New York: Oxford University Press, 1996.

———. "Our Paper and Its Prospects." In Douglass, *Life and Writings*, 1:280–82. Originally published in *North Star*, December 3, 1847.

———. "Weekly Review of Congress." In Douglass, *Life and Writings*, 2:109–15. Originally published in *North Star*, March 15, 1850.

Eckel, Leslie E. "Margaret Fuller's Conversational Journalism: New York, London, Rome." *Arizona Quarterly* 63, no. 2 (Summer 2007): 27–50. https://doi.org/10.1353/arq.2007.0009.

Fern, Fanny. "Blackwell's Island." In Fern, *"Ruth Hall" and Other Writings*, 304–06. Originally published in *New York Ledger*, August 14, 1858.

———. "Blackwell's Island No. 3." In Fern, *"Ruth Hall" and Other Writings*, 306–09. Originally published in *New York Ledger*, August 28, 1858.

———. "Family Jars." In Fern, *"Ruth Hall" and Other Writings*, 221–23. Originally published in *True Flag*, January 10, 1852.

———. "A Law More Nice than Just." In Fern, *"Ruth Hall" and Other Writings*, 299–302. Originally published in *New York Ledger*, July 10, 1858.

———. "A Law More Nice than Just, Number II." In Fern, *"Ruth Hall" and Other Writings*, 302–4. Originally published in *New York Ledger*, July 17, 1858.

———. *"Ruth Hall" and Other Writings*. Edited by Joyce W. Warren. New Brunswick, NJ: Rutgers University Press, 1986.

Fishkin, Shelley Fisher. *From Fact to Fiction: Journalism and Imaginative Writing in America*. Baltimore, MD: Johns Hopkins University Press, 1985.

Fishkin, Shelley Fisher, and Carla L. Peterson. "'We Hold These Truths to Be Self-Evident': The Rhetoric of Frederick Douglass's Journalism." In *Frederick Douglass: New Literary and Historical Essays*, edited by Eric J. Sundquist, 189–204. New York: Cambridge University Press, 1990.

Foster, Travis M. "Grotesque Sympathy: Lydia Maria Child, White Reform, and the Embodiment of Urban Space." *ESQ: A Journal of the American Renaissance* 56, no. 1 (2010): 1–32. https://doi.org/10.1353/esq.0.0045.

Fuller, Margaret. *"These Sad but Glorious Days": Dispatches from Europe, 1846–1850*. Edited by Larry J. Reynolds and Susan Belasco Smith. New Haven, CT: Yale University Press, 1991.

Giorcelli, Cristina. "A Humbug, a Bounder, and a Dabbler: Margaret Fuller, Cristina di Belgioioso, and Christina Casamassima." In Capper and Giorcelli, *Margaret Fuller*, 195–220.

Greiman, Jennifer. "'The Hangman's Accomplice': Spectacle and Complicity in Lydia Maria Child's New York." In *Democracy's Spectacle: Sovereignty and Public Life in Antebellum American Writing*, 121–56. New York: Fordham University Press, 2010.

Hartsock, John C. *A History of American Literary Journalism: The Emergence of a Modern Narrative Form*. Amherst, MA: University of Massachusetts Press, 2000.

Higginson, Thomas Wentworth. "Lydia Maria Child." In *Contemporaries*, 108–41. Vol. 2 of *The Writings of Thomas Wentworth Higginson*. Boston, MA: Houghton Mifflin, 1900.

Karcher, Carolyn L. *The First Woman in the Republic: A Cultural Biography of Lydia Maria Child*. Durham, NC: Duke University Press, 1994.

Le Sueur, Meridel. *Ripening: Selected Work*. Edited by Elaine Hedges. 1982. Rev. ed. Old Westbury, NY: Feminist Press, 1990.

McFeely, William S. *Frederick Douglass*. New York: W. W. Norton, 1991.

Mills, Bruce. Introduction to *Letters from New-York*, by Lydia Maria Child, ix–xxxi. Edited by Bruce Mills. Athens, GA: University of Georgia Press, 1998.

Mitchell, Thomas R. *Hawthorne's Fuller Mystery*. Amherst, MA: University of Massachusetts Press, 1998.

Nerio, Magdalena. "A Transcendentalist Abroad: Margaret Fuller's European Correspondence." *Prose Studies* 33, no. 2 (August 2011): 102–16. https://doi.org/10.1080/01440357.2011.632219.

Noverr, Douglas A., and Jason Stacy. "Walt Whitman's Journalism Career in New York and Brooklyn." Introduction to *Walt Whitman's Selected Journalism*, by Walt Whitman, xi–xxxvi. Edited by Douglas A. Noverr and Jason Stacy. Iowa City, IA: University of Iowa Press, 2014.

Price, Ruth. *The Lives of Agnes Smedley*. New York: Oxford University Press, 2005.

Reynolds, Larry J., and Susan Belasco Smith. Introduction to *"These Sad but Glorious Days": Dispatches from Europe, 1846–1850*, by Margaret Fuller, 1–35. Edited by Larry J. Reynolds and Susan Belasco Smith. New Haven, CT: Yale University Press, 1991.

Roberts, Heather. "'The Public Heart': Urban Life and the Politics of Sympathy in Lydia Maria Child's Letters from New York." *American Literature* 76, no. 4 (December 2004): 749–75. https://doi.org/10.1215/00029831-76-4-749.

Rowe, John Carlos. "Swept Away: Henry James, Margaret Fuller, and 'The Last of the Valerii.'" In *The Other Henry James*, 38–55. Durham, NC: Duke University Press, 1998.

Smedley, Agnes. *China Correspondent [Battle Hymn of China]*. 1943. London: Pandora Press, 1984.

———. *Daughter of Earth*. 1929. Old Westbury, NY: Feminist Press, 1973.

———. *Portraits of Chinese Women in Revolution*. Edited by Jan MacKinnon and Steve MacKinnon. Old Westbury, NY: Feminist Press, 1976.

Stacy, Jason. *Walt Whitman's Multitudes: Labor Reform and Persona in Whitman's Journalism and the First "Leaves of Grass," 1840–1855*. New York: Peter Lang, 2008.

Steele, Jeffrey. *Transfiguring America: Myth, Ideology, and Mourning in Margaret Fuller's Writing*. Columbia, MI: University of Missouri Press, 2001.

Warren, Joyce W. *Fanny Fern: An Independent Woman*. New Brunswick, NJ: Rutgers University Press, 1992.

———. Introduction to *"Ruth Hall" and Other Writings*, by Fanny Fern, ix–xxxix. Edited by Joyce W. Warren. New Brunswick, NJ: Rutgers University Press, 1986.

Whitman, Walt. "About China, as Relates to Itself and to Us." In Whitman, *Walt Whitman's Selected Journalism*, 54–57. Originally published in *Brooklyn Daily Times*, June 12, 1858.

———. "A Dialogue by Walter Whitman." In Whitman, *Walt Whitman's Selected Journalism*, 66–72. Originally published in *United States Magazine and Democratic Review*, November 1845.

———. *The Journalism*. Vol. 1, *1834–1846*, edited by Herbert Bergman, Douglas A. Noverr, and Edward J. Recchia. The Collected Writings of Walt Whitman. New York: Peter Lang, 1998.

———. "Life in New York." In Whitman, *Walt Whitman's Selected Journalism*, 187–88. Originally published in *New York Aurora*, March 14, 1842.

———. "Prohibition of Colored Persons." In Whitman, *Walt Whitman's Selected Journalism*, 51–53. Originally published in *Brooklyn Daily Times*, May 6, 1858.

———. "Scenes in a Police Justice's Court Room." In Whitman, *Walt Whitman's Selected Journalism*, 94–96. Originally published in *Brooklyn Daily Times*, September 9, 1857.

———. "Song of Myself." 1892 version. www.poetryfoundation.org/poems/45477/song-of-myself-1892-version.

———. *Walt Whitman's Selected Journalism*. Edited by Douglas A. Noverr and Jason Stacy. Iowa City, IA: University of Iowa Press, 2014.

Wright, Elizabethada A. "'Joking Isn't Safe': Fanny Fern, Irony, and Signifyin(g)." *Rhetoric Society Quarterly* 31, no. 2 (Spring 2001): 91–111. https://doi.org/10.1080/02773940109391201.

3

LITERARY JOURNALISM IN TRANSITION

The Early Memoirs of William Grimes, Mattie Jackson, and Nicholas Said

Jessie Lafrance Dunbar and Barbara McCaskill

During the nineteenth century, newspapers, journals, and other periodicals kept the American slavery question at the forefront of intellectual and popular conversations. Central to this project was the intervention of the voices of formerly enslaved African Americans, of those who had experienced firsthand the unrequited labor, separations from and sale of loved ones, and psychological and physical violence, all of which had made the institution of slavery an affront to humanity. Before the Civil War, the first-person accounts of former bondsmen and bondswomen were published in both African American and African Canadian newspapers and periodicals—for example, in New York's *Freedom's Journal* (1827–29), the first African American newspaper; in Philadelphia's long-running *A. M. E. Christian Recorder* (founded 1852); and in Ontario's *Voice of the Fugitive* (1851–54) and *Provincial Freeman* (1854–57) published by and for Canada West's fugitive slave settlements. Edited by African Americans and circulated among cosmopolitan, Afro-Diasporic subscribers, such productions participated in defining terms of citizenship and in forming communities. They made visible valuable information about employers, businesses, housing and land, places of worship, and essential institutions and people for surviving and thriving in freedom; they facilitated the exchange of advice about manners, self-help, courtship, marriage, raising families, and practicing religion; and they galvanized an international citizenry behind the antislavery cause. The collective biographies of early African American editors and journalists published by Irvine Garland Penn, Mrs. N. F. Mossell (Gertrude Emily Hicks Bustill), and Penelope L. Bullock, and recent studies of nineteenth-century African American newspapers, journals, and magazines by Benjamin Fagan, Eric Gardner, and Noliwe M. Rooks underscore how a variety of serial productions galvanized the mobile and heterogeneous African American community to take up such goals as respectability, wealth building, suffrage, and liberation.[1]

Scholars including Roberta S. Maguire, Charles A. Simmons, and John J. Pauly have noted how African Americans writing literary journalism in both the nineteenth and twentieth centuries aligned news reportage and a powerful imperative to advocate for the oppressed, disenfranchised, and silenced with critical, incisive interpretation or opinion.[2] Such critiques were delivered, as Maguire writes, via "factual writing of contemporary relevance that employs a range of literary techniques."[3] This essay pivots from thinking about the emergence of African Americans' literary journalism primarily in the early black press and instead focuses upon its early and varied interplay with, and ultimate appearance in, the mainstream press—in commercial and literary productions published primarily about and for white readers and audiences in the nineteenth-century United States. How did the first-person memoirs of three African Americans—William Grimes (pub. 1855), Mattie Jackson (pub. 1866), and Nicholas Said (pub. 1867)—intervene in the climate of mainstream journalism in which, before the Civil War, notices for the capture of runaways often appeared and, afterward, readers expressed anxieties about the prospective economic and educational burdens that over four million freedpeople imposed?

In resistance to ads, reportage, letters, and opinion pieces that dehumanized people of African descent, distorted their culture, and dismissed their aspirations, the memoirs of Grimes, Jackson, and Said participated in the slave narrative tradition. By examining their individual and distinctive arcs from servitude to freedom, they laid claim to the slave narratives' important themes of humanity and citizenship, and they lobbied for opportunities for themselves and their families and communities. Operating outside of early African American newspapers, Grimes's and Jackson's autobiographical works also worked in tandem with the black press's projects of supporting antislavery and advocating for citizenship, first by critiquing mainstream northern and southern newspapers that informed them (Grimes's *Life*) and, second, by appropriating journalistic elements of mainstream American newspapers in order to express their individual and family stories (Jackson's *Story*). Said's shortened autobiographical sketch, finally, appeared within the actual mainstream press environment as part of his post-Reconstruction black political project. Taken together, these three memoirs demonstrate a remarkable evolution. They moved from contending against and altering the mainstream press environment to embracing and engaging its themes and forms as a platform for antiracist, educational, democratic ideas.

In his 1855 narrative, which reprinted and updated his initial 1825 version, William Grimes (1784–1865), a native of Jefferson's Virginia, indirectly attacked and unpacked antebellum southern newspapers' narrow and stereotypical accounts of black bodies, whether insurgent or tractable.[4] In the 1825 edition of his *Life*, which was the first slave narrative published in the United States, Grimes introduced a style that was unusual in the nineteenth-century press yet would become a dominant convention of the slave narrative genre.[5] He wrote in a "singular, colloquial, and candid" voice, as William L. Andrews describes it, one that would come to characterize the form.[6] This candor and directness would become shorthand for the authenticity and facticity of the slave narrators' testimonies, for "the unvarnished truth"[7] of their accounts that pushed against published deceptions and smokescreens describing the benignity and orderliness of southern slavery. The 1855 edition continued this tradition by questioning reportage in both southern and northern newspapers that subscribed to the inferiority of enslaved African Americans and, to add insult to injury, that conveyed this meaning based on ostensibly objective and neutral perspectives.

Mattie Jackson (1847–1910), in her turn, crafted a postbellum memoir set in the American West and inspired by the forms and functions of mainstream newspapers. As she discussed her life in slavery by including local articles and editorial correspondence, she also disseminated Reconstruction-era themes linking education to social advancement.[8] Finally, instead of talking back to the mainstream, the abbreviated autobiographical sketch of the fugitive Nicholas Said (1836–82) appeared within it. Published in the *Atlantic Monthly*, a literary and cultural journal that, according to Sherry Lee Linkon, had made abolition "the only strongly defined political position [it] ever took"[9] (it welcomed the work of such opponents to slavery as Ralph Waldo Emerson, Thomas Wentworth Higginson, Harriet Beecher Stowe, and Frederick Douglass),[10] Said's memoir highlighted his itinerancy in eastern and western Europe in order to both embrace and critique American democratic ideals.[11]

Grimes initially printed his *Life* after the Revolutionary War, when the colonies had achieved their independence from the British monarchy, and he revised and republished it in 1855. Born in slavery in King George County, Virginia, he was passed from owner to owner. Eleven masters held him in all. His final home in bondage was Savannah, Georgia, then one of the busiest American ports of call and a rival to Charleston and New Orleans as a Deep South center for the maritime transport and exchange of cotton, rice, indigo, and black bodies up the coastal US or down to the Caribbean. The port of Savannah was also his means of escape from perpetual servitude. Aided and abetted by a sympathetic crew, he fled as a stowaway via *The Casket* bound with cotton for New York. He married, raised children, settled into business in Connecticut, and published two versions of his narrative. His enslavement returned to haunt him when one of his former Savannah masters, Francis Harvey Welman, tracked him down and demanded that he purchase his freedom or return to the South in chains. Selling his home and land, Grimes raised $500 to buy his liberation but bankrupted himself in the process.[12]

Grimes avowed to having "learned to read and write pretty well" by the time he assembled his memories and self-published his story (103). His murkiness and stealth regarding how, when, from whom, and under what circumstances he obtained literacy is a thoroughly understandable evasion shared by many formerly enslaved authors, since they endeavored to protect black and white allies still in the South and to avoid alerting slaveholders to the methods they used to acquire this powerful tool of liberation. One of Grimes's brothers, whom his master sent to school, may have secretly taught him the rudiments of literacy (31). In an early essay on Grimes's 1825 *Life*, the Hampton University English professor Charles H. Nichols stated that Grimes had "gained the rudiments of an education after his escape," and his manual employments at what is now Yale University and Yale Law School would have connected him to students and teachers who may have assisted him.[13]

What remains clear is that throughout his servitude, Grimes fortuitously obtained proximity to newspapers, presses, and journalists. One of his first duties in childhood, for example, was "to carry newspapers" from his white father (who also was his master) to the home of the physician who owned his black mother (30). Additionally, a Savannahian who purchased him in early adulthood, Philip David Woolhopter, happened to be a printer and the founding editor of the *Columbian Museum and Savannah Advertiser*. By listening to the news discussed by Woolhopter around his press, and perhaps by glimpsing various papers or collecting pages unobserved, like the character Robert Johnson in Frances E. W. Harper's *Iola Leroy* (1892),[14] Grimes also would have very likely been exposed to representations of the city's free and enslaved African Americans and their owners, which may have collided with what he knew and had endured as the realities of life in slavery. The scholar Susanna Ashton, writing about how Grimes procured knowledge of copyright practices for his *Life*, first noted that "we cannot know if he read or participated specifically in printing or binding books promoting his own bondage." What we can know, she elaborated, and "would be wise ... to consider," is how "even illiterate slaves" like Grimes would have come into contact with books, newspapers, and other printed documents through their labor in such presses as Woolhopter's.[15]

"With but few remarks," he writes in the 1855 edition of his *Life*, "I endeavor to give my readers *but a faint* representation of the hard treatment, ill usage, and horrid abuse the poor slave experiences while groaning under the yoke of bondage" (58; emphasis added). In this second printing of his memoir, which reproduces the text of his first with an additional conclusion of updated information about travels in the north and changes in family, Grimes pushes back against the negativity or outright invisibility assigned to African Americans in mainstream southern papers by employing a direct reportage laced with irony and intended to expose the humanity that the slaveholders attempted to obliterate both in rhetoric and practice. This technique refuted papered-over and deceptive reports of the inhumanity of African Americans in bondage, and it placed pressure on his readers outside of the South to confront the conditions of bondage hidden from them in white southerners' reportage. Although Grimes is not yet writing directly in the newspapers in 1855, he is writing back *to* them in a direct, fact-centric style that anticipates the literary journalism mid-nineteenth-century black writers such as Frederick Douglass and Harriet Jacobs would employ in the stories of their lives within such papers.

To undermine and counter newspaper stories that claim otherwise, Grimes's 1855 *Life*, like the 1825 edition, mobilizes the frank tone and granular details that characterize literary journalism to present the unadulterated, arduous conditions of plantation slavery. Such quantifications as the number of "hands" who have slipped away during the day's labors from a work crew or the quota exacted from one man or woman of land plowed or harvest reaped reveal the actual desperation and tedium of the enslaved. One specific example of this literary treatment is his discussion of the entrepreneurial strategy he devised for purchasing extra food in order to supplement a near-starvation diet imposed by his owner. He had planted "a small crop of rice" in a hidden parcel of land, and "when not being observed by the driver, [he would] slip in and do a little at it." As he recalls:

> After it was in a situation to cut I reaped it and carried it to town, where I sold it for $1.25 per hundred, amounting in the whole to about $5 or $6. ... I sometimes went to town where I could procure something to eat with our common allowance, (a peck of corn per week) and have often carried on my head a bundle of wood, perhaps three miles, weighing more than one hundred pounds, which I would sell for twelve cents, in order to get a supply of necessary food.
>
> *(68)*

Grimes itemizes the lengths he will go in order to satiate his hunger, however occasional and unsatisfying those meals may be. "I sometimes could steal a little provision; and after driving my master to his plantation," he writes, "I could sometimes run into the potatoe [*sic*] house, where I could find a few of them, which I ate raw. At other times I could find a bone, not quite stripped clean" (55). He is often underfed, yet by self-starvation he boldly attempts to "clear himself from the house of bondage" and to leverage his sale from a particularly cruel master (35, 50). It is a grim game of cat and mouse that the starving Grimes instigates, his health and life hanging in the balance, while his master suspects his deception yet cannot catch him red-handed in the scheme.

Such atomized descriptions spotlight Grimes's impressive capacities for memory and mathematics, organization and order, creativity, and manipulation. Additionally, they enable his self-representation as the intellectual peer of whites deemed "more enlightened" (39), as a man possessing formidable mental powers of observation and insight. This imagery opposes how the antebellum southern press frames black men, women, and children as monetized bodies valued principally for their strength, fertility, or compliance. His intention that his readers face full-on both the mental and emotional lives of enslaved persons is a forerunner of later examples of antislavery literary journalism such as the 1863 pamphlet *What Became of the Slaves on a Georgia Plantation?* published by the *New York Tribune* reporter Mortimer Thomson, whose pen name had been "Q[ueer]. K[ritter]. Philander Doesticks, P[erfect]. B[rick]." From March 2 to 3, 1859, Thomson had posed undercover at a Savannah racetrack as a prospective buyer in order to interview African American family members slated for auction by their owner Pierce Butler during what was the nation's largest slave sale.[16]

In the conclusion of the revised version of his memoir, Grimes maintains the same bittersweet tone about the limitations of his freedom as he had in 1825, when he had faced the world "destitute of property," but "no beggar," after paying his old master for his freedom.[17] This second time around, Grimes also reveals that he has maintained independence although impecunious. Finally he has become a visible presence in the New England press. After "nearly thirty years" in that part of the US, he has become "as the newspapers say, 'a fixed institution.'" He has "advertised in the public papers" to procure for himself a "perfect" copy of his 1825 memoir (104).

Additionally, to attract patrons to his New Haven, Connecticut, barbershop, he has placed "an advertisement in the paper, headed with these lines":

> Old Grimes is not dead.
> But you may see him more,
> Cleaning coats and shaving heads,
> Just as before.
> Though long old Grimes has slept,
> He only sleeps to wake;
> And those who thought him dead and gone,
> Now laugh at their mistake.
>
> (107)

In ballad-like verses, Grimes reinvents himself from a silent enslaved subject to a quietly proud Everyman hard at work earning food for the family table and joining in laughter his mirthful voice to those of his readers. Although it is uncertain that he penned these lines, they function as a kind of *ars poetica*, or as poetic encapsulation, of his work ethic and hardscrabble values of resilience, endurance, and humor. This jocular presentation of Grimes as an African American version of Washington Irving's Rip Van Winkle, as one who "has slept" yet "only sleeps to wake," gestures figuratively to his resurrection from the bondage and illiteracy that had stunted him to the experience of an autonomous, literate life, even though he suffers the indignities and uncertainties of poverty in old age. This poem's practical and down-to-earth depiction of Grimes is an apt conclusion to a memoir that has performed the work of literary journalism.

Informed and published by the Lawrence, Massachusetts, *Sentinel* one year after the Civil War, the memoir of Mattie J. Jackson offers a stark presentation of her resistance to captivity and hope for liberation, which is inspired and encouraged by the information she accesses in mainstream papers. *The Story of Mattie J. Jackson; Her Parentage—Experience of Eighteen Years in Slavery—Incidents during the War—Her Escape from Slavery. A True Story* (1866) provides a glimpse of slavery in St. Louis, Missouri, on the eve of the Confederacy's surrender. Because Jackson and her mother can read "well enough to make out the news in the papers" (10), they take full advantage of the newspapers Union soldiers tossed over plantation fences for the intended consumption of literate African Americans like themselves, who can furtively pass along information about Union victories and Confederate defeats by word of mouth to those in the enslaved community who are illiterate.

While Grimes places his memoir in conversation with mainstream papers, Jackson literally absorbs them, incorporating and repurposing actual news reportage directly into her life writing to demonstrate what DoVeanna S. Fulton identifies as "the discursive authority of a nineteenth-century black woman."[18] Her incorporation of these materials into her daily interactions with her mistress underscores a point made in Frederick Douglass's renowned 1845 *Narrative*. One of the more resonant chapters in Douglass's *Narrative* occurs when his master, Mr. Auld, scolds his wife for teaching Douglass to read. Auld hints at his worry that Douglass plans to learn to read and write as a prelude to escape. At the very least, Auld asserts, literacy will make Douglass "unfit to be a slave" and "discontented and unhappy."[19] Jackson and her mother, Ellen Turner Jackson, similarly read papers against their owners' intentions.[20] Defiantly, Jackson sits up nights reading the local papers for updates on the war's progress. She spends her days wielding the information she gathers as a weapon against her mistress.

An example of this technique occurs when she and her mother, Ellen, use information from the press to torment their white mistress, Mrs. Lewis ("Mrs. L." in the narrative), and to strike terror in her heart about a possible Union victory takeover of the outnumbered and outgunned

Confederates based at nearby Camp Jackson, named for Missouri's then governor who harbored Rebel sentiments. Jackson writes:

> I told my mistress that the Union soldiers were coming to take the camp. She replied that it was false, that it was General Kelly coming to re-enforce [sic] Gen. Frost. In a few moments the alarm was heard. I told Mrs. L. the Unionists had fired upon the rebels. She replied it was only the salute of Gen. Kelley [sic]. At night her husband came home with the news that Camp Jackson was taken and all the soldiers prisoners. Mrs. Lewis asked how the Union soldiers could take seven hundred men when they only numbered the same. Mr. L. replied they had seven thousand. She was much astonished, and cast her eye around to us for fear we might hear her.
>
> *(10)*

Here Jackson ratifies the reportage of the conventional press with her description, both factual and cutting, of what has come to be known as the Camp Jackson Affair of May 10, 1861. When Governor Claiborne Fox Jackson refused President Abraham Lincoln's command to send troops to support the Union's fight against the seceding states, it was obvious that his state of Missouri had determined to join the Confederates in battle. Jackson ordered the Missouri Volunteers, a militia comprising roughly eight hundred troops, to defend Camp Jackson. In response, Captain Nathaniel Lyon rallied volunteer Union troops to surround the camp. The commander of the Missouri Volunteer Militia, General Daniel M. Frost, surrendered, and Lyon's men transported the treasonous militiamen to prison.[21]

Beyond the historical importance of Jackson's recollection of the incident, this passage underscores a marked shift in the relationship between slave and mistress. Readers encounter a mistress expressing fear, speaking in whispers, plagued by paranoia, and fearful for the safety of her home and the security of her possessions. This cowering figure is a far cry from the slave narratives' examples of autocratic, controlling, and husband-emasculating white women such as Mrs. Flint in Harriet Jacobs's famous memoir[22] who have tormented enslaved African American women throughout the literary tradition. Jackson had acquired only a rudimentary degree of literacy, yet she demonstrates that this limitation does not diminish her ability to use the papers to obtain a psychological advantage in relation to Mrs. L. and to subvert the relationship between an owner and the human being she has claimed as property. Just as African American journalists had played activist roles in protesting racial violence against individuals and groups,[23] both Mattie and her mother, Ellen, are empowered by the papers they read to stand up for themselves against their owners' psychological and physical assaults and thereby to destabilize the master-slave relationship.

In many ways this style of subversion challenges the mainstream press's "objective" reportage of events surrounding slavery by including the personal experiences of African American people who were directly impacted by those events. By 1827, when the earliest African American periodicals appeared, it was evident that their editors, like Jackson, were intent on presenting an undeniably partisan, unified front against slavery by presenting first-person accounts and historical reflections that challenged dominant narratives of blackness, whiteness, and the institution of slavery.[24]

Jackson, like Grimes, responds to ads in the papers but pivots to the African American press to do so. In her study *'Til Death or Distance Do Us Part: Love and Marriage in Early African America* (2010), Frances Smith Foster explores how newspapers were central to black communities, and she confirms how Jackson's narrative credits newspapers for advertising to and locating family members separated in slavery and by escape. It was as common for African American newspapers and periodicals to post advertisements to locate missing family members as it was for their editors to publish accounts of parties, graduations, funerals and burials, and family visits.[25] During the

Reconstruction, the papers helped recombine literate and stable African American communities in the South and West after the dislocations caused by slavery and the Civil War.[26] As an example of how such functions filtered into the slave narratives, Jackson recollects how information collected from ads supplemented news her stepfather gathered about his missing former wife and children (27).

From the mid- to late nineteenth century, Nicholas Said intervened in the *Atlantic Monthly*'s discourses of imperialism and manifest destiny by applying admirable characteristics of autonomy and nationalistic pride to the peoples of the African continent. From its inception in 1857, the *Atlantic Monthly: A Magazine of Literature, Science, Art, and Politics* appealed to highbrow readers and canon-builders and to those, as the scholar Susan Williams identifies, who were considered "authors," because they wrote imaginatively and fictively, rather than the "writers" who focused primarily on reporting on what they observed in real life.[27] The *Atlantic* did share the mainstream press's interest in privileging the perspectives of its white American readership. In its mission statement, the *Atlantic* asserted that

> while native writers will ... be mainly relied on to fill the pages of The Atlantic, they [the publishers] will not hesitate to draw from the foreign sources at their command, as occasion may require, relying rather on the competency of an author to treat a particular subject, than on any other claim whatever.[28]

The *Atlantic Monthly* reflected preoccupations with colonialism, since most of its featured authors supported imperialism and colonialism as civilizing projects and accepted western Europe and the United States as the powers most responsible and suitable for leading this endeavor. The article "British India" (1857), for example, boasted of the superiority of Great Britain's naval forces that had facilitated the creation and ensured the protection of its vast colonial holdings. Another piece, "The Financial Flurry" (1857), suggested the superiority of Westerners who marketed and valued precious metals on the African and Asian continents in relation to the "barbaric" nations on said continents who placed more value on items such as fish bones, cowries, beads, and old rags than on such priceless natural resources. G. Reynolds's "The Late Insurrection in Jamaica" (1867) is yet another instance of the colonialist themes of many of the *Atlantic Monthly*'s articles during the nineteenth century. Reynolds links what he views as untenable social and political conditions in Jamaica to a lack of formal, Westernized education. These authors unanimously agreed that people of African descent were savages and illiterates, whose wildness needed to be domesticated and whose nations were in desperate need of the civilizing influences of Europeans' taste, culture, and aesthetic standards.[29]

Absent from these discourses on national pride, Christianity, and superiority was a postcolonial counter-narrative in the *Atlantic Monthly* that explicated the *similarities* between so-called pagan religions and Christianity, between "backward" governments and Eurocentric ones, and between people of color and white western Europeans. Said's ten-page autobiographical sketch, "A Native of Bornoo" (Bornoo is present-day Sudan), published in the October 1867 *Atlantic Monthly*, in many ways aligned itself more readily with the publication's goal to "rank itself with ... that body of men which is in favor of Freedom, National Progress, and Honor, whether public or private."[30] On one hand, Said did not totally reject Western conceptions of superiority: He indeed embraced democratic systems of governance and education, which he credited as benefiting colonized Africans and Asians. On the other hand, he tempered his assessment of the West's role in facilitating African progress with an outright rejection of the rhetoric of colonialism. Furthermore, he developed a postcolonialist strategy to address African people's omission from Westernized conceptions of history and culture.[31]

Said's "A Native of Bornoo" entered into conversation with white missionaries who proclaimed that their presence in Africa was meant to civilize its nations, yet they did not educate African peoples in any actual sense. Readers familiar with the slave narrative genre would have recognized the conventional elements in his opening *apologia*, in which he begged their gentle patience in advance for "mistakes which this article will contain" (486). Like the eighteenth-century fugitive slave memoirist and "unlettered African" Olaudah Equiano, Said "never had a teacher, nor ever was at school for the purpose of acquiring the [*sic*] English" (485).

Said was similarly conversant with African American newspapers and periodicals that endeavored, as historian Hayward Farrar writes, "to present to the world that side of the Afro-American that can be had in no other way, ... to as far as possible assist in the great uplift of the people it represents."[32] Media and communications scholar Aurora Wallace goes a step further in her observation that African American editors were intent on covering "items that were ignored in the mainstream press, primarily the news, activities, and achievements" of African Americans.[33] Said addressed racist assumptions set forth by many Western European authors—for example, those asserted by one W. Winwood Reade in his May 1867 *Atlantic Monthly* article entitled "Heroes of Central Africa." Reade critiqued findings of the British national and Protestant missionary Dr. David Livingstone (1813–73)[34] and the British explorer Sir Samuel White Baker (1821–93), who was knighted for his exploration of central Africa. According to Reade, neither was deserving of accolades because of Livingstone's attempts to abolish the slave trade in Africa through missionary work and Baker's efforts to locate the source of the Nile River. "Beyond ivory, inferior rubber, inferior ebony, and scanty supply of gold," Reade asserted, the region had delivered up nothing worthy of such white men's time and energy.[35] Reade's piece highlighted an increased European interest in the African continent, even as he disregarded the people who inhabited it.

Thus, when Said offered his own *Atlantic Monthly* account of his African origins, in which he described his native Bornoo as "the most civilized part of Soodan," even though situated in the "problematic central part of Africa, so imperfectly known to the civilized nations of Europe and America," he entered, as an African among white men, an ongoing and often heated dialogue about the merits of exploration and colonialism (485).[36] Said indirectly acknowledged a presumption of subjectivity imposed upon black writers that had not been ascribed to such so-called neutral and candid observers like Reade. Harnessing the transparent subjectivity of literary journalism, as well as a nuanced approach to questions of Eastern and Western civility, Said presented himself as a more credible reporter than his white counterparts who had merely feigned objectivity.

Other parts of Said's narrative suggested that Bornoo's history was not too dissimilar from that of the United States. The "romantic history" of Bornoo, according to Said, included the assertions of the false prophet Otman Danfodio[37] (1754–1817) that Allah had ordered him to lead the Fellatah people of Bornoo in war against Sudan and that Allah had guaranteed Bornoo's victory. The duped Fellatahs believed this Macbeth-like prophecy, and as a result, Danfodio dethroned their legitimate emperor and seized power. After enduring years of humiliation under Danfodio's rule, "the [George] Washington" of Bornoo, Mohammed el Amin el Kanemy (1776–1837),[38] "undertook to liberate his country and restore her former prestige" (486).

The actual George Washington had been very outspoken on the question of religious freedom and its centrality to the strength of the Union. In a letter to the New Jerusalem Church of Baltimore, he stated "that every person may here worship God according to the dictates of his own heart."[39] In contrast, Said's vision of a Westernized Africa did not extend to "every person" by excluding Africans who converted to Christianity from Islam. After his capture by members of the Kindill tribe and his subsequent sale to Arab and Turkish slave traders, Said had been sold to Prince Mentchikoff, Minister Plenipotentiary of Russia (1789–1869?), which had resulted in his exposure to eastern and western European cultures. Russia had not participated in the African slave trade because the czars could exploit the labor of serfs, so Said had been liberated the moment he set foot on Russian soil. He left Mentchikoff to work for Prince Nicholas Petrovich Troubetzkoy (1828–1900), who forcibly converted him from Islam to Orthodox Christianity. Said's assertion that "the way I was baptized was not right, for I think that I ought to have known perfectly well the nature of the thing beforehand" (492) invited comparison between Troubetzkoy's coercion and Danfodio's deception. He indicted both the autocracy of the Russians who forced his conversion to Orthodox Christianity and the arrogance of Europeans' colonialist missions to Africa by his additional claims that only those who could read and explain its contents were permitted to handle the Koran and that it was white visitors to the African continent who had violated this injunction out of cultural ignorance and obliviousness.

By telling a history that invoked the iconic Revolutionary hero and US founding father George Washington, Said aligned himself with American readers. Like the rebellious colonials, he questioned the divine rights of monarchs. He similarly echoed the US's republican roots by debunking the notion that any uprising against a ruler was sacrilege, even one against a monarch like England's George III. By distancing himself and the majority of his fellow Bornoo citizens from the "ignorant portion" of their nation, the Fellatahs who had succumbed to the whims of the false prophet Danfodio, Said also created his own hierarchy of African cultural norms meant to resonate with the Union's political principles. A Civil War-era analog for *Atlantic Monthly* readers of Said would have been how the Northern states ideologically distanced themselves from the seceding South, in spite of the former region's complicity in the institution of slavery, its consumption of textiles and foodstuffs cultivated by enslaved African Americans, and its political concessions to the slave states such as the Missouri Compromise of 1820 and the Fugitive Slave Law of 1850. At the core of Said's invocation of Washington, the general and patriot, finally, was the notion that even though the US was a white supremacist nation in practice, it had embraced a noble democratic project, worthy of Africans' emulation, in theory.

Said tempered his critique by conceding that African nations could learn much from Westerners about the arts and sciences while maintaining their independence in government. He thus marked an important shift in colonialist discourses that imposed a totalizing characteristic of inferiority onto people of African descent. As Said traveled with Prince Troubetzkoy, indicated by the following excerpt from his *Atlantic Monthly* essay, he became preoccupied with the idea of the US as an exemplar of what is possible for African nations, should they join forces:

> About this time I began to think of the condition of Africa, my native country, how European encroachments might be stopped, and her nationalities united. I thought how powerful the United States had become since 1776, and I wondered if I were capable of persuading the kings of Soodan to send several hundred boys to learn the arts and sciences existing in civilized countries. ... I cried many times at the ignorance of my people, exposed to foreign ambition, who, however good warriors they might be, could not contend against superior weapons and tactics in the field. I prayed earnestly to be enabled to do some good to my race.
>
> *(494)*

Said's desire to return to Africa to unify the nations on that continent and stave off European encroachments extended beyond a basic longing for the familiarity of home. He and the narrative that he produced existed in a liminal space between Westernized notions that European people are global military, religious, and intellectual leaders and postcolonial counter-narratives that underscored the viability of non-European cultures.

That Said quit his Russian employer to travel to the US, not Africa, reflected the import of that current political moment. Having fought for the Union, he had likely been emboldened to visit by America's promise of equality for black people, in spite of a Reconstruction that in many ways had not yet kept that agreement and did not altogether seem committed to it. His rather unique journey might have altered the perceptions of American audiences previously persuaded to believe in the idea of African inferiority. He thus presented the US as an exemplar of what postcolonial nations could become, and he exemplified the transformative power of access to education and social mobility for those whose ancestors once had been kidnapped into bondage. His placement of these ideas in the *Atlantic Monthly*, which published both imaginative literature and news reportage, synthesized the elements of slave memoir and journalism.

Fugitive narratives like those of Grimes, Jackson, and Said marked the moments when the genres of journalism and memoir divided and intersected. They critiqued perceptions and attitudes disseminated about African Americans and people of color by publishing outside of mainstream newspapers or periodicals (Grimes and Jackson) and then ultimately within them (Said). They also diverged from the flowery style of the nineteenth-century press (Grimes and Jackson) or emulated it (Said), as it suited their specific audiences and supported their financial, educational, or political goals. All three demonstrated how African Americans of varying degrees of literacy interacted with early print culture and recognized that print productions could be tools of both individual liberation and collective participation in democracy. These features point to how the slave narratives, and subsequent fugitive slave narratives published during and after Reconstruction, have composed a nascent literary journalism that has influenced the genre's development. In a type of literary call and response, the African American presence in early American literary journalism has been entangled with the fugitive slave's narrative. At a time when African Americans could seldom express their perspectives in commercial and mainstream newspapers without being hounded by questions of veracity or hobbled by problems of illiteracy and access, these three memoirs opened necessary spaces for black voices in American journalism.

Notes

1. Penn, *Afro-American Press*; Mossell, *Work*; Bullock, *Afro-American Periodical Press*; Fagan, *Black Newspaper*; Gardner, *Black Print Unbound*; Rooks, *Ladies Pages*.
2. Maguire, "African American Literary Journalism," 10–11; Pauly, "Literary Journalism," 73–75; Simmons, *African American Press*, 20.
3. Maguire, "African American Literary Journalism," 11.
4. Grimes, *Life*. All page references to this narrative appear parenthetically within the text, and all in-text citations refer to the Oxford edition.
5. Olney, "'I Was Born.'"
6. Andrews, introduction to *Life of William Grimes*, 13. For an additional discussion of Grimes's voice, see Andrews, *To Tell a Free Story*, 77–81.
7. Fabian, *Unvarnished Truth*, 79–116.
8. Jackson, *Story*. All page references to this work appear parenthetically within the text.
9. Linkon, "Women Writers," 3.
10. On the occasion of the Civil War's sesquicentennial anniversary, the *Atlantic* published a commemorative issue featuring selections it had published by these writers that responded to or were inspired by the war and slavery (Bennet, Civil War).
11. Said, "Native of Bornoo," 485–94. All page references to this piece appear parenthetically within the text.
12. See also McCaskill and Serafini, "William Grimes."
13. Nichols, "Case of William Grimes," 553.
14. Harper, *Iola Leroy*, 7–9. Citation refers to the Penguin edition.
15. Ashton, "Slavery, Imprinted," 137, 138.
16. Thomson, *What Became?*, 1–20; Degraft-Hanson, "Unearthing the Weeping Time"; Degraft-Hanson, "Torn Asunder," 72–75.
17. Grimes, *Life*, 68.
18. Fulton, *Speaking Power*, 54.

19 Douglass, *Narrative*, 31. Citation refers to the Norton edition.
20 Fagan, *Black Newspaper*, 12.
21 Gerteis, *Civil War St. Louis*, 93–95.
22 Jacobs, *Incidents*, 17–20. Citation refers to the Belknap edition.
23 Maguire, "African American Literary Journalism," 8–14.
24 See Maguire, 10–11.
25 Foster, *Death or Distance*, xiv–xvi, 72, 112, 132.
26 Glymph, "'This Species of Property.'" For additional discussions of black southern migrants to Kansas, Missouri, and other parts West, see Painter, *Exodusters*.
27 Williams makes this distinction specifically in the context of her discussion of nineteenth-century women authors and writers. The nineteenth-century *Atlantic Monthly* issues were dominated by men's contributions, but her reminder that these labels bore different connotations at that time is nevertheless useful (*Reclaiming Authorship*).
28 Mott, "*Atlantic Monthly*," 508.
29 "British India"; "Financial Flurry"; Reynolds, "Late Insurrection in Jamaica."
30 Mott, "*Atlantic Monthly*," 499.
31 This discussion focuses on the initial, abbreviated version of Said's narrative published in the *Atlantic* in October 1867. In 1873, he published a book-length memoir titled *The Autobiography of Nicholas Said: A Native of Bornou, Eastern Soudan, Central Africa*. In 2000, Precious Rasheeda Muhammad rediscovered his book in the archives and published an edition with historical and critical analysis.
32 Farrar, *Baltimore "Afro-American*," xii.
33 Wallace, *Newspapers*, 53.
34 Livingstone was actually born and raised in Scotland. He did not immigrate to London until he was an adult and the London Missionary Society had accepted him as a member (Jeal, *Livingstone*, 19, 23).
35 Reade, "Heroes of Central Africa," 626.
36 Various examples of this type of colonialist western European rhetoric span the mid- to late nineteenth century. An example of such rhetoric is the following observation by one Rev. C. H. Richards, writing to the *American Missionary*:

> The only permanent safety for the blacks is in their intellectual and religious education. A weak race, helpless in its ignorance and corrupted by immorality, will always be kept down. The ambitious and intense desires of those who are wiser and stronger will take advantage of its weakness, and will crowd it to the wall. No legislation can prevent the working of this natural law in the struggle for prosperity. But a strong race, with vigorous, well-disciplined minds, balanced with virtue, will always hold its own in the world. ... So when the colored man shows by his deeds that he is able to do all that a white man can do, he will hold his footing of equality secure. The race is to be tested by results.
>
> *("Communications," 20)*

37 Contemporary scholars refer to him as Uthman or Usman dan Fodio.
38 He is cited by contemporary scholars most frequently as Muhammad al-Amin al-Kanemy.
39 Washington, letter to the New Jerusalem Church.

Bibliography

Andrews, William L. Introduction to *Life of William Grimes, the Runaway Slave, Brought Down to the Present Time. Written by Himself*, edited by William L. Andrews and Regina E. Mason, 3–26. New York: Oxford University Press, 2008.

———. *To Tell a Free Story: The First Century of Afro-American Autobiography, 1760–1865*. Urbana, IL: University of Illinois Press, 1986.

Ashton, Susanna. "Slavery, Imprinted: The Life and Narrative of William Grimes." In *Early African American Print Culture*, edited by Lara Langer Cohen and Jordan Alexander Stein, 127–39. Philadelphia, PA: University of Pennsylvania Press, 2012.

Bennet, James, ed. The Civil War issue, *Atlantic*, February 2012. www.theatlantic.com/magazine/toc/2012/02/.

"British India." *Atlantic Monthly: A Magazine of Literature, Art, and Politics*, November 1857, 85–93. Hathi Trust Digital Library. https://babel.hathitrust.org/cgi/pt?id=msu.31293011014515;view=1up;seq=93.

Bullock, Penelope L. *The Afro-American Periodical Press, 1838–1909*. Baton Rouge, LA: Louisiana State University Press, 1981.
DeGraft-Hanson, Kwesi. "Torn Asunder: Savannah's 'Weepin' Time' Slave Sale of 1859." In *Slavery and Freedom in Savannah*, edited by Leslie M. Harris and Daina Ramey Berry, 72–75. Athens, GA: University of Georgia Press, 2014.
———. "Unearthing the Weeping Time: Savannah's Ten Broeck Race Course and 1859 Slave Sale." *Southern Spaces: A Journal about Real and Imagined Spaces and Places of the US South and Their Global Connections* (February 18, 2010). https://southernspaces.org/2010/unearthing-weeping-time-savannahs-ten-broeck-race-course-and-1859-slave-sale/.
Douglass, Frederick. *Narrative of the Life of Frederick Douglass, an American Slave, Written by Himself*. Edited by William L. Andrews and William S. McFeely. New York: W. W. Norton, 2017. First published 1845 by the Anti-Slavery Office (Boston, MA).
Fabian, Ann. *The Unvarnished Truth: Personal Narratives in Nineteenth-Century America*. Berkeley, CA: University of California Press, 2000.
Fagan, Benjamin. *The Black Newspaper and the Chosen Nation*. Athens, GA: University of Georgia Press, 2016.
Farrar, Hayward. *The Baltimore "Afro-American," 1892–1950*. Westport, CT: Greenwood Press, 1998.
"The Financial Flurry." *Atlantic Monthly: A Magazine of Literature, Art, and Politics*, November 1857, 112–20. Hathi Trust Digital Library. https://babel.hathitrust.org/cgi/pt?id=msu.31293011014515;view=1up;seq=120.
Foster, Frances Smith. *'Til Death or Distance Do Us Part: Love and Marriage in Early African America*. New York: Oxford University Press, 2010.
Fulton, DoVeanna S. *Speaking Power: Black Feminist Orality in Women's Narratives of Slavery*. Albany, NY: State University of New York Press, 2006.
Gardner, Eric. *Black Print Unbound: The "Christian Recorder," African American Literature, and Periodical Culture*. New York: Oxford University Press, 2015.
Gerteis, Louis S. *Civil War St. Louis*. Lawrence, KS: University Press of Kansas, 2001.
Glymph, Thavolia. "'This Species of Property': Female Slave Contrabands in the Civil War." In *A Woman's War: Southern Women, Civil War, and the Confederate Legacy*, edited by Edward D. C. Campbell and Kym S. Rice, 55–71. Richmond, VA: Museum of the Confederacy; Charlottesville, VA: University of Virginia Press, 1996.
Grimes, William. *Life of William Grimes, the Runaway Slave. Written by Himself*. New York: [William Grimes], 1825. Documenting the American South, University of North Carolina at Chapel Hill Libraries. https://docsouth.unc.edu/neh/grimes25/menu.html.
———. *Life of William Grimes, the Runaway Slave, Brought Down to the Present Time. Written by Himself*. Edited by William L. Andrews and Regina E. Mason. New York: Oxford University Press, 2008. First published 1855 by the author (New Haven, CT).
Harper, Frances Ellen Watkins. *Iola Leroy, or, Shadows Uplifted*. Edited by Hollis Robbins. New York: Penguin, 2010. First published 1892 by Garrigues Brothers (Philadelphia, PA).
Jackson, Mattie J. *The Story of Mattie J. Jackson; Her Parentage—Experience of Eighteen Years in Slavery—Incidents during the War—Her Escape from Slavery. A True Story*. Lawrence, MA: Sentinel Office, 1866.
Jacobs, Harriet. *Incidents in the Life of a Slave Girl: Written by Herself. With a True Tale of Slavery by John S. Jacobs*. Edited by Jean Fagan Yellin. Cambridge, MA: Belknap Press, 2009. First published 1861 for the author (Boston, MA).
Jeal, Tim, ed. *Livingstone*. Rev. and expanded ed. New Haven, CT: Yale University Press, 2013.
Linkon, Sherry Lee. "Women Writers and the Assumption of Authority: The *Atlantic Monthly*, 1857–1898." In *In Her Own Voice: Nineteenth-Century American Women Essayists*, edited by Sherry Lee Linkon, 3–26. New York: Garland Publishing, 1997.
Maguire, Roberta. "African American Literary Journalism: Extensions and Elaborations." *Literary Journalism Studies* 5, no. 2 (Fall 2013): 8–14.
McCaskill, Barbara, and Sidonia Serafini. "William Grimes (1784–1865)." In *New Georgia Encyclopedia*. Georgia Humanities and the University of Georgia Press. Article published February 10, 2017; last edited February 20, 2017. www.georgiaencyclopedia.org/articles/arts-culture/william-grimes-1784-1865.
Mossell, Mrs. N. F. [Gertrude Bustill]. *The Work of the Afro-American Woman*. Philadelphia, PA: G. S. Ferguson., 1908.
Mott, Frank Luther. "The *Atlantic Monthly*." In *A History of American Magazines*, 493–516. Vol. 2, *1850–1865*. Cambridge, MA: Harvard University Press, 1938.
Nichols, Charles H., Jr. "The Case of William Grimes, the Runaway Slave." *William and Mary Quarterly*, 3rd ser., 8, no. 4 (October 1951): 552–60. https://doi.org/10.2307/1916125.

Olney, James. "'I Was Born': Slave Narratives: Their Status as Autobiography and as Literature." *Callaloo: A Journal of African Diaspora Arts and Letters* 20 (Winter 1984): 46–73. https://doi.org/10.2307/2930678.

Painter, Nell Irvin. *Exodusters: Black Migration to Kansas after Reconstruction.* New York: W. W. Norton, 1992.

Pauly, John J. "Literary Journalism and the Drama of Civic Life." *Literary Journalism Studies* 3, no. 2. (Fall 2011): 73–82.

Penn, I[rvine] Garland. *The Afro-American Press and Its Editors.* Springfield, MA: Willey, 1891.

Reade, W. Winwood. "Heroes of Central Africa." *Atlantic Monthly: A Magazine of Literature, Science, Art, and Politics*, May 1867, 625–35.

Reynolds, G. "The Late Insurrection in Jamaica." *Atlantic Monthly: A Magazine of Literature, Science, Art, and Politics*, April 1866, 480–89. Hathi Trust Digital Library. https://babel.hathitrust.org/cgi/pt?id=mdp.39015030142122;view=1up;seq=492.

Richards, C. H. "Communications: Protection by Development." *American Missionary*, January 1878, 19–21.

Rooks, Noliwe M. *Ladies Pages: African American Women's Magazines and the Culture That Made Them.* New Brunswick, NJ: Rutgers University Press, 2004.

Said, Nicholas. *The Autobiography of Nicholas Said: A Native of Bornou, Eastern Soudan, Central Africa.* Edited by Precious Rasheeda Muhammad. Cambridge, MA: Journal of Islam in America Press, 2000. First published 1873 by Shotwell (Memphis, TN).

———. "A Native of Bornoo." *Atlantic Monthly: A Magazine of Literature, Science, Art, and Politics*, October 1867, 485–95. www.gutenberg.org/files/38270/38270-h/38270-.htm#A_NATIVE_ OF_BORNOO.

Simmons, Charles A. *The African American Press: A History of News Coverage during National Crises, with Special Reference to Four Black Newspapers, 1827–1965.* Jefferson, NC: McFarland, 2006.

Thomson, Mortimer [Q. K. Philander Doesticks, pseud.]. *What Became of the Slaves on a Georgia Plantation? Great Auction of Slaves at Savannah, Georgia, March 2d and 3d, 1859. A Sequel to Mrs. Kemble's Journal.* N.p., 1863.

Wallace, Aurora. *Newspapers and the Making of Modern America: A History.* Westport, CT: Greenwood Press, 2005.

Washington, George. Letter to the members of the New Jerusalem Church of Baltimore, January 27, 1793. Founders Online: Correspondence and Writing of Six Major Shapers of the United States. National Archives and Records Administration. https://founders.archives.gov/documents/Washington/05-12-02-0027.

Williams, Susan S. *Reclaiming Authorship: Literary Women in America, 1850–1900.* Philadelphia, PA: University of Pennsylvania Press, 2006.

4
AMERICAN REALISM AND THE STIRRINGS OF LITERARY JOURNALISM

Thomas Connery

By the 1890s, it had become common for American writers and journalists to seek out their material by closely observing and absorbing a city's whirlpool of life, producing a type of storytelling that emerged with the century's realistic turn and providing early examples of what we now call literary journalism, when the "drama of the present,"[1] as *Harper's Magazine* editor Henry Mills Alden put it, was demanded by many critics and readers in both literature and journalism. Stephen Crane, for example, was among those writers who would roam the Bowery and Lower East Side of New York City, soaking in the street life with its daily array of incidents and cast of characters. He then would craft sketches of what he had witnessed, such as "The Broken-Down Van," "The Men in the Storm," and "An Experiment in Misery"[2]—all works of literary journalism, though neither Crane nor his readers would call such depictions "literary journalism." They would, however, consider them genuine sketches of life being lived. When such true-life short stories started appearing in newspapers in the 1840s, they marked a broad cultural shift away from presenting life as it *should* be to depicting life as it *is*—a turn from romanticism to realism.[3]

However, this descriptor, "literary journalism," strikes some as a misnomer or a meaningless hybrid that confuses and contradicts rather than explains and defines, while others have suggested the phrase is somewhat pretentious—a claim to a higher form of journalism when it's still just journalism. But it is not *just* journalism, and while the term literary journalism is a hybrid, it is far from meaningless. By its nature, a hybrid is a mix of two species or elements that creates a new stand-alone species or element, and literary journalism contains elements of both literature and journalism. But as literary journalism scholar Joshua Roiland has explained in a perceptive research essay, attaching "literary" to "journalism" does not mean a higher quality of journalism.[4] Yet this form of journalism as literature, this hybrid, can be distinguished and identified by its specific qualities, as Roiland points out and which I emphasized twenty-five years ago when I wrote that literary journalism

> can briefly be defined as nonfiction printed prose whose verifiable content is shaped and transformed into a story or sketch by use of narrative and rhetorical techniques generally associated with fiction. The themes that then emerge make a statement, or provide an interpretation, about the people and culture depicted.[5]

Roiland provides a more recent and improved definition by declaring that literary journalism "adheres to all the reportorial and truth-telling covenants of conventional journalism, while employing rhetorical and storytelling techniques more commonly associated with fiction," giving us "journalism as literature."[6] Those rhetorical elements, the "literary" side, according to Roiland, include scene, character development, plot, dialogue, symbolism, and voice. Such stylistic elements have frequently shown up in other, earlier considerations. For instance, Norman Sims interviewed each of the writers whose work was included in his 1984 edited volume *The Literary Journalists*. Based on those interviews, Sims identified four essential elements of a work of literary journalism, two dealing with writing (voice and structure) and two dealing with reporting (immersion and accuracy). He added that literary journalists have "a sense of responsibility to their subjects."[7] In addition, in "Discovering a Literary Form," I suggested the extent to which literary journalism is storytelling, with writers avoiding formulas and shaping each story based on the topic and what has been observed and learned—in other words, the journalism side that involves "reporting" or gathering the content. The claim in this chapter is that ultimately and significantly this melding of distinct terms—this blending of forms and elements, however one assembles the elements—permits distinct depictions of observed life or depictions of *actuality* that solidly ground the writing in a specific time and place provided by the *journalistic* aspect. The *literary* aspect makes the work less ephemeral, allowing the writing to more likely stand up over time.

This move toward more realistic storytelling—toward depicting the behavior of *actual* people, places, incidents, and activities rather than their idealized or romanticized versions—that marked a "hunger for the real," to use Andrew Lawson's fitting phrase, began in the United States in the 1840s when a number of writers walked New York's streets as well as those of other major American cities, including San Francisco, Chicago, Cincinnati, Philadelphia, and Boston.[8] These writers were America's version of the flaneur, or writers who roamed the city, observing, recording, and capturing in various literary forms what was right before their eyes, explaining and showing the city and the ways of its urban dwellers who were all a part of it. Thus, these urban strollers became urban chroniclers. In other words, by the time Crane came along, there had been about fifty years of writers absorbing urban impressions in order to document this "dusty, steam-engine whirling realism," as one writer put it in 1862, placing journalism at the forefront of realism's emergence in a shift to rendering and documenting observed life.[9] Consequently, journalism wasn't merely linked to realism as it emerged in the 1800s but was a close part of a realistic movement in which all forms of expression—including poetry and fiction, art and architecture, and journalism and photography—insisted on the primacy of observed life and what one mid-nineteenth-century cultural critic called "recording realism," or writing that permitted readers to see, know, and feel the details of urban life and the experiences of their fellow citizens.[10] The focus in both journalism and literature would be on what was recent and factual or writing that produced "a rendering of felt detail," as Allen Trachtenberg put it.[11] Although the writing at this point certainly wasn't fully developed literary journalism, it is here that we find the roots of American literary journalism.

One of the most striking and accomplished of Crane's predecessors was George G. Foster, whose strolls through New York City were captured in urban sketches that regularly ran in the *New-York Tribune* from 1848 to 1850. Taking in the city at the same time as Foster was a young Walt Whitman, who would become America's iconic poet. But from 1831 to 1854, Whitman wrote for and edited eight different newspapers. In 1852, he would declare in the *New York Daily Times* that "the true poem is the daily paper."[12] Whitman's declaration arose from his strong belief that newspapers gave readers "pictures of life as it is" rather than life idealized as it might be or should be.[13] Whitman's daily walks through the streets of Brooklyn and Manhattan provided him with easy exposure to the actual and common and allowed him to absorb the urban spectacle and share in the newspaper his wonder and pleasure at the passing parade of life. Furthermore, both Whitman and Foster recognized, depicted, and often celebrated the range and diversity of New York's residents as a central characteristic of the burgeoning metropolis. Both Whitman's and Foster's writings were colored by commentary, but Foster's street observations, which ran in the *New-York Tribune* in the mid-1840s under the standing head "New York in Slices," gave readers a more concrete taste of the city and its people than did Whitman's. His "slices" were popular enough that they were published in book form in 1849 under the title *New York in Slices: By an Experienced Carver: Being the Original Slices Published in the "N.Y. Tribune," Revised, and Corrected by the Author*. Foster followed that collection with one in 1850 that contained his writings that documented his strolls through the city at night: *New York by Gas-Light: With Here and There a Streak of Sunshine*.

The *New York in Slices* sketches are worth a closer look because they clearly demonstrate the move from romance or the way life *should* be to realism and the way life *is*. Although these sketches might be best characterized today as journalism as descriptive commentary in that they mix detailed descriptions with a palpable point of view—often coupled with strong subjective judgments on the people and places depicted—nevertheless, in both Foster's approach to gathering his observations and in his writing style, we can see the roots of literary journalism as well as the early blossoming of realism. At times, Foster seemed more fascinated with the look and growth of the city, its architecture and development, rather than its diverse population. For instance, several of his sketches focus on streets such as Broadway or Wall. Those pieces are full of shops, buildings, and goods, with little mention of the people there except as broad generalizations like when he writes that "Broadway in its glory" is at 6:00 p.m. when "you will see New York's possible in the way of beautiful women, scrupulously-dressed dandies, and pretty children."[14] In this sense, Foster—and Whitman as well—was keeping with the more standard pose of the flaneur, or one who passes through the urban landscape and provides broad, sweeping, often panoramic views of the city. But when he wasn't strolling the boulevards, Foster especially enjoyed visiting one of the city's many markets. In one of his sketches, he gushes over the "varieties of human nature" in the markets, where "every face you meet is a character, every scene affords piquant contrast," and then he runs through some of the types who can be found at a market, ending his description by laughing at his own writing:

> The old huckster-woman who implores you in all weathers to buy her vegetables, although she has a handsome house at home and fifty thousand dollars out at interest, (we hope not in Moonshine Insurance Company,)—the pretty bare-armed girl who comes to buy breakfast for the mistress and must av coorse have the best of every thing—the modest mechanic's wife, who surveys the aristocratic turkey and the lordly sirloin with a sigh, and then, with a timid glance at the little stock of change, is fain to put up with a lean joint for dear John's dinner. But then it will be cooked by her own hands, and she herself will shell the peas and boil the potatoes and dress the baby; and if the mutton itself is a little tough, her glance of love as her husband enters the door, will be so tender, and will speak a heart so true, that handsome John will not miss the stall-fed luxury that his earnings would not procure, while he owns so much hearty happiness which wealth could not buy and the world cannot take away. Whew! What a sentence.[15]

Foster also gives readers a look at "the dainty cit, his boots to nicely black, and his shirt-bosom so unimpeachably white" who has "an instinct in the selection of asparagus," and the hurrying "hotel-keeper, fearful that somebody has brought something to market which he shall not see," as well as a much more detailed look at "a thin, meager, sick old lady, meanly clad, and haggard from care and anxiety," who, Foster says, has a private boarding house whose interior he specifically describes, from its mahogany chairs to its faded "Brussels carpet."[16]

In his last book of sketches, *Fifteen Minutes Around New York*, Foster's articles have far less information about a topic, far less social commentary, but more vivid descriptions of types, and overall the articles are more lively stylistically and more forward-looking than his earlier sketches. For instance, in "A General Dash at the Ferries," he describes different people entering the waiting room for the ferry, including a "lady" who "is dressed in one of those chocolate-colored, unrevealing, linen-and-cotton out-door night-gowns" and "a shirred barege bonnet of a similar hue, with a thick green veil," and "a thin, intellectual-looking woman, of thirty-five" who is not "old-maidish" but "on the strong-minded womanish order" and "thin, but not meager ... looks as if she worked hard, and still knew how to enjoy life in her own independent way," as well as "a nervous old gentleman, who is always afraid of being too late, and looks into the room timidly. ... He advertised yesterday morning in the Herald for a wife."[17]

Foster also employs a number of realistic storytelling devices appropriate to capturing the moment for his readers, including using bits of conversation or dialogue. For instance, here is an excerpt from one of the *New York in Slices* sketches, "The Pawnbrokers' Shops":

> Whom have we here? A very pale, timid-looking little man—thin to diaphony, and with large lustrous eyes that seem like jets welling up from some deep-hidden source. He staggers in under a load of books.
>
> I want a little money on these books, Sir. They are invaluable to me, and I shall be sure to redeem them as soon as my book is out.
>
> Don't want books, my good fellow—they don't pay.
>
> But, Sir, here is Byron, and Sheeley, and Bacon, and Jeremy Taylor—
>
> Who ish Cheremy Taylor? If it was Zachary Taylor, now![18]

In the same sketch, to show how expensive jewelry came to a pawnbroker's shop, Foster includes a conversation between an affluent woman and a gentleman in need of money who is willing to take the "splendidly-attired" woman's valuable jewels and pawn them for cash. In a *New York by Gas-Light* sketch, "Mose and Lize," he distinguishes between a Broadway dandy and a "b'hoy"—or a young man from a tough Lower Manhattan neighborhood—by contrasting an exchange between the dandy and a young woman with an exchange between Mose, the b'hoy, and his girlfriend, Lize:

> "Do tell me all about your fine parade with the Hoosah troup yethterday, Mither Thmith," lisped a young lady of the Upper Ten to a dandy Hussar, the other evening at a party in the Fifth Avenue.
>
> "Oh I assure you, we had a most chawming time, my deah madam—perfectly chawming."
>
> On the same evening Mose returned from a grand fireman's parade and target-excursion, and was met by Lize at the door.
>
> "Well hoss, what kind of time'd ye hev—say?"
>
> "Well now yer'd better *bleeve* we had a gallus time! Give us a buss, old gal! Guess I seen ye lookin' out er ther winder this morning—*I* did."
>
> "Oh git out—*you Mose!*"[19]

Besides conversation, Foster often employs detailed scene-setting and concrete descriptions of people, at times combining a sense for the moment or the feel of an activity with rather vivid descriptions of types as well as relatively sophisticated use of dialogue, especially in the *Fifteen*

Minutes Around New York sketches. The comical "A Plunge in the Swimming Bath," for example, begins with "Plop! Goes the fat man ... with his face red as the full moon, and his whole man appearing about to melt." The man "stripped in marvelous quick time, and glided into the water like a large lump of warm fat," compared to a "lean man" who "splashed and splutters about in the water like four sticks tied together."[20] Sprinkled throughout the sketch are snippets of conversation marked by street slang such as this exchange between a "stalwart Californian" and an "Old Fogy":

> "I say, old feller—give us a chor o'terbacker, will yer?"
> "Tobacco, sir!" Exclaims Old Fogy, Esq., aghast. "Tobacco! Do you mean to insult me?"
> "Well, I shouldn't mind, old hoss! Jest you come into this here small tin pan full of water, what they calls a simmin'-bath in these small-potatoe diggings, and ain't no objections to takin' a turn with you. Whooray! Who's afeard?"[21]

Similarly, in the previously discussed sketch about the ferry, he begins with:

> Hurra! There goes the bell! Give us the change—run—jump—dash—here we are! Thanks to a quick eye, a pair of tolerably long, if not hand-some legs, and considerable practice in the sharp work of getting around New York.[22]

Foster also would occasionally try something very different to get the "feel" of a moment as he experienced it. He did this in trying to capture the "spirit" and atmosphere of an eating-house "at high tide" by running together words and phrases to create the near-chaotic sense of motion and speed, anticipating Tom Wolfe's attempt at capturing the moment, specifically the repetitive drone of the crap dealer's voice in his opening to "Las Vegas (What?) Las Vegas (Can't Hear You! Too Noisy) Las Vegas!!!!" more than a hundred years later. Here's Foster's restaurant take followed by Wolfe's:

> "Beefsteakandtatersvegetabesnumbertwenty—In*jin*hardand sparrow-grassnumbersixteen!" "Waiter! Waiter! Wa-y-ter!" "Comingsire—while the rascal's *going* as fast as he can! "*Is* that beef killed for my porterhouse steak I ordered last week?" "Readynminitsir, comingsir, dreklysir—twosixpence, biledamand cabbage shillin, ricepudn sixpence, eighteenpence—at the barf you please—lobsaucensammingnumberfour—yes sir!" Imagine a continuous stream of such sounds as these, about the size of the Croton river, flowing through the banks of clattering plates and clashing knives and forks, perfumed with the steam from a mammoth kitchen, roasting, boiling, baking, frying, beneath the floor-crowds of animals with a pair of jaws apiece, wagging in emulation of the one wielded with such terrific effect by Samson—and the thermometer which has be-come ashamed of itself and hides away behind a mountain of hats in the corner, melting up *by degrees* to boiling heat—and you will have some notion of a New York eating-house.[23]

> Hernia, hernia, hernia, hernia, hernia, hernia, hernia, hernia, hernia, hernia, hernia, HERNia; hernia, HERNia, hernia hernia, hernia, hernia, HERNia, HERNia, HERNia, hernia hernia, hernia hernia, hernia, hernia, hernia, eight is the point, the point is eight; hernia, hernia HERNia; hernia, hernia, hernia, hernia, all right, hernia, hernia, hernia, hernia, hard eight, hernia, hernia, hernia, HERNia, hernia, hernia, hernia, HERNia, hernia, hernia, hernia, hernia.
> "What is all this *hernia, hernia* stuff?"

This was Raymond talking to the wavy-haired fellow with the stick, the dealer, at the craps table about 3:45 Sunday morning. The stickman had no idea what this big wiseacre was talking about, but he resented the tone. He gave Raymond that patient arch of the eyebrows known as a Red Hook brush-off, which is supposed to convey some such thought as, I am a very tough but cool guy, as you can tell by the way I carry my eyeballs low in the pouches, and if this wasn't such a high-class joint we would take wiseacres like you out back and beat you into jellied madrilène.[24]

As did Wolfe, and as Crane would do with "The Broken-Down Van" in the early 1890s, Foster tests the limits of language in depicting reality, pushing words in order to get as close as he could to giving readers the effect of having been there, to see, feel, and hear what he had seen, heard, and felt.

While Foster's sketches celebrate urban life, he also allows readers to see "the horrible stench of the poverty, misery, beggary, starvation, crime, filth, and licentiousness that congregate in our Large City," as he put it in the introduction to *New York in Slices*.[25] That underbelly is especially revealed in *New York by Gas-Light*. Foster makes his intentions perfectly clear in the opening sketch of *New York by Gas-Light*, "Broadway at Evening," when he declares his purpose:

To penetrate beneath the thick veil of night and lay bare the fearful mysteries of darkness in the metropolis—the festivities of prostitution, the orgies of pauperism, the haunts of theft and murder, the scenes of drunkenness and beastly debauch, and all the sad realities that go to make up the lower stratum—the under-ground story—of life in New York!

Yet he also questions his motivation "for invading these dismal realms and thus wrenching from them their terrible secrets" and responds to his concern by giving his reporting and writing a somewhat noble purpose, using language that clearly ties him to the emerging realistic sensibility: "The duty of the present age is to discover the real facts of the actual condition of the wicked and wretched classes—so that Philanthropy and Justice may plant their blows aright." What he intends to do, he says, is "to seek for and depict truth," and he invites the reader to "look and listen."[26] What, of course, is implied in such a declaration is that it is indeed possible to go out and observe people and their activities and then reality—or truth—would be revealed. What is clear as well is that such a declaration is a call to depict the "sad realities," "life," "the real facts," and the "actual condition," and to do so through observation. These words and phrases will be repeated by writers, editors, and critics for decades to come, characterizing and shaping the nineteenth century's realistic turn and the emergence of realism as the overriding sensibility in literature and other arts.

Overall, the *New York by Gas-Light* sketches involve a tour of the "under-ground," as Foster the urban explorer and guide takes the reader from one place of "infamy" to the next: notorious neighborhoods, saloons, oyster bars, billiards parlors, gambling dens, dance halls, brothels (as well as a range of other places where prostitution occurs), and "Model Artist Exhibitions," where men can view naked women under the guise of art. He shows and tells who might be present at these establishments, but he also passes judgment and points to the hypocrisy. For instance, while Foster makes the claim that the women who "eat, drink and make merry" in one type of late-night establishment, oyster cellars, "are all of one kind" (prostitutes), he notes that in contrast the men include "reverend judges and juvenile delinquents, pious and devout hypocrites, and undisguised libertines and debauchees. ... Gamblers and fancy men, high-flyers and spoonies, genteel pick-pockets and burglars." When a policeman responds to "the boisterous mirth below" and raps his stick on the pavement, Foster says, he "may be reminding a grave functionary of the city that it is time to go home to his wife and children after the discharge of his 'arduous public duties.'"[27] In this way, Foster consistently brings into focus the role of those better off, especially men, and essentially the place of class, gender, and the environment in contributing to the behavior and living conditions of this lower class.

Stuart M. Blumin certainly is correct in recognizing Foster's work as a curious mix of "indictment and celebration."[28] For instance, Foster's visit to a night market in the sketch "Saturday Night" in *New York by Gas-Light* bears some resemblance to one of his typical market strolls, beginning with his exuberant "What a squeeze—what a crowd!"[29] But as he continues, rather than capture pleasure in the market and its people, Foster allows readers to experience the crunch of a jammed and jostling market. While he still tries to give readers the "feel" of the facts, it is with a touch of humor, as he describes what it was like trying to squeeze through the crowd:

> It is not here mere elbows, and knees, and brawny chests and broad stout backs that you are to encounter. Now you stumble against a firkin, and now are overset by a bag. And there is a woman who has somehow—it is impossible to tell how—squeezed through between you and your next neighbor: but her basket, to which she clings with death-like tenacity, appears to be made of less elastic material than herself. It has assumed the position of a balloon, and forms a target for a score of noses pushed on from the rear. There is no chance of its coming through, that is certain; and the woman will *not* let go of it—that seems equally clear.[30]

As he attempts to crawl under the woman's basket, his eyes water from the "briny" mackerel at the bottom of the basket, and then a "large slice of the fat" from a piece of corned beef "reposes" on his coat collar. When he finally stands, he sees that he has been "kneeling in a basket of stale eggs," ruining his pants and causing the owner of the eggs to angrily respond:

> The Irish huckster-woman who owns them, seeing this wholesale destruction of her brood of incipient chickens, pours out a volley of abuse upon your devoted dead, and loudly demands full compensation of her irreparable loss. You gladly pay whatever she requires; and by dint of pulling and squeezing, and being pulled and squeezed, we at length make our way through the lower walk, past the butter and cheese stands, and stalls for carcasses of dead hogs and sheep, now ankle-deep in mud, and so on to the fish-market. … And see there! A fine green lobster has caught your foot in his pinchers and will be through the leather directly. You will find him the closest friend you ever had—he'll stick like a burr.[31]

While a reader might laugh at Foster's watery eyes, his collar stained by fat, his pants ruined by broken eggs, and his foot pinched by a lobster, Foster frames the sketch with poverty and want. He calls the Saturday night of the sketch "the poor man's holiday," which includes going to the market once a week for those who "work the hardest and longest, and in labors the most repulsive," who are often "cramped six days in seven for something to eat." According to Foster, "the laborer and his family, who really hold society together by the work and cunning of their hands, are often without a dinner."[32]

In several sketches in which prostitution appears, Foster depicts the prostitutes as both vixens and victims, making sure his readers understand the role of poverty, alcohol, and men of means in fostering prostitution, almost always depicting the women as fallen but blameless. In both *New York in Slices* and *New York by Gas-Light*, Foster visits the notorious Five Points section of Lower Manhattan, which he describes as a "foul and loathsome" place, and so it would remain until urban reforms in the 1890s. Here is his description of Five Points, with detail marked by repetition of words and images of decay:

> The buildings in all that neighborhood are nearly all of wood, and are so old and rotten that they seem ready to tumble together into a vast rubbish-heap. Many of them are furnished with steps, from which half the stairs are missing, and each provided with a decayed cellar-door, broken from the hinges, and ready to precipitate any one who ventures to tread upon it into the cellar below. Nearly every house and cellar is a groggery below and a brothel above. In the doors and at the windows may be seen at any hour of the afternoon or evening, scores of sluttishly-dressed women, in whose faces drunkenness and debauchery have destroyed every vestige of all we expect in the countenance of Woman, and even almost every trace of human expression. ... Here and there, digging in the foul gutters, or basking in filthy nakedness upon the cellar doors, may be seen groups of children, from the merest infancy up to the verge of premature puberty—some seeming pretty, some deformed and idiotic, and others horribly ulcerated from head to foot with that hereditary leprosy which debauchery and licentiousness entail as their curse upon their innocent offspring.[33]

Foster then takes readers inside one of the houses, into "an apartment separated by tattered blankets, suspended from the low rafters, and inhabited by several families." He continues:

> Here a mother lies dead-drunk in her squalid bed upon the floor, and her two children are fighting over her body for the bottle which she may not have drained quite to its dregs. There two women, their eyes inflamed and their faces distorted with passion, are swearing furiously at each other, and threatening a war of blows. Yonder, on a cot without a mattress or pillow, lies a paralytic old woman, looking as if living and malignant eyes had been given to a decaying wax-figure.[34]

Foster was "arguably the best and most characteristic of the New York flaneurs of the 1840s," according to Dana Brand in his significant *The Spectator and the City in Nineteenth-Century American Literature*.[35] Particularly with his *New York by Gas-Light* sketches, Foster was producing what Blumin has called "the new literary genre of nonfictional urban sensationalism" that was "rooted in the urban sketches and *romans-feuilletons*" of the early nineteenth-century French and British writers.[36] Certainly, Foster and other urban chroniclers were influenced by Charles Dickens's *Sketches by Boz*, which were published in newspapers in the 1830s in England and collected for book publication in 1836, and in which Dickens set down "the small events in the everyday life of common persons ... directing his powers of observations and description upon scenes and characters within the daily scope of any loiterer in London."[37] In one of his *New York in Slices* sketches, Foster says that "mere words can convey but a faint idea of the Five Points" and adds that what might be conveyed has already been well done by Dickens.[38] By roaming the city and writing about what he saw, Foster was "explaining the new metropolis to a society that was in so many ways affected by its development," as Blumin puts it.[39] Of particular significance, Foster, whom Blumin aptly calls a "street-wise expert," was also explaining and depicting "the realities that lie beneath the deceptive appearances of the city and its people."[40]

Those "realities" documented and interpreted so well by Foster serve to illustrate the beginning of the nineteenth century's embrace of realism and hence the local, concrete, and particular. "Heaven knows what we mean by reality," D. H. Lawrence exclaimed in *Studies in Classic American Literature*. "Telephone, tinned meat, Charlie Chaplin, Water-taps, and World-Salvation, presumably. Some insisting on plumbing, and some on saving the world: these being the two great American specialties."[41] Of course, by mapping the surface of city life, Foster provided his slice of Lawrence's tinned meat and plumbing. But at the same time, he also was a representative writer who occasionally charted the city's depths, giving readers a sense of the urban underbelly but also the actualities of urban living.

Notes

1. Alden, "Fifty Years," 959.
2. These works are collected in Crane, *Tales, Sketches, and Reports*.
3. The concept of realism and the methods and attributes assigned to realist writers have been varied and wide-ranging from the mid- to late nineteenth century to the present day. However, I choose to stick with the basic "depicting life as it is," or as the various writers claimed it was. To sample more recent attempts to define realism, see Barrish, *American Literary Realism*; Bell, *Problem of American Realism*; Kaplan, *Social Construction*; Lawson, *Downwardly Mobile*; Shi, *Facing Facts*.
4. Roiland, "By Any Other Name," 71.
5. Connery, *Sourcebook*, xiv.
6. Roiland, "By Any Other Name," 71.
7. Sims, "Literary Journalists," 8.
8. Lawson, *Downwardly Mobile*, introduction.
9. Leland, *Sunshine in Thought*, 16.
10. Connery, *Journalism and Realism*, 215.
11. Trachtenberg, "Experiments in Another Country," 278.
12. Shi, *Facing Facts*, 30.
13. Whitman, *Collected Writings*, 223.
14. Foster, *New York in Slices*, 9.
15. Foster, 40.
16. Foster, 41.
17. Foster, *Fifteen Minutes*, 27–28.
18. Foster, *New York in Slices*, 32.
19. Foster, *New York by Gas-Light*, 174.
20. Foster, *Fifteen Minutes*, 40.
21. Foster, 40.
22. Foster, 27.
23. Foster, 66–67.
24. Wolfe, "Las Vegas," 3.
25. Foster, *New York in Slices*, 4.
26. Foster, *New York by Gas-Light*, 69–70.
27. Foster, 73–74.
28. Blumin, "George G. Foster," 60.
29. Foster, *New York by Gas-Light*, 191.
30. Foster, 191.
31. Foster, 191–92.
32. Foster, 190–91.
33. Foster, *New York in Slices*, 23.
34. Foster, 24.
35. Brand, *Spectator and the City*, 74.
36. Blumin, "George G. Foster," 1.
37. Holme, introduction to *Sketches by Boz*, vii.
38. Foster, *New York in Slices*, 22–23.
39. Blumin, "George G. Foster," 11.
40. Foster, *New York by Gas-Light*, 53.
41. Lawrence, *Studies*, 226.

Bibliography

Alden, Henry Mills. "Fifty Years of Harper's Magazine." *Harper's New Monthly Magazine*, May 1900, 947–62. https://harpers.org/archive/1900/05/fifty-years-of-harpers-magazine/.

Barrish, Phillip. *American Literary Realism, Critical Theory, and Intellectual Prestige, 1880–1995*. Cambridge: Cambridge University Press, 2001.

Bell, Michael Davitt. *The Problem of American Realism: Studies in the Cultural History of a Literary Idea*. Chicago: University of Chicago Press, 1993.

Blumin, Stuart M. "George G. Foster and the Emerging Metropolis." Introduction to *New York by Gas-Light and Other Urban Sketches*, by George G. Foster, 1–62. Edited by Stuart M. Blumin. Berkeley, CA: University of California Press, 1990.

Brand, Dana. *The Spectator and the City in Nineteenth-Century American Literature*. Cambridge: Cambridge University Press, 1991.

Connery, Thomas B. "Discovering a Literary Form." In Connery, *Sourcebook*, 3–37.

———. *Journalism and Realism: Rendering American Life*. Evanston, IL: Northwestern University Press, 2011.

———, ed. *A Sourcebook of American Literary Journalism: Representative Writers in an Emerging Genre*. New York: Greenwood Press, 1992.

Crane, Stephen. *Tales, Sketches, and Reports*. Edited by Fredson Bowers. Vol. 8 of *The Works of Stephen Crane*. Charlottesville, VA: University Press of Virginia, 1973.

Foster, George G. *Fifteen Minutes Around New York*. New York: De Witt and Davenport, 1854.

———. *New York by Gas-Light and Other Urban Sketches*. Edited by Stuart M. Blumin. Berkeley, CA: University of California Press, 1990.

———. *New York in Slices: By an Experienced Carver: Being the Original Slices Published in the "N.Y. Tribune," Revised, Enlarged, and Corrected*. New York: W. F. Burgess, 1849. Reprinted by the University of Michigan Library. https://quod.lib.umich.edu/cgi/t/text/text-idx?c=moa;idno=AJA2254.

Holme, Thea. Introduction to *Sketches by Boz: Illustrative of Every-Day Life and Every-Day People*, by Charles Dickens, v–xi. London: Oxford University Press, 1957.

Kaplan, Amy. *The Social Construction of American Realism*. Chicago: University of Chicago Press, 1988.

Lawrence, D. H. *Studies in Classic American Literature*. New York: Albert and Charles Boni, 1930.

Lawson, Andrew. *Downwardly Mobile: The Changing Fortunes of American Realism*. New York: Oxford University Press, 2012.

Leland, Charles Godfrey. *Sunshine in Thought*. 1862. Gainesville, FL: Scholars' Facsimiles and Reprints, 1959.

Roiland, Josh. "By Any Other Name: The Case for Literary Journalism." *Literary Journalism Studies* 7, no. 2 (Fall 2015): 61–89.

Shi, David E. *Facing Facts: Realism in American Thought and Culture, 1850–1920*. New York: Oxford University Press, 1995.

Sims, Norman. "The Literary Journalists." In *The Literary Journalists*, edited by Norman Sims, 3–25. New York: Ballantine Books, 1984.

Trachtenberg, Alan. "Experiments in Another Country: Stephen Crane's City Sketches." *Southern Review* 10, no. 2 (1974): 265–85.

Whitman, Walt. *The Collected Writings of Walt Whitman: The Journalism*. Edited by Herbert Bergman. New York: Peter Lang, 1998.

Wolfe, Tom. "Las Vegas (What?) Las Vegas (Can't Hear You! Too Noisy) Las Vegas!!!!" In *The Kandy-Kolored Tangerine-Flake Streamline Baby*, 3–24. New York: Bantam Books, 1977. First published in 1964.

5
LITERARY JOURNALISM AND AMERICA'S NATURALISTIC WRITERS

Roark Mulligan

America's first generation of literary realists began their careers as journalists, calling for the democratic treatment of subject matter. For example, the dean of American realism, W. D. Howells, first wrote for the *Ohio State Journal*. Later, as the influential editor of the *Atlantic Monthly*, he was guided by his newspaper experience, calling for writers who "cannot look upon human life and declare this thing or that thing unworthy of notice, any more than the scientist can declare a fact of the material world beneath the dignity of his inquiry."[1] For Howells and other early realists, the fiction writer was to be a reporter, one who democratically, objectively, but also empathetically observed life and depicted it. And the *fin de siècle* naturalists who followed Howells embraced his literary precepts, employing their powers of observation when composing journalism and fiction. But a clear demarcation can also be drawn between the first generation of realists (e.g., Howells, Henry James, Mark Twain, Sarah Orne Jewett, and even Hamlin Garland) and the next generation, a group of writers described variously as new realists, gritty realists, or naturalists (e.g., Theodore Dreiser, Stephen Crane, and Frank Norris). Although early American naturalists embraced Howells's call for literary works that depicted the real, not the ideal, they went further—they rejected Howellsian morality, and they celebrated journalism, not just as a stepping-stone to a noble literary career but also as an honorable, lifelong vocation. In abandoning traditional moral standards that shunned sexuality, greed, and violence, the early naturalists were free to depict the extremes of urban life. In *Stephen Crane, Journalism, and the Making of Modern American Literature*, Michael Robertson argues this point by theoretically distinguishing the realists from the naturalists: "The varying attitudes toward journalism displayed by novelists such as Howells, James, Dreiser, and Hemingway can be seen as part of the complex, evolving relationship between 'high' and 'low' realms of cultural production."[2] Unlike the early realists, naturalists increasingly blurred the line between nonfiction and fiction, between journalism and literature, between feature stories and short stories, and between acceptable and unacceptable subject matter.

The list of possible naturalists is long and varied, not limited to a single period, and could include all of the following: Nelson Algren, Sherwood Anderson, Saul Bellow, Ambrose Bierce, Abraham Cahan, Willa Cather, Kate Chopin, Stephen Crane, Rebecca Harding Davis, Don DeLillo, John Dos Passos, Theodore Dreiser, Paul Laurence Dunbar, James T. Farrell, Harold Frederic, Henry Blake Fuller, Ellen Glasgow, Lafcadio Hearn, Ernest Hemingway, Robert Herrick, Jack London, Norman Mailer, Frank Norris, Joyce Carol Oates, Elizabeth Stuart Phelps, David Graham Phillips, Upton Sinclair, John Steinbeck, William Styron, Edith Wharton, Richard

Wright, and many others. But for this brief study, only five authors from the first generation of literary naturalists—Dreiser, Crane, Norris, Cather, and London—will serve to illustrate the evolution of literary journalism. All five were born within a six-year period (1870–76), coming of age as journalists in the 1890s, when newspapers and magazines were booming but also when belief systems were being threatened by urbanization, economic instability, scientific discoveries, and industrialization. The rise of consumer capitalism during this period conflicted with religious, agrarian, and economic ideologies of the past, so these early naturalists were uniquely positioned to witness the transformation of their society and to discover new methods for recording their experiences. In *A History of American Literary Journalism*, John Hartsock marks this transformative period as the moment literary journalism first appeared because naturalists of this period were able to "resist critical closure, or the distanced image of the absolute past, to confront the inconclusive present of an indeterminate world."[3] In their openness to the moment and through their aesthetic flexibility, the early naturalists blended literary and journalistic methods to represent and communicate gritty, sometimes brutal, experiences.

Embracing journalism as an esteemed profession with a high social purpose, this first generation of American naturalists, to varying degrees, remained reporter-novelists throughout their careers. In his autobiography *Newspaper Days* (1922), Theodore Dreiser passionately expresses his early, ardent devotion to journalism: "Because the newspapers were always dealing with signs and wonders—great functions, great commercial schemes, great tragedies and pleasure—I began to conceive of them as wonderlands in which all concerned were prosperous and happy."[4] As a reporter, Dreiser's view moderated, became realistic, but his employment of in-depth research and accurate reporting to ground literary works that illuminated the dark corners of society never ceased. He utilized literary techniques when writing journalism and journalistic techniques when composing fiction, an artistic attitude shared by Crane, Norris, Cather, and London. For this first generation of American naturalists, accepting a journalistic assignment to cover a war, a boxing match, a revolution, a labor strike, a religious movement, or an earthquake, even after they had become established writers, was a social responsibility—they were, as Dreiser imagined, ambassadors bringing news of the world to American homes. In their approach, the early naturalists were heroes sacrificing themselves for a greater good; journalism was a calling, as documented by Doug Underwood in *Chronicling Trauma* when he describes Crane as following the code of a heroic journalist who accepted assignments to test himself and to sacrifice for others.[5] During this *fin de siècle* period, Crane was not alone. Newspapers increasingly hired known authors to cover conflicts, and London, according to Underwood, took this role to the highest level, accepting hazardous assignments as a reporter so that he could experience the life-threatening struggles of his tragic heroes.[6]

In their embrace of journalism and literature, naturalists indirectly set higher prose standards for newspapers and magazines. Once they had become celebrated authors, if Crane or London were hired to cover a conflict, editors and readers expected well-written articles, detailed descriptions, and complex characterizations—they expected more than traditional journalism had previously offered, but these same readers also expected graphic fiction, including depictions of squalid poverty, amoral sexual exploits, financial greed, and violent crime. As Underwood explains in *Journalism and the Novel*:

> The journalist-literary figures that are identified as naturalists, including Stephen Crane, Norris, Dreiser, and London, are key figures in ushering in contemporary literary attitudes with their focus upon the gritty details of urban life, the brutality of warfare, and the bleak worldviews that rose out of Darwinism, industrialization, and the coming of modern imperialism.[7]

Their new approach required a reciprocity between journalism and imaginative literature, a reciprocity that resulted in literary journalism.

First observing and researching their topics, the early naturalists went beyond mere representation; they connected themselves to their subjects, like undercover agents; then they employed literary techniques (tone, setting, characterization) to express a social message. In other words, the naturalists were a bridge between the first-generation realists who called for quotidian details in literature and the New Journalists, such as Tom Wolfe, who defined literary journalism by borrowing from American naturalists.[8] Noting the influence of naturalists on his writing, Wolfe praised Dreiser and other gritty realists for following the simple principles he set forth in *The New Journalism* (1973): scene-by-scene construction, dialogue, points of view that involve the reader, and status details (the realistic artifacts of everyday life that create a rich social canvas).[9] For first-generation naturalists, as for the New Journalists, experience was gained by entering the world, usually where conflict and poverty limited people's freedom, where forces (heredity, economics, war, environment) controlled them. They observed individuals scientifically and reported their findings accurately but also artistically. In their blending of fiction and nonfiction, scientific observation and sympathetic exposition, the naturalists followed a common set of principles, but the principles were necessarily inconsistent, even contradictory, containing what Donald Pizer has described as two tensions.[10] One tension was stylistic, resulting when these authors blended their concise, journalistic prose with poetic language and tropes, creating a modern style that Cather, more than others, mastered and analyzed in theoretical essays such as "The Novel Démeublé" (1922). The second tension was ethical, resulting when naturalists experimented with narrative points of view. By shifting narrative perspective, from first person to omniscient, these authors could depict characters empathetically but also cosmically, causing the reader to care about individuals driven by forces beyond their control, a technique particularly obvious in Dreiser's journalism and fiction. Although American naturalists drew on the scientific theories of Charles Darwin, Herbert Spencer, and Joseph Le Conte, and also on the aesthetic theories of Émile Zola, they were not merely objective observers—they were caring authors who presented their subjects empathetically.

Employing these literary principles, naturalists developed a unique epistemology, a singular way of knowing the world. On the one hand, they followed the edicts of Zola, believing that writing should be based on careful observation and research. On the other, they realized that knowledge could not simply come from observation; they needed experience and involvement, which forced them into an empathetic relationship with their subjects and the social injustices that affected them. To maintain these tensions, naturalists employed an ironic attitude that they often created by shifting narrative perspectives. In other words, their naturalistic epistemology allowed them to observe individuals governed by cosmic laws but also to experience those laws as they affected the poor, the ill, and the displaced, thus to represent these human beings as suffering and caring. As David E. Shi argues, the new realists, such as Dreiser, could depict the underdog because they identified with the underdog and because they were willing to "sacrifice popularity for candor."[11] In analyzing Crane's sketch "The Men in the Storm" (1894), Thomas B. Connery illustrates this point well by noting that Crane could not depict the "affluent frolicking in the snow" without also describing "the poor standing cold and hungry in breadlines."[12] In their fiction and their journalism, first-generation naturalists developed a way of knowing and representing the world that Hartsock describes as a "truer kind of 'objectivity' because it is a discourse that inherently acknowledges its limitations and denies the spurious kind of omniscience that so-called objective journalism seems to imply."[13] As authors who immersed themselves in their subject matter, Dreiser, Crane, Norris, Cather, and London contributed to the development of literary journalism. Each shared basic journalistic and literary principles, but their methods and styles also varied, resulting in narratives that advanced literary journalism in distinctive ways: Dreiser, more than others, experimented with narrative perspective; Crane and London embraced "reportage" as a genre with an artistic and social purpose; Norris depicted characters ripped from the ordinary and driven by compulsions; and Cather defined modern prose.

Theodore Dreiser (1871–1945)

Theodore Dreiser began his career as a journalist in Chicago, where he doggedly pursued any job in the newspaper field, first securing a position in 1891 simply distributing toys for the *Chicago Herald*, then landing a place as a junior reporter at the less prestigious *Chicago Globe* after promising to sell copies of the editor's memoir door-to-door.[14] For an early *Globe* sketch, "Cheyenne, Haunt of Misery and Crime" (1892), Dreiser repeatedly visited a blighted Chicago neighborhood, observing its nightly pulse, its ethnic composition, its crowded conditions, and its domestic violence.[15] In this nonfiction sketch, Dreiser piled up realistic details, employed a sympathetic tone, but also a deterministic point of view. Realizing that he could write well, Dreiser sought greater opportunities, moving to the *St. Louis Globe-Democrat* and then to the *St. Louis Republic*, papers that allowed him to write news, reviews, and feature stories but also poetry and fiction. As a reporter for the *Republic*, Dreiser witnessed executions and a lynching, writing both unpretentious news stories and narrative features that rose to the level of literary journalism. For example, on January 12, 1894, Dreiser reported the public hanging of Sam Welsor, a bartender who killed a prostitute, but the day before the hanging, based on visits to the prison, Dreiser wrote a feature article that appeared on the front page and that detailed the life and death of Clementina Manning, the murdered prostitute, who had recently won five thousand dollars in a lottery.[16] Only a few days later, he reported the lynching of John Buckner in Valley Park, Missouri, a suburb of St. Louis. In his first article, "This Calls for Hemp" (1894), Dreiser simply describes the capture of Buckner at his home and his transportation to the sheriff's house. He filed this article before the lynching occurred and while Buckner was still held prisoner.[17] But in his second report, a long feature article, "Ten-Foot Drop" (1894), Dreiser clearly exhibits his mature narrative style, including digressions, dialogue, multiple narrative perspectives, nature imagery that counters the human tragedy, and narrative ruptures. In so doing, he describes his attempt to interview Buckner and reports his visits to the victims' families:

> The home of Miss Harrison, as well as the cabin of Mrs. Mungo, were visited last evening by a Republic reporter. Both women were found in a somewhat improved condition, it being the opinion that within a few days they would be about.[18]

Seven years later, Dreiser reshaped his coverage of the Buckner lynching into one of his earliest and most powerful short stories, "Nigger Jeff," which appeared in *Ainslee's* magazine (1901) and which he later significantly revised again for publication in his collection *Free and Other Stories* (1918).[19]

In writing his first novel *Sister Carrie* (1900), Dreiser relied not only on personal experience but also on his skills as a reporter and on previously written journalism. For example, toward the end of the novel, he incorporated "Curious Shifts of the Poor" (1899), a nonfiction sketch that depicts the nightly struggles of New York's homeless and that focuses on one particular man, the Captain, who raises money to house the displaced.[20] Even after publishing *Sister Carrie*, Dreiser followed the Captain, gathering more material so he could write a second nonfiction profile for *Success* magazine, "A Touch of Human Brotherhood" (1902), a work that illustrates Dreiser's indefatigable efforts as a journalist.[21] As Thomas P. Riggio documents in "Oh Captain, My Captain: Dreiser and the Chaplain of Madison Square," the Captain was Frederick Rotzler, a military veteran who dedicated himself to helping New York's poor. In analyzing "A Touch of Human Brotherhood," Riggio notes Dreiser's journalistic persistence: "He took to compulsively seeking out the Captain, stopping him on the street to inquire about his work in the prisons and missions."[22] In fact, Dreiser followed

Rotzler home so he could describe the Captain's austere living conditions. As a journalist, Dreiser was driven to know his subjects and to expose social problems, goals that Hartsock notes when describing literary journalism as "associated with Populist or Progressive causes."[23]

Of Dreiser's more than twenty-five book-length works, about half are imaginative literature—novels, short stories, plays, and poems—but the other half are works of nonfiction, including travel narratives, autobiographies, political diatribes, philosophical speculations, and literary criticism. And of the nonfiction works, at least four can be classified as literary journalism: two collections of urban observations, *The Color of a Great City* (1923) and *My City* (1929), and two collections of biographical sketches, *A Gallery of Women* (1929) and *Twelve Men* (1919). But even in writing his travel narratives, such as *A Traveler at Forty* (1913), *A Hoosier Holiday* (1916), and *Dreiser Looks at Russia* (1928), Dreiser worked as a literary journalist who developed a detailed knowledge of places and people. For example, as a reporter covering the Soviet Union's ten-year anniversary, Dreiser, ill with bronchitis, travelled for three months, collecting observations and experiences that appeared not only in the *New York World* (March 18–28, 1928) but also in *Dreiser Looks at Russia*, a travel narrative that varies greatly in quality, style, and content, but its best chapters ("Three Moscow Restaurants" and "Some Russian Vignettes") rise to the level of literary journalism. By accepting such arduous assignments after becoming a respected novelist, Dreiser demonstrated his lifelong commitment to journalism and social causes.

Besides *Sister Carrie*, Dreiser's other novels evidence his commitment to journalism. For example, in planning his magnum opus, *An American Tragedy* (1925), Dreiser collected news reports on more than a dozen murders.[24] Once he decided to employ, as a model, the murder of Grace Brown by Chester Gillette, Dreiser, like a reporter, visited the towns where they lived and worked, the lake where Grace was murdered, and the courthouse where Chester was convicted. To ensure the accuracy of his death row scenes, Dreiser, with the help of H. L. Mencken and the *New York World*, obtained a court order to interview Anthony Pantano, a death row inmate in Sing Sing, and while there, he witnessed the lights dimming as the electric chair was tested.[25] To depict Clyde Griffiths, the young man who murders his pregnant girlfriend, Dreiser dramatically shifts his narrative perspective throughout the novel. This is accomplished by using traditional narrative and philosophical commentary to begin most chapters, then by contrasting this overt narration with tagged or free indirect discourse that contains exclamations, broken sentences, and strange syntactical patterns, reflecting the thoughts and feelings of the protagonist. The reader is taken from a comfortable, philosophical discussion of a murderer to the warped, distorted thoughts of Clyde, a hunted animal. And this dialectic play of drastically dissimilar narrative voices allows Dreiser to sympathetically and ironically depict the protagonist not simply as a murderer but as a human being driven by forces he only partially understands. For the first time in American literature, Dreiser, experimenting with narrative point of view, voice, and time, sympathetically portrayed a convicted murderer, a literary task that Richard Wright, Truman Capote, and Norman Mailer would later accomplish in *Native Son* (1940), *In Cold Blood* (1966), and *The Executioner's Song* (1979).

Stephen Crane (1871–1900)

Like Dreiser, Stephen Crane is known today as a fiction writer, the author of works such as *The Red Badge of Courage* (1895) and "The Open Boat" (1897). And like Dreiser, Crane at a young age embraced journalism as a calling; he fell into the newspaper world, working as a summer assistant for his brother between 1888 and 1892 in Asbury Park, New Jersey, where his assignments allowed him some freedom to experiment with tone and point of view. Between 1892 and 1894, Crane lived in New York City, where he began contributing freelance pieces to New York newspapers and magazines, focusing on the street life of the Lower East Side, the

Bowery. In analyzing Crane's work as a New York novelist and journalist, Robertson suggests that Crane's career contributed to a misleading myth: "the newspaper as training ground for novelists."[26] As Robertson points out, Crane's journalism and his fiction developed along parallel tracks—he was writing New York sketches for newspapers at the same time he was writing *Maggie: A Girl of the Streets* (1893), a novella tracing the tragic fall of a girl in the Bowery. For Crane and other naturalists, the connection between the two genres was complicated and reciprocal, and this complexity is partially concealed by an incomplete knowledge of Crane's early journalism. In his authoritative biography *Stephen Crane: A Life of Fire*, Paul Sorrentino discovers close connections between Crane's physical movements and his writing. To demonstrate how his journalism affected his fiction, Sorrentino documents Crane's early sojourns into the city's slums during the fall and winter of 1891 and 1892 while he was still living with his brother in New Jersey: "[Crane] explored New York's tenement districts for background material to use in writing *Maggie*, a novel that would revolutionize American urban fiction."[27] Later as he was completing *Maggie*, Crane lived in New York, writing city sketches for newspapers, including his first known New York sketch, "The Broken-Down Van" (1892), which Robertson describes as capturing the city's street life, "the vice, crime, and sexual and economic exploitation that exist in lower Manhattan."[28]

In the spring of 1894, Crane published two well-known works of literary journalism, New York sketches titled "An Experiment in Misery" and "An Experiment in Luxury," essays that at the time were more widely read than his novel *Maggie*. For these articles, Crane, employing "saturation journalism," feigned poverty and wealth so he could experience the inequities of society. In each article, Crane highlights class structure, revealing the hardships of the poor and the advantages of the rich, but the articles are more than clever and more than polemic—they explore urban situations critically and thoughtfully, not reaching simple conclusions. Crane's growing success as a journalist opened doors—S. S. McClure, editor of *McClure's Magazine*, asked Crane to visit a mine in Pennsylvania and write "In the Depths of a Coal Mine" (1894), a journalistic work that reveals the physical conditions and economic pressures forcing workers to battle their environment (the mine) and their bosses (the owners). In this early work of literary journalism, Crane employs poetic devices to illustrate how the mine consumes the miners. As William Dow demonstrates in *Narrating Class in American Fiction*, "Crane's sympathetic feelings for the miners come through most forcefully in his descriptions of their bodies, a mode through which the reader might perceive the brute materiality of labor."[29] A year later, Crane published *The Red Badge of Courage*, a novel praised immediately as stylistically innovative in its depiction of Civil War carnage.

After the successful publication of *The Red Badge of Courage*, a critically acclaimed novel that sold well, Crane continued to accept arduous assignments as a reporter. Travelling to Mexico, the American West, England, Ireland, Florida, Greece, and Cuba, he covered both the Greco-Turkish War and the Spanish-American War. While in Cuba, he witnessed the Marines seize Guantánamo Bay. Before the United States even entered the Spanish-American War, in November 1896, Crane journeyed to Jacksonville, Florida, hoping to board a "filibustering ship" headed to Cuba (these ships supported insurgents fighting Spanish rule by transporting arms). After some delay, on December 31, 1896, he sailed on the *Commodore*, a ship carrying "forty boxes of rifles, a thousand pounds of gunpowder, more than 200,000 cartridges, three hundred machetes, and a crew of twenty-seven or twenty-eight men, with Crane listed as a seaman."[30] Shortly after setting sail, the ship's engines died, and the men boarded lifeboats; the captain, Crane, and two crewmembers departed last, on a ten-foot dinghy. Drifting for thirty hours at sea, the boat, as it neared shore, finally capsized; one of the crewmembers died in the surf. This was a traumatic experience for Crane—he spent days recovering, refusing the *New York World*'s request for an article and turning down another newspaper's offer of a thousand dollars for a thousand words.[31] But, after rest, he wrote an article, "Stephen Crane's Own Story" (1897), an excellent example of literary journalism and a work that is an early version of his pioneering short story "The Open Boat" (1897). As critical analyses of "The Open Boat" illustrate beautifully, Crane blurred the lines between journalism and literature in both works.[32] The traditional claim that Crane's newspaper article ("Stephen Crane's Own Story") is nothing more than brief reportage and that the short story is a work of high art has been questioned by Robertson and others who point out that the fact-fiction distinction cannot be applied to these two works, since both works use factual details, such as the ship's actual name, the *Commodore*, and since contemporary readers would have been aware of the actual event when reading both the article and the short story: "The generic labels traditionally assigned to these two works—fiction and nonfiction, art and reportage—obscure more than they reveal."[33] Although the short story is a more polished work of prose with a more universal theme, the newspaper article has an artistic quality based on its immediacy and its rougher prose style, such as its repetition of coordinating conjunctions. In his Crane biography, Sorrentino analyzes the artistic rendering of the subject matter, arguing that the short story, though similar to the newspaper article in facts, is drastically different in style.[34] Despite their similarities and differences, Crane's two shipwreck narratives might both be considered works of literary journalism, and this generic confusion paradigmatically evidences the blur that American naturalists created between journalism and fiction, between a newspaper story and high art. In these narratives and many others, Crane is a pioneer of reportage, a literary genre that required writers to travel to troubled places, whether urban slums or war zones, then to create a polished literary work that contains not only a factual account but also a personal response. As Pizer asserts in a recent article, "Stephen Crane was perhaps the first American writer to fully exploit the possibilities of the form [reportage] in his 1890s Bowery and war accounts."[35]

Frank Norris (1870–1902)

In 1898, as a journalist covering the Spanish-American War, Crane met a reporter named Frank Norris, a relatively unknown author who was also working for McClure's newspaper syndicate.[36] Like Crane and Dreiser, Norris began his career writing for newspapers and weekly magazines. In San Francisco, where he spent his formative years, Norris wrote for the *San Francisco Chronicle* and the *Wave* (a weekly magazine), travelling to South Africa where he reported on the Jameson Raid of Johannesburg. As a freelance journalist and later as a contributing editor to the *Wave*, Norris incorporated, even in his earliest sketches, impressionistic descriptions not only of sights but also of sounds and smells. And like Crane, his works often included a humorous or an ironic tone, as is obvious in his earliest descriptions of the Del Monte Country Club, where his mother was a member.[37] In his introduction to *Frank Norris of "The Wave,"* Oscar Lewis estimates that Norris wrote over 120 articles between 1891 and 1898, both short stories and nonfiction sketches.[38] Toward the end of his time in San Francisco, the *Wave* published, in serial form, his novel *Moran of the Lady Letty* (1898), which brought him to the attention of S. S. McClure, who hired him as a correspondent. Like Dreiser and Crane, Norris's fiction garnered him more prestigious journalism and editing assignments. Moving to New York, Norris not only wrote for McClure, but he also served as a fiction editor for the Doubleday publishing house, where he recommended Dreiser's controversial novel *Sister Carrie* for publication.

Like Dreiser and Crane, Norris blurred the line between nonfiction and fiction, drawing on his own life and his journalism when writing novels. *Blix* (1899) is particularly interesting because the novel's protagonist is a San Francisco reporter who covers the city from the waterfront, to the Presidio, to Mexican restaurants, to Chinatown, and for one assignment, the protagonist reports on a shipment of wheat, a commodity that would appear in his short story "A Deal in

Wheat" (1903) and in his unfinished trilogy *The Epic of the Wheat*, which included *The Octopus: A Story of California* (1901) and *The Pit: A Story of Chicago* (1903).[39] For another novel, *Vandover and the Brute* (1914), Norris borrowed material from San Francisco newspapers, from his own life, and from an article that he wrote for the *Wave*, "The 'Fast Girl'" (1896), which served as a character sketch of Ida, the young, pregnant woman who commits suicide. And for *McTeague* (1899), Norris appropriated material from at least two *Wave* articles: "Fantaisie Printaniere" (1897), which introduces three characters, Mr. Ryer and Mr. and Mrs. McTeague, and "Judy's Service of Gold Plate" (1897), which presents Guatemalan Judy who becomes Maria Miranda Macapa in *McTeague*.[40] Having studied art for two years in Paris before dedicating himself to writing, Norris would have learned the value of character and scene studies, a practice he employed when writing novels. And during his two years as an art student in Paris, Norris read French literature and literary theory, especially the writing of Zola. Unlike Dreiser, Crane, London, or Cather, Norris called himself a "naturalist," and he defined naturalism not as gritty realism but as a synthesis of realism and romanticism:

> Howells's characters live across the street from us, they are "on our block." We know all about them, about their affairs, and the story of their lives. One can go even further. We ourselves are Mr. Howells's characters, so long as we are well behaved and ordinary and bourgeois, so long as we are not adventurous or not rich or not unconventional.[41]

Unlike Howells's realistic characters, Norris's protagonists are extraordinary, not ordinary, the victims of passions and forces they cannot control or understand. To find inspiration for his characters and plots, Norris turned to newspapers, where he, like Dreiser, found gruesome tragedies, such as the brutal murder of a kindergarten janitress by a jealous, greedy, drunk husband, a crime on which he based the plot of *McTeague*.[42]

Willa Cather (1873–1947)

Like Crane and Norris, Willa Cather was hired by McClure, who was impressed by her short stories, and although Cather has not always been considered a naturalist, Donna Campbell in a groundbreaking work, *Bitter Tastes*, includes Cather and other women writers who do not fit the classic definition of naturalism but rather transgress "its boundaries with 'unruly' features, often present but unremarked in the work of classic male naturalism, such as sentimentalism, disability, and overt concerns with social justice."[43] Campbell's focus on "unruly naturalism" invites us not only to consider genres other than fiction, including journalism, prostitution memoirs, and early films, but also to analyze the work of Cather, whose journalism has received little critical attention. Like Dreiser, Crane, and Norris, Cather was born in the 1870s, came of age as a journalist in the 1890s, then developed a reputation as a writer of fiction; and like the other naturalists, she employed literary tropes in her journalism and journalistic methods in her fiction. Despite these similarities, Cather is seldom remembered as a literary journalist in part because she, although proud of her journalism, thought of herself as a fiction writer, and she did not sign many of her columns or articles. But Cather was a successful, professional journalist for over twenty years, landing positions that had traditionally been filled by men.

While still a student at the University of Nebraska, she was a regular contributor to the *Nebraska State Journal* and the *Lincoln Courier*, besides serving as the editor for her university's newspaper. In a long-running column that she wrote for the *Nebraska State Journal*, "One Way of Putting It," we find excellent examples of her literary journalism, including detailed character sketches and scene descriptions.[44] For example, in a single column published November 12,

1893, Cather presents six unrelated nonfiction sketches that capture the daily urban life of Lincoln: (1) a poor worker standing before a failed bank; (2) a thrifty widow bartering with a marble dealer for her husband's tombstone; (3) an old, disabled fruit vendor appearing as "humpbacked, his legs ... crooked"; (4) a prisoner visiting with his wife and son; (5) a poor, sick Swedish widow discussing her troubles with Cather; and (6) the crucifix in Lincoln's Catholic church described in great detail. The freedom that Cather had in writing "One Way of Putting It" is striking: Many articles simply review theatrical and music productions, but all are literary in their development of characters, their piling up of details, their empathy for subjects, and their personal tone. Moving to Pittsburgh in 1896, Cather, while teaching high school, wrote for *Home Monthly* (a women's magazine) and served as both the telegraph editor and drama critic for the *Pittsburgh Leader*. As Laurie S. Miller has noted in a recent dissertation, Cather's journalistic experience was extensive, and the similarities between her nonfiction and the work of the New Journalists is conspicuous.[45]

Like Norris, Cather moved to New York after she was hired by McClure, who had published her first short story collection, *The Troll Garden* (1905). As an editor and writer for McClure's syndicate, Cather edited and coauthored a biography titled *The Life of Mary Baker G. Eddy and the History of Christian Science* (1909), which appeared as fourteen installments in *McClure's Magazine* and which was the first serious examination of Eddy's life and religious work. As the principal editor of the volume, Cather worked with others, including Georgine Milmine and Burton J. Hendrick, to create a well-written biography that was praised by critics of Eddy and "Eddyism" but that was condemned by the Christian Science Church, which purchased the manuscript and the rights to its publication. Since the copyright on the biography expired, a new edition has been published (1993), sparking a critical discussion that has highlighted Cather's work as a literary journalist and as an editor who blended journalistic concision with poetic tropes.[46] In summing up Cather's years as a journalist, Carolyn Kitch states, "Between 1893 and 1912, Cather worked as a newspaper and magazine writer and editor in Lincoln, Pittsburgh, and New York. During these years she produced a body of journalism that was distinguished in both its quantity and quality."[47] After 1912, Cather focused solely on her fiction, winning a Pulitzer Prize in 1922, but even in her novels and short stories, she draws on her work as a journalist and on the people, places, and events of her childhood in Red Cloud, Nebraska, realistically and artistically capturing the struggles of Midwest pioneers and urban denizens.[48]

Excellent evidence of Cather as a naturalist influenced by journalism can be found in her short story "Paul's Case" (1905)—the title itself suggests Zola's scientific methodology, an objective study of a troubled teen who drops out of school, robs his employer, and commits suicide. In this masterful story, Cather's prose, though modern and minimal, is also poetic, a style that allows her to clinically but also empathetically depict her protagonist. Early in the narrative, Paul is described as arrogant, insolent, and difficult, as he appears before his teachers, but the drawing master questions this simplistic portrait, observing fragility unseen by others:

> His master had noted with amazement what a white, blue-veined face it was; drawn and wrinkled like an old man's about the eyes, the lips twitching even in his sleep, and stiff with a nervous tension that drew them back from his teeth.[49]

Cather's adroit use of modern prose, though evident throughout the story, is shocking in the final sentences where she describes the boy's suicide. Through this prose, which employs a mechanistic, clinical language infused with poetic figures of speech, Cather creates a graphic, but tragic, portrait of a young life lost: "Then, because the picture-making mechanism was crushed, the disturbing visions flashed into black, and Paul dropped back into the immense design of things."[50] In her writing, Cather blends factual reportage with literary minimalism, creating a style that has served as a model for all modern writers, including New Journalists. And in her essay "The Novel Démeublé," Cather describes this style, calling on others to emulate it:

> There are hopeful signs that some of the younger writers are trying to break away from mere verisimilitude, and, following the development of modern painting, to interpret imaginatively the material and social investiture of their characters; to present their scene by suggestion rather than by enumeration.[51]

In writing Paul's case, Cather modeled her protagonist on students she knew as a teacher at two Pittsburgh high schools, and she also drew on her work as a journalist, basing the main action on a crime that was covered extensively in her Pittsburgh paper.[52] But it is Cather's modern prose style that elevates a tragic news event into a forceful work of literary journalism. As Timothy Bintrim and Mark Madigan argue in "From Larceny to Suicide," "Paul's Case" illustrates beautifully Cather's attempt to blend journalism and fiction."[53]

Jack London (1876–1916)

Like Norris, Jack London was a San Francisco author, publishing an early work in the *Wave*, where Norris had been a contributing editor. But London was unlike the other naturalists in that he was a famous author of fiction before he was known as a journalist, publishing the Malemute Kid short stories, which appeared in the *Atlantic* and *Overland* magazines, then collecting these Klondike stories in *Son of the Wolf* (1900), a highly praised volume. But before 1900, London had published a few nonfiction works in periodicals and newspapers, including an excellent example of literary journalism, "The Story of a Typhoon off the Coast of Japan" (1893), based on his sealing ship experiences when he was only seventeen. Appearing in the *San Francisco Morning Call*, the short story is unique in its use of detailed descriptions and present-tense verbs.[54] In characterizing London's early writings, Jonah Raskin notes that London "learned to paint pictures with words, to fill large canvases with color, and to put himself into the picture, too, as a fictional character with the name 'Jack.'"[55] After becoming a bestselling author, London continued accepting assignments as a reporter. For example, in 1902, after a newspaper cancelled his trip to South Africa, where he was to report the aftereffects of the Boer War, he traveled to England where he wrote a shocking exposé, *The People of the Abyss* (1903), a work that has become a model for literary journalists. Even though London had grown up in poverty, he was traumatized by what he found in the East End of London. In writing *The People of the Abyss*, London gathered "facts and figures, presenting documentary evidence to buttress his case against the wealthy and the powerful," and in this process, he created a distinctive documentary work based on immersive journalism.[56] As an author, London inserted himself into the story, as both an observer and a participant. In exposing the East End's horrific living conditions, London joined a chorus of voices that shamed the United Kingdom into enacting reforms. Three years after the publication of *The People of the Abyss*, the British Liberal Party gained a massive majority and enacted numerous social reforms, which became the foundation for the modern welfare state in Great Britain.[57]

Throughout his life, London traveled extensively, not as a tourist but as a reporter and adventurer, suffering from malaria, dysentery, scurvy, numerous tropical fevers, rashes, and sores to gather experiences out of which narratives could be spun. In 1904, after publishing *The Call of the Wild* (1903), London accepted another assignment for the *San Francisco Examiner*, covering the Russo-Japanese War. He traveled to Japan and Korea, where the Japanese arrested him several times, experiences that he describes vividly in numerous articles. And in 1906, living a short distance north of San Francisco, London published an eyewitness account of the 1904 earthquake, "The Story of an Eyewitness." Even after becoming "the highest paid author in America," London continued to accept assignments as a journalist.[58] An amateur boxer and an avid fan of boxing, London, like Mailer, covered a championship match (Johnson vs. Jeffries, 1910) for the *New York Herald*. And despite ill health, until his early death in 1914, London continued to travel, write, and publish, including noteworthy works of literary journalism: *The Cruise of the Snark* (1911), "Mexico's Army and Ours" (1914), and "Our Adventures in Tampico" (1914).

Like the other naturalists, London blurred the line between fiction and nonfiction, involving himself in dangerous situations that informed all his narratives, including his fiction. His first collection of short stories and his most famous novel, *The Call of the Wild*, were based on his yearlong experiences in the Klondike Gold Rush in 1897. In writing *The Sea-Wolf* (1904), London relied on his own sailing experiences, including his time on a sealing ship, and he based the character Wolf Larsen on Captain Alex MacLean.[59] Although all of London's fiction draws on personal experiences and observations, *Martin Eden* (1909), written after London had achieved fame, is his most realistic novel, filled with autobiographical details. Raskin describes *Martin Eden* as London's "most perfectly crafted novel," a work that critiques radical individualism (the American Dream).[60] Like Dreiser, Crane, Norris, and Cather, London depicted humans in extreme conditions, but to find his inspiration, to supply his realistic details, he, more than any writer of the period, worked as a pioneer of reportage, a genre that required him to become a real-life protagonist.

Conclusion

In nonfiction works such as Crane's "In the Depths of a Coal Mine," Dreiser's *Twelve Men*, Norris's sketches for the *Wave*, Cather's *The Life of Mary Baker G. Eddy and the History of Christian Science*, and London's *The People of the Abyss*, the first generation of American naturalists developed literary journalism as a genre, embracing their roles as reporters dedicated to social causes. And in fictional works such as *An American Tragedy*, *Maggie*, *McTeague*, "Paul's Case," and *Martin Eden*, these early naturalists pushed the limits of fiction by drawing on newspaper stories, including taboo accounts of violent crime, poverty, sex, and greed, subjects that had not previously been within the purview of American fiction. In developing and expanding literary genres, in their unique amalgamations of fact and fiction, American naturalists pointed the way toward the rise of New Journalism, creative nonfiction, literary journalism, and even contemporary/postmodern naturalism, literary genres that move beyond binary divisions of fiction and nonfiction, of objective and subjective. For example, in nonfiction essays, Joyce Carol Oates, like London, Hemingway, and Mailer, has explored the world of boxing: Three long essays ("On Boxing," "On Mike Tyson," and "The Cruelest Sport") were collected in *On Boxing* (1987), a volume that draws on Oates's personal interest in boxing as symbolic of life's brutal struggles. And her historical novel *Blonde* (2000), like Dreiser's *Trilogy of Desire*, blurs fact and fiction to the extent that some readers wrongly consider the novel a biography, just as some early readers of Dreiser's financial novels considered them journalism. In a similar way, another postmodern naturalist, Don DeLillo, like early naturalists, blends fact and fiction in creative amalgamations, as in *Libra* (1988) and *Falling Man* (2007), novels based on historical events (the assassination of John F. Kennedy and the September 11 attacks). And DeLillo's nonfiction essays, like those of Oates, clearly rise to the level of literary journalism, as evidenced by a work such as "In the Ruins of the Future" (2001), which analyzes terrorism and the effects of globalization while narrating the struggles of his nephew's family as the towers of the World Trade Center collapsed. In crossing the divide between high and low culture, between fact and fiction, and in setting themselves and their characters in moments of extremity, the naturalists have helped develop literary journalism as a contemporary genre.

Notes

1. Howells, "Editor's Study," 973.
2. Robertson, *Stephen Crane*, 2.
3. Hartsock, *History*, 78.
4. Dreiser, *Newspaper Days*, 5.
5. Underwood, *Chronicling Trauma*, 139.
6. Underwood, 146.
7. Underwood, *Journalism and the Novel*, 29.
8. Wolfe, *Hooking Up*, 161.
9. Wolfe, "Seizing the Power," 31–32.
10. Pizer, "Nineteenth-Century American Naturalism," 86.
11. Shi, *Facing Facts*, 213.
12. Connery, *Journalism and Realism*, 181.
13. Hartsock, *Literary Journalism*, 23.
14. Loving, *Last Titan*, 47.
15. Dreiser, "Cheyenne," 4–6.
16. Dreiser, "At a Rope's End," 226–39.
17. Dreiser, "This Calls for Hemp."
18. Dreiser, "Ten-Foot Drop," 258.
19. Dreiser, "Nigger Jeff," 76–111. For parallels between the nonfiction and fiction works, see also Hopkins and Mulligan, "Lynching."
20. Dreiser, "Curious Shifts," 22–26.
21. Dreiser, "Touch of Human Brotherhood."
22. Riggio, "Oh Captain, My Captain," 27.
23. Hartsock, *History*, 78.
24. Swanberg, *Dreiser*, 307.
25. Swanberg, 357–58.
26. Robertson, *Stephen Crane*, 75.
27. Sorrentino, *Stephen Crane*, 88.
28. Robertson, *Stephen Crane*, 83.
29. Dow, *Narrating Class*, 68.
30. Sorrentino, *Stephen Crane*, 220.
31. Sorrentino, 226.
32. For further analysis of "Stephen Crane's Own Story" and "The Open Boat," see Robertson, *Stephen Crane*, 135; Frus, "Two Tales"; Sorrentino, *Stephen Crane*, 228, 278.
33. Robertson, *Stephen Crane*, 135.
34. Sorrentino, *Stephen Crane*, 228.
35. Pizer, "John Dos Passos," 14.
36. Sorrentino, *Stephen Crane*, 278.
37. McElrath and Crisler, *Frank Norris*, 171.
38. In his introduction to *Frank Norris of "The Wave,"* Lewis estimates that Norris's articles, during his twenty-two months as a contributing editor to the *Wave*, were about half fiction and half nonfiction (10). In their authoritative biography, *Frank Norris*, McElrath and Crisler point out that in 1896, of Norris's sixty-five contributions to the *Wave*, "only ten were short stories" (220).
39. Lewis, introduction to *Frank Norris*, 1.
40. In noticing that Ida appears in a nonfiction work before the publication of *Vandover*, McElrath and Crisler state bluntly that "Norris's description in *The Wave* of the 'Fast Girl' type in San Francisco became his characterization of Ida Wade in *Vandover and the Brute*" (*Frank Norris*, 216).
41. Norris, "Zola," 1106.
42. "Twenty-Nine Fatal Wounds," *San Francisco Examiner*, October 10, 1893, 12, cited in McElrath and Crisler, *Frank Norris*, 241.
43. Campbell, *Bitter Tastes*, 4, 7.
44. Cather, "One Way."
45. Miller in "Willa Cather's Journalism and Fiction" calls Cather a New Journalist and compares her style to Tom Wolfe's.
46. In his introduction to the 1993 edition of *The Life of Mary Baker G. Eddy*, Stouck claims that Cather should be considered the principal author of the volume. But in her article "The Standard Oil

47 Kitch, "Work," 425.
48 Ross in "Cather People" notes that Cather uses her hometown, Red Cloud, Nebraska, as a setting in six of her twelve novels (33).
49 Cather, "Paul's Case," 75.
50 Cather, 83.
51 Cather, "Novel Démeublé," 6.
52 Bintrim and Madigan, "From Larceny to Suicide."
53 Bintrim and Madigan, 121.
54 Labor, *Jack London*, 49.
55 Raskin, *Radical Jack London*, 22.
56 Raskin, 117.
57 In *A New England?*, Searle describes reform legislation enacted by the British Liberal Party, which came to power in 1906 (366–406).
58 Labor, *Jack London*, 355.
59 Throughout *Captain Alex MacLean*, MacGillivray draws parallels between the character Wolf Larsen and Alex MacLean.
60 Raskin, *Radical Jack London*, 206, 210.

Treatment," Squires questions Stouck's assertion, finding that Cather was the principal editor but only one of several coauthors. And in *Healing the Nation*, Squires dedicates an entire chapter to the Eddy biography (118–56).

Bibliography

Bintrim, Timothy W., and Mark J. Madigan. "From Larceny to Suicide: The Denny Case and 'Paul's Case.'" In *Violence, the Arts, and Willa Cather*, edited by Joseph R. Urgo and Merrill Maguire Skaggs, 109–23. Madison, NJ: Fairleigh Dickinson University Press, 2007.
Campbell, Donna M. *Bitter Tastes: Literary Naturalism and Early Cinema in American Women's Writing*. Athens, GA: University of Georgia Press, 2016.
Cather, Willa. "The Novel Démeublé." *New Republic*, April 12, 1922, 5–6.
———. "One Way of Putting It." *Nebraska State Journal*, November 12, 1893, 13. Willa Cather Archive, edited by Andrew Jewell. University of Nebraska–Lincoln. https://cather.unl.edu/j00044.html.
———. "Paul's Case: A Study in Temperament." *McClure's Magazine*, May 1905, 74–83.
Cather, Willa, and Georgine Milmine. *The Life of Mary Baker G. Eddy and the History of Christian Science*. Edited by David Stouck. Lincoln, NE: University of Nebraska Press, 1993.
Connery, Thomas B. *Journalism and Realism: Rendering American Life*. Evanston, IL: Northwestern University Press, 2010.
DeLillo, Don. *Falling Man*. New York: Scribner, 2007.
———. "In the Ruins of the Future: Reflections on Terror and Loss in the Shadow of September." *Harper's Magazine*, December 2001, 33–40.
———. *Libra*. New York: Viking, 1988.
Dow, William. *Narrating Class in American Fiction*. New York: Palgrave Macmillan, 2009.
Dreiser, Theodore. "At a Rope's End." In *Newspaper Writings*, 226–39. Originally published in *St. Louis Republic*, January 12, 1894, 1–2.
———. "Cheyenne, Haunt of Misery and Crime." In *Newspaper Writings*, 4–6. Originally published in *Chicago Globe*, July 24, 1892, 3.
———. "Curious Shifts of the Poor." *Demorest's*, November 1899, 22–26.
———. "The Hanging of Welsor." In *Newspaper Writings*, 232–39. Originally published in *St. Louis Republic*, January 13, 1894, 5.
———. *Newspaper Days*. Edited by T. D. Nostwich. Philadelphia, PA: University of Pennsylvania Press, 1991.
———. *Newspaper Writings, 1892–1895*. Edited by T. D. Nostwich. Vol. 1 of *Journalism*. Philadelphia, PA: University of Pennsylvania Press, 1988.
———. "Nigger Jeff." In *Free and Other Stories*, 76–111. New York: Modern Library, 1918.
———. "Ten-Foot Drop." In *Newspaper Writings*, 251–58. Originally published in *St. Louis Republic*, January 18, 1894, 1.
———. "This Calls for Hemp." In *Newspaper Writings*, 249–51. Originally published in *St. Louis Republic*, January 17, 1894, 1.

———. "A Touch of Human Brotherhood." In *Theodore Dreiser's Uncollected Magazine Articles, 1897–1902*, edited by Yoshinobu Hakutani, 264–70. Newark, DE: University of Delaware Press, 2003. Originally published in *Success*, March 1902, 140–41.

Frus, Phyllis. "Two Tales 'Intended to Be after the Fact': 'Stephen Crane's Own Story' and 'The Open Boat.'" In *Literary Nonfiction: Theory, Criticism, Pedagogy*, edited by Chris Anderson, 125–51. Carbondale, IL: Southern Illinois University Press, 1989.

Hartsock, John C. *A History of American Literary Journalism: The Emergence of a Modern Narrative Form*. Amherst, MA: University of Massachusetts Press, 2000.

———. *Literary Journalism and the Aesthetics of Experience*. Boston, MA: University of Massachusetts Press, 2016.

Hopkins, Patricia D., and Roark Mulligan. "Lynching the Black Male Body in Theodore Dreiser's 'Nigger Jeff': Did He 'Get It All In'?" *American Literary Realism* 45, no. 3 (Spring 2013): 229–47.

Howells, William Dean. "Editor's Study." *Harper's New Monthly Magazine*, May 1886, 972–76.

Kitch, Carolyn. "The Work That Came Before the Art: Willa Cather as Journalist, 1893–1912." *American Journalism* 14, nos. 3–4 (Summer 1997): 425–40.

Labor, Earle. *Jack London: An American Life*. New York: Farrar, Straus and Giroux, 2013.

Lewis, Oscar. Introduction to *Frank Norris of "The Wave": Stories and Sketches from the San Francisco Weekly, 1893 to 1897*, by Frank Norris, 1–13. St. Clair Shores, MI: Scholarly Press, 1972.

Loving, Jerome. *The Last Titan: A Life of Theodore Dreiser*. Berkeley, CA: University of California Press, 2005.

MacGillivray, Don. *Captain Alex MacLean: Jack London's Sea Wolf*. Vancouver: University of British Columbia Press, 2008.

McElrath, Joseph R., Jr., and Jesse S. Crisler. *Frank Norris: A Life*. Urbana, IL: University of Illinois Press, 2006.

Miller, Laurie S. "Willa Cather's Journalism and Fiction: Romancing the Facts." PhD diss., Indiana University of Pennsylvania, 2008.

Norris, Frank. *Frank Norris of "The Wave": Stories & Sketches from the San Francisco Weekly, 1893 to 1897*. Introduction by Oscar Lewis. St. Clair Shores, MI: Scholarly Press, 1972.

———. "Zola as a Romantic Writer." In *Norris: Novels and Essays*, edited by Donald Pizer, 1106–08. New York: Library of America, 1986. Originally published in *Wave*, June 27, 1896.

Oates, Joyce Carol. *Blonde*. New York: HarperCollins, 2000.

———. *On Boxing*. New York: Doubleday, 1987.

Pizer, Donald. "John Dos Passos and Harlan: Three Variations on a Theme." *Arizona Quarterly: A Journal of American Literature, Culture, and Theory* 71, no. 1 (Spring 2015): 1–23.

———. "Nineteenth-Century American Naturalism: An Essay in Definition." In *The Theory and Practice of American Literary Naturalism: Selected Essays and Reviews*, 85–101. Carbondale, IL: Southern Illinois University Press, 1993.

Raskin, Jonah, ed. *The Radical Jack London: Writings on War and Revolution*. By Jack London. Berkeley, CA: University of California Press, 2008.

Riggio, Thomas P. "Oh Captain, My Captain: Dreiser and the Chaplain of Madison Square." *Studies in American Naturalism* 11, no. 2 (Winter 2016): 23–37.

Robertson, Michael. *Stephen Crane, Journalism, and the Making of Modern American Literature*. New York: Columbia University Press, 1997.

Ross, Alex. "Cather People." *New Yorker*, October 2, 2017, 32–37.

Searle, Geoffrey Russell. *A New England? Peace and War, 1886–1918*. Oxford: Clarendon Press, 2004.

Shi, David E. *Facing Facts: Realism in American Thought and Culture, 1850–1920*. New York: Oxford University Press, 1994.

Sorrentino, Paul. *Stephen Crane: A Life of Fire*. Cambridge, MA: Harvard University Press, 2014.

Squires, L. Ashley. *Healing the Nation: Literature, Progress, and Christian Science*. Bloomington, IN: Indiana University Press, 2017.

———. "The Standard Oil Treatment: Willa Cather, *The Life of Mary Baker G. Eddy*, and Early Twentieth Century Collaborative Authorship." *Studies in the Novel* 45, no. 3 (Fall 2013): 328–48.

Stouck, David. Introduction to Cather and Milmine, *Life of Mary Baker G. Eddy*, xv–xxviii.

Swanberg, W. A. *Dreiser*. New York: Charles Scribner's Sons, 1965.

Underwood, Doug. *Chronicling Trauma: Journalists and Writers on Violence and Loss*. Urbana, IL: University of Illinois Press, 2011.

———. *Journalism and the Novel: Truth and Fiction, 1700–2000*. Cambridge: Cambridge University Press, 2008.

Wolfe, Tom. *Hooking Up*. New York: Picador, 2001.

———. "Seizing the Power." In *The New Journalism*, edited by Tom Wolfe and E. W. Johnson, 23–36. New York: Harper and Row, 1973.

6
JOURNALISTIC LITERATURE
Female Reporters and Newspaper Fiction, 1880–1930

Karen Roggenkamp

On December 19, 1912, the humor magazine *Life* presented some "Hints for Fiction Writers" seeking sure-fire advice for crafting stories that would appeal to the reading public. Writer Hinton Gilmore lays out formulas for "the different styles" and plot frameworks for "the various ... types" of popular literature, such as detective stories, hillbilly feud stories, business stories, and, finally, "newspaper stor[ies]," which Gilmore precisely outlines:

> First essential, gruff city editor. After that four "star" reporters and one unappreciated "cub." The conversation must be replete with "scoops" and "clean copy" and "throbbing presses." Let the "cub" get the big "beat" and have the story printed on the first page just as it comes from his typewriter "pulsing with human interest." On the strength of the story raise the "cub's" salary to seventy-five dollars a week. (Reminder, we are speaking of fiction.)[1]

Life's sardonic description points toward what was, in fact, a familiar though rather formulaic genre in late nineteenth- and early twentieth-century literature, narratives that fictionalized the adventures of newspaper reporters, usually authored by current or former journalists. Between 1880 and 1930, dozens of these literary works found publication in periodicals and novels—so many that *Life* could spoof the genre, secure in the knowledge that its readers would recognize the humor in describing a cliché fictional class.[2] Newspaper fiction dramatized the profession of journalism by casting reporters as heroes on the prowl for scoops, characters who braved both danger and sorrow, all for the glory of the fictionalized newspaper and adulation for the fictionalized reporter. These were representations within and about a broader type of literary journalism—termed "new journalism" and, later, "yellow journalism"—that thrived in the late nineteenth and early twentieth centuries, stories and novels that emerged out of a news style that was itself invested in the use of fictional styles and conventions that provided narratives that read like fiction itself. Inherently metatextual, newspaper fiction drew plot trajectories from news stories the author may actually have covered and toyed with the boundary between fact and fiction.

More specifically, newspaper fiction offered readers insight into an intriguing figure: the female reporter. Coinciding with the increasing employment of women at major dailies, a robust number of newspaper fictions chronicled the experiences of these professionals who were fighting their way into a male-dominated workplace. Just thirty-five women self-identified as editors or reporters in 1870, a number that grew to 288 in 1880, then exploded to 888 in 1890 and 2,193 in 1900—significant growth, though still a small proportion of that year's journalist class, which totaled 30,098.[3] Female reporters lucky enough to secure a desk in the city room faced condescension, opposition, and sometimes open hostility from their male counterparts. Editor Edward Bok, for example, declared that women could not "do the work required a reporter without undergoing a decline in the innate qualities of womanliness."[4] As journalist and fiction-writer Elizabeth Jordan complained, would-be newspaper women "stood at the door of the sanctums, so to speak, but their invitations" from men "to enter were not urgent."[5]

Newspaper fiction sought to tell the story of the women "standing at the door" by entering into the web of interactions between journalism and literature in the nineteenth century. While studies by Norman Sims, Thomas Connery, John Hartsock, and Kevin Kerrane and Ben Yagoda, among others, spotlight the place of narrative journalism within this web, newspaper fiction—which offers a look at the web from another angle—has not enjoyed the same attention. Yet newspaper fiction directly turned journalism into literature, or into a new type of "literary journalism." And the newspaper fiction of female reporters expands consideration of both this genre and the place of women within the profession. Newspaper fiction authored by women and about women bolstered the characterization of female reporters as bold and plucky professionals crafting stories to rival—and often surpass—those of their male counterparts, as all struggled to produce the kind of dramatic, engaging writing that characterizes literary journalism itself. This chapter surveys women's newspaper fiction published between 1880 and 1930 and grants insight into the profession and practice of journalism as experienced by women during a period in which they encountered shifting roles and challenging expectations within narrative-driven newsrooms. Following a discussion of fin-de-siècle new journalism and the literary nature of the era's reporting in general, I consider how the formulaic components highlight the anxieties, pressures, and self-perceptions of female journalists, as fictionalized for a mass readership.

Newspaper fiction emerged at a time when the borders between fact and fiction, journalism and literature, were particularly porous. Newspapers brimmed with stylistic conventions that were in conversation with realist fiction, which likewise teemed with details that seemed distinctly journalistic in style. Leading newspapers championed dramatic reporting that accentuated the *story* of the news, and reporters drew upon the same tools fiction writers used to craft their own work: strong characterization, vivid storytelling, engaging dialogue, strong imagery, and so on. As one writer observed, "A modern newspaper worker, to be successful, must know somewhat of the art of fiction, just as some writers of fiction need reportorial methods in the practice of their art."[6]

Renowned editor Joseph Pulitzer, first at the St. Louis *Post-Dispatch* in the 1880s and then at the New York *World* and other papers, championed this literary style, which was eventually called "new journalism." Pulitzer's reporters served up a dramatic mixture of sensationalism and human interest for a mass, urban market. The *World* and other papers still offered "hard news," but the writing drew upon detailed scene-setting, careful plotting, and vivid characterization—a format that could both "get the facts and … be colorful"—a style of literary journalism, offered daily on the pages of America's leading newspaper in the 1880s and 1890s.[7] Editors at other papers noticed Pulitzer's financial success and mimicked the *World*'s technique, so much so that by 1894, Edwin Shuman counseled future journalists that "readers will forgive a good deal of inaccuracy in your matter," provided reporters insert "sparkle" into their articles.[8]

Running throughout the discussion of new journalism was the conviction that "the art of writing well for a newspaper is the art of the plain tale"—the art of portraying life with realism, as a columnist notes in a 1907 issue of *Bookman*.[9] A natural affinity lay between reporting and the aesthetic of realist literature at the turn of the twentieth century; both aimed to capture "the real thing." While a fiction writer might represent realism through imaginary constructions, "the reporter," as one columnist put it, "is always close to life. ... He knows how man acts in passion, in stress, in joy, in hate."[10] Journalists drew upon the same creative fodder as novelists working in the realist tradition, and that overlap is particularly evident within the genre of newspaper fiction.

Newspaper fiction flourished from the 1890s through the first decades of the twentieth century. It satisfied the interest, as one book review noted in 1898, that "much of the general reading public" held for "literature which deals with the 'local color' of the editorial room, of the peculiar woes and blisses of the men and women" who reported on urban life; it placed the drama of the "city room" into literary terms.[11] Though newspaper fiction purportedly represented "what goes on in Park Row" or "Newspaper Row," the hub of New York papers and sometimes a generic term for similar hubs across America, the stories and novels described, more fundamentally, "the world a reporter sees—criminals, and other celebrities of the hour—which is visible to an artist in any walk of existence."[12]

The genre builds upon familiar themes and conventions. First, authors frequently introduce, often near the beginning, definitions of journalistic terms that may not be familiar to a general readership. A collection of newspaper stories called *Tales of the City Room*, for instance, supplies readers with a glossary of commonly used terms like "copy," "assignment," "fake," "story," and "scoop." Jordan's "Ruth Herrick's Assignment" places the nomenclature into the action of the story when the title character explains,

> A big beat ... is an important exclusive story. If it appears in your newspaper, it is the greatest journalistic feat of the year, implying the possession of superior skill, brains, and journalistic enterprise by the members of your staff. ... The reporter who brought in the story, or the "tip," gets some praise, and possibly a check. His position on the newspaper is secure—until he makes his next mistake. Tersely expressed, a "beat" is a story which only one newspaper gets, and which all the other newspapers wanted. A reporter with the right spirit will move heaven and earth to get it for the journal he represents.[13]

Jordan's passage might serve as the very definition of newspaper fiction itself. It casts a familiar set of characters, such as ambitious and unscrupulous rival reporters, earnest and devoted office boys, and gruff managing editors—"slouchy, unshaven, and profane" men "with a nose for news like a hound dog's, a rough but vivid power of expression, and an exceedingly active blue pencil."[14] The narrative's central action, however, follows a single, ambitious reporter who might face an ethical dilemma, a seemingly unsolvable mystery, dangerous situations, or the biggest story of his or her life.

Despite formulaic plots, authors of newspaper fiction faced certain challenges. As H. H. McClure noted in a 1910 *Bookman* essay, journalists sometimes "overestimate[d] the amount of glamour connected" with newspaper work "and the value of that work consequently as an exceptional basis for fiction." Subsequently, a "narrative of the intricacies of press workings proves to be tedious reading."[15] In McClure's estimation, "many of these pieces of fiction ... [fail] to reveal the journalistic sphere in its true light" given the actual grind in newsrooms.[16]

Criticism aside, newspaper fiction attracted readers between the 1890s and 1930s, and one group of novels and stories stood out: those penned by newspaper women. Coinciding with the increasing presence of women in the newsroom, a number of female reporters turned their professional experiences—and sometimes even actual news stories—into literature. If newspaper fiction overall presented familiar themes and plot conventions, women's newspaper fiction added its own set of characteristics. Read together, a collection of this fiction not only offers a composite picture of women in the newsroom but depicts their efforts to establish a gendered literary journalism.

Even as professional opportunities expanded between 1880 and 1930, newspaper women faced challenges to their status as professionals, a theme that appears frequently in the fiction as well. Stories picture male colleagues and editors who doubt women's stamina and mock a perceived sentimentality, and they grouse about an invasion into the previously masculine space. One novel's editor informs an ambitious newspaper woman, "I never count much on a woman. Women have no sustained force," while another warns that he tries "to discourage all women from attempting newspaper work."[17] If "it is hard on men," he reasons, "how can the nerves of women stand what those men rebel against?"[18] Likewise, the editor in the romping *Jennie Baxter: Journalist* scoffs that the prospect of a full-time female reporter on staff is "utterly impossible" and that, at any rate, he simply does "not believe in women journalists."[19] While the paper occasionally prints pieces written by women, they send those items in "from their own homes," presumably where they belong. Besides, the editor explains, "I have men who" can do "anything that a woman can do for a newspaper, … quite as well, if not better" than women, and "there are many things that women can't do at all which men must do."[20] In other cases, male coworkers underestimate the mettle of newspaper women by equating their femininity with weakness. The editor in a story by Jordan—the most prolific author of women's newspaper fiction between the 1890s and 1910s—contends that "you can't depend on a woman in this business."[21] More superficially, a male competitor in the 1905 novel *A Yellow Journalist* references the newspaper woman's appearance as evidence of her unsuitability, insisting that "girls with sunny hair were made" to be ladies, not reporters.[22] This attitude persists in the fiction for decades, as evidenced by a staff photographer who complains in a 1931 novel that he'd "rather work a story with ten men reporters" than one woman.[23]

Despite their doubts, male characters soon recognize their counterparts' journalistic prowess, as typified by the protagonist in an 1896 story who admits that though the "first, last, and only newspaper woman" to join his paper "was greeted with ridicule by some, and with doubt by most of us … her work soon dispelled all that; she was a natural reporter."[24] And a renowned reporter in Ernest Shriver's "A Frustrated 'Scoop'" can't help but admire his rival, who, in attempting to reach her paper first to break news about a sensational murder-suicide, furiously races for the office using that most modern form of transportation in the 1890s, the bicycle.

Admiration for the bicycling reporter points toward one of the common identities for newspaper women, both in fact and in fiction: the plucky and fearless journalist who will stop at nothing to nab a scoop for her paper—and advance her own career in the process. As Mildred Gilman's protagonist puts it, "The perfect reporter thinks of nothing but the story. The perfect reporter is happy to be rushing out to the scene of the crime, … never indignant at being torn out of a warm bed, never genuinely sad about his victim" and "happy to extract quotations from the criminal," even if it means morally questionable methods.[25] Indeed, Gilman's novel opens with an example of this ethos as the formidable reporter Jane Ray jumps a fence, sneaks into a criminal's bungalow, and dissembles in order to steal a photograph, one of her many daring—and unladylike—feats over the course of the novel. Similar journalistic daring occurs in "The Love-Making of Loo," whose reporter Miss Hartegan boasts a history of "climbing church steeples and down in diving suits to the bottom of the [San Francisco] Bay" in pursuit of a good story,[26] while the protagonist of *A Yellow Journalist* impersonates a Chinese boy to ferret out clues and solve a crime for her paper, and "The Queen" of "A Newspaper Woman's Romance" performs a whole host of feats, all for the sake of the paper:

> She interviewed a political leader in a barber's chair and a prima donna in her bath. She went up in a balloon and down in a diver's suit. … In short, she successfully carried out all the wild ideas that came into the heads of her superiors.[27]

In fact, as one editor informs his star reporter, she may need "to climb up the outside of the Woolworth Building" to secure a story, a scenario that occurs in another novel when a newspaper woman brazenly crawls along the high ledge of a building to eavesdrop and gain inside information for one of her articles.[28]

Authors frequently embroil their newspaper women in mysteries, echoing one of the most popular genres in the late nineteenth century: the detective story. Drawing upon the conventions of the form, with its intelligent sleuths and seemingly unbreakable cases, the newspaper women of fiction prove their professional mettle by uncovering hidden evidence and solving the most baffling crimes. The editor of Kate Masterson's "The Love-Making of Loo" enthuses that he has on staff a "woman writer" who is "the cleverest detective in New York."[29] A reviewer for *Jennie Baxter: Journalist* notes the same element in that novel, which is a "very clever story of an unscrupulous newspaper woman whose various and brilliant methods of getting information … are equal to many of the intricate plots of the famous Sherlock Holmes."[30]

Surprisingly, though, a common, almost inevitable, plot convention marks the *end* of the newspaper woman's career. A majority of women's newspaper fiction closes with a marriage proposal, usually uniting the female protagonist with a male colleague or rival and necessitating her resignation. In fiction, that is, the newspaper woman flees the professional world for the confines of domestic space, even if in fact the *author* of that fiction did not make the same decision in her own life. The main character of "A Frustrated 'Scoop,'" to provide one example, earns a substantial raise and the promise of a successful career after filing a sensational story, yet "she gave up journalism within the next six weeks" in order to marry her rival from another paper.[31] The title character of *May Iverson's Career* finds success working for the top New York paper yet resigns once she receives a marriage proposal from a coworker, declaring that "my professional life … lay behind me."[32] For his part, a fellow reporter saves a newspaper woman from increasingly degrading sensational journalism in "Miss Van Dyke's Best Story," and the grateful title character vows that she will gladly exchange her career for "the assignment of marriage," for, "after all, a woman's place is in the home."[33] Similarly, newspaper woman Dorothy, in "Her Best Stuff," leaves a potentially sordid journalistic career when another reporter proposes, and Arizona Victoria Harris, in "Stories of Working Girls," eventually returns West, away from New York's Park Row, "to be married," admitting that "newspaper work [is] a thing for women to let alone when they can." She will find greater joy by "turning over in [her] life's history the only Women's Page" she "will never tire of editing"—life as a wife, settled in her own domestic haven.[34] Even *Sob Sister*, a relatively risqué novel that features several sexually suggestive scenes, wraps up with a wholly conventional marriage plot.

The authors' nearly ubiquitous decision to move their female reporters from the city room to the kitchen may seem surprising, given the simultaneous celebration of women's power and professionalism within the plot trajectory. Yet these conclusions not only resolve the conflicts of the story or novel; they also gesture toward broader social anxieties about professional women and their place in a changing American landscape. If real-life newspaper women readily directed their protagonists toward lives outside journalism, they also exposed some of the darker elements of contemporary news reporting, arguably shaking the foundations on which their own, actual careers rested. This element of newspaper fiction seems to suggest, almost in keeping with what critics argued, that journalism might corrupt the very essence of femininity.

A target of the "corrupting influence" theme is reportorial inauthenticity and its negative effect on women's character, as defined by contemporary social mores. Cultural critics expressed concerns about "fake news" at the end of the nineteenth and early twentieth centuries, a period in which, again, the lines between "fact" and "fiction" were blurred on the pages of the newspaper. Fiction revealed that newspaper women were not above manufacturing news and embroidering facts in the quest to sell a more dramatic story. In some sense, the narratives imply, inauthenticity means selling not only stories but femininity as well. Jordan's "In the Case of Hannah Risser," a story that takes as its starting point a factual story Jordan published while a New York *World* reporter, features an unscrupulous reporter who simply makes up details after the subject of her story fails to provide the expected response necessary to write a successful article.[35] The drama that the writer wishes to create is more important than reality itself. Meanwhile, the anonymous author of "The Confessions of a 'Literary Journalist'" admits that "when it comes to the little things which add vividness" to a newspaper story—the things that, one might say, make it literary in nature—male and female reporters alike face the "constant temptation" to manufacture details and, in essence, turn the news into a fiction.[36] While Shuman, above, asserts that readers accept fabrication, the authors of newspaper fiction do not necessarily look upon the practice with as much confidence.

Some characters dramatize another kind of inauthenticity—faking sympathy toward the subjects of a hot story or viewing them in purely objectified terms, all so that the newspaper woman can get what she needs for the ever-important scoop. When one reporter's "sob story" about an impoverished family appears in print, her first reaction to seeing her name in a headline is self-absorbed glee rather than genuine sympathy toward the subject of her article. She adds, "hastily" and rather unconvincingly, "Of course I am not thinking of it all from my own side. I feel desperately sorry for that poor woman."[37] The protagonist of "Number Seventeen: An Episode" exhibits a similarly objectifying gaze when she searches for a patient guaranteed to die within a few hours so that she can use him or her as the subject of a story. Her editor exemplifies the ethos of the newsroom when he gives the newspaper woman her assignment: "After you've found your case, sit down beside it and—er—let it do the rest."[38] For her part, Jane Ray of *Sob Sister* uses her status as a newspaper woman to manipulate people into divulging valuable information and thereby advance her own career. "People usually didn't suspect women of being reporters," Gilman's narrator muses, "especially when they were blonde and youthful, with wide-open blue eyes and a guileless smile."[39] Ray readily learns to "promise freedom to criminals and false hope to those in distress," even "to deceive the mothers of murdered girls" so that she might "steal pictures from them" for publication in the paper.[40] Through it all, "Jane Ray, without seeming to feel anything herself, could pour more anguish into her copy, more deep emotional feeling than any other sob sister,"[41] even though, as another reporter chastises, the sympathy Ray feels "for human beings is paid sympathy."[42] The same concern toward male reporters whose sympathy is "paid" does not appear in newspaper fiction, it would seem.

The dangers of cynicism are also clear in many newspaper fictions. The title character of "Miss Underhill's Lesson: A Newspaper Story" is "a great reporter, but ... not a great lady," having been corrupted by the sensationalism of yellow journalism.[43] Another story details how that split between reporter and lady might occur: "Three years of journalistic success is bound to blunt not only the gentler attributes of femininity, but the promptings of ordinary morality" because of the "scurvy tricks" a reporter must play to win "fame and money."[44] Likewise, Jane Ray's on-again, off-again love interest charges her with being "a hard-boiled girl" who doesn't "believe in femininity, but in rushing around day and night in jails and speakeasies for murderers," with great detriment to her character.[45] A similar denigration occurs in "Miss Van Dyke's Best Story," which chronicles how a sweetly maternal newspaper woman gains an unsavory reputation in the newsroom simply by covering a wild postelection night in the Tenderloin District. She delivers a model story, but the men who once treated her with respect "now trea[t] her as one of themselves, with a good-natured camaraderie, in which, however, the deference of the old days was wholly lacking."[46] The predictable alleviation of that saucy reputation comes with marriage. Miss Van Dyke fulfills the dire prophecy of critic Edward Bok, who warned, as described above, that the newsroom would destroy "the innate qualities of womanliness."[47]

Despite—or perhaps because of—the generally tidy plots that fuel women's newspaper fiction, critics warned that the genre might lead astray any number of aspiring reporters. Eleanor Hoyt worries that newspaper fiction is "likely to put false notions into the head" of a young woman "who comes up from Podunk to try newspaper work in the great city." "If she has taken the careers of these heroines as her standard of measurement," Hoyt judges, she will be sorely disappointed by the real working conditions in the city room."[48] Newspaper stories teach that all hurdles can be overcome, though even women blessed with "good health, more than average intelligence, dogged persistence, and indomitable pluck" may not, in reality, succeed in the cutthroat world of city journalism. In contrast to the plots of countless fictions, a "prospective newspaper woman does not" simply "walk into a newspaper office, obtain, within five minutes, a position at a high salary, and depart blithely, leaving the business of the office at a standstill and the entire force paralyzed by admiration."[49] Moreover, women are not likely to discover that "within the first week" of employment, "every man on the staff, from editor-in-chief down, will fall violently in love with her"—the youngest office boy *maybe*, if she works hard at it; but everyone else? Don't count on it.[50] Nor should the aspiring reporter expect to "write the greatest story of the season within twenty-four hours after joining the staff"; indeed, the author sardonically notes, she likely will discover that an "entire week goes by without an entire first page being devoted to one of her stories and her picture."[51]

"Miss Upton's First 'Assignment,'" published by John A'Becket in the August 25, 1898, issue of *Youth's Companion*, illustrates Hoyt's point. The story, which highlights the shady line between the reality of journalism and the literary products of the profession, follows Letty Upton's grand entrance onto the public stage of Park Row. She has taken inspiration from the "long accounts" published in the Sunday papers "of very wonderful experiences to which were affixed the names, real or assumed," of female reporters—inspired, that is, by newspaper fiction. Letty determines that "she might become, in time, a writer of such signed articles" and, more to the point, "obtain high pay for them." "Could she not write as well as those women?" she wonders. After all, "from the stories in the papers, things seemed to come their way easily enough."[52] A modern young woman, Letty has nevertheless floundered in her search for a career, discarding teaching, typing, and sales as possible employment. With Letty sporting a "trim, bright little body of twenty years; pretty, in a fresh, winning way, and naturally vivacious and engaging," it seems "that this personal equipment" is, in and of itself, "a qualification for newspaper work"—or so the stories in the Sunday paper assure.[53]

Letty's grand endeavor starts off easily enough when she obtains a job through her connections with a staff writer with the *Daily Investigator*, "one of the prominent New York papers," but the workspace seems far "smaller and more 'cluttered up' than she had expected" from fictional descriptions.[54] Still, her excitement grows as her editor calls her in for her first assignment: "What would she be sent to do?" Letty wonders, breathlessly. "Oh, that her subject might be one on which she could be brilliant with ease!"[55] Somewhat disappointingly, she must instead verify the rumor that a New York socialite, Miss Harmon, is engaged to an unnamed English nobleman. Letty must find Miss Harmon's mother and dig out the details, by whatever means necessary. Problems arise from the very start. Unschooled in the most logical methods for finding subjects, Letty records the names of all Harmon families within the social register and visits each one, without success. As she travels from Harmon home to Harmon home and fails to locate the correct Mrs. Harmon, Letty grumbles that in the "'stories' of the Sunday papers there had been no preliminary failures to find the person. The reporter had always called at Mr. Whoever's and had 'been cordially motioned to a chair,' and then Mr. or Mrs. Whoever had proceeded to tell him all he wanted to know in the most friendly, considerate way."[56]

At last Letty locates—she believes—the correct Mrs. Harmon, though the woman seems far too young to have a marriageable daughter. Even so, this Mrs. Harmon answers a number of questions about English noblemen and engagement, though she declares that it is far too soon for her daughter to think of marriage. Still, satisfied that she has scooped other papers and secured salient facts about the rumored engagement, Letty confidently writes a story that will cement her reportorial triumph. But the day after her story runs, Letty receives a termination notice: The *Daily Investigator* has been made a laughingstock because while the Mrs. Harmon identified in Letty's story has a daughter, that daughter is, in fact, a baby. Letty's career, which seemed terribly easy in all the fiction she consumed, collapses before it can even begin.

A'Becket's tale delivers a sharp critique of women's newspaper fiction and of the naive readers of the genre. Yet, despite such criticism, these stories and novels offer a compelling example not only of how journalism became literary but of how women, in particular, used the stories of their own experience as source material for a "hot-breathed, pulsing realism" that blended effortlessly with other realisms of the late nineteenth and early twentieth centuries.[57] The full story of fin-de-siècle literary journalism, in all its manifestations, has yet to be written. In the papers that promoted a "new journalism," which predated the "new journalism" of the1960s and 1970s, the news often masqueraded, or at least built upon, fiction. However, the reverse was also true, and newspaper fiction provides at least one chapter in that story as it rests upon the interplay between journalism and literature in the late nineteenth and early twentieth centuries, and offers insight into the increasing—and sometimes conflicted—presence of women in the newsroom, both factually and fictionally.

Notes

1. Gilmore, "Hints for Fiction Writers," 2500.
2. A complete listing of newspaper fictions is not available, but some titles include Davis, *Gallegher and Other Stories*; Regal, "By Telephone"; McEwen, "Vengeance of Pendleton"; Pearson, "Newspaper Woman's Romance"; Shriver, "Frustrated 'Scoop'"; Madden, "Stories of Working Girls"; A'Becket, "Miss Upton's First 'Assignment'"; Williams, *Stolen Story*; Barr, *Jennie Baxter*; Masterson, "Love-Making of Loo"; Kirk, *Good-Bye, Proud World*; Balmer, "Wolf of the City"; Older, *Giants*; Michelson, *Yellow Journalist*; Michelson, *Anthony Overman*; Trites, *John Cave*; Simrall, "Her Best Stuff"; Hoyne, "Ego of the Metropolis"; Walsh, "Jane Eddington"; Powel and Carter, "Broken Wings"; Ross, *Penny Dreadful*; Gilman, *Sob Sister*.
3. For further discussion of the rise of newspaper women at the turn into the twentieth century, see Fahs, *Out on Assignment*; Lutes, *Front-Page Girls*; Roggenkamp, *Sympathy, Madness, and Crime*.
4. Quoted in Chambers, Steiner, and Fleming, *Women and Journalism*, 19.
5. Jordan, "Newspaper Woman's Story," 340.
6. "Tales," 265.
7. Schudson, *Discovering the News*, 71.
8. Shuman, *Steps into Journalism*, 66.
9. "Confessions," 371.
10. "Confessions," 376.
11. "New Books," 598.
12. Corbin, "Clever Short Stories," 255.
13. Jordan, "Ruth Herrick's Assignment," 5–6.
14. Pearson, "Newspaper Woman's Romance," 218.
15. McClure, "Inside Views of Fiction," 60.
16. McClure, 60.
17. Kirk, *Good-Bye, Proud World*, 5; Madden, "Stories of Working Girls," 213.
18. Madden, "Stories of Working Girls," 213.
19. Barr, *Jennie Baxter*, 17.
20. Barr, 17–18.
21. Jordan, "Ruth Herrick's Assignment," 29.
22. Michelson, *Yellow Journalist*, 15.
23. Gilman, *Sob Sister*, 3.
24. Pearson, "Newspaper Woman's Romance," 219.

25 Gilman, *Sob Sister*, 119.
26 Masterson, "Love-Making of Loo," 101.
27 Pearson, "Newspaper Woman's Romance," 219–20.
28 Gilman, *Sob Sister*, 66.
29 Masterson, "Love-Making of Loo," 99.
30 "Notes about New Books," 62.
31 Shriver, "Frustrated 'Scoop,'" 535.
32 Jordan, *May Iverson's Career*, 277.
33 Jordan, "Miss Van Dyke's Best Story," 231.
34 Madden, "Stories of Working Girls," 214.
35 For a detailed discussion of Jordan's "In the Case of Hannah Risser," see Roggenkamp, "Elizabeth Jordan."
36 "Confessions," 375.
37 Simrall, "Her Best Stuff," 298.
38 Jordan, "Number Seventeen," 825.
39 Gilman, *Sob Sister*, 4–5.
40 Gilman, 19.
41 Gilman, 19.
42 Gilman, 146.
43 Jordan, "Miss Underhill's Lesson," 651.
44 Masterson, "Love-Making of Loo," 101.
45 Gilman, *Sob Sister*, 145.
46 Jordan, "Miss Van Dyke's Best Story," 228.
47 Quoted in Chapman, *Gender, Citizenship and Newspapers*, 86.
48 Hoyt, "Newspaper Girl," 291.
49 Hoyt, 291.
50 Hoyt, 292.
51 Hoyt, 292.
52 A'Becket, "Miss Upton's First 'Assignment,'" 390.
53 A'Becket, 390.
54 A'Becket, 390.
55 A'Becket, 390.
56 A'Becket, 390.
57 McClure, "Inside Views of Fiction," 61.

Bibliography

A'Becket, John J. "Miss Upton's First 'Assignment.'" *Youth's Companion*, August 25, 1898, 390–91.
Balmer, Edwin. "The Wolf of the City." *Collier's Weekly*, December 23, 1905, 14–17.
Barr, Robert. *Jennie Baxter: Journalist*. New York: Frederick A. Stokes, 1899.
Chambers, Deborah, Linda Steiner, and Carole Fleming. *Women and Journalism*. London: Routledge, 2004.
Chapman, Jane L. *Gender, Citizenship and Newspapers: Historical and Transnational Perspectives*. New York: Palgrave Macmillan, 2013.
"The Confessions of 'A Literary Journalist.'" *Bookman* (New York), December 1907, 370–76.
Corbin, John. "Clever Short Stories." *Book Buyer* 16, no. 3 (April 1, 1898): 254–56.
Davis, Richard Harding. *Gallegher and Other Stories*. New York: Charles Scribner's Sons, 1891.
Fahs, Alice. *Out on Assignment: Newspaper Women and the Making of Modern Public Space*. Chapel Hill, NC: University of North Carolina Press, 2011.
Gilman, Mildred. *Sob Sister*. New York: Grosset and Dunlap, 1931.
Gilmore, Hinton. "Hints for Fiction Writers." *Life*, December 19, 1912, 2500.
Hoyne, Thomas T. "The Ego of the Metropolis." *Life*, August 5, 1915, 234–35.
Hoyt, Eleanor. "The Newspaper Girl." *Current Literature*, March 1902, 291–92.
Jordan, Elizabeth G. "In the Case of Hannah Risser." *Harper's Bazaar*, August 1902, 710–17.
———. *May Iverson's Career*. New York: Harper and Brothers, 1913.
———. "Miss Underhill's Lesson: A Newspaper Story." *Independent*, March 15, 1900, 650–57.
———. "Miss Van Dyke's Best Story." In *Tales*, 209–32.
———. "The Newspaper Woman's Story." *Lippincott's Monthly Magazine*, March 1893, 340–47.

———. "Number Seventeen: An Episode." *Harper's Bazaar*, September 1903, 825–30.
———. "Ruth Herrick's Assignment." In *Tales*, 3–29.
———. *Tales of the City Room*. New York: Charles Scribner's Sons, 1898.
Kirk, Ellen Olney. *Good-Bye, Proud World*. New York: Houghton Mifflin, 1904.
Lutes, Jean Marie. *Front-Page Girls: Women Journalists in American Culture and Fiction, 1880–1930*. Ithaca, NY: Cornell University Press, 2007.
Madden, Eva A. "Stories of Working Girls: II. The Only Woman's Page." *Youth's Companion*, May 5, 1898, 213–14.
Masterson, Kate. "The Love-Making of Loo." *Smart Set*, September 1900, 99–104.
McClure, H. H. "Inside Views of Fiction: III—The Newspaper Novel." *Bookman* (New York), March 1910, 60–61.
McEwen, Artbur. "The Vengeance of Pendleton." *Overland Monthly and Out West Magazine*, September 1895, 283–91.
Michelson, Miriam. *Anthony Overman*. New York: Doubleday, Page, 1906.
———. *A Yellow Journalist*. New York: D. Appleton, 1905.
"New Books: About Books and Authors." *Interior*, May 12, 1898, 598–99.
"Notes about New Books." *New York Observer and Chronicle*, January 11, 1900, 62.
Older, Mrs. Fremont [Cora Miranda Baggerly Older]. *The Giants*. New York: D. Appleton, 1905.
Pearson, H. C. "A Newspaper Woman's Romance." *Peterson Magazine*, February 1896, 218–21.
Powel, Harford, Jr., and Russell Gordon Carter. "Broken Wings." *Youth's Companion*, serialized August 1928–January 1929.
Regal, Francis E. "By Telephone." *Lippincott's Magazine*, January 1895, 126–35.
Roggenkamp, Karen. "Elizabeth Jordan, 'True Stories of the News,' and Newspaper Fiction in Late-Nineteenth-Century American Journalism." In *Literature and Journalism: Inspirations, Intersections, and Inventions from Ben Franklin to Stephen Colbert*, edited by Mark Canada, 119–41. New York: Palgrave Macmillan, 2013.
———. *Sympathy, Madness, and Crime: How Four Nineteenth-Century Journalists Made the Newspaper Women's Business*. Kent, OH: Kent State University Press, 2016.
Ross, Malcolm. *Penny Dreadful*. New York: Coward-McCann, 1929.
Schudson, Michael. *Discovering the News: A Social History of American Newspapers*. New York: Basic Books, 1978.
Shriver, Ernest. "A Frustrated 'Scoop.'" *Peterson Magazine*, May 1896, 531–35.
Shuman, Edwin. *Steps into Journalism: Helps and Hints for Young Writers*. Evanston, IL: Correspondence School of Journalism, 1894.
Simrall, Josephine P. "Her Best Stuff." *Lippincott's Monthly Magazine*, February 1912, 298–306.
"Tales of Trail and Town." Review of *Tales of Trail and Town*, by Bret Harte. *Critic*, April 16, 1898, 265.
Trites, William Budd. *John Cave*. London: A. Treherne, 1909.
Walsh, George Ethelbert. "Jane Eddington, Editor." *National Stockman and Farmer*, serialized December 25, 1915–February 26, 1916.
Williams, Jesse Lynch. *The Stolen Story and Other Newspaper Stories*. New York: Charles Scribner's Sons, 1899.

7
TWO GILDED AGES
Literary Muckrakers 1900s/2000s

Cecelia Tichi

Literary muckraking officially entered the US literary canon in 1930 when a leading scholar, Fred Lewis Pattee, included a chapter on "The Muck-Rake School" in his *The New American Literature, 1890–1930*. Along with discussions of genre, single authors, and urban and regional fiction, Pattee distinguished literary muckraking for its motivating premise that a "fundamentally good" citizenry, "horrified at a reign of crime or a miscarriage of justice," will collectively take remedial action, once "awakened."[1] Pattee cast literary muckrakers as instruments of a periodically revivified public conscience. Nearly a century forward from Pattee, we find that peaks of literary "muckraking" correspond with periods of social dislocation of the sort Pattee recognized in the decades following the Civil War. "The style tends to flourish in periods of grave social crisis," William Howarth observes in his examination of John Steinbeck's Depression-era investigative work, as the "traumas that fracture public trust … arouse a clamor for indisputable facts."[2] Others concur that literary journalism, itself verifiably factual within a context of narrative production, stirs most vigorously in historical periods of severe social, economic, and political dislocation in the US, which David Eason calls a periodic "breakdown in consensus about manners and morals."[3]

Scholars argue about what marks a written document as literary muckraking. The genre remains contentious in its particular traits but is bonded in its fundamental premise across time. Periods of social rupture throughout the twentieth century, notably the 1930s Great Depression and the "volcanic" years loosely called the Sixties, fostered debate over matters of style, structure, and the balance of fact to fictional techniques but consistently sustained the historical linkage to analogous root causes.[4] John Pauly cites the New Journalism of the Sixties as the successor to the muckraking Progressives of the 1910s, each distinguishable in style and structure but both responsive to the social ramifications of fractured national politics. The Vietnam War and the Civil Rights and feminist movements of the Sixties, together with the 1930s Depression, all reference such a rupture and, correlatively, reference a familiar body of literary journalism, from James Agee and Walker Evans's ironically titled *Let Us Now Praise Famous Men* (1941) to Joan Didion's equally ironic *Political Fictions* (2001).

This discussion presumes that literary muckraking is continuous from its origins in the late 1800s and early 1900s through the twentieth century and the opening decades of the twenty-first century. Historically, however, this discussion concerns the literary muckrakers whose books and articles have been responsive to two distinct Gilded Ages that are separated by a full century but aligned in their thematic concerns. The women journalists who are its practitioners invite attention to gender and its lineage in the literary muckraking tradition. Central here is the work of a progenitor, Ida M. Tarbell (1857–1944), whom Pattee cited in "The Muck-Rake School" for her "study of the oil trust … exposing to the full [its] shortcomings."[5] Tarbell's muckraking classic, *The History of the Standard Oil Company* (1904), set a standard that has been vivified most recently by Sheri Fink's *Five Days at Memorial* (2013) whose subtitle—*Life and Death in a Storm-Ravaged Hospital*—lays bare the US crisis in healthcare that was exposed when the New Orleans levees failed in the aftermath of Hurricane Katrina in August 2005. In addition, Beth Macy's *Factory Man* (2014) chronicles the dire social impact of the evisceration of US manufacturing in an era of "offshoring" (together with one individual's Herculean effort to buck the trend). The numerous US citizens deprived of proper healthcare and left in penury in their elder years are the focus of Jessica Bruder's *Nomadland: Surviving America in the Twenty-First Century* (2017), an account of impoverished legions of citizens who avoid homelessness by dwelling permanently in aging vehicles (older vans, RVs, SUVs) and who continuously travel the country in search of seasonal employment while cobbling hourly wages with Social Security funds to avoid destitution. In the newest period of a "grave social crisis" in the United States, these more recent authors, all experienced journalists, demonstrate the vitality of current literary muckraking. Their work is demonstrably the legacy of Tarbell's pioneering effort.

The very term muckraking risks overfamiliarity, so a reminder of the parameters, the genesis, and the conditions that gave rise to the phrase is useful. In tribute or in opprobrium, "muckraker" has remained current for over a century but is centered historically in the US Gilded Age of the later 1800s and early 1900s. Reformers have punctuated American history from its beginnings, but events of the post-Civil War decades fostered a growth industry in journalists' socioeconomic and political critique and laid the groundwork for literary muckraking. These years have been called the Age of Confidence, of Enterprise, of Energy, of Steel and Steam. However, the title of a novel by Mark Twain and Charles Dudley Warner furnished the enduring name—the Gilded Age—which denotes topmost golden glitter with a base metal underneath. True to the name, unprecedented wealth and opulence reigned for the titans of business and industry and their families and associates. Their names remain bywords of the era, among them Vanderbilt, Rockefeller, and Carnegie, names synonymous, respectively, with transportation, petroleum, and steel, just as J. P. Morgan signifies the era's high finance. The industrial realm that they and others created expanded opportunities for white-collar occupations in management and the professions, and a newly prosperous middle class generally valued the manufacturers of products that eased material life with such items as soap, household furnishings, and central heating.

The alarming growth of corporate behemoths and trusts, however, signaled unprecedented power and wealth concentrated at the topmost stratum of society. The legitimacy of this order depended largely on the prevalent social Darwinism distilled in the motto "survival of the fittest," a distortion of Charles Darwin's emphasis on animals' adaptation in his influential *On the Origin of Species* (1859). Many of the nearly seventy-six million persons in the US by 1900 (with the population nearly doubling since 1870) occupied the netherworld of the presumptively "unfit," and they increasingly erupted in social discord in response to irremediable poverty and perceived injustice. The notion that a contract between the worker and employer was an act of free will that was legalized between equals, as economists argued at the time, was experientially fraudulent for countless wage workers toiling in mills and factories. One leader of a charity organization warned in 1872 that these "dangerous classes"[6] needed to be taught Christian values, but a self-taught West Coast economist and journalist, Henry George, struck a social nerve in 1879 with his national bestseller *Progress and Poverty*, its title juxtaposing correlative material advance and deepened poverty. George hailed "the steamship," "the railroad train," "the reaping machine," "the throb of the engines … in obedience to human will,"[7] all meant to elevate society "from its very foundations." Instead, these "muscles of iron and sinews of steel" shackled workers in fear and the "dull, deadening pain ... involved in the words 'hard times.'"[8]

In *How the Other Half Lives* (1890), Jacob Riis, a Danish American journalist and New York *Tribune* reporter and editor, combined expository essays and photographs to bring the facts of dire slum conditions to middle-class readers, and some scholars include him in the roster of literary muckrakers.[9] Although Riis saw ethnic groups in stereotypical terms common to the time (e.g., mercenary Jews, inscrutable Chinese), he blamed slum conditions on profiteering landlords and warned that the boundary between the urban middle class and the slum-dwelling immigrant "wretched refuse" was permeable.[10] His New York case study was applicable throughout a newly urbanized and industrial America whose workforce was largely comprised of immigrant labor. Defined by rapid industrialization, urbanization, and immigration, Gilded Age America was weakened by overcrowded and squalid city slums that bred disease and crime. It was hobbled by the meager wages of men and women who worked sixty to eighty or more hours weekly but could not make ends meet—and were subject to layoffs in years of downturns as in the 1870s and 1890s. It was hampered by child labor that threatened a future of unschooled, ignorant grownups lacking job skills and likely resorting to gang life. It was roiled, in addition, by labor strikes that turned cities into war zones, at times paralyzing rail transit.

Two major rail strikes, in 1877 and 1894, were prompted by wage cuts in depression years. The first began in Martinsburg, West Virginia, and was compared by journalists to battles of the Civil War. The second, the Pullman strike in the Chicago area, shut down rail service west of Detroit. It involved 250,000 workers in twenty-seven states. In both strikes, federal troops were called to restore order. In addition, the Homestead strike of 1892 pitted Pittsburgh steel workers against the Pinkerton mercenaries hired by Andrew Carnegie and the coke baron Henry Clay Frick. Casualties mounted, and the standoff lasted for months. The year 1886, what's more, marked New York City's "Great Upheaval," when plumbers, quarrymen, bricklayers, street-railway workers, piano makers, and others struck for the eight-hour workday. That May, the much-publicized Chicago Haymarket riot sent fear rippling through the country when someone threw a bomb at a rally in support of an eight-hour workday, killing seven police officers. The rally was sponsored by anarchists, some of whom threatened massive violence against capitalists with the new explosive invented in 1866 by Alfred Nobel: dynamite.[11]

From this milieu came the muckrakers. As historian Louis Filler has written in *The Muckrakers*, "Suddenly there appeared in certain magazines a new, moral, radical type of writing by men and women who yesterday had been entirely unknown or had written less disturbingly."[12] He might have added newspapers and books, for the term has been applied to investigative narratives appearing in the press, in magazines and in books, all exposing the corruption that was rampant in US political, industrial, financial, business, religious, and social realms in the post-Civil War decades. Its texts include magazine expository articles, such as Ray Stannard Baker's "Wonderful Hawaii" (1911–12), a scathing series on the corporate monopolization of the Hawaiian sugar industry that appeared in *American Magazine*. Muckraking also includes short stories, such as Jack London's "The Apostate" (1906), an exposé of crushing child labor that was published in *Woman's Home Companion*. The best-known muckraking novel, Upton Sinclair's *The Jungle* (1906), which exposed meat contamination and horrific working conditions in the Chicago packinghouses, appeared as a bestselling book after serialization in the socialist periodical *Appeal to Reason*. Elements of muckraking surfaced, in addition, in well-regarded fiction, such as Frank Norris's *The Pit* (1903), and scholars of muckraking journalism have emphasized its centrality in the work of Stephen Crane. The roll call includes other prominent names of the time—John Fitch, William Hard, Will Irwin, C. P. Connolly, Charles Edward Russell, George Kibbe Turner, Edwin Markham, Josiah Flynt—all writers who, in Filler's words, "savagely exposed grafting politicians, criminal police, tenement eyesores" and also "attacked the church ... defended labor in disputes which in no way concerned them personally, decried child exploitation, wrote pro-suffragist articles, and described great businesses as soulless and anti-social."[13] The targeted list goes on, with "muckraking" as familiar as it is elastic in reference and usage, its boundaries expansive over a century—and perhaps blurring in definition as the term spread in casual usage.

The origin of "muckraker" merits a note on its specific introduction in journalism. On March 17, 1906, the all-male journalists' Gridiron Club in Washington, DC, prepared to hear President Theodore Roosevelt speak at its white-tie dinner. The title of Roosevelt's speech, "The Man with the Muck Rake," reminded many in the audience of their boyhood days in Sunday school, for the seventeenth-century allegory *The Pilgrim's Progress* (1678) by John Bunyan was a staple of US Protestant churches. Bunyan traced the spiritual journey of Pilgrim, a youth who encounters a roadside downcast figure who is blind to the higher spiritual life because he relentlessly rakes the muck of the material world. Roosevelt updated Bunyan in his blistering, forty-five-minute attack on a cohort of journalists he denounced as modern-day versions of the man who "fixes his eyes ... only on that which is vile and debasing."[14] In tones that reportedly "sizzled" with "moral disdain,"[15] Roosevelt acknowledged the benefits of moderate reformist publications but censured the cadre of writers whose sole focus on society's "filth" made them "one of the most potent forces for evil."[16] Collectively, they were Bunyan's modern-day "Man with the Muck Rake."

Roosevelt's gambit backfired. Within months, American popular lingo shortened the five-word phrase to "muckraker," whose work is "muckraking." His speech inadvertently specified muckrakers as specialists in a new subgenre of print media. The "literature of exposure,"[17] as these reporters termed their projects, had been in print for several years, but Roosevelt's attack, though late, was timely. No longer were certain journalists submerged in the general lot of newspaper reporters or magazine contributors (or popular fiction writers). Unwittingly, Roosevelt was skillful at branding. In the 1900s, when brand names came to the fore, "muckraker" denoted the same specificity as, say, Quaker Oats or Arrow Shirts.

The term was also gender-neutral, despite Roosevelt's reference to Bunyan's "Man." Two male-authored exposés of 1906 settled the matter of gender for the president. He was upset by the public uproar over *The Jungle* and riled by Thomas Lawson's *Frenzied Finance*, an exposé of financial chicanery in the copper industry. A self-styled reformer, Roosevelt took pride in his own efforts to uproot corruption and foster progressive action. Apprehension about the pace of reform and about the questionable legitimacy of its leadership concerned him, not gender. Nonetheless, Roosevelt's introduction of "muckraker" into the American lexicon is overlaid with irony because the gender-neutral "muckraker" opened portals to women. It permitted entry to Marie Van Vorst and her sister-in-law and coauthor, Mrs. John Van Vorst, whose *The Woman Who Toils* (1903) provided wrenching accounts of women workers in mills and factories. (Their book was prefaced with an appreciative word from Theodore Roosevelt, who promoted marriage, motherhood, and homemaking as superior to lethal wage-work toil.) The new female muckrakers also included the reporter Nellie Bly (Elizabeth Jane Cochran), who posed undercover as a mental patient in a New York insane asylum and revealed its horrors in "Ten Days in a Madhouse" (1886) in Joseph Pulitzer's New York *World*, after which, in 1889 to 1890, the paper sponsored her sensational, true-life version of Jules Verne's fictional *Around the World in Eighty Days* (1873) (with *World* sales boosted from her much-publicized seventy-eight-day circling of the globe).

Included, as well, was Ida M. Tarbell, whose *The History of the Standard Oil Company* chronicled the business brigandage that let John D. Rockefeller and his cohorts attain a near-monopoly in every aspect of the petroleum industry. She was recruited, along with Lincoln Steffens, Ray Stannard Baker, and others, when the enterprising Samuel Sidney McClure, the editor and publisher of the new *McClure's Magazine*, tapped her for what was to become the preeminent muckraking publication.

The genesis of *McClure's* within the history of US magazines warrants attention, for the rise of muckraking in US journalism is linked to the evolution of marketplace periodicals. Muckraking exposés in the 1900s appeared in *Collier's, Cosmopolitan, Hampton's, Independent, Success,* and *American,* but *McClure's* was the epicenter of US muckraking journalism. Temperamentally, the Irish-born McClure was an entrepreneur, not a reformer. From an impoverished boyhood in rural Indiana, he worked his way through Knox College, then learned business fundamentals as the editor-in-chief and business manager of a new Boston-based cycling magazine before moving to New York in 1884, when he partnered with a college classmate, John Sanborn Phillips, to start a newspaper syndicate that purchased the rights to articles and stories that they then sold to newspapers for simultaneous publication, often in Sunday supplements. Their first issue of *McClure's* appeared in June 1893, just as a catastrophic depression hit the US. Only good-faith investments (loans and a mortgage) kept *McClure's* afloat in its early years.[18]

Despite the depression of the 1890s, *McClure's* was joining a cluster of vibrant, new, low-cost American magazines in the era often called the Golden Age of American magazines. Like *Munsey's* and *Frank Leslie's*, it was affordable at fifteen cents per copy, $1.50 for a year's subscription. Like other new magazines, *McClure's* broke from the business model of the long-established *Atlantic Monthly, Harper's,* and *Scribner's,* whose readers mainly comprised the East Coast bourgeoisie and whose editors selected articles from manuscripts that arrived on their desks. The new editors did not await submissions but energetically pursued and commissioned writers to produce articles and fiction. None was more aggressive than McClure, whose restless temperament was ideal for the "hustle" necessary for the new "magazining." Like other editors of the new US periodicals, McClure had advantages that were specific to conditions of the moment. To scout writers in the US (and to distribute his magazine), he had the expansive US rail system, which added 170,000 miles of track between 1870 and 1900, totaling an outreach of 215,000 miles. To contact contributors by letter, he could rely on the extraordinarily efficient US Post Office, which, as of 1897, provided service to the most remote hamlets of the US. Magazine production also favored the newcomers as a new low-cost photo-engraving process supplanted prohibitively expensive wood engraving. The illustrations could be plentiful and cheap.

The issue that made *McClure's* synonymous with muckraking reached newsstands and homes in January 1903. By coincidence, it contained three complementary articles in the vein of exposure, including Steffens's exposé of graft in Minneapolis politics, titled "The Shame of Minneapolis," and Baker's "The Right to Work: The Story of the Non-striking Miners," an account of the hard feelings lingering in coal-mining camps when unionized strikers harassed and threatened coworkers who continued to work during the stoppage. The third article was Tarbell's "The Oil War of 1872," the third installment of her history of the US petroleum monopoly. Readers were primed for the "Oil War" from two preliminary accounts published in November and December 1902: "The Birth of an Industry" and "The Rise of the Standard Oil Company." Tarbell's series ran for nearly two years, appeared as a two-volume book in 1904, and cost *McClure's* a well-spent $50,000 (nearly $1.4 million in 2018).

Tarbell merits close attention because her work is distinguished as literary journalism and because her legacy lives in the work of literary journalists of the twenty-first century. Tarbell's personal animus toward Rockefeller's Standard Oil is well known. The business maneuvers of Standard Oil, including its collusion with the oil-shipper Pennsylvania Railroad, crushed competing oil concerns in the Tarbell family's northwestern Pennsylvania homeland, from Oil City to Titusville. Tarbell's father, an oilman, was among numerous Rockefeller business casualties. The through line from her family's oil field failure to Tarbell's muckraking, however, obscures the complex schooling that was fundamental to her singular achievement as a literary muckraker. Tarbell's exposure of Standard Oil's "shortcomings" (in Pattee's understatement) was foregrounded by extensive self-instruction, for no journalism school readied her for the monumental tasks ahead (i.e., mastering editorial duties, marshalling facts, and, crucial to literary journalism, developing the narrative structure and narrative voice that sustain the storyline that is the spine of literary journalism). The J-school advantages available to her twenty-first century heirs were nowhere in sight in the later 1800s, and Tarbell's autodidactic route to the literary narration of her Standard Oil investigation merits attention.

She had already served a journalist apprenticeship when McClure recruited her for his magazine. A graduate of Allegheny College (1880) and aspirant biologist, the Methodist-raised Tarbell first taught school then accepted an editorial post in upstate New York at the *Chautauquan*, a self-help and counselling magazine that had grown from Methodist Church annual camp meetings (chautauquas) to achieve national distribution. In 1886, Tarbell became its managing editor, acquiring the skills of editorial production and precision that were to be crucial in research for the Standard Oil investigation—from copyediting to proofreading, accurate dating, the correct spelling of names, accents, usage, and all numerals to the left and right of a decimal point. These duties, once familiar, left her feeling stalled at the *Chautauquan*, and, becoming increasingly interested in notable women in public life, she bolted for Paris in 1890 to research the career of Madame Roland, a French revolutionary. In her early thirties, preparing to become Madame Roland's biographer, Tarbell examined archival documents, a new challenge for an editor-turned-writer who must integrate secondary sources into her main text. To earn a living in Paris, she wrote occasional newspaper and magazine pieces for the US press.[19]

Tarbell's desultory (or "leisure") reading in youth helped prepare her to write the ephemeral pieces that provided her meager living in Paris. A girlhood favorite was the *Police Gazette* with its lurid tales of murders and outlaws, as were the New York *Tribune* and *Harper's Weekly*, both of which came from household subscriptions. According to Sari Edelstein's study of women's reading and writing in the nineteenth century, "American women's writing emerged through a dynamic, often critical, relationship with mainstream journalism, the most public of print discourses."[20] Edelstein continues, "Without the vote or the ability to hold public office, women writers drew on the cultural power of newspapers and co-opted journalistic techniques to telegraph their engagement with the sociopolitical world."[21] The newspapers contained character sketches, vivid descriptions, and the distilled five "W's" and one "H" of journalism: who, what, why, when, where, and how. The "vigor and brightness"[22] of late 1800s American papers impressed a British visitor, James (Viscount) Bryce, who marveled in *The American Commonwealth* (1888) that "nothing escapes them; everything is set in the sharpest, clearest light."[23] He declared US newspapers to be "influential in three ways—as narrators, as advocates, and as weathercocks."[24]

So far, Tarbell aligns with muckraking cohorts who transitioned from newspapers to magazines. Steffens, Baker, and other muckrakers such as Will Irwin, William Hard, and the Van Vorsts likewise schooled themselves in editorial protocol and norms of reportage. They too were adept at brief character sketches and alert for telling details, for interviewees' revelations, for archival documents and legislation that exposed the facts of corruption and injustice. For instance, the alleviation of "sordidness and squalor" in the lives of "working girls" who were sentenced to a "slow death" of relentless toil in Pittsburgh motivated Mrs. Van Vorst's muckraking exposé.[25] In Chicago, the "working girls" became the "cheap women of the underworld" to signal Irwin's shaming of the politically corrupt ward boss, the "large, bull-necked 'Bathhouse John' Coughlin," whom Irwin sketched in a "white shirt front" blazoned with the red sash of a parade "Grand Marshal."[26] To the east, Baker limned Pennsylvania anthracite miners by occupation when, investigating a community riven by a labor strike, he introduced a "Scotch engineer ... who had worked for twenty-three years in the place he then occupied. He was a man of high intelligence, an elder in the Presbyterian Church."[27] Baker, like his colleagues, presented numerical facts scrupulously—that seventeen thousand miners lived in the anthracite region in 1902 and that seven thousand had long occupied the area with earnings varying from $2.26 to

$3.50 daily. Steffens exploited these resources in his investigation of corruption in US cities, from the dollar-figure bribes (a $50,000 councilman in St. Louis) to the thieving "jovial pioneer doctor, Albert Alonzo Ames,"[28] of Minneapolis. He documented Ames's corruption with facsimile reproductions of a ledger listing payoffs in citywide graft. Like his muckraking colleagues, Steffens insisted that exposure of "the mercenary and selfish" was the route to social amelioration and that active citizenship would be "a power in the land."[29]

Tarbell mustered these resources but in youth also devoured lengthy prose fiction, a genre that largely eluded other muckrakers—yet proved to be as crucial for literary muckraking as it was irrelevant for newspaper reporting or magazine muckraking reportage. The contrast between Tarbell and her closest associates at *McClure's* provides a stark case in point. Steffens's *Autobiography* details a boyhood devoted to "horses, guns, [and] dogs"[30] before philosophical questions occupied him in graduate education. For his part, the youthful Baker yearned to produce the ineffable "Great American Novel," but in his autobiography, *American Chronicle*, he recorded admiration only for poets, essayists, and short story writers, not novelists. As newspaper journalists, Steffens and Baker became beat reporters producing copy for the New York *Evening Post* and the Chicago *News-Record*, respectively. Steffens in the early 1890s cultivated sources for stories on New York's municipal maneuvers and covered the warring "Bulls and Bears" of Wall Street. Baker, in Chicago, reported on "charity balls," "grand opera," and the Pullman strike of 1894. Their literary styles owed much to short fiction, and Steffens was well known for encouraging reporters at the *Commercial Advertiser* to employ a literary narrative style. Neither reporter, however, had reason to link his work with lengthy fiction. Their identities were grounded occupationally in news-gathering and reporting.[31]

Tarbell, however, was an inveterate reader of lengthy prose fiction from girlhood in the Pennsylvania oil regions. She recalled her devotion to the *Harper's Monthly* because its pages offered her memorable fiction: "Here I read my first Dickens, my first Thackeray, my first … George Eliot," and her "first Wilkie Collins" (who appeared in the *Weekly*, since detective fiction was presumably unsuited to the bourgeois *Monthly*).[32] While living in Paris, moreover, she made an admittedly "feeble and ineffectual" attempt at a novel.[33] This foray into lengthy fiction both as a reader and as a writer distinguishes Tarbell's career path from the cohort of muckrakers. Steffens neither gravitated to prose fiction in youth nor attempted to write it as an adult. Baker fantasized about authoring the Great American Novel that might gain him new respect from a father who disdained newspaper reporting and reward him financially for marriage and the support of a family. In reality, however, Baker mastered the fifteen-hundred-word essay for a newspaper series called "Shop Talk" that enlightened Chicago *Record* readers on industrial processes from "Peanut Oil" production to "Diamond Cutting."[34] He redoubled his commitment to journalism: "I began to read everything I saw in books or magazines regarding newspaper work, and even the more ambitious 'journalism,' … especially those that would confound my father by glorifying my profession."[35]

From the vantage point of Tarbell's later years, the self-deprecating reference to her aborted novel as "feeble and ineffectual" probably arose from memories of *McClure's* issues that featured the fiction of Willa Cather, Jack London, Robert Louis Stevenson, and other premier novelists and short fiction writers. Tarbell's early attempt at a novel nonetheless signals her consciousness that a storyline must be the basis of sustained narrative production. She did not list the titles of memorable novels, but Thackeray's *Vanity Fair*, Dickens's *Bleak House* and *Great Expectations*, Eliot's *Adam Bede* and *The Mill on the Floss* are probable referents, as is Wilkie Collins's *The Moonstone* (serialized in *Harper's Weekly* in 1860 as *All the Year Round*). In and of itself, extensive length is a hallmark of these and other Victorian novels, many serialized for months before book publication. (*Vanity Fair* was serialized for nineteen months, in 1847 and 1848, under the title *Pen and Pencil Sketches of English Society*.) These novels found receptive audiences in an emergent middle class with disposable cash and leisure hours for home entertainment consisting of music, board games, needlework, stereopticon viewing, letter writing—and reading.[36] The authors whom Tarbell listed appreciatively, moreover, served up the "flesh and blood" that prominent attorney Clarence Darrow called for in 1892, when he proclaimed that "the world today ... asks for facts" and implicated fiction in the "world" that "has grown tired of fairies and angels and asks for flesh and blood" and "wishes to see all; not only the prince and the millionaire, but the laborer and the beggar, the master and the slave."[37] The novelists Tarbell read showcased lengthy prose fiction as the venue for a variety of complex social issues, among them financial corruption, legal entanglements, and the snarls of social hierarchy, all in chapters replete with multiple characters, subplots, and driving storylines. These are the thematic issues and prose structures that Tarbell brought to her history of Standard Oil. The lessons gleaned from the Victorian novel became the bedrock of Tarbell's literary journalism.

Two major projects furthered Tarbell's preparation for the investigation into Standard Oil and the literary muckraking that became *The History of the Standard Oil Company*. Her 1895 series *A Short Life of Napoleon Bonaparte, together with a Sketch of Josephine, Empress of the French* shows advanced literary skills in the pacing of characterization (e.g., "At nine years of age he was a shy, proud, willful child, unkempt and untrained, little, pale, and nervous, almost without instruction, and yet already enamored of a soldier's life"[38]). Her chapters are punctuated throughout with quotations from letters and other documents that fortify her own prose account, and Tarbell's concision approaches the epigrammatic in its omission of static words (e.g., "Economy and privation were always more supportable to him than borrowing"[39]). She further sharpened research skills while working in Washington, DC, and venturing into the backwoods of Kentucky and Illinois to interview those with firsthand recollections of the long-deceased Abraham Lincoln. Doing so, she gleaned compelling details from young Abe's near-drowning in an overflowing creek to the bear meat served at Thomas Lincoln's wedding to Nancy Hanks. The four-year effort yielded a popular twenty-part series for *McClure's: The Early Life of Abraham Lincoln*. Its subtitle announced Tarbell's method: *Containing Many Unpublished Documents and Unpublished Reminiscences of Lincoln's Early Friends*. The arc of biography was powered by documentary proof and seasoned by the judiciously selected and edited spice of interviewees' memories.

McClure paid contributors generously, as they deserved, anticipating that high circulation would attract lucrative advertising to offset expenses and make *McClure's* profitable. The magazine that began at between thirty and forty thousand copies doubled in circulation with the serial publication of Tarbell's "Napoleon," which she wrote "on the gallop."[40] Her Napoleon "sketch," she said, was barely finished when McClure urged her to undertake the project on Lincoln, sensing that "people never had had enough of Lincoln."[41] Beginning serial publication in November 1895, it boosted *McClure's* circulation to a monthly quarter-million copies. The trade journal *Printer's Ink* reported that in the years 1895 to 1899, *McClure's* "carried the greatest quantity of advertising of any magazine in the world."[42]

Initially the Standard Oil project was a hard sell to a skeptical McClure who doubted that a long-running business exposé would attract readers. Tarbell, however, understood the reading public's appetite for sustained narratives, for the Victorian novels' popularity was a proven fact. She also sensed the public hunger for a fact-based narrative that cut through public confusion and anxiety—and propaganda about "prosperity"—in the face of the new monopolies and trusts that thwarted "free opportunity" and "free competition."[43] She worried, further, that credulous segments of the public were "listening in wonder and awe" to the "unctuous logic of the Mother of Trusts,"[44] Standard Oil. She vividly recalled the collapse of her father's business in a mysterious "big scheme" involving the railroads and a mysterious entity called the "South Improvement Company."[45] Persuading McClure that public interest in the machinations of big business was rising, Tarbell set to work on the project that consumed nearly a decade.

The History of the Standard Oil Company is the culmination of Tarbell's preparation for and demonstration of foundational muckraking literary journalism. Her account is replete with dates, times, and numerical and other data, and the documentary accuracy is verifiable in the included appendices of letters, court transcripts, affidavits, contracts, articles of incorporation, charters, and other papers of record, all of which invite readers to seek out these sources and determine the accuracy of the narrative for themselves. Tarbell's occasional admission of incomplete data (e.g., "there is no evidence of which the writer knows"[46]) lends credibility to her account, as does her resort to the first-person pronoun to say, "I have been able to find practically all of the important documents relating to the subject," thereafter listing the categorically inclusive "great mass of sworn testimony," "the large pamphlet literature," and the "files of daily newspapers and monthly reviews" containing "statistics and full reports."[47]

Should readers suspect the *History* to be a product solely of libraries and other archives, Tarbell includes accounts of site visits to the oil regions for interviews and to Standard Oil facilities such as its tin can factory in Long Island City, New York. Fashioned from sheets of tin and filled with petroleum, the five-gallon cans were exported, and she describes the process that "the writer" witnessed from the entrance of the facility where, for maximal efficiency, "a man was sweeping … the dirt on the floor … to be sifted for tin filings and solder dust."[48] Eyewitness to the process, Tarbell reports the thoroughgoing elimination of waste at every point. The emptied crates of tin are sold for garden planters, the cracked lids for kindling, and "laurels go to the manager who has saved the most ounces of solder, the most hours, the most footsteps."[49]

The *History* offers an episodic plotline, major and minor characters, conflicts, settings and scenes where action takes place, often in an Aristotelian structure of beginning, middle, end. Identifying herself as "the writer" and at certain points as "we," Tarbell promises a "story" and "narrative" with dramatic and pictorial elements. "The work we have in mind," she wrote to a young editor, is "a narrative history of the Standard Oil Company," "a straightforward narrative, as picturesque and dramatic as I can make it."[50] Her most forceful diction appears as though a chosen word serves precision, not authorial selection, as when she notes that a few independent refiners evaded Standard Oil's "strangulation."[51] To avoid the distracting rhetorical flamboyance of newspaper "yellow journalism" of the era, Tarbell deployed her most striking imagery sparingly and thus strategically. Her critique of the excessive oil production of 1873 prompted this censorious kinetic metaphor denoting suicide: "It seemed as if Nature, outraged that her generosity should be so manipulated … had opened her veins to flood the earth with oil."[52]

Tarbell's *History* portrays John D. Rockefeller as the commander-in-chief of a Napoleonic oil war. With a "genius for detail … very much like military genius," Rockefeller, in her terms, "saw strategic points like a Napoleon, and he swooped" upon his foes with "a suddenness of a Napoleon."[53] Her biography of Bonaparte, an obvious antecedent, must not obscure a crucial lesson about literary muckraking from Tarbell's vantage point—that it ought not to veer into the Manichaean realm of melodrama, which is to say that Tarbell kept her work clear of polemic, the one-sided position that precludes considerations of alternative viewpoints. Front and center in the *History* is the critique of the Rockefeller maneuvers in vanquishing all competition, but Tarbell concludes with a chapter on "The Legitimate Greatness of the Company." Standard Oil has secured its "privileges" by "unscrupulousness" and a "contemptuous indifference to fair play," she laments, but "privileges alone will not account for its success."[54] Tarbell commends Standard Oil for its "consummate ability," its "daring" and "brains."[55] It has always "been strong in all great business qualities—in energy, in intelligence, in dauntlessness."[56] She salutes the company for sterling management from its maintenance of equipment to its product development: "anything in the oil world … from a smoking wick in Oshkosh to the competition of Russian oil in China."[57] The Napoleon of Oil has vanquished all foes and now rules with expertise.

Tarbell's tribute to Standard Oil separates her conception and practice of literary muckraking from those of others whose critique is unalloyed by contrary or alternative viewpoints and thus becomes melodrama. In reference to literature, Peter Brooks defines melodrama as a mutually exclusive social world "charged with the conflict between light and darkness, salvation and damnation."[58] It offers no space to consider viewpoints that might temper or modify the prevailing monolithic stance of the text. Had Tarbell shaped her narrative as melodrama, she would have inserted the description of John D. Rockefeller that appeared in her autobiography, *All in the Day's Work*, in which she recounted her firsthand impression of the oil titan in the Sunday-school room of a Baptist Church in Cleveland where Rockefeller, a lifelong Baptist, delivered a homily. Recalled Tarbell, his head "riveted attention … a big, great breadth from back to front … big bumps behind the ears … with a wet look." She goes on, "The thin sharp nose was like a thorn" and "there were no lips; the mouth looked as if the teeth were all shut hard," and "there were puffs under the little colorless eyes."[59] The description exceeds the conventional terms of advanced age to approach the grotesque, the monstrous—in fact, the melodramatic, which is precisely why Tarbell would omit it from her *History*.

To cite one further case in point in regard to melodramatic literary muckraking, consider Upton Sinclair's *The Jungle*. Unlike *The History of the Standard Oil Company*, *The Jungle* critiques industrial America unrelentingly for its greed, corruption, and the murderous exploitation of workers who are treated like replaceable tools. Its excoriation of the brutal meat-packing industry and its graft-ridden political enablers, together with its portrayal of victimized workers, including women and children, channels readers unerringly toward Sinclair's sociopolitical solution: socialism. For readers of *The Jungle*, a unanimity of response is imperative, and thus interpretive debate is deliberately foreclosed. Sinclair requires a revolution, having judged capitalism in the era of industrialization to be irremediable. Tarbell, on the contrary, seeks the reform of the capitalist industrial system, which she judges to be distorted and much in need of remediation. She demands fair, open competition in the capitalist system and abhors monopoly.

***

As if to recycle history, the United States entered a second Gilded Age in the later 1900s and, accordingly, exhibited traits familiar from the post-Civil War decades. The front page of the Sunday *New York Times* of July 15, 2007, bannered this headline: "The Richest of the Rich, Proud of a New Gilded Age." The financial success of the "new tycoons," the article proclaimed, "gives them a heroic role." The father of one tycoon, Bill Gates Sr., took a less than jubilant view of the new era. With coauthor Chuck Collins, he declared in 2003, "We are now in a second Gilded Age. Instead of taking steps that would strengthen our democracy, we are heading back to the wealth inequalities of a century ago."[60] A few pundits repeat the phrase in celebration, but others, such as Nobel-winning economist Paul Krugman, strike tones of apprehension in newspapers, on TV, and in the new digital media. The *New Yorker* magazine took its book-length stance even earlier in 2000: *The New Gilded Age: "The New Yorker" Looks at the Culture of Affluence*.

A familiar range of US social, cultural, political, and economic woes hearkens to the first Gilded Age in an atmosphere of déjà vu. The TV series *Lifestyles of the Rich and Famous* aired from 1984 to 1995, succeeded in the 2010s by the Wealth Channel broadcasting sales of mansions, yachts, luxury automobiles, and jets. In protest against the amassing of wealth by the one percent of the population, the Occupy Wall Street movement began in Zuccotti Park in the fall of 2011 in New York's financial district. The occupiers' encampments were publicized by the media, and similar tent villages sprang up in city plazas nationwide, their *cri de coeur*, "We are the 99%!" Business magazines, meanwhile, hailed the splendors of globalization as corporations shuttered their US manufacturing plants to relocate them offshore in lowest-wage sites free of workplace safety regulations. Ocean-going container ships became de facto warehouses ferrying goods to US ports for distribution to the big-box stores that undercut local retailers' prices and led to the shutdown of Main Streets nationwide. Corporate support, all the while, shifted from US stakeholders in communities formerly known as company towns to shareholders and high-ranking executives who reaped a huge financial bounty.

In addition to staggering wealth inequality, the nation that prided itself from the post-World War II years on a robust middle class now experienced workplace instability, substandard housing and wages, a prohibitively expensive and corrupted prison system, political distortions, unsafe food and water, crumbling infrastructure, exorbitantly expensive yet patchy healthcare, virulent racism, unaddressed environmental threats, and a host of other critical problems that demanded the exposure that precedes remediation. In addition, just as two multiyear depressions struck in the first Gilded Age (post-1873 and post-1894), the stock market plunge of October 1987 and the near collapse of the US economy in 2008 were followed by the lingering Great Recession.

In response to new crises, a new generation of literary muckrakers has stepped forward to expose these and other problems in detail and inform the public of the urgent need for corrective measures. Cited earlier in this discussion, the current heirs of Ida Tarbell—Sheri Fink, Beth Macy, and Jessica Bruder—topically engage, respectively, the US healthcare crisis, the social impact of the abandonment of US manufacturing, and the plight of elderly Americans whose only financial recourse is a nomadic life that wards off homelessness. Fink's *Five Days at Memorial* (2013), Macy's *Factory Man* (2014), and Bruder's *Nomadland* (2017) form a triad of complementary narratives whose structural designs reprise the model that Tarbell established.

The three investigators came to their projects as bona fide, experienced journalists who had published a significant body of work, just as Tarbell approached the Standard Oil project only when her prior work on Napoleon and Lincoln had been published. Fink, a physician who has worked in disaster and conflict zones, was already a correspondent for the *New York Times* and a recipient of the Pulitzer, George Polk, and other prizes. Macy, a Nieman Foundation award winner for *Factory Man*, had been a reporter for the *Roanoke Times* for a quarter century, and Bruder, who teaches at the Columbia University Graduate School of Journalism, had already published in the *Washington Post*, *Harper's*, and the *New York Times*. Initially, the three approached their book-length projects with preliminary essays that involved them in the topics and provided footholds for their books. Fink's *Five Days at Memorial* began with "The Deadly Choices at Memorial," copublished by ProPublica and the *New York Times Magazine*, while Macy's *Factory Man* was launched with a five-thousand-word series for the *Roanoke Times* titled "Picking Up the Pieces." Bruder's investigation into the lives of elderly "road warriors" began with "a magazine story on a growing subculture of American nomads" published in *Harper's Magazine* as "The End of Retirement: When You Can't Afford to Stop Working."

Tarbell's example of extraordinarily extensive documentation is reprised in all three projects. *Five Days at Memorial* and *Factory Man* are thick with the names of interviewees, published and unpublished documents, newspaper files, and statistics. Bruder regrets the paucity of available research on the phenomenon of retirees and others living continuously on the road, but her notes for *Nomadland* span interviews, books, US government reports, newsletters, and newspaper articles, together with reference to the landmark US fiction of the road, notably *The Grapes of Wrath* (1939). She also notes the frustration that regularly besets investigative journalists: a Freedom of Information Act request arrived with names and contact information blacked out.

All three muckrakers, in addition to undertaking archival research, worked in the terrain of their projects, as did Tarbell. Realizing her need for firsthand, sustained knowledge of US nomadic life, Bruder bought a van ("a decade-old vehicle … with just 64,000 miles on the odometer"[61]) and added thousands more miles while working cross-country with her subjects and joining them in winter months in the Sunbelt, where living is cheapest. "A journalist who parachutes in for an afternoon to cover a story," she knew, "seldom gets close enough to hear any kind of truth."[62] In Galax, Virginia, Macy saw that jobless factory workers applying for retraining programs were merely a "snapshot"[63] of the unemployment crisis in the area where the furniture industry collapsed in the face of competition from China. "People seem to disappear," she realized, "like scrap lumber,"[64] and she realized she must drive deep into the "snaky corners of rural back roads"[65] to gauge the desperateness of the situation. For her part, Fink was nowhere near the flooded Memorial Hospital when it lost electrical power in the days following the New Orleans levee failures. She learned on site in the aftermath of the life-and-death struggle by hospital workers that the generators, installed in the basement when the hospital was built in the 1920s, had failed and left not only a "compromised physical infrastructure, compromised operating systems, and compromised individuals" but also "instances of heroism."[66] Fink's medical expertise and journalistic experience equipped her to convey the immediacy of the scene, as when readers are brought to the bedside of a patient breathing her last: "patients like this ... appeared to be dying cell by cell from the inside out."[67]

These three literary muckrakers far exceed their progenitor, Tarbell, in explicitly identifying themselves in their subjects' spaces. Tarbell, at the turn of the twentieth century, often resorted to the passive voice, obscuring the actuality of her work in place (e.g., manuscripts "have been examined," and "copies of affidavits ... have been made"[68]). She nonetheless stepped forward in the preface of the *History* as the "I" with access to files, the "I" who missed no episode in the Standard Oil saga, and the "I" swearing to a full account.[69] Her successors are bolder by far. Macy is "the daughter of a displaced factory worker" and a mom who "worked the graveyard shift when the economy was good."[70] But Macy, as a journalist, found it necessary to cross class lines for interviews with a corporate executive, "factory man" John Bassett III, for whom golf was a favorite outing at a private club. "The factory man and I were friendly," she reported, "but our exchanges were often fraught."[71] Bruder, joining the nomadic work force, recounts her training at a warehouse, where, together with fellow seasonal Amazon "CamperForce" workers, the journalist in her mid-thirties spent days with "a cohort of mostly elderly workers"[72] frantically scanning barcodes on everything from dildos to gun accessories to a nauseating incense. She used short breaks, she says, to make notes and "dictated observations, *sotto voce*, to an audio recorder concealed in a pen and shot video with a camera that looked like a key fob,"[73] both on the lanyard with her worker ID badge.

The author of *Five Days at Memorial* faced a different challenge situating herself in the central scene of her literary muckraking. In her epilogue, Fink's first-person "I" recounts reporting in the midst of healthcare disasters in Haiti, India, and Liberia. *Five Days at Memorial* is her report on the domestic front. Fink came to New Orleans to examine the former Memorial Hospital—more recently under new management and renamed Ochsner Baptist Medical Center—following the crisis of the flooding but also in the middle of another, ongoing crisis. To piece together the harrowing events in a modern US hospital that functioned for days without the most basic equipment, Fink interviewed numerous physicians, nurses, therapists, administrators, patients and their family members, attorneys, and city officials. When Hurricane Katrina struck and windows smashed, she learned, maintenance crews boarded them up, but the "plywood grew wet and buckled," and "water pooled on the floors."[74] As floodwaters rose on the third day after the storm and electrical power was lost, the hospital went from "assault mode" to "survival mode."[75] Some two hundred patients "needed to be brought to safety," including "around two dozen patients in the ICUs [intensive care units], a similar number in the newborn nursery, high-risk pregnant mothers, and around two dozen dialysis patients."[76] Without air conditioning or other ventilation, the air became suffocating, the walls and floors slick from moisture in high humidity. The bathrooms backed up, and potable water was limited. A hospital rooftop helipad was available for airlift, but numerous radio messages between the hospital and Coast Guard were garbled. Evacuation by boat at the emergency room ramp required workers to carry patients down pitch-black stairwells.

Compounding the crisis, Fink learned, was an investigation into the possible murder of the sickest patients, "those whose lives depended on machines." The doctors, she learned, had decided to reverse the usual protocol of prioritizing such patients. "They had decided that all patients with Do Not Resuscitate [DNR] orders would be prioritized last for evacuation."[77] Those identified as DNR, meanwhile, were injected with morphine to ease their pain and suffering. Some nurses—and a prosecutor—believed the injections deliberately euthanized these patients. A star surgeon, Dr. Anna Maria Pou, was charged with murder. Arrested, she faced a grand jury and a possible trial and conviction for murder in a nationally publicized case that garnered public support for the beleaguered physician. When the grand jury refused to indict her, Pou resumed her practice and became a spokesperson for legislation guaranteeing legal immunity to medical workers serving in disasters.

Late in her narrative, Fink situates herself directly in the scene, attending Pou's public speeches and hearings at which the surgeon testified. "I watched her as we both sat in a gallery at the Baton Rouge Capitol at a hearing," Fink says. "Ever the committed doctor, she worked on patient charts balanced on her knees as she awaited a chance to rise in support of one of three disaster immunity bills she helped write."[78]

Dr. Anna Maria Pou is the protagonist of *Five Days at Memorial*, just as the furniture manufacturer John Bassett III takes center stage in *Factory Man*, and "Linda" is central to roadway life in *Nomadland*. More than a century earlier, Tarbell understood John D. Rockefeller and the Standard Oil Company to be one and the same, and she conjoined them in a synecdoche, with each interchangeably representing the other to become the single protagonist—yet, at the same time, the antagonist—of her *History*. In the 2010s, the literary muckrakers profiled numerous major and minor characters in their narratives, as had Tarbell, but all understood that a protagonist is invaluable to the storyline. Fink's Dr. Pou is no unblemished heroine in *Five Days at Memorial* despite her sterling achievements in medicine and devotion to patients, for she equivocates in public speeches on "'ethical considerations' in disaster medicine."[79] She is sustained throughout the story, nonetheless, as its protagonist, just as Macy's Bassett is similarly positioned in *Factory Man*. No hero, Bassett is yet heroic due to the extraordinary acts that sustain his manufacturing business against formidable odds and provide livelihoods in his community. The scion of a preeminent American furniture dynasty, Bassett is irascible and stubborn, grudgingly respected by employees and hated by rival family members and some competitors and allies too. Bassett is single-mindedly bent on keeping two Vaughan-Bassett manufacturing plants open and profitable in central Virginia when the Bassett brand, along with numerous other US marquee furniture names, had been sold to Chinese manufacturers who have flooded the market with furniture produced at lower cost, even as robots replace a workforce of numerous, now-downsized American employees.

Readers of *Factory Man* glimpse one such furniture worker who has exhausted his retirement "nest egg" and now works as a gardener for an $8.50 hourly wage six days a week. He has no health insurance and recently "maxed out his credit card to have an infected tooth pulled."[80] He is thus a prime candidate for Bruder's *Nomadland*, a compatriot of her Linda who took to the road in a van after a lifetime of work as a restaurant server, a construction supervisor, a casino cocktail waitress, and a corporate clerical worker—all jobs lacking retirement or healthcare benefits. Divorcing an abusive spouse, she became a single mother raising three children who, as adults coping with their own economic ups and downs, are in no position to support their mom in her years of "retirement." Linda, as Bruder emphasizes, typifies many whose military service and lifetime of paying work have nonetheless left them "houseless." *Nomadland*'s Linda represents an American population who gamely proclaim themselves owners of "wheel estate," keeping hope alive and avoiding thoughts about the day when they no longer have the physical stamina to change a tire or bend and squat for twelve hours sorting merchandise at an Amazon warehouse before the seasonal layoff sends them back on the road (or until Amazon's increasingly automated workforce of robots lays them off permanently).

The antagonists or villains in the new literary muckraking narratives are not single individuals. There is no mastermind of a Napoleonic Rockefeller to signify and symbolize the depredation of American lives in the second Gilded Age. Instead, the new literary muckrakers collectively assign responsibility to the supporters and enablers of an economic system that rewards very few at the expense of vast numbers of their fellow citizens, a system analyzed at length in Duff McDonald's *The Golden Passport: Harvard Business School, the Limits of Capitalism, and the Moral Failure of the MBA Elite* (2017). The antagonists in Fink, Macy, and Bruder are, in sum, a US economic system whose political and social shortcomings prove devastating to the citizens who have become its unwitting casualties. Fink's heroes are the healthcare workers at Memorial Hospital who valiantly struggle to care for patients against impossible odds, sleepless and exhausted but dauntless in commitment to their work on behalf of the sick. Her prose autopsy exposes the pathology of the new Gilded Age of corporate mergers and acquisitions, when healthcare is no longer a profession but has become an industry. A faraway and mentally remote corporate executive leadership, she finds, becomes nearly paralyzed in crisis. In the post-Katrina flood, Memorial Hospital's parent company, the financially troubled Tenet Healthcare, headquartered in Dallas, proved to be useless when, for instance, a key executive who lacked any crisis management training, emailed the following to the Memorial communications leader: "Have you contacted the National Guard?"[81] Despite the scramble with phones and computers "manned by dozens of employees from various departments" at Tenet's Dallas main office, says Fink, "they had little experience in disaster management."[82] She concludes, "The bureaucratic complexities were incomprehensible to key Tenet officials and bred panic in them."[83] The struggling workforce at Memorial found they were on their own, that Tenet emails and phone calls to the company that owned theirs and other hospitals were no lifeline.

Fink's cohorts similarly disclose socioeconomic and cultural failings in the new American Gilded Age. Macy's *Factory Man* quotes Bassett's denunciation of the ideas the "MBA programs were spouting, the same ideas the free-traders … were espousing—the ones who noticed that every time they closed a factory, their stock prices went up."[84] These were the very ones, Bassett continued, "who'd awarded themselves multimillion-dollar bonuses at the same time they were putting thousands of people out of work."[85] Macy concludes that "the brunt of globalization's blow had clearly been borne by low-income American workers,"[86] a judgment proven by the portraits of Bruder's road warriors, America's new migrant workers. These nomads, Bruder insists, "can both struggle and remain upbeat simultaneously,"[87] fueled by hope and the camaraderie they share. Her protagonist, Linda, nonetheless hungers most desperately for affordable land where she can build a livable space and leave the road forever. "My time on earth," she confides to Bruder, "is short."[88]

Whether gender has recently impacted literary muckraking opens an intriguing possibility in the context of this discussion. Could the culturally traditional role of women as caregivers in families and communities influence the muckraking projects undertaken by female journalists? By males? The women writers discussed here are arguably allied with others, both women and men, in this second Gilded Age. In her undercover account of life as a non-union restaurant server, a house cleaner, and a big-box store clerk, Barbara Ehrenreich's bestselling *Nickel and Dimed: On (Not) Getting By in America* (2001) exposed the perils of physically exhausting and dangerous low-wage work with the paired terror of subpar housing. Saru Jayaraman's *Forked* (2016), allied with literary muckraking in its argument, calls for a revolution in tipped work and holds the National

Restaurant Association guilty of suppressing restaurant servers' wages for a quarter century (holding at the stubborn federal minimum of $2.13 hourly). *Forked* explodes the myth of bountiful tips (the average median for US restaurant workers settles at an hourly $9.20, from which taxes are extracted), and it calls tipped workers in the US modern-day slaves. Elizabeth Royte, meanwhile, framed a first-person narrative on the perils of privatized water in *Bottlemania: How Water Went on Sale and Why We Bought It* (2008). Yet another muckraking project, Amy Goldstein's *Janesville: An American Story* (2017), like Macy's *Factory Man*, chronicles the decline and fall of a once-flourishing US manufacturing hub. A formerly bustling Wisconsin manufacturing city and site of the first General Motors assembly plant, Janesville struggles in the aftermath of the GM plant closure and all-too-familiar laid-off workforce, the cycle of "retraining," the lower-paying but steady work in the service sector (as prison guards, as school cafeteria workers), the "gig" jobs at fractions of former union wages, the food drives, the ruptured families, and the shuttered businesses—and the civic hope against hope that somehow Janesville will get back on its feet.

Male authors are also weighing in as literary muckrakers to expose the social deficits of the second Gilded Age by framing narratives empathically allied with individual, family, and community well-being. Jonathan Harr's *A Civil Action* (1995) and Dan Fagin's *Toms River* (2013) both recount stories of family and community tragedies of leukemia and other cancers attributable to the contamination of water supplies by corporations with the legal heft to delay courtroom accountability for many years. The cost to the US of a generation of children trapped in dysfunctional communities, households, and schools is tallied in Robert Putnam's *Our Kids: The American Dream in Crisis* (2015), and Putnam's book finds its complement in Matthew Desmond's Pulitzer Prize-winning *Evicted* (2016), a case study of Milwaukee as a microcosm of the US whose laws, business practices, and housing policies enrich a few but shatter the lives of the poor. Desmond's subtitle reveals the conundrum, *Poverty and Profit in the American City*, exposing the damage—indeed, the trauma—to women, men, and children whose housing is substandard and unstable and who lack legal, financial, or political recourse for remediation.

In her preface to *The History of the Standard Oil Company*, Tarbell calls the rise of the oil trust a "national episode which has divided men's minds,"[89] one that she equated in importance to the country's recent crisis, the Civil War. Fast forward to the second Gilded Age and the US presidential election of 2016, and the US once again found itself in a period of stark, nationally divided mentalities. Whatever root causes and sources are sought and explained, the new literary muckrakers' work, like that of their predecessor Tarbell in the McClure's organization, speaks forcefully, eloquently, and subtly with narrative power and authority. Their work, like that of their predecessors in the first Gilded Age, intentionally advances social democracy in the United States and hearkens to the philosophy of another forebear, Jane Addams, a contemporary of Tarbell and her muckraking cohorts. In 1902, in *Democracy and Social Ethics*, Addams critiqued political democracy, which she felt made "little attempt to assert itself in social affairs."[90] The immediate challenge, Addams continued, was to advance the "social function of democracy on the theory that the dependence of classes on each other is reciprocal."[91] Women, in Addams's view, were uniquely qualified to meet the challenge because their role as nurturers was central to the female identity. The second Gilded Age supports Addams's position, as we see, but the recent work of male literary muckrakers indicates a new gendering of literary muckraking in the twenty-first century, an alliance of women and men in support of "the social function of democracy."

Notes

1 Pattee, *New American Literature*, 146.
2 Howarth, "Mother of Literature," 55.
3 Eason, "New Journalism," 191.

4 Pauly, "Politics," 115.
5 Pattee, *New American Literature*, 144.
6 Brace, *Dangerous Classes*.
7 George, *Progress and Poverty*, quoted in Martin and Tichi, *Gilded Age*, 44.
8 George, quoted in Martin and Tichi, 72–73.
9 Hartsock, *History*, 134; Good, "Jacob A. Riis."
10 For "wretched refuse," see Emma Lazarus's "The New Colossus," a sonnet engraved on the bronze plaque on the pedestal of "Liberty Enlightening the World" (i.e., the Statue of Liberty).
11 For detailed accounts, see Papke, *Pullman Case*. See also Green, *Death in the Haymarket*.
12 Filler, *Muckrakers*, 9.
13 Filler, 9.
14 Roosevelt, "Man with the Muck Rake," quoted in Martin and Tichi, *Gilded Age*, 180–81.
15 Morris, *Theodore Rex*, 440.
16 Roosevelt, "Man with the Muck Rake," quoted in Martin and Tichi, *Gilded Age*, 181.
17 Baker, *American Chronicle*, 31. Of this roll call of Louis Filler's muckrakers, only William Hard is included in Connery, *Sourcebook*. See Marmarelli, "William Hard." Included among literary muckrakers, one might add John A. Fitch, *The Steel Workers* (1910).
18 See Lyon, *Success Story*, 13, 32–38. See also Goodwin, *Bully Pulpit*, 157–202.
19 One short sketch by Tarbell, "The King of Paris," was purchased for ten dollars by the New York newspaper syndicate owned by Samuel McClure and John Sanborn Phillips. The memory of that newspaper piece moved McClure to recruit Tarbell for *McClure's*.
20 See Edelstein, *Between the Novel*, 2.
21 Edelstein, 2.
22 Bryce, *American Commonwealth*, 775.
23 Bryce, 775.
24 Bryce, 271.
25 Van Vorst and Van Vorst, *Woman Who Toils*, 5.
26 Irwin, "First Ward Ball," 139.
27 Baker, "Right to Work," 324.
28 Steffens, *Shame of the Cities*, 65.
29 Steffens, 26. The facsimiles appear on pp. 72, 75, and 77.
30 Steffens, *Autobiography*, 111.
31 For Steffens's career in New York news reporting, including the chapter "Bulls and Bears," see his *Autobiography*, 176–96. For Baker's account of news reporting in Chicago, see *American Chronicle*, 46–47.
32 Tarbell, *All in the Day's Work*, 13. The male muckrakers' avoidance of increasingly popular novels may also be laid to longtime US suspicions of fiction as frivolous, feminine, and thus a distraction from serious purpose. The muckrakers, questing for facts, sought quotidian information. They shunned linkage with fanciful or sentimental prose that was readily ascribed to novels. Steffens was evidently anxious lest *The Shame of the Cities* be misconstrued as a departure from muckraking journalism when his series of essay-length exposés of US urban corruption was compiled for book-length publication. "This is not a book," he insisted in the first sentence of the introduction to *The Shame of the Cities*, fearing that his "accounts as a reporter" (i.e., journalism) might be misconstrued as a project fraught with "pretensions." The "new dress" of the book was itself disturbing, and Steffens hastened to assure readers that the utilitarian, civic purpose of his essays remained intact despite hard covers. His colleague, Baker, enacted the most radical severance of journalism from fiction when, in the 1910s, he adopted the pen name of David Grayson and wrote a series of largely forgotten, unwittingly insipid novels, among them *The Friendly Road* (1913), *Hempfield* (1915), and *Great Possessions* (1917), each apparently an anodyne for escape from the harsh realities of muckraking and the First World War.

The anti-fiction bias in US literature and culture extends from the Puritan minister Increase Mather's dismissal of "vain romances" to Thomas Jefferson's censure of novels as a "mass of trash" and, for analysis, reaches to Fred Lewis Pattee's assessment of 1850s US literature as *The Feminine Fifties* (1940) and Ann Douglas's *The Feminization of American Culture* (1977). For reference to "vain romances," see Tichi, "Thespis," 101n23. For Jefferson's "mass of trash," see his letter to Nathaniel Burwell.
33 Tarbell, *All in the Day's Work*, 203.
34 Baker, *American Chronicle*, 51.
35 Baker, 52–53.
36 See Bushman, *Refinement of America*, 280–312. See also Schlereth, *Victorian America*, 201–11.
37 Darrow, quoted in Martin and Tichi, *Gilded Age*, 14.

38 Tarbell, *Short Life*, 4.
39 Tarbell, 6.
40 Tarbell, *All in the Day's Work*, 151.
41 Tarbell, 173.
42 Quoted in Mott, *History of American Magazines*, 597.
43 Tarbell, *All in the Day's Work*, 202.
44 Tarbell, *History*, 2:255.
45 Tarbell, 1:70
46 Tarbell, 1:ix.
47 Tarbell, 1:ix–x.
48 Tarbell, 2:239.
49 Tarbell, 2:239.
50 Brady, *Ida Tarbell*, 125.
51 Tarbell, *History*, 2:29.
52 Tarbell, 1:125.
53 Tarbell, 2:242.
54 Tarbell, 2:231.
55 Tarbell, 2:231.
56 Tarbell, 2:231.
57 Tarbell, 2:232
58 Brooks, *Melodramatic Imagination*, 5.
59 Tarbell, *All in the Day's Work*, 235.
60 Gates and Collins, quoted in Tichi, *Civic Passions*, 275. Muckraking at the turn of the twenty-first century (i.e., the new Gilded Age) includes Eric Schlosser's bestselling *Fast Food Nation: The Dark Side of the All-American Meal*, which alerted readers to the perils of industrial agriculture, among them meat contamination and workplace threats to health from the packinghouse to the fast-food deep fryer often operated illegally by underage workers. The book drew comparisons to *The Jungle*. Author Alex Prud'homme underscored the severity of the water crisis with *The Ripple Effect: The Fate of Freshwater in the Twenty-First Century*, as did Peter Gleick in *Sustainable Water*.

Healthcare became a central issue in the new Gilded Age, and among conflicting claims, several writers exposed the facts of the pharmaceutical business, its lobbyists, and the elected officials who collaborate in exchange for campaign contributions. Journalist Laurie Garrett warns in *Betrayal of Trust: The Collapse of Global Public Health* that national boundaries are irrelevant in a world where lethal microbes travel freely and public health systems are weak. As editor-in-chief of the *New England Journal of Medicine*, Marcia Angell, MD, expressed her alarm in *The Truth about the Drug Companies: How They Deceive Us and What to Do about It*. Her work was followed by Steven Brill's *America's Bitter Pill: Money, Politics, Backroom Deals, and the Fight to Fix Our Broken Healthcare System* and Elisabeth Rosenthal's *An American Sickness: How Healthcare Became Big Business and How You Can Take It Back*.

America's bloated prison system, both public and privatized for the profit of stockholders and top executives, has been exposed in Joseph T. Hallinan's *Going Up the River: Travels in a Prison Nation* and Marc Mauer's *Race to Incarcerate*. Michelle Alexander's title highlights its racial dimension: *The New Jim Crow: Mass Incarceration in the Age of Colorblindness*. Racial and other complexities in housing are made starkly clear in Matthew Desmond's Pulitzer Prize–winning *Evicted: Poverty and Profit in the American City*.

These are but a few of the muckraking projects of the new Gilded Age. The periodicals, preeminently *Mother Jones*, continue to publish fact-backed muckraking investigations, and the *Atlantic* and *Harper's*, among others, follow suit, both in print, online, and in film. The first Gilded Age was followed by the Progressive Era in which many glaring problems were addressed in response to public outrage. Whether the new Gilded Age may benefit from the same rebound in the twenty-first century remains an open question.
61 Bruder, *Nomadland*, 6–7.
62 Bruder, 164.
63 Macy, *Factory Man*, 236.
64 Macy, 327.
65 Macy, 327.
66 Fink, *Five Days at Memorial*, 338.
67 Fink, 215.
68 Tarbell, *History*, 1:x.
69 Tarbell, 1:xi.

70 Macy, *Factory Man*, 14.
71 Macy, 397.
72 Bruder, *Nomadland*, 194.
73 Bruder, 196.
74 Fink, *Five Days at Memorial*, 56.
75 Fink, 63
76 Fink, 74.
77 Fink, 90.
78 Fink, 435.
79 Fink, 449.
80 Macy, *Factory Man*, 336–37.
81 Fink, *Five Days at Memorial*, 77.
82 Fink, 165.
83 Fink, 168.
84 Macy, *Factory Man*, 239.
85 Macy, 239.
86 Macy, 239.
87 Bruder, *Nomadland*, 164.
88 Bruder, 240.
89 Tarbell, *History*, 1:viii.
90 Addams, *Democracy and Social Ethics*, 39.
91 Addams, 39.

Bibliography

Addams, Jane. *Democracy and Social Ethics*. New York: Macmillan, 1902.
Baker, Ray Stannard. *American Chronicle: The Autobiography of Ray Stannard Baker*. New York: Charles Scribner's Sons, 1945.
———. "The Right to Work: The Story of the Non-striking Miners." *McClure's Magazine*, January 1903, 323–36.
———. "Wonderful Hawaii—A World Experiment Station." *American Magazine*, November 1911, 28–38; December 1911, 201–14; January 1912, 328–39.
Bellamy, Edward. *Looking Backward, 2000–1887*. 1888. Reprint, New York: Penguin, 1982.
Brace, Charles Loring. *The Dangerous Classes of New York, and Twenty Years' Work among Them*. New York: Wynkoop and Hallenbeck, 1872.
Brady, Kathleen. *Ida Tarbell: Portrait of a Muckraker*. New York: Seaview/Putnam, 1984.
Brooks, Peter. *The Melodramatic Imagination: Balzac, Henry James, Melodrama, and the Mode of Excess*. New Haven, CT: Yale University Press, 1995.
Bruder, Jessica. *Nomadland: Surviving America in the Twenty-First Century*. New York: Norton, 2017.
Bryce, James. *The American Commonwealth*. Vol. 2. 1888. Reprint, New York: Macmillan, 1905.
Bushman, Richard L. *The Refinement of America: Persons, Houses, Cities*. New York: Random House, 1992.
Connery, Thomas B., ed. *A Sourcebook of American Literary Journalism: Representative Writers in an Emerging Genre*. New York: Greenwood Press, 1992.
Davis, Rebecca Harding. *Life in the Iron Mills*. 1861. Reprint, Boston, MA: Bedford, 1998.
Desmond, Matthew. *Evicted: Poverty and Profit in the American City*. New York: Penguin, 2016.
Eason, David. "The New Journalism and the Image-World." In Sims, *Literary Journalism*, 191–205.
Edelstein, Sari. *Between the Novel and the News: The Emergence of American Women's Writing*. Charlottesville, VA: University of Virginia Press, 2014.
Filler, Louis. *The Muckrakers*. 1968. Reprint, Palo Alto, CA: Stanford University Press, 1993.
Fink, Sheri. *Five Days at Memorial: Life and Death in a Storm-Ravaged Hospital*. New York: Broadway Books, 2013.
Fitch, John A. *The Steel Workers*. 1910. Reprint, Pittsburgh, PA: University of Pittsburgh Press, 1989.
Good, Howard. "Jacob A. Riis." In Connery, *Sourcebook*, 81–89.
Goodwin, Doris Kearns. *The Bully Pulpit: Theodore Roosevelt, William Howard Taft, and the Golden Age of Journalism*. New York: Simon and Schuster, 2013.
Green, James R. *Death in the Haymarket: A Story of Chicago, the First Labor Movement and the Bombing that Divided Gilded Age America*. New York: Pantheon Books, 2006.

Hartsock, John C. *A History of American Literary Journalism: The Emergence of Modern Narrative Form*. Amherst, MA: University of Massachusetts Press, 2000.
Howarth, William. "The Mother of Literature: Journalism and *The Grapes of Wrath*." In Sims, *Literary Journalism*, 53–81.
Irwin, Will. "The First Ward Ball." In *The Muckrakers*, edited by Arthur Weinberg and Lila Weinberg, 139–45. 1961. Reprint, Urbana, IL: University of Illinois Press, 2001.
Jefferson, Thomas. Letter to Nathaniel Burwell, March 14, 1818. https://founders.archives.gov/documents/Jefferson/03-12-02-0438-0001.
Lazarus, Emma. "The New Colossus." 1883. www.poetryfoundation.org/poems/46550/the-new-colossus.
London, Jack. "The Apostate." In *The Complete Short Fiction of Jack London*, edited by Earle Labor, Robert C. Leitz III, and I. Milo Shepard, 3:1112–29. Palo Alto, CA: Stanford University Press, 1993.
Lyon, Peter. *Success Story: The Life and Times of S. S. McClure*. New York: Charles Scribner's Sons, 1963.
Macy, Beth. *Factory Man: How One Furniture Maker Battled Offshoring, Stayed Local—and Helped Save an American Town*. New York: Little, Brown, 2015.
Marmarelli, Ronald S. "William Hard." In Connery, *Sourcebook*, 131–42.
Martin, Wendy, and Cecelia Tichi. *The Gilded Age and Progressive Era: Historical Explorations of Literature*. Santa Barbara, CA: ABC-CLIO, 2016.
McDonald, Duff. *The Golden Passport: Harvard Business School, the Limits of Capitalism, and the Moral Failure of the MBA Elite*. New York: HarperCollins, 2017.
Morris, Edmund. *Theodore Rex*. New York: Random House, 2001.
Mott, Frank Luther. *A History of American Magazines*. Vol. 4, *1885–1905*. Cambridge, MA: Harvard University Press, 1957.
Papke, David Ray. *The Pullman Case: The Clash of Labor and Capital in Industrial America*. Lawrence, KS: University Press of Kansas, 1999.
Pattee, Fred Lewis. *The New American Literature, 1890–1930*. New York: Century, 1930.
Pauly, John J. "The Politics of the New Journalism." In Sims, *Literary Journalism*, 110–29.
Remnick, David, ed. *The New Gilded Age: "The New Yorker" Looks at the Culture of Affluence*. New York: Random House, 2000.
Schlereth, Thomas J. *Victorian America: Transformations in Everyday Life, 1876–1915*. New York: Harper, 1991.
Sims, Norman, ed. *Literary Journalism in the Twentieth Century*. New York: Oxford University Press, 1990.
Sinclair, Upton. *The Jungle*. 1906. Reprint, New York: Norton, 2003.
Steffens, Lincoln. *The Autobiography of Lincoln Steffens*. New York: Harcourt Brace, 1931.
———. "The Shame of Minneapolis: The Rescue and Redemption of a City That Was Sold Out." *McClure's Magazine*, January 1903, 227–39.
———. *The Shame of the Cities*. New York: McClure, Phillips, 1904.
Tarbell, Ida M. *All in the Day's Work: An Autobiography*. New York: Macmillan, 1939.
———. *The History of the Standard Oil Company*. 2 vols. New York: McClure, Phillips, 1904.
———. "The Oil War of 1872." *McClure's Magazine*, January 1903, 248–60.
———. *A Short Life of Napoleon Bonaparte*. New York: S. S. McClure, 1895.
Tichi, Cecelia. *Civic Passions: Seven Who Launched Progressive America (and What They Teach Us)*. Chapel Hill, NC: University of North Carolina Press, 2009.
———. "Thespis and the 'Carnall Hypocrite': A Puritan Motive for Aversion to Drama." *Early American Literature* 4, no. 2 (Fall 1969): 86–103.
Twain, Mark, and Charles Dudley Warner. *The Gilded Age: A Tale of Today*. 1873. Reprint, New York: Penguin, 2001.
Van Vorst, Mrs. John, and Marie Van Vorst. *The Woman Who Toils*. New York: Doubleday, 1903.

8

"FEEL THE FACT"

The 1930s Reportage of Joseph North, John L. Spivak, and Meridel Le Sueur

Don Dingledine

"Something stamped the Thirties as historically different from the other times of mass hunger in America," Joseph North observes. Writing in the prologue to a 1969 anthology of works originally published during the 1930s in the American leftist magazine *New Masses*, at which he served as an editor for nearly fifteen years, North argues that what distinguished the Great Depression from the string of economic depressions that had occurred with "tragic regularity" in America before then was not the depth and severity of suffering. It was not the "assault of starvation" but "the scope and depth of the counter-attack" that made the 1930s unique. As North remembers it, the crisis was met with "a sweep, a daring, an imaginativeness ... that transcended that of any other time." Radical politics and workers' organizations fueled this unprecedented response to poverty and hunger; as North's impulse to collect poems, essays, reports, and sketches in "An Anthology of the Rebel Thirties" three decades later suggests, the revolutionary counterattack was simultaneously and inextricably a literary one. "It was the time of the Reds," North proclaims.[1] It was also the time of reportage, a genre central to the history and development of American literary journalism. Describing reportage as "the dominant literary innovation" of the 1930s, Paula Rabinowitz notes that "it affected a number of other forms. Thus fiction, poetry, and drama all sought to re-create the immediacy and power offered by the direct testimony of reportage."[2]

Surveying the contents of North's *New Masses* anthology, literary critic Maxwell Geismar singles out for praise its selection of reportage: "no decade since the Thirties has given rise to so much good writing in that genre—and raised the genre itself, at its best, to an art form."[3] Writing in 1948, North suggested that the *New Masses*' unlikely success during the Great Depression "lay in the magazine's reportage." He even claims that "the wolf howled most evilly at the door" when the *New Masses* failed to include "at least one piece of reportage in every issue." Reportage, after all, "was ever the common denominator that appealed to freshman as well as professor."[4] Close examination of the work of two journalists, John L. Spivak and Meridel Le Sueur, in the pages of the *New Masses* and elsewhere during the Great Depression, lends credence to both Geismar's and North's evaluations of the genre's merits. In addition, extended analysis of Spivak's and Le Sueur's literary strategies within the context of the period's theories of reportage, especially as articulated by North, illuminates the role of 1930s reportage in the development of American literary journalism.[5] It also reveals the genre's potential roots in two seemingly incompatible nineteenth-century literary precursors: French naturalism, with its detached observation of objective fact, and American romanticism, with its heightened sense of subjective feeling. The social relationship established between the narrator-reporter, the subject, and the reader in representative examples of 1930s reportage suggests that the subjective turn can be understood, in line with other mass movements of the era, as an embrace of the collective. In the face of crisis and widespread suffering, 1930s reportage offered readers a new sense of social responsibility and a new subjectivity—an expansive social identity, communal in nature, that defines the self in relation to others.

The Great Depression inspired a conscious effort to expand the scope of lives and experiences depicted in fiction and other art forms as well as in reportage. Organizations like John Reed Clubs—named in honor of the pioneering reporter whose first-person account of the Russian Revolution, *Ten Days That Shook the World* (1919), is an early and influential example of reportage—also aimed to nurture historically marginalized or silenced talents, thereby expanding the range of perspectives and experiences writers and artists brought to their work.[6] An anthology of *Proletarian Literature in the United States*, of which North was an editor and which includes a section devoted to reportage, was published to coincide with the first American Writers' Congress in 1935.[7] Given the lived realities of both writers and audiences in the 1930s, to "pretend to practice art for art's sake," as Joseph Freeman argues in his introduction to a collection of addresses from the second American Writers' Congress in 1937, became increasingly difficult.[8] Faith in a writer's ability to remain outside of or detached from events began to slip; some rejected it outright as a bourgeois delusion. Some wondered if inherited modes of individual artistic expression were suitable for or even capable of conveying collective experiences. Either way, even an artist with firsthand experience of working-class struggles needed to develop strategies for effectively representing suffering without turning it into spectacle. Through self-conscious adaptation and experimentation, writers searched for ways to empower working-class readers while still connecting with and informing readers from all backgrounds.[9] To be effective, a text must expose as well as transcend (or at least soften) social barriers and hierarchies.

In addition to soliciting and publishing reportage in the pages of the *New Masses*, North also defined the genre, articulated its goals, and mapped its characteristic features. North's "Reportage," a speech he delivered at the first American Writers' Congress, sheds light on the genre's role in the 1930s as well as on its place in the history of American literary journalism.[10] A time of crisis and revolution, of deep questioning and profound uncertainty, the 1930s demanded, North maintains, that hard facts and clear answers be delivered to the greatest number of readers in the fastest way possible. How a writer presents these facts to the reader, he insists, sets reportage apart from other forms of journalism. Reportage must enable readers to "feel the fact." To "answer the questions of who, why, when, where" was no longer enough. The writer of reportage "must do more than tell his reader what has happened—he must help the reader experience the event." All journalism "condenses reality," but in reaching beyond "surface observation," reportage becomes "three-dimensional reporting." Writers of reportage adopted the tools and techniques of literature, especially fiction, to help their readers experience an event and feel its facts. Noting that "boundary lines are being trampled all the time," North explains how reporters might "do their editorializing through their imagery," might "sketch a character in a few, swift strokes," or might even "get off an excellent short story." Responding to immediate concerns but crafted to stand the test of time, reportage "becomes durable literature": "The finest writers of reportage are artists in the fullest sense of the term."[11]

Despite "the almost infinite flexibility of this form," the report itself, North insists, remains the heart of reportage: "The fact, the immediate situation, dominates." What gives revolutionary reporters an edge over bourgeois reporters in North's view is that they situate facts in a network of causes and effects, with an eye to the future as well as to the past: "to the writer of reportage, the fact he is describing is no corpse; it is alive, it has its place on earth. Some phenomena have produced it; it in turn produces other phenomena." Because the best writers of reportage possess "much more than the camera eye," their works offer readers "both an analysis and an experience, culminating in an implicit course of action."[12]

The reporter's subjective response might be one way for readers to experience what is being reported. North holds up the example of Egon Erwin Kisch, whom he describes as "probably the greatest reporter in the world to-day," and whose theory and practice of reportage shaped North's conception of the genre.[13] Peter Monteath explains the theory of reportage Kisch had developed by the mid-1930s: still "demanding objectivity," it "permits and even recommends the insertion into the account of the persona of the passionate, biased reporter. The observer of action is also a participant in the action."[14] Especially when reporters' encounters with the subjects they profile are part of the story, the ethical as well as political nature of reportage becomes rooted in what philosopher Emmanuel Levinas calls *rapport de face à face*. The face-to-face encounter or relation evokes what Levinas sees as our responsibility for the Other. Levinas's ethical thought, Paul Marcus explains, identifies "a human tendency in us, an often inhibited, muted, or repressed tendency, ... to see the needs of others as more important (or at least as important as) than our own."[15] Both Spivak and Le Sueur recognize the power of the reporter's subjective presence, especially in the face-to-face encounter, to model for readers or to call forth in readers this sense of responsibility.

Although North claims reportage as a product of the twentieth century and aligns it with his era's global revolutionary currents, he also traces the genre's American roots back to Stephen Crane and Richard Harding Davis in the late nineteenth century and to the muckraking journalism of Ida Tarbell and Lincoln Steffens in the late nineteenth and early twentieth centuries. Yet the two literary figures who best illuminate what is at stake in North's definition of reportage, especially in its dual emphasis on fact and feeling, and whose influence might in fact be most palpable in Great Depression reportage, are Émile Zola and Walt Whitman.[16]

Zola's influence on 1930s American literary journalism can be seen in three areas. Most apparent is the novelist's impassioned defense of Alfred Dreyfus, a Jewish military officer falsely convicted of treason in 1894, which made Zola a model for writers committed to justice and the power of truth.[17] A second reason some literary journalists turned to Zola is best expressed by French novelist Henri Barbusse. Writing in the *New Masses* in 1934, Barbusse maintained that Zola's naturalism, following parallel developments in science, had brought "to the art of writing more and more of concrete realism, of exact materialism."[18] In theoretical writings as well as in his novels, Zola promoted a mode of fiction grounded in the rigorous and objective study of reality; naturalism thus helped quell anxieties over journalistic integrity that inevitably surfaced in response to the subjective and imaginative elements of reportage.[19] A third way in which we can trace Zola's influence on 1930s reportage is in how writers perceive the facts they investigate and report. In line with Marxist theories of dialectical and historical materialism, the ultimate focus of reportage as well as of naturalism is, as North emphasizes, the causes and effects of observable facts. "Human progress consisted during the course of the centuries in bringing," Barbusse suggests, "the reasons-for-existence and causes-behind-facts gradually from the supernatural level to the natural, from mysticism to logic, from heaven to earth."[20] Speaking at the first American Writers' Congress, Malcolm Cowley extolled this shift in thinking as the "principal gift that the revolutionary movement can make to writers": "It gives them the sense of human life, not as a medley of accidents, but as a connected and continuing process."[21] Quoting French physiologist Claude Bernard's pioneering theories of experimental medicine, Zola observes: "In the conduct of their lives men do nothing but make experiments on one another." Reform—"to master life in order to direct it"—is the shared goal of Zola's naturalism and 1930s reportage.[22]

Using Bernard's insights again—"Science has precisely the privilege of teaching us what we do not know by substituting reason and experiment for feeling"—and hailing "the coming of the physiological man," Zola proclaimed that "metaphysical man is dead."[23] Even when presenting hard facts with a naturalist slant, however, 1930s reportage was not ready to give up the "profound and warm effusions" romanticism brought to literature, especially when, as in Whitman's poetry and prose, they expressed a love of workers and of democracy.[24] "The heroic spiritual grandfather of our generation in America is Walt Whitman," declared Michael Gold, a founding editor of the *New Masses* and an early advocate of proletarian literature.[25] Yet embracing Whitman did not mean turning a blind eye to romanticism's pitfalls. Pointing to "the clouds of Whitmanism," Gold warned that the "vague, large rhetoric" of "such abstract and Olympian love" is "easily used by demagogues."[26] The challenge was to come down from the clouds while not foregoing them entirely, to bridge the "absolute cleavage" or "abyss" (as Barbusse put it) some saw between heaven and earth, between feeling and fact.[27] Successful reportage must convince readers by offering a "naturalistic view" of objective facts. It also must harness the persuasive powers of poetic sentiment, as when the reporter's engaged, subjective presence creates a bond, in the face-to-face encounter, between reporter and subject as well as among reader, reporter, and subject. Often, these personal connections are fostered through direct addresses to the reader similar in spirit and effect to those that frequently occur in Whitman's poetry.[28]

Even while their vision was being directed to the material facts of human life in the Depression, readers needed to feel something beyond these facts, something untouched or undetermined by current realities. North's lyrical account of his foundational experience as a young rivet-passer in a shipyard gives us a fertile image through which to frame this balance of romanticism and naturalism, of feeling and fact, often at the heart of 1930s reportage. North eloquently describes one harsh reality while offering a palpable glimpse of something beyond:

> I could never forget my time when I was fifteen in the smoky hold of a ship in hot July with a dozen riveting guns hammering at hard steel, the rust particles flying about like burning snowflakes, a torrent of fire, rendering everything a choky crimson that blocked the breath, filled the lung, mingled with the sweat; all this with an awareness of the God-given daylight visible through the holes in the steel the reamer had drilled, affording a telescopic-sized glimpse of the serene river, the wheeling gulls, all of which became mockery of reality, a reality that became a daily nightmare that swallowed men up.[29]

"Nobody caught that" in literature, North concludes. "But the *New Masses* did try."[30]

Calling it "a rich year" for reportage, North singles out Spivak's "series of reports on the status of 1934 America" that appeared in the *New Masses*.[31] Most were published as weekly installments in October and November, and several were included a year later in Spivak's *America Faces the Barricades*.[32] Spivak's book is organized around sections with such titles as "The Lower Depths" and "The American Worker Stirs." One piece, "A Letter to the President," merits an untitled section unto itself, coming first after a brief preface.[33] Five years before John Steinbeck's *The Grapes of Wrath* (1939), Spivak recounts his visit to a migratory workers' camp in Fresno, California. According to North, "It is as moving as any scene in contemporary American fiction."[34] Framed as a letter to President Roosevelt and written on behalf of a fifteen-year-old Mexican girl, "A Letter to the President" describes conditions found in the camp mostly in terms of their impact on the daily lives of this unnamed girl and her family. The precarious nature of their existence explains their anonymity, for the girl fears retribution—and loss of income—if her identity were revealed. Two years earlier, Roosevelt's "Forgotten Man" radio address vowed that any "real economic cure" for the Depression must put "faith once more in the forgotten man at the bottom of the economic pyramid."[35] The image conjured in most listeners' minds was a white male manual laborer or farmer, robust in the face of hard times, rather than a migrant worker—and certainly not a dark-skinned immigrant or woman, much less a teenaged girl. The "Lower Depths" in Spivak's and Le Sueur's reportage exist below the base of Roosevelt's pyramid.

Spivak takes us into the hull of North's ship when he describes the conditions he finds in the camp; he methodically documents what Zola would label an experiment, one designed to control and exploit labor, not to mention nature, solely to maximize corporate profits. Yet Spivak breaks with the supposedly objective detachment of the scientific gaze so that his readers feel and experience the facts he uncovers. How Spivak's "Letter" positions readers in relation to facts—how he implicitly enlists readers, as well as the president, in the act of investigative reporting—reveals the collective dimension of literary journalism's subjective turn in the Great Depression. North in "Reportage" rightly highlights Spivak's work as an example of reportage in which "you see the writer at grips with his subject."[36]

"A Letter to the President" reads at times like two texts in one, as if it were a hybrid of traditional journalism and reportage. Spivak presents facts as most journalists would. He also recreates for readers the encounters or experiences in which he first gathered them. For example, Spivak acknowledges in the opening paragraph that he writes on the girl's behalf "because she did not have three cents for a stamp and because she never went to school to learn how to write." "You can't go to school," he explains, "if your father is always following the rich, productive earth and needs your labor in the fields as soon as you are seven or eight years old." Spivak repeats this information a few pages later, but this time he dramatizes his first encounter with the migrant girl. "When I walked out in the field," the journalist recalls, "there was this little girl dragging a huge sack along the furrow, and stuffing the brown bolls into it. She looked so tired, so weary, and then I noticed that she was with child." He then recreates their first conversation.[37] When readers see this initial contact—the reporter's face-to-face encounter with his subject—and eavesdrop on their conversation, they feel the facts of the girl's age, her life, and her labor in a deeper way than when reading static facts and numbers in the text's opening paragraph.[38] Even the fact that the girl is pregnant, which readers learn a few paragraphs earlier, is felt in a new way—and takes on a deeper social meaning—when we meet her as the reporter first did: a child herself, with child, at work in the fields.[39]

As details accumulate and repeat throughout the text, readers not only see and feel how facts are lived but also learn to comprehend them in a web of material causes and effects. "His craft is dialectic, catching the present in its relation to the past and the future," North observes.[40] Because Spivak's text engages us directly—we, not only Roosevelt, become the "you" addressed throughout—we are active participants; as we learn to trace the patterns of exploitation in the camps, we grow to care about the people ensnared in them. Take, for example, the single electric light in the family's one-room shack. Like a tour guide, Spivak's narrator has already brought us into their dwelling, describing the bed and other objects found there. Calling attention to the "dusty bulb" in the middle of the room, he asks: "You noticed it, didn't you?" He has just explained how the baby, sick with scarlet fever, sleeps on the single bed; everyone else, six in all, sleeps on the floor. He has also pointed out a barrel of water. The family does not use it to wash themselves, only to cool the baby's fever. They must travel four miles each way by car to obtain water, and what they spend on gas cannot go toward food. Thus they go without electricity. The baby cries most at night, however, and "it's awfully hard to tend the sick baby in the darkness." The pregnant girl's sole request of the president must be understood within this web of interrelated facts: "What she wanted to ask you is if you could possibly get in touch with somebody and have them not charge them twenty-five cents for the use of the electric light—especially when somebody's sick or expecting a baby."[41]

Spivak insightfully includes a moment of misunderstanding in recounting his efforts to gain a fuller comprehension of migrant workers' lives. As noted, Spivak points out his subject's illiteracy in the opening paragraph; when he later recreates the moment he learned this fact, readers observe him miscomprehend the girl multiple times. She insists that she "no can write" the president, while Spivak insists she can—he will give her a stamp. The reporter does not comprehend the fact that this fifteen-year-old *cannot* write until she states explicitly that her work in the fields prevents her from attending school. She blushes when he first misunderstands her, and this too he misreads.[42] Spivak could simply report the fact of her illiteracy, but his goal is to acknowledge how hierarchies of power can hinder understanding. As we experience not the young girl's life but Spivak's encounter with her life, it is important to recognize that his gaps in knowledge and lapses of understanding are also ours and the president's. Of equal importance is the fact that these differences do not preclude sympathy and communication. The journalist finally comes to see the act of writing through the girl's eyes.

Spivak's text works against the traditional top-down, hierarchical relationship among reporter and reader and subject. Spivak never allows his readers or himself to lose sight of a principle sociologist Pierre Bourdieu would later identify as the driving force shaping his methodology and theory. Explaining in *The Weight of the World* (1999) how he recorded and presented interviews with French citizens who feel dispossessed and alienated from work and society, Bourdieu defines the nature of his project: "If its objective of pure knowledge distinguishes the research relationship from most of the exchanges in everyday life, it remains, whatever one does, a *social relationship*."[43] The social relationship is at the heart of Spivak's "Letter" and a defining feature of 1930s reportage. Spivak does not just recover the migrant girl and her family from the margins; he narrows the gap between himself and her, as well as between her and his readers.[44] If the text humanizes the girl, it simultaneously humanizes reporter and reader in relation to the girl; all acquire an expansive, interconnected identity.

When the girl in closing paragraphs parrots mainstream American discourse—"The President, he take care of poor people"—the reporter asks, "Is he taking care of you?"[45] Spivak's question is for readers as much as it is for the migrant girl and her family. And when she seeks Spivak's reassurance in the closing paragraphs—"You no fool me?"—her question is for readers as much as it is for him.[46] Those readers who are no longer fooled by ideologies of bootstrap individualism will recognize their own exploitation and suffering in the plight of migrant workers. We also join the reporter in his sense of duty to the girl. The only real hope she has comes when the reporter assures her that he will express her concerns while also protecting her anonymity. To return to North's ship metaphor, in her encounter with Spivak, she is granted "a telescopic-sized glimpse" of another reality, outside the camps and beyond the material realities of her daily existence, where social relationships are protective and empowering rather than exploitative.

Spivak's reportage masterfully draws readers into this type of social relationship. When the text repeats the fears that make the girl want to write a letter to the president, this time in her own words, as the reporter first heard them—"I got to have baby on floor and if it come in night, how I have baby?"—readers feel the fact exactly as Spivak did: "I nodded, unable to speak."[47] Yet he writes. The original title of Spivak's piece when it was published in the pages of the *New Masses* emphasizes the sense of collective authorship that implicitly develops over the course of its pages: "A Letter from America to President Roosevelt." In fact, Spivak's name does not appear on the issue's cover, where "A Letter from America" is listed as the first of three articles to be found inside. (The second asks, "Are Newspapermen Workers?"[48]) Through this simple, beautiful gesture, a fifteen-year-old migrant worker becomes America. And her letter becomes America's.

Six decades later, Le Sueur claimed collective authorship in *The Dread Road* (1991), published when she was ninety-one: "This is not a book written by one person. This is a communal creation."[49] The roots of Le Sueur's collective sense of self can be traced in her firsthand experiences with communal living as well as in the 1930s reportage that grew out of these experiences. Born in Iowa in 1900, Le Sueur returned to the Midwest (after stints in New York City, Hollywood, and San Francisco) just before the Great Depression. As Elaine Hedges describes it, she lived for a time in a small town in Minnesota where women would collectively bake and share bread using flour Le Sueur bought with money earned through her writing. She later lived in St. Paul "with another group of women and their children in an abandoned warehouse": "The women pooled their relief money and food and in the evenings wrote and told each other stories, with Le Sueur taking down the tales of those who could not write."[50]

Published in the January 1932 issue of the *New Masses*, "Women on the Breadlines" anticipates Spivak's "A Letter to the President" in its portrayal of individuals overlooked by dominant narratives.[51] Like Spivak, Le Sueur makes the act of recovery part of the story, starting with her intentionally misleading title. "Women on the Breadlines" is not about breadlines but about those who typically are not seen in this public display of suffering and charity. "It's one of the great mysteries of the city where women go when they are out of work and hungry," she writes. In telling women's stories, Le Sueur brings readers to consider not just the suffering they witness in the streets or read about in newspapers, but also the lives hidden from view. "There are no flop houses for women as there are for men," she explains, "where a bed can be had for a quarter or less." Nor do you "see women lying on the floor at the mission in the free flops," and women are not seen sleeping "under newspapers in the park." "A woman will shut herself up in a room until it is taken away from her, and eat a cracker a day and be as quiet as a mouse so there are no social statistics concerning her."[52]

In "Women Are Hungry" (1934), published in *American Mercury* two years later, Le Sueur goes on to argue that correcting the tally is not enough. Numbers are inadequate: "Statistics make unemployment abstract and not too uncomfortable. The human being is different. To be hungry is different than to count the hungry."[53] That difference, perhaps, accounts for a *New York Times* reviewer's ambivalent response to Spivak's *America Faces the Barricades*: "One does not doubt Mr. Spivak's facts," the reviewer concedes; bristling at the "pattern" Spivak draws in his reportage, however, he endorses instead "a journalism based on the actuarial method of computing the averages."[54] Even more successfully than Spivak, Le Sueur enables readers to feel the lived realities glossed over by statistics. "All this sounds different in the language of the banks," Le Sueur writes in 1934's "Cows and Horses Are Hungry," where she describes crop loss, cattle loss, and starving, suicidal farmers "in human terms, of life and not credit and interest."[55] And in 1937's "Women Know a Lot of Things," Le Sueur identifies an alternative way of comprehending the facts of the Great Depression, an embodied knowledge mothers acquire through the flesh and bone of malnourished children: "You don't have to read the stock reports in Mr. Hearst's paper. You have the news at its terrible source."[56]

"In a prose that is usually stark and clipped, relying on short declarative sentences and monosyllabic words," Hedges observes, "Le Sueur graphically conveys the psychology as well as the economic reality" of women's lives in the Great Depression.[57] In "Women on the Breadlines," Le Sueur's embedded narrator describes the experiences of women with whom she waits in the women's section of the city free employment bureau.[58] Tracing a dialectical pattern of causes and effects, she notes the "great exodus of girls from the farms into the city" in hopes of getting work as well as the number of middle-aged city women, many with children, whose men left in search of work and never returned: "Some such story is written on the faces of all these women."[59] Unlike Spivak, Le Sueur presents facts rather than dramatizing the encounters that uncovered them. The first profile, however, offers a tantalizing glimpse of the reporter's exchange with her subject. "Bernice sits next [to] me," Le Sueur writes. "She is a large Polish woman of thirty-five," "her great body in mounds," who "has been working in people's kitchens for fifteen years or more." Because Bernice "suffers from loneliness and lack of talk," conversation blossoms when human contact is made:

> When you speak to her her face lifts and brightens as if you had spoken through a great darkness and she talks magically of little things, as if the weather were magic or tells some crazy tale of her adventures on the city streets, embellishing them in bright colors.[60]

In this fleeting moment, poetic imagery and long, flowing sentences replace Le Sueur's sparse prose. As if through North's rivet hole, we glimpse another reality, an existence brighter, more animated, and more hopeful than a life spent waiting for employment.

The fact that readers do not hear Bernice's voice directly or eavesdrop on her exchanges with Le Sueur or with other women only intensifies our desire to do so. By the end of Bernice's profile, Le Sueur reveals that the person next to her now is a ghost of the woman who once came alive in conversation. "She comes here every day now," and the journalist bluntly informs us that Bernice "will never realize" her dreams. Readers do not know how long it has been since Bernice shared the details of her life and her dreams of a small house and some chickens, but her body documents the passage of time: "Her great flesh has begun to hang in folds," a painful contrast to the woman whose magical language once hung "heavy and thick like some peasant embroidery."[61]

The structure of "Women on the Breadlines" implies that Bernice, along with Le Sueur's narrator and all the other waiting women, will over time become the woman featured in the text's final profile: "Mrs. Grey, sitting across from me is a living spokesman for the futility of labour." Her life has been a cycle of struggle and despair; she has buried three of her six children, all raised in hunger and therefore "spare, susceptible to disease." Although Le Sueur clearly interviewed Mrs. Grey, readers see no trace of the face-to-face encounter—and certainly no glimmer of a colorful, lively conversation like the one Le Sueur's questions once sparked with Bernice. Le Sueur lays out the facts of Mrs. Grey's existence in bare-boned, minimalist prose: "Now she is fifty. Her children, economically insecure, are drifters. She never hears of them. She doesn't know if they are alive. She doesn't know if she is alive." Poverty has worn her down so completely that even Mrs. Grey's separation from her children and her self does not appear to affect her. "Such subtleties of suffering are not for her," the passage continues.[62]

Le Sueur's reportage transforms Mrs. Grey into a cautionary tale, warning not just of the bleak fate awaiting women of the Great Depression but also of the isolation that already divides them from each other.[63] Personal connections and attachments—"those subtle feelings that make a human being"—become risky if not suicidal in such an environment. Thus the women in the room avoid face-to-face, human encounters with Mrs. Grey: "We cannot meet her eyes. When she looks at any of us we look away."[64] (Here Le Sueur might be seen to anticipate *Migrant Mother, Nipomo, California*, Dorothea Lange's iconic 1936 photograph in which the subject's gaze is averted.)[65] In restoring these women to public view and in bringing to life the facts of their existence, Le Sueur refuses to let readers turn away. To do so would be to turn away from what makes us human. This fact compels Spivak in "A Letter to the President" to recreate his face-to-face encounters with those on the margins of society, and it explains why even the memory of one such encounter carries such power in Le Sueur's "Women on the Breadlines." It also suggests one reason for the enduring power of 1930s reportage.

Although they accepted "Women on the Breadlines" for publication, the *New Masses*' editors worried about its tone. Concerned that Le Sueur failed to prescribe a revolutionary cure for the ills she anatomized, they attached an "Editorial Note" acknowledging the piece as "able" and "informative" but lamenting that it was "defeatist in attitude" and "lacking in revolutionary spirit and direction."[66] Their attempt to correct this perceived flaw by urging unemployed readers to join the Communist Party and directing them to its unemployed councils falls flat next to Le Sueur's bleak and powerful piece. "We are beaten, entrapped," she writes. "There is no way out."[67] As unlikely as it might seem when reading Le Sueur's "Women on the Breadlines," "Women Are Hungry," or "Cows and Horses Are Hungry," each of which takes a decidedly naturalistic approach to documenting the impact of hunger and poverty, Whitman's romanticism is key to understanding the goals of Le Sueur's 1930s reportage as well as what keeps it from becoming as fatalistic as the *New Masses* editors feared.

A collection of Whitman's writings was at Le Sueur's bedside when she died in 1996, and Le Sueur explained Whitman's lifelong influence on her in a 1980 essay titled "Jelly Roll." She describes how his poetry spoke to the lived experiences and ideals of laborers in the agrarian Midwest and recalls how she bonded with many such individuals over Whitman's enduring song. She also emphasizes Whitman's celebration of the body: "I would have become a midwest Christian ghost without Walt Whitman. He gave me the courage to demand and get a body."[68] A painful awareness of Whitman's romantic celebration of the human body lurks behind Le Sueur's naturalistic documentation of what a life of labor and poverty and hunger does to it. (Mrs. Grey's "is a great puckered scar."[69]) If Le Sueur's reportage gives women bodies by restoring them to public consciousness, the Great Depression simultaneously threatened to strip them of their humanity by distancing them not just from the embodied pain of others but also from their own bodies. Just as they are losing the ability to meet the eyes of fellow sufferers, the youngest women she documents are starting to reject the possibility of love or marriage or children.[70]

Noting that Le Sueur viewed suffering "not as negative and passive, but as a source of solidarity," Hedges quotes a 1930 entry from her journals: "We do not know ourselves except when we suffer. ... In joy I know only myself, in sorrow I know others. ... In happiness we are seperete [sic]. ... In suffering we are fused." Le Sueur's conclusion—"given a great enough strength, suffering would open the thick substance of the world heart"—explains why she withholds any ameliorative padding when documenting suffering.[71] Le Sueur clearly hoped readers would gain a particular knowledge about themselves and their relation to others when they feel the facts of her subjects' lives. Writing in "Women Know a Lot of Things" about a Polish immigrant who works in the stockyards, Le Sueur observes: "she knows more than anybody I know, because she knows what suffering is and she knows that everyone is like herself, throughout the whole world."[72] The wisdom acquired through the suffering of isolated bodies is a deeper awareness of the social body.

Whitman "expressed the love of the land, of men and women, of children, of communality, of common grief and social and political rebellion," Le Sueur writes in "Jelly Roll."[73] "Common grief" generates love; to acknowledge it is to express love. So too are "social and political rebellion" expressions of love. Yoking rebellion to grief, Le Sueur echoes the hope of many radical writers of the 1930s: that the shared suffering of the Great Depression would spark revolution. As they saw it, the isolated suffering witnessed in "Women on the Breadlines" is the product not just of a severe economic depression but of the value system from which Whitman sought to liberate his readers, namely the individualism at the heart of America's capitalist culture.[74] As Theodore Dreiser explains in "Individualism and the Jungle" (1932), the lead article in the same issue of the *New Masses* as "Women on the Breadlines," an individual's "worship of his own private right to individual advancement, as opposed to the rights and welfare of every other," inevitably leads to alienation, disillusion, and disempowerment. If it is ever to become "a social organism worthy of the name," Dreiser insists, "society is not and cannot be a jungle." Although women's lives in the Great Depression as Le Sueur depicts them do not exhibit the competitive, "extreme and bloody individualism" of Dreiser's jungle, both she and Dreiser diagnose the breakdown of "organized society" in chillingly stark naturalistic and Darwinian terms.[75] But what drew Le Sueur and like-minded writers of the 1930s to Whitman was his warm, ecstatic celebrations of this "social organism" in action.

Le Sueur fleshes out this romantic vision in "I Was Marching" (1934), where violence against the individual gives way to a celebration of the collective. Published in the *New Masses* nearly three years after "Women on the Breadlines," "I Was Marching" is the one title by Le Sueur that North mentions in "Reportage" (alongside three pieces by Spivak), and it remains Le Sueur's best-known and most discussed piece of reportage.[76] It chronicles the Minneapolis

Teamsters Strike, which erupted in violence against strikers and their allies on Bloody Friday, July 20, 1934. Two died and sixty-seven were left wounded.[77] Without downplaying the suffering of individual bodies—she describes "whole men suddenly spouting blood and running like living sieves" and "a tall youngster, running, tripping over his intestines"—Le Sueur shifts focus to the collective body that forms in response.[78] Crowds of women and men mass together to build barricades; days later, the crowd swells into the thousands as strikers and their supporters form a defiant funeral procession. Le Sueur's narrator loses herself in the crowds, drawing strength and power from the masses as they march, "spontaneously in a movement, natural, hardy and miraculous."[79] The "I" of "I Was Marching" (the piece's title as well as its closing sentence) becomes the expansive, absorptive "I" of Whitman's first-person persona in "Song of Myself": "I am large, I contain multitudes." Le Sueur explains this "curious" feeling:

> I feel most alive and yet for the first time in my life I do not feel myself as separate. I realize then that all my previous feelings have been based on feeling myself separate and distinct from others and now I sense sharply faces, bodies, closeness and my own fear is not my own alone, nor my hope.[80]

Le Sueur's firsthand experience of the Minneapolis Teamsters Strike clearly cemented her faith in the power of collective action and communal values, and "I Was Marching" casts into sharp relief the painful isolation depicted in "Women on the Breadlines," where she exposes the forces that must be overcome for collective action to occur. "I Was Marching" might also be read as Le Sueur's response to the editors of the *New Masses*, this time giving them what they want (and then some).[81] About the act of writing as much as it is about marching, it even anticipates many of the concepts North would articulate the following year in "Reportage."

"I Was Marching" opens with a confession: "I have never been in a strike before." What follows is a first-person account of a middle-class individual's fear of joining a mass movement, one that reads like a memoir or a short story.[82] In contrast to Le Sueur's earlier reportage, where she reports from within, here the narrator is outside, anxious about going in. Although not cast explicitly as a journalist's concerns, the opening paragraph calls attention to language when the narrator informs us that she has never before joined a strike: "It is like looking at something that is happening for the first time and there are no thoughts and words yet accrued to it." Afraid to enter strike headquarters, she watches from across the street for a few days. On the third day, "with sweat breaking out on my body," she goes in. When the narrator crosses the street, she breaks away from the "artists, writers, professionals," and a photographer who have gathered to observe events from the outside, sharing as they do the narrator's desire to "remain a spectator."[83] When she crosses the street, she crosses the border between traditional journalism and reportage, between the old journalism and the new.

The hesitant narrator's fears expose what Le Sueur and other proletarian writers saw as the ideological underpinnings of the bourgeois journalist's faith in objective detachment. The narrator's confession that "I felt I excelled in competing with others," whereas the strikers "were NOT competing at all," might even be a veiled dig at the value placed on the scoop in some circles. (Indeed, "I Was Marching" chronicles events two months after the fact.) Le Sueur might have the reporter's byline in mind, or at least the values that motivate some writers in "our merchant society," when she confesses her "awful fright of mixing, of losing myself, of being unknown." She dreads the possibility "that all I had been trained to excel in would go unnoticed." Le Sueur in such passages identifies "an important psychic change that must take place in all" while simultaneously suggesting the role reportage might play in bringing it about.[84] As North would recall in the final issue of the weekly *New Masses*, its "editors sought more than muckraking or genteel side-line observation of life and letters. They sensed that history needed more than chronicling: it needed changing."[85] Once this change occurs in the writer as well as in the strategies and techniques of journalism, the hope goes, the text will not only mirror cultural shifts but might even foster change in readers by showing them the limits of individualism as well as the promises of communal values.

Le Sueur's graphic description of bodies torn apart by antilabor violence disrupts the narrator's internal struggle. "No one can be neutral in the face of bullets," she is forced to realize.[86] Several paragraphs later, we see how the narrator's pose of neutral, detached observer had already given way *before* the eruption of violence. Soon after entering the building, she sits next to a woman as they listen to a voice on loudspeakers give updates on the strike. "She took my hands," Le Sueur notes. Crying, the stranger speaks as she draws Le Sueur closer: "They've taken both my children away from me and now something is going to happen" to the strikers. Her words are framed by Le Sueur's reciprocal gesture: "I held her hands."[87] Readers feel the violence against strikers more fully because it is framed by one mother's pain, and we connect the loss of her children—was it through illness, starvation, or another form of economic violence?—with the motivation behind the strike as well as with the tactics used to block it. If Le Sueur had succeeded in retaining her "distinctly individualistic attitude, to be only partly there," her readers would not feel these facts, for the journalist would have kept herself from feeling them as a participant.[88] As writer Josephine Herbst puts it in an oft-quoted remembrance of the era, "the beauty of the thirties was its communion among people."[89] The communion Le Sueur recounts, this face-to-face encounter, is as powerful in its impact as the bullets about to fly in the streets. The individual joins the social body, which will respond en masse to intimidation and violence, and the two women's clasped hands prefigure the strength Le Sueur will discover—as a citizen and as a journalist—when she is "marching with a million hands."

Five months after "I Was Marching," the *New Masses* published "The Fetish of Being Outside" (1935), where Le Sueur argues that politics and economics cannot be approached theoretically and from afar, especially in a time of crisis. Faced with the living facts of the Great Depression, she maintains, the writer "cannot take a double course and be part of it and still apart from it."[90] In fact, the narrator's existence "apart from" the subject is illusory: she is always already "part of" the story, even before she embraces the "close reality of mass feeling."[91] Journalist, subject, and reader are alive only in relation to each other. Thus, reportage can document the life of the narrator—even the life of the reader, in a sense—without diminishing the lives of its subjects. Another "beauty of the thirties," Herbst explains, was "its chance to get out of the constricted *I* in what seemed a meaningful way."[92] When Le Sueur's narrative "I" merges with fellow marchers, the text offers readers an expansive, interdependent self in relation to and intimately connected with others through fact and feeling.[93] Age-old stories of individual lives and longings furnish "material for masterpieces," Barbusse acknowledges in "Writing and War," but "the destiny of the individual always ends depressingly: in death." Writing about a funeral procession, appropriately enough, Le Sueur takes up Barbusse's challenge: "Today we must enter into the collective drama!" he exclaims. "We must raise on the stage a new protagonist, the most imposing of all: the masses."[94]

Only when you recognize yourself as "a cellular part" of "a communal society," Le Sueur believed, will you be "able to grow and function with others in a living whole."[95] With telling irony, perhaps, some modern readers find "I Was Marching" as naïvely optimistic as the editors of the *New Masses* once found "Women on the Breadlines" bleakly pessimistic. Constance Coiner, for example, worries that the narrative arc of "I Was Marching" "seriously underestimates ideology's power and complexity" by representing it "as a false consciousness that, once recognized, can be readily discarded, shed like old skin."[96] Reportage's roots in the competing legacies of naturalism and romanticism, however, might help us see this potential blind spot as an effective strategy. North's contrast between a life spent laboring in a ship's dark hull and the beauty of the natural world as glimpsed through an unfilled rivet hole again proves useful. Like North, Le Sueur and Spivak recognized that to be effective, reform-minded reportage must paint a faithful, naturalistic portrait of life inside the ship as it is being constructed; a writer must enable readers to feel the facts of a worker's exploitation and hunger. At the same time, however, invoking the romantic ideal of getting out of one's skin (or gender or race or class) promises something beyond. Readers need to feel the fact of our shared humanity and to believe that a better world is possible, however powerful the inhumane forces bending us toward degradation and isolation might be.

In the midst of marching masses, Le Sueur's narrator in the closing paragraphs of "I Was Marching" senses but does not fully comprehend the revolutionary transformation taking place: "I only partly know what I am seeing, feeling, but I feel it is the real body and gesture of a future vitality."[97] The feeling is real even if it is not anchored in the journalist's hard facts. So too is the body she joins, even if it is only a temporary formation, and even if it does not come fully alive until a future time. To achieve this transformative vision of the social body requires us to transcend the present. To achieve a more comprehensive view of the facts being documented, sometimes our minds must float upward toward "the clouds of Whitmanism" (to return to Gold's phrase). Thus North spies not only "the serene river" but also "wheeling gulls" when he steals a glimpse of a world beyond his daily toil. And Whitman's lyrical wanderer, forever marching forward in what Le Sueur names the poet's "walking stanzas," sometimes took to the sky in poems like "The Sleepers" and "From Paumanok Starting I Fly Like a Bird."[98] Echoing Whitman's declaration of an expansive self—"I contain multitudes"—Barbusse in the pages of the *New Masses* turned to his experiences in aviation to describe the "new vision" flight "opens upon life." From a certain height, he writes, "one no longer sees a man isolated, nor a house by itself; one sees a multitude." From the heavens we gain "a true vision of the world."[99]

When the aviator returns to solid ground, when the marching ceases, or when the reader turns the page, the realities of life in the moment remain. But the best reportage enables us to see these facts anew. They come alive. We see their place in the world, in history, in a web of causes and effects. Just a glimpse of our human interconnectedness, of the feelings and facts that link our collective fates, potentially contributes to the forward march of history. This is what North had in mind when he concluded that the *New Masses* survived the Great Depression because its writers and editors "captured the spirit of the time": "We triumphed over alienation, the bleak sense of human wastefulness, of universal desolation, of primal aloneness. We took those who felt an apartheid from life by the hand and brought them to a haven of purpose." A clear-eyed survey of history—marked as it is by wars, racial and ethnic violence, economic inequality, economic depressions, recessions, and panics—is likely to judge radical writers of the 1930s as overly romantic and woefully naïve. Perhaps a more accurate way to gauge the power and promise of the decade's revolutionary culture, however, is by the intellectual capital invested in efforts to rewrite, erase, or marginalize it in subsequent years. "In the Forties they began to re-write the Thirties," North points out. "So a new generation was given an image of reality very different from the one we had who lived through it."[100]

Whether we come to embrace the 1930s as enthusiastically as Geismar does—"as the last true outburst of our social and literary creativity before the somnolence of the 1940s, the silence of the 1950s"—concentrated attention to even a small sampling of the period's reportage can outline a compelling argument for the decade's significance in the history of American literary journalism.[101] And if we follow Spivak's example when he visits a migratory labor camp, as well Le Sueur's when she uncovers the hidden lives of working-class women during the Great Depression, we realize that as important as the effort to restore 1930s reportage to its rightful place in our cultural memory is a consideration of the assumptions, anxieties, and aims that made this restoration necessary in the first place. They show us where to dig. They hint at the lessons we might draw from once-buried lives and works. Le Sueur, who (like Spivak) was blacklisted in the "Fatal Fifties" (as Geismar labels the decade), arrives at just such a conclusion—a conclusion we might echo in our assessment of 1930s reportage—when she recalls that her literary forebears were marginalized as well:

> During the McCarthy period you could not write your dissertation in Minnesota on Whitman. The southern agrarians made him a bad word, at best a naive yokel of the mob. Their fierce animosity showed how good he was for us, how dangerous, how alive.[102]

Acknowledgments

I am indebted to Nicole Ruiz for her invaluable work as a research assistant in the earliest stages of this project as well as to Ted Mulvey at the University of Wisconsin Oshkosh's Polk Library for his generous help along the way. I am also grateful to Julie Russo for her expert eye and advice and to Miles Orvell for introducing me to the rich culture of the 1930s and especially to the work of Meridel Le Sueur.

Notes

1 North, prologue, 23. North was an editor of the *New Masses* from January 1934, when it became a weekly (the monthly ceased publication the previous fall), until January 1948, when it became the quarterly *Masses and Mainstream*. North was a principal founder of the weekly *New Masses*.

2 Rabinowitz, *Labor and Desire*, 2. "The claims of history on the literature of the 1930s," Rabinowitz argues, "re-formed the generic boundaries of writing itself" (*Labor and Desire*, 2). See also Aaron, *Writers on the Left*; Entin, *Sensational Modernism*; Foley, *Radical Representations*; Shulman, *Power of Political Art*; Stott, *Documentary Expression*; Wald, *Exiles*.

3 Geismar, introduction, 7.

4 North published these comments in the final issue of the weekly *New Masses*, which began publication in the midst of the Depression, "*sans* angel, *sans* lucrative advertising. It began on a shoestring and a principle" ("And Fighting," 5, 3).

5 Wolfe acknowledges that North "had in mind a new journalism as full-bodied as anything I've been talking about," but he dismisses 1930s reportage as a worthy precursor because in his mind "most of the work degenerated into propaganda of a not very complex sort" ("New Journalism," 45). Hartsock offers a similar judgment of the *New Masses*, which he sees as "an important American venue for a literary reportage that reads much like literary journalism, ... but one that could be highly polemical in the service of political ideology" (*Literary Journalism*, 102; on reportage as a genre, see chapter 4, "The 'Elasticity' of Literary Reportage"). Elsewhere, Hartsock maintains that "literary reportage and literary journalism are much the same when they both emphasize narrative and descriptive modalities and eschew discursive polemic" ("Literary Reportage," 41).

6 During the 1930s, Entin observes, "the Left—through writers clubs, journals, magazines, and publishing houses—helped a generation of young working-class writers find their voices and put their words into print." He sees this as "one of the central accomplishments of the proletarian movement" (*Sensational Modernism*, 148).

7 The January 22, 1935, issue of the *New Masses* included a "Call for an American Writers' Congress," which promised to "be the voice of many thousands of intellectuals, and middle class people allied with the working class" ("Call"). Le Sueur, North, and Spivak are among the sixty-four sponsors who signed the call; others include Nelson Algren, Kenneth Burke, Erskine Caldwell, Malcolm Cowley, Theodore Dreiser, Josephine Herbst, Langston Hughes, Tillie Lerner, Nathanael West, and Richard Wright. The League of American Writers, affiliated with the International Union of Revolutionary Writers, was formed at the first Congress, which took place in April 1935.

8 This "once sanctimonious" phrase is now "merely ridiculous," Freeman asserts. Writers, he continues, have shared the experiences of other workers during the Depression: "Writers have been out of work; they have been on relief and on the W.P.A.; they have gone on strike for their own demands; they

have picketed not only in sympathy with workers in other fields but for themselves; they have organized mass demonstrations, been arrested and beaten; they have sent delegations to Washington and negotiated with their employers" ("Toward the Forties," 23, 16). Freeman was a founding editor of the *New Masses* as well as of the *Partisan Review*.

9. Relevant here is Entin's insightful examination of how an "aesthetic of astonishment," which mixes sensationalism with "elements of modernism, sentimentalism, and documentary," "invites readers and viewers to identify with the socially despised in ways that do not belittle, condescend, exoticize, or romanticize them" (*Sensational Modernism*, 262).

10. North also wrote the unsigned preface to the reportage section of *Proletarian Literature in the United States*, where he comments: "Some of our novelists bemoan the popularity of reportage as some bastard form passing itself off as a legally begotten son of belles lettres" ([North], preface to "Reportage," 212). North was a practitioner as well as a theorist and promoter of reportage. His best-known piece, "Taxi-Strike" (*New Masses*, April 3, 1934) is reprinted in Hicks et al., *Proletarian Literature* as well as in North's *New Masses* anthology. See Peck, "Joseph North."

11. North, "Reportage," 120–21, 123.

12. North, 122–23, 121. North's notion of facts as "alive" in proletarian reportage found a literal embodiment in the Federal Theatre Project's "Living Newspaper." Bustard notes, "these plays wove newspaper stories, speeches in Congress, sociological studies, and court records into scripts" that "dramatized contemporary social and political issues such as slum housing, industrial relations, electric power, and venereal disease" (*New Deal*, 79, 18).

13. North, "Reportage," 120.

14. Monteath, "Spanish Civil War," 76. Kisch delivered an address titled "Reportage as Form of Art and Form of Struggle" at the Paris International Congress for the Defense of Culture in 1935, the same year North presented "Reportage" at the first American Writers' Congress. For an overview of Kisch's reportage, including his influence on North, see Hartsock, *Literary Journalism*, 98–108.

15. Marcus, *In Search of the Good Life*, xii. Also see Levinas, *Entre Nous*; Levinas, *Ethics and Infinity*; Marcus, *Being for the Other*.

16. North quotes Kisch's assertion that Zola "founded modern reportage" but also suggests that "America has independently produced past masters in the art" ("Reportage," 120).

17. "*J'Accuse* ... ! Letter to the President of the Republic by Émile Zola" was published on the front page of a special edition of the French newspaper *L'Aurore* on January 13, 1898. Dreyfus was exonerated in 1906. See Bredin, *Affair*.

18. Barbusse, "Writing and War," 11. Barbusse's novel *Le feu*, about his experiences in World War I and published two years before the war ended, won France's Prix Goncourt; an English translation, *Under Fire*, was published in 1917. An English translation of Barbusse's biographical study *Zola* was published in 1933.

19. "The prestige of fact in the naturalist project," Howard observes, "is perhaps most familiarly figured in the image of the naturalist as researcher: Zola or Upton Sinclair with notebook in hand gathering material for a new novel. In naturalism the detail signifies not only reality but the rigorous investigation of reality" (*Form and History*, 147). On the connections between American literary journalism, scientific materialism, and literary naturalism in the post-Civil War era, see Hartsock, *History*, 44, 218.

20. Barbusse, "Writing and War," 11.

21. Cowley, "What the Revolutionary Movement," 64.

22. Zola, "Experimental Novel," 167, 176. Zola adapts Bernard's writings as a guide to the art of naturalist fiction, which Zola saw as bringing "the rigor of scientific truth" to the novel. Quoting Bernard, Zola distinguishes between the realist as observer and the naturalist as observer and experimenter: "Observation shows, experiment instructs" ("Experimental Novel," 162, 168). See Howard, *Form and History*; Walcutt, *American Literary Naturalism*; Becker, "Modern Realism."

23. Zola, "Experimental Novel," 175, 196. The first quotation set off by dashes is a direct quote from Bernard.

24. Barbusse, "Writing and War," 11. Rabinowitz reads the tension between fact and feeling in gendered terms, suggesting that reportage allowed the "leakage" of sentimentality "into 'the methods of science' appropriate to journalism." She argues that "reportage mediated the feminized stance of the novelist—whether male or female, the writer was viewed by the Left as effete, bourgeois—and that of the hard-boiled reporter, as tough masculine worker, because these writers did not simply report from the sidelines; they put their bodies on the line" (*Black and White and Noir*, 122–23).

25. Gold, "Towards Proletarian Art," 67. Gold engages Whitman at length in "Towards Proletarian Art," which was published in the *Liberator* in 1921. "Walt, in his poetry, had intuitively arrived at the

proletarian art," Gold suggests (68). "The American currency of the term 'proletarian literature' can be dated from the publication of this article," notes Folsom (*Mike Gold*, 62 editor's note).

26 Gold, "John Reed," 11. Gold explains the dangers of Whitmanesque rhetoric: "An Archibald MacLeish has begun to talk in such Whitman strophes, about democracy and the American people. It is a flattery designed for the purpose of using us in another imperialist war. You cannot interest the mystic MacLeishes in such lowly subjects as unemployment, rising food prices, and the segregation of the Negro Americans" ("John Reed," 11).

27 Barbusse, "Writing and War," 11. Whitman, of course, attempted to bridge this gap in his writings, as did Herman Melville.

28 Examples include "Whoever You Are Holding Me Now in Hand," "To You," and "Thou Reader." On the personal connection Lydia Maria Child, Walt Whitman, and Fanny Fern established with readers in their literary journalism, see Carolyn L. Karcher's "The Antebellum Origins of American Literary Journalism: Five Pioneers," Chapter 2 in this volume.

29 North, prologue, 22.

30 North, 22.

31 North, "Reportage," 122. North's other examples include Albert Halper's "A Morning with the Doc" and Meridel Le Sueur's "I Was Marching," both of which were published in the *New Masses*; Agnes Smedley's *China's Red Army Marches*; and John Dos Passos's *In All Countries*, parts of which had appeared in such venues as the *New Republic*, *Esquire*, *Common Sense*, and the *American Spectator*, as well as in the *New Masses*.

32 *Time*'s review of Spivak's *Europe Under the Terror* (1936) notes his "glowing reputation as 'America's greatest reporter'" ("Dictators Dissected"). In Stott's assessment, Spivak's contributions "were the best reportage in *New Masses* and brought the magazine many new readers" (*Documentary Expression*, 34). In his review of Spivak's 1940 exposé of anti-Semitic radio demagogue Father Coughlin, George Seldes declares that "Spivak remains the best reporter in the country because of his double faculty of combining evidence with interest, facts with sensation" ("Silver Charlie," 25–26). Spivak remains understudied today.

33 Spivak's "Letter" is in the March 20, 1934, issue of the *New Masses*. It appears in slightly revised form in *America Faces the Barricades* (1935). All citations refer to *America Faces the Barricades*.

34 North, "Spivak's America," 26.

35 Roosevelt, "'Forgotten Man,'" 170. "Remembering the people who had been largely forgotten during the money-mad 1920s was one of the most important manifestations of depression-era values," McElvaine writes (*Depression and New Deal*, 170).

36 North, "Reportage," 122. North compares Spivak's approach with Agnes Smedley's *China's Red Army Marches* (part of which was published in the May 22, 1934, issue of the *New Masses*). The reporter "is completely absent" in Smedley's reportage, he notes. "She feels that the subject matter is epic, history is being made by four hundred million people and does not permit the inclusion of the writer in the story" ("Reportage," 122).

37 Spivak, "Letter to the President," 15, 19.

38 Levinas's thinking is especially relevant here. As Marcus observes, his "texts are replete with references to our obligations to the vulnerable, disenfranchised and powerless clusters of people whom we are obliged, if not commanded, to honor, protect and take care of" (*Being for the Other*, 27). The title of North's 1958 autobiography is also worth noting: *No Men Are Strangers*.

39 In his examination of Spivak's reportage on southern chain gangs, Stott names this approach "vicarious or confessional" persuasion, wherein "Spivak's *example* was meant to influence his audience. The emotion he felt at going through the experience they were to share" (*Documentary Expression*, 35).

40 North, "Spivak's America," 26.

41 Spivak, "Letter to the President," 17, 18.

42 Spivak, 22.

43 Bourdieu, "Understanding," 608. Bourdieu's discussion of methodology in this passage sheds light on Spivak's inclusion of his own misunderstanding in "Letter." Bourdieu argues that a *"reflex reflexivity"*—which he sees as "based on a craft, on a sociological 'feel' or 'eye'"—enables interviewers "to perceive and monitor *on the spot*, as the interview is actually taking place, the effects of the social structure within which it is occurring" ("Understanding," 608).

44 "The purpose of literary journalism," Hartsock writes, is "to engage in a narrowing of the distance between subject and object" ("Literary Reportage," 31).

45 Spivak, "Letter to the President," 21. Spivak poses some form of this question to subjects in other pieces of reportage, notably "I See by the Papers ..." and "The Government Helps the People," both of which are included in *America Faces the Barricades*. "Despite what the 'New Deal' has really done to

the workers," Spivak concludes, "so great is the popularity of President Roosevelt, so great is the faith of the worker in his promises, that in the face of wage cuts and the government's successful efforts to settle strikes in favor of the employer while telling the workers what marvelous gains they have made, most of our people still believe that these conditions are only temporary and that before long things will get better for them" ("Government Helps the People," 84).

46 Spivak, "Letter to the President," 23.
47 Spivak, 23.
48 The title is "A Letter to the President" in *America Faces the Barricades* and "A Letter to President Roosevelt" in both *Proletarian Literature in the United States* and North's *New Masses* anthology.
49 Le Sueur, "Author's Note," 61. For a perceptive analysis of collective authorship in relation to Le Sueur's work as a writing teacher during the Great Depression, see Greer, "Refiguring Authorship."
50 Hedges, introduction, 9. Kennedy explains that the Depression "dealt especially cruelly with the Twin Cities" (*American People*, 294). "One of the most prominent women writers of the '30s," Coiner notes, "Le Sueur endured redbaiting, blacklisting, and 25 years of obscurity to become in the '70s a regional folk heroine and nearly an archetypal figure within some elements of the women's movement" (*Better Red*, 72).
51 Le Sueur, "Women on the Breadlines," 5–7. "Women on the Breadlines" was the second piece of reportage Le Sueur published in the *New Masses*; on the first, "Evening in a Lumber Town" (July 1926), see Coiner, *Better Red*, 104–05. "Women on the Breadlines" was reprinted in 1977, with slight revisions and corrections by Le Sueur, as the first Worker Writers Pamphlet published by West End Press. Titled *Women on the Breadlines*, the pamphlet also contains three other pieces about women Le Sueur wrote in the 1930s.
52 Le Sueur, "Women on the Breadlines," 6. Westin estimates that three million women were unemployed in 1932 but points out that "separate records for women were not kept" during the Depression (*Making Do*, 164). Abelson observes that women "lost jobs at a higher rate than did men in the early years of the collapse, were often unable to find other sources of income, and were routinely discriminated against in public employment" ("'Women,'" 106).
53 Le Sueur, "Women Are Hungry," 145.
54 Chamberlain, review of *America Faces the Barricades*. "Only an average hunger is left in the land" once the numbers are crunched, Judd Polk warns in "Our House Divided by Itself," a poem he published in the *New Masses* in 1940, a national census year.
55 Le Sueur, "Cows and Horses," 170.
56 Le Sueur, "Women Know," 172. Rabinowitz acknowledges as "pivotal" to her scholarship Le Sueur's "radical insistence that texts and bodies, desire and labor, be read as gendered and classed elaborations of each other" (*Labor and Desire*, 3).
57 Hedges, introduction, 11.
58 "A key aspect of Le Sueur's literary journalism during the Depression years is the degree to which, like much of her reportage, it is informed by participant, immersion research," Roberts notes ("Meridel Le Sueur," 50).
59 Le Sueur, "Women on the Breadlines," 5.
60 Le Sueur, 5.
61 Le Sueur, 5. Le Sueur cut the term "peasant" from later versions of "Women on the Breadlines." For a perceptive analysis of Bernice, see Geriguis, "Ecosomatic and Ethnological Pathologies."
62 Le Sueur, "Women on the Breadlines," 6–7.
63 In *Ripening* and in West End Press's Worker Writers Pamphlet, this isolation is mirrored by white space between each profile.
64 Le Sueur, "Women on the Breadlines," 6–7. With bitter irony, Le Sueur goes on to suggest that "the brutality of hunger and cold" works like statistical averages: "She is reduced to the least possible denominator of human feelings" (7).
65 For a comparative reading of Le Sueur and Lange, see chapter 6 of Goggans, *California on the Breadlines*.
66 "Editorial Note," 7.
67 Le Sueur, "Women on the Breadlines," 6. The editorial note perhaps explains why North does not include "Women on the Breadlines" in his *New Masses* anthology. In fact, Le Sueur is not represented in the reportage section, but her "Salvation Home" (1939) is reprinted in the section devoted to "Short Stories and Sketches."
68 Le Sueur, "Jelly Roll," 421.
69 Le Sueur, "Women on the Breadlines," 6. Between her profiles of Bernice and Mrs. Grey, Le Sueur tells the story of Ellen, a young girl who turns to prostitution to survive. Asking readers to imagine

what it would feel like to sell one's overcoat to strangers on the street, she brilliantly connects the desperate act of selling one's body with the circumstances of many American workers during the Depression: "It is even harder to try and sell one's self, more humiliating. It is even humiliating to try and sell one's labour. When there is no buyer" (6).

70 Le Sueur explains why young women "refuse to marry, refuse to rear children" in the closing paragraph of "Women on the Breadlines": "It's not the suffering, not birth, death, love that the young reject, but the suffering of endless labour without dream, eating the spare bread in bitterness, a slave without the security of a slave" (7).

71 Hedges, introduction, 11.

72 Le Sueur, "Women Know," 171. "Hunger levels all flesh," Le Sueur concludes in "Cows and Horses Are Hungry" (170).

73 Le Sueur, "Jelly Roll," 422. Le Sueur's language suggests that the love Whitman expresses is not his love of (or his love as directed toward) the people, things, places, feelings, ideas, and actions she lists but the love that emanates from them.

74 Each of the authors I discuss saw the Great Depression as a symptom of systemic socioeconomic maladies that had long plagued America. North notes "the other times of mass hunger in America that came with tragic regularity in economic depressions called the 'Panic'—1837, 1857, 1877, 1893, 1907, and now 1929" (prologue, 23). In "The Worker Thinks," Spivak quotes an African American tenant farmer from Mississippi: "Cap'n, niggers allus had old man Depression!" Another farmer laughs and chimes in: "Only now he done brought his whole family!" (165). And Le Sueur writes: "Nowhere in America are the ravages of *laissez faire* colonization so apparent as in the Middle West." Surveying the suffering caused by the displacement of midwestern families and workers, she observes: "This has been going on not only since the depression, but for seventy-five years. We have *always* been depressed" ("Proletarian Literature," 135).

75 Dreiser, "Individualism and the Jungle," 4. Dreiser insists that neither "Nature" nor "evolution" intends society to be a jungle. Levinas raises similar questions about human nature and society: "It is extremely important to know if society in the current sense of the term is the result of a limitation of the principle that men are predators of one another, or if to the contrary it results in the limitation of the principle that men are *for* one another" (*Ethics and Infinity*, 80).

76 "I Was Marching" is included in *Proletarian Literature in the United States*.

77 Kennedy explains that in 1934 the antilabor Citizens Alliance, financed by corporate interests, "outfitted what amounted to a private army to keep the predominantly Scandinavian and Irish working class in place." The Minneapolis Teamsters Strike met with violence when "teamsters cut off a truck that was provocatively trying to move under police escort through a picket line. As if on cue, the police opened fire, pouring round after round of buckshot into the backs of the scattering teamsters" (*American People*, 294–95).

78 Le Sueur, "I Was Marching," 16.

79 Le Sueur, 18.

80 Le Sueur, 18. "Only Agee in *Let Us Now Praise Famous Men* handles the 'I' with anything like Le Sueur's depth," Shulman suggests. "If John Reed and James Agee are the Tolstoys of left reportage, Le Sueur is the Chekhov of the form" (*Power of Political Art*, 67).

81 "They Follow Us Girls," published in the *Anvil* one year after "Women on the Breadlines" appeared in the *New Masses* and reprinted in the 1977 Worker Writers Pamphlet *Women on the Breadlines*, suggests that Le Sueur took the editorial comment to heart; there she presents Unemployment Councils as savior-like refuges for women on relief. For a useful analysis of Le Sueur's relationship with the Communist Party, see Pratt, "Woman Writer."

82 Entin, in fact, calls "I Was Marching" a short story (*Sensational Modernism*, 66).

83 Le Sueur, "I Was Marching," 16. "I Was Marching" is prefaced in the *New Masses* by an introduction that quotes Le Sueur: "'I have tried to put down exactly the reaction of many artists, writers and middle class to the strike here,' writes Miss LeSueur [sic] from Minneapolis. 'Although they were in great sympathy they did not know how to act, they felt frightened, timid, inferior. I do not exaggerate when I say that at the funeral ... I saw literally hundreds of them who came there, who stood outside (and many stood outside strike headquarters all the time) with all the chaos of old reactions, individualistic, special, etc.'"

84 Le Sueur, 16.

85 North, "And Fighting," 3.

86 Le Sueur, "I Was Marching," 16.

87 Le Sueur, 17.

88 Le Sueur, 18, 16.

89 Quoted in Madden, introduction to *Proletarian Writers*, xxvii.

90 Le Sueur, "Fetish of Being Outside," 22. Le Sueur published this commentary in response to poet Horace Gregory's "One Writer's Position," in which he defended his refusal to join the Communist Party. Although he supported the Party's goals, to compromise his position as an objective "outsider" and "observer," he argued, "would destroy my unique value" ("One Writer's Position," 20–21).
91 Le Sueur, "I Was Marching," 18.
92 Quoted in Madden, introduction to *Proletarian Writers*, xxvii. Le Sueur issues a similar declaration in "The Fetish of Being Outside": "I do not care for the bourgeois 'individual' that I am" (22).
93 Foley identifies this as a common trait of women's proletarian fiction from the 1930s: "By delineating individual identity as a social phenomenon, they urged their readers to rethink their assumptions about fixed male and female potentialities but also to reconsider the very notion of individuality itself, contradistinguishing it from individualism" (*Radical Representations*, 246).
94 Barbusse, "Writing and War," 11.
95 Le Sueur, "Fetish," 22.
96 Coiner, *Better Red*, 107.
97 Le Sueur, "I Was Marching," 18.
98 Le Sueur reads as distinctively American Whitman's "long line" and "walking stanzas, tonal to a man's body, walking, striding, going forward not in gloom and pessimism" but "plunging" toward "a new concept of solidarity and fraternity" ("Jelly Roll," 422).
99 Barbusse, "Writing and War," 11.
100 North, prologue, 22, 19. North finds an accurate parallel in willful distortions of the Reconstruction era.
101 Geismar, introduction, 6.
102 Le Sueur, "Jelly Roll," 424.

Bibliography

Aaron, Daniel. *Writers on the Left*. 1961. Reprint, New York: Oxford University Press, 1977.

Abelson, Elaine S. "'Women Who Have No Men to Work for Them': Gender and Homelessness in the Great Depression, 1930–1934." *Feminist Studies* 29, no. 1 (Spring 2003): 104–27.

Barbusse, Henri. "Writing and War." *New Masses*, January 9, 1934, 10–12. www.marxists.org/history/usa/pubs/new-masses/1934/v10n02-jan-09-1934-NM.pdf.

Becker, George J. "Modern Realism as a Literary Movement." Introduction to *Documents of Modern Literary Realism*, edited by George J. Becker, 3–38. Princeton, NJ: Princeton University Press, 1963.

Bourdieu, Pierre. "Understanding." In *The Weight of the World: Social Suffering in Contemporary Society*, by Pierre Bourdieu, Alain Accardo, Gabrielle Balazs, Stéphane Beaud, François Bonvin, Emmanuel Bourdieu, Philippe Bourgois, et al., 607–26. Translated by Priscilla Parkhurst Ferguson, Susan Emanuel, Joe Johnson, and Shoggy T. Waryn. Stanford, CA: Stanford University Press, 1999. Originally published as *La misère du monde* (Paris: Éditions du Seuil, 1993).

Bredin, Jean-Denis. *The Affair: The Case of Alfred Dreyfus*. Translated by Jeffrey Mehlman. New York: George Braziller, 1986.

Bustard, Bruce I. *A New Deal for the Arts*. Washington, DC: National Archives and Records Administration; Seattle, WA: University of Washington Press, 1997.

"Call for an American Writers' Congress." *New Masses*, January 22, 1935, 20. www.marxists.org/history/usa/pubs/new-masses/1935/v14n04-jan-22-1935-NM.pdf.

Chamberlain, John. Review of *America Faces the Barricades*, by John L. Spivak. *New York Times*, August 6, 1935, 15. ProQuest Historical Newspapers.

Coiner, Constance. *Better Red: The Writing and Resistance of Tillie Olsen and Meridel Le Sueur*. New York: Oxford University Press, 1995.

Cowley, Malcolm. "What the Revolutionary Movement Can Do for a Writer." In Hart, *American Writers' Congress*, 59–65.

"Dictators Dissected." Review of *Europe Under the Terror*, by John L. Spivak. *Time*, May 25, 1936. Academic Search Complete (54809366).

Dreiser, Theodore. "Individualism and the Jungle." *New Masses*, January 1932, 3–4. www.marxists.org/history/usa/pubs/new-masses/1932/v07n08-jan-1932-New-Masses.pdf.

"Editorial Note." *New Masses*, January 1932, 7. www.marxists.org/history/usa/pubs/new-masses/1932/v07n08-jan-1932-New-Masses.pdf.

Entin, Joseph B. *Sensational Modernism: Experimental Fiction and Photography in Thirties America*. Chapel Hill, NC: University of North Carolina Press, 2007.

Foley, Barbara. *Radical Representations: Politics and Form in U.S. Proletarian Fiction, 1929–1941.* Durham, NC: Duke University Press, 1993.

Folsom, Michael, ed. *Mike Gold: A Literary Anthology.* New York: International Publishers, 1972.

Freeman, Joseph. "Toward the Forties." In *The Writer in a Changing World,* edited by Henry Hart, 9–33. London: Lawrence and Wishart, 1937.

Geismar, Maxwell. Introduction to North, *New Masses,* 5–13.

Geriguis, Lina. "Ecosomatic and Ethnological Pathologies: Ethnicity, Disability, and Capabilities in Meridel Le Sueur's 'Women on the Breadlines.'" *Polish American Studies* 71, no. 2 (Fall 2014): 19–42. https://doi.org/10.5406/poliamerstud.71.2.0019.

Goggans, Jan. *California on the Breadlines: Dorothea Lange, Paul Taylor, and the Making of a New Deal Narrative.* Berkeley, CA: University of California Press, 2010.

Gold, Michael. "John Reed: He Loved the People." *New Masses,* October 22, 1940, 8–11. www.unz.com/print/NewMasses-1940oct22-00008/.

———. "Towards Proletarian Art." 1921. In Folsom, *Mike Gold,* 62–70.

Greer, Jane. "Refiguring Authorship, Ownership, and Textual Commodities: Meridel Le Sueur's Pedagogical Legacy." *College English* 65, no. 6 (July 2003): 607–25. https://doi.org/10.2307/3594273.

Gregory, Horace. "One Writer's Position." *New Masses,* February 12, 1935, 20–21. www.marxists.org/history/usa/pubs/new-masses/1935/v14n07-feb-12-1935-NM.pdf.

Hart, Henry, ed. *American Writers' Congress.* New York: International Publishers, 1935.

Hartsock, John C. *A History of American Literary Journalism: The Emergence of a Modern Narrative Form.* Amherst, MA: University of Massachusetts Press, 2000.

———. *Literary Journalism and the Aesthetics of Experience.* Amherst, MA: University of Massachusetts Press, 2016.

———. "Literary Reportage: The 'Other' Literary Journalism." In *Literary Journalism across the Globe: Journalistic Traditions and Transnational Influences,* edited by John S. Bak and Bill Reynolds, 23–46. Amherst, MA: University of Massachusetts Press, 2011.

Hedges, Elaine. Introduction to Le Sueur, *Ripening,* 1–28.

Hicks, Granville, Joseph North, Michael Gold, Paul Peters, Isidor Schneider, and Alan Calmer, eds. *Proletarian Literature in the United States.* New York: International Publishers, 1935.

Howard, June. *Form and History in American Literary Naturalism.* Chapel Hill, NC: University of North Carolina Press, 1985.

Kennedy, David M. *The American People in the Great Depression.* Part 1 of *Freedom from Fear.* New York: Oxford University Press, 2004.

Le Sueur, Meridel. "Author's Note." In *The Dread Road,* 61–62. Albuquerque, NM: West End Press, 1991.

———. "Cows and Horses Are Hungry." In *Ripening,* 166–70. Originally published in *American Mercury,* September 1934, 53–56.

———. "The Fetish of Being Outside." *New Masses,* February 26, 1935, 22–23. www.marxists.org/history/usa/pubs/new-masses/1935/v14n09-feb-26-1935-NM.pdf.

———. "I Was Marching." *New Masses,* September 18, 1934, 16–18. www.marxists.org/history/usa/pubs/new-masses/1934/v12n12-sep-18-1934-NM.pdf.

———. "Jelly Roll." 1980. In *Walt Whitman: The Measure of His Song,* edited by Jim Perlman, Ed Folsom, and Dan Campion, 421–24. 2nd ed. Duluth, MN: Holy Cow! Press, 1998.

———. "Proletarian Literature and the Middle West." In Hart, *American Writers' Congress,* 135–38.

———. *Ripening: Selected Work.* Edited by Elaine Hedges. 2nd ed. New York: Feminist Press, 1990.

———. "They Follow Us Girls." 1935. In *Women on the Breadlines,* n.p.

———. "Women Are Hungry." In *Ripening,* 144–57. Originally published in *American Mercury,* March 1934, 316–26.

———. "Women Know a Lot of Things." In *Ripening,* 171–74. Originally published in *Worker,* March 1937.

———. "Women on the Breadlines." *New Masses,* January 1932, 5–7. www.marxists.org/history/usa/pubs/new-masses/1932/v07n08-jan-1932-New-Masses.pdf.

———. *Women on the Breadlines.* Worker Writers Pamphlet. Cambridge, MA: West End Press, 1977.

Levinas, Emmanuel. *Entre Nous: On Thinking-of-the-Other.* Translated by Michael B. Smith and Barbara Harshav. New York: Columbia University Press, 1998.

———. *Ethics and Infinity.* Conversations with Phillipe Nemo. Translated by Richard A. Cohen. Pittsburgh, PA: Duquesne University Press, 1985.

Madden, David. Introduction to *Proletarian Writers of the Thirties,* edited by David Madden, xv–xlii. Carbondale, IL: Southern Illinois University Press, 1968.

Marcus, Paul. *Being for the Other: Emmanuel Levinas, Ethical Living, and Psychoanalysis*. Milwaukee, WI: Marquette University Press, 2008.

———. *In Search of the Good Life: Emmanuel Levinas, Psychoanalysis, and the Art of Living*. London: Karnac Books, 2010.

McElvaine, Robert S., ed. *The Depression and New Deal: A History in Documents*. New York: Oxford University Press, 2000.

Monteath, Peter. "The Spanish Civil War and the Aesthetics of Reportage." In *Literature and War*, edited by David Bevan, 69–85. Rodopi Perspectives on Modern Literature 3. Amsterdam: Rodopi, 1990.

North, Joseph. "And Fighting All the Way … New Masses' Journey through a Generation." *New Masses*, January 13, 1948, 3–7. www.marxists.org/history/usa/pubs/new-masses/1948/v66n03-jan-13-1948-NM.pdf.

———, ed. *New Masses: An Anthology of the Rebel Thirties*. New York: International Publishers, 1969.

———. *No Men Are Strangers*. New York: International Publishers, 1958.

———. Prologue to North, *New Masses*, 19–33.

———. "Reportage." In Hart, *American Writers' Congress*, 120–23.

———. "Spivak's America." Review of *America Faces the Barricades*, by John L. Spivak. *New Masses*, August 27, 1935, 25–26. www.marxists.org/history/usa/pubs/new-masses/1935/v16n09-aug-27-1935-NM.pdf.

———. Preface to "Reportage." In Hicks et al., *Proletarian Literature*, 211–12.

Peck, David. "Joseph North and the Proletarian Reportage of the 1930s." *Zeitschrift für Anglistik und Amerikanistik* 33, no 3 (1985): 210–20.

Polk, Judd. "Our House Divided by Itself." *New Masses*, September 10, 1940, 10. www.unz.com/print/New Masses-1940sep10-00010/.

Pratt, Linda Ray. "Woman Writer in the CP: The Case of Meridel LeSueur." *Women's Studies* 14, no. 3 (1988): 247–64. https://doi.org/10.1080/00497878.1988.9978702.

Rabinowitz, Paula. *Black and White and Noir: America's Pulp Modernism*. New York: Columbia University Press, 2002.

———. *Labor and Desire: Women's Revolutionary Fiction in Depression America*. Chapel Hill, NC: University of North Carolina Press, 1991.

Roberts, Nancy L. "Meridel Le Sueur, Dorothy Day, and the Literary Journalism of Advocacy during the Great Depression." *Literary Journalism Studies* 7, no. 1 (Spring 2015): 45–57.

Roosevelt, Franklin D. "'Forgotten Man' Radio Address." 1932. In McElvaine, *Depression and New Deal*, 170–71.

Seldes, George. "Silver Charlie." Review of *Shrine of the Silver Dollar*, by John L. Spivak. *New Masses*, March 12, 1940, 25–26. www.unz.com/print/NewMasses-1940mar12-00025/.

Shulman, Robert. *The Power of Political Art: The 1930s Literary Left Reconsidered*. Chapel Hill, NC: University of North Carolina Press, 2000.

Spivak, John L. *America Faces the Barricades*. New York: Covici Friede, 1935.

———. "The Government Helps the People." In *America Faces the Barricades*, 83–93.

———. "I See by the Papers …." In *America Faces the Barricades*, 75–82.

———. "A Letter from America to President Roosevelt." *New Masses*, March 20, 1934, 9–11. www.marxists.org/history/usa/pubs/new-masses/1934/v10n12-mar-20-1934-NM.pdf.

———. "A Letter to the President." In *America Faces the Barricades*, 15–23.

———. "The Worker Thinks." In *America Faces the Barricades*, 163–68.

Stott, William. *Documentary Expression and Thirties America*. 1973. Reprint, Chicago: University of Chicago Press, 1986.

Walcutt, Charles Child. *American Literary Naturalism, a Divided Stream*. Minneapolis, MN: University of Minnesota Press, 1956.

Wald, Alan M. *Exiles from a Future Time: The Forging of the Mid-Twentieth-Century Literary Left*. Chapel Hill, NC: University of North Carolina Press, 2002.

Westin, Jeane. *Making Do: How Women Survived the '30s*. Chicago: Follett, 1976.

Wolfe, Tom. "The New Journalism." In *The New Journalism*, edited by Tom Wolfe and E. W. Johnson, 3–52. New York: Harper and Row, 1973.

Zola, Émile. "The Experimental Novel." 1880. In *Documents of Modern Literary Realism*, edited by George J. Becker, 162–96. Princeton, NJ: Princeton University Press, 1963.

9
PERFORMATIVE CRITICISM AND THE PROBLEM OF MODERNIST CHIC
Gertrude Stein, Janet Flanner, and Dorothy Parker

Nancy Bombaci

Introduction: Popular Criticism for Cultural Aspirants

The early twentieth-century American writers Gertrude Stein, Janet Flanner, and Dorothy Parker criticized the pretensions of high modernism as they made modernist literary ideas accessible to a culturally ambitious middlebrow audience. As Janice Radway explains, the term middlebrow refers to the more accessible literary and artistic culture that emerged during the early twentieth century and continues to the present as an alternative "to high cultural tastes and proclivities" validated especially in academia.[1] Catherine Keyser emphasizes that the word middlebrow usually describes "mass-market venues and middle-class audiences" rather than a particular style of writing.[2] In books and in magazines marketed particularly toward American cultural aspirants, Stein, Flanner, and Parker wrote popular criticism for middlebrow readers receptive to the democratization of modernist elitism and the glamorization of bohemian subcultures in Europe and America. These three writers often admired but at times questioned the form and content of high modernist discourses. While their writing functions as journalism about literature and art, its fusion of reportage and satire also marks it as a distinctive form of literary journalism. When performing for their implied readers, they often evaluate modern art and literature as objects of intellectual fashion or what I term "modernist chic." As critics influenced by journalistic objectivity, they aimed to steer their readers away from the allure of modernist chic by guiding them to perceive high cultural trends with a clarity of vision.

As the high modernist style gained international prestige, it often became a fashionable aesthetic sought especially by those who desired intellectual distinction and cultural exclusivity. Pierre Bourdieu defines the acquisition of cultural capital as a means through which those aspiring to elite status emulate and appropriate upper-class tastes and values.[3] Leslie Fiedler describes many of the American promoters of modernism as men from privileged backgrounds "who sought to deny their bourgeois origins by passing into the non-class or meta-class of 'bohemians' or 'intellectuals'"—groups that had the allure of cultural superiority.[4] Male writers who practiced the high modernist aesthetic often exaggerated what Peter Middleton describes as an "inward gaze" that highlights "the authority of their subjectivity" so that "the presentation of self-consciousness was a primary and perplexing concern."[5] Middleton explains that while women modernists also experimented with the inward gaze, they render the process of self-reflection with greater subtlety.[6] In a like manner, describing the glamorization of elite tastes, Bourdieu also alludes to a gaze associated with cultural superiority:

> The naïve exhibitionism of "conspicuous consumption," which seeks distinction in the crude display of ill-mastered luxury, is nothing compared to the unique capacity of the pure gaze, a quasi-creative power which sets the aesthete apart from the common herd by a radical difference which seems to be inscribed in "persons."[7]

The overvaluation of this "pure gaze" as a mark of essential intellectual superiority led to the commodification of high modernism in terms of "modernist chic." With reference to Bourdieu, Sean Latham explains, "From the beginning [high modernists] understood that their literary art was also a social and business practice, that is, an attempt to secure both symbolic and economic capital for themselves."[8] In her analysis of the cultural significance of the Book-of-the-Month Club, Radway suggests that intellectual elitists viewed middlebrow culture as profoundly vexing since it challenged powerful but arbitrary boundaries between high and popular art forms.[9]

Recent cultural criticism has demonstrated that from the early 1930s, publishers used savvy marketing strategies to make modernist literature available to an intellectually ambitious middlebrow readership. Lise Jaillant demonstrates that under the direction of publisher Bennett Cerf, for example, the Modern Library pitched complex writers such as James Joyce and Stein toward middlebrow readers by urging them to buy cheap copies of modernist texts.[10] In *Modernism, Middlebrow and the Literary Canon*, Jaillant shows further that the Modern Library offered its readers a diversity of books that ranged from works by popular authors to valorized texts by high modernists. Despite this appeal to a variety of tastes, this publishing house attempted to sell the cultural cachet of modernist literature by offering highbrow works that editors presumed were more accessible to a middlebrow audience.[11] For example, Cerf rigorously marketed Stein's early and more accessible novel *Three Lives* (1909) toward a middlebrow audience, but in order to persuade those readers to buy her more difficult works, he pretended to find them incomprehensible.[12] Thus by feigning ignorance of Stein's modernist experimentation, Cerf opened the door for readers who may have found such work unduly intimidating.

At the same time, by differentiating the Modern Library from British publishers with more conservative tastes such as Everyman's Library and Oxford World's Classics, the editors marketed it as "the civilized minority's choice rather than the people's choice."[13] Like the American Library, magazines such as the *New Yorker* and *Vanity Fair* marketed modernism as a desirable commodity for middle-class readers eager to increase their cultural capital. The magazines and the publishing company presented "an emphasis on cultural pedagogy, a collision of different cultural tastes, and a participation in the emerging celebrity culture."[14]

Harold Ross, the editor of the *New Yorker* from 1925 until 1951, was a journalist at heart who valued precise writing and fact-based objectivity. He emphasized in his prospectus for the magazine that he had little use for the "radical" and "the highbrow."[15] Rather, he preferred a literate style that engaged the readers' intelligence without ostensibly pandering to fashionable tastes: "It will be what is commonly called sophisticated, in that it will assume a reasonable degree of enlightenment on the part of its readers. It will hate bunk."[16] Paradoxically, while Ross claimed an immunity to literary fashion, the *New Yorker*'s signature style eventually became a fashionable idiom for seekers of cultural capital. Also, by stressing that good fiction need not be highbrow, Ross created a vital space for middlebrow writers to gain an engaged readership of cultural aspirants. In her combined history and memoir about the *New Yorker*, Renata Adler explains that this magazine's heyday "was a period, culturally, of the somewhat second-rate. This would by no means detract from the magazine's achievement—might perhaps, on the contrary enhance it."[17] Adler thus suggests that the *New Yorker* enabled middlebrow writers to gain well-deserved cultural authority during this time.

As literary journalists who wrote for the *New Yorker*, Flanner and Parker challenged the sensibilities of readers who might have fallen prey to the glamorization of modernist experimentation. While Stein's abstruse style has often been derided as an exemplar of fashionable pseudo-intellectual drivel, she and her editors actually aimed to democratize modernism by gearing her more accessible writing toward middlebrow readers.[18] In their synthesis of satire and reportage, Stein, Flanner, and Parker practice a unique form of literary journalism that I term "performative criticism," a method that amuses the audience with wit—a fusion of irony and humor—as it comments on visual and performing arts as well as literature. Keyser explains that women who wrote for magazines such as the *New Yorker*, *Vanity Fair*, and *Harper's Bazaar* during the early twentieth century often used humor and irony strategically for the purpose of disclosure as well as ironic subterfuge:

> Although humor provides methods of concealment and disguise, humor and its frequent comrade, irony, also derive power from revelation, from the conceptual and critical potential of unmasking. These women writers reflected on their own personae in their work by investigating the growing publicity culture of which they were a part and symbol.[19]

As we will see, Stein, Flanner, and Parker use their performative method to criticize the culture industry, which has the power to elevate and deflate reputations in all of the arts. As literary journalists who expose and satirize the commodified inward gaze of masculine modernism, they urge their middlebrow readers to resist the allure of modernist chic.

Gertrude Stein's Democratization of Modernism

Commenting on the complex relationship between journalism and modernism, Phyllis Frus demonstrates that both journalists and fiction writers of the early twentieth century were influenced by cultural trends that viewed scientific empiricism as the most valuable intellectual discourse.[20] In this vein, she shows that important aspects of high modernist aesthetics emerged as reconfigurations of scientific and journalistic objectivity. For example, she argues that writers such as "Cather, Pound, Stein, Eliot, and other founders of modernism" transformed the utilitarian journalistic focus on the real and the objective into a high literary aesthetic that produced modes such as "Imagism, Objectivism, and objective realism."[21] Through intense experimentation with language, these writers exaggerated the empirical focus on objectivity to produce work that often seemed inscrutable and impenetrable to those unfamiliar with these techniques.

Other modernists who used more conventional, linear narrative styles challenged high cultural pretensions as they made modernist ideas accessible for popular readers. Considering the relation between journalism and modernism, David T. Humphries argues that several American modernists including Willa Cather and Ernest Hemingway aimed to appeal to mainstream readers through the use of journalistic conventions. At the same time, through their development of a "popular modernism" that fused journalistic with modernist discourses, they challenged the middle-class sensibilities of their audience.[22] Through their popular modernism, these writers also questioned the cultural fixation on objectivity by exposing the representational limits of journalism.[23]

Unlike many of her modernist contemporaries, Gertrude Stein (1874–1946) did not work directly in the field of journalism. At the same time, her unique aesthetic, which imitates and exaggerates scientific objectivity, is linked inextricably to a journalistic sensibility. For example, she advised Hemingway, who had for years been a practicing journalist, to avoid using self-reflexive remarks when writing "Big Two-Hearted River" (1925) and instead use language that mirrors the objective eye of a camera.[24] In her essays and lectures geared toward middle-brow readers, Stein explains the relation of her modernist method to journalistic empiricism. For instance, she describes her penchant for objectivity in her lecture "Poetry and Grammar" (1940), where she states her desire to represent reality with even greater lucidity than newspaper reportage:

> The newspapers tell us about it but they tell it to us as nouns tell it to us that is they name it, and in naming it, it as a telling of it is no longer anything. That is what a newspaper is by definition just as a noun is a name by definition.[25]

Stein, instead, aspires to use language that is so vivid that it can describe its object of representation without resorting to labels and generalizations: "I had to feel anything and everything that for me was existing so intensely that I could put it down in writing as a thing in itself without at all necessarily using its name."[26] While she aims to go beyond the limits of reportage, Stein expresses an affinity for the visual clarity of photography in *Everybody's Autobiography* (1937), a memoir that attempts to explain the methods of modernist art and literature to a middlebrow audience. In his analysis of Stein's more accessible style in *Everybody's Autobiography*, Loren Glass states, "Stein tries to account for and intervene in the gradual process ... whereby literary modernism, which had been developed in conscious resistance to the literary marketplace, itself became a commodity in the marketplace."[27] In this work, which presents popular criticism of literature and visual arts, Stein declares that while she "got very interested in reporters" and enjoyed conversing with them, she felt that the ideas of a young photographer were more in accord with her perspective:

> I said to the photographer you do understand what I am talking about don't you. Of course I do he said you see I can listen to what you say because I don't have to remember what you are saying, they can't listen because they have got to remember.[28]

With reference to this passage, Steven Meyer explains that Stein views herself and the photographer as having an ability to perceive language with a "*heightened consciousness of the medium.*"[29] Her entire oeuvre can be viewed as an effort to show her readers how to perceive images and ideas with greater clarity.

At the same time, while Stein values precision and objectivity, she does not equate these approaches with verisimilitude, an artistic method that she regards as dull and dated. She observes that modern artists such as Pablo Picasso disavowed simple verisimilitude to "paint with what is inside them" in order to recreate their inner lives in the work of art.[30] While this seems to validate what Middleton defines as the masculine "inward gaze" central to high modernism, she also deflates it by suggesting that writers tend not only to be focused narcissistically on their own experiences but also to be seeking an active readership: "Besides writers have an endless curiosity about themselves and anything that is written about them helps to help them know something about themselves or about what anybody says about them."[31]

When discussing the reception of art and literature, Stein presents Picasso's elitist view that even when complex artists and writers become well known, only few people can appreciate their work: "there were just about the same two or three [readers or viewers] who were really interested as when nobody knew about you, but does it make any difference."[32] Stein counters Picasso's elitism by stating that when writing *The Making of Americans* (1925), she wrote for herself and for the "strangers" who form her readership, but she has little regard for these strangers since "the earth now is covered over with people and that hearing anybody is not of any particular importance because anybody can know anybody."[33] In this humorously convoluted sentence, she suggests that the most interested readers themselves are subsumed within this mass of strangers, so she has little regard for how they or anyone else judges her work. While this sounds, on the one hand, like a snobbish disdain for mass culture, it can also be construed as a dismissal of critics by putting them on par with the ubiquitous "everyone else."

Stein herself became a celebrity through her idiosyncratic uses of language, which satirize and parody the pretensions of masculine modernism.[34] Although she had no qualms about engaging in self-promotion, she criticizes the media's tendency to use exaggeration when presenting personalities. Stein argues that popular journalism's construction of vivid personalities rivals novelists' creation of distinctive characters:

> But now well now how can you dream about a personality when it is always being created for you by a publicity, how can you believe what you make up when publicity makes them up to be so much realer than you can dream.[35]

As Stein, for a moment, shows contempt for celebrity journalism, she affirms her allegiance to the real, the true, and the objective—values associated with science, high modernism, and sophisticated journalism.

In *The Autobiography of Alice B. Toklas* (1933), Stein explains that her "passion for exactitude" is based on her desire to represent the "inner and outer reality" of her subjects in a manner that is untainted by emotion. Through the voice of Toklas, she claims that a critic likened her aestheticized precision and objectivity to mathematics and the music of Bach.[36] Despite her devotion to objectivity, she recognizes that even she inevitably infuses her work with subjective perceptions. In "The Gradual Making of *The Making of Americans*," she states that when she studied psychology with William James, she became fascinated more by her own interpretations of the people she observed than with the subjects themselves:

> I became more and more interested in my own mental and physical processes and less in that of others and all I then was learning of what made people what they were came to me by experience and not by talking and listening.[37]

When casting her critical eye toward the literature of her time in her popular essays and lectures, Stein imbues her objective method with a performative satirical perspective. This synthesis of objectivity with subjectivity is especially evident when she declares herself a genius or comments on the nature of genius in early twentieth-century culture. In *The Autobiography of Alice B. Toklas*, Stein, through the voice of Toklas, announces that she is a genius on par with Picasso and Alfred North Whitehead, masculine exemplars of modern painting and philosophy, respectively: "I have met many important people, I have met several great people but I have only known three first class geniuses and in each case on sight within me something rang. In no one of the three cases have I been mistaken. In this way my new full life began.[38] Through her humorous self-aggrandizement, Stein satirizes masculine modernism as she presents a veiled critique of its elitist, exclusionary tactics. Feigning grandiosity, she seems to be saying, if they can be considered geniuses, so could she. Deflating the myth of the masculine genius, she also declares that she was clearly the genius of her family, while her brother Leo, with whom she was competitive, clearly lacked this quality: "The only thing about it was that it was I who was the genius, there was no reason for it but I was, and he was not."[39]

Stein even humorously diminishes the prestige of genius by claiming that those who want to become one simply "have to sit around doing nothing, really doing nothing."[40] Mocking the notion of the singular modernist genius, she declares that those who have this quality are not all that different from those who are not endowed with singular creative insight:

> What is a genius. Picasso and I used to talk about that a lot. Really inside you if you are a genius there is nothing inside you that makes you really different to yourself inside you than those are to themselves who are not a genius. That is so.[41]

Stein, in fact, often suggests genius is a state of being that can be experienced by anyone who learns a mode of perception that goes beyond time in order to capture the quiddity of things.[42] For Stein, those who attain a state of genius are capable of "existing" without "any internal recognition of time"[43] and remain "eternally young."[44] She suggests that she defies time by representing people and objects in relation to a "continuous present"—a goal in line with her bent toward photography and her rejection of reportage.[45] Through her playful posturing in her performative criticism, Stein ridicules modernist chic as she makes a modernist sensibility available to the masses.

Janet Flanner's Performance of Objectivity

When writing as a critic of art, theater, and literature for the *New Yorker*, Janet Flanner (1892–1978) presents her experience of artistic works and events through her performative criticism. Using an incisive, double-edged perspective, she encourages her middlebrow readers to enjoy challenging forms of literature, visual art and theater, as she questions modernist chic. Also, her clever wit enables her to affect an objective journalistic stance, which conforms to the sensibilities of her editor, Harold Ross. Flanner developed a popular idiom that imitates objective reportage as it sets forth her subjective impressions of modern art forms.

When Flanner began writing for the *New Yorker*, Ross had her sign her pieces "Genêt," which she believed sounded like a "Frenchified" version of Janet.[46] Ross also demanded that she use a clear and objective journalistic style to present "what the French thought was going on in France" rather than her singular interpretations of artistic trends and events.[47] Her biographer Brenda Wineapple explains that Flanner aimed to convey her experience of events rather than to provide a dense critical analysis of them: "At their best, her Paris letters told not just what the French were thinking—if they did that at all—but what she thought in precisely the way she wanted her thought known, through style."[48] While Flanner defined herself as a "reporter," she was a critic at heart who could not distance herself from her subjective judgments.

In her articles for the *New Yorker*, Flanner frequently commented on the cultural value of art and literature for her audience of cultural aspirants. For example, in the following laconic comment on Léonce Rosenberg's presentation of bad taste, she provokes her readers to define for themselves whether aesthetic value is, for the most part, subjective:

Art (Semantics)
The art merchant Leonce Rosenberg is opening a show of Bad Taste, to prove his aesthetic theory that taste is largely whim.[49]

By placing the word "Semantics" next to her subtitle "Art," she hints that artistic value is not universal but contingent on the language used to define it. In this laconic, aphoristic comment, the medium becomes the message since the focus is more on Flanner's wit than the content of Rosenberg's show. While she does not describe the show in detail, she leaves it to the reader to ponder the catchy title in relation to the direct sentence, which poses as objective reportage. She does not mention that during the 1920s, Rosenberg was one of the most important promoters of cubism, a style of painting that some critics hailed as brilliant and others denounced as primitive and hideous. In many of her terse critical articles, she reserves special disdain for those she regards as poseurs and pseudo-intellectual snobs.

For example, when reporting on François Mauriac's induction into the Académie française, she finds laughable the pageantry of this event, where Mauriac "[passes] beneath the cupola to the roll of drums" as he carries a sword worth "thirty thousand francs."[50] She suggests that while Mauriac may well be a pretentious fop, his well-connected "rich and ultra-Catholic" family enabled him to get the award.[51] Flanner also cunningly distinguishes herself from most of the spectators of this event by suggesting that they are more interested in being seen at ostentatious spectacles than in interpreting and enjoying literature. These spectators include "literary and political lights, leaders from all the professions, snobs, ladies of quality, and clergy."[52] In her implicit criticism of these people, Flanner warns her readers that cultural capital cannot be gained merely by attending a fashionable happening. In fact, a persistent theme in many of her articles is the clear distinction between the pursuit of aesthetic pleasure and the quest for cultural and financial capital.

Flanner, for example, shows a particular aversion to art dealers who sell paintings by dead artists for exorbitant prices. Using her more direct, reportorial style, she discusses the resale of the John Quinn collection of modern art, which she believes "should be in a state museum."[53] During the auction, a number of artists expressed disgust that some of these works sold for ridiculously high prices. When a Matisse sold for "one hundred and one thousand francs—about thirty-two hundred dollars," and another by Rousseau sold for half a million, one old artist yelled, "This is not art but commerce. ... Rousseau died in poverty. What was he paid for this silly canvas?"[54] One can only speculate whether Flanner is reporting the witty proclamation of an "old artist," or if this in fact is her own observation. She ends this brief article with her own subjective impression. While Genêt also believes that these works should have been bought by a museum, she allows that Rousseau "would have been proud" to see one of his works reproduced in his favorite newspaper: "It was Rousseau's final triumph and the first art note that newspaper ever carried."[55] With sly wit, she suggests that this provincial and philistine journal viewed art as newsworthy only if it was part of a business exchange.

Wineapple explains that when Flanner was young, she rebelled against bourgeois conventionality in favor of a subjective approach to the arts based on the aestheticism of Walter Pater (1839–94).[56] Pater also wrote criticism for newspapers and for magazines geared toward a well-educated but nonacademic readership.[57] A Paterian aesthetic sensibility is based on a unique fusion of penetrating objective vision with incisive subjective analysis. In his major work *The Renaissance: Studies in Art and Poetry* (1893), Pater emphasizes that intellectually sensitive critics must aim to understand a work of art "as in itself it really is," as they question their subjective response to it:

> To see the object as in itself it really is, has been justly said to be the aim of all true criticism whatever, and in aesthetic criticism the first step towards seeing one's object as it really is, is to know one's own impression as it really is, to discriminate it, to realise it distinctly. ... What is this song or picture, this engaging personality presented in life or in a book to *me*? What effect does it really produce on me? Does it give me pleasure? and if so, what sort of degree of pleasure? How is my nature modified by its presence, and under its influence? The answers to these questions are the original facts with which the aesthetic critic has to do; and, as in the study of light, of morals, or number, one must realise such primary data for one's self, or not at all.[58]

When defining his aesthetics, Pater makes the unabashedly elitist argument that there is a distinction between "true humanists" who value art for its own sake and "hireling ministers of the system" who repeat officially sanctioned viewpoints:

> As always happens, the adherents of the poorer and narrower culture had no sympathy with, because no understanding of, a culture richer and more ample than their own. After the discovery of wheat they would still live upon acorns … and would hear of no service to the higher needs of humanity with instruments not of their forging.[59]

Flanner echoes this Paterian argument in *Men and Monuments* (1957), a book that presents far more detailed critiques of modern artists than her work for the *New Yorker*. In this book, Flanner states that modern art forms can be understood only by those with a superior aesthetic sensibility: Only "exceptional individuals are stimulated rather than irritated by what is importantly new and offers unexplored identifications, imagined or real."[60] Like Pater, however, she believes that this sensibility can be developed, and with reference to a "European psychiatrist," she diagnoses the rejection of modern art in terms of the fear of the unknown—a pathology exhibited by Hitler:

> Accepted and known forms are the comforting, protecting elements in civilizations; over the ages, man has found his defense and surety in religions, ceremonies, costumes, and iconography. The unfamiliar is alarming and the public recoils at identifying with it because it represents the unknown. (Hitler, not only as a bumpkin but as a dictator, feared *Entartekunsboschewismus*, or decadent Bolshevik art, as he called the Modern, because it was to him a symbol of revolution, which he feared as the unknown that could destroy him.)[61]

Through her popular criticism for the *New Yorker*, Flanner guides her middlebrow readers to view modern art forms with clarity of vision as they develop their subjective responses. When using her Paterian approach, she aims to liberate their sensibilities so that they, too, may perceive works of art with the knowledge and insight of "exceptional individuals."

Using her objective journalistic voice, Flanner positions herself in her articles for the *New Yorker* as an astute and independent-minded critic of modern art and literature—one who aims for aesthetic pleasure unsullied by intellectual snobbism and crass consumerism. On one hand, she exhibits unreserved praise for *Ulysses* (1922), perhaps the most deified modernist novel, as a work that enables readers to have an unparalleled aesthetic experience, which she compares to Pentecost.[62] Also, she refers to Joyce as "a polyglot genius" who has written "this masculine illicit masterpiece."[63] Yet despite this praise, she is more critical of Joyce's failure to acknowledge Sylvia Beach's effort in promoting his signature work.[64] She especially admires Beach for circulating a petition to numerous literary luminaries, asking them to protest Samuel Roth's attempt to infringe on her publication rights to *Ulysses*.[65] Flanner states that this petition, which includes names such as Benedetto Croce, Havelock Ellis, W. Somerset Maugham, and Rebecca West, may become an expensive "bibliophile item" someday. While this may stand as a testament to Beach's integrity and the "spirited solidarity" of dedicated writers, it may also confirm the way certain elements of the literary world seek high status artifacts to be bought and sold rather than works of art to be experienced.

Flanner agrees with French critics who caution that some readers will revel in Joyce's modernist prose because it is culturally coded as elitist, even if they fail to understand his work. With her witty, performative voice, she uses a poignant gastronomical metaphor to describe those who pretend to understand Joyce in order to feel intellectually sophisticated: "Let Monsieur Joyce beware lest he become prey of isolated commentators who fatten on high and heady dishes which even they have not properly digested."[66] A perennial paradox about *Ulysses* is that while this novel takes place in a working-class milieu, it uses the complex discourses of high modernism. Similarly, while its themes challenge the narcissism and Hermeticism often characteristic of masculine modernism, it uses literary techniques that may attract those who find such tendencies glamorous. As Latham explains, "Despite the great virtuosity of the novel, despite its telling protests against intellectual pretension, it still failed to exploit the critical potential of its own ambivalent snobbery and was appropriated by the very cultural hierarchies it sought to contest."[67]

Flanner's contemporary James Agee issues a similar warning in *Let Us Now Praise Famous Men* (1941) that readers should not be enticed by works that have gained cultural authority: "Above all else: in God's name don't think of it as Art. ... Official acceptance is the one unmistakable symptom that salvation is beaten again, and is the one surest sign of fatal misunderstanding, and is the kiss of Judas."[68] For Agee, this kiss of Judas can be interpreted as a betrayal not only of the work itself but also of the readers' and viewers' potential for greater understanding. Displaying a sensibility in line with Pater, Agee emphasizes that while perception is inherently subjective, readers and viewers must develop their sensibilities in order to perceive the essential nature of things:

> For in the immediate world, everything is to be discerned, for him who can discern it, and centrally and simply, without either dissection into science or digestion into art, but with the whole of consciousness, seeking to perceive it as it stands; so that the aspect of a street in sunlight can roar in the heart of itself as a symphony can: and all of consciousness is shifted from the imagined, the revisive, to the effort to perceive the cruel radiance of what is.[69]

With reference to Laurence Bergreen, a biographer of Agee, Humphries states that Agee, who idolized Joyce and Marcel Proust, wanted *Let Us Now Praise Famous Men* to "baffle and offend the casual reader in search of entertainment and diversion."[70] Also, by the time Agee wrote this work, he viewed journalism in terms of fraud since he had become skeptical of the objective claims of reportage. Instead, he argues that a writer's emotional reactions are far more indicative of truth.[71] Flanner, in contrast, wanted to reach and enlighten the popular reader by presenting provocative criticism in a magazine geared toward middlebrow cultural strivers.

Although Flanner showers Joyce with enthusiastic praise, she is far more skeptical of the reputations of William Faulkner, D. H. Lawrence, and Thomas Mann, all of whom she regards as overrated. When considering the French reception of Faulkner's novel *Sanctuary* (1931) (*Sanctuaire* [1933]), for example, she suggests that French critics have overhyped the book: "The sound and the fury of praise have only been less loud than the confusion."[72] Quoting André Malraux, she concurs that although the novel has banal plot elements, "the greatness of *Sanctuaire* lies not in what happens but in its somber, ardent poesy."[73] Echoing a Paterian sensibility, Flanner suggests that the astute reader who is open to profound aesthetic experiences will appreciate the elements of *Sanctuaire* that elicit poignant emotional reactions based on the beauty of the prose.

Flanner has less regard for Lawrence, whom she views as a paranoid eccentric who has gone as far as to believe that Carl Jung had plagiarized his psychoanalytic theories.[74] For Flanner, Lawrence's *coup de grâce* is the mistranslation of his novel *The Plumed Serpent* (1926) into *Serpent Dépouillé* or *The Plucked Serpent*.[75] With acerbic performative wit, she suggests that Lawrence deserves this mishap because of his pompousness. For her implied middlebrow readers of the *New Yorker*, who may not have questioned Lawrence's reputation for high seriousness, Flanner goads them to rethink his importance.

Flanner exhibits similar skepticism for Mann's literary reputation, which she regards as unduly inflated. She dismisses his publisher's description of him as "the greatest living man of letters," calling it "a carefully composed selling slogan" designed to hook a readership hungry for cultural capital.[76] Within this context, she finds amusingly inappropriate the Nazis' condemnation of Mann's novels as "degenerate art" since they put his work in the same league as "'Faust,' 'Pilgrim's Progress,' 'The Divine Comedy,' and, as a final tribute, 'Beethoven's ninth symphony.'" With "magnified detachment," Mann comments,

> I was snatched up into a whirl of success. My mailbag was swollen, money flowed in streams, my picture appeared in the papers, a hundred pens made copy of my secluded hours, the world embraced me amid congratulations and shouts of praise. ... Society took me up—in so far as I let it, for in this respect society has never been very successful.[77]

Flanner exposes how while Mann claims to resist the lure of fame and money, he simultaneously brags about his success. Aware of this paradox, she believes he presents a studied and elegant reclusion where he stays "comfortably cloistered" in upper-bourgeois trappings.[78] She takes to task his greater interest in literary characters than in "flesh and blood people," which she attributes to his hard-core narcissism.[79] She sees this narcissistic quality in his tendency to project himself into his many characters:

> Whereas narcissism of the most romantic writers leads them to use themselves as heroes, Mann's has led him to use himself as almost everything—as a hunchback, a swindler, a dilettante, as at least two overbred bourgeois youths ... and a regular bevy of authors.[80]

In her exposure of Lawrence's egotism and Mann's narcissism, Flanner presents a trenchant critique of masculine modernism, which has associations with Hermeticism and the denial of emotion.[81] She lays bare the arrogance at the heart of masculine modernism, as she questions its authority, which she locates in its appeal to the readers' shallow snobbism. For example, Flanner dismisses a coterie of Mann's female fans in Hollywood as a group of "bluestockings" who are "joined together in a cult of admiration for Mann."[82] She is even more disdainful of a Mrs. Meyer, who enables Mann to socially climb with prominent guests at her "spacious estate at Mount Kisco."[83]

While Flanner deftly uses incisive wit to expose literary and artistic pretensions, this method has limitations. Her popular criticism for the *New Yorker*, while provocative, often fails to analyze her subjects in depth. Moreover, her pithy dismissals of major modernist figures in her articles could be misread by unconfident readers as the kind of authoritative proclamations that she herself wants to avoid. Also, the glamorous Parisian veneer that she projects through her laconic observations could be easily dismissed by academic snobs as chic and intellectually insubstantial.

Flanner's British contemporary Rebecca West (1892–1983) also made trenchant assessments of masculine modernism for popular journals but with a style that combined wit with more penetrating analysis. In her long essay "The Strange Necessity" (1928), West combines highly analytical literary criticism with a performative method. She describes herself exiting a Parisian bookstore, "walk[ing] slowly down the street that leads from the Odeon to the Boulevard St. Germain," as she evaluates Joyce's reputation in exhaustive detail. During this stroll, she concludes that despite his rigorous experimentalism and essential genius, Joyce is a formulaic narcissist whose main intention is to shock and impress.[84]

Flanner, in contrast, uses laconic insights rather than dense critical detail to question modernist chic. For Flanner, the art of criticism can, in fact, be fun, while the snobbish pursuit of high culture can be ponderous and dull. She suggests, for example, when reviewing Diaghilev's ballet company that an elite Parisian audience pretentiously focused on an effete notion of high seriousness may fail to understand that modern art can in fact be "good natured" as well as complex:

> Capable of psychology in their muscles as well as in their minds, the dancers, in their geometric contrapuntal routines, facetious pantomimes, deliberate juggling of grave and gay, annually made for a complex, good-natured entertainment mistakenly offered a public which solemnly yearns for what it used to call Modern Art. As a matter of fact, it is getting it.[85]

In her literary journalism for the *New Yorker,* Flanner shows that a critic for a middlebrow magazine can simultaneously expose the pretentions of high culture while stretching the intellectual boundaries of a popular idiom. Through her fusion of an objective journalistic gaze with performative wit, she urges her readers to question the authority of masculine modernism.

Dorothy Parker's Subversion of Literary Fashion

Through her energetic performative criticism, Dorothy Parker (1893–1967) uses her sharp eye and trenchant wit to challenge modernist chic and other forms of literary snobbery. Parker writes in a style that is unabashedly chic for middlebrow readers who want to acquire cultural sophistication. A member of the Algonquin Round Table, she belonged to a group of writers noted for their modish comedic sensibility, which appealed to a mass audience. As a writer of poetry, short stories, and critical reviews for popular magazines such as *Vanity Fair,* the *New Yorker,* and *Esquire,* she uses an idiom that is usually humorous, laconic, and at times even acerbic. More caustic than Flanner, Parker creates a greater distance between her critical sensibility and the objects of her keen gaze. When Parker poses as the personification of reason, her insights are often astute, but sometimes they are shallow and unexamined, due to the terse nature of her writing. As with Flanner's performative criticism for the *New Yorker,* the genre enables the expression of keen insights, while its brevity inhibits a depth of analysis. Despite this pitfall, Parker often exploits the strengths of the genre to expose the intellectual dullness at the core of literary fashion.

When considering Parker's literary reputation, Rhonda Pettit explains that critics have dismissed her as "a modern writer who is not quite modernist" since her "work as we know it lacks radical experimentation with form."[86] Moreover, critics have judged Parker and the members of the Algonquin Round Table as mediocrities who were more concerned with commercial success than artistic distinction. Brendan Gill, for example, describes most of the members of this group as "second- and third-raters" whom Parker later dismissed as inadequate when compared to "Hemingway, Faulkner, Lardner, Fitzgerald, Dos Passos, Cather, Crane, and O'Neill," writers who did not need to attach themselves to a coterie of fashionable wits.[87] Pettit shows that while Parker eventually severed her association with this group, she and her Algonquin peers were often judged unfairly because they wrote for popular magazines:

> Reading Parker in popular magazines, or reading her with the knowledge that she published in *Vanity Fair, Life,* and *The New Yorker* rather than in *Broom, Blast,* or the *Little Review,* not only reinforces the belief that she wrote only for money, but places her contextually outside the realm of "serious" literature as we have come to define it through canonical works. One of the issues this kind of reading overlooks is the careful attention Parker paid to poetic form, itself an indicator that she took her art seriously.[88]

Parker's extreme concern with the medium of language extended to her performative criticism, where she strived for intellectual rigor as she often skewered literary fashion, using an entertaining idiom.

Her fastidious attention to language is especially evident in her negative critique of Theodore Dreiser's writing style in his 1931 memoir, *Dawn*. She regards this work as a long, ponderous tome that is filled with "monstrous bad writing."[89] She caustically adds that although Dreiser had been a journalist, "any reporter writes better and more vividly than the man who has been proclaimed the great reporter."[90] Parker has as much disdain for critics who applaud the socially relevant content of his works despite his "abominable style."[91] She uses the sarcastic neologism "the booksie-wooksies" to describe these well-regarded book critics who place a higher value on the content than the form of Dreiser's works.

During the 1920s, Parker wrote theater reviews for *Ainslee's*, a popular literary magazine that her biographer Marion Meade describes as "respectable enough but steps beneath *Vanity Fair* in both class and circulation."[92] Imitating her characteristic wit, Meade states that the editors of this publication allowed Parker to "express her opinions as bitchily as she pleased."[93] In some theater reviews for this magazine, Parker affects intellectual insecurity, as she appeals to readers who may find high culture intimidating.[94] For example, she shamelessly admits to this audience that while she enjoys reading Shakespeare's plays, she rarely enjoys watching performances of them:

> I like to tell myself that, because I enjoy reading Shakespeare, I have, in a small way, my appreciation of the beautiful, just like regular people. And naturally I don't speak right out in company and say how I feel when I go to the theatre to see *Hamlet* or *Macbeth* or even *The Merry Wives of Windsor*. ... This is just between you and me. And even in this comforting privacy I am stricken and abashed to confess that I cannot thrill to the acted plays of Shakespeare.[95]

In another article for *Ainslee's* where she declares that *As You Like It* is one of Shakespeare's least interesting plays, she affirms that she refuses to allow her perception of a literary work to be influenced by the author's reputation. Speaking of herself in the third person, she suggests that while gossips in the literary world may view her as "unrefined" even though she has a "nice husband," she is free to criticize Shakespeare since certain "big boys" or major male critics have made it acceptable to do so.[96] As she exposes and ridicules the sexism of the literary world, she declares that now she is free to confess her dislike for certain modern writers and art forms:

> It is to be hoped that this encouragement will not turn her head, but there are grave indications that, crazed with a desire for honesty, she is going to throw all to the winds any day now, and confess right out in the public square how she really feels about Cabell, Conrad, Stanislavski, T. S. Eliot, and the Russian ballet.[97]

Although she does not confess how she really feels, she implies that she finds who and what she lists overrated due to their intellectually fashionable reputations.

In "Three Rousing Cheers" (1923), she continues to appeal to an audience perplexed by modern theater. When briefly reviewing Luigi Pirandello's *Six Characters in Search of an Author* (1921), she makes clear that she agrees with a woman who "loudly proclaimed" her dislike of the play's philosophical pretensions. Parker boldly states that some viewers try to acquire cultural capital by pretending to like this play:

> Perhaps its encouraging popularity is due to the fact that, mixed with the spectator's wholehearted interest in it, is a nice, warm little feeling that he is one of the lofty few

who can appreciate such things—and a feeling like that, once in awhile, never did anyone any harm.[98]

While this feeling may, in fact, be harmless, Parker suggests that it is conducive to stupidity since it prevents the viewer from perceiving the work with more clarity. Yet as with Flanner's terse performative criticism, the genre enables Parker to get away with making comments like this that are striking but unsubstantiated.

When discussing the limits of Parker's pithy writing style, Gill compares her negatively to her contemporary Edmund Wilson, a critic who skillfully incorporated crucial details into his reviews. Gill believes that Parker was too intent on entertaining her readers with acerbic pronouncements:

> She did not have, like Wilson, a natural gift for literary journalism—where he cast the widest possible net and hauled up, to the world's astonishment, an unprecedented variety of sea monsters. Mrs. Parker dealt with books and writers on a small scale, sometimes with a facetiousness bred of unease. Evidently she feared that the praise she bestowed in her reviews would give readers less pleasure than the malicious one-line dismissals for which she was famous.[99]

Like Parker, Wilson also aimed to reveal the intellectual pretensions at the core of modernist chic, yet his criticism has more analytical depth. For example, he exposes Alfred Stieglitz as an overrated impresario whose reputation entices readers and viewers to favor certain artists and dismiss others. He explains that even his perceptions of some contemporary artists were clouded by his reverence for Stieglitz's reputation:

> My admiration for these artists was genuine, but if I had not been subjected to Stieglitz's spell, I might perhaps have discussed them in different terms. I note that there were pictures by Charles Demuth, and I do not now remember what they were; yet Demuth—as I realize today—interests me more than Marin, whose reputation I now suspect Stieglitz of having rather unduly inflated, and I might have discovered this if I had been left alone with the pictures.[100]

In her overwhelmingly positive review of Wilson's essays in *The American Earthquake* (1958), Parker describes him as "a truly wonderful reporter," one who gives "startlingly clear accounts of the idiocies and brutalities of times that were neither good nor old."[101] Yet while Wilson has the sensibility of a journalist who aims for clarity and objectivity, he goes beyond this to present subjective critical commentary.

In Parker's performative criticism, the medium often overshadows her message, but in some of her more detailed reviews, she balances her wisecracks with more substantial analysis. We see this in her incisive critique of Hemingway's works, where she lampoons both the lionization and dismissal of this writer by various critics. Parker argues that *The Sun Also Rises* (1926) was unduly overrated quickly after its publication, while *In Our Time*, his 1925 collection of short stories, failed to achieve the recognition that it deserved. She accuses H. L. Mencken and lesser critics whom she facetiously dubs "the smaller boys" as dismissing *In Our Time* because they regarded Hemingway as a lightweight, pseudo-modernist who liked to socialize with more important writers. In effect, she criticizes them for unfairly dismissing *In Our Time* as an example of modernist chic, while their tastes turned to more plebian popular writers like Bruce Barton and Mary Roberts Rinehart:

> Well, you see, Ernest Hemingway was a young American living on the left bank of the Seine in Paris, France; he had been seen at the Dome and the Rotonde and the Select and the Closerie Des Lilas. He knew Pound, Joyce, and Gertrude Stein. There is something a little—well, a little *you*-know—in all those things. You wouldn't catch Bruce Barton or Mary Roberts Rinehart doing them. No sir.[102]

Trying to assert a more incisive critical sensibility, Parker states that Hemingway's deceptively simple prose is more effective in his short stories than in his novels. She concludes that while his talent is inherently "reportorial" like that of Sinclair Lewis, it goes beyond mere reportage due to his acute ear for language: "He discards details with a magnificent lavishness; he keeps his words to their short path. His is, as any reader knows, a dangerous influence."[103] Thus according to Parker, Hemingway at his best combines a reportorial perspective with a poetic sensibility.

As a performative critic, Parker conflates reportage with terse, entertaining judgments to capture her readers' attention. Despite the limits of this genre, she, like Flanner, urges her readers to challenge the herd mentality that often plagued the literary world. In "Literary Rotarians" (1928), she ridicules critics who try too hard to win the favor of their readers by using a "chatty" and "intimate" style of writing. Covertly defending her more discerning eye, she states that while they fail to have high literary standards, they love to declare their superiority over the "Babbits."[104] Parker also disdains popular writers who use sentimental clichés to appeal to a middlebrow female readership. In her article "The Professor Goes in for Sweetness and Light," she derides Yale professor William Lyon Phelps for writing a book titled *Happiness* (1927) filled with bourgeois platitudes on the nature of contentment. Taking to task his sexist description of dull, happy women as "cows," Parker suggests that it's laughable that a mind as dull as Phelps's teaches at an esteemed university: "These are the views, this is the dogma of Professor William Lyon Phelps, pride of New Haven. I trust that my son will elect to attend one of the smaller institutions of higher education."[105]

When criticizing what she regards as the overvaluation of high modernist poetry, Parker associates the word "sophisticate" with "socialite," as she equates sophistication with "obscurity and cynicism."[106] Although she tries to make a case for light verse, she suggests that practitioners of this genre—including herself—"stayed young too long. We remained in the smarty-pants stage—and that is not one of the more attractive ages."[107] Parker's performative criticism also has a "smarty-pants" element, which proves to be both a strength and a weakness. When Parker amuses only to amuse, her medium has a callow, adolescent quality. Yet when she infuses her wit with clear observations and provocative perceptions, she goads her readers to think for themselves in order to challenge dull authorities and crass conventions.

Conclusion: The Strengths and Limits of Performative Criticism

As a variation of literary journalism, performative criticism makes interesting evaluations of works of art accessible to a middlebrow readership. Stein, Flanner, and Parker use this method to expose the pretentions of modernist chic as they challenge the great divide between high and popular culture. Writing from a journalistic tradition that values enlightened skepticism, they urge their readers to experience works of art rather than fall for the latest cultural trends. At the same time, the performative and amusing aspects of their writing style may have the effect of reducing the critical judgment of complex works of art to a few bons mots, where the medium becomes the message. While Stein, Flanner, and Parker all had a gift for producing memorable one-liners that quickly sum up their critical insights, this is both a strength and a weakness. With genuine insight into the politics of literary reputation, they warn their readers not to be swayed by the fashionable narcissism characteristic of masculine modernism. Yet performative criticism has its own narcissistic tendencies, since the performance of wit can become the self-referential and snarky province of glossy magazines read by seekers of superficial cultural sophistication. Still, Stein, Flanner, and Parker often make clear that they disapprove of snobbish readers, as they want the members of their audience to make definite distinctions between literary snobbery and the authentic pursuit of artistic experience. For Flanner and Parker, this agenda is in line with the *New Yorker*'s goals to challenge the influence of highbrow aesthetics. While Stein was herself a highbrow, her uncompromising vision was tempered by a sense of humor and a disdain for those who commodify high modernism as a chic cultural product. By stretching the critical potential of performative criticism, these writers demonstrate that an entertaining form of literary journalism can function as a vital counter discourse to high cultural trends.

Notes

1 Radway, *Feeling for Books*, 9–10.
2 Keyser, *Playing Smart*, 9.
3 Bourdieu, *Distinction*, 31.
4 Fiedler, *What Was Literature?*, 58.
5 Middleton, *Inward Gaze*, 48.
6 Middleton states: "Nothing so readily differentiates the women modernists like Dorothy Richardson and Virginia Woolf from the men as this issue. The women writers are much more flexible in their representation of self-consciousness. For the men there is a kind of all or nothing quality to it, either complete rational clarity or dark unconscious groping. The constantly negotiated emergence of self-awareness in relationships, so subtly done in *Pilgrimage* or *To the Lighthouse*, is hardly to be seen in the men writers" (48).
7 Bourdieu, *Distinction*, 31.
8 Latham, *Am I a Snob?*, 3.
9 Radway states: "It should be clear now why the book clubs and other middlebrow agencies devoted to the marketing of culture as just another consumer product proved so threatening. In packaging and selling cultural objects as if they were no different from soup, soap, or automobiles, these organizations threatened to obliterate the fundamental distinction that underwrote this entire system of privilege, that is, the distinction between the material and the immaterial, between the particularities of the body and the universality of intellect, in short, between the natural and the cultural" (*Feeling for Books*, 224–25).
10 Jaillant, "*Shucks*."
11 Jaillant, *Modernism*, 11–12.
12 When promoting *The Geographical History of America* (1936), a more experimental work by Stein, Cerf wrote, "I must admit frankly that I do not know what Miss Stein is talking about. I do not even understand the title" (Jaillant, "*Shucks*," 159). Jaillant explains that "thanks to this unconventional blurb, Stein's difficult book was widely reviewed" (159).
13 Jaillant, *Modernism*, 11–12.
14 Jaillant, 15.
15 Ross, "New Yorker Prospectus," 439.
16 Ross, 439.
17 Adler, *Gone*, 55.
18 In a 1936 article for the *New Masses* titled "Gertrude Stein: A Literary Idiot," Michael Gold states, "The literary insanity of Gertrude Stein is a deliberate insanity which arises out of a false conception of the nature of art and the function of language." See Gold, "Gertrude Stein."
19 Keyser, *Playing Smart*, 3.
20 Frus, *Politics and Poetics*, 58.
21 Frus, 73.
22 Humphries, *Different Dispatches*, 6.
23 According to Humphries, Cather in her short stories, for example, "often depicts journalists and immigrants as helping artists shape popular taste and change existing conceptions of culture, while in her later works she depicts journalism as nothing more than a form of advertising and immigrants as narrow-mindedly pursuing financial success" (23). Similarly, Hemingway subverts journalistic conventions in *The Sun Also Rises*, where he "represents the growing acceptance that it was better to acknowledge the inevitability of subjectivity than uphold an ideal of objectivity which was increasingly seen as a disabling illusion" (123).

24 Humphries, 103.
25 Stein, "Poetry and Grammar," 145.
26 Stein, 145.
27 Glass, *Authors Inc.*, 117.
28 Stein, *Everybody's Autobiography*, 218.
29 Meyer, *Irresistible Dictation*, 172.
30 Stein, *Everybody's Autobiography*, 29.
31 Stein, 31.
32 Stein, 101.
33 Stein, 101.
34 Elsewhere, I have argued that Stein in her poetry, especially, exaggerates the hermetic aspects of masculine modernism in order to satirize it: "As a literary trickster who reveled in 'doubletalk,' Stein also engaged in satire and parody by holding a mirror to aspects of masculine modernism that she found vexing. Thus, as Stein tries to make a place for herself within the patriarchal high culture, she also engages in a playful subversion of its norms and values by intensifying them" ("Performing Mindblindness," 137).
35 Stein, *Everybody's Autobiography*, 69.
36 Stein, *Autobiography of Alice B. Toklas*, 211.
37 Stein, "Gradual Making," 85.
38 Stein, *Autobiography of Alice B. Toklas*, 5.
39 Stein, *Everybody's Autobiography*, 77.
40 Stein, 70.
41 Stein, 84.
42 Barbara Will makes the case that Stein defines genius as a mode of perception available to anyone willing to make the effort: "While Stein throughout her life evinced a great interest in the extraordinary or 'vitally singular' individual producing masterpieces, she also suggested that 'genius' was a capacity anyone reading her texts could share: a decentered and dialogic, open-ended and collective mode of being" (*Gertrude Stein*, 1).
43 Stein, *Everybody's Autobiography*, 243.
44 Stein, "What Are Master-Pieces," 153.
45 Stein, "Composition as Explanation," 26.
46 Kunkel, *Genius in Disguise*, 127.
47 Flanner, *Paris Was Yesterday*, xix.
48 Wineapple, *Genêt*, 102.
49 Flanner, "Art (Semantics)," 9.
50 Flanner, "François Mauriac," 107.
51 Flanner, 108.
52 Flanner, 108.
53 Flanner, "Art (Commerce)," 9.
54 Flanner, 9–10.
55 Flanner, 10.
56 Wineapple, *Genêt*, 31.
57 Besides writing important articles for *Harper's Magazine*, an American publication, Pater published critical articles and reviews during the late nineteenth century for British journals "such as the *Oxford Magazine* and newspapers such as the *Pall Mall Gazette* and the *Guardian*" (Brake, *Subjugated Knowledges*, 77).
58 Pater, *Renaissance*, 2.
59 Pater, 10.
60 Flanner, *Men and Monuments*, xv–xvi.
61 Flanner, xvi.
62 Flanner, *Paris Was Yesterday*, x.
63 Flanner, "Infinite Pleasures of Sylvia Beach," 309.
64 Wineapple, *Genêt*, 67.
65 Flanner, "*Ulysses*," 17–18.
66 Flanner, "*Little Review*," 57.
67 Latham, *Am I a Snob?*, 168.
68 Agee and Evans, *Let Us Now Praise Famous Men*, 15.
69 Agee and Evans, 11.
70 Quoted in Humphries, *Different Dispatches*, 126.

71 Humphries states, "In making James an embodied participant reporter [in *Let Us Now Praise Famous Men*], Agee emphasizes his immediate physical sensations, sexual desires, and individual consciousness, and he tries to naturalize his language within his environment and remove it from the contested realm of culture" (133).
72 Flanner, "*Sanctuaire*," 116.
73 Flanner, 117.
74 Flanner, "D. H. Lawrence," 65.
75 Flanner, 65.
76 Flanner, "Goethe in Hollywood," 165.
77 Flanner, 166.
78 Flanner, 166.
79 Flanner, 167.
80 Flanner, 168.
81 Middleton states, "Modern literature and philosophy both manifest similar fascinations with emotional obliviousness, but unlike the popular fiction, are much more concerned to question it" (*Inward Gaze*, 195). T. S. Eliot, for example, was fascinated with the individual's potential to transcend the particularity associated with the self and "developed a poetic technology for the careful handling of emotion—impersonality" (195).
82 Flanner, "Goethe in Hollywood," 169.
83 Flanner, 169.
84 West, "Strange Necessity," 22. West states, "Such novels are written by talent or less, and *Ulysses* is written by genius, but there is in both the same narcissistic inspiration, which inevitably deforms all its products with sentimentality, since the self-image which it is the aim of narcissism to create is made not out of material that has been imaginatively experienced but out of material that has been selected as likely to please others. *Shock*. Again the values have been externally adjusted" (22).
85 Flanner, "Diaghilev's Ballet," 55.
86 Pettit, *Gendered Collision*, 23. Pettit counters this view by demonstrating that along with some of her early fiction, Parker's short story "Sorry the Line Is Busy" most notably uses aspects of modernist experimentation such as "[fragmentation], disembodied voices, irony" and the representation of "isolation, alienation, [and] frustration" (23). The work may have been overlooked by serious critics because, as Pettit suggests, it appeared in *Life*, a popular magazine, and because it was illustrated with pictures of its characters (23).
87 Gill, introduction to *The Portable Dorothy Parker*, xv.
88 Pettit, *Gendered Collision*, 35.
89 Parker, "Words, Words, Words," 522.
90 Parker, 522.
91 Parker, 523.
92 Meade, *Dorothy Parker*, 71.
93 Meade, 72.
94 See Walker, "Remarkably Constant Reader." Walker explains that Parker's tendency to feign ignorance and innocence is especially prevalent in her book reviews where she "derives her authority from seeming not to be one at all, projecting *personae* composed of enthusiasms, prejudices, and personal quirks, and developing a distinctive style—a style in which to deliver her no-nonsense opinions" (3).
95 Parker, "Three Rousing Cheers," 342.
96 Parker, "Season Plucks," 378.
97 Parker, 378.
98 Parker, "Three Rousing Cheers," 346.
99 Gill, introduction to *The Portable Dorothy Parker*, xxv.
100 Wilson, "Stieglitz Exhibition," 102.
101 Parker, "Edmund Wilson," 535.
102 Parker, "Book," 495.
103 Parker, 497.
104 Parker, "Literary Rotarians," 505.
105 Parker, "Professor," 499–500.
106 Parker, "Sophisticated Poetry," 562.
107 Parker, 562.

Bibliography

Adler, Renata. *Gone: The Last Days of "The New Yorker."* New York: Simon and Schuster, 1999.

Agee, James, and Walker Evans. *Let Us Now Praise Famous Men.* 1941. Boston, MA: Houghton Mifflin, 1969.

Bombaci, Nancy. "Performing Mindblindness: Gertrude Stein's Autistic Ethos of Modernism." *Journal of Gender Studies* 21, no. 2 (June 2012): 133–50. https://doi.org/10.1080/09589236.2012.661567.

Bourdieu, Pierre. *Distinction: A Social Critique of the Judgement of Taste.* Cambridge, MA: Harvard University Press, 1984.

Brake, Laurel. *Subjugated Knowledges: Journalism, Gender, and Literature in the Nineteenth Century.* New York: New York University Press, 1994.

Fiedler, Leslie. *What Was Literature? Class, Culture, and Mass Society.* New York: Touchstone, 1982.

Flanner, Janet. "Art (Commerce)." 1926. In Flanner, *Paris Was Yesterday*, 9–10.

———. "Art (Semantics)." 1926. In Flanner, *Paris Was Yesterday*, 9.

———. "D. H. Lawrence (1885–1930)."1930. In Flanner, *Paris Was Yesterday*, 64–65.

———. "Diaghilev's Ballet." 1929. In Flanner, *Paris Was Yesterday*, 55–56.

———. "François Mauriac." 1933. In Flanner, *Paris Was Yesterday*, 107–08.

———. "Goethe in Hollywood: Thomas Mann." 1941. In Flanner, *Janet Flanner's World*, 165–88.

———. "The Infinite Pleasure of Sylvia Beach." 1959. In Flanner, *Janet Flanner's World*, 309–14.

———. *Janet Flanner's World: Uncollected Writings 1932–1975.* New York: Harcourt, Brace, Jovanovich, 1979.

———. "Little Review." 1929. In Flanner, *Paris Was Yesterday*, 56–57.

———. *Men and Monuments: Profiles of Picasso, Matisse, Braque, and Malraux.* Introduction by Rosamond Bernier. 1957. New York: De Capo Press, 1990.

———. *Paris Was Yesterday 1925–1939.* Edited by Irving Drutman. New York: Harcourt, Brace, Jovanovich, 1972.

———. "*Sanctuaire.*" 1934. In Flanner, *Paris Was Yesterday*, 116–17.

———. "*Ulysses.*" 1927. In Flanner, *Paris Was Yesterday*, 17–18.

Frus, Phyllis. *The Politics and Poetics of Journalistic Narrative: The Timely and the Timeless.* New York: Cambridge University Press, 1994.

Gill, Brendan. Introduction to *The Portable Dorothy Parker*, by Dorothy Parker, xiii–xxviii. New York: Penguin Books, 1976.

Glass, Loren. *Authors Inc.: Literary Celebrity in the Modern United States, 1880–1980.* New York: New York University Press, 2004.

Gold, Michael. "Gertrude Stein: A Literary Idiot." Center for Programs in Contemporary Writing, University of Pennsylvania. Last modified July 18, 2007. www.writing.upenn.edu/~afilreis/88/stein-per-gold.html.

Humphries, David T. *Different Dispatches: Journalism in American Modernist Prose.* New York: Routledge, 2006.

Jaillant, Lise. *Modernism, Middlebrow and the Literary Canon: The Modern Library Series, 1917–1955.* New York: Routledge, 2016.

———. "*Shucks, We've Got Glamour Girls Too!* Gertrude Stein, Bennett Cerf and the Culture of Celebrity." *Journal of Modern Literature* 39, no. 1 (Fall 2015): 149–69. https://doi.org/10.2979/jmodelite.39.1.149.

Keyser, Catherine. *Playing Smart: New York Women Writers and Modern Magazine Culture.* New Brunswick, NJ: Rutgers University Press, 2010.

Kunkel, Thomas. *Genius in Disguise: Harold Ross of "The New Yorker."* New York: Random House, 1995.

Latham, Sean. *Am I a Snob? Modernism and the Novel.* Ithaca, NY: Cornell University Press, 2003.

Meade, Marion. *Dorothy Parker: What Fresh Hell Is This?* New York: Penguin Books, 1987.

Meyer, Steven. *Irresistible Dictation: Gertrude Stein and the Correlations of Writing and Science.* Stanford, CA: Stanford University Press, 2001.

Middleton, Peter. *The Inward Gaze: Masculinity and Subjectivity in Modern Culture.* New York: Routledge, 1992.

Parker, Dorothy. "A Book of Great Short Stories." 1927. In Parker, *Portable Dorothy Parker*, 494–97.

———. *Complete Broadway 1918–1925.* Bloomington, IN: iUniverse, 2014.

———. "Edmund Wilson: *The American Earthquake*; Jack Kerouac: *The Subterraneans*; Edna Ferber: *Ice Palace.*" 1958. In Parker, *Portable Dorothy Parker*, 533–37.

———. "Literary Rotarians." 1928. In Parker, *Portable Dorothy Parker*, 504–07.

———. *The Portable Dorothy Parker.* Edited by Marion Meade. New York: Penguin Books, 2006.

———. "The Professor Goes In for Sweetness and Light." 1927. In Parker, *Portable Dorothy Parker*, 497–500.

———. "The Season Plucks at the Coverlet." In Parker, *Complete Broadway*, 376–82. Originally published in *Ainslee's*, July 1923.

———. "Sophisticated Poetry—And the Hell with It." In Parker, *Portable Dorothy Parker*, 560–62. Originally published in *New Masses*, June 27, 1939.

———. "Three Rousing Cheers." In Parker, *Complete Broadway*, 341–48. Originally published in *Ainslee's*, February 1923.

———. "Words, Words, Words." 1931. In Parker, *Portable Dorothy Parker*, 520–24.

Pater, Walter. *The Renaissance: Studies in Art and Poetry*. 1893. Mineola, NY: Dover Publications, 1994.

Pettit, Rhonda S. *A Gendered Collision: Sentimentalism and Modernism in Dorothy Parker's Poetry and Fiction*. Madison, NJ: Fairleigh Dickinson University Press, 2000.

Radway, Janice A. *A Feeling for Books: The Book-of-the-Month Club, Literary Taste, and Middle-Class Desire*. Chapel Hill: University of North Carolina Press, 1997.

Ross, Harold. "The New Yorker Prospectus." 1924. In *Genius in Disguise: Harold Ross of "The New Yorker,"* by Thomas Kunkel, 439–41. New York: Random House, 1995.

Stein, Gertrude. *The Autobiography of Alice B. Toklas*. 1933. New York: Vintage Books, 1961.

———. "Composition as Explanation." 1926. In Stein, *Writings and Lectures*, 21–30.

———. *Everybody's Autobiography*. 1937. New York: Vintage Books, 1967.

———. "The Gradual Making of *The Making of Americans*." [1941]. In Stein, *Writings and Lectures*, 84–98.

———. "Poetry and Grammar." 1940. In Stein, *Writings and Lectures*, 125–47.

———. "What Are Master-Pieces and Why Are There So Few of Them?" 1940. In Stein, *Writings and Lectures*, 148–56.

———. *Writings and Lectures 1909–1945*. Edited by Patricia Meyerowitz. Baltimore, MD: Penguin Books, 1967.

Walker, Nancy. "The Remarkably Constant Reader: Dorothy Parker as Book Reviewer." *Studies in American Humor*, n.s., 3, no. 4 (1997): 1–14.

West, Rebecca. "The Strange Necessity." 1928. In *The Strange Necessity: Essays and Reviews*, 13–198. London: Virago Press, 1987.

Will, Barbara. *Gertrude Stein, Modernism, and the Problem of "Genius."* Edinburgh: Edinburgh University Press, 2000.

Wilson, Edmund. "The Stieglitz Exhibition." 1925. In *The American Earthquake*, 98–103. 1958. New York: Farrar, Straus and Giroux, 1979.

Wineapple, Brenda. *Genêt: A Biography of Janet Flanner*. London: HarperCollins, 2005.

10
THE NEW JOURNALISM, 1960–80

John J. Pauly

Every claim that a social phenomenon is "new" seems destined to arouse controversy.[1] Such was certainly the case with the New Journalism, a stylized, in-depth approach to reporting that took shape in American magazines like *Esquire*, *New York*, and *Harper's* in the 1960s. The term *new* had been applied before in the history of journalism—to the "yellow" journalism of Joseph Pulitzer and William Randolph Hearst in the United States, to the crusading reporting of William Stead, and to Alfred Harmsworth's mass daily newspapers in Britain.[2] As with other usages in the fifties and sixties—the New Look in fashion and design, the New Wave in cinema, the New Left in politics, the New Middle Class in sociology—the term typically signaled a felt departure from the sensibilities and assumptions of the past.

By the end of the 1970s, the upper-case term *New Journalism* would be used to reference the notable works of a select group of successful writers. But Americans' talk about a "new journalism" in the 1960s first emerged as a lower-case observation about how market forces, youth culture, political unrest, and writers' personal ambitions were challenging journalism's longstanding practices and norms. This may be the most plausible way to make sense of the meaning of the New Journalism: not as a canon of exceptional works that shared a literary style but as a shorthand commonly used to describe far-ranging changes in the mass media and American culture.[3] In the name of a new journalism, writers, editors, publishers, readers, and critics called for reporters to interpret rather than merely record the social and political chaos around them.[4] Magazines and books challenged the preeminence of the daily newspaper as a venue for journalists' best work. In-depth stories about cultural trends earned a place of respect alongside more traditional political reporting. Writers felt empowered by their readers to deploy more inventive literary techniques and even to incorporate more personal voice in their stories.[5] The new journalism seemed more attuned to the times—less beholden to the tired institutional order that daily newspapers served, less fusty in its reading of popular culture, more edgy in its style of expression. For at least a small group of exceptional writers, new journalism would make freelance reporting financially lucrative, through book contracts, college lectures, movie rights, and scriptwriting for film and television.

Scholars largely agree upon the major works that have come to be considered New Journalism.[6] The provenance often begins with Norman Mailer's *Esquire* story about the 1960 Democratic convention, "Superman Comes to the Supermart," which foretold a new approach to political reporting.[7] It then typically includes Gay Talese's celebrity profiles for *Esquire* and his books on the *New York Times* and a Mafia family; Tom Wolfe and Jimmy Breslin's features on city life for the *New York Herald Tribune*'s Sunday supplement; Truman Capote's blockbuster "nonfiction novel" about the random killing of a Kansas farm family; Hunter Thompson's ethnographic report on the Hell's Angels motorcycle gang; John Gregory Dunne's books on a grape workers' strike and the operations of a Hollywood studio; Joan Didion's vignettes of California culture; Mailer's Pulitzer Prize-winning report on the march on the Pentagon; George Goodman's parables of Wall Street, written under the pseudonym "Adam Smith"; Michael Herr and John Sack's Vietnam stories for *Esquire*; and Wolfe's books on Ken Kesey and the Merry Pranksters and on Leonard Bernstein's party for the Black Panthers.[8] Wolfe and Johnson's 1973 anthology also included works by Joe Eszterhas, Joe McGinniss, George Plimpton, Terry Southern, and Garry Wills, all of whom were occasionally cited as practitioners of the new form.[9]

Examples of an emerging new journalism were even more widely available than that, however. Commentators would variously point to stories by James Baldwin, Brock Brower, Claude Brown, Timothy Crouse, Marshall Frady, David Halberstam, Larry L. King, Seymour Krim, Thomas Morgan, Dick Schaap, Gail Sheehy, Gloria Steinem, Dan Wakefield, and Tom Wicker as examples of the trend. Nor was such work confined to the pages of *Esquire*, *Harper's*, and *New York*. The *Saturday Evening Post*, *Life*, *Look*, *Playboy*, *Atlantic Monthly*, *Sports Illustrated*, *Village Voice*, and *National Observer* occasionally tried some version of it, and *Rolling Stone* would use stories by Wolfe, Thompson, and Eszterhas to build its reputation as a venue for serious writing. By the mid-1970s, interest in the New Journalism began to fade. Wolfe vowed not to speak of it again, although he continued to tweak the New York literary establishment.[10] The editors who shepherded so much of the original work—Harold Hayes at *Esquire*, Clay Felker at *New York*, and Willie Morris at *Harper's*—had lost their positions and moved on to other projects. One last flurry of notable books appeared in the late 1970s—by C. D. B. Bryan, Herr, Wolfe, Didion, Mailer, and Talese—but by then commentators mostly considered these the latest works from mature, successful writers rather than exemplars of an emerging "new journalism."[11]

Accounts of the New Journalism often emphasize the controversy that swirled around it. But that controversy was somewhat slow to develop. Arguments about the New Journalism heated up in the late 1960s, years after its earliest and most influential examples had been commissioned, published, read, and reviewed. Early stories by Mailer, Talese, and Wolfe often elicited curiosity and respect, even from traditional journalists. The political reporter Murray Kempton sent Mailer a telegraph saying that the Kennedy campaign was circulating "Superman Comes to the Supermart" and that the piece was much admired among the Washington press corps. "I spent most of the last week with Kennedy walking around with your Esquire article forcing my brother clods to read it," Kempton wrote, "and every one of them said that it was a miracle of anticipation and quite close to the best political article that any of them had ever read."[12] Wolfe's stories about youth culture earned him invitations from press associations whose members recognized that they needed to do a better job of making their papers more contemporary. He joined advice columnist Ann Landers on a panel on "Attracting Young Adult Readers" at the 1966 annual convention of the American Society of Newspaper Editors. (He advised editors that "there is absolutely nothing in the newspaper that is of any immediate interest" to 15- to 30-year-olds, that young people did not care as much about politics and current events as the editors did, and that newspapers should cover status struggles instead.[13]) A representative of the Virginia Press Association invited Wolfe to speak to members about "where newspapers fail in their general approach to teens." He hoped that Wolfe might inspire his older reporters: "How do you tell reporters who are still milling out the same style stories popular a couple of decades ago that it's time they got with the program?"[14] References to the new style of journalism being practiced at *Esquire* and the *Herald Tribune* showed up in nationally syndicated columns. Walter Winchell praised Talese's vignettes of city life and touted him as "our choice for that paper to inherit Meyer Berger's terribly missed col'm about Manhattan. His upcoming Esquire piece, 'New York Unnoticed,' proves it."[15] Dorothy Kilgallen proposed that "Tom Wolfe ought to be given some kind of prize in journalism for his brilliantly funny account of Robert Morgenthau's tour of Coney Island."[16] Even a reporter like Breslin, so deeply identified with New York City, gained a national audience through the newspaper reviews of his books, his sports stories for the *Journal-American* and *Saturday Evening Post*, the *Herald Tribune*'s syndication of his column, and his appearances on popular network television programs like *The Tonight Show*.

Reporters and editors were willing to think about a "new journalism," in part because they themselves had spent the last decade debating the need for more interpretive reporting.[17] Since the 1930s, journalists had pondered the increasing complexity of the economic, political, and social issues confronting the nation. Covering Senator Joseph McCarthy's inquisitions and the Civil Rights Movement had forced them to admit the limitations of their commitment to objectivity and impartiality.[18] Lester Markel, the longtime Sunday editor of the *New York Times* (who would become one of the New Journalism's most caustic critics), urged journalists to acknowledge that they were more than mere recorders of events. Editors, he said, constantly made choices—about what stories to assign, how to cover them, and where to place them in the newspaper.[19] For Markel, interpretation was a basic function of journalism, standing somewhere between the recording of basic facts and the expression of editorial opinion. He believed that journalists could explain the significance of events with a measure of objectivity. Reporters, editors, and publishers would continue to debate the point from the 1950s through the early 1970s in trade publications like the *Bulletin of the American Society of Newspaper Editors* and at their annual conventions. The New Journalism, when it arrived, would offer yet another example for the profession to consider and critique.

The deepest criticisms of the New Journalism consistently emphasized two questions: the supposed originality of its storytelling techniques and the trustworthiness of its reporting. In the introduction to his anthology, Wolfe proposed a list of literary techniques that he thought distinguished his and others' work: its scene-by-scene, cinematic structuring of plot; its novelistic use of full dialogue; its effort to reconstruct a subject's interior point of view using interview materials; its immersive reporting; and its attention to symbolically significant details of setting, speech, dress, manner, and behavior (or the re-creation of what he termed the "status sphere" of a group).[20] But Wolfe himself acknowledged that such techniques had been used before in reporting.[21] *New Yorker* writers such as John Hersey, Joe Mitchell, Lillian Ross, and A. J. Liebling had employed similar techniques for decades.[22] Predecessors could even be found in late nineteenth- and early twentieth-century newspapers.[23] And although Wolfe may not have noticed it, by the late 1960s American newspapers had begun using more narrative techniques in their everyday reporting.[24] Several New Journalists continued writing both fiction and nonfiction. Breslin, Didion, Dunne, Mailer, and Southern all published novels as well as journalism in the 1960s and 1970s.[25] Capote wrote short stories for *Esquire*. Wolfe and Thompson acquired publishers' contracts for novels that they planned to write. Talese spoke often about the influence of short story writers Irwin Shaw and John O'Hara on his own writing.[26] Dunne and Didion, Southern, and Eszterhas began writing film scripts for Hollywood. And Mailer repeatedly declared to anyone who would listen that the novel was his true mistress. In short, New Journalists often imagined careers in which they would move freely between fictional and journalistic forms.

Critics worried that the New Journalism's embrace of fictional techniques came at a significant cost. Some techniques—such as reconstructing a subject's feelings and thoughts using interview responses, or Wolfe's mimicking of his subjects' voices in his own narrative—violated familiar American journalistic norms, leading critics to question the New Journalists' commitment to factual reporting and professional standards of objectivity. That criticism darkened in tone after the *New York Herald Tribune* published Wolfe's biting satire of the *New Yorker* in April 1965, during that magazine's fortieth anniversary year. His story appeared in two installments in the *Herald Tribune*'s Sunday supplement, *New York*: "Tiny Mummies! The True Story of the Ruler of 43rd Street's Land of the Walking Dead!" and "Lost in the Whichy Thicket." The first portrayed a sclerotic institution, living on its past glories. The second focused upon *New Yorker* editor William Shawn's idiosyncratic personality and management of the magazine. The uproar was immediate: an attempt by Shawn to convince *Tribune* publisher Jock Whitney not to run the second installment; news coverage that made the controversy common knowledge; broadcast interviews with Wolfe; and letters of outrage from E. B. White, J. D. Salinger, Muriel Spark, Richard Rovere, Joseph Alsop, Walter Lippmann, Murray Kempton, Ved Mehta, and Renata Adler. In the coming months, Dwight Macdonald would condemn Wolfe as a "parajournalist" who sought to exploit "the factual authority of journalism and the atmospheric license of fiction."[27] Looking back on the episode in his history of the *Herald Tribune*, Richard Kluger criticized Wolfe's reliance on "hearsay, indulgent style, and tendentiousness to carry off his performance."[28]

The intensity of the reaction reflected, in part, the *New Yorker* staff's outrage over Wolfe's targeting of Shawn. But, as importantly, Wolfe's stories had impertinently questioned New York literary life's hierarchy of style, sensibility, and social status. Of course, Wolfe was hardly the first to suggest that the *New Yorker* was in decline. A 1962 article by Krim in the *Village Voice* had mourned the *New Yorker*'s "plump-bellied complacency."[29] Responding to critics of his *Voice* article, Krim later reaffirmed his judgment that the *New Yorker* had become "the passive well-coifed little queen of rough trade cultural forces that have surpassed it in vigor, wit, pertinence, rhythm, design, excitement, surprise, illumination and selfbelief."[30] Some readers of Wolfe's piece also thought the comeuppance long overdue; southern writer William Styron, whose novel was once harshly reviewed in the *New Yorker*, quoted Corinthians: "I receive of the Lord that which also I delivered."[31] White's own protest letter admitted that "for 40 years, *The New Yorker* has employed parody, irony, ridicule and satire to deflate or diminish persons and institutions it deemed fair game."[32] It had gleefully lampooned Ernest Hemingway, Raymond Chandler, and Archibald MacLeish.[33] Most famously, in 1936 Wolcott Gibbs had mercilessly mocked *Time* style and ridiculed publisher Henry Luce's intellectual and social pretensions.[34] It was, in fact, a *New Yorker* parody of *New York* that prompted Wolfe's satire. That "Talk of the Town" item a year earlier had imagined Lippmann and theater critic Walter Kerr adopting the jangly "second-person singular" style of Breslin and Wolfe.[35]

Norman Sims has suggested that Wolfe's articles be read as social criticism rather than journalism, more akin to later works such as *The Painted Word* and *From Bauhaus to Our House*.[36] Nonetheless, critics would regularly point to Wolfe's parody as an example of the New Journalism's failure to honor professional standards of factual reporting. Over the next several years, other examples seemed to lend credence to such objections. Capote described his "nonfiction novel" *In Cold Blood* (published first in the *New Yorker* as a four-part series, then significantly revised as a book) as "immaculately factual," noting that years of research had gone into it. Capote had even bragged about his ability to recall long passages of dialogue without taking notes.[37] But an *Esquire* article cited instances of exaggeration and his invention of crucial scenes.[38] Michael Herr admitted to using composite characters in his original *Esquire* story on the battle for Hue, and years later seemed to say that he himself thought of *Dispatches* as fiction.[39] Gail Sheehy created the composite character "Redpants" for her *New York* story about prostitutes and pimps.[40] In a widely read 1980 essay, Hersey stridently condemned Wolfe, Capote, and Mailer for their misuse of fictional techniques, hoping to drive a stake through the heart of the form (although he himself had once used composite characters and would twice be credibly accused of plagiarism).[41] All these apparent blurrings disturbed journalists, who had staked the integrity and cultural authority of their profession on being factual, objective, and impersonal.[42]

A parallel version of that fact–fiction debate was emerging in literary studies at the same time. Years before Wolfe would mourn the decline of the novel and mock contemporary fiction's descent into myth and personal angst, American writers and critics were questioning whether the realist novel was up to that moment of extraordinary change. The nineteenth-century novels that Wolfe admired had taken for granted readers' sense of society's structure, manners, and morals.[43] The 1960s, however, had undercut shared assumptions about the social order, realist narrative conventions, and novelists' ability to make contemporary experience intelligible. "The American writer in the middle of the twentieth century has his hands full in trying to understand, and then describe, and then make credible much of American reality," Philip Roth wrote.[44] Many endorsed Roth's view, noting that novelists like Kurt Vonnegut, John Barth, Thomas Pynchon, and Donald Barthelme had turned to allegory, fable, and black humor instead.[45] The scholar Robert Scholes described such "fabulation" as a move away from "the pseudo-objectivity of realism toward a romance or an irony which will exploit language's distinctively human perspective on life."[46]

Journalists' discussion of fact/fiction and novelists' discussion of realism/fabulism would blend in subsequent literary criticism.[47] Some commentators sought to clarify the boundaries and purposes of factual and fictional genres.[48] Others argued that, because all writing is made and thus inherently fictional, genre distinctions are best understood as contractual agreements between writer and reader about the terms on which a writer offers a story and a reader chooses to engage it.[49] Literature scholars' growing interest in deconstruction inflected some of these discussions. Fact/fiction was just the sort of logocentric, binary thinking that deconstruction sought to destabilize.[50] Journalists' privileging of fact disguised the cultural authority being claimed in their acts of storytelling and implicitly denied fiction's power to make truth claims about the world.[51] In an influential essay, David Eason drew upon these insights to distinguish two types of New Journalists: "realists" like Wolfe and Talese, who believed that a stable, interpreting self could render the world intelligible through methods that dug more deeply beneath the surface, and "modernists" like Didion and Mailer, who found contemporary reality chaotic and indeterminate and were aware of the tentativeness of their own interpretations.[52]

There is yet another way to interpret the fact–fiction controversy, however: as an oblique commentary about the social status accorded different kinds of writing and the material conditions in which professional writers make a living. *Fact* and *fiction* denoted different literary genres, or modes of storytelling, each governed by its own narrative conventions, aesthetic standards of judgment, and reader expectations. But they were also marketing categories that implicitly referenced the institutions that published one kind of writing or the other, the kinds of readers such work attracted, the professional practices that brought such work into existence, and the assumptions editors, publishers, reviewers, and readers made about where a given work stood in relation to others in the marketplace and about the sorts of acclaim it deserved. The New Journalists had to find a home for their literary inventions within an existing system of media production, distribution, and promotion that designated some forms of writing as fact (the newspaper report) and some as fiction (the short story, the novel, and the film or television script).

A crisis in general interest magazines created new opportunities to publish the sort of stylized, longform, interpretive reporting that the New Journalists envisioned. After World War II, at the height of their influence, mass magazines such as *Collier's*, the *Saturday Evening Post*, *Life*, and *Look* suddenly found themselves squeezed on all sides. Accustomed to being the preferred platform for national consumer advertising, they now competed with television for the mass audience and with new special interest magazines for the upscale audience. The general interest magazines foolishly discounted subscriptions to retain their mass readership, but their increased overhead costs, diminished revenue from ads and subscriptions, and lower rates of renewal drove many of them deeper into debt and, soon, out of business. The new specialized publications offered a different challenge. They could narrowly tailor their editorial content and advertising material to the leisure and consumer interests of their readers.[53] Advertisers, in their turn, were willing to pay a premium to target smaller groups of readers who were demonstrably interested in their products and services. Those new magazines often cut deeply into lucrative areas of consumer purchasing, such as automobiles, travel, leisure, food, and sports.

Through the 1950s, the general interest magazines steadily reduced the number of short stories they published and sought more nonfiction prose on contemporary topics. By the early 1960s, the magazine article had emerged as a preferred venue for some American writers' best work. It had not always enjoyed such standing. For decades, the magazine article in consumer magazines had remained a serviceable but predictable form. Editors often dictated a story's angle and policed its treatment, effectively making writers somewhat interchangeable.[54] Now the magazine article offered a stage for virtuoso performance. In a widely noticed 1958 essay, Norman Podhoretz argued that writers once known for their novels were increasingly publishing nonfiction magazine articles.[55] Nor was he alone in that assessment. *Harper's* editor John Fischer called the magazine article "the characteristic literary medium of our generation," esteemed for its immediacy, national reach, and narrative flexibility.[56] For the writer Brock Brower, the article had become a vehicle for "the writer's individual intelligence and resolve" and less the product of the "corporate noodling of the journal in which it appears."[57] The ubiquity of television news encouraged readers' interest in fact-based narratives.[58] Looking back over the sixties, Ted Solotaroff saw a heightened demand for "topical writing" that emphasized "immediacy, relevance, involvement."[59] "There seems to be no important area in our national life," Solotaroff wrote,

> whether foreign policy or public welfare, family authority or community control, the city environment or the rural one, the elementary school or the university campus, the literary arts or the pop music scene—that does not bristle with the live issues of public concern.[60]

The magazine article allowed a talented journalist to develop a reputation as a shrewd cultural analyst—a role that enhanced the writer's market value as well. Organizational restrictions on subject matter, taste, and literary style had once constrained newspaper reporters, Krim observed, but when a New Journalist covered a story, he was "handling nothing less than the time in which he lives."[61] That was the opportunity that magazines such as *Esquire*, *New York*, and *Harper's* offered: for increasingly well-educated journalists to write in-depth stories on contemporary culture for sophisticated, intellectually curious readers. The newsweeklies had taken on that task, but *Time* and *Newsweek* prized organizational over personal authority; they assigned reporters to large issues but shackled them to an institutional voice. The editors of *Esquire* and *Harper's* hoped to free a writer's distinctive voice and to orchestrate each issue in a way that articulated the magazine's identity for readers and advertisers.

The publication schedules of monthly magazines favored imagination over immediacy. Magazines like *Esquire* and *Harper's* needed completed stories weeks or even months before publication, making it hard for them to seem as timely as the daily newspaper or even the weekly newsmagazine.[62] To convince readers to tackle a long story whose news value had passed, a monthly needed to emphasize the quality of its in-depth reporting, the stylishness of its writing, and its interpretive insight. A fortuitous convergence of cultural and economic forces made it financially plausible for freelance journalists to undertake such stories. As Garry Wills has noted, a magazine like *Esquire* might pay its writers a fee that seemed modest in proportion to the depth of research required, but promised a larger payoff if that article could be expanded into a book or movie script.[63] Such opportunities became more abundant in the 1960s. Postwar prosperity and the GI Bill had expanded access to higher education and fueled public interest in nonfiction. Indeed, Cornelius Ryan's 1959 bestseller about the invasion of Normandy, *The Longest Day*, demonstrated the potential popularity of saturation reporting and dramatic narrative journalism.[64] The expansion of the paperback book market meant that readers of modest means could build their own libraries. Paperbacks also found a new home as supplementary texts in college courses in the humanities and social sciences. Magazine articles could thus trigger a series of moneymaking opportunities, leading to trade book contracts and advances, paperback rights, book club editions, talk-show appearances, speeches on college campuses, and, sometimes, the sale of movie rights. Many of these collateral sources of income had been available to professional writers for decades, of course.[65] What was different in the 1960s was the power of a magazine article to command the attention of book publishers and of media conglomerates looking for blockbuster properties that they could promote across their media platforms.[66]

Book publishers' advances would subsidize much of the New Journalism. Capote set the bar (and raised eyebrows) when he received a $2 million advance for *In Cold Blood*.[67] As writers proved their marketability, their advances steadily increased. Talese received $2,500 for *New York: A Serendipiter's Journey* (1961), $11,500 for *The Kingdom and the Power* (1969), $30,000 for *Honor Thy Father* (1971), and $600,000 for *Thy Neighbor's Wife* (1980). Paperback rights for *Honor Thy Father* sold for $400,000, and the book was made into a television movie.[68] Mailer watched his advances grow, from $17,500 for *Armies of the Night* (1968) to $50,000 for *Miami and the Siege of Chicago* (1968), to $448,000 for *Of a Fire on the Moon* (1970).[69] Publishers were willing to offer such advances because they saw a series of New Journalism books make the bestseller lists in the 1960s and 1970s. Goodman's *The Money Game* (1968) sat at or near the top of the *Publishers' Weekly* nonfiction bestseller list for more than a year. McGinniss's *The Selling of the President, 1968* (1969) spent thirty-two weeks on that same list, and Talese's *The Kingdom and the Power* (1969) twenty-three weeks and his *Honor Thy Father* (1971) twenty-one weeks.[70] The popularity of New Journalism books confirmed each participant's hopes for the form. Editors demonstrated the power of their magazines to showcase a writer's work; publishers acquired book manuscripts with strong potential for paperback and subsidiary rights; and writers earned advances that enabled them to undertake long, in-depth stories.

Editors like Hayes, Morris, and Felker played a crucial role in shaping the form and tone of the New Journalism. They and their sub-editors typically did very little copy editing once a story had been assigned and written. But they aggressively participated in the early stages of a project, identifying potential topics, imagining the tone an article might take (in tune with the magazine's persona), and commissioning writers who could bring a vivid approach to the topic. They recognized that the caliber of writers they hoped to attract would be put off if asked simply to fill in the details of a piece that the editor had in mind (the arrangement long offered to many freelancers). Hayes described his approach to editing as more conceptual than mechanical. He and his staff worked closely with writers to identify the idea driving a story, then allowed those writers great leeway in the actual writing.[71] Morris was looking for journalism that felt more contemporary—less armchair philosophizing and reflection and more engagement with relevant social issues.[72] Felker insisted upon journalism that was "sharply angled," that had a distinctive point of view.[73] In each case, the editor was seeking stories that would announce his magazine's persona and make it distinctive in the eyes of readers and advertisers.

Interest in the New Journalism peaked shortly after publication of Wolfe and Johnson's anthology in summer 1973. That anthology, remembered today for Wolfe's bold introduction and its canonical selection of classic works, followed an odd and uncertain path to publication. It had begun with a proposal from Edward Johnson, then an English professor at Western Illinois University, that he and Wolfe compile a reader to be entitled *The New Nonfiction* for use in college freshman composition classes.[74] The project took almost six years to complete, delayed by discussions about which selections to include, the form Johnson's contributions should take, the departure of their book's original editor from Harper and Row, Wolfe's multiple revisions of his introduction, and his competing commitments to other articles and books. By the time the book appeared, much of Wolfe's introduction had been published in magazines.[75] In fall 1973, Wolfe announced that he would no longer talk publicly about the New Journalism.[76] He would revisit his argument about the contemporary novel's abandonment of realism in his 1978 Hopwood lecture at the University of Michigan, but without any mention of the New Journalism.[77] By the mid-1970s, the journalism profession had also turned its attention elsewhere. Bob Woodward and Carl Bernstein's reporting of the Watergate crisis encouraged skeptics' belief that the old journalism was good enough. Hard-nosed, factual, investigative reporting still had the power to inspire young reporters and make institutions quake.[78]

The New Journalism had left its mark nonetheless. It helped freelancers envision a way to support their extended, in-depth reporting. It freed journalists from the routinized forms of storytelling imposed by the daily newspaper—indeed, allowed them to imagine themselves no longer beholden to the demands of industrial news production. The New Journalism usefully complicated the aesthetic criteria that readers and critics had applied to literary works; no longer could one so easily treat journalism as a mundane carrier of fact, bereft of the creativity associated with fiction. Time and again, the New Journalists documented the power and reach of the image-worlds being created by the mass media.[79] Their exploration of that American imaginary led them to adopt the ethnographic methods of sociologists and anthropologists, in the process affirming the importance of culture as a legitimate object of reporting. Half a century after the New Journalism appeared, commentators continue to ponder its rightful place in a longer tradition of reporting.[80] But the New Journalism's parables of disorder also anticipated profound cultural conflicts that continue to vex Americans today. And that may yet prove to be its deepest contribution.

Notes

1 Tom Wolfe makes a similar observation about "the new" in "The New Journalism" (in Wolfe and Johnson, 23).
2 Roggenkamp, *Narrating the News*; Wiener, *Americanization*; Steele and de Nie, *Ireland*; Tulloch, "Eternal Recurrence."
3 I have explored that range of cultural reference in Pauly, "Politics."
4 A typical call for interpretation was Ethridge, "Meaning of the News."
5 One of the best accounts of the personalist turn remains Dan Wakefield's "The Personal Voice and the Impersonal Eye." For examples of how Wakefield managed his own stance as a reporter, see his collection *Between the Lines*.
6 To be sure, that accepted canon of works has its limits—most notably, its near exclusion of women writers. A history of women's role in the New Journalism would not only need to explore similar work by writers like Gloria Steinem, Nora Ephron, Gail Sheehy, Jane O'Reilly, Barbara Goldsmith, and Julie Baumgold but also to document the institutional practices that assigned women writers to stories of lesser scope and significance. Steinem has described her early editors refusing to assign her stories on politics and economics, despite her expertise. See Weber, *Reporter as Artist*, 80–81.
7 Mailer, "Superman."
8 Talese, *Kingdom and the Power* and *Honor Thy Father*; Wolfe, *Kandy-Kolored Tangerine-Flake Streamline Baby* and *Pump House Gang*; Breslin, *World of Jimmy Breslin*; Capote, *In Cold Blood*; Thompson, *Hell's Angels*; Dunne, *Delano* and *Studio*; Didion, *Slouching Towards Bethlehem*; Mailer, *Armies of the Night*; Smith, *Money Game*; Wolfe, *Electric Kool-Aid Acid Test* and *Radical Chic*.
9 The Wills, Sack, Herr, and Southern stories that Wolfe and Johnson chose for their anthology had also been included a few years earlier in *Esquire*'s anthology of its best nonfiction from the sixties. See Hayes, *Smiling Through the Apocalypse*.
10 Wolfe, "Literary Technique" and "Stalking the Billion-Footed Beast."
11 Bryan, *Friendly Fire*; Herr, *Dispatches*; Wolfe, *Right Stuff*; Didion, *White Album*; Mailer, *Executioner's Song*; Talese, *Thy Neighbor's Wife*.
12 Murray Kempton to Norman Mailer, telegram, [1960?], container 566.1, Norman Mailer Papers.
13 "Attracting Young Adult Readers," 170.
14 Tom Luce to Tom Wolfe, December 19, 1966, box 4, folder 2, Tom Wolfe Papers.
15 Winchell, "Broadway and Elsewhere." Inexpensive subscriptions to searchable newspaper databases like Newspaper Archive (https://newspaperarchive.com) and Newspapers (www.newspapers.com) now make it possible to track the various ways in which Americans outside of New York City might have become

aware of the emerging "new journalism." I chose these Winchell and Kilgallen examples to illustrate that general principle.
16 Kilgallen, "Broadway Bulletin Board."
17 I connect the profession's emerging discourse about interpretive reporting to the New Journalism debate in Pauly, "New Journalism."
18 On journalists' response to McCarthy, see Davies, *Postwar Decline*, 39–48. On the challenges of covering the civil rights movement, see Roberts and Klibanoff, *Race Beat*.
19 See Markel, "Case of 'Interpretation'" and "Interpretation?"
20 Wolfe explains these techniques in "The New Journalism" (in Wolfe and Johnson, 31–33). He uses the term "status sphere" in his story on Hugh Hefner, "King of the Status Dropouts." For more recent discussions of the techniques of literary journalism, see Sims, "Art of Literary Journalism"; Kramer, "Breakable Rules."
21 Wolfe, "New Journalism," in Wolfe and Johnson, 41–52.
22 Norman Sims describes that *New Yorker* tradition of literary journalism in *True Stories* (163–99).
23 Connery, "Third Way" and *Journalism and Realism*. On the historical relationship of journalism (and journalists) to fiction, see also Roggenkamp, *Narrating the News*; Robertson, *Stephen Crane*; Fishkin, *From Fact to Fiction*; Underwood, *Journalism and the Novel* and *Undeclared War*.
24 Schmidt, "Rediscovering Narrative." On the general turn to more interpretive reporting, see Forde, "Discovering the Explanatory Report"; Fink and Schudson, "Rise of Contextual Journalism"; Barnhurst and Mutz, "American Journalism." Pressman places the debate over interpretation within a broader set of changes in American newspapers in "Remaking the News."
25 Breslin, *Gang* and *World Without End*; Didion, *Run River*, *Play It*, and *Book of Common Prayer*; Dunne, *Vegas* and *True Confessions*; Mailer, *American Dream* and *Why Are We in Vietnam?*; Southern, *Blue Movie*.
26 See, for example, Talese's comments in Robinson, "New Journalism," 68–69.
27 Macdonald, "Parajournalism."
28 Kluger, *Paper*, 706.
29 Krim, "Who's Afraid," 172. Krim's original article "Who's Afraid of the *New Yorker* Now?" and his addendum are reprinted together in Krim, *Shake It*.
30 Krim, 185–86.
31 Styron, letter to the editor.
32 White, letter to the editor.
33 Menand, "Parodies Lost." The complete list of *New Yorker* parodies mentioned in Menand's essay is available in Michaud, "Reading List."
34 Gibbs, "Time … Fortune … Life … Luce." Gibbs's parody was itself a response to Ralph Ingersoll's 1934 *Fortune* story about the *New Yorker*. On the feud between Luce and *New Yorker* editor Harold Ross, see Lepore, "Untimely."
35 Purcell, "Jimmy Bennett."
36 Sims, *True Stories*, 233.
37 Plimpton, "Story."
38 Tompkins, "In Cold Fact." For recent, more detailed accounts of Capote's factual errors, see Voss, *Truman Capote*; De Bellis, "Visions and Revisions"; Axelrod, "In Cold Fact."
39 On *Esquire*'s in-house discussion of Herr's composites, see Polsgrove, *It Wasn't Pretty*, 176; Ciotti, "Michael Herr."
40 On *New York*'s in-house discussion of Sheehy's Redpants composite, see Weingarten, *Gang*, 273–76.
41 Hersey, "Legend on the License." Hersey describes his own use of composites in *Here to Stay* (107–08). Hersey's qualified apology for plagiarizing parts of Laurence Bergreen's biography of James Agee is quoted in Honan, "Hersey Apologizes." Anne Fadiman complains about Hersey's plagiarism of her parents' Bataan reporting in *Ex Libris* (109). In the 1980s, McGinniss's *Fatal Vision* would inspire Janet Malcolm's severe critique, *The Journalist and the Murderer*.
42 Weber's *Reporter as Artist* collects the most significant commentaries from the late 1960s and early 1970s. Those commentaries fairly represent the range of discussion, in those years, about fact versus fiction, objectivity versus subjectivity, and impartiality versus personalism in the New Journalism.
43 Hellmann, *Fables of Fact*, 9.
44 Roth, "Writing American Fiction," 225.
45 Roth, 10. A standard account of this turn toward fable is Scholes, *Fabulators*.
46 Scholes, *Fabulators*, 12.
47 Among the most important examples of the critical response: Murphy, *New Journalism*; Fishwick, *New Journalism*; Hollowell, *Fact and Fiction*; Zavarzadeh, *Mythopoeic Reality*; Hellmann, *Fables of Fact*;

Anderson, *Style as Argument*; Heyne, "Toward a Theory"; Eason, "New Journalism"; Lounsberry, *Art of Fact*; Frus, *Politics and Poetics*; Lehman, *Matters of Fact*; Flis, *Factual Fictions*.

48 See, for example, Murphy, *New Journalism*; Hollowell, *Fact and Fiction*; Zavarzadeh, *Mythopoeic Reality*; Weber, *Literature of Fact* and "Some Sort of Artistic Excitement." David Lodge similarly identifies empirical and fictional modes of the novel in *Novelist at the Crossroads* (3–34).

49 See, for example, Hellmann, *Fables of Fact*; Heyne, "Toward a Theory"; Lehman, *Matters of Fact*.

50 Martin McQuillan succinctly describes five key strategies used by deconstruction in *Deconstruction: A Reader* (1–43).

51 Frus, *Politics and Poetics*, and Flis, *Factual Fictions*, both follow out the implications of this deconstructive turn in their analyses of the fact–fiction binary. Though her interest is the documentary novel, Foley takes a similar tack in *Telling the Truth*.

52 Eason, "New Journalism."

53 Abrahamson, *Magazine-Made America*; Abrahamson and Polsgrove, "Right Niche," 112.

54 Hayes describes changes in the magazine article in Robinson, "New Journalism," 67–68.

55 Podhoretz, "Article as Art."

56 Fischer, "Helping Hand."

57 Brower, "Article," 138.

58 Brower, "Of Nothing but Facts."

59 Solotaroff, "Introduction," 163.

60 Solotaroff, 162.

61 Krim, "Newspaper as Literature," 181.

62 Wills, *Lead Time*, ix–x.

63 Wills, xv.

64 Shapiro, "Reporter Who Time Forgot." The popularity of Ryan's book, and of the film it inspired, also demonstrated the financial possibilities of book-length reporting.

65 West, *American Authors*.

66 Whiteside, *Blockbuster Complex*.

67 Gilroy, "Book."

68 Figures on Talese's advances are in Schwartz, "U.A. Pays $2.5 Million."

69 Information about Mailer's book advances and magazine fees can be found in containers 601.8, 834.5, and 835.5 of the Norman Mailer Papers.

70 Figures are from Justice, *Bestseller Index*.

71 Hayes explains his approach to editing in "'Spilled Coffee.'"

72 "A Prospectus (of Sorts) for Harper's Magazine," Part II, Editors' File 1944–1979, box 103, folder 2, Harper's Magazine Records.

73 Clay Felker to J. Daniels, B. Dobell, M. Glaser, T. Morgan, and S. Zalaznick, memo, September 4, 1974, New York Magazine, Editorial Memos, 1974–1976, box 3, Clay Felker Papers.

74 E. W. Johnson to Tom Wolfe, October 17, 1967, box 5, folder 1, Tom Wolfe Papers.

75 "New Journalism," *Dateline*; "New Journalism," *Bulletin*; "Birth"; "New Journalism," *New York*; and "Why They Aren't Writing."

76 Wolfe mentions his resolution not to speak publicly again about the New Journalism in "Tom Wolfe Translated from the Original."

77 Wolfe, "Literary Technique."

78 "What Ever Happened to the New Journalism?"

79 Eason, "New Journalism."

80 See, for example, Boynton, *New New Journalism*.

Bibliography

Abrahamson, David. *Magazine-Made America: The Cultural Transformation of the Postwar Periodical*. Cresskill, NJ: Hampton Press, 1996.

Abrahamson, David, and Carol Polsgrove. "The Right Niche: Consumer Magazines and Advertisers." In *The Enduring Book: Print Culture in Postwar America*, edited by David Paul Nord, Joan Shelley Rubin, and Michael Schudson, 107–18. Vol. 5 of *A History of the Book in America*. Chapel Hil, NC: University of North Carolina Press, in association with the American Antiquarian Society, 2009.

Anderson, Chris. *Style as Argument: Contemporary American Nonfiction*. Carbondale, IL: Southern Illinois University Press, 1987.

"Attracting Young Adult Readers." In *Proceedings of the 1966 Convention of the American Society of Newspaper Editors*, 168–74. Easton, PA: American Society of Newspaper Editors, 1966.

Axelrod, Daniel. "In Cold Fact, In Cold Blood: Exposing Errors, Finding Fabrication and Unearthing Capote's Unethical Behavior." *Literary Journalism: The Newsletter of the International Association for Literary Journalism Studies* 8, no. 1 (Winter 2014): 18–31.

Barnhurst, Kevin G., and Diana Mutz. "American Journalism and the Decline in Event-Centered Reporting." *Journal of Communication* 47, no. 4 (Autumn 1997): 27–52.

Boynton, Robert S. *The New New Journalism: Conversations with America's Best Nonfiction Writers on Their Craft*. New York: Vintage Books, 2005.

Breslin, Jimmy. *The Gang That Couldn't Shoot Straight*. New York: Viking, 1969.

———. *The World of Jimmy Breslin*. New York: Viking Press, 1967.

———. *World Without End, Amen*. New York: Viking Press, 1973.

Brower, Brock. "The Article." In Weber, *Reporter as Artist*, 137–48.

———. "Of Nothing but Facts." *American Scholar* 33, no. 4 (1964): 613–18.

Bryan, C. D. B. *Friendly Fire*. New York: Putnam, 1976.

Capote, Truman. *In Cold Blood*. New York: Random House, 1966.

Ciotti, Paul. "Michael Herr: A Man of Few Words: What Is a Great American Writer Doing Holed Up in London, and Why Has He Been So Quiet All These Years?" *Los Angeles Times*, April 15, 1990.

Connery, Thomas B. *Journalism and Realism: Rendering American Life*. Evanston, IL: Northwestern University Press, 2011.

———. "A Third Way to Tell the Story: American Literary Journalism at the Turn of the Century." In Sims, *Literary Journalism*, 3–20.

Davies, David R. *The Postwar Decline of American Newspapers, 1945–1965: The History of American Journalism*. Westport, CT: Praeger, 2006.

De Bellis, Jack. "Visions and Revisions: Truman Capote's *In Cold Blood*." *Journal of Modern Literature* 7, no. 3 (1979): 519–36.

Didion, Joan. *A Book of Common Prayer*. New York: Simon and Schuster, 1977.

———. *Play It as It Lays*. New York: Farrar, Straus and Giroux, 1970.

———. *Run River*. New York: Ivan Obolensky, 1963.

———. *Slouching Towards Bethlehem*. New York: Farrar, Straus and Giroux, 1968.

———. *The White Album*. New York: Simon and Schuster, 1979.

Dunne, John Gregory. *Delano: The Story of the California Grape Strike*. New York: Farrar, Straus and Giroux, 1967.

———. *The Studio*. New York: Farrar, Straus and Giroux, 1969.

———. *True Confessions*. New York: Dutton, 1977.

———. *Vegas: A Memoir of a Dark Season*. New York: Random House, 1974.

Eason, David L. "The New Journalism and the Image-World: Two Modes of Organizing Experience." *Critical Studies in Mass Communication* 1, no. 1 (1984): 51–65. https://doi.org/10.1080/15295038409360013.

Ethridge, Mark. "The Meaning of the News: The Era of Interpretative Writing." *Vital Speeches of the Day*, May 15, 1962, 472–75. Speech delivered at Marquette University, Milwaukee, WI, March 20, 1962.

Fadiman, Anne. *Ex Libris: Confessions of a Common Reader*. New York: Farrar, Straus and Giroux, 1998.

Felker, Clay. Papers. David M. Rubenstein Rare Book and Manuscript Library, Duke University, Durham, NC.

Fink, Katherine, and Michael Schudson. "The Rise of Contextual Journalism, 1950s–2000s." *Journalism* 15, no. 1 (January 2014): 3–20. https://doi.org/10.1177/1464884913479015.

Fischer, John. "Helping Hand for a Literary Upstart." *Harper's*, September 1963.

Fishkin, Shelley Fisher. *From Fact to Fiction: Journalism and Imaginative Writing in America*. Baltimore, MD: Johns Hopkins University Press, 1985.

Fishwick, Marshall, ed. *New Journalism*. Bowling Green, OH: Bowling Green University Popular Press, 1975.

Flis, Leonora. *Factual Fictions: Narrative Truth and the Contemporary American Documentary Novel*. Newcastle upon Tyne, UK: Cambridge Scholars Publishing, 2010.

Foley, Barbara. *Telling the Truth: The Theory and Practice of Documentary Fiction*. Ithaca, NY: Cornell University Press, 1986.

Forde, Kathy Roberts. "Discovering the Explanatory Report in American Newspapers." *Journalism Practice* 1, no. 2 (2007): 227–44. https://doi.org/10.1080/17512780701275531.

Frus, Phyllis. *The Politics and Poetics of Journalistic Narrative: The Timely and the Timeless*. New York: Cambridge University Press, 1994.

Gibbs, Wolcott. "Time … Fortune … Life … Luce." *New Yorker*, November 28, 1936.

Gilroy, Harry. "A Book in a New Form Earns $2-Million for Truman Capote." *New York Times*, December 31, 1965.
Harper's Magazine Records, 1847–1983. Manuscript Division, Library of Congress, Washington, DC.
Hayes, Harold, ed. *Smiling Through the Apocalypse: Esquire's History of the Sixties*. New York: McCall, 1970.
———. "'Spilled Coffee on the First Page'—How Author Regards Editor & Vice Versa." *Authors Guild Bulletin*, May–June 1968.
Hellmann, John. *Fables of Fact: The New Journalism as New Fiction*. Urbana, IL: University of Illinois, 1981.
Herr, Michael. *Dispatches*. New York: Knopf, 1977.
Hersey, John. *Here to Stay*. New York: Knopf, 1963.
———. "The Legend on the License." *Yale Review* 70, no. 1 (1980): 1–15.
Heyne, Erich. "Toward a Theory of Literary Nonfiction." *MFS: Modern Fiction Studies* 33, no. 3 (Autumn 1987): 479–90.
Hollowell, John. *Fact and Fiction: The New Journalism and the Nonfiction Novel*. Chapel Hill: University of North Carolina Press, 1977.
Honan, William H. "Hersey Apologizes to a Writer Over an Article on Agee." *New York Times*, July 22, 1988.
Ingersoll, Ralph. "*The New Yorker*." *Fortune*, August 1934.
Justice, Keith L. *Bestseller Index: All Books, by Author, on the Lists of "Publishers Weekly" and the "New York Times" Through 1990*. Jefferson, NC: McFarland, 1998.
Kilgallen, Dorothy. "Broadway Bulletin Board." *Middletown (OH) Journal*, November 2, 1962.
Kluger, Richard. *The Paper: The Life and Death of the New York "Herald Tribune."* New York: Knopf, 1986.
Kramer, Mark. "Breakable Rules for Literary Journalists." In Sims and Kramer, *Literary Journalism*, 21–34.
Krim, Seymour. "The Newspaper as Literature/Literature as Leadership." In Weber, *Reporter as Artist*, 169–87.
———. *Shake It for the World, Smartass*. New York: Dial Press, 1970.
———. "Who's Afraid of the *New Yorker* Now?" In *Shake It*, 171–86.
Lehman, Daniel W. *Matters of Fact: Reading Nonfiction over the Edge*. Columbus, OH: Ohio State University Press, 1997.
Lepore, Jill. "Untimely." *New Yorker*, April 19, 2010.
Lodge, David. *The Novelist at the Crossroads and Other Essays on Fiction and Criticism*. Ithaca, NY: Cornell University Press, 1971.
Lounsberry, Barbara. *The Art of Fact: Contemporary Artists of Nonfiction*. New York: Greenwood Press, 1990.
Macdonald, Dwight. "Parajournalism, or Tom Wolfe and His Magic Writing Machine." Review of *The Kandy-Kolored Tangerine-Flake Streamline Baby*, by Tom Wolfe. *New York Review of Books*, August 26, 1965.
Mailer, Norman. *An American Dream*. New York: Dial Press, 1965.
———. *The Armies of the Night: History as a Novel, the Novel as History*. New York: New American Library, 1968.
———. *The Executioner's Song*. New York: Little, Brown, 1979.
———. Papers. Harry Ransom Center, University of Texas at Austin.
———. "Superman Comes to the Supermart." *Esquire*, November 1960.
———. *Why Are We in Vietnam?* New York: G. P. Putnam's Sons, 1967.
Malcolm, Janet. *The Journalist and the Murderer*. New York: Knopf, 1990.
Markel, Lester. "The Case of 'Interpretation.'" *Bulletin of the American Society of Newspaper Editors*, April 1, 1953, 1–2.
———. "Interpretation?—'Yes!'" *Bulletin of the American Society of Newspaper Editors*, January 1, 1961, 1–2.
McGinniss, Joe. *Fatal Vision*. New York: G. P. Putnam's Sons, 1983.
McQuillan, Martin, ed. *Deconstruction: A Reader*. New York: Routledge, 2003.
Menand, Louis. "Parodies Lost: The Art of Making Fun." *New Yorker*, September 20, 2010.
Michaud, Jon. "Reading List: Parodies." Double Take, *New Yorker*, September 9, 2010. www.newyorker.com/books/double-take/reading-list-parodies.
Murphy, James E. *The New Journalism: A Critical Perspective*. Journalism Monographs no. 34. Lexington, KY: Association for Education in Journalism, May 1974.
Pauly, John J. "The New Journalism and the Struggle for Interpretation." *Journalism* 15, no. 5 (July 2014): 589–604. https://doi.org/10.1177/1464884914529208.
———. "The Politics of the New Journalism." In Sims, *Literary Journalism*, 110–29.
Plimpton, George. "The Story Behind a Nonfiction Novel." *New York Times Book Review*, January 16, 1966.
Podhoretz, Norman. "The Article as Art." *Harper's*, July 1958.
Polsgrove, Carol. *It Wasn't Pretty, Folks, But Didn't We Have Fun? "Esquire" in the Sixties*. New York: Norton, 1995.

Pressman, Matthew. "Remaking the News: The Transformation of American Journalism, 1960–1980." PhD diss., Boston University, 2016.
Purcell, J. Q. "Jimmy Bennett Doesn't Work Here Anymore." *New Yorker*, March 14, 1964.
Roberts, Gene, and Hank Klibanoff. *The Race Beat: The Press, the Civil Rights Struggle, and the Awakening of a Nation*. New York: Knopf, 2006.
Robertson, Michael. *Stephen Crane, Journalism, and the Making of Modern American Literature*. New York: Columbia University Press, 1997.
Robinson, Leonard Wallace. "The New Journalism: A Panel Discussion with Harold Hayes, Gay Talese, Tom Wolfe and Professor L. W. Robinson." In Weber, *Reporter as Artist*, 66–75.
Roggenkamp, Karen. *Narrating the News: New Journalism and Literary Genre in Late Nineteenth-Century American Newspapers and Fiction*. Kent, OH: Kent State University Press, 2005.
Roth, Philip. "Writing American Fiction." *Commentary*, March 1961.
Schmidt, Thomas R. "Rediscovering Narrative: A Cultural History of Journalistic Storytelling in American Newspapers, 1969–2001." PhD diss., University of Oregon, 2017.
Scholes, Robert. *The Fabulators*. New York: Oxford University Press, 1967.
Schwartz, Tony. "U.A. Pays $2.5 Million for Book by Gay Talese." *New York Times*, October 9, 1979.
Shapiro, Michael. "The Reporter Who Time Forgot: How Cornelius Ryan's *The Longest Day* Changed Journalism." *Columbia Journalism Review*, May/June 2010.
Sims, Norman. "The Art of Literary Journalism." In Sims and Kramer, *Literary Journalism*, 3–20.
———, ed. *Literary Journalism in the Twentieth Century*. Evanston, IL: Northwestern University Press, 2008. First published 1991 by Oxford University Press.
———. *True Stories: A Century of Literary Journalism*. Evanston, IL: Northwestern University Press, 2007.
Sims, Norman, and Mark Kramer, eds. *Literary Journalism: A New Collection of the Best American Nonfiction*. New York: Ballantine, 1995.
Smith, Adam [George J. W. Goodman]. *The Money Game*. New York: Random House, 1968.
Solotaroff, Theodore. "Introduction to *Writers and Issues*." In Weber, *Reporter as Artist*, 161–66.
Southern, Terry. *Blue Movie*. New York: Grove Press, 1970.
Steele, Karen, and Michael de Nie, eds. *Ireland and the New Journalism*. New York: Palgrave Macmillan, 2014.
Styron, William. Letter to the editor. *New York* [Sunday supplement of the *Herald Tribune*], April 25, 1965.
Talese, Gay. *Honor Thy Father*. New York: World Publishing, 1971.
———. *The Kingdom and the Power*. New York: World Publishing, 1969.
———. *Thy Neighbor's Wife*. Garden City, NY: Doubleday, 1980.
Thompson, Hunter S. *Hell's Angels: A Strange and Terrible Saga*. New York: Random House, 1967.
"Tom Wolfe Translated from the Original." *Bulletin of the American Society of Newspaper Editors*, July/August 1974.
Tompkins, Phillip K. "In Cold Fact." *Esquire*, June 1966.
Tulloch, John. "The Eternal Recurrence of New Journalism." In *Tabloid Tales: Global Debates over Media Standards*, edited by Colin Sparks and John Tulloch, 131–46. Lanham, MD: Rowman and Littlefield, 2000.
Underwood, Doug. *Journalism and the Novel: Truth and Fiction, 1700–2000*. Cambridge: Cambridge University Press, 2008.
———. *The Undeclared War between Journalism and Fiction: Journalists as Genre Benders in Literary History*. New York: Palgrave Macmillan, 2013.
Voss, Ralph F. *Truman Capote and the Legacy of "In Cold Blood."* Tuscaloosa, AL: University of Alabama Press, 2011.
Wakefield, Dan. *Between the Lines: A Reporter's Personal Journey Through Public Events*. Boston, MA: Little, Brown, 1966.
———. "The Personal Voice and the Impersonal Eye." In Weber, *Reporter as Artist*, 39–48.
Weber, Ronald. *The Literature of Fact: Literary Nonfiction in American Writing*. Athens, OH: Ohio University Press, 1980.
———. "Some Sort of Artistic Excitement." In Weber, *Reporter as Artist*, 13–26.
———, ed. *The Reporter as Artist: A Look at the New Journalism Controversy*. New York: Hastings House, 1974.
Weingarten, Marc. *The Gang That Wouldn't Write Straight: Wolfe, Thompson, Didion, and the New Journalism Revolution*. New York: Crown, 2006.
West, James L. W., III. *American Authors and the Literary Marketplace since 1900*. Philadelphia, PA: University of Pennsylvania Press, 1988.
"What Ever Happened to the New Journalism?" *Bulletin of the American Society of Newspaper Editors*, July/August 1974.
White, E. B. Letter to the editor. *New York* [Sunday supplement of the *Herald Tribune*], April 25, 1965.

Whiteside, Thomas. *The Blockbuster Complex: Conglomerates, Show Business, and Book Publishing.* Middletown, CT: Wesleyan University Press, 1981.

Wiener, Joel H. *The Americanization of the British Press, 1830s–1914: Speed in the Age of Transatlantic Journalism.* Basingstoke, UK: Palgrave Macmillan, 2011.

Wills, Garry. *Lead Time: A Journalist's Education.* New York: Doubleday, 1983.

Winchell, Walter. "Broadway and Elsewhere." *Logansport (IN) Pharos-Tribune*, May 31, 1960.

Wolfe, Tom. "The Birth of 'The New Journalism'; Eyewitness Report by Tom Wolfe." *New York*, February 14, 1972.

———. *The Electric Kool-Aid Acid Test.* New York: Farrar, Straus and Giroux, 1968.

———. *The Kandy-Kolored Tangerine-Flake Streamline Baby.* New York: Farrar, Straus and Giroux, 1965.

———. "King of the Status Dropouts." In *Pump House Gang*, 61–79. Originally published in *New York*, November 7, 1965.

———. "Literary Technique in the Last Quarter of the Twentieth Century." *Michigan Quarterly Review* 17, no. 4 (Fall 1978): 463–72.

———. "The New Journalism." *Bulletin of the American Society of Newspaper Editors*, September 1970.

———. "The New Journalism." *Dateline*, April 1969.

———. "The New Journalism." In Wolfe and Johnson, *New Journalism*, 1–52.

———. "The New Journalism: A la Recherche des Whichy Thickets." *New York*, February 21, 1972.

———. Papers. Manuscripts and Archives Division, New York Public Library.

———. *The Pump House Gang.* New York: Farrar, Straus and Giroux, 1968.

———. *Radical Chic and Mau-Mauing the Flak Catchers.* New York: Farrar, Straus and Giroux, 1970.

———. *The Right Stuff.* New York: Farrar, Straus and Giroux, 1979.

———. "Stalking the Billion-Footed Beast: A Literary Manifesto for the New Social Novel." *Harper's*, November 1989.

———. "Why They Aren't Writing the Great American Novel Anymore." *Esquire*, December 1972.

Wolfe, Tom, and E. W. Johnson, eds. *The New Journalism.* New York: Harper and Row, 1973.

Zavarzadeh, Mas'ud. *The Mythopoeic Reality: The Postwar American Nonfiction Novel.* Urbana, IL: University of Illinois Press, 1976.

11
ETERNAL PRESENT TENSE
The New Journalism Moved beyond Basic Needs to Tell Deeper Narratives about Chicago '68

Bill Reynolds

In this chapter, I use the 1968 Chicago Democratic National Convention as a case study to reexamine various New Journalism responses to the violence perpetrated by police officers against Yippies, hippies, antiwar protesters, and supporters of presidential candidate Eugene McCarthy, among other groups. In their crudest form, the events in Chicago that summer symbolized the confrontation between the generation that won the Second World War and its baby boomer offspring. The convention, held Monday, August 26, to Thursday, August 29, saw events spill in both directions of that time continuum. The building that housed the Democrats' convention to choose their post-Lyndon Johnson leader was the International Amphitheatre in Chicago, near the foul aroma of the stockyards. Much of the action, however, played out on downtown streets, parks, and hotel lobbies, as a fractured Democratic Party, post-Martin Luther King Jr./post-Robert F. Kennedy, struggled with uncertainty in defining its future. Mayor Richard J. Daley ensured that protesters were overmatched, harnessing a force of approximately 25,000 police officers, National Guardsmen, riot-trained federal troops, state police, county police, private security hires, and undercover agents.[1] Heads were cracked, blood was shed, and limbs were broken, but no one died, at least during convention week.

I also think it might be useful to digress from the New Journalism's response to Chicago to discuss a selection of daily news reporting. If this study's original goal was to pinpoint differences between New Journalism reportage and daily reporting by burrowing into one major event and comparing and contrasting, then I need to test my theory that the New Journalism response to Chicago was so quirky and off the wall by outlining such differences (or similarities). And the treat of this analysis might be to create an aperture to see what was implicit in being a New Journalist in the first place.

To do this, my intention here is to streamline parameters and rely on Tom Wolfe's pithy formulation that the New Journalism be written like a novel, which requires the application of just four basic techniques of fiction writing: constructing scenes, reporting telling details, capturing dialogue between characters, and creating point(s) of view.[2] About that last technique, I have come to see it as having two distinct subpoints. The first is that the author needs to have a point of view. After all, the editor who assigned and paid the New Journalist to report the story would expect the writer's "take"—otherwise, why bother to assign the long feature in the first place?

Readers may as well stick with news reports and opinion columns. The second is closer to classic Wolfe—that is, the point of view in the story might very well shift from one character to another, from one paragraph to the next. In the New Journalism mode, the writer is in no way obligated to stick to one perspective.

While restricted to this lens, I have kept in mind that so much New Journalism, and indeed literary journalism, depends on the writer's immersion in the story. Deep immersion plays such a crucial role in so many superb works of literary journalism that it is difficult to see how a reporter can deviate and find a shortcut around this onerous investment of time. This is precisely what makes the Chicago Democratic Convention of 1968 so enticing as a case study. Reporters were immersed in the battle of Chicago, whether they liked it or not. This also happens to be a weakness, since every reporter, working in no matter what medium (television, radio, newspaper, magazine, and, eventually, book), was menaced by Chicago police when covering the convention, the parks, and the hotels. Everyone, from the daily journalist to the novelist to the feature writer to the broadcaster, was boiling in the same cauldron.

Given this problem, I first examine several daily news reports (*Chicago Tribune*, *Chicago Defender*, *New York Times*, and *Globe and Mail*) for evidence of Wolfe's four techniques, or, looked at another way, nods to the then-in vogue New Journalism. (This is, after all, August 1968, three years after Wolfe's paperback *The Kandy-Kolored Tangerine-Flake Streamline Baby* awakened so many English literature students' minds to the additional horsepower that applying fiction techniques can give to nonfiction storytelling.)[3] The study then moves to analyze a collection of more likely suspects, such as author, playwright, and satirist Terry Southern, who wrote *The Magic Christian* (1959), *Candy* (1958), and *Red Dirt Marijuana* (1967); postmodernist and Beat writer William Burroughs, author of a famous counterculture novel, *Naked Lunch* (1959); author, novelist, poet, playwright, and activist Jean Genet, who wrote *The Thief's Journal* (1949) and *The Maids* (1946); and literary journalist and war correspondent John Sack, who, with his book *M* (1967), transposed the New Journalism onto war reporting. All four men were hired to report on Chicago for a November 1968 *Esquire* magazine cover package.

Also worth investigating are novelist-journalist Norman Mailer, who was writing for *Harper's* magazine (later in book form, *Miami and the Siege of Chicago* [1968]); journalist-novelist David Lewis Stein, who was writing for the *Star Weekly* and the *Toronto Star* (later in book form, *Living the Revolution* [1969]); and fiction writer and future academic John Schultz, who was writing for the *Evergreen Review* (later in book form, *No One Was Killed* [1968]). There were writers not necessarily known for being New Journalists who nevertheless brushed alongside the mode, including the journalist and future film critic Nora Sayre, reporting as New York correspondent for the *New Statesman*, the novelist/essayist William Styron, and the literary critic–fiction writer Elizabeth Hardwick, the latter two both reporting for the *New York Review of Books*. There was the television critic Michael J. Arlen filing a first-person rumination for the *New Yorker*. And, finally, there was the Gonzo journalist Hunter S. Thompson, who was in Chicago to cover events as part of his book project—working title "Death of the American Dream"—although the notes recalling his traumatic episode were not published until *Kingdom of Fear* (2003), decades later. Of this last batch, only Mailer and Thompson could be considered the real deal, although, as we will see, all of the writers discussed adopt New Journalism techniques to some degree.

For such a high-powered group of writers, thinkers, and reporters, you would think there would be more straight scene-by-scene construction, but, alas, there is not. Out of the entire batch, Stein's *Living the Revolution*, at least once the writer arrives in Chicago, contains the purest act of seeing, of actually dropping the reader into the scene, on the streets and in the parks, allowing the reader to experience the action as if she were right there with Stein, moving with the writer as he dodges mace and batons—less concerned, tellingly, with imposing his thoughts about the action on the reader than allowing the reader to absorb the action and interpret accordingly. However, this approach had the disadvantage of weakening the overall story, since such a self-imposed myopia could tell the story the writer was seeing at the time and nothing more. Stein makes fewer truth claims about what is really going on than other writers. The *New York Times* critic John Leonard, in a double book review of *Living the Revolution* and Schultz's *No One Was Killed*, harshly judged Stein's reporting for this reason (he also thought the editing execrable, but that is another story).[4]

Perhaps this is the crucial issue regarding the nature of the New Journalism. Was it about the act of getting down on page exactly what was happening, purely, with brutal honesty, without concern for what others think, without prejudice, from the subject's point of view, prejudices laid bare? Or was it a combination of criticism and opinion and on-the-ground reportage? Further, in the zeal to capture the madness in the streets in new ways—ways that generally were not allowed and/or were unthinkable in status quo reporting at the time, whatever the medium, did the New Journalists move beyond daily news reporting to achieve something more lasting and permanent?

Newspaper Coverage

The *Chicago Tribune*, one of the convention city's major newspapers, made clear its negative stance on the antiwar, anti-Hubert Humphrey protests in a page-one editorial that ran on Friday, August 30, 1968. It identified Tom Hayden of Students for a Democratic Society, David Dellinger, the "self-styled nonviolent Communist," and Youth International Party leader Jerry Rubin as "professional agitators" who influenced the "bearded, dirty, lawless rabble that followed them" and "used every sort of provocation against police."[5] The next day, the *Tribune* ran an instructive reaction story, "Police Action Draws Praise, Condemnation."[6] After the lead, the story ran five straight paragraphs of praise for the police: hosannas from Mayor Daley, the American Legion of Illinois, "hundreds" of readers who called the paper's offices in support of the editorial stand against those dirty, hairy young people, and not one but two members of something called the Greater North Michigan Avenue Association, who lauded the police's "remarkable preventive protection."[7] Yes, remarkable what follows when sticks bash heads and blood flows.

The paper then ran critical comments from three aldermen who, condemning police violence as doing "incalculable harm"[8] to the city, drafted a resolution to apologize to the demonstrators, and from one congressman who called for the prosecution of police officers who had used "terrorists tactics."[9] The following paragraph brags about city hall receiving thousands of calls and letters from citizens, ninety percent of which applauded the brutality. The Pennsylvania delegation generously donated $245 to the police pension fund. The final two paragraphs return to criticism: Sixteen religious and civil rights organizations complained about the "viciousness" of the police, and the National Council on Crime and Delinquency is given the last word, stating the obvious point that failed to register with the mayor's office—namely, there was a significant difference between a bunch of demonstrators gathered to protest and a few snipers and firebombers causing real trouble. The *Tribune* mixed reporting with crusading from the right.

The *Chicago Defender*, the influential black newspaper, which had become more conservative since its days of wide readership in the South when it advocated equal rights for blacks and cheered the Great Migration to the North,[10] nevertheless diligently covered the chaos in Chicago and its aftermath. Most of the reporting was straight news, with the natural emphasis on the black community. Occasionally, interesting detail was reported. In paragraph six of the un-bylined story "Heavy Security at Convention,"[11] readers learned that 11,835 Chicago police officers were issued riot helmets at eleven dollars each, meaning $130,185.[12] In terms of presenting the black community's point of view of the high stakes involved, "'We're Staying Put,' Rights Leaders Say," was not atypical. A black community leader was quoted:

> The police and their klansmen might try to blame any kind of uprisings on a member of the black community during the convention. Any opportunity they get will be used to implicate us and just give them the chance to kill black people.[13]

This idea was further developed nine days later in a quote from Kermit Coleman, director of the American Civil Liberties Union's ghetto project: "Now the others [meaning white protesters and journalists] will know what it's like to be brutalized."[14] Once the convention was three weeks past, the *Defender* assessed it from the black point of view in an editorial entitled "Quiet on the Black Front." Although little recognized for it, the black community had done Chicago a big favor. Black militants in general avoided the International Amphitheatre (the convention site) as well as the Loop (where cops and delegates and protesters did battle), thereby saving the black community from potential wholesale violence. These "flames of anger" could well have occurred "had not the residents of the black community realized that the convention was in the main a white man's affair with the Negro playing a non-essential role."[15]

Finally, when *Rights in Conflict*, the Walker Report on the violence in Chicago, was issued on December 1, 1968, *Defender* reporters felt obliged to solicit reactions from the black community. In "Negro Leaders React to Violence Report,"[16] militant Russ Meek was quoted as saying, "Dan Walker showed great concern about brutality toward white people, but I see no such excitement about the murder of black people—by police, which is a routine occurrence in this city."[17] Reverend Calvin Morris commented, "What happened during convention week, however, was that for a few moments white America got a glimpse of what black people must deal [with] daily."[18] The final insult came from the NAACP's Edward McClellan:

> I am deeply chagrined that Mr. Walker, who headed the same kind of investigative group probing into the April riots [post-Martin Luther King Jr.'s assassination], was unable to find kinds [sic] of travesties of justice when circumstances involved black people on the Westside.[19]

Another story, "Probe Alleged Plot to Kill HHH, Gene,"[20] focused on a *Chicago Tribune* story that accused one hundred black "extremists" of plotting to kill candidates and destroy police stations. The story had one source, an inmate of Cook County Jail. The *Defender* was also dutifully reporting various criticisms of the police hostilities from high-profile people such as the Reverend Jesse Jackson, Harry Belafonte, Democratic presidential long-shot George McGovern, and Detroit congressman John Conyers.[21]

While the *Defender* reliably reported the black point of view, it was not averse to telling its readers about police abuse of journalists. A story by staff reporter Sheryl Fitzgerald published on August 28 took an atypical turn into New Journalism territory when she recreated a scene in which two police officers beat on a photographer named Bob Black:

> It is said Black was attacked as he attempted to photograph a skirmish between police and yippie [sic] in Lincoln Park early Tuesday morning. According to reports, a policeman, who was not wearing a badge, swung at him with a club. Black protected himself by placing his camera in front of his face and the blow struck Black's camera. Seconds later another officer approached Black from the rear and struck him on his safety helmet. The force of the blow swung the photographer around and the policeman swung again, striking Black in the face and cutting his lip. Black was wearing *Sun-Times* identification on his arm band and on his safety helmet.[22]

This kind of reconstruction was rare for newspaper reporting in 1968. However brief, it is a bona fide scene because it has action in time (Tuesday morning) and place (Lincoln Park); it has telling details (cops not wearing badges, a cut lip, *Sun-Times* ID); it has a point of view, at least to some degree (as we re-experience the action through Black). Granted, there is no dialogue to enhance the scene, yet for 112 words, Fitzgerald allows her readers to become the photographer and feel the police menace.

There is a hint of a scene in "Police, Guardsmen Battle 'Yippies,'" published the next day. When two young people, identified by cops as Yippies, dove through a plate glass window into the Haymarket Lounge in the Conrad Hilton Hotel on Michigan Avenue, they were set upon and beat up by "thirty" police officers. This is a scene fragment, basically, but with a tantalizing additional enhancement tossed in: "police rushed in and knocked over a number of innocent bystanders in an effort to get to the two youths."[23] On September 3, the *Defender* published staff writer Faith Christmas's personal account of what it was like to be pushed forward in the crush of demonstrators and to arrive against the immovable object of the police line.[24] She also gave additional details of the two Yippie youths. Eyewitnesses told her the two did not dive through the window but rather were pushed. This did not concern those who were there to preserve order. "The police, 30 they said, knocked people and tables over trying to get to the Yippies. The Yippies were beaten in full view of the customers, they added."[25] The reporter's personal account deviates from white mainstream news reporting norms into impressionistic territory, yet the descriptions of various actions seem too fragmentary to become scenes.

The *Defender* published differing views on the subject, including one that defended police actions on the Wednesday night. In a first-person account titled "Writer Recalls Mob Scene Here," staff writer Bob Hunter, a local jazz scene expert, told readers he was there and wanted to write down exactly what he saw. He called the demonstrators "invaders" and "trouble seekers." He sided with the police when they retaliated for bricks being tossed at them. He managed to land the double bromide, "But the police were only trying to do their job. ... Some skulls were cracked and that is regrettable, but what were the police to do?"[26] This piece, not a news story but another personal take, is remarkable not so much for its reportage as for its defense of the "silent majority" in a black newspaper in a city where the police were not known to pamper the black community.

Meanwhile, the *New York Times* began to run bunches of stories in the last half of August. Many were standard news reports—"Chicago Police Bar TV Trucks from Parking on Street outside Hotels: Delays Foreseen in Live Coverage"[27] being a typical example—or opinion pieces like "Holding a Convention in a Garrison City."[28] The headline and deck just about tell the story, which they should. There were various angles pursued in addition to problems with media access and reporting chaos in the streets. For instance, more than 1,100 miles south of Chicago's cauldron, in Fort Hood, Texas, soldiers of the US Army's First Armored Division were put on 24-hour alert that they could be airlifted to Chicago. Sixty black soldiers protested being slated for riot control, and forty-three of them were arrested and placed in the stockade.[29] (Interestingly, the *Defender* also covered this story, saying seventy-five black soldiers protested and that forty-three "dissidents" were arrested. The *Defender* version also refreshingly ventured into descriptive, literary-journalistic territory in paragraph nine: "Some military units were bivouacked in Washington Park on the Southside of Chicago. The park had the appearance of a war encampment with barbed wire barricades and ominous-looking military equipment."[30])

In addition to copious basic reporting, the *Times* extended its toe into quasi-New Journalism territory, buying freelance articles from J. Anthony Lukas and John Kifner. Lukas reported from Bridgeport, the Chicago neighborhood Mayor Daley called home. Lukas effectively captures what the mayor's neighbors, clinging to the white-picket-fence dream, really thought about hippies and Yippies and dissidents with a colorful lead that includes a ten-year-old boy named David

Cuomo vowing, "We'll take their hippie chains and strangle them."[31] While the reporter obviously is standing there conversing with the mayor's neighbors, no action takes place. There is little scene-setting, but there are a lot of quotes. Lukas also covered the August 30 protests in Grant Park and the Conrad Hilton Hotel. Again, the story begins with a scene head fake—that is, Lukas tantalizes by placing the reader into the mob scene, where police fired more gas into the crowd, but the crowd turned away to listen to a guitarist singing Woody Guthrie's "This Land Is Your Land."[32] The lead ends, and Lukas spends the rest of his story arguing that the protesters, by rallying the peace movement, exposing liberalism's bankruptcy, and radicalizing thousands, won even though they lost the street battles to the authorities. More of a critical opinion piece couched inside an event, Lukas's take here is some distance from the New Journalism.

More promising is the story Lukas filed from the Chicago Coliseum about the Mobilization Committee to End the War in Vietnam's mockery of President Johnson's birthday.[33] Lukas situates the reader inside the "crumbling dark and drafty" building as he listens to the lineup of counterculture stars that The Fugs's Ed Sanders organized. There is the Holocaust No-Dance Band knocking out would-be classics such as "Master of Hate." There is Phil Ochs leading a sing-along of "I Ain't Marching Anymore." There are speeches from the *Esquire* magazine-assembled group of writers (Burroughs, Genet, Southern) and from Allen Ginsberg and Dick Gregory. Still, Lukas relies on reporting snippets of what was said and shortchanges the reader on atmosphere, dialogue, and off-stage action by ordinary people.

Even more promising is Kifner's "On the Road to Chicago with Some Protesters," which places the reader inside a borrowed 1962 Ford Falcon to listen to four young men, all draft resisters fully expecting to do jail time, and one young woman on their way to the Amphitheatre. Kifner is invisible. He simply records answers, captures dialogue, and offers detail—Rodney Robertson, twenty-five, is "fiercely moustached"; Sydney Hadsell, his girlfriend, the reader infers, touches his shoulder lightly; they departed from New York's Lincoln Tunnel at 2:55 p.m. the previous day for a sixteen-hour trip that includes time-outs for coffee, potato chips, and black raspberry ice cream.[34] The story might as well have been a classic Lillian Ross-style Talk of the Town piece for the *New Yorker*, where the reporter is along for the ride, stays out of the picture, and relays what happens, which allows the reader the opportunity to think about what the story means.

News Magazine Coverage

Beyond the *Times* newspaper itself, its magazine weighed in with a hefty feature two weeks after the convention was over. Tom Buckley's "The Battle of Chicago: From the Yippies' Side" recounts the events and attempts a summation. He sizes up the initial crowd of protesters that arrives: "Yet by Monday, the day the convention opened, it should have been clear to the authorities that the protest was about to fizzle."[35] He estimates that around 2,500 young protesters have come to Chicago and are eventually joined by 5,000 conventioneers and interested locals. Despite the low numbers, Mayor Daley maintains the same level of repression, vigilance, and pushback, and the reporter inserts a little personal journalism, declaring, "For me, it was like being back in Vietnam."[36] The authorities' response had been "rigid," "unimaginative," and "flatly unsuccessful."[37] The writer's assessment is soberly balanced with equally harsh words for the protest leaders. He calls them "hardline" and "militant,"[38] yet in comparison to Marxist rebels such as Che Guevara, they use "revolutionary lingo and little else."[39] After sympathizing initially, he decides they are playing a game whose stakes are not torture or death or being shipped to a gulag, but a knock on the head, a night in jail, and a photo in the paper. However, he admits that the Yippies' taunting of the police does its job: "For me, as I am sure for many observers, the continuous reference to the Mayor and the police as pigs had its psychological effect, partly because many of them tend to plumpness and thick jowls."[40]

Buckley's recounting of the week moves back and forth between event and analysis. There is no extended scene writing, although occasionally there are flourishes of illuminating detail, to wit:

> Most of the youngsters seemed to be between 17 and 21, with a slight preponderance of boys. Not more than 10 per cent were Negro. Aside from the youngsters from Chicago and its suburbs and the nearby Milwaukee area, most hailed from the Pacific Coast, Minnesota and the New York area.
>
> They seemed to be better-looking than the average, although somewhat scruffy in their hippie gear. They wore African shawls, flowered shirts, jeans and denim jackets. One young man wore a battered silk hat; another affected a tailcoat over his tee-shirt.[41]

Because of its length, more than three thousand words, Buckley's story has more depth and scope than most of the reporting on Chicago. Ultimately, though, it is still rendered in newspaper style, which is to say there is no attempt to develop characters whose actions drive the narrative. And although the writer does insert himself into the story, making it less strictly a news report, the interjection is of the "I think" variety rather than the writer himself becoming a character within an unfolding narrative.

A Northern Voice

The *Globe and Mail*, based in Toronto, mainly ran Associated Press and New York Times Service stories, although it did have one ace, journalist Michael Enright, who filed from ground zero to Toronto. Enright, although reporting, has a style that sports a strong voice. This feeling, when reading his work from 1968, may stem in part from his instantly recognizable tones during his long service on CBC radio as host of *The Sunday Edition* and other important programs, such as *As It Happens*. For instance, his story about Mobe, or the National Mobilization Committee to End the War in Vietnam, is set inside a temporary office for the convention. The reader is situated inside room 315 in an "ugly"[42] building on South Dearborn (no address given). Enright's emphasis on details—dirty floors, groaning elevator, deafening noise of elevated trains rumbling by—quickly lands the reader in the room, fly-on-the-wall style. His voice is immediately apparent: "It can best be described, oddly enough, as a war room."[43] He is invisible, but his sources' answers are quoted. He describes what he sees around him: timetables, posters, personal notes such as "David Mandell, call grandma."[44] He relays some points of view offered, but there is no real action. It's an observant story and captures a mood, but there is no narrative arc. It is a snapshot, not footage.

To pick just one more Enright story, "Politics Goes into Street" plunks the reader into the action. The first paragraph begins, "It was when the candles appeared at the north end of the hotel row along Michigan Avenue that you knew something had happened to the politics of this country."[45] Marchers, five across, walk arm in arm holding candles. It is difficult to see the people carrying the flames, so Enright focuses on the arresting image of candles marching in the dark. He has a time (August 29, four o'clock in the morning), a place (hotel row, across from Grant Park), people actually doing something, and dialogue between cops and demonstrators. Occasionally Enright inserts his voice about the calm after the terror that had occurred earlier: "And yet, in the middle of it, there was beauty, there was a strange kind of nocturnal nobility."[46] For a newspaper report, Enright's piece reads closer to storytelling, aligning it with Wolfe's ideal for the New Journalism.

The Culture Bunker I: *New York Review of Books*

The culture and current affairs fortnightly, the *New York Review of Books*, hired Elizabeth Hardwick and William Styron to report on the convention. Hardwick's essay is, in form, a standard assessment of events (the police overreact; the Democrats are in disarray) that in the second half sizes up the main contenders, Humphrey, then McCarthy, then McGovern. Her point of view is not extraordinarily different from other non-reporter types, and when she directs the reader to scenes—ones she herself is part of or witnesses—the action is bleached out with brief summations and commentary. Her mocking image of the travesty is entertaining: "A father, sweating, red-faced, unchallenged, beating up his son, 'overreacting.'"[47] Her universalizing generally works: "Few had realized until Chicago how great a ruin Johnson and his war in Vietnam had brought down upon our country."[48] And, most important, she understands the value of a joke in her effective lines: "During the raid on the McCarthy Headquarters, a girl in tears asked, 'What are the grounds?' The police answered, 'Coffee grounds,'"[49] and "Out of the meanness and hollowness, the degrading events and the worrying future, one suddenly saw a little Yippie with a sign saying, CHICAGO IS A GAS. That was transcendence, rebirth."[50] Hardwick flirts with New Journalism techniques but ultimately sticks to analysis.

On the other hand, Hardwick's *NYRB* colleague Styron, who originally had come to Chicago on official business as a "delegate challenger" for the state of Connecticut on behalf of Senator McCarthy, begins his essay in much the same fashion, as a cerebral (and funny) commentator —"When I returned as an observer to Chicago the following Sunday, the lobby of the Conrad Hilton resembled a fantasy sequence in some Fellini movie";[51] by the halfway mark, the essay shifts the reader onto the street, to the Tuesday night—"I left a party on the Near North Side … to see what was going on in nearby Lincoln Park"[52]—and then flings the reader into the ring:

> And suddenly they were there, coming over the brow of the slope fifty yards away, a truly stupefying sight—one hundred or more of the police in a phalanx abreast, in helmets and gas masks, just behind them a huge perambulating machine with nozzles, like the type used for spraying insecticide, disgorging clouds of yellowish gas, the whole advancing panoply illuminated by batteries of mobile floodlights. Because of the smoke, and the great cross outlined against it, yet also because of the helmeted and masked figures—resembling nothing so much as those rubberized wind-up automata from a child's playbox of horrors—I had a quick sense of the medieval in juxtaposition with the twenty-first century or, more exactly, a kind of science fiction fantasy, as if a band of primitive Christians had suddenly found themselves set upon by mechanized legions from Jupiter.[53]

After the literary flair, the action: Tuesday night, after midnight, not running, walking, but fast, "bleeding tear from the gas." The police "flanked us," "harrying people," spooking motorists to "collide with one another," the crowd "wailed with alarm," and then, finally "we disengaged ourselves … and made our way down Wells Street, … where in the dingy nightclubs Go-Go girls oblivious to the rout outside calmly wriggled their asses in silhouette against crimson windows."[54]

Styron's action footage in the middle of his essay might have been even more effective rendered in present tense. This would have dropped the reader, by gravitational pull, into the street and into the action, thereby feeling the mayhem and the violence.

The Culture Bunker II: *New Statesman*

Other voices include the *New Statesman*'s Nora Sayre, who introduces her Chicago article with a scene, then runs commentary, and then finishes with a personal scene, back in New York, involving having her typewriter confiscated while on deadline. When reporting from inside the maelstrom, she leads with gore: "Such blood: released from bruised and broken veins, from foreheads, scalps, and mouths, from eyesockets, shattered wrists, and skulls. Broad bloodstreaks on the sidewalks showed where the bodies had been dragged."[55] As evocative as this passage is, and

Sayre is one of the best at capturing sheer physical danger and the results of terrorizing, notice she uses "bodies" instead of body, plural instead of singular, invoking the universal. Instead of focusing on one story, she pans out to the many. In this way, the scene never achieves coalescence. Then she drops in a bit of commentary: "We all bleed inwardly from the particular atrocities we witnessed."[56] Then she testifies: "I saw seven policemen beating one girl—long after she had fallen."[57] Then the personal experience: "Gas rinses your lungs with the lash of iodine and vinegar: your own breath burns your throat."[58] Sayre moves in this way, interpreting mostly but sometimes getting out of the way, as here, in the second paragraph:

> Outside the Hilton, a little old lady patted a rebel on the chest, murmuring, "Knock the socks off them." I said, "Funny how the police seem rather powerless right now." She and I were suddenly hurled against the wall when some hundred policemen seized their blue wooden barricades to ram the crowd (mainly onlookers and press) against the building with such force that many next to me, including the old lady, were thrust through the hotel's plate glass windows. ... The police then spilled through the smashed window and clubbed those who had gone through it and some of the drinkers at the bar. Outside, people sobbed with pain as their ribs snapped from being crushed against each other. ... Soon, a line of stick-whipping cops swung in on us. Voiceless from gas, I feebly waved my credentials, and the warrior who was about to hit me said, "Oops, press." He let me limp into the hotel, where people were being pummeled into the red carpet, while free Pepsi was being timidly offered on the sidelines.[59]

The lead scene, however brief, is powerful. Sayre proceeds to give the reader a mixture of street reporting, interviewing, context, and meaning. A typical example might be, "Allen Ginsberg omming like a death rattle, his voice ravaged by the days of Hindu chants and gas."[60] She does not say when and where, exactly, just that she saw Ginsberg chanting. Much of this perceptive essay reads like this. We know she is there. We know she is in the middle of things. Yet we don't get as much of a sense of the action and movement as we might like.

The Culture Bunker III: *New Yorker*

Michael J. Arlen's story for the *New Yorker*, "The Air: A Wednesday Evening in Chicago," bounds out of the starting gate as if it were a piece of New Journalism, at least once we speed through the obligatory opening cab-driver conversation (this is a writer's temptation, to include everything). The real start reads this way: "The boy beside me, a dark-haired boy with a scraggly mustache, was dressed in Levi's and some kind of T-shirt and was called Dave, and blood was running down one side of his face."[61] The sentence runs almost one hundred words, extending itself with eight uses of the conjunction "and." The concept Didion-esque comes to mind. The long lead scene demonstrates that Arlen (who was following the New Journalism) understands the power of the four novelistic devices Wolfe highlights. Much more developed than a typical anecdotal newspaper feature lead, Arlen's "you are there" description runs just over six hundred words, and its extended footage places the reader inside the storm. He then fashions a clever hundred-word pivot to the main aim of his piece: to comment on the difference between being there, which is palpably appalling and frightening, and watching it on television, which is analytically appalling and repulsive. Big difference. Arlen, who went on to pen a response to Wolfe's essays about the New Journalism in the *Atlantic Monthly* in 1972,[62] obviously understood the power of placing the reader inside the story, but he used that knowledge for the long opening section only before reverting to standard column fare.

The Culture Bunker IV: *Esquire*

For its November 1968 cover package, *Esquire* magazine commissioned four writers,[63] two New Journalists and two noted provocateurs, to create a kind of nouveau coverage: French playwright, felon, and political activist Jean Genet; author William S. Burroughs, who employed the cut-up method of writing; Vietnam correspondent John Sack, the author of *M*; and Terry Southern, the *Candy* screenplay writer. Genet noticed the bulges in the pants of police officers while he critiqued the violent attacks. Burroughs talked of conspiracies, as Burroughs always did. Sack, with his impeccable war reporting credentials, wrote of police attitudes to the scruffy interlopers. Southern's contribution amounted to basic, solid reportage that neatly covered all of Wolfe's devices.

Southern's "Grooving in Chi" inauspiciously leads with his cab ride into the city. He reports what he is seeing, in present tense, as he sees it, moving on wheels toward his destination: a drunken black man descended upon by four prepubescent miscreants. He wonders about bad omens. Deposited into the protests, Southern gives an authentic sense of the malevolent presence in the conference zone. He uses police megaphone dialogue to build tension: "Final warning. The officers are moving in five minutes."[64] A couple of minutes later, Burroughs says, "They're coming."[65] Genet does not want to leave. Ginsberg persuades him. Later, when the team heads to the convention center, Southern says it looks like a "military installation—barbed wired, checkpoints, the whole bit"[66] and that his colleague Burroughs is "ecstatic; it was all so grotesque that at one point he actually did a little dance of glee."[67] On Wednesday, the plate-glass-window-breaking day, Southern and crew manage to escape the hordes to the bar and its "grandstand view" of the "strange, and sickening, spectator sport. ... [T]here was a certain undeniable decadence in the way we sat there, drinks in hand, watching the kids in the street getting wiped out."[68] Southern later told his biographer, "You have no idea how wild the police were. They were just totally out of control. I mean, it was a *police* riot, that's what it was."[69]

Southern employs dialogue to powerful effect. His compatriots, even *Esquire* associate editor John Berendt, also in Chicago, become characters in his recounting of the drama. His best character is saved for last, the "middle-aged man, wearing a straw hat with a Hubert Humphrey band," who watches with "distaste" as a cop lays a beating on "a thin blond boy about seventeen" at the hotel.[70] In case the reader is wondering which side the man is on, he announces, "I'd just as soon live in one of those damn police states as put up with that kind of thing."[71]

Esquire editor Harold Hayes had successfully positioned reporter Sack to hang out with a group of soldiers, M Company, from basic training to Vietnam. Sack's work on M Company was prominently displayed in the October 1966 cover story, "Oh My God—We Hit a Little Girl" and again with a follow-up piece in January 1968, "When Demirgian Comes Marching Home Again (Hurrah? Hurrah?)." For "In a Pig's Eye," he chose to focus on the contretemps from the police point of view. He employed the usual tricks of the New Journalism trade: hanging out with officers (saturation reporting, immersion), catching conversations and capturing dialogue, maintaining a certain amount of empathy for their point of view, and recording small but telling details. Like Southern, Sack mixed on-scene reportage with a bit of commentary (though far less of the latter than, say, the *Evergreen Review*'s John Schultz). The following two examples give a good idea of how Sack approached his subject. The first comes from a police officer's home front, away from the stick-swinging madness:

> Be a Chicago pig policeman! Carry a pistol and sleep until noon! Zzz ... Zzz .... On the other hand he had arrived home at four in the morning, a little mote of CS tear gas still chewing at his throat like cayenne pepper or like sunburn on his shoulders, his Irish eyes still smarting, tired: the wounds of another night of shoving the scroungers from Lincoln Park. "Yippies again" or "Hippies again," he had muttered to Mama, slipping beneath the sheets.[72]

The second excerpt neatly burrows inside the "how-would-you-like-it-if" nature of a police officer's reaction to bolder dissidents in the street:

> Sailing ever so lightly toward the squad, splashing apart on the grass, emitting an indisputable odor, the Saran bag brought a mortally horrified shout to the lips of one patrolman. "It's a bag of shit! They're shitting in bags and throwing it!" ... [T]o most of Chicago's policemen the targets of their heavy clubs were not Americans but desecrators of America's red, white and blue, not human beings but African shit-kicking chimpanzees. It was for America's most cherished beliefs—not for Nazi piggery, sadism, vengeance, relief—that the blows descended. For a young boy to resist, to argue, even to offer excuses—to Chicago's policemen this was intolerable.[73]

While Southern's and Sack's contributions fit comfortably under the New Journalism umbrella, Burroughs's "The Coming of the Purple Better One" is problematic. Like Southern and Arlen, he begins his essay with a view from a moving cab. His terse reports at times read almost police-blotter style (at the airport to see the arrival of candidate Eugene McCarthy, Burroughs notes, "Surprisingly few police. Whole scene touching and ineffectual particularly in retrospect of subsequent events"[74]). Burroughs more or less grounds his thoughts in actual events—the police brutalities committed in the park and so on—but is in a hurry. He realizes people have probably heard and read enough about the events. At about the one-third mark, Burroughs deviates from chronology and eyewitness material. He prefaces his story with a commentary on the state of the nation: "Millions of young people all over the world are fed up with shallow unworthy authority running on a platform of bullshit."[75] He lists five "questions" to be answered, namely, Vietnam, alienated youth, black power, the police and the judicial system, and something called "the disappearing dollar."[76] Then any pretense of reporting is jettisoned. He veers wildly into a fantasy about Homer Mandrill, the purple-assed baboon who is running for president. Burroughs is not a journalist seeing and reporting so much as a thought improviser riffing off basic events to portray images of what he perceives to be the rotting carcass of the American Dream and the fascistic tendencies of the ruling classes. By the end of the story, his wild fictions, and his readers, are a fair distance from New Journalism reportage (but possibly close to that specialized patch known as Gonzo—more of which later). Most New Journalists, while acknowledging that the consciousness that is performing the reporting function must also be interpreting what is being reported, on a sliding scale of subjectivity they are still reporting. That is, they do not make stuff up. Still, Burroughs qualifies as a kindred spirit.

Novelist, playwright, activist, and thief Genet's contribution, "The Members of the Assembly," is set up as a series of vignettes. As such, it is one of the better stories for having time and place stamps clearly marked throughout. In the most delightfully shocking section, "The First Day: Day of the Thighs," Genet acknowledges his lust for the "superb thighs" of the police officers while being fully aware that "they go hunting for blacks in the ghettos."[77] The title of his contribution, obviously, is a double entendre, as Genet did not mind admitting that he was distracted by the private assets contained inside the uniforms of the helmeted men in blue:

> The thighs are very beautiful beneath the blue cloth, thick and muscular. It all must be hard. The policeman is also a boxer, a wrestler. His legs are long, and perhaps, as you approach his member, you would find a furry nest of long, tight, curly hair. That is all I can see. ... America has a magnificent, divine, athletic police force, often photographed and seen in dirty books ... but the thighs are parted slightly, and through the crack which extends from the knees to the too-heavy member, I can see ... why, it's the whole panorama of the Democratic Convention."[78]

As he proceeds through the week, Genet's critique of events tips heavily in favor of the kids on the streets. Sometimes he descends into what amounts to gibberish, for example in this passage: "The Chicago police are feminine and brutal. It does not want its ladies to meekly obey their husbands whose hair is sky blue, dressed in robes of many colors."[79] In the end, he exhorts the "flower children" to unite and "fuck all the old bastards" and "go underground if necessary in order to join the burned children of Vietnam."[80] Genet was an activist-writer, not a reporter, but his funny, outrageous descriptions of real events he witnessed show that he is also a kindred spirit of the New Journalists. Both he and Burroughs wove their tangential reveries into what they were witnessing on the ground, with Genet's account being somewhat more tethered to reality and easier to follow.

Another Northern View

Canadian journalist-author David Lewis Stein was based in New York and surviving on a monthly retainer to file stories to the *Toronto Star* and *Star Weekly* magazine.[81] He was intrigued by a new band of activists labeled Yippies. He befriended leaders such as Abbie Hoffman, Jerry Rubin, and, especially, Keith Lampe. He arrived in Chicago sympathetic to their cause, eventually penning a first-person assessment for *Saturday Night* magazine in Canada, "I Think the Yippies Are the Finest People I Have Met So Far."[82] His *Toronto Star* pieces and his short book *Living the Revolution* try to portray to the reader exactly what the author was seeing that week. At times the action being described sidled Stein closer to pure New Journalism than more famous accounts. He achieved this feat by clinging to his news feature-writing training while embracing the possibilities of more in-depth, eyewitness, New Journalism prose.

Despite his friendship with Lampe—Stein phoned Lampe and told him he had secured money from his editor to cover Chicago, and to book a hotel for them—he was not necessarily blind to the group's showboating: "The people I had known as just people at Yippie meetings in New York had become stars in Chicago."[83] And, "The Yippies were depressing to watch in action. They looked ridiculous, a little band of long-haired braggarts standing in front of the Federal Building, twenty-seven stories of Mies Van Der Rohe steel girders and bronze-tinted glass."[84]

Stein also relays his growing sense of unease. He feels himself losing his reporter's distance, reflecting on his transition to openly subjective journalist:

> I decided to sit down and join the crowd. I still didn't want to get my head cracked open in Lincoln Park, but I felt I had an obligation to stay there. I was still a reporter and I had to *know* what was going to happen. But I was, in fact, turning into something more than a reporter. I was becoming a witness, in the old-fashioned, Christian sense of the word.[85]

This newfound obligation amounted to empathy for the Other. Instead of seeing the police officers as "pigs," the all-purpose flypaper moniker of the week, Stein wondered, as did Sack, what the madness in the streets looked like to the men with sticks:

> I was behind them and I could see what they were seeing. Michigan Avenue looked as if it was filled with writhing, screaming, hysterical people. I think if I had been a cop about to march into that mob, I would have been afraid for my life. And if I had been given the order, "Advance and clear the intersection," I think maybe I would have swung my club just as viciously as those cops did, just to save my own skin.[86]

Stein's empathy extends only so far, though. As his metamorphosis from reporter to would-be revolutionary takes hold, he begins to realize he has crossed a line, and it is not to the police side of the barricades:

> The Guard had formed a large semicircle guarding the Hilton and we began to pour into the park again. A kid started running at the soldiers, screaming, "Pigs! Fucking pigs!" at them. I put my arm around his shoulders and gently led him off. "Easy, brother, easy. Our time will come." Hell I was even becoming a leader.[87]

Fiction Writer as Counterculture Commentator

Out of all of the reporters covering the event, the *Evergreen Review*'s John Schultz draws the most cosmic connections from the actions in Chicago: "It is guilty, this power that lets these cops and soldiers be there in the mind and in the streets, blocking dreams, and it must die."[88] He takes the assaults personally. His long feature "Pigs, Prague, Other Democrats, Chicago and the Sleeper in the Park," published December 1968, one month after the *Esquire* package, is the most grandiose attempt to capture all the facets of the confrontation. His arresting image is "lines of blue helmets and blue shirts,"[89] which he sees when he tries to sleep at night. Schultz at every stage in his story sizes up the political cost and capital, always from a point of view: "next to party disloyalty, the major crime all over the world is killing a cop,"[90] and "They had every right to be on the sidewalk, but no one thought anymore in terms of civil rights."[91] Those sorts of statements, speaking on behalf of the left, were of one kind of value, but when Schultz begins to consider the effect of all the malice on himself, the result has a different timbre: "I'd already been hit on the head once, and I'd come to regard getting clubbed devoid of any social or political implication, a ghetto attitude."[92]

Along with the capability of self-reflection, and trying to interpret events for the reader (which he often does to the detriment of the storytelling), Schultz displays a kind of reportorial empathy. For instance, he is keen to relay a message from one of the few black protesters:

> In Lincoln Park, on that deadly-feeling Monday night behind the barricade made of picnic tables and trash cans and the bonfires and the black and red flags flying in the media headlights, a black boy suddenly stopped among the trees, as if with revelation, and screamed, "Black brothers! Black brothers! Get out of this motherfucking park! Them are *white* cops! They'll *kill* you, black brothers, they'll kill you, if they catch you in this motherfucking park!" The black brothers knew the truth of it and they were already in motion to get out of the park, except for a black Yippie leader who always stayed with whites anyway.[93]

By including this reporting, Schultz echoes the *Defender*'s work on Chicago '68. He expanded his article significantly into a book-length "documentation and meditation" the following year. The book, *No One Was Killed*, was republished on its fortieth anniversary, in 2009.

Novelist as Journalist; Journalist as Novelist

Norman Mailer, the novelist who specialized in "History as a Novel/The Novel as History" and the reporter who wrote in the third person and had been recently lauded for his spectacular feat of reportage and self-absorption in *The Armies of the Night* (1968),[94] writes an account of the Chicago cataclysm that forms the second half of his convention diptych, *Miami and the Siege of Chicago*. His journalistic methodology includes watching the police chase protesters from the nineteenth floor of his hotel, tarrying through Grant Park to bask in the adoration of multitudes of hippies and Yippies who recognize him as a bona fide star, and, as a middle-aged man, declaring his ambivalence toward the entire protest construct. Mailer tells his story as if the reality of what is happening inside his head—what he is thinking about when the police actions are happening—is as important as the action on the street. The fighting in Chicago is subservient to the larger arguments within his own turbulent psyche. This style is, following David Eason,[95] a basic type of New Journalism, attributable especially to Mailer and also Thompson. Mailer watches from the nineteenth floor of the Conrad Hilton Hotel, then quotes actual reporting. When Ginsberg is teargassed, and seventeen reporters and photographers are attacked in the melee, Mailer has to quote Nicholas von Hoffman's report for the *Post*—because he isn't there to see it.[96] When Mailer misses the second riot, just after midnight on Tuesday, August 27, he needs to quote at length Steve Lerner's report for the *Village Voice*.[97] Eight years earlier, in a profile of John F. Kennedy, Mailer had called reporters "bulldozers."[98] Now he is relying on the words of bulldozers to explain to his reader what has happened.

This sort of standing off to the side has its uses. In terms of wrestling with the idea of marching with the kids and getting his head cracked open, Mailer affords himself the opportunity to size himself up as a man among men:

> It was not that he was such a good fighter, but he was not altogether courteous either—he had broken a man's jaw in a fight not so long before, and was not certain the end of that was yet heard; it had left him nervous and edgy about fights. He was not afraid of his own violence because he necessarily thought it would be so heinous to break a policeman's jaw, good law-abiding citizen that he was! It was more that he was a little concerned with what the policeman's friends and associates might do to him immediately afterward.[99]

And Mailer continues the reverie, about whether to actually join in, whether to show solidarity with the kids, whether even to show that he could take a shot while bearing witness as a reporter; to his credit, he admits that he finds himself lacking:

> The reporter did not join [Ginsberg, Burroughs, Genet, Richard Seaver, Southern]. He had felt an unmistakable pang of fear at the thought of marching with these people through the Black Belt of Chicago or even the Polish neighborhoods in the immediate surroundings. ... [T]he thought of taking a terrible beating in this company of non-violent McCarthyites and McGovernites, shoulder to shoulder with Arthur Miller, Jules Feiffer, Theo Bikel and Jeremy Larner, no, if he was just going to take a beating, it was best to take it alone or with people he felt close to, people who were not so comparatively innocent of how to fight.[100]

In other words, Mailer is way too street punk to associate himself with these Johnny-come-lately protesters. This extreme solipsism might be better explained as a writer's sincere attempt to unmask himself before his readers—pockmarks, birthmarks, liver spots, and all. It may be terrible New Journalism, as journalism, but it is unmistakably New Journalism personified. As Louis Menand points out in his Mailer obituary note, "Mailer did not put the first person into journalism; he took it out of the closet."[101]

Coda: Gonzo and the Missed Opportunity

If anyone could have, perhaps should have, written the definitive New Journalism text of Chicago '68—but chose not to—it was Hunter S. Thompson. Two years before what is now generally considered to be the first Gonzo text, "The Kentucky Derby Is Decadent and Depraved,"[102] and one year after his well-received book on the Hell's Angels motorcycle outlaws, Thompson successfully pitched to Random House, his publishing company, a follow-up study of not just one subculture but the country in its entire exploding magnificence (or malignance). Random House accepted the proposal, "The Death of the American Dream," and he was given a $5,000 advance plus a $7,500 expense budget against future royalties.[103] Covering the Dream's expiration meant covering the Yippies, the hippies, the McCarthyites, and Mayor Daley's pig patrol in Chicago. Alas, Thompson did not write about what happened from his point of view at the Democratic National Convention until *Kingdom of Fear*. The experience had been far too traumatic, and he left town. When he finally did commit to paper his thoughts, the prose spewed volcanically in Thompson's instantly identifiable voice:

> I found myself in the middle of the pincers, with no place to run except back into the Blackstone [Hotel]. But the two cops at the door refused to let me in. They were holding their clubs out in front of them with both hands, keeping everybody away from the door.
>
> By this time I could see people getting brutalized within six feet of me on both sides. It was only a matter of seconds before I went under ... so I finally just ran between the truncheons, screaming, "I live here, goddamnit! I'm paying fifty dollars a day." By the time they whacked me against the door I was out of range of what was happening on the sidewalk ... and by some wild accidental luck I happened to have my room key in my pocket. Normally I would have left it at the desk before going out, but on this tense night I forgot, and that key was salvation—that, and the mad righteousness that must have vibrated like the screeching of Jesus in everything I said. Because I *did* live there. I was a goddamn *paying guest*! And there was never any doubt in my mind that the stinking blue-uniformed punks had no RIGHT to keep me out.[104]

Thompson's nonfiction functions best in the New Journalism mode. He is in the action, often the center of the action, an unmistakable voice, a strong point of view. Like all good solipsists, there is not much room for anyone else.

Conclusion

I chose the Democratic National Convention of 1968 to show the struggle for new ways of reporting in a turbulent time. I wanted to examine how the New Journalism, although purported to be a new way of reporting, was not simply one way of seeing. It is at least four and maybe more: the kind that throws the reader into the scene and rolls the action with little interjection on the part of the writer; the kind that throws the reader into the scene but instead of showing what happens almost immediately switches to interpreting the events being witnessed; the kind that throws the reader into the scene in a faulty narrator kind of way, with time and/or place omitted and some parts of the text being some sort of literary fabrication; and the kind where reporters thrust themselves into the scene and make the story about how they feel about the events being witnesses. But, at root, some writers are better reporters than other writers.

A fifth variation of this reporting might be the various attempts at New Journalism-style reporting in newspapers. I began with a long analysis of daily reports, some of which might conceivably be placed in the New Journalism basket. In most cases discussed, this is a stretch, although the *New York Times Magazine*'s Tom Buckley and the *Globe and Mail*'s Michael Enright come close enough to be in the overlapping section of a Venn diagram between the New Journalism and daily journalism. The *Chicago Defender* reports generally are news oriented, but news that is specifically directed at a minority community and so, by definition, has a strong point of view. And, in a few stories, that strong viewpoint is combined with equally vivid personal observation of live events—maybe not quite New Journalism but adjacent, friendly territory.

Of the magazine writers, Mailer is a terrible reporter—his DNC story is more about Mailer: how Mailer feels about RFK's death, how Mailer feels about not getting involved, how Mailer feels about this military-corporate culture. Nevertheless, Mailer is Mailer, and, content to wallow in his thoughts, he does connect. This is true of Thompson as well. Thompson's writing is unmistakably about Thompson, but his scene flow is spectacular.

Hardwick and Sayre are commentators, although Sayre begins her essay with a straight-up scene with her in it. Burroughs writes imaginative, paranoid fantasy prose. Genet treats the police as sex objects and mocks their beatings of the "beautiful" hippies. Styron brings literary flare to his version of events, as does Hardwick to a lesser degree.

Southern and Sack are the "official" New Journalists for hire. Their reports mix strange angles into scenes, details, dialogue, and point of view, à la Wolfe's classic construction. Schultz and Stein, both novelists, are reporters. The former ambitiously tries to capture events in a sweeping panorama that zooms in and out; the latter is, more or less, a Yippie imbed, his project more modest by design. Both arrive, dive into action, and report back.

Schultz finishes his long *Evergreen* story with an extended climactic scene. Until that point, his analysis tends to filter out the action and sometimes time and place, which makes it difficult for the reader to get inside the story and feel what's going on. Stein begins his book by throwing us into a scene of cops beating on demonstrators, but it's in the future, January 1969, at Nixon's inauguration. He then winds back and gives us his reason for imbedding with the Yippies (he and Keith Lampe became friends), and a compact history of the Yippies prior to the DNC. Once he's in Chicago, the book roars along chronologically, scene to scene, with Stein occasionally stepping back to assess the situation. John Leonard in the *Times* criticized Stein for not knowing what was going on half the time. Schultz saw more and mixed in more reporting when he wasn't there to directly see. In terms of how the New Journalism actually works, Stein's prose functions more as unfiltered reality; Schultz prefers to intermingle his cogitations on reality with the reports of what is actually happening. Not for nothing did he subtitle his book "Documentation and Meditation"—at times the solemn prose and unending, undifferentiated detail read like anti-storytelling.

Did the New Journalists report on Chicago '68 with the kind of depth unavailable to daily reporters? The short answer is yes. Why? Well look, the prose is more ambitious. The story scope both pans a large canvas of late sixties protest and focuses on detailed stories within the larger frame. The scenes place the reader inside the crowd, or in the bar, or in the hotel lobby, or on the street, fleeing, ducking, wincing from blows. This inside view affords the reader an opportunity to feel like she is there. When this happens, the writer has led the reader to develop a palpable stake in the story—a stake that, I would argue, is much greater and more valuable than simply being amazed or appalled or revulsed by the images being witnessed on television. Mainly this is because scene-setting almost by definition sets up a walk-a-mile-in-my-shoes kind of intimacy. At this juncture, some of the New Journalism's finest achievements are still a long way off—Thompson's *Fear and Loathing: On the Campaign Trail '72* (1973), Joan Didion's *The White Album* (1979), Wolfe's *The Right Stuff* (1979)—yet the New Journalists have already gone well beyond reporting the news to capture a vibrant narrative history.[105] In so doing, their stories, while retaining a whiff of the slang and word usage of the times, are not stale, old news reports. They remain impervious to age, refreshingly alive, etched in an eternal present tense.

Notes

1 Biles, *Richard J. Daley*, 151–52. Biles breaks down the numbers like so: "Arrayed against the anti-war activists, in addition to the twelve-thousand-member Chicago Police Department, the mayor commanded five thousand Illinois National Guardsmen, six thousand riot-trained federal troops, hundreds of state and county police, a private security force deployed at the convention site, and a large

contingent of secret service agents. The military claimed that one of every six demonstrators was an undercover federal agent. By most estimates, the forces for law and order outnumbered the dissidents five to one. As Mike Royko observed, 'Never before had so many feared so much from so few.'"

2. Wolfe, introduction to *The New Journalism*, 31–32.
3. Wolfe, *Kandy-Kolored Tangerine-Flake Streamline Baby*.
4. Leonard, "Bloody Melodrama," 27.
5. "Chicago: A Great City," 1.
6. Wolfe, "Police Action," 7.
7. Wolfe, 7.
8. Wolfe, 7.
9. Wolfe, 7.
10. Thornton, "'Dangerous' *Chicago Defender*," 40.
11. "Heavy Security at Convention," 3.
12. Adjusted for inflation to 2018 dollars, the cost would be $927,257.63, according to www.usinflationcalculator.com (accessed February 26, 2018).
13. "'We're Staying Put,'" 3. That wasn't the only expense. "Superintendent Conlisk equipped each officer with a riot helmet and a teargas dispenser and placed a shotgun in every squad car" (Biles, *Richard J. Daley*, 151).
14. "Judge Cracks Down," 2.
15. "Quiet on the Black Front," 10.
16. Mosby, "Negro Leaders."
17. Mosby, 3.
18. Mosby, 3.
19. Mosby, 28.
20. "Probe Alleged Plot," 3.
21. Christmas, "Rev. Jackson," 3.
22. Fitzgerald, "Black Newsmen," 3.
23. "Police, Guardsmen Battle 'Yippies,'" 2.
24. Christmas, "Reporter Tells of Bloodbath," 4.
25. Christmas, 4.
26. Hunter, "Writer Recalls," 4.
27. "Chicago Police," 23.
28. Janson, "Holding a Convention," E4.
29. Kifner, "Politics," 71.
30. "Black Soldiers," 4.
31. Lukas, "Mood Is Hostile," 20.
32. Lukas, "Outlook after Chicago Violence," 11.
33. Lukas, "Johnson Mocked," 31.
34. Kifner, "On the Road," 22.
35. Buckley, "Battle of Chicago," 130–31.
36. Buckley, 131.
37. Buckley, 131.
38. Buckley, 131.
39. Buckley, 131.
40. Buckley, 132.
41. Buckley, 133.
42. Enright, "Military Might Marcher's Concern," 4.
43. Enright, 4.
44. Enright, 4.
45. Enright, "Politics Goes into Street," 8.
46. Enright, 8.
47. Hardwick, "Chicago," 5.
48. Hardwick, 5.
49. Hardwick, 5.
50. Hardwick, 7.
51. Styron, "In the Jungle," 12.
52. Styron, 12.
53. Styron, 12.

54 Styron, 12.
55 Sayre, "Democratic Death-In," 23.
56 Sayre, 23.
57 Sayre, 23.
58 Sayre, 23.
59 Sayre, 23–24.
60 Sayre, 28.
61 Arlen, "Air," 109.
62 Arlen, "Notes."
63 *Esquire* editor Harold Hayes sent a letter, dated January 30, 1968, to William Burroughs in London, inviting him to become part of a "house network" that would report on the Chicago convention and, originally, on the Republican National Convention being held in Miami, August 5–8, 1968. The concept called for Terry Southern to cover the Democrats' nomination process while the other three would fan out to "cover developments in the headquarters of Ronald Reagan, George Romney and Richard Nixon." Hayes told Burroughs that Southern had already been hired and, it seems from the letter, so had two well-known, avant-garde, absurdist playwrights, the French Romanian Eugene Ionesco and the Englishman Harold Pinter. Ionesco and Pinter must have declined, for it was Jean Genet and John Sack who completed the network. Instead of covering both conventions, the network focused on the Democratic National Convention. And instead of fanning out, three of the four writers, Genet, Southern, and Burroughs, generally stuck together while Sack split off to cover the police officers' point of view (Hayes, Letter to William Burroughs). (Thanks to John J. Pauly.)
64 Southern, "Grooving in Chi," 84.
65 Southern, 84.
66 Southern, 84.
67 Southern, 84.
68 Southern, 86.
69 Hill, *Grand Guy*, 176.
70 Southern, "Grooving in Chi," 86.
71 Southern, 86.
72 Sack, "In a Pig's Eye," 91.
73 Sack, 94.
74 Burroughs, "Coming," 89.
75 Burroughs, 89.
76 Burroughs, 90.
77 In the Harold T. Hayes archives, there is a wonderful letter from a disgruntled London, UK, reader that begins, "I have never read a more perverted article. … I knew that *Esquire* was subtitled 'The Magazine for Men' but I think of that epithet now as colored with connotations of the wrong sort" (Letter to the Editor).
78 Genet, "Members of the Assembly," 87; second and third ellipses in the original.
79 Genet, 87.
80 Genet, 89.
81 This author was surprised to realize two admittedly useless but nevertheless interesting facts. One: Stein and Thompson were the youngest writers discussed here. In August 1968, they were thirty-one years old. Sayre was thirty-five, Schultz thirty-six, Arlen thirty-seven, Sack thirty-eight, Styron forty-three, Southern forty-four, Mailer forty-five, Hardwick fifty-two, Burroughs fifty-four, and Genet fifty-seven. And two: except for Stein and Arlen, they are all dead (Genet died in 1986, Southern in 1995, Burroughs in 1997, Sayre in 2001, Sack in 2004, Thompson in 2005, Styron in 2006, Hardwick and Mailer in 2007, and Schultz in 2017).
82 Stein, "I Think."
83 Stein, *Living the Revolution*, 34.
84 Stein, 35.
85 Stein, 103.
86 Stein, 118–19.
87 Stein, 137–38.
88 Schultz, "Pigs," 27.
89 Schultz, 27.
90 Schultz, 28.
91 Schultz, 28.

92 Schultz, 29.
93 Schultz, 30.
94 The subtitle, of course, refers to Mailer's previous book about the march on the Pentagon, October 21–23, 1967, which was first published as "The Steps of the Pentagon," *Harper's*, March 1968, 47–142, then expanded to book form as *The Armies of the Night* (New York: New American Library, 1968), and published on May 1, 1968, well before convention season.
95 David Eason's point is that writers like Mailer (along with Joan Didion and Hunter Thompson) "describe what it feels like to live in a world where there is no consensus about a frame of reference to explain 'what it all means'" (Eason, "New Journalism," 192).
96 Mailer, *Miami*, 149.
97 Mailer, 170. Actually, Mailer quotes three paragraphs of a *Times* story by Lukas, a paragraph from a Steve Lerner story in the *Village Voice*, and six hundred words from a Jack Newfield story, also in the *Voice*.
98 Mailer, "Superman."
99 Mailer, *Miami*, 145–46.
100 Mailer, 184–85.
101 Menand, "Postscript."
102 Thompson, "Kentucky Derby," 1–12.
103 Adjusted for inflation to 2018 dollars, the $5,000 advance would be $35,613.07 and the $7,500 expense account would be $53,419.61 for a total of $89,032.69, according to www.usinflationcalculator.com (accessed February 27, 2018).
104 Thompson, *Kingdom of Fear*, 80.
105 I'm borrowing a phrase from William Langewiesche, who used it to describe his methodological approach to reporting on the post-9/11 cleanup of debris and gathering of human remains at the World Trade Center site. In the afterword to the paperback edition of *American Ground*, Langewiesche wrote that he wanted to "approach the narrative as if I were looking back on current events from several decades into the future. The result would be, I hoped, like a 'history in the present tense'" (204). I doubt the New Journalists were looking back from far into the future—that was not their project—but the urgency of their narratives does suggest a kind of eternal present tense.

Bibliography

Arlen, Michael J. "The Air: A Wednesday Evening in Chicago." *New Yorker*, September 7, 1968, 109–13.

———. "Notes on the New Journalism." *Atlantic Monthly*, May 1972. Accessed March 2, 2018. www.theatlantic.com/magazine/archive/1972/05/notes-on-the-new-journalism/376276/.

Biles, Roger. *Richard J. Daley: Politics, Race, and the Governing of Chicago*. DeKalb, IL: Northern Illinois University Press, 1995.

"Black Soldiers Say No to Demo Parley Duty." *Chicago Defender*, August 26, 1968, 4.

Buckley, Tom. "The Battle of Chicago: From the Yippies' Side." *New York Times Magazine*, September 15, 1968, SM28+.

Burroughs, William. "The Coming of the Purple Better One." *Esquire*, November 1968, 89–91.

"Chicago: A Great City." Editorial. *Chicago Tribune*, August 30, 1968, 1.

"Chicago Police Bar TV Trucks from Parking on Street Outside Hotels: Delays Foreseen in Live Coverage." *New York Times*, August 23, 1968, 23.

Christmas, Faith. "Reporter Tells of Bloodbath." *Daily Defender*, September 3, 1968.

———. "Rev. Jackson Raps Daley for Calling Up Troops." *Chicago Defender*, August 26, 1968, 3.

Eason, David. "The New Journalism and the Image-World." In *Literary Journalism in the Twentieth Century*, edited by Norman Sims, 191–205. Evanston, IL: Northwestern University Press, 2008.

Enright, Michael. "Military Might Marcher's Concern." *Globe and Mail*, August 26, 1968, 4.

———. "Politics Goes into Street." *Globe and Mail*, August 30, 1968, 8.

Fitzgerald, Sheryl. "Black Newsmen Bore Brunt of Cops' Attack." *Chicago Defender*, August 28, 1968, 3.

Genet, Jean. "The Members of the Assembly." *Esquire*, November 1968, 86–89.

Hardwick, Elizabeth. "Chicago." *New York Review of Books*, September 26, 1968, 5–7.

Hayes, Harold. Letter to William Burroughs, January 30, 1968. Box 7, Folder 6, MS596, Harold T. P. Hayes Papers. Special Collections and Archives, Z. Smith Reynolds Library, Wake Forest University, Winston-Salem, NC.

"Heavy Security at Convention." *Chicago Defender*, August 5, 1968, 3.

Hill, Lee. *A Grand Guy: The Art and Life of Terry Southern*. New York: HarperCollins, 2001.
Hunter, Bob. "Writer Recalls Mob Scene Here." *Chicago Defender*, September 4, 1968, 4.
Janson, Donald. "Holding a Convention in a Garrison City." *New York Times*, August 25, 1968, E4.
"Judge Cracks Down on Police Abuse." *Chicago Defender*, August 31, 1968, 1–2.
Kifner, John. "On the Road to Chicago with Some Protesters." *New York Times*, August 23, 1968, 22.
———. "Politics: Thousand of U.S. Troops Mobilized for Guard Duty at Democratic Convention." *New York Times*, August 25, 1968, 71.
Langewiesche, William. *American Ground: Unbuilding the World Trade Center*. New York: North Point Press, 2003.
Leonard, John. "Bloody Melodrama." Review of *No One Was Killed*, by John Schultz, and *Living the Revolution*, by David Lewis Stein. *New York Times*, November 27, 1969, 27.
Letter to the Editor. November 28, 1968. MS596, Harold T. P. Hayes Papers. Special Collections and Archives, Z. Smith Reynolds Library, Wake Forest University, Winston-Salem, NC.
Lukas, J. Anthony. "Johnson Mocked as a 'Freak' at 'Unbirthday Party.'" *New York Times*, August 28, 1968, 31.
———. "Mood Is Hostile in Back of the Yards Area." *New York Times*, August 24, 1968, 20.
———. "Outlook after Chicago Violence." *New York Times*, August 31, 1968, 11.
Mailer, Norman. *Miami and the Siege of Chicago: An Informal History of the Republican and Democratic Conventions of 1968*. New York: Donald I. Fine, 1986.
———. "Superman Comes to the Supermarket." *Esquire*, December 8, 2009. Accessed February 17, 2018. www.esquire.com/news-politics/a3858/superman-supermarket/. Originally published November 1960.
Menand, Louis. "Postscript: Norman Mailer." *New Yorker*, November 19, 2007. Accessed February 21, 2018. www.newyorker.com/magazine/2007/11/19/norman-mailer.
Mosby, Donald. "Negro Leaders React to Violence Report." *Chicago Defender*, December 4, 1968, 3, 28.
"Police, Guardsmen Battle 'Yippies.'" *Chicago Defender*, August 29, 1968, 2.
"Probe Alleged Plot to Kill HHH, Gene." *Chicago Defender*, August 24, 1968, 3.
"Quiet on the Black Front." Editorial. *Chicago Defender*, September 21, 1968, 10.
Sack, John. "In a Pig's Eye." *Esquire*, November 1968, 91–94.
Sayre, Nora. "Democratic Death-In: Chicago, August 1968." In *Sixties Going on Seventies*, 23–32. New York: Arbor House, 1973. Originally published as "On the Battlefield," *New Statesman*, September 6, 1968. Republished May 22, 2008. Accessed February 17, 2018. www.newstatesman.com/society/2008/05/chicago-police-vietnam-history.
Schultz, John. *No One Was Killed: Documentation and Meditation: Convention Week, Chicago—August 1968*. Chicago: Big Table Publishing, 1969.
———. *No One Was Killed: The Democratic National Convention, August 1968*. With a new foreword by Todd Gitlin and a new afterword by the author. Chicago: University of Chicago Press, 2009.
———. "Pigs, Prague, Other Democrats, Chicago and the Sleeper in the Park." *Evergreen Review*, December 1968, 26+.
Southern, Terry. "Grooving in Chi." *Esquire*, November 1968, 83–86.
Stein, David Lewis. "I Think the Yippies Are the Finest People I Have Met So Far." *Saturday Night*, July 1969, 31–34.
———. *Living the Revolution: The Yippies in Chicago*. New York: Bobbs-Merrill, 1969.
Styron, William. "In the Jungle." *New York Review of Books*, September 26, 1968, 11–13.
Thompson, Hunter S. "The Kentucky Derby Is Decadent and Depraved." *Scanlan's Monthly*, June 1970.
———. *Kingdom of Fear: Loathsome Secrets of a Star-Crossed Child in the Final Days of the American Century*. New York: Simon and Schuster, 2003.
Thornton, Brian. "The 'Dangerous' *Chicago Defender*: A Study of the Newspaper's Editorials and Letters to the Editor in 1968." *Journalism History* 40, no. 1 (Spring 2014): 40–50.
Walker, Daniel. *Rights in Conflict: The Violent Confrontation of Demonstrators and Police in the Parks and Streets of Chicago during the Week of the Democratic National Convention of 1968*. Philadelphia, PA: Braceland Brothers, 1968.
"'We're Staying Put,' Rights Leaders Say." *Chicago Defender*, August 22, 1968, 3.
Wolfe, Sheila. "Police Action Draws Praise, Condemnation." *Chicago Tribune*, August 31, 1968, 7.
Wolfe, Tom. Introduction to *The New Journalism*, edited by Tom Wolfe and E. W. Johnson, 3–52. New York: Harper and Row, 1973.
———. *The Kandy-Kolored Tangerine-Flake Streamline Baby*. New York: Farrar, Straus and Giroux, 1965.

12
LITERARY JOURNALISM AND ALTERNATIVE MEDIA

Susan Keith

During the 1960s and 1970s, a new world of alternative media exploded in the United States, enabled by a revolution in offset printing technology[1] and coalescing around social change: opposition to the war in Vietnam, an eruption of youth culture, and activism for the rights of African Americans, women, gay and lesbian individuals, and Native Americans.[2] These publications—a wide range of newspapers, magazines, and pamphlets that have come to be known as the "alternative," "radical," "underground," or "progressive" press—rejected many of the contemporary conventions of mainstream journalism: a focus on traditional news topics, a privileging of official institutional sources, and a detached, objective stance. Instead, they trumpeted causes, reveled in the first person, and critiqued and tweaked the Establishment.

Some also used techniques often ascribed to literary journalism or one of its subgenres, the "New Journalism" beginning to make tentative inroads into some mainstream journalism outlets about the same time.[3] Although different writers have approached literary journalism and New Journalism differently,[4] these techniques generally have been defined as including immersion in the scene, focus on dramatic detail and the writer's experience, novelistic storytelling, and emphasis on dialogue in recounting events.[5] This essay examines the use of these techniques in two types of "outside-the-mainstream" US media of the 1960s and 1970s: counterculture newspapers and local journalism reviews, publications in which journalists critiqued their own profession and the performance of news media outlets.[6] This work is important for two reasons. First, it addresses a gap in scholarship at the intersection of literary journalism studies and scholarship on the US alternative press of the Vietnam War.[7] Second, examining these two types of publications, the essay illuminates how techniques of literary journalism were embraced by writers who might initially appear quite different—mainstream media insiders and amateurs with a cause—but were united in a sense that new types of media could change their worlds.

Understanding "Alternative Media"

Before addressing how the alternative press employed literary journalism in the 1960s and 1970s, I must explain how I am using "alternative media," a term as resistant to easy definition as "literary journalism."[8] British media scholar Chris Atton writes that to be considered "alternative," media must be economically and organizationally different from mainstream commercial media, "radical in the sense that they are opposed to hierarchical, elite-centered notions of journalism as a business."[9] He also sees such media as characterized by participatory practices that create "horizontal and dialogic communication."[10] Many of the radical publications of the 1960s and 1970s fit that bill, according to John McMillian, author of *Smoking Typewriters: The Sixties Underground Press and the Rise of Alternative Media in America*. "Many of these papers were run communally," he told the *New Yorker* magazine, by people who "were suspicious of leadership, hierarchies, and authority." As a result, "some underground papers practically made it an editorial policy not to edit."[11]

Marisol Sandoval and Christian Fuchs, however, caution that being participatory and noncommercial is not enough to make a media outlet "alternative."[12] They suggest that whether media are "alternative" should rest instead on their content, whether it is critical and "questions dominative social relations."[13] Taking these definitions together, we might then say that the term "the alternative press," in the context of the United States in the 1960s and 1970s, applies to print media from that period with content that is critical or radical, which are likely to but not required to be participatory and noncommercial.

As works by James Hamilton and Lauren Kessler demonstrate, outlets that fit, at least loosely, the description of "the alternative press" have existed since the American Revolution.[14] As a result, that term encompasses both more types of media and more specific media than could reasonably be examined for a chapter like this one. To narrow the field, this chapter will focus on the 1960s and 1970s—a period that encompasses student protests in the US and Europe and is often associated in popular imagination with rebellion against authority.[15] It will also be confined to two types of alternative press publications from that period: the counterculture/underground/antiwar press and local journalism reviews published by working journalists.

The former group of antiestablishment publications included such newspapers as the *Los Angeles Free Press*, published weekly from 1964 to 1978; the *Paper*, published in East Lansing, Michigan, from 1965 to 1969;[16] the *Berkeley Barb*, a weekly published in Berkeley, California, from 1965 to 1980; the *East Village Other*, a biweekly printed in New York City from 1965 to 1972;[17] and the *Fifth Estate*, launched in 1965 in Detroit[18] and still publishing online as of spring 2018.[19] These five publications were the original members of the Underground Press Syndicate, a loose content-sharing network that, along with the similar Liberation News Service, was responsible for an explosion of critical and radical media across the US. By advocating sharing of material, they gave any local publisher who wanted to start an alternative publication a ready supply of copy to publish in it.[20]

Together, these alternative newspapers, which have been widely analyzed,[21] are often referred to as the "underground press." Their creators repurposed this term from its original use as a name for media published in secret in totalitarian or occupied societies, such as Nazi-occupied France in World War II, even though the publications of the 1960s and 1970s were, for the most part, neither clandestinely produced nor secretly distributed. It is difficult to know for certain how many newspapers, magazines, and pamphlets might be considered part of this group of counterculture publications—focused on anti-Vietnam War activism, music, youth culture, and sometimes drugs—but the number seems to have been in at least the low thousands. By 1969, relatively early in the period, the Underground Press Syndicate had ninety-eight members, and far from all underground papers belonged to that network.[22] The University of Washington's "Mapping American Social Movements" project estimates that there were more than two thousand "underground, alternative, and other kinds of unorthodox publications" in the United States between 1965 and 1975.[23]

The second group of publications considered here, local journalism reviews of roughly the same period, are less often studied. They might be considered the less well-known relatives of two long-lived US journalism reviews with national scope and highly professional standards: *Columbia Journalism Review*, founded in 1961 at the Columbia Graduate School of Journalism in New York City and still publishing (though mostly online with just two or three print editions a year),[24] and *American Journalism Review*, published from 1977 to 2015, the first sixteen years under the title *Washington Journalism Review*[25] and the last twenty-eight years under the auspices of the University of Maryland.[26] These reviews have been the subject of several scholarly studies,[27] but only a few of the twenty-five to forty local journalism reviews published in the United States between 1968 and 1980[28] have received significant academic scrutiny.

The first of the local reviews was an annual publication created in 1958 at the Montana School of Journalism, which was originally titled simply *Journalism Review* and, later, *Montana Journalism Review*. For twenty years, it provided readers with articles on press criticism, Montana journalism history, journalism-related research done by the school's master's students, and what sometimes amounted to public relations for the Montana Newspaper Association. It was revived, on its fiftieth anniversary, as a publication of a Montana School of Journalism course.[29]

The local journalism review movement did not gain steam, however, until the 1968 founding of *Chicago Journalism Review*, started by journalists dismayed by Chicago newspapers' characterizations—once national media had left town—of violence that had taken place outside the Democratic National Convention. That publication was, as Steve Macek notes, something new: "a journalism review with a local focus, published not by academics but by members of the working press, and devoted to candidly examining the constraints imposed on journalists by the corporate structure of the media."[30] *Chicago Journalism Review* published for seven years, with 9,000 subscribers across the country.[31]

A number of those subscribers were other journalists, who were inspired by *Chicago Journalism Review* to create journalism reviews in their own cities. Eventually, reviews blossomed around the country, including *Ball and Chain*, *Black Journalism Review*, *Buncombe: A Review of Baltimore Journalism*, *Dallas Journalism Review*, *Hawaii Journalism Review*, *Houston Journalism Review*, *Northwest Journalism Review*, *Overset: A Review of Newspaper Journalism*, *Philadelphia Journalism Review*, *San Francisco Journalism Review*, *St. Louis Journalism Review*, *Thorn: A Connecticut Valley Journalism Review*, *Twin Cities Journalism Review*, the *Unsatisfied Man* in Denver, *Wisconsin Journalism Review*,[32] and *[MORE]* in New York City, a review arguably more national in scope than its peers.[33] These reviews varied widely in content and degree of radicalization. All, however, met Sandoval and Fuchs's alternative media definition of having critical content, and all except perhaps *[MORE]* met Atton's definition of being participatory and nonprofit. Most, in fact, survived only a short time because they lacked a robust financing model and were "staffed" by contributors who already had full-time jobs in the news media.

Although examining these two types of publications together may seem, at first, counterintuitive, there are reasons for doing so. First, local journalism reviews were, in some ways, related to radical alternative newspapers. Like the radical newspapers that had grown up in college towns and major cities to record an explosion of youth culture, the journalist-produced local reviews that followed *Chicago Journalism Review* were reacting to questions about how journalists should define themselves in relation to the institutions for which they worked. The issue to resolve, *Chicago Journalism Review* managing editor Ron Dorfman suggested, was: "Were we mere employes [sic], who could be told what to write about and how to write it, or did we have some professional status and the attendant responsibility to portray the world as we saw and understood it?"[34] Second, the two types of publications occupied the same time, with what is generally considered the earliest of the major radical newspapers, the *Los Angeles Free Press*, having been founded in 1964,[35] just four years before the first of the reporter-produced journalism reviews, *Chicago Journalism Review*. In addition, some of the journalists contributing to the reviews were young reporters, people who were exactly the target audience, at least in age, of the counterculture publications. It seems quite possible that some people were reading both types of publications.

Literary Journalism: A Rare Approach

It is risky to make sweeping claims about a group of publications that contains twenty-five to forty titles (the journalism reviews of the 1960s and 1970s), much less a group that contains perhaps two thousand examples (the US radical press of the same period)—especially since some issues of both types of publications have been lost to time. It is probably fair, however, to suggest that true literary journalism in either type was the exception. Both counterculture alternative media and local journalism reviews had missions that could make passion more important than writerly style,[36] which led to a number of straightforward journalistic approaches.

One early issue of the *Berkeley Barb*, for example, offered this run-of-the-mill inverted pyramid-style lede on an article about the detention of three women involved in the Free Speech Movement: "Three female FSM jailees spent their last five days at Santa Rita prison farm in isolation 'lock up' cells, the BARB learned in an exclusive interview Tuesday nite [sic]."[37] Similarly, an article about a dinner honoring a civil rights activist in a 1967 issue of the *Fifth Estate* took a straightforward approach that would have been at home in any mainstream newspaper: "More than 200 peace, civil rights and church activists honored David M. Gracie at a testimonial dinner Friday, July 21, as the Rev. Gracie prepared to leave Detroit for a new job with the Episcopal Diocese of Pennsylvania."[38] And a 1967 issue of the *Los Angeles Free Press* had a front-page story headlined "Poverty Board Elections to be Held March 5th"[39] that could have run in the mainstream *Los Angeles Times*.

Similarly, most of the writing in local journalism reviews also was far from literary. For example, an article in a 1970 edition of the *Unsatisfied Man: A Review of Colorado Journalism* about gendered hiring practices in Denver newsrooms began with a rather conventional feature approach:

> If you ask men who do the hiring, there is no discrimination in the newsrooms of either *The Denver Post* or *The Rocky Mountain News*. Both insist they hire the best man—oops, the best person—for the job. But talk to the one woman working cityside at the News or any number of women at *The Post* and the answer is different.[40]

Similar approaches were used in articles on news media coverage of gender and public policy and foreign news in *St. Louis Journalism Review*;[41] looting by American soldiers during the Vietnam War in *A. P. Review*, published by Associated Press staff members in New York;[42] and President Nixon's veto of the Comprehensive Child Development Bill in *Philadelphia Journalism Review*.[43]

The rarity of literary journalism in both types of publications in the 1960s and 1970s is, however, in many ways not surprising. The journalists writing for the journalism reviews would have used such straightforward approaches in their day jobs, and writers in counterculture newspapers would have seen such straightforward approaches, no doubt, in their own reading. So it may have seemed natural to use such approaches even in publications that challenged mainstream thinking about society or journalism. (Using such writing styles, of course, did not make either the counterculture publications of the 1960s and 1970s or the journalism reviews "mainstream," rather than alternative. As some scholars of alternative media have noted, journalism practices are not binary, either alternative or mainstream, but exist in what Tony Harcup referred to as "a continuum, with people, ideas and practices moving along this continuum, in both directions."[44])

A lack of familiarity with how to practice literary journalism may also have been an issue, although works that are rightly considered icons of the literary journalism movement known as the "New Journalism" were being published during this period[45] and surely were read by at least some counterculture writers and journalists publishing in journalism reviews. But merely reading literary journalism does not teach one how to report and write it well. As Thomas R. Schmidt has pointed out in his study of the embrace of literary journalism in the Style section of the *Washington Post* in the 1970s—part of the period under consideration in this chapter—literary journalism was just beginning to appear in well-funded mainstream US media.[46] So it is likely that many writers contributing work to counterculture media or local journalism reviews in the 1960s and 1970s were inexperienced at practicing the form.

Another factor may have been that very few alternative/antiwar/radical media publications or local journalism reviews compensated their writers. A 1969 survey reported that only 72 percent of underground newspapers made a profit,[47] and the *Berkeley Barb* paid some writers nothing and others fifty cents an inch, "with reductions for fractions of an inch."[48] Meanwhile, only the best-funded of the local journalism reviews, *Chicago Journalism Review*, which had some foundation grants,[49] and *[MORE]*, bankrolled by the private banking inheritance of publisher and former *New York Post* reporter Woody Woodward, seems to have had the ability to pay staff members. Even *[MORE]*, its historian Kevin Lerner notes, "rarely had enough money to pay its contributors well (or sometimes at all)," meaning that the writers "often turned in some of their less-thorough work."[50] So writers with the skills to produce literary journalism may have been reluctant to spend the considerable time necessary to do so for these types of outlets, especially if they had full-time "day" jobs, as many journalism review contributors did.

In addition, both types of media had limited space—sometimes as little as eight quarterfold pages—and audience members who expected a variety of content. Some of the counterculture publications filled cover space with cartoons, such as those by illustrator R. Crumb on the *East Village Other*,[51] or psychedelic swirls, such as those by designer Gary Grimshaw on early editions of the *Ann Arbor Sun*.[52] Some of the journalism reviews devoted covers to political cartoons, such as those by *Chicago Sun-Times* Pulitzer Prize-winner Bill Mauldin on *Chicago Journalism Review*[53] and *Philadelphia Inquirer* cartoonist Tony Auth on *Philadelphia Journalism Review*.[54]

Inside the publications, space was often reserved for content that didn't lend itself to literary journalism treatment. For example, significant parts of the *Paper* of East Lansing, Michigan, consisted of attacks on Michigan State University, its student government, or the official campus newspaper, the *State News*, where the editor of the *Paper*, Michael Kindman, had been a staff member.[55] Several of the journalism reviews devoted a page or more to "winners and sinners" columns of media praise and pans modeled on *Columbia Journalism Review*'s Darts and Laurels column.[56] Some of the local journalism reviews also devoted space to summarizing the work of their peers,[57] keeping up with counterculture alternative publications,[58] or reprinting copy from other local journalism reviews or journalism-related publications. For example, *Overset*, a journalism review published in San Diego, frequently republished essays from the *Grassroots Editor*, the publication of the International Society of Weekly Newspaper Editors. *Overset* noted that an article in its fifth issue was "a milestone … the first article written specifically for this magazine."[59]

Literary Journalism: Finding a Home

Some alternative media publications and local journalism reviews, however, employed at least some literary journalism techniques. Others produced what might reasonably be called literary journalism. They published the work of writers who embedded themselves in stories that used innovative narrative structures and the techniques of literary fiction.

In the Counterculture Media

A 1973 issue of *Borrowed Times*, a newspaper published in Missoula, Montana, from 1972 to 1980, for example, recounted a visit to the University of Montana by Nelson Rockefeller (then New York Governor), not by discussing what he said, but by describing how he was protested. The activists gathered below the campus's Montana Room and reenacted the 1971 riot at New York's Attica State Prison, which left thirty-nine dead and eighty hurt and prompted Rockefeller to tell President Gerald Ford, "That's life."[60] Then, the demonstrators "surged upstairs."

> They gained entrance to the dining room through the kitchen, sending Rock's security guards into a frenzy almost matched by the nervousness of U.M. President Robert Pantzer and some of the other guests. During the next hour, Rockefeller was continually fielding questions from the hostile crowd that surrounded the banquet tables. He attempted to maintain the composure of a man used to such inquisitions by deflecting questions and talking around the real issues. ...
>
> Although the press and many of the Missoula elite tried to ignore the confrontation, some seemed genuinely pleased that real questions were being raised and that they didn't have to sit through another boring and empty lecture.
>
> One of the people sympathetic to the demonstrators was the luncheon's second guest of honor—Carroll O'Connor, the Archie Bunker of "All in the Family." No great fan of Rockefeller himself, O'Connor said the luncheon demonstration was "marvelous" and praised those who packed the dining room to push Rocky up against a wall.[61]

The unnamed writer recounting the scene seems to have been with the protesters downstairs. By following the events from their view, he or she kept Rockefeller silent until the tenth paragraph. The author thus privileged over a sitting governor a group of protesters who likely would have been marginalized in Missoula's mainstream media outlets.

Sometimes when radical media used literary journalism techniques, the sense of participation of the author was relatively restrained, as with a 1968 Q&A-style interview with guitarist Jimi Hendrix in the *Great Speckled Bird*, an alternative newspaper published in Atlanta, Georgia, from 1968 to 1985. After describing two lackluster Hendrix shows on August 17 at Atlanta Municipal Auditorium, the unidentified author wrote:

> Then there is the interview—Hendrix sits on the 21st floor of the Regency Hyatt House and does not want to be interviewed. ... We begin slowly, phones ring, doors knock, the rest of the band comes in, and they are good people in a better mood than Hendrix, we stone, we spray aerosol cans, we indeed finish slowly with Hubert Humphrey's red and blue face on the color tube.[62] We leave stepping over four or five Afro kids in the hall by the star's door—strange—the elevators are a gas though. We stop at every floor and freak for Regency guests.[63]

The writer then transitions into a rather unremarkable Q&A, in which Hendrix complained that he was tired before the show and that audiences had come to expect him to burn his guitar.

In other alternative media accounts, the narrative was as chaotic as the scene. Take, for instance, the Liberation News Service dispatch on the occupation of promoter Bill Graham's Fillmore East venue in New York City by members of Up Against the Wall, Motherfucker,[64] a radical Lower East Side collective headed by Ben Morea and known for protesting the war in Vietnam by "unfurling banners of Napalmed children during High Mass in St. Patrick's Cathedral"[65] and throwing cow blood on US Secretary of State Dean Rusk. The scheduled feature at the Fillmore on October 22, 1968, was Judith Malina and Julian Beck's Living Theater performance of *Paradise Now*,[66] a show that featured "controlled improvisation involving nudity and audience participation,"[67] staged as a fund-raiser for students arrested during the occupation of Columbia University the previous April.[68] "The night began ominously enough with the first skit getting booed off the stage," the author writes in a copy of the dispatch published in the Seattle alternative newspaper *Helix*. Then Yippie Abbie Hoffman "goofed through days and nights in jails in Washington and Chicago" and "everybody crowded into the lobby to see the Sixth Street Players, who got crowded out onto Second Avenue." Next:

> The actors stripped down the [*sic*] jock straps and bikinis in the middle of the crowded stage and people climbed up curtains, speakers, scaffolds and ropes. Women's Liberation contributed a huge red silk banner serpentined through the crowd ... art, audience, action, politics, pretense became nearly one. The players called for a free theater. "Open the Doors. Bring in the people. Occupy the theater" and non-violence. "Don't seize power. Don't kill. You're the pigs, Pigs." and [*sic*] from the audience, "Kill the Pigs! Revolution! Class War! ... Ben Morea and Tom Newman ran down Graham [about] how he lived off the community's culture at prices they couldn't pay.[69]

The author quoted Graham as saying in response, "If you want to take this theater by force, you'll have to kill me first."[70]

> Then there was an hour of confused peripatetic negotiation. Graham would go from group to group flanked by promoters and aides ... All through it people are goofing from the stage, waving, singing, throwing bread, burning money. Finally, Graham promises to open up the Fillmore next Wednesday for a town meeting of the "community," and Ben Morea says, "If it takes us ten hours, everybody in this theater is going to get to say what he wants."[71]

Although perhaps not terribly literary in voice or grammar—the Liberation News Service article, as published in *Helix*, was missing occasional words, and lacked conventional writerly control—the report provided a point of view and placed readers within the scene, as the best literary journalism does.

In Local Journalism Reviews

Of all the local journalism reviews, *[MORE]*, located in New York, where it had access to writers working in the country's largest media market, had the greatest chance to publish work that clearly met the definition of literary journalism. For example, nonfiction writer and memoirist Barbara Grizzuti Harrison took readers to the National Religious Broadcasters Convention in Washington, DC, to observe the rise of the religious and political right in an article titled "The God Band: Coast to Coast with the Holy Ghost." As a device, Harrison—a more accomplished writer than many journalism reviews were able to draw—used the view of a French television journalist covering the event:

> It was his first day in America. French broadcasting had sent him over with a camera crew to do a coast-to-coast story on born-again Christians. He had survived a press conference with Anita Bryant and a futile search for the elusive Larry Flynt (said to be lurking in the halls of the Washington Hilton or sulking in his room, where the ubiquitous

strains of "Yes, Jesus Loves Me," piped like Muzak throughout the convention exhibition halls, presumably could not reach him).

Now he was listening to Anita Bryant sing to an evening audience of 1,100 evangelicals who had gathered in Washington for the National Religious Broadcasters 35th annual convention. Bryant sang, red-leather bible in her hand, in a white, rose-splattered gown with floating chiffon petals. ...

"Are all Americans like this?" the gentleman from French broadcasting asked. "Are religion and patriotism and show business the same thing in your country?"

"I came here," he said, summoning up his best English, "thinking I was a Christian. Now I discover I'm only a Catholic. That doesn't count?" Then Bryant segued from the "The Battle Hymn of the Republic" to the "Florida Sunshine Tree" jingle. The Frenchman surreptitiously made the sign of the cross.[72]

Harrison, who seems to have read at least some of the New Journalism—she famously attacked the prose of Joan Didion, author of an acclaimed book of New Journalism essays,[73] as "a bag of tricks"[74]—put the reader in the shoes of an outsider, showing what that person would have experienced. An accomplished essayist who went on to write about her own religious upbringing as a Jehovah's Witness,[75] Harrison knew that having someone else express concerns about religion in the United States made the critique of the religious right stronger than if she herself had leveled it.

Chicago Journalism Review used a different type of literary journalism approach in its December 1969 issue,[76] a special report on the December 4 shooting deaths of Black Panthers Fred Hampton, 21, and Mark Clark, 22, in an apartment on West Monroe Street in Chicago occupied by at least nine people.[77] The review's challenge in covering the story, as a monthly publication, was to find a way to out-report the city's four mainstream daily newspapers. Fortunately for *Chicago Journalism Review*, the dailies had made several mistakes. First, *Chicago Today* had simply accepted the early police version that the men died in a gun battle with police—using the headline "Panther Bosses Killed in Cop Shootout"[78]—when the reality turned out to be quite different. Then the *Sun-Times* buried an article reporting that the bullet holes in the apartment, portrayed in wrenching *Chicago Journalism Review* cover art by Bill Mauldin,[79] were not located where they would be if the police version of events was correct, while editors initially discouraged reporters from digging deeper.[80] In eight articles, a column, a chart displaying contradictions among various accounts of the fatal raid, and a diagram of the apartment, the journalism review explained how police accounts of the deaths shifted.

Perhaps the most literary approach was taken by Brian Boyer, a former *Sun-Times* reporter whom *Chicago Journalism Review* identified as "the first newsman to discover the discrepancies between the police account and the physical condition of the apartment."[81] According to an editor's note, he was asked to explain in the journalism review how and why the raid occurred and how prosecutors felt about the wave of criticism they had received. He did so by drawing readers into the life of a minor player in the controversy, starting a standard past-tense account of the shootings and events that led to them with a separate, italicized present-tense emotive narrative:

> The phone number at the State Attorney's office is 542-2900. If you call that number and ask for the boss, Edward V. Hanrahan, or his assistant, Dick Jalovec, you get a slight man with a Mr. Chips' voice. His name is Mel Mawrence, and now he is the public relations man for the office. ... Mel has not been feeling well these pleasant, early winter days because the man he calls his master has not been feeling well. It has not been ill health that has stricken his preoccupied master ... . What's made a former

acolyte like Ed feel so bad is that his own number one man, [Chicago Mayor] Dick Daley, hasn't been going out front to tell the people how much he's behind him.[82]

After explaining Hanrahan's initial accounts of the shootings to the press, Boyer returned several times, in italics, to Mawrence:

> There is a lot of mail on Mel's desk and some of it is for Mr. Hanrahan and some of it is against him but he's thoroughly sick of all of it. … Mel keeps wondering what is going on in that apartment on Madison Street with all the people going through and the Panther kids telling all of them the bulletholes show that Fred got murdered in his sleep. He'd like to go through himself even though Mr. Hanrahan's a good man and wouldn't lie if he could help it. Mel thinks there's something going on and in all his life he's never seen anything like it before.[83]

Indeed, the deaths of Hampton and Clark made a mark on Chicago and the nation. There were protests in Chicago and as far away as Oregon, and Hampton was eulogized by the Reverend Ralph Abernathy, the heir to the nonviolent civil rights crusade of the Reverend Martin Luther King Jr. After the slayings, it was revealed that Hampton had in fact died in his sleep, drugged by his teenage bodyguard, William O'Neal, an FBI informant who had infiltrated the Panthers. After Hanrahan and the police raiders were indicted but acquitted by a Chicago jury, the Panthers filed a civil suit against the federal government, which was eventually settled by giving Hampton's family and others $1.8 million.[84] Hanrahan lost his bid to be reelected as state's attorney, and Hampton's Black Panther associate Bobby Rush eventually became a politician earning election to the Chicago City Council and the US House of Representatives.[85]

Other articles in local journalism reviews used at least touches of literary approaches, such as extended dialogue, immersion into a scene, or dramatic detail. For example, in a *San Francisco Journalism Review* article examining whether Bay-area media had under-covered the trial of Ruchell Cinque Magee, a San Quentin inmate and alleged accomplice of Angela Davis, radio reporter Mark Schwartz used first-person details and colorful language to explain how security at the courthouse attempted to intimidate reporters. Schwartz wrote that one officer, "6 feet, 8 inches of Aryan arrogance, once pulled me over and said, 'We know what you're up to Mr. Schwartz. You know I'd love to throw you out of here.'" In the face of such threats, Schwartz wrote, "there was no one to turn to except the radio audience. The Police Chief sent you to the Sheriff, the Sheriff sent you to the judge, and … [the judge]—who was responsible for the whole thing—was unapproachable."[86] Schwartz's use of specific detail, colorful phrases, repetition, and a first-person approach created the opportunity for an emotional connection with the reader.

Potential Advantages of Literary Approaches

Reaching readers emotionally was only one potential outcome of the use of literary journalism techniques in the alternative press and local journalism reviews, but it was an important potential outcome. Many underground publications, McMillian writes, were "barely solvent,"[87] and local journalism reviews were full of pleas for readers to subscribe and donate—requests that often noted a review's nonprofit, tax-exempt status.[88] There were death knells and resurrections. The board of *Philadelphia Journalism Review*, for example, voted to kill the review in late 1973 or early 1974 but then kept it going, saying that the publication was "gasping, coughing, struggling for life like a patient in an intensive care unit."[89] So counterculture media and local journalism reviews could use all the emotional appeal they could get.

In addition, use of the most basic of literary journalism techniques—immersion into the scene, focus on dramatic detail, and attention to the writer's experience—also had the potential to help brand counterculture media and local journalism reviews as something distinct from everyday reporting in mainstream newspapers and run-of-the-mill features in magazines. Both radical publications and local journalism reviews depended for survival on readers who had not had the chance to build long associations with these relatively new products. So use of particularly literary reporting and writing techniques could have helped identify these publications, though there is little evidence editors and publishers took that into account.

Individual writers also could brand themselves through the ways they reported and wrote their contributions to counterculture media and local journalism reviews. The fact that material from radical publications was shared among those who were members of the Underground Press Syndicate and Liberation News Service might have served to spread a contributor's fame beyond his or her own city. Similarly, writers who contributed to local journalism reviews had the chance to display their writing prowess to peers and potential hiring managers beyond those who followed their usual beat.

Conclusion

There were an estimated two thousand alternative counterculture newspapers, magazines, and pamphlets in the United States during the 1960s and 1970s, a period when twenty-five to forty journalism reviews—depending on what one considers a journalism review—also were published. Analyzing every article in each issue of all of those publications was beyond the scope of this chapter. This chapter has established, however, that literary journalism techniques and full-blown literary journalism approaches were used by some—though evidence suggests far from the majority—of writers in the two types of non-mainstream publications examined here.

This work could usefully be extended in several ways. First, a more systematic examination of counterculture publications—starting, perhaps, with those that were successful enough to be part of the Liberation News Service and the Underground Press Syndicate—might reveal the frequency with which writers in so-called underground publications employed literary techniques. Writers for these publications could have been familiar from high school or college literature courses with the work of nineteenth- and early twentieth-century authors who wrote literary nonfiction as well as novels, including Charles Dickens, Stephen Crane, and Willa Cather.[90] Second, future research might delve more deeply into the more manageable archive of journalism reviews—an understudied type of US media production—to determine not only how frequently they used literary journalism approaches but also, more broadly, what prose and rhetorical strategies they employed.

An even more ambitious project might use interviews with contributors to alternative media or journalism reviews to trace the impetus for using techniques of literary journalism. It would be interesting to know, for example, whether practitioners of 1960s and 1970s journalism were influenced by their reading of New Journalism practitioners such as Gay Talese, Joan Didion, and Tom Wolfe. It would also be worthwhile to understand whether literary journalism approaches in late twentieth-century and early twenty-first-century media were tied to the creation of courses about New Journalism or literary journalism from as early as the 1980s.[91] As this work stands, however, it indicates yet another place in the panoply of media production where literary journalism approaches have taken hold.

Notes

1 McMillian, *Smoking Typewriters*.
2 Lewis, *Outlaws of America*.

3   Schmidt, "Pioneer of Style"; Wolfe, "Birth."
4   Eason, "New Journalism."
5   Sims, *Literary Journalists*.
6   Bertrand, "Look at Journalism Reviews."
7   There *has* been some scholarship on literary impulses in what might be called "alternative media." See, for example, Choonoo, "Sophiatown Generation." But little of that work has substantively addressed US alternative media of the Vietnam War era.
8   Richard Lance Keeble refers to "literary journalism" as a "highly contested term, its essential elements being a constant source of debate" ("Literary Journalism").
9   Atton, "What Is 'Alternative' Journalism?" 268.
10 Atton, *Alternative Media*, 154.
11 Blake, "Ask an Academic."
12 Sandoval and Fuchs, "Towards a Critical Theory."
13 Sandoval and Fuchs, 147.
14 Hamilton, "Theory Through History"; Kessler, *Dissident Press*.
15 McMillian, *Smoking Typewriters*.
16 "About *The Paper*."
17 NYU Arthur L. Carter Journalism Institute and The Local East Village, "East Village Other."
18 Gholz, "*Fifth* at 40."
19 *Fifth Estate*.
20 Charnigo, "Prisoners of Microfilm"; Guida, "East Village Other"; Lewes, "Underground Press in America."
21 See, for example, Glessing, *Underground Press in America*; Hume, "Past as Persuader"; Levin and Spates, "Hippie Values"; Mount, "Grasp the Weapon"; Stewart, *On the Ground*.
22 Lewes, "Underground Press in America," 382.
23 "Mapping the Underground."
24 Arana, "Columbia Journalism Review"; Pope, "Note from the Editor."
25 Robertson, "Life and Times."
26 Hoyt, "End of *American Journalism Review*."
27 See, for example, Haas and Steiner, "Fears of Corporate Colonization." The article offers an examination of the coverage in *Columbia Journalism Review* and *American Journalism Review* of the public journalism movement.
28 The lower number was given in Bertrand, "Look at Journalism Reviews." The higher number comes from Klotzer and Block, "Critiquing the Mainstream Media."
29 Keith, "Montana Journalism Review." *Montana Journalism Review* was published until 1978 and was resurrected—with content focusing on Montana issues, rather than journalism—as an undergraduate class project in 2008.
30 Macek, "Reporters' Rebellion."
31 Anderson and Benjaminson, *Investigative Reporting*, 12.
32 Keith, "Examining the Critics' Criticism."
33 Lerner, "Gadfly to the Watchdogs."
34 Lerner, 187–88, 189.
35 McMillian, *Smoking Typewriters*, 37.
36 Writing about media produced by Students for a Democratic Society, John McMillian notes that "through the organization's various permutations, melodramatic zeal was rarely in short supply; reticence was" (*Smoking Typewriters*, 14).
37 Kauffman, "Women FSM Jailees'," 1.
38 Murphy, "Two Hundred."
39 Basing, "Poverty Board Elections," 1.
40 Tharp, "Unsatisfied Broads," 10.
41 Jones, "Sex and Public Policy Coverage," 6; Minogue and Pearson, "St. Louis Dailies," 7.
42 "Covering the War."
43 Rovner, "Nixon's Daycare Veto."
44 Harcup, "'I'm Doing This,'" 370. See also Downing, *Radical Media*, viii–ix.
45 Tom Wolfe's book of essays, *The Kandy-Kolored Tangerine-Flake Streamline Baby*, was published in 1965 and his *The Electric Kool-Aid Acid Test* came out three years later. Truman Capote's "non-fiction novel" *In Cold Blood* was published in 1966, and Norman Mailer's similarly labeled *Miami and the Siege of Chicago: An Informal History of the Republican and Democratic Conventions of 1968* came out in 1968. Joan Didion's book of reportorial essays about California, *Slouching Towards Bethlehem*, was also published in 1968.

46 Schmidt, "Pioneer of Style."
47 McMillian, *Smoking Typewriters*, 7.
48 Stephens, "Berkeley's Own Don Quixote."
49 Macek, "Reporters' Rebellion."
50 Lerner, "(MORE) Guided Journalists."
51 See, for example, Crumb, "Okay, Lady," 1.
52 Grimshaw, "Love-In Detroit," 1.
53 DePastino, *Bill Mauldin*.
54 See, for example, Auth, "Barlett and Steele," 1.
55 For example, Kindman, "As We Begin"; Kindman, "MSU"; Jolles, "Morality at MSU"; "Here We Go Again."
56 For example, *Chicago Journalism Review* used a "Tidbits" roundup column to call out the *Chicago Tribune* for identifying suspects in the beating of two police officers as "all Negroes" when a policy of avoiding identifying the race of suspects unless it was relevant to a crime had been in place for fifteen years ("Tidbits," 13). *San Francisco Journalism Review* published "Poops and Scoops," a roundup of short items about local media foibles, such as the *San Francisco Chronicle* publishing the word *schmuck* in a photo caption, apparently unaware that the word is Yiddish for "penis" ("Poops and Scoops," 18). The *Unsatisfied Man: A Review of Colorado Journalism* used its Laurels and Hardlies column to slap the hand of the Rocky Mountain News sports desk for letting through a reference in a columnist's copy to a team's "makeshit lineups" ("Laurels and Hardlies," 14–15).
57 "Tidbits"; Hendrickson, "Reviewing Those Other Reviews."
58 Deleon, "Somehow."
59 Stanger, "Er … ," 9.
60 Clines, "Postscripts."
61 "Rockin' Rocky," 6.
62 It is not clear where Hendrix and the author would have seen Vice President Hubert Humphrey, then a Democratic candidate for president. Although Humphrey gave a speech on August 17, 1968, to the New York state Democratic delegates at the Waldorf Astoria Hotel in New York City, less than two weeks before he would receive his party's nomination at the Democratic National Convention in Chicago, there were no national TV newscasts on that night, a Saturday. See Humphrey, "Vice President Hubert Humphrey's Address."
63 "Experience," 8.
64 McMillian, "Garbage Guerrilla."
65 McMillan, 532.
66 Neumann, *Up Against the Wall*, 105.
67 Neumann, 105.
68 Cronin, *Time to Stir*.
69 Liberation News Service, "Graham Is Crackers," 2. *Helix* was published from 1967 to 1970.
70 Liberation News Service, 2.
71 Liberation News Service, 2.
72 Harrison, "God Band."
73 Didion, *Slouching Towards Bethlehem*.
74 Harrison, "Joan Didion," 115.
75 Harrison, *Visions of Glory*.
76 "Death of Fred Hampton."
77 Bloom and Martin, *Black Against Empire*; Haas, *Assassination of Fred Hampton*; McPherson, "Fred Ain't Dead."
78 "Panthers," 3.
79 Mauldin, "Death of Fred Hampton," 1.
80 "Panthers," 3.
81 Boyer, "Who, What, Where, When," 14.
82 Boyer, 14.
83 Boyer, 14–15.
84 Kifner, "Nation," 4.
85 Grossman, "Fatal Black Panther Raid."
86 Schwartz, "Bay Area Media," 15–16.
87 McMillian, *Smoking Typewriters*, 7.
88 "Do You Believe," 16.

89 "We Need You Now," 2.
90 Hartsock, *History*; Keeble and Wheeler, *Journalistic Imagination*.
91 Edy, "Getting the Story."

Bibliography

"About *The Paper*. (East Lansing, Mich). 1965–1965." Chronicling America: Historic American Newspapers. https://chroniclingamerica.loc.gov/lccn/sn94053428/.

Anderson, David, and Peter Benjaminson. *Investigative Reporting*. Bloomington, IN: Indiana University Press, 1976.

Arana, Gabriel. "*Columbia Journalism Review* Isn't Going Anywhere, Editor Vows." Huffington Post, October 15, 2015. www.huffingtonpost.com/entry/columbia-journalism-review-future_us_ 562016c2e4b06462a13b672b.

Atton, Chris. *Alternative Media*. Thousand Oaks, CA: Sage, 2002.

———. "What Is 'Alternative' Journalism?" *Journalism: Theory, Practice, and Criticism* 4, no. 3 (2003): 267–72. https://doi.org/10.1177/14648849030043001.

Auth, Tony. "Barlett and Steele." *Philadelphia Journalism Review* 4, no. 1 (Summer 1974): 1.

Badertscher, John M. "Ethics and Professional Practice in News Journalism: A Study of the *Chicago Journalism Review*." PhD diss., University of Chicago Divinity School, 1975.

Basing, Mary. "Poverty Board Elections to Be Held March 5th." *Los Angeles Free Press*, December 15–22, 1967.

Bertrand, Claude-Jean. "A Look at Journalism Reviews." Paper no. 19. Columbia, MO: Freedom of Information Center, 1978.

Blake, Meredith. "Ask an Academic: The Sixties Underground Press." *New Yorker*, May 3, 2011. www.newyorker.com/books/page-turner/ask-an-academic-the-sixties-underground-press.

Bloom, Joshua, and Waldo E. Martin Jr. *Black Against Empire: The History and Politics of the Black Panther Party*. Berkeley, CA: University of California Press, 2016.

Boyer, Brian. "Who, What, Where, When—and Why." *Chicago Journalism Review* 2, no. 12 (December 1969): 14–16.

Capote, Truman. *In Cold Blood: A True Account of a Multiple Murder and Its Consequences*. New York: Random House, 1966.

Charnigo, Laurie. "Prisoners of Microfilm: Freeing Voices of Dissent in the Underground Newspaper Collection." *Progressive Librarian*, no. 40 (Fall/Winter 2012): 41–90.

Choonoo, R. Neville. "The Sophiatown Generation: Black Literary Journalism during the 1950s." In *South Africa's Alternative Press: Voices of Protest and Resistance, 1880s–1960s*, edited by Les Switzer, 252–65. New York: Cambridge University Press, 1997.

Clines, Francis X. "Postscripts to the Attica Story." *New York Times*, September 18, 2011. www.nytimes.com/2011/09/19/opinion/postscripts-to-the-attica-story.html.

"Covering the War." *A. P. Review* 1, no. 2 (September 1970): 1, 4.

Cronin, Paul, ed. *A Time to Stir: Columbia '68*. New York: Columbia University Press, 2018.

Crumb, R. "Okay, Lady, Now Let's Just Say that This Dirt Is Your Conscious Mind …." Cartoon. *East Village Other*, October 25, 1968, 1.

"The Death of Fred Hampton: A Special Report." *Chicago Journalism Review* 2, no. 12 (December 1969): 1–16.

Deleon, Clark. "Somehow, the Drummer Keeps Marching On." *Philadelphia Journalism Review* 2, no. 2, 8–9.

DePastino, Todd. *Bill Mauldin: A Life Up Front*. New York: W. W. Norton, 2008.

Didion, Joan. *Slouching Towards Bethlehem*. New York: Farrar, Straus and Giroux, 1968.

Downing, John D. H. *Radical Media: Rebellious Communication and Social Movements*. Thousand Oaks, CA: Sage, 2001.

"Do You Believe Everything You Read (See, Hear)? Neither Do We." *Twin Cities Journalism Review* 4, no. 4 (March/April 1977): 16.

Eason, David L. "The New Journalism and the Image-World: Two Modes of Organizing Experience." *Critical Studies in Mass Communication* 1 (1984): 51–65. https://doi.org/10.1080/15295038409360013.

Edy, Carolyn. "Getting the Story: A Study of the State of Literary Journalism in the American Academy." *Literary Journalism: The Newsletter of the International Association for Literary Journalism Studies* 3, no. 4 (Fall 2009): 5–6.

"Experience." *Great Speckled Bird* (Atlanta, GA), August 30, 1968, 8–9.

Fifth Estate, no. 400 (Spring 2018). www.fifthestate.org/archive/400-spring-2018/.

Gholz, Carleton S. "Fifth at 40." *Detroit Metro Times*, February 23, 2005. www.metrotimes.com/detroit/fifth-at-40/Content?oid=2180779.

Glessing, Robert J. *The Underground Press in America*. Bloomington, IN: Indiana University Press, 1971.

Grimshaw, Gary. "Love-In Detroit." Cover art. *Ann Arbor Sun*, April 1, 1967, 1.

Grossman, Ron. "Fatal Black Panther Raid in Chicago Set off Sizable Aftershocks." *Chicago Tribune*, December 4, 2014. www.chicagotribune.com/news/history/ct-black-panther-raid-flashback-1207-20141206-story.html.

Guida, Jeremy. "The East Village Other." Reveal Digital, March 10, 2017. http://revealdigital.com/digging-the-underground/the-east-village-other/.

Haas, Jeffrey. *The Assassination of Fred Hampton: How the FBI and Chicago Police Murdered a Black Panther*. Chicago: Lawrence Hill Press, 2011

Haas, Tanni, and Linda Steiner. "Fears of Corporate Colonization in Journalism Reviews' Critiques of Public Journalism." *Journalism Studies* 3, no. 3 (2002): 325–41. https://doi.org/10.1080/14616700220145579.

Hamilton, James. "Theory Through History: Exploring Scholarly Conceptions of U.S. Alternative Media." *Communication Review* 4 (2001): 305–26. https://doi.org/10.1080/10714420109359472.

Harcup, Tony. "'I'm Doing This to Change the World': Journalism in Alternative and Mainstream Media." *Journalism Studies* 6, no. 3 (2005): 361–74. https://doi.org/10.1080/14616700500132016.

Harrison, Barbara Grizzuti. "The God Band: Coast to Coast with the Holy Ghost." *[MORE]* 8, no. 3 (March 1978): 12–18.

———. "Joan Didion: Only Disconnect." In *Off Center: Essays by Barbara Grizzuti Harrison*, 113–24. New York: Dial Press, 1980.

———. *Visions of Glory: A History and Memory of Jehovah's Witnesses*. New York: Simon and Schuster, 1978.

Hartsock, John C. *A History of American Literary Journalism: The Emergence of a Modern Narrative Form*. Amherst, MA: University of Massachusetts Press, 2001.

Hendrickson, Peter. "Reviewing Those Other Reviews." *Thorn: Connecticut Valley Media Review*, no. 1 (June 1971): 6–7.

"Here We Go Again: Another Agonized Editorial." *Paper* (East Lansing, MI), May 19, 1966, 1, 5. https://docs.google.com/viewer?url=http%3A%2F%2Fmsupaper.org%2Fissues%2FThe_Paper_1966-05-19.pdf.

Hoyt, Mike. "The End of *American Journalism Review* and What It Means for Media Criticism." *Columbia Journalism Review*, August 24, 2015. www.cjr.org/analysis/american_journalism_review_no_more.php.

Hume, Janice. "The Past as Persuader in *The Great Speckled Bird*." *Journalism History* 41, no. 4 (Winter 2016): 182–90.

Humphrey, Hubert H. "Vice President Hubert Humphrey's Address to New York State Democratic Delegates, August 17, 1968, Waldorf-Astoria, N.Y. (Gold Room)." www2.mnhs.org/library/findaids/00442/pdfa/00442-02676.pdf.

Jolles, Char. "Morality at MSU: The Inhuman Comedy." *Paper* (East Lansing, MI), February 10, 1966, 3. https://docs.google.com/viewer?url=http%3A%2F%2Fmsupaper.org%2Fissues%2FThe_Paper_1966-02-10.pdf.

Jones, E. Terrence. "Sex and Public Policy Coverage." *St. Louis Journalism Review* 4, no. 22 (May 1976): 6.

Kauffman, George. "Women FSM Jailees' 5 Days in 'Solitary.'" *Berkeley Barb*, August 27, 1965, 1.

Keeble, Richard Lance. "Literary Journalism." In *Oxford Research Encyclopedia of Communication*. Oxford: Oxford University Press, 2018. https://doi.org/10.1093/acrefore/9780190228613.013.836.

Keeble, Richard, and Sharon Wheeler, eds. *The Journalistic Imagination: Literary Journalists from Defoe to Capote and Carter*. New York: Routledge, 2007.

Keith, Susan. "Examining the Critics' Criticism: A Bibliographic Essay on Journalism Review Research." Paper presented at the annual conference of the Association for Education in Journalism and Mass Communication, Washington, DC, August 2013.

———. "*Montana Journalism Review*: The Big Sky Beginning of the Local Journalism Review Movement." Presentation at the Joint Journalism Historians Conference, sponsored by the American Journalism Historians Association and the History Division of the Association for Education in Journalism and Mass Communication, City University of New York Graduate Center, New York, March 13, 2010.

Kessler, Lauren. *The Dissident Press: Alternative Journalism in American History*. Beverly Hills, CA: Sage, 1984.

Kifner, John. "The Nation: Informers: A Tale in Itself." *New York Times*, January, 22, 1995, 4.

Kindman, Michael. "As We Begin: A Loyalty Oath." *Paper* (East Lansing, MI), December 3, 1965, 1. https://docs.google.com/viewer?url=http%3A%2F%2Fmsupaper.org%2Fissues%2FThe_Paper_1965-12-03.pdf.

———. "MSU – The Closed Society." *Paper* (East Lansing, MI), December 10, 1965, 2. https://docs.google.com/viewer?url=http%3A%2F%2Fmsupaper.org%2Fissues%2FThe_Paper_1965-12-10.pdf.

———. *My Odyssey Through the Underground Press*. Edited by Ken Wachsberger. Voices from the Underground. East Lansing, MI: Michigan State University Press, 2011.

Klotzer, Charles L., and Eleanor S. Block. "Critiquing the Mainstream Media: A Case Study of the *St. Louis Journalism Review*." *Serials Review* 19, no. 1 (Spring 1993): 7–26. https://doi.org/10.1080/00987913.1993.10764120.

"Laurels and Hardlies." *Unsatisfied Man: A Review of Colorado Journalism* 2, no. 1 (September 1971): 14–15.

Lerner, Kevin. "(MORE) Guided Journalists during the 1970s Media Crisis of Confidence." *Columbia Journalism Review*, May 10, 2018. www.cjr.org/the_profile/more-journalism-review.php.

———. "Gadfly to the Watchdogs: How the Journalism Review [MORE] Goaded the Mainstream Press toward Self-Criticism in the 1970s." PhD diss., Rutgers University, 2014.

Levin, Jack, and James L. Spates. "Hippie Values: An Analysis of the Underground Press." *Youth and Society* 2, no. 1 (September 1970): 59–73. https://doi.org/10.1177/0044118X7000200104.

Lewes, James. "The Underground Press in America (1964–1968): Outlining an Alternative, the Envisioning of an Underground." *Journal of Communication Inquiry* 24, no. 4 (October 2000): 379–400. https://doi.org/10.1177/0196859900024004003.

Lewis, Roger. *Outlaws of America: The Underground Press and Its Context: Notes on a Cultural Revolution*. Baltimore, MD: Penguin Books, 1972.

Liberation News Service. "Graham Is Crackers or Try to Find the Wall." *Helix* (Seattle, WA), October 31, 1968, 2.

Macek, Steve. "The Reporters' Rebellion." Area Chicago, no. 7 (n.d.). http://areachicago.org/the-.reporters%E2%80%99-.rebellion/.

Mailer, Norman. *Miami and the Siege of Chicago: An Informal History of the Republican and Democratic Conventions of 1968*. New York: Random House, 1968.

"Mapping the Underground/Alternative Press 1965–1975." Mapping American Social Movements Through the 20th Century. University of Washington. http://depts.washington.edu/moves/altnews_map.shtml.

Mauldin, Bill. "The Death of Fred Hampton: A Special Report." Cover art. *Chicago Journalism Review* 2, no. 12 (December 1969): 1.

McMillian, John. "Garbage Guerrilla: The Mystery Man Behind the East Village Art Gang with the Unprintable Name." In *Resistance: A Radical Social and Political History of the Lower East Side*, edited by Clayton Patterson, 532–42. New York: Seven Stories Press, 2007.

———. *Smoking Typewriters: The Sixties Underground Press and the Rise of Alternative Media in America*. New York: Oxford University Press, 2011.

McPherson, Craig S. "Fred Ain't Dead: The Impact of the Life and Legacy of Fred Hampton." Master's thesis, Georgia State University, 2015.

Minogue, Thomas, and Frederic Pearson. "St. Louis Dailies Give Readers Distorted View of the World; Offer Similar Foreign News Coverage in Quantity and Coverage, Survey Shows." *St. Louis Journalism Review* 4, no. 22 (May 1976): 7.

Mount, Andre. "Grasp the Weapon of Culture! Radical Avant-Gardes and the *Los Angeles Free Press*." *Journal of Musicology* 32, no. 1 (Winter 2015): 115–52. https://doi.org/10.1525/JM.2015.32.1.115.

Murphy, Patricia. "Two Hundred Honor Rev. Gracie." *Fifth Estate*, no. 35 (August 1–15, 1967). Available, in part, at www.fifthestate.org/archive/35-august-1-15-1967/two-hundred-honor-rev-gracie/.

Neumann, Osha. *Up Against the Wall, Motherf**ker: A Memoir of the '60s, with Notes for Next Time*. New York: Seven Stories Press, 2008.

NYU Arthur L. Carter Journalism Institute and The Local East Village. "The East Village Other: Blowing Minds; 1965–1972: The Rise of Underground Comix and the Alternative Press." 2012. http://eastvillageother.org.

"The Panthers and the Rest of Us." *Chicago Journalism Review* 2, no. 12 (December 1969): 3.

"Poops and Scoops." *San Francisco Journalism Review* 2, no. 1 (April 1973): 18.

Pope, Kyle. "A Note from the Editor." *Columbia Journalism Review*, Fall 2017. www.cjr.org/special_report/a-note-from-the-editor.php.

Robertson, Lori. "The Life and Times of AJR." *American Journalism Review*, October 12, 2013. http://ajr.org/2013/10/12/history-of-ajr/.

"Rockin' Rocky." *Borrowed Times* (Missoula, MT), April 18, 1973, 6–7.

Rovner, Ruth. "Nixon's Daycare Veto: A Matter of Press Distortion." *Philadelphia Journalism Review* 2, no. 2 (February 1972): 11–12.

Sandoval, Marisol, and Christian Fuchs. "Towards a Critical Theory of Alternative Media." *Telematics and Informatics* 27, no. 2 (2010): 141–50. https://doi.org/10.1016/j.tele.2009.06.011.

Schmidt, Thomas R. "Pioneer of Style: How the *Washington Post* Adopted Literary Journalism." *Literary Journalism Studies* 9, no. 1 (Spring 2017): 34–59.

Schwartz, Mark. "How Bay Area Media Ignored and Important Trial." *San Francisco Journalism Review* 2, no. 2 (July–August 1973): 15–16.

Sims, Norman. *The Literary Journalists*. New York: Ballantine Books, 1984.

Stanger, Robert R. "Er ... Mind If I Look Over Your Shoulder While I Type?" *Overset* 1, no. 5 (July–August 1972): 9.

Stephens, Diana. "Berkeley's Own Don Quixote." *Berkeley Barb*, n.d. www.berkeleybarb.net/stories-diana.html.

Stewart, Sean, ed. *On the Ground: An Illustrated Anecdotal History of the Sixties Underground Press in the U.S.* Oakland, CA: PM Press, 2011.

Tharp, Marty. "The Unsatisfied Broads." *Unsatisfied Man: A Review of Colorado Journalism* 1, no. 3 (November 1970): 10.

"Tidbits." *Chicago Journalism Review* 3, no. 11 (November 1970): 13.

"We Need You Now So We'll Be Here When You Need Us." *Philadelphia Journalism Review* 4, no. 1 (Spring 1974): 2.

Wolfe, Tom. "The Birth of 'The New Journalism': Eyewitness Report by Tom Wolfe." *New York Magazine*, February 14, 1972. http://nymag.com/news/media/47353/.

———. *The Electric Kool-Aid Acid Test*. New York: Farrar, Straus and Giroux, 1968.

———. *The Kandy-Kolored Tangerine-Flake Streamline Baby*. New York: Farrar, Straus and Giroux, 1965.

13

FROM MAGAZINES TO NEWSPRINT

How Literary Journalism Went "Mainstream"

Jim Collins

> It was late in 1966 when you first started hearing people talk about "the New Journalism" in conversation, as best I can remember. ... It was no "movement." There were no manifestos, clubs, salons, cliques; not even a saloon where the faithful gathered, since there was no faith and no creed. At the time, the mid-Sixties, one was aware only that all of a sudden there was some sort of artistic excitement in journalism, and that was a new thing in itself.[1]
> —From the introduction to *The New Journalism*, by Tom Wolfe

The 1973 publication of *The New Journalism* by Tom Wolfe and E. W. Johnson marked a watershed moment in the history of literary journalism. Other books in the early seventies—by Everette Dennis, Michael Johnson, Nicolaus Mills, and others[2]—noted the exciting new brand of nonfiction bursting into books and magazines, primarily from writers in their thirties, primarily writing for New York publishers. But it was Wolfe's forty-nine-page introduction, incorporating material from articles he'd written for *Esquire* and *New York* magazine, that publicly christened the movement and declared its name, its precepts, and its definition. He traced its historical roots and antecedents and announced its arrival as the new force in American literature. He observed how its leading practitioners didn't see themselves as part of an emerging genre but that they were keenly and competitively aware of each other's writing. Wolfe gave them, and others who aspired to be in their company, a collective way to self-identify.

Naming the movement was instantly controversial. Many observers, citing the same historical roots and antecedents, pointed out that the genre wasn't new.[3] Others questioned whether there was even a movement at all. Jack Newfield, who wrote for the *Village Voice*, argued that "New Journalism" did not exist: "It is a false category. There is only good writing and bad writing, smart ideas and dumb ideas, hard work and laziness," he wrote. "I suspect it is nothing more profound than a lot of good writers coming along at the same time."[4]

But the essential ingredients Wolfe labeled helped create a working definition for reporters and writers interested in crafting a more literary brand of journalism. The ingredients included the novelist's tools of scene-by-scene construction, dialogue, third-person point of view, and special attention paid to the small, revealing details of ordinary life.

Importantly—in terms of influence, perhaps more importantly—Wolfe's book drew attention to writers who wrote with individual, idiosyncratic voices. In their writing, they presented themselves as authorities. They wrote as informed observers, giving hints of their own personalities and values, unafraid of breaking conventions. They wrote with attitude, humor, anger, frankness, style. They incorporated a wider set of emotions than what was allowed in conventional journalism, which needed to appeal to (and not offend) a wide, diverse audience.[5] They used their voices for literary effect. Readers—and other writers—discovered that the individual voices gave the writing power.

Historically, writers have developed their craft by discovering and studying exemplars of the craft.[6] The nonfiction pieces Wolfe selected for the anthology served as powerful new models. In announcing its arrival, Wolfe suggested that this new form was poised to sweep into the mainstream of American journalism. Of course, "mainstream" is a blurry term. Of the twenty-three pieces anthologized in *The New Journalism*, all but a handful had first appeared in books or in magazines. Six of them came out of *Esquire* alone. A small number of publications, or, more accurately, a small cadre of experimental, ambitious editors—notably Harold Hayes at *Esquire*, Clay Felker at *New York* magazine, Jann Wenner at *Rolling Stone*, William Shawn at the *New Yorker*, Willie Morris at *Harper's*—played an outsized role in assigning and publishing the new brand of journalism that Wolfe described. If there were a contagion leading to the spread of this new journalism, it was that group of editors.

Their combined audience was influential—but it remained a niche next to the sixty-three million people who read American daily newspapers in 1973.[7] If there was a "mainstream" in journalism, or at least its most powerful current, the daily paper was it. The breadth and scale of the daily newspaper audience was spread across the country, in cities and towns of all sizes. Newspapers' influence in the marketplace of ideas, more difficult to quantify, was deep and multiplicative. Decades later, as newspapers everywhere were struggling for survival against the onslaught of digital media, Clay Shirky, a journalism professor at New York University, captured an essential part of that influence in a 2009 blog entry. Print media, he asserted,

> does much of society's heavy journalistic lifting, from flooding the zone—covering every angle of a huge story—to the daily grind of attending the City Council meeting, just in case. This coverage creates benefits even for people who aren't newspaper readers, because the work of print journalists is used by everyone from politicians to district attorneys to talk radio hosts to bloggers.[8]

In other words, newspaper reporting was where mainstream America got informed.

And the prevailing newspaper culture in 1973 was, in Wolfe's opinion, not ready or not willing to adopt a new kind of reporting and writing. "Newspaper people were better than railroad men at resisting anything labeled new," he wrote. "The average newspaper editor's idea of a major innovation was the Cashword Puzzle."[9] In a 2011 interview at Harvard, Gay Talese echoed the point, recalling his early career in the 1960s. "When I worked on the *New York Times* in the old days," he said,

> those guys that got it right weren't necessarily lyrical figures in the world of literature—they were boring. They got it right, but they were the paper-of-record people. If you weren't a dazzling stylist it didn't make a bit of difference; in fact they suspected anyone who might be called a stylist in those days.[10]

Newspaper style, in fact, wasn't monolithic and unchanging. Journalism throughout history had displayed many of the literary elements Wolfe described. The earliest printed newspaper story in Louis Snyder and Richard Morris's *A Treasury of Great Reporting* (1949), from the *London Spy* in

January 1699, is a literary, first-person account by reporter Ned Ward of a tour he and a friend took at Bedlam, the city's asylum. "We were admitted in through an iron gate," Ward wrote.

> We turned in through another iron barricade, where we heard such a rattling of chains, drumming of doors, ranting, hollering, singing, and running that I could think of nothing but Don Quevedo's vision, where the damned broke loose, and put hell in an uproar.[11]

Indeed, throughout the eighteenth and nineteenth centuries, much of the best newspaper journalism in Europe and America consisted of reports dispatched by individuals, describing characters scene by scene, in daily life, with dialogue and close observation, the exact ingredients Wolfe had noted in *The New Journalism*. Longform reporting and serially published articles totaling tens of thousands of words were immensely popular with the reading public. The accounts were literary, in many cases, because their writers were steeped in literary techniques. Writers who became known for their poetry and fiction—including Charles Dickens, Walt Whitman, Mark Twain, Stephen Crane, and Rudyard Kipling—commonly wrote for newspapers.[12]

The conventions of American newspaper reporting and writing abruptly changed in 1845 with the invention of the telegraph. At a time when it took a letter two days to travel from Washington, DC, to New York, or a dispatch a month by stage from the West Coast to the East, the telegraph's effect on mass communication was revolutionary. News reporting suddenly—from any corner—could include breaking news and near-real-time updates. As chronicled in Christopher Scanlan's *Reporting and Writing: Basics for the Twenty-first Century* (1999), the telegraph not only impacted the timeliness of the reporting but the very form the reporting took:

> The telegraph had a drawback. It was expensive to use: One of the first charges was a penny a character. Newspapers spent hundreds of thousands of dollars in telegraph costs to report the Civil War. That economic pressure more than anything else influenced a new kind of writing that departed from the flowery language of the nineteenth century—it was concise, stripped of opinion and detail. Fueling the shift in writing style was a new type of news organization, named the "wire service" after the technology used to transmit the news.[13]

The fledgling Associated Press at one of its first meetings established the trend with an agreement that stories would be brief, tailored for a national audience and deliberately stripped of the partisanship that characterized American newspapers until that time. This technology—the telegraph and the lingo of its transoceanic partner, the cable—provided "the underlying structure for one of the most influential literary styles of the twentieth century."[14]

Thus was conceived the "inverted pyramid" formula that became a hallmark of newspaper journalism. Reporters were urged—and soon taught in journalism schools—to efficiently lead with the most important, newsworthy information, with no ornamentation or attempt at style, then follow with decreasingly important news and finally with background information, in short paragraphs. The brevity saved newspapers thousands of dollars in telegraph costs. The form allowed readers to scan articles quickly for information. It allowed editors to cut copy easily, simply starting with the least important paragraph at the bottom of the file and trimming back from there.[15]

In time, the Associated Press's informal guide used by member reporters became formalized. Along with consistent grammar and punctuation, the unadorned, objective-voiced who-what-when-where approach to writing became a part of "AP Style." The style defined one side of a widening rift between just-the-facts editors and a succession of stylists who had kept the narrative, storytelling form alive in many of the country's best newspapers, including fiction crossovers Damon Runyon, John Steinbeck, Jack London, Willa Cather, and Ernest Hemingway.[16]

By the 1950s, the just-the-facts camp prevailed. The *AP Stylebook* was the most popular English-language reference used by news bureaus throughout the world.[17] The mannered, institutional voice—seemingly objective, detached from emotion—mirrored society's growing trust of science and the scientific method. Accuracy, facts, and analysis became the press's guiding bywords. The topics that constituted "legitimate" news coalesced around cops, courts, finance, and civic life, with the necessary information provided by official sources and those in positions of power.[18]

In his "Notes on the New Journalism," published in the *Atlantic* in response to Wolfe's manifesto, Michael Arlen described the conventional news reporting this way:

> In those days, when something happened, an event, a hotel fire, for example, newspapers generally gave you certain facts, embedded in an official view. No matter that the reporter himself, personally was a hotshot, a drinker, a roarer, an admirer of Yeats, a swashbuckler of the city room; in most instances he gave you the official view of the fire. Where it was. How many people got burned. How much property got damaged. What Fire Commissioner Snooks said of the performance of his men.[19]

In 2002, looking back a half century, journalist Jon Franklin was quoted in Harvard's narrative nonfiction newsletter, *Nieman Reports*:

> The quality of journalistic writing was devastated by the demise of the short story apprenticeship. When journalism turned away from literature, newspaper and magazine writing lost its luster. Nonfiction wasn't as good a training ground as the short story had been because it emphasized subject over form and rewarded reporting skills at the expense of writing technique.[20]

Preparing a chapter for his 2011 book *Storycraft*, the *Oregonian*'s long-time managing editor Jack Hart observed:

> By the mid-1950s, bureaucratization, uniformity, and the "it's-not-news" ethic had driven narrative storytelling from the American newsroom. Newspaper staffs became regimented machines with interchangeable parts. Smoke Hale, city editor at the *Los Angeles Times*, said, with perverse pride, "All news stories are essentially the same. Reporting consists largely of getting the names sorted out and spelled right."[21]

In addition to style and approach, journalistic conventions had also coalesced around an accepted set of emotional stances that were appropriate for a civic voice writing for a mass audience. As Mark Kramer, writer and professor at Boston University, later described, they included

> anger at crime in the streets; fury when they're raping our women; disapproval of criminals; swelling heart when you see the flag; thankfulness for the boys in blue; pride in our sports teams; civic strength in the face of adversity. Try to write with "voice" and keep to these emotions, and you end up with sentimental, mawkish journalism. To get away from that, you need to expand the emotion set.[22]

Such was the newspaper landscape that Wolfe, Talese, Jimmy Breslin, Joan Didion, and other "new" journalists stood out against in the 1960s, both in form and in topic. And such were the conventions blocking Wolfe's prediction that a more literary journalism would burst into the mainstream in the 1970s.

Many editors and publishers in the conservative newspaper establishment saw the new writing that was enlivening books and magazines and pushed back against what they saw as subjective reporting and the elevation of style to the same level as substance. It was sociology, it was entertaining, it was atmospheric—but it wasn't journalism. Where was the attribution? On whose authority? Where was the *news*? Columnists dismissed the entire literary genre by questioning the facts in the reporting of Truman Capote and Hunter S. Thompson. They condemned the composite-character approach that *New York* writer Gail Sheehy famously used in her reporting on the city's subculture of prostitution.[23] More than one critic suggested that literary journalists played with the facts in order to serve their storytelling—that the novelist's techniques were perfectly suited to fiction, but that fiction had no place in American newspapers.

To be clear, personal-voice, ordinary-life journalism was already part of newspapers when Wolfe's book was published. Most prominently, though, that writing appeared in the alternative weeklies—the *Village Voice* in New York, Boston's *Phoenix*, where Kramer was getting his start, Portland's *Willamette Weekly*, where Susan Orlean was getting hers—and in the Sunday supplements and the so-called Women's and Style pages of the dailies.[24] Most people in the business disdainfully referred to those articles as "features." The real-life features were dismissed as soft news, often about ordinary people, not the hard, consequential news of the newsroom and worthy of page 1. Outside of magazines and books, much of America's most brilliantly reported and written longform journalism was quietly appearing in newspapers alongside recipes and fashion and society news.

A handful of pioneering editors such as Ben Bradlee at the *Washington Post*, Marj Paxson at the *St. Petersburg Times*, Dorothy Jurney at the *Miami Herald*, and Vivian Castleberry at the *Dallas Times Herald* were recalibrating the limits of Women's pages and creating the room for writing of substance.[25] They ventured into politics, race, and domestic abuse. Late in her career, legendary Texas political reporter Molly Ivins said that Castleberry and her stable of writers on the *Times Herald*'s Living section "got away with murder because the male editors never bothered to read it. They were writing about birth control. Abortion. But it wasn't considered 'real news.'"[26]

Through the early and mid-1970s, aside from the weeklies and Style sections and Sunday magazines, though, mainstream examples of literary journalism swirled to the surface only in pockets, and just as quickly subsided. The establishment's mistrust of the form—coupled with the entrenched newsroom hierarchies and structures—made publishers and editors reluctant to experiment or deviate from the status quo. Economically, there was no incentive to mess with it. The newspaper industry was enjoying a banner run. In 1970, according to the Newspaper Association of America, the industry's combined advertising and circulation revenues reached just over $8.3 billion. Six years later—driven in large part by growth in local and classified advertising—total revenues approached $14 billion and were increasing exponentially.[27] Advances in technology had created great savings in printing costs, driving the growth of net income even faster. The Washington Post Company, entering its hundredth year in 1977, was enjoying record profit on its way to a 16 percent increase in revenues and 45 percent increase in net income. Its annual report that year noted that operating income gains were broadly spread across the company's broadcasting and publishing divisions but that the most dramatic change occurred in the newspaper division, where the *Washington Post* more than doubled its operating income in a single year.[28]

But the growing profitability masked troubling trends. In an industry that was notoriously tradition bound and shortsighted, a new force threatened the status quo with a longer view: market research. At its annual meeting in Honolulu in May 1977, the American Society of News Editors (ASNE) took a hard look at a disorienting landscape. Leo Bogart, an experienced research director with the Newspaper Advertising Bureau, presented his initial findings from the Newspaper Readership Project, a groundbreaking, quantitative, multiyear survey aimed at understanding newspaper reader behavior and preferences. Across the country, hidden beneath the record revenues and profits, circulation across all levels of newspapers was actually lagging behind population growth and in several cities had even begun to decline. In the face of television news broadcasts, afternoon-edition newspapers were disappearing altogether.[29]

As a group, ASNE had agreed to help fund the study, though many of the editors were skeptical that statistical analysis could inform the nuanced, intuitive, complex business of putting out the daily news. Even so, and despite the healthy economics of the industry, Bogart's data worried them. They showed that American newspaper readers were aging. Those readers were spending fewer minutes reading newspapers each day. They were growing less trustful of print journalism. A growing percentage of them were turning to radio and television for their main sources of news.

The ASNE editors represented the brain trust of the mainstream press. The association had been formed back in 1922 to codify the industry's ethics and practices and, according to its bylaws, "to interchange ideas for the advancement of professional ideals and for the more effective application of professional labors, and to work collectively for the solution of common problems."[30] It had become an effective, influential body. In the spring of 1977, the brain trust acknowledged that it had a common problem.

Over four days at the Sheraton Waikiki Hotel, the editors heard reports and shared ideas. As the lead researcher on the reader project, Bogart had also sent out a survey to 1,300 working newspaper editors. He later explained,

> All the information we were collecting about readers' responses to content would make sense only if it could be compared with editors' expectations and assumptions. If an incongruity existed between the reality of the public's tastes and editors' notions of them, a playback of this incongruity to the editors would provoke discussion, provide insight, and thereby improve the attractiveness of newspapers.[31]

Interestingly, Bogart's preliminary data showed that successful, middling, and unsuccessful papers alike were all operating with more or less the same editorial philosophy and standards. The forces contributing to losses in circulation—marketing, pricing, distribution, changes in population and demographics—appeared unrelated to a newspaper's actual content. "When I presented this conclusion to the ASNE convention," recalled Bogart,

> it might have seemed likely to evoke the editors' delight. They had just been let off the hook. But most of them had the opposite reaction. To accept my conclusion would have reduced their self-importance, their sense of full responsibility for the fortunes of the papers they directed. They wanted to take the blame, since only by doing so could they be left with the illusion that they had full control over their newspapers' destinies.[32]

Indeed, the editors gathered in Honolulu felt compelled to mess with the status quo. Some of their ideas—how to incorporate more color, more graphics—were aimed directly at the competition coming from television news. But the most animated discussions centered on the uncomfortable admission that books and magazines were simply out-reporting and out-writing newspapers.[33]

Coming on as president of ASNE that year was Eugene "Gene" Patterson, the editor of the *St. Petersburg Times*. Patterson was one of the boldest and most writerly newspaper editors of the era. He had won a Pulitzer for editorial writing while he was executive editor of the *Atlanta Journal* and *Atlanta Constitution*. As managing editor of the *Washington Post*, under intense pressure from the White House not to do so, he had published the documents of the Pentagon Papers, which detailed the history of American involvement in Vietnam, including how President Lyndon Johnson had withheld key information from the US Congress. In St. Petersburg, Patterson would go on to inspire the likes of Howell Raines, Rick Bragg, Tom French, Anne Hull, and Lane DeGregory, all Pulitzer Prize winners known for their dedication to the craft of writing.[34]

At the meeting in Honolulu, Patterson challenged his colleagues to improve the depth of reporting and the literary quality of newspaper writing. If literary journalism was to become a part of America's mainstream, perhaps the headwaters were found there, in Hawaii, in two of the ideas that Patterson pushed, one involving mentors, the other, models. The first idea—hiring professional writing coaches—Patterson implemented at his own paper later that year. He hired a young professor of writing and literature from Auburn University named Roy Peter Clark to spend a year at the *St. Petersburg Times* to interview the paper's reporters, gather information about their methods, and help them improve their craft. It was a radical idea, bringing an outsider into the newsroom like that, specifically to focus on improving the quality of the paper's writing. Patterson was impressed by the difference Clark made—and by the positive response from readers. He invited Clark to present his findings at the following year's ASNE convention.[35] The report was persuasive. The idea of professional development in service of a more literary journalism took root.

At the *Boston Globe*, editor Tom Winship and Sunday editor Jack Driscoll brought on former Pulitzer Prize winner and University of New Hampshire English professor Donald Murray as a paid editorial consultant to work directly with *Globe* writers. Murray coined the role "writing coach." He preached the process method, a step-by-step approach that demystified the act of writing and gave reporters a scaffolding they could build on: *idea, collect, focus, order, draft, clarify*. He encouraged the journalists to talk with each other about their approaches and methods, to share drafts, and, especially, to revise. He coached editors on how to get the best writing from their reporters.[36] (Writing in the April 1981 *Bulletin of the American Society of News Editors*, Murray said,

> Most writers are non-organizational men and women, self-absorbed, self-doubting to the point of false confidence, exceptionally sensitive to their own problems and insensitive to their editors' problems. But if editors want good writing, they're going to have to nurture and support writers.[37])

Murray consulted with other metro papers, joining the payroll as a writing coach at the Raleigh *Times*, the Raleigh *News and Observer*, and the *Providence Journal-Bulletin*. The *Journal-Bulletin* brought Murray into a culture already in the vanguard of nurturing high-quality writing. Under the leadership of managing editor Joel Rawson and news editor Len Levin, the paper offered regular writing workshops, weekly critique sessions, and working brown-bag lunches where reporters were encouraged to talk shop. They had their writers read "Drama in Real Life" stories from *Reader's Digest* to use as models of dramatic pacing. In 1977, the paper had hired a young reporter named Christopher "Chip" Scanlan, who had once dreamed of writing fiction. Early on at the *Journal-Bulletin*, Scanlan stumbled onto the news of a teenager who had died from a drug overdose, and on his own time dug into it. He proposed the piece to editor Judy Stark. Stark handed him a copy of *The New Journalism*, told Scanlan to read Wolfe's introduction, and to take his drug overdose story into the deep end. "That book gave me a master class," Scanlan recalled later. "And I can't believe I was the only reporter who read that book and thought, 'Holy shit! You can write that?' Of course, you needed editors above you who were open to it. At the *Pro-Jo* we had those editors." Scanlan not only rewrote the piece, he rereported it to get the richer detail he needed. "I was given the chance to write a *story*," said Scanlan. "It launched my career as a journalist."[38]

After hiring Murray, the *Journal-Bulletin* started a weekly writing contest, open to all departments, with a prize of twenty-five dollars. The judging was done by a panel of writers, consisting of previous winners of the weekly contests. The rules required each winner to submit an account of how he or she reported and wrote the story, which was then posted in all departments and bureaus. In 1986, Scanlan collected the best of those stories and how they were written and published them in an anthology, *How I Wrote the Story*, and Murray's mentoring got disseminated.[39]

With the industry raking in record profits, editors across the country had unprecedented resources to invest in their news reporting. Loren Ghiglione, editor and publisher of the *News* in Southbridge, Massachusetts, wrote an essay for the *Bulletin of the American Society of News Editors* in 1982 in which he described how that investment was turned toward creating "four-color writing" that could compete with television's fireworks and boost sagging circulation. "Newspapers hired writing coaches to work with reporters," he wrote. "Editors attended writing seminars. Papers appointed assistant managing editors whose primary responsibility was to overcome the second half of Oscar Wilde's line about the difference between literature and journalism: 'Literature is not read and journalism is unreadable.'"[40]

A few years after Clark's report at the 1978 ASNE convention, some sixty writing coaches were working at papers across the country, from Murray in the East to Bob Baker at the *Los Angeles Times*, from Alaska to Florida. Editors at other papers, such as Steven Lovelady at the *Philadelphia Inquirer*, served without official titles as staff writing coaches or story doctors. (Lovelady had come over from editing the brilliant, splendidly written, often off-beat "A-hed" features that ran down the middle of the front page of the *Wall Street Journal*.[41] In 2002, some of the best of those features would be anthologized in a collection titled *Floating Off the Page*.)

Clark became the industry's first national writing coach through the Poynter Institute in St. Petersburg, a new nonprofit dedicated to improving the quality of American journalism. Clark was responsible for creating Poynter's academic program. One of his initiatives, under an umbrella called the National Writers Workshops, was organizing conferences on narrative and literary journalism, most of them scheduled conveniently over weekends, at affordable rates geared toward working beat reporters. He took his model from the Wilmington Writers' Workshop, launched in 1992 by managing editor John Walston and writing coach John Sweeney of the Delaware-based *News Journal*. In time, nine regional conferences would attract more than 5,000 writers annually, from Seattle to Hartford to Charlotte. They helped spread literary practices and joined practitioners in a broad, informally connected network.[42] "Those early experiments went so well," Clark recalled, "that a lot of newspapers became focused on training—they invested in better interviewing, better reporting, better deadline writing, better story telling."[43]

Around the same time, literary nonfiction courses spread across college and university campuses. Early pioneers such as Melvin Mencher at the Columbia School of Journalism and Wilmott Ragsdale, whose literary journalism class was famous at the University of Wisconsin in the 1960s, were joined by Jessica Mitford at San Jose State University, John McPhee at Princeton, Noel Perrin at Dartmouth, Mark Kramer at Smith, Jon Franklin at the University of Oregon, and a host of others—many of them stellar writers without traditional academic credentials. One of Ragsdale's students, Jack Hart, went on to teach journalism at the University of Oregon and become an editor and influential writing coach at the *Oregonian*, which emerged as one of the nation's best-written papers under his influence. Among other devices, Hart taught reporters classic narrative plot structures, introducing concepts of rising action, climax, and dénouement. A new generation of nonfiction writers emerged with literary tools and ambition. Many of them entered a profession that increasingly provided mentors who would support their ambition.[44]

Patterson's other seminal idea coming out of that 1977 ASNE convention recognized the importance of visible, high-profile literary models—in the form of competition. Along with charging Clark to study the newsroom habits at the *St. Petersburg Times*, Patterson tasked Clark with creating an annual contest: ASNE's Distinguished Writing Awards. The awards included categories for deadline writing and non-deadline writing. The winning entries were published in a yearly anthology along with behind-the-scenes interviews with their creators. "This book," said Clark, should help dispel persistent myths about newspaper writing in America: that there is no room in newspapers for good writing; that reporting and writing are mutually exclusive skills; that deadlines make good writing impossible; that governmental or international news is, by definition, unreadable; that good writing can only be found in powerful papers with enormous resources.[45]

The awards created an instant buzz in the profession and set a bar for aspiring journalists. Jacqui Banaszynski, who won a Pulitzer in 1988, said, "Yeah, the Pulitzer ... But among working journalists, winning an ASNE award—that was the *bomb*."[46]

Accepting the first ASNE Distinguished Writing Award in 1978, journalist Everett Allen captured a sense of the award's meaning:

> When I was about to graduate from college, one of my English professors, who apparently thought quite well of me, called me to his office. He said, "I believe that you have some ability to write and I am therefore most depressed to learn that you have decided to go into journalism."
>
> At the moment, I was in no position to reply, but I resented the remark. In part, that may have been why I made such an effort, from the very beginning, to inject the very best writing of which I was capable into such news stories as were assigned to me.
>
> I believe I am the only newspaper reporter who deliberately and successfully inserted in a general-alarm fire story a perfect iambic line. I was so titillated at being able to do it—and getting it past the copy desk, and you know how copy desks are about perfect iambic lines—that even though it was something like 38 years ago, I remember it perfectly.
>
> The line was, "Ten pumpers roared throughout the night in Sawyer Street." Now, if 13 pumpers had shown up at the fire, or if the fire had been, let us say, in Brock Avenue, I would have had to either (a) change the meter of the line, or (b) respectfully decline to cover the fire.
>
> Happily, I did not have to make either choice. And since that time, I have persisted in attempting to introduce creative writing into the news columns whenever possible and, in these latter years, that has meant encouraging the young to do likewise.
>
> I am most pleased that my peers, the prestigious leadership of ASNE, have, through the creation of these awards, moved to provide a fresh and important incentive to those on American newspaper staffs who can and wish to write creatively.[47]

In 2001, Clark and Scanlan (by then on the faculty at the Poynter Institute) published selections from more than twenty years of ASNE prize winners, along with commentary and instruction, under the title *America's Best Newspaper Writing*. It became a bible in newsrooms everywhere. More models. More dissemination.

In 1979, one year after the inaugural ASNE awards, in a move that must have gratified many Sunday and Women's page editors, the Pulitzer Prize committee added a new category in journalism: Feature Writing. Jurors would honor a "distinguished example of feature writing giving prime consideration to high literary quality and originality."[48] Franklin of the *Baltimore Evening Sun* won the category the first year for "Mrs. Kelly's Monster," a haunting narrative account of a brain surgery. The piece, dramatically rendered at 3,500 words, had scared the editors of the paper because it was unlike and longer than anything else they had run before. Worried that readers wouldn't stay engaged with such a lengthy article, the editors decided to run it over two issues, in the paper's Features section. Long before the Pulitzer jurors validated the experiment, those at the paper knew: The switchboard at the *Evening Sun* lit up after the first installment and kept lighting up. Hundreds of readers called in, wanting to know how the story ended.[49]

The genre was gathering strength. Several papers—the *Philadelphia Inquirer* under Gene Roberts, the *Wall Street Journal*, the *Washington Post* (the Style section, especially), section 6 of the *New York Times*—were already running longform journalism, narratives of 10,000 words or more. Others around the country—the *Miami Herald*'s Sunday magazine *Tropic* under Gene Weingarten, the *Virginian-Pilot* under Sandy Rowe, Foster Davis's writers at the *Charlotte Observer*, Mike Pride's at New Hampshire's *Concord Monitor*—would soon join them. Everywhere, "extraordinary stories about ordinary people" (as Rawson liked to put it) moved off the Green Sheet of the *Milwaukee Journal* and onto page 1, moved out of the Sunday editions of the *Detroit Free Press* and the *St. Paul Pioneer Press* and into the daily news. Everyday life moved in on the cops, courts, and finance.[50]

To the confluence of money and ambitious editors and mentors and models, another stream emerged that added momentum to the genre: women. Following Franklin, women were awarded four of the next six Feature Writing Pulitzers: Madeleine Blais of the *Miami Herald*, Theresa Carpenter of the *Village Voice*, Nan Robertson of the *New York Times*, and Alice Steinbach of the *Baltimore Sun*. Their subjects included a murder—but also an account of an eighty-three-year-old veteran seeking justice and a ten-year-old boy who had been blind since birth. Writing on the Poynter Institute website in 2016, Clark devoted a column to the thirty-eight women who at that point had won or been finalists for the Pulitzer feature-writing prize:

> The journalism produced by these women brought to their publications concerns and issues that may not have been on the radar screens of their male counterparts—such as the welfare of children. But, as their stories reveal, they would not be confined to topics that were the product of some women's ghetto in the newsroom. They wrote about crime and punishment. They wrote about war and peace. Far from the days when feature departments confined themselves to recipes and celebrities, these writers turned these sections into the most fertile habitat for longform journalism.[51]

In a profile in a 2007 issue of the *Southwestern Historical Quarterly*, Castleberry recalled how

> an editor approached her in a hallway and asked what happened to the "little girl" they had hired who had "really believed in God, country, motherhood, and apple pie." She responded: "You hired me and you sent me out to see what the real world was like. And I found out that the stories do not happen at the Petroleum Club and the Dallas Country Club."[52]

In the January 1988 ASNE Bulletin, Jean Gaddy Wilson reported that women made up 13 percent of directing editors, a small but influential number that included editors such as Geneva Overholser at the *Des Moines Resister* and Deborah Howell at the *St. Paul Pioneer Press*. Howell had been a city editor at the *Minneapolis Star* with a reputation for being tough when she moved to the *Pioneer Press* in 1979. (In 1990, when Howell announced she was leaving the *Pioneer Press* to become chief of the Newhouse newspaper group's Washington bureau, she explained, "I'm feisty and aggressive and the *Pioneer Press* is feisty and aggressive."[53])

Under Howell's aggressive leadership, the *Pioneer Press* won a Pulitzer for feature writing in 1986 for John Camp's five-part series exploring the life of an American farm family. Two years later, the paper won the prize again for Banaszynski's landmark four-part series, "AIDS in the Heartland." Howell had challenged Banaszynski to find a powerful way to cover the complicated topic of the AIDS epidemic and gave her a year to find the right subject and do the necessary reporting for an immersive diagnosis-to-death story.[54]

Elsewhere, writers such as Ellen Goodman, Molly Ivins, Georgie Anne Geyer, Dorothy Gilliam, and Anna Quindlen moved from the society and op-ed pages onto the more "serious" sections of the paper. In her 1995 essay "Wrinkling the Fabric of the Press," Norma M. Schulman credited female columnists with having expanded conventional definitions of what counted for news. She called their work "a refreshing trend—one that already shows signs of spreading to their male colleagues: integrating commentary on public affairs with insights into the human condition." Schulman, in what could have described a key tenet of literary journalism, went on to assert that the columns allowed room for "the full range of emotional tones, the distinctive (even idiosyncratic) authorial voice, and the progressive discovery-by-analogy that mark some of the most outstanding examples of women's journalism in the United States today."[55]

In an industry still flush with cash, publishers routinely paid for writing seminars. Editors let writers devote months to single projects. The *Virginian-Pilot* had a dedicated narrative team. *Washington Post* reporters did so much field work and travel that the paper employed two full-time in-house travel agents to make arrangements.[56] Papers of all sizes published special reports and multipart series, in personal-voiced reporting with dialogue and scene-by-scene construction. In the *Oregonian*, narratives appeared in Metro, Sports, Living, and News—even on the same day. Reporters there sometimes could hear executive editor Peter Bhati asking, "Okay, Hart … What's the dénouement on that one?"[57]

Through the 1980s and into the 1990s, more books came out—more anthologies, still more models, still more dissemination—and new gatherings emerged, notably the annual conference on narrative journalism convened by Kramer for Boston University and for Harvard's Nieman Foundation. Leading literary nonfiction writers crossed between books and magazines and newspapers and discussed their craft in formal and informal settings. A shared vocabulary deepened, a lingua franca, an agreed-upon set of conventions and ethics. More narrative and literary courses were being taught in colleges, in J-schools. The form increasingly showed up in dailies even on deadline, even in twenty-inch stories. If there was a point when literary journalism joined the mainstream of American media, it was probably around then, unremarked on at the time, when it slipped into the newsroom to stay. The culture had been changed.

And then, of course, the culture changed again. The emergence of a more literary journalism may have forestalled the inevitable, but it hadn't reversed the worrying circulation trends that had so concerned the newspaper editors in Honolulu back in 1977. Even as advertising revenues continued to grow during the spread of coaching and workshops and prizes for great writing, the daily circulation of American newspapers remained flat. In the 1990s, readership declined gradually—and then sharply. At the turn of the twenty-first century, average weekday readership fell below 56 million people; by 2017, it slid to just above 30 million—less than half the number it was in 1973 when Wolfe's manifesto was published.[58] And as Kramer noted, "Once it became clear that narrative journalism wasn't the clotting agent for hemorrhaging readership, interest among editors just dropped off."[59]

The dramatic loss of newspaper advertising revenues (display advertising to direct mail and the internet, classified ads to Craigslist) devastated the industry. Number of pages shrank. Newsrooms cut staff. Across the country, paper after paper folded. Writing budgets, writing coaches, annual anthologies, and (except in a handful of well-funded, one-class papers such as the *New York Times* and *Los Angeles Times*), serials and multi-thousand-word features faded away. "The habitat for narrative writing in newspapers," said Clark, "disappeared."[60]

And yet.

Longform narrative journalism sites emerged on the internet, where space was no limit. Bloggers and podcasters proliferated, many of them narrative storytellers. The tools of intimate voice, scene-by-scene construction, inventive structure, and immersive, detailed reporting flourished in magazines and books, in riveting, eclectic radio programs, and in novel, multimedia combinations of words, images, and sound.

The streams of influence that could so clearly be traced from the New Journalists of the 1960s to the newspaper reporters of the 1970s and 1980s had grown diffuse. The pockets of excellence multiplied and overlapped; the currents mixed, became impossible to distinguish. Historians of the future, looking back at the subject of literary, narrative journalism in the mainstream of American media, would have a hard time making a clear case. They might note that in 2018, Pulitzer prizes were awarded for powerful storytelling and stylish writing to newspapers ranging from the *New York Times* and the *Washington Post* to the *Cincinnati Enquirer* and *Arizona Republic*, from the *Des Moines Register* to the *Press Democrat* of Santa Rosa, California. By 2018, however, less than one in ten Americans under the age of fifty was getting his or her daily news from a printed newspaper. For citizens younger than thirty, it was less than one in twenty.

Literary, narrative journalism was established across the media, for good. It was the mainstream that was disappearing.

Notes

1 Wolfe and Johnson, *New Journalism*, 23.
2 Applegate, *Literary Journalism*, xiv.
3 Murphy, *New Journalism*.
4 Newfield, "Is There a New Journalism?," 45.
5 Kramer, "Narrative Journalism."
6 Christopher Scanlan, phone interview with the author, September 1, 2017.
7 "Newspapers Fact Sheet."
8 Shirky, "Newspapers."
9 The popular cash-paying crossword puzzle, syndicated by Superior Features Syndicate, made its debut in mid-1956 ("Spotlight on Fred Fredericks").
10 Gay Talese, "Gay Talese has a Coke."
11 Snyder and Morris, *Treasury of Great Reporting*, 6.
12 Applegate, *Literary Journalism*, 55, 63, 267; "Published Works"; Engle, "Rudyard Kipling."
13 Scanlan, *Reporting and Writing*, excerpted in Scanlan, "Birth."
14 Scanlan, *Reporting and Writing*, excerpted in Scanlan, "Birth." See also Carey, *Communication as Culture*.
15 Scanlan, *Reporting and Writing*, excerpted in Scanlan, "Birth."
16 Fishkin, *From Fact to Fiction*, 3.
17 "AP Stylebook."
18 Kramer, "Narrative Journalism."
19 Arlen, "Notes."
20 Jon Franklin, quoted in Lepore, "Historical Writing."
21 Hart, "Story for the Ages."
22 Mark Kramer, email interview with the author, October 26, 2016.
23 Murphy, *New Journalism*.
24 Kramer, interview, 2016.
25 Jacqui Banaszynski, interview with the author, September 13, 2017.
26 Molly Ivins, quoted in Jaffe, "From Women's Page."
27 "Newspapers Fact Sheet."
28 Washington Post Company, *Annual Report*.
29 Bogart, *Preserving the Press*, 107–08.
30 "Formation."
31 Bogart, *Preserving the Press*, 108.
32 Bogart, 108.
33 Roy Peter Clark, phone interview with the author, July 21, 2017.
34 Roy Peter Clark, email exchange with the author, May 21, 2018.
35 Clark, interview.
36 Clark.

37 Murray, *Bulletin*.
38 Scanlan, interview.
39 Scanlan, interview; follow-up email exchange, May 21, 2018.
40 Ghiglione, *Bulletin*.
41 Clark, email exchange.
42 Jackson and Sweeney, *Journalist's Craft*, introduction.
43 Clark, interview.
44 Kramer, interview, 2016; Jack Hart, phone interview with the author, July 10, 2017.
45 Roy Peter Clark, quoted in Woods, "Poynter."
46 Banaszynski, interview.
47 Clark and Scanlan, *America's Best Newspaper Writing*, xv.
48 "1979 Pulitzer Prize Winner."
49 Williams, "Jon Franklin."
50 Clark, interview; Banaszynski, interview; Scanlan, interview.
51 Clark, "Where Are All the Women?"
52 Vivian Castleberry, quoted in Voss, "Vivian Castleberry," 515–16.
53 Miller and Tuss, "Deborah Howell."
54 Banaszynski, interview.
55 Schulman, "Wrinkling the Fabric," 55.
56 Kramer, interview, 2016.
57 Hart, interview.
58 "Newspapers Fact Sheet."
59 Kramer, interview, October 10, 2018.
60 Clark, email exchange.

Bibliography

"The 1979 Pulitzer Prize Winner in Feature Writing." Pulitzer Prizes, Columbia University. Accessed August 12, 2018. www.pulitzer.org/winners/jon-d-franklin.
Applegate, Edd. *Literary Journalism: A Biographical Dictionary of Writers and Editors*. Westport, CT: Greenwood Press, 1996.
"AP Stylebook." Wikipedia. Accessed August 12, 2018. https://en.wikipedia.org/wiki/AP_Stylebook#History.
Arlen, Michael J. "Notes on the New Journalism." *Atlantic*, May 1972.
Bogart, Leo. *Preserving the Press: How Daily Newspapers Mobilized to Keep Their Readers*. New York: Columbia University Press, 1991.
Carey, James W. *Communication as Culture: Essays on Media and Society*. Rev. ed. New York: Routledge, 2009.
Clark, Roy Peter. "Where Are All the Women Writing Longform? Check the History of the Pulitzer Prizes." Poynter Institute, May 24, 2016. www.poynter.org/news/where-are-all-women-writing-longform-check-history-pulitzer-prizes.
Clark, Roy Peter, and Christopher Scanlan, eds. *America's Best Newspaper Writing*. Boston, MA: Bedford/St. Martin's, 2001.
Engle, George. "Rudyard Kipling: The Young Journalist (1882–89)." Kipling Society. Accessed August 12, 2018. www.kiplingsociety.co.uk/facts_journo.htm.
Fishkin, Shelley Fisher. *From Fact to Fiction: Journalism and Imaginative Writing in America*. Baltimore, MD: Johns Hopkins University Press, 1985.
"Formation of the American Society of News Editors." American Society of News Editors. Accessed August 12, 2018. www.asne.org/asne-history.
Ghiglione, Loren. *Bulletin of the American Society of News Editors*, June 1982.
Hart, Jack. "A Story for the Ages." Unpublished chapter prepared for *Storycraft: The Complete Guide to Writing Narrative Nonfiction* (Chicago: University of Chicago Press, 2011).
Jackson, Dennis, and John Sweeney. *The Journalist's Craft: A Guide to Writing Better Stories*. New York: Allworth Press, 2002.
Jaffe, Sarah. "From Women's Page to Style Section." *Columbia Journalism Review*, February 19, 2013.
Jones, Chris. "Gay Talese: New York Observer." *Nieman Reports*, Spring 2012.
Kramer, Mark. "Narrative Journalism Comes of Age." *Nieman Reports*, Fall 2000.
Lepore, Jill. "Historical Writing and the Revival of Narrative." *Nieman Reports*, Spring 2002.

Miller, Pamela, and Vince Tuss. "Deborah Howell, Prominent Editor, Killed in Car Accident." *Star Tribune* (Minneapolis, MN), January 2, 2010.

Murphy, James E. *The New Journalism: A Critical Perspective*. Journalism Monographs 34. Lexington, KY: Association for Education in Journalism, 1974.

Murray, Donald J. *Bulletin of the American Society of News Editors*, April 1981.

Newfield, Jack. "Is There a New Journalism?" *Columbia Journalism Review*, July–August 1972, 45–47.

"Newspapers Fact Sheet." Pew Research Center, June 13, 2018. Accessed August 12, 2018. www.journalism.org/fact-sheet/newspapers/.

"Published Works." Walt Whitman Archive. Accessed August 12, 2018. https://whitmanarchive.org/published/periodical/journalism/index.html.

Scanlan, Christopher. "Birth of the Inverted Pyramid: A Child of Technology, Commerce and History." Poynter Institute, June 20, 2003. www.poynter.org/news/birth-inverted-pyramid-child-technology-commerce-and-history.

———. *Reporting and Writing: Basics for the 21st Century*. New York: Oxford University Press, 1999.

Schulman, Norma M. "Wrinkling the Fabric of the Press: Newspaper Opinion Columns in a Different Voice." In *Women and Media: Content, Careers, and Criticism*, edited by Cynthia M. Lont, 55–67. Belmont, CA: Wadsworth, 1995.

Shirky, Clay. "Newspapers and Thinking the Unthinkable." *Clay Shirky* (blog), March 13, 2009. www.shirky.com/weblog/2009/03/newspapers-and-thinking-the-unthinkable/.

Snyder, Louis Leo, and Richard Brandon Morris, eds. *A Treasury of Great Reporting*. New York: Simon and Schuster, 1949.

"Spotlight on Fred Fredericks – Other Comics – New Jersey Patriots." MandrakeWiki, last modified February 13, 2018. www.mandrakewiki.org/index.php?title=Spotlight_on_Fred_Fredericks_-_Other_Comics_-_New_Jersey_Patriots#cite_note-1.

Voss, Kimberly Wilmot. "Vivian Castleberry: An Editor Ahead of Her Time." *Southwestern Historical Quarterly* 110, no. 4 (April 2007): 514–32. https://doi.org/10.1353/swh.2007.0055.

Washington Post Company. *Annual Report*. Washington, DC: Washington Post Company, 1977.

Williams, Paige. "Jon Franklin and 'Mrs. Kelly's Monster.'" Nieman Storyboard, August 24, 2012. http://niemanstoryboard.org/stories/line-by-line-mrs-kellys-monster-how-jon-franklin-wrote-a-classic/.

Wolfe, Tom, and E. W. Johnson, eds. *The New Journalism*. New York: Harper and Row, 1973.

Woods, Keith. "Poynter, ASNE Release 'Best Newspaper Writing 2003.'" Poynter Institute newsletter, August 14, 2003.

14
LITERARY JOURNALISM AT THE CENTER
A Process of Maturation

Miles Maguire

At various times in its history, literary journalism has been viewed as a subversive mode of expression,[1] "a bastard form,"[2] and a threat to traditional journalism and its values.[3] But in the twenty-first century, at least in the United States, literary journalism has become safely ensconced within the mainstream. Recipients of major prizes, from the MacArthur Foundation "genius grants" to the gold standard of American reporting, the Pulitzer Prizes, have frequently employed the techniques of literary journalism in their winning work. In a landmark ruling, *Masson v. New Yorker*,[4] the Supreme Court endorsed a key technique of literary journalism, the compression and editing of quotations to replicate actual dialogue. Other indicators of how thoroughly literary journalism has been accepted include the institution of annual professional conferences on its practice and an established presence in the university curriculum. Literary journalism has advanced so far that it has become the focus of a learned society, the International Association for Literary Journalism Studies, which publishes a biannual peer-reviewed journal on the subject. While all this recognition for literary journalism and its related fields (such as narrative journalism, gonzo journalism, and creative nonfiction) may be viewed as a healthy development, such newfound acceptance and respectability may also come at a price of diminished impact and reduced levels of innovation for a genre that boasts a long history of social critique and advocacy on behalf of marginalized groups and points of view. This chapter will trace the way that the status of literary journalism has changed from outsider to insider and explore the implications of this evolution.

Award-Winning Journalism

The gold medal for public service awarded each year by the Pulitzer Prize Board is widely viewed as the epitome of journalistic achievement, "the most coveted prize of all,"[5] and can serve as a useful benchmark to demonstrate how the standards for judging quality journalism have changed over time. A good place to start to see how literary journalism has moved from the margins to the mainstream is 1973, which was the year that the *Washington Post* received the Pulitzer gold medal for public service in recognition of the newspaper's Watergate investigation, probably the single most significant feat of American journalism in the twentieth century. That was also the year when Tom Wolfe published *The New Journalism*, laying out his case for how and why reporting was changing.

The *Post*'s findings were conveyed in articles that used a direct, understated style of simple sentences and declarative statements to describe the blockbuster discoveries of two young reporters, Carl Bernstein and Bob Woodward. For example, an article that was published on September 29, 1972, begins with this sentence: "John N. Mitchell, while serving as U.S. Attorney General, personally controlled a secret Republican fund that was used to gather information about the Democrats, according to sources involved in the Watergate investigation."[6] The story then proceeds, using the inverted-pyramid structure, to provide specific dates and amounts, denials and other comments from those implicated, and additional background information. Their prize-winning writing matches closely the prescriptions for news journalism as contained in textbooks of the day. "The distinguishing characteristics of the news story are immediate factuality and objectivity," notes Paul V. Sheehan in his 1972 *Reportorial Writing*. "The primary purpose of this type of story is to provide the timely information of interest and significance to the reader. Usually the news story tells what happened or took place."[7]

Wolfe, by contrast, was practicing and advocating a kind of journalism with a different goal, namely to achieve what he called the "unique" and "extraordinary power" of the realistic novel, "variously known as its 'immediacy,' its 'concrete reality,' its 'emotional involvement,' its 'gripping' or 'absorbing' quality."[8] Wolfe went on to identify "four devices"[9] that journalists could use to this end: scene-by-scene organization, dialogue rather than isolated quotations, source-based point of view, and the inclusion of details with symbolic relevance. While these four techniques are not the only way to define literary journalism, they do serve as a useful marker of the genre and how far it has come into widespread acceptance.

Wolfe's early experiments with this new form of journalism and his manifesto on the topic were met with considerable skepticism. Some questioned whether a form that was essentially literary could be classified as journalism.[10] Other criticisms targeted the subjectivity of the form as well as the way that at least some practitioners adopted questionable techniques, such as the use of composite characters, that could serve to undermine the veracity and validity of a report.[11] Scholars who investigated the new journalism phenomenon, however, came to the conclusions that this kind of reporting wasn't particularly new, did not necessarily threaten the standards and ethics of the field, and could usher in a new era of "freer and better journalism."[12]

These views began to take hold in the profession, and in 1979, the Pulitzer competition created a new category, feature writing, to accommodate the kind of approach that Wolfe was arguing for. Not surprisingly, this category has been dominated by literary journalism since it was established in 1979, with the award going that year to Jon Franklin, a pioneer in the field of creative nonfiction. In the words of the Pulitzer judges, the new prize was to recognize "a distinguished example of feature writing giving prime consideration to high literary quality and originality."[13] But the public service category continued to be dominated by the straight-ahead presentation of facts, as illustrated by the *Point Reyes Light* investigation of Synanon, winner in 1979;[14] the Gannett News Service exposé of the Pauline Fathers, winner in 1980;[15] and the *Charlotte Observer*'s in-depth reporting on brown lung disease, winner in 1981.[16]

Over the following decades, the literary style of journalism, with its emphasis on narrative, dialogue, close observation, and omniscience, continued to merit recognition in the Pulitzer's feature category, although in two years, 2004 and 2014, no award was given. Some notable examples of Pulitzer-caliber feature writing include Ron Suskind's 1994 account in the *Wall Street Journal* about inner-city students in Washington who struggle to fulfill their academic potential[17] and Sonia Nazario's 2002 reporting in the *Los Angeles Times* about a Honduran boy's illicit travels aboard the tops of freight trains to reach his mother in the United States, for which Nazario herself recreated his journey by riding aboard boxcars through Mexico.[18]

A clear sign of how the literary approach to news reporting was accepted as a legitimate means of covering serious issues came in 1989. In that year, a series of reports about conditions in South Africa written by David Zucchino for the *Philadelphia Inquirer* won the Pulitzer for feature writing. The articles had originally been entered in the international category, where the judges found themselves with two other pieces of work that they wanted to recognize. But rather than let Zucchino's work, a series of profiles of black South Africans, get passed over, the judges exercised their prerogative to move Zucchino's entry, which they described as a "richly compelling series,"[19] into the features category.[20]

The stature of literary technique in the news profession has continued to rise, and narrative forms have been recognized in many Pulitzer categories. The technique can be seen, for example, in the 1997 winner in the explanatory category, a five-part series in the *Philadelphia Inquirer* about terminally ill patients seeking to die with dignity.[21] The same tools can be detected in the 2001 winning work in national reporting, an intensive examination of race relations in the United States published by the *New York Times*.[22]

In *The New Journalism*, Wolfe had argued that the key to narrative was the ability to develop a story through scenes: "The basic reporting unit is no longer the datum, the piece of information, but the scene."[23] Today the idea of using scenes to convey important news stories is such a mainstream concept that the technique is consistently employed in those reporting projects that are rewarded with Pulitzer gold. But this is not a new phenomenon. As early as 1988, the *Anchorage Daily News* introduced its award-winning series on alcoholism and despair among the native population with a description of a young man who walked out on the tundra and shot himself in the heart:

> The sound of the shot rolled across the flat delta land through the supper time darkness of a cold spring day. It breached the walls and windows of the wooden houses, marking the moment as a beginning, for Louie Edmund had begun a 16-month suicide epidemic that ended the lives of eight young villagers.[24]

The use of the other techniques aside from narrative in the public service category, although less apparent, has also become more common. For example, in 2000 the *Washington Post* was cited for its coverage of group homes for people with intellectual disabilities where residents were abused and neglected. The judges noted in particular the writing of Katherine Boo. While she necessarily employs expository writing techniques to present statistics and other background information, she introduces the series with the story of a particular abuse victim: "Tiny, half-blind, mentally retarded, 39-year-old Elroy."[25] Not only does Boo present Elroy through a series of scenes, including his bedroom and the basement laundry where he goes to clean bedsheets after being sexually assaulted, she also describes status details, such as "the leatherette Bible he can't read; the Norman Rockwell calendar of family scenes he hasn't known."[26] Perhaps most significantly for a daily newspaper journalist, she tells at least parts of her story from Elroy's perspective, in Wolfe's words, "giving the reader the feeling of being inside the character's mind and experiencing the emotional reality of the scene as he experiences it."[27] At the end of Boo's first article, Elroy visits a friend in jail and then goes back to his home: "Bible to stare at. Bedsheets to wash."[28]

These markers of literary journalism have almost become the price of admission for reporters whose work is entered in the public service category. To be sure, blockbuster scoops, like the one about secret government surveillance that earned Pulitzer gold medals for both the *Guardian US* and the *Post* in 2014,[29] may still be told in the simple, direct writing style that Woodward and Bernstein used in the early 1970s. But the public service Pulitzers that were awarded in the three subsequent years all incorporated some techniques of narrative, while exploring hard-news topics such as domestic assault, labor conditions, and unfair evictions. For example, in 2017 ProPublica and the *New York Daily News* shared a gold medal for reporting on how eviction rules were being applied unfairly, especially to minorities.[30] The first story begins by describing a police raid on the home of a woman named Jameelah El-Shabazz.

The article opens with scene-by-scene reconstruction to advance the narrative: first the view from an apartment window, then a retreat to the bedroom, and then a switch to what's happening at the front door. In the bedroom, the reader is invited to consider a series of status details as El-Shabazz is seen feeding her newborn, worshipping before a shrine made up of "candles and carvings,"[31] and then engaging in a cleansing ritual using finely crushed eggshells. The reporter goes further, providing the third-person point of view of El-Shabazz. This is done by including descriptions that are specifically attributed to El-Shabazz, traceable to some documentary evidence. By subtly inserting attributions to these documents in the interiors of sentences, the writer emphasizes the emotional experience of her subject while still maintaining a degree of distance and accountability.

If there is one narrative technique that appears less often in the Pulitzer competition, it is the use of back-and-forth dialogue among multiple sources rather than simple quotations from one source after another. As Wolfe pointed out, getting to a place where a journalist can incorporate dialogue—as opposed to mere quotations—requires "extraordinary feats of reporting" whereby reporters invest the time to "actually witness the scenes in other people's lives as they took place."[32] While this New Journalism technique is not common among Pulitzer winners outside the feature category, it can be found. For example, the 2014 prize in explanatory journalism was won by the estimable Eli Saslow, for articles about the widespread use of food stamps following the recession, and the technique is on display there.[33] Now that all Pulitzer categories have been opened to magazine writers,[34] one may see more dialogue in the future.

While the Pulitzer Prize competition enjoys a high profile and great esteem within the journalism profession, it is not the only prize competition or even the richest. That distinction goes to the MacArthur Fellows Program, which is sponsored by the John D. and Catherine T. MacArthur Foundation. As of 2017, it awarded a stipend of $625,000, compared to the $15,000 that is awarded in most Pulitzer categories (public service winners receive a gold medal).[35] The MacArthur program does not publicize specifics about its selection criteria and is notoriously secretive about how it makes its awards, but a 2011 study showed that the adroit use of literary journalism techniques appears to play a role in the choice of MacArthur fellows.[36] In the first thirty years of the program, half of the journalists who were named as fellows could be described as engaging in literary journalism, particularly if it is defined in a more expansive way to focus on the use of a literary style. Some of these MacArthur fellows had merely incorporated narrative techniques into otherwise standard works of traditional newspaper and magazine reporting, but most of them had produced full-length works of literary journalism. They applied the writing techniques that Wolfe took note of and also the immersive methods of reporting that are required to be able to apply these techniques.

The first reporter to be named a MacArthur fellow, in 1981, was Richard Critchfield, a onetime newspaper reporter who covered the Vietnam War for the *Washington Star* but decided he wanted to break out from the restrictions of daily journalism. Critchfield studied the participant–observer methods of anthropologist Oscar Lewis and applied them in his study of an Egyptian village, which he described through the eyes of one particular young man, Shahhat. The book is structured like a novel and is replete with intense, literary descriptions. At one point, Shahhat may have attempted to commit suicide by throwing himself at the feet of a charging band of horsemen. Critchfield describes

> the horses' plunging hooves and the white tunic and the clouds of thick yellow dust all rolled over and over again together slowly, the white turning red, and the slowly pounding hooves and the yellow dust, rolling over and over again slowly.[37]

Other MacArthur journalism fellows who are known for their narrative journalism include the Pulitzer winner Boo, who won a National Book Award in 2012 for *Behind the Beautiful Forevers: Life, Death, and Hope in a Mumbai Undercity*; Adrian Nicole LeBlanc, author of *Random Family: Love, Drugs, Trouble, and Coming of Age in the Bronx*; David Isay, the radio documentarian who cites Joseph Mitchell as a primary influence on his subject matter and technique;[38] and Alma Guillermoprieto, who published a book based on her immersion into the dance culture of the shantytowns of Rio de Janeiro, including her performance as part of a samba school at Carnival.[39] In 2012, when MacArthur selected David Finkel of the *Washington Post* as a fellow in the communications and journalism category, the foundation made clear how much value it places on literary techniques, especially narrative. MacArthur described Finkel as a "journalist pushing beyond the constraints and conventions of traditional news writing to craft sustained narratives that heighten the reality of military service and sacrifice in the public consciousness."[40]

Another awards program that regularly recognizes literary journalism techniques is one sponsored by a group called Investigative Reporters and Editors, or IRE. This development is notable given that literary journalism techniques were once considered suspect and unreliable by mainstream opinion makers in the profession, and yet investigative journalism, which typically involves charges of wrongdoing by powerful persons or interests, has to be what reporters sometimes call "bulletproof,"[41]—that is, able to stand up to the harshest scrutiny. To be sure, the vast amount of investigative work recognized in the annual IRE awards is based on quantitative methods such as computer-assisted reporting or the analysis of documents obtained through freedom of information requests, but—particularly when it comes to reporting on drugs and on Latin America—literary journalism techniques for information gathering can be found. Literary journalism techniques for presentation, such as the use of narrative, are also commonplace throughout the awards program.

One of the key reporting techniques of literary journalism—the one that is required if reporters are to gather the information necessary to present status details, dialogue, and an omniscient point of view—is immersion.[42] Journalists who engage in immersion commit to spending long periods of time with their subjects, along the way developing a level of trust that allows those subjects to behave naturally and speak honestly. In some cases, reporters reveal their identities as reporters; in other cases, they do not. Under some circumstances, personal safety is a key reason reporters disguise their identities or true goals, but another reason they do go undercover is to get a closer, and presumably a more honest, look at their subjects. But the undercover approach also carries with it questions of ethics and fairness. For reporters with established reputations or those working for a prominent news outlet, the undercover approach may not be an option at all because they are too well known.

In 2009, Shane Liddick, a writer for *San Diego Magazine*, received from IRE the Tom Renner Medal, which is given for outstanding reporting on organized crime.[43] To get his story, Liddick infiltrated a human trafficking ring, which in turn provided him entrée to illegal drug cartels. The IRE judges said in their comments:

> Liddick's reporting in *San Diego Magazine* dispels the stereotypes we have about corrupt Mexican cops and instead shows us a system at least partially populated by honest officers risking—and losing—their lives in the fight to keep some semblance of civilization in their hometown. Liddick chronicles his five years of work on this story in a gritty style that matches the gritty conditions in which he lived to do the reporting.[44]

Another example of literary journalism being seen as investigative journalism came in 2013, when Alberto Arce of the Associated Press was recognized for his dispatches from Honduras,[45] which at the time was considered the most violent country in the world.[46] Unlike the typical investigative journalist who relies on documentary sources, Arce had to deal with the fact that Honduras had no public records law.[47] Instead, he developed an extensive range of human sources, including in the military, courts, prisons, and criminal gangs. His winning dispatches were typically tightly written narratives of specific horrors. In one, for example, he described the day of a police officer's assassination at a busy intersection in broad daylight, shifting his account back and forth from the perspective first of the killers and then of their victim. The article ends with an anecdote showing how the cycle of violence continues full circle and with a quotation from the son of the dead officer, who declares that when he grows up, "I want to be a policeman and kill those gang members."[48]

While journalists and scholars were arguing the relative merits of literary journalism, a parallel argument was playing out in the courts, a story that has been admirably recounted in Kathy Roberts Forde's *Literary Journalism on Trial*. Her book tells the story of the long-running legal battle between Jeffrey Masson, a Sanskrit scholar turned custodian of the Sigmund Freud archives, and the *New Yorker* along with one of its star writers, Janet Malcolm. Forde argues that the ultimate outcome of that case was a blow to First Amendment freedoms.

But another reading of the Supreme Court's decision is a vindication of one of the key methods of literary journalism, the use of extended dialogue instead of discrete quotations.[49] Malcolm defended her use of altered quotations by arguing that such changes were only in the form of "compression" and "translation" and were actually in the service of more accurately portraying her subject.[50] To convey a realistic rendering of Masson, Malcolm maintained, it was necessary to compress quotations spoken on different occasions into a single statement and to make adjustments when translating spoken language into writing.

Masson took issue with six specific quotations and filed a federal lawsuit. He lost at the trial level, and in August 1989, the Ninth Circuit Court of Appeals rejected Masson's argument as well. Masson contended that he had been libeled in the magazine and that Malcolm had demonstrated actual malice because she had altered the wording of comments he made to her. But the appeals court said that it was acceptable to change direct quotations so long as the final wording was a "rational interpretation" of the speaker's original speech.[51]

On further appeal to the Supreme Court, Masson finally achieved a legal victory when the justices decided that his case should go to trial. In backing Masson, the court narrowed the "rational interpretation" standard in a way that has been seen by Forde and others as a limit on the media's First Amendment rights. But the court also made clear that journalists need not be bound by the idea that direct quotations had to be the exact words of a speaker. The majority opinion, written by Justice Anthony Kennedy, did in effect endorse the method that was employed by literary journalists at the *New Yorker* and elsewhere, the modification of the exact record of speech to achieve a desired effect. Words that were presented as quotations were not to be held to the standard of being an exact transcription of what had been spoken. The court ruled:

> The existence of both a speaker and a reporter; the translation between two media, speech and the printed word; the addition of punctuation; and the practical necessity to edit and make intelligible a speaker's perhaps rambling comments, all make it misleading to suggest that a quotation will be reconstructed with complete accuracy.[52]

Altered quotations are acceptable so long as there is no "material change in meaning"[53] from the actual spoken words.

The dissenting opinion would have struck a serious blow to literary journalism because it contended that any intentional alteration to a direct quotation is the same as "reporting a known falsehood" and therefore "sufficient proof of malice."[54] If the court had ruled in this way, the American system of libel law, with its high walls of protection for journalists, would have been altered drastically. A journalist who used dialogue reconstructed from notes and memories, under this theory, would almost automatically be guilty of libel if any of that dialogue could be shown to be defamatory to the speaker.

The recognition of literary devices as powerful tools for telling journalistic stories, as demonstrated by the acceptance of literary journalism in prestigious professional awards programs, was accompanied by a movement in academic circles to study and promote the practice of literary journalism. By the mid-1980s, creative nonfiction, a variant term for the genre, was the fastest-growing part of writing programs on campuses across the country.[55] In 1990, Norman Sims published the seminal *Literary Journalism in the Twentieth Century*, which was, among other things, an attempt "to bring some of the insights from contemporary theory to bear on the works of literary journalists,"[56] and a decade later John Hartsock came out with *A History of American Literary Journalism: The Emergence of a Modern Narrative Form*, which was inspired by a scholar's surprise discovery that no such history existed.[57] In 1994, the literary journal *Creative Nonfiction* was started with an exclusive focus on narrative nonfiction. Its founding editor was Lee Gutkind, who started a pioneering master of fine arts program with an emphasis on narrative nonfiction at the University of Pittsburgh.[58]

In 1998, Mark Kramer, who was writer-in-residence at Boston University at the time, organized a conference called "Aboard the Narrative Train." Three years later, the conference moved to Harvard University,[59] where it became the cornerstone of the Nieman Foundation Program on Narrative Journalism, an offshoot of perhaps the most prestigious and selective fellowship program in the field. By virtue of its association with Harvard and the Nieman Foundation, literary journalism had clearly established itself as central to the practice of news reporting and critical to the future of the profession. In announcing the creation of the narrative program, Nieman's director Bob Giles stated, "Narrative journalism builds a newspaper's franchise for the long term. It plays to the strengths of print journalism—space and considered reporting—adding value that no other medium can duplicate."[60]

Such an assessment was quite a turnabout from the criticism of New Journalism that emerged in the 1960s and 1970s, but this optimism was not borne out by subsequent developments affecting the economics of the industry. As cutbacks trimmed the ranks of newspaper reporters, attendance at the Nieman conference fell, and the conference returned to Boston University in 2010. Nieman has continued to promote literary journalism, however, most notably with the Nieman Storyboard, an online publication that "showcases exceptional narrative journalism and explores the future of nonfiction storytelling."[61]

In 2005, while the Nieman conference was declining, a second major conference on the practice of literary journalism was started at the Frank W. and Sue Mayborn School of Journalism at the University of North Texas. The Mayborn Literary Nonfiction Conference "serves to enhance the quality of nonfiction writing, encourage innovation, and create a community of factual storytellers who maintain an unflinching faith in the narrative craft."[62] One of the attractions of Mayborn is that it offers a range of writing competitions with cash awards and the opportunity to be published in book or magazine form. Other narrative conferences have sprung up at institutions from coast to coast, including a program called "Thread at Yale"[63] and the Berkeley Narrative Journalism Conference.[64] Coursework and full-fledged degree programs in literary journalism are widely available, such as the Literary Reportage program at New York University.[65]

The recognition of literary journalism as a core element of the discipline and one that was worthy of serious scholarly attention was made clear in May 2006, with the inaugural meeting of the International Association for Literary Journalism Studies (IALJS). The beginnings of this group were inauspicious, with a call for papers that attracted just three replies. But a revised call netted a group of fourteen scholars from Canada, Scotland, Portugal, the United States, Australia, France, and England, who agreed to meet in Nancy, France.[66] The group has continued to meet on an annual basis, and its membership has grown to 159. While membership represents twenty-seven countries, nearly half of all members are from the United States.[67] In spring 2009, the association began publishing a scholarly journal, *Literary Journalism Studies*. The journal has an international focus, but it is published in English and frequently features articles about American practitioners of literary journalism.

One result of the mainstreaming of literary journalism is that its fortunes are tied to the future of mainstream journalism, a future that is much in question. As Nicholas Lemann, the distinguished writer and former dean of the Columbia School of Journalism, noted in his keynote speech at the tenth annual conference of IALJS, "Literary journalism needs money and strong institutions."[68] The simple fact is that literary journalism takes time to produce, so much so that John McPhee once argued that literary journalism actually has little in common with standard journalism.[69] Today the traditional supporters of literary journalism—magazines and book publishers initially and more recently newspapers—have struggled financially, making investments in literary journalism more challenging. In Lemann's view, the old forms of institutional backing can be supplanted by a new support network based in "universities, nonprofit organizations old and new, writers' colonies, struggling new publications, and elsewhere."[70]

Clearly, literary journalism, as measured by its recognition in award competitions, legal rulings, conferences, classrooms, and scholarly research, can no longer be viewed as a fringe phenomenon. For proponents and enthusiasts of the form, this situation is a significant achievement, one that Wolfe was not completely sure would occur. In fact Wolfe expressed doubts whether this would be a positive development. "With any luck at all the new genre will never be sanctified, never exalted, never given a theology," he wrote in his *New Journalism* manifesto. "I probably shouldn't even go around talking it up the way I have in this piece."[71] As Lemann pointed out, literary journalism has demonstrated its value in accomplishing the primary missions of journalism, discovering the truth and finding stories to communicate that truth. But communicating depends upon getting the attention of an audience, which may be more difficult to achieve now that literary journalism has become a part of the conventional journalistic tool box. Nazario may have won the Pulitzer for her account of the struggles of Central American immigrants, but a dozen years later, political debates rage on related issues, little informed by what she had to say. Today when journalists try new approaches, "they can find their experiments in form greeted with a mixture of faint praise, puzzlement, or outright hostility,"[72] as Christopher P. Wilson has noted. Compare this reaction to the one that Norman Mailer received for his 1968 nonfiction novel, *The Armies of the Night*. Writing in the *Times*, the critic Alfred Kazin described how the book demonstrated Mailer's conviction "that the times demand a new form." Moreover, Kazin wrote, Mailer "has found it."[73] For better or worse, literary journalism has lost some of its power to shock and motivate change so long as it contents itself with incremental advances within an established and well-accepted framework. As Wolfe suggested, it may be time to look for some "glorious chaos"[74] out of which "may come, from the most unexpected source, in the most unexpected form, some nice new fat Star Streamer Rocket that will light up the sky."[75]

Notes

1 Hartsock, *History*, 77.
2 Macdonald, "Parajournalism," 3.
3 Iggers, *Good News, Bad News*, 78.
4 Masson v. New Yorker Magazine, Inc., 501 U.S. 496 (1991).
5 Harris, *Pulitzer's Gold*, 1.
6 Bernstein and Woodward, "Mitchell Controlled," A1.
7 Sheehan, *Reportorial Writing*, 117.

8   Wolfe, *New Journalism*, 31.
9   Wolfe, 31.
10 Murphy, *New Journalism*, 34.
11 Murphy, 13.
12 Murphy, 38.
13 "Pulitzer to Be Given."
14 Pulitzer Prizes, "1979 Pulitzer Prize Winner."
15 Pulitzer Prizes, "1980 Pulitzer Prize Winner."
16 Pulitzer Prizes, "1981 Pulitzer Prize Winner."
17 Pulitzer Prizes, "1995 Pulitzer Prize Winner."
18 Pulitzer Prizes, "2003 Pulitzer Prize Winner."
19 Pulitzer Prizes, "1989 Pulitzer Prize Winner."
20 Randolph, "Alaska Paper Wins Pulitzer."
21 Pulitzer Prizes, "1997 Pulitzer Prize Winner."
22 Pulitzer Prizes, "2001 Pulitzer Prize Winner."
23 Wolfe, *New Journalism*, 50.
24 Toomey, "Alakanuk's Suicide Epidemic," 6.
25 Boo, "Forest Haven Is Gone."
26 Boo.
27 Wolfe, *New Journalism*, 32.
28 Boo, "Forest Haven Is Gone."
29 Pulitzer Prizes, "2014 Pulitzer Prizes."
30 Pulitzer Prizes, "2017 Pulitzer Prize Winner."
31 Ryley, "NYPD."
32 Wolfe, *New Journalism*, 31.
33 Saslow, "'I'm Not Ready.'"
34 Pulitzer Prizes, "Pulitzer Prizes Open."
35 MacArthur Foundation, "About MacArthur Fellows Program."
36 Maguire, "Literary Journalism."
37 Critchfield, *Shahhat*, 222–23.
38 Maguire, "Literary Journalism," 65.
39 Guillermoprieto, *Samba*.
40 MacArthur Foundation, "David Finkel."
41 Investigative Reporters and Editors, "Watchdog Workshops."
42 Wolfe, *New Journalism*, 31.
43 Investigative Reporters and Editors, "2009 IRE Awards Winners."
44 Investigative Reporters and Editors.
45 Investigative Reporters and Editors, "2013 IRE Award Winners."
46 Sherwell, "Welcome to Honduras."
47 Investigative Reporters and Editors, "2013 IRE Award Winners."
48 Arce, "Teens' Thievery," 6.
49 Forde, *Literary Journalism on Trial*, 202.
50 Forde, 209.
51 Forde, 143.
52 *Masson*, 501 U.S. at 515.
53 *Masson*, 516.
54 *Masson*, 527.
55 Hesse, "Place of Creative Nonfiction."
56 Sims, *Literary Journalism*, vi.
57 Hartsock, *History*, ix.
58 "Lee Gutkind."
59 Boston University, "Power of Narrative."
60 Nieman Foundation, "Nieman Foundation Establishes Program."
61 "About."
62 Frank W. and Sue Mayborn School of Journalism, University of North Texas, "About."
63 Yale University, "Thread at Yale."
64 Graduate School of Journalism, University of California, Berkeley, "Berkeley Narrative Journalism Conference."

65 Arthur L. Carter Journalism Institute, New York University, "Literary Reportage."
66 Bak, "President's Letter," 1.
67 Abrahamson, "2017 IALJS," 7.
68 Lemann, "Journalism in Literary Journalism," 57.
69 Sims, *True Stories*, xvii.
70 Lemann, "Journalism in Literary Journalism," 57.
71 Wolfe, *New Journalism*, 35.
72 Wilson, "Chronicler."
73 Kazin, "Trouble He's Seen."
74 Wolfe, *New Journalism*, 36.
75 Wolfe, 36.

Bibliography

"About." Nieman Storyboard. Accessed December 4, 2017. http://niemanstoryboard.org/about-storyboard/.

Abrahamson, David. "2017 IALJS Annual Business Meeting." *Literary Journalism: The Newsletter of the IALJS* 11, no. 3 (Summer 2017): 7.

Arce, Alberto. "Teens' Thievery Turns Tragic for Honduran Cop." Associated Press, December, 27, 2013.

Arthur L. Carter Journalism Institute, New York University. "Literary Reportage." Accessed November 19, 2017. https://journalism.nyu.edu/graduate/programs/literary-reportage/.

Bak, John. "President's Letter." *Literary Journalism: The Newsletter of the IALJS* 1, no. 1 (Summer 2007): 1+.

Bernstein, Carl, and Bob Woodward. "Mitchell Controlled Secret GOP Fund." *Washington Post*, September 29, 1972, A1+.

Boo, Katherine. *Behind the Beautiful Forevers: Life, Death, and Hope in a Mumbai Undercity*. New York: Random House, 2012.

———. "Forest Haven Is Gone, but the Agony Remains." *Washington Post*, March 14, 1999, A1. Accessed November 29, 2017. www.washingtonpost.com/wp-srv/local/daily/march99/grouphome14.htm.

Boston University. "The Power of Narrative." Accessed December 4, 2017. www.bu.edu/com/narrative/about.html.

Critchfield, Richard. *Shahhat: An Egyptian*. Syracuse, NY: Syracuse University Press, 1978.

Forde, Kathy Roberts. *Literary Journalism on Trial: "Masson v. New Yorker" and the First Amendment*. Amherst, MA: University of Massachusetts Press, 2008.

Frank W. and Sue Mayborn School of Journalism, University of North Texas. "About." Mayborn Literary Nonfiction Conference. Accessed November 19, 2017. www.themayborn.com/about.

Graduate School of Journalism, University of California, Berkeley. "The Berkeley Narrative Journalism Conference." Accessed November 19, 2017. https://events.journalism.berkeley.edu/narrative/speakers/.

Guillermoprieto, Alma. *Samba*. New York: Alfred A. Knopf, 1990.

Harris, Roy J., Jr. *Pulitzer's Gold: Behind the Prize for Public-Service Journalism*. Columbia, MO: University of Missouri Press, 2007.

Hartsock, John C. *A History of American Literary Journalism: The Emergence of a Modern Narrative Form*. Amherst, MA: University of Massachusetts Press, 2000.

Hesse, Douglas. "The Place of Creative Nonfiction." *College English* 65, no. 3 (January 2003): 237–41. https://doi.org/10.2307/3594255.

Iggers, Jeremy. *Good News, Bad News: Journalism Ethics and the Public Interest*. Boulder, CO: Westview Press, 1998.

Investigative Reporters and Editors. "2009 IRE Award Winners." Accessed December 4, 2017. https://ire.org/awards/ire-awards/winners/2009-ire-awards-winners/#renner.

———. "2013 IRE Award Winners." April 3, 2014. Accessed December 4, 2017. https://ire.org/media/uploads/2013_ire_press_release_with_links.pdf.

———. "Watchdog Workshops." Accessed December 4, 2017. www.ire.org/events-and-training/watchdog-workshops/.

Kazin, Alfred. "The Trouble He's Seen." Review of *The Armies of Night*, by Norman Mailer. *New York Times*, May 5, 1968. Accessed July 2, 2018. https://archive.nytimes.com/www.nytimes.com/books/97/05/04/reviews/mailer-armies.html?_r=1&oref=slogin.

LeBlanc, Adrian Nicole. *Random Family: Love, Drugs, Trouble, and Coming of Age in the Bronx*. New York: Scribner, 2003.

"Lee Gutkind." *Creative Nonfiction*. Accessed December 4, 2017. www.creativenonfiction.org/authors/lee-gutkind.

Lemann, Nicholas. "The Journalism in Literary Journalism." *Literary Journalism Studies* 7, no. 2 (Fall 2015): 50–58.

MacArthur Foundation. "About MacArthur Fellows Program." Accessed December 2, 2017. www.macfound.org/programs/fellows/strategy/.

———. "David Finkel." Accessed December 3, 2017. www.macfound.org/fellows/865/.

Macdonald, Dwight. "Parajournalism, or Tom Wolfe and His Magic Writing Machine." Review of *The Kandy-Kolored Tangerine-Flake Streamline Baby*, by Tom Wolfe. *New York Review of Books*, August 26, 1965, 3–5.

Maguire, Miles. "Literary Journalism as a Key to Reporting's Richest Prize." *Literary Journalism Studies* 3, no. 1 (Spring 2011): 53–71.

Murphy, James E. *The New Journalism: A Critical Perspective*. Journalism Monographs 34. Lexington, KY: Association for Education in Journalism, 1974.

Nieman Foundation. "Nieman Foundation Establishes Program on Narrative Journalism." August 17, 2001. Accessed December 4, 2017. http://nieman.harvard.edu/news/2001/08/nieman-foundation-establishes-program-on-narrative-journalism/.

Pulitzer Prizes. "The 1979 Pulitzer Prize Winner in Public Service." Accessed November 26, 2017. www.pulitzer.org/winners/point-reyes-light.

———. "The 1980 Pulitzer Prize Winner in Public Service." Accessed November 26, 2017. www.pulitzer.org/winners/gannett-news-service.

———. "The 1981 Pulitzer Prize Winner in Public Service." Accessed November 26, 2017. www.pulitzer.org/winners/charlotte-nc-observer.

———. "The 1989 Pulitzer Prize Winner in Feature Writing." Accessed November 27, 2017. www.pulitzer.org/winners/david-zucchino.

———. "The 1995 Pulitzer Prize Winner in Feature Writing." Accessed November 26, 2017. www.pulitzer.org/winners/ron-suskind.

———. "The 1997 Pulitzer Prize Winner in Explanatory Journalism." Accessed November 28, 2017. www.pulitzer.org/winners/michael-vitez-april-saul-and-ron-cortes.

———. "The 2001 Pulitzer Prize Winner in National Reporting." Accessed November 28, 2017. www.pulitzer.org/winners/staff-50.

———. "The 2003 Pulitzer Prize Winner in Feature Writing." Accessed November 26, 2017. www.pulitzer.org/winners/sonia-nazario.

———. "2014 Pulitzer Prizes." Accessed November 29, 2017. www.pulitzer.org/prize-winners-by-year/2014.

———. "The 2017 Pulitzer Prize Winner in Public Service." Accessed November 29, 2017. www.pulitzer.org/winners/new-york-daily-news-and-propublica.

———. "Pulitzer Prizes Open All Journalism Categories to Magazines." October 19, 2016. Accessed December 2, 2017. www.pulitzer.org/news/pulitzer-prizes-open-all-journalism-categories-magazines.

"Pulitzer to Be Given for Feature Writing." *New York Times*, April 19, 1978, A17.

Randolph, Eleanor "Alaska Paper Wins Pulitzer." *Washington Post*, March 31, 1989. Accessed November 27, 2017. www.washingtonpost.com/archive/politics/1989/03/31/alaska-paper-wins-pulitzer/4757cc11-4ea9-4851-ba99-6bbfbe9b0f07/?utm_term=.6c4bb4b8e3f5.

Ryley, Sarah. "The NYPD Is Kicking People Out of Their Homes, Even If They Haven't Committed a Crime." ProPublica, February 4, 2016. Accessed November 29, 2017. www.propublica.org/article/nypd-nuisance-abatement-evictions.

Saslow, Eli. "'I'm Not Ready to Sign Up for This Yet.'" *Washington Post*, April 24, 2013. Accessed November 29, 2017. www.pulitzer.org/winners/eli-saslow.

Sheehan, Paul V. *Reportorial Writing*. Philadelphia, PA: Chilton Book, 1972.

Sherwell, Philip. "Welcome to Honduras, the Most Dangerous Country on the Planet." *Telegraph*, November 16, 2013. Accessed December 4, 2017. www.telegraph.co.uk/news/worldnews/centralamericaandthecaribbean/honduras/10454018/Welcome-to-Honduras-the-most-dangerous-country-on-the-planet.html.

Sims, Norman, ed. *Literary Journalism in the Twentieth Century*. New York: Oxford University Press, 1990.

———. *True Stories: A Century of Literary Journalism*. Evanston, IL: Northwestern University Press, 2007.

Toomey, Sheila. "Alakanuk's Suicide Epidemic." In *The Pulitzer Prizes 1989*, edited by Kendall J. Wills, 6–9. New York: Simon and Schuster, 1989.

Wilson, Christopher P. "The Chronicler: George Packer's *The Unwinding*." Post45, May 5, 2017. Accessed July 2, 2018. http://post45.research.yale.edu/2017/05/the-chronicler-george-packers-the-unwinding-2013/.

Wolfe, Tom. *The New Journalism*. New York: Harper and Row, 1973.

Yale University. "Thread at Yale." Accessed November 19, 2017. https://thread.yale.edu/#thread.

15
COMING OF AGE AS A WRITER IN THE SIXTIES
Realizations about Voice

Mark Kramer

Here are the two main elements of narrative journalism: The factual, structured, and populated string of scenes and related digressions, which all seem to the reader (or viewer, or listener) to be heading toward some destination—that part is the story. And then there's the story*teller*, the voice who is the reader's companion and guide. The storyteller is not quite "the author," but (most often) a handier, simplified character, like the author, with human sensibility intact, but many traits sidelined that aren't useful for storytelling. In the common practice of narrative journalism, retaining that human sensibility is what opens the content to wide exploration—to whatever concerns people in conversation, from breaking news events to the small happenings of individual experience. This is how narrative journalism differs from other nonfiction.

This minimal human voice, unlike the voice of daily journalism or academic papers, or business memos, or partisan essays, is in particular not the voice of someone official, and does not represent or speak on behalf of an organization—does not speak for a newsroom, an academic discipline, a fire department, a foundation, a corporation, or a political movement. It's a friend of the reader, speaking on his or her behalf.

I've taught breaking-news print and broadcast journalists from many countries for decades, and virtually all have been trained to write the day's news in a particular, similar voice. Except in columns and op-eds (which may be more personal), this voice for imparting the day's news speaks with the authority of the organization. "News voice" seems, like bureaucracy itself, to be a cross-cultural universal. It sounds to the casual reader about the same in other nations as it does in the US—a voice purposively de-selfed—emptied of human sensibilities. Readers can't detect anything about the personality of whoever the teller of a news story might be. The result is of course stilted, but usefully stilted; it comes across as authoritative, factual, and straightforward for news articles and broadcasts, precisely because it both restricts most emotional content and because it addresses, with a sense of distanced impartiality, its audience of citizens. It adheres to civic fact with a diction ("blaze" and "no reported casualties") that mobilizes the "citizen" portion of readers' shared identity, and skips the deep, contradictory, emotion-filled, disaffiliated and singular concerns that also occupy (and complicate and differentiate) the minds of each idiosyncratic reader. News voice is a remarkable, useful invention, perfected over a few centuries. It's the voice of newspapers in the world's freest countries—with more strictures in less-free countries—that links press and government.

News voice solves some of the political difficulties candor presents for writing news shared by multi-cultural, multi-class, multi-ideological, and multi- and non-denominational populations, whose members' perspectives vary widely. In these areas, one reader's gospel truth may be another's heresy or irrelevant fantasy. In part because of its lack of personhood, news voice accomplishes the crucial work of keeping disparate citizens informed about many shared concerns. Like a sentinel or town crier or clarion or tribune or guardian or courier or herald (the de-selfed, impartial informant's role has lent its name to many newspapers), it functions to alert citizens to approaching danger ("Powerful Storm Predicted") and to commend acts of social cohesion ("Neighbors Open Their Doors to Blast Survivors"). It increases social cohesion in disparate populations by framing common concerns.

News voice is a regular part of our lives; we read and hear it every morning. It reports, with authority, often reliably, official information of record—address of the blaze, number of casualties, a hospitalized victim's medical status, a perpetrator's criminal record, a judge's verdict. This voice frames alarming events as perturbations of what's usual and adequately handled by appropriate authorities.

News voice is also often up to the task of speaking truth to power when that helps restore civic equilibrium. In many crises, it conveys gravitas while addressing public concerns. News voice is a specialized, well-developed diction of news bureaucracies, and accomplishes the organization's mostly beneficial work of normalizing or remediating what has disturbed the status quo.

But if you listen closely, it's an odd voice, handy and usual in the morning paper, but preposterous in a conversation in everyday life. A neighbor, chatting with me, would never describe a house burning down on our street by saying, "Mark, a fire yesterday at 123 Elm Street destroyed a three-story, wood-framed house. The cause of the early-morning blaze is under investigation. There were no reported casualties, according to Assistant Fire Chief Charles J. O'Mally." If your neighbor did speak that way, you'd think he or she had turned strange. News voice omits much of human concern that you'd expect to hear about in a friendly conversation. The constrained expressiveness of the voice is its constant subtext; its delimited selection of official facts and its usefully narrow emotional range abet its functional authority, but also make it unsuited for neighborly chats.

News voice delivers only a thin, standardized stratum of civic information (routine stories can now be composed by a computer), while not readily turning to the turbulent, rich, interpersonal, extra-institutional reality that flares with human complications with every burning house—from the brutal actuality of witnessing fierce combustion physics to the coolness and cautious boldness of the firefighters driving back the flames, while bewildered, displaced tenants cry real tears and cats leap from windows. It does not regularly address such inherent political questions as, for example, how much life-saving can a city budget afford? or are building codes as prudently enforced for tenements and for mansions? The emotional and political range of fire-related events is usefully underreported—they fall beyond the reporting of the civic management of a combustion event.

For many sorts of stories, and with many sorts of neighbors, the voice of informal chat includes more layers of emotional and political complexity. Such information goes easily into, and even drives, stories offered by storytellers with human sensibility. Scenes on a human scale (the hissing and roaring of flames, the stench of sooty steam, the cries of kids, the attending police officers' dispassionate side conversation about upcoming vacations) fit into stories that offer insights beyond civic concerns. Such stories do show up as features or special projects in newspapers, and they are regularly published in books and in magazines such as the *New Yorker* or the *Atlantic* or *Esquire*. And they show up in narrated podcasts and video pieces. As the voice describing a fire shifts from civic to intimate, from depersonalized to having human sensibility, scenes become more specific and sensory. The ranges of facts and of emotions that can be imparted expand greatly. Empathy and complexity of characterization, and even irony, become part of such reporting, as they may be part of the conversations of neighbors discussing a fire. And the reader plays a different role—not just that of a citizen, but as someone whose whole sensibility, intellectual and emotional, can be addressed and brought into play by the text.

Without a formal affiliation, a skilled, human-voiced storyteller develops credibility on his or her own behalf. That sensible voice needn't be obtrusive. The default common-practice voice in quality narrative nonfiction usually is intimate, but it doesn't put an authorial "I" center stage. Because it's a reduction of the writer's self to the minimum needed for opening up unofficial, human topics and for portraying relationships, it offers a way of including subtle and complex interrelationships that exist beyond shared civic facts—a whole other world of factual material.

The few narrative nonfiction writers who succeed with an intrusive, flashy voice shape topics in which a cool-dude-on-the-scene voice adds ironic perspective to official goings-on—like Tom Wolfe's voice in *The Right Stuff* (1979) or Hunter Thompson's in *Fear and Loathing on the Campaign Trail '72* (1973). But it's not the usual voice of such writing. More typically, a minimal but sufficient human voice, perhaps one with an informal sensibility but no first-person pronouns at all, works best for exploring non-civic topics and scenes that would seem out of place in news voice.

***

I did not know much of this in 1969, when I started writing nonfiction for publication, and I'm sure most other young nonfiction writers didn't either. We were on the cusp of the major expansion of interest in and publishing opportunities for what came to be known as narrative nonfiction or narrative journalism, or literary journalism, or creative nonfiction, or the nonfiction novel.

I was, by upbringing and disposition, outside what I saw as the mainstream. I'd moved from New York City to a hill farm in rural Massachusetts that dirt-poor Depression-era farmers had abandoned—the fields were too small, infertile, and tilted for the post-horse world. The place became my topic; I wrote a column every other week about rural life for the *Phoenix*, the cultural weekly newspaper in Boston, a few hours to the east. Back-to-the-landers were suddenly of special interest to the *Phoenix*'s liberal, yuppyish readership. I described the thirty-cow dairy farm where I'd found work, and the farmer who'd become my rural mentor, and the communards who were settling nearby and were my friends.

This was the time that narrative journalism first took flight, though it had been gathering force and occasionally bursting forth for several hundred years before that, without a widely shared label or marketplace. I was twenty-five, a newcomer to rural life and to print. Country people and their situations became my beat, in stories written for my precise, affluent urban, politically awakened audience. I was an intermediary, decoding what I was learning out there about how the nation worked. I'd grown up in a curious, talkative, humorous, liberal, psychologically oriented, and politicized family. The voice of my *Phoenix* columns was the voice spoken at my family's table (at its best), reflecting our authority-questioning, naively privileged social niche. It was not the academic voice of my grad school sociology papers. It was not "covering farming" in news voice. For my topics, news or academic voice didn't come to mind. The major culture-changing events and attitudes of that late 1960s era led to my writing in a voice that could encompass whole, complex situations. From the perspective of someone who ended up deeply immersed in the subgenre of narrative journalism—writing books and articles, teaching, and helping build conferences on the topic—looking back on how I came to its informal voice may say something about how a literary form coalesces. My experience was typical enough to be a case in point.

In the late 1960s, the haze of easy, assumed patriotism in which I'd grown up lifted. The country was engaged in a war that, to ever-more citizens, didn't make sense. Conventional media got there slowly, but meanwhile, a commercially sufficient supply of younger readers disillusioned about something as life-framing as our national purpose came to identify as independent of the mainstream and its careers and materialism. They sought alternative newspapers and books and singers. Pete Seeger sang a popular tune renouncing the homes we'd heedlessly aspired to in middle-class suburbia:

> And they're all made out of ticky tacky
> And they all look just the same.[1]

These readers wondered more and more how "the system" really worked and had attitudes that went with coming to doubt the very civic authority that spoke news voice. Many hungered for things basic—including my stories about milking cows and making hay and a summer solstice commune party and slaughtering pigs raised on farm for meat and fixing tractors and about why family farms were slipping away in a national transition toward corporate agriculture. The columns proved popular; many readers wrote letters, and a few arrived from book editors offering to publish the collected columns. Those years, the late 1960s and early 1970s, were just when storytelling journalism exploded as a publishing category. Its writers were working out skills of a personal-voiced journalism before we had a good term for it.

Later, I understood that I'd chanced, circumstantially, upon a setup that made for open, enjoyable narrative journalism: I was writing for a specific, frank, new-reality hungry audience, a demographic that welcomed an amiable, informal but reliable voice exploring a newly crucial and socially relevant foreground topic (moving to a simpler life and family farming in hard times) that was unfamiliar, intriguing, and directly relevant to that audience (I wrote, "there's the draft, taxes for evil uses, rape of nature, drug laws," but "a farm with friends is a very pleasant street corner to hang out on while waiting for the bomb to fall").[2] The columns offered rich, small, symbolic foreground stories (a storm's coming, and in a field leased by the farmer I work for, cut hay needs baling and stacking in the barn) that pointed toward the tectonic social change (the corporatization of our food supply and the displacement of rural traditions) playing out in the daily lives of cool characters, exurban and rural.

Without much thought, I fell into a usual and sturdy structure for narrative journalism: Explanatory digressions interrupted engrossing scenes. That informal, unofficial voice that defines narrative journalism kept the reader company. It acknowledged readers' whole human natures, certainly not just the citizen part. Voice and reader were presumptive friends with shared values (I wore mine on my sleeve), and the reader was predisposed to learn more. There was no breaking news. The pieces showed rural people and recent refugees from the city working at something like parallel play as traditional society came apart and the war in Vietnam raged far away.

I felt my way along, developing the topics weekly, so those letters of inquiry from publishers amazed me. I was years away from developing a formulated understanding about voice, scene-setting, character development, style, pace, digressive placement, or framing themes. I was simply chatting with like-minded friends who shared the fascinations I had. No notion of writing "objectively" came to mind, or of making things up. It simply seemed meaningful to me that I tell true stories. I tried for clarity and geniality and a plain writing style.

I'd absorbed some precedents for these aspirations but hadn't realized it then. Back in high school, in about 1960, I'd read *Hiroshima*—John Hersey had reported it for the *New Yorker* in 1946, just months after we'd A-bombed Japan. His precise and personal voice stuck with me as an aspiration.

During college, I'd read Lincoln Steffens's 1902 colloquial exploration (in *McClure's Magazine*) of the machoest guy at the rodeo, "The American Man on Horseback: The Bronco-Busting Contest at Denver for the Championship of the World"—an immersion in a scene showing the dwindling cowboy culture.

And on the farm, in 1971, I'd devoured Ed Sanders's new book, *The Family* (1971). It seemed obvious as I read it that it was different from what newspapers had offered on the recent murders by Charlie Manson's sad, nasty followers.

The papers ran lurid glimpses of mayhem in the summer of 1969, and then again near Christmas, when Manson was captured. The *New York Times* (in news voice) wrote, on December 3, that "the persons accused ... lived a life of indolence, free sex, midnight motorcycle races and apparently blind obedience to a mysterious guru."[3] United Press International's arrest story, "Hippie Clan Is Suspect in Killing Sharon Tate," had said, with stereotypical civic sensibility: "A weird hippie band called 'the Manson Family' burst into the Sharon Tate estate and brutally killed five persons because the home was a 'symbol of rejection' to the cult's leader, a member of the family has told police."[4] And the local paper near my farm ran an Associated Press wirephoto of Manson's hairy face, with the headline "Cult Leader?" The photo text read: "Charles Manson, 34, was described today by the Los Angeles Times and attorney Richard Caballero as the leader of a quasi-religious cult of hippies."[5]

Sanders's book didn't do that. Sanders expanded my understanding of news and of humankind by retelling the story in an informal voice. He had written as a hip, curious, politically aware, and thorough friend of readers. I was really excited by his way of doing it; I wanted to write that way.

Sanders distilled the opening chapter, "A Poor Risk for Probation," mostly from Manson's extensive probation report following a prior seven-year imprisonment:

> Manson announced that he was going to live with his mother on Harkinson Avenue in Los Angeles. This was the first of twenty addresses Manson would have in this particular year and eight months' stretch of freedom.
>
> The parole office gave him some employment leads. His employment pattern for the following months reads like a struggling novelist's. But Manson was just struggling, working as a bus boy, bartender, frozen-food locker concessionaire, canvasser for freezer sales, service station attendant, TV producer and pimp.
>
> On January 1, 1959,[6] an irate father complained to the Los Angeles police department that Manson was making attempts to turn his daughter Judy out into the streets to hustle.[7]

There it was. Fact by fact, in a relaxed, savvy, sensible, human voice, he most unofficially described personalities and situations. The voice engaged my own savvy about life and trusted me as a reader to "get" the ironic comparison of Manson's job-shifting to the part-time work of a "struggling novelist." Sanders had bothered to count those twenty addresses and assumed that we readers could understand Manson, that we weren't dull, cult-endangered citizens but were engaged by discovering what's what with this psychopath who'd been shaped by the society that had locked him up. Sanders's authority grew from hard research, poise, and his own outsiderhood—he was, for example, a member of a cool and somewhat famous band called The Fugs.

Sanders was one of us, the one who'd gone backstage and accomplished what the crime beat reporters' voices fell short of achieving. They'd conventionalized Manson followers, squeezing them within a framework of civic concerns, as a "weird hippie band" and "hippie clan"—terms that failed to connect the hideous crime with the spectrum of human behavior that stretched from Manson to me and everyone else who hadn't committed bloody murder. The literate, puzzled, disoriented, authority-doubting audience that had come of age in the 1960s was a market of readers hungry for human-scale, non-official explanations and portrayals. Writers had begun to satisfy the need for human-voiced storytellers.

Tom Wolfe declared an emerging "New Journalism" then. That was the title of his article, "The Birth of 'The New Journalism'; Eyewitness Report," in a February 1972 issue of *New York* magazine (then an insert in the *Herald Tribune*).[8] I read it sitting in a battered wicker rocker before a wood stove.

As I'm sure many other writers of the era did, I understood at once that I was writing, and wanted to keep writing, in the sort of voice Wolfe described. I felt instructed and grateful. I saw that my columns were part of this newish genre. He'd named it and declared its seemingly obvious and appropriate practices an innovative trend.

It was a way of approaching material and of writing that was opening up as a profession, published at that point almost entirely in books and magazines. It would gain wider entry to newspapers about a decade later. It would be identified by still more labels then—not just literary journalism, narrative journalism, creative nonfiction, and the nonfiction novel, but enterprise reporting and feature writing—all describing the same elephant.

Its development was accelerated by specific editors, including Clay Felker, who cofounded *New York* magazine in 1968, Harold Hayes at *Esquire*, John Bennett at the *New Yorker*, and Dick Todd at the *Atlantic Monthly*. They all got it early and acquired stables of protégés.

In the *Atlantic Monthly*, Todd reviewed *Mother Walter and the Pig Tragedy* (1972), the anthology of my *Phoenix* (and *Real Paper*) columns that Knopf published. I wrote him a note and, at his invitation, drove across the state and met him for lunch at the Ritz.

Having found an editor, and a genre label, and a sense of style and informal approach to official topics, I'd touched down as a writer of narrative journalism. Todd took a few farm-related pieces of mine for the *Atlantic Monthly* and signed on to edit *Three Farms: Making Milk, Meat and Money from the American Soil* (1980) and, later, *Invasive Procedures: A Year in the World of Two Surgeons* (1983). I am fortunate to have had his mentorship through the ensuing forty years.

Colleges awakened to the subgenre slowly. I became one of the first writers-in-residence in the field, teaching a course called Writing about Society at Smith College for a decade, starting in 1980. I moved on to a professorship in journalism at Boston University for another decade and then was founding director and writer-in-residence of the Nieman Program on Narrative Journalism at Harvard. I learned to verbalize how the form works by teaching it. Teachers joined those early editors as vectors of contagion.

I wrote more books and coedited two anthologies of representative pieces and *Telling True Stories*, an anthology of advice by practitioners for narrative journalists, and began several decades of organizing conferences for working narrative journalists in the US and abroad (including extant annual conferences in London, Amsterdam, and Bergen, Norway).

The experience of reading this human-voiced, candid, and humane subgenre builds on the writer's individual authority, candor, companionship, and compassionate focus on people in ordinary but revealing situations. It has become a vital sector of journalism, especially suited for witnessing specific situations nested in their social contexts. It's a form that has emerged and grown to match the demands of a readership glad to have more intimate insight, from more varied sources of authority, portraying how the non-civic aspects of our increasingly complex world work.

If the market for articles and books in the genre is now narrowing, it seems also to be well established for proven writers and occasional upstarts. When the best-seller lists occasionally do contain books by or about people not famous from television, movies, pop music, or high government office, those books are almost always works of narrative journalism. While it's hard for many people to make good livings from the genre, the same is true of writers of fiction, drama, and verse. There's a bit of room on the reporting staffs of a few newspapers, and there are opportunities to teach and write. This does not seem to daunt my current (2019) seminar members (young working writers, for the most part), who are as fascinated with the creative and informative potential of the form as were my brilliant Smith College undergraduates in the 1980s, and my graduate students at BU in the 1990s, and the Nieman fellows in my seminars in the 2000s. The current Boston-area professional writers who have joined my "kitchen workshop" are increasingly interested, of course, in adapting the genre to digital media—videos, podcasts, online mixed-media magazines, and e-books. And the subgenre translates to these media well, its authoritative and informal voice intact.

Notes

1. Seeger, "Little Boxes."
2. Kramer, "Country Radicals," 6, 7.
3. Roberts, "3 Suspects," 37.
4. "Hippie Clan."
5. "Cult Leader?"
6. The date is January 16, 1959, in the 1971 E. P. Dutton edition of *The Family*.
7. Sanders, *Family*, 5.
8. Wolfe, "Birth."

Bibliography

"Cult Leader?" *Fitchburg (MA) Sentinel*, December 3, 1969, 1.

"Hippie Clan Is Suspect in Killing Sharon Tate." *Russell (KS) Daily News*, December 3, 1969. Also available at www.cielodrive.com/archive/5-killed-as-symbol-cultist-member-says/.

Kramer, Mark. "Country Radicals." In *Mother Walter and the Pig Tragedy*, 3–8. New York: Alfred A. Knopf, 1972.

Roberts, Steven V. "3 Suspects in Tate Case Tied to Guru and 'Family.'" *New York Times*, December 3, 1969, 37+.

Sanders, Ed. *The Family*. 1971. New York: Thunder's Mouth Press, 2002.

Seeger, Pete. "Little Boxes." Lyrics by Malvina Reynolds. 1962.

Wolfe, Tom. "The Birth of 'The New Journalism'; Eyewitness Report." *New York*, February 14, 1972. http://nymag.com/news/media/47353/.

PART II

Themes, Venues, and Genres across Time

16
OF TROOPS AND TROPES
US Literary War Journalism from the Civil War to the War on Terror

John S. Bak

His soldiers weren't yet calling him the Lost Kauz behind his back, not when this began. The soldiers of his who would be injured were still perfectly healthy, and the soldiers of his who would die were still perfectly alive. A soldier who was a favorite of his, and who was often described as a younger version of him, hadn't yet written of the war in a letter to a friend, "I've had enough of this bullshit." Another soldier, one of his best, hadn't yet written in the journal he kept hidden, "I've lost all hope. I feel the end is near for me, very, very near." Another hadn't yet gotten angry enough to shoot a thirsty dog that was lapping up a puddle of human blood. Another, who at the end of all this would become the battalion's most decorated soldier, hadn't yet started dreaming about the people he had killed and wondering if God was going to ask him about the two who had been climbing a ladder. ... Those dreams would be along soon enough, but in early April 2007, Ralph Kauzlarich, a U.S. Army lieutenant colonel who had led a battalion of some eight hundred soldiers into Baghdad as part of George W. Bush's surge, was still finding a reason every day to say, "It's all good."[1]

So opens *The Good Soldiers* (2009), David Finkel's account of his eight months in Baghdad as an embedded journalist with the US Army's 2nd Battalion, 16th Infantry, or the 2–16 Rangers.[2] Caustic in subjunctive mood, disturbing in image, ironic in tone, and not a little over-sensationalistic in detail—what nonfiction book about war cannot be?—Finkel's literary war journalism is both unique and derivative of nearly all American war reportage of the past century or more.

It is unique not only because Finkel's voice is his own but also because his micro-reporting looks at the tribulations specific to *these* soldiers in *this* war; it is derivative because these soldiers' acts of heroism and futility are universal enough to have been plucked from any war that American soldiers have been engaged in and that journalists have reduced to byte-sized kernels of palpable truth. For while the wars' fronts have migrated and the tools by which they have been fought and recorded have evolved over time, three elements have remained constant in US literary war journalism (perhaps *all* literary journalism about war): the irony through which a war is rendered, the understatement by which it is judged, and the sensationalism in which it is captured. At once rhetorical strategy and literary trope, irony and understatement allow the literary journalist to report and editorialize simultaneously, to faithfully reveal the facts of war and spin them at the same time. Sensationalism, in the hands of a lesser journalist, becomes newsporn, but when balanced in a text alongside the sobering effects of irony and understatement, it can, like salt and pepper or vinegar and oil, season the story in a way that whets a reader's appetite. And nowhere in the canon of American literary journalism has this equilibrium been achieved as frequently, and as effectively, as in its war reporting.

Literary war journalism has had, in fact, a rich—and sadly—long tradition in the United States. Each war in which the nation has found itself ensnared has produced its own brand of journalism, from the sensationalist "yellow" journalism of the Spanish–American War (1898–99) to the embedded "new" journalism of the War on Terror. If war journalism traditionally fluctuates between the statistic-hungry reporting of the mass media, televised or written, and the jingoistic newspeak of state-run propaganda machines, *literary* war journalism has often tried to fill the void that lies in between, intermingling historical and contemporary contexts and political commentary with human interest stories involving soldiers and noncombatants alike. In the United States in particular, this literary war journalism began forming around the time of the Civil War (1861–65), though historian Alfred E. Cornebise dates it as early as 1782 when Nathanael Greene's colonial troops published the soldier newspaper *South Carolina Gazette*.[3] Regardless of the actual birth date of American literary war journalism, nearly all scholars agree that it came of age during the Spanish–American War, suffered its first major crisis during World War I (1914–18), and then went underground for a time, only to re-emerge on foreign soil during the Spanish Civil War (1936–39). As forerunners to today's literary war journalism in America, these early accounts nonetheless marked the nation's early efforts to document the human side of war—not just the victory marches celebrated or the trenches taken and retaken, but also the mundane and the sundry, from the reconciliation of southern debutantes toward Yankee officers to the varieties of mud that mired soldier advances in the Somme.[4]

If the nineteenth century laid the groundwork for literary war journalism in America, with its unique admixture of local-color vernacular and Zolaesque naturalism, it was during the twentieth century that American literary war journalists acquired international status. From the literary reportages of the Great War to those of the Spanish Civil War, the most important American literary journalism was literary *war* journalism. War, perhaps more than any topic covered in the news, was inherently charged with gut-wrenching emotionalism and opposing idealisms and thus an easy cauldron in which to experiment with stories, just as immigration and poverty were at the fin de siècle. With competing journalistic media in photography and then film and television, written war journalism had little place to go other than toward the literary, lest it lose its momentum and credibility. While objective war reporting eventually replaced the literary in the major American dailies after World War I, literary war journalism from the second half of the twentieth century to the start of the twenty-first went from cutting to bearing its teeth, always advancing the genre's aesthetic and emotional appeal but forever negotiating its way through the plethora of sensationalist images and ironic portrayals that have traditionally demarcated "yellow" from "new" journalism. John Hersey's opus *Hiroshima* (1946), Michael Herr's *Dispatches* (1977) about the Vietnam War, Mark Bowden's daily bylines on the Battle of Mogadishu (1997), and Sebastian Junger's dispatches on the war in Afghanistan (2008)—today, these authors are taught in literature classes for their aesthetics as often as they are in journalism and history programs for their faithfulness to fact and astute political commentary.

This chapter covers a century and a half of literary war journalism produced by American writers about citizens and soldiers involved in a native or foreign war. In providing a panorama of literary war journalism from the Civil War to the current War on Terror, this chapter demonstrates how American literary war journalism, as an alternative to war literature and traditional war journalism, as well as to the historical legacies that have emerged from or given rise to both, has sought different ways to perceive and capture the aesthetics of the war experience. And yet, among the litany of voices, what makes them recognizably American by the twenty-first century is their admixture of detached irony and understatement and sensationalism.[5] Too much of one or the other, and literary journalism risks becoming an op-ed or turning "yellow." If less is more, as the adage goes, then none is arguably the most, and the best of America's later literary war journalism relies precisely upon the unspoken, the insinuation, and even the silence among the cacophony in order to be heard. It may not have been "all good" in the history of American war involvement, as Finkel intimates, but it has been "all good" in the history of American war reportage.

US Literary Journalism from the Civil War to the Spanish–American War: A Press Divided

Both Norman Sims and John C. Hartsock situate the dawn of US literary journalism in the second half of the nineteenth century, with most significant developments occurring around the fin de siècle rise of mass communication. "The core of nineteenth-century literary journalism," Sims writes, "can be found in a simple, widespread prose device used in the newspapers—the sketch. ... It permitted newspaper reporters to be writers, playing with voice and perspective and challenging readers to evaluate the text."[6] Sims argues that local-color sketches evolved into a realist literary journalism evident in the Anglo-American press, such as in the works of Jack London, Stephen Crane, Richard Harding Davis, and John Reed.[7] Hartsock expands upon the role of the sketch and suggests that rhetorical, literary, and professional factors were also emerging around this time that provided the framework for a later literary journalism.[8] While Hartsock admits that literary elements could also be found in early American journalistic work, it was not until the late nineteenth century that the professional field of journalism became a mass-circulation phenomenon, one that gave rise to national newspapers and necessitated a certain neutral standard of reporting that every region could identify with. Literary journalism gave local reporters and journalists the ability to be journalistically accurate but vernacularly identifiable to local readerships. It would not be wrong, then, to suggest that the American Civil War, and the era of Realism that accompanied it, is partly responsible for having precipitated these changes that Sims and Hartsock describe.

Concerning the journalism produced around the time of the American Civil War, David B. Sachsman and others have detailed in *A Press Divided: Newspaper Coverage of the Civil War* (2017) the impact that Northern and Southern presses had on the mediatization of the Civil War, in particular how both sides' lack of objective reporting on the people and events leading up to, during, and following the war captures a nation not simply divided but wholly fragmented.[9] Ford Risley, in *Civil War Journalism*, similarly demonstrates that journalism at the time was more than simply writing *about* people and events; it was also about writing *for* the people—civilians and soldiers alike—who are central to any civil war.[10] Presses from the North and South did so not out of any political or journalistic ideology but out of the humanist need to speak to one's own people behind the lines, emphasizing individuals' stories over bipartisan agendas. Since many accounts of the Civil War come from the American soldiers themselves, who captured their daily lives in the troop newspapers published on both sides of the Mason–Dixon Line, journalism historians are recognizing the need to widen the scope of war reporting to literary journalism. Donagh Bracken even claims in *The Words of War* that Civil War reporting has laid the foundation for modern American journalism and that the war shaped the press as much as the press shaped the war.[11]

Another source of early literary war journalism can be found in the newspapers that the Union and Confederate soldiers published themselves. Alfred Cornebise examined nearly three hundred titles from the American Civil War that enjoyed print runs of up to four thousand, including *The Soldiers' Journal* and *The Cripple*, and while they lack the signature irony of American war reportage, they do carry a certain amount of understatement, if only because they were heavily censored by the army brass. Earle Lutz, one of the first scholars to have studied these soldier papers, writes extensively of the "extracurricular work of the soldier typographer and editor who seemingly never lost an opportunity to stack his army shooting stick in the corner of some obscure, abandoned newspaper office to resume temporarily the use of his beloved printer's shooting stick."[12] "Never before," Lutz continues,

> had the common soldier had his own organ in which to give expression to the American ideal of freedom of thought and speech. From these examples of the enterprise of Billy Yank and Johnny Reb sprang the frank-speaking *Stars and Stripes* so familiar to every veteran of World Wars I and II.[13]

American literary journalism in general, and literary war journalism in particular, advanced apace from the Civil War to the end of the nineteenth century, and while some writers exploited the local-color voices of their regions and others delved into the naturalism of inner-city reporting, newspapers became havens for war journalism that had literary flare. That flare would eventually become excessive in the yellow journalism and the muckraking journalism of the fin de siècle. And with a new war on the horizon, literary journalism was once again poised to evolve. Newspaper magnates Joseph Pulitzer and William Randolph Hearst are often credited with (or blamed for) drawing the nation into the Spanish–American War with their sensationalist stories or outright half-truths. The most famous example of the exaggeration is the apocryphal story that artist Frederic Remington telegrammed Hearst to tell him all was quiet in Cuba and "There will be no war." Hearst responded, according to reporter James Creelman, "REMINGTON, HAVANA: Please remain. You furnish the pictures, and I'll furnish the war."[14]

Two of the most significant literary journalists during this war were Stephen Crane and Richard Harding Davis. As Thomas Connery notes of Crane's New York City sketches, "Crane used a host of literary techniques, including contrast, dialogue, concrete description, detailed scene setting, careful word selection that built a repetition of imagery, and irony."[15] It was this type of writing that nourished his literary journalistic piece about the Spanish–American War. From the summer of 1898 until the end of the war, he wrote dozens of stories for the *New York World* and then the *New York Journal*, but his most famous war piece is undoubtedly "Stephen Crane's Own Story," published in the *New York Press* on January 6, 1897, only five days after the sinking of the *Commodore*, on which he was a passenger accompanying a filibustering shipment of arms to Cuba:

> Jacksonville, Fla., Jan. 6.—It was the afternoon of New Year's. The Commodore lay at her dock in Jacksonville and negro stevedores processioned steadily toward her with box after box of ammunition and bundle after bundle of rifles. Her hatch, like the mouth of a monster, engulfed them. It might have been the feeding time of some legendary creature of the sea. It was in broad daylight and the crowd of gleeful Cubans on the pier did not forbear to sing the strange patriotic ballads of their island.[16]

The journalistic piece's notable understatement of gloom prevails from the opening lines, as is typical of American literary naturalism, which attempts to show nature's and the gods' indifference to humankind. The account later appeared in Crane's well-known novella "The Open Boat," first published in *Scribner's Magazine*, which colors the narrative with an even heavier dose of objective naturalism. In the novella, as factual as we can tell based on the few survivors of the wreck, the sea takes on more of an antagonistic role, turning the story from a failed attempt at filibustering to a struggle for survival.

Along with the artist Remington, Hearst sent writer Richard Harding Davis to Cuba in 1896 to cover the rebellion against the Spanish. Davis had spent several months in Latin America, a period he described in his nonfiction book *Three Gringos in Venezuela and Central America* (1896), and he contributed literary journalistic pieces about several other wars, including the Boer War, the Russo–Japanese War, and World War I. But perhaps his most memorable literary journalistic contribution to war reporting was a 2,500-word article from Cuba about the execution by firing squad in early 1897 of the Cuban rebel Adolfo Rodríguez:

> He had a handsome, gentle face of the peasant type, a light, pointed beard, great wistful eyes and a mass of curly black hair. He was shockingly young for such a sacrifice, and looked more like a Neapolitan than a Cuban. You could imagine him sitting on the quay at Naples or Genoa, lolling in the sun and showing his white teeth when he laughed. He wore a new scapula around his neck, hanging outside his linen blouse.
>
> It seems a petty thing to have been pleased with at such a time, but I confess to have felt a thrill of satisfaction when I saw, as the Cuban passed me, that he held a cigarette between his lips, not arrogantly nor with bravado, but with the nonchalance of a man who meets his punishment fearlessly, and who will let his enemies see that they can kill but can not frighten him.[17]

As Edd Applegate notes about Davis's literary war journalism, "Whenever he covered a war he looked for action that could be described sensationally; in short, it had to be dramatic so that he could write vivid, picturesque scenes easily visualized by the reader."[18] Though fin de siècle literary war journalism often maintained its ironic tone, understatement was frequently replaced with sensationalist overstatement, a trait typical of yellow journalism evident in Davis's words here.

US Literary Journalism from World War I to the Spanish Civil War: Their Wars, Our Words

In the opening years of the twentieth century, literary journalism moved underground, largely because yellow journalism, and muckraking journalism after it, had pushed the genre to such sensationalist ends that space was created for a more objective journalism to occupy the middle ground of news reporting. But the Great War tarnished these early years of objective reporting because state-sponsored censorship plagued every nation reporting on the fighting. As journalism historian Philip Knightley famously quipped about World War I journalism, "More deliberate lies were told than in any other period in history."[19] One of the consequences of this censorship resulted in the journalistic reporting—some of it literary, most of it humorous, nearly all of it ironic—by the soldiers themselves in the hundreds of trench journals they produced on all war fronts.[20] A second consequence was that a literary-inspired journalism at the time moved off the front page of the dailies and into weekly or monthly journals, such as the *Masses* (and later the *New Masses*), the *Coming Nation*, and the *Crisis*, to name just a few, or developed into longform journalism sold to New York publishing houses. These first-person impressions of the war were meant to combat the propaganda machine that Knightley describes, which kept the horrific truths of trench warfare hidden from the public. Literary journalism, like investigative journalism in general, is nourished by the smoke screens, red herrings, lies, and roadblocks it confronts. Denying journalists the right to report from the front only helped to foment their drive to get the story, and to get it right. As Andrew Griffiths and Sara Prieto rightly note, "Under these circumstances, the reporters were forced to look for alternative strategies to narrate the war. Literary journalism offered a means to overcome the barriers imposed by the censors and by the brutal realities of the war."[21] Literary war journalism had now swapped roles with traditional news reporting, inserting a more sober and objectified voice (even when written in the first person) to offset the jingoistic, even sensationalistic reporting produced by the warring nations to win over their respective audiences. It was a major shift from the "yellow" literary journalism of just a decade earlier, one which would set the stage for the irony-driven reportages of the thirties onward.

But a secondary aim, particularly for the articles that appeared in *Masses* and *Crisis*, was to stoke its targeted readerships' ideologies—proletarian and Pan-African, respectively—and inform them of the shaping revolutions, political and cultural alike, facing the American nation. For example, John Reed—a major literary war journalist of the period who was partly groomed just out of college by another literary journalist, Lincoln Steffens—gained celebrity in the years just prior to the war. In 1913, Reed covered the Mexican Revolution for *Metropolitan Magazine* and the *New York World* and even interviewed rebel leader Pancho Villa, accompanying his peasant soldiers south to La Tropa, where he witnessed their massacre by the federal troops. In his dispatches over the four-month period, Reed nearly single-handedly swayed American sympathies in favor of Villa's revolution. Reed collected these articles into *Insurgent Mexico* (1914), a riveting piece of war journalism, though perhaps not entirely untainted by what Daniel Wayne Lehman calls "his manipulating presence throughout the text."[22]

The *Metropolitan* then sent Reed, born into wealth but who acquired socialist leanings while at Harvard, to report from the Western front once World War I had broken out in 1914. Revolted by capitalist interests in the Great War, Reed concluded the unsigned piece entitled "The Traders' War," published in the September 1914 issue of the *Masses*: "This is not Our War."[23] He later perfected the sardonic tone of his reportage writing in his masterpiece on the Bolshevik Revolution, *Ten Days That Shook the World* (1919), evident in the following exchange between a Marxist theorist and a Leninist pragmatist:

> "You are a fool! Why, my friend, I spent two years in Schlüsselburg for revolutionary activity, when you were still shooting down revolutionists and singing, 'God Save the Tsar!' ... And I am opposed to the Bolsheviki, who are destroying our Russia, our free Revolution. Now how do you account for that?" The soldier scratched his head.
>
> "I can't account for it all. ... To me it seems perfectly simple—but then, I am not educated. It seems like there are only two classes, the proletariat and the bourgeoisie—"[24]

Marxist writers like Reed saw freedom in the European brand of politicized reportage, which they later imported to magazines like Joseph North's *New Masses*. This reportage literature, North famously said, "is three-dimensional reporting. The writer not only condenses reality, he helps the reader feel the fact. The finest writers of reportage are artists in the fullest sense of the term. They do their editorializing through their imagery."[25]

Similar war "impressions" at this time were often told in the same detail-driven travelogue voice that dominates much of the literary war journalism of World War I: Irvin S. Cobb in *Paths of Glory: Impressions of the War Written At and Near the Front* (1915), Richard Harding Davis in *With the Allies* (1914) and later *With the French in France and Salonika* (1916), Mary Roberts Rinehart in *Kings, Queens and Pawns: An American Woman at the Front* (1915), Will Irwin in *A Reporter at Armageddon* (1918), and Edith Wharton in her nonfiction-based novel *The Marne* (1918).[26]

With the Allies is Davis's early firsthand account of the war and of his movements around the Somme with Allied armies, and, in a literary style that is more polemical than ironic, Davis pulls no punches with open attacks on German aggression and affronts to humanity.[27] Although he understood President Wilson's hesitancy to enter the war, given the significant number of German American citizens, Davis makes a distinct claim between Germans and German technocrats in his book's preface:

> The loss of hundreds of thousands of lives, the wrecking of cities, and the laying waste of half of Europe cannot be brought home to people who learn of it only through

newspapers and moving pictures and by sticking pins in a map. Were they nearer to it, near enough to see the women and children fleeing from the shells and to smell the dead on the battle-fields, there would be no talk of neutrality.[28]

The book thus reads more like a book-length op-ed demanding American involvement than a feature story about trench warfare and, as such, is ripe with the yellow journalistic traits he learned during his reporting on the Spanish–American War:

> The day before the Germans had sentenced Louvain to become a wilderness, and with German system and love of thoroughness they left Louvain an empty, blackened shell. The reason for this appeal to the torch and the execution of non-combatants, as given to Mr. Whitlock and myself on the morning I left Brussels by General von Lutwitz, the military governor, was this: The day before, while the German military commander of the troops in Louvain was at the Hôel de Ville talking to the burgomaster, a son of the burgomaster, with an automatic pistol, shot the chief of staff and German staff surgeons. ...
>
> "Fifty Germans were killed and wounded," said Lutwitz, "and for that Louvain must be wiped out—so!" In pantomime with his fist he swept the papers across his table.
>
> "The Hôtel de Ville," he added, "was a beautiful building; it is a pity it must be destroyed."
>
> Were he telling us his soldiers had destroyed a kitchen-garden, his tone could not have expressed less regret.[29]

Mary Roberts Rinehart was sent to the Belgian front by the *Saturday Evening Post* in early 1915. Traveling under the auspices of the American Red Cross, which needed reports on hospital supplies, Rinehart had access to the front, and she captures her experiences in *Kings, Queens and Pawns: An American Woman at the Front*, an admixture of reporting, observation, and editorializing about the condition of the soldiers. As she writes in her chapter "Night in the Trenches,"

> When I had been thawed out they took me into the trenches. Because of the inundation directly in front, they are rather shallow, and at this point were built against the railroad embankment with earth, boards, and here and there a steel rail from the track. Some of them were covered, too, but not with bombproof material. The tops were merely shelters from the rain and biting wind.[30]

Of the book, biographer Jan Cohn writes, "It is not a narrative of her experiences so much as a report, personal and affecting, of the war, of the men who were fighting it, and of the men who were lying in the hospitals."[31] In sum, it is an encomium to these young men, a diatribe to those governments responsible for the deaths, and a plea to Americans to do something about it.

Muckraker journalist Will Irwin was also sent to Europe to report on World War I in August 1914, and his stories appeared in *Collier's* and the *American Magazine*.[32] He, too, confronted firsthand the struggle for reporters to get to the front; when he saw that the stories being told by those who eventually did make it to the front were not always accurate, Irwin returned to Europe later and traveled to neutral countries like Spain and Switzerland to find evidence of the untold war. That voyage led to his book *A Reporter at Armageddon*. Written "in the fashion of a late 19th-century travelogue," as Andrew Griffiths and Sara Prieto inform us, it takes advantage of "elements of different literary genres to build a tale of the war that moves beyond factual reporting and the combat-centric perspective that characterized much of the writing of the period."[33]

A decade later, the jingoistic censorship of World War I had largely tested readers' continued faith in the dailies, and literary journalism became a potential antidote to fact-manipulated news reporting. In the years of peace and laissez-faire government following the Great War, serious literary war journalists either left America to cover the wars elsewhere, as John Reed had done, or focused on the "cultural" wars at home. For instance, the postbellum Great Migration that spread African American culture north, with Harlem becoming the center of a Renaissance of the arts, sparked the writing of several pieces of literary journalism. While one of the Harlem Renaissance's mouthpieces, the *Crisis*, published poetry, stories, essays, political tracts, editorials, and art, there was the occasional nonfiction piece, such as the anonymous "The Waco Horror" or "Mariannhill: The Work of the Catholic Trappists in South Africa" by Father M. Thomas, RMM.[34] With the exception of W. E. B. Du Bois's July 1918 editorial, "Close Ranks," which called upon US blacks to put aside their differences and fight in the war, the *Crisis* was by and large silent about the Great War, since US Pan-Africans did not consider the war as their own and had other battles to fight at home, but Emmett Jay Scott's 1917 piece, "The Negro and the War Department,"[35] did begin a debate in the journal about blacks in the war. The June 1918 issue was dedicated as the "Soldiers Number" and contains several short pieces influenced by a literary style of journalism without actually being literary journalism, and these may have sparked Du Bois's famous editorial in the following month's issue. The topic perhaps culminated in a 1919 piece by Du Bois, whose work is often aligned with literary journalism, entitled "The Black Man in the Revolution of 1914–1918," a detailed account of the role black soldiers played in saving European civilization.[36] By and large, Zora Neale Hurston, another writer from the Renaissance, dabbled in literary journalism,[37] and the form certainly influenced Langston Hughes, who traveled to Spain in July 1937 to join the Popular Front and serve as a political correspondent for the *Baltimore Afro-American*.

In the context of any civil war in pedigreed nations—countries that coalesced after centuries of strife and compromise and were not merely cobbled together through modern treaties or post-colonial reconstitutions—journalists are faced with the paradox of covering the war's tragedies and simultaneously celebrating its victories in some national narrative typical of grand war reporting. When brothers are killing brothers, however, whom do you choose to support and can you ethically demonize the Other? The way journalism evolved during and after the American Civil War influenced the treatment of information in wars to come, from the Great War to the Spanish Civil War a few decades later. It is not by chance, then, that literary journalism as a genre appropriate for war reporting evolved and expanded over time, evidenced in the accounts of the Spanish Civil War by literary authors of international fame, from Ernest Hemingway in *For Whom the Bell Tolls* (1940) to George Orwell with *Homage to Catalonia* (1938), and from prominent Irish socialist Peadar O'Donnell in *Salud! An Irishman in Spain* (1937) to anti-communist Eoin O'Duffy with his *Crusade in Spain* (1938). When the fascists in Spain overthrew the democratically elected Republican government, sparking the Spanish Civil War, these war reportage writers found new material to write about that did not (yet) directly have an impact upon their neutral nations. Writing to readers who did not initially take an interest in a foreign civil war, however, allowed these many literary journalists to close their own ranks per the dichotomous politico-religious ideologies that would soon plunge the world into a second World War, while forcing them to adopt different strategies in their writing, such as understatement, inference, and metonymy, to turn disinterested readers into disappropriated world citizens who should care about what was happening in Spain. When the Self cannot identify itself in the suffering of the Other, war journalism generally fails to raise empathy, even by sensationalist means. By turning these Spanish Others, especially to American readers, into fathers, mothers, sisters, and brothers and by making the land itself an injured protagonist in the war, as most of these writers had done, literary war journalism had effectively turned what was deemed a Spanish conflict into a universal struggle between us and them, good and evil. In fact, the Spanish Civil War was by and large the golden era of literary war journalism, and many countries took part in the reporting, making it one of the most international movements of literary war journalism ever. In terms of American literary journalists who covered the Spanish Civil War, there are many—Hemingway, of course, but also Martha Gellhorn, John Dos Passos, and Langston Hughes, just to name the most celebrated.[38]

In an article dating back to 1959, Richard Freedman looked into the "little-known newspaper dispatches" that Hemingway wrote from Spain for the North American News Alliance (NANA) "in the hope of shedding some light on a rather obscure aspect of this controversial author's career." These dispatches, he writes, "some cabled, some sent air mail, were to be features, written, as [editor] Wheeler told Hemingway, 'in your colorful style,' rather than drily factual spot news stories."[39] Hemingway the literary journalist is evident in these heavily ironic dispatches, especially Dispatch 19, which, as Herbert Mitgang notes, was written, cabled, and then edited down for publication:

> Handwritten field notes, saved by Hemingway, begin this way:
> "pink of almond blossoms—grey dusty green of the olives—planting plane trees along the road during the great battle—planes—the ditch—the olive trees—Reus—the bombing—clouds of smoke dust—brown dust."
> Then, in a typewritten second draft—he changed or added 213 words from his first draft of a 778-word dispatch—Hemingway wrote in cablese:
> "twas lovely false spring when we started for front smorning stop last night incoming barcelona tad been grey and foggy and dirty and sad but today twas bright and warm and the pink of almond blossoms coloured the grey hills and brightened the dusty green rows of olive trees stop."
> Taking what was already a slightly altered cable, the NANA editors translated it into standard journalistic language:
> "It was a lovely false spring day when we started for the front this morning. Last night, coming to Barcelona, it had been grey, foggy, dirty and sad, but today it was bright and warm, and pink almond blossoms colored the gray hills and brightened the dusty green rows of olive trees."[40]

As Mitgang rightly concludes:

> The meaning of the two sentences remains unchanged, but Hemingway's rhythm in the second sentence is broken and the color impressions have been altered by an editor. The original Hemingway text preserves his intended rhythms and phrases, and sounds more like the novelist.[41]

Hemingway's literature, persona, and exploits in Madrid during the Spanish Civil War still attract more attention, scholarly and otherwise, than his literary journalism, but his dispatches are striking examples of the form's development from World War I in that they are less discursive, more poetic, and less didactic, and editorializing is made implicit in their imagery. The conclusion to the NANA dispatch entitled "Loyalists Await Tortosa Assault" (April 19, 1938), represents, arguably, the best literary journalism Hemingway wrote about the Spanish Civil War, replete with his signature irony, foreshadowing, understatement, and metonymy:

> Artillery was picking up a little now. Two shells came in at a fairly useful place, and, as the smoke blew away ahead and settled through the trees, you picked an armful of Spring onions from a field beside the trail that led to the main Tortosa road. They were

the first onions of this Spring and, peeling, one found they were plump and white and not too strong. The Ebro Delta has a fine rich land, and, where the onions grow, tomorrow there will be a battle.[42]

The only other literary journalist writing during the Spanish Civil War who could match Hemingway's eloquence and accuracy captured here was Martha Gellhorn, whose own exploits with Hemingway while they were encamped in the Hotel Florida in Madrid would, unfortunately, often overshadow her writing. Since she had no official connection with a newspaper or magazine covering the Spanish Civil War, Gellhorn was given a letter announcing her as a special correspondent for *Collier's*.[43] Unlike Hemingway, she spoke no Spanish and relied on the help of others to get her *diem* travel documents to reach the front. She was a writer, she notes, but not yet a war correspondent, and she was pleasantly surprised when told by a friend to write an article, which she did, and *Collier's* eventually published it. Thus began her career as a war journalist, as she describes it in *The Face of War*, which also reproduces three literary journalistic pieces about the civil war: "High Explosive for Everyone" (July 1937), "The Besieged City" (November 1937), and "The Third Winter" (November 1938). "The Third Winter" opens with a Hemingwayesque dose of irony and understatement that sets up the tone for the rest of the story:

> In Barcelona, it was perfect bombing weather. The cafés along the Ramblas were crowded. There was nothing much to drink; a sweet fizzy poison called orangeade and a horrible liquid supposed to be sherry. There was, of course, nothing to eat. Everyone was out enjoying the cold afternoon sunlight. No bombers had come over for at least two hours.
> The flower stalls looked bright and pretty along the promenade. "The flowers are all sold, Señores. For the funerals of those who were killed in the eleven o'clock bombing, poor souls." ...
> It was cold but really too lovely and everyone listened for the sirens all the time, and when we saw the bombers they were like tiny silver bullets moving forever up, across the sky.[44]

Similar to a screenplay, Gellhorn's piece intercuts the lengthy exchanges she has with the Hernández family (whom she has come to see as the father is a carpenter and she needs a picture frame for a friend of hers) with her own observations, descriptions, and commentaries about the struggles all families are facing daily in Barcelona. The jump cuts between scenes help not only to build up tension (readers are warned that this was a perfect day for bombing and then, later, are introduced to the daughter who works in a munitions factory) but also to generate pathos, as when she visits a children's hospital: "The children looked like toys until you came closer—tiny white figures propped up with pillows, swathed in bandages, the little pale faces showing, the great black eyes staring at you, the small hands playing over the sheets."[45] The volley of simple adjectives, a style that here demarcates her writing from Hemingway's, creates a rhythm in the sentence that sounds like feet marching—or bombs punctuating the ground one after another as they are released from a plane, just as she had foreshadowed in the piece's opening sentence.

John Dos Passos's literary journalistic contribution to the civil war was his work with Hemingway as a screenwriter for their documentary *The Spanish Earth* (1937), directed by Dutch filmmaker Joris Ivens. Like Hemingway and Gellhorn, Dos Passos admired the Spanish commoners as much for their struggle to overcome poverty and starvation during wartime as for their resisting Franco's advances. Unlike Hemingway, though, Dos Passos quickly soured to the communist struggle against fascism when his friend José Robles Pazos, whom Dos Passos had met in the US and who translated Dos Passos's work into Spanish, was accused of treason and shot by the Red Army (Dos Passos considered it the beginning of Stalin's purges against his own supporters). It was this disillusionment that Dos Passos harbored which created (or at least consolidated) the acrimony between the two authors. Dos Passos was no stranger to war or to war reporting, having also served in the American Red Cross during World War I, an experience that provided him material for two war novels, *One Man's Initiation—1917* (1920) and *Three Soldiers* (1921). As his erstwhile friend Hemingway did after him with *Death in the Afternoon* (1932), Dos Passos used his literary skills and his war experiences to produce an important piece of literary journalism about Spain and Spanish culture, *Rosinante to the Road Again* (1922).[46] It was this book that captured his early love for the country, quickly turning to disgust when he saw firsthand what the fascists and communists were doing to it.

Another literary journalist who grew disillusioned with the political struggle for the soul of Spain (and, as it would play out, of Europe) was Langston Hughes, although his disillusionment stemmed from a different source of personal and political frustration. Hughes faced these personal issues in the spring of 1937, when he traveled to Spain and witnessed other black soldiers from North Africa fighting for the fascists, which meant that they were also fighting against America's Lincoln Battalion, a battalion of white and eighty-five African American soldiers who had volunteered to come to Spain to fight on behalf of the Republican Loyalists. These soldiers, who were part of the XV International Brigade, became the subjects of Hughes's sixteen dispatches for the *Baltimore Afro-American* newspaper, many running over 1,500 words.[47] Given the Pan-African Renaissance in which Hughes participated back in Harlem, he came to Spain to celebrate universal blackness and to provide stories of heroic African Americans during the war, who saw echoes of their own struggles against white supremacists and Jim Crow at home in the Republicans' struggles against Franco, given the recent incursions of Mussolini into East Africa.[48] The Spanish Civil War for many black Americans was as much a war of opposing ideologies as it was of opposing races. As Hughes writes in the *Afro-American* on December 18, 1937, "Give Franco a hood and he would be a member of the Ku Klux Klan, a kleagle."[49] In October 1937, the *Afro-American* began publishing

> the series of dispatches Hughes sent back from Spain, and the first article, embellished with a dramatic "EXCLUSIVE!!!" label, carried this "precede": From war-torn Spain, Langston Hughes, celebrated American novelist and poet, brings exclusively to AFRO-AMERICAN readers a vivid and accurate picture of the bitter struggle that is now going on. This interesting series and the accompanying photographs will appear only in the AFRO-AMERICAN.[50]

The dispatch, entitled "Hughes Bombed in Spain: *Tells of Terror of Fascist Raid—Women, Children Huddled in Fear as Bombs Explode*," describes Hughes's "entry into wartime Spain, his impressions, and the terror of war, the relative scarcity of food (which was to become more acute as he moved toward Madrid), and, always, the presence of dark people."[51] The titles given to his dispatches show his and the paper's racial-political intentions: "Hughes Finds Moors Being Used as Pawns by Fascists in Spain" (October 30, 1937); "Organ Grinder's Swing" Heard Above Gunfire in Spain—Hughes: *Lunceford, Calloway and Ellington Already Known There; Ability, Not Color Found to Count Most* (November 6, 1937); "Madrid's Flowers Hoist Blooms to Meet Raining Fascist Bombs: *Soldiers Go to School in Trenches, Which Ziz-zag through Gardens, and Shell-Torn Homes*" (November 27, 1937); "Fighters from Other Lands Look to Ohio Man for Food" (January 8, 1938); "Pittsburgh Soldier Hero, but Too Bashful to Talk" (January 15, 1938); "Howard Man Fighting as Spanish Loyalist" (February 5, 1938). And we can hear the distinct politico-poetic voice of his poetry coming through his journalistic prose:

> Like frightful modernistic drawings, the mangled houses lifted their broken walls and torn roofs to the cool blue sky, and trenches cut through rooms where once families

had lived and children had played. In one house, or rather a portion of a house—for one whole side had been blown away—we paused and were shown up a broken staircase to the second floor.[52]

Hughes, unlike the majority of the foreign literary journalists in Spain during the war, spoke fluent Spanish, so there is a sense of authority in his dispatches when he paraphrases an exchange with a Republican soldier in the trenches around Madrid or when he quotes a person verbatim in translated English. That trust level is, perhaps, attained in Hemingway's dispatches as well, though there is a sense in reading him that it might not be one hundred percent accurate, given his penchant for hard-boiled drama and self-aggrandizement. In the case of "The Third Winter," however, Gellhorn is not as forthcoming in her dialogue. She does not speak of a translator accompanying her on this visit, and yet it is unlikely that she was fluent enough in Spanish, or even Catalan, to have recorded the dialogue as it was spoken to her, and it is even less likely that the peasants spoke any English. In terms of the foreign literary war journalism produced in Spain at this time, one wonders just how accurate the pieces really are, and how much interpolation by the writers is present in the texts. One of the most challenging questions remains from these pieces written during the civil war: How much was journalistic integrity sacrificed for literary excellence? In other words, literary war journalism by the late 1930s was vastly different from what was produced earlier, but was literary war journalism in America becoming journalistic war literature?

US Literary Journalism and the (Post-)World War II Experience: The Rise of New (War) Journalism

While Hemingway, Gellhorn, and *New Yorker* correspondent A. J. Liebling—whose war dispatches, like Ernie Pyle's, have been eclipsed by those of the glamorous couple—were very much the celebrities of literary war journalism at the end of World War II, there were other writers whose stars were on the rise. Tom Wolfe would collectively call them the New Journalists. Wolfe even singled out John Hersey as one of Wolfe's "Not Half-Bad Candidates"[53] for his *New Yorker* piece "Hiroshima." It is with Hersey that post-World War II US literary war journalism rightfully begins. Winning the 1944 Pulitzer Prize for his novel *A Bell for Adano* about the Allied occupation of Italy, Hersey had also penned that year two noteworthy literary journalistic pieces: "Joe Is Home Now," on how traumatized GIs adapted to home life, and "Survival," his account of the sinking of Kennedy's PT-109. Yet it is for *Hiroshima* (1946), which New York University lists as the greatest piece of American journalism of the twentieth century,[54] that he is most recognized.

Hiroshima recounts the traumatic hours, days, and weeks of six people following the atomic blast on the morning of August 6, 1945. In researching the story, Hersey, who, according to Ben Yagoda, "had a novelist's eye and ear and a reporter's work ethic,"[55] interviewed two doctors (Dr. Masakazu Fujii and Dr. Terufumi Sasaki), two clergymen (Reverend Kiyoshi Tanimoto and Father Wilhelm Kleinsorge), and two women (Toshiko Sasaki and Hatsuyo Nakamura). The powerful narrative intercuts between the six survivors' experiences from when they awoke to what they were doing at the moment the bomb hit, and from the hours immediately following the blast to the next several days, weeks, and months. Hersey, whose consistent understated tone allows him to editorialize through his imagery, manages to capture some of the most frightening scenes of the aftermath without the over-sensationalizing often linked to earlier war journalism. In one passage, for example, Hersey writes,

> Mr. Tanimoto ... reached down and took a woman by the hands, but her skin slipped off in huge, glove-like pieces. He was so sickened by this that he had to sit down for a moment. Then he got out into the water and, though a small man, lifted several of

the men and women, who were naked, into his boat. ... He had to keep consciously repeating to himself, "These are human beings." It took him three trips to get them all across the river. When he had finished, he decided he had to have a rest, and he went back to the park.[56]

Tanimoto, who had worked himself into exhaustion by pulling people to safety on the banks of the Ōta River, falls asleep, having failed to account for the tide, and Hersey concludes on a simple, understated but gut-wrenching image:

When he awoke, in the first light of dawn, he looked across the river and saw that he had not carried the festered, limp bodies high enough on the sandspit the night before. The tide had risen above where he had put them; they had not the strength to move; they must have drowned. He saw a number of bodies floating in the river.[57]

There were to be, unfortunately, many wars following World War II, and many war books, but US literary journalism over the next two decades focused on the culture "wars" at home: civil rights, counter-culture, feminism, Stonewall, and the hippy generation. The works produced during the golden age of New Journalism are, nonetheless, worth citing: Norman Mailer's 1948 novel *The Naked and the Dead* and its influence on the nonfiction novel *The Armies of the Night* (1968), his attack against false liberalism during the October 1967 March on the Pentagon; Joan Didion's subtle but scathing critique of California as the land of milk and honey and, specifically, of the Haight-Ashbury crowd in *Slouching Towards Bethlehem* (1968); and Hunter S. Thompson's gonzo look into the failed American Dream in *Fear and Loathing in Las Vegas* (1971).

Among all of these important post-World War II books of literary (war) journalism cited above, Michael Herr's *Dispatches* (1977) stands out as being the most significant in terms of the impact it has had on a generation of writers and journalists that followed. Published ten years after Herr covered the Vietnam War as a correspondent for *Esquire*, *Dispatches* remains the iconic representation not just of a new type of war but also of a new type of soldier fighting in it. Like the movies *Apocalypse Now* (1979) and *Full Metal Jacket* (1987), both influenced by Herr's documented experiences during the war and to which Herr contributed material for their screenplays, *Dispatches* documents the ever-growing rift palpable between the enlisted and the officer in modern-day warfare, a rift that David Finkel describes in *The Good Soldiers*. As Wolfe posits, Herr did not make the book autobiographical but "penetrate[es] the psyche ... of the line troops themselves," accurately recording their thoughts and their voices.[58] His ability to write in first and third person throughout the book weaves his voice among the soldiers and even the readers long after the war had ended. Like novelist Tim O'Brien in *Going After Cacciato* (1978), but working from a nonfiction canvas, Herr manages to capture the zeitgeist of the post-traumatic seventies, evidenced in this extract from the chapter "Khe Sanh":

And the grunts themselves knew: the madness, the bitterness, the horror and doom of it. They were hip to it, and more: they savored it. It was no more insane than most of what was going down, and often enough it had its refracted logic. "Eat the apple, fuck the Corps," they'd say, and write it up on their helmets and flak jackets for their officers to see. ... They even wrote a song, a letter to the mother of a dead Marine, that went something like, "Tough shit, tough shit, your kid got greased, but what the fuck, he was just a grunt ..." They got savaged a lot and softened a lot, their secret brutalized them and darkened them and very often it made them beautiful. It took no age, seasoning or education to make them know exactly where true violence resided.[59]

Notably different from previous literary war journalism is the language, of course, with its "hallucinogenic, disjointed rock-n-roll prose," but also of note is the writer's perspective, which draws readers closer to the soldier and pushes them further from the brass: "He might ape the soldiers in their speech, but is never condescending."[60] In an early example of an embedded journalist, Herr is perceived by the soldiers he shadows not as a war correspondent after the facts and, perhaps, the emotions of battle, but as a soldier fighting right alongside them, firing off images instead of bullets, armed with black humor instead of an M-16, and protected by a flak jacket of irony. As one soldier says, in pleading with Herr near the end of the book for him to reveal the true story of the Vietnam War experience: "Okay, man, you go on, you go on out of here cocksucker, but I mean it, you tell it! You tell it, man. If you don't tell it …"[61]

Herr's journalistic rapport with the soldiers and the brass had brought literary war journalism into its own.[62] Hemingway had stood alongside soldiers in the heat of battle and more than likely fought with them at times, but early literary war journalists like him were more about capturing the experience of battle or the suffering of the noncombatants. Hemingway's pieces were ultimately about Hemingway. If Herr's *Dispatches* is also about Herr and his experiences, it is all the more penetrating because Herr manages to merge his experiences, his perceptions, and his angst with those of the soldiers. He is not reporting *on them*; he *is* them and reporting on himself through them, and on them through himself. It was an impressionistic style of literary war journalism that would influence the New New Journalists who soon followed.

US Literary Journalism and the *New* New Journalism: Alas, Not a Final Salute[63]

In the introduction to *The New New Journalism* (2005), Robert S. Boynton picks up where Wolfe left off and describes the next generation of literary journalists. This new breed of writers, Boynton suggests, owes as much to the New Journalists of the 1960s as they do the nineteenth-century "new" journalists (Lincoln Steffens, Jacob Riis, Stephen Crane) in terms of their ethics in immersion reporting, loyalty to their subjects, and trust in the power of irony and understatement. But these *New* New Journalists do not have the same hang-ups about being nonfiction writers as their predecessors had: "When experimenting with narrative and rhetorical techniques, they conceive of themselves as working wholly within the nonfiction genre, rather than parsing the philosophical line between fact and fiction."[64] Just as their more traditional styles of writing distinguish them from their predecessors, so too do the ways in which they get their stories: "Their most significant innovations have involved experiments with reporting, rather than the language or forms they used to tell their stories."[65] In terms of literary war journalism, there are certainly more embedded journalists than foreign correspondents writing about the experience of US troops overseas, but there are also some capturing the war from the safe distance of time and space. And while there are a number of exceptional New New Journalistic pieces about war—and perhaps a few *New* Yellow Journalistic pieces as well—and its aftermath, two works are worth discussing at length here not just because they were both bestsellers but also because they demonstrate a return to the sensationalist reportage writing of a century ago: Mark Bowden's *Black Hawk Down* (1997) and Sebastian Junger's *War* (2010).

> Late in the afternoon of Sunday, October 3, 1993, attack helicopters dropped about 120 elite American soldiers into a busy neighborhood in the heart of Mogadishu, Somalia. Their mission was to abduct several top lieutenants of Somalian warlord Mohamed Farrah Aidid and return to base. It was supposed to take about an hour.[66]

So begins Bowden's first of twenty-nine installments for the *Philadelphia Inquirer*, one a day for nearly a month, during the winter of 1997, on what has come to be known as the two-day Battle of Mogadishu. Bowden interviewed more than seventy people in the years following the battle and consulted thousands of pages of official and, at times, classified documents. Because of the stories' immense popularity (and the interactive, hyperlink multimedia website that accompanied them, providing access to the interviews Bowden conducted, radio transmissions between the US forces and their commanders, the Pentagon's video of the raid, diagrams of the city, explanations of the weapons used, etc.),[67] they were later collected to form the book *Black Hawk Down* (published by Penguin Books in 1999) and later made into a successful and rather controversial Hollywood blockbuster by director Ridley Scott.

Actually, the above citation was, in fact, the *second* installment (published on the same day). The first story that ran on November 16 began this way:

> Staff Sgt. Matt Eversmann's lanky frame was fully extended on the rope for what seemed too long on the way down. Hanging from a hovering Blackhawk helicopter, Eversmann was a full 70 feet above the streets of Mogadishu. His goggles had broken, so his eyes chafed in the thick cloud of dust stirred up by the bird's rotors.
>
> It was such a long descent that the thick nylon rope burned right through the palms of his leather gloves. The rest of his Chalk, his squad, had already roped in. Nearing the street, through the swirling dust below his feet, Eversmann saw one of his men stretched out on his back at the bottom of the rope.
>
> He felt a stab of despair. *Somebody's been shot already!* He gripped the rope hard to keep from landing on top of the guy. It was Pvt. Todd Blackburn, at 18 the youngest Ranger in his Chalk, a kid just months out of a Florida high school. He was unconscious and bleeding from the nose and ears.[68]

This gripping, cold open is a trait of more recent literary war journalism that wants to plant its hooks into the reader before retreating to provide needed context. While understatement might have been sacrificed here, irony is not, and Bowden uses it to his advantage to comment on the absurdity of American foreign policy behind the brief, albeit bloody, battle. Written five years after the event, Bowden nonetheless manages here and elsewhere to "get it right"—that is, write about the military so accurately that even the military put its stamp of approval on the work. His access to the soldiers who survived, as well as the interviews he conducted with several Somalians present during the attack, lend the story its historical accuracy. Its division into rapidly paced short chapters—that are themselves interpolated with scenes that frequently jump cut between the various soldiers in the heat of multiple battles and the command center giving them their orders—supplies its film-like quality, which made *Black Hawk Down* an easy mark for Hollywood producers. Although Bowden's goal was to follow the tragic and heroic stories of the US forces, he was also sympathetic to Somalia's nearly five hundred killed and thousands wounded, including women and children, a detail neglected in the film adaptation and fully ignored in the video game that followed, attesting to the potential current dangers with successful literary war journalism in the US.[69]

Unlike Bowden, whose story was reconstructed after months of painstaking research, Sebastian Junger composed his reportage *War* while in the white-hot cauldron of battle. And also unlike Bowden, who does try to explain, and perhaps justify, US involvement in Somalia, Junger shows little interest in contextualizing the war in Afghanistan, an extension of the War on Terror against the Muslim extremist Taliban. According to Dexter Filkins, Junger's purpose was to create more of a "laboratory to examine the human condition,"[70] which Junger himself confirms in the book's second chapter:

> I'm not interested in the Afghans and their endless, terrible wars; I'm interested in the Americans. I'm interested in what it's like to serve in a platoon of combat infantry in the U.S. Army. The moral basis of the war doesn't seem to interest soldiers much, and its long-term success or failure has a relevance of almost zero.[71]

Embedded with the Second Platoon, B Company, while on assignment for *Vanity Fair* from June 2007 to June 2008, Junger was assigned to the Korengal Valley in the eastern part of the country, about twenty-five miles from the Pakistani border and a hotbed of violent incursions until US forces withdrew in the spring of 2010. During his five month-long trips to the valley, Junger was stationed at a remote outpost called Restrepo (named after Juan Restrepo, a platoon medic killed in 2007; it is also the name of Junger's 2010 documentary film co-directed with his friend and photojournalist Tim Hetherington, footage from which helped him to capture accurately everything he writes in the book) and tries to capture for his readers what it is like for a soldier to live in a bunker that would incur up to four attacks per day:

> Summer grinds on: a hundred degrees every day and tarantulas invading the living quarters to get out of the heat. Some of the men are terrified of them and can only sleep in mesh pup tents, and others pick them up with pliers and set them on fire. The timber bunkers at Phoenix are infested with fleas, and the men wear flea collars around their ankles but still scratch all day long. First Squad goes thirty-eight days without taking a shower or changing their clothes, and by the end their uniforms are so impregnated with salt that they can stand up by themselves. The men's sweat reeks of ammonia because they've long since burned off all their fat and are now breaking down muscle.[72]

And while the war in Afghanistan is significantly different from the one waged in Vietnam four decades earlier, the "modern" aspects to Junger's prose are similar to Herr's: Understatement is traded for sensationalism; narrative focus is locked onto the soldiers' experiences alone; and irony, which is kept intact, targets the absurd situation more than the policies that created it. In a 2010 op-ed about the US withdrawal from the valley, Junger writes:

> War is a complex endeavor that has no predictable outcome: ill-equipped militias can defeat modern armies, huge battles can hinge on luck or bad weather. Expecting commanders to make strategically correct decisions every time is not a realistic criterion for evaluating the war.[73]

Both of the writers of these late twentieth- and early twenty-first-century examples of American literary war journalism discussed here have had to negotiate their way through the nation's two opposing traditions in war nonfiction: from the sensationalist reporting of yellow journalism at the fin de siècle to the caustic editorializing of modernist literary journalism that peaks with the New Journalism of the sixties and seventies. Avoid affect altogether in a story about a soldier's or a civilian's life during war, and you risk boring modern readers of longform journalism; provide too many sensationalist details, and you risk being labeled a tabloid journalist. Avoid irony and understatement in that same story, and you insult your discerning readers' intelligence about the complexities of international conflict; overuse both, and you ostracize them. New New Journalists, then, have had a fine line to walk when writing about war, and that line is likely to grow even finer as the century progresses. As the nature of war evolves, so too will the expectations of readers (and editors) to render those experiences on paper.

Conclusion

Literary war journalism in the US this past century and a half has varied widely for reasons linked as much to the evolution of weaponry and battle tactics as to the blurring ethics of war reporting. But one constant can be found in each of the war reportages, dispatches, and literary journalism stories discussed here, and it is that which makes them all timeless: through its potent and poignant use of irony and understatement, be it from the nineteenth, twentieth, or twenty-first century, each story elevates the reader's emotive response above the sensationalist titillation typically associated with the death that war inevitably brings. Newspapers can list casualty figures, outline policy, and perhaps even offer context. Over time, history can extend commentary to what the press accomplishes and even try to justify the war's endgame. Literature can add affect and aesthetics to the other media's assets. Literary journalism can do *all* of that.

If war literature has one noted difference with respect to literary war journalism, it is this: Novels about wars—past, present, or future—still deal with mostly fictive deaths. Literary war journalism, for all the beauty it brings to readers in its haunting tales of heroics and defeats, is still premised on death, real and unimagined. To add to this canon of US literary war journalism, unfortunately, means to add to the number of people, soldiers and civilians alike, displaced, traumatized, or killed by all of the wars we have still yet to wage.

Notes

1 Finkel, *Good Soldiers*, 3.
2 Although embedded journalism technically began with the 2003 US invasion of Iraq, as the Pentagon's response to criticism emerging from the media about its low-level access to the 1991 Gulf War and the 2001 invasion of Afghanistan, historically literary war journalists have stood beside the soldiers they have reported on since the nineteenth century. See, for instance, Pfau et al., "Embedding Journalists."
3 Cornebise, *Ranks and Columns*, 2–3. See also his *The Stars and Stripes: Doughboy Journalism in World War I*.
4 Mud was one of the watchwords of the war experience, and nearly every recollection from World War I makes damning references to it. The anonymous author of the article "Muds I Have Met" (1917) that appeared in the *Listening Post*, a Canadian/British Columbia trench journal, makes metaphorical use of the omnipresent mud as a way to criticize or honor his fellow combatants and their national character or stereotype.
5 What distinguishes American literature from the other literatures of the world is also what separates American literary journalism, especially its war journalism, from other nations' war reportages—namely, its struggle with an uncertain historicity in the national narrative; its sense of moral rectitude per the Other, especially when that Other is the Self writ large; its inevitable confluence of racial, religious, and regional concerns with political identities, etc. Much of the world's classic literary war journalism, from Orwell's *Homage to Catalonia* (1938) to Walsh's *Operación Massacre* (1957) to Alexievich's *Boys in Zinc* (1989), contains to a certain extent the same sensationalism, understatement, and irony that American literary war reporting has, but each also bears the traces of its author's own nation's literary past, be it Britain's specter of colonialism, Argentina's political instability, or Russia's culture of clandestine reprisals.
6 Sims, *True Stories*, 44.
7 Sims, 44–86.
8 Hartsock, *History*, 23.
9 Sachsman, *Press Divided*, xi–xii.
10 Risley, *Civil War Journalism*.
11 Bracken, *Words of War*.
12 Lutz, "Soldier Newspapers," 373.
13 Lutz, 374–75.
14 Creelman, *On the Great Highway*, 178.
15 Connery, "Third Way," 7.
16 Crane, "Stephen Crane's Own Story," 85.
17 Davis, *Cuba in War Time*, 65.
18 Applegate, *Literary Journalism*, 60.

19 Knightley, *First Casualty*, 84.
20 For more on soldier newspapers and trench journals, see Cornebise, *Stars and Stripes* and *Ranks and Columns*; Nelson, "Soldier Newspapers"; Seal, *Soldiers' Press*; Bak, "'Paper.'"
21 Griffiths and Prieto, introduction to *Literary Journalism*, 6.
22 Lehman, *John Reed*, 96.
23 Reed, "Traders' War," 17.
24 Reed, *Ten Days*, 186–87.
25 North, "Reportage," 121.
26 Edith Wharton's *The Marne* (1918) is a novella, and although it is based on her war experiences as an ambulance driver, since it is not literary war journalism, it will not be discussed here.
27 Examples of Davis's anger, not just toward German aggression but also its complete disregard for human life and property, can be found throughout the book. In one example, Davis writes: "Village after village had been completely wrecked. In his march to the sea Sherman lived on the country. He did not destroy it, and as against the burning of Columbia must be placed to the discredit of the Germans the wiping out of an entire countryside" (*With the Allies*, 85–86).
28 Davis, *With the Allies*, viii.
29 Davis, 87–88.
30 Rinehart, *Kings, Queens and Pawns*, 122.
31 Cohn, *Improbable Fiction*, 91.
32 Applegate, *Muckrakers*, 86.
33 Griffiths and Prieto, introduction to *Literary Journalism*, 8.
34 "Waco Horror"; Thomas, "Mariannhill."
35 Scott, "Negro," 76.
36 Du Bois, "Black Man."
37 See Maguire, "From Fiction to Fact."
38 Lillian Hellman was also a literary journalist writing about the Spanish Civil War, but Hellman's journalism in *An Unfinished Woman* (1969) was largely discredited by Gellhorn as fabricated sensationalism. For instance, Gellhorn found Hellman's facts about certain aerial bombings fictitious and her chronology of several historical events (that placed Hellman in Moscow, Vienna, and Spain at the same time) erroneous.
39 Freedman, "Hemingway's Spanish Civil War Dispatches," 171.
40 Mitgang, "Hemingway on Spain."
41 Mitgang.
42 Hemingway, "Loyalists Await Tortosa Assault," 12.
43 Gellhorn, *Face of War*, 15.
44 Gellhorn, 37.
45 Gellhorn, 43.
46 Applegate, *Muckrakers*, 68.
47 *Essays on Art, Race, Politics, and World Affairs*, volume 9 of *The Collected Works of Langston Hughes*, reproduces only thirteen of Hughes's dispatches for the *Baltimore Afro-American*. Articles missing include "They Deserve a Hand" (February 5, 1938, p. 10); "Cuban Newspaperman Covers Spanish War" (February 26, 1938, p. 5); and "Tonight" (February 19, 1938, p. 11). For a detailed study of Hughes's Spanish Civil War literary journalism, see Joshua Roiland's excellent article "'Just People' Are Just People: Langston Hughes and the Populist Power of African American Literary Journalism."
48 Soto, "'I Knew,'" 137.
49 Hughes, "Soldiers from Many Lands," 181.
50 Quoted in Presley, "Langston Hughes," 483.
51 Presley, 483.
52 Hughes, "Madrid's Flowers," 175.
53 Wolfe, "New Journalism," 45–46.
54 "Top 100 Works."
55 Yagoda, *About Town*, 185.
56 Hersey, *Hiroshima*, 45.
57 Hersey, 49.
58 Wolfe, editorial note to "Khesanh," 85.
59 Herr, *Dispatches*, 102–03; second ellipses in the original.
60 "Michael Herr."
61 Herr, *Dispatches*, 207; ellipses in the original.

62 See also Bowden, *Hue 1968.*
63 This subheading alludes to Jim Sheeler's Pulitzer Prize–winning story, "Final Salute," published in the *Rocky Mountain News* in 2005, an excellent recent example of literary war journalism not discussed here for reasons of space.
64 Boynton, *New New Journalism*, xii.
65 Boynton, xiii.
66 Bowden, "A Defining Battle."
67 See Bowden, table of contents for "Black Hawk Down."
68 Bowden, "Reliving a Firefight." It is worth noting that in the final book version, the start is different: "At liftoff, Matt Eversmann said a Hail Mary." See Bowden, *Black Hawk Down*, 4.
69 The rise in popularity these past couple of decades has seen its unique blend of realistic storytelling ripe of Hollywood's blockbuster economics, and indeed the list of bestselling nonfiction books to have made a splash is not insignificant. As Boynton rightly notes, "The New New Journalism is big business on a scale never before seen by serious literary journalism" (*New New Journalism*, xxx). But with literary war journalism comes responsibility. Bowden, who saw *Black Hawk Down* significantly altered when it was adapted for the big screen—to say nothing of the videogame that spun off from it—also understood the "Faustian bargain" that writing a bestselling literary journalistic piece implies, as he noted in a reply to a series of write-in Q&As at the *Philadelphia Inquirer* about the *Black Hawk Down* articles:

> I will do my best with the movie. The producer and director have said they want to be accurate, and have hired me to write the screenplay, which means I'll at least start out with a shot at some control. But movies are the ultimate collaborative art form, and I can't promise I will even be happy with what is ultimately done. The good news is that whenever a big movie is made about a book, it promotes sales of the book like nothing else in this world. So it's kind of a Faustian bargain. Even if the movie gets it wrong, more people end up reading the book, which I can stand fully behind. Any mistakes there will be my very own fault.
>
> *("Round 20")*

No one would wish to deny literary journalists their right to make money, and very good money sometimes, but the ethics of literary journalism imply an unwritten contract between the journalist and his or her often downtrodden subject and between the journalist and his or her reader that the story was written because the writer felt it needed to be told and not that he or she thought it might land a six-figure contract in Hollywood. And literary war journalism in particular is sensitive here since Hollywood has never satiated its appetite for war films, especially those based on real events.

70 Filkins, "'Nothing to Do,'" BR13.
71 Junger, *War*, 25.
72 Junger, 53.
73 Junger, "Farewell to Korengal," A27.

Bibliography

Applegate, Edd. *Literary Journalism: A Biographical Dictionary of Writers and Editors*. Westport, CT: Greenwood Press, 1996.

———. *Muckrakers: A Biographical Dictionary of Writers and Editors*. Lanham, MD: Scarecrow Press, 2008.

Bak, John S. "'The Paper Cannot Live by Poems Alone': World War I Trench Journals as (Proto-) Literary Journalism." In *Literary Journalism and World War I: Marginal Voices*, edited by Andrew Griffiths, Sara Prieto, and Soenke Zehle, 13–48. Nancy, France: Presses Universitaires de Nancy–Éditions Universitaires de Lorraine, 2016.

Bowden, Mark. *Black Hawk Down: A Story of Modern War*. New York: Grove Press, 1999.

———. "A Defining Battle." *Philadelphia Inquirer*, November 16, 1997. Accessed July 14, 2018. http://inquirer.philly.com/packages/somalia/nov16/rang16.asp.

———. *Hue 1968: A Turning Point of the American War in Vietnam*. New York: Atlantic Monthly Press, 2017.

———. "Reliving a Firefight: Hail Mary, Then Hold On." *Philadelphia Inquirer*, November 16, 1997. Accessed October 14, 2017. http://inquirer.philly.com/packages/somalia/nov16/default16.asp.

———. "Round 20 of Q&A." *Philadelphia Inquirer*. http://inquirer.philly.com/packages/somalia/ask/ask20.asp.

———. Table of contents for "Black Hawk Down." *Philadelphia Inquirer*. Accessed October 14, 2017. http://inquirer.philly.com/packages/somalia/sitemap.asp.

Boynton, Robert S. *The New New Journalism: Conversations with America's Best Nonfiction Writers on Their Craft*. New York: Vintage, 2005.

Bracken, Donagh. *The Words of War: The Civil War Battle Reportage of the "New York Times" and the "Charleston Mercury" ... and What Historians Say Really Happened*. Palisades, NY: History Publishing, 2007.

Cohn, Jan. *Improbable Fiction: The Life of Mary Roberts Rinehart*. Pittsburgh, PA: University of Pittsburgh Press, 1980.

Connery, Thomas B. "A Third Way to Tell the Story: American Literary Journalism at the Turn of the Century." In *Literary Journalism in the Twentieth Century*, edited by Norman Sims, 3–20. New York: Oxford University Press, 1990.

Cornebise, Alfred Emile. *Ranks and Columns: Armed Forces Newspapers in American Wars*. Westport, CT: Greenwood Press, 1993.

———. *The Stars and Stripes: Doughboy Journalism in World War I*. Westport, CT: Greenwood Press, 1984.

Crane, Stephen. "Stephen Crane's Own Story." In *Reports of War: War Dispatches: Great Battles of the World*, edited by Fredson Bowers, 85–94. Vol. 9 of *The University of Virginia Edition of the Works of Stephen Crane*. Charlottesville, VA: University of Virginia Press, 1971. Originally published in *New York Press*, January 7, 1897.

Creelman, James. *On the Great Highway: The Wanderings and Adventures of a Special Correspondent*. Boston, MA: Lothrop Publishing, 1901.

Davis, Richard Harding. *Cuba in War Time*. With illustrations by Frederic Remington. New York: R. H. Russell, 1897.

———. *With the Allies*. 1914. Toronto: Copp Clark, 1915.

Du Bois, W. E. B. "The Black Man in the Revolution of 1914–1918." *Crisis*, March 1919, 218–23.

Filkins, Dexter. "'Nothing to Do but Kill and Wait.'" Review of *War*, by Sebastian Junger. Sunday Book Review, *New York Times*, May 14, 2010, BR13.

Finkel, David. *The Good Soldiers*. New York: Farrar, Straus and Giroux, 2009.

Freedman, Richard. "Hemingway's Spanish Civil War Dispatches." *Texas Studies in Literature and Language* 1, no. 2 (Summer 1959): 171–80.

Gellhorn, Martha. *The Face of War*. 1959. New York: Atlantic Monthly Press, 1986.

Griffiths, Andrew, and Sara Prieto. Introduction to *Literary Journalism and World War I: Marginal Voices*, edited by Andrew Griffiths, Sara Prieto, and Soenke Zehle, 1–12. Nancy, France: Presses Universitaires de Nancy–Éditions Universitaires de Lorraine, 2016.

Hartsock, John C. *A History of American Literary Journalism: The Emergence of a Modern Narrative Form*. Amherst, MA: University of Massachusetts Press, 2000.

Hemingway, Ernest. "Loyalists Await Tortosa Assault." *New York Times*, April 19, 1938, 12.

Herr, Michael. *Dispatches*. New York: Alfred A. Knopf, 1977.

Hersey, John. *Hiroshima: A New Edition with a Final Chapter Written Forty Years after the Explosion*. New York: Vintage, 1989.

Hughes, Langston. *Essays on Art, Race, Politics, and World Affairs*. Edited by Christopher C. De Santis. Vol. 9 of *The Collected Works of Langston Hughes*. Columbia, MO: University of Missouri Press, 2002.

———. "Madrid's Flowers Hoist Blooms to Meet Raining Fascist Bombs." In Hughes, *Essays on Art*, 173–76. Originally published in *Baltimore Afro-American*, November 27, 1937.

———. "Soldiers from Many Lands United in Spanish Fight." In Hughes, *Essays on Art*, 178–81. Originally published in *Baltimore Afro-American*, December 18, 1937.

Junger, Sebastian. "Farewell to Korengal." *New York Times*, April 20, 2010, A27.

———. *War*. New York: Twelve, 2010.

Knightley, Philip. *The First Casualty: The War Correspondent as Hero, Propagandist and Myth-Maker from the Crimea to Iraq*. 1975. London: André Deutsch, 2003.

Lehman, Daniel Wayne. *John Reed and the Writing of Revolution*. Athens, OH: Ohio University Press, 2002.

Lutz, Earle. "Soldier Newspapers of the Civil War." *Papers of the Bibliographical Society of America* 46, no. 4 (Fourth Quarter 1952): 373–86.

Maguire, Roberta S. "From Fiction to Fact: Zora Neale Hurston and the Ruby McCollum Trial." *Literary Journalism Studies* 7, no. 1 (Spring 2015): 16–34.

"Michael Herr, *Dispatches* (Knopf, 1977)." *Portfolio*. Arthur L. Carter Journalism Institute, New York University. Accessed October 13, 2017. https://journalism.nyu.edu/publishing/archives/portfolio/home.html.

Mitgang, Herbert. "Hemingway on Spain: Unedited Reportage." *New York Times*, August 30, 1988. Accessed October 15, 2017. www.nytimes.com/1988/08/30/arts/hemingway-on-spain-unedited-reportage.html.

"Muds I Have Met." *Listening Post*, no. 22 (February 15, 1917): 146.

Nelson, Robert L. "Soldier Newspapers: A Useful Source in the Social and Cultural History of the First World War and Beyond." *War in History* 17, no. 2 (2010): 167–91. https://doi.org/10.1177/0968344509357127.

North, Joseph. "Reportage." In *American Writers' Congress*, edited by Henry Hart, 120–23. New York: International Publishers, 1935.

Pfau, Michael, Michel Haigh, Mitchell Gettle, Michael Donnelly, Gregory Scott, Dana Warr, and Elaine Wittenberg. "Embedding Journalists in Military Combat Units: Impact on Newspaper Story Frames and Tone." *Journalism and Mass Communication Quarterly* 81, no. 1 (Spring 2004): 74–88. https://doi.org/10.1177/107769900408100106.

Presley, James. "Langston Hughes, War Correspondent." *Journal of Modern Literature* 5, no. 3 (September 1976): 481–91.

Reed, John. *Ten Days That Shook the World*. New York: Boni and Liveright, 1919.

———. "The Traders' War." *Masses*, September 1914, 16–17.

Rinehart, Mary Roberts. *Kings, Queens and Pawns: An American Woman at the Front*. New York: George H. Doran, 1915.

Risley, Ford. *Civil War Journalism*. Santa Barbara, CA: Praeger, 2012.

Roiland, Joshua M. "'Just People' Are Just People: Langston Hughes and the Populist Power of African American Literary Journalism." *Literary Journalism Studies* 5, no. 2 (Fall 2013): 15–35.

Sachsman, David B., ed. *A Press Divided: Newspaper Coverage of the Civil War*. 2014. London: Routledge, 2017.

Scott, Emmett Jay. "The Negro and the War Department." *Crisis*, December 1917, 76.

Seal, Graham Patrick. *The Soldiers' Press: Trench Journals in the First World War*. Basingstoke, UK: Palgrave Macmillan, 2013.

Sheeler, Jim, and Todd Heisler. "Final Salute." *Rocky Mountain News*, November 11, 2005, 1S–14S.

Sims, Norman. *True Stories: A Century of Literary Journalism*. Evanston, IL: Northwestern University Press, 2007.

Soto, Isabel. "'I Knew that Spain Once Belonged to the Moors': Langston Hughes, Race, and the Spanish Civil War." *Research in African Literature* 45, no. 3 (Fall 2014): 130–46. https://doi.org/10.2979/reseafrilite.45.3.130.

Thomas, M. "Mariannhill: The Work of the Catholic Trappists in South Africa." *Crisis*, December 1922, 63–65.

"The Top 100 Works of Journalism in the United States in the 20th Century." Accessed October 12, 2017. www.nyu.edu/classes/stephens/Top%20100%20page.htm.

"The Waco Horror." Supplement, *Crisis*, July 1916, 1–8.

Wolfe, Tom. Editorial note to "Khesanh," by Michael Herr. In *The New Journalism*, edited by Tom Wolfe and E. W. Johnson, 85–115. New York: Harper and Row, 1973.

———. "The New Journalism." In *The New Journalism*, edited by Tom Wolfe and E. W. Johnson, 3–52. New York: Harper and Row, 1973.

Yagoda, Ben. *About Town: The "New Yorker" and the World It Made*. New York: Scribner, 2000.

17
LITERARY JOURNALISM AND SOCIAL ACTIVISM

Nancy L. Roberts

Social and political activism has a rich, extensive history in the United States, starting in the colonial period with the Puritan John Winthrop's famous concept of America as "a city upon a hill."[1] The founders envisioned a model society that would be a beacon to the world. Since then, innumerable citizens have sought to promote social, political, economic, and other types of reform and radical societal change. Among the myriad causes that have compelled them are peace advocacy, racial equality, workers' rights, woman suffrage, fair housing, and, in the nineteenth century, the abolition of slavery and temperance. These activists have undertaken picketing, public speaking, street marches, strikes, sit-ins, and civil disobedience, among other forms of activism. The First Amendment of the US Constitution's unparalleled support of freedom of expression has empowered them to communicate often controversial ideas in the press and elsewhere. Thus, writing (and other forms of communication, such as photojournalism) has become another form of activism.[2]

Journalism flourishes in times of crisis, when people are eager for news. An early American example is the period of the Revolutionary War, when political unrest stimulated considerable press development.[3] Not surprisingly, activism also thrives in such crisis periods, as does literary journalism. Thomas B. Connery has noted literary journalism's ascendancy in three times of great social, political, and economic upheaval—the period from about 1890 to 1912, the Great Depression of the 1930s, and the 1960s. It is during these "times of massive change and reform ... [that] progressive ideas come to the front, wars are fought, big changes in media occur."[4] When all society's constants are seemingly changing, literary journalism offers not just the who, what, where, and when—but also the why and the backstory context and analysis that conventional journalism omits. The latter two elements require, for example, immersion research that is often beyond the scope of time-limited, conventional straight news stories. Further, literary journalism is singularly able to provide what Norman Sims, quoting the literary journalist Richard Rhodes, has called "symbolic realities,"[5] dramatizing a narrative with metaphor and simile and using all appropriate techniques of literary writing (including transcending conventional news' inverted pyramid for other, more complicated structures), while remaining scrupulously faithful to facts. And as Connery has observed, literary journalists depict reality "by attempting to recreate the feel and look of life and experience." Thus, literary journalism "informs at a level common to fiction, attempting to give not just the facts but the 'feel' of the facts."[6] More than merely providing an in-depth treatment of a subject, literary journalism can offer the consummate *visceral* understanding of it, achieved through a powerful alchemy of reason and emotion.

No wonder that some of our most passionate social and political activists have turned to literary journalism as a way to persuade others to adopt and to act upon their heartfelt convictions. This chapter explores the link between literary journalism and activism, focusing primarily on Jacob Riis, who practiced a literary journalism of advocacy (in both text and pictures) in the late nineteenth and early twentieth centuries, and on Barbara Ehrenreich, who has been writing literary journalism to advance social reform since the 1970s. Both of these writers make literary journalistic techniques and styles central to their activism, a characteristic that binds them across more than a century's time. In particular, I explore these two journalists' vision of journalism—its aims and purposes vis-à-vis societal change—and their conception of their roles as journalists/activists (gleaned from their journalism, autobiographical writing, and personal interviews).

To provide a context, this chapter also addresses the work of the environmentalist writer Henry David Thoreau (1817–62) in the mid-nineteenth century and the socialist activist writer John Reed (1887–1920) in the World War I era. Both wrote literary journalism to foment social change.

A Danish immigrant, Jacob Riis (1849–1910) had worked for fourteen years as a police reporter for the *New-York Tribune* before he published his best-known work, *How the Other Half Lives*, in 1890. With its text, fifteen stark half-tone photographs, and fifteen drawings based on Riis's photographs, along with facts and statistics he gathered through his police reporting connections, the book revealed the sordid conditions of the slums during this time of unprecedented urbanization and industrialization. Howard Good, one of the earliest scholars to study Riis as a literary journalist, has called his book *How the Other Half Lives* "easily the most popular and influential of the nineteenth century on the subject."[7] Here, Riis brings home the sights, sounds, and smells of a Ludlow Street sweater's shop (sweatshop) on a typical Sunday:

> Up two flights of dark stairs, three, four, with new smells of cabbage, of onions, of frying fish, on every landing, whirring sewing machines behind closed doors betraying what goes on within, to the door that opens to admit the bundle and the man. A sweater [sweatshop], this, in a small way. Five men and a woman, two young girls, not fifteen, and a boy … are at the machines sewing knickerbockers, "knee-pants". … The floor is littered ankle-deep with half-sewn garments. … The faces, hands, and arms to the elbows of everyone in the room are black with the color of the cloth.[8]

He also reports on an early-morning police raid on a stale-beer dive. The denizens, "a foul and ragged host of men and women," crowd into a small room "covered with a brown crust that, touched with the end of a club, came off in shuddering showers of crawling bugs."[9] In another of his books, *The Children of the Poor* (1892), Riis describes how "when, recently, one little Italian girl, hardly yet in her teens, stayed away from her class in the Mott Street Industrial School so long that her teacher went to her home to look her up, she found the child in a high fever, in bed, sewing on coats, with swollen eyes, though barely able to sit up."[10]

Riis was no stranger to poverty, overcrowding, and tenement life. The third of fourteen children of a Danish schoolteacher and his wife, he saw all but two of his siblings die young, including six from tuberculosis. Then, as a young immigrant to New York in 1870, he struggled for several years to find adequate work and was often homeless and destitute. In his autobiography *The Making of an American* (1901), he describes traveling through New Jersey, New York State, and the Midwest, working in lumber mills, ice houses, and shipyards and selling books, furniture, and flat irons. He knew hunger and uncertainty firsthand, and undoubtedly that fueled his passion to document the injustices suffered by the poor in the tenements of the Lower East Side.[11] He was also motivated to do so by the social injustices he had investigated during his years as a police reporter and by his strong ethic of Christian charity.

Immersing oneself in this kind of extended participant-observation (not just the standard reportorial tactic of adopting a different lifestyle for a fortnight in order to write about it) is a hallmark of the literary journalism of advocacy seen most thoroughgoingly, for example, in the work of Dorothy Day and Meridel Le Sueur during the 1930s and beyond. Day (1897–1980) lived in voluntary poverty among the homeless at the Catholic Worker house of hospitality and soup kitchen on the Lower East Side from 1933 until her death; Le Sueur (1900–96) also lived in communities of workers and women. These firsthand experiences with poverty gave a unique authenticity and authority to their literary journalism, much as Riis's early life of poverty informed his later writing about the subject.[12]

Another strong influence on Riis was the writing of Charles Dickens, which he read as a boy learning English in his native village of Ribe in Denmark. Dickens, touted by Victorian-era newspaper editors to inspire their feature reporters, wrote not only fiction but also literary journalism that deftly characterized the struggles of the poor and powerless in works such as "The Great Tasmania's Cargo" (1860). Good suggests that "in the process of puzzling out the words, [Riis] may have absorbed something of Dickens's literary style and humane spirit."[13]

Riis took the long view of social change, explaining in his autobiography:

> No chance was allowed to pass of telling the people of New York what they were harboring. They simply needed to know, I felt sure of that. And I know now that I was right. But it takes a lot of telling to make a city know when it is doing wrong. However, that was what I was there for. When it didn't seem to help, I would go and look at a stonecutter hammering away at his rock perhaps a hundred times without as much as a crack showing in it. Yet at the hundred and first blow it would split in two, and I knew it was not that blow that did it, but all that had gone before together ... and the walls did fall, though it took nearly twice seven years. But they came down, as the walls of ignorance and indifference must every time, if you blow hard enough and long enough, with faith in your cause and in your fellow-man. It is just a question of endurance. If you keep it up, they can't.[14]

Similarly, Day held a gradualist view of social change, often repeating her cofounder of the Catholic Worker movement Peter Maurin's personalist dictum that change in society begins with change in individuals.[15]

Riis worked tirelessly to advance slum reform through his literary journalism of advocacy. He plunged fearlessly into the new and hazardous urban frontier of tenement poverty with its hunger, poor sanitation, overcrowding, and disease, whose existence was becoming impossible for middle- and upper-class society to deny. Riis's view was "that such conditions were not inevitable and due to the natural immorality of certain ethnic groups, but to their environment and specifically to their awful living conditions."[16] He quickly recognized the possibilities inherent in the revolutionary new invention of photographic flash powder in 1887, which allowed much faster shutter speeds in low light or even darkness, and he harnessed it to create a visual reinforcement of his advocacy writing. With a handheld camera, he explored New York's Lower East Side slums "like an industrial-age Meriwether Lewis," one scholar has written,[17] documenting children's deaths from diphtheria epidemics and sleeping men's fatal slips off the tenement roofs where they had gone to escape the scorching summer heat. The images he produced are timeless and haunting, such as "Police Station Lodgers," depicting the West 47th Street Station's lodging room for women.[18] Here careworn women without the comfort of any bedding sleep on the stained wooden floor, trying to warm themselves by a potbelly stove. Perhaps this photograph's impact stems from our sad familiarity with its subject, across the ages. It may remind us that many homeless people today still struggle to endure cold, inclement weather with only meager resources. Indeed, in a 1997 introduction to an edition of *How the Other Half Lives*, Luc Sante writes:

The book haunts us because so much of it remains true. While its lasting social effects were many—there are no more windowless rooms, double-decker tenements, cellar apartments, dwellings accessible via alleys, doughnut bakeries in basements, sweatshop franchises in slum flats—the living conditions of the poor remain abominable. ... The sweatshop is as much a feature of the recent immigrant's daily hell as it was in 1890.[19]

Another unforgettable image is a portrait of nine-year-old Katie, who when Riis asked, "What kind of work do you do?" replied, "I scrubs."[20] She stands against a brick wall, hands folded, gazing grimly at the camera with a face far older than her years. Katie is one of the "little mothers" that Riis frequently found in the tenements, themselves children, caring for younger siblings to enable their mothers to go to work. "Minding the Baby" is Riis's emblematic portrayal of this practice in a tenement in Gotham Court. It shows a small girl clasping another, still smaller child, while squatting on a cracked, dirty stone floor. The angle of the camera, from above, emphasizes the twin vulnerability of the baby and her diminutive minder. In Riis's accompanying words, "Of Susie's hundred little companions in the alley—playmates they could scarcely be called—some made artificial flowers, some paper-boxes, while the boys earned money at 'shinin' or selling newspapers. The smaller girls 'minded the baby.'"[21]

Riis felt deeply the tragedy of child labor and degradation, as this passage from *How the Other Half Lives* demonstrates:

> Evening has worn into night as we take up our homeward journey through the streets, now no longer silent. The thousands of lighted windows in the tenements glow like dull red eyes in a huge stone wall. From every door multitudes of tired men and women pour forth for a half-hour's rest in the open air before sleep closes eyes weary with incessant working. Crowds of half-naked children tumble in the street, and on the sidewalk, or doze fretfully on the stone steps. As we stop in front of a tenement to watch one of these groups, a dirty baby in a single brief garment—yet a sweet, human little baby despite its dirt and tatters—tumbles off the lowest step, rolls over once, clutches my leg with an unconscious grip, and goes to sleep on the flagstones, its curly head pillowed on my boot.[22]

This deeply affecting literary journalistic interaction of words and photographs is pathbreaking. Riis was typically humble about his photographs, writing in his autobiography that "I am no good at all as a photographer."[23] While some may have accepted this comment at face value,[24] others have recognized the artistic quality of Riis's photographs. In his preface to Alexander Alland Sr.'s *Jacob Riis: Photographer and Citizen* (1974), Ansel Adams praised Riis's "expressive ... expression of people in misery, want and squalor. These people live again for you in the print—as intensely as when their images were captured on the old dry plates of ninety years ago. Their comrades in poverty and suppression live here today, in this city—in all cities of the world." Adams also wrote, "the quality of his flash illumination is extraordinary; the plastic shadow-edges, modulations and textures of flesh, the balance of interior flash and exterior daylight—what contemporary work really exceeds it in competence and integrity?"[25] A powerful example of such a photograph is "Tenement Baby," which Riis explains depicts a small child "standing with its back against the public sink in a pool of filth that overflowed on the floor." Heading up the "dark stairs" in such old gloomy buildings, he often encountered such scenes, "but I never was able to get used to it." Indeed, when the Gilder Tenement House Committee reported that "one in five of the children in the rear tenement into which the sunlight never comes was killed by the house," Riis notes, "It seemed strange, rather, that any survived."[26]

Riis excelled at what are today called environmental portraits, photographs of people in their material surroundings. Compositions such as "Men's Lodging Room in the West 47th Street

Station" illuminate the condition of poverty through careful depiction of its accoutrements—newspapers laid upon hard floors for bedding, piles of scrap wood flanking the rusty, ash-covered potbellied stove, and battered wooden chairs and planks serving as beds.[27] These images speak volumes, as do many of Walker Evans's Depression-era photographs of the Alabama sharecroppers' humble dwelling interiors in *Let Us Now Praise Famous Men* (1941). Riis took up photography, he wrote, "never" as a "pastime" but because he "had use for it."[28] It was a way to reinforce the message inherent in his writing, that poverty's destructive force affected not just the indigent but all of us. A viewer who gazes into the eyes of Riis's subjects will have a hard time denying the humanity evoked there. Riis's literary journalism, both writing and photography, inspires making that all-important connection from the one (the Other) to the all (of us). Historians have interpreted Riis as an early muckraker and as a pioneering documentary photographer, but as Good has shown, he was a literary journalist as well:

> He is a link in a chain that stretches backward to [Charles] Dickens's *American Notes* and forward through [Stephen] Crane's and [Theodore] Dreiser's sketches of New York low life and Jack London's *The People of the Abyss* to George Orwell's *Down and Out in Paris and London* and James Agee and Walker Evans's *Let Us Now Praise Famous Men*.[29]

The thread of these classic explorations of poverty is intriguing.[30] The link to Evans is noteworthy and bears brief comment. Evans and Agee's *Let Us Now Praise Famous Men* is similarly and simultaneously a work of textual and visual literary journalism. However, Evans's accompanying photographs do not seem to result from any desire to directly inspire social change.[31] Evans was not aiming toward directly inspiring concern and reform to better the lives of the "other half," in this case Alabama sharecroppers and their families. Reflecting upon his life and work, Evans said:

> The problem is one of staying out of Left politics and still avoiding Establishment patterns. I would not politicize my mind or work. ... I don't think an artist is directly able to alleviate the human condition. He's very interested in *revealing* it.[32]

By contrast, the literary journalism of Barbara Ehrenreich, in the 1960s and beyond, is inseparable from her advocacy for social reform and even radical change. Born in Butte, Montana, in 1941, Ehrenreich is a journalist, book author, social critic, and activist who may best be known for her celebrated 2001 book, *Nickel and Dimed: On (Not) Getting By in America*, which recounts her experiences trying to live on minimum-wage work. For three months, she worked variously as a waitress, hotel maid, house cleaner, nursing-home aide, and Wal-Mart associate. Here is how she describes her restaurant workplace:

> The kitchen is a cavern, a stomach leading to the lower intestine that is the garbage and dishwashing area, from which issue bizarre smells combining the edible and the offal: creamy carrion, pizza barf. ... The floor is slick with spills, forcing us to walk through the kitchen with tiny steps, like Susan McDougal in leg irons. Sinks everywhere are clogged with scraps of lettuce, decomposing lemon wedges, water-logged toast crusts. Put your hand down on any counter and you risk being stuck to it by the film of ancient syrup spills, and this is unfortunate because hands are utensils here, used for scooping up lettuce onto the salad plates, lifting out pie slices, and even moving hash browns from one plate to another.[33]

Ehrenreich's method of participant-observation is intensive and well thought through.[34] She acknowledges her status as only a "visitor"—and one with a graduate degree, a PhD in cell immunology from Rockefeller University, no less—to the working-class world:

> With all the real-life assets I've built up in middle age—bank account, IRA, health insurance, multiroom home—waiting indulgently in the background, there was no way I was going to "experience poverty" or find out how it "really feels" to be a long-term low-wage worker. My aim here was much more straightforward and objective—just to see whether I could match income to expenses, as the truly poor attempt to do every day.[35]

Ultimately Ehrenreich discovers that it is impossible to work at minimum-wage jobs and shelter, feed, and clothe herself at the most basic levels, even when working at two jobs, seven days a week. She concludes that

> the "working poor," as they are approvingly termed, are in fact the major philanthropists of our society. They neglect their own children so that the children of others will be cared for; they live in substandard housing so that other homes will be shiny and perfect; they endure privation so that inflation will be low and stock prices high. To be a member of the working poor is to be an anonymous donor, a nameless benefactor, to everyone else.[36]

Nickel and Dimed has been compared to Michael Harrington's *The Other America* in the forcefulness of its evocation of poverty. Harrington, who had edited Dorothy Day's *Catholic Worker* in the early 1950s, published *The Other America* in 1962 and saw it spark President John F. Kennedy's plan for a "War on Poverty," which was carried on by his successor Lyndon B. Johnson. Ehrenreich's book, while perhaps not quite as influential, made her a household name and galvanized many across the country to push for a living wage. Ehrenreich has also written considerable cultural criticism, such as her book *Bright-Sided: How the Relentless Promotion of Positive Thinking Has Undermined America* (2009). There she discusses everything from the positive-thinking ideas of Norman Vincent Peale, Martin Seligman, and motivational business seminars to her own experiences with "the pink ribbon culture" as a breast cancer patient. The latter section is based on participant-observation, of course. She observes:

> You can dress in pink-beribboned sweatshirts, denim shirts, pajamas, lingerie, aprons, loungewear, shoelaces, and socks; accessorize with pink rhinestone brooches, angel pins, scarves, caps, earrings, and bracelets; brighten up your home with breast cancer candles, stained glass pink-ribbon candleholders, coffee mugs, pendants, wind chimes, and nightlights; and pay your bills with Checks for the Cure™.[37]

Ehrenreich is all for being open about one's struggle with illness and mortality but points out "that the existential space in which a friend had earnestly advised me to 'confront [my] mortality' bore a striking resemblance to the mall."[38] Later she harnesses her background as a biologist to point out the flaws in research studies that claim that cancer patients who maintain a positive attitude and attend support group meetings actually extend their longevity.

As William Dow and Leonora Flis have observed, much of Ehrenreich's work demonstrates her ability to masterfully engage in literary activity, using literary techniques in the creation of character, e.g., the rapid-fire character sketches of the McLean Bible Church career ministry in *Bait and Switch*; the reconstructions of dialogue, such as the ironic exchanges between the narrator and Marge and Holly in *Nickel and Dimed*; and in the use of figurative language, such as the many metaphorical constructions and explanations … in *Living with a Wild God*.[39]

Her style in the aforementioned works and elsewhere is to marshal the relevant facts through thick description and then to underscore a point with a bomb of dry wit. For instance, she writes:

> In the most extreme characterization, breast cancer is not a problem at all, not even an annoyance—it is a "gift," deserving of the most heartfelt gratitude. One survivor turned author credits it with revelatory powers, writing in her book *The Gift of Cancer: A Call to Awakening* that "cancer is your ticket to your real life. Cancer is your passport to the life you were truly meant to live."

In this view, Ehrenreich adds, cancer becomes transformed into a "rite of passage," "a normal marker in the life cycle, like menopause or grandmotherhood."[40] In *Blood Rites: Origins and History of the Passions of War* (1997), Ehrenreich observes:

> our incestuous fixation on combat with our own kind has left us ill prepared to face many of the larger perils of the situation in which we find ourselves: the possibility of drastic climatic changes, the depletion of natural resources, the relentless predations of the microbial world.

Yet, she counsels pithily, "Any anti-war movement that targets only the human agents of war—a warrior elite or, in our own time, the chieftains of the 'military-industrial complex'—risks mimicking those it seeks to overcome."[41] The quick wit of that aside nails her point.

Ehrenreich's inclination to write literary journalism that is strongly imbued with advocacy seems influenced by her childhood in Butte, Montana. Her father was a miner there, and in a 2015 interview, she recalled being exposed at a young age to union principles such as "standing by other people, and sticking together." She continued, "When I get involved with a subject, often there's an activist component for me." She cited the example of her involvement in efforts to raise the minimum wage after writing *Nickel and Dimed*, saying, "I don't see how I could do otherwise, as a moral person."[42] This approach to reform, motivated by personal moral principles, echoes that of Riis, who turned his bleak photos of slum life into magic lantern slides that he used in his lectures at churches, YMCAs, and other institutions as a way to inspire public action. Starting in 1888, he became a popular speaker around the country, his photographs and lectures a seamless means of inspiring social action. The same can be said for Day, whose writing flowed boundlessly from her lecturing and civil disobedience actions; all were the interrelated components of her staunch activism. Le Sueur, too, wrote authentically of her participation in social movements and political action, for example in her influential piece "I Was Marching," her reportage about the deadly 1934 Minneapolis truckers' strike:

> We were moving spontaneously in a movement, natural, hardy, and miraculous. We passed through six blocks of tenements, through a sea of grim faces, and there was not a sound. There was the curious shuffle of thousands of feet, without drum or bugle, in ominous silence, a march not heavy as the military, but very light, exactly with the heartbeat. I was marching with a million hands, movements, faces. … As if an electric charge has passed through me, my hair stood on end. I was marching.[43]

Ehrenreich, also, is a longstanding activist who participated, for example, in the spring 1966 anti–Vietnam War demonstrations in Washington, DC.[44] "My political instincts were, and remain, resolutely populist," she writes in *Living with a Wild God: A Nonbeliever's Search for the Truth about Everything* (2014),[45] her memoir. She has explained:

> with the birth of my first child in 1970, I underwent a political, as well as a personal, transformation. Bit by bit, I got involved with what we then called the "women's health movement," advocating for better health care for women and greater access to health information than we had at that time.[46]

This work was the catalyst for her widely read pamphlet (coauthored with Deirdre English), *Witches, Midwives and Nurses: A History of Women Healers* (1973). She then wrote columns for *Ms.* and *Mother Jones* in the 1980s and for *Time* in the 1990s and the *New York Times* in the 2000s, and worked to end the Vietnam War and to further feminism, particularly women's reproductive health rights. Today, she explains on her website, she continues to write opinion journalism "mostly on themes related to social injustice and inequality" and books related to her deep intellectual interests, particularly the historical.[47] Her third major endeavor, she notes, is activism focusing on "such issues as health care, peace, women's rights, and economic justice. I have never seen a conflict between journalism and activism: As a journalist, I search for the truth. But as a moral person, I am also obliged to do something about it."[48] In a 2015 interview, Ehrenreich said:

> My stance is not optimism. My stance is that the realities are really grim, yet we have to work hard. My stance is not that we will overcome and have a wonderful, fair, loving, kind world. It might not be possible, but I'll die trying.[49]

This perspective emphasizing one's beliefs and one's advocacy links Ehrenreich to Riis, Day, and Le Sueur as well as to other advocacy journalists. In their landmark sociological study of journalists, *The News People* (1976), John W. C. Johnstone, Edward J. Slawski, and William W. Bowman pointed to ideology as the "cornerstone" of advocacy journalism as practiced by Liberation News Service (New York, NY) and the *Great Speckled Bird* (Atlanta, GA). Such advocacy journalism, they concluded, also emphasized "substance over technique."[50] But this is certainly not true of the literary journalism of advocacy produced by Riis, Ehrenreich, Day, and Le Sueur. These journalists all sought to open people's hearts and minds to the problems faced by society's most vulnerable—the poor and the homeless—through a literary journalism of advocacy that illuminated both the facts (substance) and the "feel of the facts." They recognized such communication's potential to inspire the contemplation and creation of solutions for society's greatest problems.

Further examination of literary journalism as a form of activism should start with an inventory of its practitioners. Of largely unrecognized significance is Gloria Steinem (1934–), who is usually given short reference in standard histories of literary journalism as a New Journalist.[51] Much more attention is paid to her long leadership role in the feminist movement, for example as the editor of *Ms.* As Ashlee Nelson notes:

> it is the overpowering image of Steinem as the figurehead of feminism … which has led many to not look past her role as an advocate of feminism to the critical importance of her role as a journalist and advocate and practitioner of New Journalism.[52]

Nelson has shed welcome light on Steinem's literary journalism about the presidential campaign of 1972, demonstrating its strong message of social change. Among the other major journalists reporting on the campaign were Norman Mailer, Timothy Crouse, and Hunter S. Thompson, but Steinem's writing most clearly articulated her "secondary agenda," which was feminism. This is not surprising, given that Steinem helped found the National Women's Political Caucus (NWPC) in 1971 with an eye toward influencing the 1972 campaign; furthermore, the NWPC elected her to serve as its spokesperson at the 1972 Democratic Convention. New Journalism itself grew out of the commitment to spark social change, and for Steinem, writing it seems to have been an extension of her activism.

The same might be said of the socialist activist writer John Reed (1887–1920) in the World War I era.[53] And even earlier, in 1854, Henry David Thoreau (1817–62) produced *Walden* as a kind of literary journalistic call to action for environmental preservation. For both, activism and producing literary journalism were inseparable endeavors. As early as 1937, Thoreau was recognized as a writer of literary journalism, by Edwin H. Ford in his groundbreaking *A Bibliography of Literary Journalism in America*.[54] Indeed, Thoreau strongly condemned superficiality and other limitations of conventional news reporting and sought in *Walden* to find a different way to achieve thoughtful, in-depth writing.[55] As Mark Canada explains, "Reporting on nature ... was Thoreau's own form of truth-telling, one that he explicitly and implicitly contrasts with [the limits of conventional] journalism."[56] Choosing to live for more than two years in the simple cabin he built near Walden Pond, Thoreau sought to capture the universal significance of everyday natural phenomena, such as warring ants, the calls of whip-poor-wills, and the seasonal freezing and thawing of the pond. *Walden* is his passionate, prescient critique of how Western society's consumerist culture not only detaches it from the natural world, but even causes the destruction of that world. It could be called the first literary journalism of environmental advocacy.

Reed grew up in a middle-class family in Portland, Oregon, then went to Morristown Academy in New Jersey and graduated from Harvard in 1910. Living in Greenwich Village, a bohemian hotbed, seems to have propelled him toward radicalism. By early 1913, Reed became a managing editor and contributor to the *Masses*, Max Eastman's lively leftist magazine that critiqued capitalist culture with literary panache. That spring he covered striking silk workers in Paterson, New Jersey, which landed him in jail for four days and reinforced his commitment "to cover firsthand ... violent struggles of the poor against political injustice," as Robert E. Humphrey has noted.[57] The following year, Reed hit his stride as a literary journalist of advocacy while covering the Mexican Civil War for *Metropolitan* magazine. "It was the radical point of view, namely, a sympathy for lowly Mexicans and an antipathy for Americans, that distinguished Reed from the typical correspondent," Humphrey observed. Still, Reed's account eschewed propaganda, because while he idolized Pancho Villa, the Mexican revolutionary and guerilla leader, "he showed that selfish and materialistic as well as idealistic motives induced Mexicans to join the fight."[58] And while other reporters focused on the usual military aspects, such as strategies and tactics, Reed told stirring stories of individual peons on the battlefield whom he interviewed in the midst of the action, much like Ernie Pyle illuminated the experiences of ordinary rank-and-file soldiers.[59] Ultimately, Reed's reporting of the Russian Revolution of 1917, which was published as a popular and influential book, *Ten Days That Shook the World* (1919), overshadowed his Mexican reporting. But his Russian reporting is closer to propaganda because as "Reed sailed into the eye of the political storm, his writing became less personal."[60] In fact, he became an exponent of Communism, viewing the Bolshevik Revolution as the start of the utopian society he had hoped for. Rather, it is Reed's earlier Mexican reporting that most fully embodies his literary journalism of advocacy. As a participant–observer, "he rode with [Villa's men] all day and drank and danced all night."[61] He sought in his writing to humanize the Mexican, disavowing Americans' defamatory stereotype of "an undersized, treacherous little half-breed fit to kick around on a section gang, but really not worth much."[62]

What seems common to Thoreau and Reed—and to Riis, Ehrenreich, Day, and Le Sueur—is a palpable, deep-seated sense of moral concern about societal problems, often developed over a period of years through immersion in firsthand experiences. It is also important to note that because so few poor people have the resources to write about their situations, it has often fallen to others to tell their stories. Unfortunately, too often these accounts objectify the destitute. But because Day and Le Sueur and, to a lesser degree, Thoreau, Riis, Reed, and Ehrenreich "walked the talk," their accounts offer original insights. They share an unwavering commitment to foment social change through a literary journalism of advocacy emphasizing the unique viewpoints of the participant–observer. All, particularly during times of crisis, produced timeless literary journalism as a central means of expressing their activism.

Notes

1. Winthrop (1588–1649) used these words in his famous speech, "A Model of Christian Charity," which he gave aboard the *Arabella* in 1630, shortly before landing in New England. See Miller, *American Puritans*, 83.
2. See Roberts, *American Peace Writers*.
3. Emery, Emery, and Roberts, *Press and America*, 35.
4. Connery, "Research Review," 211. See also Hartsock, *History*, 167–69; Sims, *True Stories*, 91.
5. Sims, introduction to *The Literary Journalists*, 23–24.
6. Connery, "Third Way," 6; Connery, *Sourcebook*, 11; Connery, *Journalism and Realism*, 10.
7. Good, "Jacob A. Riis," 81.
8. Riis, *How the Other Half Lives*, 96.
9. Riis, 59, 58.
10. Riis, *Children of the Poor*, 21.
11. Riis subscribed to many of the racial and ethnic prejudices of his day, but still he was "fundamentally tolerant to a degree that far surpassed his contemporaries," concludes Edward T. O'Donnell, who studied Riis's entire career and written work ("Pictures vs. Words?," 7). See also Lamunière, "Sentiment as Moral Motivator."
12. Roberts, "Meridel Le Sueur," 50.
13. Good, "Jacob A. Riis," 83.
14. Riis, *Making of an American*, 163–64.
15. Roberts, *Dorothy Day*, 8.
16. Connery, *Journalism and Realism*, 172.
17. Morris, "Poverty of the Imagination," 96.
18. Riis, "Vice Which Is Unchecked," quoted in Alland, *Jacob A. Riis*, 62.
19. Sante, introduction to *How the Other Half Lives*, xiii.
20. Riis, *Children of the Poor*, 61, quoted in Alland, *Jacob A. Riis*, 142–43.
21. Riis, *Children of the Poor*, 114, 111, quoted in Alland, *Jacob A. Riis*, 140–41.
22. Riis, *How the Other Half Lives*, 102.
23. Riis, *Making of an American*, 171.
24. See, for example, Yochelson, "Jacob A. Riis."
25. Adams, preface to *Jacob A. Riis*, 6, 7.
26. Riis, *Peril and the Preservation of the Home*, quoted in Alland, *Jacob A. Riis*, 120.
27. Riis, "Vice Which Is Unchecked," quoted in Alland, *Jacob A. Riis*, 82–83.
28. Riis, *Making of an American*, 171.
29. Good, "Jacob A. Riis," 87–88.
30. See, for example, McClay and Alspaugh, "Thinking about the Poor."
31. Paul Ashdown has argued convincingly that Agee wrote literary journalism in this, his opus, and elsewhere (see "James Agee" and introduction to *James Agee*, ix).
32. Mellow, *Walker Evans*, 308.
33. Ehrenreich, *Nickel and Dimed*, 29–30.
34. Carolyn Betensky has criticized Ehrenreich's practice of participant observation in *Nickel and Dimed* as an example of the "enduring experience of make-believe powerlessness among the dominant classes in Western cultures." She argues that this "practice of impersonating the poor in their own milieu" is a source of pleasure for "people in positions of power [who] often enjoy pretending that they are powerless" and that "the enjoyment of powerlessness is, in some sense, the enjoyment of power" ("Princes as Paupers," 130). Yet this perspective ignores Ehrenreich's many years of social and political activism, including her literary journalism, all of which are spurred by her own moral compass (as will be shown).

35 Ehrenreich, *Nickel and Dimed*, 6.
36 Ehrenreich, 221.
37 Ehrenreich, *Bright-Sided*, 22.
38 Ehrenreich, 23.
39 Dow and Flis, "Scholar-Practitioner Q&A," 152.
40 Ehrenreich, *Bright-Sided*, 29.
41 Ehrenreich, *Blood Rites*, 239–40.
42 Quoted in Court, "Barbara Ehrenreich,"
43 Le Sueur, *Ripening*, 165.
44 Ehrenreich, *Living with a Wild God*, 194.
45 Ehrenreich, 186.
46 Ehrenreich, "Bio."
47 Ehrenreich.
48 Ehrenreich. See also Ehrenreich, "Class Matters."
49 Dow and Flis, "Scholar-Practitioner Q&A," 157.
50 Johnstone, Slawski, and Bowman, *News People*, 174–75, 178, 171.
51 For example, as Ashlee Nelson notes ("A New Feminism in New Journalism"), a history of New Journalism by Marc Weingarten, *Who's Afraid of Tom Wolfe? How New Journalism Rewrote the World*, mentions Steinem's participation in the founding of *New York* magazine but does not really address her important role as a New Journalist. Kevin Kerrane and Ben Yagoda's anthology of literary journalism, *The Art of Fact*, leaves out Steinem entirely.
52 Nelson, "New Feminism," 2.
53 See, for example, Humphrey, "John Reed"; Knudson, "John Reed"; Frazier, "John Reed's Unblinking Stare"; Shafer, "O'Neill, Glaspell, and John Reed."
54 Ford noted that the literary journalist "refashions and evaluates the world about him," doing this "through the medium of the sketch or essay, of the literary or humorous column, of verse, or of critical comment" (foreword to *A Bibliography of Literary Journalism*, i). See also Hartsock, *History*, 23, 130–31.
55 Canada, *Literature and Journalism*, 87–97.
56 Canada, 92.
57 Humphrey, "John Reed," 153.
58 Humphrey, 155, 156.
59 Knudson, "John Reed," 59.
60 Humphrey, "John Reed," 159.
61 Knudson, "John Reed," 63.
62 Reed, "Bandit in Mountains Can Hold His Retreat against Bigger Force," *New York American*, March 13, 1916, quoted in Knudson, "John Reed," 63.

Bibliography

Adams, Ansel. Preface to *Jacob A. Riis: Photographer and Citizen*, by Alexander Alland Sr., 6–7. Millerton, NY: Aperture, 1974.

Alland, Alexander, Sr. *Jacob A. Riis: Photographer and Citizen*. Preface by Ansel Adams. Millerton, NY: Aperture, 1974.

Ashdown, Paul. Introduction to *James Agee: Selected Journalism*, edited by Paul Ashdown, xxx-xliv. Knoxville, TN: University of Tennessee Press, 1985.

———. "James Agee." In Connery, *Sourcebook*, 197–204.

Betensky, Carolyn. "Princes as Paupers: Pleasure and the Imagination of Powerlessness." *Cultural Critique*, no. 56 (Winter 2004): 129–57. https://doi.org/10.1353/cul.2003.0055.

Canada, Mark. *Literature and Journalism in Antebellum America: Thoreau, Stowe, and Their Contemporaries Respond to the Rise of the Commercial Press*. New York: Palgrave Macmillan, 2011.

Connery, Thomas B. *Journalism and Realism: Rendering American Life*. Evanston, IL: Northwestern University Press, 2011.

———. "Research Review: Magazines and Literary Journalism, an Embarrassment of Riches." In *The American Magazine: Research Perspectives and Prospects*, edited by David Abrahamson, 207–16. Ames, IA: Iowa State University Press, 1995.

———. *A Sourcebook of American Literary Journalism: Representative Writers in an Emerging Genre*. Westport, CT: Greenwood Press, 1992.

———. "A Third Way to Tell the Story: American Literary Journalism at the Turn of the Century." In Sims, *Literary Journalism*, 3–20.
Court, Emma. "Barbara Ehrenreich: 'When I Get Involved with a Subject, Often There's an Activist Component for Me.'" *Dallas Morning News*, July 15, 2015.
Dow, William, and Leonora Flis. "Scholar-Practitioner Q&A: An Interview with Barbara Ehrenreich." *Literary Journalism Studies* 7, no. 1 (Spring 2015): 146–58.
Ehrenreich, Barbara. "Bio." *Barbara Ehrenreich*. http://barbaraehrenreich.com/barbara-ehrenreich-bio/.
———. *Blood Rites: Origins and History of the Passions of War*. New York: Henry Holt, 1997.
———. *Bright-Sided: How the Relentless Promotion of Positive Thinking Has Undermined America*. New York: Henry Holt, 2009.
———. "Class Matters." *Anglican Theological Review* 98, no. 1 (Winter 2016): 15–21.
———. *Living with a Wild God: A Nonbeliever's Search for the Truth about Everything*. New York: Twelve, 2014.
———. *Nickel and Dimed: On (Not) Getting By in America*. New York: Henry Holt, 2001.
Ehrenreich, Barbara, and Deirdre English. *Witches, Midwives and Nurses: A History of Women Healers*. Old Westbury, NY: Feminist Press, 1973.
Emery, Michael, Edwin Emery, and Nancy L. Roberts. *The Press and America: An Interpretive History of the Mass Media*. 9th ed. Boston, MA: Allyn and Bacon, 2000.
Ford, Edwin H. Foreword to *A Bibliography of Literary Journalism in America*, 1–68. Minneapolis, MN: Burgess, 1937.
Frazier, Ian. "John Reed's Unblinking Stare." *American Scholar* 71, no. 3 (Summer 2002): 29–39.
Good, Howard. "Jacob A. Riis." In Connery, *Sourcebook*, 81–89.
Harrington, Michael. *The Other America: Poverty in the United States*. New York: Macmillan, 1962.
Hartsock, John C. *A History of American Literary Journalism: The Emergence of a Modern Narrative Form*. Amherst, MA: University of Massachusetts Press, 2000.
Humphrey, Robert E. "John Reed." In Connery, *Sourcebook*, 151–60.
Johnstone, John W. C., Edward J. Slawski, and William W. Bowman. *The News People: A Sociological Portrait of American Journalists and Their Work*. Urbana, IL: University of Illinois Press, 1976.
Kerrane, Kevin, and Ben Yagoda, eds. *The Art of Fact: A Historical Anthology of Literary Journalism*. New York: Simon and Schuster, 1998.
Knudson, Jerry W. "John Reed: A Reporter in Revolutionary Mexico." *Journalism History* 29, no. 2 (Summer 2003): 59–68.
Lamunière, Michelle. "Sentiment as Moral Motivator: From Jacob Riis's Lantern Slide Presentations to Harvard University's Social Museum." *History of Photography* 36, no. 2 (May 2012): 137–55. https://doi.org/10.1080/03087298.2012.658694.
Le Sueur, Meridel. *Ripening: Selected Work, 1927–1980*. New York: Feminist Press, 1982.
McClay, B. D., and Leann Davis Alspaugh. "Thinking about the Poor: A Bibliographical Essay." *Hedgehog Review* 16, no. 3 (Fall 2014): 82–91.
Mellow, James R. *Walker Evans*. New York: Basic Books, 1999.
Miller, Perry, ed. *The American Puritans: Their Prose and Poetry*. Garden City, NY: Anchor Books, 1956.
Morris, James McGrath. "Poverty of the Imagination." Review of *The Other Half: The Life of Jacob Riis and the World of Immigrant America*, by Tom Buk-Swienty. *Wilson Quarterly* 32, no. 4 (Autumn 2008): 96–97.
Nelson, Ashlee. "A New Feminism in New Journalism: Gloria Steinem and the 1972 U.S. Presidential Election." Paper presented at the Annual Conference of the International Association for Literary Journalism Studies, Halifax, Nova Scotia, Canada, May 2017.
O'Donnell, Edward T. "Pictures vs. Words? Public History, Tolerance, and the Challenge of Jacob Riis." *Public Historian* 26, no. 3 (Summer 2004): 7–26. https://doi.org/10.1525/tph.2004.26.3.7.
Reed, John. "Bandit in Mountains Can Hold His Retreat against Bigger Force." *New York American*, March 13, 1916.
Riis, Jacob A. *The Children of the Poor*. New York: Garrett Press, 1970. Photographic copy of the original edition published in 1892 by Charles Scribner's Sons (New York).
———. *How the Other Half Lives: Studies among the Tenements of New York*. With an introduction and notes by Luc Sante. Penguin Classics ed. New York: Penguin Books, 1997. Originally published in 1890 by Charles Scribner's Sons (New York).
———. *The Making of an American*. New York: Macmillan, 1901.
———. *The Peril and the Preservation of the Home*. Philadelphia, PA: George W. Jacobs, 1903.
———. "Vice Which Is Unchecked in Police Station Lodging-Houses." *New-York Tribune*, January 31, 1892, 13.

Roberts, Nancy L. *American Peace Writers, Editors, and Periodicals: A Dictionary.* Westport, CT: Greenwood Press, 1991.

———. *Dorothy Day and the "Catholic Worker."* Albany, NY: State University of New York Press, 1984.

———. "Meridel Le Sueur, Dorothy Day, and the Literary Journalism of Advocacy during the Great Depression." *Literary Journalism Studies* 7, no. 1 (Spring 2015): 44–57.

Sante, Luc. Introduction to *How the Other Half Lives: Studies Among the Tenements of New York*, by Jacob A. Riis, ix–xxii. New York: Penguin Books, 1997.

Shafer, Yvonne. "O'Neill, Glaspell, and John Reed: Antiwar, Pro-American Reformers." *Eugene O'Neill Review*, no. 32 (2010): 70–85.

Sims, Norman, ed. *Literary Journalism in the Twentieth Century.* New York: Oxford University Press, 1990.

———. Introduction to *The Literary Journalists*, edited by Norman Sims, 3–25. New York: Ballantine Books, 1984.

———. *True Stories: A Century of Literary Journalism.* Evanston, IL: Northwestern University Press, 2007.

Weingarten, Marc. *Who's Afraid of Tom Wolfe? How New Journalism Rewrote the World.* London: Aurum Press, 2005.

Yochelson, Bonnie. "Jacob A. Riis, Photographer 'After a Fashion.'" In *Rediscovering Jacob Riis: Exposure Journalism and Photography in Turn-of-the-Century New York*, by Bonnie Yochelson and Daniel Czitrom, 121–227. New York: New Press, 2007.

18
LITERARY JOURNALISM AND AMERICAN MAGAZINES

Doug Underwood

The leftist critic Mary McCarthy was three-for-three as a magazine literary journalist when she authored a scathing review of David Halberstam's *The Best and the Brightest* (1972), his "new" journalism account of the Kennedy administration's "whiz kids" who led the United States into the Vietnam War. A war critic herself, McCarthy—her literary reputation long made as a bestselling novelist, a cleverly acerbic book reviewer, and a writer of her own narrative nonfictional accounts of the US military quagmire in Vietnam—complained that Halberstam's book induced in her a "stupefied boredom" with its "fluency of cliché" and its "deafness to idiom and grammatical incomprehensibility."[1] "What is the purpose of this book?" she wrote in 1973 in the *New York Review of Books*:

> Six hundred and eighty-eight pages of "colorful" narrative that … except for the portions that appeared in magazines, never [seemed] to have been touched by an editorial pencil wielded by the author or anybody else. … The book's success is a mystery to this reader, who was unable to stay awake for more than a few paragraphs at a go.[2]

McCarthy's three-fold demonstration of the art of literary journalism captures the common historical definitions of the term: In her own writings, she was a successful practitioner of the newly popular mode of long-form narrative (or what was then called "new") journalism; she was a critic of a fellow writer in her role as a book reviewer; and she wielded her already established reputation in a literary forum (in this case, a magazine or review) that showcased literary production and criticism.

Magazines and periodicals have been crucial platforms for the evolution and development of American literary journalism.[3] This has happened within the context of the various definitions of the term—the narrative and storytelling forms of nonfictional writing, as well as book reviewing and periodical essay writing, notably by a person with an already established literary reputation—that have been applied at different points in time. As an older writer skeptical of what was being touted as a path-breaking trend in nonfictional writing, McCarthy was reluctant to put herself in the camp of Halberstam or other "new" journalists who were promoting their dramatic and colorfully textured narrative techniques as the latest "big" thing in literature. However, there is a good deal of historical irony imbedded in McCarthy's criticism of Halberstam. Along with her reputation as a reviewer, her own narrative, nonfictional accounts of the conflict in Southeast Asia, *Vietnam* (1967), *Hanoi* (1968), *Medina* (1972), and *The Seventeenth Degree* (1974)—portions of which were written for the *New York Review of Books* before they were published as books—have made her a precursor figure to the "new" or what scholars in the 1980s and 1990s renamed and pulled in under the historic label of literary journalism.[4] In this, she can be seen as the embodiment of the shifting meaning of a term that scholars have attached to writers' efforts to produce and critique—and sometimes hope that they might be remembered for—their own and/or others' writing, including journalism and magazine writing, that might be deemed worthy of being elevated to the ranks of literature.[5]

Historical Complexities in the Development of Literary Journalism in Magazines: Defining the Terrain

The framework for this survey of the role of magazines as a venue for literary journalism will draw upon the term as it has been used by writers and scholars in American literary history—as storytelling and narrative forms of nonfiction writing; as book reviewing and literary criticism for periodicals; and as essays and nonfiction by writers with already established reputations in the fields of fiction, poetry, and drama. In examining the way that periodicals have launched, nourished, and promoted the careers of literary journalists, a strong case can be made that magazines are so intertwined with the emergence and evolution of literary journalism that they exist in a near symbiotic relationship with the creative nonfiction forms that they have helped to spawn. From their origins, many magazines have welcomed strong opinion, original expression, and experimental writing techniques—as well as resisted the fixed writing formulas and repetitive news framing judgments that have long dominated the industrialized newspaper business. Although newspapers have been open to printing forms of what can be called literary journalism, it has been general circulation magazines of literature and commentary that have continued to serve as primary outlets for nonfictional content that sometimes has been considered too inventive, iconoclastic, or outspoken to fit into the made-to-order formats of ordinary journalism.[6]

First, I will be discussing the term literary journalism as it has been applied by the contemporary scholars who have embraced the richly stylistic, storytelling forms of the "new" journalism of Halberstam, Tom Wolfe, Truman Capote, Terry Southern, Joan Didion, Norman Mailer, Gay Talese, Michael Herr, Frances FitzGerald, Hunter S. Thompson, Gail Sheehy, and other narrative nonfictionists whose landmark works—often first appearing in magazine and periodical formats—were published during the social and political ferment of the 1960s and 1970s. Many scholars and anthologists of this genre, including Norman Sims, Thomas Connery, John Hartsock, Mark Kramer, Edd Applegate, Arthur J. Kaul, Kevin Kerrane, and Ben Yagoda, have chosen to use the term literary journalism as a synonym for the 1960s- and 1970s-style narrative "new" journalism and then extended the definition backward into history to find examples of older writing with similarities to the forms developed by modern narrative journalists. This analysis will include antecedent writers—McCarthy, Mark Twain, Stephen Crane, Ambrose Bierce, Jack London, James Agee, Edith Wharton, Richard Wright, Martha Gellhorn, A. J. Liebling, John Hersey, Joseph Mitchell, Lillian Ross, James Baldwin—who have been studied by scholars and historians of narrative literary journalism and were seen as historical models (often in their writing for magazines) by Wolfe and his cohorts as they marketed their boundary-pushing, narrative nonfictional techniques.

A second equally storied tradition—which has been called literary journalism in Britain and the US of the mid-to-late nineteenth and throughout the twentieth- and twenty-first-centuries—includes the production of critical reviews and essays for general circulation magazines of literature and commentary, as well as for the book review pages of major newspapers such as the *New York Times*, the *Times* of London, the *Washington Post*, the *Guardian*, and a handful of others. These discursive and expository activities—although sometimes viewed as too informational and prosaic to be called literature—have included thoughtful, wit-laden, and often provocative contributions by such notable American public critics and essayists as McCarthy, Baldwin, Margaret Fuller, James Russell Lowell, Oliver Wendell Holmes Sr., Bayard Taylor, Ralph Waldo Emerson, Henry David Thoreau, Henry Adams, Charlotte Perkins Gilman, W. E. B. Du Bois, H. L. Mencken, E. B. White, Dorothy Parker, Edmund Wilson, Lionel and Diana Trilling, and Ralph Ellison. In the course of the research for this chapter, the term has been found to refer to discursive writing and criticism in American literary periodicals as early as in the 1840s, as well as in the writings of twentieth- and twenty-first-century American critics and literary commentators (Wilson, Granville Hicks, Christopher Lasch, Jonathan Alter, Eliot Weinberger, Jeffrey Meyers), literary scholars (Allen Tate, Edwin Cady, Gerald Graff, D. G. Myers, Patrick Collier, Carla Mulford, Louis Menand), and literary authors (T. S. Eliot, Saul Bellow, John Updike, Paul Auster).[7]

Finally, as the fictional novel's influence grew in the nineteenth century and journalism increasingly became seen as the domain of the industrialized news organizations that sought mass readership and marketplace success, there developed yet another use of the term literary journalism—that is, for the discursive (and occasionally narrative) nonfiction of authors who had established their reputations as poets, dramatists, or fictional novelists but also engaged in magazine and periodical reviewing and other forms of essay writing. These writers ranged from Edgar Allan Poe, William Dean Howells, and Henry James as nineteenth- and/or early- twentieth-century figures to Eliot, whose critical viewpoints made him a leading voice among literary studies scholars of the twentieth century. Celebrated examples of modern novelists operating in the critic's role in magazines or periodicals include Wright's accusing Zora Neale Hurston of writing with the "minstrel technique" in *Their Eyes Were Watching God*; Hersey's excoriation of the "new" journalism tactics of Capote, Wolfe, and Mailer; and novelist Jane Smiley's accusing Twain of racial insensitivity in *The Adventures of Huckleberry Finn*.[8] Others who are best known for their fictional and poetic artistry—John Updike, John Gardner, Kenneth Rexroth, Edmund White, Joyce Carol Oates—also have made influential nonfictional contributions with their essays and literary reviews in general circulation periodicals.[9]

Amanda Claybaugh suggests that the literatures of the Anglo-American world never have been entirely distinct—and this has been the case in the study of literary journalism.[10] One of the challenges in analyzing literary journalism in magazines is dealing with the different ways that the term is today used by many contemporary American and British critics, reviewers, and writers. After the coming of the Wolfe-style, narrative journalism movement, many journalists and scholars in the US—and particularly so ex-journalists teaching in academic communication departments—have largely used the term literary journalism to apply to Wolfe's storytelling forms of nonfiction. Meanwhile, most British periodical critics—along with some scholars in British literary studies departments—have continued to use the historical definition of the term as book reviewing and discursive criticism. Some have tried to solve this problem by simply referring to "British literary journalism" as the literary reviewing and periodical essay writing tradition and "American literary journalism" as the narrative, storytelling tradition.[11] Although this somewhat fits with the contemporary treatment of the term, it is complicated not only by historical factors but also by the ways that today's British and American critics and writers are far from consistent in this usage. For example, a Nexis search of 630 articles in recent British and American periodicals and newspapers found 82 percent of the authors of articles in US publications using the term literary journalism in its narrative meaning and 18 percent in its discursive and book reviewing form; in turn, 78 percent of those writing articles in British publications used the term in its discursive and 22 percent in its narrative meaning.[12] This state of affairs—where a portion of both British and American critics and writers are using the terminology in reverse form to what others treat as their national tradition—sometimes has led to confusion in the critical discourse about journalism's overall impact upon Anglo-American literature.[13]

This situation is additionally complicated by how rarely scholars in literary studies departments in either Britain or the US actually apply the term "literary" to journalism in their academic studies and scholarly journal articles about magazines and other general circulation periodicals. William Dow has noted how seldom academic narrative theorists treat journalism as literature in the higher meaning of the term and how unusual it is to find chapters or references to literary journalism in literary anthologies or compilations of canonical texts edited by researchers in English studies departments.[14] This same phenomenon holds true in magazine research and scholarship about narrative and discursive literary journalism in both countries. An examination of Anglo-American scholarship about magazines and periodicals shows the term literary journalism appearing only occasionally, with literary studies scholars, in particular, preferring to use the term literary criticism and avoiding the label literary journalism altogether.[15] This fits with John Hartsock's observations about the "marginalization" of journalism as a traditional focus of literary scholarship and the way that literary studies scholars' views of journalism as a "sub-literary" discipline have persisted into present times.[16] It also means that the term literary journalism is much more likely to be found in journalistic publications and much less so in scholarly ones.[17]

Magazines and the Narrative, Storytelling Forms of Nonfiction

American magazines have been favorite outlets for some of the most celebrated examples of narrative nonfiction, including *In Cold Blood*, which first appeared in 1965 in the *New Yorker*, and a version of Wolfe's groundbreaking "Kandy-Kolored Tangerine-Flake Streamline Baby" (1963) in *Esquire*. Because so many of the best-known works of narrative literary journalism are now read in book form, it is sometimes forgotten how important magazines have been as incubators of new and inventive forms of creative nonfiction, not only in the 1960s and 1970s but earlier within the heritage of American literature. During the "new" journalism period of Wolfe and Capote, this can be seen in the magazines that were publishing such narrative nonfiction as Southern's "Twirling at Ole Miss" (*Esquire*, 1963); Didion's "Some Dreamers of the Golden Dream" (*Saturday Evening Post*, 1966); Herr's "Hell Sucks" (*Esquire*, 1968); Wolfe's "Radical Chic" (*New York*, 1970); Thompson's "The Kentucky Derby Is Decadent and Depraved" (*Scanlan's Monthly*, 1970); and Sheehy's "The Secret of Grey Gardens" (*New York*, 1972). Iconic books of narrative literary journalism that also appeared originally in magazines (often in compressed form) include Mailer's *The Armies of the Night* (1968) in *Harper's* and *Of a Fire on the Moon* (1969, 1970) in *Life*; Talese's *Fame and Obscurity* (1970) and Herr's *Dispatches* (1977) in *Esquire*; Thompson's *Fear and Loathing in Las Vegas* (1972) and Timothy Crouse's *The Boys on the Bus* (1973) in *Rolling Stone*; Jon Krakauer's *Into Thin Air* (1997) in *Outside*; and Susan Sheehan's *Is There No Place on Earth for Me?* (1982), Neil Sheehan's *A Bright Shining Lie* (1988), Janet Malcolm's *The Journalist and the Murderer* (1990), and Jill Lepore's *Joe Gould's Teeth* (2016) in the *New Yorker*.[18]

In similar fashion, works that are considered historical predecessors of the Wolfe-style "new" journalism published in American magazines (and thus not likely written by authors with a conscious sense that they were writing in a new genre that was not named and defined until sometime after the mid-1960s) include Twain's *Life on the Mississippi* (1883)—a portion of which was published as "Old Times on the Mississippi" (1876) in the *Atlantic*—Bierce's "What I Saw of Shiloh" (1881) in the *Wasp*; London's "The Story of an Eye-Witness" (1906) and Gellhorn's "The Third Winter" (1938) in *Collier's*; Crane's "The Open Boat" (1897) in *Scribner's Magazine*; Wright's "Joe Louis Uncovers Dynamite" (1935) in *New Masses*; and Hersey's "Hiroshima" (1946), Ross's "Picture" (1952), Liebling's "The Earl of Louisiana" (1960), Baldwin's "Letter from a Region in My Mind" (1962), and Mitchell's "Joe Gould's Secret" (1964), all in the *New Yorker*.

Magazines and the Discursive Forms of Literary Journalism

The production of literary journalism by reviewers, essayists, and critical and cultural commentators in the pages of magazines, public journals, and other periodicals exploded with the industrial expansion of modern printing and publishing technologies. This discursive type of literary journalism—much of it aimed at general audiences and appearing in publicly circulated periodicals as they grew in scope and ambition throughout the nineteenth century and beyond—has been produced by both notable and less remembered writers. The application of the term to the general activity of periodical book reviewing would encompass the work of Van Wyck Brooks, Bernard DeVoto, Gilbert Seldes, Malcolm Cowley, Maxwell Geismar, and Clifton Fadiman—all important American public critics in their day but who sometimes have been dismissed by specialist scholars for taking a biographical, impressionistic, and/or historically focused approach rather than one emphasizing theory and close textual readings.[19] However, a number of noted examples of high quality reviewing by important journalist-literary figures have been published by American general circulation magazines, including Mencken's "Ring W. Lardner" (*American Mercury*, 1924); Parker's criticism of A. A. Milne's *House at Pooh Corner*, "Far from Well," where (using her "Constant Reader" by-line) she wrote "Tonstant Weader fwowed up" (*New Yorker*, 1928); Wilson's "Hemingway: Gauge of Morale" (*Atlantic*, 1939); Lionel Trilling's "Willa Cather" (*New Republic*, 1937); Diana Trilling's "Eudora Welty's *Delta Wedding*" (*Nation*, 1946); Dwight Macdonald's "Parajournalism, or Tom Wolfe & His Magic Writing Machine" (*New York Review of Books*, 1965); and Menand's "The Norman Invasion: The Crazy Career of Norman Mailer" (*New Yorker*, 2013).

Although sometimes less recognized in this role, American magazine editors in their behind-the-scenes activities also have supported and highlighted advances in discursive prose literature. In addition to their own critical writings, Lowell and Adams have received scholarly attention as editors of the *North American Review*, along with such early nineteenth-century editors as Sarah Hale at *Ladies' Magazine* and *Godey's Lady's Book*; Charles Fenno Hoffman and Lewis Gaylord Clark at the *Knickerbocker*; Lydia Maria Child as the first editor of the *National Anti-Slavery Standard*; and Fuller and Emerson as editorial leaders of the transcendentalist magazine the *Dial*. This also has been the case during the later nineteenth and early twentieth centuries with Howells and Thomas Bailey Aldrich as editors of the *Atlantic Monthly*; Elizabeth Jordan's editorship of *Harper's Bazaar*; Pauline Hopkins's tenure as editor of the *Colored American Magazine*; Charlotte Perkins Gilman's founding editorship of *Forerunner* magazine; Du Bois's longtime editorship of the *Crisis*; Mencken and George Jean Nathan in top editorial positions at the *Smart Set* and the *American Mercury*; Harold Ross and William Shawn as editors of the *New Yorker*; John H. Johnson's lengthy regime as publisher of *Ebony* and *Jet* magazines; and Willie Morris's and Lewis H. Lapham's guiding editorial leadership of *Harper's*.[20]

If they use the term, today's scholars of literary journalism—particularly literary studies scholars in England who study discursive journalism as well as some in the US—often will apply it to both the high-profile discursive essayists who wrote before and during the Victorian period and twentieth- and twenty-first-century book reviewers whose primary concern has been cultural and intellectual discussions carried on in the literary pages of general circulation publications.[21] And yet, as the meaning of literary journalism has expanded over the decades, the British scholars Jeremy Treglown and Bridget Bennett, in *Grub Street and the Ivory Tower: Literary Journalism and Literary Scholarship from Fielding to the Internet* (1998), claim that the term has become so broad and varied in its application that it soon may have to be abandoned in the traditional sense. Especially in the US, they say, the term is often applied to any journalism thought of as having lasting value—including journalism that is discursive, but more typically narrative, in structure and contains literary features associated with the fiction-writing tradition.[22]

Magazines and Literary Journalism by Celebrated Literary Figures

A good way for journalists to make their literary mark has been to do so in the traditionally more respected fields of poetry, drama, and fiction writing—although many also continued to write journalism and nonfiction throughout their careers. The novelist Henry James, for example, is often viewed as a bridge figure between the American realist and the high modernist movements in literature—but he also dabbled in newspaper travel writing and wrote a good deal of discursive nonfiction for magazines and periodicals. Like Poe, Howells, and T. S. Eliot, James has become as prominent in certain quarters for his sophisticated critical writings as he is for his prolix, intricately constructed fiction. James wrote one of his early critical statements—"The Noble School of Fiction"—for the first issue of the *Nation* magazine in 1865, and this was followed by his best-known critical work, the "Art of Fiction," for *Longman's Magazine* in 1884, which joined many of his serialized novels (*The American, The Portrait of a Lady, The Reverberator, The Bostonians*) as contributions to general circulation magazines. Poe, Howells, and Eliot also made their living for a time as reviewers at and editors of public periodicals, even though they tended to denigrate popular journalism and hold elitist views about what was meant by quality literature. However, in the case of Poe and Howells, their positions at magazines worked in important ways to broaden their literary reach and reputations beyond their fiction—Poe as the high-profile advocate for importing the sword-clashing and invective reviewing style of such prominent British literary periodicals as *Blackwood's*, the *London Magazine, Fraser's*, and the *Edinburgh Review* to America and Howells in establishing himself in top editorial posts at the *Atlantic* and *Harper's* magazines as the "dean" of later nineteenth- and early-twentieth-century literature, which provided him a forum for promoting the careers of Twain, Adams, Crane, James, Frank Norris, and other writers with backgrounds as journalists. While also working as a reviewer at the *Times* of London, where he practiced what he called "literary journalism," Eliot became a much acclaimed poet and a vanguard figure in the modernist movement, where stylistic experiments and innovative literary themes and structures aimed at knowledgeable audiences grew to be the measure of literary excellence. In founding his own literary magazine in 1922, Eliot and his followers in literary studies departments were drawing hard lines between popular journalism in the commercial marketplace and Eliot's concept of "difficult" literature—which included, as he defined it in the *Criterion*, "minority journalism" that appealed to a small but discriminating readership.[23] Much of the mission of the *Criterion* would soon be subsumed into the content of the academic literary journals that were cropping up during the expansion of the American university system in the late nineteenth- and twentieth-centuries and moving the focus of literary criticism from commercial magazines to the academic English department, as important American literary scholars such as Tate, John Crowe Ransom, Cleanth Brooks, and R. P. Blackmur, known as the "New Critics," hoped to do.

Today there are academics who use the term literary journalism to contrast their scholarship with the work of general periodical critics. Stefan Collini has written that since the rise of modernism and the New Criticism in the early to mid-twentieth century, literary criticism has come to be at the heart of the academic study of literature. During this period, the use of the term literary journalism for writing "about" books as a synonym for literary criticism became a contested one. For many contemporary British and American literary studies scholars, Collini says, criticism "seems to change sides in any contrast between the academic and the journalistic, and 'literary criticism' then becomes counterposed to 'book reviewing.'"[24] And yet, there are still examples of high quality essay and review writing in general circulation magazines and periodicals by important journalist-literary figures that stand out for their literary qualities. Examples of these would include Norris's "Hunting Human Game" (*Wave*, 1897); Du Bois's "Again, Lincoln" (*Crisis*, 1922); Wright's "I Tried to Be a Communist" (*Atlantic Monthly*, 1944); E. B. White's "Here Is New York" (*Holiday*, 1948); Nelson

Algren's "One Man's Chicago" (*Holiday*, 1951); Susan Sontag's "Notes on 'Camp'" (*Partisan Review*, 1964); Kurt Vonnegut Jr.'s "In a Manner That Must Shame God Himself" (*Harper's*, 1972); and David Foster Wallace's "Consider the Lobster" (*Gourmet*, 2004).

The Historical Appearance of Literary Journalism within Magazines and Periodicals

It is helpful to any discussion of magazines and literature to examine the changing platforms and practices of journalists and the critical frameworks of analysis used by scholars in the study of non-fiction throughout American history.[25] In the mid-to-late-eighteenth and the early decades of the nineteenth centuries, "literature"—if the term was applied beyond the traditional genres of poetry and drama—tended to be seen as the discursive essays produced for general circulation publications of literary and political commentary. These "magazines" grew out of the early forms of newspapers, "miscellany" and "item" publications, and literary periodicals (often including in the title "museum" or "repository") of essays and commentary that developed in Britain and then spread to the American colonies. Before the Revolutionary War, American editors—often owners of print shops—were content with reprinting material from British publications as a way to satisfy the literary needs of colonial readers. For example, content from reprinted English periodicals, such as Richard Steele's *Tatler* and Steele's and Joseph Addison's *Spectator* newspapers (founded in 1709 and 1711, respectively), greatly appealed to the youthful Benjamin Franklin, who would copy them verbatim as a way of developing his literary style. As the publisher of the *General Magazine* (founded in 1741), one of the earliest magazines in America, Franklin consciously framed his format and content upon the model of the *Spectator*, as well as Edward Cave's *Gentleman's Magazine* (1731), another pioneering British periodical, which was one of the first to print literary reviews and an early writing home for the influential English essayist and critic Samuel Johnson.[26]

Some scholars prefer to call the publications that imitated Addison's and Steele's newspapers "essay" or "literary" periodicals since they were filled with short narratives (often invented), satire and caricature, commentary about manners and conduct, gossip and innuendo, political discussion, and contributions from readers more than they were "news" (the occasional compilation of trading information or ships in harbor, letters from travelers and correspondents in other countries, dated accounts of war and battlefield action, chronicles of fires, disease, executions, etc.).[27] In this respect, the modern magazine of literature and commentary became the inheritor of these sometimes ponderous, sometimes witty publications of the early-to-mid 1800s that often combined literary discourse with the material featured in popular digests such as Charles Brockden Brown's the *American Register or General Repository of History, Politics, Science*; the *Magazine of Useful and Entertaining Knowledge*, edited for a time by Nathaniel Hawthorne; and *Merry's Museum for Boys and Girls* of editor Louisa May Alcott. This published potpourri has provided historians with a variety of literary forms that have been incorporated into "magazines"—thus making them metaphorically a storehouse (the English word magazine is derived from the French term, which in turn is derived from the Arabic word for storehouse). The genre was well enough established in the early American republic that it was praised by George Washington as an "easy" vehicle of knowledge "more happily calculated than any other, to preserve the liberty, stimulate the industry and meliorate the morals of an enlightened and free people."[28]

By the twentieth century, journalism historian Frank Luther Mott defined a magazine as a "bound pamphlet issued more or less regularly … containing a variety of reading matter and … a strong connotation of entertainment."[29] However, in the context of what literary journalism has come to mean, many early American historians and literary studies scholars tended to focus on the periodicals that featured such "high letters" figures as Emerson, Holmes, Lowell, Thoreau, and Fuller. In the early stages of their development, many of these publications printed submissions anonymously or pseudonymously, as was the case with Franklin's spirited and satirical contributions to his brother's *New-England Courant* (founded in 1721)—published under the pseudonym "Silence Dogood"—that were later imitated under the monikers of Washington Irving ("Diedrich Knickerbocker"), Charles Farrar Browne ("Artemus Ward"), Sara Payson Parton ("Fanny Fern"), and Finley Peter Dunne ("Mr. Dooley") in their magazine and newspaper writings. Although lowbrow humor and slashing polemics have been a persisting feature of periodicals in the United States—particularly during the peak period of the partisan, party press era of politically subsidized publications (the 1770s to 1830s) and as regional humor columns spread in popularity—these forms of popular colloquy aimed at the populist marketplace increasingly have been distinguished from the magazines and literary reviews that have published "intelligent" reading material for a cultivated audience. In recognizing the class elements and historical connections between these aspirational publications and the higher meaning of the term literary journalism, historian John Tebbel, for example, has called the *New Yorker* a "twentieth century version of the great literary magazines of the nineteenth century."[30]

A Survey of the Magazine as a Forum for Literary Journalism in the US

A close look at the history of literary journalism finds its development deeply interwoven with the evolution of the magazine in the US. Early magazines that appealed to an informed and civic-minded audience were described by historian Harold Herd as a "new kind of periodical journalism that was to develop into the modern weekly review … a two-page, thrice-weekly paper intended to reflect in particular the more urbane outlook and interests of those who frequented coffee-houses."[31] Magazines founded before the Revolutionary War that fit this mold included, besides Franklin's *General Magazine*, Andrew Bradford's the *American Magazine*, Jeremiah Gridley's the *American Magazine and Historical Chronicle*, William Livingston's *Independent Reflector*, Isaiah Thomas's the *Royal American*, and the *Pennsylvania Magazine*, edited for a time by Thomas Paine (who it is said contributed his best "pungent, vigorous prose" when under the influence of his third glass of brandy).[32] Although often forthright about political, cultural, and social matters, these first American editors were hesitant to produce literary criticism beyond what was reprinted from British publications, with Tebbel crediting Noah Webster as the first to do anything in that direction in his own *American Magazine* (founded in 1787). While excerpts from plays, poems, and a few sentimental stories were printed, the heavily political focus of these publications founded in the eighteenth century can be recognized by the contributions from many of the country's early American political figures, such as Paine, John Jay, Alexander Hamilton, Benjamin Rush, Francis Hopkinson, and Philip Freneau.[33]

After the American break from Britain, and as the US entered the party press era, magazines appeared that were intended to give literary-oriented readers a break from the seemingly relentless polemical nature of print discourse. Joseph Dennie's *Port Folio* was published with a circle of literary friends, and—although simultaneously editing Hamilton's Federalist *Gazette of the United States* (founded in 1789)—he managed to include a good deal of literary material in its pages. During this period, Freneau, a poet as well as a partisan Democratic-Republican, became editor of the rival Jeffersonian *National Gazette* before retiring—exhausted from print wrangling—at age fifty-one to the countryside to write poetry and essays (including a poem called "On Retirement," where he embraced "a hermit's house beside a stream" and found "more real happiness … than if I were a monarch crowned").[34] Freneau and Hopkinson, another poet of the Revolutionary War period, both published poetry in Mathew Carey's the *American Museum* (founded in 1787), which in its first edition reprinted Paine's *Common Sense* (1776) and the proposed Constitution of the US—thus perhaps achieving the melding of politics and literature that solicited the tribute of Washington (who was a subscriber) to the greatness of magazines in reflecting the new nation's life.[35]

As the Industrial Age brought forth the steam-powered printing press, American magazines founded in the early decades of the nineteenth century emerged that reflected the coming era of specialization by focusing upon literary topics—along with such subjects as manners, social affairs, professional and home life, business, farming, travel, and the relationship of the sexes. What would come to be called literary journalism appeared in such publications as Brown's *American Review and Literary Journal* and his *Literary Magazine and American Register*; Irving and James Kirke Paulding's lampooning *Salmagundi* magazine and the Irving-edited *Analectic Magazine*; the *North American Review* of Nathan Hale and later edited by Lowell, Adams, and Charles Eliot Norton; the *Saturday Evening Post*, which would reach its height of influence in the twentieth century under the editorship of George Horace Lorimer; and the *Southern Literary Messenger* and *Graham's Magazine*, which helped to launch and sustain the literary career of Poe.

With the romantic movement (and the anti-romantic countermovements of American literary "realism" and "naturalism") in full swing by the mid-to-late 1800s, some of the best-known US magazines of literature and commentary were established, with many surviving to this day. These included the contemporary vestige of *Harper's Monthly*, the *Atlantic*, and *Cosmopolitan*, along with the *Nation* of E. L. Godwin and Robert La Follette's the *Progressive* of the early twentieth century. *Harper's*, the *Atlantic*, and *Cosmopolitan*—although a very different magazine from what it is today—were all edited by or employed Howells at different points in time. The *Atlantic*, which was cofounded by Emerson, Holmes, Harriet Beecher Stowe, and John Greenleaf Whittier in 1857, and first edited by Lowell, has included such diverse contributors through the years as Twain, Oates, Frederick Douglass, William Parker, Julia Ward Howe, Charles Chesnutt, Charles W. Eliot, William Allen White, Gloria Emerson, William Greider, Tracy Kidder, Bobbie Ann Mason, James Fallows, Andrew Sullivan, and Ta-Nehisi Coates. Once important literary magazines founded in the late Victorian period but that are no longer in print include *Scribner's Magazine*, which first published such literary journalism classics as Jacob Riis's "How the Other Half Lives" (1889), Wharton's "A Tuscan Shrine" (1895), Richard Harding Davis's "The Battle of San Juan Hill" (1898), and Ernest Hemingway's *Green Hills of Africa* (1935); the *Galaxy*, where Twain briefly served as editor of the humor department and which published the journalism and literature of Taylor, Rebecca Harding Davis, Walt Whitman, Bret Harte, and Joaquin Miller; *Lippincott's*, which was a publishing forum for James, Lafcadio Hearn, and Paul Laurence Dunbar; the *Century Magazine*, where the persuasive editor Richard Watson Gilder talked Twain into letting him print pre-publication excerpts of *Huckleberry Finn* (1884) and *Pudd'nhead Wilson* (1894). The now-deceased "muckraking" periodicals of reform and investigative journalism included *Collier's* (founded in 1888), which also was a serial publishing and literary journalism home for such figures as Norris, London, Lardner, Vonnegut, James Whitcomb Riley, Damon Runyon, John O'Hara, Zona Gale, Stephen Vincent Benét, Sinclair Lewis, and J. D. Salinger; and, perhaps most famously, *McClure's* (founded in 1893), with its staff of the muckrakers Dunne, Lincoln Steffens, Ida Tarbell, Ray Stannard Baker, William Allen White, and Will Irwin. *McClure's* pages also were filled with contributions from Crane, O. Henry, Joel Chandler Harris, and one-time managing editor of the magazine, Willa Cather, who served as the ghostwriter of S. S. McClure's autobiography.

Historians have blamed the demise of muckraking on a host of historical factors—not the least of which were the specialty and more entertainment-oriented magazines that crowded into the post-World War I marketplace.[36] These publishing trends also pushed existing magazines in more commercialized directions (think *Cosmopolitan*'s heritage as the publisher of David Graham Phillips's "The Treason of the Senate" [1906]—which led to President Theodore Roosevelt tagging Phillips and his fellow reform journalists with the label "muckrakers"—followed by the editorial reign of Helen Gurley Brown, who in the 1960s transformed "*Cosmo*" into a sex and fashion magazine under the ownership of the Hearst Corporation). Although many of these pre—and post-World War I magazines continued to publish literary journalism—including Lorimer's *Saturday Evening Post*, which carried journalism and literature by Hurston, Conrad Richter, John P. Marquand, and Carl Sandburg; and the humor magazines *Puck* and its competitor *Judge*, briefly edited by Harold Ross and which published Lardner, Heywood Broun, and S. J. Perelman; the mass market *Munsey's Magazine*, edited by John Kendrick Banks, which in 1929 was merged with the "pulp" magazine *Argosy*; the semi-urbane *Ainslee's* and its imitator *Esquire*—they soon had moved the magazines that sought a large, "middlebrow" audience a considerable distance from the American magazine's roots in the "high" literary periodicals of Emerson and Fuller, Lowell and William Cullen Bryant, and Adams and Norton.[37] The 1920s saw the birth of Mencken's *American Mercury* and the *New Yorker* of Ross—with Ross's publication proving to have longevity, a worshipful following of readers and a stable of notable contributors, and a reputation for such high-quality essays, reviews, and short stories that some have called it literature in and of itself.[38]

The shock and deprivation that came with the stock market crash of 1929 led to an upsurge of literary journalism in magazines and periodicals—often produced by well-known novelists and established literary figures—who felt a powerful need to explore and protest the plight of those suffering in the Great Depression. Sherwood Anderson's *Puzzled America* (1935) was a collection of magazine articles he wrote while visiting downtrodden communities and unemployed workers around the country, as were essays in Wilson's *The American Jitters* (1932), which he produced during his leave as literary editor from the *New Republic* magazine. Other radicalized literary journalists saw important works shut out from mainstream magazine publication—Agee's *Let Us Now Praise Famous Men* (1941), about the dire circumstances of sharecroppers in the South, was rejected in magazine form by Henry Luce's *Fortune*; Theodore Dreiser's *Tragic America* (1932) included a number of the left-oriented essays that he unsuccessfully tried to get published in the *American Spectator*; and John Steinbeck's newspaper journalism about the Oklahoma Dust Bowl migrant farmers in central California was turned down by a number of eastern magazine outlets. Protest literary journalists had better luck placing material in leftist, socialist, and Marxist magazines—Floyd Dell's "Were You Ever a Child?" (1918) and John Reed's "Soviet Russia Now" (1921) in Max Eastman's the *Liberator*; Parker's "Not Enough" (1939), Meridel Le Sueur's "Women on the Breadlines" (1932), and Anna Louise Strong's "Inside China" (1941) in Mike Gold and Granville Hicks's *New Masses*; Baldwin's "Everybody's Protest Novel" (1949) in Philip Rahv's *Partisan Review*, and Agnes Smedley's "How Chiang Was Captured" (1937) in Freda Kirchwey's the *Nation*. But some of these writers also paid a price during the Espionage Act trials of World War I and the anti-communist backlash of the Red Scare and the blacklisting of writers after World War II. Historians have seen literary nonfiction given a boost by these writers who, in deciding that true stories could be more powerful than fictional ones, set aside their novel writing or other literary activities to involve themselves in social justice movements and were willing to suffer for it.

By the 1940s and 1950s, the national magazines that survived the Depression rode high during the post-World War II recovery and return to "normalcy," but for a number, this prosperity was short-lived. Luce's *Life* and the Cowles family's *Look*, which printed literary journalism amid the pictorials, attained peak national circulation figures but still were headed for oblivion based upon declining advertising, the competition of television, and the explosion of specialty publications serving niche audiences. *Commentary* and the *New Republic*, *Vogue* and *Playboy*, *McCall's* and the *Ladies Home Journal*—all published through World War II or were founded soon after, and all became homes for writers who produced what has been labeled literary journalism. The magazine contributors who saw themselves as countercultural critics of the complacency of the post-World War II years and aligned themselves with the "beat," "hippy," and sexual and women's revolution movements of the 1950s, 1960s, and 1970s (Rexroth, Jack Kerouac, William S. Burroughs, Gary

Snyder, Allen Ginsberg, Charles Bukowski, Michael McClure, Gregory Corso, Thomas Pynchon, Rita Mae Brown, Vivian Gornick, Kate Millett, Adrienne Rich, Anne Waldman, Erica Jong, Ken Kesey, Tom Robbins, Richard Brautigan) wrote for a variety of social adversary and "underground" magazines. These included Paul Krassner's the *Realist*; Lawrence Ferlinghetti's *City Lights*; the *Outsider* and *Open City*, which were Bukowski publishing favorites; along with more dressed-up versions such as the *Village Voice*, with Mailer as a cofounder and columnist; Clay Felker's *New York* magazine, which was important in building the reputations of a number of literary journalists, including his wife, Gail Sheehy, as well as Nora Ephron and the movie reviewer Judith Crist; and George A. Hirsch's *New Times*, which featured the social investigative commentators and literary journalists Jack Newfield, Mike Royko, Jimmy Breslin, J. Anthony Lukas, Studs Terkel, and Nicholas von Hoffman.

As carried on from the 1960s and 1970s to today at *Harper's* and the *New Yorker*, which have published Ellison, Baldwin, Langston Hughes, Albert Murray, Maya Angelou, N. Scott Momaday, Louise Erdrich, Richard Rodriguez, Colson Whitehead, and Hilton Als, the historical role often served by magazines—as platforms for women, minority, gay, and other once marginalized writers to find expression in the practice of literary journalism—has widened considerably from the days when Du Bois and Wright debated with Mencken and Burton Rascoe about why it was so difficult to get honest writing by black authors into mainstream magazines.[39] The opportunities for gay or minority writers have expanded in recent decades with the publication of literary journalism by such figures as Elvis Mitchell, with his "Psycho Shopper" (1989) in the *Village Voice*; Amy Tan's "Mother Tongue" (1990) in the *Threepenny Review*; Edmund White's "Appropriate Stupidity" (2003) in the *Stranger*; Charles R. Johnson's "The King We Need" (2005) in *Shambhala Sun*; and Victor Villaseñor's "Rain of Gold" (2015) in *Literal Magazine*. In their role as publishers of diverse voices, these magazines, both large and small, have deviated dramatically from the eras when politics, prejudice, and audience sensitivities foreclosed the possibilities for the expression of viewpoints about race, gender, and sexual identity that ran counter to majority attitudes. However, given the risks of radical speech, many alternative and underground magazines have lived short lives, evolved into the "build-the-better-bagel" publications of chain-owned city magazines, or joined the "little" magazines that have forsaken commercialism to help maintain arts and culture discourse as a counterpoint to prevailing national viewpoints about war, economics, and the life of the less privileged.

The social and political turbulence of the 1960s and 1970s saw the rise of other countercultural magazines, with a few ceasing publication, such as Warren Hinckle and Robert Scheer's *Ramparts*, but others showing staying power—including Jann Wenner's *Rolling Stone*, Charles Peters's *Washington Monthly*, Gloria Steinem's *Ms. Magazine*, Richard Parker and Adam Hochschild's *Mother Jones*, and the conservative countervoices, William F. Buckley, Jr.'s *National Review* and R. Emmett Tyrrell Jr.'s revived *American Spectator*—that spoke with their literary journalism to the cultural and political mood that came with the Vietnam War, Watergate, and the civil rights protest years. Although the subjective form of narrative nonfiction sometimes has been called "personal" or "conversational" journalism, some of the first generation of "new" journalists who wrote in a flamboyant, freewheeling "I" voice—including Southern, Mailer, Thompson, Sheehy, and Herr—have fallen out of fashion with critics and journalists who have swung back the pendulum to more conventional modes of literary journalism expression. These initial experiments in pushing against conventional fact-fiction boundaries have precipitated professional scandals at such magazines as *New York*, the *New Republic*, and *Rolling Stone* and led to a chastening of the movement and a more tempered approach to the production of factually based literary journalism in recent decades.[40] Even so, the full spectrum of what is and has been called literary journalism is thriving in general, even while some of its historical magazine purveyors struggle economically in the digital media marketplace, and the second generation of narrative literary journalists that Robert Boynton has called the "new new" journalists (Michael Lewis, Adrian Nicole LeBlanc, Susan Orlean, Leon Dash, Jonathan Harr, etc.) has been pushed forward by an even newer generation of American literary journalists (Kathryn Schulz, Annalee Newitz, James McWilliams, John Jeremiah Sullivan, Leslie Jamison, Michelle Orange, Luke Dittrich, Robert Sanchez) and those who review them. Today, one is as likely to find high quality literary nonfiction at Longform.com or the *Atlantic*'s Conor Friedersdorf's annual blog of one hundred exceptional works of journalism or by clicking on *Slate* or *Aeon* as in the pages of the *New Yorker* or *Harper's* or *Esquire*. That is a tribute to the longevity and adaptability of George Washington's "easy" and "happily calculated" agent of knowledge and the concept of the magazine as literary journalism's vessel and catalyst.

Notes

1 McCarthy, "Sons of the Morning."
2 McCarthy.
3 Connery, "Research Review," 209–10, 213.
4 By narrative nonfiction, narrative literary journalism, or what Tom Wolfe called "new" journalism, I mean nonfictional writing that uses literary and stylistic devices often borrowed from the fictional tradition to advance a plot, tale, or account of connected events. One reason that scholars relabeled the 1960s and 1970s-style "new" journalism was that Wolfe's term was not really new. They noted that "new" journalism has an older meaning in the British and the turn-of-the-twentieth-century American journalistic tradition. The term "new" journalism in the British tradition dates back to the 1880s, when it was used by W. T. Stead for his colorful editorial strategies in the *Pall Mall Gazette* but was criticized by the poet and critic Matthew Arnold as "full of ability, novelty, variety, sensation, sympathy, generous instincts; its one great fault is that it is *feather-brained*" (Collier, *Modernism on Fleet Street*, 34). Stead's chatty, easy-to-browse journalism had some of the features of the "new" journalism of Wolfe and his 1960s American cohort; its clever use of colloquial language was designed to attract regular readers while at the same time raise the stature of journalistic narrative by incorporating storytelling techniques traditionally associated with realistic fiction. American editors of this period, such as Joseph Pulitzer, William Randolph Hearst, Charles Dana, and Frank Munsey, who also mixed high-minded motives with low market tactics, saw their sensationalistic content called "new" journalism until it was tagged with the label "yellow journalism" (described by historian Ted Curtis Smythe as "new" journalism" carried "to an extreme" [Smythe, *Gilded Age Press*, 210]), which it is better known as today. For more discussion of the historical relationship of journalism to literature and the evolution of the terms associated with it, see Underwood, *Journalism and the Novel*, 1–31; Underwood, *Undeclared War*, 1–27; Smythe, *Gilded Age Press*, 182–83, 206–07.
5 One of the difficulties in using the appellations "literary" or "literature" is that the dictionary definitions can have more than one meaning. In *Merriam Webster*, for example, the term literature is defined as simply "writing in prose or verse" but also writing that has "excellence of form or expression" and is of "permanent or universal interest." Because what has been called literary journalism can include writing of various degrees of quality and accomplishment, this sometimes has led to different interpretations of their understanding of the genre by journalists, scholars, and critics. For more discussion of this matter, see Underwood, *Undeclared War*, 68–84.
6 While American newspapers published such narrative and/or humorous literary journalism as Stephen Crane's about his shipwreck on the way to Cuba ("Stephen Crane's Own Story,"[*New York Press*]); Finley Peter Dunne's Mr. Dooley stories (*Chicago Post*), and John Steinbeck's "The Harvest Gypsies" (*San Francisco News*), as well as literary reviews and discursive essays by Margaret Fuller, Edgar Allan Poe, Washington Irving, Kate Chopin, Willa Cather, John O'Hara, T. S. Eliot, and others, most of the best-known narrative works published in newspapers by important journalist-literary figures were fictional short stories or serialized novels, often distributed by newspaper syndicates (Johanningsmeier, "Where the Masses," 113, 167; Underwood, *Undeclared War*, 113–15).
7 By discursive nonfiction or discursive journalism, I mean the use of written prose to formulate and exchange thoughts, ideas, and opinions. By expository writing, I mean the use of print language to explain abstract concepts and/or to convey information. D. G. Myers has pointed to authors, critics, and scholars from the mid-1800s as well as an unsigned 1842 editorial in the *Yale Literary Magazine* and an 1859 *Southern Literary Messenger* article (which welcomed two reviewers entering "fully upon the career

of literary journalism") who have continued to describe book reviewing and discursive essay writing in general circulation publications as literary journalism. Myers's other quoted comments about the historical use of the term include those of T. S. Eliot (who described "literary journalism" as a "precarious means of support for all but a very few"), Allen Tate (who suggested resisting "the organized literary journalism of New York"), Granville Hicks ("the responsible literary journalist must be prepared to judge a political novel on more than one level"), Christopher Lasch (who described Oswald Garrison Villard as "one of the last great eccentrics who distinguished American literary journalism"), Saul Bellow (who complained of the universities and mass media having "swallowed up literary journalism"), and Paul Auster ("I never thought of myself as a critic or literary journalist, even when I was doing a lot of critical pieces") (Myers, "Decline and Fall").

In other works found in the research for this chapter, the terms "literary journalist" and/or "literary journalism" are used to refer to discursive periodical reviewing and essay writing in the works of American literary scholars (Mulford, "Benjamin Franklin," 26–28, 34, 36, 41, 43; Menand, "Missionary"; Collier, *Modernism on Fleet Street*, 48, 58; Cady, *Howells as Critic*, 59; Graff, *Professing Literature*, 84); critics and biographers (Edmund Wilson's description of the work of Samuel Johnson, Edgar Allan Poe, H. L. Mencken, G. K. Chesterton, and Hilaire Belloc in Wilson, *Literary Essays and Reviews*, 671, 813; Meyers, *Edmund Wilson*, 76; Alter, "Revolt against Tradition"); and literary writers (Eliot's description of Charles Whidbey's "Musings without Methods" for *Blackwood's* magazine as "the best sustained piece of literary journalism" that "he knew of in recent times" [www.primidi.com/charles_whibley/later_career_as_a_writer]; Eliot's reference to "a high summer of literary journalism" [quoted in Whitworth, "Enemies of Cant," 366]; and John Updike's discussion of questions about the novel raised by "literary journalists" in Updike, *Picked-Up Pieces*, 17).

8   Wright, "Between Laughter and Tears"; Hersey, "Legend on the License"; Smiley, "Say It Ain't So, Huck."

9   Critic and literary essayist Eliot Weinberger in offering this interpretation of literary journalism said in many cultures, the term, "if it is used at all," would mean the journalism written by poets and fiction writers who have used it for income and employment. He pointed to Kenneth Rexroth and Joseph Roth as two practitioners of the form, which he says involves "free-form combinations of observation, anecdote, and rumination" (Athitakis, "NBCC Reads").

10 Claybaugh, *Novel of Purpose*, 12–14, 27, 31, 154.

11 American-born scholar John Bak refers to a "British usage of literary journalism as about literature" that differs from the contemporary American narrative tradition. While calling for an "elastic enough" definition to cover literary journalism traditions from around the globe, Bak argues that literary journalism is not a genre but a discipline and that no nation's tradition developed independently of others (Bak and Reynolds, *Literary Journalism across the Globe*, 3, 8, 18, 19n3; Keeble and Wheeler, *Journalistic Imagination*, 2–4). One can see the variations between these British and American traditions at work in the *Encyclopedia of Journalism* (2009) where British literary journalism scholar Richard Keeble in his chapter, "British Literary Journalism," defines it as the "journalism of authors, poets, and playwrights" and does not directly discuss distinctions between narrative and discursive forms (1:196), while in her chapter, "Literary Journalism," in the same publication, American journalism scholar Kathy Roberts Forde treats literary journalism as narrative journalism solely and discusses almost exclusively American writers of literary journalism in the narrative mode (3:854–58). Also see more discussion of the British way of treating literary journalism as reviews, essays, and writing about literature in Treglown and Bennett, *Grub Street*, 70, 74, 151–60, 263; Collier, *Modernism on Fleet Street*, 48, 58; and Keeble and Wheeler, *Journalistic Imagination*, 4, 6, 29–30, 34–38, 40–41.

12 A Nexus search of 630 articles (380 in US publications, 250 in British publications) for the twenty-year period from August 19, 1998, to August 19, 2018, found these results: 310 articles in US general circulation periodicals and newspapers and 54 in British ones that used the term literary journalism in its narrative, storytelling form; 196 articles in British publications and 70 in US ones using the review writing and discursive essay meaning of the term.

13 Only in recent years has there been much public discussion about these distinctions among scholars who study literary journalism within its different meanings and contexts. In 2012, Ohio State and Texas A&M English studies scholar Myers—himself also a critic for *Commentary* magazine—called for returning to the original meaning of the term. "Literary journalism is periodical writing about literature," Myers said, adding that for over a century it "meant this and only this" (Myers, "Decline and Fall"). In response, Norman Sims attributed his use of the term in its narrative form to University of Minnesota professor Edwin Ford, the author in 1937 of *A Bibliography of Literary Journalism in America*, where Ford includes examples of literary journalism by American writers of what can be classified as narrative

nonfiction but also fictional, semi-fictional, discursive, critical, and other forms of journalistically influenced writing (Ford, *Bibliography of Literary Journalism*). Myers debate about this with Sims, who in his anthologies of the 1980s and 1990s was the leading figure in relabeling Wolfe's narrative "new" journalism as literary journalism, was carried out in *Commentary* and *Critical Mass*, the blog of the board of the National Critics Circle. Mark Athitakis, "NBCC Reads: Norman Sims on Literary Journalism," *Critical Mass: The Blog of the National Book Critics Circle Board of Directors*, June 8, 2012, http://bookcritics.org/blog/archive/nbcc-reads-a-last-word-on-literary-journalism-from-norman-sims; Athitakis, "NBCC Reads: Cultural Views." See also Norman Sims, ed., *The Literary Journalists* (New York: Ballantine, 1984); Norman Sims, ed., *Literary Journalism in the Twentieth Century* (New York: Oxford University Press, 1990); Norman Sims and Mark Kramer, eds., *Literary Journalism: A New Collection of the Best American Nonfiction* (New York: Ballantine, 1995); Sims, *True Stories*; Myers, "Decline and Fall."

14 Dow, "Reading Otherwise."

15 A search of indexes of some of these major critical and scholarly works about American magazine journalism contained no mention of the term literary journalism by the following American scholars: Mott, *History of American Magazines*, 5 vols.; James Playsted Wood, *Magazines in the United States* (1949; repr., New York: Ronald Press, 1971); Theodore Peterson, *Magazines in the Twentieth Century* (Urbana, IL: University of Illinois Press, 1964); Lyon N. Richardson, *A History of Early American Magazines, 1741–1789* (New York: Octagon Books, 1966); James L. C. Ford, *Magazines for the Millions: The Story of Specialized Publications* (Carbondale, IL: Southern Illinois University Press, 1969); Neal L. Edgar, *A History and Bibliography of American Magazines* (Metuchen, NJ: Scarecrow Press, 1975); Elliott Anderson and Mary Kinzie, eds., *The Little Magazine in America: A Modern Documentary History* (New York: Pushcart Press, 1978); William H. Taft, *American Magazines for the 1980s* (New York: Hastings, 1982); Edward E. Chielens, *American Literary Magazines: The Eighteenth and Nineteenth Centuries* (New York: Greenwood Press, 1986); Edward E. Chielens, *American Literary Magazines: The Twentieth Century* (New York: Greenwood Press, 1986); Sam G. Riley, *Magazines of the American South* (New York: Greenwood Press, 1986); David E. E. Sloane, *American Humor Magazines and Comic Periodicals* (New York: Greenwood Press, 1987); Nancy K. Humphreys, *American Women's Magazines: An Annotated Historical Guide* (New York: Garland, 1989); Alan Nourie and Barbara Nourie, eds., *American Mass-Market Magazines* (New York: Greenwood Press, 1990); Matthew Schneirov, *The Dream of a New Social Order: Popular Magazines in America, 1893–1914* (New York: Columbia University Press, 1994); Kathleen L. Endres and Therese L. Lueck, eds., *Women's Periodicals in the United States: Consumer Magazines* (Westport, CT: Greenwood Press, 1995); Mary Ellen Zuckerman, *A History of Popular Women's Magazines in the United States, 1792–1995* (Westport, CT: Greenwood Press, 1998); Nancy A. Walker, *Women's Magazines, 1940–1960: Gender Roles and the Popular Press* (Boston, MA: Bedford/St. Martin's, 1998); Nancy A. Walker, *Shaping Our Mothers' World: American Women's Magazines* (Jackson, MS: University Press of Mississippi, 2000); Tom Pendergast, *Creating the Modern Man: American Magazines and Consumer Culture* (Columbia, MO: University of Missouri Press, 2000); Amy Aronson, *Taking Liberties: Early American Women's Magazines and Their Readers* (Westport, CT: Praeger, 2002); Carolyn Kitch, *Pages from the Past: History and Memory in American Magazines* (Chapel Hill, NC: University of North Carolina Press, 2005); Robert Scholes and Clifford Wulfman, *Modernism in the Magazines: An Introduction* (New Haven, CT: Yale University Press, 2010); David E. Sumner, *The Magazine Century: American Magazines Since 1900* (New York: Peter Lang, 2010); Gardner, *Early American Magazine Culture*; Heather A. Haveman, *Magazines and the Making of America: Modernization, Community, and Print Culture, 1741–1860* (Princeton, NJ: Princeton University Press, 2015); Ian Morris and Joanne Diaz, eds., *The Little Magazine in Contemporary America* (Chicago: University of Chicago Press, 2015); Eric Bulson, *Little Magazine, World Form* (New York: Columbia University Press, 2017). The non-use of the term literary journalism also held true for these works discussing magazines by British literature-oriented scholars and researchers: Cynthia L. White, *Women's Magazines, 1693–1968* (London: Michael Joseph, 1970); Brian Braithwaite and Joan Barrell, *The Business of Women's Magazines* (London: Associated Business Press, 1979); Jeremy Tunstall, *The Media in Britain* (New York: Columbia University Press, 1983); Dominic Strinati and Stephen Wagg, eds., *Come on Down? Popular Media Culture in Post-War Britain* (London: Routledge, 1992); Brian Braithwaite, *Women's Magazines: The First 300 Years* (London: Peter Owen, 1995); David Reed, *The Popular Magazine in Britain and the United States, 1880–1960* (London: British Library, 1997); Anna Gough-Yates, *Understanding Women's Magazines: Publishing, Markets and Readerships* (London: Routledge, 2003); Faith Binckes, *Modernism, Magazines, and the British Avant-Garde* (Oxford: Oxford University Press, 2010); Martin Conboy, *Journalism in Britain: A Historical Introduction* (London: SAGE, 2011); Howard Cox and Simon Mowatt, *Revolutions from Grub Street: A History of Magazine Publishing in Britain* (Oxford: Oxford University Press, 2014). Magazine and periodical scholars in the

United Kingdom who use the term literary journalism for book reviewing and discursive writing include Jason Harding, "The Idea of a Literary Review: T. S. Eliot and *The Criterion*," in *Oxford Critical and Cultural History*, ed. Brooker and Thacker, 347; Sean Matthews, "'Say Not the Struggle Naught Availeth …': *Scrutiny* (1932–53)," in ibid., 847; David Finkelstein, "Literature, Propaganda, and the First World War: The Case of *Blackwood's Magazine*," in *Grub Street*, ed. Treglown and Bennett, 91–92, 106, 111; and Daly, "William Hazlitt," 29–30, 34, 36–38, 40–41.

16 Hartsock, "Critical Marginalization"; Hartsock, *History*, 6.

17 Examples of the use of the term literary journalism abound in contemporary American newspapers and journalistic and literary periodicals as it is applied to discursive essay writing and reviewing. For example, *Washington Post* critic and reviewer Michael Dirda discusses literary journalism in its discursive form on multiple occasions, including in referring to T. S. Eliot's literary journalism in the *Washington Post* of July 2, 2000, and the literary journalism of Clifton Fadiman, W. H. Auden, and Henry James (*Washington Post*, November 1, 2007). Louis Menand in the *New Yorker* and James Wood, the British-born critic of the *New Republic* and the *New York Times*, call Edmund Wilson a literary journalist (*New Yorker*, August 8, 2005; *New Republic*, September 26, 2005). In addition, the following figures are referred to as practitioners of discursive literary journalism in American publications: Daniel Defoe (*Publishers Weekly Review*, July 14, 2014); William Hazlitt (*New York Times*, May 18, 2009); Leigh Hunt (*Weekly Standard*, October 19, 2009); Thomas Hardy (*New Republic*, February 26, 2007); V. S. Pritchett (*New York Times*, January 12, 2005); Irving Howe (*New Yorker*, May 8, 2000); Frank Kermode (*Slate*, August 26, 2010); John Updike (*Weekly Standard*, July 2, 2001); Joyce Carol Oates (*Kirkus Reviews*, December, 2004); Giles Foden (*Washington Post*, July, 2, 2000); and Walter Kirn (*New York Times*, October 16, 2005). In publications of the British Isles, these journalist-literary figures are called writers of discursive literary journalism: William Hazlitt (*Independent*, October 17, 2008); Charles Dickens (*Glasgow Herald*, October 3, 2009); Wilkie Collins (*Prospect*, February 23, 2012); Virginia Woolf (*Evening Standard*, March 31, 2011); George Orwell (*Irish Times*, June 7, 2003); Anthony Powell (*Irish Times*, April 1, 2000); Craig Raine (*Guardian*, October 17, 2009); and Salman Rushdie (*Guardian*, November 23, 2002).

18 Wolfe, "Birth," 1–11. See also Underwood, *Journalism and the Novel*, 155, 236n5; Underwood, *Undeclared War*, 7–8, 13–14, 30–31, 33, 36–37, 45–46, 60.

19 For example, in articles from the *New York Times*'s archives, these critics' own critics refer to them as a synthesizer and old-fashioned (Brooks), too opinionated and invective in style (DeVoto), a defender of popular entertainment and an opponent of "arty" works (Seldes), a taste-maker and cross-pollinator (Cowley), a popularizer and anthologist (Fadiman), and a historian (Geismar). William H. Prichard, "Not to Write Was Not to Be Alive," *New York Times* archives, November 1, 1981 (Brooks); Malcolm Cowley, "The Uneasy Chair," *New York Times* archives, February 10, 1974 (DeVoto); Dwight Garner, "In Letters, a Literary Force Lets Readers In," *New York Times* archives, February 11, 2014, and Christopher Benfey, "Malcolm Cowley Was One of the Best Literary Tastemakers of the Twentieth Century," *New Republic*, March 1, 2014 (Cowley); and Leon Edel (September 27, 1953), Benjamin DeMott (November 8, 1970), C. Gerald Fraser (July 25, 1979), and Richard Severo (June 20, 1999) in articles in the *New York Times* archives (Geismar and Fadiman).

20 Examples of this scholarly, critical, and biographical attention include Henry Adams, *Sketches for the North American Review*, ed. Edward Chalfant (Hamden, CT: Archon, 1986); Joseph Michael Sommers, "*Godey's Lady's Book*: Sarah Hale and the Construction of Sentimental Nationalism," *College Literature* 37, no. 3 (Summer 2010): 43–61; George William Curtis, "The Shrouded Portrait," in *The Knickerbocker Gallery: A Testimonial to the Editor of "The Knickerbocker" Magazine [i.e. Lewis Gaylord Clark]* (1855; repr., https://searchworks.stanford.edu/view/8417255); Kent P. Ljungquist, ed., *Antebellum Writers in New-York, Second Series*, vol. 250 of *Dictionary of Literary Biography* (Detroit, MI: Gale, 2002); Anne Righton Malone, "Sugar Ladles and Strainers: Political Self-Fashioning in the Epistolary Journalism of Lydia Maria Child," in *Women's Life-Writing: Finding Voice/Building Community*, ed. Linda S. Coleman (Bowling Green, OH: Popular Press, 1997), 239–56; David M. Robinson, "The Movement's Medium: Fuller, Emerson, and the *Dial*," *Revue française d'études américaines* 140 (2014): 24–36; Ellery Sedgwick, *A History of the "Atlantic Monthly," 1857–1909: Yankee Humanism at High Tide and Ebb* (Amherst: University of Massachusetts Press, 1994); Karen Roggenkamp, "Elizabeth Jordan, 'True Stories of the News,' and Newspaper Fiction in Late-Nineteenth-Century Journalism," in *Literature and Journalism*, ed. Canada, 119–41; Yu-Fang Cho, "Cultural Nationalism, Orientalism, Imperial Ambivalence: The *Colored American Magazine* and Pauline Elizabeth Hopkins," *Journal of Transnational American Studies* 3, no. 2 (2011), https://cloudfront.escholarship.org/dist/prd/content/qt6x5280hq/qt6x5280hq.pdf; Ann Heilmann, *Feminist Forerunners: New Womanism and Feminism in the Early Twentieth Century* (Chicago:

Pandora, 2003); Amy Helene Kirschke and Phillip Luke Sinitiere, eds., *Protest and Propaganda: W. E. B. Du Bois, the "Crisis," and American History* (Columbia, MO: University of Missouri Press, 2014); Alfred A. Knopf, "H. L. Mencken, George Jean Nathan and the *American Mercury* Venture," *Menckeniana* 78 (Summer 1981): 1–10; Thomas Kunkel, *Genius in Disguise: Harold Ross of "The New Yorker"* (New York: Carroll and Graf, 1996); Ved Mehta, *Remembering Mr. Shawn's "New Yorker": The Invisible Art of Editing* (Woodstock, NY: Overlook Press, 1998); Jason Chambers, "Presenting the Black Middle Class: John H. Johnson and *Ebony* Magazine, 1945–1975," in *Historicizing Lifestyle: Mediating Taste, Consumption and Identity from the 1900s to 1970s*, ed. David Bell and Joanne Hollows (Burlington, VT: Ashgate, 2012); Berkley Hudson and Rebecca Townsend, "Unraveling the Webs of Intimacy and Influence: Willie Morris and *Harper's* Magazine, 1967–1971," *Literary Journalism Studies* 1, no. 2 (Fall 2009): 63–78.

21 Some examples of the use of the term literary journalism for discursive writing and literary reviewing among British scholars can be found in such works as and/or essays in Treglown and Bennett, *Grub Street*; Italia, *Rise of Literary Journalism*; Daly, "William Hazlitt"; Collini, "Trilling's Sandbags"; and Miller, *Dark Horses*. Similar usages among American scholars of discursive literary journalism can be found in Mulford, "Benjamin Franklin"; Menand, "Missionary"; Collier, *Modernism on Fleet Street*; and Graff, *Professing Literature*. There also are American scholars who discuss literary journalism in both its narrative and discursive forms (Forde, *Literary Journalism on Trial*, 8, 40; O'Brien, *Selected Literary Journalism*; and Hartsock, *History*, 9–11, 113–14, 136–38).

22 Treglown and Bennett, *Grub Street*, ix.

23 See Collier, *Modernism on Fleet Street*, 48, 55, 58, 68–69; White, "Literary Journalism"; Myers, "Decline and Fall."

24 Collini, "Critic as Journalist," 152–53.

25 Maguire, "Literary Journalism."

26 Gardner, *Early American Magazine Culture*, 38, 48, 57–58; Holmes and Nice, *Magazine Journalism*, 3, 8–9; Underwood, *Journalism and the Novel*, 35.

27 Allen, *Addison and Steele*, v–vii, x, xii–xiii, xv; Spector, *English Literary Periodicals*, 249; McCrea, *Addison and Steele*, 11–12, 14; Roberts, "Literary Journalism." Roberts says Addison and Steele developed the "informative or persuasive essay as a major form" and encouraged Benjamin Franklin and others to "craft journalism that was factual, interesting, and written with literary panache" ("Literary Journalism," 270).

28 Tebbel, *American Magazine*, 1.

29 Mott, *A History of American Magazines, 1741–1850*, 7.

30 Tebbel, *American Magazine*, 235; Altick, *Victorian People and Ideas*, 67–68.

31 Herd, *March of Journalism*, 52–53.

32 Tebbel, *American Magazine*, 12.

33 Tebbel, 6–12; Gardner, *Early American Magazine Culture*, 47.

34 Freneau, "On Retirement."

35 Tebbel, *American Magazine*, 10, 17.

36 See Wilson, "Circulation and Survival"; Wilson, *McClure's Magazine*; Filler, "Muckrakers and Middle America," 35.

37 Abrahamson, *Magazine-Made America*, 16, 19, 25.

38 Kathy Roberts Forde describes the *New Yorker* as long having "a reputation as a stronghold of literary journalism in American culture" and quotes the critic Edmund Wilson as praising the magazine as "elegant and literate" (*Literary Journalism on Trial*, 9–10, 40–41). The *New Yorker* also has been called "the most desirable literary magazine in the world" (Cameron, "*New Yorker* Rejects Itself") and "the gatekeeper for literature" (Carr and Kirkpatrick, "Gatekeeper for Literature"), as well as a "totem for the educated American" and a repository for high standards of "English prose, taste, conscience, and civility" (Yagoda, *About Town*, 24).

39 Wright, *Richard Wright Reader*, 55; Du Bois, *W. E. B. Du Bois*, 519.

40 Three of the most highly publicized controversies involving factual inaccuracies, the questionable use of reporting methodology, and the blurring of fact-fiction boundaries occurred with articles that were offered as narrative literary journalism at these three magazines. These included Gail Sheehy's presentation of a composite portrait of a street hooker in a 1971 story in *New York*; a series of falsely constructed stories by Stephen Glass in the *New Republic* in the 1990s; and a narrative investigation of an alleged rape on a college campus that turned out to have relied on problematic sources and reporting techniques by *Rolling Stone* in 2014 (Weingarten, *Gang*, 273–76; Hiltzik, "Stephen Glass"; Somaiya, "Rolling Stone Article").

Bibliography

Abrahamson, David, ed. *The American Magazine: Research Perspectives and Prospects*. Ames, IA: Iowa State University Press, 1995.

———. *Magazine-Made America: The Cultural Transformation of the Postwar Periodical*. Cresskill, NJ: Hampton Press, 1996.

Abrahamson, David, and Marcia R. Prior-Miller, eds. *The Routledge Handbook of Magazine Research: The Future of the Magazine Form*. New York: Routledge, 2015.

Allen, Robert J., ed. *Addison and Steele: Selections from "The Tatler" and "The Spectator."* 1957. Reprint, New York: Holt, Rinehart, and Winston, 1970.

Alter, Robert. "The Revolt against Tradition: Readers, Writers, and Critics." *Partisan Review* 58, no. 2 (Spring 1991): 282–94.

Altick, Richard. *Victorian People and Ideas*. London: J. M. Dent, 1974.

Athitakis, Mark. "NBCC Reads: Cultural Views on Literary Journalism." *Critical Mass* (blog), June 7, 2012. http://bookcritics.org/blog/archive/nbcc-reads-critical-views-on-literary-journalism.

Bak, John S., and Bill Reynolds, eds. *Literary Journalism across the Globe: Journalistic Traditions and Transnational Influences*. Amherst, MA: University of Massachusetts Press, 2011.

Brooker, Peter, and Andrew Thacker, eds. *The Oxford Critical and Cultural History of Modernist Magazines*. Vol. 1, *Britain and Ireland, 1880–1955*. Oxford: Oxford University Press, 2009.

Cady, Edwin H., ed. *W. D. Howells as Critic*. London: Routledge, 1973.

Cameron, David. "The *New Yorker* Rejects Itself: A Quasi-Scientific Analysis of Slush Piles." Review Review. www.thereviewreview.net/publishing-tips/new-yorker-rejects-itself-quasi-scientific-a.

Canada, Mark, ed. *Literature and Journalism: Inspirations, Intersections, and Inventions from Ben Franklin to Stephen Colbert*. New York: Palgrave Macmillan, 2013.

Carr, David, and David D. Kirkpatrick. "The Gatekeeper for Literature Is Changing at New Yorker." *New York Times*, October 21, 2002. www.nytimes.com/2002/10/21/business/the-gatekeeper-for-literature-is-changing-at-new-yorker.html.

Claybaugh, Amanda. *The Novel of Purpose: Literature and Social Reform in the Anglo-American World*. Ithaca, NY: Cornell University Press, 2007.

Collier, Patrick. *Modernism on Fleet Street*. Aldershot, UK: Ashgate, 2006.

Collini, Stefan. "The Critic as Journalist: Leavis after *Scrutiny*." In Treglown and Bennett, *Grub Street*, 151–76.

———. "Trilling's Sandbags: Lionel Trilling's Critical Essays." *Nation*, December 3, 2008. www.thenation.com/article/trillings-sandbags-lionel-trillings-critical-essays/.

Connery, Thomas. "Research Review: Magazines and Literary Journalism, an Embarrassment of Riches." In Abrahamson, *American Magazine*, 207–16.

Daly, Kirsten. "William Hazlitt: Poetry, Drama and Literary Journalism." In Keeble and Wheeler, *Journalistic Imagination*, 29–43.

Dow, William. "Reading Otherwise: Literary Journalism as an Aesthetic Narrative Cosmopolitanism." *Literary Journalism Studies* 8, no. 2 (Fall 2016): 119–36.

Du Bois, W. E. B. *W. E. B. Du Bois: A Reader*. Edited by David Levering Lewis. New York: Henry Holt, 1995.

Filler, Louis. "The Muckrakers and Middle America." In *Muckraking: Past, Present, and Future*, edited by John M. Harrison and Harry H. Stein, 25–41. University Park, PA: Pennsylvania State University Press, 1973.

Ford, Edwin. *A Bibliography of Literary Journalism in America*. Minneapolis, MN: Burgess, 1937.

Forde, Kathy Roberts. "Literary Journalism." In *Encyclopedia of Journalism*, vol. 3, edited by Christopher H. Sterling, 854–58. Los Angeles, CA: SAGE, 2009.

———. *Literary Journalism on Trial: "Masson v. New Yorker" and the First Amendment*. Amherst: University of Massachusetts Press, 2008.

Freneau, Philip. "On Retirement." http://famouspoetsandpoems.com/poets/philip_freneau/poems/15615.

Gardner, Jared. *The Rise and Fall of Early American Magazine Culture*. Urbana, IL: University of Illinois Press, 2012.

Graff, Gerald. *Professing Literature: An Institutional History*. Chicago: University of Chicago Press, 1987.

Hartsock, John C. "The Critical Marginalization of American Literary Journalism." *Critical Studies in Media Communication* 15, no. 1 (1998): 61–84. https://doi.org/10.1080/15295039809367033.

———. *A History of American Literary Journalism: The Emergence of a Modern Narrative Form*. Amherst, MA: University of Massachusetts Press, 2000.

Herd, Harold. *The March of Journalism: The Story of the British Press from 1622 to the Present Day*. London: Allen and Unwin, 1952.

Hersey, John. "The Legend on the License." *Yale Review* 70 (Winter 1980): 1–25.
Hiltzik, Michael. "Stephen Glass Is Still Retracting His Fabricated Stories—18 Years Later." *Los Angeles Times*, December 15, 2015. www.latimes.com/business/hiltzik/la-fi-mh-stephen-glass-is-still-retracting-20151215-column.html.
Holmes, Tim, and Liz Nice. *Magazine Journalism*. Thousand Oaks, CA: SAGE, 2012.
Italia, Iona. *The Rise of Literary Journalism in the Eighteenth Century: Anxious Employment*. London: Routledge, 2005.
Johanningsmeier, Charles. "Where the Masses Met the Classes: Nineteenth- and Early-Twentieth-Century American Newspapers and Their Significance to Literary Scholars." In Canada, *Literature and Journalism*, 143–67.
Keeble, Richard Lance. "British Literary Journalism." In *Encyclopedia of Journalism*, vol. 1, edited by Christopher H. Sterling, 196–99. Los Angeles: SAGE, 2009.
Keeble, Richard, and Sharon Wheeler, eds. *The Journalistic Imagination: Literary Journalists from Defoe to Capote and Carter*. London: Routledge, 2007.
Maguire, Miles. "Literary Journalism: Journalism Aspiring to Be Literature." In *The Routledge Handbook of Magazine Research: The Future of the Magazine Form*, edited by David Abrahamson and Marcia R. Prior-Miller, 362–74. New York: Routledge, 2015.
McCarthy, Mary. "Sons of the Morning." Review of *The Best and the Brightest*, by David Halberstam. *New York Review of Books*, January 25, 1973. www.nybooks.com/articles/1973/01/25/sons-of-the-morning/.
McCrea, Brian. *Addison and Steele Are Dead: The English Department, Its Canon, and the Professionalization of Literary Criticism*. Newark, DE: University of Delaware Press, 1990.
Menand, Louis. "Missionary: Edmund Wilson and American Culture." *New Yorker*, August 8, 2005.
Meyers, Jeffrey. *Edmund Wilson: A Biography*. Boston, MA: Houghton Mifflin, 1995.
Miller, Karl. *Dark Horses: An Experience of Literary Journalism*. London: Picador, 1998.
Mott, Frank Luther. *A History of American Magazines*. 5 vols. Cambridge, MA: Belknap, 1968.
———. *A History of American Magazines, 1741–1850*. Cambridge, MA: Harvard University Press, 1930.
Mulford, Carla. "Benjamin Franklin, Literary Journalism, and Finding a National Subject." In Canada, *Literature and Journalism*, 25–46.
Myers, D. G. "The Decline and Fall of Literary Journalism." *Commentary*, June 8, 2012. www.commentarymagazine.com/2012/06/08/literary-journalism-then-now.
O'Brien, Fitz-James. *Selected Literary Journalism, 1852–1860*. Edited by Wayne R. Kime. Selinsgrove, PA: Susquehanna University Press, 2003.
Roberts, Nancy L. "Literary Journalism." In *Encyclopedia of American Journalism*, edited by Stephen L. Vaughn, 270–72. New York: Routledge, 2008.
Sims, Norman. *True Stories: A Century of Literary Journalism*. Evanston, IL: Northwestern University Press, 2007.
Smiley, Jane. "Say It Ain't So, Huck." *Harper's Magazine*, January 1996.
Smythe, Ted Curtis. *The Gilded Age Press, 1865–1900*. Westport, CT: Prager, 2003.
Somaiya, Ravi. "Rolling Stone Article on Rape at University of Virginia Failed All Basics, Report Says." *New York Times*, April 5, 2015. www.nytimes.com/2015/04/06/business/media/rolling-stone-retracts-article-on-rape-at-university-of-virginia.html.
Spector, Robert Donald. *English Literary Periodicals and the Climate of Opinion during the Seven Years' War*. The Hague: Mouton, 1966.
Sterling, Christopher H., ed. *Encyclopedia of Journalism*. Los Angeles: SAGE, 2009.
Tebbel, John. *The American Magazine: A Compact History*. New York: Hawthorn, 1969.
Treglown, Jeremy, and Bridget Bennett, eds. *Grub Street and the Ivory Tower: Literary Journalism and Literary Scholarship from Fielding to the Internet*. Oxford: Clarendon Press, 1998.
Underwood, Doug. *Journalism and the Novel: Truth and Fiction, 1700–2000*. Cambridge: Cambridge University Press, 2008.
———. *The Undeclared War between Journalism and Fiction: Journalists as Genre Benders in Literary History*. New York: Palgrave Macmillan, 2013.
Updike, John. *Picked-Up Pieces*. New York: Alfred A. Knopf, 1975.
Weingarten, Marc. *The Gang That Wouldn't Write Straight: Wolfe, Thompson, Didion, and the New Journalism Revolution*. New York: Crown, 2006.
White, Peter. "Literary Journalism." In *T. S. Eliot in Context*, edited by Jason Harding, 93–104. Cambridge: Cambridge University Press, 2011.
Whitworth, Michael H. "Enemies of Cant: *The Athenaeum* (1919–21) and *The Adelphi* (1923–48)." In Brooker and Thacker, *Oxford Critical and Cultural History*, 364–88.

Wilson, Edmund. *Literary Essays and Reviews of the 1930s and 40s*. New York: Library of America, 2007.
Wilson, Harold S. "Circulation and Survival: *McClure's Magazine* and the Strange Death of Muckraking Journalism." *Western Illinois Regional Studies* 11, no. 1 (1988): 71–81.
———. *"McClure's Magazine" and the Muckrakers*. 1970. Reprint, Princeton, NJ: Princeton University Press, 2015.
Wolfe, Tom. "The Birth of 'The New Journalism.'" *New York*, February 14, 1972. http://nymag.com/news/media/47353/.
Wright, Richard. "Between Laughter and Tears." Review of *Their Eyes Were Watching God*, by Zora Neale Hurston. *New Masses*, October 5, 1937.
———. *Richard Wright Reader*. Edited by Ellen Wright and Michael Fabre. New York: Harper and Row, 1978.
Yagoda, Ben. *About Town: The "New Yorker" and the World It Made*. New York: Scribner, 2000.

19
LITERARY JOURNALISM'S HISTORICAL LINEAGE
In Defense of Mencken

Stacy Spaulding

As the history of American literary journalism has taken shape over the last half century, Lincoln Steffens's tenure at the *Commercial Advertiser* has emerged as a fulcrum in the development of modern narrative nonfiction. In 1897 Steffens became city editor of what was then New York's oldest newspaper; though with a circulation of only 2,500, it was a "wreck" with "no influence."[1] Steffens championed an innovative, literary newsroom that soon discovered that "a newspaper can be saved—to sell again."[2]

Steffens wrote in his autobiography that he desired to achieve "the true ideal for an artist and for a newspaper: to get the news so completely and to report it so humanly that the reader will see himself in the other fellow's place."[3] He preferred hiring Harvard graduates who saw journalism as a brief interlude in a writing career—a way to gather short story and novel material.[4] Steffens set no style rules or news beats for his writers,[5] instead making general assignments on abstract topics such as "How Grief Is Expressed" or inviting reporters to "look for one instance of gayety in New York," promising "to report it in the paper as conspicuously as a murder."[6] Steffens did not expect his reporters to get the news first—the Associated Press took care of that. Instead, he demanded that writers "beat the other papers only in the way they presented the news."[7] The goal was to make a newspaper with "literary charm as well as daily information, mood as well as sense, gayety as well as seriousness."[8]

To the contemporary ear, such literary experiments may sound like a forerunner of magazines such as the *New Yorker*. Indeed, the *Commercial Advertiser* is often cited as a notable development in the history of modern literary journalism. But it is an unsatisfying one. Steffens's experiment lasted only two years. His literary approach to news "was not generally accepted even in [his] own office."[9] And once the paper was profitable, owners and managers grew conservative, according to one Steffens biographer: "Now that the paper was finally turning a profit they were no longer interested in supporting a city room conducted as a literary experiment and a writer's conference."[10] On the verge of a nervous breakdown,[11] Steffens moved on to *McClure's Magazine*, where he became a key figure among Progressive Era muckrakers.

Nevertheless, the *Commercial Advertiser*'s literary experiments rank highly in historical accounts of literary journalism. Only recently has the history of this marginalized and underexplored genre been recovered and positioned within the context of American philosophical and literary movements, thanks to the work of scholars such as John C. Hartsock and Thomas B. Connery, among others.[12]

Yet this critical reinvigoration also casts doubts on the scope and impact of Steffens's approach. Connery has written that the genre's earliest works "may not suggest a direct influence on future literary journalists,"[13] and John J. Pauly has suggested that New Journalism and "the entire history of literary nonfiction ... to some degree" has been primarily a "New York phenomenon."[14]

Guided by Pauly's argument that literary journalism is not only an aesthetic discourse but also a social discourse in which "writers finesse their relationships with the marketplace, sources, and readers,"[15] this chapter examines the commercial influences upon literary journalism at the turn of the century. Rather than focusing on its literary developments, might tracing the genre's commercial trail through the marketplace provide a more satisfying link between the modern emergence of the form and literary journalism today? The resulting chapter is neither comprehensive nor exhaustive. Yet it highlights two areas deserving of further investigation: the content strategies deployed by evening newspapers during the turn-of-the-century newspaper boom and the editorial influence of H. L. Mencken.[16]

From the Penny Press to a Clash of Paradigms

The direct antecedents to the modern American form are most clearly visible in the development of the Penny Press during the nineteenth century, "the papers to which modern journalism clearly traces its roots."[17] As early as the 1830s, editors such as Horace Greeley of the *New-York Tribune*, James Gordon Bennett of the *New York Herald*, and Benjamin Day of the *New York Sun* pioneered a "commercial revolution,"[18] shunning political affiliation and subsidies in favor of a market-based income from circulation and advertising. These editors pioneered smaller, cheaper newspapers and a "fresh and vigorous"[19] concept of news. This included paying reporters to search for human-interest stories, the "most characteristic feature" of the Penny Press.[20]

The human-interest story was particularly identified with Charles A. Dana, who became editor and part owner of the *New York Sun* in 1868. By "the prime years of the Dana period"[21] in the 1870s and 1880s, the *Sun* came to be known as "the newspaperman's newspaper"[22] for its fresh approach to capturing city life:

> Human interest! It is an old phrase now, and one likely to cause lips to curl along Park Row. But the art of picking out the happenings of every-day [sic] life that would appeal to every reader, if so depicted that the events lived before the reader's eye, was an art that did not exist until Dana came along. Ben Day knew the importance of the trifles of life and the hold they took on the people who read his little *Sun*, but it remained for Dana to bring out in journalism the literary quality that made the trifle live. Whether it was an item of three lines or an article of three columns, it must have life, or it had no place in the *Sun*.[23]

Though Dana built a reputation on these techniques, he was by no means the only editor to exploit them. The press of this era—the Civil War through the 1890s—is regarded today as the "the first period of *modern* narrative literary journalism in the United States."[24] Newspapers were generally open to publishing narrative, with "sufficient evidence that the practice of a narrative literary journalism by professional journalists was more extensive than has been accounted for."[25]

By the 1890s, Steffens's narrative experiments at the *Commercial Advertiser* constituted one of three models battling for dominance of the New York newspaper market, according to W. Joseph Campbell. In *The Year That Defined American Journalism* (2006), Campbell argues that three paradigms clashed in 1897: the "journalism of action,"[26] known popularly as yellow journalism and identified most visibly with William Randolph Hearst's *New York Journal* and Joseph Pulitzer's *New York World*; the more objective, detached model of Adolph S. Ochs and the *New York Times*; and the narrative model developed by Lincoln Steffens at the *Commercial*

Advertiser. Though he judged it to be an "idiosyncratic"[27] and "off-beat experiment [that] produced curious if uneven results,"[28] Campbell's work is notable for elevating Steffens's "eccentric"[29] approach to the level of paradigm, an "anti-journalistic"[30] alternative to the yellow press. Such positioning harmonizes with the work of literary journalism scholars who have explored Steffens's literary approach as a response to an "epistemological crisis"[31] caused by the clash of yellow journalism and objectivity. Campbell's work also opens up a new vein for literary journalism historians to explore: In an era that reframed newspapers "as a business rather than a political tool,"[32] Steffens's narrative model was a response to a dramatic marketplace shift and a mass commercialization of news.

Steffens was cognizant of, but not quite comfortable with, the transformation he saw occurring around him. In an 1897 *Scribner's* article, he described the work of the "commercial journalists"[33] whose goal was to provide readers with sensational reading in order to increase circulation and advertising. "The new journalism," Steffens concluded, "is the result of a strictly commercial exploitation of a market,"[34] a trend that editors "deplored" and business managers "rejoiced at."[35] Yet privately, in letters to his father, Steffens was an eager student of business matters who hoped to demonstrate that he was "not so incompetent as you think in a business way."[36] His ambivalent feelings are visible in his autobiography. He clearly saw—and exploited—the link between good copy and increased circulation. Local controversies, he wrote, meant "good journalism and good business,"[37] and coverage of big stories such as the Spanish–American War, the Boer Wars, and Tammany Hall increased sales.[38] But he also claimed an editorial ignorance of newspaper operations: "There were other departments ... but we rarely noticed them and nobody asked us to. Even the business office did not bother us much."[39]

Of the three "new journalism" paradigms observable in the 1897 landscape of New York journalism, Steffens's model saw some commercial success. But it was also the first to wither away, introducing doubt of its long-term influence upon successive narrative efforts.

An Alternate Lineage?

Two years after that 1897 clash of paradigms, eighteen-year-old H. L. Mencken began working as a reporter at the *Baltimore Herald*. From this entry-level position, he built a career as one of the most famous journalists of the twentieth century, writing an estimated ten million words in his lifetime,[40] a number that includes over thirty books and as many as three thousand newspaper columns published over six decades.[41] His work as editor, columnist, literary critic, satirist, cultural commentator, and memoirist continues to attract the attention of scholars, biographers, and publishers today.[42]

Mencken claimed that his chief influence was not Steffens, Pulitzer, Hearst, nor Ochs—but rather Dana's *New York Sun*. This paper, he wrote, outranked all other newspapers as the "grandest, gaudiest newspaper that ever went to press,"[43] his "daily scripture reading"[44] as a young reporter in 1899. Each day after the *Herald*'s telegraph editor scoured the *Sun* for copy, Mencken salvaged and devoured it on the trolley car home.[45] He clipped favorite columns and pasted them into a notebook along with fragments of incidents, dialogue and slang, and records of the magazines to which he submitted stories.[46] The *Sun* was "the Bible of all the ambitious young journalists of that era, and particularly of those with literary aspirations,"[47] Mencken claimed, "your daily food and drink, your pastor and your bootlegger, your dream and your despair."[48]

The *Sun*, Mencken wrote, had long been ignored by "the dull professors who write literary histories"[49] and "the decayed editorial writers and unsuccessful reporters who teach in schools of journalism."[50] This is perhaps because Dana's reputation had suffered by the time of his death in 1897, when he had accumulated many enemies in failed wars against the Associated Press, Hearst's *New York Journal* and Pulitzer's *New York World*.[51] Today, the *Sun* of the 1890s is seen by scholars as "past [its] prime"[52] compared to the rip-roaring work of Pulitzer and Hearst. Yet Mencken claimed that even then,[53] the *Sun*'s influence upon American literature was greater than any other paper, creating what he called "a sophisticated and highly civilized point of view," while ridding its writers of "the national fear of ideas:"[54]

> What Dana and his aides taught these youngsters was double: to see and savor the life that swarmed under their noses, and to depict it vividly and with good humor. Nothing could have been at greater odds with the American tradition. The heroes of the Stone Age were all headed in other directions. The life of their place and time interested them very little, especially the common, the ordinary life, and depicting things vividly was always far less their purpose than discussing them profoundly.[55]

Of course, one of the reporters freed by this point of view was Mencken himself. In 1899, Mencken began his reporting and editing apprenticeship at the Baltimore *Herald*, a paper that valued human interest and bright writing noticeably more than one of its stodgiest competitors, the *Baltimore Sun*. Mencken rose through the *Herald*'s editorial ranks quickly, serving as drama critic, Sunday *Herald* editor, and *Morning Herald* city editor before helping launch the *Evening Herald* in 1903 and becoming its managing editor in 1905. As one scholar has noted, "No matter how much Mencken … admired the New York *Sun*, he could not have used it as his model if the *Herald* policies had not encouraged him to do so."[56] A careful reading of *Herald* clippings in Mencken's scrapbooks suggests that this model wasn't merely a function of literary style; it was a deliberate and widespread strategy used to market evening newspaper start-ups during the country's greatest newspaper boom.

The Commercial Strategies of Evening Newspapers

The turn of the century was a period of tremendous growth for American newspapers. By 1909, there were 2,600 daily English language newspapers in the United States—an all-time high that would decline throughout the twentieth century.[57] This growth was powered by sweeping changes in the decades after the Civil War. New technologies such as linotypes, typewriters, and telephones emerged as the US population grew urbanized and literate.[58] The telegraph forced competing morning publishers to print afternoon and extra editions to cover breaking news, and the installation of gas and electric lights in the home meant new evening leisure hours that could be spent reading. By 1910 many newspapers were using high-speed presses, color ink, linotypes, and halftones to produce multiple editions per day, generating a "twenty-four-hour news cycle" long before the term found its way into our modern vocabulary.[59]

Evening newspapers accounted for much of this growth,[60] a significant but often overlooked fact given that a scholarly historical account of the evening newspaper in America has yet to be written.[61] Yet in 1880 there were more evening newspapers than morning newspapers, and their numbers continued to increase rapidly with the establishment of 518 evening newspapers by 1899 and another 580 by 1910.[62]

This dramatic marketplace expansion points toward a shift in newswriting and marketing strategies. Though evening newspapers had previously confined themselves to printing the day's news "briefly and brightly … leav[ing] the morning paper to amplify," by 1897 these papers began to print all of the day's news "as completely and carefully as the morning paper, yet with that lightness of touch that is characteristic of the evening paper."[63] This was "America's second wave of 'penny' sensationalism, its second big 'subscribers' market' in editorial policy."[64] In part, this growth was fueled by afternoon street sales to bustling crowds of shoppers, theater goers, and homeward-bound workers. Women emerged as a key audience—they were thought to have more leisure in the afternoons and were targeted by the fat advertising budgets of department stores.[65]

These evening newspapers exploited a growing backlash to the era's most sensational news practices and deployed marketing and content strategies aimed at increasing circulation by touting their suitability for the home. Key to this content mix, according to an 1897 survey of newspaper editors and business managers, was "a great quantity of good miscellany,"[66] and stories for "every member of the home circle."[67] Newspapers across the country such as the *New York Evening Post*, the *New York Journal*, the *Detroit Free Press*, the Chicago *Dispatch*, and the *San Francisco Chronicle* boasted of employing "literary men"[68] to create literary Sunday editions,[69] write human-interest stories that "will be read first in a pageful of almost any kind of newspaper matter,"[70] and furnish "literary matter to the people who do not have books."[71] This mix of news, stories, sketches, reviews, and editorials was so common that by 1899—the year that Mencken began his reporting career in Baltimore—a proposal for a newspaper that printed nothing but condensed news was considered by the trade magazine the *Journalist* to be a "radical departure."[72]

Like other evening newspaper start-ups, Baltimore's *Evening Herald* marketed itself as a lively paper that was also suitable for the home. A series of advertisements published between November and December 1905 shows that the *Evening Herald* portrayed itself as a "growing" newspaper that was neither "a roaring yellow journal" nor "dull and gloomy."[73] The paper claimed to provide reading material suitable for the entire family, aiming to "reach its readers at a time when they have leisure to read—after the evening meal. They want the day's news and they want pleasant reading of other sorts—stories, articles for women, clean fun—and good pictures."[74] These advertisements are pasted into Mencken's scrapbooks along with other articles and editorials he penned. As managing editor, he certainly took part in adapting and deploying this increasingly popular content strategy.

A "Home Paper" Apprenticeship

This was a period Mencken remembered in his memoirs as an "extraordinarily fateful and interesting one for American journalism" in which "newspapers became more prosperous than they had ever been before."[75] And his many memoirs show that Mencken was an attentive student of business tactics throughout these "apprenticeship" years.[76]

As city editor when the *Evening Herald* launched in 1904 and managing editor in 1905, he wrote of monitoring advertising and circulation reports and being "drawn deeper and deeper" into the paper's operations and gloomy finances.[77] When the *Evening Herald* folded in 1906, Mencken worked briefly at the *Baltimore Evening News*, where "the setting of ads pretty well occupied its composing-room all morning."[78] Some days, so much advertising flowed in that it couldn't all be set, leaving "little room on the linotypes for editorial copy."[79] Within a few weeks, Mencken jumped to the more prosperous—and less lively—*Sunpapers*. As editor of the Sunday *Sun* from 1906 to 1910, he wrote of his frustration that the owners refused to share circulation numbers and business reports with its editors, leaving him with no data with which to "figure out how it was going."[80]

When Charles H. Grasty purchased the *Sunpapers* in 1910, Mencken helped launch the Baltimore *Evening Sun*, a paper one admirer later called "the house that Mencken built."[81] In his self-titled position of "prime minister without portfolio," Mencken was given "free rein" to create a "more outspoken and radical" newspaper with livelier headlines than the "stodgy, ultraconservatism" the *Sunpapers* was known for.[82] Mencken borrowed freely from his experience at the *Evening Herald*, and soon the *Evening Sun* touted itself as a "home paper"[83] and "interesting to the family circle."[84] Bucking tradition, the *Evening Sun* upon its launch printed circulation numbers on the masthead for all to see, according to a history of the *Sunpapers* written in part by Mencken.[85]

Mencken's experiences in Baltimore with the *Herald* and *Sunpapers* amount to an education in the interrelated strategies of marketing, circulation, and content. Mencken drew on this education as he built an influential career as a magazine editor, beginning at *Smart Set*, a magazine that has come to be known as "the first *New Yorker*."[86] Mencken began contributing literary reviews to the magazine in 1908, championing realism in "striking and original"[87] prose and building a reputation as one of the nation's leading critics. These reviews positioned Mencken as "the leader of the forces for realism,"[88] a movement rooted in turn-of-the-century journalism.[89]

With coeditor George Jean Nathan, Mencken edited *Smart Set* from 1914 to 1923, together using their editorial and business insight to develop and sell successful pulp magazines on the side,[90] generating "more money than they had ever touched before."[91] When Mencken eventually tired of *belles-lettres* and began to desire a more "dignified forum,"[92] he shifted his focus from literature to public affairs as editor of *American Mercury* from 1924 to 1933. The *Mercury* expanded the scope of a monthly review to include "constant consideration of American politics, American governmental problems, American industrial and social relations, and American science" with an "element of novelty," attempting "a realistic presentation of the whole gaudy, gorgeous American scene."[93]

Poetry and drama took a backseat to essays, book reviews, and editorials that examined "political, religious, psychological, medical and journalistic subjects."[94] Fiction was present, but subordinate to "debunking and satirical essays"[95] in which the *Mercury* made a regular habit of "breaking heads"[96] to capture attention. It was a successful attention-getting tactic rooted in Mencken's newspaper experience. As he noted:

> I often wonder that so few publishers of periodicals seem aware of the psychological principle here exposed. It is known to every newspaper publisher of the slightest professional intelligence; all successful newspapers are ceaselessly querulous and bellicose. They never defend any one [sic] or anything if they can help it; if the job is forced upon them, they tackle it by denouncing some one [sic] or something else. The plan never fails.[97]

The *Mercury* prized the contributions of undiscovered writers, who appeared alongside noted scholars and journalists from across the nation (reporters were the "most published writers in the magazine"[98]). In an editorial celebrating the magazine's fifth anniversary, Mencken boasted that the *Mercury* "has given a great deal more space to something quite different, namely, to introducing one kind of American to another," allowing them all to "tell their own stories."[99] Such "slice of life writings"[100] included Jim Tully's adventures as a hobo, convict Ernest Booth's descriptions of robbing a bank, and Mary Austin's accounts of Native American life, among many others.[101] In a similar vein, the *Mercury*'s fiction stressed a brand of "quiet" realism that drew upon personal experiences.[102] This resulted in a blurring of the "reality boundary,"[103] as it was often difficult to tell the magazine's fiction apart from its autobiographical essays: "What began as an essay would sometimes blend into fiction, and fiction ... was later declared to have been nonfiction."[104]

Both *Smart Set* and *American Mercury* dramatically extended Mencken's influence throughout the magazine world of the 1920s.[105] The effect of the *Mercury*, wrote Mencken biographer Carl Bode, "was more than a breath of fresh air; it was a gust that once or twice grew to a gale."[106] Mencken's influence extended to the early years of the *New Yorker*, an "early and consistent champion of narrative literary journalism."[107] Harold Ross and Jane Grant, his wife and cofounder, studied a number of magazines while formulating the business plan for the *New Yorker*.[108] The *Smart Set* was the primary model,[109] and the *New Yorker* is considered to be its successor.[110]

The *New Yorker* launched in 1925, one year after *American Mercury*. Though Ross and Grant developed their own audience strategy, style, and humor,[111] Mencken's influence was nevertheless obvious. Early issues of the *New Yorker* commented regularly on the *Mercury*.[112] The *New Yorker's* regular feature Newsbreaks resembled *American Mercury's* Americana column, which was originally a feature of the *Smart Set*.[113] The *New Yorker's* Talk of the Town bore similarities to the *Mercury's* Clinical Notes.[114] Even the *New Yorker's* famous profile was "born in the office of the *Mercury*,"[115] claimed *Mercury* managing editor Charles Angoff. Both Mencken and Ross prized "character sketches that seized the essence of a personality," featuring "significant detail" and "revealing trivia."[116] The difference between the two editors was that Ross favored "kindly" profiles, while "Mencken could enjoy printing a portrait etched in acid."[117] As editors, Mencken and Ross "privilege[d], on the whole, literature with affinities to journalism."[118] Wrote Joseph Mitchell: "In those days, two magazines were reporter's bibles, *The New Yorker* and the *American Mercury*."[119]

In Defense of Mencken

Today, Mencken is "generally neglected"[120] in journalism histories and classrooms. It's a puzzling omission, given that critic Edmund Wilson, writing for the *New Yorker*, judged him as "without question, since Poe, our greatest practicing literary journalist."[121] It's a description that one biographer stated was "if anything … an understatement."[122] If so, why do Mencken's contributions to the emerging history of literary journalism remain unexamined?

Historically, definitions of literary journalism often included work by humorists, novelists, short-story writers, poets, essayists, and critics,[123] a genre that Mencken-as-writer sits comfortably within. But contemporary definitions of the genre have shifted, with scholars today generally focusing on the long-marginalized narrative mode. This focus, Hartsock writes, "tends to move to the margins"[124] so-called "discursive"[125] essayists and columnists like Mencken. It also altogether ignores his influential role as editor, as this chapter has shown.

Though he is careful *"not* to suggest that what Mencken wrote is *not* literary journalism,"[126] Hartsock is cautious and precise in differentiating Mencken's discursive prose from the narrative mode.[127] Hartsock argues that recognizing discursive essays as literary journalism is problematic for a number of reasons, chief among them the following: The boundaries between the modes are often difficult to distinguish, and the narrative mode is in danger of again being overshadowed by its "better-known discursive sibling."[128] Also, elevating the discursive mode "risks critical rebuke from elitist literary circles for reducing to the lowly level of a journalism what … once was viewed as having a pedigree and lineage worthy of poetry and drama."[129] But this is a curious rationale given that such judgments have long marginalized journalism as a literary genre. They are also precisely the sort of affectations that Mencken-as-literary-critic intended to "blow up."[130] Mencken wrote of his work: "Whether it appears to be burlesque, or serious criticism, or mere casual controversy, it is always directed against one thing: unwarranted pretension."[131] As a champion of modernism and realism, Mencken's literary criticism emphatically enforced a break with such pretensions, a move that facilitated the blending of journalism into a modernist milieu.

Mencken's contributions to the history of literary journalism deserve reappraisal. His writings and scrapbooks show that as a young reporter, he devoured the *New York Sun*, one of the most prominent innovators of the human-interest story. As a young newspaper editor, he was involved in developing and promoting the content strategies of two evening newspaper start-ups during a turn-of-the-century newspaper boom, a period in which newspapers across the nation deployed narrative and literary content strategies to exploit a backlash against sensationalism. Mencken's memoirs show that he studied the connections among advertising, circulation, and copy during his apprenticeship and drew upon that education as editor of two highly influential magazines, *Smart Set* and *American Mercury*. There, he adapted newspaper practices and championed realism, creating a blend of literature and journalism that deeply influenced magazines such as the *New Yorker*, an "important mainstay for the form."[132] Mencken did not run a newsroom as a writer's workshop, as Steffens did. Nevertheless, Mencken provides a more tangible link—both stylistically and commercially—between the newspapers of literary journalism's first modern period and its twentieth-century migration to magazines. Though he might sneer at the pretension, this rich literary and journalistic legacy positions Mencken as one of the genre's most influential editors.

Notes

1 Steffens, *Autobiography*, 311.
2 Steffens, 311.
3 Steffens, 317.
4 Steffens, 317.
5 Steffens, 315, 317.
6 Steffens, 321.
7 Steffens, 317.
8 Steffens, *Letters*, 130.
9 Steffens, *Autobiography*, 317.
10 Kaplan, *Lincoln Steffens*, 95.
11 Steffens, *Autobiography*, 353.
12 Hartsock, *History*; Connery, *Sourcebook*; Connery, *Journalism and Realism*.
13 Connery, "Third Way," 18.
14 Pauly, "Politics," 120.
15 Pauly, 124.
16 The author would like to thank Mencken biographer Marion Elizabeth Rodgers for her comments on an early draft of this essay and Vincent Fitzpatrick, curator of the H. L. Mencken Collection at the Enoch Pratt Free Library in Baltimore, for his research assistance.
17 Schudson, *Discovering the News*, 60.
18 Schudson, 17.
19 Hudson, *Journalism*, 408.
20 Schudson, *Discovering the News*, 23–24, 27.
21 Mitchell, *Memoirs of an Editor*, 157.
22 Mitchell, 157.
23 O'Brien, *Story of "The Sun,"* 245.
24 Hartsock, *History*, 22; italics in the original.
25 Hartsock, 33.
26 Campbell, *Year*, 75–87.
27 Campbell, 70.
28 Campbell, 101.
29 Campbell, 6.
30 Campbell, 7.
31 Hartsock, *History*, 60.
32 Baldasty, *Commercialization of News*, 139.
33 Steffens, "Business of a Newspaper," 448.
34 Steffens, 460.
35 Steffens, 448.
36 Steffens, *Letters*, 131.
37 Steffens, *Autobiography*, 318.
38 Steffens, 327.
39 Steffens, 338.
40 Other credible estimates run from five to fifteen million words (Mencken, *Diary*, 367; Shafer, "Mencken's Millions").
41 Fitzpatrick, "H. L. Mencken," 182.
42 Recent works include Mencken, *Saturnalia of Bunk*; Mencken, *Days Trilogy*; Mencken, *Prejudices*; Joshi, *H. L. Mencken*; Harrison, *A.K.A. H. L. Mencken*; Rodgers, *Mencken*; Fitzpatrick, *H. L. Mencken*; Teachout, *Skeptic*.
43 Mencken, "Library," 505.

44. Mencken and Nathan, "Clinical Notes," 310. The section under "Clinical Notes" that this is taken from is "Constructive Suggestion," which scholars agree was written solely by Mencken. This applies also to citations in notes 47 and 53 below.
45. Rodgers, *Mencken*, 58.
46. Rodgers, 64.
47. Mencken and Nathan, "Clinical Notes," 310.
48. Mencken, "Library," 505.
49. Mencken, 505.
50. Mencken, 506.
51. Campbell, *Year*, 23–25.
52. Campbell, 72.
53. Mencken specified: under the leadership of Edward P. Mitchell and William M. Laffan (Mencken, "Library," 505; Mencken and Nathan, "Clinical Notes," 311).
54. Mencken, "Library," 506.
55. Mencken, 505.
56. Stenerson, "Mencken's Early Newspaper Experience," 155.
57. Lee, *Daily Newspaper in America*, 65.
58. Sloan, *Media in America*, 224–26.
59. Historians trace the roots of the twenty-four-hour news cycle to James Gordon Bennett and the antebellum *New York Herald*, a legacy that fed the frenetic new journalism of the 1880s and 1890s and the emergence of the modern era of newspapering in the 1910s and 1920s (Sloan, *Media in America*, 226–27).
60. Lee, *Daily Newspaper in America*, 65.
61. Much of the scholarship on this era has analyzed newspapers through the biographical lens of owner, publisher, or editor, thereby aggregating morning and evening products together. Few books examine only evening newspapers. One trade example is Benjaminson, *Death in the Afternoon* (W. Joseph Campbell, email message to author, June 23, 2016).
62. Lee, *Daily Newspaper in America*, 65; Mott, *American Journalism*, 447.
63. Bates, *American Journalism*, 241–42.
64. Lee, *Daily Newspaper in America*, 65.
65. Mott, *American Journalism*, 447.
66. Bates, *American Journalism*, 107.
67. Bates, 107.
68. Bates, 27.
69. Bates, 322.
70. Bates, 99.
71. Bates, 176.
72. "News Only," 396–97.
73. Mencken, *Editorials*, 145.
74. Mencken, 135–36.
75. Mencken, *Thirty-Five Years*, 5.
76. According to Vincent Fitzpatrick, Mencken bibliographer, biographer, and curator, this apprenticeship spans from 1899, the date of Mencken's first newspaper article, to 1908, when he began reviewing books for *Smart Set* (*H. L. Mencken*, 28).
77. Mencken, *Days Trilogy*, 398–99.
78. Mencken, *Thirty-Five Years*, 8.
79. Mencken, 8.
80. Mencken, "Thirty-Five Years," 34–35.
81. Norton, "Mencken's Heart."
82. Villard, "Baltimore *Suns*," 392–93.
83. Johnson et al., *Sunpapers of Baltimore*, 299; Mencken, *Thirty-Five Years*, 32.
84. Johnson et al., *Sunpapers of Baltimore*, 299.
85. Johnson et al., 316.
86. Hamilton, "First *New Yorker*!," 90.
87. Mott, *History of American Magazines*, 268.
88. Nolte, introduction to *Mencken's "Smart Set" Criticism*, xxxi.
89. Connery, *Journalism and Realism*, xx.
90. Hamilton, "First *New Yorker*!," 96.
91. Rodgers, *Mencken*, 150.

92 Mott, *History of American Magazines*, 270.
93 *American Mercury Publisher's Prospectus*, 1, 3.
94 Singleton, *H. L. Mencken*, 82.
95 Singleton, 65.
96 Mencken, "American Magazine," 106.
97 Mencken, 106.
98 Singleton, *H. L. Mencken*, 137.
99 "Editorial," 408.
100 Singleton, *H. L. Mencken*, 75.
101 Several can be found in *The American Mercury Reader*.
102 Singleton, *H. L. Mencken*, 77.
103 Sims, "Problem and the Promise," 11.
104 Singleton, *H. L. Mencken*, 75.
105 Singleton, *H. L. Mencken*, 181–82; Bode, *Mencken*, 259–62.
106 Bode, *Mencken*, 258.
107 Hartsock, *History*, 169.
108 Grant, *Ross*, 212; Yagoda, *About Town*, 35.
109 Hammill, "*The New Yorker*," 25.
110 Hamilton, "First *New Yorker!*," 101.
111 Hammill, "*The New Yorker*," 26.
112 Hammill, 19.
113 Hammill, 25.
114 Bode, *Mencken*, 260.
115 Angoff, "Inside View," quoted in Singleton, *H. L. Mencken*, 182.
116 Bode, *Mencken*, 259.
117 Bode, 260.
118 Hammill, "*The New Yorker*," 28.
119 Yagoda, *About Town*, 137.
120 Harrison, "Mencken," 61.
121 Wilson, "Mencken," 112.
122 Teachout, *Skeptic*, 10.
123 See, for example, Mott, *New Survey of Journalism*, 306–08.
124 Hartsock, *History*, 136.
125 Hartsock, 137.
126 Hartsock, 138; italics added.
127 Hartsock, 137.
128 Hartsock, 137.
129 Hartsock, 136–37.
130 Mencken wrote: "ideas—i.e., the follies and imbecilities of men—interest me. Blowing them up is the noblest of human occupations" (*Letters*, 190).
131 Mencken, *Letters*, 188.
132 Hartsock, *History*, 156.

Bibliography

The American Mercury Publisher's Prospectus and Three Editorials by H. L. Mencken. New York: Alfred A. Knopf, 1924–28. Portfolio 343, no. 17. Printed Ephemera Collection. Rare Book and Special Collections Reading Room, Library of Congress, Washington, DC.

The "American Mercury" Reader. Edited by Lawrence E. Spivak and Charles Angoff. Philadelphia, PA: Blakiston, 1944.

Angoff, Charles. "The Inside View of Mencken's Mercury." *New Republic*, September 13, 1954.

Baldasty, Gerald J. *The Commercialization of News in the Nineteenth Century*. Madison, WI: University of Wisconsin Press, 1992.

Bates, Charles Austin. *American Journalism from the Practical Side*. New York: Holmes, 1897.

Benjaminson, Peter. *Death in the Afternoon: America's Newspaper Giants Struggle for Survival*. Kansas City, MO: Andrews, McMeel and Parker, 1984.

Bode, Carl. *Mencken*. Baltimore, MD: Johns Hopkins University Press, 1986.

Campbell, W. Joseph. *The Year That Defined American Journalism: 1897 and the Clash of Paradigms.* New York: Routledge, 2006.

Connery, Thomas B. *Journalism and Realism: Rendering American Life.* Evanston, IL: Northwestern University Press, 2011.

———. *A Sourcebook of American Literary Journalism: Representative Writers in an Emerging Genre.* New York: Greenwood Press, 1992.

———. "A Third Way to Tell the Story: American Literary Journalism at the Turn of the Century." In *Literary Journalism in the Twentieth Century*, edited by Norman Sims, 3–20. Evanston, IL: Northwestern University Press, 2008.

"Editorial." *American Mercury*, December 1928.

Fitzpatrick, Vincent. *H. L. Mencken.* Macon, GA: Mercer University Press, 2004.

———. "H. L. Mencken." In *American Magazine Journalists, 1900–1960*, edited by Sam G. Riley, 179–204. Vol. 137 of *Dictionary of Literary Biography*. Detroit, MI: Gale Research, 1994.

Grant, Jane C. *Ross, "The New Yorker," and Me.* New York: Reynal, 1968.

Hamilton, Sharon, "The First *New Yorker*! The *Smart Set* Magazine, 1900–1924." *Serials Librarian* 37, no. 2 (1999): 89–104. https://doi.org/10.1300/j123v37n02_06.

Hammill, Faye. "*The New Yorker*, the Middlebrow, and the Periodical Marketplace in 1925." In *Writing for "The New Yorker": Critical Essays on an American Periodical*, edited by Fiona Green, 17–35. Edinburgh: Edinburgh University Press, 2015.

Harrison, S. L. *A.K.A. H. L. Mencken.* Miami, FL: Wolf Den Books, 2005.

———. "Mencken: Magnificent Anachronism." *American Journalism* 13, no. 1 (Winter 1996): 60–78. https://doi.org/10.1080/08821127.1996.10731793.

Hartsock, John C. *A History of American Literary Journalism: The Emergence of Modern Narrative Form.* Amherst, MA: University of Massachusetts Press, 2000.

Hudson, Frederic. *Journalism in the United States from 1690 to 1872.* New York: Haskell House, 1968.

Johnson, Gerald W., Frank R. Kent, H. L. Mencken, and Hamilton Owens. *The Sunpapers of Baltimore 1837–1937.* New York: Alfred A. Knopf, 1937.

Joshi, S. T. *H. L. Mencken: An Annotated Bibliography.* Lanham, MD: Scarecrow Press, 2009.

Kaplan, Justin. *Lincoln Steffens: A Biography.* New York: Simon and Schuster, 2004.

Lee, Alfred McClung. *The Daily Newspaper in America: The Evolution of a Social Instrument.* New York: Macmillan, 1937.

Mencken, H. L. "The American Magazine." In *Prejudices: First, Second, and Third Series*, edited by Marion Elizabeth Rodgers, 101–06. New York: Library of America, 2010.

———. *The Days Trilogy.* Edited by Marion Elizabeth Rodgers. Expanded ed. New York: Library of America, 2014.

———. *The Diary of H. L. Mencken.* Edited by Charles A. Fecher. New York: Alfred A. Knopf, 1989.

———. *Editorials, Dramatic Reviews and Other Pieces, Baltimore Morning and Evening "Herald" 1904–1906.* Folio A59. H. L. Mencken Collection. Enoch Pratt Free Library, Baltimore, MD.

———. *The Letters of H. L. Mencken.* Edited by Guy J. Forgue. New York: Alfred A. Knopf, 1961.

———. "The Library." *American Mercury*, December 1924.

———. *Prejudices: The Complete Series.* Edited by Marion Elizabeth Rodgers. New York: Library of America, 2010.

———. *A Saturnalia of Bunk: Selections from the Free Lance, 1911–1915.* Edited by S. T. Joshi. Athens, OH: Ohio University Press, 2017.

———. "Thirty-Five Years of Newspaper Work." 1942. H. L. Mencken Collection. Enoch Pratt Free Library, Baltimore, MD. Original manuscript.

———. *Thirty-Five Years of Newspaper Work.* Baltimore, MD: Johns Hopkins University Press, 1994.

Mencken, H. L., and George Jean Nathan. "Clinical Notes." *American Mercury*, November 1924.

Mitchell, Edward Page. *Memoirs of an Editor: Fifty Years of American Journalism.* New York: Charles Scribner's Sons, 1924.

Mott, Frank Luther. *American Journalism: A History 1690–1960.* New York: Macmillan, 1962.

———. *A History of American Magazines.* Vol. 5, *Sketches of 21 Magazines, 1905–1930.* Cambridge, MA: Harvard University Press, 1968.

Mott, George Fox. *New Survey of Journalism.* New York: Barnes and Noble, 1953.

"News Only." *Journalist* 25, no. 21 (1899): 396–97.

Nolte, William Henry. Introduction to *H. L. Mencken's "Smart Set" Criticism*, by H. L. Mencken, xi–xxxvii. Ithaca, NY: Cornell University Press, 1968.

Norton, John. "Mencken's Heart Belonged to Baltimore Paper." *New York Times*, September 22, 1995.

O'Brien, Frank Michael. *The Story of "The Sun."* New York: George H. Doran, 1918.

Pauly, John J. "The Politics of the New Journalism." In *Literary Journalism in the Twentieth Century*, edited by Norman Sims, 110–29. Evanston, IL: Northwestern University Press, 2008.

Rodgers, Marion Elizabeth. *Mencken: The American Iconoclast*. New York: Oxford University Press, 2005.

Schudson, Michael. *Discovering the News: A Social History of American Newspapers*. New York: Basic Books, 1978.

Shafer, Jack. "Mencken's Millions: Exactly How Many Words Did the Sage of Baltimore Write?" *Slate*, January 1, 2006. Accessed August 15, 2014. www.slate.com/articles/news_and_politics/press_box/2006/01/menckens_millions.html.

Sims, Norman. "The Problem and the Promise of Literary Journalism Studies." *Literary Journalism Studies* 1, no. 1 (Spring 2009): 7–16.

Singleton, Marvin Kenneth. *H. L. Mencken and the "American Mercury" Adventure*. Durham, NC: Duke University Press, 1962.

Sloan, Wm. David. *The Media in America: A History*. Northport, AL: Vision Press, 2011.

Steffens, Lincoln. *The Autobiography of Lincoln Steffens*. New York: Harcourt, 1931.

———. "The Business of a Newspaper." *Scribner's Magazine*, October 1897.

———. *The Letters of Lincoln Steffens*. Edited by Ella Winter and Granville Hicks. New York: Harcourt, 1938.

Stenerson, Douglas C. "Mencken's Early Newspaper Experience: The Genesis of a Style." *American Literature* 37, no. 2 (May 1965): 153–66. https://doi.org/10.2307/2922990.

Teachout, Terry. *The Skeptic: A Life of H. L. Mencken*. New York: HarperCollins, 2002.

Villard, Oswald Garrison. "The Baltimore *Suns*—A Notable Journalistic Resurrection." *Nation*, April 5, 1922, 390–93.

Wilson, Edmund. "Mencken through the Wrong End of the Telescope." *New Yorker*, May 6, 1950.

Yagoda, Ben. *About Town: "The New Yorker" and the World It Made*. New York: Scribner, 2000.

20
A SHORT, COMPREHENSIVE HISTORY OF LITERARY SPORTS JOURNALISM

Ted Geltner and Ted Spiker

Introduction

On September 29, 1954, a little-known writer named Arnold Hano took the D-train from the Bronx to downtown New York, bought a two-dollar-and-ten-cent ticket for seat number 1662, and climbed the steps toward the right-centerfield bleachers in the Polo Grounds, home park of the New York Giants. He got to his seat a few hours before the first pitch, in time to take in batting practice, see the great Willie Mays shag flies, and watch as the seats around him slowly filled up. It was Game 1 of the World Series between the Giants and the Cleveland Indians. Hano went as a fan, there to enjoy a game, but as the afternoon progressed, his fan persona began to recede and the writer in him took over.

Then, in the top of the eighth inning, with the game tied 2–2, Cleveland outfielder Vic Wertz hit a long drive to centerfield. The Polo Grounds had a famously expansive centerfield, 483 feet at the wall, and a ball that would have been a home run in most every other ballpark in America hung over the field of play as Mays gave chase. He finally caught up to it at about 460 feet, cradled it in his glove with his back still facing home plate, then whirled and fired the ball back to the infield, saving a run and creating one of the most indelible images in the history of the national pastime.

For Hano, however, the story was not just "The Catch." That was just one of the many elements that had coalesced over the course of the day to create the possibility of literature in his mind. What had awoken the writer in him that day was the scene, of which he was a part, that played out over the course of the afternoon in the right-centerfield bleachers above the Polo Ground outfield. He decided on the subway ride home that he would write about his day.

"Actually, I thought I could write a magazine article," said Hano fifty-five years later:

> I expanded the ballgame into ten thousand words. The only magazine that published stuff like that was the New Yorker … So I brought it down to the New Yorker and some kid came out. I said, "Here's an article, it's about a baseball game that took place, and if you publish it you'll have to publish it right away." The kid listened, and he said, "Okay, I'll have them read it." He went upstairs, an hour later he comes back to me and says they liked it, but it wasn't right. I took it home and I read it, and it *wasn't* right. They were absolutely right that it wasn't right. So I decided, what the hell, I'll make it a book.[1]

The book, *A Day in the Bleachers*, was, for its time, a sparkling work of technical innovation. Hano found characters in the stands and on the field, built tension related to the action of the game interlaced with vignettes that created personal connections to the players involved, and exponentially expanded on details that at first glance would have seemed far too incidental for mention in immediate news coverage of the game. "The Catch" became a chapter unto itself, built entirely around Mays's pursuit of Wertz's towering shot and the subsequent throw.

Today, it's easy to recognize *A Day in the Bleachers* for what it is: longform literary journalism, or narrative nonfiction, of the highest order. Hano was writing, however, before Tom Wolfe coined the term "New Journalism" in the early 1970s, before researchers began to categorize what is and what isn't literary journalism, and before book publishers and booksellers knew that readers would purchase writing by authors who could tell gripping narrative stories that were based on actual reporting. The fact that he was writing in a genre that had yet to be named was something that Hano would soon find out.

Hano was also placing his byline in another, parallel journalistic tradition: He was using the world of sports as the canvas upon which to create his literary innovation. Throughout the development of journalism in America, writers have found in athletic endeavor the ingredients and interest to practice their craft. Jimmy Cannon is the writer most often credited with coining the saying "the sports department is the toy store of life," but many other writers who have made their names in the sports pages have been associated with it as well. Perhaps that is because the idea it represents, that the rules that existed in the news pages were relaxed for the no-consequence, just-for-entertainment realm of sports coverage, has allowed creativity to flourish to an immense degree and produced some of the finest craftsmen in the grand tradition of American literary journalism. The names and publications and sports and events have varied through the eras, but when the conditions were right, the creation of art through sports reporting has flourished, leaving a deep record of innovation in its wake.

The Golden Era

The development of sports journalism mirrored the rise of spectator sports in America, a phenomenon that emerged in the mid-nineteenth century but exploded a century ago,[2] due to both the increase in recreational time for middle-class Americans and the continued rise of the newspaper, as well as the advent of radio as a mass-market medium. The growth started at the turn of the century and crested during the 1920s, the Golden Age of Sports. Newspapers prospered as they had never before, and the publishers and editors of these money machines searched for subjects that would make good copy and keep the profits rolling in. They found those subjects in the stadiums and arenas of America's growing cities, which supplied ready-made heroes—Babe Ruth and Jack Dempsey and Red Grange and Man o' War. All the editors needed was somebody with a typewriter who could turn the drama into good copy. Those who could truly excel at that job became as rich and nearly as famous as the heroes they used their typewriters to create.[3] The writers who left the deepest impressions did so because they were able to create literature with an element of permanence.

Most of these craftsmen used sports as a launching pad, finding even greater success once they abandoned the newspaper sports page. Ring Lardner was one who took that path, beginning his career writing about baseball for the *Chicago Tribune* and the *Chicago Examiner*, among others. Baseball writers during that era travelled with their subjects, taking extended train rides from city to city, all the while drinking, eating, playing cards, and bantering with the ballplayers they wrote about. Lardner found in these men the voice of American individualism. He honed his skills at the observation and re-creation of rural Midwestern vernacular. Eventually, out of his day-to-day baseball coverage emerged the character of Jack O'Keefe, a bush-league ballplayer at the center of

Lardner's most famous work, *You Know Me Al*, a book "filled with the glow of an earlier and rural American scene."[4] Both Ernest Hemingway and F. Scott Fitzgerald were devotees of Lardner. Hemingway's earliest writing was filed under the pen name Ring Lardner Jr.[5]

The lasting contribution of the writer Paul Gallico was a story he wrote when he was a twenty-four-year-old reporter for the *New York Daily News*. Jack Dempsey held the heavyweight belt and was at the height of his fame when Gallico talked the champ into sparring with him. Gallico landed the first punch; Dempsey landed the rest. One minute and thirty-seven seconds later, Gallico was unconscious.[6] An hour later, he was writing a first-person account of his cup of coffee in the ring with the Manassa Mauler. If Dempsey, by achieving a level of sports celebrity that had not previously been attained, was a harbinger of a future where the heavyweight champion of the world would also be the most famous person on the globe, then Gallico, by putting himself into the story and allowing the reader to feel the action from the writer's point of view, was also blazing a trail, inventing a story form that sports journalists would be refining for the next century.

The gamblers, hustlers and gangsters who would populate Damon Runyon's tales of a certain type of Prohibition-era Broadway lifestyle made their first appearances in his work as a newspaper sports writer, covering baseball and boxing for the *New York American*. Runyon's first subjects were mythical New York sports figures such as John McGraw and Bugs Raymond. A "Damon Runyon character," in literary parlance, denoted somebody with an overpowering New York accent who was both morally and grammatically compromised. The skills he utilized to create the colorful portraits that put flesh to the term, a keen power of observation trained on those he encountered as a denizen of the streets, were honed in the press-box and at the ballpark.[7] Literary-minded sports writers after Runyon knew to look beyond the headlines and mine the subjects who lived their lives out of view of the paying spectators.

Of all the sports writers to come out of the first half of the twentieth century, the name that remains, indeed the name that has come, in the modern era, to symbolize the fedora-and-overcoat wearing, typewriter lugging newspaperman, is Grantland Rice. It was even chosen as the moniker for the website created by ESPN to house its literary-flavored content (though reportedly over the initial objections of Bill Simmons, the engine behind the site, which eventually went the way of its namesake).[8] Rice was a prolific writer of both sports poetry and commentary, and as famous in his day as Simmons today, if not more so. He wrote in a florid, overdrawn, and unfailingly positive style that a biographer wrote would have doomed him to weekly newspaperdom had he been born after 1930, but in his time he outshone his peers.[9] His lead, "Outlined against the blue-grey October sky, the Four Horsemen rode again," stands both as the most famous line of sportswriting and the perfect symbol of the style of Rice the writer, a style that feels dated today but nonetheless remains as an artifact of the literature of sports from an earlier era of American journalism.

The Columnists

Rice redefined the vision of the sports columnist during his time. Feature syndicates had come into existence in the early part of the century, supplying columns on a wide variety of topics to newspapers across the country, including politics, art, music, and sports. The job of local sports columnist grew concurrently and would come to be what Frank Deford termed each newspaper's "high priest of games," occupying the symbolic place of greatest importance.[10] Within Rice's lifetime, no newspaper could be without one, and most had a handful. These writers were usually fashioned in the mold of Rice, a cheerleader and chronicler who could be counted on to appear on the front of the sports page each day, attend and provide analyses from the Masters, the Kentucky Derby, the World Series, and all the iconic national sporting events, and offer what would today be called their "take" on the fortunes of each particular city's athletes and teams. These writers were the best of each newspaper, and a few of them used the post to create a truly unique voice and to take the 800-word daily structure into the realm of literature, to transcend the banality of the daily sports page and increase the collective understanding of games and how they related to the day's human existence. Newspapers were the leading medium of sports journalism for most of the twentieth century, and sports columnists were also given the freedom to both explore and create with little control exerted from editors, as long as they met deadline.

The most influential columnists honed a distinctive style, were widely read and syndicated nationally, and imitated by peers and those who followed them. Red Smith wrote deftly crafted, literary-minded columns for fifty years in St. Louis, Philadelphia, and New York. His best read like stand-alone short stories worthy of Hemingway or Fitzgerald. As lead sports columnist at the *Los Angeles Times* for nearly forty years, Jim Murray became known as the king of the one-liner, but his style transcended his brilliant humor, and eventually his name and voice became synonymous with Southern California sports. Jimmy Cannon walked the streets of New York to find material for his one-sentence nuggets of wisdom that filled his Nobody Asked Me, But columns. Comfortable to remain the dean of the New York back pages, Cannon liked to say, "It's true that I have solved little of my country's dilemma, but the statesmen also have failed."[11] Murray Kempton also wrote columns from New York for half a century, adhering to the sportswriting adage that the best stories are found in the losers' locker room, most famously when he ventured to that very place to interview Sal Maglie, the losing pitcher in baseball's only World Series perfect game.[12]

Today, the job of sports columnist at a major metropolitan daily newspaper is often viewed as a stepping stone to more lucrative jobs in radio and television. However, writers who focus their talents on the particular skill of the 800-word daily sports column do it as well as their predecessors. Sally Jenkins of the *Washington Post*, Mitch Albom of the *Detroit Free Press*, Christine Brennan of *USA Today*, and William C. Rhoden of the *New York Times* have devoted most of their energy toward the craft of column writing and have continued to breathe life into the fading art.

New Journalism

When Tom Wolfe opened an issue of *Esquire* in 1962, he found a story that he would identify as the start of the era of New Journalism—the merging of journalism with literary techniques of novelists. The story was a sports piece by Gay Talese called "Joe Louis: The King as Middle-Aged Man." Wolfe noticed that the story opened with "the tone and mood of a short story, with a rather intimate scene; or intimate by the standards of magazine journalism in 1962."[13] The opener featured dialogue between the boxing great and his wife, and the piece, Wolfe said, featured many scenes that showed the private life of a sports hero.[14] Wolfe and Talese were two of the first writers to be credited with launching a longform, literary approach to journalism. They used techniques found regularly in novels—scene-setting, dialogue, metaphor, point of view, and fly-on-the-wall reporting—to tell stories in ways that newspapers and magazines typically did not. Wolfe said what interested him most was that it was possible in journalism to "use any literary device, from the traditional dialogisms of the essay to stream-of-consciousness, and to use many different kinds simultaneously, or within a relatively short space ... to excite the reader both intellectually and emotionally."[15]

While Wolfe credits the Louis piece in *Esquire* as one of the first times he consciously recognized the form of storytelling, some will point to Talese's "The Silent Season of a Hero," published in *Esquire* in 1966, as one of the founding documents of New Journalism.[16] In this story, Talese follows the life of Yankees great Joe DiMaggio after his retirement with up-close details about DiMaggio's character. He uses DiMaggio in ordinary scenes, rather than sports highlights, to give insight into his character, such as a passage in which he comes down for breakfast with his sister, wearing a bathrobe, and yawns.[17] Jonathan Seitz, of Nieman Storyboard, says that these minutiae make it a powerful story: "Those ordinary moments ... serve as the springboard for a series of flashbacks that Talese uses to bring out the character of DiMaggio."[18]

Talese said he was drawn to sports because reporters get to witness the events—and the aftermath—as it unfolds, unlike other genres in which reporters rely on others to tell them what has happened.[19] He was also interested in failure "and those who can rise from the floor," he said, adding:

> That's why [boxer] Floyd Patterson was an ideal subject. He was so honest in moments of triumph and moments of defeat. Patterson got knocked down more than anybody in the history of boxing, but he got up more than anybody, and that is a real achievement. What I write about is perseverance more than anything else.[20]

The New Journalists—like Wolfe, Talese, and Hunter S. Thompson—were drawn to sports because of the drama that unfolded and the scenes that could be re-created from both the competition and the human side of sports. Gonzo journalist Thompson, more well known for his takes on guns, politics, and drugs, often wrote about sports, even finishing his career writing for ESPN. His most famous sports-related piece was "The Kentucky Derby Is Decadent and Depraved," published in 1970 in the antiestablishment magazine *Scanlan's*.[21] Thompson got the assignment when he called his editor's home at three thirty in the morning three days before the Derby. Thompson told his editor, "Goddammit, *Scanlan's* has to cover the Derby. It's important."[22] Thompson's story focuses little on the actual race, with the exception of a quick passage in which he writes, "The race itself was only two minutes long, and even from our super-status seats and using 12-power glasses, there was no way to see what was really happening."[23] Instead, most of the piece centers on his invasion into Louisville, with references to drinking and overall madness:

> The rest of that day blurs into madness. The rest of that night too. And all the next day and night. Such horrible things occurred that I can't bring myself even to think about them now, much less put them down in print.[24]

Starting in the 1960s, literary journalists paved the way for journalists to go into untapped areas for nonfiction writers. Whereas much of sportswriting revolved around the games, players, and scores, the New Journalists opened up the playing field for the audience—as the writers took readers to places they never had access to before: into people's homes and conversations, behind previously closed doors, and inside the minds of people whom readers cared about. This level of detailed and point-of-view reporting and writing would be the springboard for today's longform narrative pieces.

The Bonus Piece

Years before Jim Murray became the king of one-liners, he was one of a small group of Time Inc. employees who were called to New York in the early 1950s to create a secret new publication, known only as Project X. *Time* and *Life* were both profit machines for the company at the time, and founder Henry Luce believed sports was the next great subject to be covered by his journalistic machine. Project X was eventually christened *Sports Illustrated* and was unleashed on the American public in the fall of 1954. The magazine would take ten years to reach profitability,[25] but it quickly became the pinnacle of American sports journalism.

From the beginning, the project had a literary bent. In its first three years, the magazine ran pieces by Ernest Hemingway on hunting, John Steinbeck on fishing, Robert Frost on the Major

League Baseball All-Star Game, and William Faulkner on the Kentucky Derby.[26] When the position of managing editor was passed to a man named Andre Laguerre, *Sports Illustrated* became the beating heart of literary sports journalism. One of Laguerre's most innovative moves was the establishment of a permanent place within the design of the magazine for extended literary articles. This feature was to become known as "the bonus piece" and would be *Sports Illustrated*'s showcase for its most literate and accomplished writing, a work of what would in the twenty-first century be called "longform" journalism, as the final feature in each weekly edition. Laguerre viewed this as a crucial aspect for his vision for the magazine. In his book about the history of *Sports Illustrated*, Michael MacCambridge wrote: "The bonus piece, 52 weeks a year, would provide a longer, literary minded takeout on some person in or aspect of the sports world, often running between 6,000 and 8,000 words, sometimes longer."[27]

The bonus piece became the breeding ground for those who would become the magazine's A-list writers. Frank Deford is the name most associated with longform writing for *Sports Illustrated*, but Dan Jenkins, Curry Kirkpatrick, Mark Kram, and many, many others emerged as top sports journalists of the day,[28] largely because they were given the time, resources, and freedom to write and to experiment. The result was a weekly piece of writing that aimed for the highest reaches of literary quality. George Plimpton built on the tradition started by Paul Gallico and used the slot to write experiential pieces that achieved wide notoriety.[29] Editors hunted for the perfect writer, on staff or not, to match with subjects. Topics varied wildly from week to week. Any idea from a writer or editor, provided it was at least tangentially related to sports, was fair game for a bonus piece. (Sometimes, the relationship to sports was difficult to determine, as when Deford famously profiled Jerry Malone, a man who traveled the country showing off his twenty-ton, thirty-eight-foot frozen dead whale named Little Irvy.)[30] Mainstream sports and personalities were mixed in with off-beat topics, from cricket to yachting to quail hunting. Techniques varied from week to week, writer to writer. Narratives, works of immersion journalism, essays, first-person memoirs, and in-depth profiles all appeared regularly. Often, original artwork was commissioned to run with the pieces. The freedom originated with Laguerre's vision. "His genius as an editor was that he made you want to please him, but he wanted you to do it by writing in your own distinct way," said Deford.[31] That guidance allowed *Sports Illustrated* to become the incubator for at least two generations of literary journalists. Though Laguerre was gone from the magazine within a decade, the bonus piece remained his defining legacy.

Gary Smith

When *Sports Illustrated* senior writer Gary Smith made a guest appearance via Skype in a sports media class at the University of Florida, he was asked about what he thought of modern, digital journalism—with all the links and access to so many nuggets of information. This was a good question, considering that Smith was a winner of four National Magazine Awards (and a ten-time finalist) and was once called by *Slate* not just the greatest sportswriter in America, but the greatest magazine writer in America.[32] Smith had made his career in longform narrative writing—the antithesis to today's quick-hit, sound-bite media culture. Smith answered by saying that while he had great respect for all kinds of information and journalism, he didn't want his stories to have "exit ramps"—links to other stories, distractions, and other ways to get a reader *off* of a page. Instead, he wanted readers to stay on the road—the road of the story that he was telling—so that the reader could be immersed in that journey, not distracted in it.[33]

That has been a hallmark of Smith's storied career; his readers have followed him on the tales he has told about both the famous and not-so-famous people in the world of sports. Smith has written about Mike Tyson, Muhammad Ali, Jim Valvano, Pat Summitt, Mia Hamm, and many others. Some of the stories that many consider to be his best work are about people most sports fans do not know. "Shadow of a Nation" focused on a Crow Indian Reservation in Montana. "Damned Yankee" centered on a former Yankees minor leaguer who held a tragic family secret for decades—about his responsibility in the death of a relative when they were both young boys. "Rapture of the Deep" is a tragic love story about two of the world's best freedivers.

Smith's typical work cycle was to write four in-depth stories a year.[34] Smith told the *New York Times* that he did not pass judgment on his subjects, even if they had done things that would be looked down upon by the public. His job, he said, was about journey, not judgment. "Each person's life is a problem to be solved, and I try to get a grasp of what problem they're solving," Smith said. "You're doing stories about people who do extraordinary things, and that usually comes out of extraordinary pressures and frictions. That's what I try to understand."[35]

Smith, who retired in 2014, was known for his ability to do immersive reporting and poetic, literary writing. Smith's stories very rarely have many direct quotes, yet he still reports on what people are *thinking*. "In a Smith piece, you rarely see a quote until the backstretch, when he's got his narrative hooks into you and can afford to plunk in some background info via direct testimony," wrote Ben Yagoda in *Slate*.[36] Smith is able to do this by spending so much time with his subjects.[37] In Smith's piece about North Carolina State basketball coach Jim Valvano, who died of cancer shortly after giving the now-famous "never give up" speech at the ESPYs, Smith captures the complex emotions that come with celebrity death. This is the opening to "As Time Runs Out":

> He entered the arena with his wife on his arm and a container of holy water from Lourdes in his black leather bag. His back and hips and knees ached. That was the disease, they told him. His ears rang and his stomach turned and his hands and feet were dead. That, they said, was the cure. Each step he took brought a rattle from his bag. Twenty-four tablets of Advil were usually enough to get him through the day.
>
> He braced himself. No doubt someone would approach him this evening, pump his hand and say it. Strangers were always writing it or saying it to him: "We're pulling for you, Vee. You can do it. Nobody thought you had a prayer against Houston in that national championship game in '83, and you pulled that off, right? Keep fighting, Vee. You can do it again."
>
> *No.* Not in the same breath. Not in the same sentence, not in the same paragraph, not in the same magazine or book could the two be uttered: a basketball opponent and a cancer eating its way through the marrow and bone of his spine. A basketball opponent and death. *No.* In their fear of dying, people didn't make it larger than it was. They shrank it, they trivialized it. Vee versus metastatic adenocarcinoma. Vee versus Phi Slamma Jamma. Go get 'em, baby. Shock the world, Vee.
>
> *No.* No correlation, baby, he longed to tell them sometimes. *None.*[38]

Smith, who started in newspapers before joining *Sports Illustrated* in 1982, has said that the key to constructing such scenes is by "asking a zillion questions":

> When I sense a scene could really be a compelling one, a revealing one, an important one, I'll just think of a million little questions about what that moment was like. I talk to other people who might have had some glimpse into it as well. It's basically painstaking questioning, really.[39]

While he is sometimes criticized for the overuse of certain devices, such as rhetorical questions and purposeful repetition,[40] Smith is often revered as one of the greatest storytellers of the modern era—with sports being just the backdrop for stories about universal truths about the human condition.[41]

Jemele Hill, of ESPN, interviewed Smith for the Poynter Institute when one of the two anthologies of his work came out. She asked Smith what makes a story compelling. Smith said:

> I have to smell that there's ripples to it, that the thing has some dramatic arc to it. To go 8,000 or 9,000 words, it's got to have a couple twists and turns and somersaults to it. If it speaks to something larger, better still.[42]

Personal Narratives

Longform sports stories often feature a variety of themes, subjects, and reporting techniques. The genre that perhaps lends itself most to narrative technique is that of the personal narrative—a deep dive into the life of one person to help understand the complex layers of the moments and emotions that form the cocktail of the person we see on the field and on our screens. These can be complex reporting projects, depending on the level of access that is granted. In the case of Gary Smith's pieces, he uses open access—and upfront disclosure that the project will take a lot of time on the part of the subject. In the case of Gay Talese's Joe DiMaggio piece, it starts out with Talese having no access at all and DiMaggio (kindly) shutting the door on Talese's wish to work on a story about him.

These personal narratives can fall into the category of either the people we know or the people we don't. The so-called sports celebrity profile is one that has been taken on by the literary-journalist giants, starting with Talese. In June 1986, Richard Ben Cramer wrote "What Do You Think of Ted Williams Now?" which fits a similar theme to Talese's "Silent Season" in that it focuses on the waning days of a long-ago star.

> These days, there are no crowds, but Ted is watched, and why not? What other match could draw a kibitzer's eye when Ted, on the near court, pounds toward the net, slashing the air with his big racket, laughing in triumphant derision as he scores with his killer drop shot, or smacking the ball twenty feet long and roaring, "SYPHILITIC SON OF A BITCH!" as he hurls his racket to the clay at his feet?[43]

Today, it is not uncommon to see intimate stories about some of the biggest names in sports. J. R. Moehringer wrote a signature piece about maligned baseball superstar Alex Rodriguez, focusing on his controversial past (suspension for performance-enhancing drugs) and his strained relationship with his father.[44] Wright Thompson, of ESPN, spent time with Michael Jordan; the opening scene depicts Jordan bantering with a fellow basketball executive over the phone.[45] In the *New York Times*, John Branch profiled Golden State Warriors head coach Steve Kerr, starting the story with a striking account of Kerr's father being assassinated in Beirut.[46] Many media outlets have invested in this type of storytelling. That includes traditional outlets, such as the *New York Times*, ESPN, and *Sports Illustrated*, as well as newer digital platforms such as the Bleacher Report and the now-defunct Grantland.

Other personal narratives focus on sports figures whom the mainstream public may not know as well. "The Shot That Saved Lives" by Thomas Lake of *Sports Illustrated* tells the story of a basketball player who made a shot to force overtime that kept the crowd inside the Georgia Dome. If he had missed it and the game was over, those fans all would have been outside when a tornado struck a few minutes later.[47] The point of these personal narratives is to give readers information, emotion, and levels of depth that they don't get in a diet of fast-moving media feeds.

The Future

Judging by recent pieces in longform sports journalism, it appears that media outlets are willing to invest resources in this intensive reporting and writing process. One of the most notable recent pieces is by ESPN's Wright Thompson, called "The Secret History of Tiger Woods." Thompson takes readers deep inside Woods's life (something rarely done before of this notoriously private public figure). Readers get detailed scenes of Woods on a private plane going to and from his father's funeral. They see him training with Navy SEALs (one of Woods's obsessions), and they see him in the carpool line at his kids' school. Here's the kicker: Tiger Woods didn't give Thompson interviews or access: "(Woods' camp declined to comment for this story.)"[48] That sentence makes the story that much more powerful, from an execution point of view, in that Thompson provides readers extensive access to these scenes. Another current piece, "The Greatest, At Rest," written by Tom Junod for ESPN, takes readers inside the intimate process of planning Muhammad Ali's funeral. A passage:

> The plane is a 737 leased from the San Francisco Giants. It is the large plane the man in the hold wanted it to be. There are not quite 30 passengers. Although they are scattered around the cabin, they all have something in common. It is no accident that they are together; it is no surprise that they are here. To the extent that they know one another, they know one another because for years they were bound to the same secret: Long before Muhammad Ali died, they were chosen to lay him to rest.[49]

As long as media outlets invest in writers who can report these detailed pieces, it appears that the future of traditional longform sports stories will continue strongly. But it is interesting to think about how the sports narrative will develop. Will there be literary podcasts that are more in the sports genre, like the mega-popular *Serial*? And certainly, we will continue to see development of visual longform stories, as evidenced by ESPN's *30 for 30* series of documentaries.

Perhaps the most interesting development in narrative journalism will be about a possible shift from being writer-centric to player-centric. The launch of the Players' Tribune—a site founded by former Yankee Derek Jeter—now provides athletes a mainstream place to tell their own stories and in their own voices, without the media as gatekeeper. While some may choose to announce retirements, explain why they tweeted something silly, or speak out on special issues, others may take advantage of the platform to tell longform stories. "Dark, Dark, Dark, Dark, Dark, Dark, Dark, Dark" was written by Corey Hirsch, a retired NHL goalie. It starts with a scene of him contemplating suicide by driving off a cliff and it later goes into detail about his battle with mental health issues. It's told in the style of literary journalism—balancing powerful and emotional scenes with explanation (it should be noted that it's unclear if Hirsch wrote it himself or used a ghostwriter).[50]

If more players and coaches choose to tell their stories using this platform (or similar platforms, like Medium, or personal blogs), it does raise the question about the future of literary storytelling. What role does the reporter/writer serve, and why is that person a necessary part of storytelling? How does one's story change when it's told by oneself, or by someone who is looking at it from the outside, often interviewing other people and doing more research to include various perspectives?

An Ever-Evolving Art

Back in 1954, Arnold Hano had trouble finding a place for his work based on that memorable day in the stands of the Polo Grounds watching Game 1 of the World Series. His publisher of choice, Crown Publishing, turned him down, saying the book wouldn't sell because there was nowhere in the bookstore to sell it. The sports aisle was where fathers went to buy presents for little boys, and nobody would buy a sports book out of the nonfiction aisle. Hano took it to Thomas Y. Crowell Company, who agreed to publish it, only to find out that Crown was right. "It sold," Hano said, "like cold cakes." Despite rave reviews from the *New York Times*, the *Herald Tribune*, and others who saw the literary merits of his work, the book was a flop: "Suddenly I was famous, to 12 people."[51] The readership eventually caught up with the writer, and today *A Day in the Bleachers* is recognized as one of the classics of baseball literature. Like James Agee's *Let Us Now Praise Famous Men*, it was an experiment that, when first conducted, appeared to be a complete and utter failure. It took a change in the culture for the experiment to be judged a success.

It is as a laboratory for just this type of experimentation that sports coverage has been allowed to play a critical role in the development of American literary journalism. Sports emerged as part of American life in the nineteenth century and thereafter continued to claim a larger and larger share of interest and attention among its citizens. Writers and readers followed, and celebrated practitioners emerged to be studied and idolized, only to be replaced as circumstances changed. Tomorrow's literary innovators will no doubt have new technologies that they will incorporate in their efforts to best tell the stories of the victory and defeat on and off the field of play.

The bleachers that Hano wrote about in 1954 are long gone, as is the team that the denizens of those bleachers cheered on that day. *A Day in the Bleachers* was rereleased on its fiftieth anniversary in 2004.[52] The passage of time had changed it from an epic failure to a classic of sports literature. The words on the page were exactly the same. The story that appeared in the mind of Arnold Hano that day in the stands was just as clear to him in 2004 as it was in 1954. It was the rest of us who had caught up. "I wrote a book," he said. "I wrote a book about a day, and this is the day."

Notes

1. Waddles, "Bronx Banter Interview."
2. Betts, *America's Sporting Heritage*, 250.
3. Garrison, *Sports Reporting*, 230.
4. Geismar, *Ring Lardner Reader*, xviii.
5. Fenton, *Apprenticeship*, 24.
6. Holtzman, *No Cheering*, 63–64.
7. Clark, *World of Damon Runyon*, xi, 49.
8. Biasotti, "Bill Simmons."
9. Fountain, *Sportswriter*, 3.
10. Deford, *Over Time*, 102–05.
11. Anderson, "Jimmy Cannon."
12. Halberstam, *Best American Sports Writing*, 170.
13. Wolfe, "Birth."
14. Wolfe.
15. Wolfe.
16. Simon, "Sports Reporting Hero."
17. Talese, "Silent Season."
18. Seitz, "'Why's This So Good?'"
19. Deitsch, "Q&A Gay Talese."
20. Deitsch.
21. Thompson, "Kentucky Derby."
22. MacCambridge, "Director's Cut."
23. Thompson, "Kentucky Derby."
24. Thompson.
25. Elson, *World of Time Inc.*, 353–54.
26. Faulkner, "Kentucky: May: Saturday," 22–24. Faulkner's lead: "Three days before. This saw Boone: the Bluegrass, the virgin land rolling westward wave by dense wave from the Allegheny gaps, unmarked

then, teeming with deer and buffalo about the salt licks and the limestone springs whose water in time would make the fine bourbon whiskey; and the wild men too—the red men and the white ones too who had to be a little wild also to endure and survive and so mark the wilderness with the proofs of their tough survival—Boonesborough, Owenstown, Harrod's and Harbuck's Stations; Kentucky: the dark and bloody ground."

27 MacCambridge, *Franchise*, 108.
28 Fleder, *Sports Illustrated*, 7.
29 Aldrich, *George, Being George*, 161–70.
30 Deford, "Little Irvy."
31 Deford, *Over Time*, 172.
32 Yagoda, "Going Deep."
33 Personal interaction, University of Florida, November 10, 2011.
34 Pérez-Peña, "Sports Whisperer."
35 Pérez-Peña.
36 Yagoda, "Going Deep."
37 Personal interaction, University of Florida, November 10, 2011.
38 Smith, "As Time Runs Out."
39 Hill, "'Going Deep.'"
40 Yagoda, "Going Deep."
41 Personal interaction, University of Florida, November 10, 2011.
42 Hill, "'Going Deep.'"
43 Cramer, "What Do You Think."
44 Moehringer, "Education of Alex Rodriguez."
45 Thompson, "Michael Jordan."
46 Branch, "Tragedy."
47 Lake, "Shot That Saved Lives."
48 Thompson, "Secret History."
49 Junod, "Greatest, At Rest."
50 Hirsch, "Dark."
51 Waddles, "Bronx Banter Interview."
52 Hano, *Day in the Bleachers*.

Bibliography

Aldrich, Nelson W., Jr., ed. *George, Being George: George Plimpton's Life as Told, Admired, Deplored, and Envied by 200 Friends, Relatives, Lovers, Acquaintances, Rivals—and a Few Unappreciative Observers*. New York: Random House, 2008.

Anderson, Dave. "Jimmy Cannon, Columnist, Dies; Sportswriter Ranged Far Afield." *New York Times*, December 6, 1973. Accessed August 21, 2018. www.nytimes.com/1973/12/06/archives/jimmy-cannon-columnist-dies-sportswriter-ranged-far-afield-protege.html.

Betts, John Rickards. *America's Sporting Heritage: 1850–1950*. Reading, MA: Addison-Wesley, 1974.

Biasotti, Tony. "Bill Simmons Is Leaving Grantland. Can the Site Survive without Him?" *Columbia Journalism Review*, May 11, 2015. Accessed August 20, 2018. www.cjr.org/analysis/bill_simmons_is_leaving_grantland_can_the_site_survive_without_him.php.

Branch, John. "Tragedy Made Steve Kerr See the World Beyond the Court." *New York Times*, December 22, 2016, SP1.

Clark, Tom. *The World of Damon Runyon*. New York: Harper and Row, 1978.

Cramer, Richard Ben. "What Do You Think of Ted Williams Now?" *Esquire*, June 1986. Accessed August 20, 2018. www.esquire.com/sports/a5379/biography-ted-williams-0686/.

Deford, Frank. "Little Irvy." *Sports Illustrated*, August 11, 1969, 50–57.

———. *Over Time: My Life as a Sportswriter*. New York: Atlantic Monthly Press, 2012.

Deitsch, Richard. "Q&A Gay Talese." *Sports Illustrated*, May 29, 2006, 29.

Elson, Robert T. *The World of Time Inc.: The Intimate History of a Publishing Enterprise*. New York: Atheneum, 1973.

Faulkner, William. "Kentucky: May: Saturday." *Sports Illustrated*, May 16, 1955, 22–24.

Fenton, Charles. *The Apprenticeship of Ernest Hemingway*. New York: Farrar, Straus & Young, 1954.

Fleder, Rob, ed. *Sports Illustrated: Fifty Years of Great Writing*. New York: Time, 2004.

Fountain, Charles. *Sportswriter: The Life and Times of Grantland Rice*. New York: Oxford University Press, 1993.
Garrison, Bruce. *Sports Reporting*. Ames, IA: Iowa State University Press, 1985.
Geismar, Maxwell, ed. *The Ring Lardner Reader*. New York: Charles Scribner's Sons, 1963.
Halberstam, David, ed. *The Best American Sports Writing of the Century*. New York: Houghton Mifflin, 1990.
Hano, Arnold. *A Day in the Bleachers: The 50th Anniversary of "The Catch."* Cambridge, MA: Da Capo Press, 2004.
Hill, Jemele. "'Going Deep' with *Sport Illustrated*'s Gary Smith." Poynter, October 7, 2008. Accessed August 20, 2018. www.poynter.org/news/going-deep-sports-illustrateds-gary-smith.
Hirsch, Cory. "Dark, Dark, Dark, Dark, Dark, Dark, Dark, Dark." Players' Tribune, February 15, 2017. Accessed August 20, 2018. www.theplayerstribune.com/en-us/articles/corey-hirsch-dark-dark-dark.
Holtzman, Jerome. *No Cheering in the Press Box*. New York: Henry Holt, 1995.
Junod, Tom. "The Greatest, At Rest." ESPN, June 12, 2017. Accessed August 20, 2018. www.espn.com/espn/feature/story/_/id/19409912/the-planning-muhammad-ali-funeral.
Lake, Thomas. "The Shot That Saved Lives." *Sports Illustrated*, March 16, 2009, 56–64.
MacCambridge, Michael. "Director's Cut: 'The Kentucky Derby Is Decadent and Depraved,' by Hunter S. Thompson." Grantland, May 3, 2013. Accessed August 20, 2018. http://grantland.com/features/looking-back-hunter-s-thompson-classic-story-kentucky-derby/.
———. *The Franchise: A History of "Sports Illustrated" Magazine*. New York: Hyperion, 1997.
Moehringer, J. R. "The Education of Alex Rodriguez." ESPN, February 18, 2015. Accessed August 20, 2018. www.espn.com/espn/feature/story/_/id/12321274/alex-rodriguez-return-new-york-yankees.
Pérez-Peña, Richard. "The Sports Whisperer, Probing Psychic Wounds." *New York Times*, September 15, 2008, E1.
Seitz, Jonathan. "'Why's This So Good?' No. 24: Gay Talese on Joe DiMaggio." Nieman Storyboard, December 13, 2011. Accessed August 21, 2018. http://niemanstoryboard.org/stories/whys-this-so-good-no-24-gay-talese-joe-dimaggio-jon-seitz/.
Simon, Scott. "Sports Reporting Hero Speaks of 'Silent Season.'" National Public Radio, October 2, 2010.
Smith, Gary. "As Time Runs Out." *Sports Illustrated*, January 11, 1993, 10–25.
Talese, Gay. "The Silent Season of a Hero." *Esquire*, July 1966, 40.
Thompson, Hunter S. "The Kentucky Derby Is Decadent and Depraved." *Scanlan's Monthly*, June 1970.
Thompson, Wright. "Michael Jordan Has Not Left the Building." ESPN, February 22, 2013. Accessed August 20, 2018. www.espn.com/espn/feature/story/_/page/Michael-Jordan/michael-jordan-not-left-building.
———. "The Secret History of Tiger Woods." ESPN, April 21, 2016. Accessed August 20, 2018. www.espn.com/espn/feature/story/_/id/15278522/how-tiger-woods-life-unraveled-years-father-earl-woods-death.
Waddles, Hank. "Bronx Banter Interview: Arnold Hano Part II." *Alex Belth's Bronx Banter*, September 28, 2009. Accessed August 20, 2018. www.bronxbanterblog.com/2009/09/28/bronx-banter-interview-arnold-hano-part-ii/.
Wolfe, Tom. "The Birth of 'The New Journalism'; Eyewitness Report by Tom Wolfe." *New York*, February 14, 1972.
Yagoda, Ben. "Going Deep." Slate, June 30, 2003. Accessed August 20, 2018. www.slate.com/articles/sports/sports_nut/2003/06/going_deep.html.

PART III

Theorizing American Literary Journalism

Disciplinary Intersections

21
AMERICAN LITERARY JOURNALISM AND BOOK HISTORY
Crossing the Divide

Kathy Roberts Forde

As a recognized form of news reportage, American literary journalism dates at least to the late nineteenth century. But as a recognized field of academic study, it is only a few decades old, occupying a borderland between literary studies and journalism studies. It's not surprising, then, that topical concerns and approaches from these two fields have shaped the study of American literary journalism thus far.[1] American literary journalism has much to discover in terms of subject matter as well as methods, concepts, and theories from other allied fields.

An especially promising field is *histoire du livre*, or the history of the book and print culture, which can be traced in the US context to the publication of Isaiah Thomas's *The History of Printing in America* in the early nineteenth century, a book that gave special attention to journalism, particularly newspapers.[2] When David D. Hall gave the inaugural Wiggins Lecture at the American Antiquarian Society (AAS) in 1983, he not only announced the formal establishment of the AAS Program in the History of the Book in American Culture but also set the agenda for a developing field that understood its purview as the history of *all* print culture, including newspapers and magazines, forms many scholars had formerly viewed as too lowbrow to be worthy of study (with the notable exception of scholars in university journalism programs). Hall opened his lecture with a story about his earliest credentials "as a historian of the book": his job delivering newspapers at age eleven in Alexandria, Virginia.[3]

Isaiah Thomas, an eighteenth-century printer and publisher of the newspaper *Massachusetts Spy*. David Hall, a twentieth century newspaper boy. Two seminal figures in the history of the book in America. And both had deep connections to the world of journalism.

It's curious, then, that after more than three decades, journalism history and book history are, as David Paul Nord has written, "still largely nonintersecting academic fields."[4] Nord, one of the few journalism historians who has built intellectual bridges to the neighboring field of book history, has been especially keen to demonstrate the ways reading the news was an act of community formation at different times and places in the American experience. "Communities are built, maintained, and wrecked in communication," he wrote in the introduction to his path-breaking book *Communities of Journalism: A History of American Newspapers and Their Readers*.[5] And journalism has almost always been at the center of such activity. Yet scholars of journalism—including scholars of literary journalism—have largely pursued their work with little recourse to the critical concepts, models, and concerns of book history.[6]

In this essay, I review in broad brushstrokes the emergence and development of both literary journalism studies and book history as distinct fields of study in the US context and suggest particular ideas and approaches from book history that can enrich the study of literary journalism. In addition, I review the several studies that have merged the fields of literary journalism and book history. Finally, I highlight two social theories of democracy that, when joined with approaches from book history, can help us understand and explain the actual influence and work of literary journalism in American public life, both in the past and in our present moment. After all, to study literary journalism is to study journalism, a particular form of public communication central to civic life in the United States, protected by law and widely understood to be a tool of democracy.[7] While historians of the book privilege the "reader," historians of any form of journalism necessarily conceive of readers as publics. As Michael Schudson has written, "What print means to people is what matters most" for the history of American print culture.[8] And what literary journalism means to the public is what matters most for literary journalism studies.

Beyond personal enrichment and fulfillment, what does literary journalism as a cultural, social, and political product offer the public? How has a given work informed public discussion and understanding of important social and political issues and even public policy? What role, if any, has literary journalism played in helping groups of people associate and imagine themselves as communities?[9] What meanings do readers make out of particular works of literary journalism, and how do they use these meanings in their lives? These are the kinds of questions we can begin to answer when we study literary journalism from the perspective of book history.

American Literary Journalism Studies

Long before *literary journalism* became an accepted term, and long before the form and its practitioners became accepted subjects of academic study, Edwin H. Ford, a journalism professor at the University of Minnesota, was busy writing and teaching about the "literary aspects of journalism." In 1937, he published two separate works attempting to describe and validate the form as a professional craft and literary-journalistic product suited for academic study. Taken together, "The Art and Craft of the Literary Journalist" and *A Bibliography of Literary Journalism in America* constitute the first known attempt in American higher education to bring literary journalism into the purview of journalism scholarship and education.[10]

A long winter followed Ford's work. It was more than three decades before other scholars became interested in literary journalism and literary journalists. The catalyst for this interest was the emergence of the New Journalism as a recognizable social and aesthetic movement in American public life and the challenges it posed not only to the practices and standards of conventional journalism but also to the realistic novel. In 1973, Tom Wolfe, an important spokesperson for and practitioner of the New Journalism, along with E. W. Johnson published *The New Journalism*, an apology for the journalistic form and a collection of readings—inaugurating a critical response that continues today.[11] In 1974, a spate of scholarly works on the New Journalism appeared, constituting what can be considered the first wave of literary journalism scholarship.[12]

These early examinations of the New Journalism as a unique phenomenon in American social life and print culture of the 1960s and early 1970s established several topical and critical trends that have shaped, and continue to shape, the field of literary journalism studies. First, most attempted to name and to define through reference to established literary and journalistic genres what was generally perceived as a new form of writing. Second, these works identified key "New Journalism" writers—including Wolfe, Lillian Ross, Gay Talese, Jimmy Breslin, Truman Capote, and Norman Mailer—and described and critiqued their work with a focus on narrative and reportorial techniques and style. Third, some of this early work provided an early social history of the New Journalism.

When literary journalism scholarship emerged again in the second half of the 1980s and in the 1990s, it received a much broader historical treatment than the previous bracketed treatments of the New Journalism. A key effort in this second wave of scholarship was to name and define the object of study. Thomas Connery offered particularly influential critical discussions with terms, concepts, and historical periodization that have become central to the field.[13] More than anyone, Connery established "literary journalism" as the preferred term of art to describe "a third way to tell the story" that emerged in the late nineteenth century as a hybrid of the fictional story and the factual news report popular in American print culture of the time. He also provided a provisional yet durable periodization of American literary journalism: the first period in the late nineteenth and early twentieth centuries; the second from the 1930s to the 1940s; and the third the New Journalism of the 1960s and 1970s. John Hartsock, in the first book-length history of American literary journalism, adopted this periodization as well as the term "literary journalism."[14] Much of this second-wave scholarship identified key works, authors, and publications of American literary journalism across a century of production and undertook either traditional literary analysis of the works or profiles of the writers and publications or both.[15] A literary-biographical approach remains favored in literary journalism studies, particularly in the recovery of women literary journalists from the shadows of history.[16] This scholarship also collectively served to identify and reify particular writers and texts in what has become "the canon" of literary journalism—that pantheon of works commonly understood to be the most enduring, prototypical, and influential in the greater historical body of literary journalistic texts.[17] Finally, this formative scholarship introduced social and cultural histories of the expressive forms and professional practice of literary journalism as well as theoretical examinations of genre and literary journalistic texts from a range of perspectives, most notably the postmodern and political.[18]

History of the Book and Print Culture in America

Book history studies, although arguably practiced for hundreds of years, emerged as a recognizable academic field in the first half of the twentieth century with the "New Bibliography" school, a scholarly movement focused on identifying authentic, authoritative original texts. How could one establish, for example, a "true" version of a Shakespearean play from a "corrupted" version when printing practices of the era were notoriously nonuniform? The point was to uncover the author's original text and thus intended meanings. This strain of analytical bibliography devoted to the study of printing was preoccupied with the material conditions of a book's production and became a fixture in many English graduate programs in the United States and Great Britain.[19]

But as with so many fields of study in the social sciences and humanities in the 1970s and 1980s, intellectual ferment unseated what came before. The so-called cultural turn challenged the assumption that positivist social science and objectivist history could provide stable, reliable explanations of social life. Social arrangements, beliefs, texts, and languages constructed reality so thoroughly, many scholars came to believe, as to make the study of culture a necessary correlate to social understanding. In the field of analytical bibliography, the idea that "true" or fixed meanings could be recovered from a text printed according to an author's original intent came to seem rather naive. Enter Don McKenzie's concept of the "sociology of the text," which emphasized the importance of forces external to a given text if one was to determine its meanings and understand how it came to be produced and received by readers.[20]

McKenzie's intellectual move placed new concerns about production and reception at the center of the study of printed texts. The publication of Robert Darnton's essay "What Is the

History of Books?" in 1982 and Hall's inaugural AAS Wiggins Lecture marking the birth of the AAS's Program in the History of the Book in American Culture in 1983 initiated a flurry of scholarly activity in the American context. The field we now call "the history of the book" in the United States came into being.[21]

Darnton introduced the concept of "the communication circuit" to help historians of the book map the field and the place of their work within it. A printed book (or any printed text), he suggested, went through a circuit of communication typically moving from "the author to the publisher … the printer, the shipper, the bookseller, and the reader." It was a model describing the creation, distribution, and reception of books and the multiple actors involved, with attention to the economic, political, social, and cultural forces at work within the circuit. For Darnton, the point of book history was "to understand how ideas were transmitted through print and how exposure to the printed word affected the thought and behavior of mankind."[22] Hall, who viewed "the history of the book as the history of culture and society," suggested four topics the new history of the book should explore: 1) the cultural values shaping the material production of texts; (2) readers and reading, particularly how people responded to and used texts in their lives; (3) the texts of popular culture; and (4) the materiality of texts that was the specialty of analytical bibliographers. For Hall, the point of book history was to better understand how cultural "processes and artifacts"—such as the production and reception of texts and the material texts themselves—influenced "the shape and exercise of power."[23]

Book history developed its empirical studies largely following the pathways Darnton and Hall identified in the early 1980s. To provide a sense of the rich topical terrain covered in this scholarship, I list here a few of the more influential works. In *Revolution and the Word*, Cathy Davidson mined the account books of publishers, library lending registers, letters, diaries, and even readers' marginalia in novels to examine the role of the novel—its production and reception as well as popular fears surrounding it—in negotiating ideas of nation and identity in early America.[24] In *The Nature of the Book*, Adrian Johns explored the making of early modern print culture by examining the production, distribution, and reading of books in London and the relationship of this process to the creation of scientific knowledge.[25] In *Reading the Romance*, Janice Radway examined the publication, distribution, and reading of romance novels; she conducted ethnographic interviews with a large group of romance readers in a Midwestern town and found these women read both to escape and to protest the patriarchal systems constraining their own lives.[26]

This modest review of several landmark studies of book history suggests topics, concepts, and approaches for literary journalism scholarship that have scarcely been touched. How have works of literary journalism—newspaper series, magazine articles, books, radio shows, documentaries, and, more recently, digital forms such as podcasts and multimedia stories—circulated through the communication circuit and with what consequences? How have readers made sense of such works and used them to negotiate their lives, both private and public? How have particular institutions nurtured or challenged the production and distribution of literary journalism and for what reasons and with what effects for social, political, and economic life in America? How have literary journalistic works introduced particular ideas into public conversations and discourses and with what consequences? How have institutions, authors, and readers of literary journalism influenced, as Hall put it, "the shape and exercise of power"?

Crossing the Border: Book History in Literary Journalism Studies

In literary journalism studies, we have few models that employ the insights and approaches of book history. The only works with which I'm familiar are my own, which variously document and analyze the publication and communication circuit of John Hersey's *Hiroshima* and the publication and reception of James Baldwin's *The Fire Next Time*.[27] The Baldwin article is part of a much bigger project, a book-in-progress that self-consciously attempts to build bridges between literary journalism studies and the history of the book. How did Baldwin's two social protest essays published in the liberal magazines the *New Yorker* and the *Progressive* in late 1962, and as the book *The Fire Next Time* by Dial Press in early 1963, operate within the public sphere of political and social action and in the private realm of personal belief during a pivotal moment of the US Civil Rights Movement? In other words, how did Americans—political, social, and cultural leaders as well as ordinary citizens—read, appropriate, negotiate, and use Baldwin's writing on race relations during the active phase of the Civil Rights Movement and, indeed, up to the present moment? My research examines how these essays and book came to be written and published, how they circulated in the communications circuit, how and why they were read, and what changes they effected in the sphere of racial beliefs, attitudes, and actions through their readers' negotiation of meaning across time. I argue that *The Fire Next Time* played a meaningful and ongoing role in helping Americans "achieve our country" (to borrow Baldwin's phrase from the book) through expanding the country's collective racial consciousness. My sources are rich and varied: the institutional records of the *New Yorker* (which include a trove of reader letters), the *Progressive*, and Dial Press; the personal papers of Baldwin (which also include reader responses), his literary agents, and others in his orbit; various collections at the John. F. Kennedy Presidential Library and the Lyndon B. Johnson Presidential Library; press reports of the period; and more.

Although there is little work in literary journalism studies that demonstrates empirically how book history can ventilate our field, there is a modest range of work that blends book history with journalism history. These works provide much food for thought for the literary journalism scholar. Two works have served as particularly helpful guides as I have considered how book history can help me answer questions about the role of literary journalism in public life: Nord's *Communities of Journalism* (briefly discussed earlier) and Priscilla Coit Murphy's *What a Book Can Do: The Publication and Reception of "Silent Spring."*[28] Murphy's book, which first introduced me to the field of book history, has provided many fruitful avenues of exploration for my work on Baldwin.[29] Both Rachel Carson, author of *Silent Spring*, and Baldwin published their work first in the *New Yorker*; both quickly republished their magazine articles in book form; both books circulated widely and quickly in the communication circuits of their era; both inflected national conversations about public policy and ultimately public policy itself; and both were seminal texts of major social movements, Carson's of the environmental movement and Baldwin's of the Civil Rights Movement.

Another notable work that joins book history with journalism history is Charles Johanningsmeier's *Fiction and the American Literary Marketplace: The Role of Newspaper Syndicates in America, 1860–1900*.[30] In the transitional period between 1860 and 1900, newspaper readers encountered syndicated fiction as a matter of course. As the author explains, "Newspaper editors during this time created intertextual printed salad bowls where non-fiction stories and advertisements mixed on the pages with syndicated fiction."[31] Throughout the late nineteenth century, most newspapers carried syndicated fiction, and most major fiction authors published in newspapers using the literary syndicates. In researching newspaper syndicates, about which little was previously known, Johanningsmeier consulted the institutional records of various leading syndicates, trade publications like the *Journalist* and the *Writer*, and nineteenth-century newspapers, among other sources. How might literary journalism scholars adopt similar approaches to interrogate the complex institutional practices in print marketplaces and the social and cultural work the blending of fiction and news forms has historically effected in the public sphere?

Theorizing the Power of Journalism in Public Life

While book history's focus on communication networks, particularly readers and reception, can help us understand how particular works of print culture have influenced public life, scholars of journalism have often turned to social theory.[32] Literary journalism scholars can do the same, even as they use the tools of book history. Consider, for example, my work on Baldwin's *The Fire Next Time*. I discovered that Baldwin's text reached all the way into the executive branch of government and influenced the Kennedy administration's decision to pursue what became the Civil Rights Act of 1964. To explain how that happened, and its consequences for American political and social life, I was forced to think more explicitly about the operation of media power in democratic struggle. So I turned to sociology—where the study of journalism was born—to find a macro-level social theory that could convincingly account for the role Baldwin's text played in democratic decision-making.[33] I found it in Jeffrey Alexander's concept of the civil sphere, which he thoroughly theorizes, empirically grounds, and defends in his masterwork *The Civil Sphere*.[34]

Civil sphere theory is concerned with the creation and maintenance of civil society and democratic life and the achievement of justice. "This book is about justice," Alexander writes in *The Civil Sphere*'s opening sentence, "and about the democratic institutions and beliefs that can sustain justice in our massively complex and highly stratified world."[35] Civil sphere theory accounts for the processes by which democratic societies simultaneously pursue social solidarity and social oppression and exclusion, how they manage, at their best, to expand the "circle of we" at the heart of civil society and, at their worst, to build exclusionary, hierarchical, antidemocratic societies. Journalism and media are at the center of this process, representing and interpreting the narratives competing groups use as they struggle for inclusion in democratic society. An oppressed group gains inclusion when it is able to control the dominant public narrative and thus induce the in-group to recognize its claim. This process, as Alexander argues, is a matter of "symbolic recognition," not "factual knowledge," "of understanding, not information."[36]

Let me return to my Baldwin project. I focused my analysis on readers of Baldwin in the Kennedy administration as they reacted to a massive national social and political struggle for civil rights and racial justice. And I uncovered sources that pointed toward the key conceptual categories and workings of civil sphere theory. Given the centrality of justice and social movements to Alexander's conception of the civil sphere, and the moral awakening and empathetic identification I found Baldwin's ideas inspired in key actors in the Kennedy administration as it was contemplating whether to commit to civil rights legislation, I found civil sphere theory a fitting explanatory framework.

But civil sphere theory is simply one among many social theories that may prove useful to historians of the book, scholars of literary journalism, and those who work across the boundaries of these fields. Jürgen Habermas's theory of the public sphere has been of immense interest to communication and journalism studies scholars.[37] As complex and contested as public sphere theory is,[38] the well-known classic formulation can be expressed in fairly straightforward terms. A free press and a self-regulated communication system provide a dispersed yet egalitarian public with the information and means to engage in rational, critical debate on matters of common interest, and the resulting public opinion influences political and policy decision-making, thus operating as a control on market and state power. This space of public-opinion formation is the Habermasian public sphere.[39] Given the theory's emphasis on the role of a free press in democratic deliberation and decision making—the centerpiece of most press theory—it is no wonder it has proven to be of such interest and utility in communication and journalism studies.

Book historians, too, have invoked public sphere theory as a means for interrogating and explaining the role of print culture in public life. For example, Murphy's *What a Book Can Do*, discussed earlier, engages public sphere theory to interrogate the role of Carson's *Silent Spring* in informing and stimulating robust public debate about the harmful effects of pesticides—and ultimately prompting the creation of new environmental policy. Michael Warner's *The Letters of the Republic: Publication and the Public Sphere in Eighteenth-Century America* uses the concept of the public sphere to demonstrate how print media (especially newspapers), a republican political culture, and a vibrant public sphere developed symbiotically in the eighteenth century, creating a nation of citizen-readers who understood their claim to citizenship as emanating from reading and discussion.[40] Put another way, newspaper culture helped constitute the nation-state and notions of citizenship in the early US experience.

Both public sphere theory and civil sphere theory have the potential to help scholars explain, given fitting empirical evidence, how literary journalism operates in public life. Such explanation has been a notable weakness in literary journalism scholarship to date; when studies make claims about the public effects and outcomes of literary journalism, they often simply assume and assert their existence. Rather, we must demonstrate how literary journalism matters in public life. With its emphasis on the role of print culture in public life, book history, coupled with sensitive theorizing, gives us the tools to do exactly that. Other theories attentive to counterpublics can help us in this project, too: critical race theory and intersectional theory, to name just two.[41]

Conclusion

A scholarly community is designed by many minds and built by many hands. The community that literary journalism studies has been building is international in scope, multidisciplinary in design, and accommodating of diverse topics, theoretical perspectives, and methodological approaches. As the building continues, I hope some scholars will take on the critical task of exploring how works of literary journalism—and the authors, editors, publishers, institutions, readers, and contexts associated with them—have not only reflected but also shaped social, cultural, and political life in particular communities, nations, and regions of the world, including the United States. The history of the book can help us understand and explain why literary journalism matters.

Notes

1 Sims, "Problem and the Promise"; Connery, "Research Review."
2 Thomas, *History*.
3 Hall, "On Native Ground," 313.
4 Nord, "History of Journalism," 162.
5 Nord, *Communities of Journalism*, 2.
6 Nord, "Historical Readership Studies," 86–87.
7 Barnhurst and Nerone, *Form of News*, 1.
8 Schudson, "Enduring Book," 20.
9 See Anderson, *Imagined Communities*, the influential book that shaped the study not only of nationalism but also of mass communication products, processes, and institutions.
10 Ford, "Art and Craft"; Ford, *Bibliography*. For interesting discussions of Ford's contributions to the field of literary journalism, see Connery, "Third Way," 16; Hartsock, *History*, 19–20, 241–42; Sims, *True Stories*, 8.
11 Wolfe and Johnson, *New Journalism*.
12 Dennis and Rivers, *Other Voices*; Hellman, *Fables of Fact*; Hollowell, *Fact and Fiction*; Mills, *New Journalism*; Weber, *Reporter as Artist*; Weber, *Literature of Fact*.
13 Connery, "Third Way"; Connery, "Discovering a Literary Form."
14 Hartsock, *History*, 14.
15 Fishkin, *From Fact to Fiction*; Frus, *Politics and Poetics*; Lounsberry, *Art of Fact*; Sims, *Literary Journalism*.

16 See, for example, Lauters, *Rediscovered Writings*; Thorne, "Developing a Personal Style"; Whitt, *Settling the Borderland*.
17 These canonical works and writers remain of considerable interest to literary journalism scholars today. See, for example, discussions of Tom Wolfe in Sims, *True Stories*, and Zdovc, *Literary Journalism*, and discussions of Truman Capote in Sims, *True Stories*, and Keeble and Wheeler, *Journalistic Imagination*.
18 See, for example, Frus, *Politics and Poetics*, and Pauly, "Politics."
19 Finkelstein and McCleery, *Introduction to Book History*, 8.
20 Finkelstein and McCleery, 8–11; Bonnell and Hunt, introduction to *Beyond the Cultural Turn*; Berger and Luckmann, *Social Construction of Reality*; McKenzie, *Bibliography*, 14.
21 Darnton, "What Is the History?"; McDonald, "*Semper Aliquid Novi*"; Gura, "'*Magnalia Historiae Libri Americana.*'"
22 Darnton, "What Is the History?," 65.
23 Hall, "On Native Ground," 336.
24 Davidson, *Revolution and the Word*.
25 Johns, *Nature of the Book*.
26 Radway, *Reading the Romance*.
27 Forde, "Profit and Public Interest"; Forde and Ross, "Radio and Civic Courage"; Forde, "*Fire Next Time.*"
28 Nord, *Communities of Journalism*; Murphy, *What a Book Can Do*. Based on deep investigation, *Silent Spring* reported on pesticide manufacturing and use and its environmental impacts.
29 Forde, "'Dozen Best.'"
30 Johanningsmeier, *Fiction*.
31 Johanningsmeier, 4.
32 For a robust discussion of such theories, see Christians et al., *Normative Theories*.
33 Benson, "Shaping the Public Sphere."
34 Habermas, *Structural Transformation*; Alexander, *Civil Sphere*.
35 Alexander, *Civil Sphere*, 13.
36 Alexander, "On the Interpretation," 648.
37 Habermas, *Structural Transformation*.
38 See, for example, Fraser, "Rethinking the Public Sphere," 123–25.
39 Habermas, *Structural Transformation*; Habermas, *Theory of Communicative Action*. For a review of the prominence of public sphere theory in journalism studies, see Hess and Gutsche, "Journalism." For a discussion of Habermas's contribution to media sociology and communication, see Benson, "Shaping the Public Sphere."
40 Warner, *Letters of the Republic*. Joanna Brooks has usefully challenged Warner's assumption that black Americans had no place in the early American public sphere in "The Early American Public Sphere and the Emergence of a Black Print Counterpublic."
41 Delgado and Stefancic, *Critical Race Theory*; Lykke, *Feminist Studies*.

Bibliography

Alexander, Jeffrey C. *The Civil Sphere*. New York: Oxford University Press, 2006.
———. "On the Interpretation of *The Civil Sphere*: Understanding and Contention in Contemporary Social Science." *Sociological Quarterly* 48, no. 4 (2007): 641–59. https://doi.org/10.1111/j.1533-8525.2007.00095.x.
Anderson, Benedict. *Imagined Communities*. London: Verso, 1983.
Barnhurst, Kevin G., and John Nerone. *The Form of News: A History*. New York: Guilford Press, 2001.
Benson, Rodney. "Shaping the Public Sphere: Habermas and Beyond." *American Sociologist* 40, no. 3 (2009): 175–97. https://doi.org/10.1007/s12108-009-9071-4.
Berger, Peter L., and Thomas Luckmann. *The Social Construction of Reality: A Treatise in the Sociology of Knowledge*. Garden City, NY: Anchor Books, 1966.
Bonnell, Victoria E., and Lynn Hunt. Introduction to *Beyond the Cultural Turn*, edited by Victoria E. Bonnell and Lynn Hunt, 1–34. Berkeley, CA: University of California Press, 1999.
Brooks, Joanna. "The Early American Public Sphere and the Emergence of a Black Print Counterpublic." *William and Mary Quarterly* 62, no. 1 (2005): 67–92. https://doi.org/10.2307/3491622.
Christians, Clifford G., Theodore L. Glasser, Denis McQuail, Kaarle Nordenstreng, and Robert A. White. *Normative Theories of the Media: Journalism in Democratic Societies*. Urbana, IL: University of Illinois Press, 2009.
Connery, Thomas B. "Discovering a Literary Form." In *A Sourcebook of American Literary Journalism: Representative Writers in an Emerging Genre*, edited by Thomas B. Connery, 3–37. New York: Greenwood Press, 1992.

———. "Research Review: Magazines and Literary Journalism, an Embarrassment of Riches." In *The American Magazine: Research Perspectives and Prospects*, edited by David Abrahamson, 207–16. Ames, IA: Iowa State University Press, 1995.

———. "A Third Way to Tell the Story: American Literary Journalism at the Turn of the Century." In *Literary Journalism in the Twentieth Century*, edited by Norman Sims, 3–20. New York: Oxford University Press, 1990.

Darnton, Robert. "What Is the History of Books?" *Daedalus* 111, no. 3 (1982): 65–83.

Davidson, Cathy N. *Revolution and the Word: The Rise of the Novel in America*. New York: Oxford University Press, 1986, republished with new introduction 2004.

Delgado, Richard, and Jean Stefancic. *Critical Race Theory: An Introduction*. 3rd ed. New York: New York University Press, 2017.

Dennis, Everette, and William L. Rivers. *Other Voices: The New Journalism in America*. San Francisco, CA: Canfield Press, 1974.

Finkelstein, David, and Alistair McCleery. *An Introduction to Book History*. New York: Routledge, 2005.

Fishkin, Shelley Fisher. *From Fact to Fiction: Journalism and Imaginative Writing in America*. Baltimore, MD: Johns Hopkins University Press, 1985.

Ford, Edwin H. "The Art and Craft of the Literary Journalist." In *New Survey of Journalism*, edited by George Fox Mott, 304–13. New York: Barnes and Noble, 1950. Originally published as *Journalism Outline* in 1937.

———. *A Bibliography of Literary Journalism in America*. Minneapolis, MN: Burgess, 1937.

Forde, Kathy Roberts. "'A Dozen Best': Top Books for the Journalism Historian Exploring the History of the Book." *American Journalism* 26, no. 2 (2009): 140–49. https://doi.org/10.1080/08821127.2009.10677723.

———. "*The Fire Next Time* in the Civil Sphere: Literary Journalism and Justice in America 1963." *Journalism* 15, no. 5 (2014): 573–88. https://doi.org/10.1177%2F1464884914523094.

———. "Profit and Public Interest: A Publication History of John Hersey's 'Hiroshima.'" *Journalism and Mass Communication Quarterly* 88, no. 3 (2011): 562–79. https://doi.org/10.1177%2F107769901108800306.

Forde, Kathy Roberts, and Matthew W. Ross. "Radio and Civic Courage in the Communications Circuit of John Hersey's 'Hiroshima.'" *Literary Journalism Studies* 3, no. 2 (2011): 31–53.

Fraser, Nancy. "Rethinking the Public Sphere: A Contribution to the Critique of Actually Existing Democracy." In *Habermas and the Public Sphere*, edited by Craig Calhoun, 109–42. Cambridge, MA: MIT Press, 1992.

Frus, Phyllis. *The Politics and Poetics of Journalistic Narrative: The Timely and the Timeless*. Cambridge: Cambridge University Press, 1994.

Gura, Philip F. "'*Magnalia Historiae Libri Americana*'; or, How AAS Brought the History of the Book into the New Millennium." *Proceedings of the American Antiquarian Society* 114, part 2 (2004): 249–80.

Habermas, Jürgen. *The Structural Transformation of the Public Sphere: An Inquiry into a Category of Bourgeois Society*. Cambridge, MA: MIT Press, 1989.

———. *The Theory of Communicative Action*. Boston, MA: Beacon Press, 1984.

Hall, David D. "On Native Ground: From the History of Printing to the History of the Book." *Proceedings of the American Antiquarian Society* 93, part 2 (1983): 313–36.

Hartsock, John C. *A History of American Literary Journalism: The Emergence of a Modern Narrative Form*. Amherst, MA: University of Massachusetts Press, 2000.

Hellman, John. *Fables of Fact: The New Journalism as New Fiction*. Chicago: University of Illinois Press, 1981.

Hess, Kristy, and Robert E. Gutsche Jr. "Journalism and the 'Social Sphere.'" *Journalism Studies* 19, no. 4 (2017): 483–98. https://doi.org/10.1080/1461670X.2017.1389296.

Hollowell, John. *Fact and Fiction: The New Journalism and the Nonfiction Novel*. Chapel Hill, NC: University of North Carolina Press, 1977.

Johanningsmeier, Charles A. *Fiction and the American Literary Marketplace: The Role of Newspaper Syndicates in America, 1860–1900*. Cambridge: Cambridge University Press, 1997.

Johns, Adrian. *The Nature of the Book: Print and Knowledge in the Making*. Chicago: University of Chicago Press, 1998.

Keeble, Richard, and Sharon Wheeler, eds. *The Journalistic Imagination: Literary Journalists from Defoe to Capote and Carter*. London: Routledge, 2007.

Lauters, Amy Mattson, ed. *The Rediscovered Writings of Rose Wilder Lane, Literary Journalist*. Columbia, MO: University of Missouri Press, 2007.

Lounsberry, Barbara. *The Art of Fact: Contemporary Artists of Nonfiction*. Westport, CT: Greenwood Press, 1990.

Lykke, Nina. *Feminist Studies: A Guide to Intersectional Theory, Methodology and Writing*. New York: Routledge, 2012.

McDonald, Peter D. "*Semper Aliquid Novi*: Reclaiming the Future of Book History from an African Perspective." *Book History* 19 (2016): 384–98. https://doi.org/10.1353/bh.2016.0011.
McKenzie, D. F. *Bibliography and the Sociology of Texts*. 1984. Reprint, Cambridge: Cambridge University Press, 1999.
Mills, Nicolaus, ed. *The New Journalism: A Historical Anthology*. New York: McGraw Hill, 1974.
Murphy, Priscilla Coit. *What a Book Can Do: The Publication and Reception of "Silent Spring."* Amherst, MA: University of Massachusetts Press, 2005.
Nord, David Paul. *Communities of Journalism: A History of American Newspapers and Their Readers*. Urbana, IL: University of Illinois Press, 2001.
———. "Historical Readership Studies: A Methodological and Autobiographical Note." *American Journalism* 33, no. 1 (2016): 86–97. https://doi.org/10.1080/08821127.2015.1134976.
———. "The History of Journalism and the History of the Book." In *Explorations in Communication and History*, edited by Barbie Zelizer, 162–80. London: Routledge, 2008.
Pauly, John J. "The Politics of the New Journalism." In *Literary Journalism in the Twentieth Century*, edited by Norman Sims, 110–29. New York: Oxford University Press, 1990.
Radway, Janice A. *Reading the Romance: Women, Patriarchy, and Popular Literature*. Chapel Hill, NC: University of North Carolina Press, 1984, republished with new introduction 1991.
Schudson, Michael. "The Enduring Book in a Multimedia Age." General introduction to *The Enduring Book: Print Culture in Postwar America*, edited by David Paul Nord, Joan Shelley Rubin, and Michael Schudson, 1–22. Vol. 5 of *A History of the Book in America*. Chapel Hill, NC: University of North Carolina Press, 2009.
Sims, Norman, ed. *Literary Journalism in the Twentieth Century*. New York: Oxford University Press, 1990.
———. "The Problem and the Promise of Literary Journalism Studies." *Literary Journalism Studies* 1, no. 1 (2009): 7–16.
———. *True Stories: A Century of Literary Journalism*. Evanston, IL: Northwestern University Press, 2007.
Thomas, Isaiah. *The History of Printing in America*. Albany, NY: Joel Munsell, 1874.
Thorne, Ann. "Developing a Personal Style: Janet Flanner's Literary Journalism." *American Journalism* 23, no. 1 (2006): 35–62. https://doi.org/10.1080/08821127.2006.10677996.
Warner, Michael. *The Letters of the Republic: Publication and the Public Sphere in Eighteenth-Century America*. Cambridge, MA: Harvard University Press, 1990.
Weber, Ronald. *The Literature of Fact: Literary Nonfiction in American Writing*. Athens, OH: Ohio University Press, 1980.
———, ed. *The Reporter as Artist: A Look at the New Journalism Controversy*. New York: Hastings House, 1974.
Whitt, Jan. *Settling the Borderland: Other Voices in Literary Journalism*. Lanham, MD: University Press of America, 2008.
Wolfe, Tom, and E. W. Johnson. *The New Journalism*. New York: Harper and Row, 1973.
Zdovc, Sonja Merljak. *Literary Journalism in the United States of America and Slovenia*. Lanham, MD: University Press of America, 2008.

22

EXPLORING THE REFERENTIALITY OF NARRATIVE LITERARY JOURNALISM

John C. Hartsock

At a fundamental level, narrative literary journalism is about the ambition to recover the aesthetics of everyday experience. On that basis, we can discern much about the nature of the genre's referentiality, I would suggest. This includes how such an aesthetics contributes, at its most compelling, to what could be described as a threshold of cognitive disruption inviting new interpretive opportunities that challenge our secular mythologies. It also includes a paradox central to understanding the genre in which the seemingly tangible of experience—what conventionally we describe as "real life"—is a lot less tangible than one might expect, resulting in a genre forever in a state of becoming.[1]

Of course, in one sense the ambition to recover the aesthetics of everyday experience must fail, because as science historian Peter Dear has noted, "the singular experience could not be evident" or fully constituted in the mediation. That said, he adds an important qualifier: "but it could provide evidence," in this case of what contributed to constituting the mediation.[2] And that qualifier makes all the difference in perceiving the nature of the genre's referentiality. Implicit, too, in such an examination is the issue of the "reality boundary," articulated by Norman Sims, which exists between conventional fiction and a narrative literary journalism.[3] Such a boundary, however, is not so much a hard-and-fast divide, I would propose, but rather a space of complex relationships.

What is said here, I would add, may have application to other documentary or nonfictional forms. But to maintain a reasonable focus, I have restricted my examination to narrative literary journalism.

* * *

In defining "aesthetics" in the "aesthetics of experience," I do not mean "the beautiful" as is often associated with the term by refined aesthetes who have assumed the term for their own ends (that truth is beauty and beauty truth, altogether missing the irony of Keats's poem). Instead, the aesthetics of experience comes closer to the Greek original, referring to a phenomenal experience that prompts a sensory response, a viewpoint revived in the concept of the "aesthetics of the everyday" that makes aesthetes of us all in our responses to experience, whether lowbrow or highbrow—and the variations in between. As Tom Leddy notes, when we engage in the everyday experience of life—such as taking a walk—"all of the senses are involved." The result is a "sensuous or imaginative apprehension. ... The properties appreciated in everyday aesthetics are neither wholly objective nor wholly subjective. They are properties of experienced things, not of physical objects abstracted from our experienced world."[4]

Consider, for example, a passage from Michael Paterniti's "Driving Mr. Albert," his account (originally published in *Harper's*) of hospital pathologist Thomas Harvey taking a road trip across the country with Albert Einstein's brain in preservative in a Tupperware bowl. Harvey removed Einstein's brain after the world-famous physicist's death in 1955, reportedly without either Einstein's or the Einstein family's permission. Harvey did so ostensibly for scientific research (he did send out cross sections on slides to other pathologists and neuroscientists). In the passage that follows, the eighty-four-year-old Harvey, accompanied by Paterniti, arrives in Lawrence, Kansas. There, Harvey meets his former New Jersey neighbor, the now octogenarian writer William S. Burroughs of Beat Generation fame who is likely best remembered for his novel *Naked Lunch*:

> Shuffling across the front porch now, Harvey clasps the old writer's hand, enunciating loudly, believing that the eighty-three-year-old Burroughs is equally deaf, which he isn't, then climbs up his arm until they are in a startled embrace, the two of them as pale as the marble of a Rodin sculpture. "REAL, REAL GOOD TO SEE YA!" Later, Harvey quaffs glasses of burgundy until he turns bright red; Burroughs, himself a bowed and hollowed cult hero and keeper of the Secret—his cheeks dimpled as if by the tip of a blade, a handgun in a holster over his kidney—drinks five Coke and vodkas after taking his daily dose of methadone.
>
> "Have you ever tried morphine, Doctor?" he asks Harvey.
>
> "NO. NO, I HAVEN'T," yells Harvey earnestly.[5]

We recognize the reflected or mediated evidence of the aesthetics of experience, partial to be sure as Dear noted, in such descriptors as "shuffling," "clasps," "enunciating loudly," "climbs up his arm," "startled embrace," both "pale as ... marble," among other examples. To this can be added the aesthetics of sound as Harvey, compensating for his deafness, yells at Burroughs.

Such examples of the aesthetics of everyday experience, commonplace if not outright banal, provide only a starting point, however. This is because it is all too easy to overlook the nature of the originating phenomenal status of an aesthetic experience amid the accumulated clutter of abstract constructions of consciousness, constructions that nonetheless make powerful claims to our existential condition such as "peace," "love," "war," "death," among others. It is an originating nature located at the intersection of a unique and distinctive time and space. At that intersection we find what critic Mikhail Bakhtin characterized as the chronotope. In the chronotope, time (chronos) and space (topos) are inseparable.[6] Their intersection is distinctive because the two can never occur again in the same combination. Time alone assures this, as well as the vicissitudes of any one location in space over time, both of which are fundamentally fluid, slipping away even as we attempt to grasp their evidence.

The concept of the chronotope has provided much inspiration for literary scholars. What is clear is that the concept has been privileged as literary gesture.[7] But it is not privileged exclusively because Bakhtin identifies the point of departure for the chronotope: phenomenal experience, which is followed by the aesthetic response. "Out of the actual chronotopes of our world (which serve as the source of representation) emerge the reflected and created chronotopes of the world represented in the work (in the text)."[8] The kind of chronotope at work in a narrative literary journalism, or what could also be called a "narra-descriptive journalism" given the dominant modalities, takes its cue from this observation: It is "reflected," however imperfect, incomplete and distorted a reflection might prove. The literary chronotope is one that openly acknowledges and is indeed inspired by the phenomenal or empirical as it is negotiated by the linguistic, and maintains a claim of direct relationship to the phenomenal. This is a more difficult claim for fiction to make if we speak of fiction as make-believe and wholly invented. Then there are the troubling accounts in between. I will examine this issue in greater detail when I discuss Victor Hugo's *Les Misérables*.

What we can see in such an approach to a narrative literary journalism is a dynamic process, not a static intellectual concept, which Bakhtin acknowledges: While emphatically cautioning against confusing phenomenal experience and linguistic expression, he says, "they are nevertheless indissolubly tied up with each other and find themselves in continual mutual interaction; uninterrupted exchange goes on between them."[9] It is in the mutual interaction, in the uninterrupted exchange, that the distinctiveness of the aesthetic moment extracted from time and space arises.

There are, moreover, additional epistemological consequences when we respond aesthetically and select or pluck a singular detail from the fluidity of the time-space continuum. Here I return to Friedrich Nietzsche's seminal "On Truth and Falsity in Their Ultramoral Sense" (also often translated as "On Truth and Lying in an Extra Moral Sense"), which has provided much critical fodder for the postmodernist positions. Briefly, Nietzsche cites an example of how a leaf of the kind found on a tree or bush is distinctive and therefore discrete from every other distinctive leaf (each derived of different times and spaces, so to speak). Thus each reflects "differentiating qualities" within its own species. Referentially, each constitutes a discrete "concrete metaphor," to use Nietzsche's characterization, in which a fundamental "inequality" exists between them. However, the human mind has a natural inclination to erase such inequalities in an effort to construct generalizations, in this case of trees or bushes having generic "leaves" in what Nietzsche characterizes further as a linguistic "volatilisation."[10] This is only a beginning, however, because erasing the differences presents still additional points of departure, ones engaged in constructing still broader "concepts" or generalizations. Eventually "volatilization" results in the kinds of concepts or totalizations (again, think peace, love, war, death) we reify although they are only abstractions, but abstractions powerful enough that they reflect our taken-for-granted assumptions and expectations, or take on the power of secular mythologies we are unlikely to challenge. As Nietzsche says, we attach the allegorical "ship" of our lives to them, granting them an occult quality or power over us, which he identifies as a "*qualitas occulta.*"[11]

To the contrary, the rhetorical ambition of a narrative literary journalism is to resist (but not necessarily successfully) the abstracting inclination by maintaining a claim to the distinctiveness and integrity of discrete intersections in time and space.[12] We detect this in the mediated evidence derived from the aesthetics of everyday experience—"shuffling," "clasps," "enunciating loudly," "climbs up his arm," "startled embrace," both "pale as ... marble"—because they are distinctive to a singular time and place-in-space.

Clearly, such a resistance to abstraction and ultimately reification has implications for any discourse making a referential claim to the phenomenal world. Interpretations of the continental philosophers of language in the last century tended to focus on the metaphoric or literary nature of the concrete metaphor given the noun. But as the term implies, Nietzsche (like Bakhtin) did not lose sight of what prompted the metaphor: concrete experience.

* * *

The presence of the concrete metaphor in narrative literary journalism invites comparison with other similar forms or genres to understand how they differ. To be sure, chronotopes of experience can exist in more conventional models of journalism such as the hard news story and the conventional feature story. But the treatment, compared to a narrative literary journalism, is different. The same is the case with conventional fiction, which I will also examine.

As explored in greater detail elsewhere,[13] the rhetorical ambition of the hard news model, known as the inverted pyramid, digresses from the narrative and descriptive modalities that dominate in a narrative literary journalism by emphasizing discontinuity in which the specificity and distinctiveness of the chronotopes selected from discrete times and spaces descend in a growing detail relegated to a decreasing order of importance so that what is discrete—what resists volatilization into abstract ether—has a declining claim to cognitive value. Fundamentally, the inverted pyramid digresses in an expository direction, the digression into exposition migrating or evolving away from narrative. Here I use the most basic of definitions of narrative as "a sequence of events," one decipherable as a passage of time.[14] The inverted pyramid violates that chronicity because it is subject to an overarching ambition: "What is most newsworthy here?" The intent, then, is analytically digressive (and moves in an expository direction). Concrete metaphors are selected according to what is deemed most important, and they can be extracted from anywhere in the chronicity. Hence the discontinuity.

In such a movement away from traditional narrative chronicity, the inverted pyramid confronts a problem identified in psychological research: "The results of these studies are compatible with the claim that narrative text is recalled approximately twice as well as expository text and is read approximately twice as fast."[15] This is because of what cognitive psychology characterizes as an increased sense of psychological "transportation" into the story world of narrative as a sequence of events.[16] Such a "transportation" is "defined as an integrative melding of attention, imagery, and feelings, focused on story events."[17] For these reasons, traditional narrative storytelling reflects how the brain naturally enquires into the world.[18] A narrative literary journalism—or again a "narra-descriptive journalism" given the dominant modalities—is then more cognitively accessible.

Regarding the relationship between a narrative literary journalism and more conventional feature writing, the latter, too, can be invested with chronotopes that are descriptive and narrative in the form of scene construction.[19] However, unlike a narrative literary journalism, such scene construction usually serves the purpose of illustrating an expository—and abstract—claim.[20] In other words, the chronotopes in conventional feature writing—as well as in the inverted pyramid, hard news story—are in thrall to the digressing and abstracting rhetorical ambition or volatilization.

The resistance to such volatilization in narrative literary journalism can be noted, for example, in a 2002 article by Paula Bock, a reporter for the *Seattle Times*. The article examines the AIDS epidemic in sub-Saharan Africa. At the beginning of the article, Bock poses an epistemological challenge—a problem of knowledge or of what we believe we can know—when she notes: "Listen to Ruth's mother cry, and you'll never think of the number 2.3 million in the same distant way." Three sentences later, she reiterates: "Two million three hundred thousand. A number too big to get your arms around, a number easier to calculate than to comprehend." And again, after an explanatory paragraph describing the AIDS epidemic, she writes: "If you've ever wondered whether 2.3 million deaths make any single death less painful, listen. Imagine wind moaning, tires screeching, goats being strangled."[21] So she embarks into the world of the narrative as a traditional story, this in an examination of one singularly dying life in Harare, Zimbabwe. In the one dying life lies the differentiating qualities of the concrete metaphors.

What is revealing is how Bock squarely took aim, in the mantra-like refrain of "2.3 million," at conventional reportorial models according to which the story of the AIDS epidemic in Africa generally has been reported, models that might read abstractly like this: "Some 2.3 million Africans died of AIDS in 2001, according to the World Health Organization." Bock and her editors sensed the limitations implicit in the objectivist paradigm so long dominant in journalism practice, namely that it only interprets the world in "a distant way," as she defined the issue, or as a constative report, as reader-response theory would. Bock's account seeks escape, then, from the *qualitas occulta* of linguistic abstraction inadequate for examining one dying life.

Nor is she the only journalist to expose this epistemological problem. One sees it in literary journalist Michael Herr's *Dispatches*, his account of the Vietnam War. As he notes of conventional reporting about the war, "The press got all the facts (more or less); it got too many of them. But it never found a way to report meaningfully about death, which of course was really what it was all about."[22] Stephen Crane made a similar observation. While perhaps best remembered as the author of the fictional *Red Badge of Courage*, he was a capable literary journalist in his own right in the 1890s.[23] As he noted in 1898 while reporting on the Spanish–American War, an American battle casualty "will achieve a temporary notoriety, figuring in the [casualty] lists for one brief moment in which he will appear to the casual reader mainly as part of a total, a unit in the interesting sum of men slain."[24] In the "part of a total, a unit in … the sum" lies the "volatilized" abstraction of death.

We find, then, three literary journalists over the course of more than a century who sensed the problem of an objectifying "objective" journalism abstracted and detached from the concrete metaphors of the aesthetics of everyday experience, experience that clearly appeals at a more visceral level. The normative journalistic rhetoric they resisted had become what was expected, and it took on a kind of occult quality that readers so often uncritically read, substituting information for experience. Bock, Herr, and Crane were trying to resist the attempt to elide the differences, the inequalities, between the distinctive concrete metaphors as unique entities each in its own time and space in the attempt to recover the aesthetics of everyday experience.

Then there is narrative literary journalism's relationship to conventional fiction, given that a common (if imprecise) definition for literary journalism has long been a journalism that "reads like a novel" or "short story."[25] The effort to escape from the *qualitas occulta* of linguistic abstraction is one that solely traditional and conventional fictional accounts cannot so comfortably make. This is because traditional fictions in terms of stories made up solely from the imagination are fundamentally and only allegorical since they are severed from claims of phenomenal referents located in distinctive, one-of-kind phenomenal times and spaces. This is not to dispute the imaginative power of fictional novels. One reason, as David Herman observes, is that the fictional world is a self-contained or "sovereign world."[26] Because of its "sovereign" nature, it provides a greater cognitive freedom for creation and interpretation. But we must bear in mind that traditional fiction draws from the generalized "representativeness" of experience. If it does not, we say it is not "real to life," meaning that our conceptions of what is reality are determined in advance. In comparison, the claims of narrative literary journalism are more modest because they are only referential to distinctive, one-of-a-kind phenomenon—like Nietzsche's distinctive, one-of-a-kind leaf. Given fiction's detachment from such distinct chronotopes located in time and space that, I would emphasize, exist outside the cover of books, fiction can only be prospective or hypothetical.[27] Liberated from such distinctive phenomenal chronotopes, fiction has only one ambition in which consciousness, drawn by the vacuum, can proceed: in the centrifugal direction of allegory, the *qualitas occulta*. When literature is discussed as transcendent, it is allegorized, from which arises, in an illustration of an abstracting "volatilization," claims to the bromide of the universal truth of literature, one to which the fustian littérateur attaches the allegory of the "ship" of his or her life.[28]

In a narrative literary journalism, a chronotope can aspire to having a generalized or volatilized representativeness. (This, after all, was Nietzsche's point, that it is part of the natural human inclination to "volatilize" the distinctiveness of experience and the concrete metaphors of such experience into generalizations no longer claiming a direct referentiality to what exists outside the covers of books. The degree of the "concreteness" in the concrete metaphor has become untethered from a distinctive time and place-in-space. It has become, by degrees, more fictional, given that all text is a kind of fiction or mediation.) But as long as a narrative literary journalism makes a claim to being located uniquely in one time and location in space, an inherent resistance arises in the chronotope to volatilization, given the inequalities of the differences. In a sense, the aspiration of a more conventional fiction to a generalized or volatilized representativeness remains tied to the cultural assumptions or secular mythologies of what it is not willing to free itself from, just as the aspiration of a narrative literary journalism remains tied to a one-of-a-kind distinctiveness it is unwilling to free itself from.

* * *

One reason an understanding of the dynamic nature of the chronotope as both phenomenon and metaphor is necessary in appreciating the peculiar nature of a narrative literary journalism is perhaps obvious: We do need to acknowledge our phenomenal world in an epistemological act, given that the epistemological act is the only recourse available for conveying to others the experience of our existential condition. Simply, we cannot avoid acknowledging existential consequences. Herein lies perhaps one of the clearest differences between such a narrative literary journalism and conventional fictions. Journalism (and more broadly documentary) deals in the end with phenomenal consequences. But again fiction deals with imagined allegorical prospects or hypotheticals (which is not to dismiss that there can be value to such prospects or hypotheticals). This is the case until fiction attempts to crib on the terrain of documentary.[29] If the latter, then one can, arguably, note that fiction becomes a bastard genre. At the least, it has lost its integrity as a true fiction because it has engaged in a con by pretending to deny phenomenal origins. The result is a kind of confused identity unable to decide what it is. (But then arguably the same can be said of a claimed journalism that engages in fictional make-believe.)

In a narrative literary journalism—fundamentally narra-descriptive in its inseparable compound modality—we are caught in a compromise because the testimony of the senses must be reflected in language. But even if we concede that all discourse is a kind of "fiction," not all fictions, it should be emphasized, are equal. Rather, there are qualitative differences because there are those mediated forms that subscribe to reflecting, however imperfectly, phenomenal consequences located outside the covers of books. Conventional fictions in the way of made-up stories denying referentiality to distinctive one-of-a-kind phenomenal times and spaces are only metaphorical or allegorical, or exist at a greater symbolic remove from phenomena. They are, to cite Nietzsche again, the "paler" and "cooler" ideas of generalization because they deny the phenomenal status of the attempt to reflect the aesthetics of everyday experience.[30] The word "chair" is referential; but without existing in a distinctive and one-of-a-kind phenomenal time and place, with the distinctive grain of the wood similar to Nietzsche's leaf with its distinctive one-of-a-kind structure (the petiole, the midrib, the veins, all of a distinctive cellular structure), such a fictional chair is only allegorically referential.

Such a distinction has significant consequences for readers in terms of their reaction to what conventionally we describe as the "real" in the referencing of a distinctive phenomenon. The more "real" stories are perceived, as neuroscience research suggests, the more actively the brain responds to them.[31] Furthermore, as Jean-Marie Schaeffer notes, "Developmental psychology and comparative ethnology have shown that the distinction between representations having truth claims and 'make-believe' representations is crucial in the ontogenetic development of the cognitive structure of the infant psyche."[32] In other words, the brain responds differently to truth claims of the "factual" mediation than to fictional make-believe, and a narra-descriptive discourse referential to phenomenon existing in time and space captures the imagination in a way that more abstract and allegorical models of discourse cannot.

Inevitably, we do not deny, nor can we afford to deny, the claims of the phenomenal world. As Schaeffer observes, "In real-life situations, the distinction between factual and fictional narrative seems to be unavoidable, since mistaking a fictional narrative for a factual one (or vice versa) can have dramatic consequences."[33] In other words, those consequences can be existential consequences. In such consequences lies part of the unique influence over the imagination of documentary accounts because we understand that we could in a phenomenal world face similar existential consequences. In acknowledging that such consequences could apply to us in our phenomenal world, as opposed to the hypothetical or prospective reflected in the allegory of fiction, we cannot, in an act of our own denial, assume that similar differentiating qualities of phenomenal experience will not rise up and devour us. With the unambiguously fictional (meaning allegorical), we can always deny it—or as I would say as a seven-year-old in the late 1950s watching Grade B horror movies starring Vincent Price while holding my father's hand for reassurance, "Oh, this isn't real." This is not a claim one can (for existential reasons) so comfortably make with accounts referential to phenomena.

Our response is also enhanced cognitively and viscerally when reading "real life" stories because of the mirror neuron, discovered at the University of Parma in the 1990s. The mirror neuron permits the observer to feel a similar response when observing someone else who is confronting an existential threat.[34] One example would be Søren Kierkegaard's ice skater eliciting from his audience the visceral thrill of the dangerous when skating closer and closer to thin ice.[35] In other words, we do have the capacity to see ourselves in the other person's existential predicament and have a similar neurological response. This, in turn, is fostered and nurtured by means of the psychological transportation of the more traditional and cognitively accessible narrative model, which is how we naturally inquire into the nature of the world. (Of course, there is the other interpretation to Kierkegaard's parable, namely that the audience engages in the vicarious experience as an existential escape that they can later smugly dismiss while deluding themselves they experienced it.)[36]

* * *

Conventional fiction can, of course, reference historical events, which lay claim to a location in time and place-in-space. It is beyond the scope of this essay to examine the relationship between history and narrative literary journalism, although clearly there is one as reflected in the aphorism "journalism is the first draft of history." But given the claim that narrative literary journalism is different from traditional or conventional fiction (since, again, all mediated communication is a kind of fiction, but, and I continue to emphasize, not all fictions are equal), it is important to understand the relationship between the two when fiction appears to be making a claim to referencing a location in time and space.

Hugo's *Les Misérables* serves as an example. In recent years much has been made by critics that the novel is a kind of history, or at least contributes to a collective historical memory.[37] But as with the inherent fictive nature of any mediation, there is history and there is history, and not all histories are the same. In *Les Misérables*, the historical events are subordinated or in thrall to the fictional—and allegorical. True, Hugo provides a historical account of the 1815 Waterloo battle in *Les Misérables*. He also witnessed the arrest of a beggar who had stolen a loaf of bread, which has long been considered part of the inspiration for the main character Jean Valjean.[38] But the resulting character of Valjean, around whom the novel revolves, is not the same as that beggar who existed in a time and place-in-space. And the Battle of Waterloo is, in the end, only a contextual backdrop for Valjean and the other fictional characters such as Javert. Such historical accounts lend authenticity in providing social context for the characters. But therein lies the problem because the characters do not exist except as allegory. They provide the break with the historical chain of phenomenal evidence—the concrete metaphors of phenomenal experience—that persuades us we are reading history. While it would be tempting to dismiss the plainly fictional, such as Valjean, as ancillary to the history in order to establish historical credentials, few would dispute that a fictional character like him is central to the project of the conventional fictional novel. In effect, the allegory filters and subverts or undermines the power and authority of history. In providing the historical context, it is like saying, "Believe me, believe me, even though I'm not real." The result is a faux-historical authenticity.

Moreover, Valjean and other fictional characters serve, in turn, the larger (fictional) purpose of the "schema," as Nietzsche called it, which motivated Hugo. It is no secret that republican Hugo wrote on behalf of social change for the benefit of the "*misérables*," the dispossessed of society. Hence, Hugo had locked up the meaning of those historical events in an allegorical nostrum to serve a social cause (or the "paler, cooler" idea, Nietzsche further termed it, of the *qualitas occulta*). History, then, has been abducted not to illustrate demonstrable consequences but rather to present a hypothetical or prospective allegory.

Whether intentionally or not, this movement toward the exclusively allegorical is reflected in one recent account firmly placing Hugo as historian, William VanderWolk's *Victor Hugo in Exile: From Historical Representations to Utopian Vistas*. The subtitle reveals the kind of "volatilization" Nietzsche predicted: The historical evidence migrates toward allegory because it is subservient to illustrating the fictional (the "utopian"), much the way concrete description in conventional feature writing serves the larger idea. Indeed, VanderWolk's fifth chapter is entitled "*Les Misérables*: The Novel as Historical Allegory." Hugo is fundamentally Hegelian in his ambition. Paul Ricoeur, who provides an important theoretical basis for VanderWolk's position that Hugo is a historian, nonetheless observes, "Only history can claim a reference inscribed in empirical reality, inasmuch as historical intentionality aims at events that have actually occurred."[39] (And here Ricoeur's stated position recalls the similar positions of Nietzsche and Bakhtin in not losing sight of phenomenal or empirical realities.) What Ricoeur said of history can be applied to journalism and other documentary accounts (which problematizes Ricoeur's adjective "only"). The allegory of fiction like *Les Misérables* cannot be inscribed in historical reality given the break with the historical chain of phenomenal evidence.

What can be examined is how and why the fiction was prompted and created against the personal and cultural backdrop of the moment, and to a certain extent that is reflected in the position Hugo scholars take. But that does not establish the fiction as inscribed in empirical reality, only the process of its creation. And the why of Hugo was to promote his republican politics and shed light on social conditions. In the case of *Les Misérables*, it should also be emphasized that Hugo was often in error in his history, given that it served the fiction of his ambition. As Alan B. Spitzer has observed of Hugo's historical accounts, "He got so much wrong."[40]

Finally, the claim that Hugo was a historian in *Les Misérables* can, to some extent, be taken for granted if it is not telling the obvious. All authors, whether they write great historical (fictional) novels or graffiti in public restrooms, are in a sense historians, reflecting the history and culture of their era.

This, however, is not to dispute the distinctive power over the imagination of *Les Misérables*.[41] Nor can one disagree that all texts reflect their own kind of history that contributes to a collective historical memory. As Kathryn M. Grossman observes, "Hugo offers a collective *fictional* (but not fictitious) version of the past."[42] But, and this makes the difference, it is a "fictional" history. Of course, one cannot help but suspect an inconsistency in a history that can be fictional but not fictitious. And one detects an acknowledgment of the faux historical authenticity.

Then there is the problem when dealing with nontraditional narrative works often viewed as fiction or presented as poetry that have more complex historical and referential issues. Again, a lengthy examination is beyond the scope of this chapter. But, and as I noted earlier, the resistance to abstraction and reification and, I would add, allegory, especially as an extended metaphor of representativeness, has implications for any discourse making a referential claim to the phenomenal world. I would suggest that perception will undoubtedly continue to be central to how readers receive such accounts, as neuroscience and developmental psychology tell us. We respond differently if we believe an account is real in referencing phenomenal time and space, as opposed to what we receive as make-believe without those referents. In that may lie one approach for dealing with such issues in nontraditional narratives. This also may account, at least in part, for why a modern narrative literary journalism emerged, because of the perception, rightly or wrongly, that older forms or genres such as fiction and poetry were inadequate to the task. The larger issue is whether the chain of evidence in the concrete metaphors is perceived as being interrupted by the solely allegorical such as a character or voice without a location in time and space.

* * *

The need to acknowledge the aesthetics of everyday experience as reflected in the chronotope has further and more complex implications for a narrative literary journalism, or a narra-descriptive journalism given the dominant modalities. For any work to be literary, it must, Bakhtin suggests, escape what he describes as the "distanced image of the absolute past" in which the meaning is tied up in and determined by previous models. The "distanced image of the absolute past" could include the predictability of the classical epic reflecting the cultural expectations of its era, or the modern equivalent of the contemporary superhero movie that inevitably must have the clichéd ending of "the triumph of good over evil," again reflecting the cultural expectations of its era. For literature to renew itself, it must embrace what Bakhtin described as the "inconclusive present."[43] This is because when one is receptive to the "novel" or unpredictable unfolding of the aesthetics of everyday experience, there is no guarantee that such experience will conform in lockstep to the earlier models framed in the distanced image of an absolute past. Hence we have Bakhtin's concept of the "carnivalesque" of experience inherent in the chronotope. And hence we also have the notion that reality can be stranger than fiction; at best, fiction, because it depends on fictional models, too often subscribes to the illusion of what a reality is believed to conform to.

Clearly, "differentiating qualities" in phenomena can pose profound challenges to our preconceptions and assumptions, or the "paler, cooler ideas" of the *qualitas occulta* in linguistic abstraction.[44] Such differentiating qualities provide the basis for what could be characterized as a cognitive or imaginative disruption. Joseph H. Kupfer observes of the aesthetic response to everyday experience:

> From an aesthetic promontory, we can see comprehensive reformulations of experience, reformulations that remain hidden when we think strictly within social, moral, political, or educational categories. The aesthetic runs through all of these domains of life and so seems an especially promising entrance into their interstices, interdependencies, and common problems. Because the aesthetic speaks with a radically different voice to the values cultivated in these various domains, it may uncover radically different approaches to their realization.[45]

In other words, the "radically different approaches" are prompted because they reach a threshold of cognitive disruption. Kupfer further notes, "the varieties of aesthetic experience variously nurture a panoply of human values,"[46] which we, as individuals and a community, seek to share or reject in our assessments of those experiences. But there is no requirement that the varieties of aesthetic experience—the carnivalesque of the chronotopes—have to fit existing shared (and abstract) values, or Nietzsche's "schema" or "concepts," or the secular mythologies as I characterize them.[47] Therein lies the inherently subversive nature of a narrative literary journalism, but one nonetheless different from conventional fiction and conventional journalism because it is grounded in neither the allegory of fiction nor the level of abstraction inherent in the more conventional models of journalism (which arguably are their own kind of allegory—if not fiction —given their levels of expository digression disconnected from chronicity). Rather, the subversive nature of a narrative literary journalism is found in the referential distinctiveness or inequality of each phenomenal experience to which one responds aesthetically. And such distinctiveness or inequality can sound dissonant, disruptive notes.

For example, to return to the Paterniti passage, the two octogenarians are engaged in the kind of discussion one often expects octogenarians to engage in: an exchange about the current medications they are taking and what they have or have not found of benefit. To this is added that Harvey is hard of hearing and, like the multitude of other seniors who have had their hearing deteriorate in old age, has to yell because he projects on to others his own deafness, which others do not necessarily suffer from.[48] But it is one thing to swap information about medications such as Diovan (the high blood pressure medication) or Viagra. It is another to hear that someone in his eighties is taking methadone (mixed with alcohol in a chemically life-threatening combination): Burroughs was a heroin addict. For anyone who knows of Burroughs's life, this is no secret. But to the uninitiated, it is a jarring moment that can disrupt what we tend to expect of octogenarians: It is unlikely that most of us will recall our grandparents being heroin addicts. (However, given the current opioid epidemic in the United States, such a perspective may change, hence the carnivalesque that can disrupt assumptions about how grandma and grandpa are expected to conduct themselves.)

Moreover, in a play on words, Paterniti describes Burroughs, again one of the beacons of the Beat Generation, as "hollowed" rather than "hallowed." He is, in other words, an old, frail, and empty icon of what the author of *Naked Lunch* once was, "bowed" by age and no longer bowing to acclaim.

So we find ourselves estranged from what had once been familiar, to invoke Viktor Shklovsky's concept that literature attempts to make the familiar unfamiliar.[49] But as the reader should bear in mind, what we have is a collection of details or chronotopes derived of the phenomenal world that began to accumulate earlier when one discovered that the remains of Einstein's brain, the brain of what many would say was the most brilliant scientist of the twentieth century, is kept in preservative in a Tupperware bowl. Tupperware is plastic kitchenware, but equally important, it is a symbol of the domestic culture of the traditional American housewife from the 1950s and 1960s who would invite other housewives over for "Tupperware parties" in order to supplement the family income by selling Tupperware to her guests. Imagine a housewife saying: "You see. You can even keep Albert Einstein's brain in Tupperware." Such is what the brilliant mind has been reduced to. Moreover, his brain has been consigned to a car trunk along with the spare tire. One can reasonably assume that most people do not drive around with human brains in a plastic bowl in their car trunk. We detect again one way in which the carnivalesque of unexpected phenomenal evidence reaches a threshold of cognitive disruption. And it is here that we also detect the importance of the seemingly commonplace or banal detail. Usually, we are inclined to take the commonplace or banal for granted, whether it is Tupperware ("Put the egg salad in the Tupperware bowl, please"), the car trunk, or the spare tire ("Would you get the spare tire from the trunk, please?"), and we give them little thought because of such familiarity. But their ironic juxtaposition poses the disruption: The banal details of everyday life are keeping company with Einstein's brain. Of course, the celebrity of Einstein's brain especially invites such ironic juxtaposition. But the same can be said of the porch scene. We see two former neighbors (although they were not close friends) meeting each other after many years on that cultural symbol of American family familiarity and neighborly civility, the front porch.[50] But instead of the octogenarians discussing the banalities of Diovan and Viagra, they discuss morphine. And instead of drinking lemonade on the front porch (amid pleasing orchestral phrases of "somewhere over the rainbow" in Dorothy's Kansas), Burroughs drinks Coke and vodka as a chaser for methadone while wearing a handgun in a holster over his kidney (here in Capote's land of cold blood). What we detect is an assault on secular mythologies, which has long been a central impulse to some of our most compelling narrative literary journalism.[51]

To be sure, the familiar made unfamiliar can exist in fiction, too, and that was Shklovsky's intent, even though he exemplified it in his own version of literary journalism, *A Sentimental Journey* (borrowing the title from Laurence Sterne's 1768 volume of the same name), which is a factual account of the Russian Revolution and civil war.[52] The difference from fiction is that a narrative literary journalism acknowledges its phenomenal referents existing outside the covers of books that make the familiar unfamiliar possible. Or, again, "reality" can appear stranger than fiction. Similarly, the familiar can be made unfamiliar in more conventional forms of journalism. But in these, the potential of the familiar as unfamiliar is subjugated once again to the constative act of exposition because it is digressively detached from the original narrative containing the initial inconclusive present as genuinely carnivalesque.

We should bear in mind, too, a fundamental shortcoming to the telling of conventional fictional narratives. The literary Darwinist informs us that the telling of stories is part of a survival strategy in which we can share in the experiences of someone else, experiences we might not otherwise be exposed to as experience.[53] So we learn from someone else how to kill a sabertoothed tiger or a mastodon with the result that such stories serve as surrogates and learning tools. But it is easy to overlook that stories can, in addition, appeal to what we seek to escape from as reflected in the distanced image of an absolute past we are more comfortable embracing. (This, again, was Kierkegaard's point regarding the audience for the daring ice skater. The audience was engaged in a kind of pornography, enjoying the experience only for its vicarious nature, which it could then smugly dismiss.) For example, Spider-Man can appear miraculously to cast his web and tie up the saber-toothed tiger and mastodon, which can then be returned to the safety of their zoo cages. In other words, stories can serve as much for avoidance as for learning about new—and potentially dangerous—experiences. This is a claim that is more difficult to make, and uncomfortably so, when confronting phenomenal consequences that serve as an existential threat as opposed to confronting allegorical hypotheticals or prospects one can more easily deny as I had done as a seven-year-old watching Vincent Price horror movies.

How do the concrete metaphors get selected? What are the motivations for doing so? It is here that the full complexity of cultural and individual influences come into play. I do not mean to privilege phenomenal referentiality over cultural and individual influence in the construction of a narrative. But similarly it is important not to privilege the cultural and the individual over the phenomenal. All are, to borrow from Bakhtin, involved in mutual exchange. From the vantage point of a narrative literary journalism, what is important in the exchange is when the referentiality of the newly observed phenomenon establishes the disruptive threshold that challenges the constructed personal and cultural assumptions, or, again, our secular mythologies. Einstein's brain is an example. Most people would likely find it unusual to carry around human brains in a Tupperware bowl in the trunk of a car, no less Einstein's. Naturally one's openness to exploring the inconclusive present, whether as author or reader, depends on the degree of receptivity the individual has to such disruptions. This is because, as Hans Robert Jauss has observed, a text "is not an object that stands by itself and that offers the same view to each reader in each period." Instead, the "context of experience of aesthetic perception" will be applied differently by each.[54] But as readers we will be less inclined to reject what has had consequences in the phenomenal world because of our greater openness to what we believe is "real."

* * *

The focus on the aesthetics of everyday experience results, I would suggest, in a narrative literary journalism that tends toward avoiding closed or global meanings. This is, in part, because on closer examination we discern that the concrete metaphor of the chronotope is a lot less solid and stable—a lot less "concrete"—and more ambiguous in phenomenal status than we may initially think or wish when we are first introduced to it. This was Dear's important qualifier to his observation about how "the singular experience could not be evident" or fully constituted in the mediation, but at the same time "it could provide evidence."[55]

It is here that we confront the paradox inherent to the perceived tangible, and the implications such a paradox has for a narrative literary journalism. While the seeming tangible we characterize as "real life," which we take so much for granted, serves to reveal the phenomenal, it can also blind us, serving as a kind of euphemism that disguises the phenomenal beyond our knowing. It was Tom Wolfe, of course, who emphasized that the attraction of the New Journalism of the 1960s and 1970s—one variation and historical chapter of literary journalism—was that it showed "real life."[56] His observation reflected the belief that one could trust the testimony of one's senses. But clearly such a trust is problematic. Nor is this only because we may be mistaken in the initial perceptions of memory.[57] There is that, too. But additionally, the reality of the "real" of the phenomenal world is that the seemingly plain and simple concrete metaphor not only speaks to what exists phenomenally but also serves (often unconsciously) as a marker for what is not included in the recognition.

Implicit but unstated to the claim negotiated between the phenomenal and language is that there is something always left out. Few would dispute that there is much beyond our knowing. At the same time, there is always the allure of turning "real life" into a comforting habit of seeing, or an expectation, or an assumption, which can rise to the level of a platitude in the form of what we take for granted as common sense. Like all platitudes, "real life" lulls us into acceptance as a kind of Nietzschean *qualitas occulta* to which we attach the "ship" of our lives, one holding the promise of existential command, which we are only too eager to embrace in our hubris masking the neurosis of our existential fear: "I'm in control … I'm in control … I assure you I am in control."

One has to consider what the act of making selections about the phenomenal implies; it must result in incompleteness since something is excluded, either intentionally as part of the selection process or because it is unobserved. The evidence Dear said could be detected is incomplete in our observation. The epistemological reality is that there are those phenomenal differentiating qualities that are beyond the momentary apprehension of the perception of the aesthetics of everyday experience. Another way of putting it is that there is the unassimilated beyond our perceptions. Those who are receptive enough to acknowledge as much understand that there is always something we cannot know—at least for the moment. Then there are readers who will be unquestioning in the tendency to accept at face value the platitude or euphemism of "real life" as elementary and fundamental to their expectations or "habits of seeing."[58]

As Mary Poovey notes, the idea of the unassimilable is not new: "Ciceronian skepticism was essentially epistemological, for he held that the frailty of the human senses renders certainty about the natural impossible."[59] We are, then, talking about the excess beyond our knowing. As Poovey further observes, in a discussion of the emergence of the concept of the "modern fact" during the late Renaissance as a result of the Baconian scientific method,

> If one had to resist premature generalization, after all, and if one could produce systematic knowledge only by reasoning from the phenomena one observed, then it was imperative to know how one moved from the particulars one saw to knowledge that was sufficiently general to explain things one had not seen.[60]

"Things one had not seen" is the hidden flaw in the Baconian formulation of the scientific method, she notes. It leaves out the unassimilated or excess of what we do not know. It was ironic that Bacon's intent was to try to address the peculiar, the anomalous, the abnormal that did not fit so comfortably into the Aristotelian commonplaces that constituted the "norm" at the time, whether it was a secular or theological norm—or "habit of seeing"—in the hope that eventually the result would be general deductive laws. Thus the concept of the modern fact was born, Poovey suggests, but was inherently flawed and contradictory from the outset.[61] Bacon never squared induction with deduction, or the "imperative to know how one moved from the particulars one saw to knowledge that was sufficiently general to explain things one had not seen." On this, Poovey notes, he was vague.

The implications should be clear: A narrative literary journalism favors a more inductive approach better attuned to the distinctive carnivalesque that can challenge our deductive laws—or habits of seeing. Can we conclude that the excess or the unassimilated phenomenal can never be assimilated? No. Nor can we conclude that all differentiating qualities of the excess can be assimilated. What we have then is a recognition of our limitations attached not only to the concrete metaphor but also to what about the concrete metaphor we do not know.

Studies on modern narrative have also intuited to varying degrees the concept of the unassimilated. Wolfgang Iser cites Arnold Bennett's observation that "you can't put the whole of a character into a book," then adds, "[H]e was thinking of the discrepancy between a person's life and the unavoidably limited form in which that life may be represented."[62] The same observation has been made of history. In quoting and interpreting German historian Johann Gustav Droysen, Jauss observes that what we believe about narrative

> is the illusion of the complete process. Although every historian knows that our knowledge of history must always remain incomplete, the prevailing form of the narrative creates "the illusion and wants to create it, that we are faced with a complete process of historical things, a finished chain of events, motives and purposes."[63]

In the illusion to create a complete process lies the inherent flaw.

The result is that the vague notion of the unassimilated or the excess of the aesthetics of the everyday cognitively hangs suspended as an absence and out of reach of consciousness, at least temporarily, this as opposed to the selected description, or originary concrete metaphors of the text. To assimilate all differentiating qualities is impossible, given the nature of cognitive reductionism that must end increasingly in an abstract realm in the form of subatomic particles well beyond the common sense-appeal of the shared common senses, or the personal aesthetics of everyday experience. Our knowledge of the phenomenal is inevitably indeterminable because of the limitations of the testimony of the senses.

* * *

It is not easy (or perhaps it is not "convenient") to grasp the concept of the "unassimilated" since it is beyond our knowing. For a genre making a referential claim to the seeming solidity of the phenomenal—to "real life"—this is epistemologically unsettling. Built into our expectations is that the phenomenal does have a solidity that an abstract totalization does not have. It is unsettling because any referent to real life is, after all, always reflective of incompleteness. There is not only "inequality," as Nietzsche termed it, within the "concrete metaphor," but there are the potential specters of inequalities in the incompleteness of what lies beyond our conception of the concrete metaphor. In this we can perceive the fuller paradox of the correspondence of the referential, however imperfect its attempt at reflection, to the phenomenal or tangible we perceive. Despite what we may want to believe, "real life" is forever playing a kind of hide-and-seek with our perceptions.

A consequence of this paradox is that a narrative literary journalism is potentially always in a state of becoming because such accounts can continue to evolve in a way fiction cannot since the unassimilated of phenomenal experience can continue to emerge. The virtue of fiction is that it presents in its allegory a totality—again what Herman described as a "sovereign world."[64] As Iser notes, "the disordered multiplicity of everyday life" provides the basis for a fictional narrative's "harmonious form."[65] In the idea that the form can be harmonious is revealed the desire for a platonic totality according to which a story must comply because everything will fit in a harmonious manner. He adds further, "contingencies and complexities are reduced to a meaningful structure."[66] What is "structured" is, implicitly, a reflection of what is self-contained. This is a variation that goes back to what Aristotle said in his *Poetics* about mimesis having a beginning, middle, and end making, finally, for a "whole."[67] Hence the structure. Keith Oatley, in his own translation of Aristotle, notes, "A poetic mimesis, then, ought to be … unified and complete."[68] We recognize the attempt at closure in the "whole," or the "unity," or the "harmonious form," or the "sovereign world." (We see this, too, in medieval allegory and the religious need at the time to provide a spiritual ideology; fiction, being inherently allegorical, evolved to some extent out of that experience resulting in the belief in a transcendent literature.) In contrast, the structure or unity of a narra-descriptive journalism can never be complete because the constituent concrete metaphors referential to phenomena are never complete.

An example (one, I would emphasize, that is disruptive) is when a detail hangs suspended and unexplained, teasing the reader with what he or she does not know and will never know. Consider Joan Didion's "Some Dreamers of the Golden Dream," which has been described as iconic.[69] In Didion's tale of adultery and murder, Lucille Miller, who is charged with killing her husband, is convicted and goes to prison pregnant. While the legal defense in the court case suggested that the pregnancy was a result of Miller's wanting to mend her marriage with her husband (thus making her more sympathetic in the eyes of the court), one cannot help having doubts, given her adultery and that Miller faked her husband's fiery death as an accident.[70] Didion leaves this ambiguity from real life unanswered for the reader, and presumably she did not have the answer. As Jonathan Harr has noted, after completing his monumental *A Civil Action*, "The facts of a real event sometimes don't occur in a way that lends itself to narrative elegance."[71] In narrative "elegance" lies the ambition for the perfect story; part of that perfection is tying up the loose ends of the details. One sees this in Anton Chekhov's admonition: If you introduce a gun (or rifle) onstage, you should fire it.[72] In other words, foreshadowing should not be gratuitous. Instead, the expectations aroused in the audience should be fulfilled. The result is the conventional portrait of reality deriving from conventional causal verisimilitude: We can believe it when the gun is fired because it was there as part of the foreshadowing. In a narrative literary journalism, there is too much that can go unaccounted for, too much that must remain unassimilated.[73] But is that necessarily a fault? Or is it—uncomfortably—"reality"?

Consider, also, conclusions in a narrative literary journalism. They are only temporary. For example, John Hersey added a significant sequel to his volume *Hiroshima*, which was about how six Japanese survived the atomic bombing of that city in 1945. In the sequel, he picked up where he left off with the first version. In the first version published in 1946, he ended with the immediate aftermath of the dropping of the atomic bomb. But forty years later, Hersey added a new chapter after returning to Japan to find out what happened to the survivors.[74] The revised paperback edition with the additional chapter adds sixty-two pages to the original account, extending the book by more than two-thirds.[75] Decidedly, this was a significant sequel. (The work is more like a novella in length because it was originally published in the *New Yorker*, taking up the entire contents of the issue.)[76]

Nor is *Hiroshima* the only work of a narra-descriptive journalism that has prompted sequels, given that there can never be an ultimate conclusion because of the continuing emergence of the once unassimilated. We see this in James Agee and Walker Evans's *Let Us Now Praise Famous Men*, their account of hardscrabble white tenant farmers in Depression-era Alabama. In 1989, Dale Maharidge and Michael Williamson published a sequel, *And Their Children after Them*, which explored what happened to the tenant farmers' families some fifty years later. (The book won a Pulitzer Prize.) Among them, we learn about the death of "Maggie Louise Gudger" (Agee had changed the subjects' names), who was a ten-year-old blonde girl in a woven straw hat with what is perhaps a puzzled though not hostile expression on her face in one of Evans's accompanying photographs in *Let Us Now Praise Famous Men*.[77] At the age of ten, she had the ambition to escape her family's poverty as tenant farmers picking cotton by getting an education. She never did. In the Maharidge and Williamson volume, the reader discovers that she killed herself in 1971 by drinking rat poison.[78]

The journalistic "follow-up" is a venerable tradition, of course. But epistemologically the follow-up is about the failure of the "end" of the previous narrative. Nor must all sequels be written as a traditional narra-descriptive journalism. This was the case with the 1999 *Black Hawk Down*, an account of the shooting down of an American helicopter in Mogadishu, Somalia, and the disastrous attempt to rescue American military personnel in a firefight.[79] What the website for the story series, which appeared originally in the *Philadelphia Inquirer*, reveals is an even less defined and structured account, with additional videos, audios, and interviews with participants.[80]

There is, clearly, a corollary to this. If there is no final conclusion in a narra-descriptive journalism, or if it is only a temporary conclusion, then the same can be said of beginnings, that there is no true beginning, or at best just temporary beginnings.

Fiction may be perceived as more superior because it is sovereign and self-contained (while lacking referents to unfolding locations in phenomenal time and space). But consider: Is self-containment how life's stories really play out? Or is narrative unity itself a fiction with which we can deceive ourselves by believing we have a global view? Again, there will be those who will prefer the distanced image of an absolute past they can more comfortably embrace and retreat into ("Spider-Man will rescue me"; "Deus ex machina will rescue me"). When you finish reading a work of narra-descriptive journalism, you know at some level, conscious or otherwise, that the story does not end. Life goes on, and this provides new material for disrupting "the illusion of the complete process," as Droysen said of history.[81]

* * *

We detect a threshold of disruption in the conclusion to Paterniti's "Driving Mr. Albert." At the end of the story, Harvey has left the brain temporarily in Paterniti's care. Among other details, the author places the Tupperware container with the brain on a pillow next to his on a bed in a cheap motel room (the "Flamingo Motel"—painted pink, naturally, drawing us in with an appeal to one of our secular mythologies, pink flamingoes).[82] He will return the brain to Harvey. But in the concluding paragraphs, Paterniti reflects philosophically about the energy of the universe of which the brain has become so emblematic, which he is now holding in his hands in the Tupperware bowl. End of story. What happens to the brain? Outrageously, we do not find out. (Today most remaining pieces of the brain are at the National Museum for Health and Medicine in Silver Spring, Maryland. Some remnants are at the Mütter Museum in Philadelphia. Not all of the brain has been accounted for.)[83] But in another example of how a narrative literary journalism is always in a state of becoming, Paterniti in the future expanded on the article and turned it into a book with the addition of a subtitle.[84]

Such is how the aesthetics of everyday experience can provide chronotopes that establish new thresholds of disruption to conventional habits of seeing. Then there is what is outside the initial perception that has yet to be perceived that always has the potential to further emerge, thus providing additional thresholds of disruption, and undoing the lie of "real life" as a comfortable platitude. Therein lies an ethical dimension to such work: the potential to challenge false gods. And such gods are by nature make-believe fictions. This is why we need a narrative literary journalism, or narra-descriptive journalism, drawing from the aesthetics of everyday experience as a chain of uninterrupted if imperfectly collected evidence whose referential concrete metaphors refer to what was once a location at the distinctive intersection of phenomenal time and space. To cite Kupfer again, we can from the aesthetics of such everyday experience detect reformulations of our values, "reformulations that remain hidden when we think strictly within social, moral, political, or educational categories."[85] So a narrative literary journalism provides us important thresholds for gazing—if at times uncomfortably—on new "realities."

Notes

1 I initially explored the role of the aesthetics of experience in narrative literary journalism in *Literary Journalism and the Aesthetics of Experience*. Here I expand on the examination and address more directly the issue of the genre's referentiality. On "secular mythologies," I borrow from Mircea Eliade, the distinguished scholar of mythology, and explore the issue in chapter 3, "The Death of the Dream of Paradise," in *Literary Journalism and the Aesthetics of Experience*. See also Eliade, *Myths, Dreams and Mysteries*, 28.

   Also, by a narrative literary journalism, I mean a journalism in which the narrative and descriptive modalities predominate. Often it has been described as a journalism that reads like a fictional novel or short story. But as I note in *Literary Journalism and the Aesthetics of Experience*, such a description is imprecise. I would refer readers to the volume (5–6).
2 Dear, *Discipline and Experience*, 25.
3 Sims, "Promise," 8.
4 Leddy, "Nature of Everyday Aesthetics," 4, 7; emphasis added.
5 Paterniti, "Driving Mr. Albert," 123.
6 Bakhtin, *Dialogic Imagination*, 84. Ironically, at least for Paterniti's account, Bakhtin borrowed the basic idea from Einstein's theorizing on time and space in the latter's relativity theories.
7 See, for example, Bemong et al., *Bakhtin's Theory*.
8 Bakhtin, *Dialogic Imagination*, 253.
9 Bakhtin, 253–54.
10 Nietzsche, "On Truth and Falsity," 179–81. I have often belabored this point. See, for example, *History*, 48–49. I do so for two reasons. First, Nietzsche's insight into how "concrete metaphors" evolve into abstract concepts seems to me to provide one of the best explanations for how a narrative literary journalism insists on the distinctive integrity of experience thus revealing what it sets itself up in opposition to. Second, literary journalism scholars are a diverse group from different disciplines and with different experiences and expectations. Nietzsche's essay, from my observation, is not widely known in all sectors of the academy.
11 Nietzsche, 179–81.
12 Bakhtin takes a similar if slightly different position: "All the novel's abstract elements—philosophical and social generalizations, ideas, analyses of cause and effect—gravitate toward the chronotope and through it take on flesh and blood" (*Dialogic Imagination*, 250).
13 Hartsock, *Literary Journalism*, 10–18.
14 See Genette, "Frontiers of Narrative," 127; Scholes, "Language," 205.
15 Graesser, Olde, and Klettke, "How Does the Mind," 240.
16 Green, "Transportation into Narrative Worlds," 247, 257, 260, 262; Gerrig, *Experiencing Narrative Worlds*, 136.
17 Green, "Transportation into Narrative Worlds," 248.
18 See Boyd, *On the Origin*, 181, 131.
19 Hartsock, *Literary Journalism*, 10–18.
20 For a fuller examination, see Hartsock, *Literary Journalism*, 12–14.
21 Bock, "In Her Mother's Shoes."
22 Herr, *Dispatches*, 214–15.
23 Hartsock, *History*, 25.

24. Crane, "Regulars Get No Glory," 171.
25. Hartsock, *Literary Journalism*, 3, 6–7. I cite Wolfe for this definition, although he was not the only one to use it. I also explore in the citation how imprecise it is in attempting to define a narrative literary journalism.
26. Herman, *Storytelling*, 98.
27. I borrow the expression (and its variants) "outside the cover of books" from Zavarzadeh, *Mythopoeic Reality*, 226.
28. Hartsock, *History*, 48.
29. This is ably explored by Davis in *Factual Fictions*, 151–61. I also explore the issue in *History*, 81–90, 111–20.
30. Nietzsche, "On Truth and Falsity," 181.
31. Mar et al., "Detecting Agency," 204.
32. Schaeffer, "Fictional vs. Factual Narration."
33. Schaeffer.
34. See, for example, Ferrari and Rizzolatti, "Mirror Neuron Research."
35. Kierkegaard, "Present Age," 33–36.
36. The full dimensions of the mirror neuron have not been fully plumbed, and research is ongoing. There was initially some resistance, but Ferrari and Rizzolatti's subsequent issue of *Philosophical Transactions of the Royal Society B: Biological Sciences* helped to allay much of those concerns and increase acceptance.
37. Among others, see Grossman, *Later Novels*; VanderWolk, *Victor Hugo in Exile*; Metzidakis, "On Rereading French History"; Spitzer, "Reflections of Historical Remembering"; de la Carrera, "History's Unconscious."
38. Bellos, *Novel of the Century*, 6–7.
39. Ricoeur, *Time and Narrative*, 87.
40. Spitzer, "Reflections of Historical Remembering," 145, 146–47.
41. This writer no less so. As reader response has taught us, we all have our reasons for responding the way we do to *Les Misérables*.
42. Grossman, *Later Novels*, 210.
43. Bakhtin, *Dialogic Imagination*, 39.
44. Hartsock, *Literary Journalism*, 27.
45. Kupfer, *Experience as Art*, 192–93.
46. Kupfer, 192.
47. Nietzsche, "On Truth and Falsity."
48. Or, as my wife says, "You don't have to yell. I'm not deaf."
49. Shklovsky, "Art as Technique," 12.
50. Of the front porch as American cultural symbol, Crowder writes, "The classic image of a front porch filled with family and friends on a hot summer evening has long been a symbol of traditional American values," adding elsewhere, "The image of the front porch remains 'as one of the few semi-public outdoor spaces associated with community and neighborliness,' says Victor Deupi of the Institute of Classical Architecture. Porches link us to an idealized past—one before e-mail (or even the telephone), when face-to-face interaction formed the core of communities." See also Kahn and Meagher, *Preserving Porches*.
51. As a central impulse, see again chapter 3, "The Death of the Dream of Paradise," in my *Literary Journalism*.
52. Shklovsky, *Sentimental Journey*. For a discussion of his *A Sentimental Journey* and the familiar made unfamiliar, see Hartsock, *Literary Journalism*, 112–14.
53. Boyd, *On the Origin*, 131, 181.
54. Jauss, *Toward an Aesthetic*, 21, 23.
55. Dear, *Discipline and Experience*, 25.
56. Wolfe, "New Journalism," 33.
57. I explored the frailties of memory in Samuel Johnson's and James Boswell's two separate accounts of a walking tour they took together in Scotland in 1773. See Hartsock, *Literary Journalism*, 47–48.
58. I borrow the expression "habits of seeing" from the German writer Ernst Jünger (*Storm of Steel*, 23).
59. Poovey, *History*, 40.
60. Poovey, 15; emphasis added.
61. Poovey, 15.
62. Iser, *Act of Reading*, 125.
63. Jauss, *Toward an Aesthetic*, 53. Jauss's Droysen quotation derives from the latter's *Historik*, 35.

64 Oatley, "Why Fiction," 101–17; Herman, *Storytelling*, 98.
65 Iser, *Act of Reading*, 125.
66 Iser, 70.
67 Aristotle, *Poetics*, 1450b27.
68 Oatley, "Why Fiction," 7.
69 For "iconic," see Ulin, "What Happened Here?"
70 Didion, "Some Dreamers," 22, 23, 26.
71 Quoted in Boynton, *New New Journalism*, 126.
72 Rayfield, *Anton Chekhov*, 203; Simmons, *Chekhov*, 190. Over the years, I have heard many variations on this axiom, including that the gun was, no less, a cannon (this from an undergraduate literature class). Chekhov was known to repeat the axiom in many variations.
73 As I noted in *History*, David Bromwich makes a not dissimilar observation about the seemingly contingent in rearticulating a viewpoint of Irving Howe: "The detail we call irrelevant or gratuitous has a way of seeming peculiarly right, so that we think it belongs just where it occurs, though strictly speaking it lacks any formal and dramatic warrant" (*History*, 174). See also Bromwich, "What Novels Are For," 7.
74 Hersey, *Hiroshima* (Bantam, 1986), title page.
75 Hersey, *Hiroshima* (Milestone Editions, 1946). Compared to the Bantam edition in the previous note. In this first edition, the text of the story is 123 pages long. In the Bantam edition, the text of the original story of the Milestone Editions concludes on page 90. The Bantam edition is 152 pages long.
76 Forde and Ross, "Radio and Civic Courage," 31–38.
77 Agee and Evans, *Let Us Now Praise Famous Men*, n.p. (unnumbered sixth photograph counting from first photograph at the beginning of the book). See also Evans, *Lucille Burroughs*. The photograph is also in the collection of the Library of Congress.
78 Maharidge and Williamson, *And Their Children*, iv.
79 Bowden, *Black Hawk Down* (Atlantic Monthly Press, 1999).
80 Bowden, *Black Hawk Down* (Philadelphia Inquirer, 1997).
81 Jauss, *Toward an Aesthetic*, 53.
82 Paterniti, "Driving Mr. Albert," 157.
83 Falk, Lepore and Noe, "Cerebral Cortex," 11.
84 Paterniti, *Driving Mr. Albert*.
85 Kupfer, *Experience as Art*, 192–93.

Bibliography

Agee, James, and Walker Evans. *Let Us Now Praise Famous Men*. Boston, MA: Houghton Mifflin, 1941.

Aristotle. *Poetics*.

Bakhtin, Mikhail M. *The Dialogic Imagination*. Edited by Michael Holquist. Translated by Caryl Emerson and Michael Holquist. Austin, TX: University of Texas Press, 1981.

Bellos, David. *The Novel of the Century: The Extraordinary Adventure of "Les Misérables."* New York: Farrar, Straus and Giroux, 2017.

Bemong, Nele, Pieter Borghart, Michel De Dobbeleer, Kristoffel Demoen, Koen De Temmerman, and Bart Keunen, eds. *Bakhtin's Theory of the Literary Chronotope: Reflections, Applications, Perspectives*. Ghent, Belgium: Academia Press, 2010.

Bock, Paula. "In Her Mother's Shoes." *Seattle Times*, December 1, 2002.

Bowden, Mark. *Black Hawk Down: A Story of Modern War*. New York: Atlantic Monthly Press, 1999.

———. *Black Hawk Down*. *Philadelphia Inquirer*, November 16–December 14, 1997. Accessed July 22, 2017. http://inquirer.philly.com/packages/somalia/sitemap.asp.

Boyd, Brian. *On the Origin of Stories: Evolution, Cognition, and Fiction*. Cambridge, MA: Harvard University Press, 2009.

Boynton, Robert S. *The New New Journalism*. New York: Vintage, 2005.

Bromwich, David. "What Novels Are For." Review of *A Critic's Notebook*, by Irving Howe. *New York Times Book Review*, October 30, 1994, 7.

Crane, Stephen. "Regulars Get No Glory." 1898. In *Reports of War: War Dispatches: Great Battles of the World*, edited by Fredson Bowers, 170–73. Vol. 9 of *The University of Virginia Edition of the Works of Stephen Crane*. Charlottesville, VA: University Press of Virginia, 1971.

Crowder, Kate. "History of Old-House Porches." *Old House Journal Online*, June 27, 2011. www.oldhouseonline.com/articles/history-of-old-house-porches.

Davis, Lennard J. *Factual Fictions: The Origins of the English Novel*. Philadelphia, PA: University of Pennsylvania Press, 1996.
Dear, Peter. *Discipline and Experience: The Mathematical Way in the Scientific Revolution*. Chicago: University of Chicago Press, 1995.
de la Carrera, Rosalina. "History's Unconscious in Victor Hugo's *Les Misérables*." *MLN* 96, no. 4 (May 1981): 839–55. https://doi.org/10.2307/2905840.
Didion, Joan. "Some Dreamers of the Golden Dream." In *Slouching Towards Bethlehem*, 3–28. New York: Farrar, Straus and Giroux, 1968.
Droysen, Johann Gustav. *Historik, Vorlesungen über Enzyklopädie und Methodologie der Geschichte*. Edited by Rudolph Hübner. Munich: Oldenbourg, 1967.
Eliade, Mircea. *Myths, Dreams and Mysteries: The Encounter between Contemporary Faiths and Archaic Realities*. Edited by Ruth Nanda Anshen. Translated by Philip Mairet. New York: Harper and Row, 1963.
Evans, Walker. *Lucille Burroughs, Hale County, Alabama / Maggie Louise Gudger*. 1936. Photograph. J. Paul Getty Museum. www.getty.edu/art/collection/objects/40413/walker-evans-lucille-burroughs-hale-county-alabama-maggie-louise-gudger-american-1936/.
Falk, Dean, Frederick E. Lepore, and Adrianne Noe. "The Cerebral Cortex of Albert Einstein: A Description and Preliminary Analysis of Unpublished Photographs." *Brain* 136, no. 4 (April 2013): 1304–27. https://doi.org/10.1093/brain/aws295.
Ferrari, Pier Francesco, and Giacomo Rizzolatti. "Mirror Neuron Research: The Past and the Future." *Philosophical Transactions of the Royal Society B: Biological Sciences* 369, no. 1639 (April 2014). www.ncbi.nlm.nih.gov/pmc/articles/PMC4006175/.
Forde, Kathy Roberts, and Matthew W. Ross. "Radio and Civic Courage in the Communications Circuit of John Hersey's 'Hiroshima.'" *Literary Journalism Studies* 3, no. 2 (Fall 2011): 31–53.
Genette, Gérard. "Frontiers of Narrative." In *Figures of Literary Discourse*, translated by Alan Sheridan, 127–44. New York: Columbia University Press, 1982.
Gerrig, Richard J. *Experiencing Narrative Worlds: On the Psychological Activities of Reading*. New Haven, CT: Yale University Press, 1993.
Graesser, Arthur C., Brent Olde, and Bianca Klettke. "How Does the Mind Construct and Represent Stories?" In *Narrative Impact: Social and Cognitive Foundations*, edited by Melanie C. Green, Jeffrey J. Strange, and Timothy C. Brock, 229–62. New York: Psychology Press, 2002.
Green, Melanie C. "Transportation into Narrative Worlds: The Role of Prior Knowledge and Perceived Realism." *Discourse Processes* 38, no. 2 (2004): 247–66. https://doi.org/10.1207/s15326950dp3802_5.
Grossman, Kathryn M. *The Later Novels of Victor Hugo: Variations on the Politics and Poetics of Transcendence*. Oxford: Oxford University Press, 2012.
Hartsock, John C. *A History of American Literary Journalism: The Emergence of a Modern Narrative Form*. Amherst, MA: University of Massachusetts Press, 2000.
———. *Literary Journalism and the Aesthetics of Experience*. Amherst: University of Massachusetts Press, 2016.
Herman, David. *Storytelling and the Sciences of the Mind*. Cambridge: MIT Press, 2013.
Herr, Michael. *Dispatches*. New York: Vintage, 1991.
Hersey, John. *Hiroshima*. New York: Milestone Editions, 1946.
———. *Hiroshima*. 1946. New ed. New York: Bantam, 1986.
Iser, Wolfgang. *The Act of Reading: A Theory of Aesthetic Response*. Baltimore, MD: Johns Hopkins University Press, 1978.
Jauss, Hans Robert. *Toward an Aesthetic of Reception*. Translated by Timothy Bahti. Minneapolis, MN: University of Minnesota Press, 1982.
Jünger, Ernst. *The Storm of Steel: From the Diary of a German Storm-Troop Officer on the Western Front*. Translated by Basil Creighton. 1929. New York: Howard Fertig, 1975.
Kahn, Renee, and Ellen Meagher. *Preserving Porches*. New York: Henry Holt, 1990.
Kierkegaard, Søren. "The Present Age." In *The Living Thoughts of Kierkegaard*, edited by W. H. Auden, translated by A. Dru and W. Lowrie, 31–55. Bloomington, IN: Indiana University Press, 1971.
Kupfer, Joseph H. *Experience as Art: Aesthetics in Everyday Life*. Albany, NY: State University of New York Press, 1983.
Leddy, Tom. "The Nature of Everyday Aesthetics." In *The Aesthetics of Everyday Life*, edited by Andrew Light and Jonathan M. Smith, 3–22. New York: Columbia University Press, 2005.
Maharidge, Dale, and Michael Williamson. *And Their Children after Them*. New York: Pantheon, 1989.
Mar, Raymond A., William M. Kelley, Todd F. Heatherton, and C. Neil Macrae. "Detecting Agency from the Biological Motion of Veridical vs Animated Agents." *Social Cognitive and Affective Neuroscience* 2, no. 3 (2007): 199–205. https://doi.org/10.1093/scan/nsm011.

Metzidakis, Angelo. "On Rereading French History in Hugo's *Les Misérables*." *French Review* 67, no. 2 (December 1993): 187–95.

Nietzsche, Friedrich. "On Truth and Falsity in Their Ultramoral Sense." In *Early Greek Philosophy and Other Essays*, edited by Oscar Levy, translated by Maximilian Mügge, 171–92. Vol. 2 of *The Complete Works of Friedrich Nietzsche*. 1911. New York: Russell and Russell, 1964.

Oatley, Keith. "Why Fiction May Be Twice as True as Fact: Fiction as Cognitive and Emotional Stimulation." *Review of General Psychology* 3, no. 2 (June 1999): 101–17. https://doi.org/10.1037//1089-2680.3.2.101.

Paterniti, Michael. "Driving Mr. Albert." In *Love and Other Ways of Dying*, 104–159. New York: Dial Press, 2016.

———. *Driving Mr. Albert: A Trip across America with Einstein's Brain*. New York: Dial Press, 2001.

Poovey, Mary. *A History of the Modern Fact: Problems of Knowledge in the Sciences of Wealth and Society*. Chicago: University of Chicago Press, 1998.

Rayfield, Donald. *Anton Chekhov: A Life*. New York: Henry Holt, 1998.

Ricoeur, Paul. *Time and Narrative*. Vol. 1. Chicago: University of Chicago Press, 1984.

Schaeffer, Jean-Marie. "Fictional vs. Factual Narration." *The Living Handbook of Narratology*, revised September 20, 2013. Accessed February 11, 2018. www.lhn.uni-hamburg.de/article/fictional-vs-factual-narration.

Scholes, Robert. "Language, Narrative, and Anti-narrative." In *On Narrative*, edited by W. J. T. Mitchell, 204–12. Chicago: University of Chicago Press, 1981.

Shklovsky, Victor. "Art as Technique." In *Russian Formalist Criticism: Four Essays*, edited and translated by Lee T. Lemon and Marion J. Reis, 3–24. Lincoln, NE: University of Nebraska Press, 1965.

———. *A Sentimental Journey*. Translated by Richard Sheldon. Ithaca, NY: Cornell University Press, 1970.

Simmons, Ernest J. *Chekhov: A Biography*. Chicago: University of Chicago Press, 1970.

Sims, Norman. "The Problem and the Promise of Literary Journalism Studies." *Literary Journalism Studies* 1, no. 1 (Spring 2009): 7–16.

Spitzer, Alan B. "Reflections of Historical Remembering: 'The Year 1817,' *Les Misérables*, Part I, Book III." *Literature and History* 14, no. 2 (Fall 1988): 143–59.

Ulin, David L. "What Happened Here?" *Columbia Journalism Review*, March/April 2010. www.cjr.org/second_read/what_happened_here.php?page=all.

VanderWolk, William. *Victor Hugo in Exile: From Historical Representations to Utopian Vistas*. Lewisburg, PA: Bucknell University Press, 2006.

Wolfe, Tom. "The New Journalism." In *The New Journalism*, edited by Tom Wolfe and E. W. Johnson. New York: Harper and Row, 1973.

Zavarzadeh, Mas'ud. *The Mythopoeic Reality: The Postwar American Nonfiction Novel*. Urbana, IL: University of Illinois Press, 1976.

23
IMMERSION JOURNALISM AND THE SECOND-ORDER NARRATIVE

Christopher P. Wilson

INTERVIEWER: Is reporting abroad different from reporting in the U.S.?
FINNEGAN: Yes.
INTERVIEWER: How?
FINNEGAN: You need a passport.
—William Finnegan in an interview by Robert S. Boynton

What do we talk about when we talk about "immersion" journalism? And what criteria do we use when we try to categorize those reporters who seem—as if applying William Finnegan's half-comic analogy between immersion and international border-crossing, above—to "cross over" into American worlds of poverty, class or racial subjugation, or criminality, while providing retrospective accounts of their journey?[1] Because we often talk across different texts, different historical periods, and even different academic disciplines—well, it's inevitable that we sometimes talk at cross-purposes.

To illustrate this point, let's start with just such a classic instance of immersion—strikingly *literal* immersion—described by the American reporter Nellie Bly in her famous *New York World* exposé, "Ten Days in a Mad-House" (1887). Bly, of course, posed as a down-on-her-luck, bedraggled, and unstable young workingwoman in order to be committed to the infamous Blackwell's Island asylum in New York City. Her goal, as with so many immersion narratives, was to arrive at what it feels like to *be* the subjected women she wrote about—to share their perceptions, their fears, even their sense of powerlessness—and, moreover, to inaugurate that exchange of subjectivities with the reader that John Hartsock has said is often at the heart of narrative journalism.[2] But the particular scene I'm thinking of takes place about a third of the way into Bly's account, when she is stripped naked and dumped—one is liable to say *quite* ceremoniously—into a tub of water:

> The water was ice-cold, and I again began to protest. How useless it all was! ... I was at last past seeing or speaking, although I had begged that my hair be left untouched. ... My teeth chattered and my limbs were goose-fleshed and blue with cold. Suddenly I got, one after the other, three buckets of water over my head—ice-cold water, too—into my eyes, my ears, my nose and my mouth. I think I experienced some of the sensations of a drowning person as they dragged me, gasping, shivering and quaking, from the tub. For once I did look insane. ... Unable to control myself at the absurd picture I presented,

> I burst into roars of laughter. They put me, dripping wet, into a short canton flannel slip, labeled across the extreme end in large black letters, "Lunatic Asylum, B. I., H. 6." The letters meant Blackwell's Island, Hall 6.[3]

Here, true to the sensational tradition's emphasis on extreme bodily states, Bly represents herself as a fully observed physicality, reduced to her skin and hair and teeth—as if, in fact, the flannel gown so labeled by Blackwell's Island signifies her full submission to the institution's identity: She is, as it were, baptized. Bly thereby captures the loss of bodily control so characteristic of classical immersion narratives, as the very organs of perception (eyes, ears, nose, mouth, skin) are flooded and overwhelmed. Indeed, we might notice that even though she comically declares her success at merely looking insane, Bly's laughter seems suffused with the fear of actually *becoming* the imprisoned subject whose experience she means to emulate—of crossing over, but perhaps never coming back. Immersing herself in the subjectivity of the inmates at Blackwell's seems to come, powerfully, with the risk of succeeding too well.

And yet, as classical as it seems, this scene also typifies some of the ways our definitions of immersion start to become a little crossed up. Even calling Bly's account an "immersion narrative" does not clarify just what we mean to refer to. Scholars of a formalist or textual bent, for instance, are liable to use "immersion" as a genre label, and thus to put literary effects uppermost in their readings. In short, by "immersion narrative," these scholars mean to identify a set of conventions, stylistic signatures, and literary effects: typically, first-person narration, deeply sensate reporting, rich detailing of subjective experience. In fact, this stylistic emphasis is generally understood to connect to the intuition that the label "immersion" also encompasses the experience of *reading* such a text—or, again as Hartsock suggests, the reader's feeling of being imaginatively transported away from his or her immediate context.[4]

However, practitioners and scholars closer to the journalism trade itself often use "immersion" a bit differently. That is, they tend to use the term to refer not to style or readerly experience at all but to the physical social practices ostensibly *producing* such a text. In short, immersion is in what Bly *does*, not what she writes. For instance, to unpack another layer of the joke from William Finnegan in my epigraph, this usage connects to the way we speak of being immersed in the culture of another country—to have engaged that culture in a time-extensive, participatory mode that takes one beyond mere observation or tourism. And thus, in turn, journalists and scholars alike have recently used this meaning to suggest that immersion journalism should be thought of as akin to practices made famous by classical anthropological fieldwork.[5]

To an extent, of course, each of these meanings of immersion is revealing in its own way. Nevertheless, we should pause before assuming they all line up easily with each other. For instance, practicing journalists will often disagree about what really constitutes immersion in the practical, logistical sense. Many, for example, will rarely if ever use "immersion" to refer, as in Bly's vivid exemplum, to going *undercover*, much less to losing one's identity while observing. Rather, these practitioners simply use "immersion" to mean doing legwork, traveling, or interviewing, or again inhabiting a given milieu for an extended period of time. More to the point, a given narrative style can never really be connected directly to the journalistic *modus operandi* ostensibly behind it. For example, the Hemingway-inspired style of the fly-on-the-wall observer, readapted by John Hersey in *Hiroshima* (1946) and used to strikingly similar effect by David Finkel in *Thank You for Your Service* (2013), actually results from different on-the-ground methods: Finkel was ever-present and immersed with his often-traumatized subjects; Hersey obviously could not have been. Leon Dash, to take up a third example, also characterizes his *modus operandi* in works like *Rosa Lee* (1996) as "anthropological" fly-on-the-wall observation. But stylistically, he not only writes in the first person; moreover, he recreates his own real-time presence in the narrative unfolding before us. Contrary to Bly, one learns, Dash regards undercover imposture as the professional, practical, and even moral *antithesis* of what others call immersion.[6]

One cannot hope, then, to untangle these many different usages. Instead, in this essay, I want to examine a few instances where, as readers, we encounter these rival meanings of "immersion" seemingly in play simultaneously—that is, in a single performance of literary journalism. Indeed, I want to go further, and to suggest that this happens because many of our most canonical immersion texts, in Bly's family tree and beyond it, do not simply present themselves as depictions of their given journalistic topics (poverty, low-wage life, and so on). Rather, many of these texts also weave in, collaterally, what we might call a *second-order* narrative: that is, a coexisting literary story about *how* the text we're reading ostensibly came to be researched and written. As if comingling and contrasting the usages I have just described, in other words, these texts propose themselves as both accounts of *being* immersed and *how* such immersion was enacted.

I'm interested, then, in how (as readers or critics) we distinguish and/or coordinate these two narrative levels. However, to my first propositions, I also want to append a final, perhaps countervailing one. At first blush, this second-order dimension would seem to have a great deal to do, in the first place, with whether or not we accede to what we often call a given text's ethnographic authority; as I've already suggested, that's why analogies between anthropological and journalistic immersion have seemed to proliferate of late—as they should. Nevertheless, I also want to caution us about adopting this seemingly ready-made analogy too quickly; in fact, I want to take a moderately contrarian path. That is, I mean to show that many of our finest contemporary second-order narratives—texts I would call "*post*ethnographic," actually—turn out to trouble such analogies to the norms of classical fieldwork, and with that, they challenge some of our current intuitions about observers' and/or readers' imaginative transport into a putatively "alternate" reality (poverty, a different class experience, and so on). Indeed, I will suggest that it may even be a bit imprecise to call these particular narratives "participant-observation" accounts. Rather, I will argue that these postethnographic journalistic narratives also ask us—as one anthropologist has put it, about her own work—to observe their participation.[7]

Indeed, it is with the matter of the journalistic transcription of poverty or subjection, I think, where this turnabout becomes most germane to how readers and critics might conceive of immersion in the first place. Of course it is understandable that—given descriptions like Bly's—we tend to think of immersion as an all-or-nothing enterprise; conditions of powerlessness or submission can indeed feel much like drowning. Yet it is perhaps the *literal* force of Bly's metaphor for her practice—being immersed in a tub of water—that should actually bring us up short. When we really think about it, societies or cultures or subcultures may not always possess properties of "inside" and "outside" as physically distinct as a human's breathing boundary between air and water. That is, if we're talking about cultural transcription of a radically different world, foreign or domestic, a reflection of class or supposed racial difference, and so on—well, when is one ever fully immersed, exactly? When has one arrived at a cultural ground zero, a place of equivalence with the perceptions of the ostensibly native subjects of that culture?[8] Leaving aside that not all inhabitants of any culture are native to it, *is* there such place? Or, to turn things around, have we ourselves ever been in such a place, as inhabitants of our *own* cultures—never apart, never feeling self-conscious, never sensing our difference from those around us?

And so, by looking at the Victorian roots of immersion practices and then at three contemporary variations on this tradition, I mean to address several interrelated questions. First, what are the conventions of this older tradition, and what are the critiques that literary critics and ethnographers themselves mounted against it? Second, what would it mean to consider classic immersion texts' second-order narratives not merely as transparent renderings of the actual practices behind a given work of reporting but as literary and indeed meta-texts readers must unpack? And, finally, what can critical attention to these second-order narratives suggest to us about how to read these newer, postethnographic texts of immersion journalism, these days?

* * *

I say "these days" because describing the styles or practices of immersion necessarily involves some historicizing. Bly's exposé, so rooted in Joseph Pulitzer-style stunt journalism and the long-standing aesthetics of sensationalism, can now seem to us very Victorian in its stock casting, emphasis on shocking bodily violation, and emotional overload. Indeed, from the late nineteenth through the mid-twentieth century, immersion journalism's ethos of direct witnessing often connoted not only unmediated seeing or "being present to" but a moral imperative taking possession of the viewer's body. In Bly's era, as William Dow has put it, immersion journalists often focused on telling "the story of a body's entrance into meaning."[9] And the range of this ethos was considerable. For instance, writers who, in the words of Eric Schocket, "conceived of their own bodies both as objects of social forces" and as "sites of social knowledge" included amateur criminologists like Josiah Flynt, experimental impressionists like Stephen Crane, and early professional sociologists such as Annie MacLean.[10] Meanwhile, in activist works like Ida B. Wells's *Red Record* (1895)—which might stylistically not seem like an "immersion narrative" at all—the harrowing accumulation of reports of lynching was nevertheless framed in a manner akin to Christian testimonial traditions, in which one's own being carried the moral weight (or the terrors) of standing in for the victimized. With different political variations, traces of these testimonial traditions would remain evident in the border-crossing immersions of writers like radicals John Reed, Agnes Smedley, or Margaret Randall.[11] And in immersion narratives new and old, the implicit argument is often that the simple demands of sustaining an undercover identity can close the gap with one's subjects: As Barbara Ehrenreich writes in her introduction to *Nickel and Dimed* (2001), "There's no way … to pretend to be a waitress; the food either gets to the table or not."[12] Bly, likewise, is treated as what she is pretending to be, and she is going to get her bath.

Oddly, however, even those contemporary journalists who seem most indebted to these traditions—Ehrenreich, for one—can also claim not really to be going there.[13] And that's because, or so the story goes, many in the journalism mainstream have now deemed these immersion traditions too partisan, too rhetorical, or just plain unprofessional. As I've said, among some journalists, going undercover can be itself regarded as an unethical deception practiced on one's subjects. In some situations, it can even be seen as criminal (involving, for instance, trespassing, abetting illegal immigration, committing fraud, and more).[14] Indeed, some famous examples of narrative journalism, even those that reflect deep *logistical* immersion, omit what I have called a second-order narrative altogether. Instead, in varieties of what is sometimes labeled "ethnographic realism"—Alex Kotlowitz's *There Are No Children Here* (1991), Adrian Nicole LeBlanc's *Random Family* (2003), or David Simon and Edward Burns's *The Corner* (1997) come to mind—the presence of the reporter (or even a first-person voice) is confined to postscripts and methodological notes so as to retain the illusion of novelistic wholeness in the main narrative, and thus seamless integration with the informant's world and worldview.[15] This tradition of ethnographic realism has been surprisingly resilient within sociological texts as well. For example, in recent crossover books like Matthew Desmond's *Evicted* (2016) or Alice Goffman's *On the Run* (2014), a lengthy and even deeply confessional methodological reflection may be *appended* to a text resulting from immersion practice, even though it often seems that the appendix is precisely what allows the main narrative to elide the observer and maintain realist protocols. (A similar byplay is evident in *LA Times* reporter Sonia Nazario's *Enrique's Journey* [2006]: After a prologue recounting the author's five-year, high-risk immersion in the world of border-crossing—including riding on the top of freight cars, imperiled by gangsters and traffickers and physical dangers of all kinds—Nazario herself disappears as the book starts up again with a chronological recasting of her protagonist's odyssey.) And thus, as if without saying so, the aura of narrative objectivity and professional rigor is preserved, even though it is logistical immersion that has partly established methodological street cred.

Nevertheless, these disavowals cannot obscure the fact that many of the literary conventions established in the late Victorian and early modern era have persisted well beyond their apparent expiration date. As in Bly's narrative, for example, the account of moving into poverty can still be rendered as an initiation story; that is, writers often recount the disorientation or shock they initially feel, often followed by a breakthrough moment of understanding or acceptance or comfort. The supposed crossing over is itself often characterized as the entry into another "world" or "country" even when that is not literally so; not uncommonly the universe is "halved" or made into an "other" America, much like it was in Jacob Riis's work. A series of half-comic inversions have also become conventional, whereby an upper-world education and training (as, for instance, in Lincoln Steffens's *Autobiography* [1931]) prove useless in this underworld: Up proves to be down, while culturally acquired preconceptions (for instance, the notion that the police will protect you) turn out to be profoundly inapt. At the end of the immersion writer's journey, it also isn't uncommon to find the author recounting a kind of reverse disorientation or culture shock.[16]

Of course, drawing attention to the persistence of such literary conventions within *journalistic* practice might also generate an uneasiness in us. That is, to suggest that journalists follow a literary convention can imply that such devices may have overruled their perceptions as reporters. In other words, drawing attention to such metaphorical structures or discursive inheritances can seem to implicitly cut against the empiricist standards the trade has traditionally inculcated and that readers often expect from journalists.

Even more fundamentally, the critical-historical attention to class, race, and ethnicity has also generated a recurrent series of critiques of immersion as an interpretive practice. For example, scholars have raised important questions about the privilege these early immersion journalists imported into the field: privileges of race, of education, or simply of having the leisure to look at those who do not. As Christopher Herbert has shown, for example, the idea that a "culture" of poverty—a holistic and coherent symbolic order available to what we would call "thick," realistic description—is at least as old as Victorian investigators of the London poor in the 1840s. And yet, to Herbert, those very same investigators were merely "projecting [their] own values and discursive categories upon exotic others ... in order to render [such] experience intelligible" and make it into an object of study in the first place. (One feature of being poor, we might say, was that you could count on being categorized and enumerated.)[17] Indeed, Herbert's history of the British roots of ethnographic practice should be bracing for scholars of immersion journalism, since he argues that its classically organizing gambit—again, the idea that poverty constituted a distinct "culture" or world unto itself into which one could be deeply immersed—was merely an interpretive "fiction" that "has been in crisis"[18] practically from its inception.[19]

Similarly, within US cultural history, the common critique is that the crossing over of a hypothetical social boundary, even when the goal is to empathize or identify with one's journalistic subject, often merely ends up by reifying that very boundary. As Jean Marie Lutes has brilliantly shown, for example, Bly positioned herself as the champion of the immigrant and the working poor only by creating, simultaneously, the sensational figure of the intrepid female reporter. To be sure, Bly skillfully mocked male medical authority both at the asylum and in the legal system by performing the role of a female hysteric in a way her readers often found, well, hysterical.[20] But by suggesting it was all an act, Bly also conveyed "a self-assured, sexually attractive but emphatically virginal self" who protected her more privileged readers from the dangers of over-identification with the less fortunate segments of the urban population by carefully preserving the respectability of her physical self, and by reiterating her middle-class white identity through the posture of modesty and beauty.[21]

In other words, despite her newspaper's "triumphant claims that she impersonated insanity,"[22] Bly simply re-instantiated some of the class and ethnic differences she proposed to transcend.

These problems hardly disappear in later immersion accounts. For instance, a book like John Howard Griffin's *Black Like Me* (1961), in which a "white" Southern journalist dyed his skin attempting to "pass" as "black," can seem little more than an updated slave narrative, wherein a "white" amanuensis frames and thereby legitimates a supposedly unreliable slave's testimony. Griffin also carried with him racist, primitivist, and class-based notions of the "Negro" that deeply undermined his supposedly scientific experiment. Indeed, by the very strategy of immersive disguise, writers often unwittingly suggested that those being witnessed are somehow unable to testify on their own. That is, the reporter's own experience seems to be offered in place of those being simulated.[23]

However, we should not simply be ready to give up the ghost of immersion entirely—and here is where considering the second-order narrative as a literary text we imbibe comes into play. All too often, my sense is that the idea of immersion's imaginative transport or bodily simulation is predicated on a naïve or romantic reader who doesn't notice what the critic does—for instance, a reader who somehow forgets Bly's or Griffin's whiteness, education, or middle-class status.[24] Alternatively, Kate Baldwin has reminded us that the journalist's own identity is in fact always implicitly present to the reader's eye, even when a reporter claims to be immersed or undercover (as far as his or her informants are concerned). That is, as readers, we actually sustain a sense of the original identity of the reporter and thus rarely lose sight of immersion's fundamentally performative mode. As Baldwin puts it in her essay on Griffin:

> At the same time that the author attempts to inscribe himself within a "black" persona, his narrative creates a disjunctive space where his "whiteness" always persists in framing his blackness. ... The dissembling space of Griffin's passing produces a continual "error" of identity that [the reader] is always intended to register.[25]

In other words, when we are reading Jack London's *The People of the Abyss* (1903) or Norah Vincent's *Self-Made Man* (2006), we are often *intended*—that's the interesting word—to be in on the simulation. We may admire the skill of the performance or we may not. But Baldwin's larger point, I think, is that there is a special privilege accorded the reader in being able to see both layers at once, since the actual subjects under investigation (the insane, "Negroes," and so on) almost never can. Conversely, I would add that we are rarely fooled into believing that the reporter has actually *become* his or her subject. In fact, as Mark Pittenger has observed, there are several ways the journalist can effectively inoculate him- or herself against that interpretive error by the reader, not the least of which is showing oneself running off to "a secluded spot" to scribble some notes.[26]

It's not, then, that there aren't moments of connection and empathy—there are. However, they sometimes arise in unscripted places, in momentary "contact zones" or marginal scenes. Let's return, for instance, to Lutes's own discussion of the bathtub scene with which I began. Even while Lutes is quite critical of Bly's claims of immersion, she also has a different way to read that moment of the journalist's dunking in the bath:

> [Here] Bly placed herself, both mentally and physically, on the margins of sanity. Her difference was obliterated, for a moment. Her narratives gained force from moments like these, from the tension created by doubt about her ability to maintain a coherent

self as she crossed and re-crossed social lines: "for once" she did look insane, if only once, only for a moment, only after she had been robbed of her unflappable calm by the gross violation of a forced public bath.[27]

As with Baldwin's proviso, this is a fundamental insight with which our discussions of immersion need to contend. What Lutes suggests is that, paradoxically, Bly is never closer to her subjects than when she *fails* at becoming the invisible, privileged observer. In other words, precisely because of the lack of control that can come with immersion, moments of insight come into view—all the while, as Baldwin suggests, we as readers are made aware that the improbability of immersion, tellingly, exposes a rift between the first- and second-order narratives.

In my final section, I explore the way these ideas might reshape our understanding of three instances of recent US literary journalism—instances, in fact, that might at first seem simple adaptations of classical immersion practices but which all invite a reading of their second-order dimension. But first, a few words on the field of ethnography's own recent paths.

* * *

The question of what modifications might be made on standard immersion practice has, in fact, preoccupied the fields of anthropology, qualitative sociology, and cultural studies for some time now. In the 1970s and 1980s, these fields both mounted critiques of time-honored ethnographic practices—critiques that in many ways informed the cultural histories I have summarized above—and began to fashion new alternatives. Scholars and practitioners have cobbled together a toolkit of less holistic, more collaborative, and admittedly partial ways of describing and executing the classical immersive approach. Analysts now describe their approach, for example, as fundamentally "interpretive" or "dialogic" at its core (rather than a simple act of transcription by an observer); as "studying up" (looking at dominant structures rather than the oppressed, in isolation); as "polymorphous engagement" or "multisite" ethnography (recognizing that cultures express themselves in different locations and through different media, rather than through a "deep," singular event ostensibly at a society's core); or as learning how to "interface" with one's informants (rather than assuming one can cross over into their identities or worldview).[28] The point has not been to abandon immersion wholesale or—if I can venture one last pun—to throw out Bly with the bathwater. Rather, the idea is to subject traditional immersion to a more self-reflexive, less holistic, and even candidly improvisational approach that both acknowledges the social-structural differentiation within the culture(s) being observed and admits to the partiality of the observer's own representations (that is, both the invested nature of any portrait and its incompleteness).[29] In genre terms, as Janice Radway once usefully put it, the goal has often been not to emulate the seamlessness of realism—or, in effect, to make the writer seem to have fully "crossed over"—but to foreground the interpretive and experiential seams *between* the analyst and his or her informants.[30]

Suppose, for instance, we take a look at *Coyotes* (1987), by Ted Conover, a former anthropology major at Amherst College who has typically invited analogies between his immersion style and ethnographic fieldwork. On the whole, *Coyotes* indeed seems like a traditional undercover-immersion account of Mexican immigration into and across the US, a participant-observation attempt to get inside these migrants' culture and consciousness. The book contains, appropriately enough, a first-chapter initiation into illegally crossing the US border; a series of chapters in which Conover explores migrant labor, including one entitled "Deep in the Orchard"; moments when he uses his immersion to reverse-other the consumer world oblivious to that work (for instance, calling Phoenix-area farmworkers "reverse snowbirds"[31])—and so on. *Coyotes* can thus seem—like the two other accounts I will discuss in closing here—a direct lineal descendant of its Victorian forbears, a story of tramping with the poor and of losing oneself in their struggles.

And yet, as such, *Coyotes* may also end up seeming vulnerable to much of the critique to which I have already alluded. Despite the deft portraiture Conover provides, for example, he often seems to treat his (almost exclusively male) informants' personal traits as representative of a supposedly characteristic "Mexican" temperament. Or, on the flip side—betraying a kind of Eurocentric paternalism—he likes to emphasize the likeness of these Mexicans' aspirations to American immigrants of the past, without much historical documentation about either side of his parallel. Indeed, as if content merely to conjure up the spirits of Josiah Flynt, Jack London, or Jack Kerouac, Conover can seem all too ready to enfold the story of Mexican migration into his own romantic notions of tramping, riding the rails, and having a rollicking personal adventure. In the entire book, however, we witness Conover himself undertaking the backbreaking labor done by migrants only once—otherwise, he is assigned roles as a teacher, a guide on a plane trip to Los Angeles, and a driver on a wild cross-country escapade. His Mexican informants can, reciprocally, too often seem like comic figures, even sidekicks. In fact, Conover's subject often seems as much Kerouac's road as it is Mexican migration as such. And it's not that these limitations are easily explained away. Nevertheless, if we shift our readerly attention to the second-order narrative, we might see something else also going on.

In part, I would suggest, we might begin to see that at least some of this seeming *lack* of immersion on Conover's part is, once again, something we are intended to see. From his very first chapter, for example, Conover casts himself as a white gringo, his racial designation an inescapable anomaly at the border and everywhere else he goes. His immersion, as even his recent "how to" book suggests, is actually partial.[32] As a result, the reporter we read about must negotiate the very tactics of his immersion with the understanding that he will always stand out in the scenes he recreates. And thus, rather than always going "deep," even into that orchard, Conover must actually move across the surfaces of the US-Mexico borderlands, before circling back to Mexico in what I feel is *Coyotes'* finest chapter, its fifth. In this important turn, Conover goes back into Northern Mexico to live for a time in a feeder village for the migration: a small municipality known as Ahuacatlán. He interrupts, in other words, the restless impulse of the road, and immersion stops being a matter of merely crossing over and returning home.

And in that fifth chapter, Conover's self-presentation becomes, in fact, even more emphatically self-reflexive. Gradually, we begin to see that this persona *in* the first-order text, this "Ted" or "Teodoro," is himself an object of *Coyotes'* observation, evaluated at a second remove by the older narrator and even by Ahuacatlán itself. Nor is this village presented as the primitive oasis of, say, the towns in John Reed's *Insurgent Mexico* (1914), as a lost world poised on the precipice of modernity.[33] Rather, as a local priest tells us, Ahuacatlán is well *over* that precipice, its social structure already fractured by the pressures of migration. For instance, Conover sees that the enticements of Mexican migration, illusory as he believes them to be, has split the men of the village along generational lines, thus threatening to subvert its structures of patriarchal authority. Like the "Ted" we've been following, its young men are drawn into the thrill of adventure they anticipate will happen when they go north, not recognizing the humiliations and dangers the older men (and the elder narrator) know they are certainly going to face. ("Make like one who's been abused," one informant had advised Conover, about how to disguise oneself when crossing the border.)[34] And this internal quarrel in the village redounds upon "Ted's" own identity. That is, Conover recognizes in retrospect that his own identity had risked functioning, while he was in Ahuacatlán, as a visible embodiment of the very forces of humiliation and degradation that these migrants so often face. The chapter thus culminates in a quite profound epiphany. As "Ted" witnesses the village drained of its young as they head north, ironically leaving Conover himself behind, he is taken into a small house by a local woman who, lamenting the lives of the men who will leave *her* behind, too, asks "Teodoro" to "look after" them in the US (an assignment at which, in the next and final chapter, he will fail). And in one final, rather morose, seriocomic toast, the woman gives him a lollipop—"[f]or the road."[35] But of course what has happened is that "the road," and the literary architecture with which "Ted" had arrived, has itself been undone. The road has turned into an enticement and a privilege that only accentuates the differences between the observer and the observed.[36]

This kind of second-order, postethnographic inversion is also visible in Barbara Ehrenreich's *Nickel and Dimed*. Immersing herself among the waitresses, maids, and Wal-Mart associates of the emerging US service class, Ehrenreich—or "Barb," as she calls herself in the identity she travels under—seems, like "Teodoro," never to achieve the immersion we might have expected of her. A sarcastic, sharp-tongued narrator and in-text persona, this "Barb" preserves certain privileges for herself while supposedly on her immersion mission: retiring to her laptop at night, cutting financial corners to retain some semblance of her professional identity, and more. Moreover, her self-mocking wit is often redirected, outwards, into condescending remarks about the workers around her (for instance, gratuitous comments on their appearance or, more generally, their passivity in the face of degradation by their employers). Indeed, it's not clear we can call them "informants" at all, because Ehrenreich seems to focus more on her own bodily woes, fatigue, and even class prejudices rather than sufficiently *listening* to her subjects or portraying their fuller lives. Although supposedly undertaking very serious subjects—exploitation, class subordination, working poverty—the book can read very much like a picaresque comedy, as "Barb" trips from job to job, tilting at windmills in each institution but ultimately giving up on one job after another.

Again, however, we might consider that the second-order story we get is *about* Ehrenreich's failing at her supposed mission. That is, the very point may be that even the secretly literate, highly educated Ehrenreich ("Barb" has a PhD in cellular immunology, it so happens) cannot marshal the skill or the bodily endurance to sustain herself in such service-class roles, even as we recognize that those who are already there have no choice but to keep trying to. Every way that "Barb" fails shows us in stark detail what the costs might be merely to survive. On this score, the *picaro/a* figure here may hold yet another key. Not only intended as a placeholder of interpretive errors or sarcasm, "Barb" turns out to be the name given to her by her father, a union man and organizer who had risen through the ranks of the mining industry, and whose dedication and labor pulled his daughter out of the very persona we've been following. "Barb," in other words, is the multilayered literary construction, a *persona* who, indeed like the classic *picaro/a*, travels through a world of decaying institutions—here, in the revised Marxian tradition on which Ehrenreich draws, the manufacturing sector and blue-collar force that are being eviscerated by the new tourism and service sector itself. Or, we might say, the error we witness is Ehrenreich's falling back into "Barb" when that identity actually has little place anymore in the service world she witnesses. Moreover, the chance to *see* this error of immersive arrogance has payoffs for readers as well. For instance, upper-middle- and upper-class readers are positioned outside of their (our) customary role as consumers, losing the privilege to tip or to make dismissive comments behind the server's back. In turn, the episodic nature of the picaresque may actually tell us about the inconstancy of service employment itself: the arbitrary coming and going of what used to be a steadier shop-floor experience. In other words, the second-order narrative is where the book's more explicit argument about class passivity meets the personal, for "Barb" and perhaps for us.

Of course, Conover and Ehrenreich each operate at what I have suggested is the undercover end of the immersion spectrum—their second-order inversions can often appear impulsive, "out of step" with professional norms. William Finnegan, by contrast, seems closer to the mainstream trade notion of immersion. Rather than adopting a disguise, Finnegan seems like a guy who simply likes to "hang" with his subjects—no more so than in *Cold New World* (1998), the book in which he recounts his travels across four regions of the US to depict at-risk young adults and their families confronting poverty, drugs, and violence in a post-Cold War, deindustrialized nation. However, I say "guy" intentionally, because who those informants meet is also—like "Barb" and "Teodoro"—a persona, here denominated as "Bill," a laid-back, born-in-California character who will drink Scotch in a New Haven kitchen, give a teenager a ride while the kid talks about drug dealing or girls or rap music, and openly admit to having "failed to keep [his] journalistic distance" by sporadically helping out those young people with money, a job application, and more.[37] (When he's being mildly obstreperous during jury duty in a related essay, Finnegan finds himself slugged in the arm by a watchful fellow juror—"c'mon, Bill," she says. She chooses the familiar.)[38]

"Bill" also wears what he thinks and feels on his sleeve: He thinks out loud *in* the action we read, even when he's wrong or acting on an impulse or just plain fed up. Here are two examples from his voyages—the first, reacting to the New Haven ghetto that opens *Cold New World*; the second, to the skinhead world of the Antelope Valley in California that closes it:

> Someone, I realize, is always telling me what someone else's problem is. ... [They] sense that I want an explanation: what is wrong. *Something* is wrong: why else would I be coming around?[39]

> "I know him," Mindy said. "He likes me."
> ["Bill"]: "No, he doesn't. ... He's a psychopath. He may want to sleep with you, but that's different from liking you."[40]

Much as in *Coyotes* and *Nickel and Dimed*, these impulsive, in-the-moment recreations might easily make us feel this is *not* really immersion; that is, the informality of it all, the constant marking of the observer's actions and reactions, seems to cut against the grain of conventions that require subordinating one's identity and remaining "objective" on scene. Indeed, sometimes when I teach the original *New Yorker* essays on which Finnegan's book is based, I xerox them directly from the magazine so that my classes will see the glitzy ads, the sly or snide cartoons, the entire upper-class aura encasing Finnegan's grim depictions. My students have little trouble pointing to the apparent contradictions: a critic of underclass hyperconsumerism reporting his fieldwork on poverty to American elites, the privilege of distanced irony embedded in the *New Yorker*'s cosmopolitan disposition, and so on. Sometimes my students will discover along the way—as his award-winning memoir *Barbarian Days* (2016) has recently told us—that "Bill" was, for his early adult life, primarily a surfer. Hardly, one should think, an apprenticeship for the serious work of reporting.

By now, of course, my own reader will expect that I think about all of this quite differently. It doesn't take long to discover, for example, that Finnegan is in fact a highly literate intellectual, well versed in sociological and ethnographic theory, whose surfing excursions had eventually landed him in South Africa, where he became a teacher in the homelands of apartheid, a witness to the emerging political struggle, and gradually a foreign correspondent who would write about postcolonial conflicts all around the globe. In *Cold New World*, "Bill's" experience in South Africa, in particular, slides underneath the obvious shocks felt by what we soon realize is a returning American prodigal, overwhelmed by the cold violence of rap music, awed by US consumerism, and dumbstruck by domestic poverty when he gets home. For instance, Finnegan writes that though some scenes remind him of the South African homelands, he "rarely, if ever" saw scenes "any more desolate" than he does in New Haven.[41] Seeing the black-nationalist or skinhead ideologies suffusing the young and the poor, Finnegan also thinks back on more authentic and more violent African or European versions, as the Old World pops into the New—a cold "New World" that he can't help but see with eyes that have made him older, out of time in several senses of the word.[42] And as a result, it is the culture clash *in the observer's work* that is very much Finnegan's second- and first-order subject—as it has been mine.

Although Finnegan has been open to friendly analogies to anthropology offered by interviewers,[43] in practice he emphasizes more what James Clifford has termed the predicament of the ethnographic position. Primarily, Finnegan emphasizes that his informants do not occupy a separate or distinct culture of poverty and that his sense of eerie estrangement when crossing over into such a world results as much from his own experience of re-immersing himself back in the US. In one sense, he comes to believe that "the moral authority of the social order that once might have allowed me to pass unambivalent judgments on the lives of poor Americans"[44] has itself proved bankrupt. After all, the larger point of *Cold New World* is that the new world disorder only *reproduces* itself *in* the lives of these young people: in joblessness, in the anomie of families, in undereducation, and yet—another twist of the knife—in a hyperconsumerism that reinforces poverty and dead-end criminality. Conversely, however, Finnegan also undercuts the idea of using as the foil to these othered communities the supposedly peaceable kingdom of the middle-class suburb. Instead, he comes to see that the disintegration of that very ground is part of the same story he is telling.[45] And so, Finnegan writes, "I've tried to keep one eye on my limitations as observer and analyst, and to reflect, where possible, the densely freighted power relations between me and some of my subjects."[46]

Elsewhere in the interview with Boynton from which I've taken my epigraph, Finnegan elaborates on what this awareness means for his practice:

> Omniscience is really not a possibility. My fallibility, my presumptuousness, have to be acknowledged. ... The right of the characters in the piece to tell their *own* stories seems much greater. I feel compelled to show how I am constructing the story, how my opinions are just my opinions, how the people I'm writing about may have different opinions, and how this is all about not simply *their* lives, but my interactions with them—and their efforts to understand me.[47]

Even more than Conover and Ehrenreich, in fact, Finnegan tries to implement a postethnographic practice *in* the tissues of his style, not just by foregrounding the subjectivity of his protagonist-persona. For example, we can see that "Bill," in all his flaws, is also an intricate result of Finnegan's adroit manipulation of the devices of retrospection and interior reflection, carefully marked when such reflection originally happened in the moment and when it did not. And, as in the passages I quoted earlier, Finnegan will often signal that he had little control of his personal reactions by using the past present tense, thus carefully delineating the time frame of his own perceptions and conclusions, and not whiting out the errors he made then or now. Moreover, he goes beyond simply exhibiting the limits of his own middle-class or forty-something interpretations; where he can, he tries to collaborate with the argot and the ritualistic displays and the asides of his subjects[48] by feeding them into his own analysis, for instance, when a New Haven petty drug dealer says of the streets, "That's a Terrordome in there,"[49] or when a gang member who says of an antagonist who sneers when he is stabbed, "That's cool. They can have their story."[50] As if circling in and around such orations or performances, Finnegan's retrospection does not, any more than the direct witnessing of the real time "Bill," fully underwrite any claim to omniscience.[51] Instead, Finnegan's paragraphs often fluctuate: Hypotheses are proposed and undone; closure ends up as anything but. That surfer, rather than diving deep, catches a wave but cuts back against it, willing to accept that a crash may await the end of interpretive privilege.

In *Cold New World*, the ultimate endpoint of what Finnegan actually calls "my own generation's crash site"[52] ends up being, in fact, the now-transformed California of his own youth. Finnegan thus quite literally circles back to the ground of his second-order narrative. And here the intention seems to go beyond conventional journalistic irony. Rather, to use a word at the very end of his book on war in Mozambique, Finnegan creates—and here I must credit Robert Boynton—more precisely an *aporia*, a moment quite like the disorientation when a clueless traveler encounters a word in a foreign language, or a category, or a classification for which he or she has no equivalent.[53] Indeed, if an *aporia* classically referred to perplexity or an interpretive impasse, in Finnegan's hands it often appears as something he has actively sought. Going beyond a personal double take or mere self-consciousness, that is, Finnegan's *aporia* breaks the seams between the journalist's explanations and those with whom he or she may not ever be fully immersed. In closing *Cold New World*, Finnegan even pauses to admit that "as for [his] own analysis ... none of these kids could much relate to it," and they were nonplussed or put off any time he would try to voice his ideas to them. "Fortunately for all concerned," Finnegan concludes laconically, "my job was to listen."[54]

So, of course, is ours. In the larger, ongoing task of rethinking immersion, we should perhaps start by echoing Finnegan's modesty here. Moreover, we should do so in order to avoid falling back into the simpler conclusion that one or the other, informant or observer, is right or wrong, or more at the center of a world that is, these days, indeed often ruthless, cold, and splintered by forces both new and old. And that is because, as I have also suggested, we need to avoid thinking of status or economic differences or racial designations as creating separate and distinct worlds, things in themselves between which we build a bridge and can stand back and look. Rather, if the meaning of power or class dominance is in how such things are exercised or performed *in relation* to other citizens—well, that is indeed what the immersed postethnographic observer often re-performs, makes us aware of, makes us come to terms with. The power to interpret is a privilege, but it is not always a power that ends up with anything but partial insight in its hands.

Nor is this cautionary reading principle necessarily an idea incompatible with journalism's larger professional mission, or its traditions. On the contrary: Modesty, pragmatism, even the cultivation of doubt (one of Finnegan's favorite terms)—if we think about it, all that sounds quite resonant with well-established journalistic principles.[55] As is, of course, the idea of listening to informants who have their own observations, including about those who observe them. In the future, we might simply immerse ourselves in such exchanges, and as we do, hold our breath.

Notes

1 The quotation above is from an interview with Finnegan (quoted in Boynton, *New New Journalism*, 88).
2 Hartsock actually prefers to call this a "narrowing" of the distance between reader and what is depicted; see his *Literary Journalism*, 71.
3 Bly, *Ten Days in a Mad-House*, chap. 11.
4 Hartsock, *Literary Journalism*, 19.
5 See especially Cramer and McDevitt, "Ethnographic Journalism"; Hermann, "Temporal Tipping Point." Citing a remark by Clifford Geertz, Hermann elides the differences between journalistic immersion and what reporters like to call "hanging out" (see 497ff).
6 Dash, quoted in Boynton, *New New Journalism*, 64–71; for Dash's explicit invocation of anthropology and participant observation, see 70.
7 Tedlock, "From Participant Observation."
8 Tedlock quotes Bronislaw Malinowski's *Argonauts of the Western Pacific* (1922) on the goal of classical anthropology: "to grasp the native's point of view, his relation to life, to realize *his* vision of *his* world" (as quoted in "From Participant Observation," 69–70).
9 Dow, *Narrating Class*, 83.
10 Schocket, "Undercover Explorations," 110.
11 This witnessing ethos can be felt even in the tradition of liberal exposé. For a discussion of Jacob Riis's use of Christian iconography and rhetoric, for example, see Jackson, "Cultivating Spiritual Sight."

12. Ehrenreich, *Nickel and Dimed*, 9. In his interview in Boynton (*New New Journalism*, 13), Ted Conover also speaks of having had no choice but to be "100 percent" a guard in his research for *Newjack: Guarding Sing Sing*.
13. See, for instance, Ehrenreich's introduction to *Nickel and Dimed*, where she states flatly that "this is no death-defying 'undercover' adventure" (6), or Ted Conover's assertion in *Immersion: A Writer's Guide to Going Deep* that "I don't think of it as being incognito when I immerse, and I really don't like the phrase undercover, as it has overtones of a law enforcement investigation into illicit activity" (58).
14. See, for instance, Schwartz, "Is Undercover Over?"; Kurtz, "Undercover Journalism"; Lisheron, "Lying to Get the Truth." Several of these refer to the controversies surrounding Kenneth Silverstein's undercover operation, recounted in "Their Men in Washington."
15. "Ethnographic realism" is a term used a bit differently across disciplines; contrast, for example, David Eason's "The New Journalism and the Image-World: Two Modes of Organizing Experience" and James Clifford's introduction to *Writing Culture: The Poetics and Politics of Ethnography* (23–25). My own thinking draws heavily on James Clifford's *The Predicament of Culture*.

    Footnotes, as William Dow has pointed out to me in an email exchange, can provide this kind of split voice as well—notably, for instance, in *Nickel and Dimed*, where Ehrenreich's formal academic training is much more in evidence than in her narrative.
16. I have discussed the resurfacing of these conventions in "'Out There'" and in *Learning to Live with Crime*.
17. Herbert, *Culture and Anomie*, 204.
18. Herbert, 17.
19. This tendency occurs most notoriously, of course, within the so-called culture of poverty hypothesis. See Goode, "How Urban Ethnography."
20. Lutes, "Into the Madhouse"; Pittenger, "World of Difference." Lutes summarizes those scholars "who have argued that cross-class investigators at the turn-of-the-century forged a pernicious dynamic that reified class and race hierarchies under the guise of challenging them" ("Into the Madhouse," 228).
21. Lutes, "Into the Madhouse," 222.
22. Lutes, 232.
23. And though I cannot consider the subject fully here, literary journalism scholars also need to interrogate the role of ethnic and racial difference within the very formulation of an immersion tradition. Does even the label "immersion" intrinsically connote, for instance, the observer's mainstream status? Is a white journalist who cultivates novelistic invisibility in his or her text, as do (say) Alex Kotlowitz or Adrian Nicole LeBlanc, more or less "immersed" than (say) black journalist Leon Dash, who consciously makes himself visible in the text? In some cases, journalists of color, if they write about a culture to which they have affiliations, are seen as writing "memoirs," not exposés. See especially Kim, "Reluctant Memoirist."
24. Prisoners call Ted Conover "Barney Fife," for instance, thus making his whiteness visible to us as readers (*Newjack*, 226, 255). As I discuss in *Learning to Live with Crime*, Conover's Sing Sing is situated as a so-called downstate prison, meaning that many of its corrections officers are from the New York metropolitan area—and thus, unlike Conover, nonwhite (141).
25. Baldwin, "Black Like Who?," 114.
26. Pittenger, "World of Difference," 15.
27. Lutes, "Into the Madhouse," 244.
28. For my summary of these transformations, along with relying on Clifford and Marcus, I have depended on Tedlock, "From Participant Observation"; Ortner, "Access"; Venkatesh, "Reflexive Turn"; Lewis and Russell, "Being Embedded"; Hannerz, "Being There."
29. On this double sense anthropologists have used the term "partial." See Clifford, introduction to *Writing Culture*, 7.
30. Radway, "Identifying Ideological Seams."
31. Conover, *Coyotes*, 32.
32. Conover's *Immersion*, for instance, talks about immersion as inviting different parts of his identity rather than a singular one (58–59).
33. I discuss Reed's immersion in "Plotting the Border."
34. Conover, *Coyotes*, 232.
35. Conover, 188.
36. There is even the possibility that Conover's title, *Coyotes*, is self-reflexive. That is, the observer may be part of the forces that, on both sides of the border, compel migrants north only to exploit them.
37. Finnegan, *Cold New World*, xv.
38. I'm referring to an exchange in William Finnegan's "Doubt."

39 Finnegan, *Cold New World*, 54.
40 Finnegan, 312.
41 Finnegan, 66.
42 Finnegan's title and book epigraph allude to *The Tempest*, particularly the exchange between Prospero and Miranda on how the "new world" seems new only to the eyes of the young. I have written about Finnegan's transnational observations in "'Out There.'"
43 See the interviews with Finnegan quoted in Hermann, "Temporal Tipping Point," 495.
44 Finnegan, *Cold New World*, xvi.
45 Finnegan, 344.
46 Finnegan, xvi.
47 Quoted in Boynton, *New New Journalism*, 90.
48 Cf. Finnegan, *Cold New World*, xv.
49 Finnegan, 20.
50 Finnegan, 333.
51 Here as elsewhere I am indebted to Barbie Zelizer's observations that journalistic authority shuttles *between* direct witnessing and retrospection. See Zelizer, "On 'Having Been There.'"
52 Finnegan, *Cold New World*, 337.
53 Finnegan, *Complicated War*, 263. Boynton singles out this quality in Finnegan (*New New Journalism* 73, 78).
54 Finnegan, *Cold New World*, 350.
55 Here again I follow Zelizer, who has suggested that the dissonant and even contradictory dimensions of mainstream trade practices need greater visibility in our analysis. See Zelizer, *Taking Journalism Seriously*, 189–90ff.

Bibliography

Baldwin, Kate. "Black Like Who? Cross-Testing the 'Real' Lines of John Howard Griffin's *Black Like Me*." *Cultural Critique* 40 (Autumn 1998): 103–43. https://doi.org/10.2307/1354469.

Bly, Nellie. *Ten Days in a Mad-House*. New York: Ian L. Munro, [1887]. http://digital.library.upenn.edu/women/bly/madhouse/madhouse.html.

Boynton, Robert S. *The New New Journalism: Conversations with America's Best Nonfiction Writers on Their Craft*. New York: Vintage, 2005.

Clifford, James. Introduction to *Writing Culture: The Poetics and Politics of Ethnography*, edited by James Clifford and George E. Marcus, 1-26. Berkeley, CA: University of California Press, 1986.

———. *The Predicament of Culture: Twentieth-Century Ethnography, Literature, and Art*. Cambridge, MA: Harvard University Press, 1988.

Conover, Ted. *Coyotes: A Journey through the Secret World of America's Illegal Aliens*. New York: Vintage, 1987.

———. *Immersion: A Writer's Guide to Going Deep*. Chicago: University of Chicago Press, 2016.

———. *Newjack: Guarding Sing Sing*. New York: Vintage, 2000.

Cramer, Janet M., and Michael McDevitt. "Ethnographic Journalism." In *Qualitative Research in Journalism: Taking It to the Streets*, edited by Sharon Hartin Iorio, 127–43. Mahwah, NJ: Lawrence Erlbaum, 2004.

Dow, William. *Narrating Class in American Fiction*. New York: Palgrave, 2009.

Eason, David L. "The New Journalism and the Image-World: Two Modes of Organizing Experience." *Critical Studies in Mass Communication* 1, no. 1 (1984): 51–65. https://doi.org/10.1080/15295038409360013.

Ehrenreich, Barbara. *Nickel and Dimed: On (Not) Getting By in America*. New York: Metropolitan Books, 2001.

Finnegan, William. *Cold New World: Growing Up in a Harder Country*. New York: Random House, 1998.

———. *A Complicated War: The Harrowing of Mozambique*. Berkeley, CA: University of California Press, 1992.

———. "Doubt." *New Yorker*, January 31, 1994.

Goode, Judith. "How Urban Ethnography Counters Myths about the Poor." In *Urban Life: Readings in the Anthropology of the City*, edited by George Gmelch and Walter P. Zenner, 185–201. Prospect Heights, IL: Waveland Press, 2002.

Hannerz, Ulf. "Being There … and There … and There! Reflections on Multi-site Ethnography." *Ethnography* 4, no. 2 (June 2003): 201–16. https://doi.org/10.1177/14661381030042003.

Hartsock, John C. *Literary Journalism and the Aesthetics of Experience*. Amherst, MA: University of Massachusetts Press, 2016.

Herbert, Christopher. *Culture and Anomie: Ethnographic Imagination in the Nineteenth Century*. Chicago: University of Chicago Press, 1991.

Hermann, Anne Kirstine. "The Temporal Tipping Point: Regimentation, Representation and Reorientation in Ethnographic Journalism." *Journalism Practice* 10, no. 4 (2016): 492–506. https://doi.org/10.1080/17512786.2015.1102605.

Jackson, Gregory S. "Cultivating Spiritual Sight: Jacob Riis's Virtual-Tour Narrative and the Visual Modernization of Protestant Homiletics." *Representations* 83, no. 1 (Summer 2003): 126–66. https://doi.org/10.1525/rep.2003.83.1.126.

Kim, Suki. "The Reluctant Memoirist." *New Republic*, June 27, 2016. https://newrepublic.com/article/133893/reluctant-memoirist.

Kurtz, Howard. "Undercover Journalism." *Washington Post*, June 25, 2007.

Lewis, S. J., and A. J. Russell. "Being Embedded: A Way Forward for Ethnographic Research." *Ethnography* 12, no. 3 (2011): 398–416. https://doi.org/10.1177/1466138110393786.

Lisheron, Mark. "Lying to Get the Truth." *American Journalism Review*, October/November 2007.

Lutes, Jean Marie. "Into the Madhouse with Nellie Bly: Girl Stunt Reporting in Late Nineteenth-Century America." *American Quarterly* 54, no. 2 (2002): 217–53. https://doi.org/10.1353/aq.2002.0017.

Ortner, Sherry B. "Access: Reflections on Studying Up in Hollywood." *Ethnography* 11, no. 2 (June 2010): 211–33. https://doi.org/10.1177/1466138110362006.

Pittenger, Mark. "A World of Difference: Constructing the 'Underclass' in Progressive America." *American Quarterly* 49, no. 1 (1997): 26–55. https://doi.org/10.1353/aq.1997.0009.

Radway, Janice. "Identifying Ideological Seams: Mass Culture, Analytical Method, and Political Practice." *Communication* 9 (1986): 93–123.

Schocket, Eric. "Undercover Explorations of the 'Other Half,' or the Writer as Class Transvestite." *Representations* 64 (Autumn 1998): 109–33. https://doi.org/10.2307/2902934.

Schwartz, Aaron. "Is Undercover Over?" *Extra!*, March/April 2008, 28–30.

Silverstein, Ken. "Their Men in Washington: Undercover with D.C.'s Lobbyists for Hire." *Harper's*, July 2007.

Tedlock, Barbara. "From Participant Observation to the Observation of Participation: The Emergence of Narrative Ethnography." *Journal of Anthropological Research* 47, no. 1 (Spring 1991): 69–94. https://doi.org/10.1086/jar.47.1.3630581.

Venkatesh, Sudhir Alladi. "The Reflexive Turn: The Rise of First-Person Ethnography." *Sociological Quarterly* 54, no. 1 (2013): 3–8. https://doi.org/10.1111/tsq.12004.

Wilson, Christopher P. *Learning to Live with Crime: American Crime Narrative in the Neoconservative Turn*. Columbus, OH: Ohio State University Press, 2010.

———. "'Out There': Transnationalism and the Other America." In *Through the Looking Glass: American Studies in Transcultural Perspective*, edited by Hans Krabbendam and Jaap Verheul, 244–57. Amsterdam: VU University Press, 1999.

———. "Plotting the Border: John Reed, Pancho Villa, and *Insurgent Mexico*." In *Cultures of United States Imperialism*, edited by Amy Kaplan and Donald E. Pease, 340–64. Durham, NC: Duke University Press, 1993.

Zelizer, Barbie. "On 'Having Been There': 'Eyewitnessing' as a Journalistic Key Word." *Critical Studies in Media Communication* 24, no. 5 (December 2007): 408–28. https://doi.org/10.1080/07393180701694614.

———. *Taking Journalism Seriously: News and the Academy*. Thousand Oaks, CA: Sage, 2004.

24
CONCEPTUALIZING AN ECOLOGICAL APPROACH TO ETHICAL LITERARY JOURNALISM

Lindsay Morton

Well into the twenty-first century, it has become commonplace to observe the disruptive impact technological advances have made on the media landscape. Innovations in modes of gathering, processing, and distributing the news have produced crises ranging from the breakdown of traditional business models to fears about the decline of quality journalism.[1] Along with these issues has come the erosion of public trust in media institutions in general and journalism in particular, necessitating a renewed discussion about communication ethics.[2] A number of factors complicate a discussion of ethics in this field, including a lack of certainty over who is—or who identifies as —a literary journalist; the broad range of genres the field participates in and their particular demands; and choices regarding the extent to which voice, style, subjectivity, transparency, and testimony infuse or inform practitioners' work. Central to this discussion is the complex web of relationships among practitioners, subjects, texts, and readers that gives rise to issues ranging from the ethics of belief to the ethics of advocacy.

While work has been done toward creating ethical rules, codes, and guidelines for narrative literary journalists,[3] this chapter takes a different approach by outlining and advocating what is essentially an ethical posture toward the practice of literary journalism: *ecological thinking*. This approach is informed by Lorraine Code's text *Ecological Thinking: The Politics of Epistemic Location* (2006). Code's approach is "a revisioned mode of engagement with knowledge, subjectivity, politics, ethics, science, citizenship, and agency that pervades and reconfigures theory and practice."[4] That is, *Ecological Thinking* literally re-visions epistemology in an ecological conceptual paradigm. Drawing insights from feminist and postcolonial theories, among others, the approach explicitly critiques Western epistemologies that perpetuate inequality and marginalization of minority groups by privileging particular ways of knowing. The term "ecological" functions both literally and metaphorically: It emphasizes that projects of inquiry are always *located*, not only geographically but also historically, politically, and socially, and that the social-physical world both enables and constrains ethical ways to act and claims of what can be known.[5] Specifically, it encourages consideration of the political issues around ethical injunctions, such as the first principle of the Society of Professional Journalists' (SPJ) Code of Ethics: "Seek truth and report it."[6] While SPJ interprets this in part as a requirement to find verifiable, accurate content; to identify sources clearly; and to "give voice to the voiceless,"[7] an ecological approach might pose further questions: "Truth according to whom?" "Whose perspective is to be represented here?" and "How might the journalist's position affect what can and cannot be 'seen' in this situation?" These are key ethical concerns as they involve interaction with—and representation of—sources, subjects, the self, and truth claims to readers. Ecological thinking invites deeply reflexive critical engagement with existing journalistic ethical codes such as those of SPJ, the US Press Association, and the American Media Council.[8] It encourages knowledge seekers to think politically about the assumptions embedded in universal imperatives. And critically, it challenges the empirical concept of "facts," demonstrating that "statements of fact … acquire or fail to achieve factual status *situationally*."[9] Ecological thinking probes the assumptions on which existing journalistic ethical codes are based, and invites a re-visioning of ethical engagement among author, subject, and reader—in regards to gender, race, education, environment, and privilege—as part of "a commitment to responsible ideals of citizenship and preservation of the public trust."[10]

Epistemology and Ethics

In a special edition of *Journalism* focusing on literary journalistic ethics, epistemology is identified as the first of three ethical dimensions relevant to the field.[11] Epistemology, or the study of knowledge and how it can be substantiated, is a key area for exploration, given the highly disputed territory of literary journalism's truth claims, and is the focus of this chapter. Ecological thinking highlights the political dimensions of knowledge production. It critiques orthodox epistemologies and ethical theories that work on an "ethos of mastery" and result in oppression for the marginalized and powerless.[12] This is a key idea that informs ecological thinking: The way in which knowledge is conceived and justified *is* ethical and generates ethical consequences. As Code explains:

> Theories of knowledge shape and are shaped by dominant social-political imaginaries. … [I]n ordinary, everyday epistemic lives, assumptions that emanate from these theories participate in the structural ordering of societies, large and small, according to uneven distributions of authority and expertise, power and privilege.[13]

As a result, ecological thinking contains an ethical imperative that asks inquirers to re-vision what knowledge is, critique the structures that perpetuate oppression, and address inequities perpetuated by rationalist-empiricist ways of knowing.

In 2012 Richard Keeble wrote that literary journalists "claim the real," which in essence is "an assertion about truthfulness to verifiable experience, an adherence to accuracy and sincerity which practitioners assert are the crucial features that distinguish their narratives from 'fiction.'"[14] Ecological thinking does not dismiss the possibility of making truth claims but views the processes of knowledge creation as inductive rather than deductive.[15] This reorientation is a moral matter: It emphasizes the limitations of what can be known; it privileges the particular in order to deconstruct stereotypes; and it is critical of terms such as "statement of fact" to the extent that they are often embedded in power discourses.[16] Again, a key assertion from an ecological perspective is that facts "acquire or fail to achieve factual status *situationally*, according to the patterns of authority and expertise constitutive of the institution(s) of knowledge production in whose discursive spaces they circulate."[17] While this is a potentially controversial point, consider rules of law, admissibility of evidence, and kinds of knowledge validated or denied by particular institutions. Or the world of science, where knowledge is hierarchically organized—for example, fact is privileged over anecdote, and observation over narrative.[18] These norms are constructed and reproduced as "rational" ways of knowing, but an ecological approach, alive to the ways knowledge is both enabled and constrained by these positions of power, or "epistemologies of mastery,"[19] works to take "subjectivity, cognitive agency, and geographical-material-historical-cultural location seriously into account."[20]

The discipline of verification has been cited by Bill Kovach and Tom Rosenstiel as "what separates journalism from entertainment, propaganda, fiction, or art."[21] Does the situated nature of knowledge release a literary journalist from the obligation of verification? Ecological thinking does not discredit the need for verification but rather requires a practitioner to think more deeply about the situation from which that "fact" or "truth claim" was produced. It recognizes that while there are facts that can be empirically verified—such as thermometer readings, DNA samples, and fingerprinting[22]—many of the knowledge claims made emerge outside of rational-intellectual endeavor from "the messiness, confusion, and concerns of the everyday."[23] Much has been written about controversies generated by truth claims that did not take the subjects' environment into account. Internationally, the cases of Åsne Seierstad and Richard Critchfield expose the limits of verification and highlight the ways that facts can be constituted by their cultural context and vice versa.[24] Closer to home, North American literary journalists display various degrees of awareness about the situated nature of knowledge claims. Those with a background in anthropology raise this issue in discussions of their works: Ted Conover and William Langewiesche, who have degrees in the field, appear to be sensitive to the way knowledge is mediated, located, and embodied.[25] Langewiesche describes his experience of working on the beaches of India and Bangladesh:

> It became obvious that the workers on the beach had a completely different viewpoint—a different cosmology, really—from the world I was used to. I mean this in a very immediate sense. It was not just that they had different political views or ideologies from my own, but they had a completely different sense of the experience we were sharing at the moment. There were times when it seemed amazing to me that we were capable even of breathing the same air. We were animals of the same species, of course, but our understanding of the room in which we were sitting, or the field in which we were standing, or the bus we were riding in, was completely different.[26]

From an ecological approach, this is an example of inquiry located "'down on the ground' where knowledge is made, negotiated, circulated; and where the nature and conditions of the particular 'ground' ... have claims to critical epistemic scrutiny equivalent to those of allegedly isolated, discrete propositional knowledge claims."[27]

Rather than being relativist in nature, ecological thinking is related to "strong objectivity."[28] Michael Schudson has defined objectivity as "the belief that one can and should separate facts from values,"[29] but *strong objectivity* works in the other direction. It includes interests, assumptions, presuppositions, and personal values, and considers them as worthy of analysis as other types of knowledge.[30] As Linda Steiner writes, *strong objectivity* acknowledges that "cultural identities have epistemic status: They 'enable us to read the world in specific ways.'"[31] This is a similar ethical position to that advocated by practitioners such as Leon Dash. Dash, an experienced and influential literary journalist, writes that his time in the Peace Corps taught him about cultural relativity, and that as a result, "I teach my students that you can't be a journalist if you are going to be judgmental."[32] While Dash here is rightly warning about making moral or value judgments from a standpoint where particular class or race values are the norm,[33] ecological thinking asks inquirers to go further by using their own values, expectations, and judgments as objects of analysis, and by being as open to critical evaluation as those of their subjects. This calls for critical consciousness and reflexivity, both of which require "*learning* to see what is ordinarily invisible: to see from below, from the margins, and—self-critically—from the center."[34]

This kind of reflexivity is exemplified by a number of North American practitioners; in addition to those cited above, William Finnegan observes the following about writing about minority groups in the United States:

> So when I come to write about the lives of poor black Americans in New Haven, my options for choosing a narrative voice are not the same as they would have been forty years ago, nor are they the same ones I have when it comes to writing about Mozambique. Omniscience is really not a possibility. My fallibility, my presumptuousness, have to be acknowledged. My own implication in the lives of the people I'm describing is just so much greater. The right of the characters in the piece to tell their *own* stories seems much greater. I feel compelled to show how I am constructing the story, how my opinions are just my opinions, and how this is all about not simply *their lives*, but my interaction with them—and their efforts to understand me. It all requires a much greater degree of self-reflexivity than writing about Mozambique does. It also requires more originality.[35]

In this scenario, Finnegan demonstrates a self-critical awareness that when he is writing at home, he is writing from the center, and that his truth and knowledge claims are *located*: geographically, culturally, economically, historically, and politically. This self-awareness both enables and limits what he can represent and the form his knowledge claims make (that is, truth claims, opinion, etc.). Ideally, strong objectivity leads to a deeper sense of responsibility, care, and caution, as is evident in this case. However, it is interesting to note that this self-reflexivity does not extend to Finnegan's international subjects in the same way. He says:

> In Mozambique, I traveled around the country, interviewing a lot of people, often with a translator. And I found that pretty much everybody, even the most oppressed, illiterate peasants, understood perfectly well what I was doing: I was a foreigner, interviewing them so as to understand something about their country. The journalistic conventions held steady. Nobody seriously questioned the purpose of what I was doing, or my right to be doing it. Of course, I could never make the same kinds of generalizations about my own country, if only because my readers—Americans—know too much about it already—it's their country—and would therefore know endless exceptions to any big, gauche generalization I might throw out there.[36]

Given that strong objectivity "demands a breadth of scrutiny encompassing, at minimum, the standpoint of the knower and the 'nature' of the known,"[37] both the interactions with and representations of Finnegan's subjects in this example suggest less reflexivity and caution in this scenario. While even the most oppressed, illiterate peasants may well understand the purpose of the reporting, a few issues here include the unacknowledged power dynamic between reporter and subjects, the limits of what can be known and claimed, and the role of general or dislocated knowledge claims that may perpetuate patterns of "Othering" and, hence, imbalances of power.

As well as acknowledging the located nature of facts and evidence, ecological thinking encourages openness to a wider range of evidence than traditional journalistic–epistemic models. An ecological approach argues that to truly know well, it is important to include "the messiness, confusion, and concerns of the everyday" in order to represent reality in the fullest—and most objective—sense.[38] Barbie Zelizer puts it this way:

> There exists a whole slew of material out there in the world that seems to have no evidentiary value because it does not fit that mindset, and so it gets largely discounted.

Messiness, hesitation, emotions, imagination, contingency, contradiction, qualification all often go under the radar of the evidentiary envelope, even if they exist plentifully in the world. This means that the evidence we pay attention to does not always best reflect what is; nor does it signal how partial that evidence remains. In fact, in many cases, evidence reflects more about things as we want them to be than about how things are on their own terms.[39]

This approach closely reflects the critical stance of literary journalism: While a healthy respect for facts is clear, literary journalists seek out details to create a fuller, more representative description of reality than a denatured account. Lawrence Weschler uses an ecological metaphor to make this point: "It is very important that conversations take place in *places*. That they *take place*. This is another problem with the traditional, pyramid-style journalism that uses free-floating quotes that just kind of hang there. They pop out of nowhere."[40] This is another example of working toward "strong objectivity." While "journalists regularly migrate away from the noise, tentativeness and incongruity in the circumstances they cover,"[41] literary journalists recognize how their subjects' environment is often composed of these elements and that acknowledging a range of evidence—including physical, political, and emotional environments—in fact creates more responsible representations of reality than those that admit only rationalist-empiricist ways of knowing.

For literary journalists, this list of "under the radar" evidence includes acknowledging gaps and "not-knowing" as much as knowledge claims. One literary journalist asks:

> Does one perspective bring you closer to truth than another? Not necessarily. Sometimes being there can distort your perspective; sometimes it gives you unique insights. ... Putting your cards on the table as the narrator—your doubts, your hesitations, your conflicting thoughts and impressions—is often more honest than third-person writing.[42]

Incorporating incongruity and even uncertainty is commonplace in literary journalism for writers ranging from Joan Didion to Tracy Kidder to Rebecca Skloot[43] and in practice is part of what Steiner calls a "strong ethics" for a "strong journalism."[44] In line with ecological thinking, recognizing contradiction and conflict is as defensible and responsible in an objective description of reality as rational-intellectual, empirically verifiable inquiry. Rather than undermining the concept of objectivity, this kind of transparency points toward the possibility of strong objectivity. By acknowledging gaps and uncertainties, the inquirer reinforces the ultimate aim to know well—and epistemic shortcomings are represented as part of the lived experience. "Strong ethics" suggests an obligation to acknowledge one's location and limitation in regard to human knowledge and encourages incorporating the research process and epistemic justification into journalism.[45]

The Ethics of Advocacy

As John Hartsock observes, many figures in the history of North American literary journalism were propelled by their epistemic questions into moral and political action. Hartsock names Stephen Crane, Edmund Wilson, and James Agee as among those who found that when "narrative ambition in their literary journalism attempted to more openly acknowledge the relationship between subjectivity and a phenomenal world, they ... could not stay detached ... and that would make activists of them."[46] Indeed, their experience closely reflects an impulse driving ecological thinking, which "focuses as closely on the exemplary possibilities of knowing other people—in everyday and social scientific contexts—as on those traditionally derived from knowing 'facts' about the world."[47] Experiments with narrative representation are driven by a range of reasons, but literary journalism's ambition "to narrow the gulf between subject and object"[48] is arguably one of advocacy.

Code acknowledges advocacy's roots in legal usage where one argues on behalf of another but extends this within *Ecological Thinking*

> from the courtroom to everyday lives, where it has to do with defending or espousing a cause by arguing in its favour; speaking on behalf of, supporting, vindicating, ... representing someone/some group in order to counter patterns of silencing, discounting, incredulity, and other egregious harms.[49]

With Crane, Wilson, and Agee, many contemporary literary journalists also display an orientation of advocacy toward marginalized subjects. Alex Kotlowitz, Ron Rosenbaum, Jane Kramer, and others report choosing subjects who are "heretical outsiders," who live "along the margins," or who replicate their own "distance from the center."[50] Kramer's epistemic stance is aligned with an ecological ethos as she reflects on her subject choice:

> I like writing about people who, by most "news" standards, would be considered marginal. I find that the perspective from the margins is usually much more telling—if you're interested in how power works—than any number of conversations with politicians and especially with important ones like presidents and prime ministers. I thought a lot about this when I was exploring people in the margins of established bourgeois life for my book *Unsettling Europe*. I think I must have realized back then the extent to which my fascination with margins had to do with women of my generation being, almost by definition, marginal to power, too. We had looked at the world from our own very marginal perspective.[51]

Kramer here demonstrates awareness of the impact epistemic location has on what can be known and how people in positions of power can limit both access to knowledge and what counts *as* knowledge. While advocacy—or arguing the case of another—is strongly associated with rhetoric, an ecological approach observes how orthodox epistemologies undermine an assertion of "neutral logic and pure language" by means of claiming "that there is no need for rhetoric"—which in itself is a rhetorical maneuver.[52] In fact, Code proposes that "*practices of advocacy often make knowledge possible* within hierarchical distributions of autonomy and authority and in institutional divisions of intellectual labor in western societies."[53] Code's point here is that the knowledge claims of marginalized individuals are often not heard because they are not recognized as knowers whose claims to know are to be taken seriously.[54] Their evidence—most often testimony—is not valued to the extent that rational-intellectual evidence (such as statistics) is valued; therefore, because they lack cultural capital, they also lack epistemic autonomy and legitimacy. For this reason, "advocacy carries epistemological force within the power and privilege structures of hierarchical societies: as a cluster of liberatory practices whose goal is to (re)enfranchise epistemically disadvantaged, marginalized, disenfranchised Others."[55] Advocacy journalism therefore has two important epistemic functions: In addition to bringing knowledges of marginalized Others into epistemic legitimacy, it also highlights the impossibility of making claims from an epistemically neutral location. Knowledge claims that are made within orthodox epistemic frameworks may *appear* to be neutral, but in fact they may perpetuate (in)equality simply by belonging to a particular discourse, as will be illustrated below.

Advocacy as an epistemically emancipatory act raises some interesting ethical issues about representation. One of these is the extent to which literary journalists appear as subjects in their writing. Ecological thinking's commitment to strong objectivity and beyond, which "demands reimagining standpoints and subjectivities in order to investigate the specificities of place, habitat, habitus, and ethos in the construction of putative knowledge,"[56] would seem to require transparency about the location of literary journalists in their work. Yet practitioners have a range of approaches to disclosing their location—physical, social, epistemic, etc.—each of which has epistemic-ethical implications. Writers such as Lawrence Wright appear to work out of an ethos that privileges their subject. Wright explains: "I don't put myself into the narrative unless there's a damn good reason. I want to enhance the reader's appreciation of the subject, and if being there accomplishes that—or is impossible to avoid—then I'll do it."[57] Gay Talese and Calvin Trillin hold similar positions.[58] But despite the desire to "get out of the way of the narrative,"[59] this intention arguably reveals

> a taken-for-granted, rarely articulated or interrogated empiricist-realist stance—almost a *naïve* realism—[which] implicitly allows most standard moral theories to work with a picture of knowledge for which right perception is alike in all moral agents, who therefore can readily "put themselves in anyone else's shoes."[60]

This stance, Code argues, belies the range of justifiable beliefs—many of which are held by the disenfranchised—and the complexity of moral choices that face would-be knowers. The point is not that third-person narratives are unethical but rather that not acknowledging epistemic location may reinforce a myth of "right perception" that can perpetuate social and political inequity. An approach more in line with ecological thinking can be found in Weschler's reflections:

> I'm a very big advocate of first-person journalism—which is to say the use of an "I" narrator—not out of megalomania, but out of modesty. In fact, I would argue that those stories that *don't* have the first person are the ones that are megalomaniac. ... The "I" doesn't have to show up every five sentences; in fact it is better if it doesn't. But there had better be an individual voice that says, "This is just one person's view, based on one series of experiences."[61]

The belief articulated here does not discount the possibility of knowing a subject or object in itself but acknowledges limitations in what can be known and claimed about such knowledge. The result is arguably a more complex, responsible, and deliberative approach to knowing well. This ethos is in line with "democratic, deliberative, negotiative practices of epistemic responsibility, approaches to knowing meticulous in their attention to evidence, yet cognizant of the extent to which evidence is multiply interpretable, with wide-ranging human and ecological consequences."[62]

An interesting example of the ethical implications involved in literary journalists representing themselves in their narratives was raised by JoAnn Wypijewski, herself a practitioner of both daily and longform journalism, in a review of Adrian Nicole LeBlanc's *Random Family* (2003). In her critique, Wypijewski is primarily concerned with the ethical issues raised by LeBlanc's relationship with her subjects, a Puerto Rican clan living in a poor neighborhood in the Bronx in the 1990s. But Wypijewski also is critical of LeBlanc's absence in the 404-page book: She "wrote herself out of the story, becoming in the process its most provocative character: the voyeur who is everywhere and nowhere, watching and telling as things fall apart." Further, "It is only by accident, in the acknowledgements, that the book finally confronts the reader with the 'American experience of class injustice' that is ostensibly its subject."[63] Like a number of the literary journalists cited above, LeBlanc's aim was to convey the lived experience of her subjects.[64] In an interview with the *Guardian*, she defends her rationale: "I didn't want it to be the white girl's journey into the ghetto: there have been other books like that. I didn't want to bounce the reporting off that. This is a subject worthy of close scrutiny on its own."[65] But the lack of an interpreting presence or critical consciousness in the text is, for Wypijewski, an ethical failure that calls into question the text's truth claims. The truths in the text are drowned in "the onrush of personal detail": "'even living right was just another precarious hold'; that 'success was less about climbing than about not falling down'; … and family generosity, however defeating, might be the only bulwark between awfulness and horror." The issue of "truth" and "truths" here invite epistemic scrutiny. In an ecological approach, "Truth" gives way to

> a textured, responsive conception of "truth to," as knowing moves transversely across geographical and social landscapes, following along the ground the trajectories of diverse habitat-constitutive or obstructive lines of evidence: mapping their paths and surrounds; showing how they can generate interpretive/coherent understandings that may bear analogously on other features of the habitat. … Physical, social, or other location, then, functions neither as a backdrop nor context, but as constitutive of the *Lebenswelt*, and the *Leben* within it, shaping possibilities of knowing, and demanding, themselves, to be known.[66]

From this perspective, the heavy detail is not only defensible but in fact necessary to demonstrate how the subjects' experiences were constituted by their location and how their agency was limited by the physical, social, political, and cultural landscapes they inhabited. Wypijewski's criticism that the text essentializes the subjects' experience[67] is met by thick description, or what Hartsock calls "a critical precipitation because of its focus on the concrete particular—scene construction and dialogue, for example—as applied to a certain time and place." Further, "Because such particulars are distinctive, they can make no claim to critical closure or totalized volatilization and thus must continue to exist in resistance to such volatilization."[68]

LeBlanc's position is signaled in the epigraph where the text is framed as a work of advocacy for those who experience class injustice. Combined with the author's note, these elaborate LeBlanc's epistemic location—how she has informed herself, what her interests are, her relationship with her subjects—that establishes her knowledge claims about her subjects. In the narrative, LeBlanc offers multiple locations from which her subjects' situations can be viewed and includes a range of knowledge claims such as: "The word that came to Sister Christine's mind whenever she thought of Coco was *enmeshed*. Coco would have said that she had heart."[69] Examples like these show how complex knowledge claims can be and how an individual's knowledge is constituted by the "specificities of place, habitat, habitus, and ethos"[70] even as the individual shapes these elements. As an example of ecological thinking, LeBlanc's literary journalism works toward strong objectivity by reimagining the possibility of knowledge from epistemic locations other than her own, and locating inquiry

> 'down on the ground' where knowledge is made, negotiated, circulated; and where the nature and conditions of the particular 'ground,' the situations and circumstances of specific knowers, their interdependence and their negotiations, have claims to critical epistemic scrutiny equivalent to those of allegedly isolated, discrete propositional knowledge claims.[71]

LeBlanc maps "the complex network of locations and relations, whether social, historical, material, geographical, cultural, racial, sexual, institutional, or other, where organisms—human or nonhuman—try to live well, singly and collectively."[72]

Limitations

Despite a strong positive reception of Code's work, there are some difficulties in applying *Ecological Thinking* to the literary journalistic context. The first is by virtue of its nature: Code has gone to great lengths to avoid developing a theory or system to replace orthodox epistemologies; instead, Code refers to her work as "a revisioned *mode of engagement* ... that pervades and reconfigures theory and practice."[73] *Ecological Thinking* cannot be reduced to rules or ethical codes; rather, it might be characterized as *a way of thinking* about and critiquing such journalistic codes. Code avoids criticism of replacing one epistemology of mastery with another, but *Ecological Thinking* consequently lacks foundational principles that are common to—and useful for—training in journalistic ethics. Steiner puts it bluntly: "Journalists get no simple recipe here. Applying [an alternate] epistemology requires a complex reorientation among and across individual journalists of all kinds, as well as systematic transformation in the thinking and structure of news organizations."[74]

Ecological Thinking calls for demanding levels of critical consciousness. As one scholar asks of progressive epistemology:

> Can journalists, who are privileged by virtue of background, education, professional authority, and affiliation within corporate organizations, legitimately write and speak about social outsiders? After all, even public, progressive activist, advocacy, and feminist journalists reproduce traditional sex, class and racial biases.[75]

Literary journalists may not have the corporate affiliations of mainstream journalists, but the point stands that bias is often unintentionally perpetuated or reinforced because it is invisible; this makes *re-educating vision*[76] a challenge at the very least, and perhaps aspirational for some. As Miles Maguire puts it: "After all, journalists are trained to report what they know, not what they don't know."[77] This type of re-visioning of the social-moral-political landscape may appear to be at odds with the discipline of verification ingrained in the journalistic imaginary, which allows for judgments and verifications on an empirical basis. *Ecological Thinking* calls not only for a wider range of evidence to be admitted as knowledge but also for a more rigorous and critically conscious assessment of the environment in which that knowledge was produced.

Another critique can be raised in response to *Ecological Thinking*'s aims, which are based on democratic values and the preservation of public trust.[78] Michael Ryan believes that the goals of progressive journalism are admirable but argues that they can become problematic in specific cases. "For example," he asks, "whose view about what constitutes 'improvement' should prevail?" He goes on to question:

> Who decides when the view of the dominant insiders must be counterbalanced by the views of the marginalized? Also, who decides which views of which marginalized groups should be considered first? ... Everything depends on whose definition of *freedom* or *public good* or *approved marginalized group* holds sway.[79]

Code herself is critical of naïve theories in which "perception is alike in all moral agents, who therefore can readily 'put themselves in anyone else's shoes.'"[80] But the counter issue is not resolved: In an approach that "distances itself from ... transcendent principles and truths,"[81] who arbitrates between parties when knowledge and action are located in particular environments and disputes arise over what is in the public's best interest?

Kara Barnette makes an analogous observation: While Code aims to identify and examine structures of power in her approach to knowledge construction, her work on advocacy does not have sufficient methodology to resolve conflicts between differing testimonies.[82] Code writes that "ecological thinking requires principled adjudication of incompatible claims"[83] and gives detailed examples of ecological thinking at work in a range of contexts, but Barnette argues that ecological thinking rests "on the assumption that at some point in the knowledge-making process the parties involved will be able to recognize the truth"[84] and concludes that ecological thinking needs deeper and more rigorous methods of detecting error and arbitrating between testimonies.[85]

Conclusion

Despite these limitations, an ecological approach to literary journalism has much to recommend it. Perhaps the strongest reasons are the similarities that already exist between ecological thinking and literary journalism. Both respect but go beyond positivist-empiricist understandings of what constitutes knowledge; both are inclusive of physical, emotional, affective, and subjective elements as holding epistemic status; and both are motivated by a desire to know "the real world" in all its richness and complexity. Ecological thinking calls for an ethical response to knowing well. It locates the ecological subject within a dynamic system of power structures and cultural, historical, and physical locations, and asks subjects to be responsive to each unique environment's features that constrain and enable truth claims. It pays attention to context and subjectivity, and respects formalized ethical codes while calling for a deeper assessment of the epistemic foundations of these codes. Conceptualizing literary journalists as ecological subjects places the practitioner at the locus of moral responsibility for ethical behavior and representation but recognizes the interdependence of individuals and their environment to negotiate legitimate terms and responsible representation of their subjects. An ecological approach to literary journalism is ideally responsive to the demands of moral and epistemic responsibility across a range of social-cultural-political terrains and engaged in a project "to produce 'faithful accounts of the real world' by working through genealogical, power-, and situation-sensitive inquiry."[86]

Notes

1 See Curran, "Future of Journalism"; Singer, "Getting Past the Future"; Van Tuyll, "Past Is Prologue."
2 Christians, "Ethical Theory," 3.
3 Berning, "Toward a Critical Ethical Narratology"; Ricketson, *Telling True Stories*; Harrington, "Toward an Ethical Code."
4 Code, *Ecological Thinking*, 5.
5 Code, 5.
6 "SPJ Code of Ethics."
7 "SPJ Code of Ethics."
8 See "US Press Association"; "Code of Ethics."
9 Code, *Ecological Thinking*, 99.
10 Code, 4.
11 Greenberg and Wheelwright, "Literary Journalism," 512.
12 Code, *Ecological Thinking*, 6.
13 Code, 4–5.
14 Keeble, introduction to Keeble and Tulloch, *Global Literary Journalism*, 7.
15 Code, *Ecological Thinking*, 7.
16 Code, 118.
17 Code, 99.
18 Code, 51.
19 Code, 47.
20 Code, 89.
21 Kovach and Rosenstiel, *Elements of Journalism*, 71.

22. Code, *Ecological Thinking*, 96.
23. Code, 118.
24. See McKay, "Åsne Seierstad"; Maguire, "Richard Critchfield."
25. Code, *Ecological Thinking*, 118.
26. Langewiesche, quoted in Boynton, *New New Journalism*, 210.
27. Code, *Ecological Thinking*, 5–6.
28. Code, 61–62.
29. Schudson, *Discovering the News*, 5.
30. Code, *Ecological Thinking*, 62.
31. Steiner, "Less Falseness," 116.
32. Dash, quoted in Boynton, *New New Journalism*, 60.
33. Dash, quoted in Boynton, 60.
34. Code, *Ecological Thinking*, 118–19.
35. Finnegan, quoted in Boynton, *New New Journalism*, 89–90.
36. Finnegan, quoted in Boynton, 88.
37. Code, *Ecological Thinking*, 177.
38. Code, 118.
39. Zelizer, "Why Journalism," 32.
40. Weschler, quoted in Boynton, *New New Journalism*, 424.
41. Zelizer, "Why Journalism," 39.
42. Rosenbaum, quoted in Boynton, *New New Journalism*, 339.
43. See Hartsock, *History*, 199; Sims, *True Stories*, 5; Skloot, *Immortal Life*.
44. Steiner, "Less Falseness," 113.
45. Steiner, 113.
46. Hartsock, *History*, 78, 169.
47. Code, *Ecological Thinking*, 61.
48. Hartsock, *History*, 59.
49. Code, *Ecological Thinking*, 165.
50. See Boynton, *New New Journalism*, 324, 131, 188.
51. Kramer, quoted in Boynton, 188–89.
52. Code, *Ecological Thinking*, 175.
53. Code, 165; italics in the original.
54. Code, 165.
55. Code, 165.
56. Code, 177.
57. Wright, quoted in Boynton, *New New Journalism*, 453.
58. See Boynton, 376, 400.
59. Trillin, quoted in Boynton, 400.
60. Code, *Ecological Thinking*, 209.
61. Weschler, quoted in Boynton, *New New Journalism*, 418.
62. Code, *Ecological Thinking*, 62.
63. Wypijewski, "No Way Out."
64. LeBlanc, quoted in Boynton, *New New Journalism*, 236.
65. Bedell, "Eleven Years."
66. Code, *Ecological Thinking*, 8.
67. Wypijewski further writes: "It seems the destiny of Jessica's and Coco's daughters to follow in their paths. It seems the destiny of young Puerto Rican men to go to jail. ... It seems the destiny of the whole community to live with extraordinary drama" ("No Way Out").
68. Hartsock, *History*, 48.
69. LeBlanc, *Random Family*, 148.
70. Code, *Ecological Thinking*, 177.
71. Code, 5–6.
72. Code, 91.
73. Code, 5; italics added.
74. Steiner, "Less Falseness," 113.
75. Steiner, 126.
76. Code, *Ecological Thinking*, 118–19.
77. Maguire, "Richard Critchfield," 18.

78 Code, *Ecological Thinking*, 4.
79 Ryan, "Journalistic Ethics," 15; italics in the original.
80 Code, *Ecological Thinking*, 209.
81 Code, 5.
82 Barnette, "Necessary Error," 31.
83 Code, *Ecological Thinking*, 6.
84 Barnette, "Necessary Error," 31.
85 Barnette, 33.
86 Code, *Ecological Thinking*, 112.

Bibliography

Barnette, Kara E. "Necessary Error: Josiah Royce, Communal Inquiry, and Feminist Epistemology." PhD diss., University of Oregon, 2012.

Bedell, Geraldine. "Eleven Years in the Bronx." *Guardian*, October 18, 2003. www.guardian.co.uk/world/2003/oct/19/usa.politicsphilosophyandsociety?INTCMP=ILCNETTXT3487.

Berning, Nora. "Toward a Critical Ethical Narratology for Literary Reportages: Analyzing the Story Ethics of Alexandra Fuller's *Scribbling the Cat*." *Interférences Littéraires/Literaire Interferenties*, no. 7 (November 2011): 189–221.

Boynton, Robert S. *The New New Journalism: Conversations with America's Best Nonfiction Writers on Their Craft*. New York: Vintage Books, 2005.

Christians, Clifford G. "Ethical Theory in Communications Research." *Journalism Studies* 6, no. 1 (2005): 3–14. https://doi.org/10.1080/1461670052000328168.

Code, Lorraine. *Ecological Thinking: The Politics of Epistemic Location*. Oxford: Oxford University Press, 2006.

"Code of Ethics of the Media Council." Accountable Journalism. Accessed February 14, 2018. https://accountablejournalism.org/ethics-codes/US-Media-Council.

Curran, James. "The Future of Journalism." *Journalism Studies* 11, no. 4 (August 2010): 464–76. https://doi.org/10.1080/14616701003722444.

Greenberg, Susan, and Julie Wheelwright. "Literary Journalism: Ethics in Three Dimensions." *Journalism* 15, no. 5 (July 2014): 511–16. https://doi.org/10.1177/1464884914529210.

Harrington, Walt. "Toward an Ethical Code for Narrative Journalists." In *Telling True Stories: A Nonfiction Writers' Guide from the Nieman Foundation at Harvard University*, edited by Mark Kramer and Wendy Call, 170–72. New York: Plume, 2007.

Hartsock, John. *A History of American Literary Journalism: The Emergence of a Modern Narrative Form*. Amherst, MA: University of Massachusetts Press, 2000.

Keeble, Richard Lance, and John Tulloch, eds. *Global Literary Journalism: Exploring the Journalistic Imagination*. 2 vols. New York: Peter Lang, 2014.

Kovach, Bill, and Tom Rosenstiel. *The Elements of Journalism: What Newspeople Should Know and the Public Should Expect*. New York: Three Rivers Press, 2001.

LeBlanc, Adrian Nicole. *Random Family: Love, Drugs, Trouble, and Coming of Age in the Bronx*. New York: Scribner, 2004.

Maguire, Miles. "Richard Critchfield: 'Genius' Journalism and the Fallacy of Verification." *Literary Journalism Studies* 1, no. 2 (Fall 2009): 9–21.

McKay, Jenny. "Åsne Seierstad and the Bookseller of Kabul." In Keeble and Tulloch, *Global Literary Journalism*, 1:175–90.

Ricketson, Matthew. *Telling True Stories: Navigating the Challenges of Writing Narrative Non-fiction*. Sydney: Allen & Unwin, 2014.

Ryan, Michael. "Journalistic Ethics, Objectivity, Existential Journalism, Standpoint Epistemology, and Public Journalism." *Journal of Mass Media Ethics* 16, no. 1 (2001): https://doi.org/10.1207/S15327728JMME1601_2.

Schudson, Michael. *Discovering the News: A Social History of American Newspapers*. New York: Basic Books, 1981.

Sims, Norman, ed. *True Stories: A Century of Literary Journalism*. Evanston, IL: Northwestern University Press, 2007.

Singer, Jane B. "Getting Past the Future: Journalism Ethics, Innovation, and a Call for 'Flexible First.'" *Comunicação e Sociedade* 25 (2014): 67–82. https://doi.org/10.17231/comsoc.25(2014).1860.

Skloot, Rebecca. *The Immortal Life of Henrietta Lacks*. New York: Crown Publishers, 2010.

"SPJ Code of Ethics." Society of Professional Journalists, 2012. www.spj.org/ethicscode.asp.

Steiner, Linda. "Less Falseness as Antidote to the Anxieties of Postmodernism." In *Assessing Evidence in a Postmodern World*, edited by Bonnie Brennen, 113–36. Milwaukee, WI: Marquette University Press, 2011. http://epublications.marquette.edu/marq_fac-book/133/?referer=https%253A%252F%252Fscholar.google.com.au%252F.

"US Press Association - Journalist Code of Ethics." US Press Association. Accessed February 14, 2018. http://uspressassociation.org/page.php?57.

Van Tuyll, Debra Reddin. "The Past Is Prologue, Or." *Journalism Studies* 11, no. 4 (August 2010): 477–86. https://doi.org/10.1080/14616701003638343.

Wypijewski, JoAnn. "No Way Out." *Guardian*, December 13, 2003. www.guardian.co.uk/books/2003/dec/13/featuresreviews.guardianreview24.

Zelizer, Barbie. "Why Journalism Has Always Pushed Perception Alongside Reality." In *Assessing Evidence in a Postmodern World*, edited by Bonnie Brennen, 31–40. Milwaukee, WI: Marquette University Press, 2011. http://epublications.marquette.edu/marq_fac-book/133/?referer=https%253A%252F%252Fscholar.google.com.au%252F.

25

THE ETHNOGRAPHIC IMPULSE

Bruce Gillespie

As a relatively young field of study, American literary journalism is still coming into its own, and scholars from a range of disciplines are working to establish its center of focus as well as its boundaries. This involves not only deciding which types of work may qualify as American literary journalism but also coming to a consensus on which concerns and questions are central to its study. One way to chart a young discipline's trajectory toward complete academicization is to compare it with that of a similar field of study. In doing so, we may be better able to assess its progress and highlight some of the possible challenges that lie ahead. As such, I will compare the field of American literary journalism with the field of autoethnography, a relatively young, uniquely American branch of ethnography. The two fields make for a worthwhile comparison for three key reasons. First, they are both new fields of study, having emerged in the past twenty or thirty years, predominantly in the United States. Second, they share a background in conventional news reporting and a dissatisfaction among their practitioners with the limits and strictures of conventional, objective research. Third, the two fields share a number of similarities with respect to their aim and style, to the extent that some works of autoethnography are almost indistinguishable from works of American literary journalism.

Previously, I have analyzed the similarities between autoethnography and literary journalism in terms of their goals, form, and style. In short, both genres are based on in-depth, qualitative research, highlight lived experience, and employ a range of literary techniques, such as narrative arc, conflict, and point of view, to appeal to a wide, general audience.[1] Here, then, I will expand the scope of that analysis in two ways: first, by examining the shared journalistic roots of American literary journalism and autoethnography, and, second, by comparing some of the common critiques of both fields.

As its name suggests, the genre of autoethnography may be traced back to ethnography, which is itself a branch of anthropology. Generally speaking, ethnography is the study of people, cultures, and customs, which usually involves long-term fieldwork observing and listening to ordinary people go about their daily routines and producing detail-rich accounts of that research. As Karen O'Reilly explains, ethnography has roots in both British social anthropology and American cultural anthropology.[2] For our purposes, it is most useful to concentrate on the genre's American genealogy. What is now recognized as ethnography developed from the work of scholars at the University of Chicago in the early twentieth century, who later became known as the Chicago School. Included in this group was Robert E. Park, who played a key role in pioneering this distinct style of sociological research and influencing how students and future scholars understood the focus, methods, and goals of the field. Interestingly, and tellingly for our purposes, Park was a journalist long before he became a sociologist. As Rolf Lindner argues, "The orientation of urban research represented by Park ultimately owes its origins to the reporting tradition. ... This influence is directly reflected both in the areas he investigated and the techniques he used in his research."[3] According to biographer Winifred Raushenbush, Park graduated with a degree in philosophy from the University of Michigan in 1887 and then spent the next eleven years working as a newspaper reporter and editor as a way to see the world in a variety of different postings, including Minneapolis, Detroit, Chicago, and eventually New-York.[4] He was interested in examining the life of the city through the experiences of the ordinary people who lived and worked there. A great deal of his reporting focused on issues of social concern, such as stories about gambling houses and opium dens. He also wrote stories that, for example, positioned alcoholism as a disease rather than a personal failing.[5] He credited these muckraking stories as the beginnings of his interest in sociological matters.

In 1898, at the age of thirty-four, Park left the newsroom to attend graduate school, first at Harvard University and later in Germany, where he hoped to learn more deeply about the sorts of issues he wrote about for the newspaper. "He wanted to understand communication and collective behavior and had imagined that social psychology as taught at Harvard would give him the answers. It did not," writes Raushenbush.[6] After returning to the United States, he became an assistant in Harvard's Department of Philosophy and, at the same time, worked as the editor of the Sunday edition of a Boston newspaper and did publicity work as secretary of the Congo Reform Association, which organized against human rights abuses in that country under Belgian rule.[7] As Raushenbush explains, Park rarely felt settled with his work, vacillating between the abstract world of academia and the "real world" of the newsroom:

> His impulses toward thought and action were equally powerful and his whole life was a rhythm of moving back and forth from one to the other. Having spent four years in universities, he was eager for action, but not action merely. He yearned to do something worthwhile.[8]

As Park himself wrote, "I wanted to get back into the world of men. I had never given up the ambition I gained from reading Faust—the ambition to know human nature, know it widely and intimately."[9]

This mindset helps explain the next stage of Park's career. While working for the Congo Reform Association, Park was introduced to African American leader Booker T. Washington, whom he impressed with his work on behalf of the organization. Washington invited Park to work for him as a publicist-cum-fundraiser for the Tuskegee Normal and Industrial Institute, a training school for African Americans in Alabama, which he accepted.[10] This was a pivotal moment for Park. During the seven years that he worked for Washington, he, as a Caucasian man, had an unparalleled opportunity to observe the living and working conditions of African Americans in the South firsthand, of which he knew very little. Travelling with Washington on his fundraising speaking tours, Park met ordinary people, took notes, and wrote up their life histories. Much as a reporter has a special license to visit places and people that may not traditionally be open or welcoming to outsiders, travelling with Washington gave Park a window into African American life he would not have had otherwise, as well as the opportunity to practice the in-depth, observational style of reporting that would become the foundation of the Chicago School's ethnographic research methods.

As a teacher, Park sought to inspire in his students a passion for understanding the nature of urban life beyond Main Street and the halls of power. For Park, there were two kinds of knowledge essential to this type of research: "'Acquaintance with' is the knowledge one acquires through experience at first hand, whereas 'knowledge about' means systematic knowledge, that which replaces concrete reality by concepts."[11] This was quite similar to how he worked as a reporter, gaining experiential knowledge by walking through a neighborhood and hanging out with its inhabitants before using secondary resources to develop broader, more systematic knowledge. As Raushenbush explains:

> [Park] had discovered that he did his most joyous and creative thinking by exposing himself to new situations and people and thus getting insights, having hunches, evolving fresh hypotheses. At this point the process which might lead to "knowledge about" could begin.[12]

Park encouraged his students to spend time in parts of the city that were unfamiliar to them and get to know the local residents deeply over a long period of time. He believed strongly that American cities, and the lives of its ordinary inhabitants, were worthy of study at a time when most anthropologists were concerned with distant, indigenous populations:

> The same patient methods of observation which anthropologists like Boas and Lowie have expended on the study of the life and manners of the North American Indian [sic] might be even more fruitfully employed in the investigation of the customs, beliefs, social practices, and general conceptions of life prevalent in Little Italy on the lower North Side in Chicago, or in recording the more sophisticated folkways of the inhabitants of Greenwich Village and the neighborhood of Washington Square, New York. We are mainly indebted to writers of fiction for our more intimate knowledge of contemporary urban life. But the life of our cities demands a more searching and disinterested study.[13]

According to Mary Jo Deegan, the legacy of Park and the Chicago School is both a focus on revealing the everyday life of ordinary citizens and a style of writing that, because it was written for an audience of undergraduate students, was conversational and informal compared to much of the sociological theory emerging from Europe at the time, which was abstract and complex.[14]

Park's legacy was not confined to his own discipline; his ethnographic impulse may also be tracked across the genre of modern American literary journalism in works such as Adrian Nicole LeBlanc's *Random Family* (2003). The book is a coming-of-age story of two ordinary women in the Bronx in the mid-1980s and their struggles to establish lives for themselves with limited education and resources, set against a backdrop of addiction, violence, and the drug trade. By Park's standards, they are ideal objects of study, meant to be representative of the community in which they live. Their experiences, as young women of color raised in the inner city, trying to make a living outside of the drug trade, provide a home and food for their children and extended families, and stay out of jail in the face of a justice system and society that seem indifferent at best, are not unique. As LeBlanc explains in her author's note at the end of the book:

> My decision to write about Coco's daily struggles baffled her neighbors, family, and friends. "Why Coco?" I was asked again and again. "Coco's just regular," people said. "Plenty of girls is worse off." Certainly, I have found this to be true. The hardships of these young people and their families are not unusual in their neighborhoods. Neither are their gifts.[15]

LeBlanc spent eleven years working on the book, building a level of rapport and trust with her subjects that eventually gave her access not only to the stoops and street corners where they socialized but to more intimate locations as well, including their shared tenement bedrooms and prisons where they would visit their loved ones. Her "acquaintance with" her subjects, to use Park's words, is evident from the depth of her access into their lives and the countless details she is able to include, such as when Coco prepares for a fight: "She doubled up on T-shirts to avoid giving the street a free show. She tucked razor blades in her ponytail and rubbed her face with her trusty Vaseline."[16] LeBlanc also writes in a style that is familiar to ethnography—narrative and evocative but, ultimately, impersonal. She never appears as a character in the book or comments on the action in her own voice, with the exception of the author's note, so that the reader feels like an omniscient observer of her subjects' lives. Her book is no less engaging for doing so, but it does highlight one of the key differences between an ethnographic approach and an autoethnographic approach.

The genre of autoethnography emerged from ethnography in the late 1990s in the United States and came into its own as a popular, discipline-spanning genre in the early twenty-first century (the term "autoethnography" first appeared in the late 1970s but described something different from what it is commonly accepted to mean today).[17] Much like literary journalism, autoethnography developed partly out of a desire by its practitioners to move beyond the strictures of their field and its impersonal, positivist leanings. They wanted to write in a more personal, emotional, and narrative way than was normally allowed in formal writing that was subject to peer review. It also evolved from the larger crisis of representation in the social sciences, in which subjects questioned the rights of researchers to tell and interpret their stories and life experiences, as did an increasing number of researchers themselves. Additionally, it was a response to how some voices had been marginalized in the extant literature, as Robin Boylorn (writing about herself in the third person) experienced as a graduate student learning about ethnography under Bud Goodall:

> She was intrigued by ethnography but still felt lost in what felt like exclusive white male gazes and interpretations. With Goodall's leading she began to write her own narratives, from her particular raced, classed, gendered, sexed positionality, identifying the distinctions between how and why she viewed the world through her lens and what made it different from others.[18]

Autoethnography as we know it today was popularized by Carolyn Ellis and Arthur Bochner of the University of South Florida, initially through various journal articles and the launch of their Ethnographic Alternatives book series for AltaMira Press in 1998. The genre exploded after the 2004 publication of Ellis's "methodological novel" about autoethnography, which served as both an example of and a guide to the form.[19] Ellis's conception of autoethnography has shifted slightly over the years, but most recently, she describes it this way:

> One characteristic that binds all autoethnographies is the use of personal experience to examine and/or critique cultural experience. Autoethnographers do this in work that ranges from including personal experience within an otherwise traditional social scientific analysis ... to the presentation of aesthetic projects—poetry, prose, films, dance, photographic essays, and performances—as autoethnographic research. ... While all personal writing could be considered examinations of culture, not all personal writing is autoethnographic; there are additional characteristics that distinguish autoethnography from other kinds of personal work. These include (1) *purposefully commenting on/critiquing of culture and cultural practices,* (2) making *contributions to existing research,* (3) *embracing vulnerability with purpose,* and (4) *creating a reciprocal relationship with audiences in order to compel a response.*[20]

It is a popular genre today, used in such diverse fields as education, communication studies, business, health studies, and social work in addition to sociology and anthropology.

Autoethnographies typically take one of two forms: first, as an entirely impressionistic piece of narrative that reads like a memoir and makes little to no mention of the standard content one would expect to find in peer-reviewed research, such as a literature review, data collected from research subjects or studies, or theory development. An example of this type of autoethnography is Ellis's "Katrina and the Cat" (2007), published in the SAGE journal *Cultural Studies ↔ Critical Methodologies*. In this piece, she juxtaposes her experience of finding a dying cat in her front yard and wondering if and how she can help it with the feelings of helplessness and frustration she feels while simultaneously watching the news unfold about the millions of people affected and displaced along the Gulf Coast by Hurricane Katrina, including her sister and brother-in-law, and the lack of appropriate, timely government assistance. Weaving these two narrative threads together, Ellis creates a richly descriptive, emotionally engaging story about how society deals with those whose lives are considered expendable and how people cope with and react to natural disasters. The fourteen-page story is written in the first person, with only five in-text citations: one that refers to one of Ellis's previous works, two that provide complete references to news reports from which she quotes, and near the end of the story two that refer to articles about how people cope with disaster. The piece is composed of long sections of reconstructed dialogue and scenes as well as shorter sections of description and personal reflection. Eschewing the formal essay structure used in many academic articles, Ellis's piece has a strong narrative, in that it has a clear beginning, middle, and end, that relies on the tension of unanswered questions—Who will take responsibility for the dying cat? Do Ellis's family members survive the hurricane?—to keep readers engaged until the very end. The writing is evocative, descriptive, and, importantly for a piece of autoethnography, personal and reflexive, as seen in the example below:

> I pull vines with a vengeance, raging against pain and death. Then, I sit beside the cat, but I can stand its agony only so long. I pour more water on the maggots. Back and forth, in the house, to the cat, back to the vines. What kind of person am I? How would I have reacted if I had been in New Orleans? I guess I could be a lot worse. Where's the person who ran over the cat? Where are its "owners"?
>
> Someone should be with the cat in its last moments. I speak my final words to the cat. "Someone's coming to get you. It's going to be okay. Help is on the way." I speak lies.[21]

The second type of autoethnography looks like a more conventional piece of academic writing, except that it is more conversational in tone, uses the researcher's own personal experiences as a focal point, includes the researcher's emotional reactions to his or her research, and features long sections of narrative writing, such as Tony Adams's *Narrating the Closet* (2011), his study of coming-out narratives. In the book, each chapter is a mix of conventional academic writing and narrative writing. He alternates sections that examine and critique theory and peer-reviewed research with sections of anecdotal evidence from his own research subjects, which he crafts in a vivid, scenic way. Included in each chapter, serving as a narrative through line for the book, are scenes from Adams's own coming-out story, relayed in chronological order, as he comes to grips with his sexuality. The scenes are evocative, vivid, and, in many cases, written in an almost stream-of-consciousness style:

> "Stay in bed," he says. "I'll be back in a few hours." You like sleeping in his bed and enjoy being around him but find him too comfortable with men, too gay. When he returns he takes you to an isolated waterfall, a place where the two of you kiss. With the exception of skin-tight white boxer briefs, he removes his clothes and asks to remove yours, a request adamantly refused after looking at and admiring his smooth,

toned body. You know the work he does to maintain it and wish you had such discipline but then feel uncomfortable looking lustfully at a man, a man who likes you, who cares, whose heart you'll soon break. In a few weeks you'll meet another man you like, or think you like, and tell this beautiful, caring man that you don't want to see him anymore, because he's too openly gay and likes to please you too much and doesn't worry about what others think about men dating and loving men.[22]

Thus, it is easy to appreciate the similarities between autoethnography and literary journalism. Writers of both genres employ a range of techniques normally associated with literary storytelling to make their work vivid, evocative, and engaging, including plot, characterization, tension and conflict, and dialogue as well as rich description and scenes. The desired result is prose that reads as much like a novel as possible, as opposed to a piece of conventional academic or news writing.[23] One key difference between the two genres relates to point of view—autoethnographers must, almost by definition, write in the first person, while literary journalists may choose to write in a personal, reflexive voice or use the third person. A piece of literary journalism such as the book *Random Family* has more in common with conventional ethnographic writing, as it is told in the third-person omniscient, while Ted Conover's classic piece of literary journalism *Rolling Nowhere* (1984), which is told in the first person and features personal reflection as well as conventional reporting, has more in common with autoethnography. Notably, Conover originally wrote his story about crisscrossing the country with hoboes on freight trains as an undergraduate anthropology thesis, so the techniques involved in immersion reporting and participant observation were familiar to him.[24] But if we examine his book for the characteristics that Ellis argues distinguish autoethnography, we can see that it holds up both as a piece of literary journalism and autoethnography. First, *Rolling Nowhere* makes an original contribution to the extant literature and critiques the hobo subculture in which Conover becomes a participant-observer. The book is a call to action of sorts, as can be seen in its final pages when Conover writes:

> We are no richer than the poorest among us. If we are not going to make room for tramps inside society, we can at least make allowances for their presence outside it. We can repeal laws against victimless crimes such as public intoxication and vagrancy, and we can make sure that no one is denied food, warm clothing, and shelter, all of which are basic human rights.[25]

Second, as Ellis suggests is crucial for autoethnography, the focus of Conover's book is a personal one, although he also discovers and shares a great deal of information about hobo culture. He demonstrates a high level of reflexivity in the book, such as when he openly questions the ethics of some of his research tactics, such as buying alcohol for the hoboes he rides with in order to make them more willing to be photographed.[26] He also embraces his own vulnerability as a researcher and a human being, as is evident toward the end of the book, when Conover grapples with how his work has affected him:

> I did not want to be a hobo anymore. The life was too horrible. And horrible within me was the realization that I had gotten so good at getting along with hoboes that I was having a hard time remembering where they ended and I began. My own unusual talent, as I had thought of it, had turned against me. My hobo identity was now a trap. The only release I could imagine was to be in the presence of somebody who knew who I *really* was.[27]

Thus, it is clear that highly reflexive literary journalism and the more narrative style of autoethnography have much in common in terms of their goals and styles.

One of the main differences between the two genres is where they are published and, relatedly, how they are written and perceived. For while all types of autoethnography are published in an increasingly wide range of peer-reviewed journals, literary journalism is not. Today, a number of leading journals, including *Cultural Studies ↔ Critical Methodologies, Journal of Contemporary Ethnography, Qualitative Inquiry,* and *Qualitative Research,* publish autoethnography, including pieces that are highly personal, narrative, and impressionistic, as well as articles that critique autoethnography.[28] The latter are written as conventional peer-reviewed journal articles, using the third person and adopting a formal tone, devoid of personal anecdotes or reflection, and focused on academic critique and analysis. Conversely, peer-reviewed journals that publish articles about literary journalism do not publish actual works of literary journalism, preferring instead to critique, analyze, or theorize about the genre at a remove. These articles are written in the conventional academic form, using the third person and formal essay structure, and relying on research and analysis as opposed to personal experience and reflection.[29] Even *Literary Journalism Studies,* the international journal devoted to the genre, makes a clear distinction in its submission guidelines that its goal is to publish scholarly work *about* literary journalism rather than works *of* literary journalism, with the exception of short examples "of previously published literary journalism accompanied by a scholarly gloss about or an interview with the writer who is not widely known outside his or her country."[30] Other journals that publish scholarly research about literary journalism, such as *Journalism, Journalism Practice,* and *Journalism Studies,* would have to change their aims and scopes significantly to accept actual works of journalism, which seems unlikely. This illustrates a key discrepancy between the two genres and their relative acceptance within the academy. Scholars in the humanities and social sciences have largely accepted autoethnography, even at its most personal and narrative, as a valid and meaningful type of qualitative research on par with conventional scholarly theorizing, critiquing, and researching. Journalism scholars have not arrived at the same conclusion and see the production of journalism, including literary journalism, as distinct from the production of scholarly research and criticism. While the former may contain interesting research and be worthy of study, it is, in and of itself, not viewed as equivalent to scholarly research.

As noted above, I have previously analyzed the similarities between autoethnography and literary journalism in terms of their goals, form, and style. Here, I will examine three significant critiques often levelled against autoethnography as a way to expand the comparison of the two fields. The three critiques are, first, that autoethnography is too self-absorbed to be considered valid scholarly research; second, that autoethnographers play fast and loose with the truth and are not adequately transparent with their readers about their methodological and narrative choices; and third, that autoethnographers often act unethically when it comes to gaining informed consent from some of the people who appear in their works.

Since the emergence of autoethnography, critics have argued that it is too personal and narrow in scope to be considered serious scholarly research. Of all three critiques of autoethnography, this is the most common. Leon Anderson, for example, was among the early critics of the genre and argued in favor of a type of "analytic autoethnography," writing that autoethnography could only be taken seriously if it included analysis and engaged in the development of theory, as opposed to the narrative and impressionistic type of personal memoir that Ellis wrote.[31] He has revised his critique slightly since then, explaining that while he prefers a model of ethnography that includes personal elements but is more conventional in style and approach to conventional scholarly writing, he recognizes that increased reflexivity about the researcher's own experiences may enrich all ethnographic undertakings and that there is room for both types of research and writing within the field.[32] Sara Delamont remains less convinced, arguing that "autoethnographic self-obsession" on writers' personal lives and feelings has little or nothing to say about the topic being researched; indeed, many article-length autoethnographies read more like personal, therapeutic writing than conventional research or theory development.[33] Delamont also worries that autoethnographers are taking the easy way out of the strenuous fieldwork and data collection for which ethnography is known, opting instead for introspection, which she considers a poor substitute.[34] Similarly, she questions the value of using the methods of ethnography, designed to explore lesser-known, insular communities, on social scientists themselves, who pose no accessibility issues. As she writes,

> The social worlds of pupils, of prisoners, of jazz musicians and of *capoeira* teachers are interesting and worth researching. [But] autoethnography focusses on social scientists who are not usually interesting or worth researching. The *minutiae* of the bodies, families or households of social scientists are not likely to provide analytic insights for social science.[35]

Even a cursory look through results in a database search for autoethnography reveals how common such work continues to be, from pieces about how professors decide when to start having children[36] and becoming vegan[37] to ruminations on being a university proctor[38] or a nursing teacher.[39] As I have argued previously, this fault may lie at least partly with Ellis, whose model autoethnographies focus on her life as a professor and are filled with extraneous details and dialogue in an attempt to create an engaging, immersive narrative.[40]

American literary journalism has faced similar criticism for not being "objective" and, in many cases, seeming too personal, particularly with respect to first-person writing, such as the work of Joan Didion. But of the three main criticisms we are discussing, this is the easiest one to dismiss, largely because of the inherent differences between academic and trade publishing. Editors are deeply involved with works of literary journalism, often from the moment of assignment, to ensure that they are relevant and interesting to a wide range of consumers, who, after all, are expected to pay for them. This is obviously not the case with academic publishing, as peer reviewers are not the same as editors. Still, the debate in autoethnography suggests some valuable avenues of research for literary journalism scholars, such as how one might distinguish between what is a personal memoir and what is a piece of literary journalism that happens to have a personal focus. Can works such as novelist Ann Patchett's *Truth & Beauty* (2004),[41] a literary, nonfiction story of her friendship with poet Lucy Grealy, be considered literary journalism, even though she would probably not identify herself as a journalist? Where are the boundaries of the genre when it comes to personal writing? Similarly, it would be valuable to the genre for scholars to engage in a debate about the academic value of literary journalism. If scholars across a wide variety of sociological fields, as well as many others, accept personal writing (i.e., autoethnography) as a scientifically valid type of research that can pass peer review and be published in a journal, why don't journalism scholars? Are journalism scholars falling behind the times in terms of what the academy deems acceptable, meaningful research, or is there a reason to maintain a distinction between journalistic and scholarly research?

The second critique made against autoethnographers concerns their relationship with truth and accuracy. For example, Ellis supports autoethnographers being able to use composite characters in their work, as she herself did in *The Ethnographic I* (2004). She also supports collapsing separate events into one scene and altering the chronological order of reported events for the sake of creating a more engaging reading experience. In her view, this is no different from how traditional ethnographers interpret their fieldwork and research notes, choosing which quotations to use and applying their own interpretation to a custom or event they have observed.[42] These critiques are likely to sound familiar to scholars of American literary journalism and suggest areas of further study. Questions of accuracy commonly arise in the field, as well as how much, if any, leeway writers have to create composite characters and conflate events, as well as how to work with memories versus notes taken firsthand, and how to recreate dialogue. As Mark Kramer notes, it was common for New Journalists of the mid-twentieth century to employ the techniques Ellis uses, but he argues that as the genre has grown, writers and readers have developed a clearer, stricter stance on what is considered acceptable:

> no composite scenes, no misstated chronology, no falsification of the discernible drift or proportion of events, no invention of quotes, no attribution of thoughts to sources unless the sources have said they'd had those very thoughts, and no unacknowledged deals with subjects involving payment or editorial control.[43]

This area seems ripe for more examination by scholars of literary journalism, such as undertaking a study of publications that produce literary journalism—what processes, if any, do they have in place to verify the work? This seems more pressing now than ever when even the blandest of daily reporting may be labelled "fake news"; if the standards for literary journalism are different from those for other types of journalism, what are they? Similarly, we need more research to understand how the expectations of literary journalists, their publishers, and their readers may differ in order to develop guidelines or best practices, and scholars of autoethnography have demonstrated how to do this.

The third major critique made against autoethnography concerns how autoethnographers deal with the issue of informed consent when it comes to the people who become characters in their work, who are often the writers' students, colleagues, and/or family members. Martin Tolich argues that in many cases, the rights of those people are overlooked and that few practical guidelines exist to help autoethnographers navigate issues surrounding consent.[44] In his analysis of three autoethnographies by leaders in the field, including Ellis, he identifies one work in which twenty-three people appear who would not have known about their inclusion in it and, from all accounts, were not asked in advance of publication for their consent.[45] In such cases, autoethnographers, at the request of institutional research ethics boards, often try to seek retrospective consent, but Tolich questions whether that is ethical: "Identifying retrospective informed consent as potentially coercive is foundational for autoethnographers; it creates a natural conflict of interest between an author's publication and the rights of persons mentioned, with the author's interest unfairly favored over another."[46]

He also argues that autoethnographers should make a more concerted effort to be transparent with readers about the various ethical and narrative choices they make in their work. While he notes that there is some evidence of the writers in his study doing this, such explanations fall short of what is expected of scholarly research in terms of clarity and depth.[47] These critiques appear frequently in the extant literature, and it is clear that they are having an effect on the norms of the young genre. For example, particularly in book-length autoethnography, writers are devoting more space to a discussion of the methodological and ethical considerations involved in their research and narrative choices. In Adams's book, for example, a nineteen-page appendix examines issues of method, criticism, and representation, including when and why he chose to protect the privacy and identity of some of his research subjects, and when and why he chose to alter the chronology of events.[48] Similarly, autoethnographers appear to be taking the issue of informed consent more seriously than they used to. Both Tolich and Jillian Tullis have developed clear codes of ethics for autoethnographers to follow, drawing from existing codes in ethnography and other types of human-focused qualitative research.[49] In addition, the expanding number of books published about how to undertake autoethnographic projects regularly feature chapters about how to navigate ethical issues; for example, D. Soyini Madison's guidebook has three chapters devoted to ethics: ethics in relationships with research participants, ethics with respect to doing fieldwork, and case studies in ethical dilemmas.[50]

Literary journalists have also been the subjects of critique concerning their transparency with their readers. While they often note when they give people pseudonyms to protect their privacy, they rarely discuss how they navigated any of the ethical challenges involved in reporting difficult stories and, in many cases, exposing the lives of marginalized people. For example, in Tracy Kidder's *Among Schoolchildren* (1989), there is a two-line author's note explaining that the children featured in the book, along with one student teacher and one other character, have been given pseudonyms, but it is on the copyright page, where many readers might fail to notice it. There is also no discussion of how he obtained the consent of the children or their parents to take part in his research. In LeBlanc's *Random Family*, she explains in a one-and-a-half-page author's note that she has changed the names of some of her characters but neglects to say which ones or why, and that she has avoided using composite characters or conflating events.[51] But once again, it falls short of providing any insight into how she negotiated access with her sources, many of whom lived in poverty and were involved in criminal activity, or the possible consequences of their becoming involved in her project. This trend suggests an opportunity for scholarly exploration: What is the norm when it comes to how transparent literary journalists are with their readers? If, as seems to be the case, they are far less transparent about their methodological, ethical, and narrative choices than autoethnographers, why is that the case? How does this lack of transparency affect literary journalists' relationships with their readers? Similarly, what is the effect of having no set of common guidelines for literary journalists to follow?

As shown, there are significant similarities between American literary journalism and autoethnography in terms of their origins, their methodologies and styles, and even the common critiques levelled against them. This presents a valuable opportunity for literary journalism scholars to learn from how autoethnographers have engaged with their critics to help expand their field and achieve complete academicization. Despite the serious criticisms that have been levelled against autoethnography since its inception, including questions about its value as serious research, the field has only grown in acceptance and popularity across a range of disciplines. This is due in no small part to the willingness of autoethnographers to engage with their critics, address their concerns directly, and evolve the genre. If scholars of American literary journalism, which is travelling along a similar trajectory as a burgeoning young field, are able to do the same, then they stand to achieve the same level of success in establishing their field of study in the academy.

Notes

1. Gillespie, "Building Bridges."
2. O'Reilly, *Key Concepts in Ethnography*, 3.
3. Lindner, *Reportage of Urban Culture*, 3.
4. Raushenbush, *Robert E. Park*, 15.
5. Raushenbush, 15–16.
6. Raushenbush, 30.
7. Raushenbush, 37–40.
8. Raushenbush, 41.
9. Quoted in Raushenbush, 41.
10. Raushenbush, 39.
11. Lindner, *Reportage of Urban Culture*, 38.
12. Raushenbush, *Robert E. Park*, 122.
13. Park, "City," 3.
14. Deegan, "Chicago School of Ethnography," 14.
15. LeBlanc, *Random Family*, 406.
16. LeBlanc, 85.
17. Reed-Danahay, introduction to *Auto/Ethnography*, 4.
18. Boylorn and Orbe, introduction to *Critical Autoethnography*, 13.
19. Ellis, *Ethnographic I*.

20 Jones, Adams, and Ellis, "Coming to Know Autoethnography," 22; italics in the original.
21 Ellis, "Katrina and the Cat," 199.
22 Adams, *Narrating the Closet*, 76.
23 Gillespie, "Building Bridges," 70–71.
24 Walters, "Ted Conover," 10.
25 Conover, *Rolling Nowhere*, 281.
26 Conover, 208–09.
27 Conover, 219; italics in the original.
28 See, for example, Chang, "Autoethnography in Health Research"; Lapadat, "Ethics in Autoethnography"; Peterson, "Case."
29 See, for example, Hartsock, "Literature in the Journalism"; Morton, "Rereading Code"; Schmidt, "Pioneer of Style."
30 "Submission Information."
31 Anderson, "Analytic Autoethnography."
32 Anderson and Glass-Coffin, "I Learn by Going," 64.
33 Delamont, "Only Honest Thing," 58.
34 Delamont, 60.
35 Delamont, 59–60; italics in original.
36 Tillman, "Labor Pains."
37 Andreatta, "Being a Vegan."
38 Walford, "Finding the Limits."
39 Wright, "Searching One's Self."
40 Gillespie, "Building Bridges," 75–76.
41 Patchett, *Truth & Beauty*.
42 Ellis, *Ethnographic I*, 125–26.
43 Kramer, "Breakable Rules," 25.
44 Tolich, "Critique of Current Practice," 1599–600.
45 Tolich, 1600.
46 Tolich, 1601.
47 Tolich, 1601.
48 Adams, *Narrating the Closet*, 153–71.
49 Tullis, "Self and Others."
50 Madison, *Critical Ethnography*.
51 LeBlanc, *Random Family*.

Bibliography

Adams, Tony E. *Narrating the Closet: An Autoethnography of Same-Sex Attraction*. Walnut Creek, CA: Left Coast Press, 2011.

Anderson, Leon. "Analytic Autoethnography." *Journal of Contemporary Ethnography* 35, no. 4 (August 2006): 373–95. https://doi.org/10.1177/0891241605280449.

Anderson, Leon, and Bonnie Glass-Coffin. "I Learn by Going: Autoethnographic Modes of Inquiry." In *Handbook of Autoethnography*, edited by Stacy Holman Jones, Tony E. Adams, and Carolyn Ellis, 57–83. New York: Routledge, 2016.

Andreatta, Maria Marta. "Being a Vegan: A Performative Autoethnography." *Cultural Studies ↔ Critical Methodologies* 15, no. 6 (2015): 477–86. https://doi.org/10.1177/1532708615614025.

Boylorn, Robin M., and Mark P. Orbe. Introduction to *Critical Autoethnography: Intersecting Cultural Identities in Everyday Life*, edited by Robin M. Boylorn and Mark P. Orbe, 13–26. New York: Routledge, 2016.

Chang, Heewon. "Autoethnography in Health Research: Growing Pains?" *Qualitative Health Research* 26, no. 4 (2016): 443–51. https://doi.org/10.1177/1049732315627432.

Conover, Ted. *Rolling Nowhere: Riding the Rails with America's Hoboes*. New York: Vintage, 2001.

Deegan, Mary Jo. "The Chicago School of Ethnography." In *Handbook of Ethnography*, edited by Paul Atkinson, Amanda Coffey, Sara Delamont, John Lofland, and Lyn Lofland, 11-25. Thousand Oaks, CA: SAGE Publications, 2001.

Delamont, Sara. "The Only Honest Thing: Autoethnography, Reflexivity and Small Crises in Fieldwork." *Ethnography and Education* 4, no. 1 (2009): 51–63. https://doi.org/10.1080/17457820802703507.

Ellis, Carolyn. *The Ethnographic I: A Methodological Novel about Autoethnography*. Walnut Creek, CA: AltaMira Press, 2004.

———. "Katrina and the Cat: Responding to Society's Expendables." *Cultural Studies ↔ Critical Methodologies* 7, no. 2 (2007): 188–201. https://doi.org/10.1177/1532708606288652.

Gillespie, Bruce. "Building Bridges between Literary Journalism and Alternative Ethnographic Forms: Opportunities and Challenges." *Literary Journalism Studies* 4, no. 2 (2012): 67–79.

Hartsock, John. "The Literature in the Journalism of Nobel Prize Winner Svetlana Alexievich." *Literary Journalism Studies* 7, no. 2 (2015): 37–49.

Jones, Stacy Holman, Tony E. Adams, and Carolyn Ellis. "Coming to Know Autoethnography as More than a Method." Introduction to *Handbook of Autoethnography*, edited by Stacy Holman Jones, Tony E. Adams, and Carolyn Ellis, 17–47. New York: Routledge, 2016.

Kidder, Tracy. *Among Schoolchildren*. New York, Harper Perennial, 1989.

Kramer, Mark. "Breakable Rules for Literary Journalists." In *Literary Journalism: A New Collection of the Best American Nonfiction*, edited by Norman Sims and Mark Kramer, 21-34. New York: Ballantine Books, 1995.

Lapadat, Judith C. "Ethics in Autoethnography and Collaborative Autoethnography." *Qualitative Inquiry* 23, no. 8 (2017): 589–603. https://doi.org/10.1177/1077800417704462.

LeBlanc, Adrian Nicole. *Random Family: Love, Drugs, Trouble, and Coming of Age in the Bronx*. New York: Scribner, 2003.

Lindner, Rolf. *The Reportage of Urban Culture: Robert Park and the Chicago School*. Cambridge: Cambridge University Press, 1996.

Madison, D. Soyini. *Critical Ethnography: Method, Ethics, and Performance*. Thousand Oaks, CA: SAGE Publications, 2005.

Morton, Lindsay. "Rereading Code: Representation, Verification, and a Case of Epistemic (Ir)responsibility." *Literary Journalism Studies* 8, no. 1 (2016): 35–50.

O'Reilly, Karen. *Key Concepts in Ethnography*. Thousand Oaks, CA: SAGE Publications, 2009.

Park, Robert E. "The City: Suggestions for the Investigation of Human Behavior in the Urban Environment." In *The City*, edited by Robert E. Park, Ernest W. Burgess, and Roderick D. McKenzie, 1–46. Chicago: University of Chicago Press, 1967.

Patchett, Ann. *Truth & Beauty: A Friendship*. New York: HarperCollins, 2004.

Peterson, Ashley L. "A Case for the Use of Autoethnography in Nursing Research." *Journal of Advanced Nursing* 71, no. 1 (2015): 226–33. https://doi.org/10.1111/jan.12501.

Raushenbush, Winifred. *Robert E. Park: Biography of a Sociologist*. Durham, NC: Duke University Press, 1979.

Reed-Danahay, Deborah E. Introduction to *Auto/Ethnography: Rewriting the Self and the Social*, edited by Deborah E. Reed-Danahay, 1–17. Oxford: Berg, 1997.

Schmidt, Thomas R. "Pioneer of Style: How the *Washington Post* Adopted Literary Journalism." *Literary Journalism Studies* 9, no. 1 (2017): 35–59.

"Submission Information." *Literary Journalism Studies* 9, no. 1 (2017): 4.

Tillmann, Lisa M. "Labor Pains in the Academy." *Cultural Studies ↔ Critical Methodologies* 11, no. 2 (2011): 195–98. https://doi.org/10.1177/1532708611401338.

Tolich, Martin. "A Critique of Current Practice: Ten Foundational Guidelines for Autoethnographers." *Qualitative Health Research* 20, no. 12 (2010): 1599–610. https://doi.org/10.1177/1049732310376076.

Tullis, Jillian A. "Self and Others: Ethics in Autoethnographic Research." In *Handbook of Autoethnography*, edited by Stacy Holman Jones, Tony E. Adams, and Carolyn Ellis, 244–61. New York: Routledge, 2016.

Walford, Geoffrey. "Finding the Limits: Autoethnography and Being an Oxford University Proctor." *Qualitative Research* 4, no. 3 (2004): 403–17. https://doi.org/10.1177/1468794104047238.

Walters, Patrick. "Ted Conover and the Origins of Immersion in Literary Journalism." *Literary Journalism Studies* 9, no. 1 (2017): 9–33.

Wright, Jane. "Searching One's Self: The Autoethnography of a Nurse Teacher." *Journal of Research in Nursing* 13, no. 4 (2008): 338–47. https://doi.org/10.1177/1744987107088046.

26

FROM MAJOR TO MINOR

Literary Journalism and the First Person

Lisa A. Phillips

Conventional journalism, on the page, renders the journalist invisible. One of the first things journalism students learn is not to use the first person in their articles. Though first-person commentary and essays have proliferated in the era of digital news,[1] daily breaking news reports still rarely include the pronoun "I," holding to standards of objectivity that evolved from the rise of wire services and mass circulation newspapers in the nineteenth century. But these standards have always coexisted with literary journalism, a genre whose emphasis on subjectivity not only permits the first person but also privileges it. Literary journalists often overtly enter the narrative, their presence meant to give, at minimum, insight into the subject at hand and, at maximum, a narrative of self-discovery, combining the personal essay and deep reporting.[2] The first person also offers immediacy and intimacy, a way for the reader to identify with the writer as a fellow thinking, feeling human being. The use of the first person in literary journalism calls attention to the presence of the writer, both as the investigator of the truth—the reporter—and as the truth teller, or narrator, who intentionally crafts a story for the reader's consumption. The first person illuminates the ways the omniscient third-person point of view of conventional journalism is an enabling fiction: The reporter reports, the reporter writes, and as such shapes the story, yet the reporter's "I" is not there on the page, an erasure that makes it seem like there is no wizard, so to speak, behind the curtain. The discussion that follows will examine the role the first person plays in defining literary journalism as a genre, review how the first person has evolved historically in literary journalism, and explore the range of issues that emerge when the "I" makes its presence known. While the "I" can foster transparency of method, narrative tension, and reader empathy and intrigue, the first-person point of view, like the disembodied omniscient third person of conventional journalism, is a construct with a marked impact on the journalistic imperative to "seek truth and report it." The first person shapes the framing, content, and structure of the narrative, helping us perceive certain claims to truth and excluding others, affecting the work's emotional, moral, and thematic impact. While use of the first-person point of view is an acknowledgment of the inherent subjectivity of the reporting process, it also underscores subjectivity's limits.

The "I" of literary journalism, as described by Tracy Kidder and Richard Todd, exists on a spectrum. At one end is the "first-person minor," or the restricted first person, used by Kidder himself in *The Soul of a New Machine* (1997) and other works. The first-person minor narrator's presence is light and utilitarian, an observer rather than a protagonist in the story. At the other end of Kidder and Todd's first-person continuum is the first-person major, when the "I" is a dominating presence on the page[3] and often the central character in the story, using the tools of journalism to investigate the narrator's own life. Plenty of works of literary journalism don't use the first person at all. Yet the idea of the first person—that there is always a human being behind the reporting process and in the creation of the text—is integral to the genre of literary journalism. Whether written in the first person or the third, works of literary journalism are distinguished by the sense of being told in "the individual and intimate voice of a whole, candid person."[4] Conventional news and academic writing, in contrast, emphasize objectivity, facts, and the suspension of judgment. The first-person point of view underscores what these more neutral forms render invisible: the reflectiveness, experiences, and authority of the writer as fact finder and witness. The first person gives the impression of forthrightness, of nothing held back.

Entwined with the emphasis on candor are other key features of the genre of literary journalism: plot, character, and theme. The first person in literary journalism, in short, must be the narrator of a good *story*. In this way, first-person literary journalism, in particular the first-person major, intersects with the human impulse toward autobiography—making the material of the self cohere into a storyline. Philosopher Daniel Dennett calls the self at the center of the storyline a "fictional object," something we use to make sense of ourselves and our world, less a "true" self than a way of communicating and controlling the otherwise unruly and disorganized reality of who we are.[5] J. David Velleman takes this stance one step further: A first-person narrator may be a "fictional apparatus," but as such it guides the decisions of the self and becomes integral to the creation of the self. Constructing a first-person account is what makes us "the characters whom we invent," our actions determined by whether they are a coherent continuation of the story of ourselves.[6] Though literary journalism seeks to convey subject matter and human experience beyond the purely autobiographical, Velleman's stance has particular relevance to the genre. If the first-person narrator is a constructed persona, it is the persona of a journalist, tasked with a distinct professional duty: to fact find. This quest for verifiable truths becomes a coherent and engaging storyline in itself as the narrator engages in the reporting process: seeking out and interviewing sources, witnessing scenes, and experiencing moments of discovery and conflict. The drama of the fact-finding journey is one of the reasons journalists-as-protagonists hold such appeal not only in literary journalism but also in novels and films, such as *All the President's Men* (1976) and *Spotlight* (2015). Yet in nonfiction, this narrative coherence should also make us wary of the constructed nature of storytelling and what kinds of information it permits and what it excludes. David Shields reminds us to be skeptical of the idea that the journalist's duty is to tell us what "really happened." Once writers engage in the construction of a narrative, they force order onto the inherent messiness of life, imagination, and memory, omitting what seems irrelevant or inconvenient: "The story takes hold. It begins to determine what goes in and what's left out."[7]

The Evolution of the "I" in Literary Journalism and the Paradox of Objectivity

Literary journalism evolved out of a variety of forms of nonfiction prose that predate conventional objective journalism: diaries, travelogues, and sensational early reporting on crime, politics, and domestic conflicts. John Hartsock identifies Mary White Rowlandson's 1682 memoir of her captivity among Native Americans during King Philip's War as a text with qualities that would eventually help define literary journalism as a genre: detailed descriptions, a strong plotline, and a subjective point of view.[8] We also see in her account an example of the first-person narrator as a constructed character, shaping a storyline of Christ-like redemption to convey a deliberately shaped reality. Her moralistic approach minimizes the humanity of her Native American captors in the service of dogmatism, as she interprets her own suffering from the "savageness" of captivity as the Lord's way to "scourge and chasten" her.[9]

The eighteenth and nineteenth centuries saw the rise of journalism about social concerns, with works that described everyday life, society, and its woes through thickly detailed travelogues, sketches, letters, and reports. Narratives of encounters with the people suffering from social ills—the poor, the imprisoned, the oppressed, the foreigner, the mistreated—often used the first person. The narrator of J. Hector St. John de Crèvecoeur's *Letters from an American Farmer* (1782) is a farmer named James, writing to an English gentleman about farming practices, wildlife, American identity, and other aspects of life in the British colonies in the years before the Revolutionary War. This fabricated first-person narrator and scenario are in line with other early works of literary journalism, such as the spy narrator in Ned Ward's *The London Spy* sketches (1703), which blurred the line between fiction and fact, particularly when it came to narrative personae. Readers did not expect the illusion of total authenticity, yet the "I" of these early works functioned much as it does today—as a means to share the act of witnessing with readers as fellow human beings and evoke an emotional response. In "Letter IX: Description of Charles-Town; Thoughts on Slavery," the most vivid and historically significant chapter in an otherwise wandering and diffuse text, James describes his encounter in South Carolina with an enslaved African American man held in a cage for killing his overseer. The man had been savagely beaten, his eyes pecked out by birds, and was on the verge of death. Horrified, James passes the man some water, and the man begs him to "pute some poison and give me." The slave explains that he has been suffering from his injuries for two days and "no die." This interaction underscores the cruelty of the man's lot and, quite graphically, the limits of James's pity and attempts to help; no one-time act of kindness will be enough to assuage the evil of slavery. The first-person point of view amplifies the narrative of the man's suffering. The enslaved man will soon die, but James the narrator will live on, changed, his mind "oppressed since I became witness to it" and compelled to recount what he saw.[10]

In the nineteenth century, subjective first-person journalism was rivaled by the rise of the ideal of objectivity, a phenomenon driven by technological, economic, and cultural forces. The Enlightenment had set the stage with its emphasis on reason, rationality, and science, particularly as tools to question religious dictates and monarchal authority. Facts and empiricism gained authority. Realism replaced Romanticism as the guiding cultural aesthetic, with increasing interest in the details of everyday working-class people. The invention of the steam-driven printing press drove the price of newspapers down, creating a "penny press" of tabloid-style newspapers. A new form of brief, objective news writing helped newspapers build mass circulation audiences instead of targeting partisan niches, as their hand-crafted, costly predecessors had. In 1835, the *New York Herald* adopted a policy of political independence, laying the foundation for a more neutral reporting style in the press. In 1840, the invention of the telegraph led to the launch of the Associated Press and, eventually, other wire services, which issued stories written in a spare, neutral style. The approach satisfied two needs, one commercial, the other practical: The objective stance could serve a wider range of audiences and a greater number of newspapers, and short articles had a better chance of transmitting before a glitch in the telegraph line.[11] An objective news style, Robert Miraldi points out, satisfied emerging philosophical views of the function of the press: to provide the information that a rational public needed to make public policy decisions.[12] The press won't tell the public what to think, only what to think about.

Narrative form and first-person journalism did not fade away as these changes transpired—in fact, quite the opposite. As the objectivity ideal gained traction in newsrooms, so did literary journalism and related feature forms; good storytelling, just like political independence, had commercial appeal. A number of big city dailies cultivated reporters who could do both, such as Lincoln Steffens, who was a police reporter for the *New York Evening Post*, and Stephen Crane, who wrote for the *New York Press*. Crane's 1894 sketch "When Man Falls, a Crowd Gathers," a seminal work of narrative literary journalism, illustrates the tensions between the conventions of objective news and literary journalism. The sketch has a strong narrative thrust yet is written in the third person, the default point of view for objective news. The narrator depicts the voyeuristic men "crowded savagely" around an Italian man who has collapsed on the street. The narrator's vantage point is at first outside the crowd but eventually moves so close as to see the froth on the collapsed man's chin.[13] Witness to the man's fit, the narrator participates in the voyeurism, but his participation is obscured behind the third person; he can ironically detail the crowd's lust to see blood without being transparent about the fact that he himself is right in the thick of the scene, likely a participant in the shoving. Though the third person in this case evokes the emerging conventions of neutrality, as the narrative progresses it can be understood to reveal a shortcoming of the conventions: They erase the fact that a reporter who digs deeply into a story is likely to play a role in it. The sketch is a fascinating illustration of what Rosalind Coward calls the paradox of objectivity: Articles should read as if the journalist were invisible and omniscient, yet the very act of reporting depends on the reporter's subjective presence as an interviewer and witness.[14] The third person fails to answer the question of *how* the news was gathered, what the reporter did to gather it, who the reporter is, and what forces frame the reporter's perspective on the events at hand.

A far less enigmatic narrator can be found in the work of pioneering reporter Nellie Bly, née Elizabeth Jane Cochrane. Her high profile "first-person major" stunt journalism in *Around the World in Seventy-Two Days* (1890)—featuring Egyptian alligator hunting, an offer of marriage, a private train, and competition from another female journalist—created a showy serial narrative for readers that did more to provide insight into the publicity-seeking tactics of the *New York World* than it did to give insight into the exotic locales she sped through. But "Ten Days in a Mad-House" (1887), an earlier series of articles for the *World*, makes very different use of the first-person major. Bly goes undercover as a mentally ill woman in the notorious Blackwell's Island Insane Asylum. In her masquerade, she is the central protagonist of a high-narrative account. Inasmuch as this endeavor is also a "stunt," it is a stunt meant to fulfill a central tenet of reporting: to tell the stories of those who can't readily tell (and disseminate) them themselves. She is not staging a globe-trotting show for entertainment. She is putting her body on the line so her readers will know how awful the conditions in the asylum are and how it feels to be trapped helplessly inside. She is at the center of the story because she must be. There is no other way to thoroughly report what goes on in a mad-house, a point she underscores at a several junctures when reporters come around, "untiring in their efforts to get something new,"[15] and fail to discover much of importance. Yet Bly is also, in Velleman's terms, a character of her own invention. On a literal level, she is a woman in disguise. But even the Bly underneath the mask is a construct, making decisions to heighten the drama of her situation, the challenges of truth seeking, and the paradoxes of mad-house life. After she is admitted to Blackwell, she decides to no longer act insane. She strategically underscores the Catch-22 of the inmate's situation by making persistent requests to be released. The staff interprets her efforts as even more evidence of "delusions," and they refuse to grant her request.[16] This strategy adds an additional complication to the plotline of uncovering the inhumane conditions at Blackwell's Island. The reader is invited not only to pity the inmates but also to identify with them. If asylum staff can't tell the insane from the sane, who is really safe from being deemed crazy?

In narratological terms, first-person narrators are referred to as homodiegetic, meaning they participate as characters in the story they tell. Their point of view can be "internally focalized"—they know only as much as one character can know. Inasmuch as the degree of their presence—where they fall on the minor to major continuum—is an important factor, so is how they narrate the story and how they participate as characters. Bly's career sets forth some of the issues: How much is the story about the narrator, and how much is it about the subject she's covering? Can narrators see outside their own perspectives and concerns to direct reader empathy away from themselves? Cecilia Aare offers some tools for assessing these questions. A homodiegetic narrator, who as the "first-person major" main character of the story focuses tightly on the narrator/reporter's own experiences, creates a consonant narration, without ex-post, or backward-looking, reflection that evaluates the experience. This type of narrator, Aare argues, offers fewer opportunities for reader empathy, as other characters tend to be seen from the outside, potentially in generalized terms. Yet when a homodiegetic narrator who is the central protagonist tells a story *with* retrospective reflection, a separation, or "dissonance," occurs between the reporter/protagonist's immediate, internally focalized experience and the narrator's broader understanding. A dissonant first-person narration allows for a more complex portrayal of the other characters in the story and offers more opportunity for reader empathy.[17] In Velleman's terms, the "characters whom we invent" in creating a first-person narrative persona have a range of options for how their experience can be conveyed, with varying degrees of immediacy, reflection, knowingness, and ability to generate empathy.[18] Bly, for example, maintains an awareness of her privilege as a reporter whose suffering in the mad-house is relatively limited. She confesses her terror of being trapped behind the ward's locked doors if a fire breaks out, then acknowledges that her risk is only temporary; she deflects reader empathy toward her fellow inmates, who must dwell indefinitely with such hazards: "Unless there is a change there will some day be a tale of horror never equaled."[19]

The Self-Conscious First Person in the Twentieth Century

The twentieth century saw the emergence of a more overtly individual first-person major narrator in American literary journalism, a figure that mined the emotions of the reporter-source relationship as material in and of itself. In *Let Us Now Praise Famous Men* (1941), an account of the lives of three white sharecropper families in rural Alabama during the Great Depression, James Agee's first-person presence is searingly self-conscious. He is full of self-doubt, fretting over the possibility that his work will be little more than voyeuristic entertainment.[20] His highly personal approach defies what Paul Ashdown calls "the very reductivist substance of journalistic modernism: a scientific obsession with facts and documentation in pursuit of objective reality."[21] Agee opens the book with a listing of a "cast of characters," including himself as a "spy, traveling as a journalist,"[22] suggesting that his role is inherently invasive and limited. His dissonant homodiegetic narration underscores how he as the journalist-spy, inasmuch as he may strive to depict reality, alters that reality as soon as he enters the scene with his thoughts, neuroses, shortcomings, and dreams. A journalist, in this way, is *always* "first-person major," even when posing as a minor figure or hiding behind a veil of omniscience; Agee is simply one who stopped pretending. Yet for all this self-consciousness and cynicism, Agee's narrative persona also embraced emotional connection with his subjects in what Dale Maharidge called "method journalism"—total immersion in his sources' world, just as method acting demands a complete immersion in a character.[23]

To what extent does Agee's dissonant narration direct attention toward an empathetic portrayal of his subjects? It is hard to say. He depicts George Gudger as a holy figure in overalls and his daughter Emma, married off at sixteen to a jealous older man, as being attracted to Agee and his photographer, Walker Evans, both sexually and "as symbols or embodiments of a life she wants and knows she will never have."[24] It is unclear to what extent Agee is sensing something real, and to what extent he is using his subjects for his own spiritual and erotic fantasies. Agee gives his subjects little agency. We know them only through his point of view, with little evidence that Agee's impressions of them have anything to do with what they are actually thinking or feeling. Emma's desire, for example, is surmised only through her "sudden and subtle but unmistakable expressions of the eyes, or ways of smiling."[25] Skeptical as he is of reductive and exploitative journalistic fact finding, Agee's highly subjective approach also imposes a restrictive frame on his subjects. He is such an obsessive chronicler of his reactions to his subjects that they rarely speak for themselves. There is very little quoted dialogue or any other sign that Agee's subjects have disclosed much about themselves.

The preoccupied "I" of *Let Us Now Praise Famous Men* foreshadows what John Pauly calls the "personalism" of the New Journalism in the 1950s and 1960s, as much a political style as a literary one. This new wave of writers imagined themselves not as dispassionate observers, obligated to repress their reactions, but as connected to the people and events they covered. They believed that "personal involvement and immersion were indispensable to an authentic, full-blooded account of experience."[26] Their rebellion against editorial traditions was in keeping with other crises of authority in American society, primarily the Vietnam War and the Generation Gap. For some writers, the New Journalism's personalism was about telling stories in a distinctive style, not necessarily from a first-person point of view. Tom Wolfe, in his seminal essay on New Journalism, was notably antagonistic to putting the "I" at the center of a story, calling it "very limiting for the journalist, since he can bring the reader inside the mind of only one character—himself—a point of view that often proves irrelevant to the story and irritating to the reader."[27] Getting an accurate portrayal of the minds of one's characters meant interviewing them extensively about their thoughts and reactions, earning the ability to reconstruct reactions and depict mind states.

Wolfe, along with Gay Talese, Truman Capote, and others, produced what David Eason calls "ethnographic realism," in which the reporter uncovers the underlying reality of a subculture—such as Ken Kesey's Merry Pranksters or Capote's rural small-town Kansas—that previously was known only in superficial façade. The reporting presents the subculture as an "object of display," with the reporter and the reader seeing that object with an assumed, shared set of values.[28] Works of ethnographic realism typically use either a heterodiegetic narrator—an omniscient third-person narrator who is not a character in the story, as in *In Cold Blood* (1966)—or the first-person minor, the "I" appearing in the text when the reporter's interactions with sources or environment offer insight and information that could not be easily conveyed otherwise. In "How Do You Like It Now, Gentlemen?" (1950), Lillian Ross (a writer who, it should be noted, prefigures New Journalism; she resisted the association with the movement while being credited with defining it) suggests to a clearly uncomfortable Ernest Hemingway that he see a doctor, only to get the retort: "I never trust a doctor I have to pay."[29] The exchange between Ross and Hemingway underscores his resistance to coping with his illness, along with his self-protectiveness and his willingness to take advantage of caretakers who kowtow to his fame. We also get a glimpse of her narrator persona as a kind of guardian of normalcy, who sees Hemingway's frailty as he refuses to.

For another faction of New Journalism writers, "personalism" was all about asserting the self in full-fledged "first-person major." Cultural phenomenology—the term Eason uses to describe the modernist texts of Joan Didion, Norman Mailer, Hunter S. Thompson, and others—is similar to ethnographic realism in that both rely on the creation of texts that read like fiction, with scenes, dialogue, and narrative tension. Yet in cultural phenomenology, reporting is not a quest to find an objective reality but rather a way to "[join] writer and reader together in the *creation* of reality," which will always be riddled with uncertainty.[30] In "Slouching towards Bethlehem" (1967), for example, Didion presents herself as part of a ruined world—"at some point we had aborted ourselves and butchered the job"—and too disoriented by it to even know what she was seeking. She was drawn to San Francisco because it was where the "social hemorrhaging was showing up," an image of humanity as unsalvageable, and ultimately unknowable, waste.[31] In this way, works of cultural phenomenology won't definitively state "the way things are" or fact find in the traditional sense of the word. When Didion acts like a reporter, seeking information from the police or trying to score an interview with a source who will help her understand runaway youths, her efforts to fact find dead end. The police tell her little, and sources, such as the elusive Deadeye, are too dissipated to make sense. The self she constructs is guided not by the quest for truth but instead by "the story of the writer's efforts to impose order" on what she's witnessed.[32] Though the text presents Didion as a dissonant narrator, engaging in a considerable degree of retrospective reflection, her use of the first person does not necessarily generate empathy or present her subjects in detailed characterization; there are so many sources, and they are difficult to get to know. The decisions of the self Didion creates are motivated more by her quest to build a moral argument against the society that incubated the San Francisco drug culture than by a journalistic fact-finding mission. She enters the text overtly troubled by the hippie scene and finds no shortage of evidence to support her initial impressions. She finds chaos, aimlessness, and altered states everywhere. She structures her impressions of Haight-Ashbury to culminate in a final scene revealing the neighborhood's troubling legacy: young children who take acid in "high kindergarten," start fires, and chew on electrical cords.

Cultural phenomenology's emphasis on imposing order on a slippery and uncertain reality allows for the first person to thrust itself into the forefront of a story with unbridled subjectivity. Thompson is a first-person major showman, his actions creating the story from whole cloth through the intensity, humor, and outlandishness of his "center-stage participatory manner."[33] His narrating style is self-dramatized and highly consonant, focused on immediacy and personal experience, with the idea that the closer you get to the material, the better you understand it. As with Didion, empathy is not a priority for Thompson. His journalism is what he encounters on the way to the bar at the race track, or what he sees on his portable television in between laps in the hotel pool. Sometimes it's what he makes up, or hallucinates. Yet the centrality of his persona does not necessarily mean his stories are only "about him"—his antics are in service of making sense of a culture "where the real has become so permeated by the fantastic that knowledge and ethics have become problematic in new ways."[34] Thompson reports on what's on the poolside television because he is no closer to reality there than he would be at the White House, where every move is scripted and packaged for the media.

The Quest: The Self as Material

Cultural phenomenology's "I," defined by the struggle to grapple with an unknowable reality, gradually gave way to the late twentieth/early twenty-first century obsession with authenticity—the memoir boom of the 1990s, the rise of reality television, and eventually the rise of the confessional essay as click bait in the content ecosystem. This "reality hunger," as Shields puts it, depends on the illusion that we *can* successfully portray real life by writing about it: "The moment you put pen to paper and begin to shape a story, the essential nature of life—that one damn thing after another—is lost."[35] Yet the appeal of the personal narrative also can be seen as a reaction to the same thing that inspired cultural phenomenology: skepticism about objectivity and the questioning of authority. Both history and conventional journalism have fallen short in communicating the truth of the varieties of human experience, so we need the inherent subjectivity of memoir to help us make headway into the "stories of ourselves."[36]

The zeal for memoir influenced the tastes of readers and editors of journalism, who increasingly welcomed a first-person perspective in reporting. This could mean a more elaborate take on a first-person minor approach. In *Into the Wild* (1996), Jon Krakauer shared his own reckless experiences from his youth to suggest that his subject, Christopher McCandless, wasn't necessarily suicidal to venture alone into the Alaskan wilderness.[37] Other writers used a hybrid of memoir and reporting I call the quest narrative: work that applies the tools of journalism to investigate a matter of personal importance to the journalist. Inasmuch as the "I" may be motivated to gather information to help with self-understanding as well as with the forces that have shaped the writer's life, the inquiry still uses traditional reporting methods to uncover more broadly applicable insights for readers. The question isn't just "Why did X happen to me?" but "Why does X *happen*?" A foundational quest narrative is Sara Davidson's *Real Property* (1980), which uses her search for a place to live as a means to explore greed, spirituality, politics, and community in the booming real estate market of Venice, California. In *Salvation on Sand Mountain* (1995), Dennis Covington's search for his Southern and spiritual roots illuminates the ecstatic Christian subculture of snake handlers and faith healers in his native Alabama. "The Cost of Life" (2014), *Sarasota Herald-Tribune* reporter Justine Griffin's multipart account of becoming an egg donor, is a work of first-person multimedia literary journalism with a strong investigative bent. Andrew Solomon's *Noonday Demon: An Atlas of Depression* (2001) was launched by Solomon's own Herculean struggle with the disease. My own book, *Unrequited: Women and Romantic Obsession* (2015), an investigation into why loving someone who won't love you back can be so all-consuming, was prompted by an acute obsession from my past.

The interplay between the personal and the reportorial is crucial to all of these works, as is the ability to provide the retrospective reflection entailed in dissonant narration. The combination of fact-finding and self-disclosure guides the decisions of the quest's first-person narrator persona, a hybrid of inquisitive reporter and vulnerable confessor whose experiences shape the narrative and serve as journalistic evidence in themselves. In her Pulitzer Prize–winning 2017 *GQ* article, "A Most American Terrorist," Rachel Kaadzi Ghansah uses the first-person point of view in her profile of Dylann Roof, the white man who murdered eight black parishioners and their pastor at Mother Emanuel AME Church in Charleston. She emphasizes that she has little choice but to bring herself into the narrative, because any guise of neutrality or objectivity is impossible: "This black body of mine cannot be furtive. It prevents me from blending in."[38] Her first-person narrator persona is on a quest to use both her subject—Roof and his world—and her self—a black woman in that world—to expose the extent of the racism that motivated him to kill, making him "not an outlier at all … but rather emblematic of an approaching storm."[39] She highlights moments when her presence following Roof's footsteps reveals what might have fed his hatred. In his family's all-white church, she is scrutinized "like a shoplifter trying to steal from their God."[40] At a historical plantation Roof once visited to honor the Confederacy, she must reckon with the sight of "stuffed enslaved-people dummies Roof posed with in some of his pictures."[41] As she stood next to the figures, which "are supposed to represent black people in their deepest ignominy,"[42] she listened to a group of young white women gushing over how beautiful the plantation was. The delusion that Roof's massacre had little to do with systemic racism is one her first-person narrator can't abide, and, she maintains, neither should we.

Forging Ahead with the First Person: Enduring Dilemmas

The first person continues to thrive in the contemporary news ecosystem. First-person articles of all kinds, from personal essays to op-eds to literary journalism, attract clicks and shares. The first person is a common presence on publications' "most shared" and "most popular" lists of trending stories. In an essay in the *Washington Post*, journalist Eve Fairbanks expresses concerns about the escalating popularity of personal essays, which have moved from niche sites, columns, and blogs into the main arteries of legacy news organizations such as CNN and the *New York Times*. In an era of newsroom budget slashing and sped-up deadlines, "plumbing the depths of your own life seems to be the only way to spend time on a topic … to draw 'reporting' from a wider time frame than this morning's press conference,"[43] Fairbanks writes. The focus on writers' lives, however interesting, may distract from the duty of journalism to tell stories about the lives of people who can't or won't readily write their own. With its expectations of immersive reporting, first-person literary journalism is a different animal from both the personal essay and the related genre of autobiographical, or confessional, journalism. Yet Fairbanks raises an apt point: Is the self as source a troubling shortcut, albeit a compelling one?

In *The Journalist and the Murderer* (1990), an account of the lawsuit brought by convicted murderer Jeffrey MacDonald against Joe McGinniss, the author of a book about the case, Janet Malcolm notably calls the "I" in a work of journalism the only character that is invented. The "I" is "an over reliable narrator, a functionary to whom the crucial task of narration and argument and tone have been entrusted, an ad hoc creation, like the chorus of a Greek tragedy."[44] The journalist, she explains, has total control over self-depiction. In one scene in *Fatal Vision* (1983), McGinniss describes MacDonald, then accused of murdering his wife and young children, callously throwing darts at a photograph of a government prosecutor. Yet McGinniss, according to court testimony, also participated in the dart throwing, a fact he tellingly leaves out of his book —an important omission, as during the reporting process McGinniss led MacDonald to believe that he was on his side and would depict him as innocent. Just as the third person puts the journalist out of the frame in conventional objective journalism, the first-person approach also imposes a frame. Journalists decide when to show up and when not to, exercising control over their own presence in ways their subjects cannot. This element of control remains no matter how central journalists are to their narratives and how much they disclose about themselves. We may think we are getting "everything"—or at least everything we need—about journalists who write in the first-person major, but are we? When journalists become the central sources in their reporting, how devoted will they be—indeed, *can* they be—to pursuing the truth about themselves?

Notes

1. Fairbanks, "How Personal Essays."
2. Harrington, "When Writing," xvii.
3. Kidder and Todd, *Good Prose*, 24–26.
4. Kramer, "Breakable Rules," 29.
5. Velleman, "Self as Narrator," 57–58.
6. Velleman, "Self to Self," 204–06.
7. Shields, *Reality Hunger*, 65.
8. Hartsock, *History*, 108.
9. Rowlandson, *Narrative*.
10. St. John de Crèvecoeur, *Letters*.
11. Coward, *Speaking Personally*, 12–16.
12. Miraldi, *Muckraking and Objectivity*, 153–54.
13. Crane, "When Man Falls."
14. Coward, *Speaking Personally*, 20.
15. Bly, *Ten Days*.
16. Bly.
17. Aare, "Narratological Approach."
18. Velleman, "Self as Narrator," 58.
19. Bly, *Ten Days*.
20. Agee, *Let Us Now Praise*, 7.
21. Ashdown, "James Agee," 198.
22. Agee, *Let Us Now Praise*, 4.
23. Maharidge, "Close Enough to Hurt," 56.
24. Agee, *Let Us Now Praise*, 55.
25. Agee, 56.
26. Pauly, "Politics," 114.
27. Wolfe, *New Journalism*, 32.
28. Eason, "New Journalism," *Literary Journalism*, 192–93.

29   Ross, "How Do You Like It Now."
30   Eason, "New Journalism," *Literary Journalism*, 192–93; emphasis added.
31   Didion, "Slouching towards Bethlehem," 85.
32   Eason, "New Journalism," *Literary Journalism*, 200.
33   Weber, *Reporter as Artist*, 20.
34   Eason, "New Journalism," *Critical Studies*, 55.
35   Shields, *Reality Hunger*, 66.
36   Armistead, "My Life."
37   Boynton, *New New Journalism*, 179.
38   Ghansah, "Most American Terrorist."
39   Ghansah.
40   Ghansah.
41   Ghansah.
42   Ghansah.
43   Fairbanks, "How Personal Essays."
44   Malcolm, *Journalist and the Murderer*, 160.

Bibliography

Aare, Cecilia. "A Narratological Approach to Literary Journalism: How an Interplay between Voice and Point of View May Create Empathy with the Other." *Literary Journalism Studies* 8, no. 1 (Spring 2016): 107–39.

Agee, James. *Let Us Now Praise Famous Men*. New York: Mariner, 2001.

Armistead, Claire. "My Life as a Story." *Guardian*, January 26, 2001. www.theguardian.com/books/2001/jan/27/biography.

Ashdown, Paul. "James Agee." In *A Sourcebook of American Literary Journalism: Representative Writers in an Emerging Genre*, edited by Thomas B. Connery, 197–204. Westport, CT: Greenwood Press, 1992.

Bly, Nellie. *Ten Days in a Mad-House*. New York: Ian L. Munro, n.d. http://digital.library.upenn.edu/women/bly/madhouse/madhouse.html.

Boynton, Robert S. *The New New Journalism*. New York: Vintage, 2005.

Coward, Rosalind. *Speaking Personally: The Rise of Subjective and Confessional Journalism*. New York: Palgrave Macmillan, 2013.

Crane, Stephen. "When Man Falls, a Crowd Gathers." In *Stephen Crane: Prose and Poetry*, 600–04. New York: Library of America, 1984.

Didion, Joan. "Slouching towards Bethlehem." In *Slouching towards Bethlehem*, New York: Farrar, Straus and Giroux, 2008.

Eason, David L. "The New Journalism and the Image-World: Two Modes of Organizing Experience." *Critical Studies in Mass Communication* 1, no. 1 (1984): 51–65. https://doi.org/10.1080/15295038409360013.

———. "The New Journalism and the Image World." *Literary Journalism in the Twentieth Century*, edited by Norman Sims, 191–205. Evanson, IL: Northwestern University Press, 2008.

Fairbanks, Eve. "How Personal Essays Conquered Journalism—and Why They Can't Cut It." *Washington Post*, October 10, 2014. www.washingtonpost.com/posteverything/wp/2014/10/10/how-personal-essays-conquered-journalism-and-why-they-cant-cut-it/?utm_term=.ecdb2879e88c.

Ghansah, Rachel Kaadzi. "A Most American Terrorist: The Making of Dylann Roof." *GQ*, August 21, 2017. www.gq.com/story/dylann-roof-making-of-an-american-terrorist.

Harrington, Walt. "When Writing about Yourself Is Still Journalism." Preface to *The Beholder's Eye: A Collection of America's Finest Personal Journalism*, edited by Walt Harrington, xv–xxii. New York: Grove Press, 2005.

Hartsock, John C. *A History of American Literary Journalism: The Emergence of a Modern Narrative Form*. Amherst, MA: University of Massachusetts Press, 2000.

Kidder, Tracy, and Richard Todd. *Good Prose: The Art of Nonfiction*. New York: Random House, 2013.

Kramer, Mark. "Breakable Rules for Literary Journalists." Nieman Storyboard, January 1, 1995. https://niemanstoryboard.org/stories/breakable-rules-for-literary-journalists/.

Maharidge, Dale. "Close Enough to Hurt." *Columbia Journalism Review*, January/February 2005, 54–57.

Malcolm, Janet. *The Journalist and the Murderer*. New York: Vintage, 1990.

Miraldi, Robert. *Muckraking and Objectivity: Journalism's Colliding Traditions*. Westport, CT: Greenwood Press, 1990.

Pauly, John J. "The Politics of the New Journalism." In *Literary Journalism in the Twentieth Century*, edited by Norman Simns, 110-129. Evanson, IL: Northwestern University Press, 2008.

Ross, Lillian. "How Do You Like It Now, Gentleman?" *New Yorker*, May 13, 1950. www.newyorker.com/magazine/1950/05/13/how-do-you-like-it-now-gentlemen.

Rowlandson, Mary. *Narrative of the Captivity and Restoration of Mrs. Mary Rowlandson*. [1682]. Project Gutenberg, 2009. Accessed October 20, 2017. www.gutenberg.org/files/851/851-h/851-h.htm#link2H_4_0020.

Shields, David. *Reality Hunger*. New York: Alfred A. Knopf, 2010.

Sims, Norman, ed. *Literary Journalism in the Twentieth Century*. Evanston, IL: Northwestern University Press, 2008.

Solomon, Andrew. *The Noonday Demon: An Atlas of Depression*. New York: Scribner, 2001.

St. John de Crèvecoeur, J. Hector. *Letters from an American Farmer*. Accessed July 2, 2018. http://avalon.law.yale.edu/18th_century/letter_09.asp.

Velleman, J. David. "The Self as Narrator." In *Autonomy and the Challenges to Liberalism: New Essays*, edited by John Christman and Joel Anderson, 57–76. Cambridge: Cambridge University Press, 2005.

———. "Self to Self." *Philosphical Review* 105, no.1 (January 1996): 39–76. www.jstor.org/stable/2185763.

Weber, Ronald. *The Reporter as Artist: A Look at the New Journalism Controversy*. New York: Hastings House, 1974.

Wolfe, Tom. *The New Journalism*. Edited by Tom Wolfe and E. W. Johnson. London: Picador, 1975.

PART IV

New Directions for Scholarly Inquiry

27
THE "BLACK DIFFERENCE" IN AFRICAN AMERICAN LITERARY JOURNALISM

Roberta S. Maguire

That literary journalism is a hybrid genre partaking of techniques and aims associated with both fiction and journalism is an axiom that scholars of the genre share, even if the specific techniques and aims—and balance between them—can vary widely. How literary journalism combines those genres has received considerable attention over the last several decades as the scholarly field has matured. Yet just as literary journalism is a combination of literature and journalism, the ways in which it differs from both—and so becomes a hybrid—have also been the focus of significant research. And as is the case with any field, the generalizations promulgated by this scholarship have tended to become accepted premises, helping to guide the kinds of questions scholars ask even as the field expands.

I offer the above as a necessary starting point for this chapter on African American literary journalism, an area I have been researching for nearly a decade. Using the insights of scholars before me about what literary journalism shares with creative writing, especially fiction, and with journalism, including its fidelity to actuality, I have identified such a quantity of writing by African Americans from the nineteenth century to the contemporary moment that I am convinced a compelling tradition exists to be traced out.[1] But I am increasingly recognizing that this tradition that is beginning to come into focus, while it of course comes under the umbrella of American literary journalism, must be approached on its own terms—or, rather, that it matters that the widely accepted generalizations regarding American literary journalism, derived primarily from stories produced by majority, or mainstream, writers, are not wholly applicable to the work produced by African Americans. It matters because those generalizations serve as the foundation for the kinds of theorizing scholars undertake to understand the form and function of literary journalism, so when those generalizations are not applicable, then the related theorizing will likely miss the import of the material studied.

Now to concretize this: As suggested above, part of the work that such founding scholars in the field as Thomas Connery, Norman Sims, John Hartsock, and others have undertaken has been to delineate the markers of literary journalism by distinguishing it from what has variously been described as "standard," "classic," "conventional," and "traditional" journalism.[2] A number of traits associated with fiction writing in particular, from scene-by-scene construction and status details, named by Tom Wolfe in the 1970s when referencing the New Journalism, to symbolism and ambiguity, traits emphasized by Sims and Hartsock, respectively,[3] have been put forward as among the non-journalistic characteristics of literary journalism. Another trait that is often given special prominence, even serving as the trait from which the others follow, is subjectivity. Connery, in his 1992 volume *A Sourcebook of American Literary Journalism: Representative Writers in an Emerging Genre*, sums up the "goal of the literary journalist" as "to recreate the feel and look of life and experience from a single, subjective point of view,"[4] which thereby separates such writing from "purely journalistic work" whose goal is "to convey information, primarily facts and authoritative viewpoints, clearly and efficiently."[5] Both Sims and Mark Kramer, who together edited *Literary Journalism: A New Collection of the Best American Nonfiction* (1995), in their separate introductions to the volume also highlight subjectivity as a key trait differentiating it from "standard reporting." Sims points out that such reporting "hides the voice of the writer," whereas "literary journalism gives that voice an opportunity to enter the story,"[6] in turn allowing writers to serve "as participants or witnesses, rather than as distanced onlookers."[7] Building on that, Kramer calls the literary journalist's voice "intimate" and sets it in opposition to the "seemingly objective and factual, judgment-suspending, orthodox informant" encountered in "newswriting."[8] The intimate voice, he asserts, "is a key characteristic of literary journalism and is indeed something new to journalism."[9]

Kevin Kerrane and Ben Yagoda in their *The Art of Fact: A Historical Anthology of Literary Journalism* (1997) identified such subjectivity as a corrective to the objectivity of "classic journalism," which they termed "a kind of flimflam" perpetrated by a "disembodied measured voice," adding that "the pure objectivity [that voice] implies is probably unattainable by humans."[10] Unattainable, perhaps, but Kerrane and Yagoda remind readers, "anyone who has ever taken Journalism 101 knows" that having the reporter be "at the forefront" of a story "violates not only a formula but one of the guiding principles of the profession" of journalism.[11] Sharing that view of objectivity as a common denominator of "conventional" journalism even as it is a "pretense,"[12] Hartsock in *A History of American Literary Journalism* (2000)—a text that continues to be vital for scholars new to the field—claims that "modern literary journalism ... fundamentally has been a reaction in this century against the alienating gulf created by the objectification of news in the American mainstream press," an objectification that "makes a claim to critical closure." Likening that claim to "the emperor's invisible clothes," Hartsock insists "subjectivity alone undoes the lie."[13] And while taking up other matters beyond the scope of *A History* in his second book on the genre, *Literary Journalism and the Aesthetics of Experience* (2016), Hartsock retains a focus on subjectivity as a key marker differentiating literary journalism from "mainstream models of journalism."[14] He highlights the point in his concluding chapter, claiming that "one of the hallmarks" of literary journalism

> is that it is a much more subjective form (inflected with a more personal voice) than the more objectifying conventional models of journalism dominant in American practice even if the subjectivity is merely reflected in the shaping consciousness of the author selecting descriptive details.[15]

The subjective voice, however, is not something that distinguishes African American literary journalism from the conventional journalism produced by the US black community. And that is because subjectivity is at the heart of the African American journalistic tradition, which begins in 1827 with Samuel Cornish and John Russwurm's weekly *Freedom's Journal*.[16] The paper's goal—"We wish to plead our own cause. Too long have others spoken for us"[17]—itself indicates that subjectivity, or personal views standing in for a community's views, was a critical dimension of its journalism. A fiercely abolitionist paper, *Freedom's Journal* set in motion the African American press's primary role as advocate on behalf of the nation's black population.

Post-slavery, the need for advocacy was unabated as Reconstruction led to Black Codes restricting the freedom of African Americans, especially in the labor market, which were followed later in the nineteenth century by Jim Crow (segregation) laws, notoriously upheld by the Supreme Court case *Plessy v. Ferguson* and not overturned until the middle of the twentieth century. As Patrick Washburn explains in *The African American Newspaper: Voice of Freedom* (2006), in the face of growing limitations on black freedoms in the new century, the African American press made a "continual push for more black rights ..., using a powerful and compelling form of advocacy journalism rather than the standard objective style found in most white-owned papers."[18] Writing that was "highly charged with emotion"—shunned by the mainstream press as it increasingly embraced objectivity in the twentieth century—was "the heart and soul"[19] of the journalism produced by African Americans. Phyllis Garland, who wrote for two black publications, the *Pittsburgh Courier* and *Ebony*, and later taught journalism at Columbia University, summed up the orientation of the black press in this way: "The black press was never intended to be objective because it didn't see ... the white press being objective. It often took a position. It had an attitude. This was a press of advocacy."[20]

And it was also the press that attended to black accomplishments in education, business, and the professions, as well as to the ordinary concerns the community had about such matters as health, child-rearing, and personal relationships. It was "the main source of the black citizen's information and comment about his or her life,"[21] given that such information was systematically excluded from the mainstream press until late in the twentieth century's Civil Rights Movement.[22] The function of this internal focus on the community has historically been to promote race pride and solidarity, bolstering African Americans' views of themselves in the face of discrimination and racism. And the internal focus continues to serve an important function today even as the mainstream press is no longer so thoroughly segregated: The African American community still needs the black press, David Love recently pointed out, because it continues to publish stories "with underrepresented points of views, that would otherwise go missing—and do not necessarily reflect the white men who dominate the industry."[23]

That summary of the twin functions of the black press—external advocacy and internal community building—speaks to a complexity inherent in African American journalism that, related to subjectivity, sets it apart from the history of mainstream US journalism: It has longstandingly had a radically double audience. The components of that audience have been the black community itself, to be sure, but also the full spectrum of the white majority, ranging from those sympathetic to black causes to those antagonistic to the community's appeals. Beginning with *Freedom's Journal* in 1827 and continuing with other publications through the Civil War, the black press provided encouragement for the black community while also seeking to "impress" the white community with positive stories about African Americans in an effort to eliminate the "stigma of inferiority" that dogged the race.[24] After the Civil War and well into the twentieth century, while the black press became increasingly indispensable to African Americans for documenting their lives, which were ignored by the white press unless something sensationally terrible could be reported, its editors and publishers did not and could not ever completely ignore the white majority. Inclined to highlight injustices while advocating for greater equality yet alert to efforts by local officials and, especially during World War II, federal authorities to silence their publications, black journalists were navigating a mixed and at times treacherous terrain.[25]

Compounding those differences between mainstream and African American journalism is the profound effect twentieth-century segregation has had on the black press, from who wrote for it to how they wrote. Part of the scholarly project researchers interested in American literary journalism have undertaken has been to identify mainstream writers more readily known in the academy for their fiction and poetry, such as Mark Twain, Stephen Crane, and Ernest Hemingway, and more recently Walt Whitman and Willa Cather, as contributors to the literary journalism canon. They have been treated largely individually, with analysis often focused on the relationship between their own creative and journalistic writing. But as Fred

Carroll argues in *Race News: Black Journalists and the Fight for Racial Justice in the Twentieth Century* (2017), segregation led to a profound synergy between journalism and literature generally in African American writing: Having "constrained black writers' careers and earnings," segregation "often compelled authors, poets, scholars, and activists to publish alongside working reporters," producing a "willingness to shift genres" among them. As a result, "black journalism [evolved] with an unexpected cultural vibrancy and cosmopolitan character," which in turn helped create a "progressive reporting style not tolerated in white-owned daily newspapers."[26] Carroll provides a list of black writers "work[ing] at the fulcrum of literature and journalism" in the twentieth century that includes such canonical literary figures as Langston Hughes, W. E. B. Du Bois, James Weldon Johnson, Pauline E. Hopkins, Claude McKay, Alice Childress, and Lorraine Hansberry, while noting "many more" names could be added to his list, which I have only partially represented here.[27]

To sum up: Due to the specific history of the black community in the US, in the twentieth century lively writing and storytelling, along with a subjectivity ranging from first-person perspectives to general advocacy, remained commonplace in the conventional black press even as such elements were lost in the mainstream press's quest for objectivity. The kind of contrast set up between literary and conventional journalism that has been used to help delineate the twentieth-century tradition of literary journalism in the US, which has served as a basis for theorizing about it, therefore does not wholly translate to an African American tradition. And when we combine those differences with the double audience the black press has had from its beginnings, which carries over to black writing generally, it has become clear to me that in bringing theory to bear on the hybridized writing produced by African Americans that we call literary journalism, we must attend to what Henry Louis Gates Jr., the eminent scholar of African American literature, has called the "black difference."[28]

Henry Louis Gates Jr. and the "Black Difference" in African American Writing

In his 1985 essay "Writing, 'Race,' and the Difference It Makes," Gates outlines African Americans' historically complicated relationship to writing, which grew out of the Enlightenment's emphasis on literacy and in particular on the idea that writing was "the *visible* sign of reason"[29] and, therefore, humanness. Africans were not fully human and so could be enslaved in the New World, the logic went, because they lacked a written tradition that would provide the sign of reason. Teaching a slave to read and write was outlawed in many slaveholding states of the early Republic, indicating how unsupportable the logic sustaining slavery was. Nonetheless, to prove humanness US blacks had to write, and in doing so they took on the challenge of using a "language in which blackness is a sign of absence" in order to establish the black presence.[30] As a result, black writing, rather than "obliterat[ing] the difference of 'race'"—the very difference underlying slavery—has from its beginnings "preserved" it. Theorizing about the African American literary tradition, Gates was coming to realize, required "turn[ing] to the black tradition itself," specifically the "cultural differences" that have been preserved and "inscrib[ed]" in black writing as it relates to, comments upon, and challenges the Western, or mainstream, tradition.[31] Two years later, in his introduction to *Figures in Black: Words, Signs, and the "Racial" Self* (1987), Gates crystallized what his earlier essay pointed to:

> This is the challenge of the critic of Afro-American literature: not to shy away from literary theory, but rather to translate it into the black idiom, renaming principles of criticism where appropriate, but especially naming indigenous black principles of criticism and applying these to explicate our own texts.[32]

Taking my cue from Gates, in the remainder of this essay my aim is to show how his two-pronged prescription for analyzing African American literature—using mainstream theory that has been revised to respect black difference as well as theory derived from the black tradition—is similarly appropriate for scholars of African American literary journalism. Doing that I think not only highlights the critical black difference that distinguishes those texts from mainstream literary journalism but also helps pave the way for articulating the parameters, qualities, and purposes of this distinctive segment of literary journalism produced in the US. To start this effort I have turned to the mid-twentieth-century Civil Rights Movement because that is an era when the complexities I have outlined above are particularly acute.

The Civil Rights Era

Following *Brown v. Board of Education*, the 1954 Supreme Court case that overturned *Plessy v. Ferguson*, Carroll finds that "America's racial problems [finally] emerged as a prominent national [news] story."[33] But even as white-owned publications began to cover those issues, they were inclined neither to integrate their staff nor to take a particularly sensitive approach to the black community—a point emphasized in the 1968 report produced by the National Advisory Commission on Civil Disorders, commonly known as the Kerner Commission. Charged by President Lyndon B. Johnson following the especially traumatic summer of 1967 during which racial tensions erupted into violence in cities across the country, the commission identified many contributing factors to racial unrest and singled out the media for "its failure to report adequately on race relations and ghetto problems" as well as its reluctance "to bring more Negroes into journalism."[34] These failures had ill-served both its white and black readers, the commission concluded, depriving white readers of insight into the "the difficulties and frustrations of being a Negro in the United States" and black readers of a recognizable representation of themselves, due to white editors' and reporters' lack of "understanding or appreciation of … Negro culture, thought, or history."[35] Because of those failures of the mainstream press, black publications during this time of upheaval were necessarily the primary source for journalism representing a black perspective: "While white editors treated African Americans as news subjects, black reporters wrote about them as citizens pushing for social change," Carroll explains.[36] And yet during this time, there were a few black journalists who had joined the staff of white-owned publications. As the first black hires on the editorial side—and typically hired to cover the "race" beat—they were often the only such hires for years. This position heightened the challenge of having a dual audience that black journalists had historically faced; instead of working under like-minded black editors committed to advocacy, these "firsts" had white editors typically with limited exposure to and understanding of the black community and its causes.

Ted Poston and Charlayne Hunter-Gault were two such journalists during the Civil Rights Movement whose writing reveals the "black difference" while negotiating the line between literature and journalism and among multiple audiences. Poston was hired by the *New York Post* as its first black reporter in 1937, where he covered the "race beat" for thirty-five years.[37] Hunter-Gault was the first black staffer hired by the *New Yorker* in 1963, where she began as an editorial assistant but within the year had been promoted to staff writer;[38] she left the magazine in 1968 when she began reporting for the *New York Times*.[39] To demonstrate how Gates's approach to African American literature is transferable to the literary journalism produced by US blacks, I have selected an installment of Poston's series "Prejudice and Progress: The Negro in New York," published in the *Post* in April 1956, and Hunter-Gault's "A Trip to Leverton," which appeared in the *New Yorker* in April 1965. (At that time Hunter-Gault was writing as Charlayne Hunter.) The venues for the stories are quite different, as the former, a daily newspaper, has not typically been credited for being in the vanguard of the era's literary journalism, while the latter venue—the magazine, and especially the *New Yorker*—has long been seen as a hospitable environment for such writing. What the specific venues share, of course, is their status as mainstream, white-owned publications. And the two writers on one hand are quite different in terms of gender and generation—Poston was born in 1906 while Hunter-Gault was born in 1942—but on the other hand they share an important history: Both were profoundly shaped by their experiences writing for black-owned publications, Poston at the *Pittsburgh Courier* and *Amsterdam News* and Hunter at the *Atlanta Inquirer*,[40] before they went on to be firsts at white-owned publications.

Ted Poston and "You"

As Poston's biographer Kathleen A. Hauke explains it, in coming to the *Post*, Poston "aimed to expose racial conditions and race relations accurately"—he once was quoted as saying "I explain black folks to white people and white folks to black people"[41]—but he also knew "his material had to be agreeable to publishers."[42] That meant that early on at the *Post*, he used "amusing stereotypes of blacks," appeasing his publisher and the paper's mainstream readers, but at the same time he made sure to represent the black community "not as victims" but as "inventive" and in control of their lives and actions, which appealed to the paper's black readers: "Harlemites were delighted to read about their own community in the mainstream daily press, written by a trusted reporter from an authentic black background."[43] Being the only black reporter on the staff of the paper, however, and often isolated from the fraternity of white reporters due to racism, Poston continued to rely on his contacts in the black press,[44] which likely fueled his increasing confidence throughout the Civil Rights Movement in using his own voice in his reporting for the *Post*.

A particularly interesting dimension of Poston's voice in the "Prejudice and Progress" series—which appears in the *Post* two years after *Brown v. Board of Education*, six months after fourteen-year-old Emmett Till was murdered in Mississippi, and four months after Rosa Parks refused to give up her seat on an Alabama bus—is his use of the second person. First-person reporting in literary journalism has received significant attention, including in this volume (see Chapter 26 by Lisa Phillips), as it highlights the writer's subjectivity. Use of the second person is far less common, and its effects are complicated, especially in the hands of an African American journalist writing for a major metropolitan daily in the middle decades of the twentieth century. To show how Poston uses the second person, I turn first to narrative theory as developed by white theorists and typically applied to texts by majority writers, but, following Gates, I am tweaking it to address the "black difference."

First, some mainstream narrative theory: In a first-person narration, "I" is the controlling, subjective narrator, whereas in a third-person narration, the distancing pronouns "he," "she," and "they" dominate, suggesting a degree of objectivity. When the second person is used in narration, "you" functions as the controlling consciousness. Matt DelConte proposes that second person has historically been problematic for scholars studying narration because it doesn't function in the same way as first and third person, which are both defined by who is speaking. In terms of the speaker, second person inevitably overlaps with either first or third person. That leads DelConte to define second-person narration in this way: It is "a narrative mode in which a narrator tells a story to a (sometimes undefined, shifting, and/or hypothetical) narratee—delineated by *you*—who is also the (sometimes undefined, shifting, and/or hypothetical) principal actant in that story."[45] The critical difference highlighted is that a second-person narration functions as a "point of reception" whereas a first- or third-person narration functions as "a point of seeing or speaking."[46] Analysis of the second person, then, requires a focus on the "distinctive rhetorical effects" it produces.[47]

Alert to "the very diversity of second-person forms" that results from what DelConte identifies as the different focus of that narrative model, Monika Fludernik focuses on "the instability within individual second-person texts,"[48] an instability that serves a writer's purpose: "The decision to employ the second person in a narrative text is … a highly self-conscious one," she argues, "much more self-conscious and fraught with significance than the choice between the first- or third-person form."[49] The resulting instability "can, and frequently does, correlate with great emotional depth since the dialogic relationship it puts at its very center allows for an indepth treatment of human relationships, especially of relationships fraught with intense emotional rifts and tensions."[50] Another narrative theorist, Brian Richardson, calls this instability "unsettling" and attributes it to second-person narration's potential to collapse the distinction between the "protagonist/narratee"—and here the narratee is the *story's* designated listener—and the "actual or implied reader."[51] Calling it "arguably the most important technical advance in fictional narration since the introduction of … stream of consciousness," Richardson further describes second person as "a playful form, original, transgressive, and illuminating," one that is "conscious of its own status and often disguises itself, playing on the boundaries of other narrative voices."[52] Because of its boundary-crossing, transgressive properties, second-person narration, Richardson continues, might be "a useful vehicle for minority writers to foreground a subjectivity typically excluded from common, unexamined notions of 'you' and 'us,'"[53] a proposition beyond the scope of his work.

Now to Poston: In the second installment of his "Prejudice and Progress" series, for which he served as the writer with some background research provided by white coworkers, Poston employs the second person as a "useful vehicle" to heighten the black difference of double-consciousness, a concept defined by W. E. B. Du Bois at the beginning of the twentieth century as a dual identity, a two-ness, that US blacks experience. Ostensibly "American" but denied full citizenship because of prejudice and racism, US blacks, according to Du Bois, see the two components of their identity—racial and national—as incompatible in the eyes of the majority culture and therefore themselves. In Du Bois's words, "always looking at [themselves] through the eyes of others," black Americans had "two souls, two thoughts, two unreconciled strivings; two warring ideals in one dark body."[54] This also meant they were "gifted with second-sight"[55] and thus able to envision themselves as *both* American and black—and therefore have special insight into white Americans—but such a gift was more often overtaken by the debilitating effects of racism, leading to alienation from each part of the dual identity.

Race as both gift and handicap is at work in Poston's piece, which opens with a question: "How does one go about preparing a series of articles on segregation and discrimination against Negroes in the largest—and reputedly most liberal—city in the nation?"[56] This question is addressed to an indeterminant audience—perhaps the readers, or perhaps the writer, as in Poston himself. The use of the indefinite pronoun "one" also keeps a reader off balance as to who is being written about and who is the actant undertaking the preparation of the series. It theoretically could be anyone. But immediately thereafter Poston switches to the second person: "You and your coworkers search out the race relations experts, the Negro and white leaders, and examine all the data available in public and private agencies throughout the city" (109). That sentence serves to draw readers in, even as it clarifies that the "one" actant is not just anyone, but rather a specific group at the *Post*—the coworkers—that includes a "you" and others. The narrowing continues; by the next sentence, the coworkers are gone, and it is just "you" undertaking the work: "You visit the slums, talk to the people in their homes, churches, barber shops, gin mills and other places of public assembly" (109). The reader has been conflated with Poston; both reader and Poston are undertaking the actions. But then "you" is placed in a different context: "You also visit other sections of the city less frequented by Negro New Yorkers and watch the reactions of people there to this stranger in their midst" (109). "You" has now been narrowed to black, distinguished from non-Negro, New Yorkers. But even more striking—and destabilizing à la Richardson—"you" further becomes a "stranger," displaced from the reader and the writer as well.

With the movement from third person to second person and back to third person in the sentences quoted above, Poston dramatizes the alienation that is the end result of Du Bois's concept of double-consciousness. And he continues to invoke the concept in the next section of the article when he recalls how the project began: His editor had asked him, "How does it feel to be a Negro in New York?"[57]—a question that echoes Du Bois's own "real question, How does it feel to be a problem?" posed in "Of Our Spiritual Strivings," the essay in which he defines double-consciousness.[58] Poston offers this answer to his readers: "So you try to recall when it was that you started feeling like a New Yorker first and a Negro second, after your youthful arrival here in 1928 from Hopkinsville, Ky."[59]

The rest of the article moves through selected recollections, addressed to a "you" who is both the actant/narrator of the recollected stories and the narratee, allowing the piece to negotiate the newspaper's largely mainstream readership as well as its critical mass of black readers, with both functioning as the actual or implied readers. One recollection takes Poston and his readers back to 1938 when he went for dinner at a café and was denied service because he was black. Poston recreates the scene, this time collapsing actant, narratee, and reader. All are New Yorkers first: "You are an old New Yorker now and sure of your rights." Black and white readers, united, engage with the next sentence: "So you explain to [the café proprietor], patiently, that she can be locked up under the amended Civil Rights law for refusing a Negro service because of his race or color."[60] At that moment the reader, who has identified with the New Yorker "you" and so has been denied service, experiences the illogic of Jim Crow segregation—common for black readers, unprecedented for white readers. "Negro" becomes entirely separable from New Yorker; a New Yorker with "rights" would not be denied service, but nonetheless someone who is black is. As in Du Bois's double-consciousness, two identities are in conflict.

This pattern of conflating actant and readers irrespective of race, then separating them based on race, and rejoining them once again holds throughout other incidents Poston recalls, including one involving his father who came to visit after spending nearly his entire life in Kentucky "su-[ing] every Jim Crow agency in the state."[61] Father and son go to a Broadway show, and afterwards, when no cab will pick them up, they turn to the subway. Using second person and the present tense, Poston recreates how he and his father manage the subway scene:

> You dash into the car to save a seat for him and he sinks into it with audible relief.
>
> You are startled a minute later when he leaps suddenly to his feet and takes the strap beside you.
>
> He'd only realized then that the seat you had saved for him was next to a white woman.
>
> You look at each other and look away ashamed. You both remain silent for the long ride to Brooklyn.
>
> *(113–14)*

Poston's use of "you" allows all his readers to ride that subway and experience the son's momentary confusion and then his and his father's humiliation. He recaps the recitation with this: "How can one say to a father who has fought all his life for equality that: 'The crackers got you anyway'" (114). As in the article's beginning, the rhetorical question starts with an abstract address to "one"—anyone—but with a "you" embedded now in quotation marks, clearly not inclusive of white readers. This humiliation, Poston shows, is not the mainstream reader's experience, even as he shares it with his black readers. The reality of the division between white and black caused by the irrationality of racism comes into relief. And when in the article's penultimate sentence Poston declares, "You may never be able to determine when you became a New Yorker first and a Negro second—if, indeed, you ever did" (115), it is an indetermination white readers also experience, as they have crossed the color line, if only momentarily, a crossing made possible by the indeterminate second person and the second sight of double-consciousness that Poston's black readers share.

Charlayne Hunter-Gault's Signifyin(g)

By the time Charlayne Hunter-Gault's story "A Trip to Leverton" was published in the *New Yorker* nine years after Poston's series in the *Post*, the Civil Rights Movement was at its height, with marches, sit-ins, and other peaceful demonstrations having led to such gains as the Civil Rights Act of 1964. Yet violent backlashes—bombings, assassinations, and physical attacks on demonstrators—also intensified during this time. Compounding all of that were racial disturbances in cities and towns, disturbances that became more frequent later in the decade, finally leading to the Kerner Commission. Hunter-Gault had herself played a significant role in the movement, having been asked by the Atlanta Committee for Cooperative Action (ACCA) to apply to the University of Georgia in 1959 in an effort to desegregate the school. She and a fellow high school classmate, Hamilton Holmes, who was also recruited by the ACCA to apply, were denied admission, which provoked a suit that ultimately resulted in their enrollment at the university in 1960. There Hunter-Gault majored in journalism and began to write for the *Atlanta Inquirer*, an alternative black paper that had its beginnings in covering the city's student-led protests in support of civil rights[62] and prided itself on telling the stories ignored by both the city's white press and the conventional black press. The experience was formative; in Hunter-Gault's words, "That may have been the most important education I received."[63] Working alongside the paper's managing editor, Julian Bond, who was fast becoming a national leader of the Civil Rights Movement, she learned that "journalists can be servants of the people." Bond would continue to influence her: Shortly after she began at the *New Yorker*, following a speech he had delivered in New York, he admonished her, "You can't stop fighting. You have to go back to your communities and work there."[64]

Bond's advice undergirds "A Trip to Leverton," Hunter-Gault's recollection of taking her grandmother to the town where she had raised her family and where her husband, Hunter-Gault's grandfather, was buried. While not stated in the piece, the year would be 1960, when Hunter-Gault was attending Wayne State University in Detroit, Michigan, after having been initially denied admission at the University of Georgia. It is set during one spring morning when Hunter-Gault is home on spring break. The night before, we learn, she stayed out late with friends from high school who, deeply involved in the Atlanta Civil Rights Movement, had drafted a manifesto they were seeking to publish in local newspapers.

To see how the "black difference" is at work in the story, I turn to Gates's theory of Signifyin(g), which is built on the idea that writing produced by US blacks is inherently double-voiced: As Gates explains in his introduction to *The Signifying Monkey: A Theory of African-American Literary Criticism* (1988), where he first outlines his theory, "Black writers ... learn to write by reading literature, especially canonical texts of the Western tradition. Consequently, black texts resemble other, Western texts. These black texts employ many of the conventions of literacy form that comprise the Western tradition." In other words, black writers repeat in their work what they find in canonical—white—literature. Even so, Gates continues, such "black formal repetition always repeats with a difference, a black difference that manifests itself in specific language use."[65] This mode of repetition and revision, Gates argues, is deeply embedded in black culture. To show this, Gates looks to two separate but ultimately related trickster figures, Esu-Elegbara, derived from Yoruba cultures, and the Signifying Monkey, an African American creation. Both tricksters share the "tendency to reflect on the uses of formal language."[66] Esu is a messenger between the gods and humanity, a translator of language. As a trickster, this messenger also employs language that can convey opposite meanings simultaneously (which is suggested by the figure having two mouths)[67] and so is radically double-voiced. The Signifying Monkey operates by playing on language, using punning and pastiche, and in doing that stands for repetition and reversal. The two modes, Gates argues, suggest the black difference in writing by African Americans, as together they point to a complex intertextuality—black writing responding to dominant culture writing, to be sure, but also repeating tropes specific to black writing—and a distinctive US black tradition in letters.

In "A Trip to Leverton," we can see both double-voicedness and repetition and revision at work. While the story is today one of Hunter-Gault's best-known pieces, it echoes another famous story featuring a graveyard and an elderly black figure that appeared in the *New Yorker*, Joseph Mitchell's "Mr. Hunter's Grave." Published in the September 22, 1956, issue of the magazine, the piece focuses on "a bespectacled, elderly Negro man"[68]—Mr. George H. Hunter—who, living in the black community of Sandy Ground on Staten Island, gives Mitchell a tour of the local graveyard. Recognized as "one of the most enduring and defining stories of [Mitchell's] career," "Mr. Hunter's Grave," Thomas Kunkel points out in his recent biography, "pull[s] together almost all the great themes [Mitchell had] been writing about, and thinking about, for a quarter century."[69] The result, Kunkel concludes, is "an affecting allegory, on mortality specifically and the human condition generally."[70] While it reaches for those timeless themes, the piece might also be read as being out of time, given that by September 1956, the newsman in Mitchell would have been well aware of the developing Civil Rights Movement that the mainstream press had finally begun to attend to following *Brown v. Board of Education*. Invisible in the story is the social and political reality of being black in the US. Mitchell reports that "for years, [he] kept intending to find out something about" Sandy Ground, which "was something of a mystery" to him.[71] What he finally does learn has little to do with a sociohistorical context for understanding the community beyond that it was founded by free blacks from Maryland after the Civil War and that Mr. Hunter's mother was born a slave in 1849 but "didn't like to talk about it, and she didn't like for [her family] to talk about it" (525). Instead, the story's focus is largely on how the community has deteriorated, "is just a ghost of its former self" (522), with the impetus for Mitchell's travel to the community—a search for wildflowers that he undertakes in Staten Island cemeteries "when things get too much for" him (594) in urban Manhattan—woven throughout.

Hunter-Gault's story, by contrast, uses the frame of the contemporary Civil Rights Movement. She opens it by recalling how at school in Michigan she "kept up with the news" of the student protests that had begun with the Greensboro, North Carolina, sit-in on February 1, 1960, yet her distance from the action had left her feeling "useless." So back home in Atlanta on spring break, she "tried to lend" her friends, who were attending college locally and in the thick of drafting their manifesto, "support—mostly moral—wherever and whenever [she] could."[72] After staying up late with her friends one Friday night excitedly discussing their work, she had a restless sleep, "so it was not hard for me to snap awake" (96), Hunter-Gault explains, when her grandmother entered her bedroom Saturday morning with a request for a ride to Leverton.

Like Mitchell's Mr. Hunter, who appears to know everyone in Sandy Ground, Hunter-Gault's grandmother, whose name we eventually learn is Frances Wilson, "had an easy acquaintance with all the townspeople."[73] And like Mr. Hunter, she is devoted to her church; both elders keep track of who is sick, visit with them, are generous in their support. And, finally, both are part of the first generation post-slavery, each having had mothers who were born into it. But there the similarities end. If Mr. Hunter is alert to tensions between the black and white communities on Staten Island, they are not revealed in the story. Instead, any problems are attributed simply to impersonal economics. In the early days, Mr. Hunter tells Mitchell, the black residents were poor—"everybody had had to work"; the men labored "for the white oystermen" while the women "washed for white women."[74] But by the 1880s, when Mr. Hunter arrived, "that had all changed." The community was "quite a prosperous little place," welcoming all to its social events: White oystermen and their families came to summer church camp meetings; everyone, from the "big oyster captains" to anyone living on the South Shore, came to Sandy Ground's barbecues (521). In the story the community's decline is attributed to the end of the oyster business, begun by suspicion that the beds were diseased and finalized by a Department of Health injunction, which in turn led to a lack of community spirit. Mr. Hunter complains that the current residents "sit inside, and keep to themselves, and listen to the radio or look at television," yet are also obsessed with keeping up with their neighbors: "whenever something new comes out, if one family gets one, the others can't rest until they get one too" (523). The graveyard, in its disarray, reflects the town's lack of community spirit.

"A Trip to Leverton" provides a significant repetition of and revision to the form and content of "Mr. Hunter's Grave." As noted above, the frame for the trip to the cemetery, unlike the frame for Mitchell's story, is focused on the historical moment, and in particular race relations. But like Mitchell's story, the frame's theme is woven throughout the piece. While Hunter-Gault's relationship to Atlanta's student protest movement provides the details for the frame, what emerges in the interior story—the actual trip to Leverton and to the graveyard—are seemingly small moments that underline the inequality and disrespect that have given rise to those protests. What prompts Hunter-Gault's grandmother's request to be taken to Leverton is a bill she had received from the city for upkeep of her cemetery lot, a bill that if not paid, she is informed, will result in the city claiming the property. As readers we have learned that the city is not in fact maintaining the property at all; the black section of the cemetery is treated as a disposal area for cut branches, leaves, and grass from the white section. This has led Mrs. Wilson to hire a longtime friend and resident of Leverton, Mr. Will, to maintain her lot. When grandmother and granddaughter arrive at the lot, they find evidence of Mr. Will's handiwork, as

> hardly a grain of sand [is] out of its place. In the left-hand corner was a budding little tree, surrounded by neatly blocked hedges and green grass that looked like a carpet. The simple headstone that marked the grave was clean and white, and the mound of earth beneath it was neat and solid. In this peaceful space, one could momentarily shut out the ugly jungle that surrounded it.[75]

After visiting the lot, the two women travel to the city office responsible for sending the bill. As they enter the office and find one young clerk at work, Hunter-Gault's grandmother whispers, "That's Ella Mae Stevens. I remember when she was born."[76] Always polite, Mrs. Wilson greets her as "Miss Stevens" and offers her name, Frances Wilson, in case the young woman had forgotten her. In return, the clerk addresses the elderly woman as "Frankie"—illustrating the "habit" that earlier in the story Hunter-Gault attributes to the town's white men of "addressing every Negro, regardless of age, by his or her first name," a habit that leads Hunter-Gault, "whenever possible, … to avoid them" (106). The clerk's rudeness, combined with an unsatisfactory exchange that follows, renders Hunter-Gault "hardly able to contain [her]self" as she witnesses, yet stays silent out of respect for her grandmother, how "everything [her friends at home] stood for" and were demanding in their manifesto "was being compromised" (112). While this can be read as a revision of Mitchell's cemetery story, in which any need for challenging the racial status quo is absent, Hunter-Gault's revised repetition might also be a nod to what Mr. Brock, the Staten Island cleric in "Mr. Hunter's Grave" tells Mitchell even as he encourages him to seek out

Mr. Hunter to learn about the area. After asserting that "the man to speak to is Mr. George H. Hunter," and explaining who he is and why he would know so much about Sandy Ground, Brock adds this caveat: "Not that he'll necessarily tell you what he knows, or even a small part of it."[77] Perhaps there is a kind of knowledge Mr. Hunter does not share with Mitchell, knowledge that is foregrounded in Hunter-Gault's story.

But to return to the unsatisfactory exchange between the clerk and grandmother: With that exchange plus Hunter-Gault's friends' manifesto, "A Trip to Leverton" engages with what Gates has called the "trope of the Talking Book," a trope that is repeated and revised within the black literary tradition itself. It has its beginnings in slave narratives, in which black writers challenge their legal status as "objects" through asserting themselves as "speaking subjects."[78] Gates traces the first instance of the trope to *A Narrative of the Most Remarkable Particulars in the Life of James Albert Ukawsaw Gronniosaw, an African Prince, as Related by Himself*, which first appeared in 1770.[79] Thinking he was going to embark on an adventure to a new land, Gronniosaw is actually captured and, after a voyage to the Caribbean, purchased by a New York businessman. As a slave, he learns to read and write in English, and on another sea voyage, he recalls his master reading aloud from a book to the ship's crew. This astonished him, as he thought the book itself was speaking. He recalls in his narrative how later, alone with the book and hoping to hear its voice, "I opened it, and put my ear down close upon it, in great hopes that it would say something to me; but I was very sorry and greatly disappointed, when I found that it would not speak."[80] This trope of the talking-then-silent book appears in a number of antebellum slave narratives, and in revised form, it periodically reemerges in black literature. What the trope does initially, Gates explains, is demonstrate that "the silent book"—representing the Western tradition—"did not reflect or acknowledge the black presence before it."[81] Its implication beyond that is the need for black writers to "make the white written text speak with a black voice,"[82] which in turn sets in motion a tension between orality and literacy, speech and writing, which is at the heart of the African American literary tradition.

Mrs. Wilson's encounter with the young clerk in "A Trip to Leverton" coupled with Hunter-Gault's friends' written manifesto can be read as a signifyin(g) continuation of the trope of the Talking Book. Signfiyin(g), as noted above, arises out of black oral culture. It is a "rhetorical strategy" that plays with rather than reinforces or confirms received meaning.[83] A means of "making a point by indirection and wit," signifyin(g) "presupposes an 'encoded' intention to say one thing but to mean quite another," and in that way is radically double-voiced.[84] In Hunter-Gault's story, the trope of the Talking Book emerges with the bill her grandmother receives, which is a text that does not speak to her and that she is determined to revise. Hunter-Gault recalls her grandmother explaining on the way to Leverton how the basis for the bill—that she was not necessarily the rightful owner of the cemetery lot—is wrong, since she owned the lot free and clear, having received it as "a gift":

> My mother was a slave before I was born, and the man whose farm she lived on, Mr. John Robert Henry, gave it to her just before he died. Later, she was freed and the people on the farm knew about the gift. They didn't need to see any legal papers as long as Mr. John Henry had given his word. And they knew he had. My mother gave me the land later on.[85]

When Mrs. Wilson begins explaining to the clerk the reason for her visit with "I received this notice," she is cut off by the clerk: "'Yes, I know,' Ella Mae Stevens said. 'Have you got your proof of ownership?'" In the exchange that follows, Mrs. Wilson repeats to Miss Stevens the information she has shared with her granddaughter, stressing the value of John Robert Henry's word and the fact that the city had not fulfilled its obligation to maintain her lot. Miss Stevens brushes these assertions aside with "all I know" and "I don't know anything about that," concluding their conversation with "I do know that you're going to have to pay this bill and continue to pay the city as long as you claim to hold title to the property" (110).

Through the conversation, Hunter-Gault shows how invoking a white man's word to challenge the base of the inequity the city's written bill perpetuates has no effect, which further demonstrates the precarious position of African Americans nearly one hundred years after slavery had ended: Speech delivered by a white man on behalf of a black woman, when recounted by another black woman, can be ignored, and writing produced by the white majority can deny the black reality. The disconnect that Gronniosaw experienced between himself and the Talking Book recurs.

Another attempt at revising the text is tied to the manifesto Hunter-Gault's friends had been writing, and to which she returns near the story's end. Anxious to see the manifesto claiming equal rights for her generation in the paper, she gets a copy not long after she and her grandmother return home. What she finds in the paper reinforces the day's experience in Leverton. Harkening back to the antebellum era, when slavery was justified by the black community's supposed inability to write, is the governor's response to her friends' work: "He had said that the students' manifesto had not been written by students in the Georgia school system—or even adults in this country, for that matter."[86] The effort to rewrite the "book" that denies the black presence is once again dismissed.

But the story ends with an important revision. We are told early on that Hunter-Gault's grandmother had been experiencing memory lapses due to arteriosclerosis, which at times made her irrational and irascible, causing great distress for her family. We also learn that the distress is best alleviated by Mrs. Wilson herself, once her mind is cleared and she is able to laugh at what has occurred. After discovering the governor's dismissal of her friends' demands, Hunter-Gault is approached by her grandmother. In the midst of another memory lapse and so having forgotten the trip to Leverton earlier in the day, she tells her granddaughter:

> I had planned to ask you to take me to Leverton to see about a bill the city sent me yesterday. But it's too late today. ... Maybe next week. Early on Saturday morning we'll go. Yes, I think next week will do fine.[87]

Once again, Hunter-Gault's grandmother is the reliever of distress, as her words end the story, delivering a double-voiced message with wit and indirection: Efforts to change how black Americans are treated and viewed—efforts to change the controlling text—must be and will be repeated until achieved. This is a critical message in the Civil Rights era, foregrounding for all of the *New Yorker*'s readers the legitimacy of the black difference.

Conclusion

The rise of modern literary journalism in the US has been understood as a response to traditional journalism's homage to objectivity in the twentieth century, suggesting different functions as well as aesthetics for the two. The development of African American literary journalism, however, cannot be framed in the same way, given the specific history of writing in the US black community, which is triggered by the claim of white Europeans and their descendants in the New World that Africans lacked a written tradition and so were not fully human. Writing, therefore, begins as an act of advocacy in the African American tradition, and this is especially true of its journalism. Advocacy indicates subjectivity, so the notion of an "objective" press has been to a large degree anathema to US black journalists. This in turn means that to read African American literary journalism as a reaction against a traditional press does not hold. Similarly, the differences that arise from that basic distinction between objectivity and subjectivity also do not apply. The function, for example, of American literary journalism has frequently been framed in terms of bridging gaps—between the writer's subjectivity and an objectified world,[88] between a reader of some privilege and a disparaged, invisible, or disenfranchised "other." By contrast, however, because African American journalism arose not only as a means to advocate on behalf of the black community but also to tell the stories of that community that the mainstream press ignored, the divide between writer and subject in the journalism, literary and otherwise, has not been so stark. Race and its attendant realities in US culture profoundly link writer and subject and reader as well.

African American literary journalism, then, requires different paradigms than what scholars have been using to understand and explicate mainstream US literary journalism, paradigms that reflect not only the history outlined above but also the complicating factor of readership. If the black press arose in response to the white press's failure to represent the black community fairly or even at all, the twentieth century's civil rights movements slowly, if imperfectly, changed that, as mainstream papers and magazines hired black writers in response to gains in and protests for civil rights. Henry Louis Gates Jr. argues that the literature produced by African Americans is inherently double-voiced. As I have endeavored to show in my readings of an installment of Poston's "Prejudice and Progress in New York" and Hunter-Gault's "A Trip to Leverton," this holds true for the literary journalism as well and is especially acute when African Americans are writing in white-owned publications. Focusing on the dimension of double-voicedness itself helps bring to light a "black difference" in literary journalism: the need to negotiate the writer/reader relationship, a negotiation that has implications for both the function and aesthetics of the work, and which exists apart from the subject/object division we have seen to be so central to mainstream American literary journalism.

Notes

1 African American literary journalism in the nineteenth century reasonably includes antebellum slave narratives as well as writing by women especially during Reconstruction and beyond. Jennie Carter's work for the *Elevator* and Ida B. Wells's for the *New York Age* are two examples of the latter category.
2 See Sims's introduction to *Literary Journalism*, Kerrane and Yagoda's *The Art of Fact*, Hartsock's *A History of American Literary Journalism*, and Connery's *A Sourcebook of American Literary Journalism*, respectively, for these descriptors of non-literary journalism.
3 See Wolfe, *New Journalism*, 31–33; Sims, *Literary Journalists*, 4; Sims and Kramer, *Literary Journalism*, 5; Hartsock, *History*, 239; and Hartsock, *Literary Journalism*, 5.
4 Connery, *Sourcebook*, 11.
5 Connery, 15.
6 Sims and Kramer, *Literary Journalism*, 3.
7 Sims and Kramer, 14.
8 Sims and Kramer, 28.
9 Sims and Kramer, 30.
10 Kerrane and Yagoda, *Art of Fact*, 16.
11 Kerrane and Yagoda, 16.
12 Hartsock, *History*, 198.
13 Hartsock, 202, 203.
14 Hartsock, *Literary Journalism*, 4.
15 Hartsock, 151.
16 Washburn, *African American Newspaper*, 11.
17 Washburn, 18.
18 Washburn, 8.
19 Washburn, 9.
20 Nelson, *Black Press*.

21 Wolseley, *Black Press*, 17.
22 Washburn, *African American Newspaper*, 51.
23 Love, "Why the Black Press."
24 Washburn, *African American Newspaper*, 36.
25 See Washburn, *Question of Sedition*.
26 Carroll, *Race News*, 3–4. Carroll cites W. E. B. Du Bois, Langston Hughes, and Ida B. Wells as three writers whose work shifted among a range of genres—formal essays to columns, poetry to columns, and memoir to news reporting, respectively.
27 Carroll, 4.
28 Gates, "Writing, 'Race,'" 1144.
29 Gates, 1138.
30 Gates, 1142.
31 Gates, 1142.
32 Gates, *Figures in Black*, xxi.
33 Carroll, *Race News*, 140.
34 *Report of the National Advisory Commission*, 210.
35 *Report of the National Advisory Commission*, 210.
36 Carroll, *Race News*, 119.
37 Hauke, introduction to Poston, *A First Draft of History*, xxii.
38 Hunter-Gault, *In My Place*, 241.
39 Streitmatter, *Raising Her Voice*, 132.
40 Hauke, introduction to Poston, *A First Draft of History*, xx–xxi; Carroll, *Race News*, 158.
41 Moore, "Quietly, Heroic 'Alibi Negro,'" 28.
42 Hauke, *Ted Poston*, 76.
43 Hauke, 77.
44 Carroll, *Race News*, 68.
45 DelConte, "Why *You* Can't Speak," 207.
46 DelConte, 208.
47 DelConte, 204.
48 Fludernik, "Second-Person Narrative," 455.
49 Fludernik, 467.
50 Fludernik, 466.
51 Richardson, "Poetics and Politics," 312.
52 Richardson, 327, 314.
53 Richardson, 327.
54 Du Bois, "Of Our Spiritual Strivings," 8–9.
55 Du Bois, 8.
56 Poston, "Prejudice and Progress," 109.
57 Poston, 110.
58 Du Bois, "Of Our Spiritual Strivings," 7.
59 Poston, "Prejudice and Progress," 110.
60 Poston, 110.
61 Poston, 113.
62 Hunter-Gault, "Surviving School Desegregation."
63 Hunter-Gault, "I Remember," 7.
64 Hunter-Gault, "Legendary Journalist."
65 Gates, *Signifying Monkey*, xxii–xxiii.
66 Gates, xxi.
67 Gates, xxv.
68 Mitchell, "Mr. Hunter's Grave," 510.
69 Kunkel, *Man in Profile*, 190.
70 Kunkel, 190.
71 Mitchell, "Mr. Hunter's Grave," 506.
72 Hunter, "Trip to Leverton," 95.
73 Hunter, 106.
74 Mitchell, "Mr. Hunter's Grave," 518–19.
75 Hunter, "Trip to Leverton," 109.
76 Hunter, 109.

77 Mitchell, "Mr. Hunter's Grave," 509.
78 Gates, *Signifying Monkey*, 129.
79 Gates, 132.
80 Gates, 136.
81 Gates, 136.
82 Gates, 131.
83 Gates, 46–47.
84 Gates, 78, 82.
85 Hunter, "Trip to Leverton," 106.
86 Hunter, 113.
87 Hunter, 113.
88 See, for example, Hartsock, *History*, 41–79.

Bibliography

Carroll, Fred. *Race News: Black Journalists and the Fight for Racial Justice in the Twentieth Century*. Urbana, IL: University of Illinois Press, 2017.

Connery, Thomas B., ed. *A Sourcebook of American Literary Journalism: Representative Writers in an Emerging Genre*. New York: Greenwood Press, 1992.

DelConte, Matt. "Why *You* Can't Speak: Second-Person Narration, Voice, and a New Model for Understanding Narrative." *Style* 37, no. 2 (Summer 2003): 204–19.

Du Bois, W. E. B. "Of Our Spiritual Strivings." In *The Souls of Black Folk*, 7–15. New York: Vintage Books, 1990.

Fludernik, Monika. "Second-Person Narrative as a Test Case for Narratology: The Limits of Realism." *Style* 28, no. 3 (Fall 1994): 445–79.

Gates, Henry Louis, Jr. *Figures in Black: Words, Signs, and the "Racial" Self*. New York: Oxford University Press, 1987.

———. *The Signifying Monkey: A Theory of African-American Literary Criticism*. New York: Oxford University Press, 1988.

———. "Writing, 'Race,' and the Difference It Makes." In *The Critical Tradition: Classic Texts and Contemporary Trends*, edited by David H. Richter, 1132–44. Shorter 3rd ed. Boston, MA: Bedford St. Martin's, 2016. Originally published in *Critical Inquiry* 12, no. 1 (Autumn 1985): 1–20.

Hartsock, John C. *A History of American Literary Journalism: The Emergence of a Modern Narrative Form*. Amherst, MA: University of Massachusetts Press, 2000.

———. *Literary Journalism and the Aesthetics of Experience*. Amherst, MA: University of Massachusetts Press, 2016.

Hauke, Kathleen A. Introduction to *A First Draft of History*, by Ted Poston, xvii–xxvii. Athens, GA: University of Georgia Press, 2000.

———. *Ted Poston: Pioneer American Journalist*. Athens, GA: University of Georgia Press, 1998.

Hunter, Charlayne. "A Trip to Leverton." *New Yorker*, April 24, 1965.

Hunter-Gault, Charlayne. *In My Place*. New York: Farrar, Straus and Giroux, 1992.

———. "I Remember." *Change* 11 (October 1979): 6–7, 76. https://doi.org/10.1080/00091383.1979.10569704.

———. "Legendary Journalist Charlayne Hunter-Gault Reflects on the Day She Desegregated the U. of Georgia." Interview by Amy Goodman. *Democracy Now!*, March 2, 2018. www.democracynow.org/2018/3/2/legendary_journalist_charlayne_hunter_gault_reflects.

———. "Surviving School Desegregation, and Finding Hope in #NeverAgain." *New Yorker*, February 28, 2018.

Kerrane, Kevin, and Ben Yagoda, eds. *The Art of Fact: A Historical Anthology of Literary Journalism*. New York: Scribner, 1997.

Kunkel, Thomas. *Man in Profile: Joseph Mitchell of "The New Yorker."* New York: Random House, 2015.

Love, David. "Why the Black Press Is More Relevant than Ever." CNN Opinion Series, November 30, 2017. www.cnn.com/2017/11/30/opinions/newsroom-diversity-mainstream-media-opinion-love/index.html.

Mitchell, Joseph. "Mr. Hunter's Grave." In *Up in the Old Hotel and Other Stories*, 504–36. New York: Pantheon Books, 1992. Originally published in *New Yorker*, September 22, 1956.

Moore, Keith R. "Quietly, Heroic 'Alibi Negro' Integrates City Newsroom." Review of *Ted Poston: Pioneer American Journalist*, by Kathleen A. Hauke. *New York Observer*, April 12, 1999, 28.

Nelson, Stanley, Jr., dir. *The Black Press: Soldiers without Swords*. Arlington, VA: PBS, 1999. Transcript available at www.pbs.org/blackpress/film/fulltranscript.html.

Poston, Ted. "Prejudice and Progress: The Negro in New York II." In *A First Draft of History*, edited by Kathleen A. Hauke, 109–15. Athens, GA: University of Georgia Press, 2000.

Report of the National Advisory Commission on Civil Disorders. Washington, DC: US Government Printing Office, 1968.

Richardson, Brian. "The Poetics and Politics of Second Person Narrative." *Genre* 24 (Fall 1991): 309–30.

Sims, Norman. *The Literary Journalists*. New York: Ballantine Books, 1984.

Sims, Norman, and Mark Kramer, eds. *Literary Journalism: A New Collection of the Best American Nonfiction*. New York: Ballantine Books, 1995.

Streitmatter, Rodger. *Raising Her Voice: African-American Women Journalists Who Changed History*. Lexington, KY: University Press of Kentucky, 1994.

Washburn, Patrick S. *The African American Newspaper: Voice of Freedom*. Evanston, IL: Northwestern University Press, 2006.

———. *A Question of Sedition: The Federal Government's Investigation of the Black Press during World War II*. New York: Oxford University Press, 1986.

Wolfe, Tom. *The New Journalism*. New York: Harper and Row, 1973.

Wolseley, Roland E. *The Black Press, U.S.A.* 2nd ed. Ames, IA: Iowa State University Press, 1990.

28
METABOLIZING GENRES
American Poetry and Literary Journalism

William E. Dow

As Andrea Pitzer has recently pointed out, "When people talk about journalism tottering off into quaint irrelevance, there is a tendency to compare journalism to poetry."[1] Alongside actual combinations of poetry and journalism, such comparisons, particularly in reference to twentieth-century and contemporary American poetry, ask some hard questions for literary journalism studies. Can a poetic use of literary journalism create an ethos that might be arrived at in a fashion that strikes the imagination and makes observation a little richer than what it was? Can poetry be a more direct narrative mode than has been historically imagined for narrative journalism? How can scholars best confront the fact that contemporary American poets are increasingly writing "documentary" poems that "report" on events and that journalists are resorting to poetic prose in order to convey perspectives that cannot be presented in any other form?[2] "Poetry seems unlikely to replace standard print narratives and even less likely to supplant the inverted pyramid," as Pitzer argues, but "the future of poetry and the future of news"[3] may be intertwined more tightly than critics have previously recognized. "Not static or universal but situational, contextual, shifting depending on the other [nonpoetry discourses] engaged,"[4] poetry certainly deserves its place in debates on genres within literary-journalistic texts and on notions of representations and stylistic innovations in journalism.[5]

The poets Charles Reznikoff (1894–1976), Muriel Rukeyser (1913–80), Mark Nowak (b. 1964), C. D. Wright (1949–2016), and Claudia Rankine (b. 1963) did, or are doing, some of their best and most influential work in long poems that encompass a large documentary and literary-journalistic picture. These poets offer a range of versions of how poetry and journalism have evolved together and work together in narrative reporting while at the same time showing the variety of possibilities open to poets about the uses of journalism. Each poet specializes in reconciling the language of information with the language of art through their poetic discourses and each sheds much light on the question of what poetry is—or perhaps what it does or might do. In the tradition of American poets who employ literary-journalistic and documentary devices in their poetry and/or integrate distinctly poetic forms into their journalism (e.g., Walt Whitman, Adrienne Rich), these five poets show representative meeting points in an American tradition of experimental poetry and journalism.[6]

For Reznikoff, his distinct and direct correlation between the news and poetry was derived from the testimonials of the Nuremberg and Eichmann trials, as documented in *Holocaust* (1975), and from court cases, as in the multivolume project about the United States, *Testimony: The United States (1885–1915)* (1934). *Testimony* will be discussed later in this chapter. Rukeyser's most famous example of news-poetry concerns the two thousand miners who contracted silicosis in the 1930–31 Gauley Bridge disaster, as depicted in her long poem *The Book of the Dead* (1938). Nowak's poetry-news testimonies are composed from the present-day disenfranchised of America's rust belt and postindustrial culture, as chronicled in *Revenants* (2000), *Shut Up Shut Down* (2004), and *Coal Mountain Elementary* (2009). For Wright, her journalistic-poetic method in *One Big Self: An Investigation* (2003) and *One with Others* (2010) is an accretion of images, a registering of a bevy of voices, and an engagement with politics, daily life, journalism (sometimes fictionalized), and the personal lyric. Rankine's *Don't Let Me Be Lonely: An American Lyric* (2004) and *Citizen: An American Lyric* (2014) share stylistic and thematic preoccupations with Reznikoff, Rukeyser, Nowak, and Wright, especially in Rankine's journalistic-poetic insistence on the relations of trauma and racism to the American psyche. Taken together, these five poets, in attempting to do justice to both poetry and journalism, can be seen as significant players in the history of American poetry's relation to American journalism.

In the context of some of their most important long poems, this chapter will examine how these five poets get the news *into* their poems and how they transform human suffering, racial segregation, and industrial tragedies into a new political poetic based on case histories and profiles of families, communities, industries, prisoners, and victims of hate crimes. A common thread that emerges in the work of Reznikoff, Rukeyser, Nowak, Wright, and Rankine is their fidelity to the voices of others: how these poets serve as a poetic witness to witnesses; how they stress the reported characters of events through legal testimony, reportage, interviews, mixed media, and newspapers; and how they alternate between poetry and prose to create their profiles.[7]

In *Testimony*, *Book of the Dead*, *Shut Up Shut Down*, *One Big Self*, *One with Others*, and *Citizen*, these voices of others, many extracted from newspaper accounts, refracted through the very different lenses of newspaper and poetry, underscore the idea that "truth" does not come only through direct, non-figurative, un-ornamented language. Their poetic profiles implicitly acknowledge and interrogate the limitations of language. At the same time, the truth of human suffering cannot fit into an everyday language (the tacit assumption of journalism) because human truth surpasses fact. By incorporating poeticity into their profiles—through interstices opened up by figurative language, ambiguity, symbol, sound relationships, visuals, and rhythmic patterns—the five poets get the reader beyond simply absorbing facts and into a responsive engagement with them because that (emotional, affective) engagement is a crucial part of the truth. With a special focus on how their profiles respond to cultural and personal catastrophes from Depression-era to contemporary America, this chapter examines the presence of such discourses as part of a largely unrecognized American poetic tradition.

My argument is also a response to what I see as an inadequate taxonomy regarding certain "social forms" of experimental American poetry from the 1930s to the present. Nowak, a contemporary American poet, can usefully be seen as extending the legacy and poetic traditions of such poets from the American 1930s and 1940s as Rukeyser, Edwin Rolfe, Sol Funaroff, Kenneth Fearing, and Reznikoff. The taxonomy that I'll take issue with is the grouping of such writers as documentary or "modern mass media" poets[8]—or mere "extenders of the document."[9] Although these poets were working out of a documentary culture that had infiltrated modernist fiction—especially following the economic events of 1929—their poetry is much more than "juxtapos[ed] snatches of discourse drawn from diverse registers and locations."[10] Rather, there are hard strains of objective journalistic discourse in their profiles that resist the inclusive categories of "documentary style" or a "documentary (post-)modernism" to which their poetry is frequently assigned.[11]

Charles Reznikoff

Suburb
If a naturalist came to this hillside,
He'd find many old newspapers among the weeds
to study.[12]

Charles Reznikoff's short poem "Suburb" (1934) suggests the importance he gave to the materials of daily life, such as "old newspapers among the weeds to study." But for his poetry, he focused foremost on legal testimonies, which he edited and transformed into journalistic-like literary materials. To this end, Reznikoff was obsessed with the discursive properties of official records, an obsession that underlies his tradition as a documentarian, social protester, and poet as journalist.[13] *Testimony* and *Holocaust* demonstrate how Reznikoff uses the objective language of such records to create his poetic profiles. Thus, in accord with such an aesthetic, he belonged to a group of poets known as the "Objectivists" (which included Louis Zukofsky, George Oppen, Basil Bunting, and others)—poets who were "commit[ted] to poetry as a mode of epistemology and an ethical or political praxis."[14] "Objectivism represents an emphasis on the 'detail, not mirage' of energies in the larger world," as Michael Davidson has argued, and its poetics "stresses exactitude and sincerity, visual immediacy over introspection and irony."[15] Relying on such Objectivist applications, *Holocaust* and *Testimony* are a direct result of Reznikoff's work in a legal publishing house summarizing court records in the 1930s. Originally published as a prose text, *Testimony* was transformed into a lengthy two-volume meditation on the United States that Reznikoff finished in 1975.

Testimony is Reznikoff's declaration that national history, rather than being written from "the standpoint of an individual … could be written from every standpoint—as many standpoints as were provided by the witnesses themselves."[16] Like Rukeyser, Nowak, and Wright, Reznikoff was part of a documentary culture that wished to repurpose traditional journalism and "objective" discourse into an alternative materialist history based on what can be termed journalistic and sociological findings, but ultimately resembling a kind of poetic journalism. Reznikoff relies on an objectification that does not disclaim empathy but rather provides historical surfaces that can capture reader identification. To this end, his multiple-perspective history is not meant to be absolutist or comprehensive but rather evocative and suggestive. Here is Reznikoff on his composition process for *Testimony*:

> But I throw out an awful lot to achieve my purpose. It's not a complete picture of the United States at any time, by any means. It's only a part of what happened, a reality that I felt as a reader and could not portray adequately in any other way.[17]

This method funnels into the poetic devices behind Reznikoff's profiles in *Testimony*: his specific reliance on individual figures whose testimonies are based usually not on feelings but on what the speaker "saw or heard."[18] Largely derived from "bare facts"[19] and a paring and intensifying of such facts, his profiles establish a "linguistic production within the realm of law."[20] But crucially, Reznikoff prioritizes the evidential or communicative aspects of language over any of its metaphorical or figural qualities.[21] Culled from criminal court transcripts, his profiles come directly from the voices of victims, witnesses, and perpetrators—but are ungrounded in specific historical references. In effect, as if placing the reader in the middle of a described action for which the historical context has not been given (though general timeframes and regions—e.g., West, North, South, 1885–1890—are provided), Reznikoff ahistoricizes the facts.[22]

Testimony chronicles these perpetual facts of human suffering, cruelty, and mistreatment in a world beset by class inequalities, racism, violence, and poverty. Divided under such headings as "social life," "domestic scenes," "boys and girls," "property," "negroes," "persons and places," "market," "railroads," and "machine age," these profiles, in journalistic terms, resemble the general categories of crime reporting and human-interest stories.[23] But Reznikoff's poeticity transforms such documents into a distinctive perceptual field that focuses on portraying human encounters and conflicts in sharp, evocative ways. He uses imagistic techniques in such a way as to construct complex ways of perception.[24] In so doing, Reznikoff relies on the language of common speech, the presentation of images that are concrete and definite, and avoids offering complete statements or interpretations. As he affirms in a 1969 interview,

> In *Testimony* the speakers whose words I use are all giving testimony about what they actually lived through. … What I wanted to do was to create by selection, arrangement, and the rhythm of the words used as a mood or feeling.[25]

While providing social narratives that stress the poeticized discursiveness of official records, Reznikoff attempts to translate raw data into feeling and perception.

Unlike the standard newspaper profile that uses the background of a particular person as a stepping stone for another focus, for Reznikoff, biographical fact is neither backgrounded nor foregrounded but is of equal value to everything else he describes in the profile. Conversely, Reznikoff's biographical sketches (and this pertains to most of the *Testimony* profiles: e.g., "Episode in the Life of a Laundress"; "Death of a Salesman"; "A Divorce") almost always include, like the standard journalistic profile, some of the major elements of hard news stories: murder, physical abuse, domestic disputes, crime, betrayal, theft, and so on. Fusing a journalistic authenticity (e.g., "She had been cut by a razor on her right forearm and across the/right shoulder"[26]) with an imagistic starkness and condensation ("although the boy kept begging him to stop,/until he was interrupted again—/by the boy's death"[27]), he has it both ways.

In fact, in evoking such hard news, Reznikoff's profiles adhere to the standard tenets of journalistic objectivity (e.g., fairness, disinterestedness, factuality, and nonpartisanship); they exude a pervasive neutrality, however poeticized they might be. At the same time, his profiles offer a mode of relatedness[28] that depends on a denotative rather than a connotative relationship to his material[29] and, in some cases, include an implicit interview structure (an alternative to that commonly found in journalistic profiles).

Testimony's cumulative impact is much more than an objectified materialist history. The referenced actions spreading across a range of social spheres and institutions—and with the social actors mostly stripped of psychological gloss—suggest how the collection is an indictment of industrial destructiveness, purposefully set in a period (1885–1915) in which America was changing from an agrarian republic to an industrial superpower. But while writing a poetry that refuses the spirit of transcendence so as to focus on the brutality of the commonplace and everyday, Reznikoff allows the residual outlines of the original plaintive appeals to appear in their ahistorical significance—albeit with a renewed social purpose. He follows the textual traces without trying to eliminate their archival aura, thus creating a cumulative history of diverse profiles based on daily-occurring criminal aberrations and transgressions. Significantly, like successful "objective" journalistic profiles, the profiles in *Testimony* make a point about their subjects (many of whom come off as strong-willed, ineffectual, avenging, indifferent, and cruel), although in a fragmented, discontinuous, and partial way. The recorded disputes are often based on petty grievances and minor altercations that become dramatic and deadly. Yet, as Stephen Fredman argues, "Reznikoff writes a poetry that shows us 'where danger lies' and how an awareness of it can cut through self-delusion and open us to humane encounters beyond the bounds of the social group with which we identify."[30] In doing so, I would add, Reznikoff invites us into these variously absurd and tragic worlds in which decisive moments transpire.

But it is Reznikoff's craft in composing or "editing" the profiles more than the content itself that produces such effects. These brief and assorted profiles, monotonal in pitch, are not about direct objective witnessing but rather about *re*-witnessing—or witnessing differently—in a poeticized way; they are not mere photographic juxtapositions but rather suggestions for the necessity of interpretation and for opening the profiles into a social world of language. As Reznikoff has argued, "[Ideal poetic language] is restricted almost to the testimony of a witness in a court of law,"[31] his way of creating, as Louis Zukofsky puts it in his poem, "A"-6, "a desire for what is objectively perfect."[32]

Muriel Rukeyser

Like Charles Reznikoff's *Testimony*, C. D. Wright's *One with Others*, and Mark Nowak's *Shut Up Shut Down*, Muriel Rukeyser's *The Book of the Dead* announces the continuing significance of experimental American poetry in relation and in response to objectified news in the twentieth and twenty-first centuries.[33] Documenting an outbreak of silicosis in Gauley Junction, West Virginia, and its effect on miners working for Union Carbide and Carbon Corporation, *The Book of the Dead* was first published in Rukeyser's 1938 collection, *U.S. 1*. The historic tragedy at Gauley Junction, the most serious industrial accident in the United States up to that time, led to a class-action suit and congressional investigation. In the poem, Rukeyser draws on legal documents, interviews, scientific reports, documentary film techniques, and journalistic devices to create her profiles of ordinary people. Along with her first collection, *Theory of Flight* (1935), and early journalism, this volume has contributed most strongly to giving Rukeyser the moniker of activist and poet-journalist, prompting Adrienne Rich to call her "poet journalist pioneer mother."[34]

But Rukeyser's work as an actual investigative reporter began long before the Gauley Bridge disaster with her coverage of the 1932 Scottsboro trial in which nine young black men were accused of raping two white women. Through her journalistic efforts, she also supported the Spanish Loyalists during the Spanish Civil War in the 1930s and various Vietnam protest campaigns in the 1970s.[35] As Julius Lobo has argued in reference to the journalistic coverage of Gauley Bridge,

> By 1935, news of the Gauley Bridge disaster began to circulate, at first in radical venues such as the *People's Press* and *New Masses*. But as *Time*, *The Nation*, and *The New York Times* began to take notice, especially in the wake of the House subcommittee hearings in early 1936, the death at Gauley Bridge became national news.[36]

Rukeyser's *The Book of the Dead* is her poeticized "journalistic" response to the disaster.

In basing her profiles on such contemporary news events as the Gauley disaster, Rukeyser found one of her most powerful natural expressions in the combinative form of poetry and news. *The Book of the Dead* juxtaposes lyric forms and modernistic and mythic structures (i.e., the Egyptian Book of the Dead, featuring a cyclic structure of burial and rebirth, and a journey to an underworld) with the discursive forms of objective journalism. Moreover, Rukeyser's version of *in medias res*—relating her news from the midpoint rather than the beginning of a testimony (paralleling Reznikoff)—signals her artistry of conjoining dramatic effect with the documents she acquired as an investigative reporter. These documents included those from Indiana representative Glenn Griswold, the chairman of the subcommittee investigating Gauley Bridge, and the April 1,

1936, *Congressional Record*.[37] Through such techniques, Rukeyser makes her poeticized profiles—pared down and presented through her "editing"—essential to her news component.

The collection's free-verse style, like that of *Testimony*, is best suited to what is heard and the representation of living speech that Rukeyser, like Reznikoff, had an uncanny capacity for capturing. In line with this position, Rukeyser believed there were essentially two kinds of poems: one of

> unverifiable facts, based in dreams, in sex, in everything that can be given to other people only through the skill and strength by which it is given; and the other kind being the document, the poem that rests on material evidence.[38]

With a heightened emphasis on recorded speech and aural forms, Rukeyser's writing connects these two worlds.

Yet the reader must also play her part. Like Reznikoff, Rukeyser conceived of her reader foremost as a "witness." As she states in *The Life of Poetry* (1949), "I should like to use another word: 'audience,' or 'reader' or 'listener' seems inadequate. I suggest the old word 'witness,' which includes the act of seeing and knowing by personal experience, as well as the act of giving evidence."[39] In writing *The Book of the Dead* as a "journalistic narrative," with the reader as a central witness,[40] Rukeyser might have "forfeited some of the advantages of journalism (immediacy of impact, accessibility, and the presumption of objectivity),"[41] but she compensates for this by creating a kind of poetry that highlights a richness and density of voice, a subjective authorial engaged perspective, and an alternative modernistic discourse. Most specifically, her sense of modernity, rejecting many of the premises of high modernism, envisioned shared problems of human existence at the same time that it sought to recover—as did Langston Hughes, Meridel Le Sueur, Richard Wright, and others—an ethical and social function within literary modernism.

A profile from *The Book of the Dead* that perhaps most insists on an innovative binary form of poetry and journalism is "Statement: Philippa Allen." But even the introductory poem to the collection, "The Road," which is cast in the form of direct address, already suggests the importance of journalism—"reading the papers with morning inquiry"—for preparing to "take the road into your own country."[42] Along with "bring[ing] down the maps," "select[ing] the mountains," and "travel[ing] the passes," the poem's speaker implies that a knowledge of the news is also necessary if one is to be "tied" to the meaning of the road.[43]

Following this introductory poem and its companion piece, "West Virginia," the collection's first profile, "Statement: Philippa Allen," is a mixture of recorded human speech, testimonial interviews, and statistical evidence. Based on the actual transcripts of Philippa Allen's 1936 testimony at the hearing before the House of Representatives Subcommittee on Labor, the poem introduces the reader to the history and present circumstances of the Gauley Bridge disaster through Rukeyser's interview and first-person testimonial structure. Echoing the interview techniques of *Testimony*, Rukeyser makes a verbatim use of the congressional transcripts, but her editing changes the order of Allen's testimony and transposes it into a question-and-answer format to enhance dramatic intensity and effect.[44] Allen's statements establish the basic information about the Gauley tunnel disaster: "The rock through which they were boring was of a high/silica content. … The tunnel is part of a huge water-power project/begun, latter part of 1929/direction: New Kanawha Power Co./subsidiary of Union Carbide & Carbon Co."[45]

The Allen testimony sets up the kind of poetic-journalistic mixtures Rukeyser uses throughout *The Book of the Dead*: interviews with and first-person testimonies of local witnesses, workers, and their families; juxtapositions of lyric and didactic modes; and juxtapositions of matter-of-fact statistical information ("2000 men were/employed there/period, about 2 years/drilling, 3.75 miles of tunnel"[46]) with personal observations and interpretations ("I was doing social work/down there, I first heard of what we were pleased to call the/Gauley tunnel tragedy").[47]

Similar in objective to *Testimony*, *The Book of the Dead* becomes a public language fused with a private discourse. Rukeyser's poeticized journalistic diagnostics give way to a demand for accountability that echoes through the dramatic monologues of all her profiles, including those of George Robinson and Juanita Tinsley. As David Kadlec has argued, Rukeyser, though effusive in her praise of government photographers like Dorothea Lange, Walker Evans, and Ben Shahn, was "shar[p] in her poetic condemnation of conventional documentary images" and wished to expand the perspective of "the New Deal documentary apparatus."[48] Rukeyser's (partisan) poetic profiles, perhaps less a mode of expressing the world than statements of being in it, allowed her to move quickly in this direction.

Mark Nowak

Following in the steps of Reznikoff and Rukeyser, Mark Nowak creates poetry that is political *and* textual. Nowak relies on various contexts and forms—photographs, personal testimonials, hip-hop, rap music, etymological questionings, and lyric—for his narrative story. By doing so, he both "emphasiz[es] that all documents, including photographs and including his own poems, are always incomplete" and demonstrates that "knowledge, experience, and understanding are necessarily framed and necessarily limited."[49] But although Nowak, as David Ray Vance argues, shows us the limitations of such individual forms, he also reveals, in the tradition of Reznikoff and Rukeyser, that poetry "should be based on the materials being written about."[50] While extending and responding to the poetic legacies of such politically engaged poets as Kenneth Fearing and Rukeyser, Nowak writes not only about the news but experiments with his own versions of "writing like a newspaper,"[51] of conceiving of the news, in Michael Schudson's sense, as "a form of culture [that] incorporates assumptions about what matters, what makes sense, what time and place we live in, what range of considerations we should take seriously."[52]

Nowak experimentally assigns to the news an interpretive function in his poems that it lacks in its original state; in this sense and in many others, he reveals new possibilities for a poetry that has more in common with literary-journalistic expression than with documentary genres. Along with the work of such contemporary poets as Kenneth Goldsmith, Vanessa Place, and the French poet Franck Leibovici, Nowak's poetry shows the limitations of applying the same conceptualizations and categories to twenty-first-century poetic forms that one might use for examining 1930s documentary texts.

A poet and labor activist, Nowak is the author of three poetry collections: *Revenants*, *Shut Up Shut Down*, and *Coal Mountain Elementary*, the first of which I'll focus on in my discussion of his profiles. In *Shut Up Shut Down*, Nowak, while demonstrating the political necessity for remembering—and reconceiving the past creates a confluence of counter-narratives: first-person working-class testimonials set against articles from such publications as *Harper's Magazine*, *U.S. News and World Report*, and the *Nation*; unpeopled photographs of abandoned factories and construction sites weighing against internal corporate memos and sound bites from politicians; etymological and grammatical explanations juxtaposed with the common and pedagogical use of such words as *capitalization* and *unemployment*.

Shut Up Shut Down, like his most recent work, *Coal Mountain Elementary*, has the aim of securing emotional truths that go far beyond any neoliberal views or mass cultural representations.[53] Nowak's subjects are inseparable from the systems—industrial, corporate, technological, historical, stylistic—that have evolved to account for and represent the people he depicts.[54] Nowak provides counter-narratives to such systems presenting the material facts and everyday tribulations of his subjects by evoking a "close, continuing participation/in the lives of others."[55] This practice relates directly to Nowak's sense of "authorship." As he states in a recent interview, "I'm less and less interested in single authorship and more and more interested in the potential for new forms of collaboration."[56] With such an objective in mind, *Shut Up Shut Down* extends beyond documentary conventions to explore dialogic relations that suit Nowak's creative repurposing and the integration of journalistic texts into his poetry. He uses factual journalism in his verse in ways that create his distinctive profiles of moral inquiry between self and society.

A representative profile in the first chapter from *Shut Up Shut Down*, "$00/LINE/STEEL/TRAIN," is that of the disenfranchised Frank Albert. In this poem, Nowak layers Joseph L. Galloway's report, "True Grit in a Steel Town" on the difficult times in Steelton, Pennsylvania,[57] with his own visually resonant lines. The poem is intersticed with contrastive and complementary sensory representations:

> Read the writing on the Wal-Mart. **The town has never been the same, says Frank Albert, 71 … whose home fell to the bulldozers.** In the U.S. Steel Gary Works yard, someone spray painted "House of Pain" on an empty coal car. **We lost a lot of people when the West Side went. There just weren't enough homes for those who wanted to stay.** Under the (Capital) cover of darkness the "HALT!" signs go unread. **Albert is still president of the West Side Hose Co., the volunteer fire department of a neighborhood that no longer exists.** Doors (scrape), doors (stain), doors (including or only their frames). **We still have meetings, he says.**[58]

The phrases in bold face are taken from Galloway's report. While such phrases serve as distinct and unaltered components to Nowak's poetry, they also function as interstices between visual markers ("spray painted 'House of Pain,'" "'HALT!' signs") and auditory evocations ("Doors (scrape)"). The story of Frank Albert is contextualized as tragically typical of the dismemberment of American industry ("U.S. Steel") and the corporate exploitation of workers ("Wal-Mart"). The speaker of the poem urges us to "read" the visual markers accompanied by the case of Albert, specifically the bulldozing of his home, as a metonym for the demise of Steelton ("the government bought and bulldozed 452 West Side houses, displacing more than 2,000 people. Few of them could find new homes in Steelton, hemmed in as it is by the mill and the river and other town boundaries").[59] In this way, the text, constantly pulling toward some kind of objectivity, is haunted, even subsumed, by the news reports and nonfictional excerpts that it deploys in the poem or refers to outside of it.

Nowak uses his sources as basic components of his poetry making them bridge into social interpretations. In the first part of *Shut Up Shut Down*, they include books on American labor (e.g., "Arnowitz, Stanley. *From the Ashes of the Old: American Labor and America's Future*. Boston: Houghton Mifflin, 1998"), studies of female steel workers (e.g., "Deaux, Kay and Joseph C. Ullman. *Women of Steel: Female Blue-Collar Workers in the Basic Steel Industry*. New York: Praeger, 1983"), analyses of race and class (e.g., "Roediger, David. *The Wages of Whiteness: Race and the Making of the American Working Class*. London: Verso, 1991") as well as reports culled from newspapers and magazines (e.g., "Galloway, Joseph L. 'True Grit in a Steel Town.' *U.S. News and World Report*. June 12, 1995: 30, 32")—all of which serve to document the industrial closures he interprets. In conventional and modernist documentary fiction (e.g., works by Theodore Dreiser, Émile Zola, John Dos Passos, James T. Farrell), the author presents the document to the reader "seem[ing] to sa[y] make of it what you will."[60] Taking a different tack, although not giving parenthetical citations or footnotes for his quoted material, Nowak inclusively identifies each source he uses in the "Works Cited" pages at the end of each of the five parts of the volume. He highlights his citations as fundamental, irreplaceable *sources* for his poetic project.

The nonfictional forms in *Shut Up Shut Down* seem to be inherently poetic, just as the poetic forms seem to be inherently prose-like. This is a tribute collection in which the profiled subjects are reflected in taxonomies (i.e., the term *employment*), worker testimonials, sociological statistics, and lyric ruminations. Similar to Reznikoff, Nowak uses prose paragraphs and verse forms to produce an *indirect* emotional effect rather than using an authorial commentary or engaging in a metaphorical discourse or relying on abstractions. In effect, Nowak creates his visceral and experiential effects through an assortment and juxtaposition of nonfictional sources and a verbatim quoting of these sources. Such is not the documentary poetics of a Muriel Rukeyser, in whose *The Book of The Dead* a strong central voice controls the contents and direction of the poem. Nor does it follow the tradition of James Agee's *Let Us Now Praise Famous Men* (1941), in which all documentary material is carefully sifted into personal interpretation and editorialized by a first-person narrator. Nowak's poetry differs as well from Reznikoff's "transcriptions of reality" as expressed in *Testimony* in which Reznikoff edits and changes the language of the original source material. Instead, Nowak creates in a very dispassionate, undidactic way what might best be seen as a twenty-first-century poetic praxis that comes much closer to a contemporary literary-journalistic aesthetic than conventional or "modernistic" documentary forms.

C. D. Wright

C. D. Wright, a poet from Arkansas, has been interpreted as a Southern writer and an experimentalist.[61] She is both but much more as well. In her introduction to *One Big Self*, she states, "The popular perception is that art is apart. I insist it is a part of."[62] In this regard, *One Big Self* is an ethical and political project, but Wright also identifies it, via the book's subtitle, as an "investigation": a gathering of evidence and a "resistance to the conventions of evidentiary writing."[63] While veering toward documentary conventions and investigative journalism, it comes close to a kind of poetry that draws on the personal lyric, quotation, found material, and a multiplicity of voices and tones to underline the poem's major motif: "nothing will be settled or made easy."[64] Although sometimes following the montage aesthetic of Rukeyser and the collage-based writings of John Dos Passos, Langston Hughes, and Kenneth Fearing, Wright also departs from this aesthetic by offering no reasoned solutions or facile judgments to the problems she exposes in the book. As Wright states in a recent interview, "I am attempting to write the text [*One Big Self*] for what turns out to be a very intimate form of portraiture. ... I would not want to distort what we see to suit what I want to say."[65] Originally published in 2003, featuring photographs by Deborah Luster, *One Big Self* portrays the prisoners, from four prisons in Louisiana, whom Luster and Wright photographed and wrote about.

While getting the news into her poetry through direct testimony (accrued during her visits), bumper stickers, road signage, prison data, inmate correspondence, and larger social conditions ("What they hold in common, their poverty"[66]), Wright presents a skepticism about poetry's documentary abilities. Alternating between a display of hard facts (e.g., a prisoner's crime, his or her earlier family life, a privatized prison industry driven by profit) in which Wright attempts to report what she sees (though to tell it slant) and an outswelling of fragments, lists, and lyrical passages, Wright's method reframes the totalizing awareness and omniscient qualities of documentary fiction, especially that from the 1930s.

In this regard, by creating her own "anti-genre" of the news and by "resisting poetry as an aestheticized escape from living history,"[67] Wright relies on a dialectic of reportage and lyrical abstraction. As Jennie Berner has argued, "The poem in particular deploys a kind of abstraction that violently wrenches readers from lived experience and locates them in a formal space. ... [I]t simultaneously solicits and forbids the viewer's [/reader's] identification with its subjects."[68] At the same time, however, Wright is coolly astute about the pragmatic "truths" she turns to and formulates. As she concedes in her introduction, "The obvious truth, people are people. Equally, the damage is never limited to perpetrator and victim. Also, that the crimes are not the sum of the criminal any more than anyone is entirely separable from their acts."[69] And Wright relies on a meticulous hyper-realistic display of detail in evoking the daily lives/profiles of the prisoners, from their language to their religious beliefs, from their reading to their favorite television series. Her outward-directed mimeticism is turned inward toward a lyrical present-mindedness, a ritual recursiveness, and a constant self-questioning ("We left before visiting hours ended. It wasn't our place to be there. It really wasn't in us to be there"[70]). To this end, her dialectic in *One Big Self* combines anecdotal forays with a rigorous and quantified analysis—"Not to idealize, not to judge, not to exonerate, not to aestheticize immeasurable levels of pain"—and with her more difficult task of "lay[ing] out the real feel of hard time."[71]

One with Others continues the kind of quirky, eclectic documentary collage technique that Wright established in *One Big Self*. Fusing lyric with evidentiary fact, the book chronicles events occurring in Arkansas at the time of a protest march (a four-day March against Fear, from West Memphis to Little Rock) led by Sweet Willie Wine, a Memphis activist. But the poem's primary purpose is to offer a memorial profile of Wright's friend, Margaret Kaelin McHugh, who participated in the march and was ostracized by her community because of it. The book, as Dan Chiasson contends, "retakes for poetry some of the 'real life' ground that it long ago ceded to other art forms."[72]

But *One with Others* can perhaps best be understood as animating a spectrum of discursive possibilities between the news and poetry. The collection alternates such historical moments and figures as Martin Luther King (33), the Los Angeles riots (39), Sonny Liston (51), and Vietnam war protests (99) with emotive sense data and the poet's elegiac impulses. Wright profiles V. by describing events through V.'s perspective, as in her feelings during the March against Fear:

> V: We had the water and the shoes in my car. There was a black man named/Stiles. [He was a midget.] He kept that water good and cold [for the marchers]. ... V: It was invigorating. It was the most alive I ever felt in my life.[73]

In this book of partly fictionalized journalism, much of it reading as a montage of recorded accounts and facts about an actual person, Wright loads the poetic onto a journalistic prose. By doing so, she demonstrates the possibility of generating a coherent aesthetic and form that recalibrates social fact while opening up fresh possibilities for literary-journalistic poetry.

Claudia Rankine

Similar to Nowak, Claudia Rankine in her collections *Don't Let Me Be Lonely* and *Citizen* disrupts the boundaries of the lyric to question facile political frameworks promulgated by mass media. Like Wright, Rankine creates an investigative poetry that pieces together documentary, reportage, and the poet's imagination—including testimonials, cultural documents, news reports, photos, sketches, graphs, facts, and statistics—and takes the form of a third-person and first-person lyrical prose. Still further, based on "subjectivity produced by the experience of identifying or being interpolated as 'black' in the U.S. ... in the context of a racist society,"[74] Rankine's poetic style can be aligned with an experimental African American poetry that includes Sonia Sanchez, Gwendolyn Brooks, Ed Roberson, and Harryette Mullen. In both *Don't Let Me Be Lonely* and *Citizen*, Rankine is at once a reporter, a collector of cultural artifacts, and an assembler of the diverse materials she presents.

The open mixed-genre form of *Don't Let Me Be Lonely* is particularly conducive to Rankine's investigative purposes and her relationship to the reader. As Tana Jean Welch argues,

"Rankine's poetic form requires active reading, while her subject—a first-person speaker's interaction with mass media—conveys the need to critically and actively read all forms of social media."[75] While positioning the contents of her volume (pharmaceutical abuses, the distribution of AIDS medication, the wars in Afghanistan and Iraq, concentration camp numbers, Mahalia Jackson, the United States Postal Service, etc.) between headline news and innovative experimentation, Rankine typically fragments her texts into short news stories. But as Christopher Nealon asserts, she "maintains a lyric attitude"[76] throughout the stories—or more precisely, establishes the "lyric" as a master category meant to be powerful enough to resist the intrusions of mediated representations and the "makeshift reality"[77] she comments on in her prose paragraphs.[78]

The profiles in *Don't Let Me Be Lonely* fit into this resistance by disclosing the insubstantiality of the broader cultural regimens, identifications, narratives, and definitions that underlie the dot-com boom of the 1990s and the Bush administration. The profile of Timothy McVeigh, "the boy next door," for instance, ends in a discussion of "forgiveness," something that was "not necessary to him."[79] The speaker concludes that forgiveness "is simply a death, a dying down in the heart, the position of the already dead."[80] The profile of James Byrd Jr., murdered by three white supremacists in 1998, is associated with "caring" and not caring:

> All the non-reporting is a distraction from Bush himself, the same Bush who can't remember if two or three people were convicted for dragging a black man to his death in his home state of Texas. *You don't remember because you don't care.*[81]

Those of Abner Louima, assaulted and sexually brutalized by NYC police officers in 1997; Amadou Diallo, shot forty-one times by four NYC police officers in 1998 ("All the shots, all forty-one never add up, never become plural, and will not stay in the past"[82]); and Mahalia Jackson are linked respectively to fear, loss, and spirituality. Juxtaposed to each profile is often the narrator's bodily reaction to the effects the profiled person has produced on her. In the case of Abner Louima, for example, the speaker states: "Sometimes I look into someone's face and I must brace myself—the blow on its way."[83] Through such profiles, the narrator hopes to compensate for the "non-reported" facts by providing a competing bodily (and historical, intellectual, and racial) register among the images and news stories she presents.

Citizen follows *Don't Let Me Be Lonely* in that it reads both as poetry and journalism.[84] The two works share a stylistic and thematic focus, relying on testimonies, featuring reproductions of artworks and photographs, incorporating media images into a written text, and combining quotations from artists, writers, and critics in order to examine, through the speaker's personal experiences, racial injustice in the US. Nick Laird notes in the *New York Review of Books* that "*Citizen* suggests that racial harmony is superficial—skin deep—and Americans revert readily and easily to their respective racial camps."[85] But Rankine's conversations on race depend on refashioning the lyric to lean towards the language of prose, "plain, direct, conversational, though simultaneously uncanny and reverberant."[86] Indeed, her work is on the cusp of poetry and an innovative journalistic-like critique: She does not depend on mere presentation but instead, in the grain of Rukeyser and Nowak, displays an ethical-political position that is meant to serve as social evidence and fact.

Most of her anecdotes and short news stories in *Citizen* originate from the profiles of racially coded, abused, and slain African Americans. Serving as sources and explanations, these profiles—both personal to the poet herself and widely recognized cultural and news images—are essential to an understanding of the book. In her profile of Serena Williams, Rankine raises the question of who speaks for her and through her:

For years you attribute to Serena Williams a kind of resilience appropriate only for those who exist in celluloid. Neither her father nor her mother nor her sister nor Jehovah her God nor NIKE camp could shield her ultimately from people who felt her black body didn't belong on their court, in their world.[87]

Through accretion and repetition, and use of the present tense—techniques found throughout the book—Rankine shows Williams as someone whose self-identification and individuation have been culturally stolen: "Serena's frustrations, her disappointments, exist within a system you understand not to try to understand in any fair-minded way because to do so is to understand the erasure of the self as systematic, as ordinary."[88] For Rankine, Williams is an analogue to black anger and daily experience ("American culture provokes black rage and then demonizes it when it is expressed"[89]) to which her addressed "you" must identify: "Every look, every comment, every bad call blossoms out of history, through her, onto you."[90]

Rankine's profiles in *Citizen* constantly challenge the legitimacy of media images that come to stand in for reality. As the speaker emphasizes in her assessment of Hurricane Katrina, "The fiction of the facts assumes innocence, ignorance, lack of intention, misdirection; the necessary conditions of a certain time and place."[91] As opposed to such images that "assum[e] randomness and indeterminancy,"[92] Rankine wishes to individuate and personalize her subjects, and does so, for example, by memorializing their deaths. The profile of Trayvon Martin, a seventeen-year-old African American shot by a neighborhood watch volunteer in 2012, takes the form of an emotive script in which the speaker pays tribute to Martin by emphasizing the possibility of multiple interpretations. Similarly, in her profile of James Craig Anderson, murdered in a hate crime in Jackson, Mississippi, she provides, in the form of a lyrical tribute, her interpretation of the events. For her profile of Mark Duggan, a black British man shot and killed by police in Tottenham, north London, in 2011, the speaker emphasizes the humanly tangible: "Grief comes out of relationships to subjects over time and not to any subject in theory."[93] Rankine thus retells media narratives in her own journalistic-lyrical way, suggesting that we need to interrogate our perceptions and interpretations of a mediated world. To put this another way, as Wright asserts in *One Big Self*, referring to the Heisenberg principle: "you change what you observe / EVERYTHING IS PERSONAL."[94]

Conclusion

The news-oriented poems of Reznikoff, Rukeyser, Nowak, Wright, and Rankine are meant to testify to the often unheard voices of people struggling to survive in the face of unspeakable violence, displacement, poverty, economic exploitation, and racism. The assortment of journalistic and nonfictional material in these poems[95] cannot be said to be wholly or exclusively discursive or polemical because this material contains within it a cohesive string of visceral, experiential, and affective language. In their profiles, all five poets make a journalistic language read like poetry, the end result of which asks some hard questions about the categorizations and conceptualization of poetic forms. In other words, thinking of the poem as a form of journalism can be vitally expansive because the status of poetry is then located within "the generic democracy of the written—[as] *a piece of writing*," undercutting any Romantic or "elitist aura of the Poem."[96] But, to push this point further, Reznikoff, Rukeyser, Nowak, Wright, and Rankine treat all the language in their cited documents as expressive features; in the poems under discussion, they tend to conceive of poetic language as factual expressions.

In the context of the profiles of these five poets, a vital question needs to be posed in literary journalism studies: Can literary journalism both inform and take the form of poetry? This group of poets demonstrates that it can. Although they were certainly not the first to do so—they are working from a long poetic tradition that includes Walt Whitman, Anna Louise Strong, Langston Hughes, W. C. Williams, Melvin Tolson, and Kenneth Fearing—they might very well be the most important twentieth- and twenty-first-century examples of poets who work historical documents, artifacts, and the news into their poetry.[97] They have developed narrative forms that create something qualitatively different from either poetry or nonfiction or what has been overtaxed (and oversimplified) as documentary or media poetry. Their poetry responds to cultural and personal stories, by beginning with a conception of the poem in relation to its social motivation. Without belaboring the point, I think the taxonomic distinction does make a difference: It points the way both to the past and to the future of social poetry itself, to such poetries that are willing to discard the existing poetry audience by creating works—and imagining alternative poetic lineages (e.g., based on nonfictional forms)—that call into being new kinds of language re-production and combination, and, perhaps most importantly, new methods of reading.

Notes

1 Pitzer, "Poetry as Narrative Journalism?"
2 See Garton, "Take Me to the Intersection."
3 Pitzer, "Poetry as Narrative Journalism?"
4 Ramazani, *Poetry and Its Others*, 60.
5 Too vague and static, most baseline definitions of journalism do not adequately consider journalism's transformations and possibilities for innovations (see Adam, *Notes*; Zelizer, *What Journalism Could Be*). And as Tom van Hout and Peter Burger have noted, "the craft of journalism is no longer exclusively defined by reporting. Instead, for a large majority of journalists, making news now means navigating dense information flows" ("Mediatization").

 In its treatment of journalism, this chapter centers on its possible values in relation to poetic forms. According to the American Press Institute, the value of journalism flows from its purpose to provide people with verified information they can use to make better decisions, and its practices, the most important of which is a systematic process—a discipline of verification—that journalists use to find not just the facts, but also the "truth about the facts" ("What Is the Purpose").

 In the discussion that follows, journalism, as distinct from nonfiction, can be defined, in its historicized forms, not only as assessing, creating, and presenting news and information, but in the sense that Zeliger gives it: "the very essence of journalism is creating an imagined engagement with events beyond the public reach." In the broadest sense, while journalism employs established forms and methods, nonfiction, as it offers provable fact, uses a much fuller range of techniques, some of which it shares with literature.

 The group of poets I discuss here interact with journalism on a wide discursive spectrum, engaging with journalism's mimeticism and its emphasis on actuality, while intensifying and expanding its temporal engagement—most specifically its orientation to the present. In so doing, I argue, these poets create new epistemic values for journalism and its possible narrative blendings, transformations, and new directions.
6 In such an interactive context, Barbie Zelizer's argument on journalistic practices is especially enlightening: "much journalism scholarship keeps alive the discussion of multiple news practices that are no longer pertinent to journalism. These include overused notions of neutral, objective and impartial journalism … a repeated regard for journalism as autonomous and revolutionary rather than a phenomenon that works incrementally and slowly with other forces of the environment … and [a perspective that] treats multi-platform stories and multi-media journalism as curiosities rather than evolutionary necessities" (*What Journalism Could Be*, 214). A bit eerily, most of the poets under discussion here, in their poetry, have either anticipated or confirmed such current conditions and innovations.
7 This chapter develops an earlier argument I presented in "Profiles of Lived Experience."
8 Kalaidjian, *American Culture*, 201.
9 Thurston, review of *The Objectivist Nexus*, 171.
10 Thurston, 173.
11 See Thurston, review of *The Objectivist Nexus*, and Kalaidjian, *American Culture*.
12 Reznikoff, *Poems*, 101. This line is taken from section 41 entitled "Suburb" contained in the larger poem, "Jerusalem the Golden" (1934). All quotations of Reznikoff's poetry, with the exceptions of those taken from *Testimony* and *Holocaust*, come from *The Poems of Charles Reznikoff, 1918–1975*.

13 Although this chapter points to Reznikoff's leftist politics, my concern here is principally with the genre and forms of his poetry. For a fuller discussion of his political positions, see Davidson, *Ghostlier Demarcations*, 135–70.
14 Thurston, review of *The Objectivist Nexus*, 344–45.
15 Davidson, *Ghostlier Demarcations*, 23.
16 Reznikoff, *Testimony* (New York: Objectivist Press, 1934), xii. As the editor of the Black Sparrow Book edition of *Testimony* (1978), Seamus Cooney has noted, "*Testimony: The United States* originally was prepared in four parts. The first, covering the years 1885–90, was published by New Directions in 1965. The second, covering 1891–1900, was published by the author in a small private edition of 200 copies in New York in 1968. The third part, 1901–10, is a book length typescript prepared by the author for publication before his death, and the final part, 1911–15, is a brief typescript found among his papers after his death with a letter showing it to have been completed before May 1975" (7). In the Black Sparrow Book edition, these parts were consolidated into two volumes. The citations of *Testimony* in this chapter will refer to the updated 2015 edition.
17 Reznikoff, "'Objectivist' Poet," 202.
18 Reznikoff, 202.
19 Franciosi, "'Detailing the Facts,'" 243.
20 Listoe, "'With All Malice,'" 112.
21 Seen everywhere in *Testimony*, this prioritizing can be linked to Reznikoff's fascination with courtroom testimony in which what matters are "the facts of the case, not what the witness saw and heard, nor the witnesses' feelings about, or interpretations of those facts" (Weinberger, introduction to *Testimony*, xiii). See, for example, the various incarnations of "Labor Troubles," "Domestic Scenes," "Social Life," "Property," "Whites and Blacks," and "Thefts—and Thieves" in the first four sections of *Testimony*.
22 Eliminating from his narratives most identifying information, Reznikoff focuses in on the narrative itself, and not historical markers per se. See, for example, such poems in Part Two of *Testimony* as "Sounds and Smells" (158), "Domestic Scenes" (175), "Negroes" (204), and "The Lodger" (223) in which what counts is not who does the telling, or when the scene takes place, but the personal testimony, the concrete details of a given sketch or profile. Put another way, the cumulative effect of *Testimony* resembles something of a "natural history," almost awaiting interpretation and prognosis. On this point, see Listoe, "'With All Malice.'"
23 See Watson, "Reznikoff's *Testimony*."
24 Throughout *Testimony*, Reznikoff relies on imagistic techniques to describe horrific violence or the effects of such a violence. Staying within an evidentiary frame, "Machine Age," for example, uses clear, precise language that depends on imagistic condensation (e.g., "the night was cold with a fall of snow"; "there was a steep grade and a reverse curve in the track," 24).

Rezinkoff's imagistic entries, covering a wide spectrum of social spheres and sociological data, challenge the reader's perceptual capacities because of their multiplicity in content and form. His poetics is one of observation that draws on a realist, anti-mythological worldview but at the same time includes, as Mark Scroggins has argued, "the sonorities of the King James Bible ... [and] the formal precisions of the Imagists and William Carlos Williams" ("Objectivists and the Left," 735).
25 Reznikoff, "'Objectivist' Poet," 202.
26 Reznikoff, *Testimony*, 159.
27 Reznikoff, 119.
28 Altieri, "Objectivist Tradition," 5.
29 Reznikoff's poetic denotativeness is reflected in his process of working with documentary sources in which he selectively pares and intensifies the affective power of supposedly actual facts.
30 Fredman, *Menorah for Athena*, 22.
31 Clover, "Words Pithy and Plain," 13.
32 Bernstein, introduction to *Louis Zukofsky*, xii.
33 Commenting on the hybridity of *The Book of the Dead*, a 1938 *Time* review chastised it as "part journalism, part lyricism, part Marxian mysticism" ("Rukeyser 2," 63). The journalistic aspects of the poem have received little critical attention, an area this chapter hopes to address.
34 Rich, "Atlas," 150.
35 See Lowney, *History*, 34; Vassar Encyclopedia.
36 Lobo, "From 'The Book of the Dead,'" 78.
37 Lobo, 78.
38 Rukeyser, "Education of a Poet," 226.
39 Rukeyser, *Life of Poetry*, 175.

40 For *The Book of the Dead* insisting on reader engagement for social purposes and positioning its reader as an active witness, see Lowney, *History*, 38–41.
41 Dayton, *Rukeyser's "The Book of the Dead,"* 21.
42 Rukeyser, *Book of the Dead*. All quotations from *The Book of the Dead* will be taken from an annotated electronic edition.
43 Rukeyser, *Book of the Dead*.
44 For details on Rukeyser's reordering Allen's testimony, see Shulman, *Power of Political Art*, 190.
45 Rukeyser, *Book of the Dead*.
46 Rukeyser.
47 Rukeyser.
48 Kadlec, "X-Ray Testimonials," 29.
49 Vance, "Mark Nowak," 348, 347.
50 Kees, "Fearing's Collected Poems," 266.
51 Barnard, *Great Depression*, 42.
52 Schudson, *Power of News*, 14.
53 This is so because in *Shut Up Shut Down* Nowak consistently captures working-class speech in its historicity and current forms; in so doing, he creates a counterpoint to the epistemologies and truth claims of neoliberalism and to such representations. See especially the poems in the section "Francine Michalek Drives Bread," 89–128.
54 In Nowak's poetry, the systems and the subjects "speak," which is why there is rarely any mediating author-narrator in his texts. See Shea, "Forms of Affiliation."
55 Nowak, *Revenants*, 92.
56 Nowak, "Interview," 463.
57 Galloway, "True Grit."
58 Nowak, *Shut Up Shut Down*, 24.
59 Galloway, "True Grit," 30, 32.
60 Hinken, "Documentary Fiction."
61 Goodman, "Politics," 41.
62 Wright, *One Big Self*, xiv.
63 Wright, ix.
64 Wright, 77.
65 Wright, "Looking for 'One Translatable Song.'"
66 Wright, *One Big Self*, 23.
67 Ramazani, "American Poetry."
68 Berner, "From Stenotype to Tintype."
69 Wright, *One Big Self*, xi.
70 Wright, xi.
71 Wright, xiv.
72 Chiasson, "Southern Discomfort."
73 Wright, *One with Others*, 5; square brackets in the original.
74 Shockley, *Renegade Poetics*, 9. Rankin's work, especially her long poems, counters many previous considerations of experimental poetry and poetics that limit their study to white poets, reductively assessing what an avant-garde can do or is. On this matter, see Reed, *Freedom Time*.
75 Welch, "*Don't Let Me Be Lonely*," 129.
76 Nealon, *Matter of Capital*, 152.
77 Rankine, *Don't Let Me Be Lonely*, 18.
78 The essayistic-journalistic style of the book is intended to mimic the form of newspaper columns and typeface. See Rankine, interview by Leonard Lopate.
79 Rankine, *Don't Let Me Be Lonely*, 47.
80 Rankine, 48.
81 Rankine, 21.
82 Rankine, 57.
83 Rankine, 56.
84 What can be useful in understanding Rankine's use/creation of journalism is the poet's strategy of intervention into topical news stories, most of which, in *Citizen*, for example, involve race and racial tensions. Chronicling the affective landscape of black life, she radically breaks rules of storytelling to stage a necessary disruption of the news by foregrounding the complex connections between private experience and larger social directions. Her tactics of converting "journalism" into a radical formalism involve

ways of articulating social relations that are often concealed within conventional modes and standards of journalism.
85 Laird, "New Way."
86 Laird.
87 Rankine, *Citizen*, 26.
88 Rankine, 32.
89 Domestico, "Bookmarks," 35.
90 Rankine, *Citizen*, 32.
91 Rankine, 83.
92 Rankine, 85.
93 Rankine, 117.
94 Wright, *One Big Self*, 32.
95 If this material can be considered as a conception of the world (of largely what actually occurred and its representations), then the group of poets under discussion can be said to provide a critical understanding and commentary on this conception in their poetry.
96 Bernstein, *Attack*, 169.
97 This is an extension of the earlier list.

Bibliography

Adam, G. Stuart. *Notes towards a Definition of Journalism: Understanding and Old Craft as an Art Form*. St. Petersburg, FL: Poynter Institute for Media Studies, 1993.
Altieri, Charles. "The Objectivist Tradition." *Chicago Review* 30, no. 3 (Winter 1979): 5–22. https://doi.org/10.2307/25303858.
American Press Institute. "What Is the Purpose of Journalism?" www.americanpressinstitute.org/journalism-essentials/what-is-journalism/purpose-journalism/.
Barnard, Rita. *The Great Depression and the Culture of Abundance: Kenneth Fearing, Nathanael West, and Mass Culture in the 1930s*. Cambridge: Cambridge University Press, 1995.
Berner, Jennie. "From Stenotype to Tintype: C. D. Wright's Technologies of 'Type.'" *Postmodern Culture* 22, no. 2 (January 2012). www.pomoculture.org/2013/04/07/from-stenotype-to-tintype-c-d-wrights-technologies-of-type/.
Bernstein, Charles. *Attack of the Difficult Poems: Essays and Inventions*. Chicago: University of Chicago Press, 2011.
———. Introduction to *Louis Zukofsky: Selected Poems*, edited by Charles Bernstein, xiii–xxvii. New York: Library of America, 2006.
Chiasson, Dan. "Southern Discomfort: C. D. Wright's 'One with Others.'" *New Yorker*, January 3, 2011. www.newyorker.com/magazine/2011/01/03/southern-discomfort-dan-chiasson.
Clover, Joshua. "'Words Pithy and Plain.'" Review of *The Poems of Charles Reznikoff, 1918–1975*, edited by Seamus Cooney. *New York Times Book Review*, January 22, 2006, 13–15.
Davidson, Michael. *Ghostlier Demarcations: Modern Poetry and the Material World*. Berkeley, CA: University of California Press, 1997.
Dayton, Tim. *Muriel Rukeyser's "The Book of the Dead."* Columbia, MO: University of Missouri Press, 2003.
Domestico, Anthony. "Bookmarks: How Racism Speaks." *Commonweal*, August 14, 2015. www.commonwealmagazine.org/node/37465/37465.
Dow, William. "Profiles of Lived Experience: Charles Reznikoff, Muriel Rukeyser and Mark Nowak." In *Profile Pieces: Journalism and the "Human Interest" Bias*, edited by Sue Joseph and Richard Lance Keeble, 116–36. New York, Routledge, 2016.
Franciosi, Robert. "'Detailing the Facts': Charles Reznikoff's Response to the Holocaust." *Contemporary Literature* 29, no. 2 (Summer 1988): 241–64. https://doi.org/10.2307/1208439.
Fredman, Stephen. *A Menorah for Athena: Charles Reznikoff and the Jewish Dilemmas of Objectivist Poetry*. Chicago: University of Chicago Press, 2001.
Galloway, Joseph L. "True Grit in a Steel Town." *U.S. News and World Report*, June 12, 1995, 30, 32.
Garton, Jane Dwyre. "Take Me to the Intersection of Poetry and Journalism." Huffington Post, February 17, 2009. www.huffingtonpost.com/jane-dwyre-garton/take-me-to-theintersecti_b_155276.html.
Goodman, Jenny. "Politics and the Personal Lyric in the Poetry of Joy Harjo and C. D. Wright." *MELUS* 19, no. 2 (Summer 1994): 35–56. www.doi.org/10.2307/467724.

Hinken, Michael. "Documentary Fiction: Authenticity and Illusion." Review of *The Historian*, by Elizabeth Kostova, and *The Lake, the River and the Other Lake*, by Steve Amick. *Michigan Quarterly Review* 45, no. 1 (Winter 2006): 218–25. http://hdl.handle.net/2027/spo.act2080.0045.128.

Kadlec, David. "X-Ray Testimonials in Muriel Rukeyser." *Modernism/Modernity* 5, no. 1 (1998): 23–47. www.doi.org/10.1353/mod.1998.0020.

Kalaidjian, Walter. *American Culture between the Wars: Revisionary Modernism and Postmodern Critique*. New York: Columbia University Press, 1993.

Kees, Weldon. "Fearing's Collected Poems." Review of *Collected Poems of Kenneth Fearing*, by Kenneth Fearing. *Poetry* 57, no. 4 (January 1941): 264–70.

Kovach, Bill, and Tom Rosenstiel. *The Elements of Journalism: What Newspeople Should Know and the Public Should Expect*. Updated ed. New York: Three Rivers Press, 2007.

Laird, Nick. "A New Way of Writing about Race." Review of *Citizen: An American Lyric*, by Claudia Rankine. *New York Review of Books*, April 23, 2015. www.nybooks.com/articles/2015/04/23/claudia-rankine-new-way-writing-about-race/.

Listoe, Daniel. "'With All Malice': The Testimonial Objectives of Charles Reznikoff." *American Literary History* 26, no. 1 (Spring 2014): 110–31. https://doi.org/10.1093/alh/ajt068.

Lobo, Julius. "From 'The Book of the Dead' to 'Gauley Bridge': Muriel Rukeyser's Documentary Poetics and Film at the Crossroads of the Popular Front." *Journal of Modern Literature* 35, no. 3 (Spring 2012): 77–102.

Lowney, John. *History, Memory, and the Literary Left: Modern American Poetry, 1935–1968*. Iowa City, IA: University of Iowa Press, 2006.

Nealon, Christopher. *The Matter of Capital: Poetry and Crisis in the American Century*. Cambridge, MA: Harvard University Press, 2011.

Nowak, Mark. "An Interview with Mark Nowak." By Steel Wagstaff. *Contemporary Literature* 51, no. 3 (Fall 2010): 453–76.

———. *Revenants*. Minneapolis, MN: Coffee House Press, 2000.

———. *Shut Up Shut Down*. Minneapolis, MN: Coffee House Press, 2004.

Pitzer, Andrea. "Poetry as Narrative Journalism? You'd Be Surprised." Nieman Storyboard, January 21, 2010. https://niemanstoryboard.org/stories/poetry-as-narrative-journalism-youd-be-surprised/.

Ramazani, Jahan. "American Poetry, Prayer, and the News." In *The Oxford Handbook of Modern and Contemporary American Poetry*, edited by Cary Nelson. Oxford Handbooks Online, November 2012. www.doi.org/10.1093/oxfordhb/9780195398779.013.0017.

———. *Poetry and Its Others: News, Prayer, Song, and the Dialogue of Genres*. Chicago: University of Chicago Press, 2013.

Rankine, Claudia. *Citizen: An American Lyric*. Minneapolis, MN: Graywolf Press, 2014.

———. *Don't Let Me Be Lonely: An American Lyric*. Minneapolis, MN: Graywolf Press, 2004.

———. Interview by Leonard Lopate. *Leonard Lopate Show*, October 4, 2004. www.wnyc.org/story/50183-claudia-rankine.

Reed, Anthony. *Freedom Time: The Poetics and Politics of Black Experimental Writing*. Baltimore, MD: Johns Hopkins University Press, 2014.

Reznikoff, Charles. "The 'Objectivist' Poet: Four Interviews." By L. S. Dembo. *Contemporary Literature* 10, no. 2 (Spring 1969): 193–202. https://doi.org/10.2307/1207760.

———. *The Poems of Charles Reznikoff, 1918–1975*. Edited by Seamus Cooney. Jaffrey, NH: Black Sparrow Book, 2005.

———. *Testimony: The United States (1885–1915): Recitative*. New York: Objectivist Press, 1934.

———. *Testimony: The United States (1885–1915): Recitative*. Introduction by Eliot Weinberger. Jaffrey, NH: Black Sparrow Book, 2015.

Rich, Adrienne. "An Atlas of the Difficult World." 1991. In *Adrienne Rich's Poetry and Prose*, edited by Barbara Charlesworth Gelpi and Albert Gelpi, 142–48. New York: Norton, 1993.

Rukeyser, Muriel. *The Book of the Dead*. 1938. *Muriel Rukeyser: A Living Archive*. http://murielrukeyser.emuenglish.org/2018/12/07/the-book-of-the-dead/.

———. "The Education of a Poet." 1976. In *The Writer on Her Work*, edited by Janet Sternburg, 213–17. New York: Norton, 1992.

———. *The Life of Poetry*. 1949. New York: Current Books, 1996.

"Rukeyser 2." Review of *U.S. 1*, by Muriel Rukeyser. *Time*, March 28, 1938, 63.

Schudson, Michael. *The Power of News*. Cambridge, MA: Harvard University Press, 1996.

Scroggins, Mark. "The Objectivists and the Left." In *The Cambridge History of American Poetry*, edited by Alfred Bendixen and Stephen Burt, 728–49. Cambridge: Cambridge University Press, 2014. https://doi.org/10.1017/CHO9780511762284.036.

Shea, Anne. "Forms of Affiliation in Mark Nowak's *Coal Mountain Elementary*." *Contemporary Literature* 58, no. 1 (Spring 2017): 82–115. https://doi.org/10.3368/cl.58.1.82.

Shockley, Evie. *Renegade Poetics: Black Aesthetics and Formal Innovation in African American Poetry*. Iowa City, IA: University of Iowa Press, 2011.

Shulman, Robert. *The Power of Political Art: The 1930s Literary Left Reconsidered*. Chapel Hill, NC: University of North Carolina Press, 2000.

Thurston, Michael. Review of *The Objectivist Nexus: Essays in Cultural Poetics*, edited by Rachel Blau DuPlessis and Peter Quartermain. *Modernism/Modernity* 7, no. 2 (April 2000): 344–45. https://doi.org/10.1353/mod.2000.0048.

Vance, David Ray. "Mark Nowak, Radical Documentary Praxis [Redux]." In *American Poets in the 21st Century: The New Poetics*, edited by Claudia Rankine and Lisa Sewell, 336–52. Middletown, CT: Wesleyan University Press, 2007.

Van Hout, Tom, and Peter Burger. "Mediatization and the Language of Journalism." In *The Oxford Handbook of Language and Society*, edited by Ofelia García, Nelson Flores, and Massimiliano Spotti. Oxford Handbooks Online, December 2016. https://doi.org/10.1093/oxfordhb/9780190212896.013.9.

Vassar Encyclopedia. "Muriel Rukeyser." 2014. https://vcencyclopedia.vassar.edu/alumni/muriel-rukeyser.html.

Watson, Benjamin. "Reznikoff's *Testimony*." *Legal Studies Forum* 29, no. 1 (2005): 67–94.

Weinberger, Eliot. Introduction to *Testimony: The United States (1885–1915): Recitative*, by Charles Reznikoff, ix–xiv. Jaffrey, NH: Black Sparrow Book, 2015.

Welch, Tana Jean. "*Don't Let Me Be Lonely*: The Trans-corporeal Ethics of Claudia Rankine's Investigative Poetics." *MELUS* 40, no. 1 (Spring 2015): 124–48. https://doi.org/10.1093/melus/mlu060.

Wright, C. D. "Looking for 'One Translatable Song': C. D. Wright on Poetics, Collaboration, American Prisoners, and Frank Stanford." Interview by Kent Johnson. *Jacket*, December 2001. http://jacketmagazine.com/15/cdwright-iv.html.

———. *One Big Self: An Investigation*. Port Townsend, WA: Copper Canyon Press, 2007.

———. *One with Others*. Port Townsend, WA: Copper Canyon Press, 2010.

Zelizer, Barbie. *What Journalism Could Be*. Cambridge: Polity Press, 2017.

29
THE REVIVIFYING FLAMES OF ROCK AND ROLL JOURNALISM

Todd Schack

Preface: Awopbopaloobop! Sex, Danger, and Secret Magic

When Nik Cohn, a precocious young Irishman, secluded himself on the blustery coast of West Ireland to write the "history of rock and roll" as he saw it, he figured he was writing a eulogy to a dying form of music that had burned furious and bright, only to extinguish itself in fantastic flames a few short years from its birth. The year was 1968. Cohn was twenty-two years old. However, instead of eulogizing rock and roll, he initiated a new subgenre of writing. What he did most of all, and before many others, was bring a writer's skill, a first-person point of view, a passion for music, and an unflinching look at the cultural, political, and social landscape of the era. The result, *Awopbopaloobop Alopbamboom: The Golden Age of Rock* (1969), became a cornerstone on which future decades of music journalism would be built as a cry for authenticity, a wailing against pretense, and a solemn panegyric to the death of art in the face of corporate capitalism.

Cohn recalls that rock and roll at this point (*1968!*) was "a doomed romance, a passionate beating against the tides."[1] The "tides" against which rock beat were of course commerce and capital, and ultimately he wrote of the betrayal of rock (an "outlaw trade") for a corporate product. He writes further:

> My purpose was quite simple: to catch the feel, the pulse of rock, as I had found it. Nobody, to my knowledge, had ever written a serious book on the subject before, so I had no precursors to inhibit me. ... I simply wrote off the top of my head, whatever and however the spirit moved me. Accuracy did not seem of prime importance (and the book, as a result, is a morass of factual errors). What I was after was guts, and flash, and energy, and speed. Those were the things I'd treasured in music. Those were the things that I tried to reflect as I left.[2]

Going after guts, flash, energy, and speed was, of course, a very rock and roll thing to do. And necessary, if the prose were to match the subject. He relates the moment rock and roll took hold of his ten-year-old self, an electric-jolt epiphany that another world was possible:

> Across the street I had heard Little Richard singing *Tutti Frutti* on a coffee-bar jukebox. Watched the local teen hoods—Teddy Boys, they were called—with their duckass

haircuts and drainpipe jeans, jiving in plain day. Had my first glimpse of sex, and danger, and secret magic. And I had never been healthy since.[3]

Perhaps he was never healthy since, but what he sensed in the sex, danger, and secret magic was the importance of the moment, the tectonic cultural and political shift that rock and roll signified, the fact that essentially, fundamentally, music *mattered*. And so did writing about it. And this prefigured what came after: an entire generation of music journalists who wrote as if their lives depended on it—because in their eyes, it did.

Rock and Roll Journalism vs. Criticism, and the Problem with Canons

Thus Cohn, on his side of the Atlantic, initiated a subgenre of music journalism that was born at the same time as the US was having the New Journalism moment of the late 1960s, and to which it bears striking similarities. However, before we situate the "literary" legacy within the larger field of music journalism, a bit of situational context is necessary. What follows is, first and foremost, not meant to be a comprehensive attempt at creating a music journalism (or even a "rock and roll journalism") canon. Such an attempt would be both overbearingly voluminous and notoriously problematic on multiple fronts.[4] Nor is it the purpose of this chapter to engage in a discussion of the problematics of canonical work, on the familiar grounds of exclusionary sexist or "rockist" practice, both of which are legitimate and merit discussion.[5]

Second, some historical context is warranted in that the claim above, that Cohn "initiated" a subgenre of music writing, might be laughable to those who rightfully point to the earlier work of jazz enthusiasts, critics, and writers such as Ralph Ellison, Ralph Gleason, and Amiri Baraka (who wrote as LeRoi Jones), and all of whom pre-dated Cohn by at least twenty years. This is entirely understandable, and without a doubt the writers who will be considered here as beginning the legacy of *literary journalism* within the genre of music writing (and further, the subgenre of rock and roll journalism) were certainly traveling a path that was originally broken by jazz writers, critics, and journalists such as Ellison, Gleason, and Baraka. So much so, in fact, that just as rock and roll was beyond question a cultural appropriation by the white, mainstream culture of the blues, so is "rock writing" itself an appropriation of jazz writing, and undoubtedly these three are rightfully the godfathers, as it were, of the form.[6]

Further, this piece will draw an admittedly nebulous line between music writers who are first and foremost critics and those who are journalists, a distinction sometimes found in the final product: the writing itself. Thus, certain well-known writers—*critics*—will be purposefully left out of the discussion below, most notably Robert Christgau and Ellen Willis, because suddenly, just prior to the time Cohn was penning his eulogy in 1968 to rock and roll's death, when the genre was in its infancy (detailed below), what mattered was not so much *critique* but *story*. While certainly higher forms of critique move beyond the mere drawing lines of distinction (high vs. low, good vs. bad, buy vs. don't buy), and into the realm of situating the musical artifact within the cultural and political sphere, and situating the artist within society, this form of critique is more sociology, or even ethnomusicology, than it is journalism.

Demonstrating this perfectly are the sharp social critiques of Willis, one of the early greats, who could write circles around most of the men in the genre from the late 1960s until the early 1980s, when she quit writing about music altogether. When she was at her fiercest, nobody could write what amounted to the sociology of music like she could or situate rock and roll *simultaneously* as a function of both liberation and oppression; as a vehicle advancing both equality between the sexes and misogyny; as both cultural revolution and conspicuous consumption; as an expression of both democracy and fascism.[7] But despite the fierceness and importance in the sociopolitical realm of her writing on music, she was not writing literary journalism, which will be considered here:

> She was not a high stylist, not obtuse or literary. Unlike her gonzo peers and followers, she wasn't trying to make her language re-create the experience of the music. Likewise, her first-person voice promoted ideas, not herself. Her style was almost invisible, and if all her fans and mentees would use one word to describe it, that word would be *clear*.[8]

The same holds (mostly) true for other writers such as Christgau (mentioned above), Paul Nelson, Dave Marsh, and Jon Landau, some of whom played fundamental roles in the history of music writing and will be discussed immediately below. Finally, two other genres of music writing that will not be considered are musicians writing about their own music and music biography. Both of these, while worthy of their own discussion, fall beyond the purview of this piece, because while they may certainly contain some elements that will be considered below (first-person point of view in particular), they are altogether a distinctive category within the sub-genre of music writing.

Thusly, turning our attention to the examples of music writing that will be considered, we see that the traditional devices of the New Journalism as outlined by Tom Wolfe, such as scene-by-scene construction, dialogue, status details, and immersive reporting, are present in most, if not all, of what we will consider exemplary music journalism.[9] But at their best, music journalists also carry on literary traditions that go beyond Wolfe's checklist of devices, and these traditions are the subjects of this chapter: (1) writing that makes the music make sense: it situates the musical moment culturally, socially, politically—and helps create the "rock mythologies" that will come to define a certain moment in time; (2) writing that makes the reader "hear" or, even better, "feel" the music—a form of synesthesia and the most difficult to pull off; and (3) a first-person, even gonzo-style point of view that both situates the reader in the moment and establishes the authority of the writer's voice. Together, these traditions make the genre and are what literary music journalism does best: It provides a context for, and as such a historical understanding of, what music means to us in a sociopolitical sense.

When it is done well, using the stylistic devices and writing techniques of the best of *literary* music journalism, it does so with an importance and an immediacy that situates music as a cultural endeavor that matters vitally. The best writers in this genre—Lester Bangs, Richard Meltzer, Nick Kent, Greil Marcus, Nick Tosches, to name the most obvious—knew this during the early years of rock and roll, but this fact also forces the question: Has music journalism survived or, even, *can* it survive in the modern era, and *who* carries on the traditions today? Who, if anyone, is today's Lester Bangs?

Culture as Ecstatic Disruption:
The Writing that Made the Music Make Sense

The early days of music writing are invariably tied up in the early days of music magazines, and in England two long-standing magazines existed where writers could publish works on music: *Melody Maker*, the oldest, founded in 1926, and *New Musical Express*, founded in 1952. But in the US, writers needed to take things into their own hands and print what amounted to self-published zines. The first of these, *Little Sandy Review*, founded in 1959 by Paul Nelson, is widely regarded as the first serious outlet for music journalism, and Nelson the first serious writer on the subject of music: "A pioneer of rock criticism, and one of its most talented practitioners, Nelson ... wound up changing the way people listened to music, while helping to launch a 'New Journalism' that barely exists anymore."[10] Nelson would later move on to become

Rolling Stone's most important record-review editor, but let's not get ahead of ourselves. Next in line in both chronology and importance was the founding of *Crawdaddy!* in 1966, by Paul Williams, who, according to John Harris, was one of the most influential of the early writers:

> The history of rock writing begins around 1966 when, with what was once mere "pop" being taken seriously, the American writer Paul Williams published a journal-cum-fanzine titled *Crawdaddy!*, which aimed to bring to rock music the kind of cerebral writing long devoted to folk and jazz. Other currents were swirling around the more educated bits of the US counterculture, among them the expressive precedents set by the Beats and the possibilities suggested by New Journalism.[11]

Indeed, cerebral writing was the purpose, as evidenced from the first issue, which read, "You are looking at the first issue of a magazine of rock and roll criticism. *Crawdaddy!* will feature neither pin-ups nor news-briefs; the specialty of this magazine is intelligent writing about pop music."[12] This was certainly a cultural shift, as up to this point both "rock" and "pop" were considered not worth writing about, or at least not seriously, as were classical, orchestral, jazz, and even folk music. But things changed with *Crawdaddy!*, as Harris, quoting future great Marcus, writes:

> And so a new idea spread: as Marcus puts it, the notion of writing about music "passionately … as if it was the most important thing in the world, as if the stakes were high, as if everything mattered. There were no rules. There was nobody there to tell you, 'This is silly, this doesn't make sense, this is too long, why are you connecting this with that?' There was no procedure. There was no such term as 'rock criticism', really. No one knew what they were doing."[13]

Next came *Circus*, founded in 1966 as *Hullabaloo*, which featured early writings by Nelson, but it was the launch in 1967 of *Rolling Stone* by founder Jann Wenner that solidified the genre's importance, as now serious music journalism had multiple, competing outlets that together considered the importance culturally, socially, and politically of rock and roll. Author Joe Levy writes,

> Over the next few years, *Rolling Stone* would become a defining voice in a rapidly changing form of writing that lifted the tools of literary criticism, film-auteur theory and sociology to create a living document of the counterculture overtaking the mainstream, album by album.[14]

And while it was at *Rolling Stone* that many of the greatest music writers would practice their craft, it would be remiss not to include Rolling Stone's archrival *CREEM*, founded in 1969, on this list of seminal publications.

Indeed, when Bangs was fired by Wenner at *Rolling Stone*, he became editor of *CREEM* in 1971, and the list of writers who would end up writing for both, but with more creative freedom at *CREEM*, includes Christgau, Meltzer, Tosches, Marcus, and many, many others. Thus, where *Rolling Stone* is certainly essential to considering this legacy of music writing and the stylistic conventions that were being formulated, in terms of the larger cultural forces that were at play, namely artistic integrity and authenticity versus corporate "product" and commercial mainstreaming, *CREEM* represented the former and *Rolling Stone* the latter. And while most of the best names in music writing had a stint at *Rolling Stone*, they were mostly culled from the roster by a celebrity-obsessed, corporate-friendly Wenner. Both magazines, however, played a critical role in the early formation of music journalism's most celebrated (and cursed) trio, dubbed "The Noise Boys": Lester Bangs, Richard Meltzer, and Nick Tosches.

According to Christgau (the self-ordained "Dean of Rock Criticism"), Bangs, Meltzer, and Tosches "were all partisans of rock at its noisiest—culture as ecstatic disruption."[15] That is, they saw their role as writers to be as disruptive to culture as their rock and roll heroes, and no editor, magazine, or other authority should stand in their way. Seen in this light, the various writings of "The Noise Boys" can be understood as a constant struggle against pretense, a constant search for authenticity, and constantly distraught when former rock and roll heroes are found to be wanting.

Here is where music journalism approaches the heart of rock and roll itself, because here it's about what matters, what's at stake, and why we as a culture should care. It's also about the writing itself and the use of language that is itself very rock and roll: "Lester's writing—his self-mocking confessionals, left-field generalizations, free-form metaphors, effortless epithets, and boffo laugh lines, all flowing like a river of Romilar or a Coltrane solo—touched readers in a place his legend never reached."[16]

A very important point, and while the "legend" of Bangs casts a shadow to this day, it is the writing itself that is the most important element of music journalism, the one that makes the entire genre culturally relevant. That is, how music journalists situate the artist and his or her time, how they are able to know before anyone else does the importance—politically, socially, culturally—of a music movement, or a particular band, singer, or performance, which speaks to the ability of the journalist to *make the music make sense*.

For instance, Cohn, crystalizes the sociocultural importance of Elvis in the late 1950s and the fact that rock and roll was, in fact, always about sex:

> Always, he came back to sex. ... Elvis was blatant. When those axis hips got moving, there was no more pretense about moonlight and hand-holding; it was hard physical fact. ...
>
> [With Elvis] it's all been down to mainline sexual fantasy. Sitting in concert halls, schoolgirls have screamed, rioted, brawled and fainted. They've wet themselves and they've masturbated. ... They've done all kinds of outrageous stuff that they'd never do anywhere else and they've been so uninhibited because there has always been a safety belt, because the pop singer himself has been unreachable, unreal, and nothing could actually happen.
>
> In this way, it's all been sex in a vacuum—the girls have freaked themselves out, emptied themselves, and then they've gone back home with their boy-friends and played virgin again. As rituals go, it's not been beautiful but it's been healthy, it's acted as a safety valve. Screaming at Elvis or the Beatles or the Rolling Stones, has been as good as saying confession or going to an analyst.[17]

Or when Bangs writes the following passage shortly after witnessing for the first time the Clash perform in England. Here, he is back at their hotel and duly amazed at how well they treat their fans—not patronizing, not bored or jaded, but truly interested in what they have to say. Bangs speaks for them, for their entire generation, and for all their desires, political or otherwise:

> The politics of rock and roll, in England or America or anywhere else, is that a whole lot of kids want to be fried out of their skins by the most scalding propulsion they can find, for a night they can pretend is the rest of their lives, and whether the next day they go back to work in shops or boredom on the dole or American TV doldrums in Mom 'n' Daddy's living room nothing can cancel the reality of that night in the revivifying flames

when for once if only then in your life you were blasted outside of yourself and the monotony which defines most life anywhere at any time, when you supped on lightning and nothing else in the realms of the living or dead mattered at all.[18]

But what is more important than this feeling, penned by Bangs, that music meant that at least for one moment you could step outside yourself and "sup on lightning," an explosive feeling of absolute freedom and youth, is what this feeling meant socially, culturally, and politically. What it meant, of course, when it was true was revolution. It meant the rejection of mainstream culture, a condemnation of consumerism and the "American TV doldrums." It also meant, of course, a new culture, new community, and a place to belong to especially if you rejected the mainstream. Another writer in the pantheon, Nick Kent, also writes of this same feeling as he watched the New York Dolls:

> The music is raw and alive, played with reckless abandon until it becomes a joyous celebration of the whole "be young, be foolish, be happy" school of thought. Believe me, the records don't even begin to capture the special magic of the Dolls on a good night playing in a pissy little club to their elite little crowd of mascara-daubed misfits and vagrant vamps. Misty glitzy memories of the way we were. So cute. So vital. So star-crossed.[19]

Rejecting the mainstream and belonging to like-minded individuals of the counterculture were especially important tropes in music journalism. Equally important, and another form of "making the music make sense," was the flipside of revolution: consumerism. That is, what it meant when the music was sold out, washed up, and dead. Cohn, one of the first to call out rock and roll as a corporate "product," writes:

> Heady days. But not, by their nature, made to last. Even as I was pigging out on the moment, rock & roll was already changing. The world that I knew and adored was essentially an outlaw trade, run by a motley of adventurers, snake-oil salesmen, and inspired lunatics. But their time was almost over. With each passing season, the scene was becoming more industrial. Corporate fat cats and accountants were driving out the wild men. The new buzzword was *product*. It would not be long, I came to realize, before rock was just another branch of commerce, no more nor less exotic than autos or detergents.[20]

Similarly, Bangs eulogizes the Beatles in 1975, saying the unthinkable—that if anything, our reverence of the Beatles amounts to nostalgia through rose-tinted glasses, and if something else, nothing more than the buzzword "*product*" that Cohn spoke of:

> The death of the Beatles as a symbol or signification of anything can only be good, because like the New Frontier their LOVE nirvana was a stimulating but ridiculous, ephemeral and ultimately impractical mass delusion in the first place. If the Beatles *stood* for anything besides the rock and roll band as a communal unit suggesting the possibility of mass youth power, which proved to be a totally fatuous concept in short order, I'd like to know what I have missed by not missing the Beatles. They certainly didn't stand for peace or love or true liberation or the brotherhood of humankind, any more than John Denver stands for the protection of our natural resources. On the other hand, like Davy Crockett hats, zoot suits, marathon dances, and bootleg alcohol, they may well have stood for an era, so well as to stand out from that era, totally exhumed from it in

fact, floating, light as dandelions, to rest at last on the mantle where, neighboring your dead uncle's framed army picture, they can be dusted off at appropriate intervals, depending on the needs of Capitol's ledgers and our own inability to cope with the present.[21]

Dancing about Architecture: Writing about Music

For music journalists, one special challenge has always been the representation of the musical performance in written prose. This is most likely the reason Elvis Costello famously quipped in an interview, "Writing about music is like dancing about architecture—it's a really stupid thing to want to do."[22] By far the most difficult aspect to pull off is to make the readers actually *feel* the music, and when it is done properly with literary style, the writer strikes a delicate fine point, using a sort of synesthetic detailing with descriptive language, making us "hear" the music through words.

This is where it becomes possible to tell who the best writers of the genre are, due to musical acumen, the knowledge of what the musician is doing on stage or on record, and the command of language, the ability to translate sound to printed word. Certainly, the standard was set by the likes of Bangs, Marcus, Tosches, Meltzer, and Kent, as their ability to spot musicians' craft and turn it into art on the page was what set them apart. For example, when Bangs wrote about Nico's *The Marble Index*, which he called "the greatest piece of avant-garde classical serious music of the last half of the twentieth century so far," he wrote of the song "Frozen Warnings":

> Through a pale morning's arctic sunlight glinting dimly off the snow, a bank of violas emits one endless shrill note which eventually becomes electronically distorted by points of ice panning back and forth through the space between your ears, descending and then impossibly ascending in volume and ineluctable intensity until they're almost unbearable though infinitely graceful in their beauty; at length they wind off into the skies trailing away like wisps of fading beams.[23]

Or Kent, describing the way Iggy Pop and his band The Stooges play when at their best:

> They were hell-bent on taking a time capsule right back to the darkest ages of music they could hope to sink into, back to that dim time when the world was one big, pulsating swamp which shook with the terrible thunderous rhythms of nature's raw elemental power. To this end they beat out this muddy, brutal, ecstatic music that grabbed anyone in its path roughly by the scruff of the neck and hurled them headlong onto the very wilderness of the senses that lies stretched out just beyond man's deepest primordial fears. For some, like myself, being exposed to music this raw and alive had a profoundly liberating effect.[24]

Sometimes, however, it is not the music itself that is the most important but the atmosphere of place or the demeanor of the artist that tells us the most about the musical moment. For instance, in the following passage by Marcus, "With the Sex Pistols on Stage," he writes:

> ... everything changed. Slumping like Quasimodo under heavy air, Johnny Rotten cut through the curiosity of the crowd with a twist of his neck. He hung on to the microphone

stand like a man caught in a wind tunnel; ice, paper cups, coins, books, hats, and shoes, flew by him as if sucked up by a vacuum. ...

Sid Vicious was there to bait the crowd; two fans climbed on to the stage and bloodied his nose. A representation of a representation, even streaked with his own gore, his arm bandaged with a self-inflicted gouging, he was, in a strange way, hardly there at all: this was actually not happening. ...

Paul Cook was hidden behind his drums. Steve Jones sounded like he was playing a guitar factory, not a guitar; it was inconceivable that there were only three instruments on stage. The stage was full of ghosts; song by song, Johnny Rotten ground his teeth down to points.[25]

Similarly, Tosches captures the spirit, dark as it is, of Jerry Lee Lewis:

He was the Killer and he was immortal—damned to be, for as long as there were good and evil to be torn between in agony. He would sit backstage in a thousand dank nightclubs, and he would know this, and he would swallow more pills and wash them down with three fingers more of whiskey, and he would know it even more. He would walk like a man to the stage, with his Churchill in one hand and his water glass of whiskey in the other, and he would pound the piano and sing his sinful songs, and he would beckon those before him, mortals, made not as he to destruction from the womb; he would beckon them to come, to stand with him awhile at the brink of Hell. Then he would be gone into the ancient night, to more pills and more whiskey, to where the black dogs never ceased barking and dawn never broke; he would go there.[26]

Thus, contrary to Costello's surmise that writing about music is a "stupid thing to want to do," what the best of the writing is able to accomplish is to situate the reader in the music itself and, as importantly, to situate the music within the cultural, political moment. Without the likes of Tosches, Marcus, Kent, Bangs, and others, we would not know, unless we were both there in the moment and hyperaware of the larger cultural importance, of the liberating effect of the Stooges, taking their audience to that "wilderness ... just beyond man's deepest primordial fears," or how the Sex Pistols' Sid Vicious, "streaked with his own gore," was a "representation of a representation," or of the nightly struggle over The Killer's soul by God and Devil, while he beckoned his audience "to stand with him awhile at the brink of Hell."

Rock-Writer Gonzo

For music journalists aspiring toward the literary, the use of first-person voice is essential. Since the writer is relegated to the sidelines anyway, the general rule of thumb is to make his or her stance on those sidelines as interesting as possible. Hence the similarity to Hunter S. Thompson's gonzo style—that is, if they can't *be* the music, at least they could *be there*, and that presence becomes a focal point.

Of course, in the early days of *Rolling Stone*, *CREEM*, and *Circus*, the writing was as much about living and delivering the rock and roll lifestyle as it was about the music. The pioneers of rock journalism went to extraordinary lengths of Thompson-esque excess, all of which bought them a sort of street credibility—both with readers and, more importantly, with the aristocrats of rock themselves. Most famous along these lines were Lester Bangs and Richard Meltzer, about whom Patti Smith said, "Rock and roll is anything Richard Meltzer does."[27]

Meltzer arguably was the first great rock journalist, and he argues as much himself: "Before Lester Bangs was, I am (and he's dead). Which, heck, I dangle as neither credit nor debit—just my way of saying hi." Never one to allow an opportunity for self-aggrandisement to pass unseized, Melzer displays in the following quote exactly the sort of make-yourself-the-story, gonzo style of writing he became famous for in "Rock-Crit Blood 'n' Guts":[28]

> I was always a fucking zealot. The giddiest smartass to hold the banner high. This is among *writers* we're talking; the rock-roll flag of whatever. (Something to do with the night.) We'd all be at this party, for inst, for the fabulozoolous Rolling Stones at some fussy French—or was it Italian?—New York eatery. After '72 at the Garden. There's this huge fountain, *indoors*, this incredible fountain—so who's gonna JUMP in the thing? I look around, I don't see no candidates, Mick's asleep face-down on a table. So it's gotta be me—*got* to, right? 'Cause if not, if the option's so clear and *nobody* does it, rock-roll as we um uh know it will um uh *perish*, y'know? ... that sort of trip.
> So I jump and they give me the boot, a big security jerk on each arm. ... you get the idea: I once really, truly *gave a shit*; I cared religiously.[29]

Which is to say he was more than willing to make himself the story in order to have a story, a very gonzo thing to do. In this, his archrival was beyond question the incorrigible Bangs. In perhaps one of the most oft-quoted interviews in the genre, the hilariously titled "Let Us Now Praise Famous Death Dwarves," Bangs does not so much interview Lou Reed as he uses Reed as a sounding board for his own obsessive ideas and to showcase his writing acrobatics:

> I decided to change my tack again. "Lou, we're gonna have to do it straight. I'll take off my sunglasses if you'll take off yours." He did. I did. Focus in on shriveled body sprawled on the bed facing me ... Lou's sallow skin almost as whitish yellow as his hair, whole face and frame so transcendently emaciated he had indeed become insectival. His eyes were rusty, like two copper coins lying in desert sands under the sun all day. ... Anyway, I was ready to ask my Big Question, the one I'd pondered over for months.[30]

Suffice it to say, the "Big Question" was more about Bangs than it was about Reed:

> "Do you ever resent people for the way that you have lived out what they might think of as the dark side of their lives for them, vicariously, in your music or your life?" He didn't seem to have the slightest idea what I was talking about, shook his head.[31]

This was what made Bangs so great: He was able to make the audience care just as much about his own rock and roll writer persona as those of the famous rock and rollers he wrote about.

Other legendary gonzo moments abound in the history of rock journalism, such as the famous "Masked Marauders" hoax, penned by Marcus. Tired of the rock and roll fad of "supergroups" being formed solely for promotional success, not to mention the overly gushing reviews that such supergroups garnered (a situation that betrayed both the corporatization of rock and the complicity of music journalism), Marcus wrote a review, under the pseudonym T. M. Christian, of a nonexistent album put out by a new supergroup, The Masked Marauders, formed by Bob Dylan, Mick Jagger, John Lennon, Paul McCartney, and George Harrison. The result: a hoax so effective that *Rolling Stone* was flooded by requests from the public, radio stations, and music retailers for access to the new album; the music press picked up the story and ran with it; and, finally, "Marcus decided that things had gone so far they had to go much further"[32]—so he hired a real band to record his fake songs and released them to the radio. After this, when Marcus and his friends, carrying the hoax even further still, wanted to actually press vinyl but balked at the price, they contacted Warner Brothers for an advance ... which netted the hoaxers $15,000!

Tosches, not to be outdone, not only reviewed an album that did not exist (he did that, too) but colluded with Meltzer to write reviews under each other's bylines. Here Meltzer himself details the idea being born, under the influence of whiskey (and coconut ice cream) at a Commander Cody performance:

> So here's where the gig ended. ...
>
> Nick Tosches and I were at a press party for the album, the band; plenty of whiskey. I remember coconut ice cream. The Commander played and we had so much fun we agreed to each review the thing. ... Nick was so buzzed he took the first mental step down a path that would lead inexorably to the writing of *Country*—still the definitive overview of cowpoop music—and *Hellfire*, one of the great music bios of the last 200 years. ... But before any of that we decided to both review the Commander—under each other's byline.
>
> I secured the *Fusion* assignment, which he then wrote in my name; he pulled off the likewise with *Rolling Stone*, and I wrote that in his. When [John] Landau somehow found out, he was furious. For our little bitty "gag," our flaunting of low-level "kicks," our breach of I dunno, whatever it was a breach of, he booted us both.[33]

And so ended the tenure of both Tosches and Meltzer at *Rolling Stone*. But did they care? Meltzer:

> All told, I was done with this sorry, useless publication in less than two years. People I run into still hit me with: "Ooh, didn't you write for *Rolling Stone*?" "Yeah," I say, "but at least I've had the smarts never to stick my pecker in a garbage disposal."[34]

Which is, of course, a very rock and roll thing to say.

Conclusion: Disturbing the Peace

With such an interesting cadre of writers, personalities, and subject matter, it would make sense if the history of music journalism continued to this day unabated, but it hasn't, really. The following is a fair question to ask: Whatever happened to music journalism since the heady days of "The Noise Boys"? In many ways, the trend has mirrored that of other forms of literary journalism, as both are tied to an industry that has seen multiple technological, financial, and cultural challenges. Certainly, *Wired* magazine noted: "As music has become ubiquitous, music critics, and the magazines they write for, have become collateral damage, bypassed on the digital highway by cheap and instant gratification."[35] And, in a technophile conclusion, suggested that "perhaps it won't be long until we'll be able to install iTunes Genius, The Lester Bangs Edition." God knows what Bangs himself would think of such a development.

As for the technological challenges, these are straightforward: With the internet, magazines have ceased being the territory where the various publics find their music information including both criticism and journalism. Harris points out that

> Whereas music writing was once the province of a few hundred thousand fans and a handful of writers, usually in specialized magazines, it's now in the bookshop ... the blogosphere and beyond. The result too often suggests a very modern combination of

abundance and short weight. To put it another way: how is it that writing about music now is everywhere, and yet seems to be nowhere at all?[36]

Even more to the point is this question: Now that writing about music is everywhere, where is the writing about music that matters, that is unique, even *literary*? Now that those magazines have been replaced by blogs, and where the magazines exist at all, they are mere shells of their former existence (e.g., *Rolling Stone*, which rarely publishes music journalism of any literary quality at all) as publishers and editors seem to have decided that their audiences only want to be told which CD to buy—or rather, which songs to download; and writers, where they exist at all, write neither beautifully nor as if their lives depend on it, because, frankly, the audience does not depend on it as it used to. Harris continues, pointing out: "When the main event is only a click away, there isn't always much point to rhapsodies or forensic critiques."[37] That is, when a person's favorite band has YouTube videos, a Facebook page, and a Twitter feed only one click away, who needs to read a longform narrative about that band, no matter how literary?

Coupled with the technological challenges to music journalism are of course the economic pressures that have caused near total disruption across all publishing industries since the rise of the internet. As newspapers, magazines, and indeed the entire music industry itself has witnessed, it is increasingly difficult to sustain the type of investment that producing quality content demands—no less in terms of music as in longform journalism, no matter the genre, music journalism included. Asking precisely the question, "What is the future of long-form music journalism?" *Decibel* editor J. Andrew Zalucky writes:

> Any music publication looking to keep long-form journalism alive and economically viable faces—and has always faced—the following reality: demand for reading material about music must be high enough, and targeted effectively to get cash flowing into the system to pay for the publication to generate the supply at a reasonable price AND then pay its writers in enough wages or stipends to compete for their time. This was hard enough before the digitization of news media and the demand-destroying effects of the 2008 recession. In 2017, the challenge seems even greater.[38]

While this is certainly the situation, it is also an economic reductionism. What has become apparent, however, is that while music journalists of the old breed are indeed an endangered species, the reasons for this are both structural (i.e., economic and technological) *and* cultural.

Certainly, some of the cultural developments are wrapped up in new technologies, in that we simply consume music in ways that are vastly different from how it was done before, and that includes music discovery that is freed from a knowledgeable curator (music journalist) writing for an interested audience in a common source (magazine). Harris also notes, "Rock culture has turned even more impatient, promiscuous and scatterbrained. Apart from anything else, music is now free and easy to download. For many listeners, songs simply shuffle away on an iPod, liberated from any context."[39] Thus, by consuming music divorced from social or political context, the audience—and the artists—is reduced from active participant to passive product. This, combined with the fact that the music industry *in toto* has become a finely tuned public-relations machine, makes journalism a mere platform for ad copy.

Asking "how rock writing has changed since the days when [Lester Bangs's] pieces were done,"[40] John Morthland, himself a music journalist, writes in an introduction to a collection of Bangs's writings:

> This subject is debated virtually any time two or more rock critics wind up in the same room ... the arguments usually revolve around the fact that there are so many more

music writers than ever before; around the way it's become a recognized profession ... and geared, not coincidentally, toward consumerism and the music industry's notion of publicity rather than toward journalism and/or criticism; around how much more difficult it's become, and the concessions a writer has to make to the PR machine, to get face time with interview subjects; around how effortlessly music journalism mutated into celebrity journalism. These are all good and true insights, ... but the single factor that strikes me most after months of immersion in Lester's work is that rock critics don't fantasize these days. Period.[41]

So if arguments based solely on economics or technology, while true, are also merely two aspects of the larger issue, which is that music is now a fully integrated and captured market, and if Morthland's description above of journalism's failure of imagination is also true, this might bring us to a larger question. It is not so much "who is today's Lester Bangs?" not "what has happened to rock writers?" but rather "what has happened to rock and roll?" That is, perhaps rock journalism doesn't matter anymore because rock doesn't matter anymore. Perhaps the politics and cultural and social importance of the form have been so thoroughly corporatized, packaged, sold, and resold that the need for writers to make the music make sense has disappeared into industry-friendly celebrity journalism. If this is the case, then perhaps the place to find music journalism that still matters would be in the only musical form with a politics, a social and cultural relevance, and that would arguably be hip-hop. And even though hip-hop is itself neither young and vital nor free from corporate pressure to produce "*product*," there is one writer who without a doubt would be a contender for today's Lester Bangs, and that is Greg Tate.

A truly unique voice, a writer's writer who makes the music make sense, as he does in the following piece entitled "Hip-Hop Turns Thirty," Tate does so with language that mirrors the staccato beats of the form itself:

> Because at heart, hip-hop remains a radical, revolutionary enterprise for no other reason than its rendering people of African descent anything but invisible, forgettable, and dismissible in the consensual hallucination-simulacrum twilight zone of digitized mass distractions we call our lives in the matrixized, conservative-Christianized, Goebbelsized-by-Fox twenty-first century.[42]

Tate can produce the synesthetic quality of writing that makes music come alive in written form. Writing from a compelling first-person point of view, he situates the musical moment socially, culturally, and politically perhaps better than even the legendary "Noise Boys" of the golden era of rock writing. Witness this excerpt from "The Zeitgeist Reloaded," a fiercely written homage to the Icelandic singer Björk:

> James Baldwin liked to say "Artists are here to disturb the peace." True that, Jimmy, true that. But when those rowdies are really on their game, they also rip folks out of mortal time and the fear of extinction. Lunge them away from their circadian lockstep and into the white-water roller-coaster rush of mythicized ritual frenzy, becoming mad, redemptive angel-banshees on the loose, casting wide nets, screaming love on that ass.
>
> A lifetime of loving Miles Davis and Ornette Coleman prepares you to love Björk and the way she worries the notes, stresses tonality until it cracks not because she can't help it but because she lives to crucify a pretty melody with her own brand of wounded, buck-wild, Middle Earth dissonance. She has become this century's zeitgeist artist for that reason, that alarming sonic tongue she uses to zap her diversity-conference audience's sense of emergency, fragility, and pure animal panic. She also operatically exalts and

exudes that most elusive and fanciful of human desires: untrammeled, untamable freedom, laid out to the pomo techno-tribalist beat all you earthbound E.T.'s now call home.[43]

And finally, in "Hip-Hop Turns Thirty," ever sensitive to the larger forces at play, he eulogizes the form in almost precisely the same way Cohn eulogized rock and roll in 1968:

> Hip-hop may have begun as a folk culture, defined by its isolation from mainstream society, but being that it was formed within the America that gave us the coon show, its folksiness was born to be bled once it began entertaining the same mainstream that had once excluded its culture … from the moment "Rapper's Delight" went platinum, hip-hop the folk culture became hip-hop the American entertainment-industry sideshow. … Problem today is that where hip-hop was once a buyer's market in which we, the elite hip-hop audience, decided what was street legit, it has now become a seller's market in which what does or does not get sold as hip-hop to the masses is whatever the boardroom approves.[44]

So while the question "what is the future of music journalism?" remains, as always, no matter if it is 1968 or 2018, the answer must be found in the writing itself. That is, *quality*, *literary* writing, by those writers who can make the music make sense, those who care religiously, those who are "fucking zealots" as Meltzer was, must be the future. And maybe they won't be writing about rock and roll, because such a thing has ceased to exist as a political force. But as long as there are youth who seek in music the "revivifying flames" against the monotony of life, and writers such as Bangs, who can describe the primal desire to sup—even for one night—on lightning, there is a future for music journalism. As Baldwin said, it takes an artist "to disturb the peace," and when musicians are making music that matters, no matter the genre, and writers are making that music make sense—socially and politically—the culture is rightly disturbed. And that's a very rock and roll thing to do.

Notes

1. Cohn, *Awopbopaloobop Alopbamboom*, 6.
2. Cohn, 6.
3. Cohn, 4.
4. For an excellent example of one such volume, I refer the reader to *Shake It Up: Great American Writing on Rock and Pop from Elvis to Jay Z*, edited by Jonathan Lethem and Kevin Dettmar.
5. For an excellent discussion of why such attempts are doubly myopic in terms of too much focus on white male writers and too much focus on "rockism," or "the conviction that the highest forms of popular music are created by (mostly white, male) practitioners of guitar-based music who are intrepidly following in the footsteps of Dylan, the Beatles, and the Boss," I refer the reader to Jack Hamilton's *New Yorker* article "The Trouble with Building a Rock-Writing Canon."
6. Ellison, *Living with Music*; Ellison, "Golden Age"; Gleason, *Music in the Air*; Baraka, *Black Music*.
7. Willis, *Out of the Vinyl Deeps*.
8. Carr and Nagy, "Raise Your Hand," 226.
9. Wolfe, *New Journalism*.
10. Ward, "What Ever Happened."
11. Harris, "Don't Look Back."
12. Williams, *Crawdaddy!*
13. Harris, "Don't Look Back."
14. Levy, "For the Record."
15. Christgau, "Impolite Discourse."
16. Christgau.
17. Cohn, *Awopbopaloobop Alopbamboom*, 26–27.

18 Bangs, *Psychotic Reactions*, 239.
19 Kent, *Dark Stuff*, 165–66.
20 Cohn, *Awopbopaloobop Alopbamboom*, 5.
21 Bangs, "Dandelions in Still Air."
22 Costello, "Man Out of Time," 52.
23 Bangs, *Mainlines*, 212.
24 Kent, *Dark Stuff*, 245.
25 Marcus, *Lipstick Traces*, 79.
26 Tosches, *Hellfire*, 188–89.
27 Meltzer, *Whore Just Like the Rest*.
28 Meltzer, 3.
29 Meltzer, 3.
30 Bangs, *Psychotic Reactions*, 178.
31 Bangs, 178.
32 Christgau, "Album of the Year."
33 Meltzer, *Whore Just Like the Rest*, 144.
34 Meltzer, 144.
35 Van Buskirk, "Can Device Integration."
36 Harris, "Don't Look Back."
37 Harris.
38 Zalucky, "What Is the Future."
39 Harris, "Don't Look Back."
40 Morthland, introduction and acknowledgements to *Mainlines*, xiv.
41 Morthland, xiv.
42 Tate, "Hip-Hop Turns Thirty," 250.
43 Tate, "Zeitgeist Reloaded."
44 Tate, "Hip-Hop Turns Thirty," 247.

Bibliography

Bangs, Lester. "Dandelions in Still Air: The Withering Away of the Beatles." *CREEM*, June 1975.
———. *Mainlines, Blood Feasts, and Bad Taste: A Lester Bangs Reader*. New York: Anchor Books, 2003.
———. *Psychotic Reactions and Carburetor Dung*. New York: Anchor Books, 2003.
Baraka, Amiri. *Black Music*. New York: AkashiClassics, 2010.
Carr, Daphne, and Evie Nagy. "Raise Your Hand." Afterword to *Out of the Vinyl Deeps: Ellen Willis on Rock Music*, edited by Nona Willis Aronowitz, 225–32. Minneapolis, MN: University of Minnesota Press, 2001.
Christgau, Robert. "Album of the Year." *Village Voice*, January 8, 1970. www.robertchristgau.com/xg/rock/album-70.php.
———. "Impolite Discourse." *Village Voice*, July 4, 2000. www.robertchristgau.com/xg/rock/noiseboy-00.php.
Cohn, Nik. *Awopbopaloobop Alopbamboom: The Golden Age of Rock*. New York: Grove Press, 1969.
Costello, Elvis. "A Man Out of Time Beats the Clock." Interview by Timothy White. *Musician*, October 1983, 44–53.
Ellison, Ralph. "The Golden Age: Time Past." *Esquire*, January 1, 1959. https://archive.esquire.com/issue/19590101.
———. *Living with Music: Ralph Ellison's Jazz Writings*. New York: Modern Library Classics, 2002.
Gleason, Ralph J. *Music in the Air: The Selected Writings of Ralph J. Gleason*. New Haven, CT: Yale University Press, 2016.
Hamilton, Jack. "The Trouble with Building a Rock-Writing Canon." *New Yorker*, June 8, 2017. www.newyorker.com/books/page-turner/the-trouble-with-building-a-rock-writing-canon.
Harris, John. "Don't Look Back." *Guardian*, June 26, 2009. www.theguardian.com/music/2009/jun/27/music-writing-bangs-marcus.
Kent, Nick. *The Dark Stuff: Selected Writings on Rock Music*. Cambridge, MA: Da Capo Press, 2002.
Lethem, Jonathan, and Kevin Dettmar, eds. *Shake It Up: Great American Writing on Rock and Pop from Elvis to Jay Z*. New York: Library of America, 2017.
Levy, Joe. "For the Record." *Rolling Stone*, April 20, 2017.

Marcus, Greil. *Lipstick Traces: A Secret History of the Twentieth Century*. Cambridge, MA: Harvard University Press, 1989.

Meltzer, Richard. *A Whore Just Like the Rest: The Music Writings of Richard Meltzer*. Cambridge, MA: Da Capo Press, 2000.

Morthland, John. Introduction and Acknowledgements to *Mainlines, Blood Feasts, and Bad Taste: A Lester Bangs Reader*, by Lester Bangs, xiii–xviii. New York: Anchor Books, 2003.

Tate, Greg. "Hip-Hop Turns Thirty." In *Flyboy 2: The Greg Tate Reader*, 246-252, Durham, NC: Duke University Press, 2016.

———. "The Zeitgeist Reloaded." *Village Voice*, May 1, 2007. www.villagevoice.com/2007/05/01/the-zeitgeist-reloaded/.

Tosches, Nick. *Hellfire: The Jerry Lee Lewis Story*. New York: Grove Press, 1982.

Van Buskirk, Eliot. "Can Device Integration Save Music Journalism?" *Wired*, October 7, 2009. www.wired.com/2009/10/music-magazine/.

Ward, Steven. "What Ever Happened to Rock Critic Paul Nelson." RockCritics.com, March 2000. https://rockcritics.com/2013/01/28/from-the-archives-interview-with-paul-nelson/.

Williams, Paul. *Crawdaddy!*, February 7, 1966.

Willis, Ellen. *Out of the Vinyl Deeps: Ellen Willis on Rock Music*. Edited by Nona Willis Aronowitz. Minneapolis: University of Minnesota Press, 2001.

Wolfe, Tom. *The New Journalism*. New York: Harper and Row, 1973.

Zalucky, J. Andrew. "What Is the Future of Long-Form Music Journalism?" *Decibel*, August 1, 2017. www.decibelmagazine.com/2017/08/01/what-is-the-future-of-long-form-music-journalism/.

30
LITERARY JOURNALISM AND THE PEDAGOGY OF LIBERAL EDUCATION

Jeffrey C. Neely and Mitzi Lewis

In his keynote address at the 2016 annual conference for the International Association for Literary Journalism Studies, William Dow adapts an argument from author David Shields by proposing that literary journalism "permits and encourages readerly knowledge in a way that is less indirect than fiction and less contrived and more open than conventional journalism."[1] Ron Rosenbaum describes literary journalism as helping us to investigate "the nature of human nature and its place in [the] cosmos,"[2] and David Abrahamson has referred to it as exploring the human condition.[3] Miles Maguire points out that literary journalism "conforms to Dewey's call to combine the 'highest and most difficult kind of inquiry' with a 'subtle, delicate, vivid, and responsive art of communication.'"[4]

In this chapter, we suggest first that these definitions point to the potential for literary journalism to be understood as answering the charge of a liberal education, a "system for organizing and understanding the known world—human beings, societies, nature,"[5] that has in recent years been expressly embraced by over 1,300 institutes of higher education in the United States.[6] Second, we argue that literary journalism's support of a liberal education may offer a pathway to helping departments that teach literary journalism in the US to secure and even grow their places on campus. While our primary focus is on higher education in the United States, we also suggest that with educators from more than twenty-seven countries represented in the information we share, the value of a liberal education—and literary journalism's value in bolstering it—can be seen as transferable and adaptable to the specific cultural dynamics that present themselves across international boundaries. We do this by examining survey data and interviews with postsecondary instructors and illustrating linkages of the pedagogy of literary journalism to the framework of the Liberal Education and America's Promise (LEAP) essential learning outcomes developed by the Association of American Colleges and Universities (AAC&U).[7]

A Brief Look at Enrollments

The need for pedagogical texts that are both sophisticated and artful, that can blend rich intellectual curiosity with deep real-world reporting, is arguably more critical now than ever as journalism and English programs alike face declining enrollments. In their "2015 Survey of Journalism and Mass Communication Enrollments," Melissa R. Gotlieb, Bryan McLaughlin, and R. Glenn Cummins found that while enrollments in strategic communications programs have increased in recent years, enrollments in the field of mass communication as a whole have gone down, and "decline among undergraduate student enrollments was particularly prevalent in journalism sequences."[8] A 2014 study conducted by the University of Georgia's Grady College of Journalism and Mass Communication found that enrollments at the University of Missouri School of Journalism, as just one of many anecdotal examples, were down 9 percent between 2011 and 2013, leading the university to increase financial aid to attract more students to the school.[9] English programs have seen similar declines. Over the last five years, English enrollments at the University of Minnesota, for example, have dropped 32 percent. The University of Wisconsin–Stevens Point announced in March 2018 that English was among thirteen majors proposed to be cut in favor of programs with "clear career pathways."[10]

At the same time, however, there is increasing evidence that college graduates with a liberal education are highly desirable among employers because they are "agile thinkers."[11] In the context of journalism education, we suggest that by pairing hands-on skills (e.g., writing, reporting, editing, digital media) with a liberal arts foundation—both of which can be fostered through literary journalism—students can leave college with the discrete skills and a broader intellectual foundation that will serve them in the near and distant future. In October 2013, a Carnegie-Knight Initiative on the Future of Journalism Education report opened with this well-known quote from Carnegie President Vartan Gregorian:

> Journalists should be cultured people who know about history, economics, science. Instead they are learning what is called nuts and bolts. Like schools of education, journalism schools should either be reintegrated intellectually into the university or they should be abolished.[12]

Although the Carnegie-Knight report focused specifically on recommendations for *graduate* programs, Gregorian's point, originally published in a 1997 *New York Times Magazine* article, referred to journalism schools more broadly.[13] The nuts and bolts are important, but journalism educators must also help students understand how these skills fit into a more holistic understanding of the world.

On the other hand, in the context of English programs, an ad hoc committee at the 2017 annual convention of the Modern Language Association reported findings from their investigation of forty-five English programs around the country, which included trends away from traditional survey courses (e.g., Shakespeare, British literature) and toward more writing-focused courses.[14] This has naturally raised concerns among English educators who recognize the enduring value of a common knowledge base for English majors; however, it is also a reflection of the on-the-ground expectations of their students, many of whom want to pursue writing careers.

In this space, poised between conflicting perspectives and the perceived choice of a liberal education *or* practical skills, sits literary journalism. The genre offers an opportunity to demonstrate that a liberal education can offer an appreciation of the arts and humanities, *as well as* factual information applicable to the world outside of academe, *as well as* hands-on, practical skills that graduates can apply in the workplace.

LEAP Essential Learning Outcomes

LEAP was launched in 2005 by the AAC&U as "a national advocacy, campus action, and research initiative"[15] to promote the importance of a liberal education in the twenty-first century. Among the central strategies of LEAP are its essential learning outcomes, which were the product of a multiyear dialogue among hundreds of colleges and universities, aimed at equipping students with "the broad knowledge, higher order capacities, and real world experience they need to thrive both in the [national] economy and in a globally engaged democracy."[16] The essential learning outcomes apply to *all* higher learning students, regardless of program of study. These outcomes are listed in Figure 30.1.

Across the country, initiatives based on or informed by LEAP have been launched at the state, system, and institutional levels to revise, restructure, and redirect curriculum and assessment for higher education. In Kentucky, for example, postsecondary administration is guided by a strategic plan known as Stronger by Degrees. This plan centers its objectives on LEAP principles, "including authentic assessment of student learning and preparation for twenty-first-century challenges by strengthening essential learning outcomes (ELOs)."[17] In Texas, LEAP initiatives have been used to support efforts to prepare college graduates through the state's recent revision of the Texas Core Curriculum, Texas's general education requirements. The Texas Undergraduate Education Advisory Committee "considered carefully" the LEAP initiative,[18] and the resulting core curriculum changes are already having an impact on institutions' communication curriculum offerings across the state.[19]

Anecdotally, one of the authors' departments, the Department of Mass Communication, has needed to add a lecturer position to accommodate the increased demand for its core course offerings. Several students in these core courses have changed their major to mass communication after their introduction to the field. Similar stories of how LEAP is driving deep curricular changes can be found in states such as California, North Dakota, Oregon, Massachusetts, Wisconsin, Virginia, and Utah, among others, all of which point to the wide-reaching influence this initiative is having on higher education in the United States. Thus, identifying ways in which teaching literary journalism aligns with the goals of LEAP may help instructors and administrators recognize the relevance of the genre in a much broader curricular context.

In 2008, the AAC&U collaborated with multiple education research and advocacy organizations, along with nearly one hundred colleges and universities, to develop an assessment initiative that corresponded to the LEAP essential learning outcomes. This initiative, the Valid Assessment of Learning in Undergraduate Education (VALUE), employed rubrics developed by teams of faculty and other education professionals. In 2014, the VALUE initiative was used by institutions in thirteen states across a three-year period to assess student performance in three selected LEAP outcomes from the "Intellectual and Practical Skills" category: written communication, critical thinking, and quantitative literacy.[20] Results of this aggregate assessment suggest that in the area of written communication, students seem to be doing quite well in developing content with an understanding of purpose, along with a command of syntax and mechanics. However, the results suggest that students continue to struggle in their abilities to incorporate evidence and sources in their writing across differing genres and conventions. With respect to critical thinking, students perform well in their abilities to explain issues, but they are less adept at drawing conclusions and understanding why these issues are important in a broader context.[21]

The study of literary journalism is poised to help address these challenges. One value of studying literary journalism is that it is informative, but it is also interpretive.[22] It uses rhetorical tools like scene, symbolism, point of view, and characterization to confront us with not just facts but also their importance. It invites us to consider a text in terms of its rhetorical situation, which is on the whole more accessible to us as readers than it is in fiction because we understand that the text is firmly situated in a concrete, factual, reported reality.[23] The study of literary journalism not only illustrates to students concrete ways to improve their own written and oral communications, but it offers myriad opportunities for them to develop other intellectual and practical skills; to grow in cultural and intercultural knowledge; to internalize a sense of personal and collective responsibility for social, environmental, civic, and ethical concerns; and to consider how these skills and considerations intersect with their other academic and professional pursuits. In the sections that follow, we suggest—based on results from surveys and interviews with instructors of

The Essential Learning Outcomes

★ ★ ★ ★ ★ ★ ★ ★ ★ ★ ★ ★ ★ ★ ★ ★ ★

Beginning in school, and continuing at successively higher levels across their college studies, students should prepare for twenty-first-century challenges by gaining:

★ Knowledge of Human Cultures and the Physical and Natural World

- Through study in the sciences and mathematics, social sciences, humanities, histories, languages, and the arts

Focused by engagement with big questions, both contemporary and enduring

★ Intellectual and Practical Skills, including

- Inquiry and analysis
- Critical and creative thinking
- Written and oral communication
- Quantitative literacy
- Information literacy
- Teamwork and problem solving

Practiced extensively, across the curriculum, in the context of progressively more challenging problems, projects, and standards for performance

★ Personal and Social Responsibility, including

- Civic knowledge and engagement—local and global
- Intercultural knowledge and competence
- Ethical reasoning and action
- Foundations and skills for lifelong learning

Anchored through active involvement with diverse communities and real-world challenges

★ Integrative and Applied Learning, including

- Synthesis and advanced accomplishment across general and specialized studies

Demonstrated through the application of knowledge, skills, and responsibilities to new settings and complex problems

Note: The Essential Learning Outcomes were identified through a multiyear dialogue with hundreds of colleges and universities about needed goals for student learning; analysis of a long series of recommendations and reports from the business community; and analysis of the accreditation requirements for engineering, business, nursing, and teacher education. The findings are documented in previous publications of the Association of American Colleges and Universities: *Greater Expectations: A New Vision for Learning as a Nation Goes to College* (2002), *Taking Responsibility for the Quality of the Baccalaureate Degree* (2004), and *Liberal Education Outcomes: A Preliminary Report on Achievement in College* (2005). *Liberal Education Outcomes* is available online at www.aacu.org/leap.

LEAP

Figure 30.1 LEAP essential learning outcomes.

Source: Reprinted with permission from *The LEAP Vision for Learning*. Copyright 2011 by the Association of American Colleges and Universities.

literary journalism—that the pedagogical value of literary journalism study aligns closely with the objectives of all four LEAP essential learning outcomes and contributes to a foundational liberal education that will serve students well as future professionals and lifelong learners.

Method

The results presented in this chapter are based on a multimethod study that brings together five years of web-based surveys and twenty-six interviews of literary journalism teachers. The surveys began in 2011 and have progressed each year with the exception of 2013. They were developed to inform teaching panels created for the annual International Association for Literary Journalism Studies (IALJS) conference, and some have been shared at the annual Association for Journalism and Mass Communication conference.[24] The number of survey respondents has varied from year to year, with a range of 44 respondents in 2012 to 110 respondents in 2014. While over two-thirds of survey respondents teach in the United States, educators in twenty-seven other countries also contributed. The respondents are an experienced group: over one-third have been teaching twenty or more years and over one-half have been teaching fifteen or more years. Almost all respondents teach undergraduate students.

Additionally, semi-structured, in-depth interviews with twenty-four postsecondary instructors of literary journalism were conducted by phone and video call from January to May 2017. The average duration of each interview was fifty-three minutes. An additional two instructors responded to questions via email, resulting in a total sample of twenty-six instructors (fourteen female and twelve male) from eleven countries. Participants ranged in their teaching experience from graduate students to retired faculty at institutions with student body populations ranging from roughly 1,000 to more than 33,000. Interview participants taught literary journalism at both the graduate and undergraduate levels and came from a variety of disciplinary departments (e.g., journalism, English, creative writing, and language).

Results

Results from both surveys and interviews with postsecondary instructors of literary journalism suggest that the pedagogical interests of teaching in this genre intersect with each of the LEAP essential learning outcomes in specific ways.

Knowledge of Human Cultures and the Physical and Natural World

When asked "What do you want students to learn through reading [literary journalism]?" in the 2011 survey for this study, instructors indicated that they want students to gain knowledge about "the world they live in" and learn how the world "is supposed to work and how it actually does (n't)."[25] Instructors surveyed also indicated that when selecting texts to read in their classes, one of their considerations was subject matter. Specifically, instructors noted that they considered characteristics such as timeliness, diversity of origin, and classical status, among other criteria, when selecting their texts.

To see evidence of how these goals in text selection intersect with the LEAP objective of acquiring knowledge, we can peruse some of the titles that literary journalism instructors surveyed in 2012 reported assigning in their classes. From the biological, economic, and ethical considerations of John Valliant's *The Golden Spruce*; to the nuances of cultural and political history in Joe Sacco's *Palestine*; to the gritty sociological insights on urban life and youth development in Adrian Nicole LeBlanc's *Random Family*; to the counterculture chronicles of Tom Wolfe, David Lewis Stein, Joan Didion, and others, literary journalism dives deep into the factual world and the implications of our actions for the world around us. Moreover, instructors almost always use these texts as points of classroom discussion, which allow students to gain a greater understanding of these topics by hearing the perspectives of their peers.

Interviews with instructors bear out these intersecting objectives of literary journalism and LEAP. In applying literary journalism to teaching students composition in her French program at Fordham University in New York, Kari Evanson said she has students do immersive writing exercises about their first-hand observations in New York City.[26] Students often come back with insightful reflections on issues like poverty, income inequality, racism, and discrimination, she said. Additionally, she noted that reading French literary journalism texts, such as Henri Béraud's *Le flâneur salarié* or Joseph Kessel's *Marchés d'esclaves*, offers students an opportunity beyond sociological research to confront current and historical social challenges—questions of immigration, labor, race, gender, exoticism, and orientalism.

Intellectual and Practical Skills

Perhaps the most explicit intersection of teaching literary journalism with LEAP outcomes is found in the shared aim of developing intellectual and practical skills. Surveyed instructors indicated that, along with knowledge about the world around them, they want students to learn to think deeply and critically, to become better writers, and to become better reporters. Literary journalism is employed in a variety of classroom contexts, which shape certain pedagogical emphases. Among respondents to the 2015 survey, just under one-quarter (23.3%) reported teaching primarily the *study of* literary journalism, just over one-quarter (27.4%) of respondents reported teaching primarily the *practice of* literary journalism, and the remaining half (49.3%) reported teaching both. Additionally, some postsecondary instructors teach classes wholly devoted to the study of literary journalism—either academically or as praxis—while other instructors employ literary journalism as an *instrument* in teaching courses with other primary subject matter.

These responses suggest that, among other benefits, literary journalism instruction offers a concrete means of incorporating outside sources to write across genres, which has been identified through AAC&U research as a continuing challenge.[27] At face value, bringing together *literary* and *journalism* offers students an opportunity to learn from the conventions and styles of these two oft-segregated traditions to understand, for example, how we might consider texts along a spectrum that straddles literature and nonfiction. On the website for his project *Reading Narrative Journalism*, Christopher Wilson points out that reading and analyzing the genre brings together critical thinking approaches that cannot be accomplished through examining texts from traditional journalism or literary fiction alone. Specifically, Wilson suggests that literary journalism offers us four approaches to reading and understanding a work of literary journalism: (1) reading for news content, (2) reading for the narrative story-form, (3) reading for the legwork, or the story of how the journalist collected the information and put it together in the text, and (4) reading for the subject, or the stories of the people about whom these works are written.[28] Wilson argues that "works of [literary] journalism are especially unique and challenging precisely because, unlike many other kinds of texts we encounter, arriving at a critical reading typically involves thinking about these four crucial dimensions, often at the same time."[29]

Wilson further notes that this genre asks us to reconsider, or "unlearn," some of our existing ideas about "objectivity" as an inherent requirement of journalism or as categorically opposed to the narrative construction that we often associate with literature. That is, first, literary journalism presents audiences with works that may or may not conform to an objective *approach* in the writer's obtaining information but which nonetheless are understood as *factually accurate* accounts of the people and events they portray. Second, regardless of whether a writer ascribes to an objective method of researching the story, the narrative is nonetheless a construction—a *lens*—that asks us to see the world in a certain way.[30]

Thus, it is exactly these kinds of complications of both form and content, along with the multidimensional interplay of research and presentation, that make literary journalism an optimal field of study for students to develop the critical intellectual skills that LEAP identifies as essential for a liberal education. While the qualities of journalism alone and the qualities of literature alone both offer great opportunities for developing abstract analytical skills, only literary journalism brings the qualities of these two forms together in a synergistic blend to simultaneously broaden our factual and conceptual knowledge. At the same time, the genre forces readers (e.g., students) to wrestle with conventional expectations of a given text. It is not simply that we must read for story, journalistic legwork, character, and content; often we must read in all of these ways at the same time—or as Wilson says, to read in "4-D."[31] We must recognize that the text was borne out of these simultaneous expectations put upon the writer, and we are likewise expected to understand the text in these factual and literary contexts simultaneously. In doing so, our critical capabilities become more attuned to textual qualities, such as journalistic limitations imposed upon a literary flourish or the accentuated vividness produced through a real-life metaphor.

Along with this enhanced engagement with primary texts of literary journalism, whether students engage in the academic study or the practiced craft of the genre, they are introduced to a variety of ways to incorporate outside sources in their own written work. Biographical and historical secondary source material might inform rhetorical analysis of a text, while primary source material collected from students' interviews may be used to create their own works of literary journalism.

Interview results also supported this broad applicability of literary journalism and its value for improving writing skills. Barry Siegel, who won the 2002 Pulitzer Prize for feature writing and went on to direct the literary journalism program at the University of California, Irvine, likened his applied literary journalism students to auto mechanics:[32] They take apart great literary journalism texts to see how they work. Learning to apply these techniques to their own writing is empowering, Siegel said: "I've had so many students say at the end of the process, 'I never thought I could do this.'" Kate McQueen, who taught literary journalism to prison inmates as part of the Education Justice Project at the University of Illinois at Urbana–Champaign, said literary journalism offers students alternatives to the narrative frames they encounter in mainstream media.[33] McQueen gave her students the opportunity to explore self-portrayals through writing their own personal narratives, which would often then be published in a newsletter distributed to other inmates at the prison as well as people at the University of Illinois. Other instructors likewise noted that students frequently had their work published in various ways and that this kind of reward provides motivation for students to actually care about their writing, to see it as an extension of themselves and not merely a blunt tool to get a job done.

With respect to critical thinking skills, results of this study align with observed challenges in students' abilities to draw conclusions and understand why various issues are important in a broader context.[34] One interviewee, who asked not to be identified in this study, suggested that, particularly with the current emphasis on standardized testing in primary and secondary schools, students are not being adequately prepared with the critical thinking skills expected of them when they arrive in college.[35] Prior to college, the interviewee explained, "It's about basically repeating the question and using a quote and summarizing." However, literary journalism, the instructor said, offers students a way to move beyond this superficial formula and to think critically about modern media. In a time when content producers are competing for our attention with soundbites and clickbait, literary journalism lets us slow down and consider what may be missing from, or misleading about, the popular narratives presented through mainstream media.

Instructors also suggested in interviews that we should not lament or be surprised that young college students do not yet bring the same level of critical thinking to the subject as someone with more life experience or more previous exposure to the genre. Rather, literary journalism instructors should seize the opportunity that the genre affords to help *build* these critical-thinking skills. Robert Boynton, the director of New York University's literary reportage concentration, said literary journalism introduces students to texts, ideas, methods, and techniques that they were unaware of.[36] He tells them, "Here's a whole set of ideas and techniques and ways to look at reality and people that you may have not known really were even available to you."

In these responses, we see where teaching literary journalism brings writing and critical thinking to bear on developing other dimensions of intellectual and practical skills identified explicitly in this second LEAP essential learning outcome. In comparing media narratives, for example, we see arable ground for developing information literacy. Through courses that teach the reporting skills necessary to produce original works of literary journalism, we see immediate opportunities for developing primary research skills in inquiry and analysis. At the same time, courses that pursue a more academic treatment of literary journalism texts offer opportunities to develop higher-level research skills necessary for learning in a more scholarly context.

LEAP also suggests that intellectual and practical skills should be "practiced extensively, across the curriculum."[37] Over half of the respondents to the 2016 survey reported assigning book-length readings (54.5%), and comments included encouraging students to read widely and assigning readings frequently. Most educators (85.0%) said they assign substantial writing assignments, up to 240 pages in a semester. Reported assignments using teamwork have included up to fourteen students working together on the same project. Resulting writings have evolved into published books and magazines, and the work sometimes develops over more than one semester. Additionally, respondents hailed from a range of departments across the curriculum with forty-seven different names. While eighteen of these names included the word "journalism," there was notable variation. Twenty-nine names did not include the term journalism and instead used other words such as English; American Studies; Media and Cultural Studies; Philology and Communication; Romance Literature and Languages; and Culture, Politics and Society.

Personal and Social Responsibility

Instructors responding to the 2011 survey question "What do you want students to learn through reading [literary journalism]?" said also that they want students to "feel appreciation and joy for reading" and to "become better readers." In a 2015 article in *American Educator*, Daniel Willingham suggests that many students avoid reading because they think of it as work, not pleasure.[38] Robert Leamnson similarly argues that reading, as well as writing, will become an effective learning experience only when associated with a certain level of emotional involvement, or interest.[39]

In interviews, many instructors noted their own love of literary journalism as their motivation to teach it. Furthermore, many indicated that the descriptive, narrative qualities of literary journalism make this genre appealing to students. Paul Ashdown, a retired journalism professor from the University of Tennessee, said he once had a Danish student who, after reading the literary journalism anthology *The Art of Fact*, went back and compiled his own anthology of Danish literary journalism.[40] Other students have sent him pictures of literary journalism books they began reading after they left his courses. However, Ashdown noted that many times students have the will to read but do not have the mindset to set aside significant blocks of time to do it. The academic context of literary journalism courses offers students extrinsic motivation (i.e., getting a good grade) that can be translated into intrinsic motivation (i.e., pleasure of reading) if they are presented with literary journalism texts that they can connect with personally and emotionally.[41]

Some instructors interviewed suggested that the traditional emphasis on New Journalism and other "canonical" works might not be working for today's students. Amy Lauters, chair of the Department of Mass Media at Minnesota State University, Mankato, said her literary journalism students regularly complain that some of the texts are too dated.[42] Kent State University journalism professor Jacqueline Marino also said she recognizes this desire among students for readings that are more current and relatable.[43] Much of this work is now found online, she said, and may incorporate multimedia storytelling that is both engaging and instructional for students. To realize the potential of literary journalism in fostering a liberal education, instructors who rely only on classically heralded works of the genre might consider also incorporating newer material.

Other dimensions of this third LEAP outcome include "ethical reasoning and action" and "intercultural knowledge and competence." Here again, text selection can be a critical component in achieving these goals. Reading Djuna Barnes's "How It Feels to Be Forcibly Fed" confronts students with ethical questions on human volition and the right to die in the context of the early twentieth-century women's suffrage movement. John Hartsock, a professor in the Communication and Media Studies Department at SUNY Cortland, listed a number of texts from non-American writers that he regularly uses in his classroom, such as the autobiography *I Am Nujood, Age 10 and Divorced* by Nujood Ali and Svetlana Alexievich's *Zinky Boys*, which offer students a more globalized perspective.[44] "I've decided to put the focus on something that gives them content," Hartsock said, "that gives them a true liberal arts education, that helps to get them more broadly educated so that they can understand other cultures better, including their own." Exposure to this kind of reading asks students to internalize a certain social responsibility—to recognize that suffering, oppression, and other social ills are not nearly as removed from our own lives as we often believe—yet also recognize the various complexities (e.g., cultural, psychological, gendered) of such challenges.

Personal and social responsibility components are also addressed beyond class readings. Writing assignments reported in the 2016 survey included a variety of cultural and civic topics. Extended survey responses included one professor stating she asks students to compare "how the two Native American writers Thomas King and Linda Hogan approach the telling of national, tribal, and personal histories and how their storytelling deviates from conventional historiography or the discourse we associate with the discipline of history." Cheryl Bacon, chair of the Department of Journalism and Mass Communication at Abilene Christian University, noted in her survey response that she requires students to reach "outside their cultural comfort zone." Resulting stories have featured a local Mexican American soccer league, a trade mission project to Honduras by the local Black Chamber of Commerce, a Japanese student spending a day with a ranch hand hauling hay, and a French student covering a goat cook-off. At the same time, while students need to be challenged, they also need to be personally invested. Another educator attributed project success to student interest. Some topics students have selected included a nonprofit that conducted a gang intervention for kids and their families; an after-school visual learning course in a South Central LA housing project; and "the fifth-year anniversary of the Haiti earthquake and how education, local business and faith were part of the comeback in that country."

Integrative and Applied Learning

Clearly, courses focused on developing the skills of applied literary journalism afford opportunities to meaningfully synthesize "connections among experiences outside of the formal classroom."[45] Student journalism of all kinds requires reporters to go into the field for interviews, observations, and background research. However, the *immersive* reporting required for literary journalism experiences magnifies these out-of-class learning experiences. Instructors regularly have students dissect works of literary journalism to consider how they, too, might apply similar techniques of capturing dialogue, scene-setting, detailed observation, or character description in their own stories. Berkley Hudson, a journalism professor at the University of Missouri, said in an interview that he takes students on field trips to practice immersive reporting.[46] For one exercise, he assigns each student one of the five senses to focus on, and write about, as they walk around—and then into—a state park cave.

Additionally, many respondents in the 2014 survey indicated that their students are increasingly incorporating digital, multimedia technologies in producing their original works of literary journalism. One respondent likened the various digital media platforms to tools in a toolbox, stating, "The more tools one has to work with, the better the story will be." Another respondent stated, "Expanding to include motion and sound and text and graphics adds incredible depth to stories." In the 2016 survey, roughly three out of ten respondents (68.6%) reported they include social media in their assignments. Among other ways these technologies are being implemented, students are using social media to share about their experiences in immersive reporting, find sources for their stories, publish their work, and engage with a community of their readers. Thus, students are able not only to develop multimedia skills that they will likely use in their professional and personal lives beyond the classroom but also to connect to audiences beyond their immediate classmates in the process of employing these technologies in their assignments.

Outside of the immediate application of learning to report and write original works of literary journalism, either traditionally or as complemented by digital media, classes focused on a more academic dissection of texts likewise offer opportunities for integrative learning. A number of instructors interviewed noted that their courses often draw students from disciplinary concentrations outside of literature, journalism, or writing. For example, the study of history has a natural intersection with the study of literary journalism, which chronicles many of the most significant moments in modern civilization. Students of sociology or anthropology are attracted to the accessible ethnographic methodology that literary journalism requires.

Shared Purpose and Shared Outcomes

The results of this study suggest a clear intersection between the purposes of teaching literary journalism and the AAC&U's purpose to promote liberal education through the LEAP essential learning outcomes (see Figure 30.2).[47] The charge to focus students' knowledge of human cultures and the physical and natural world through engaging them with "big questions, both contemporary and enduring," maps directly onto responses from journalism educators regarding what they want students to learn. Through reading and discussing texts that are both interesting and informative, along with thoughtfully chosen writing assignments, students are invited to wrestle with big issues—from ongoing environmental concerns, to social justice challenges, to international and intracultural conflict.

Aligning with the effort to develop intellectual and practical skills among students, literary journalism, as employed across a variety of disciplines, offers flexibility to adapt according to instructors' expectations in terms of pedagogical objective, subject matter, and skill level. The genre is being used to teach students in classes ranging from first-year composition courses, to upper-level writers' workshops, to graduate seminars in literary analysis. Depending on their goals, instructors may find literary journalism to be an effective tool for developing communication skills, information literacy, critical and creative thinking, and inquiry and analysis.

Of course, with this flexibility comes the responsibility of instructors to carefully assess how to best utilize literary journalism in their courses. Younger undergraduate students with less life experience cannot be expected to bring the same sophistication to their reading or writing as, say, graduate students who are ten years their senior. Similarly, students coming from a journalism program would be already well versed in the skills and work necessary to produce originally reported work and, therefore, likely have an advantage in an applied literary journalism

Literary Journalism and Pedagogy

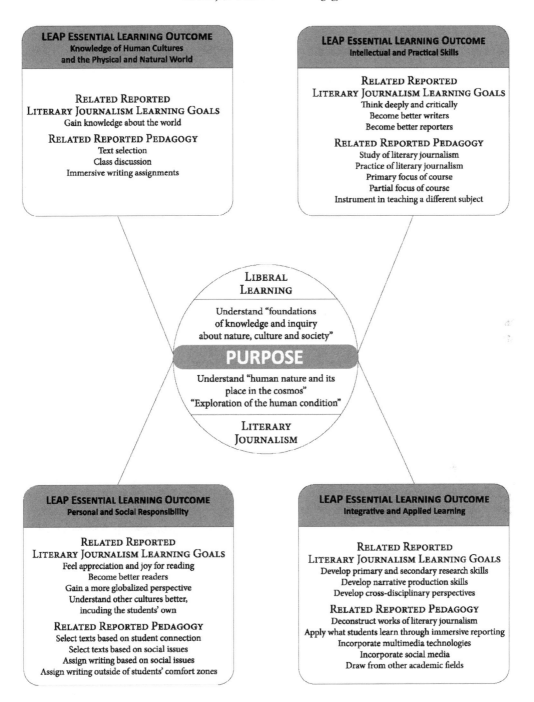

Figure 30.2 Purpose and learning outcomes shared by LEAP and literary journalism.

course over students coming from an English program, for example, where most of the coursework had focused on a more academic treatment of texts.

LEAP suggests that the third essential learning outcome, personal and social responsibility, should be "anchored through active involvement with diverse communities and real-world challenges." Here again, the potential for applied student work offers strong opportunities for "active involvement." However, more academic courses in literary journalism also offer fertile ground to consider and address real-world challenges because the "journalism" of the genre insists on a foundation in nonfiction. Thus, for example, students who learn of the *factual* abuses experienced by a young Yemeni girl forced into marriage (in *I Am Nujood, Age 10 and Divorced*) may be more apt to get involved with an on- or off-campus women's rights organization. Students who read David Finkel's *The Good Soldiers* or *Thank You for Your Service* may find their way to volunteering with a veteran's organization or seek out research opportunities in PTSD. Many students will not, of course, but active involvement can be prompted by the full, deep awareness afforded by literary journalism.

Lastly, the results of this study show that literary journalism courses draw students from a variety of disciplines to integrate learning across a range of academic and applied contexts. For example, University of Lisbon Language School Director Isabel Soares said she uses literary journalism texts to "counterbalance the official political discourse of empire-building."[48] Applied in the context of an American classroom, this postcolonial approach to teaching the genre might offer students new ways of understanding the mainstream historical narratives of our nation and its place on the geopolitical stage. Such courses might attract students of history, cultural studies, political science, and numerous other disciplines. Additionally, other studies have noted that literary journalism texts have been applied in teaching students transcultural nursing skills.[49] So the potential for literary journalism to reach across disciplines is deep and wide.

A Couple of Journalism Program Exemplars

While the preceding discussion has noted that the teaching of literary journalism frequently reaches into various disciplinary domains and is employed in a variety of classrooms and programs, it is worth taking a moment to examine a couple of notable examples of academic programs around the US that explicitly emphasize or center on literary journalism. The academic landscape presents a veritable cornucopia of quality literary journalism education offered throughout the country, and we present only two examples here as a means of highlighting some of the strong pedagogical potential that is already being realized in American higher education. There are, of course, many other programs that could be included in this discussion. With the intersection and overlap of terms like "literary journalism," "narrative journalism," "creative nonfiction," and "literary reportage" employed in teaching literary journalism, one could spend a career identifying and discussing the best programs and their practices. The brief discussion below considers just two notable examples—one at the graduate and one at the undergraduate level. (Readers interested in diving further into postsecondary offerings for literary journalism studies might also look at institutions such as Boston University, the University of Oregon, the Medill School at Northwestern University, the Mayborn School at the University of North Texas, Columbia University, Washington University in St. Louis, Goucher College, and the University of North Carolina Wilmington, among many others.)

One of the most striking distinctions in postsecondary literary journalism education is in the stark contrast between the number of existing graduate versus undergraduate programs that focus directly on literary journalism. While master's-level programs abound, undergraduate programs are nearly nonexistent. However, one university stands out as an exception. The University of California, Irvine, offers its students both a major and a minor in the study of literary journalism. Directed by Barry Siegel, mentioned earlier as an interviewee for this study, the program includes courses such as Introduction to Literary Journalism, Immersion Journalism, History and Theory of Literary Journalism, Immigrant Narratives, and Literature of Law. Along with being perhaps the only undergraduate US program completely focused on literary journalism, this program stands out for its rich instructional blend of applied practice and theoretical, conceptual perspective. Students gain hands-on experience reporting longform narratives in written and multimedia forms, but they also interrogate the ethics of "covenants with readers versus covenants with subjects; fundamental truth versus factual accuracy; the blurred lines between fiction and journalism; entering the minds of your characters; reconstructing past events; imposing meaning by seeing/stories/in situations."[50] Moreover, the program demonstrates the potential for literary journalism to contribute to a broad-based liberal education through its collaborative forums and lecture series, which it holds in conjunction with UCI's history department and law school.

At the graduate level, the Literary Reportage program at New York University certainly stands out. Starting with the program's director, Robert Boynton (also interviewed for this study), NYU's master's concentration in literary reportage boasts a faculty of professional A-listers such as Ted Conover and its Distinguished Writer in Residence, James McBride. Its students are regular contributors to publications like *Harper's*, the *Guardian*, and the *Nation*, and with its additional emphasis on "audio reportage," student work is also found in places such as the nationally syndicated public radio news show *Here & Now*, as well as various podcasts. The NYU program is explicitly professional in its emphasis, as are many master's-level programs. (Academic study of literary journalism at the graduate level seems, anecdotally, most often conducted in doctoral studies according to the specific interests of individual students.) Its website reads: "Journalism schools produce good reporters; MFA programs train beautiful writers. In Literary Reportage, we combine the best of both. We will teach you how to transform your passions into well reported, thoroughly researched, beautifully expressed journalism."[51] In the course of learning to become strong literary journalists, students are also required to take elective courses that may include "Undercover Reporting: The Truth about Deception," "Magazines of the Twentieth Century," or "The Journalism of Empathy." Thus, within the distinct frame of applied reportage, students are drawn into ethical, historical, and sociological discussions, all of which again point to the value of literary journalism study for a liberal education.

Limitations and Closing Thoughts

In this chapter, we have suggested that studying literary journalism offers a rich and wide range of opportunities to promote students' liberal education. We have sought to map as closely as possible the findings of our research with the specific objectives of the LEAP essential learning outcomes and the rigorous empirical work that is being done through this initiative. However, this is not to suggest that literary journalism is right for every teacher and every course. Educators must gauge their own interest in the genre, as well as that of their unique student populations, and decide for themselves if it will be useful in meeting their own pedagogical goals. Additionally, the results presented here represent the perceptions only of instructors, not of students. Future research would do well to explore the latter area.

Nonetheless, this research and discussion derives from a robust multiyear, ongoing project that has yielded insights regarding the promises and challenges of teaching literary journalism. Based on input from instructors in the field, we believe that this genre affords a great deal of malleability in realizing the pedagogical goals of a liberal education within a wide range of instructional and disciplinary contexts. Others' work in this area may help deepen understanding and provide additional examples of how literary journalism pedagogy can support LEAP learning outcomes.[52] Explicitly sharing this connection with others may help those not "in the know" to better understand the didactic value of our field. We hope this conversation continues.

Notes

1. Dow, "Reading Otherwise," 119.
2. Rosenbaum, "Ron Rosenbaum," para. 72.
3. Abrahamson, "Narrative of Collegial Discovery," 93.
4. Maguire, "Literary Journalism," 56.
5. Scheuer, "Critical Thinking," 37.
6. Association of American Colleges and Universities, "AAC&U Members."
7. National Leadership Council for Liberal Education and America's Promise, *College Learning*.
8. Gotlieb, McLaughlin, and Cummins, "2015 Survey," 139.
9. Lynch, "State," para. 2.
10. Strauss, "University of Wisconsin Campus," para. 2.
11. Mendler, "Why Startups," para. 3.
12. Folkerts, Hamilton, and Lemann, *Educating Journalists*, quoted in Lynch, "State," para. 11.
13. Dreifus. "It Is Better."
14. Redden, "Changing English Major."
15. Association of American Colleges and Universities, *Introduction to LEAP*, para. 1.
16. Association of American Colleges and Universities, "About LEAP," para. 3.
17. Dunkum and Knowles, "Embracing LEAP in Kentucky," para. 3.
18. Texas Higher Education Coordinating Board, *Revising*, 7.
19. Henschel et al., "Trends."
20. Association of American Colleges and Universities, *On Solid Ground*, 12.
21. Association of American Colleges and Universities, 4.
22. Anderson, *Style as Argument*.
23. Clifford, "Reader's Text."
24. John Hanc and Mitzi Lewis have led these survey research efforts with valuable input from David Abrahamson, John Capouya, Hannah Hofmann, Jeffrey Neely, Scott Ramsey, Robin Reid, and Christopher Wilson.
25. Lewis and Hanc, "Encouraging Students," 16.
26. Kari Evanson, interview by Jeffrey C. Neely, March 30, 2017, audio recording.
27. Association of American Colleges and Universities, *On Solid Ground*, 12.
28. Wilson, "Chapter 1," paras. 41–49.
29. Wilson, para. 51.
30. Wilson, paras. 53–64.
31. Wilson, para. 51.
32. Barry Siegel, interview by Jeffrey C. Neely, March 30, 2017, audio recording.
33. Kate McQueen, interview by Jeffrey C. Neely, March 23, 2017, audio recording.
34. Association of American Colleges and Universities, *On Solid Ground*, 4.
35. Anonymous, interview by Jeffrey C. Neely, February 6, 2017, audio recording.
36. Robert Boynton, interview by Jeffrey C. Neely, March 2, 2017, audio recording.
37. Association of American Colleges and Universities, *LEAP Vision for Learning*, 7.
38. Willingham, "For the Love," 6.
39. Leamnson, *Thinking about Teaching*, 77.
40. Paul Ashdown, interview by Jeffrey C. Neely, April 6, 2017, audio recording.
41. Leamnson, *Thinking about Teaching*, 77.
42. Amy Lauters, interview by Jeffrey C. Neely, February 2, 2017, audio recording.
43. Jacqueline Marino, interview by Jeffrey C. Neely, April 6, 2017, audio recording.
44. John Hartsock, interview by Jeffrey C. Neely, February 24, 2017, audio recording.
45. Association of American Colleges and Universities. "Integrative Learning VALUE Rubric."
46. Berkley Hudson, interview by Jeffrey C. Neely, February 14, 2017, audio recording.
47. The AAC&U statement on liberal learning provides further insight into the underlying goals of LEAP. The statement includes the following:

    > Liberal education requires that we understand the foundations of knowledge and inquiry about nature, culture and society; that we master core skills of perception, analysis, and expression; that we cultivate a respect for truth; that we recognize the importance of historical and cultural context; and that we explore connections among formal learning, citizenship, and service to our communities. … The ability to think, to learn, and to express oneself both rigorously and creatively, the capacity to understand ideas

and issues in context, the commitment to live in society, and the yearning for truth are fundamental features of our humanity.

48 Isabel Soares, email correspondence with Jeffrey C. Neely, April 6, 2017.
49 Anderson, "Teaching Cultural Competence."
50 Literary Journalism Program, "Course Descriptions," para. 2.
51 Arthur L. Carter Journalism Institute, "About the Program," para. 1.
52 See, for example, Christopher Wilson's *Reading Narrative Journalism: An Introduction for Students (1st ed.)* project (https://mediakron.bc.edu/readingnarrativejournalism) that teaches students how to read and interpret literary journalism in a way that is different from reading fiction and journalism and in a way that addresses LEAP learning outcomes distinctly.

Bibliography

Abrahamson, David. "A Narrative of Collegial Discovery on Some Conceptual Essentials." *Literary Journalism Studies* 2, no. 2 (Fall 2010): 85–95.
Anderson, Chris. *Style as Argument: Contemporary American Nonfiction*. Carbondale, IL: Southern Illinois University Press, 1987.
Anderson, Kathryn L. "Teaching Cultural Competence Using an Exemplar from Literary Journalism." *Journal of Nursing Education* 43, no. 6 (2004): 253–59.
Arthur L. Carter Journalism Institute, New York University. "About the Program." Accessed February 7, 2018. https://journalism.nyu.edu/graduate/programs/literary-reportage/.
Association of American Colleges and Universities. "AAC&U Members." Accessed November 1, 2017. http://secure.aacu.org/iMIS/AACUR/Membership/MemberListAACU.aspx.
———. "About LEAP." Accessed June 12, 2017. www.aacu.org/leap.
———. "Integrative Learning VALUE Rubric." Accessed September 19, 2017. www.aacu.org/value/rubrics/integrative-learning.
———. *An Introduction to LEAP*. Accessed February 23, 2018. www.aacu.org/sites/default/files/files/LEAP/IntroToLEAP2015.pdf.
———. *The LEAP Vision for Learning: Outcomes, Practices, Impact, and Employers' Views*. Washington, DC: Association of American Colleges and Universities, 2011. Accessed July 17, 2018. www.aacu.org/sites/default/files/files/publications/LEAP_Vision_Summary.pdf.
———. *On Solid Ground: VALUE Report 2017*. Washington, DC: Association of American Colleges and Universities, 2017. www.aacu.org/OnSolidGroundVALUE.
Clifford, John. "The Reader's Text: Responding to Loren Eiseley's 'The Running Man.'" In *Literary Nonfiction: Theory, Criticism, Pedagogy*, edited by Chris Anderson, 247–61. Carbondale, IL: Southern Illinois University Press, 1989.
Dow, William. "Reading Otherwise: Literary Journalism as an Aesthetic Narrative Cosmopolitanism." *Literary Journalism Studies* 8, no. 2 (Fall 2016): 118–37.
Dreifus, Claudia. "It Is Better to Give Than to Receive." *New York Times Magazine*, December 14, 1997. Accessed July 17, 2018. www.nytimes.com/1997/12/14/magazine/it-is-better-to-give-than-to-receive.html.
Dunkum, Molly, and Tracy Knowles. "Embracing LEAP in Kentucky." *Peer Review* 19, no. 3 (Summer 2017). Accessed July 7, 2018. www.aacu.org/peerreview/2017/Summer/Kentucky.
Folkerts, Jean, John Maxwell Hamilton, and Nicholas Lemann. *Educating Journalists: A New Plea for the University Tradition*. New York: Columbia Journalism School, 2013.
Gotlieb, Melissa R., Bryan McLaughlin, and R. Glenn Cummins. "2015 Survey of Journalism and Mass Communication Enrollments: Challenges and Opportunities for a Changing and Diversifying Field." *Journalism and Mass Communication Educator* 72, no. 2 (June 2017): 139–53. https://doi.org/10.1177/1077695817698612.
Henschel, Sally, Mitzi Lewis, Kelly Calame Wade, and Danielle Schwertner. "Trends in Undergraduate General Education in the U.S., the Texas Core Curriculum, and Communication Course Requirements." *Texas Education Review* 6, no. 1 (April 2018): 84–101.
Leamnson, Robert. *Thinking about Teaching and Learning*. Sterling, VA: Stylus, 1999.
Lewis, Mitzi, and John Hanc. "Encouraging Students to Be Readers: Survey Results of Successful Practices." *Teaching Journalism and Mass Communication* 2, no. 1 (2012): 12–20.
Literary Journalism Program, University of California, Irvine. "Course Descriptions." Accessed February 7, 2018. www.humanities.uci.edu/litjourn/program/courses.php.

Lynch, Dianne. "The State of American Journalism Education." In *Above & Beyond: Looking at the Future of Journalism Education*. Miami, FL: John S. and James L. Knight Foundation, 2015. Accessed July 16, 2018. https://knightfoundation.org/features/je-the-state-of-american-journalism-education.

Maguire, Miles. "Literary Journalism as a Key to Reporting's Richest Prize." *Literary Journalism Studies* 3, no. 1 (Spring 2011): 53–71.

Mendler, Adam. "Why Startups Should Hire Liberal Arts Graduates." *Inc.*, January 24, 2018. Accessed July 17, 2018. www.inc.com/young-entrepreneur-council/why-startups-should-hire-liberal-arts-graduates.html.

National Leadership Council for Liberal Education and America's Promise. *College Learning for the New Global Century: A Report from the National Leadership Council for Liberal Education and America's Promise*. Washington, DC: Association of American Colleges and Universities, 2007. Accessed July 17, 2018. www.aacu.org/sites/default/files/files/LEAP/GlobalCentury_final.pdf.

Redden, Elizabeth. "The Changing English Major." Inside Higher Ed, January 11, 2017. Accessed July 17, 2018. www.insidehighered.com/news/2017/01/11/amid-enrollment-declines-speakers-consider-shape-english-major.

Rosenbaum, Ron. "Ron Rosenbaum." Interview by Tim Cavanaugh. Feed, April 2011. Accessed October 21, 2017. https://web.archive.org/web/20010418031539/http://www.feedmag.com/re/re196_master2.html.

Scheuer, Jeffrey. "Critical Thinking and the Liberal Arts." *Academe* 101, no. 6 (2015): 35–39.

Strauss, Valerie. "A University of Wisconsin Campus Pushes Plan to Drop 13 Majors—Including English, History and Philosophy." *Washington Post*, March 21, 2018. Accessed July 17, 2018. www.washingtonpost.com/news/answer-sheet/wp/2018/03/21/university-of-wisconsin-campus-pushes-plan-to-drop-13-majors-including-english-history-and-philosophy.

Texas Higher Education Coordinating Board. *Revising the State Core Curriculum: A Focus on 21st Century Competencies*. Austin, TX: Texas Higher Education Coordinating Board, 2011.

Willingham, Daniel T. "For the Love of Reading: Engaging Students in a Lifelong Pursuit." *American Educator* 39, no. 1 (2015): 4–13.

Wilson, Christopher. "Chapter 1: Introduction." In *Reading Narrative Journalism*. Accessed September 5, 2018. https://mediakron.bc.edu/readingnarrativejournalism/table-of-contents/chapter-1-introduction-new.

31
FROM MAGIC LANTERN SLIDES TO VIRTUAL REALITY

Tracing the Visual in and around American Literary Journalism

Jacqueline Marino and Susan Jacobson

In the late nineteenth century, newspaper readers were captivated by stories of immigrants living in New York City's Five Points slums. Unlike many reporters who wrote those accounts, Jacob A. Riis was no tourist to this netherworld of stinking garbage, rampant crime, and sick children; he used to live there. Before he was a reporter, Riis sometimes worked as a carpenter and a handyman, but he always found himself back in Mulberry Bend, an outbranch of Five Points, sleeping in doorways and police lodging houses, barely managing not to starve.[1] A Scandinavian immigrant who came to the United States in 1870, Riis developed a strong mission to help the poor as he settled into a career reporting on the police beat in the late 1870s.[2] Unlike the work of many other reporters of the time, Riis's writing was empathetic, crafted so readers would identify with immigrants as human beings, establishing him firmly among American literary journalists of the nineteenth century.[3] It was not Riis's heartfelt stories, however, but how he paired those stories with photographs in his landmark 1890 text-and-picture book *How the Other Half Lives* that distinguished him among the literary journalists of his time.

With this work, a literary journalistic relationship between words and images found its footing. Over the next 130 years, visual journalists often occupied the contested fronts of journalism's changing norms, interjecting convention-bending practices on the edges of the mainstream. Visual and literary journalism appeared on the same media platforms, sometimes even in the same publications, and were affected by the same business and social influences. Using examples from five major periods, this chapter traces some of the ways in which the craft of visual journalism—which now encompasses photo, video, and multimedia—has evolved, from recording visual "facts" to incorporating the techniques of narrative film, multimedia, and virtual reality to document the human condition, and how these techniques have often blended with American literary journalism.

Writing and the visual have always commingled. "The visual and the verbal are interwoven in the way we decode everyday messages," although the meaning of the visual is not organized in the logical, structured methods of written language but rather "requires an active synthesis of interpretive and emotional skills from the viewer."[4] W. J. T. Mitchell observes that language is not the "paradigmatic" way that meaning is conveyed. He argues that "there are no visual media. ... [A]ll media are mixed media" and that the complex mixing of media, interactions, and influences can be understood through the notion of "braiding," in which two or more media appear together to create a combined meaning.[5]

When words and images are "braided," they can relay the kind of deeper meaning that has attracted readers to traditional literary journalism on the printed page. To understand today's digital literary journalism, then, it's helpful to examine the traditions of those who have made enduring photographs in conjunction with enduring texts, ones that were original in their time. Kevin Kerrane and Ben Yagoda's definition of literary journalism can be applied to this photojournalism: "thoughtfully, artfully and valuably innovative."[6] Photojournalists striving to produce this sort of work have been affected by some of the same factors that have impacted the way "literary stylists" working in journalism outlets have crafted their own work of lasting value and deep purpose. According to Thomas B. Connery, the form of literary journalism has changed depending on journalism's role in society, cultural expectations of the public, and the owners of the media in which literary journalism has been published.[7] Similarly, the role of the photograph in society, cultural expectations of photojournalists, and demands of publishers have affected the way photojournalists have told their visual stories and applied their advancing technologies with the goal of documenting not just the way people lived and the events that shaped their lives but the entirety of the human condition. The most influential among the photojournalists with this mission are the ones who followed their own creative instincts and social consciences, pushing hardest against accepted norms to innovate their craft.

Jacob Riis's Mission for the Photograph of Fact in the Late 1800s

During late-night raids with the sanitary police, Riis lugged his cumbersome photography equipment to the slums and produced a visual record of what he saw and described.[8] To accompany one photograph of an unsmiling family of an English coal-heaver, for instance, he wrote, "A patched and shaky stairway led up to their one bare and miserable room, in comparison with which a white-washed prison-cell seemed a real palace."[9] Riis used photographs like these, called "magic lantern slides," in lectures where he made the case for improving conditions in the slums, which were especially meaningful to the church groups that invited him.[10] It was at one of these lectures where he was asked to write about his work for the *Christian Union*. Soon afterward, *Scribner's* magazine published "How the Other Half Lives: Studies Among the Tenements," an eighteen-page article with twenty illustrations drawn from Riis's photographs.[11] The article led to *How the Other Half Lives*.

Even though engravings made from news-event photographs have been produced in America as far back as 1844, illustrated weeklies established in the 1850s "made photographs and other visual materials equal partners of the printed word in the reporting of news."[12] *Frank Leslie's Illustrated Newspaper* was especially popular, setting in place the audience demand for photographic coverage of the Civil War, the first American conflict systematically documented by photographers.[13] It wasn't until the halftone process was invented in 1880, however, that newspapers and magazines were able to reproduce actual photographs, which became commonplace in big-city newspapers by the end of the nineteenth century.[14] (Small-town newspaper editors didn't publish photographs much until World War I. They couldn't afford the expensive equipment for photo-engraving or the kind of printing press they needed.)[15] The public grew to see photography as "the most accurate way to capture reality."[16] Photographs were thought to provide a factual basis for the events, places, and people journalists covered. In 1886, the *New York Times* art manager Stephen H. Horgan said he believed photographs would help the newspaper relay the news of the day: "The newspaper aims to give a faithful picture of current history," he said. "How much more truthful would that record be if it were made by the unprejudiced and impartial camera[?]"[17]

In late nineteenth-century newspapers, photography emerged as a corrective measure "to the excess of the partisan press."[18] The "sketches" of everyday lives, the literary journalism of the day, stood in contrast to the objectivity of the camera. These sketches were short, colorful accounts of everyday life that could be factual or fictional.[19] Reporters often wrote in the voice of the character and were not concerned about whether audiences took what was reported as fact.[20] During this time, audiences did not know whether they could trust the news reports, which were often sensationally reported, unverified, or falsified altogether. With few exceptions, such as Lincoln Steffens's *New York Commercial Advertiser* in 1897, the rise of photography accompanied a decline in literary journalism sketches in American newspapers as the twentieth century approached.[21]

Reporting with photography became known as photojournalism. The simple definition of photojournalism is to "report visually."[22] According to the National Press Photographers Association's Code of Ethics, photojournalists have a duty

> to report visually on the significant events and varied viewpoints in our common world. Our primary goal is the faithful and comprehensive depiction of the subject at hand. ... [W]e have the responsibility to document society and to preserve its history through images.[23]

In addition to documenting the human condition, Claude Cookman argues that three other traditions have shaped photojournalism in America: to record important events and people, to promote social reform, and to adjust to the evolution of photographic technology.[24] Riis was the first literary journalist to use photographs to fulfill the same goals as his writing, and his work laid the groundwork for all these traditions, especially social reform. Ironically, Riis, who didn't regard himself as a skilled photographer, set the practice of documentary photography in its tracks: not arranging his subjects or their backgrounds to force a point of view but simply photographing a wide enough array of the "other half" to relay an authentic message.[25]

Walker Evans's Publishing Failure of the 1930s

Between the late nineteenth century and mid-twentieth century, photojournalism techniques evolved from Riis's "photography of fact" to encompass a documentary aesthetic. By the 1930s, the photograph became used for more than relaying factual information to the specialized audiences of newspapers, magazines, and books. Photographic technology was now accessible for mass consumption, and the perceived objectivity of the camera made it a powerful force with which to influence others politically.

The documentary text-and-picture books of the Depression display the many ways to pair photographs and words in service of particular messages, evoking Mitchell's notion of "braiding." In the 1930s Depression era, photographers did not have to prove the "other half" existed, but they were often called upon to document their lives in service of a political agenda. Specifically, in order to drum up support for Franklin D. Roosevelt's New Deal programs, the Farm Security Administration (FSA) funded a small number of photographers to document the farming poor of America. Like European artists in the late nineteenth century, some Depression-era American photographers followed the course charted by novelists, creating "the black-and-white artistic equivalent to the novels of John Dos Passos, John Steinbeck, Richard Wright and Tillie Olsen."[26] This effect may also be seen in reverse, as the written stories of John Dos Passos, John Steinbeck, and James Agee were influenced by the visual work of Sergei Eisenstein, Dorothea Lange, and Walker Evans.

The work of these 1930s-era photographers was paired with writing. Although the documentary text-and-picture book was not new—Riis first used works of words and photographs to document the poor—it resonated with the audiences of the Great Depression.[27] Experiments with these photo-and-text explorations abounded, and history has treated some of those experiments better than others. Richard Wright's *12 Million Black Voices*, published in 1941, is lauded as "a folk history of Black America."[28] In contrast, the 1937 book *You Have Seen Their Faces* by Erskine Caldwell and Margaret Bourke-White has been criticized for its use of sensational photographs, some shot at odd angles or using filters, to make sharecropper subjects look as pitiful as possible.[29]

Yet *You Have Seen Their Faces*, which confirmed the dominant view of the farming poor by portraying them as wretched and pathetic, was a commercial success, while Evans and Agee's 1941 *Let Us Now Praise Famous Men*, which contradicted popular perceptions by showing the dignity with which their subjects lived despite their poverty, was a publishing disappointment. Evans, an FSA-supported photographer, had taken time off in order to work with Agee on an assignment for *Fortune* magazine, though it was with the understanding that the government would own his photographs. For three weeks in 1936, the two men lived with one of the three sharecropper families who became the focus of their work. Agee describes the family members' lives in painstaking detail, as well as their interactions, tense moments, and even Agee's own romantic attraction to one of the women. Through this work, Evans's greatest contribution was the unobtrusive and dignified way in which he documented the human condition, even though that treatment went against societal expectations and publishers' directives.

Self-taught and fiercely independent, Evans fought against the political propaganda intentions of the FSA. He didn't believe pictures should be used to further any political goals.[30] "To Evans, the word 'documentary' has a definite and crucial significance," wrote William Stott. "It means that the reality treated is in no way tampered with."[31] About his Depression photographs, he said, "I suppose I was interested in calling attention to something and even shocking people, but I don't think I had the purpose of improving the world. I like saying what's what."[32]

Fortune rejected the article, and Agee and Evans published it as a book. Agee said they produced their work as a book "by necessity. More seriously, it is an effort in human actuality, in which the reader is no less centrally involved than the authors and those of whom they tell."[33] Agee explains:

> If I could do it, I'd do no writing at all here. It would be photographs; the rest would be fragments of cloth, bits of cotton, lumps of earth, records of speech, pieces of wood and iron, phials of odors, plates of food and of excrement. ... A piece of the body torn out by the roots might be more to the point.[34]

Agee's goal of relaying actual human life in all its dignity and suffering through exhaustive documentation was unobtainable, but he strived to achieve it anyway. He recognized the necessity of the photographs—specifically Evans's photographs—to the telling. Unlike how news photographs were conventionally used, Evans's photos were not meant merely to illustrate the text. Rather, Agee writes, "They, and the text, are coequal, mutually independent, and fully collaborative."[35] In an unpublished note, Evans says his "objective picture of America in the 1930's was neither journalistic or political in technique and intention. It was reflective rather than tendentious and, in a certain way, disinterested."[36] Evans's way of documenting the human condition pushed photojournalism beyond its status as a relayer of fact or a vehicle of political propaganda. By showing people as they were, not as victims, villains, heroes, or any other "type" of character, he didn't further any point of view or political agenda. The lack of editorial direction was an invitation to look at the photo subjects as they would be seen at any day and time in the places where they lived and worked. In the 1960s, the *Let Us Now Praise Famous Men* "publishing failure" was rediscovered and deemed a classic.[37]

W. Eugene Smith's Defiance of the *Life* Establishment in the 1940s and 1950s

Although there were no government agencies deploying photojournalists to serve a political agenda in the 1940s and 1950s, some publishers pressured them to confirm dominant social ideologies. This was a golden period for photojournalism, before the rise of television news.[38] World War II diverted the focus from features to hard news. Society expected to see the reality of the conflict through the photojournalist's eye, and this resulted in great feats of bravery in both the actions and the perspectives photojournalists took. War correspondents risked their lives; they now had the technology (smaller cameras, faster shutter speeds) to make photographs reward those efforts. Although their work wasn't often published with literary journalism, as it was in the text-and-picture books of the 1930s, photojournalists did focus on ordinary lives. This was the first war where photographers made pictures from the vantage points of the soldiers and the victims. Robert Capa, a friend of Ernest Hemingway, was known to say, "If your pictures are not good enough, you aren't close enough."[39]

Life magazine was the publication most responsible for this shift in photojournalistic tradition—and for supplying the pressure to confirm dominant social ideologies. While American newspapers sided ever more closely with objective reporting, *Life* highlighted mainstream American values.[40] Photographers and writers were expected to make a judgment about the subjects they covered,[41] and the magazine's photo-driven stories were consumed, at its peak circulation, by twenty-four million readers per week.[42] *Life* covered ordinary people, like its readers.[43] Its first issue showed a naked baby boy just after his birth. Generally, its content seemed to champion Republican politics, patriotism, and American exceptionalism. Many scholars have criticized the magazine for perpetuating mainstream conservative American values over truthful portrayals of the 1950s and 1960s.[44]

The work of William Eugene Smith, who began at *Life* as a war correspondent—one seriously wounded in combat—stands apart from this characterization, however. *Life* published three picture stories from him that broke the *Life* formula. The first, "Country Doctor," published in 1948, focused on Dr. Ernest Ceriani, the only physician in a town of two thousand people. Over twenty-three days, Smith shot pictures of Ceriani attending to every serious medical need, from stitching a child's forehead to amputating a veteran's leg.[45] Smith resisted the heavy-handed editing direction of *Life*'s picture editor, Wilson Hicks, and did not make his deadlines.[46] To capture Ceriani's Herculean job, Smith followed him as he worked, as unobtrusively as possible, similar to the fly-on-the-wall reporting technique of Lillian Ross. Once the pictures were made, Smith worked to portray his character realistically, without placing him into the magazine's predetermined frame. He likened laying out a photo story to writing an essay, "with each picture in relationship to the others."[47] His photographs led the viewer to a specific overall impression, like an essay writer does through the choice and arrangement of facts, observations, and insights.

Some historians have heralded "Country Doctor" as *Life*'s best photo story and a pioneering work of photojournalism. In later works, he went from resisting editorial control—an attribute he shared with Evans in the 1930s—to challenging the journalistic ideal of objectivity. He became more personally involved in the lives of his subjects, including donating blood to an infant while working on a story about a black midwife in South Carolina and eating the same mercury-poisoned fish as the Japanese villagers suffering from neurological problems and birth defects caused by industrial pollution.[48] Smith said he was "always torn between the attitudes of the journalist who is a recorder of facts and the artist who is necessarily at odds with the facts. My principal concern is for honesty, above all, honesty with myself."[49]

Unlike Evans before him, however, he was not concerned simply with showing "what's what." According to Smith's biographer, Jim Hughes, "Gene had managed to produce, for a mass-circulation magazine, a true essay in visual language that successfully combined the fictive power of the short story narrative with the verisimilitude of the camera as witness."[50] Like the short story writer (and many literary journalists), Smith wanted to bring about social change. But unlike Riis, who shared that mission in his documentation of the human condition, Smith felt he needed to manipulate both the environment in which he made photographs and the prints themselves to do that.[51] He didn't believe a photograph was an objective fact, and with "Nurse Midwife" and "Spanish Village," both published in 1951, he manipulated backgrounds and the lighting of prints.[52] He was transparent and even vocal about these decisions, explaining in a letter to his daughter, "Facts just do not tell truth without poetry and drama."[53]

Diane Arbus's Visual Voice of the 1960s

By the 1960s, almost no human subject had evaded the photojournalists. Over the decades, they captured images of people in poverty and war, on city streets and remote countries, and in realms of both the powerful and the powerless. The photograph evolved from being perceived—and treated—as fact to propaganda to essay. Diane Arbus pushed the photograph further into essayistic territory through her portrayals of people on society's fringes, those whom society tends to ignore or ostracize. An Arbus portrait doesn't just challenge dominant ideologies about the human condition; it expands the boundaries of it.

In the 1960s and 1970s, the big picture magazines, such as *Life* and *Look*, were winding down in popularity, losing to television's ability to broadcast moving pictures into people's living rooms. Piling up on their coffee tables, however, were magazines. The vanguard of nonfiction writing was the *New Yorker*, which published groundbreaking works that would go on to fill college reading lists, such as John Hersey's *Hiroshima* (1946), Truman Capote's *In Cold Blood* (1966), and works by John McPhee and Lillian Ross. Meanwhile, literary journalists like Gay Talese, Norman Mailer, and Hunter S. Thompson were turning magazines like *Esquire*, *Harper's* and *Rolling Stone* into must-reads. In 1970, Tom Wolfe would bestow a new title on these writers and others who applied the techniques of fiction writing to journalism, the New Journalists. The decades of the 1960s and 1970s were filled with images of news events, such as the Civil Rights Movement and the Vietnam War. For photojournalists who had documentary goals, however, there was the book—or the route blazed by Arbus in mainstream magazines, such as *Esquire* and *Harper's Bazaar*.

No one before or since has documented the human condition like Arbus. Born into a wealthy Jewish family in New York, she began taking fashion photographs for magazines in the 1940s with her husband Allan Arbus. In 1956, Diane Arbus set off on her own, photographing people on the street, children, passersby, and people at Coney Island. But it was at Hubert's Museum, a flea circus in the basement of a penny arcade on 42nd Street, where she first found the subjects on whom she would build her career: carnival performers, female impersonators, nudists, the obese, and the odd. (Coincidentally, Hubert's was where, less than two decades earlier, literary journalist Joseph Mitchell had found Lady Olga, the bearded lady about whom he wrote for the *New Yorker* in 1940.) Arbus was more than fascinated with her subjects; she seemed to revere them. "Most people go through life dreading they'll have a traumatic experience," she said. "Freaks were born with their trauma. They've already passed their test in life. They're aristocrats."[54]

Like some New Journalists, Arbus threw herself into her subjects' lives, often spending weeks or even years getting to know them. But unlike Joseph Mitchell, Hunter S. Thompson, and other journalists who sometimes chose to profile people on the fringes of society, Arbus became a target of great criticism for her subject choices—and for how she secured their cooperation, which sometimes included sexual intimacy.[55] Arbus wasn't attempting to help the viewer empathize with her subjects or document their lives, in the tradition of Smith or Evans, respectively. In her photographs, Eddie Carmel, "the Jewish Giant," towers over his pained parents. A female impersonator is made up but shirtless under harsh bare-bulb dressing-room lights. Girls at a camp for overweight kids stare angrily into the camera. In Arbus photographs, subjects reveal their hidden selves confidently, even confrontationally. She used frontal light, often shooting with a flash, to deliver this effect.[56] Susan Sontag lambasted Arbus's work for being grotesque and exploitative:

> In their acceptance of the appalling, the photographs suggest a naïveté that is both coy and sinister, for it is based entirely on distance, on privilege, on a feeling that what the viewer is asked to look at is really *other*.[57]

Sontag was not alone in her view of Arbus's work. After Mailer saw photographs she shot of him for *Esquire* in 1963, he said, "Giving a camera to Diane Arbus is like putting a live grenade in the hands of a child."[58] Other critics have been kinder. Robert Hirsch, for instance, wrote that "Arbus unblinkingly pictured people on the margins of society so that their images were no longer about them as individuals but about them as archetypes of human circumstances."[59] And Arthur Lubow, Arbus's most recent unauthorized biographer, has offered this assessment: "It wasn't just truth she was after but Truth. She wanted her pictures to reveal profound verities, to pry out what was invisible to the casual eye."[60]

Arbus's dedication to her subjects is apparent in the text she wrote to accompany her photographs. These narratives lend context, depth, and detail to her portraits. For "The Full Circle," portraits of five eccentric people she photographed for *Harper's Bazaar* in 1961, she includes many poignant details and keen observations, similar in nature to those Joseph Mitchell used to describe Lady Olga.

> Jack Dracula, the Marked Man, is embellished with 306 tattoos (estimated value: $6,000) and although this work in progress conspicuously distinguishes him, he is living in seclusion and I have solemnly sworn not to reveal his whereabouts. There are 28 stars on his face as well as 4 eagles in various postures. … He can outstare any stranger and causes a sensation on the subway, looking loud, proud, aloof, predominantly blue-green, like a privileged exile.[61]

Some of Arbus's magazine work was featured in the now famous *New Documents* exhibition, the 1967 show at the Museum of Modern Art that credited her, along with Garry Winogrand and Lee Friedlander, with creating a new documentary journalistic style, one that was personal instead of bent on raising social consciousness and bringing change. Curator John Szarkowski, MoMA's department of photography director, writes, "Their aim has been not to reform life but to know it, not to persuade but to understand."[62]

The show was groundbreaking but not lucrative. Arbus sold few portraits to collectors.[63] Winogrand found work at a university, and Friedlander made books. Arbus kept developing her style through magazines, managing to do so without straying from her own creative vision. Arbus had 250 photographs published in seventy magazines beginning with portraits of six New Yorkers in *Esquire* in 1960 and ending with photographs of Ozzie and Harriet Nelson and their sons' families in 1971,[64] the year she died by suicide at forty-eight years old. Her photographs of people on society's fringes are evidence of the photograph's remarkable versatility. In addition to its factual value, photographs can be used to serve not just political and social missions but the personal visions of the photographer as well.

The *New York Times*'s Shift to Immersive Journalism and Virtual Reality in the 2010s

In the early twenty-first century, photojournalism's reach and influence are greater than ever. Mitchell Stephens argues that video is on the rise as reading is in decline, providing as an example the televisions that are on everywhere we go, from doctors' offices to airports. People are watching in places where they used to be reading.[65] We now consume more than half of all video on mobile devices,[66] playing video wherever we can bring our phones. Instead of looking for pictures to illustrate the words, literary journalists who wish to reach wide, contemporary audiences must include visual elements in their work. Indeed, audiences look for photographs, videos, and illustrations to do more than "help tell the story." They expect the visual to be part of the story. The words are still read, supplementally, by audiences who want a deeper understanding of a subject, audiences who can find this work more easily than ever thanks to social media and digital presentation.[67] Within the visual, words are also spoken and implied: According to Seth Gitner, "A true visual storyteller must think about what is in front of the camera, and possibly even more importantly, why it is there."[68]

In the second decade of the twenty-first century, video, social media, virtual reality, and other technologies have enabled photojournalism to expand beyond the journalistic standards established at the beginning of the professionalization of the field.[69] Unlike the other time periods discussed in this chapter, we cannot single out any one trailblazer of the 2010s. The innovators in this decade have been teams of journalists, particularly at the *New York Times*, but also at other news outlets, such as the *Guardian*. These teams of photojournalists, developers, and designers are forging a new literary journalism anatomy, one of words and visual parts coming together in what is intended to be one body of storytelling for the audience. Filmmakers and scholars have bent the format of nonfiction narrative toward documentary film first defined by John Grierson as "the creative treatment of actuality."[70] Bill Nichols identifies four modes of documentary film: expository, which creates a narrative arc similar to fiction film, often with a "voice of god" commentary to keep the story on track; observational, which seeks to capture recordings of unstaged encounters in real life; interactive, where the perspective of the filmmaker is made more present through the use of techniques like interviews with the documentary subjects; and reflexive, a technique that is designed to make the process of filmmaking more transparent to the viewer.[71] Some of these techniques are transmutable to digital literary journalism. For example, eyewitness video, often recorded by citizens using their cell phones, has featured prominently in works like "Snow Fall," published in 2012 by the *New York Times*, and "Firestorm," published in 2013 by the *Guardian*, a technique that may have parallels in observational documentary. *Grantland*'s 2013 "Out in the Great Alone" is told from the perspective of the reporter, Brian Phillips, who unmasks the process of creating the multimedia piece through the use of first-person reporting in text, photos, and videos, resulting in storytelling that has elements of both interactive and reflexive documentary.

Paula Rabinowitz describes documentary film as a combination of history, memory, and documents, piling "wreckages upon wreckages" that require editing to evoke meaning.[72] "Images themselves are 'dumb,'" Rabinowitz writes, echoing the words of artist Martha Rosler.[73] Images need sound, text, and the use of montage to create context, to create meaning. "The camera's view is disembodied and so dehistoricized," Rabinowitz writes, citing the use of raw footage from Nazi death camps as an extreme example.[74] While the images are haunting and grisly, by themselves, they do not tell a story. The British government hired master filmmaker Alfred Hitchcock to craft a narrative from the images, and the result was considered so inflammatory it was shelved and remained unviewed for forty years.

Miles Maguire invokes the concept of "borderlands" when analyzing multimedia journalism, finding that, like literary journalism, multimedia representation borrows conventions from several traditions, including film, photography, and design. But there are differences. Maguire examines the multimodal retelling of David Isay's 1998 "Sunshine Hotel" as written text, radio program, and photo book, and discovers that the retelling in different media is not the same:

In the radio version, the hotel residents ... take on symbolic roles in an exploration of the human psychology of failed lives or unfulfilled promise. The newspaper returns the residents to their places in an urban drama that is in all essentials realistic. ... In the book version of their story, the residents are transformed into objects of art, haunting images of human existence that are woven together with fragmentary texts.[75]

As journalism moved onto the internet, one of the earliest examples of literary journalism heavily integrated with digital multimedia components was the *Philadelphia Inquirer*'s "Blackhawk Down." Over twenty-eight days in 1997, Mark Bowden unfurled the story of a battle between American Rangers and armed Somalian citizens that took place when a US helicopter crashed in Mogadishu in 1993. The piece features maps, a photo gallery, audio, and video interviews, among other elements woven into Bowden's riveting narrative. It received hundreds of thousands of views and won the *Editor and Publisher* award for best journalistic series on the internet.[76]

However, the digital longform genre never really caught on until the end of 2012, when the *New York Times* published "Snow Fall: The Avalanche at Tunnel Creek." The story, which drew millions of viewers and won the Pulitzer Prize for feature writing in 2013, spawned an industry of in-depth reporting projects integrated with multimedia elements and literary journalism techniques, including works like "Firestorm" by the *Guardian*, "Out in the Great Alone" by *Grantland*, and "The Prophets of Oak Ridge" by the *Washington Post*.[77] In "Snow Fall," this is achieved from the opening page, which features a full-screen video loop of snow falling on a desolate mountainside that dissolves into textual passages to immediately thrust the reader into the heart of the story: "The snow burst through the trees with no warning but a last-second whoosh of sound, a two-story wall of white and Chris Rudolph's piercing cry: 'Avalanche! Elyse!'"[78]

The piece was so successful that journalists across the country starting asking: "Can we 'Snow-Fall' this?"[79] The news-reading public was apparently ready for the digital innovations that "Snow Fall" popularized: the "parallax scroll," a technique that allows the background of a digital screen to move more slowly than the foreground, creating a 3D effect;[80] video loops, which stand in for still images and "serve to give a sense of place, time or character in the story";[81] and a seamless integration of these multimedia elements within the "cognitive container" of a single, scrolling page of text.[82] In short, "Snow Fall" pressed the boundaries and reaffirmed that it was possible not to "just rely on text to tell the story."[83]

But why was "Snow Fall" successful in launching a new field of digital literary journalism when earlier works like "Blackhawk Down" were less so? By 2013, when "Snow Fall" won the Pulitzer Prize, more than 80 percent of Americans received their news in some kind of digital format.[84] This is in contrast to the 25 percent of US households with internet access in 1997, when "Blackhawk Down" was published.[85] In 2013, the technical infrastructure of the internet and the digital literacy of most Americans created an environment that was hospitable for works like "Snow Fall" to grow, while the technical terrain of 1997 was still too uncultivated for "Blackhawk Down" to seed many offspring.

The divergent influences of "Snow Fall" and "Blackhawk Down" remind us that, while each new media technology brings with it the promise of revolution,[86] sometimes the revolution is unrealized or delayed. Marshall McLuhan observed that the first content of a new medium is an old one, and we can see an example in the digital editions of the early 2000s that consisted of newspapers "repurposing" their print content on the web.[87] Emerging technologies lack a sense of context and history and are often "clumsy."[88] Even the glory of "Snow Fall," heralded for its immersive bells and whistles in 2012 and 2013, faded as newer presentations, such as the *Washington Post*'s "A New Age of Walls," published in 2016, emerged. These stripped-down presentations were designed with cell phone consumption in mind to encourage "linearity" and "the deep reading of the literary mind."[89] Researchers have found that the lack of user choices in works with considerably less infused technology than "Snow Fall" may allow for a less distracting reading and viewing experience.[90]

At the end of the 2010s, immersive technologies emerged as new forms of journalistic expression. Platforms, production processes, and playback devices have evolved rapidly, as is often the case with new technology, and few producers have emerged as leaders in the new form, although the work of the *New York Times* and Nonny de la Peña stand out as having received multiple awards[91] and using different approaches to immersive storytelling.

Journalist-producers of virtual reality, on the other hand, are trying to command the audience's attention with different tools and toward another end. Upon entering "The Displaced," one of the first virtual reality presentations of the *New York Times*, published in 2015, users are thrust into a 360-degree video scene that shows the remains of a school in war-torn Syria.[92] Textual fragments, like museum wall plaques, serve to contextualize the scene, and subtitle translations of the child war refugees' commentary is placed, somewhat awkwardly, at different points in the 360-degree videos. In one such scene, young boys clamber over the remains of desks and bookcases in a bombed-out classroom. As the user looks around, the subtitles appear superimposed, at different points, over the rubble and the boys: "Before, when the teachers would yell at us, we'd say," one fragment reads, followed by "Wouldn't it be cool if the school blew up?" "We would never say that now," the text concludes.[93] This sequence of events plays with the audience's expectations of a news story, frustrating the assumption that all of the pertinent who-what-where-when-why information will be easily accessible to them at a glance, rather than revealed in the spatial metaphor of a 360-degree virtual reality environment.

Virtual reality (VR) is one of the more recent developments in media technology that may also propel digital literary journalism to move beyond the written word and even beyond the visual storytelling techniques pioneered by "Snow Fall." As with "Snow Fall," the *New York Times* has taken an early lead among news organizations producing works for the new medium, beginning with "The Displaced." That project and subsequent *Times* VR works incorporate 360-degree video, audio, text fragments, and "hotspot" navigation points that serve to propel the viewer into the story. Viewers must download a special VR player app to view the projects on a smartphone, which may be attached to an inexpensive viewer.

The contemporary term "virtual reality" dates back to the "goggles and gloves"-era originated by Jaron Lanier at VPL Research in 1987,[94] but its roots go deeper, to the first head-mounted displays developed in the 1960s, the first flight simulators in the 1930s, and even stereoscopic photo viewers of the 1830s.[95] But like "Snow Fall" before it, "The Displaced" emerges with a few advantages that may help create a nourishing environment for virtual reality's sustainability. For one thing, Millennials and Generation Xers are deeply involved with their screens, for better or for worse,[96] so experiencing media in a virtual headset may not be too cumbersome for them. Furthermore, it has become much less costly to consume and produce virtual reality. In 2014, Google produced Google Cardboard, an inexpensive device for viewing immersive 360-degree photos and videos with a cell phone. Earlier devices were hundreds of dollars more expensive. Many inexpensive apps have emerged for viewing and producing 360-degree photos and videos on cell phones. While the quality of the inexpensive tools can be spotty, it is likely to improve.[97]

To date, VR work by the *New York Times* and other mainstream news organizations has emphasized 360-degree video, a technique that places users at the center of a visual environment where they are free to look around by moving their heads, if using a headset, or by swiping left, right, up, or down on a smartphone screen. But the promise of VR is as an immersive, multisensory experience that gives the audience the impression of being in a whole new world, incorporating three-dimensional visual objects and freedom of movement by the users.[98] The dual concepts of "immersion" and "presence" are key to many discussions of virtual reality. Janet Murray describes the features of the *Star Trek* holodeck, perhaps the ultimate virtual reality machine, as immersive: "the sensation of being surrounded by a completely other reality."[99] However, Burcu Dogramaci and Fabienne Liptay point out that the term "immersion" may also describe "a sensation that can equally arise while reading a book, watching a film, visiting an exhibition, or playing a computer game."[100] "To tell a story, you must first of all build a world," the novelist Umberto Eco famously wrote.[101] The difference in immersion that one experiences with virtual reality is that immersion is technically realized: It is "the illusion of *participation* in a synthetic environment rather than an external *observation* of such an environment," as Christian Stein explains.[102] Several theorists have linked an increased level of immersion with an increased perception of "presence,"[103] defined by Matthew Lombard and Theresa Ditton as "an illusion that a mediated experience is not mediated."[104] It is also suggested that the perception of presence engendered by virtual reality may increase the level of empathy that news audiences feel for the subjects of news stories, particularly when compared to news stories conveyed in other media.[105]

But while the visual plays a central role in creating a sense of immersion and presence in virtual reality, it does not have to be perfectly realized to be effective.[106] Perhaps the leading practitioner to emerge from the nascent realm of virtual reality storytelling is de la Peña, whose 2007 work "Gone Gitmo" was created in the online 3D environment Second Life. In this interactive "docu-game," the user plays a prisoner in a 3D rendering of the infamous detention camp and comes in contact with re-creations of documented artifacts of life there. For example, users may overhear the interrogation of a prisoner in another cell, the text of which is based on transcripts of an actual incident.[107] De la Peña's more recent work has included the 2012 "Hunger in Los Angeles," which recreates an incident where a man collapsed in a food bank line; "Use of Force," which depicts a tragic story of deportation and domestic violence; and "Project Syria," a work commissioned by the World Economic Forum in 2014 that combines citizen video with a 3D environment to convey the plight of Syrian children experiencing a street bombing in Aleppo.[108] In all of these works, the user dons a virtual reality headset and is an eyewitness to a re-creation of events that unfolded, as documented by witnesses or in published reports.

The storytelling devices of literary journalism continue in VR but play out differently. Wolfe was only examining the written work of the New Journalism when he identified four devices that distinguished it: (1) constructing scenes through which the story is told; (2) including dialogue; (3) relaying the story through the point of view of characters; and (4) recording such details as possessions, gestures, mannerisms, etc., that symbolize the "status life" of the characters.[109] Scenic depiction in a virtual reality is already occurring. "The Displaced," for example, immediately recreates the world of child war refugees, with the participant as a witness or an observer. Dialogue is easily reproduced in the limited VR world of "Gone Gitmo," where the audience can "overhear" the interrogation of a prisoner. Characterization is created in part by what film theorists Natalie Zemon Davis and Robert Rosenstone would call the authenticity of local people, dressed in their own garb, moving and interacting with their own environment.[110] For example, "Under a Cracked Sky,"[111] a 360-degree video created in 2017 by the *New York Times*, gives users a view of the world of Antarctic divers, who enter the water through a hole in the ice and traverse crystal-clear water populated by stalactites and seals. The "cracked sky" refers to the solid sheet of ice above them. Status details are observed. For example, Alejandro González Iñárritu's VR installation *Carne y Arena* (Flesh and Sand), which premiered at the 2017 Cannes Film Festival, plunges audience members into the world of immigrants seeking to cross over into the United States from Mexico. While hailed for its use of multisensory elements (sounds of gunshots, gusts of wind from helicopter blades, freezing temperatures, sandy floors), users travel with a group of immigrants whose expressions and mannerisms were rendered with motion-capture technology.

Journalists today are trying to figure out how virtual reality and other powerful new visualization tools can and should help their journalistic mission, just as they did in the late nineteenth century when it became possible to publish photography in newspapers and magazines. Unlike in Riis's time, however, today's journalists are trying to do so while upholding widely accepted journalistic standards, including the idea that journalists should not influence the people, situations, or places they cover.[112] Riis used his camera much in the same way he used his writing—to awaken the conscience of his readers and bring about social change. Today's journalists are experimenting with new and increasingly powerful visual tools to increase the public's awareness of "how the other half lives," but the technical requirements and the nature of how one experiences these presentations are challenging. For example, setting up 360-degree cameras and rigging setups can be cumbersome, and producers often must turn the field where journalists record news into what amounts to a movie set. In "The Displaced," for instance, journalists were transparent about needing to delay one of the boys so they could set up the camera on his bicycle. They also had to coordinate some actions with their subjects or have them repeat them.[113] De la Peña and Iñárritu both use motion-capture techniques to create 3D characters in their virtual reality presentations. Journalism ethicists may question the authenticity of what's being witnessed, whose story the journalists have chosen to tell, and what degree of reconstruction is acceptable. As Thomas Kent explains it,

> In some cases, VR producers have operated somewhat as directors, shooting and re-shooting scenes until they get what they want. When that happens there can be question [sic] about whether the project is truly capturing reality at all, or using the people in the scene as extras in a movie.[114]

The literary journalists of the twentieth century heard similar criticism about their practices of reconstruction and choosing points of view, of subject choice and motivation. They were challenging expectations and pushing technological boundaries. Today's photojournalists are doing the same. "Visual media expands while norms are slow to change,"[115] and, therefore, virtual reality and other visual storytelling techniques will attempt to fulfill literary goals in ways we cannot completely predict. For now, literary journalism still features words, artfully arranged, often infused with multimedia online and sometimes (as with "The Displaced") near a link where one can download the accompanying VR story. Both digital literary journalism and VR immerse audiences in their own way, showing distinctive "windows that never provide a complete view of reality."[116] Their audiences come to them for the same purpose, however, to find snapshots of life, as it is lived by someone somewhere, that will lead them to their own meaning.

Notes

1. Sante, introduction to *How the Other Half Lives*, xvi.
2. Kobre, *Yellow Press*, 34.
3. Connery, *Sourcebook*, 87.
4. Mitchell, *Picture Theory*; McCannon, "Towards the Hybrid Essay," 134.
5. Mitchell, "There Are No Visual Media," 9.
6. Yagoda, preface to *The Art of Fact*, 14.
7. Connery, "Literary Aspects of Journalism," 316–17.
8. Connery, *Journalism and Realism*, 174.
9. Riis, *How the Other Half Lives*, 131.
10. Connery, *Journalism and Realism*, 174–75.
11. Connery, 175.
12. Carlebach, *Origins of Photojournalism*, 7, 63–65.
13. Carlebach, 62.

14 Dooley, *Technology of Journalism*, 10.
15 Carlebach, *American Photojournalism*, 40.
16 Connery, *Journalism and Realism*, 122.
17 Campbell, *Year*, 22.
18 Alexander. "'Right Kind of Eyes,'" 21.
19 Sims, *True Stories*, 46, 48.
20 Sims, 54.
21 Sims, 59.
22 Newton, "Photojournalism."
23 National Press Photographers Association, Code of Ethics.
24 Cookman, *American Photojournalism*, 3.
25 Hirsch, *Seizing the Light*, 269.
26 Rabinowitz, "1930s Documentary."
27 Sims, *True Stories*, 139.
28 Polite, "Classic Review."
29 Sims, *True Stories*, 149–50.
30 Cookman, *American Photojournalism*, 117.
31 Stott, *Documentary Expression*, 269.
32 Getty Museum, "Walker Evans."
33 Agee, *Let Us Now Praise Famous Men*, 9.
34 Agee, 28.
35 Agee, 8.
36 Nordeman, "Introduction."
37 Cookman, *American Photojournalism*, 120.
38 Hirsch, *Seizing the Light*, 329.
39 Hirsch, 331.
40 Hirsch, 319.
41 Cookman, *American Photojournalism*, 176.
42 Hirsch, *Seizing the Light*, 319.
43 Cookman, *American Photojournalism*, 150.
44 Cookman, 176.
45 Cookman, 162–64.
46 Cookman, 164.
47 Hirsch, *Seizing the Light*, 332.
48 Cookman, *American Photojournalism*, 169.
49 Rothstein, *Documentary Photography*, 85.
50 Quoted in Cookman, *American Photojournalism*, 165.
51 Hirsch, *Seizing the Light*, 333.
52 Cookman, *American Photojournalism*, 167.
53 Cookman, 169.
54 Davies, "Diane Arbus."
55 Lubow, *Diane Arbus*.
56 Hirsch, *Seizing the Light*, 382.
57 Sontag, "Freak Show."
58 Belth, "Portrait of Diane Arbus."
59 Hirsch, *Seizing the Light*, 382.
60 Lubow, *Diane Arbus*.
61 Arbus, *Diane Arbus*, 17.
62 Museum of Modern Art, *New Documents* press release.
63 Pett, "Photographers Who Exposed America."
64 Arbus, *Diane Arbus*, 152.
65 Stephens, *Rise of the Image*, 8.
66 Roettgers, "More Than Half."
67 Marino, Jacobson, and Gutsche, *Scrolling for Story*.
68 Gitner, *Multimedia Storytelling*, 10.
69 Becker, "Visual Cultures of Journalism"; Schwalbe, Silcock, and Candello, "Gatecheckers."
70 Grierson, "First Principles of Documentary," 147.
71 Nichols, *Representing Reality*, 32–34.

72 Rabinowitz, *They Must Be Represented*, 16.
73 Rabinowitz, 17.
74 Rabinowitz, 21.
75 Maguire, "Literary Journalism," 61.
76 Jacobson, Marino, and Gutsche, "Digital Animation," 530.
77 Jacobson, Marino, and Gutsche.
78 Branch, "Snow Fall."
79 Dowling and Vogan, "Can We 'Snowfall' This?"; Sullivan, "Who Gets to 'Snow-Fall'?"
80 Greenfield, "Good"; Jaffe, "Snow Fail."
81 Jacobson, Marino, and Gutsche, "Digital·Animation," 539.
82 Dowling and Vogan, "Can We 'Snowfall' This?," 3.
83 Asakawa, "'Snow Fall.'"
84 "Key Indicators."
85 "1994–2008—14 Years of Web Statistics."
86 Cuban, *Teachers and Machines*; Postman, *Technopoly*; Steensen, "Online Journalism."
87 McLuhan, *Understanding Media*.
88 Steensen, "Online Journalism"; Oppenheimer, "Virtual Reality Check," 27–28.
89 Dowling, "Toward a New Aesthetic," 108.
90 Jacobson, Marino, and Gutsche, "Should There Be an App?"
91 The *New York Times*'s "The Displaced" won the Cannes Lions International Festival of Creativity's Entertainment Grand Prix in 2016. "Under a Cracked Sky" won first prize in immersive storytelling in World Press Photo's 2018 Digital Storytelling Contest. "David Bowie in Three Dimensions" was a finalist in 2018 in the Excellence in Immersive Storytelling category of the Online Journalism Awards.
92 Sirkkunen et al., "Journalism in Virtual Reality."
93 Silverstein, "Displaced,"
94 "Who Coined the Term?"
95 "History of Virtual Reality."
96 Nielsen Company, *2016 Nielsen Social Media Report*; Alter, *Irresistible*.
97 Aronson-Rath et al., *Virtual Reality Journalism*; Sirkkunen et al., "Journalism in Virtual Reality."
98 Stein, "Virtual Reality Design"; Warnke, "On the Spot."
99 Murray, *Hamlet on the Holodeck*, 99.
100 Dogramaci and Liptay, "Immersion," 9.
101 Eco, *Name of the Rose*, 512.
102 Stein, "Virtual Reality Design," 53.
103 Aronson-Rath et al., *Virtual Reality Journalism*; Domníguez, "Going Beyond"; Sirkkunen et al., "Journalism in Virtual Reality."
104 Lombard and Ditton, "At the Heart."
105 Aronson-Rath et al., *Virtual Reality Journalism*; Nuwer, "Journalism's New Reality"; Sirkkunen et al., "Journalism in Virtual Reality."
106 Murray, *Hamlet on the Holodeck*.
107 Domínguez, "Going Beyond."
108 Nuwer, "Journalism's New Reality."
109 Wolfe, *New Journalism*, 46–47.
110 Davis, "'Any Resemblance'"; Rosenstone, *Visions of the Past*.
111 Corum and Roberts, "Under a Cracked Sky."
112 Mullin, "Virtual Reality."
113 Mullin.
114 Kent, "Virtual Reality Journalism."
115 Becker, "Visual Cultures of Journalism."
116 Connery, *Journalism and Realism*, 213.

Bibliography

"1994–2008 – 14 Years of Web Statistics at UVa." University of Virginia, 2009. Accessed June 27, 2017. www.virginia.edu/virginia/archive/webstats.html.

Agee, James. *Let Us Now Praise Famous Men*. Compiled by Michael Sragow. New York: Literary Classics of the United States, 2005.

Alexander, Robert. "'The Right Kind of Eyes': *Fear and Loathing in Las Vegas* as a Novel of Journalistic Development." *Literary Journalism Studies* 4, no. 1 (Spring 2012): 19–36.

Alter, Adam. *Irresistible: The Rise of Addictive Technology and the Business of Keeping Us Hooked*. New York: Penguin Press, 2017.

Arbus, Diane. *Diane Arbus Magazine Work*. New York: Aperture, 1984.

Aronson-Rath, Raney, James Milward, Taylor Owen, and Fergus Pitt. *Virtual Reality Journalism*. New York: Tow Center for Digital Journalism, 2016. https://towcenter.gitbooks.io/virtual-reality-journalism/content/.

Asakawa, Gil. "'Snow Fall' Set Gold Standard. Now What?" *Quill*, April 10, 2013. Accessed June 27, 2017. www.spj.org/quill_issue.asp?ref=1993.

Becker, Karin. "Visual Cultures of Journalism." Paper presented at the annual meeting of the International Communication Association, San Francisco, CA, May 23, 2007. http://citation.allacademic.com/meta/p168725_index.html.

Belth, Alex. "A Portrait of Diane Arbus at *Esquire*." June 7, 2016. Accessed July 7, 2018. http://classic.esquire.com/editors-notes/diane-arbus/.

Branch, John. "Snow Fall: The Avalanche at Tunnel Creek." *New York Times*, 2012. Accessed June 29, 2017. www.nytimes.com/projects/2012/snow-fall/#/?part=tunnel-creek.

Campbell, Joseph W. *The Year That Defined American Journalism: 1897 and the Clash of Paradigms*. New York: Routledge, 2006.

Carlebach, Michael L. *American Photojournalism Comes of Age*. Washington, DC: Smithsonian Institution Press, 1997.

———. *The Origins of Photojournalism in America*. Washington, DC: Smithsonian Institution Press, 1992.

Connery, Thomas B. *Journalism and Realism: Rendering American Life*. Evanston, IL: Northwestern University Press, 2011.

———. "Literary Aspects of Journalism." In *History of the Mass Media in the United States: An Encyclopedia*, edited by Margaret A. Blanchard, 316–17. Abingdon, UK: Fitzroy Dearborn, 1998.

———. *A Sourcebook of American Literary Journalism: Representative Writers in an Emerging Genre*. Westport, CT: Greenwood, 1992.

Cookman, Claude. *American Photojournalism: Motivations and Meanings*. Evanston, IL: Northwestern University Press, 2009.

Corum, Jonathan, and Graham Roberts. "Under a Cracked Sky." *New York Times*, May 18, 2017. Accessed July 10, 2018. www.nytimes.com/interactive/2017/climate/antarctica-virtual-reality.html.

Cuban, Larry. *Teachers and Machines: The Classroom Use of Technology Since 1920*. New York: Teachers College Press, 1986.

Davies, Lucy. "Diane Arbus: A Flash of Familiarity." *Telegraph*, May 6, 2009. Accessed February 5, 2018. www.telegraph.co.uk/culture/photography/5250229/Diane-Arbus-a-flash-of-familiarity.html.

Davis, Natalie Zemon. "'Any Resemblance to Persons Living or Dead': Film and the Challenge of Authenticity." *Historical Journal of Film, Radio and Television* 8, no. 3 (1988): 269–83. https://doi.org/10.1080/01439688800260381.

Dogramaci, Burcu, and Fabienne Liptay. "Immersion in the Visual Arts and Media." Introduction to *Immersion in the Visual Arts and Media*, edited by Fabienne Liptay and Burcu Dogramaci, 1–17. Leiden, Netherlands: Koninklijke Brill, 2016.

Domínguez, Eva. "Going Beyond the Classic News Narrative Convention: The Background to and the Challenges of Immersion in Journalism." *Frontiers in Digital Humanities* 4 (2017). https://doi.org/10.3389/fdigh.2017.00010.

Dooley, Patricia L. *The Technology of Journalism: Cultural Agents, Cultural Icons*. Evanston, IL: Northwestern University Press, 2007.

Dowling, David. "Toward a New Aesthetic of Digital Literary Journalism: Charting the Fierce Evolution of the 'Supreme Nonfiction.'" *Literary Journalism Studies* 9, no. 1 (Spring 2017): 100–16.

Dowling, David, and Travis Vogan. "Can We 'Snowfall' This? Digital Longform and the Race for the Tablet Market." *Digital Journalism* 3, no. 2 (2015): 209–24. https://doi.org/10.1080/21670811.2014.930250.

Eco, Umberto. *The Name of the Rose*. New York: Harcourt Brace, 1983.

Getty Museum. "Walker Evans in His Own Words." February 2, 2012. Accessed February 5, 2018. www.youtube.com/watch?v=DlXfbixbGG8&list=PL5HEzzxHD17s9poabkVA13ORqoY22KsNA&t=0s&index=2.

Gitner, Seth. *Multimedia Storytelling for Digital Communicators in a Multiplatform World*. New York: Routledge, 2015.

Greenfield, Rebecca. "The Good, the Bad, and the Downright Ugly of Parallax Web Design." *Wire*, July 23, 2013. Accessed June 27, 2017. www.thewire.com/technology/2013/07/good-bad-and-downright-ugly-parallax-web-design/67234/.

Grierson, John. "First Principles of Documentary." In *Grierson on Documentary*, edited by Forsyth Hardy, 147. London: Faber and Faber, 1966.

Hirsch, Robert. *Seizing the Light: A History of Photography*. Boston, MA: McGraw-Hill, 2000.
"History of Virtual Reality." Virtual Reality Society, 2017. Accessed June 27, 2017. www.vrs.org.uk/virtual-reality/history.html.
Jacobson, Susan, Jacqueline Marino, and Robert E. Gutsche Jr. "The Digital Animation of Literary Journalism." *Journalism* 17, no. 4 (2016): 527–46. https://doi.org/10.1177/1464884914568079.
———. "Should There Be an App for That? An Analysis of Interactive Applications within Longform News Stories." *Journal of Magazine Media* 18, no. 2 (Spring 2018). Accessed July 3, 2018. https://aejmcmagazine.arizona.edu/Journal/Spring2018/JacobsonMarinoGutsche.pdf.
Jaffe, Eric. "Snow Fail: Do Readers Really Prefer Parallax Web Design?" *Fast Company*, December 19, 2013. Accessed June 27, 2017. www.fastcodesign.com/3023690/evidence/snow-fail-do-readers-really-prefer-parallax-web-design.
Kent, Thomas. "Virtual Reality Journalism." Online News Association. Accessed June 27, 2017. https://ethics.journalists.org/topics/virtual-reality-journalism-2/.
"Key Indicators in Media and News." Pew Research Center, March 26, 2014. Accessed July 6, 2018. www.journalism.org/2014/03/26/state-of-the-news-media-2014-key-indicators-in-media-and-news/.
Kobre, Sidney. *The Yellow Press and Gilded Age Journalism*. Tallahassee, FL: Florida State University Press, 1964.
Lombard, Matthew, and Theresa Ditton. "At the Heart of It All: The Concept of Presence." *Journal of Computer-Mediated Communication* 3, no. 2 (September 1997). https://doi.org/10.1111/j.1083-6101.1997.tb00072.x.
Lubow, Arthur. *Diane Arbus: Portrait of a Photographer*. Kindle ed. New York: Ecco, 2016.
Maguire, Miles. "Literary Journalism on the Air: What David Isay's Travels in the Footsteps of Joseph Mitchell Can Tell Us about the Nature of Multimedia." *Literary Journalism Studies* 6, no. 1 (Spring 2014): 47–64.
Marino, Jacqueline, Susan Jacobson, and Robert Gutsche Jr. *Scrolling for Story: How Millennials Interact with Long-Form Journalism on Mobile Devices*. White paper. Columbia, MO: Donald W. Reynolds Journalism Institute, University of Missouri, July 22, 2016. Accessed July 3, 2018. www.rjionline.org/stories/scrolling-for-story-how-millennials-interact-with-long-form-journalism-on-m.
McCannon, Desdemona. "Towards the Hybrid Essay: The 'Visual Essay Project.'" *Journal of Writing in Creative Practice* 4, no. 2 (2011): 131–40. https://doi.org/10.1386/jwcp.4.2.131_1.
McLuhan, Marshall. *Understanding Media: The Extensions of Man*. Cambridge, MA: MIT Press, 1994.
Mitchell, W. J. T. *Picture Theory*. Chicago: University of Chicago Press, 1994.
———. "There Are No Visual Media." In *The Visual Culture Reader*, edited by Nicholas Mirzoeff, 9. 3rd ed. New York: Routledge, 2013.
Mullin, Benjamin. "Virtual Reality: A New Frontier in Journalism Ethics." Poynter Institute, January 6, 2016. Accessed June 29, 2017. www.poynter.org/2016/virtual-reality-the-next-frontier-in-journalism-ethics/390280/.
Murray, Janet. *Hamlet on the Holodeck: The Future of Narrative in Cyberspace*. Cambridge, MA: MIT Press, 1998.
Museum of Modern Art. *New Documents* press release. February 28, 1967. www.moma.org/documents/moma_press-release_391564.pdf.
National Press Photographers Association. Code of Ethics. 2017. Accessed July 3, 2018. https://nppa.org/code-ethics.
Newton, Julianne H. "Photojournalism." In *The International Encyclopedia of Communication*. July 9, 2013. Accessed February 4, 2017. https://onlinelibrary.wiley.com/doi/abs/10.1002/9781405186407.wbiecp035.pub2.
Nichols, Bill. *Representing Reality*. Bloomington, IN: Indiana University Press, 1991.
Nielsen Company. *2016 Nielsen Social Media Report*. New York: Nielsen Company, 2017. Accessed June 27, 2017. www.nielsen.com/content/dam/corporate/us/en/reports-downloads/2017-reports/2016-nielsen-social-media-report.pdf.
Nordeman, Landon. "Introduction." *Walker Evans Revolutionizes Documentary Photography*. American Studies Group, University of Virginia, February 28, 2007. http://xroads.virginia.edu/~ug97/fsa/intro.html.
Nuwer, Rachel. "Journalism's New Reality." *Pacific Standard*, November 18, 2015. Accessed June 27, 2017. https://psmag.com/environment/journalisms-new-reality.
Oppenheimer, Todd. "Virtual Reality Check." *Columbia Journalism Review*, March/April 1996, 27–29.
Pett, Shaun. "The Photographers Who Exposed America: Arbus, Goldin, Winogrand." *Guardian*, April 30, 2016. Accessed July 3, 2018. www.theguardian.com/artanddesign/2016/apr/30/diane-arbus-nan-goldin-garry-winogrand-photography-exhibition.
Polite, Marc W. "Classic Review: *12 Million Black Voices* – 70th Anniversary." Polite on Society, February 20, 2011. Accessed June 26, 2017. www.politeonsociety.com/2011/02/20/classic-review-12-million-black-voices-70th-anniversary/.

Postman, Neil. *Technopoly: The Surrender of Culture to Technology*. New York: Vintage, 1993.

Rabinowitz, Paula. "1930s Documentary and Visual Culture." In *The Wiley Blackwell History of American Film*. November 13, 2011. Accessed July 3, 2018. https://onlinelibrary.wiley.com/doi/abs/10.1002/9780470671153.wbhaf026.

———. *They Must Be Represented: The Politics of Documentary*. London: Verso, 1994.

Riis, Jacob A. *How the Other Half Lives*. New York: Penguin, 1997.

Roettgers, Janko. "More Than Half of All Video Viewing Now on Mobile, Tablet Viewing Flat." *Variety*, December 6, 2016. Accessed July 3, 2018. http://variety.com/2016/digital/news/mobile-video-viewing-stats-1201934907/.

Rosenstone, Robert A. *Visions of the Past: The Challenge of Film to Our Idea of History*. Cambridge, MA: Belknap Press, 1996.

Rothstein, Arthur. *Documentary Photography*. Boston, MA: Focal Press, 1986.

Sante, Luc. Introduction to Riis, *How the Other Half Lives*, by Jacob A. Riis. New York: Penguin, 1997.

Schwalbe, Carol B., B. William Silcock, and Elizabeth Candello. "Gatecheckers at the Visual News Stream: A New Model for Classic Gatekeeping Theory." *Journalism Practice* 9, no. 4 (2015): 465–83. https://doi.org/10.1080/17512786.2015.1030133.

Silverstein, Jake. "The Displaced." *New York Times Magazine*, November 5, 2015. Accessed June 27, 2017. www.nytimes.com/2015/11/08/magazine/the-displaced-introduction.html.

Sims, Norman. *True Stories: A Century of Literary Journalism*. Evanston, IL: Northwestern University Press, 2007.

Sirkkunen, Esa, Heli Väätäjä, Turo Uskali, and Parisa Pour Rezaei. "Journalism in Virtual Reality: Opportunities and Future Research Challenges." In *Academic Mindtrek '16: Proceedings of the 20th International Academic MindTrek Conference*, Association for Computing Machinery, Tampere, Finland, October 17–18, 2016. https://doi.org/10.1145/2994310.2994353.

Sontag, Susan. "Freak Show." *New York Review of Books*, November 15, 1973. Accessed July 3, 2018. www.nybooks.com/articles/1973/11/15/freak-show/.

Steensen, Steen. "Online Journalism and the Promises of New Technology: A Critical Review and Look Ahead." *Journalism Studies* 12, no. 3 (2011): 311–27. https://doi.org/10.1080/1461670x.2010.501151.

Stein, Christian. "Virtual Reality Design: How Upcoming Head-Mounted Displays Change Design Paradigms of Virtual Reality Worlds." *MediaTropes eJournal* 6, no. 1 (2016): 52–85.

Stephens, Mitchell. *The Rise of the Image, the Fall of the Word*. Oxford: Oxford University Press, 1998.

Stott, William. *Documentary Expression and Thirties America*. Chicago: University of Chicago Press, 1986.

Sullivan, Margaret. "Who Gets to 'Snow-Fall' or 'Jockey' at the Times and Why?" *New York Times*, August 20, 2013. Accessed June 29, 2017. https://publiceditor.blogs.nytimes.com/2013/08/20/who-gets-to-snow-fall-or-jockey-at-the-times-and-why/.

Warnke, Martin. "On the Spot: The Double Immersion of Virtual Reality." In *Immersion in the Visual Arts and Media*, edited by Fabienne Liptay and Burcu Dogramaci, 204–13. Leiden, Netherlands: Koninklijke Brill, 2016. https://doi.org/10.1163/9789004308237_010.

"Who Coined the Term 'Virtual Reality'?" Virtual Reality Society, 2017. Accessed June 27, 2017. www.vrs.org.uk/virtual-reality/who-coined-the-term.html.

Wolfe, Tom. *The New Journalism*. London: Picador, 1975.

Yagoda, Ben. Preface to *The Art of Fact: A Historical Anthology of Literary Journalism*, edited by Kevin Kerrane and Ben Yagoda, 14. New York: Touchstone, 1997.

32
LITERARY JOURNALISM AND ECOCRITICISM

Robert Alexander

Introduction

Since it appeared in her introduction to the landmark volume *The Ecocriticism Reader* in 1996, Cheryll Glotfelty's definition of ecocriticism as "the study of the relationship between literature and the physical environment"[1] has provided a durable conceptual framework for the flourishing field it helped produce. That this field has been more open than most areas of literary studies to accord works of nonfiction the consideration typically reserved for fiction and poetry is consistent with the longstanding relationship that has existed between nonfiction genres and environmental writing, particularly in America.[2] And while within ecocriticism, literary journalism continues to draw less critical attention than other nonfiction genres, this chapter will argue that Glotfelty's definition, along with a few of its subsequent variations, offers useful guidelines for an examination of the way some of literary journalism's most distinctive features allow it to articulate the two terms of the ecocritical relationship—literature and the physical environment—in a manner unique among genres. First, the slow, immersive reporting techniques of literary journalism are well suited to the incremental pace of environmental change. Second, the genre's preoccupation with everyday subjects of modest scale attracts it to the seemingly small, supposedly non-newsworthy environmental events that are collectively transforming the planet. And third, literary journalism's capacity to link those instances to larger contexts and to do so in a discourse that combines factual rigor with emotional impact makes it a potent force in the efforts to address the current ecological crisis.

Ecocriticism has also, however, subjected its main terms—literature and the physical environment—to considerable scrutiny, and the results pose challenges to several key assumptions that have typically helped characterize literary journalism. One of ecocriticism's main projects, for example, has been to critique and disrupt the anthropocentric framework that renders the natural world always only in relation to the human. Journalistically, this stance manifests itself in the anthropocentric bias silently inscribed in objectivity and the hallucination of (in Diane Ackerman's words) the "extraterrestrial" perspective it bestows upon its human agents.[3] Ecocriticism reminds us that there is no such position—that "there is no Away," as ecocritic Timothy Morton says[4]—and this recognition complicates any notion that "immersion" might be a genre-defining exception rather than an unacknowledged norm of journalism.

Ecocriticism and Literary Journalism: Slow Violence … Slow Journalism

While the ideas to be explored in this chapter stem from Glotfelty's early definition of ecocriticism, they are also conditioned by the nuance and complexity added to it by subsequent, sometimes overlapping waves of scholarship, just a few of the variations of which I will try to acknowledge here.[5] Generally, as Kate Rigby says, ecocriticism seeks "to restore significance to the world beyond the page."[6] In its first years, it offered itself as what Pippa Marland describes as an "earth-centred"[7] corrective to the work of literary critics overly enamored, it was believed, by theories of textuality. As Glotfelty famously observes in her introduction to *The Ecocriticism Reader*,

> If your knowledge of the outside world were limited to what you could infer from the major publications of the literary profession, you would quickly discern that race, class, and gender were the hot topics of the twentieth century, but you would never suspect that the earth's life support systems were under stress. Indeed, you would never know that there was an earth at all.[8]

Over time, however, ecocriticism's initial aversion to critical theory has given way to a fruitful "re-engagement"[9] with feminist, Marxist, and postcolonial ideas as well as to an invigorating receptiveness to developments in philosophy, science studies, anthropology, geography, the natural sciences, and other fields. Like journalists, ecocritics continue to make Rigby's "world beyond the page" a priority in their work; in doing so, however, as Stacey Alaimo and Susan Hekman observe, these critics "build on rather than abandon the lessons learned in the linguistic turn,"[10] elaborating a range of theoretical challenges to anthropocentric thinking by offering new ways to conceptualize the human relationship with what David Abram has called the "more-than-human" world.[11]

These developments, which have made ecocriticism one of the most diverse and rapidly expanding areas of contemporary literary and cultural scholarship, are acknowledged in Marland's recent redefinition of ecocriticism as

> an umbrella term for a range of critical approaches that explore the presentation in literature (and other cultural forms) of the relationship between the human and the nonhuman, largely from the perspective of anxieties around humanity's destructive impact on the biosphere.[12]

Like Glotfelty, Marland reminds us, in the destructive agency she here assigns to "the human," of the etymological link between criticism and crisis. In her revision of the basic terms of Glotfelty's definition, however, from "the relationship between literature and the physical *environment*" to "the presentation in literature … of the relationship between the human and the *nonhuman*,"[13] that is, of the word "environment" to "the nonhuman," she also signals a crucial shift in the way that relationship and its key terms have come to be imagined in ecocriticism. The reintroduction of theory into ecocritical discourse helped displace the "celebratory"[14] and "devotional"[15] attitude towards nature (usually regarded as "wilderness," out there, remote, removed, and away from the lives of most readers) and such canonical American nature writers as John Muir, Mary Austin, and Edward Abbey[16] with critical paradigms that took into consideration the complex entanglements among the textual, cultural, and material spheres. The word "environment," for example, with its roots in the French *environs* (surroundings) suggests nature as a simple background against which human activity plays out. "The nonhuman," on the other hand, despite its negative prefix, literally includes and involves "the human" in a way "the environment" does not, suggesting, as we shall see in the work of a writer like David Ewing Duncan, a more deeply imbricated relationship than what we find in Glotfelty's formulation.

Ecocriticism's potential to reshape literary studies, including literary *journalism* studies, suggested here, becomes explicit in the "working definition" with which Timothy Clark prefaces *The Cambridge Introduction to Literature and the Environment*: "A study of the relationship between literature and the physical environment, usually considered from out of the current global environmental crisis and its revisionist challenges to given modes of thought and practice."[17] While Clark retains the word "environment" in his definition, the instability of the term is suggested in the emphasis he places on the unsettling effects of ecocritical theory on established patterns of "thought and practice." One example Clark provides of such a "revisionist challenge" has particularly suggestive implications for journalism and its literary counterpart. Clark writes that "environmental thinking ... changes the priorities as to what issues are more significant than others: a *small* fungus necessary to the life of a tree may be more *lastingly* decisive than the *sensational* diaries of a *leading* politician."[18] Environmental thinking, in other words, encourages a shift in values from those privileging the human, the prominent, and the sensational (and thus, presumably, the fleeting) to others that acknowledge the overlooked and unremarkable (but ultimately indispensable) slow-moving things of the nonhuman world.

In this turn from the sensational to the everyday, we can recognize something analogous to the shift from the timeliness we associate with mainstream journalism to the "timeless" quality Truman Capote identified as an important feature of his own version of literary journalism, "the nonfiction novel."[19] The shift entails matters of both scale and temporality. Concerning scale, Mark Kramer notes that the subjects of literary journalism are typically far more commonplace than the high-profile personalities and explosive events that dominate mainstream news. The reason for this preference is a practical one: "The ecology of convenient access impels literary journalists toward routine events, not extraordinary ones,"[20] Kramer writes in "Breakable Rules for Literary Journalists." The ordinariness of a subject, however, does not imply its lack of interest or significance. You may not have heard, for example, of the mycologist (fungus expert) Paul Stamets, but the 2015 *Vice* profile in which he is featured makes a good case for his claim that mushrooms can "cure disease, soak up toxins, kill unwanted pests, heal our chronically suffering bodies, prevent further sickness [and] taste good in pasta."[21]

Furthermore, just as we find with many ecological subjects, questions of scale in literary journalism are bound up with matters of temporality.[22] The literary journalist is drawn to humble subjects not simply because of barriers to access but also because the sort of intimate stories he or she wishes to tell demand "*long-term*, frank access" to those subjects.[23] The most distinguishing temporal feature of literary journalism involves the immersion techniques writers use to get at the "felt life"[24] of their subjects, and immersion, like the processes of nature, takes time. "Literary journalists," Kramer writes, "hang out with their sources for months and even years"[25]—one is tempted to say, like the "small fungus" Clark describes on that tree to whose life it is so "lastingly decisive."[26]

These twin, entangled features of scale and time are neatly captured by Susan Greenberg in her notion of "slow journalism," which she describes as "essays, reportage and other nonfiction writing that takes its time to find things out, notices stories that others miss, and communicates it all to the highest standards" and which she contrasts with the "fast news" of print, broadcast, and online cultures.[27] Greenberg's concept also, however, has a powerful parallel in ecocriticism in Rob Nixon's influential book *Slow Violence and the Environmentalism of the Poor* (2011). Nixon explores the toxic mismatch between the frenzied pace of the contemporary news cycle and the creeping destructive force of "climate change, the thawing cryosphere, toxic drift, biomagnification, deforestation, the radioactive aftermaths of wars, acidifying oceans, and a host of other slowly unfolding environmental catastrophes."[28] All, he writes, are examples of "slow violence"—"a violence that occurs gradually and out of sight, a violence of delayed destruction ... that is typically not viewed as violence at all."[29] Lacking the spectacular violence and explicit conflict that commands mainstream news, shaping public opinion and thus influencing legislation, and with its harm disproportionately inflicted on people out of the media spotlight in the Global South, slow violence faces "formidable representational obstacles."[30] Nixon asks,

> How can we convert into image and narrative the disasters that are slow moving and long in the making, disasters that are anonymous and that star nobody, disasters that are attritional and of indifferent interest to the sensation-driven technologies of our image-world? How can we turn the long emergencies of slow violence into stories dramatic enough to arouse public sentiment and warrant political intervention, these emergencies whose repercussions have given rise to some of the most critical challenges of our time?[31]

He finds an answer to these questions in what are, in literature departments anyway, the long-marginalized genres of creative nonfiction. Nonfiction, Nixon writes, "possesses" the "robust adaptability, imaginative and political," as well as the "information-carrying capacity and … aura of the real"[32] necessary to deal in a compelling way with the representational problems posed by the unwieldy spatial and temporal scales typical of slow violence. Curiously, though, literary journalism gets relatively short shrift in Nixon's book. Despite references to his own work as a journalist,[33] the main focus of the critical attention to nonfiction in his book is to activist memoirs such as those by Ken Saro-Wiwa and Wangari Maathai and the polemical essays of Arundhati Roy.

However, although he doesn't single it out, literary journalism is no less equal to the representational challenges of slow violence than those genres in "nonfiction's broad domain" he does explicitly identify.[34] In literary journalism, nonfiction's capacity to engage the imagination while delivering the facts is pointed to in a characteristic Kramer identifies as the "mobile stance" authors of the genre take in relation to their subjects.[35] While the literary journalist tells a story, he or she, Kramer says, "isn't trapped within the events"[36] portrayed but may freely digress at any moment to offer background, personal recollection, and reflection. Such apparent diversions may risk breaking the dream John Gardner said that the fictional narrative creates in the reader's mind,[37] but they do so only to add depth, context, and perspective to the story, giving weight and substance—Nixon's "aura of the real"[38]—to that narratively induced dream. (Perhaps literary journalism is narrative's *lucid* dream.) Literary journalism is, above all, a rhetorically capacious genre that allows smooth passage among a variety of discursive modes—narration, exposition, argumentation, description—as well as between what rhetorical genre theorists call "high" and "low-levels of generality," that is, "from the highest, most abstract concepts through general concepts down to specific details."[39] For example, in the first volume of *Carbon Ideologies* (2018), William T. Vollmann's epic work of environmental reportage, the author combines voluminous pages of background, definitions, and tables with descriptions and personal accounts of his interactions with the people he meets as he explores the contaminated zones of Fukushima, Japan, in the aftermath of the 2011 earthquake, tsunami, and subsequent reactor meltdowns.[40] Linking the abstract and the concrete is the steady stream of numbers Vollmann reads into his narrative from the dosimeter and scintillation counters he carries with him to measure his radiation exposure: "the best way for me to complete my word-pictures of the red zones," Vollmann writes, "is to overlay my descriptions with numbers. Here is how the meadow appeared … and in that meadow a plume of pampas grass was emitting so many nasty microsieverts."[41] His friend Jay remarks, "'It's like having another sense!'"[42]

The full effects of this wedding of exposition, argument, and description with narrative are eloquently detailed in Kramer's discussion of the text he uses to illustrate literary journalism's "mobile stance,"[43] science writer David Quammen's mixed-genre account of the "death-defying"[44] properties of ice, "Strawberries Under Ice" (1988):

He entertains by telling you a good winter camping tale, immersing you in it so you feel the immediacy of it, its past, its impending future, and the ongoing "now" of it. He also guides you, his presumptive social intimate, through his evaluation of it, exiting from story to informative digressions about glaciers and his psychology, then reentering action.[45]

Quammen's text combines narrative with judgment, abstraction with detail, information with experience, and logos with pathos in a way that corroborates the claim *New Masses* editor Joseph North made in 1935 that the writer of such stories "not only condenses reality, he helps the reader feel the fact."[46] It is also apparent, however, in Kramer's references to the "past," "future," and the "ongoing 'now'" of the narrative, that Quammen's story accommodates multiple time frames, from "the forward-moving leading edge of [the] narrative"[47] to the *longue durée* of glaciological time, an integration that stands in sharp contrast to the incommensurability Nixon describes between the slow but ineluctable—indeed glacial—movement of environmental destruction and the spectacular scenes that attract mainstream news media.

Literary journalism's ability to mobilize a range of rhetorical modes and the ease with which it can shift between abstract and concrete levels of information and, through them, to assimilate disparate scales of time and space is also evident in *Every Day We Live Is the Future*, Douglas Haynes's 2017 account of two families living in the slums of contemporary Managua. The book powerfully demonstrates literary journalism's potential to realize the promise of nonfiction Nixon describes in *Slow Violence*. Over five years, Haynes observed the lives of Dayani Baldelomar and Yadira Castellón, two Nicaraguan women who live with their children in "The Widows," a squalid shantytown "squeezed between a drainage ditch and putrid Lake Managua."[48] In what is a sort of Nicaraguan *Random Family*, Haynes follows these women from the impoverished rural communities they flee to the jobs they create for themselves in Managua's sprawling Mercado Oriental and, with other family members, as waste pickers, salvaging recyclable material from La Chureca, an open-air dump "about the size of fifty soccer fields."[49] With the lives of its subjects frequently turned upside down by the floods that inundate The Widows, the book provides a grueling sense of the attritional and exponentially expanding violence[50] of climate-aggravated poverty and its cascading consequences of discomfort, depression, sickness, hunger, and death: Misery is inflicted on Haynes's subjects from a thousand related sources, only a small number of which are directly identifiable as environmental.

But in a world where everything is against you, "natural" disasters like floods can rub raw the vulnerabilities exposed by class inequities, lax municipal regulations, poor urban design, and inadequate social services. The compounding pressures of these trials can break a family and a nation and perhaps a planet, a point Haynes makes at various moments in the book when he steps back from the scenes he narrates to provide historical context and research-based commentary, ultimately extrapolating the experiences of his subjects to a global scale. He remarks, for example, in a way that recalls Nixon's description of the unseen nature of the "slow violence" of the poor, that "every day in cities around the world, the gradual confluence of inequality, urbanization, and climate change causes events that are just as calamitous for individuals as media-hyped crises."[51] Haynes also, however, extends the book's images of desperate lives *temporally*, into the future, when he presents us with the shattering assertion that "the United Nations predicts that by 2050 three billion people might live in shantytowns and favelas—almost half the world's projected urban population."[52]

Hyperobjects, Nonhuman Animals, *Umwelten*, and Trans-corporeality: Toward a Non-anthropocentric Journalism

Through literary journalism's mobile stance, Haynes links the abstract, invisible, statistical fact of climate change to the actual lives of specific individuals whose experience becomes both an example of the current plight of a global population of urban poor and a herald of a deepening future crisis in which their numbers will only increase. With these links, the distinction between local and global begins to blur as does the line separating present from future. For example, while global warming deniers consistently dispute the threat of imminent climate collapse, some recent works of literary journalism position themselves in the space of a future we have yet to acknowledge as having already arrived. In her account of the Chernobyl disasters, Nobel Prize-winning literary journalist Svetlana Alexievich concludes about the many interviews she conducted with those who witnessed the blast and its aftermath, "These people had already seen what for everyone else is still unknown. I felt like I was recording the future."[53] In *Carbon Ideologies*, Vollmann addresses his apologia for why he and his contemporaries did so little to avert environmental disaster to the audience of a "hot dark future":[54] "In the course of a century," he writes, accumulations of carbon dioxide "might alter our future, but I was pushing 60; I'd soon be dead. As for you, reader, *you* must have begun to sweat ..."[55]

Literary journalism's ability to shift among various rhetorical modes, between different spatial and temporal scales, and to link the abstract and unseen with the concrete is clearly a powerful resource. For example, Rachel Carson's *Silent Spring* (1962) combined empirical accounts of the systematic abuse of commercial toxins with descriptions of their often-devastating effects on human and nonhuman species to produce a work commonly credited with inspiring changes to laws governing pesticide use around the world but also with inaugurating the environmental movement.[56] Since *Silent Spring*, literary journalism's commitment to the felt fact has allowed writers such as Erik Reece, Elizabeth Kolbert, Naomi Klein, and others to provide disturbing accounts of the many dimensions of the environmental crises we currently face. At the same time, the immersion techniques that characterize the genre, along with its openness to the subjective experience of its writers, have enabled literary journalists like Charles Siebert and John Vaillant to represent their nonhuman subjects in ways that not only defy what John Hartsock has identified as the alienating effects of journalistic objectivity[57] but also the anthropocentrism inherent in many journalistic conventions.

Indeed, the sheer fact, magnitude, and complexity of the current ecological crisis challenges, as Clark said, our "given modes of thought and practice,"[58] including those that underlie journalism, both mainstream and literary. The contents of the contemporary newspaper, for example, like its broadcast and online counterparts, are organized around a well-regulated principle of sectionalisation. In the newspaper I collect from my doorstep every day,[59] hard news is clearly separated from Entertainment, Sports, and Life as well as from the content the newspaper's index identifies as "regular features, puzzles," where one finds such diversions as bridge, comics, crosswords, Sudoku, TV listings, and, tucked away on the last page of the Sports section, Weather. Increasingly, however, the lists of temperatures as well as the highs, lows, and isotherms of the colorful daily weather map have been breaching the editorial wall that had historically sequestered them from the hard news pages. Weather is no longer a "regular feature": with rising numbers of extreme heat events, typhoons, hurricanes, wildfires, floods, and droughts, their effects all heightened by climate change, weather is now frequently headline news. Or, to put it another way, that which had been a background feature in our lives is increasingly thrusting itself with a puzzling and concerning regularity into the foreground. Not only that: Global warming is also the unacknowledged subtext of a growing number of news stories with no obvious connection to climate. A 2018 *New York Times* Opinion column by Lauren Markham, who writes on "issues of forced migration,"[60] argues, for example, that beyond the widely reported reasons for unauthorized immigration to the United States there lurks another:

> The hundreds of migrants I've interviewed in the past few years—whether from Gambia, Pakistan, El Salvador, Guatemala, Yemen or Eritrea—are often leaving because

of some acute political problem at home. But I've also noticed something else in my years of reporting. If you talk to these migrants long enough, you'll hear about another, more subtle but still profound dimension to the problems they are leaving behind: environmental degradation or climate change.

... The more out of whack our climate becomes, the more people up and leave their homes. As our world heats up and sea levels rise, the problem of forced migration around the world is projected to become far worse.[61]

Just as our changing environment is unsettling longstanding distinctions between what is "news" and what is a "regular feature" (or a "puzzle") and asserting itself as the hidden ground of an increasing number of those stories, so too is it playing havoc with the sort of detachment that has traditionally characterized the journalist's relationship with his or her sources. The notion of journalistic objectivity, for example, with its corollary, however loosely subscribed to by its practitioners, that it is possible for one subject (human or, indeed, nonhuman as we shall see) to stand entirely exterior to another, is contradicted by Morton's concept of "the hyperobject." "The term hyperobject," Morton writes, "refers to things that are massively distributed in time and space relative to humans,"[62] so massively distributed, in fact, that they are only indirectly perceptible. Things like the nuclear fallout from the Chernobyl disaster, the current reserves of fossil fuels, the sum of all the plastic waste contaminating the oceans, or, of course, global warming—these things "so massively outscale us," Morton says, that "we can't point to them directly."[63] You can't, for example, perceive "climate change" as such, although you can argue its bleak reality on the basis of statistical evidence or feel its effects in the sweat on the back of your neck on yet another unseasonably warm fall day. Hyperobjects are so large, in fact, that it is impossible to discern their proper boundaries. As such, the possibility of exiting the hyperobject and observing it from some Archimedean point of pure externality is doubtful as is, because of this all-encompassing scope, "the possibility of devising a metalanguage that could account for things while remaining uncontaminated by them."[64] Indeed, one of the various qualities Morton attributes to hyperobjects is their "viscosity": "I do not access hyperobjects across a distance, through some transparent medium," he writes. "Hyperobjects are here, right here in my social and experiential space,"[65] sticking to us, as it were, like the sweat on your skin or, in the case of the anthropogenic chemical toxins for which Ewing was tested for his 2006 *National Geographic* article "The Pollution Within," *under* your skin. Hyperobjects, in other words, dramatize the basic ecological axiom, already suggested by Nixon, that "there is no Away"—spatially, temporally, or, indeed, rhetorically.[66]

For literary journalism, this revelation implies that anything other than immersion, or at least an *acknowledgment* that we are necessarily immersed in the current environmental crisis and necessarily bear a responsibility for it, amounts to borderline denialism. At every turn of *Carbon Ideologies*, for example, Vollmann concedes his unthinking participation in advancing the climate catastrophe afflicting his imagined future audience. In response to the question that propels the book, "What was the work for?" (where "work" is the force extracted by the conversion of "chemical energy to mechanical energy" by, for example, burning coal[67]), Vollmann notes how, among the many carbon-generating activities that comprised his day, he liked a nice shower:

> If it was already rising hour, I strolled to the bathroom and showered to my heart's content. In those days I saw nothing wrong in letting a stream of hot water tingle the back of my neck even when I was clean; it did wonders for grogginess. One of my womanfriends loved to shower just to think. If you from the future are the losers for this, I am sorry. I think we felt a kind of grandness to have so many energies at our call, even if we rarely thought about our situation. Why shouldn't they serve us faithfully?[68]

Nothing makes one's involvement, however unimagined, in a problem more obvious than being forced to face its consequences. There is no ethical refuge when one confronts, as Vollmann does, the future with which our present decisions are bound up and the prospect of generations who will pay the price for our mindless carbon habits. In the time of hyperobjects, such immersion is more obviously than ever a fact of life, and to regard it as some exceptional journalistic position is to fail to recognize the complex entanglements such as those of present, past, and future, and their representation that ecocritical concepts like "the hyperobject" articulate. Explaining his own, sometimes "iterative, circling" style,[69] Morton remarks, "I am one of the entities caught in the hyperobject I here call *global warming*. ... Thus, no discourse is truly 'objective,' if that means that it is a master language that sits 'meta' to what it is talking about."[70]

Morton's concern with one's discursive situation is part of a larger effort to address the anthropocentrism he and many other ecocritics regard as a crucial factor in our fraught relationship with the nonhuman world. Like others in the "speculative realism" movement in philosophy (and the "object-oriented ontology," or OOO, branch with which he identifies his work), Morton's book amounts to a critique of the manner in which Western philosophy since at least Kant has conceived objects always only in terms of their *relation* to the human rather than in their own right.[71] The effect of this tradition of what Quentin Meillassoux has termed "correlationism" is an impoverished experience of the universe of things that, nonetheless, preserves "the human" at its center.[72]

In journalistic discourse, this humanistic bias manifests itself in the anthropocentric privilege presumed by journalistic objectivity itself, particularly in its central conceit that it occupies (or aspires to occupy) the "extraterrestrial" perspective Ackerman describes and embodies a mode of representation somehow "outside of nature,"[73] including, one may assume, outside the limits imposed by our specifically *human* nature. The notion of such a transcendental discourse manifests itself most conspicuously in mainstream reporting on animals. Julia B. Corbett has observed that the news typically concerns itself with animals only when they cross the "boundary that is supposed to separate them from humans."[74] This genre is recognizable as the "deer-in-the-living-room" story or its "poultry-on-the-freeway" or "moose-loose-in-the-mall" variants.[75] As with animal stories generally, such accounts are dominated by "industry and government" perspectives from police and wildlife officials rather than the views of spokespeople for conservation or environmental groups.[76]

According to the authors of a paper that appeared in *Journalism Studies* in 2011, such reporting consistently neglects to acknowledge the "interests, desires, and cognitive, emotional and moral intelligences" of animals.[77] As the paper's lead author Carrie Packwood Freeman argues, in failing to represent animals from anything but a human perspective, such stories are not only anthropocentrically biased but also inaccurate: In assuming for journalistic objectivity a perspective that transcends the limits of its human origins, mainstream reporting effaces the animal perspective in a way that naturalizes their marginalization and, ultimately, their exploitation.

Freeman offers a variety of strategies she says will help journalists incorporate the nonhuman animal (NHA) "voice as a legitimate source or perspective" in their stories.[78] Literary journalists have proven adept at intuiting and acting on these cues, probably because Freeman's suggestions resemble some of the main techniques they have developed since the late nineteenth century to gain access to and represent the "felt lives" of their human subjects. Freeman suggests, for example, that journalists should "observe, listen to, and try to communicate with NHAs in their own environments,"[79] advice that recalls the immersion techniques typically employed by literary journalists. Second, acknowledging the undeniable fact that access to animals' perspectives is difficult, Freeman urges journalists to "interpret NHA behaviour and communication and/or consult an expert for interpretation."[80] Here it is hard not to think of the paradigmatic example of Gay Talese interviewing "everyone he could, friends and managers, bodyguards, a wigmaker"[81] for their impressions of the famously uncooperative subject of "Frank Sinatra Has a Cold." Third, like the importance Tom Wolfe placed on "New Journalists" observing the status details of their subjects' lives,[82] Freeman says journalists should "learn the cultural cues and codes of animal societies with which they are unfamiliar."[83] Finally, in Freeman's general suggestion that reporters should "consider and incorporate the NHAs' perspective and interests,"[84] we hear a call for the sort of informed, empathic engagement at which literary journalism excels and with it an encouragement to resist the tendency to reductive characterizations that in mainstream news can transform a singular subject into a stereotype.

Although Freeman's article does not note it, there are instructive precedents for such a perspective. In this regard, the work of the early twentieth-century Estonian biologist, ethologist, and proto-zoosemiotician Baron Jakob von Uexküll (1864–1944) stands out, particularly because of his influential notion of *umwelt*. According to Uexküll, the experience of each species in the world is determined by the environmental "signs" or "carriers of meaning"[85] that species is equipped to perceive. The tick, for example, is uniquely sensitized to a set of smells (butyric acid), a temperature (37°C), and textures (spots on mammals' skin free of hair) that allow it to identify, drop onto, and feed upon the blood of passing mammals. The complex of signs it perceives constitutes the tick's specific experience of the world—what Uexküll calls its *umwelt* and characterizes as a sort of soap bubble enclosing the animal that he says represents the limits of "each animal's [subjective] environment and contains all the features accessible to the subject."[86]

The *umwelt* of every species is distinct, and though many species may inhabit a single general environment, each will experience that environment according to the cues to which their specific *umwelt* is fitted. Furthermore, while members of one species may possess some grasp of the *umwelt* of another species—such interspecies understanding is essential to successful predation—this access is never absolute. Nor may any species escape from or transcend its own *umwelt*. This rule applies to nonhuman and human animals alike, that is, to both ticks and journalists. It was with Uexküll in mind that the philosopher of science Georges Canguilhem noted, "As a living being, man does not escape from the general law of living beings. ... Yet man as scientist and bearer of knowledge constructs a universe of phenomena and laws that he holds to be an absolute universe."[87] But, as Carlo Brentari explains, rather than achieving an "absolute objectivity," such an abstracting operation "does not lead to anything except the construction of a specific environment that seems to enjoy the luxury of a sort of illusory 'privilege.'"[88]

There are two points relevant to literary journalism that we can take from this argument. First, as the example of Uexküll's rigorously researched narratives of the lives of other species including such "uncharismatic" creatures as sea cucumbers, sea urchins, and paramecia demonstrate, it is possible to engage with some precision the *umwelten* of nonhuman animals. Second, the fact that one cannot escape one's own species' *umwelt* prohibits one's ability to occupy in any absolute way the *umwelt* of some other species. Nor is it possible to burst the bubble of one's *umwelt* to gain access to the objective world. (To recall Morton's claim, there is no *meta-umwelt*.) Indeed, in the eyes of contemporary scholars, one of the most significant aspects of Uexküll's work is that it "gives the lie to the idea of scientific objectivity divorced from the perspectival, perceptual subjectivity of the observers themselves and the signs they use."[89] As Paul Bains notes in a special volume of *Semiotica* devoted to Uexküll, "The idea of an independently existing external reality divorced from minds occurs only within minds,"[90] which is to say that the concept of objectivity is itself part of the human *umwelt* but nothing more. To argue anything else is necessarily to adopt an anthropocentric position of human exceptionalism.

In their immersive engagement with their subjects, Uexküll's narrative forays into the "felt life" of animals offer literary journalists a guide as to how one might write in a non-anthropocentric manner about nonhuman species. There are, in fact, a large number of works of literary journalism that bear evidence of the spirit if not the letter of Uexküll's work. Vaillant's representation of the Amur tiger in his 2010 book *The Tiger* is explicitly informed by Uexküll's ideas. One may also think, however, of David Foster Wallace's "Consider the Lobster" (2006), where a detailed description of that species's "exquisite tactile sense," including its extreme susceptibility to minute changes in temperature and the absence in its system of the opioids that help moderate "intense pain,"[91] leaves the reader with a distressing impression of the agony these creatures must feel when dropped alive into a pot of boiling water. Freeman herself recommends Siebert's "Watching Whales Watching Us" for its attention to its nonhuman animal subjects as well as the agency it accords them.[92] A similar attitude is evident in the intuition Sy Montgomery expresses in the opening pages of *The Soul of an Octopus* (2015): "I've often had the feeling that the octopus I was watching was watching me back, with an interest as keen as my own."[93]

These works and others like them demonstrate literary journalism's potential to challenge prevailing anthropocentric representations and thus, according to Freeman, to "test the bounds of journalistic objectivity and fairness more so than perhaps any other social reform."[94] And just as a literary journalist's long exposure to a source can reveal uncanny resemblances between the two,[95] these examples of nonhuman subjects "looking back" suggest that immersion can unsettle the anthropocentric privilege of writer and reader, provoking an uncanny sense of kinship with even a species as "completely alien" as the octopus from whose evolutionary line humans separated "more than half a billion years ago."[96]

A heightened awareness of the impact of environmental destruction and a mindful resistance to anthropocentric habits of thought can also turn the gaze of the literary journalist back on that journalist's self. Just as ecocritics focusing on nonhuman animals have dismissed as crude the line said to divide them from humans,[97] feminist critics working in the area known as "material ecocriticism" have recently questioned the prevailing disregard of "matter" in critical theory and philosophy. And like concepts such as the hyperobject and *umwelten*, material ecocriticism (like the interdisciplinary area of "new materialism" with which it is associated) confronts anthropocentrism in a manner that poses distinct challenges as well as possibilities for literary journalism.

The "new materialism" arises from a growing sense that feminist thought, steeped in social constructionist and discourse theories, had encouraged a disdain of nature, the materiality of which had been pejoratively associated with the female body. The result of this neglect, according to Alaimo, has been to "bracket or minimize the significance, substance, and power of the material world."[98] But matter, Alaimo and Hekman argue in the introduction to their important volume *Material Feminisms* (2008), "is agentic—it acts and those actions have consequences for both the human and nonhuman world."[99] Materiality is something the human and nonhuman have in common, and this sharing, according to Marland, "renders obsolete the distinction between human and environment."[100] Once again, we find the nonhuman background against which human activity supposedly plays out asserting its unruly agency and breaching a foreground previously sealed off as "the human." In material feminist theory, Alaimo and Hekman contend that nature is "an agentic force that interacts with and changes the other elements in the mix, including the human."[101] Alaimo calls these material flows and interactions evidence of the "trans-corporeality" of matter, and in her book *Bodily Natures* (2010), she focuses explicitly on those points in theoretical and literary works as well as in social practices and political culture,[102] where the porous interface of human bodies and the environment is represented.

The notion of "trans-corporeality" achieves several things. First, it mounts one more challenge to the association that dominated early ecocriticism of "the environment" as something "out there" and brings it into "homes, schools, workplaces, and neighborhoods."[103] Second, trans-corporeality "entails a rather disconcerting sense of being immersed within incalculable interconnected material agencies that erode even our sophisticated modes of understanding."[104]

The relevance of such "immersion" to literary journalism becomes most evident in Alaimo's analysis of what she calls "material memoirs"—autobiographical texts in which the writer's "sense of selfhood is transformed by the recognition that the very substance of the self is interconnected with vast biological, economic, and industrial systems that can never be entirely mapped and understood."[105] Works such as Audre Lorde's feminist account of her experience of cancer, *The Cancer Journals*, are exemplary here, but Alaimo also gives brief, critical attention to Duncan's *National Geographic* story "The Pollution Within" (2006), a work recognizable as literary journalism.

In this article, Duncan recounts the results of tests he underwent to determine the chemicals he had picked up through his interactions with his environment. Of the 320 chemicals for which he was tested, 165 showed up in results, everything from metals, PCBs, phthalates, pesticides, and PFAs to high concentrations of PBDEs, the compounds widely used as flame retardants in such products as fabrics, building materials, carpets, and electronics. Duncan's readings are like luggage labels of this journey through life, chemical souvenirs of, for example, the Kansas dump where he played in the 1960s, innocent of the knowledge that it would later be declared an EPA superfund site, or of his college years spent on the Hudson River, downstream from where GE "legally dumped excess PCBs,"[106] or of the 200,000 air miles he had logged the year he wrote the article, unaware that for safety reasons, the interior of airplanes are "drenched in flame retardants."[107] The load of chemicals he carries within him, moreover, connects his biography to postwar American industrial history (GE, 3M, Ford, Colgate-Palmolive, the Kansas Power and Light Company, and Bayer are among the corporations named in the story) and a regulatory regime that seems always to arrive a bit late to the inferno. Despite the horrifying photos that accompany the story and a general sense that researchers "don't know"[108] the full range of the effects of many of these chemicals, the piece, as Alaimo notes, is curiously "upbeat."[109] One toxicologist, for example, assures Duncan that "dose is everything,"[110] while others agree that "the miniscule smidgens of chemicals inside us are mostly nothing to worry about."[111] In the article's final sentence, Duncan confesses, somewhat ambivalently that he will "never feel quite the same about the chemicals that make life better in so many ways."[112] The sentence reflects the angle he used to approach the experiment: He underwent the tests, he writes, "searching for a way to think about risks, benefits, and uncertainty—the complex tradeoffs embodied in the chemical 'body burden' that swirls around inside all of us."[113] But such a balanced approach does not dispel the horror implied in his opening paragraph when he declares that these chemicals "are where they should not be: inside my body."[114] It seems evident that Duncan's selfhood has been "transformed," as Alaimo says, by a new sense of its connections to "vast biological, economic, and industrial systems,"[115] an awareness that serves as a reminder, consistent with the tenor of ecocritical thought, that the "environment is not located somewhere out there, but is always the very substance of ourselves."[116]

Duncan is a literary journalist writing about disturbing news. That news, however, is not simply someplace "out there": it is breaking inside his own body. In doing so, it's also breaking a barrier that journalists have typically assumed distinguished their perspective from those of the subjects on which they report. The reporter, we're told, should never be the story. But in a time of hyperobjects, and in an era marked by the sort of increasing awareness of the instability of such previously reliable coordinates as near and far, present and future, inside and outside, background and foreground, self and other, human and nonhuman, which a thoughtful, clear-sighted engagement with the current environmental crisis compels—in such times, it is difficult to imagine doing otherwise. Literary journalism's unique complex of journalistic and rhetorical features equips it better perhaps than any other genre to meet the representational challenges of this new world. And as writers continue to explore the ways in which the surprising resources of both journalism and literariness are fitted to the exigencies of that new world, they are sure as well to influence the future of ecocriticism and, one hopes, the planet.

Acknowledgments

I would like to thank the members of English 5V78, "Literary Journalism and Ecocriticism," which I taught at Brock University in Winter 2018. I hope something of their great insight and enthusiasm is conveyed here.

Notes

1. Glotfelty, "Literary Studies," xviii.
2. Timothy Clark discusses the privileged place nonfiction has occupied in ecocriticism, remarking in *The Cambridge Introduction to Literature and the Environment* that "to open any issue of *Interdisciplinary Studies in Literature and the Environment*, the journal of the Association for the Study of Literature and the Environment, is to still find at least as many studies of creative non-fiction as the novel and poetry" (35).
3. In *The Moon by Whale Light*, Diane Ackerman comments on being called a "nature writer": "How curious that label is, suggesting as it does that nature is somehow separate from our doings, that nature does not contain us, that it's possible to step *outside* nature, not merely as one of its more promising denizens but objectively, as a sort of extraterrestrial voyeur" (xiv).
4. Morton, *Hyperobjects*, 31.
5. For a concise summary of ecocriticism, see Marland, "Ecocriticism."
6. Rigby, "Ecocriticism," 154–55.
7. Marland, "Ecocriticism," 847.
8. Glotfelty, "Literary Studies," xvi.
9. Marland, "Ecocriticism," 851.
10. Alaimo and Hekman, "Emerging Models," 6.
11. Abram, *Spell of the Sensuous*, 7.
12. Marland, "Ecocriticism," 846.
13. Marland, 846; emphases added.
14. Head, "Ecocriticism and the Novel," quoted in Marland, 849.
15. Phillips, *Truth of Ecology*, ix.
16. In *The Environment and the Press*, Mark Neuzil argues that, while the works of these canonical American nature writers bear some journalistic elements such as research and observation (98), their relationship with environmental journalism has been primarily one of "influence" (xv). Exceptions do exist, however, mainly in the work of women writers: Neuzil notes that Mary Austin had a substantial background in magazine journalism (123) and Rachel Carson's writing appeared in the *New Yorker* (124).
17. Clark, *Cambridge Introduction*, xiii.
18. Clark, *Cambridge Introduction*, 5; emphases added.
19. Plimpton, "Story."
20. Kramer, "Breakable Rules," 27.
21. Cannon, "This Man."
22. For a thoughtful treatment of the complex temporality of literary journalism, and particularly the implications of its frequently "belated" relationship to the events it relates, see Wilson, "Journalist." The environmental stories of literary journalists are often caught in the same trap of "belatedness" that Wilson describes. Indeed, in the case of a work like John McPhee's geological history of North America, *Annals of the Former World*, this "belatedness" may extend to billions of years. But such retrospective narratives are also often accompanied by an urgent *prospective* focus in which the writer predictively describes the likelihood of the dire future consequences of current ecological realities and practices. In John H. Richardson's 2015 *Esquire* article "Ballad of the Sad Climatologists," for example, that future fact is registered in psychiatrist Dr. Lise Van Susteren's diagnosis of the profound "sadness, ... fear and anger" currently experienced by climate activists as a version of posttraumatic disorder she calls "'pre-traumatic' stress" (85). Even more dire is the blunt message Roy Scranton delivers in *Learning to Die in the Anthropocene*: that it's no longer a question of when this grim new climate reality will arrive but rather "how we are going to adapt" now that it has (17).
23. Kramer, "Breakable Rules," 27; emphasis added.
24. Kramer, 23.
25. Kramer, 22.
26. Clark, *Cambridge Introduction*, 5.

27 Greenberg, "Slow Journalism."
28 Nixon, *Slow Violence*, 2.
29 Nixon, 2.
30 Nixon, 2.
31 Nixon, 3.
32 Nixon, 25.
33 In Chapter 6 of *Slow Violence*, Nixon recalls his visit during the 1994 South Africa general election to the game reserve of "wildlife entrepreneur" J. P. Kleinhans (177). The vivid narrative that follows, complete with exposition, description, scenes, and dialogue, is readily recognizable as literary journalism.
34 Nixon explicitly mentions "memoirs, essays, public science writing, polemics, travel literature, graphic memoirs, manifestos and investigative journalism" (25).
35 Kramer, "Breakable Rules," 31.
36 Kramer, 31.
37 Gardner, *Art of Fiction*, 31.
38 Nixon, *Slow Violence*, 25.
39 Giltrow et al., *Academic Writing*, 303.
40 Vollmann, *Carbon Ideologies*.
41 Vollmann, 399.
42 Vollmann, 399.
43 Kramer, "Breakable Rules," 31.
44 Quammen, "Strawberries Under Ice," 267.
45 Kramer, "Breakable Rules," 31.
46 Sims, *True Stories*, 9–10.
47 Kramer, "Breakable Rules," 41.
48 Haynes, *Every Day*, cover copy.
49 Haynes, 59.
50 Nixon, *Slow Violence*, 2.
51 Haynes, *Every Day*, 238.
52 Haynes, 9.
53 Alexievich, *Voices from Chernobyl*, 236.
54 Vollmann, *Carbon Ideologies*, 13.
55 Vollmann, 172; ellipses in the original.
56 Commenting on the original *New Yorker* articles that formed the basis of Carson's famous book, Priscilla Coit Murphy notes in *What a Book Can Do: The Publication and Reception of "Silent Spring*,*"* "Overall, the effect and the rhythm of the pieces were—appropriately—that of a [sic] investigative, journalistic feature, beginning with dramatic themes and anecdotes, supporting the middle mainly through the accuracy and lucidity of Carson's explanations of scientific phenomena, and concluding with philosophic commentary" (10).
57 Hartsock, *History*, 42.
58 Clark, *Cambridge Introduction*, xiii.
59 References are to the *Toronto Star*.
60 Markham, "Warming World."
61 Markham.
62 Morton, *Hyperobjects*, 1.
63 Morton, 12.
64 Morton, 2.
65 Morton, 27.
66 Morton, 31.
67 Vollmann, *Carbon Ideologies*, 25.
68 Vollmann, 25–26.
69 Morton, *Hyperobjects*, 4.
70 Morton, 3–4.
71 Sheldon, "Form/Matter/Chora," 193–94.
72 Sheldon, 193–94.
73 Ackerman, *Moon by Whale Light*, xiv. See Note 3 here for the full quotation.
74 Corbett, *Communicating Nature*, cited in Freeman, Bekoff, and Bexell, "Giving Voice," 593.
75 For an example, see "Two Moose."

76 Freeman, Bekoff, and Bexell, "Giving Voice," 593.
77 Freeman, Bekoff, and Bexell, 590.
78 Freeman, Bekoff, and Bexell, 596.
79 Freeman, Bekoff, and Bexell, 596.
80 Freeman, Bekoff, and Bexell, 596.
81 Kellogg, "Inside."
82 Wolfe, "New Journalism," 32.
83 Freeman, Bekoff, and Bexell, "Giving Voice," 598.
84 Freeman, Bekoff, and Bexell, 598.
85 Von Uexküll, *Foray*, 139.
86 Von Uexküll, 43.
87 Canguilhem, *Knowledge of Life*, quoted in Brentari, *Jakob von Uexküll*, 211.
88 Brentari, 211.
89 Sagan, "Umwelt after Uexküll," 26.
90 Bains, "*Umwelten*," paraphrased in Sagan, 26.
91 Wallace, "Consider the Lobster," 250.
92 Freeman, Bekoff, and Bexell, "Giving Voice," 599.
93 Montgomery, *Soul of an Octopus*, 1.
94 Freeman, Bekoff, and Bexell, "Giving Voice," 598.
95 Alexander, "'My Story.'"
96 Montgomery, *Soul of an Octopus*, 2.
97 Clark, *Cambridge Introduction*, 186.
98 Alaimo, *Bodily Natures*, 8.
99 Alaimo and Hekman, "Emerging Models," 5.
100 Marland, "Ecocriticism," 856.
101 Alaimo and Hekman, "Emerging Models," 7.
102 Alaimo, *Bodily Natures*, 3.
103 Alaimo and Hekman, "Emerging Models," 9.
104 Alaimo, *Bodily Natures*, 17.
105 Alaimo, 23.
106 Duncan, "Pollution Within," 128.
107 Duncan, 122.
108 Duncan, 133.
109 Alaimo, *Bodily Natures*, 108.
110 Duncan, "Pollution Within," 122.
111 Duncan, 122.
112 Duncan, 133.
113 Duncan, 121.
114 Duncan, 122.
115 Alaimo, *Bodily Natures*, 23.
116 Alaimo, 4.

Bibliography

Abram, David. *The Spell of the Sensuous: Perception and Language in a More-Than-Human World*. New York: Vintage, 1996.

Ackerman, Diane. *The Moon by Whale Light and Other Adventures among Bats, Penguins, Crocodilians, and Whales*. New York: Vintage, 1991.

Alaimo, Stacy. *Bodily Natures: Science, Environment, and the Material Self*. Bloomington, IN: Indiana University Press, 2010.

Alaimo, Stacy, and Susan Hekman. "Emerging Models of Materiality in Feminist Theory." Introduction to *Material Feminisms*, edited by Stacey Alaimo and Susan Hekman, 1–19. Bloomington, IN: Indiana University Press, 2008.

Alexander, Robert. "'My Story Is Always Escaping into Other People': Subjectivity, Objectivity, and the Double in American Literary Journalism." *Literary Journalism Studies* 1, no. 1 (Spring 2009): 57–66.

Alexievich, Svetlana. *Voices from Chernobyl: The Oral History of a Nuclear Disaster*. Translated by Keith Gessen. New York: Picador, 2006.

Bains, Paul. "Umwelten." *Semiotica*, no. 134 (July 2001): 137–67.

Brentari, Carlo. *Jakob von Uexküll: The Discovery of the Umwelt between Biosemiotics and Theoretical Biology*. Dordrecht, Netherlands: Springer, 2015.

Canguilhem, Georges. *Knowledge of Life*. Translated by Stefanos Geroulanos and Daniela Ginsburg. New York: Fordham University Press, 2008.

Cannon, Frances B. "This Man Believes Mushrooms Can Solve Virtually All of Humanity's Problems." *Vice*, June 5, 2015. https://munchies.vice.com/en_us/article/d75e4y/this-man-believes-mushrooms-can-solve-virtually-all-of-humanitys-problems.

Carson, Rachel. *Silent Spring*. New York: Houghton Mifflin, 1962.

Clark, Timothy. *The Cambridge Introduction to Literature and the Environment*. Cambridge: Cambridge University Press, 2011.

Corbett, Julia B. *Communicating Nature: How We Create and Understand Environmental Messages*. Washington, DC: Island Press, 2006.

Duncan, David Ewing. "The Pollution Within." *National Geographic*, October 2006, 116–37.

Freeman, Carrie Packwood, Marc Bekoff, and Sarah M. Bexell. "Giving Voice to the 'Voiceless': Incorporating Nonhuman Animal Perspectives as Journalistic Sources." *Journalism Studies* 12, no. 5 (2011): 590–607. https://doi.org/10.1080/1461670X.2010.540136.

Gardner, John. *The Art of Fiction: Notes on Craft for Young Writers*. New York: Vintage, 1983.

Giltrow, Janet, Richard Gooding, Daniel Burgoyne, and Marlene Sawatsky. *Academic Writing: An Introduction*. 2nd ed. Peterborough, ON: Broadview Press, 2009.

Glotfelty, Cheryll. "Literary Studies in an Age of Environmental Crisis." Introduction to *The Ecocriticism Reader: Landmarks in Literary Ecology*, edited by Cheryll Glotfelty and Harold Fromm, xv–xxxvii. Athens, GA: University of Georgia Press, 1996.

Greenberg, Susan. "Slow Journalism." *Prospect*, February 2007. www.prospectmagazine.co.uk/magazine/slowjournalism.

Hartsock, John C. *A History of American Literary Journalism: The Emergence of a Modern Narrative Form*. Amherst, MA: University of Massachusetts Press, 2000.

Haynes, Douglas. *Every Day We Live Is the Future*. Austin, TX: University of Texas Press, 2017.

Head, Dominic. "Ecocriticism and the Novel." In *The Green Studies Reader: From Romanticism to Ecocriticism*, edited by Laurence Coupe, 235–41. London: Routledge, 2000.

Kellogg, Carolyn. "Inside the Legendary Gay Talese Story 'Frank Sinatra Has a Cold.'" *Los Angeles Times*, October 9, 2013. www.latimes.com/books/jacketcopy/la-et-jc-inside-the-legendary-gay-talese-story-frank-sinatra-has-a-cold-20131009-story.html.

Klein, Naomi. *This Changes Everything: Capitalism vs. the Climate*. New York: Simon and Schuster, 2014.

Kolbert, Elizabeth. *The Sixth Extinction: An Unnatural History*. New York: Picador, 2014.

Kramer, Mark. "Breakable Rules for Literary Journalists." In *Literary Journalism: A New Collection of the Best American Nonfiction*, edited by Norman Sims and Mark Kramer, 21–34. New York: Ballantine Books, 1995.

Markham, Lauren. "A Warming World Creates Desperate People." *New York Times*, June 29, 2018. www.nytimes.com/2018/06/29/opinion/sunday/immigration-climate-change-trump.html.

Marland, Pippa. "Ecocriticism." *Literature Compass* 10, no. 11 (2013): 846–68. https://doi.org/10.1111/lic3.12105.

McPhee, John. *Annals of the Former World*. New York: Farrar, Straus and Giroux, 1998.

Montgomery, Sy. *The Soul of an Octopus: A Surprising Exploration into the Wonder of Consciousness*. New York: Atria, 2015.

Morton, Timothy. *Hyperobjects: Philosophy and Ecology after the End of the World*. Minneapolis, MN: University of Minnesota Press, 2013.

Murphy, Priscilla Coit. *What a Book Can Do: The Publication and Reception of "Silent Spring."* Amherst, MA: University of Massachusetts Press, 2005.

Neuzil, Mark. *The Environment and the Press: From Adventure Writing to Advocacy*. Evanston, IL: Northwestern University Press, 2008.

Nixon, Rob. *Slow Violence and the Environmentalism of the Poor*. Cambridge, MA: Harvard University Press, 2011.

Phillips, Dana. *The Truth of Ecology: Nature, Culture, and Literature in America*. Oxford: Oxford University Press, 2003.

Plimpton, George. "The Story Behind a Nonfiction Novel." *New York Times*, January 16, 1966. https://archive.nytimes.com/www.nytimes.com/books/97/12/28/home/capote-interview.html?_r=2.

Quammen, David. "Strawberries Under Ice." 1988. In *Wild Thoughts from Wild Places*, 253–67. New York: Scribner, 1998.

Reece, Erik. *Lost Mountain: A Year in the Vanishing Wilderness: Radical Strip Mining and the Devastation of Appalachia*. New York: Riverhead Books, 2006.

Richardson, John H. "Ballad of the Sad Climatologists." *Esquire*, August 2015, 82–89.

Rigby, Kate. "Ecocriticism." In *Introducing Criticism in the 21st Century*, edited by Julian Wolfreys, 151–78. Edinburgh: Edinburgh University Press, 2002.

Sagan, Dorion. "Umwelt after Uexküll." Introduction to *A Foray into the Worlds of Animals and Humans*, by Jakob von Uexküll, 1–34. Minneapolis, MN: University of Minnesota Press, 2010.

Scranton, Roy. *Learning to Die in the Anthropocene: Reflections on the End of a Civilization*. San Francisco, CA: City Lights Books, 2015.

Sheldon, Rebekah. "Form / Matter / Chora: Object-Oriented Ontology and Feminist New Materialism." In *The Nonhuman Turn*, edited by Richard Grusin, 193–222. Minneapolis, MN: University of Minnesota Press, 2005.

Siebert, Charles. "Watching Whales Watching Us." *New York Times Magazine*, July 8, 2009. www.nytimes.com/2009/07/12/magazine/12whales-t.html?pagewanted-5.

Sims, Norman. *True Stories: A Century of Literary Journalism*. Evanston, IL: Northwestern University Press, 2007.

"Two Moose Invade Calgary—One Shot and Killed." Global News, December 5, 2014. https://globalnews.ca/video/1712031/two-moose-invade-calgary-one-shot-and-killed.

Vollmann, William T. *Carbon Ideologies*. Vol. 1, *No Immediate Danger*. New York: Viking, 2018.

Von Uexküll, Jakob. *A Foray into the Worlds of Animals and Humans*. Translated by Joseph D. O'Neil. Minneapolis, MN: University of Minnesota Press, 2010.

Wallace, David Foster. "Consider the Lobster." In *Consider the Lobster and Other Essays*, 234–54. New York: Black Bay Books, 2006.

Wilson, Christopher P. "The Journalist Who Was Always Late: Time and Temporality in Literary Journalism." *Literary Journalism Studies* 10, no. 1 (Spring 2018): 113–38.

Wolfe, Tom. "The New Journalism." In *The New Journalism*, edited by Tom Wolfe and E. W. Johnson, 1–52. New York: Harper and Row, 1973.

33
THE DISCLOSURE OF DIFFERENCE
Literary Journalism and the Postmodern

Pascal Sigg

Although the postmodern incredulity toward the possibility of the objective representation of reality has almost become a cliché in literary journalism studies,[1] the issue has largely remained untouched. This is not surprising because the question of its relationship to reality pierces to the core of literary journalism's identity, which according to a recent definition "works on a spectrum or continuum that ... results in either an increasingly alienated objectified world on the one hand or, on the other, a solipsistic subjectivity in the most personal of memoirs."[2] If the postmodern's primary concern is "to point out that those entities that we unthinkingly experience as 'natural' ... are in fact 'cultural,'"[3] it is certainly at odds with literary journalism as a "cognitively efficient"[4] narrative realism that takes the unhindered representation of reality for granted. Recently, however, writers of literary journalism have experimented with modes of realist representation that question the limits of the subjectivity/objectivity dichotomy and show influences of postmodern ideas of knowledge and communication.

Since shortly before the turn of the millennium, there was an emergence of experimental literary journalism that works against solipsism precisely because of its communication of the writer's subjectivity. Understood as an intensification of New Journalism's self-consciousness, the literary journalism of David Foster Wallace, John Jeremiah Sullivan, Mac McClelland, and George Saunders is aware of itself as a mode of aestheticized speech. Unlike many texts of New Journalism, however, it does not claim to be able to represent reality itself. Exhibiting an acute awareness of the split between language and reality, it rather works as a conscious contribution to a collective conversation about reality. In my analyses of Sullivan's "Getting Down to What Is Really Real," which shows how reality TV invites cast members to explore different identities; McClelland's "Can the Ivory-Billed Woodpecker Be Found in Cuba?," which shows the difficult conditions under which bird conservationists aim to establish facts; and Saunders's "Buddha Boy," which centers on the possibility of a boy's different human physicality, I aim to show that the writers' particular subjectivities not only emphasize the ubiquity of difference but also convey generative senses of what cannot be represented and thus reflect postmodern ideas of knowledge and language in a specific mode of experimental realist representation that understands communication as a disclosure of difference rather than as an exchange of meaning.[5]

Literary Journalism and the Postmodern

As previously noted, few scholars have connected literary journalism with ideas of the postmodern. The few affiliations that have occurred illustrate the difficulties in connecting the two. Both John Hellmann and Leonora Flis reduce the postmodern to a rather general concept that promoted fictionality and focused on literary journalism's alleged generic hybridity.[6] Hellmann explicitly uses the term "postmodern journalism" for works of New Journalism, which he argues sought to overcome realism's "inadequacies in the face of the fragmenting, changing world of the postmodern"[7] and claimed it possessed "a greater verisimilitude in presenting a reality pervaded by fictions."[8] Although Hellmann is right to identify clearly fictional elements in the works of Norman Mailer or Hunter Thompson, he creates a theoretical impasse by equating the postmodern with an understanding of fiction that at once opposes and includes works of journalism.

Relating literary journalism to the postmodern more specifically requires acknowledging that the postmodern is a discursive, plural, and conflicted theoretical construct with at least three main versions or distinct meanings.[9] In a 1985 essay, the French philosopher Jean-François Lyotard identified a critical formation containing three different and contradictory versions of the postmodern that he sees at work simultaneously. In his view, the postmodern can not only be understood as a new period following modernity but also as a sense of loss of faith in progress that characterizes the narratives of modernity and the continual analysis of modern society, thought, and culture.[10] According to Hans Bertens, this third version, an ongoing analysis of modernity—in which I would argue literary journalism takes part—has found its expressions in largely two spheres: first in the "reflection of the complex of social and cultural perspectives—the so-called socio-cultural formation" of Marxist critics such as Fredric Jameson and, second, in a development predominantly confined to the field of literature, "a reaction against the literary realism of the 1950s and against the modernism of the inter-war period."[11]

Importantly, this distinction between critical analysis and aesthetic expression corresponds to the split between journalistic reporting and the communication of the resulting facts in artful prose that has defined literary journalism since the coinage of the term. This contrast between practice and product must be viewed in light of the sharp distinction between literature and other uses of language. Grouping together all types of literature and rhetoric regardless of their referentiality, the categorization promoted by thinkers such as Jürgen Habermas places literature and rhetoric in opposition with "the specialized languages of science and technology, law and morality, economics, political science, etc.,"[12] in which "the tools of rhetoric are subordinated to the discipline of a distinct form of argumentation."[13] Joshua Roiland challenges this very hierarchy that also elevates literature over journalism in a recent attempt to redefine literary journalism. In lieu of understanding the adjective "literary" as a value judgment or ploy for legitimacy, Roiland argues, it "denotes the use of rhetorical elements ranging from scene, character development, plot, dialogue, symbolism, voice, et cetera."[14] Rather than a category separate from journalism, the literary with its specific rhetorical manifestations is thus viewed as a quality of journalistic work itself. Consequently, in relation to the postmodern, works of literary journalism must be read as both reactions against earlier modes of realism and reflections of complex social and cultural perspectives that investigate modernity using tools of both rhetoric and argumentation.

In postmodern debates, hierarchical binary distinctions such as the one between rhetoric and argumentation were questioned by French philosopher Jacques Derrida in his broader critique of structuralism. Derrida presented the highly influential and transforming concept of *différance* and the technique of deconstruction with its continuous reiteration of the instability of meaning and emphasis on temporality. In Derrida's view, meaning is based on relations of infinite differences and thus regarded as always in the process of becoming and never fully realized until encountering an impasse.[15] Indebted to Edmund Husserl's phenomenology and likely also Mikhail Bakhtin's writings on dialogism,[16] Derrida's idea of realist representation entails a wide and encompassing understanding of text and writing as "that which enables the sense and the truth-value of statements or propositions to be communicated from one context to the next."[17] Despite still-popular accusations of relativism, scholars have shown that Derrida did not deny the existence of material reality. More importantly, he emphasized the inevitable differentiation and relationality inherent in our perception of it.[18] In this view, then, all thought, language, and hence also argumentation could be seen as rhetorical. This, however, does not mean that they are all regarded as fictional, but rather that a potential distinction between fiction and nonfiction is necessarily only negotiated within a text itself.

Acknowledging the instability of meaning, Lyotard formulated an influential idea of knowledge and art based on perpetual experimentation. Rather than grand metanarratives that preserve the status quo, postmodern texts were to seek "new presentations, not in order to enjoy them but in order to impart a stronger sense of the unpresentable."[19] These texts, essays rather than fragments, were concerned not with the supply of reality but with "allusions to the conceivable which cannot be presented."[20] However, with his emphasis on the unrepresentable, Lyotard did not aim to promote relativism. He rather perceived a chance for humanity to defend itself against threatening inhuman capitalist forces. In order to counter these forces, Lyotard conceived an imaginary inhuman: a "potential for being taken hold of by surprising and uncanny transformative possibilities that cannot be predicted, explained or mastered by technologically based systems of reason."[21] The human, he argued, is the product of the conflict between the very real capitalist and the imaginary transformative inhuman forces. Lyotard saw it as "the task of writing, thinking, literature, arts, to venture to bear witness to it."[22]

Literary scholars have argued that postmodern literature took up this task in a specific way that is best understood as an intensification of rather than a break from modern literature. They have described this intensification as a concern of postmodern literature with world-navigation and world-making rather than the world-witnessing of modern literature. Compared to their predecessors, postmodern writers appear more interested in questions about the interrelation and creation of worlds of being rather than understanding.[23]

A general concern with creation could also be located in New Journalism, the literary journalism that emerged in the 1960s and 1970s when Derrida formulated his ideas. New Journalism has been read as a direct response to the capitalist forces described by Lyotard. Despite their different theoretical frameworks, scholars such as John Hellmann, Chris Anderson, Phyllis Frus, David Eason, and Jason Mosser share the conclusion that New Journalism's emphasis on language or style was mainly a response to a media industry whose primary mode of representation was an industry-driven objectivity more akin to images than texts. In Anderson's view, the New Journalists' style, their very use of language as a stubborn "belief in the power of language to order and create" is itself the argument.[24] Mosser claims that written language in works of New Journalism could attain a rhetorical power that was able to generate a sense of presence.[25] In general, New Journalism has been credited with thus undermining "the authoritative versions of reality created by conventional journalism."[26]

In the texts themselves, however, scholars have located different degrees of experimentation. Frus, for instance, argues that a text such as Tom Wolfe's *The Right Stuff* (1979)—similar to works of traditional realism—represses its own temporal aspects, its "own structures of representation," or "processes of coming into being."[27] Incorporating Frus's point to some degree, Eason claims that New Journalism could emphasize two forms of texts that he called either realist or modernist: "In realist reports, the dominant function of the narrative is to reveal an interpretation; in modernist reports it is to show how an interpretation is constructed."[28] Realist texts, according to Eason's analysis of writings by Wolfe, Gay Talese, and Truman Capote, "organize the topic of the report as an object of display, and the reporter and reader ... are joined in an act of observing that assures conventional ways of understanding still apply."[29] What Eason calls modernist reports, however, "focus instead on the contradictions that emerge at the intersection of various maps of experience."[30] Their phenomenological impetus, Eason argues, "is revealed in the multilayered questioning of communication, including that between writer and reader, as a way of making a common world."[31] As they tell stories of how writers try to make sense of their experiences of reality, the writers of such experimental texts of the 1960s and 1970s mainly highlight the impossibility of directly accessing meaning in a culture and society increasingly perceived as fantastic. By merely emphasizing that meaning "is created and recreated in acts of interpretation and expression"[32] through a particular style, however, writers associated with New Journalism do not yet locate the obstacles to meaning-making that thinkers such as Derrida pointed to in style or language itself.

David Foster Wallace's Call to Communication

A further intensification of the literary journalist's self-consciousness that extended focus to the role of language itself could be observed roughly thirty years after the emergence of New Journalism. On one hand, poststructuralist theory had successfully argued that the ability of language to represent reality ought to be viewed more critically. On the other hand, there could also be observed an increased segmentation of US society and culture.[33] If the US media landscape had seen a major shift toward homogenization with the emergence of mass broadcasting, the development of new media technology such as satellites, cable TV, personal computers, and ultimately the internet had different effects. As media historian John Durham Peters noted in 2001, such new technology fragmented the media's audience and raised "fear that media segmentation will cause citizens to retreat to a cocoon of private egoism."[34] On the other hand, he also observed that a "chief feature of modern interpersonal life is its mediation—by mail, phone, e-mail, and so on."[35] Human interaction, he claimed, "has become precisely something to be managed, not a natural reciprocity."[36] He thus pointed to a major concern of postmodern thinkers. Derrida, for instance, had criticized an idealization of instantaneity in the news media and emphasized the mediated character of presence or actuality in contemporary culture in 1996.[37]

In such a historical context of fragmented and mediated experiences of reality, the writer David Foster Wallace argued that "the classical Realist form is soothing, familiar and anesthetic; it drops us right into spectation."[38] In its place, he sought to imagine a different realism that countered the mere function of entertainment by focusing more explicitly on communication and reader engagement. Wallace was known not only for his short fiction and his magnum opus *Infinite Jest* (1996) but also for his substantial trove of innovative but controversial reportage, essays, and commentary published between 1992 and 2008, which have influenced and inspired other writers of literary journalism.[39] For John Jeremiah Sullivan, Wallace "got his finger into a certain wound and was moving it around," and Leslie Jamison claimed that the "multiplicity of [his] perspectives feels almost like an ethical stance; the refusal of the single view."[40] An experimental fiction writer, Wallace had no journalistic training, and he never claimed to be a reporter. He preferred the writings of George Orwell or Joan Didion to those of Wolfe or Thompson, whose texts—except for *Hell's Angels* (1967)—he found "naïve and narcissistic."[41] Furthermore, particularly in his early career, Wallace seemed uncertain about where and how he wanted to draw the line between fact and fiction.[42]

In his arguably most popular piece of literary journalism, "A Supposedly Fun Thing I'll Never Do Again,"[43] he tells the story of a cruise as an experience of alienation and displacement in which the promised vacation from everyday life becomes itself an alienating and saddening experience. As Roiland notes, this trope of escape, "supplanting everyday reality with fantasy," is prominent in Wallace's nonfiction.[44] Unlike Wolfe or Thompson, he not only describes the replacement of reality with fantasy with increased subjectivity and potentially fictional elements; he also problematizes this replacement itself as a disconnecting and insincere effect of consumerism. With a sensitive kind of objective subjectivity that is aware of itself as such, Wallace exposes fantastic elements of reality manifested in the insincerity of the cruise personnel or a PR brochure. As he thus raises suspicion about language's own ability to represent reality and consequently his own text, he presents his critique to readers with what Roiland calls an "imperative to be present."[45]

Compared to experimental works of New Journalism, Wallace's text does more than offer a multilayered questioning of communication or reveal how an interpretation of reality is constructed. Additionally, the excess of speech that Eason observes in New Journalism is heightened. With his display of irony, direct reader address, and experimental use of formal features such as footnotes, Wallace asks the reader rather explicitly to engage in a communicative process about the meaning of his experience of reality.[46] Clare Hayes-Brady shows that this "fundamentally political process, offering the potential liberation of the late-capitalist subject, necessitates a deliberate act of will"[47] and "works to alleviate the symptoms of both narcissistic and solipsistic self-referentiality by simultaneously seeking to recognize the other *and* reinforcing the primacy of the individual."[48] As Wallace conceptualizes this necessarily open-ended process of meaning-making between both writer and material reality as well as writer and reader, similar to Derrida's concept of deconstruction, he resists closure and seeks to preserve the possibility of plurality.[49]

Difference, Connection, and Possibility in Contemporary Texts

In works of literary journalism by John Jeremiah Sullivan, Mac McClelland, and George Saunders, all published between 2005 and 2016, a similarly heightened self-consciousness can be observed. They all tie the possibility of the representation of reality not primarily to a belief in style but more fundamentally to intended, open-ended processes of communication. These writers thus reflect their texts not as constitutional but only as complicit in the making of the meaning of reality. Sullivan and McClelland write personal, reported texts on cultural, social, and political themes with a focus on cultural understanding. They have repeatedly been recognized as finalists for the American Society of Magazine Editors' yearly award in feature writing (Sullivan won the prize in 2003). Saunders may be primarily known for his short fiction and his recent experimental novel, *Lincoln in the Bardo* (2017). However, he has published five pieces of literary journalism, three of which were republished in his essay collection, *The Braindead Megaphone*, in 2007. His most recent piece on Donald Trump's supporters was nominated for an ASME award in feature writing in 2017.

In their texts, these writers expose their experience of reality as deeply mediated. They find meaning both in the more primal stage of their bodies' responses to material reality and in the mere existence of conversations between themselves and their subjects and readers about the meaning of reality. As they lay bare the contradictions inherent in their own perceptions of reality as well as the communal, discursive, and unstable character of meaning, their texts are self-reflexive products concerned with the making of reality and the self through ongoing physical and linguistic interaction rather than definitive interpretation.

Sullivan's playful "Getting Down to What Is Really Real"[50] (2011), for instance, which describes his examination of the lives of three former cast members of *The Real World: Back to New York* (2001), is an example of careful negotiation and playful suspension of the author's connections with both his readers and his subjects. In the text, Sullivan depicts himself as fundamentally different from his readers, as he plays with imagined reader expectations, which he claims to both fulfill and disappoint, thus refusing to identify himself clearly. As he imagines that the readers "know how it [reality TV] works ... this being the twenty-first century and reality having long surpassed our fictions,"[51] he uses an assumption of shared knowledge of reality TV to create a sense of complicity that implies no need for further explanation. Although this connection appears pre-established, Sullivan nevertheless openly claims to violate it in favor of his affection for his subjects. Imagining that his readers expect him to unmask the inauthenticity of reality TV, for example, he pretends to ask one of the characters, "the Miz," whether his lifestyle took a toll on his soul, only to unmask the question itself as a prank on the reader.[52] Similarly, referring to meeting the former cast members, Miz, Coral, and Melissa, he initially claims that he "was curious to see if they were real," only to acknowledge that he could not confirm this possibility because he "got distracted."[53] What here appears as an inability to get to the core of the issue he later acknowledges more openly: "I wish—for your sakes—that the Miz, Coral, and Melissa had turned out to be more fucked-up, as people. I have a vague sense of owing the reader that."[54] These humorous assumptions about the readers' expectations, however, indicate that Sullivan enjoys his writing and that he feels he is very much able to make sense of reality if only he manages to convince his readers.

In the case of this text, what Sullivan claims to be real, then, is that while reality TV "has successfully *appropriated reality*,"[55] it paradoxically also "made things more real."[56] Rather than vilifying the cast members' appropriation of reality, he notices a "shift toward greater self-consciousness, this increased awareness of complicity in the falseness of it all."[57] It is this awareness of falseness that Sullivan values higher than a potential access to "real" reality because it feels good. Sullivan claims that the perpetual acting he observes in the Miz, who tours from party to party and who "never really leaves *The Real World*,"[58] has given him "so much joy over the years"[59] and established a bond between them that Sullivan depicts as more important than what is real. Sullivan appears to liken this connection between the Miz and his viewers (and hence himself) to his own acting in his relationship with readers. In absence of a direct access to reality, he and his readers still have the relationship between themselves in order to make sense of reality. Consequently, Sullivan's ending is an inclusive suspension of these relationships that converge in one moment of joyful connection. After Sullivan observes the Miz dancing with one of his viewers, he addresses his readers as "bros" with the final word of the text.[60] Rather than decrying the Miz's freezing of time in a moment when the "whole idea of being a young American seemed fun"[61] as inauthentic, Sullivan celebrates him for enjoying it. This dynamic interplay among writer, readers, and reality emphasizes the possibilities in which reality can be made through the exploration of identities and human communication.

Similar to Sullivan's text, McClelland's "Can the Ivory-Billed Woodpecker Be Found in Cuba?" (2016), a deconstruction of the exploration narrative, examines ways in which reality is both explored and shaped by its very exploration. In the piece, McClelland describes this process as an end in itself with her subjects' mere experience of a connection between themselves and material reality as reward. The physical stakes in her narrative, however, are much higher than in Sullivan's. In order to prove the existence of an exotic bird, the characters she portrays do not merely attempt to suspend time but perpetually risk the ending of time as they imperil their very lives. McClelland's physical exposure to the experience of the trip through remote parts of Cuba's rainforest with two conservationists functions as an argument for the authenticity of the story itself as well as for the conservationists' efforts. Different from Sullivan's direct addresses, McClelland's relationship with her readers becomes apparent in her ironic distancing both from herself—she refers to herself as "the writer"—and from the other participants in the expedition. While her self-distancing is further signified as ironically objective by a fundamental lack of emotion, the distancing from her fellow male travelers occurs mainly through the description of her desire for more comfort and safety. Unlike her companions, for instance, McClelland expresses a "wish that there were seatbelts,"[62] uses modern water-filtration and UV-sterilization equipment,[63] and openly expresses resentment of men who boast about their experiences of bad times.[64]

Despite those expressions of difference, McClelland claims similarity with the explorers on a deeper level. The reality they encounter, McClelland posits, is a reality that is made through human experience. Like the birders who are on a quest to hear and see a possibly extinct bird, as a writer she has to expose her body to reality in order to first create experience in order then to write about it. As McClelland argues, the conservationists' acts aim to preserve the possibility that the world is still wild and unknown.[65] A similar argument could be made for the writer McClelland herself, who struggles using excessive speech in an abundance of stylistic features to preserve the possibility of the plurality of meaning and freedom of signification. Very much like Sullivan, then, despite all the differences between her and her subjects, McClelland finds a connection in the very acknowledgment of these differences that necessitates the active, willful making of reality in the shared experience of their trip through remote parts of Cuba. Unlike the reality in Sullivan's text, however, the reality of the exploration for McClelland is not pleasurably fantastic. It is disturbingly fantastic because the human effort to prove the existence of the bird threatened by abstract forces of capitalism—logging and mining—is both perilous and unsuccessful.

First published in 2006, George Saunders's "Buddha Boy" explores the possibility of a fundamentally different physicality of a Buddhist teenager. Confronted with the rumor of a boy who allegedly had been meditating for seven months without eating or drinking, Saunders travels to Nepal to find out for himself. Similar to Sullivan, Saunders anticipates his readers' responses to this rumor. He divides the readers into "Believers" and "Realists," while he himself resists any response or closed judgment, declaring simply: "This I have to see."[66] As the narrative progresses, however, this distinction gets porous as Saunders imagines possibilities of more complexity to the story. For instance, Saunders implies that he serves as a stand-in for readers. He asks them to imagine a potential scheme by the villagers to make money off the meditating boy;[67] he claims that they sense what he senses[68] or supposes that they generally "know that feeling at the end of the day."[69] Saunders contrasts this imagined identification with a kind of transparent subjectivity that makes clear that Saunders's experience is affected by intention. For instance, Saunders notes that the boy "makes me feel (or I make me feel)"[70] or he catches himself engaged in wishful thinking.[71] Saunders thus suggests that he is both like his readers but also different from them, and what connects them is imagination.

Compared to Saunders's readers, however, the boy appears to be more fundamentally alien to Saunders. Saunders establishes the difference between himself and the boy when he engages in an experiment to control his own desires and consequently his body and fails.[72] He makes it evident when he goes on a frenzy of over-interpretation and dreaming during the bitterly cold night he spends at the boy's enclosure, ponders his own "limited mind,"[73] and concludes that what the boy does is an act of strong will or "something even stranger."[74] Saunders, however, does not go on to conclude that the boy is doing something impossible. He rather humanizes him as he connects the boy's meditation to the general human desire to master physicality. Thus, Saunders entertains the thought that the boy "makes this fight in a new way."[75] In Saunders's text, it is this very acceptance of the possibility of difference that has the potential to make a connection. This is not only manifested in the scene in which Saunders and Prem, the boy's friend, "have a moment" after Saunders has tried "to communicate [his] basic acceptance of the possibility"[76] that the boy is an incarnation of God. It is also signified with the overall hope that the boy's difference could help the divided nation threatened by civil war.[77] Similar to Sullivan's and McClelland's texts, reality appears fantastic based on the underlying premise that it is made by humans. The human transgression that Saunders witnesses, however, is neither an act of successful appropriation nor a unsuccessful rebellion, but a hardly imaginable control of human desire itself.

Conclusion: Generative Differences

As I have sought to demonstrate, a certain experimental type of contemporary literary journalism seeks to impart senses of Lyotard's unpresentable or unknowable through an emphasis on difference between the writers and certain aspects of the realities they seek to represent in their texts. This mode of experimentation is akin to the ways in which postmodern knowledge and postmodern fiction have been conceptualized. However, in the literary journalistic texts analyzed here, the act of making, which has been associated with fictional discourse, is always already and necessarily part and parcel of both reality and its textual representation. More to the point, these texts are interested in the very specific ways in which humans—writers, their subjects, and their readers—ultimately communally represent reality in telling, acting, exploring, and thinking. This communal act of representation makes visible possible connections between both readers and subjects, enabling "uncertainty to appear as something other than a negative form of knowing."[78] Difference, these texts thus claim, is not an obstacle to be overcome in a quest for sameness and efficiency but a fundamental trait of humanity and driver of collaboration and communication.

If this body of literary journalism can be understood as an intensification of New Journalism, it operates mainly through this increased reflection of the possibilities of its own communicative workings and functions. Consequently, with its emphasis on communication, this intensely self-conscious literary journalism insists that, as Peters has stated, communication "is more basically a political and ethical problem than a semantic or psychological one."[79] It thus highlights the qualities and deficiencies of its own human ways of giving meaning to reality based on the premise that there is no knowledge independent of self-knowledge. However, this basic insight does not mean that humans are bound to lead solipsistic lives in isolation but rather that they are invited to collaborate on the never-ending task of giving meaning to their shared realities.

Notes

1 In his introduction to *Literary Journalism across the Globe*, John Bak observes a "postmodern incredulity toward objective reality" in recent works on American literary journalism (4).
2 Hartsock, *Literary Journalism*, 3.
3 Hutcheon, *Politics of Postmodernism*, 2.
4 Hartsock, *Literary Journalism*, 150; Kramer, "Narrative Journalism."
5 See Peters, *Speaking into the Air*, 20–21 for distinctions between these ideas of communication.
6 See, for instance, Hellmann, *Fables of Fact*; Hellmann, "Postmodern Journalism"; Flis, *Factual Fictions*.
7 Hellmann, "Postmodern Journalism," 52–53.
8 Hellmann, 53.
9 In need of a concise and accessible introduction to the postmodern, I was very grateful for Malpas, *Postmodern*.
10 Lyotard, "Note on the Meaning of Post-," 76–80.
11 Bertens, "World Literature and Postmodernism," 204.
12 Habermas, *Philosophical Discourse of Modernity*, 209.
13 Habermas, 209–10.
14 Roiland, "By Any Other Name," 71.
15 Cuddon, "Post-Structuralism."
16 See Kristeva, "Word, Dialogue and Novel"; MacCannell, "Temporality of Textuality"; Sempere, *Influence of Mikhail Bakhtin*.
17 Norris, "Truth in Derrida," 26; Marder, *Event of the Thing*; Mooney, "Derrida's Empirical Realism."
18 Deutscher, *How to Read Derrida*, 34–36.
19 Lyotard, *Postmodern Condition*, 81.
20 Lyotard, "Answering the Question," 149–50.
21 Malpas, *Postmodern*, 76.
22 Lyotard, *Inhuman*, 7.
23 Connor, "Postmodernism and Literature," 65–66.
24 Anderson, *Style as Argument*, 180.
25 Mosser, *Participatory Journalism*, 44.
26 Mosser, 54.

27 Frus, *Politics and Poetics*, 233.
28 Eason, "New Journalism," 199.
29 Eason, 192.
30 Eason, 192.
31 Eason, 192.
32 Eason, 202.
33 Rodgers, *Age of Fracture*.
34 Peters, "Media and Communications," 22.
35 Peters, 28.
36 Peters, 29.
37 Derrida and Stiegler, *Echographies de la télévision*.
38 McCaffery, "Interview," 138.
39 On Wallace's influence, see most recently and explicitly Roiland, "Derivative Sport." See also Lewis-Kraus, "Viewer Discretion"; Lorentzen, "Rewriting"; Sullivan, "Too Much Information."
40 Roiland, "Derivative Sport."
41 Jacob, "Interview," 153–54.
42 Roiland, "Fine Print."
43 Wallace, "Supposedly Fun Thing." The story was first published titled "Shipping Out" in *Harper's Magazine* in January 1996.
44 Roiland, "Getting Away."
45 Roiland, 31.
46 Hoffmann makes a similar claim in his analysis of Wallace's "postironic" writing (*Postirony*, 171).
47 Hayes-Brady, *Unspeakable Failures*, 6.
48 Hayes-Brady, 11.
49 Hayes-Brady, 25–26.
50 An earlier version of "Getting Down to What Is Really Real" was published in GQ in 2005, titled "Leaving Reality."
51 Sullivan, "Getting Down," 92.
52 Sullivan, 95.
53 Sullivan, 100.
54 Sullivan, 103.
55 Sullivan, 97.
56 Sullivan, 98.
57 Sullivan, 98.
58 Sullivan, 93.
59 Sullivan, 102.
60 Sullivan, 108.
61 Sullivan, 108.
62 McClelland, "Ivory-Billed Woodpecker," para. 3.
63 McClelland, para. 9.
64 McClelland, para. 48.
65 McClelland, para. 81.
66 Saunders, "Buddha Boy," 212.
67 Saunders, 231.
68 Saunders, 221.
69 Saunders, 224.
70 Saunders, 226.
71 Saunders, 227, 236.
72 Saunders, 213–15.
73 Saunders, 243.
74 Saunders, 244.
75 Saunders, 243.
76 Saunders, 230.
77 Saunders, 221.
78 McCarthy, "Suspension," 23.
79 Peters, *Speaking into the Air*, 269.

Bibliography

Anderson, Chris. *Style as Argument: Contemporary American Nonfiction*. Carbondale, IL: Southern Illinois University Press, 1987.

Bak, John S. Introduction to *Literary Journalism across the Globe: Journalistic Traditions and Transnational Influences*, edited by John S. Bak and Bill Reynolds, 1–20. Amherst, MA: University of Massachusetts Press, 2011.

Bertens, Hans. "World Literature and Postmodernism." In *The Routledge Companion to World Literature*, edited by Theo D'haen, David Damrosch, and Djelal Kadir, 204–12. London: Routledge, 2012.

Connor, Steven. "Postmodernism and Literature." In *The Cambridge Companion to Postmodernism*, edited by Steven Connor, 62–81. Cambridge: Cambridge University Press, 2004.

Cuddon, John Anthony. "Post-Structuralism." In *A Dictionary of Literary Terms and Literary Theory*, 690–93. 4th ed. Oxford: Blackwell, 1998.

Derrida, Jacques, and Bernard Stiegler. *Échographies de la télévision: Entretiens filmés*. Paris: Galilée, 1996.

Deutscher, Penelope. *How to Read Derrida*. London: Granta Books, 2005.

Eason, David. "The New Journalism and the Image-World." In *Literary Journalism in the Twentieth Century*, edited by Norman Sims, 191–205. Evanston, IL: Northwestern University Press, 2008.

Flis, Leonora. *Factual Fictions: Narrative Truth and the Contemporary American Documentary Novel*. Newcastle upon Tyne, UK: Cambridge Scholars Publishing, 2010.

Frus, Phyllis. *The Politics and Poetics of Journalistic Narrative: The Timely and the Timeless*. Cambridge: Cambridge University Press, 1994.

Habermas, Jürgen. *The Philosophical Discourse of Modernity: Twelve Lectures*. Translated by Frederick Lawrence. Cambridge, MA: MIT Press, 1987.

Hartsock, John C. *Literary Journalism and the Aesthetics of Experience*. Amherst, MA: University of Massachusetts Press, 2016.

Hayes-Brady, Clare. *The Unspeakable Failures of David Foster Wallace: Language, Identity, and Resistance*. New York: Bloomsbury, 2016.

Hellmann, John. *Fables of Fact: The New Journalism as New Fiction*. Urbana, IL: University of Illinois Press, 1981.

———. "Postmodern Journalism." In *Postmodern Fiction: A Bio-Bibliographic Guide*, edited by Lawrence McCaffery, 51–61. Westport, CT: Greenwood Press, 1987.

Hoffmann, Lukas. *Postirony: The Nonfictional Literature of David Foster Wallace and Dave Eggers*. Bielefeld, Germany: Transcript, 2016.

Hutcheon, Linda. *The Politics of Postmodernism*. 2nd ed. New York: Routledge, 2002.

Jacob, Didier. "Interview with David Foster Wallace." In *Conversations with David Foster Wallace*, edited by Stephen J. Burn, 152–57. Jackson, MI: University Press of Mississippi, 2012.

Kramer, Mark. "Narrative Journalism Comes of Age." Nieman Storyboard, October 1, 2001. http://niemanstoryboard.org/stories/narrative-journalism-comes-of-age/.

Kristeva, Julia. "Word, Dialogue and Novel." In *The Kristeva Reader*, edited by Toril Moi, 34–61. New York: Columbia University Press, 1986.

Lewis-Kraus, Gideon. "Viewer Discretion: The Trajectory of Writer-Worrier David Foster Wallace." Review of *Both Flesh and Not*, by David Foster Wallace. *Bookforum*, 2012. www.bookforum.com/inprint/019_03/10012.

Lorentzen, Christian. "The Rewriting of David Foster Wallace." Vulture, June 30, 2015. www.vulture.com/2015/06/rewriting-of-david-foster-wallace.html.

Lyotard, Jean-François. "Answering the Question: What Is Postmodernism?" In *Modernism/Postmodernism*, edited by Peter Brooker, 140–50. New York: Longman, 1992.

———. *The Inhuman: Reflections on Time*. Translated by Geoffrey Bennington and Rachel Bowlby. Cambridge: Polity Press, 1991.

———. "Note on the Meaning of 'Post-.'" In *The Postmodern Explained*, translated by Don Barry, Bernadette Maher, Julian Pefanis, Virginia Spate, and Morgan Thomas, 75–80. Minneapolis, MN: University of Minnesota Press, 1992.

———. *The Postmodern Condition: A Report on Knowledge*. Translated by Geoff Bennington and Brian Massumi. Minneapolis, MN: University of Minnesota Press, 1984.

MacCannell, Juliet Flower. "The Temporality of Textuality: Bakhtin and Derrida." *MLN* 100, no. 5 (1985): 968–88. https://doi.org/10.2307/2905440.

Malpas, Simon. *The Postmodern*. New York: Routledge, 2005.

Marder, Michael. *The Event of the Thing: Derrida's Post-Deconstructive Realism*. Toronto: University of Toronto Press, 2009.

McCaffery, Lawrence. "An Interview with David Foster Wallace." *Review of Contemporary Fiction* 13, no. 2 (1993): 127–50.

McCarthy, Anne C. "Suspension." In *Jacques Derrida: Key Concepts*, edited by Claire Colebrook, 23–30. New York: Routledge, 2015.

McClelland, Mac. "Can the Ivory-Billed Woodpecker Be Found in Cuba?" *Audubon*, May–June 2016. www.audubon.org/magazine/may-june-2016/can-ivory-billed-woodpecker-be-found-cuba.

Mooney, Timothy. "Derrida's Empirical Realism." *Philosophy and Social Criticism* 25, no. 5 (1999): 33–56. https://doi.org/10.1177/0191453799025005002.

Mosser, Jason. *The Participatory Journalism of Michael Herr, Norman Mailer, Hunter S. Thompson, and Joan Didon: Creating New Reporting Styles*. Lewiston, NY: Edwin Mellen Press, 2012.

Norris, Christopher. "Truth in Derrida." In *A Companion to Derrida*, edited by Zeynep Direk and Leonard Lawlor, 23–41. Chichester, UK: Wiley Blackwell, 2014.

Peters, John Durham. "Media and Communications." In *Blackwell Companion to Sociology*, edited by Judith R. Blau, 16–29. Malden, MA: Blackwell, 2001.

———. *Speaking into the Air: A History of the Idea of Communication*. Chicago: University of Chicago Press, 1999.

Rodgers, Daniel T. *Age of Fracture*. Cambridge, MA: Belknap Press, 2011.

Roiland, Joshua. "By Any Other Name: The Case for Literary Journalism." *Literary Journalism Studies* 7, no. 2 (Fall 2015): 60–89.

———. "Derivative Sport: The Journalistic Legacy of David Foster Wallace." Longreads, December 2017. https://longreads.com/2017/12/07/derivative-sport/.

———. "The Fine Print: Uncovering the True Story of David Foster Wallace and the 'Reality Boundary.'" Review of *Both Flesh and Not: Essays*, by David Foster Wallace. *Literary Journalism Studies* 5, no. 2 (Fall 2013): 148–61.

———. "Getting Away from It All: The Literary Journalism of David Foster Wallace and Nietzsche's Concept of Oblivion." In *The Legacy of David Foster Wallace*, edited by Samuel Cohen and Lee Konstantinou, 25–52. Iowa City, IA: University of Iowa Press, 2012.

Saunders, George. "Buddha Boy." In *The Braindead Megaphone: Essays*, 211–50. New York: Riverhead Books, 2007.

Sempere, Julio Peiró. *The Influence of Mikhail Bakhtin on the Formation and Development of the Yale School of Deconstruction*. Newcastle upon Tyne, UK: Cambridge Scholars Publishing, 2014.

Sullivan, John Jeremiah. "Getting Down to What Is Really Real." In *Pulphead: Dispatches from the Other Side of America*, 89–108. London: Vintage, 2012.

———. "Leaving Reality." *GQ*, 2005. www.gq.com/story/john-jeremiah-sullivan-leavin-reality-gq-july-2005-reality-tv-star-future.

———. "Too Much Information." *GQ*, March 31, 2011. www.gq.com/story/david-foster-wallace-the-pale-king-john-jeremiah-sullivan.

Wallace, David Foster. "A Supposedly Fun Thing I'll Never Do Again." In *A Supposedly Fun Thing I'll Never Do Again: Essays and Arguments*, 256–353. London: Abacus, 1997.

34
BEYOND COMPARISON
American Literary Journalism in a Global Context

Isabelle Meuret

An American Trademark

Since its inception, American literary journalism has reflected the cultural, political, economic, and social history of the American people. The genre has always existed in the DNA of America and still serves as a barometer of its moral, spiritual, and constitutional health. In addressing a wide range of issues, it illuminates the uniqueness of the American experience, where nation and narration nicely dovetail. However, the polymorphous nature and global presence of literary journalism today question its allegedly American pedigree. Arguably, literary journalism has exceeded its generic frontiers to become a discipline,[1] while its international reach bespeaks immense possibilities for both practitioners and scholars. Treading out of familiar precincts raises legitimate concerns as the contours of this protean genre are constantly being redrawn. This chapter identifies the stakes for American literary journalism in a globalized world and examines its ramifications abroad. It also reflects upon the state of international literary journalism by looking beyond the collation and constellation of its occurrences to its most urgent challenges in terms of research, development, and education.[2] Finally, the chapter explores future endeavors with a view to affirming the purposes of and prospects for literary journalism in a global context.

The categorization of literary journalism as a form, genre, and discipline has been discussed widely. Using the right labels is an arduous task, now aggravated by the internationalization of literary journalism. The International Association for Literary Journalism Studies,[3] an ever-expanding learned society, attests to the existence of numerous traditions subsumed under the "literary journalism" moniker. Ironically, elusiveness has come to characterize a once oxymoronic appellation that still bears the standard of its dual essence. The juxtaposition of both terms is not necessarily common in other cultures, which resort to a wide array of denominations contingent on the evolution of the genre in contexts fashioned by political, economic, cultural, and social mores. In France, for instance, literature and journalism used to coexist as two parallel universes, whose mutual scrutiny eventuated in fruitful cross-fertilization.[4] While journalists critiqued literary work in the press, renowned authors wrote in the papers, and publishing houses launched prestigious collections of reportages.[5] However, *journalisme littéraire* today still sounds like an awkward bricolage, whereas *grand reportage* or *écriture du réel* have become common parlance to categorize the work of its best (and not exclusively American) representatives.[6]

The origination of the "literary journalism" label has been tracked down by Thomas B. Connery to *A Bibliography of Literary Journalism in America*, published in 1937 by Edwin H. Ford.[7] Then defined as a practice "fall[ing] within the twilight zone that divides literature from journalism," the term did not catch on successfully despite its many occurrences in the first half of the twentieth century.[8] The term "nonfiction" was generally preferred in studies published in the late 1970s and into the 1980s, which significantly advanced the knowledge of the genre. Among those studies are Mas'ud Zavarzadeh's *The Mythopoeic Reality: The Postwar American Nonfiction Novel* (1976), John Hollowell's *Fact and Fiction: The New Journalism and the Nonfiction Novel* (1977), Ronald Weber's *The Literature of Fact: Literary Nonfiction in American Writing* (1980), John Hellmann's *Fables of Fact: The New Journalism as New Fiction* (1981), Norman Sims's *The Literary Journalists* (1984), Shelley Fisher Fishkin's *From Fact to Fiction: Journalism and Imaginative Writing in America* (1985), Barbara Foley's *Telling the Truth: The Theory and Practice of Documentary Fiction* (1986), and Barbara Lounsberry's *The Art of Fact: Contemporary Artists of Nonfiction* (1990).[9] These critical texts consolidated literary journalism as a subject in its own right in the Anglo-American academy.[10]

In *From Fact to Fiction*, Fishkin interestingly notes that a number of writers in the US were first reporters of facts before they turned to fiction. She also insists that although "the phenomenon is not uniquely American the frequency with which it has occurred in this country is."[11] The primacy of the American experience was essential to those who initially experimented with the genre, and their dabbling in journalism was paramount in honing their technical skills as "documenters of fact."[12] Fishkin contends that prominent authors felt the need to be freed from the shackles of conventional journalism so as to engage readers intellectually and emotionally through storytelling. Among the distinctive tools, techniques, and themes of literary journalism, a particular "narrative impulse"[13] and a brilliant marriage of substance and style are often singled out by critics. More recently, David Samuels has affirmed that "weaving narratives around an armature of verifiable facts is a literary strategy invented by American writers."[14] A regular contributor to major magazines of the genre, Samuels lauds their critical role as breeding grounds where talented writers can express their unique and authoritative American cachet.

John C. Hartsock locates the emergence of American literary journalism at a decisive moment in the nineteenth century, when stories were needed to make sense of the extraordinary changes shaping the country.[15] Since then, the genre has been riding a bumpy road, with its nadirs and climaxes, but has always been rebooted with innovative experiments triggered by cultural, social, and political disruptions,[16] hence the revival of interest and another swath of anthologies published in the 1990s and 2000s, including Sims's *Literary Journalism in the Twentieth Century* (1990) and *True Stories: A Century of Literary Journalism* (2007), Connery's *A Sourcebook of American Literary Journalism: Representative Writers in an Emerging Genre* (1992), Edd Applegate's *Literary Journalism: A Biographical Dictionary of Writers and Editors* (1996), and Hartsock's *A History of American Literary Journalism: The Emergence of a Modern Narrative Form* (2000).[17] Other books have drilled down the American substratum, such as Jan Whitt's *Settling the Borderland: Other Voices in Literary Journalism* (2008), Connery's *Journalism and Realism: Rendering American Life* (2011), and Hartsock's *Literary Journalism and the Aesthetics of Experience* (2016).[18] These milestones contribute to establishing a canon and, consequentially, have sanctioned the genre at home and abroad.

American literary journalism is a port of entry to understanding the cultural history of the country and to feeling its *zeitgeist*.[19] Historical depth and substance, imbued with emotional and elegant style, characterize the craft. The American exceptionalism attached to literary journalism is no conceited appropriation. Robert Boynton traces its ancestry back to "reportorial journalism" adorned with "literary quality," which he identifies as "a distinctively American phenomenon."[20] Quoting practitioners of the genre, in particular Jane Kramer, Boynton points to its capability to fathom the vibrant energy of quintessential America and to its insatiable storytelling drive.[21] It is a truism that a specific tradition in literary journalism was born in the US and boasts a unique *savoir faire* leavened with local, regional, or national ferments, to wit the relentless production and thriving criticism. Indeed, literary journalism has always been a staple of journalism in the US, as most notably practiced by an outstanding group of writers, from Mark Twain to Joan Didion to Ted Conover. Conversely, this is less the case in other countries, and especially in France, where literary journalism has been a less vivacious or mainstream entity and more a peripheral or anecdotal genre, whose popularity is more dependent on the vagaries of the times. The aforementioned anthologies and collections also testify to the academic relevance of literary journalism studies in the US, for that matter. Consequently, permanence and prevalence make it a decidedly American genre. Samuels wryly calls it "the only indigenous American literary form."[22] There even exists a literary journalism proper to the *New Yorker*, a "cathedral" for the high priests of the genre,[23] represented by the likes of Joseph Mitchell or Gay Talese, who lent it credibility and fortified both the magazine and US literary journalism. However, inasmuch as literary journalism is profoundly American, it also acknowledges legitimate forebears in European realism and naturalism,[24] and the éclat of some esteemed writers rested on their international affiliations.[25]

Boynton's *The New New Journalism: Conversations with America's Best Nonfiction Writers on Their Craft* (2005) proposes both a sequel and a response to Tom Wolfe's seminal *The New Journalism* (1973).[26] The volume focuses on the methods and philosophy of a new generation of nonfiction writers who "represent the continued maturation of American literary journalism."[27] From his interviews with contemporary practitioners, Boynton infers that their reportorial and literary accomplishments draw from a twofold heritage: They share the thematic concerns of nineteenth-century pioneers and tap into the bold stylistic experiments of the New Journalists. In so doing, they "synthesiz[e] the best of these two traditions."[28] Ted Conover, Jon Krakauer, Susan Orlean, William Langewiesche, Adrian Nicole LeBlanc, and Eric Schlosser appear among those ranking high in Boynton's new pantheon. American literary journalism has thus been rejuvenated due to these prolific writers who have "revived the tradition to a more popular and commercial level" than previously hoped, Boynton insists.[29] However, the claim that this new generation "may well be the most popular and influential development in the history of American literary nonfiction," due to their journalism being "rigorously reported, psychologically astute, sociologically sophisticated, and politically aware," is disputable.[30] William Dow justly interrogates such affirmation, which fails to historicize the movement and, I would add, disregards other significant nonfiction writers not bracketed in Boynton's potentially exclusionary movement.[31] Moreover, Boynton further asserts that "drilling down into the bedrock of ordinary experience" implicitly adds an "activist dimension" questionably absent from Wolfe's New Journalism.[32] While I acknowledge the—albeit unsystematic—societal commitment of the so-called New New Journalists, I also argue that the multimedia and multilingual circulation of the genre partakes in its fortunate dissemination today. Storytelling morphs into scrollytelling: Literary journalism is now widely read online and in translation.[33]

A Global Brand of Storytelling

The online and global renaissance of literary journalism presents two major risks to the American tradition. First, new technologies and the internet have enlarged its sense of possibilities; yet by reducing literary journalism to a commodity labeled as a "new brand of storytelling,"[34] Josh Roiland cautions, the risk is that it will be removed from its most notable and original—literary and journalistic—attributes.[35] There is no denying that the new lease on life experienced by nonfiction on the web is a propitious springboard for literary journalism's "multimedia features," constituting the "driving force" behind further developments.[36] If there be any danger in rebranding the genre to meet web-age needs and make it sound more trendy or profitable, it lies in uprooting it from its historical background. American literary journalism harks back to a period of time in which two types of journalism were cohabiting and reflects the schism that took place in journalism at the end of the nineteenth century.[37] Relinquishing the term "literary journalism" may eventuate in a whole historical chapter sinking into oblivion. By the same token, Dow denounces a glaring omission in recent literary histories that simply ignore and thereby condemn the genre to immateriality if not invisibility. For etymological reasons, literary journalism and its "related incarnations" have their *raison d'être*.[38] Therefore, the "infrequency" and lack of "traction" of the term in US culture beg questions as to the acceptance of literary journalism as a legitimate discipline in the academy and as a necessary historiographic category, Dow observes.[39]

Aggregating stories is part of the scholarly effort to advance literary journalism studies. Roiland lists popular American websites that promote the best reads and echoes the polemic that has recently been raging around the "longform" qualifier.[40] Anything "long" is the new fad, but quantity does not mean quality. The publishing industry is capitalizing on the renewed interest in a literature of the real. It is not incidental either that our post-truth era of fake news and alternative facts has spawned its own counterforce, an increasingly vocal Fifth Estate more inclined to read and share online rather than engage with print magazines. While generating infinite possibilities, the internet is also a showcase for the latest trends and whimsicalities that may jeopardize good literary journalism. However, Susan Greenberg welcomes the fact that "slow" journalism[41] is vying for online space. Greenberg provocatively supports the innovative wherewithal of the internet, a "surprisingly textual place."[42] She evaluates the liberating force of the "narrative turn"[43] taken by the web for both users and producers of content. While new editing and verification constraints emerge in "the digital fast lane," working patterns have also been affected in a positive way, maximizing mobility and creativity for "slow" journalists, thanks to reading apps that facilitate the distribution of stories, new formats launched by publishers, and crowdsourcing intervention.[44]

The second threat posed to the genre, when apprehended as a "new brand of storytelling," to use Roiland's phrase again, is that it may be stretched to accommodate a growing number of subgenres related to literary journalism but not always quite the same. Stretched too thin, the "brand" becomes diluted and arouses suspicion as to the quality of the genuine product. As a result, scholars may find themselves in uncharted territories, dealing with objects that have few stylistic features in common. An overly inclusive approach could transform literary journalism into a ragbag of nonfiction stories, deprived of any original flavor and blended in some supposedly bankable, homogenized goop. Subsuming too many byproducts under the literary journalism genre undoubtedly alters its substance and erodes its value. Whereas in the past the many denominations revealed preoccupations with veracity (creative nonfiction, nonfiction novels) and artistry (arts journalism, literary reportage), or blatantly flaunted its hesitations (faction, journalit), the confusion today also resides in the vast array of visual and audio cultures that are increasingly aligned under the banner of literary journalism. The paradox that "disciplinary blind spots" persist and a "canon" is still missing in literary journalism[45] is evidence of the intellectual complexity of a professedly nascent discipline that coincidentally suffers from indiscipline in its painstaking maturation out of blended genres and reconstituted traditions.

The *literariness* in literary journalism elicits either admiration or contempt, and critics disagree as to its epistemic value. "Literary" is rarely claimed as a signature by practitioners lest they be considered conceited at best, fusty at worst. Nicholas Lemann warns that the social function and the serious reporting inherent in literary journalism should not be shunned for the benefit of artistry.[46] Roiland, for his part, regrets the misapprehension of the term whose creative potential is often pitted against the "accuracy" of professional journalism. As mentioned above, he also makes the case for "literary" as a historical marker, which the "longform" moniker obliterates, as it rebrands literary journalism as a neoliberal commodity.[47] That it should be "literary" speaks volumes about the American venues that initially welcomed the genre and about the renowned writers that ensured its prosperity. Now that the journalistic imagination is a territory coveted and cornered by mainstream journalism, it is essential for literary journalism to redefine its competitive *literary* edge. Haun Saussy's suggestion that literariness be envisaged not exclusively in relation to written texts but rather as "reading *literarily*," meaning "with intensive textual scrutiny, defiance," applies to literary journalism,[48] whose *literary* descriptor is no dead letter. Dow too interpellates our reading practices and cautions that some tenets should be reevaluated due to the "formalistic and ontological" nature of the genre.[49]

Notwithstanding somewhat blinkered views that "once again, America's is the story the world wants to read about,"[50] opportunities to test new grounds, put out the feelers, and exploit the already dense terrain of American literary journalism *sensu stricto* must of course be encouraged by both scholars and writers. The many comprehensive studies of its patrimony, which provide an invaluable inventory of outstanding practitioners and precursors,[51] combined with the bustling online platforms and print magazines that routinely post exemplary pieces, point to the value in perpetuating a tradition, the understanding of which is increasingly broadened by researchers working on insufficiently uncovered corpuses, such as African American[52] or women's literary journalism.[53] These variations within US literary journalism, in light of the advances in global journalism and world literature studies, will enjoy the collateral benefits of "shifting focal points."[54] Out of subtle forays into transnational texts and contexts, unexpected connections and correlations surface, prompting new readings and revised interpretations. The US scholarship is often used as a yardstick to evaluate other national productions, but the emergence of literary journalistic texts and academic research in other contexts inevitably leads to rearrangements in terms of credits and influences. Joining an international conversation inevitably affects the balance of power and offers mutual resistance to hegemonic understandings of literary journalism.

But for all the attempts at encouraging non-US traditions to come to the fore, the likes of Truman Capote, Tom Wolfe, and Joan Didion are still touted as examples to emulate. Back in 2010, the national weekly supplement to *Le Monde* was drawing parallels between newly translated US authors and major French writers-cum-journalists.[55] Five years later, an article in the newspaper *Le Nouvel Observateur* excitingly announced the "landing" of "narrative journalism *à l'Américaine*."[56] To take the example of France again, the shelves of bookshops are now heavy with translations of authors well known to US readers and new editions of French reportages that had been forgotten.[57] Publishers today capitalize on the renewed interest in the genre. A case in point is the remarkable Éditions du Sous-Sol (Underground Publishing), which showcases only foreign reportage in translation. Oscillating between "creative" and "narrative nonfiction" or even *"littérature active,"* a term borrowed from Pierre Mac Orlan,[58] their flagship magazine, *Feuilleton*, tunes its pitch to Wolfe's oft-quoted phrase—journalism "that reads like a novel"—and branches out into muckraking, stunt, gonzo, and investigative journalism. While aligning the rich American heritage with the French tradition, they also integrate a vast array of pieces and authors from other countries and continents.

American literary journalism is flourishing, to wit the many hospitable online and print venues that host estimable pieces by literary journalists whose big books routinely top best-seller lists. International literary journalism studies have shed light on the immensity of the field, adopting both synchronic and diachronic perspectives. Albeit literary, the journalistic component also brings the genre back to its main responsibilities and burning issues (i.e., to cover and report wars and conflicts, climate change, economic downturns, political debacles, and immigration and refugees, to name just a few).[59] While some find it "regrettable" or even "reprehensible" that "researchers in journalism have thus far failed to concertedly theorize and empirically examine" such issues, dependent on their treatment by international media, I believe that scholars in *literary* journalism would be well inspired to question their "global cosmopolitan outlook."[60] As Simon Cottle suggests, I would further recommend that we must also "come of global age" in literary journalism studies and gain augmented insight by adopting transnational perspectives. Assuming such a critical stance would enable literary journalism scholars to be more inclusive in their examination of world crises or global conflicts that span different times and climes. For instance, the treatment of the refugee crisis in landmark projects such as "Fractured Lands" (*New York Times*), "Refuge" (*Washington Post*), "The Refugee Crisis" (*Granta*), or *Réfugiés* (Arte),[61] although hosted by major Western media outlets, also involves film directors, photographers, cartoonists, and refugees themselves. It thereby illuminates our understanding of complex realities and invites us to question the way stories are written, framed, and interpreted.

Transnational Perspectives

Making the case for literary journalism as an American household term does not deprive or bar the rest of the world from studying it. With the center-margin dichotomy long evaporated, an inclusive approach to scholarship is now favored. Abundant research is being conducted on the roots and routes of literary journalism, although many are still missing the conversation.[62] Scholars who propose definitions of international literary journalism aim neither to hierarchize traditions nor to vie for popularity along national lines.[63] We are thus not dealing with mutually exclusive categories. While the genre has been flourishing worldwide, engaging in a global conversation proves both problematic and promising, Sims warns, given the many variations in form and the specificities of each context of production.[64] John Bak insists that "any definition of international literary journalism must be elastic enough to account for its cultural variances."[65] Each tradition must be considered in its local crucible as it is shaped by its production and reception. Understandably, Bak also raises questions regarding the toolbox we use to identify and describe texts that may vary substantially.[66] At the crossroads between two disciplines that have developed comparative approaches and transcultural perspectives, literary journalism is grappling with its own aggravations. Methodological and epistemological quandaries inevitably result from transnational and translational considerations. The challenge of devising proper methods to compare corpora with full knowledge of their political, historical, and cultural depths is exacerbated by the genre's disciplinary hybridity. Such an ambitious project makes for compelling observations and fertile exchanges, but the ultimate end for such work is still undetermined.

Literary journalism scholars have thus far delineated the contours and characteristics of different traditions from a variety of locations using comparative approaches and multicultural perspectives. They have commendably been cataloging instances of literary journalism across the globe and compiling invaluable resources. The many denominations used to refer to the genre are a testament to its creative potential and journalistic relevance. In current international research, as published in *Literary Journalism Studies* and in several recent books, scholars do not look to ostracize or prioritize different traditions. Rather, they weave together a vast backdrop for identifying synergetic patterns and contact zones while detecting networks of activity or resistance. Also, scholars encourage close readings of experiential reportages and experimental formats and stimulate the examination of crossbreeding processes, be they textual hybridizations, international collaborations, or transmedia productions. Most importantly, they are pointing to the creative opportunities presented by new technologies and the internet at large, which have eroded national borders and facilitated, or complicated, dialogues between local cultures. Literary journalism studies has gained in scope, visibility, and pertinence.

Both journalism and literary studies have international organizations and learned societies. Neither academic field is immune to multicultural exchanges and transnational challenges; practitioners were actively involved in global networks and on international fronts long before the academy took an interest in them. They crossed geographic borders and generic boundaries before scholars established disciplines and tagged them as international, global, world, planetary, or comparative domains of knowledge. As a result, the world is literary journalism's oyster. Research opportunities abound as literary journalists are agents of hybridization and cross-fertilization. With the growing interest in international manifestations of the genre, critical volumes have appeared, all commendable in their intent on collating remarkable examples of literary journalism. John S. Bak and Bill Reynolds took the lead with *Literary Journalism across the Globe: Journalistic Traditions and Transnational Influences* (2011), followed by two volumes of *Global Literary Journalism: Exploring the Journalistic Imagination* (2012, 2014), edited by Richard Keeble and John Tulloch.[67] These editors deserve credit for bringing to worldwide attention the many literary journalistic endeavors that exist outside the United States.

Defining literary journalism—a favorite, even obsessive name game among international scholars—has been a matter of concern, if not a bone of contention. The spadework of unpacking and unpicking the genre was a prerequisite for outlining a coherent field, engaging in consistent research, and connecting with a global community of researchers. The conceptual theorization efforts have undoubtedly been worthwhile—to wit the unabated enthusiasm for the genre and the plethora of publications. Bak's notable efforts to elevate literary journalism to a discipline and his recommendation not to tinker further with terminology have not fallen on deaf ears. Keeble and Tulloch, for their part, prefer to talk of a "*field* where different traditions and practices of writing intersect," with "an assertion about truthfulness to verifiable experience"[68] as its backbone. However, "discipline" and "field" fail to embrace the subtleties of language at work in literary journalism and to fathom its poetic affects and organic effects. Albeit tantalizing, the disciplinary designation tends to offer a deceptively safe space depriving the genre from exacting examination relative to its ontological dimensions and inventive aspirations. Addressing literary journalism as a discipline may alienate it from its very object and relinquish close examinations of its core material, texts that encapsulate the gist of the genre. Keeble, for that matter, highlights major incursions into unchartered territories, values "rescue" operations of estimable works fallen into oblivion, and praises meticulous readings and groundbreaking explorations of past heritages.

These laudable exertions in bringing examples of local practices to global attention show that sharing and comparing are most instructive when exceeding the definitional and descriptive levels. Approaching international corpora requires creative methodologies, as paradigmatic shifts bring their own share of intricacies. Beyond the impressionistic collage of texts and contexts, a wider framework is needed to problematize transnational and translational concerns and to encompass parameters such as authorial and publishing strategies, reception studies, generic cross-breeding, and cultural transfers. Opening windows onto a multitude of traditions fantastically widens our perspectives and enlightens our expertise, and scholars have meticulously aggregated the sum of existing scholarship to that effect.[69] Collecting and considering the rich corpora of texts is a *sine qua non* for developing literary journalistic communities. Sims encouragingly sensitizes us to such endeavors and their collateral benefits. "Experimental border crossing can result in innovation,"[70] he observes. Definitely so, provided the three dimensions he proposes—cultural borders, mental boundaries, and the barrier of time—do not work to consolidate the US position as the epicenter but, rather, work to draw lines of flight in a complex rhizomatic system that may indeed acknowledge European ancestors and American masters while spotlighting earlier and future invigorating forces from other continents and further shores.

Sims's exhortation to adopt a cultural approach, rather than compartmentalized disciplinary perspectives, is the first step in formulating specifically literary journalistic hermeneutics. The process of devising adequate heuristic tools and establishing a holistic model of interpretation can gain from procedures undertaken in parent and parallel disciplines, but it must innovate in proposing its own homegrown methodology.[71] Collaborative enterprises with other domains are instrumental to forging new paradigms.[72] Literary journalism studies would benefit from a strategy feeding on its interdisciplinary genealogy and multicultural history and aiming toward an organic taxonomy and integrative destiny. Research in global journalism has identified challenges that correlate with those encountered in international literary journalism.[73] Skewed assumptions of a supposedly theoretical universalism must be overcome just as conceptual clarifications cannot be dispensed with, Thomas Hanitzsch notes.[74] Inasmuch as normative views were originally favored to apprehend heterogeneous corpora, pluralistic methods must now be substituted for self-referential and exclusionary strategies. Although motivated by the noblest intentions, comparative research in journalism has limitations. Establishing common frames of reference and measurements proves daunting due to the multitude of intellectual traditions and media histories within and across cultures.

Likewise, the tools honed within the field of comparative literature studies shed light on dilemmas literary journalism studies is contending with. They are conducive to examining productions that emanate from different times and climes. But debates have been raging in a discipline oscillating between multiple appellations. Albeit coopted by other fields, the comparative yardstick has increasingly invited criticism due to inevitable power struggles. In a landmark conversation with Gayatri Chakravorty Spivak on the state of the discipline, David Damrosch warns against the risks of being "culturally deracinated, philologically bankrupt, and ideologically complicit with the worst tendencies of global capitalism."[75] Comparative adumbrations may indeed create obstacles for exploration, expression, and education in literary journalism. For the sake of comparison, we need to hone tools and wield concepts that are graspable by a majority; we must create a communication system hospitable to all and avoid the risk of losing touch with original texts and local contexts. Terminological trials and tribulations are inspirational, yet "planetary," "cosmopolitan," "world," or "global" qualifiers are not exactly interchangeable. They markedly interrogate disciplinary presuppositions and may disclose "surprising cognitive landscapes hailing from inaccessible linguistic folds."[76]

Not immune to criticism, comparative literature studies, Saussy contends, has "benefited from intense self-scrutiny and proposals for renewal."[77] Like postcolonial studies, it foregrounds the need to deconstruct hierarchical relations and debunk colonial representations. Concepts coined in the field—hybridity, *métissage*, creolization, subaltern, strategic essentialism—are perfectly suited to scrutinizing texts on their operational and interactive levels. Such a multilayered approach is coextensive with that supported by the "cultural transfer" theory and *histoire croisée* ("crossed," "connected," or "shared history" in English), which acknowledges that cultural contacts involve partners not necessarily on a par for social, political, or economic reasons.[78] The insistence on considering reciprocity, knowing that it may imply asymmetry and conduce to self-reflexivity, potentiates the dynamic forces at play in recognizing that some partners in literary journalism studies may be more vulnerable than others, while leaving all participants with room for participation.[79] Mads Rosendahl Thomsen proposes a mapping of world literature congruent with such prerogatives. Devising constellations, he suggests, enables scholars to change viewpoints and highlight the complexities and potentialities of texts, their circulation and networks included. In sum, comparative work and cultural transfer theory or shared history offer useful methods provided we fine-tune our objectives.

Collations and Constellations

Epistemological and conceptual challenges drive scholars to reevaluate domestic productions, this time enlightened by transcultural exchanges, endowed with new insights, wider angles, and an augmented depth of field. Literary journalism studies has devoted well-invested time theorizing and exemplifying the genre, despite a tendency to effacement in the "larger history of academic culture," a shortcoming Dow attributes to multiple factors, ranging from terminological haziness to lack of disciplinary status, at least in the American context.[80] But, as language and culture influence our apprehension of the world, literary journalism empowers readers to expand their cognitive frames as they encounter idiosyncratic specificities emerging from diverse contexts. Saussy's premise that world literature should be the locus of "interchange" prone to creative "investment in methods" is helpful, as the very point of comparative literature "as a discipline is precisely defined by its proper objects" and the location of such objects through history are paramount in delineating the discipline.[81] While geographical and temporal benchmarks provide a frame, the dynamics within that space constitute the very promise of a transcultural conversation. Beyond these interstitial spaces, texts congregate or coalesce, independently from any formal or disciplinary accreditation. As Thomsen aptly notes, such constellations make it possible for works to connect that were not meant to in the first place, simply because "the canonical imperative directs the gaze" to other works, or because their "coherence" rests on incidental features rather than on "central attributes."[82]

Such a blueprint revolving around complex mappings exposes literary journalism studies to the same travails as those aggregated under "the indiscipline of comparison." Jacob Edmond hails the sustained efforts of scholars who blaze a trail toward "an age of post-discipline comparison" in their conceiving of imaginative approaches that avert Euro-American centrism.[83] *Histoire croisée*, for that matter, sensitizes us to the collisions and collusions resulting from cultural contacts. Crucial to this latter conceptual framework are the intercrossing and multidimensional principles that favor an active and relational approach. These, Michael Werner and Bénédicte Zimmerman argue, "stand in contrast to the static framework" initially proposed by comparative studies.[84] Applying such an approach to literary journalism means that its constitutive elements, be they cultural traditions, literary techniques, journalistic practices, publishing contexts, or academic theorizations, need to be carefully examined with a view to scales of comparison, multiple points of view and crossings, and conceptual historicizations. The task may look daunting, but such complexification will inevitably enrich literary journalism studies by disentangling its intertwined histories and devising its mixed destinies. Thomsen's premise that globalization will soon be an internalized notion supports his constellation model, which pleads for a fluid approach to works' trajectories.[85] His study of migrant writing is a case in point and can be easily applied to literary journalism, which abounds in stories of refugees and by exiles.[86]

A transatlantic examination of two traditions serves as a good starting point to anatomize such evolving literary journalism. While American literary journalism and its French counterpart boast long histories and equally impressive stables of writers, their trajectories have at times run parallel, intersected, or diverted. The fairly recent use in French of a collocation to designate the object of study—*journalisme littéraire*—faithfully mirrors the Anglo-American terminology. Indeed, the substantial research in the Anglo-American world provides the glue to fill the cracks in a long literary journalistic tradition in France and also leads to new criticism in the field.[87] *Journalisme littéraire*, which results from joint research and increased exposure to international scholarship, does not obliterate existing categories of nonfiction or bar alternative terms. Each nation has its preferred appellations to designate the genre, and France is no exception. The uncommon appellation of *journalisme littéraire* shows attempts at rapprochement and legibility on a transnational level. However, words are loaded with historic significance, and the split between journalism and literature in postwar France accounts for the lack of cohesion between the two sides that did not merge into a hybridized genre or form at that moment. More recently, Lionel Ruffel has proposed *narrations documentaires* as a relevant term to designate contemporary reportages that are documenting the real. Interestingly enough, the references he uses to illustrate these narratives are not limited to French authors.[88]

Scholars in France have worked extensively at documenting examples of literary journalism produced in the nineteenth and twentieth centuries. Myriam Boucharenc's *L'écrivain-reporter au cœur des années trente* (2004) and Marie-Ève Thérenty's *La littérature au quotidien: Poétiques journalistiques au XIXe siècle* (2007) are two major contributions to the field. While Thérenty delineates and conceptualizes a literary matrix in the press, Boucharenc resurrects decades of reportage and attributes its failure at gaining literary legitimacy to a lack of codification. Marc Martin unearths a collection of *grands reporters*—Pierre Giffard, Jules Huret, Henri Béraud, Fernand Xau—fervent supporters of a "new journalism" *à la Française* during the *Belle Époque* (1871–1914). Not impervious to American influences, they nevertheless censured the US model and rejected any parentage due to what they deemed was a lack of artistry and their certainty that they could outshine their American counterparts.[89] Today, networks of researchers are excitingly rebooting a tradition thanks to the ever-expanding conversation engaged with an international community. They have established an archaeology of French literary journalism and are launching new projects with a view to exploring how the genre has sprawled, resisted, impacted, and benefited from intercultural contacts.[90]

A comparative approach to literary journalism could start from contexts—conflicts, revolutions, colonization—and examine texts and consider the individual itineraries of literary journalists (e.g., their background, affiliation, or reception). To epitomize the merits of such a rhizomatic perspective, we can turn systematically to instances taken from such conflicts as the Spanish Civil War, to which literary journalists from all over the world rushed and from which they reported personal, albeit highly political, stories, depending on their origins, allegiances, readership, and life paths.[91] As for revolutions, the 1960s yielded much coverage, with variations in angles, depending on the volatile crucibles from which they erupted, be they the May 1968 protest in Paris or the countercultural movements in the US.[92] When it comes to colonization, it is a mystery why some of the most prominent French writers in the thirties—Albert Londres and Joseph Kessel—are hardly known in the Anglo-American world, since they were doing the kind of muckraking typical of the Progressive Era by holding their governments to account. While these celebrities are not famous beyond French borders, it is equally fascinating that Joan Didion was first published in French only in 2005 and that Wolfe's *New Journalism* has not been translated. However, Ted Conover and Adrian Nicole Leblanc can be read in French because they benefit from the genre's regeneration and forceful marketing today.

As mentioned above, publishers in France bank on this exciting phenomenon and publish not only first translations of Nellie Bly's immersion journalism but also republish reportages written by women in France in the early twentieth century. Maryse Choisy's immersion journalism is a case in point,[93] but there is little chance she will ever be translated into English. Another telling example, where a trend is reflected or, rather, deviated from or refracted is the case of gonzo in the 1970s. While gonzo established itself as a brand associated with Hunter S. Thompson, it morphed into music and sports journalism in the francophone sphere.[94] Conversely, the *mook* windfall that has been reinvigorating journalism in France for more than a decade has hardly any US equivalent.[95] The first to make this risky wager, called XXI, turned out to be an overnight sensation and was instantly emulated by an avalanche of others, but it remains a French (and also Belgian, Quebecer, or Swiss) exception. A connected history approach thus shows that struggles for influence do not take place across the board, and interaction does not necessarily imply reciprocity. However, self-reflexivity prompts rich creativity on international, transcultural, and media levels, with cross-pollination producing many ingenious developments, opportune revivals, and unexpected bonanzas for writers, publishers, and educators.

Conclusively, through reflection and "refraction," literary journalism is taking new directions in France, both in terms of scholarly research and journalistic production.[96] The timely revival of and renewed interest in nonfiction or *écriture du réel* are a saving grace for professionals and the academic world, which is now increasingly turning to inventive methods in pedagogy. While classes in creative writing have existed for decades at Anglo-American universities, they are only now surfacing in French institutions. That really is a revolution in a culture still impregnated by the genius of the French language, where one either had the talent of an *écrivain* or was at best an *écrivant*.[97] Creative writing was not taught in higher education for two main reasons: First, good writing was considered a gift or innate faculty; second, pupils had already been trained in the art of rhetoric and essay writing at school, as they were bracing themselves for the *baccalauréat*. Undergraduate students had supposedly acquired such technical skills prior to going to university. We are thus living at a watershed moment with universities creating a variety of trainings in communication and composition. Classes in *création littéraire* energize teaching programs by emulating and ostensibly flaunting their Anglo-American model.[98]

Werner's *histoire croisée* and Thomsen's constellation models can thus be fruitfully adapted to literary journalism. In structurally and dynamically articulating global instances of literary journalism, scholars may sketch convergences and divergences into multidimensional patterns of signification. Such constellations are more than mere constructions; they are "realistic, innovative, pluralistic, and didactic,"[99] Thomsen concludes. Pedagogical ventures are indeed essential among the preoccupations of literary journalism studies. Not only creative writing but also literary journalism courses have been missing from academic programs, except in the Anglo-American world. Keeble nevertheless notes that literary journalism emerged very late in British universities, despite a long tradition going back to Daniel Defoe.[100] There is obviously an urgent need to teach courses in literary journalism, which is another reason, perhaps, why the genre is increasingly claimed as an academic discipline. Why not then promote creative, collaborative, and even curative cultures? The recent visit of Pascal Verbeken, a Flemish writer, to our class on narrative journalism at our French-speaking university in Brussels was both a humbling and uplifting experience. *La terre promise* (2010), first published in Dutch and barely noticed in the southern, French-speaking, part of Belgium, tells the story of a mostly ignored chapter in the history of the country, that of Flemish immigration to a then-prosperous Wallonia.[101] Its explanatory depth and aesthetic mastery reveal the invisible wounds of a country that still needs healing. Verbeken's oeuvre repairs the missing link and enlightens the cultural history of a divided nation.

Of Roots and Routes

Without erring on the universalist side, we must nevertheless avert any evolutionary cultural homogenization while simultaneously celebrating a diversity of practices sprouting from different locations. Our ability to kindle local imaginations and see how they impact a global context is of paramount importance. It is not just at the level of creative production but also at the level of critical reception that literary journalism studies must expand, solidify its academic pedigree, and finesse its most pressing agendas. Beyond comparison, scholars must leave the thresholds of their safe spaces and explore unfamiliar settings or paths. Pushing the boundaries of a phenomenological approach is possible by constructing an exhaustive anatomy of literary journalism that questions our traditional selection criteria and escapes canonical diktats that may hide precious works that have so far escaped the academic radar. Even more than an archeology, a complete architecture of the genre is needed, designed as a comprehensive interpretative apparatus. Mapping transnational and translational roots and routes is vital to drawing a cartography of literary journalism; probing the textual and philological material is pivotal for such a critical project.

Attempts at devising such networks exist, to wit some ambitious wagers to apprehend cross-cultural and transnational texts that reveal the challenges, assets, but also failings of wide-ranging and broad-spectrum approaches. Marie-Ève Thérenty and Alain Vaillant's *Presse, nations et* *mondialisation au XIXe siècle* (2010), the third volume of a series devoted to the relationships between journalism and literature, examines the mutualizing of influences, be they hybridizations or appropriations, and an awareness of the hegemony of some press industries. The models of reportage, sensational scoops, and good stories, imported from America, cannot be denied. *Journalisme et mondialisation: Les ailleurs de l'Europe dans la presse et le reportage littéraires (XIXe–XXIe siècles)* (2017), edited by Marie-Astrid Charlier et Yvan Daniel, deals with the many instances in which globalization permeated both the literary and journalistic fields in the last two centuries. It focuses on French writers' peregrinations through and representations of Africa, America, and Asia in the French press and literature as well as on colonial reportage. These volumes, formidable bridges between cultures, do not investigate the genre we call American literary journalism per se, yet they analyze cultural transfers and crucially shed light on Americanisms found in the French literary and journalistic imaginations.

Other attempts at crossing perspectives exist in the francophone domain, such as *Littérature et reportage* (2001) and *Roman et reportage* (2015), both edited by Myriam Boucharenc.[102] In 2016, a special issue of *Literary Journalism Studies* devoted to francophone literary journalism, published in English, proved a significant move to reach a wider audience and acknowledge the work of women journalists, as well as efforts by indigenous voices to make themselves heard in newspapers during the colonial period.[103] Literary journalism is here understood in a much broader sense than that of a genre that "reads like a novel," although the literary presence of reportages printed in the press is proof of the constant cross-pollination between both fields. The gender and postcolonial angles favored in the issue reveal an attention to embracing global concerns to which an international community is particularly sensitive. In so doing, we no longer otherize but rather authorize those that are un-, under- or misrepresented in literary journalism, at least to a certain extent. Indeed, a much more inclusive approach must be promoted and space allocated to examples not about but from francophone Africa or Asia, hence the importance of starting from contexts to better identify how, and by whom, true stories are told.

In addition to finding forebears and identifying intersections and discrepancies, scholars and researchers continue to discover uncharted territories, map new routes, devise unprecedented itineraries, and connect new networks. On that account, it would be remiss not to cite the huge potential of digital humanities for expanding literary journalism studies. By way of illustration, the ambitious Numapresse project, under the aegis of Thérenty, aims at mapping constellations of literary journalists and their works over centuries and at identifying their trajectories and contacts with other cultures.[104] The digitalization of the press makes it possible to aggregate massive data and to outline cartographies that were not previously visible. Such technological advances reveal unexpected matrices and articulations that give a new boost to research in literary journalism. Numapresse shares similarities with Ryan Cordell and David Smith's Viral Texts project, in which computational means and methods (data mining and visualization) actualize impressive webs of circulation and reprinting of newspapers.[105] The project epitomizes the full capability of Thomsen's constellation model: In making extensive antebellum texts legible to the academic eye today, Cordell reveals the immense potential digitized corpora and "textual clusters" hold for understanding patterns of hyperconnected networks of the past.[106] With the caveat that we should not be mesmerized by alluring graphics and sleek presentations, there is no denying that digital tools are a bonanza to parse forgotten corpora and highlight unexpected configurations.

The transformative experience of reading international corpora eventuates in rejuvenation for scholars across the world. Through crisscrossing and crossbreeding, we affect each other, effect changes, and reinvent ourselves. However, challenges posed by multicultural, multilingual, multimedia, and multigeneric texts are real. Ignoring them would see the work of our academic community doomed to Babelian failure, elicited by linguistic misunderstandings and terminological conundrums. This is why the case for a philological adventure is commensurately imperative to canvas questions and parse documents. Too many pieces of literary journalism go unnoticed because they do not exist in translation. It would be remiss not to mention the huge responsibility resting on the shoulders of publishers, translators, and educators, who discover talents, provide access to indispensable works, and disseminate criticism. Courses and conferences must be organized that include readings and sessions in several languages, and publishing ventures must be encouraged to share salient texts. As for multilingual scholars and practitioners, they are invaluable go-betweens, whose vantage point gives them access to primary and secondary sources, which are crucial for global criticism.

Venturing out of the canon of American literary journalism into discomfort zones where foreign languages and cultures thrive is both a stimulating and challenging endeavor. This tentative dislocation of cultures, provided it be akin to Spivak's strategic essentialism or Thomsen's shifting focal points, is a transient passage allowing for adjustment, comprehension, and empathy. Likewise, the *histoire croisée* approach is a saving grace to make sense of similitudes and differences. In drawing cultures closer together, it weaves productive networks and devises innovative reflexive practices. Such a principle goes beyond comparison in yielding a dynamic transitory space for imagining original methodologies. While comparative and transfer studies hinge their advances on juxtaposition and intersection, *histoire croisée* departs from their essentially "historically constituted formations" to propose an inventive approach grounded in the multiplicity of perspectives not just of languages and cultures, but also "terminologies, categorizations and conceptualizations, traditions and disciplinary usages."[107] Erasing or rebranding the many subcategories of literary journalism is not an option. The constant reassessments are necessary, but such reevaluations can take place while avoiding historical misrepresentations or distortions.

Damrosch's caveats against cultural uprooting and linguistic meltdown have the virtue of hinting at attendant potential hazards, which can be discarded provided we embrace literary journalism in its historicity and diversity. As for the risks of capitalist ideology permeating academic endeavors or of pretensions to Americanize literary journalism, there is no denying that the genre is still excitingly thriving in the US, but also elsewhere. Few would be discontented with such a boon, despite the fragility brought by technological innovations with regard to print. Conversely, digital tools and computational developments stimulate research in literary journalism. In this chapter, I have resisted the temptation of listing examples from different literary journalistic traditions—except for the francophone Western world—as doing so would have meant impossible choices and blatant omissions. The complexity of our multiple heritages does not alleviate the difficulty of interpreting texts, subtexts, and contexts. Misconceptions might ruin our efforts at developing fruitful collaborations, trigger counterproductive feuds, and obscure our understanding of the genre.

In *What Journalism Could Be*, Barbie Zelizer insists on the creative capabilities and obligations of journalism. She champions "a new audacity of the imagination,"[108] prompted by craft but also political, technological, economic, and moral considerations, conducive to a more active and empowering process. Taking our cue from Zelizer, we would be well advised to question the prospects of *literary* journalism. In today's post-truth world, where traditional media have been upended, fake news disseminated, and political powers polarized, it is worth asking whose true stories we should turn to and whose *literary* authori(ali)ty should be acknowledged. In the face of adversity, we are aptly reminded that "the license of literary journalism"[109] helps comprehend unimaginably perilous moments and combat vanities. Literary journalism provides the wherewithal to defeat the dearth of talent and the paucity of language with critical acumen and rhetorical audacity. Beyond the respect for ancestral traditions and the excitement at the current diversity of form and content, we must foster collaborative, creative, and possibly curative cultures. As an antidote to blatant falsehood and ignorant bigotry, longform narratives may prove to be a *pharmakon* of choice. Cultivating a methodological approach that favors sharing and caring epistemologies is what literary journalism *should be*, or *could do*, at a global level.

Notes

1. Bak, introduction to *Literary Journalism*, 18. More on the disciplinary question later in the chapter.
2. By "collation," I mean the collection and comparison of examples of literary journalism; by "constellation," I am referring to the composition and configuration of such occurrences into patterns of signification. The terms "collation" and "constellation" will be thoroughly discussed in the fourth section of this chapter.
3. See the association's website at www.ialjs.org. This international learned society is a unique forum dedicated to the development of scholarly research and education in literary journalism. The association organizes annual conferences and publishes a biannual journal, *Literary Journalism Studies*.
4. France has a long tradition of *grand reportage*. Examples thereof can be found in the special issue on "francophone literary journalism" in *Literary Journalism Studies* 8, no. 2 (2016), featuring articles on Colette, Françoise Giroud, and writers from Belgium and Quebec, such as Marie Gevers and Gabrielle Roy, as well as an interview with Jean Hatzfeld. Particularly noteworthy in France is the scholarly work of Myriam Boucharenc, Marie-Ève Thérenty, and Alain Vaillant, presented later in this chapter.
5. Major French publishers launched collections of reportages in the interwar period (e.g., "Cahiers verts" [Grasset] and "Documents bleus" [Gallimard]). See Martin, *Les grands reporters*, 311–12.
6. The term *écriture du réel* (writing of the real) was notably used by journalist Nelly Kaprièlian to discuss new nonfiction writing in French. See Kaprièlian, "Au-delà du réel," 4–5.
7. Connery, "Discovering a Literary Form," 16.
8. Sims, *True Stories*, 9.
9. Zavarzadeh, *Mythopoeic Reality*; Hollowell, *Fact and Fiction*; Weber, *Literature of Fact*; Hellmann, *Fables of Fact*; Sims, *Literary Journalists*; Fishkin, *From Fact to Fiction*; Foley, *Telling the Truth*; Lounsberry, *Art of Fact*. More examples can be found in Dow, "Center and Beyond."
10. Literary journalism has featured in American university curricula as a distinctive class, course, or even program for decades. The University of California, Irvine, notably has a full program in literary journalism.
11. Fishkin, *From Fact to Fiction*, 3.
12. Fishkin, 7.
13. Sims, "International Literary Journalism," 36; also in Sims, *True Stories*, 11.
14. Samuels, "Literary Reportage."
15. Hartsock, *History*, in particular, the first chapter, "Locating the Emergence of Modern Narrative Literary Journalism," 21–40.
16. Sims, *True Stories*, 20; see also Sims, "Evolutionary Future," 85.
17. Sims, *Literary Journalism*; Sims, *True Stories*; Connery, *Sourcebook*; Applegate, *Literary Journalism*.
18. Whitt, *Settling the Borderland*; Connery, *Journalism and Realism*; Hartsock, *Literary Journalism*. Whitt noticeably and unprecedentedly features a significant number of women in her comprehensive study.
19. Sims infers that point from James W. Carey's insistence on the consciousness preempting and prompting events in cultural history ("Problem and the Promise," 7, 15).
20. Boynton discusses the alleged American exceptionalism in his introduction to *The New New Journalism* (xx–xxii). On page xxi, he refers more specifically to John A. Kouwenhoven's *Made in America* (1948).
21. More specifically, Boynton cites Chris Anderson, *Style as Argument* (Carbondale, IL: Southern Illinois University Press, 1987), 2; Jane Kramer, in Boynton, *New New Journalism*, 202–03; and Richard Preston, "The Fabric of Fact" (Princeton University dissertation, 1983), 6. All sources in Boynton, *New New Journalism*, xxi.
22. Mueller, "Conversation with David Samuels."
23. Sims, "Evolutionary Future," 87. On the importance of the *New Yorker* as a hub for literary journalists, see, for example, Sims, "Joseph Mitchell," 82–109 and *True Stories*, 10, 20.
24. See Kerrane and Yagoda, *Art of Fact*. Their anthology gathers sample texts by British and American precursors and pioneers of the genre.
25. See Thomsen, *Mapping World Literature*, 41–43. Thomsen shows that the national canonization of some writers of the 1920s was to some extent predicated upon international recognition. Crucially, he notes that the triumph of high caliber writers of the Lost Generation—incidentally also literary journalists—

boomeranged back home and dislodged British literature from its monopolistic position in the US academia.

26 Wolfe and Johnson, *New Journalism*.
27 Boynton, introduction to *New New Journalism*, xi.
28 Boynton, xi.
29 Boynton, xxx.
30 Boynton, xi, xii. Also quoted in Dow, *Narrating Class*, 161.
31 Dow, 161–62.
32 Boynton, introduction to *New New Journalism*, xv.
33 By way of illustration, the market of nonfiction translations is expanding in France. Not all, but a vast selection of books by the authors mentioned in Boynton's *The New New Journalism* exist in French: Conover, Langewiesche, LeBlanc, Schlosser, Krakauer, Talese, Lewis, to name just a few.
34 Roiland, "By Any Other Name," 63.
35 Roiland writes, "Calling or tagging a story #longform (or #longread) divorces it from the rich lineage of literary journalism in America" ("By Any Other Name," 65).
36 Jacobson, Marino, and Gutsche, "Digital Animation," 528. On the creative potential and opportunities of online literary journalism, see also Greenberg, "Slow Journalism in the Digital Fast Lane"; Lassila-Merisalo, "Story First."
37 Hartsock, *History*, 17.
38 Dow, "Reading Otherwise," 123.
39 Dow, "Center and Beyond."
40 Roiland, "By Any Other Name," 70–72.
41 Greenberg, "Slow Journalism," 15–16.
42 Greenberg, "Slow Journalism in the Digital Fast Lane," 383.
43 Greenberg, 383.
44 Greenberg, 388–90.
45 Dow, "Center and Beyond."
46 Lemann, "Journalism in Literary Journalism."
47 Roiland, "By Any Other Name," 69, 70.
48 Saussy, "Exquisite Cadavers," 23.
49 Dow, "Center and Beyond."
50 Boynton, introduction to *New New Journalism*, xxix.
51 As in Sims, Hartsock, Connery, Kerrane and Yagoda.
52 See R. Maguire, "African American Literary Journalism," a special issue of *Literary Journalism Studies*, in particular her "African American Literary Journalism: Extensions and Elaborations."
53 See, for instance, Flis, "Women and Literary Journalism," a special issue of *Literary Journalism Studies*, in particular her introduction, "On Recognition of Quality Writing." See also Whitt, *Settling the Borderland*.
54 Thomsen, *Mapping World Literature*, in particular Chapter 2, "Shifting Focal Points in the International Canons," 33–60.
55 Birnbaum, "Du journalisme," 1, 6–7.
56 Caviglioli, "Attention."
57 The Éditions Stock, for instance, has recently reprinted Maryse Choisy's *Un mois chez les filles*, an immersion reportage in a brothel initially published in 1928. The Éditions du Sous-Sol has published the undercover journalism of Nellie Bly in French.
58 The Éditions du Sous-Sol, now a department of Éditions du Seuil, in Paris, came to prominence with the launch of a first magazine, called *Feuilleton*, entirely dedicated to the best foreign literary nonfiction. They now publish other literary magazines and translations of major books written by literary journalists. Their presentation leaflet is a tribute to US literary journalists and nonfiction at large ("La plaquette"). Worth consulting is their special edition celebrating the fifth anniversary of *Feuilleton*, a unique collection in French of self-reflexive essays and interviews by and with the most prominent representatives of the genre: Joan Didion, Gay Talese, Ted Conover, David Samuels, Roberto Saviano, Gabriel García Marquez, Emmanuel Carrère, and others (see www.editions-du-sous-sol.com/publication/feuilleton-18/).
59 Richard Lance Keeble also suggests that literary journalism studies tend to focus on its positive achievements and successful treatment of complex issues "while marginalizing the political economy of the media and a *critical consideration* of ideological bias" ("Literary Journalism").
60 Cottle, "Journalism Studies," 309, 311.

61 Anderson, "Fractured Lands"; Davidson and Sullivan, "Refuge"; "Refugee Crisis"; "Réfugiés."
62 On the need to expand geographically and include scholars from Asian and African countries, see Trindade, "What Will the Future Bring?," 102–04.
63 See part I of Bak and Reynolds, "Toward a Theory of International Literary Journalism," in *Literary Journalism across the Globe*, 23–94. This section has contributions by Hartsock, McCay, Reynolds, Abrahamson, and Sims.
64 Sims, "Problem and the Promise."
65 Bak, introduction to *Literary Journalism*, 10.
66 Bak points to the particularly rich heritage of Anglo-American literary journalism, which encompasses a number of subcategories such as "literary reportage, narrative journalism, creative nonfiction, and New Journalism." Conversely, he argues, other traditions may not use such a large repertoire and thus keep using American literary journalism as a standard to discuss their own production (7).
67 Bak and Reynolds, *Literary Journalism*; Keeble and Tulloch, *Global Literary Journalism*.
68 Keeble and Tulloch, *Global Literary Journalism*, 1:6–7.
69 For a comprehensive cataloging of sources and examples, see M. Maguire, "Literary Journalism." See also M. Maguire, "Recent Trends," 144–45; R. Maguire and M. Maguire, "Recent Trends."
70 Sims, "International Literary Journalism," 33.
71 Dow insists on the need for "mutual recognition of other disciplines," including, for example, sociology, gender studies, literary criticism, and visual studies, to help literary journalism studies flourish. See Dow, "Reading Otherwise," 122. Also in Dow, "Center and Beyond."
72 A point also made earlier by Sims, "Problem and the Promise," and Dow, "Center and Beyond."
73 See, for instance, Löffelholz, Weaver, and Schwarz, *Global Journalism Research*, in particular, Weaver and Löffelholz, "Questioning Boundaries," 3–12; Hanitzsch, "Comparing Journalism," 93–105; Singer, "Journalism Research," 145–57; Reese, "Theorizing a Globalized Journalism," 240–52.
74 Hanitzsch, "Comparing Journalism," 96, 99–101.
75 Spivak and Damrosch, "Comparative Literature/World Literature," 365.
76 Apter, *Against World Literature*, 2. Also published as "Against World Literature (2013)," 346.
77 Saussy, preface to *Comparative Literature*, xiii.
78 Werner and Zimmermann, "Beyond Comparison." See also Werner and Zimmermann, "Penser l'histoire croisée."
79 The term "vulnerable" is to be understood as Judith Butler defines it (i.e., with a potential for resistance, not victimization). See Butler, "Rethinking Vulnerability and Resistance." By "vulnerable" here, I mean less advanced in scholarship because new or coming later to the field, or where the latter is ignored or unacknowledged; or where there is limited access to primary, academic, or online resources; or where free speech is repressed.
80 Dow, "Center and Beyond."
81 Saussy, "Exquisite Cadavers," 11, 12.
82 Thomsen, *Mapping World Literature*, 140.
83 Edmond, "No Discipline," 652.
84 Werner and Zimmermann, "Beyond Comparison," 38.
85 Thomsen, *Mapping World Literature*, 97. Thomsen argues that globalization might even become an obsolete concept, since it will be increasingly internalized, which does not mean that "local" and "global" will become irrelevant, but they will be part of a wider web of elements.
86 Thomsen asserts that in migrant writing, "ideas of place, nation, and identity are more complex than ever" and that "migrant writing stands out and forms a constellation of its own, due to the simple fact that the writers have a different relation to languages and book markets than most other writers" (*Mapping World Literature*, 100, 101).
87 Meuret, Aron, and Thérenty, "Francophone Literary Journalism," 10.
88 While studying a number of contemporary French writers, such as François Bon, Jean Hatzfeld, Jean Rolin, and Philippe Vasset, Ruffel also mentions William T. Vollmann, Svetlana Alexievich, and Roberto Saviano. See Ruffel, "Un réalisme contemporain."
89 Martin, *Les grands reporters*, 32–35.
90 Among the most significant work on French literary reportage or journalism, see Boucharenc, *L'écrivain-reporter*; Thérenty, *La littérature au quotidien*; Thérenty and Vaillant, *Presse, nations et mondialisation*; Kalifa et al., *La civilisation du journal*; Boucharenc, Martens, and van Nuijs, "Croisées de la fiction"; Aron and Gemis, "Le littéraire."
91 See, for instance, Roiland, "'Just People'"; Meuret, "Rebels with a Cause."
92 See, for instance, Harbers, Van den Broek, and Broersma, *Witnessing the Sixties*.

93 Choisy, *Un mois*. Choisy was a reckless journalist who spent one month at a brothel and published this book ("One month with the girls," 1928) on the prostitution milieu in France. She then spent a month undercover at a monastery, pretending she was a male monk. Her reportage was published as *Un mois chez les hommes* in 1929. A new edition of the former was released in 2015; the latter has not been reprinted to this date.
94 Meuret, "Le journalisme littéraire." On gonzo journalism, see Alexander and Isager, *Fear and Loathing Worldwide*.
95 Mooks—a portmanteau word that merges "magazine" and "book"—are classy or glossy magazines sold in bookshops (not at newsagents) that combine longform reportages, photojournalism, and occasionally graphic journalism. See, for instance, Alvès and Stein, *Les mooks*. On *mooks*, see Neveu, "Revisiting Narrative Journalism."
96 The term "refraction" (as deviation, or deflection) is used in comparative literature, namely by Damrosch.
97 Barthes, "Écrivains et écrivants (1960)."
98 The University of Le Havre was the first to launch a master's degree in creative writing in 2012. Others have now followed suit (Paris 8 Saint-Denis and Toulouse, for example). The launch of these programs is typically pitched with references to the Anglo-American model of creative writing classes.
99 Thomsen, *Mapping World Literature*, 139, and 139–42 for further development of these four arguments.
100 Keeble, "Literary Journalism."
101 Verbeken, *Arm Wallonië*; for the French translation, see Verbeken, *La terre promise*. Verbeken discussed his book at Université libre de Bruxelles, Belgium, on March 9, 2018.
102 Boucharenc and Deluche, *Littérature et reportage*; Boucharenc, *Roman et reportage*.
103 See Meuret, "Francophone Literary Journalism," a special issue of *Literary Journalism Studies*.
104 Numapresse is the name of a consortium developing the international project From Paper to Screen: Cultural Exchanges, Generic Transfers, and Mediapoetics of the French Press, funded by the ANR (Agence Nationale de la Recherche) in France. The project coordinator is Marie-Ève Thérenty, and the partners are French, Belgian, and Canadian scholars. Pierre-Carl Langlais and Julien Schuh are in charge of the digitalization, data mining, and visualization of the project, which started in October 2017. See the project website at www.agence-nationale-recherche.fr/Projet-ANR-17-CE27-0014.
105 Cordell and Smith, *Viral Texts*.
106 Cordell, "Reprinting," 422, 430.
107 Werner and Zimmermann, "Beyond Comparison," 31, 32.
108 Zelizer, *What Journalism Could Be*, 8.
109 Siegel, "Time of Many Questions."

Bibliography

Alexander, Robert, and Christine Isager, eds. *Fear and Loathing Worldwide: Gonzo Journalism Beyond Hunter S. Thompson*. New York: Bloomsbury, 2018.

Alvès, Audrey, and Marieke Stein, eds. *Les mooks: Espaces de renouveau du journalisme littéraire*. Paris: L'Harmattan, 2017.

Anderson, Scott. "Fractured Lands: How the Arab World Came Apart." *New York Times Magazine*, 2016. www.nytimes.com/interactive/2016/08/11/magazine/isis-middle-east-arab-spring-fractured-lands.html.

Applegate, Edd, ed. *Literary Journalism: A Biographical Dictionary of Writers and Editors*. Westport, CT: Greenwood Press, 1996.

Apter, Emily. *Against World Literature: On the Politics of Untranslatability*. London: Verso, 2013.

———. "Against World Literature (2013)." In *World Literature in Theory*, edited by David Damrosch, 345–62. Malden, MA: Wiley-Blackwell, 2014.

Aron, Paul, and Vanessa Gemis, eds. "Le littéraire en régime journalistique." *COnTEXTES* (November 2012). http://journals.openedition.org/contextes/5296.

Bak, John S. Introduction to Bak and Reynolds, *Literary Journalism*, 1–20.

Bak, John S., and Bill Reynolds, eds. *Literary Journalism across the Globe: Journalistic Traditions and Transnational Influences*. Amherst, MA: University of Massachusetts Press, 2011.

Barthes, Roland. "Écrivains et écrivants (1960)." In *Essais critiques*, 147–54. Paris: Seuil, 1964.

Birnbaum, Jean. "Du journalisme comme laboratoire littéraire." Dossier spécial, Cahier du *Monde*, May 7, 2010, 1, 6–7.

Boucharenc, Myriam. *L'écrivain-reporter au cœur des années trente*. Villeneuve d'Ascq, France: Presses Universitaires du Septentrion, 2004.

———, ed. *Roman et reportage: Rencontres croisées*. Limoges, France: Presses Universitaires de Limoges, 2015.

Boucharenc, Myriam, and Joëlle Deluche, eds. *Littérature et reportage*. Limoges, France: Presses Universitaires de Limoges, 2001.

Boucharenc, Myriam, David Martens, and Laurence van Nuijs. "Croisées de la fiction: Journalisme et littérature." *Interférences littéraires / Literaire interferenties* 7 (November 2011): 9–19.

Boynton, Robert S. Introduction to Boynton, *New New Journalism*, xi–xxxii.

———, ed. *The New New Journalism: Conversations with America's Best Nonfiction Writers on Their Craft*. New York: Vintage Books, 2005.

Butler, Judith. "Rethinking Vulnerability and Resistance." In *Vulnerability in Resistance*, edited by Judith Butler, Zeynep Gambetti, and Leticia Sabsay, 12–27. Durham, NC: Duke University Press, 2016.

Caviglioli, David. "Attention, le journalisme narratif débarque en France." *Le Nouvel Observateur*, June 28, 2015. http://bibliobs.nouvelobs.com/actualites/20150626.OBS1646/attention-le-journalisme-narratif-debarque-en-france.html.

Charlier, Marie-Astrid, and Yvan Daniel, eds. *Journalisme et mondialisation: Les ailleurs de l'Europe dans la presse et le reportage littéraires (xixe–xxie siècles)*. Rennes, France: Presses Universitaires de Rennes, 2017.

Choisy, Maryse. *Un mois chez les filles*. Paris: Stock, 2015.

Connery, Thomas B. "Discovering a Literary Form." In Connery, *Sourcebook*, 3–37.

———. *Journalism and Realism: Rendering American Life*. Evanston, IL: Northwestern University Press, 2011.

———, ed. *A Sourcebook of American Literary Journalism: Representative Writers in an Emerging Genre*. New York: Greenwood Press, 1992.

Cordell, Ryan. "Reprinting, Circulation, and the Network Author in Antebellum Newspapers." *American Literary History* 27, no. 3 (Fall 2015): 417–45. https://doi.org/10.1093/alh/ajv028.

Cordell, Ryan, and David Smith. *Viral Texts: Mapping Networks of Reprinting in 19th-Century Newspapers and Magazines*. 2017. http://viraltexts.org.

Cottle, Simon. "Journalism Studies: Coming of (Global) Age?" *Journalism* 10, no. 3 (2009): 309–11. https://doi.org/10.1177/1464884909102573.

Davidson, Linda, and Kevin Sullivan. "Refuge: 18 Stories from the Syrian Exodus." *Washington Post*, 2013. www.washingtonpost.com/sf/syrian-refugees/story/refuge/.

Dow, William. "The Center and Beyond: The Expansion of American Literary Journalism Studies." *Famecos* 23 (October 2016). https://doi.org/10.15448/1980-3729.2016.s.25142.

———. *Narrating Class in American Fiction*. New York: Palgrave Macmillan, 2009.

———. "Reading Otherwise: Literary Journalism as an Aesthetic Narrative Cosmopolitanism." *Literary Journalism Studies* 8, no. 2 (Fall 2016): 118–36.

Edmond, Jacob. "No Discipline: An Introduction to 'The Indiscipline of Comparison.'" *Comparative Literature Studies* 53, no. 4 (2016): 647–59.

Fishkin, Shelley Fisher. *From Fact to Fiction: Journalism and Imaginative Writing in America*. Baltimore, MD: Johns Hopkins University Press, 1985.

Flis, Leonora. "On Recognition of Quality Writing." In "Women and Literary Journalism." Special issue, *Literary Journalism Studies* 7, no. 1 (Spring 2015): 7–14.

———, ed. "Women and Literary Journalism." Special issue, *Literary Journalism Studies* 7, no. 1 (Spring 2015).

Foley, Barbara. *Telling the Truth: The Theory and Practice of Documentary Fiction*. Ithaca, NY: Cornell University Press, 1986.

Greenberg, Susan. "Slow Journalism." *Prospect*, February 2007, 15–16.

———. "Slow Journalism in the Digital Fast Lane." In Keeble and Tulloch, *Global Literary Journalism*, 1:381–93.

Hanitzsch, Thomas. "Comparing Journalism across Cultural Boundaries: State of the Art, Strategies, Problems, and Solutions." In *Global Journalism Research: Theories, Methods, Findings, Future*, edited by Martin Löffelholz and David Weaver, with Andreas Schwarz, 93–105. Malden, MA: Blackwell Publishing, 2008.

Harbers, Frank, Ilja Van den Broek, and Marcel Broersma, eds. *Witnessing the Sixties: A Decade of Change in Journalism and Literature*. Leuven, Belgium: Peeters, 2016.

Hartsock, John C. *A History of American Literary Journalism: The Emergence of a Modern Narrative Form*. Amherst, MA: University of Massachusetts Press, 2000.

———. *Literary Journalism and the Aesthetics of Experience*. Amherst, MA: University of Massachusetts Press, 2016.

Hellmann, John. *Fables of Fact: The New Journalism as New Fiction*. Urbana, IL: University of Illinois Press, 1981.

Hollowell, John. *Fact and Fiction: The New Journalism and the Nonfiction Novel*. Chapel Hill, NC: University of North Carolina Press, 1977.

Jacobson, Susan, Jacqueline Marino, and Robert E. Gutsche Jr. "The Digital Animation of Literary Journalism." *Journalism* 17, no. 4 (2016): 527–46. https://doi.org/10.1177/1464884914568079.

Kalifa, Dominique, Philippe Régnier, Marie-Ève Thérenty, and Alain Vaillant, eds. *La civilisation du journal: Histoire culturelle et littéraire de la presse française au XIXe siècle*. Paris: Nouveau Monde Éditions, 2011.

Kaprièlian, Nelly. "Au-delà du réel." Special issue, Nouvelles littératures françaises, *Les Inrockuptibles* (2010): 4–5.

Keeble, Richard Lance. "Literary Journalism." In *Oxford Research Encyclopedia of Communication*. July 2018. https://doi.org/10.1093/acrefore/9780190228613.013.836.

Keeble, Richard Lance, and John Tulloch, eds. *Global Literary Journalism: Exploring the Journalistic Imagination*. Vol. 1. New York: Peter Lang, 2012.

———, eds. *Global Literary Journalism: Exploring the Journalistic Imagination*. Vol. 2. New York: Peter Lang, 2014.

Kerrane, Kevin, and Ben Yagoda, eds. *The Art of Fact: A Historical Anthology of Literary Journalism*. New York: Touchstone Books, 1998.

Lassila-Merisalo, Maria. "Story First—Publishing Narrative Long-Form Journalism in Digital Environments." *Journal of Magazine and New Media Research* 15, no. 2 (Summer 2014): 1–15.

Lemann, Nicholas. "The Journalism in Literary Journalism." *Literary Journalism Studies* 7, no. 2 (Fall 2015): 51–58.

Löffelholz, Martin, and David Weaver, with Andreas Schwarz, eds. *Global Journalism Research: Theories, Methods, Findings, Future*. Malden, MA: Blackwell Publishing, 2008.

Lounsberry, Barbara. *The Art of Fact: Contemporary Artists of Nonfiction*. New York: Greenwood Press, 1990.

Maguire, Miles. "Literary Journalism: Journalism Aspiring to Be Literature." In *The Routledge Handbook of Magazine Research: The Future of the Magazine Form*, edited by David Abrahamson and Marcia R. Prior-Miller, with a foreword by Bill Emmott, 362–74. New York: Routledge, 2015.

———. "Recent Trends and Topics in Literary Journalism Scholarship." *Literary Journalism Studies* 8, no. 1 (Spring 2016): 141–51.

Maguire, Roberta S., ed. "African American Literary Journalism." Special issue, *Literary Journalism Studies* 5, no. 2 (Fall 2013).

———. "African American Literary Journalism: Extensions and Elaborations." In "African American Literary Journalism," edited by Roberta Maguire. Special issue, *Literary Journalism Studies* 5, no. 2 (Fall 2013): 8–14.

Maguire, Roberta S., and Miles Maguire. "Recent Trends and Topics in Literary Journalism Scholarship." *Literary Journalism Studies* 9, no. 1 (Spring 2017): 119–28.

Martin, Marc. *Les grands reporters: Les débuts du journalisme moderne*. Paris: Éditions Louis Audibert, 2005.

Meuret, Isabelle, ed. "Francophone Literary Journalism." Special issue, *Literary Journalism Studies* 8, no. 2 (Fall 2016).

———. "Le journalisme littéraire à l'aube du XXIe siècle: Regards croisés entre mondes anglophone et francophone." *COnTEXTES* (November 2012). http://journals.openedition.org/contextes/5376.

———. "Rebels with a Cause: Women Reporting the Spanish Civil War." *Literary Journalism Studies* 7, no. 1 (Spring 2015): 79–98.

Meuret, Isabelle, Paul Aron, and Marie-Ève Thérenty. "Francophone Literary Journalism: Exploring Its Vital Edges." *Literary Journalism Studies* 8, no. 2 (Fall 2016): 9–13.

Mueller, Ben. "A Conversation with David Samuels." *New Journal*, September 8, 2012. www.thenewjournalatyale.com/2012/09/a-conversation-with-david-samuels/.

Neveu, Erik. "Revisiting Narrative Journalism as One of the Futures of Journalism." *Journalism Studies* 15, no. 5 (2014): 533–42. https://doi.org/10.1080/1461670X.2014.885683.

"La plaquette." Éditions du Sous-Sol. www.editions-du-sous-sol.com/le-sous-sol/.

Reese, Stephen D. "Theorizing a Globalized Journalism." In Löffelholz, Weaver, and Schwarz, *Global Journalism Research*, 240–52.

"The Refugee Crisis." *Granta*, September 7, 2015. https://granta.com/the-refugee-crisis/.

"Réfugiés." *Arte Reportage*. 2016. www.arte.tv/sites/refugies/.

Roiland, Josh. "By Any Other Name: The Case for Literary Journalism." *Literary Journalism Studies* 7, no. 2 (Fall 2015): 60–89.

Roiland, Joshua M. "'Just People' Are Just People: Langston Hughes and the Populist Power of African American Literary Journalism." *Literary Journalism Studies* 5, no. 2 (Fall 2013): 15–34.

Ruffel, Lionel. "Un réalisme contemporain: Les narrations documentaires." *Littérature*, no. 166 (2012): 13–25.

Samuels, David. "Literary Reportage." *Villa Gillet*, March 2, 2011. https://villagillet.wordpress.com/2011/03/02/literary-reportage/.

Saussy, Haun. "Exquisite Cadavers Stitched from Fresh Nightmares." In *Comparative Literature in An Age of Globalization*, edited by Haun Saussy, 3–42. Baltimore, MD: Johns Hopkins University Press, 2006.

———. Preface to *Comparative Literature in An Age of Globalization*, edited by Haun Saussy, vii–xiii. Baltimore, MD: Johns Hopkins University Press, 2006.

Siegel, Lee. "In a Time of Many Questions, Literary Journalism Provides an Answer." *Columbia Journalism Review*, December 5, 2016. www.cjr.org/special_report/literary_journalism_trump_president.php.

Sims, Norman. "The Evolutionary Future of American and International Literary Journalism." In Bak and Reynolds, *Literary Journalism*, 85–94.

———. "International Literary Journalism in Three Dimensions." *World Literature Today* 86, no. 2 (March/April 2012): 32–36. https://doi.org/10.7588/worllitetoda.86.2.0032.

———. "Joseph Mitchell and *The New Yorker* Nonfiction Writers." In Sims, *Literary Journalism*, 82–109.

———. *Literary Journalism in the Twentieth Century*. New York: Oxford University Press, 1990.

———, ed. *The Literary Journalists*. New York: Ballantine Books, 1984.

———. "The Problem and the Promise of Literary Journalism Studies." *Literary Journalism Studies* 1, no. 1 (Spring 2009): 7–16.

———. *True Stories: A Century of Literary Journalism*. Evanston, IL: Northwestern University Press, 2007.

Singer, Jane B. "Journalism Research in the United States: Paradigm Shift in a Networked World." In Löffelholz, Weaver, and Schwarz, *Global Journalism Research*, 145–57.

Spivak, Gayatri Chakravorty, and David Damrosch. "Comparative Literature/World Literature: A Discussion (2011)." In *World Literature in Theory*, edited by David Damrosch, 363–88. Malden, MA: Wiley-Blackwell, 2014.

Thérenty, Marie-Ève. *La littérature au quotidien: Poétiques journalistiques du XIXe siècle*. Paris: Seuil, 2007.

Thérenty, Marie-Ève, and Alain Vaillant, eds. *Presse, nations et mondialisation au XIXe siècle*. Paris: Nouveau Monde Éditions, 2004.

Thomsen, Mads Rosendahl. *Mapping World Literature: International Canonization and Transnational Literatures*. 2008. London: Continuum, 2010.

Trindade, Alice Donat. "What Will the Future Bring?" *Literary Journalism Studies* 4, no. 2 (Fall 2012): 101–05.

Verbeken, Pascal. *Arm Wallonië: Een reis door het beloofde land*. 2007. Antwerp, Belgium: De Bezige Bij, 2014.

———. *La terre promise: Flamands en Wallonie*. Translated by Anne-Laure Vignaux. Bègles, France: Le Castor Astral, 2010.

Weaver, David, and Martin Löffelholz. "Questioning National, Cultural, and Disciplinary Boundaries: A Call for Global Journalism Research." In Löffelholz, Weaver, and Schwarz, *Global Journalism Research*, 3–12.

Weber, Ronald. *The Literature of Fact: Literary Nonfiction in American Writing*. Athens, OH: Ohio University Press, 1980.

Werner, Michael, and Bénédicte Zimmermann. "Beyond Comparison: *Histoire Croisée* and the Challenge of Reflexivity." *History and Theory* 45, no. 1 (2006): 30–50. https://doi.org/10.1111/j.1468-2303.2006.00347.x.

———. "Penser l'histoire croisée: Entre empirie et réflexivité." In *De la comparaison à l'histoire croisée*, edited by Michael Werner and Bénédicte Zimmerman, 15–49. Paris: Seuil, 2004.

Whitt, Jan. *Settling the Borderland: Other Voices in Literary Journalism*. Lanham, MD: University Press of America, 2008.

Wolfe, Tom, and E. W. Johnson, eds. *The New Journalism*. London: Picador, 1975.

Zavarzadeh, Mas'ud. *The Mythopoeic Reality: The Postwar American Nonfiction Novel*. Urbana, IL: University of Illinois Press, 1976.

Zelizer, Barbie. *What Journalism Could Be*. Cambridge: Polity Press, 2017.

35
LITERARY JOURNALISM IN THE DIGITAL AGE

David O. Dowling

At the dawn of the internet age in 1997, the online publication of Mark Bowden's celebrated "Black Hawk Down" marked the advent of literary journalism in the digital age. Originally appearing in twenty-nine daily installments in the print edition of the *Philadelphia Inquirer*, the online version of this harrowing story, which was later made into the motion picture that propelled the reporter to world fame, is a relic of the earliest days of Web 2.0. Its clunky hyperlinks—many of which have fallen prey to internet ephemerality known as link rot—render maps and images in staccato succession in an arduous, click-heavy reading experience, with Bowden's sterling prose indelicately shoveled onto the page. Skirting the left margin under a tiny navigation bar are supplemental multimedia clustered into utilitarian categorical boxes labeled video, audio, photos, maps, and full text.[1] Although an unprecedented achievement in 1997, decades later the visually disjointed transition-less design now feels more like a Wikipedia page or a database of raw information in sharp contrast to the latest immersive multimedia narratives designed for mobile audiences. Now at the forefront of digital longform, "a relatively new species undergoing a gradual but fierce evolution" according to Harvard's Nieman Journalism Lab,[2] are the *Washington Post*'s "A New Age of Walls" and "The Waypoint," along with the *New York Times*'s "Greenland Is Melting Away." These 2016 legacy media publications have become the new standard bearers whose design has distinctly improved upon the landmark achievement of the *Times*'s Pulitzer Prize-winning "Snow Fall: Avalanche at Tunnel Creek" in 2012.

This brief but fierce evolution is in part attributable to the shift from an audience with notoriously short attention spans on the early web to one more deeply engaged than ever in the new immersive online ecosystem. Mobile users now spend twice the engaged time with longform articles than shortform, according to the latest Pew research.[3] Skyrocketing social media use has escalated interest in highly sharable digital narratives, as the majority of longform readers arrive at their stories from Facebook and Twitter.[4] Through a rising number of aggregators such as Longreads and Longform, tablet and expanded smartphone users now flock to online-only platforms specializing in narrative nonfiction such as Byliner, the Big Roundtable, the Atavist Magazine, and Epic Magazine. Legacy media including the *Washington Post*, T Brand Studio, and WSJ Custom Studios (the latter two being the respective content marketing producers for the *New York Times* and the *Wall Street Journal*) have redoubled their efforts to out-Snowfall "Snow Fall," the feature that revolutionized multimedia digital design. Technical innovations have encouraged bold investments from industry to capitalize on unprecedented mobile reader engagement, a movement that has ushered in the current golden age of digital literary journalism, which Robert Boynton has heralded "the supreme nonfiction."[5]

In pursuit of the new gold standard of reader engagement measured by time on site rather than pageviews, where literally every additional second that users remain with the story is handsomely rewarded, publishers at the industry's leading edge have leveraged new storytelling technologies for mobile audiences to capture and maintain their attention.[6] The purpose of this chapter is to demonstrate how the latest developments in digital longform now offer a reading experience calibrated to reduce reader distraction and encourage focus on narrative, thus fueling the most potent forms of literary journalism in the genre's brief history. Narrativity is treated in this chapter as a multimodal phenomenon that in combining visual and written modalities produces an effect distinct from standard writer or visual narrative. I examine what Martin Conboy and Scott Eldridge call "the mix of trepidation and exuberance with regard to new technologies" and business models behind this renaissance in nonfiction digital storytelling—today's fastest growing literary genre—marked by high-end productions that function to build prestige and express brand values for their respective publishers and, in the case of content marketing, corporate sponsors.[7] Atavist has grown from a boutique publisher to a mainstream force, just as the Big Roundtable and Narratively have escalated their readership through longtail marketing. The most powerful pieces to follow "Snow Fall" are increasingly commissioned by corporate entities, as seen in Netflix's partnerships with WSJ Custom Studios to promote its streaming series *Narcos* through the Webby Award-winning "Cocainenomics," and T Brand Studio on behalf of *Orange Is the New Black* to create the "Snow Fall"-inspired "Women Inmates: Why the Male Model Doesn't Work." Other content marketing partnerships delivered stunning digital longform documentary journalism in Epic's "Beyond the Map" and "Moon Shot," both Google promotional interactive documentaries.

This study bears important implications for both industrial and technological media convergence. Traditional print media has converged with digital storytelling to enrich and expand what John Hartsock defines as literary journalism's distinctive narra-descriptive aesthetic, particularly its chronotopic capacity to transport the reader to a specific time and place.[8] Rather than losing readers the way "jumps" did in print newspapers by directing them to inside pages to continue stories, digital works like the *Guardian*'s "Firestorm" immerse them in the story world with sequenced visuals animated as they rise into view on the screen, in effect rewarding readers for advancing the linear narrative. Today's multimedia narratives are built upon such absorbing templates, which render profoundly different reading experiences from the inherently distracting ones associated with the superannuated jump in newspaper stories or the primitive digital design of Bowden's web edition of "Black Hawk Down." Now when readers encounter an image, video, or charts in stories like the *New York Times*'s "Greenland Is Melting Away," these elements are directly tied to the text on the previous screen not as mere ancillary decoration but as vital components of a carefully orchestrated symphony of verbal and visual communication modalities known as ekphrasis.[9] As with print reading, users may access any of the movements within that symphony, as it were, by way of navigation through sections and chapters. Once within the space of the story, however, they follow a linear thread distinctly choreographed according to Aristotelian narrative progression from rising action to a key turning point (*peripeteia* in the original Greek) and falling action to the denouement where order is restored, or disturbed, as in the case of overtly political pieces such as "A New Age of Walls."[10] With more cinematic power than ever, multimedia elements realize the meaning of the written text with the heft and dynamism of lived experience, whether from satellite or drone footage taken from thousands of feet in the air as in "Greenland." Such innovations also capitalize on the power of these pieces to induce the reader's empathy through a more immersive, integrated design, marking a distinct advance beyond the original iconic scene of a surviving skier discovering the bodies of his companions through a GoPro in "Snow Fall."

The following contextualizes the technological developments that have led to the current multimedia narrative designs, while providing a review of recent research in the digital animation of literary journalism, multimodal communication in longform digital journalism, and industrial news branding. Discussion then addresses legacy media and independent start-ups that have implemented industrial innovations in production, including the move away from single-author bylines toward eclectic creative development teams.

Literary Journalism's Digital Design

Whatever Bowden's prototype of digital literary journalism may lack in polished production features it compensates for in its vast archive of data contextualizing the story of the 1993 raid on Mogadishu. As critics of online reading voiced concern that the overflow of data could create undue distraction in the reading experience and thus pose a threat to the narrative integrity of digital longform, Bowden pushed back against the tide of skepticism, publishing his second multimedia text, "The Desert One Debacle," in 2006.[11] Although he had forged his reputation in print—the medium through which his journalistic art drew praise from the iconic Tom Wolfe in his 2010 acceptance speech for the National Book Lifetime Award as one of the two journalists to watch along with Michael Lewis—Bowden made his preference for digital publishing clear.[12] When asked about the difference, he proclaimed, "The online presentation is a lot richer than the written text." To him, enabling the reader to drill down into the reporter's rich archive of research made that difference: "The reader/viewer/listener can delve as deeply into the material as he wishes. On the Internet, the writer can provide a new service to the readers." In this manner, readers "can make sense of the writer's material themselves, digest the sources, and draw their own conclusions."[13] Hyperlinks to material on the open web and supplemental multimedia elements, however, typically jettison the reader to another website, detracting from a linear reading experience of Bowden's main narrative thrust.[14] Reader autonomy is now honored through navigability between chapters and sections *within* the story in today's design.

Four years after "The Desert One Debacle," Apple's release of the iPad in 2010 introduced design features to remedy this scattershot horizontal reading experience with a different kind of immersion, one operating on a vertical axis drawing the reader deeper into the drama of the story. Smartphones and tablets not only raised professional standards for news production through the new app economy but also helped build value for publishers by encouraging higher-quality content to restore profitability for professional top-down information. This benefit of higher production standards and more professional content, however, comes at the loss of generative media content, since the app economy's bundled and tethered content cannot be remixed into new material.[15] It is telling of the mobile reading revolution for literary journalism that the inauguration of this new era of multimedia storytelling with ESPN's "The Long, Strange Trip of Dock Ellis," which preceded "Snow Fall" by several months in 2012, and the *Guardian*'s "Firestorm," which followed it in 2013, all bear a distinctive app feel for the reader yet are free on the open web as brand identifiers and loss leaders driving traffic back to their respective monetizing websites.[16] This first wave of digital longform still was less effective at capturing mobile audiences than the current generation of publications bearing leaner designs. "Greenland," for example, does not clutter smaller screens with tap-activated embedded multimedia as "Snow Fall" does.

Unlike Bowden's early digital story, elements from visuals and graphics to video loops and maps activate automatically and are unveiled with the magic of parallax scrolling or "the curtain effect" as the reader advances the narrative. Now the expanding size of smartphones—many are five to six inches, approaching the size of a seven- to eight-inch tablet—and lengthening user engagement have evolved into streamlined storytelling free from the clutter swamping last century's web layouts like "Black Hawk Down."[17] Immersed in the new mobile cognitive containers, readers have a disincentive to exit the space of the story. Portals to outside drillable data sources have been replaced by interactive infographics where supplemental information is more easily accessed and carefully embedded in the text, unlike the data glut that overwhelms the reader in "Black Hawk Down." Digital journalism has now entered the realm of immersive media as designs enable a more fluid professional polish. Audio effects and music combine with visuals—both static and dynamic images shot with 360-degree cameras, VR, satellites, and drone technology—to play a more central role in the narrative.

Since the release of the tablet, the template for longform storytelling has undergone a revolution. The writer's source materials now appear seamlessly woven into digital longform narratives, providing visual transitions between text screens in the manner of the print *New York Times Magazine* or *Esquire*. The reader autonomy of Bowden's original vision now manifests itself in the users' ability to move through the various sections or chapters of each piece and to dwell on any of the embedded multimedia features. The crucial difference lies in the embedded quality of these features, which now automatically activate as they scroll onto the screen. Story navigation is more intuitive and efficient. Interactives illuminate more relevant data without the click-heavy hyperlinks that may compromise or disperse attention. Bowden has acknowledged in his most recent publication that "the Internet affords, if anything, a superior platform for every kind of journalism, and I have no doubt that long-form narratives will remain essential."[18]

Rather than one medium among many providing "a singular and dominating continuity to which the others are adjuncts," digital design now enables stories to use any combination of visual and written communication modalities without losing readers to distracting elements that vie for their attention.[19] Hartsock worries about the loss of literary narrative given the increasing role of visuals in digital journalism, wondering "what is lost cognitively if the image dominates and reading abilities decline."[20] His concern reflects how the larger "discourse of fear of language decay surrounding [online] media" is a reaction to both "the growing informality of public life" and the radical hybridization of online communication blending informal conversation and writing with the image, especially "formal elements of film, television, music videos, and photography, and other genres and practices," as Nancy Baym observes.[21] Amy Mitchell et al.'s 2016 Pew study indicates that readers are spending more time on stories containing a greater number of words than their shorter counterparts and that they access each with equal frequency.[22] This means the majority of time reading on mobile phones has swung toward longform rather than the opposite. The finding, along with the evidence detailed in this chapter on the evolution of digital longform, underlines the need to dispel old notions of digital culture as a deterrent to reading written text. The rise of digital longform is one of many recent signs in online culture suggesting that reports of the death of literary culture—as seen in Loren Ghiglione's comment, "Despite what we newspaper Neanderthals wish to believe about the majesty of print, the age of literate readers—readers of newspapers, serious literature, and books—is passing," having "fallen prey to television, computers, videos and Nintendo"[23]—have been greatly exaggerated.

Countering Ghiglione's view is Henry Jenkins. Writing on the impact of *Moby-Dick* on the lives of youth when wedded to their online practices, he argues that "it is simplistic to assume that technologies can support only one mindset" and thus "wrong-headed to assume that the internet's intellectual ethic is in direct and total opposition to that associated with books" and literary culture.[24] Just as Herman Melville's magnum opus now takes on new life with new audiences in the digital age, narrative journalism's roots in print literary culture now extend across media platforms, expanding its storytelling prowess to meet the diverse literacy of twenty-first century audiences.

Renewing the New Journalism Revolution Online

Digital longform of 2017 is more carefully edited and less cluttered with gratuitous interactives than it was five years earlier during the first wave of "Snow Fall"-inspired works such as Grantland's "Out in the Great Alone." The latest generation of digital longform publications confirms the possibility Hartsock entertains that if "a 'reader' is still focused on a journalistic story derived from the intersection of one time and place, research may yet show an efficacy to such various efforts" demanded of that reader in multimedia narrative.[25] Digital longform is now hardly so arduous to consume in terms of the cognitive processing of multimedia and written text. Certainly Michael Shapiro, founder of the digital magazine the Big Roundtable, saw the internet as no detriment to his audience's attention span when he disclosed the platform's "mission to renew the promise of the New Journalism revolution that started and then sputtered a few decades ago, connecting techniques of great fiction with the discipline and thrill of serious reporting."[26] Regarding that ambition's articulation in a multimedia online format, empathy becomes a major epistemological and phenomenological consequence for the genre of literary journalism and literary journalism studies in general. Digital longform's new cinematic qualities have achieved the feat of becoming both more immersive in terms of a sensory experience and social in terms of their shareable nature through social media. At the individual levels, multimedia elements combine with text to weave narrative that can potentially draw the reader deeper into the text itself, and potentially identify with the individuals it portrays. It is especially potent as a form of advocacy journalism in its power to elicit empathy. But the intensity of that aesthetic and emotional response now can circulate online among other readers faster and more efficiently than ever, spawning vast networks of longform reading communities. Both the multimodal narrativity and online reading communities, therefore, present ideal subjects for further exploration in literary journalism studies.

It is crucial that critics and scholars of digital longform not assume that its converged media represent the multitasking Clifford Nass proved in his Stanford labs to be deleterious to cognitive function. The lost train of thought in Nass's studies occurs during task switching, specifically between two totally unrelated activities in different visual and cognitive environments such as texting and driving a car. Texting in this case would be the "irrelevant environmental stimuli" distracting the driver, rather than stimuli such as speedometers and rear view mirrors—analogous to thematically coherent stimuli of multimedia longform—designed to enhance the driving experience.[27] The research carries fewer implications for in-app reading/watching of news than it does in disproving the assumption among many millennials that multitasking empowers them with greater efficiency and productivity, an issue that is now currently besieging classrooms as undergraduates insist on having laptops open during lectures. Nass was interested in how *competing* streams of electronic information compromised cognitive function by overloading the executive function of the brain rather than how multimedia could be designed to relieve the executive portion of the brain and thus enhance deep reading by complementing each other's reinforcement of a single coherent narrative through line. Juggling disparate tasks—the essence of multitasking—impaired the cognition of those attempting "to switch from one job to another in comparison to those who prefer to complete one task at a time."[28] There is no overarching narrative or theme meaningfully connecting the unrelated tasks Nass's experimental subjects were asked to juggle. By contrast, multimedia in digital longform function as connective tissue integrated with written text.

Tellingly, Nass's studies were all published in 2009, one year before the release of the iPad and well before mobile news apps became widely used. The point therefore should not be confused with multimedia elements readers increasingly encounter in linear succession alternating with text-filled screens activated by the scroll function that rivet attention on a vertical downward trajectory. Moving horizontally through the various portals and archives of "Black Hawk Down" could indeed be construed as a distracting process akin to task switching. But in today's digital longform, "multimedia is at the heart of its narrative structure" rather than simply being a display of technological prowess, according to the most recent research into the genre's multimodality.[29] As such, it is immersive rather than distracting, as stories unfold by harnessing and combining the narrative powers of documentary cinema with the feature magazine. Text and video rise onto the screen, actively encouraging extended engagement, focus, and time on site. The variety of media in such stories, if carefully embedded, only functions to absorb the reader in the narrative. This new design is the fullest technological realization of ekphrasis in journalistic storytelling, converging written and visual media into new dimensions from its print origins, a dynamic exemplified by the synergy between James Agee's narrative and Walker Evans's photographs in *Let Us Now Praise Famous Men*.

Evidence from industrial practice and user trends suggests that the written word is not pitted in a zero-sum game with technological advancements in visual media. Literary journalism studies should be responsive to the current era of technological and industrial media convergence and not view media systems in isolation from each other. The current inevitable degree of hybridity arising from producers and audience suggests that "the field of media studies and the subfield of media narratology can only progress by embracing transmedia and transnational perspectives," as Anthony Pearson and Roberta Smith claim.[30] As platforms such as Atavist and the Big Roundtable have shown, digital longform publishers have now expanded into the market for print books, a form of convergence in which old media play crucial roles in new media. "One medium does not displace another," Jenkins explains, "but rather, each adds a new cultural layer, supporting more diverse ways of communicating, thinking, and feeling, and creating than existed before."[31] Digital longform typifies this enriching effect of new media's impact on narrative nonfiction.

Recent research in digital longform journalism has reinforced how the genre is reworking existing media in new ways to elicit completely different, and decidedly more immersive, reading experiences. Multimodal theory, for example, offers valuable insight into how digital longform situates and sequences different modes of communication to captivate the audience. News on the web made a great leap forward in its evolution when "Snow Fall" broke the storytelling template. Specifically, digital longform must handle both time- and space-based organizational structures, according to Tuomo Hiippala's findings.[32] Video plays out in time, whereas spatial media such as still graphics, charts, and text exploit layout space. Susan Jacobson, Jacqueline Marino, and Robert Gutsche have demonstrated that both can combine to accentuate literary techniques found in traditional nonfiction narrative. Rather than confronting readers with competing messages that might demand task switching, digital longform instead builds on the means by which print and television journalists embed social and cultural meaning in their stories through visual and verbal messages that audiences interpret simultaneously. For the literary journalist interested in probing the boundaries of the medium's conventional uses, it is important to underscore that all media bear the qualities of those that preceded them and thus are inherently mixed media. This process "can be understood through the notion of 'braiding,' in which two or more media appear together to create combined meaning," thus enabling new modalities of storytelling.[33] Traditional media thus combine in new ways to build multimedia narratives beyond their early 2000s (pre-smartphone and tablet) existence as stories shoveled from print to the web, after which they were supplemented with slideshows, interactives, and videos.

Studies now confirm the new narrative power achieved through harnessing and combining news media and aesthetic forms. Disparate semiotic modes of media appeal to diverse literacies of twenty-first century audiences because they effectively "synthesize and integrate the older conventions of the printed text-and-image page and the dynamic image-and-sound streams of film, video, and animation," as Lemke describes of film.[34] Print literary journalism's signature elements of scene, dialogue, characterization, and dramatic tension now find new enhanced, even "supreme" as Boynton would have it, modes of expression through the latest digital longform designs. The digital interface unleashes new powers of aesthetic expression by enabling new combinations of communication modalities, which my research with Travis Vogan suggests.[35] "Snow Fall" not only functioned as a brash statement by the *New York Times* of the possibilities of digital journalism and thus a proclamation of the organization's industrial dominance, but it also provided a point of departure for further development of online narrative nonfiction. Whereas its prototype set the template, design innovations have made storytelling methods leaner, more distilled, and immersive.

Longform after "Snow Fall"

A case in point illustrating the stunning leap forward is to compare "Snow Fall" with the *Times*'s next best digital storytelling, "Greenland Is Melting Away," which does not use parallax scrolling, the technique many assumed would be a staple ingredient for the genre. Its screens are less cluttered with either text or visual dominating each so that smaller mobile screens do not become overcrowded with tiny graphic add-ons lurking in the margins. Users are invited to do one task per screen for ease of use on mobile devices. The first is a brief orienting video, a convention borrowed by film known as the establishing shot, providing stunning aerials taken with a drone of the vast frozen ice sheet and the multiple rivers and streams carving its surface. Scrolling downward brings into view several paragraphs of text, free of hyperlinks or multimedia elements of any sort. The language is unmistakably literary, as the reader confronts a surreal, destabilizing "midnight sun" that "still gleamed at 1 a.m.," a chronotopic device transporting the reader to this remote setting where we enter the world of doctoral student Brandon Overstreet "picking his way across the frozen landscape," thus entering the narrative through his third-person-limited subjectivity.[36]

This transfixing and surreal aura is established primarily through written text, as the two-minute drone video functions like the video loop at the beginning of "Snow Fall," only with far greater visual effect. The key difference is that it does not play automatically but instead allows the reader to skip it. Death in a vast icy abyss, interestingly, is invoked in "Greenland" just as it is in "Snow Fall." Overstreet climbs precariously on the ridge of an icy river rushing inexorably toward a "giant sinkhole," where, if he were to fall in, "the death rate is 100 percent."[37] Description of the scientific project of measuring the rate at which the ice sheet is melting invests the characters with agency and purpose. With narrative tension established, the text then gives way by scrolling to a screen providing what appears to be a static satellite map of Greenland. Scrolling further, however, reveals one of the piece's most stunning effects: Brief passages of written text then pass in and out of the screen from bottom to top as the maps zoom in with a red box indicating the rapidly decreasing square miles until the tents of scientists' base camp below come into view. The subjectivity of Overstreet and his team now comes into sharp focus, as the zooming satellite dramatically intimates precisely its own preferred mode of consumption marked by increasingly distilled focus, rapid transport through time and space, and the undeniable gravitational pull of plunging into the narrative's lived experience from high above. The vertical pull of the story is profound, even stronger than in "Snow Fall," which by comparison carries a composition layout that appears cramped on smaller phones.

The *Times*'s 2015 "Greenland" carries significant implications that build on previous research by Jacobson, Marino, and Gutsche, establishing that "long-form multimedia journalism represents a new wave of literary journalism."[38] Their content analysis of fifty multimedia narratives is limited to samples published in 2012 and 2013. As such, they represent the first wave of "Snow

Fall"-inspired digital longform, thus featuring video loops and the use of parallax and single-page scroll as alternatives to earlier modes of digital storytelling that relied on hypertext. Their findings show that video loops establish scenes and that parallax and single-page scroll "created a more centered, more linear presentation of the narrative."[39] Transitions now link textual components together through many more methods than video loops or parallax scrolling as "Greenland" demonstrates. Yet the point that "the integration of technology in storytelling holds literary purposes of its own" deserves emphasis here, as new methods continue to augment the literary techniques of narrative journalism.[40] The dissolve, for example, a technique borrowed from film, does not always signify the passage of time but depends on the previous and succeeding shots for its meaning. Similarly, in written text, context cues enable the reader to make meaning of abstract figures of speech such as synecdoche and metonymy.

Looping video in the case of "Snow Fall" indeed functions as a transition between texts, but in other stories such as the *Guardian*'s "Firestorm," it is more essential in carrying the narrative forward. This is because, according to the perspective of Steve Duenes, the graphic arts department head and assistant editor of "Snow Fall," "the dominant stream of content on any platform is still copy—is still text—we still employ hundreds of reporters and writers and still express ourselves fully" with the objective of being "articulate with language."[41] By contrast, the video loops at the head of each section of "Firestorm" are essential artifacts that not only support the story with interesting color but also build upon the narrative with the substantiating evidence of the surviving family's own raw video footage and testimonials that fill the entire screen. What sets "Snow Fall" apart from "Firestorm," however, is what Richard Koci Hernandez and Jeremy Rue call its classification as "Continuous-Comprehensive" digital storytelling with immersive elements but whose linear narrative progression is driven primarily by the text.[42] Other entries into digital longform have adopted more even blends of text and visual to great effect. A recent new wave of interactive documentaries has now appeared, expanding digital longform further across media platforms and hybridizing the control of print reading's self-paced autonomy with the audio-visual immersion of documentary cinema.

The user experience uniting the various forms of digital longform that now includes podcasting and interactive documentaries is visible in their immersive seamless narratives that "stand in stark contrast to other journalistic genres, such as landing pages, photo galleries and news stories," as Hiippala observes.[43] To establish and maintain reader attention, digital longform—in which written text is prominent rather than functioning as mere captioning as in Animal Planet's "Blood and Water"—tends to feature videos with a limited number of shots. No lengthy, complex videos appear in these pieces because they would distract from, rather than support, the main text. The extreme complexity of hierarchical organization in filmic narrative thus reflects a constraint to multimodal storytelling, as Hiippala points out.[44] Yet that constraint has been successfully circumvented by companies like Google, which partnered with the Epic Magazine digital production team to create an interactive digital documentary featuring a self-guided tour through the favelas, or shantytowns, of Brazil's Rio de Janeiro. Each of the videos in "Beyond the Map" are constructed like feature profile stories, each adding a new dimension to our understanding of the cultural geography of the place and the compelling aspirations of its denizens, from an aging surfing instructor to an aspiring teenage ballet dancer who faces discrimination and abuse for his gender orientation. Each is far more complex in terms of its hierarchical semantics of multiple shots and scenes than a video clip appearing on text-driven digital longform.

This explains in large part why the video components of "Snow Fall" were so effective. Not only were they skillfully embedded in the text to complement John Branch's prose, but they also typically never extended beyond several minutes and contained no more than several shots. Indeed, the GoPro footage from "Snow Fall" is uncut and raw, a single shot made more powerful because its unscripted simple narrative structure augments the complex textual one by bringing the reader directly into the scene. From the point of view of the skier, whose camera lens functions as his eyes, the reader enters both the scene and—in the most direct manner possible given this film technology—the skier's subjectivity. Never before in literary journalism have we been able to enter into a figure's subjectivity through this medium that enables such depth and intimacy. The emotion is overwhelming, but given the raw authenticity of the discovery of his friend's body via the haunting metonymic ski pole resting on the surface of the snow, the scene cannot be accused of being maudlin, sentimental, or melodramatic. Although the scene carries profound emotional complexity, its single-shot structure ensures that the reader "does not have to resolve complex layout structures commonly featured in page-flow, as engaging in this kind of interpretive process would likely distract the reader from the linearly unfolding narrative."[45] The *Times*'s "Greenland" builds on this effect with an even cleaner design structure that directs and distills reader attention vertically down the page rather than horizontally across the page as in any major newspaper's landing page, where structure and organization of space into hierarchies prevail.

From a production standpoint, it is essential to approach digital longform from the vantage point of both a literary artist and a filmmaker. The "mechanistic expository style of hard news stories" is anathema to the distinctly creative aesthetic driving digital longform narrative, as Megan Le Masurier explains of slow journalism's departure from breaking news.[46] Digital longform works differently to exploit available semiotic modes and combine them in provocative and aesthetically meaningful sequences, all activated by scrolling—a movement previously reserved for interacting with a single screen—which triggers a variety of transitions between conjoined and contiguous screens.[47] The genre is designed for sharing and discussing on social media, as evidenced by the frequent use of social web panels to encourage the posting of not only each story in its entirety but its component parts, from its written paragraphs to its data visualizations, photos, and videos.[48] "The accessibility and shareability of [digital longform] stories bring about new possibilities for reaching readers and creating conversations," according to Maria Lassila-Merisalo.[49] These news products represent media hybridity with topics ranging from pressing contemporary issues of learned debate such as immigration and global warming to entertainment topics such as video gaming and sports. Most are treated in a sophisticated way that leverages multimedia elements to extend the "multireferential plane"[50] while abiding by core journalistic principles such as "the reality boundary."[51] Users are as captivated by text as video according to an industry report by Marino, Jacobson, and Gutsche on eye-tracking and digital longform, which found that total fixation was relatively even between the two. Yet of vital importance was their finding that participants expressed greater levels of enjoyment and satisfaction in the text and photography in several cases than they did in videos. Indeed, many were bored by videos they found were "too long," attesting to Hiippala's theory that longform prefers shallow formatted videos that function to establish the "cognitive container" that has become the signature feature of the genre. Followed closely by text, well-edited photographs, by contrast, provoked the most specific comments indicating pleasure and satisfaction of all the multimedia elements. "Firestorm" carried the greatest impact visually, as its photos and videos were seen as essential, rather than accessory, to the immersive eyewitness quality of the reportage. Readers of digital longform, according to their report, also preferred autonomous navigation, as they disliked the locked-in progression of chapters in "Rebuilding Haiti."[52] Their findings suggest that autonomous navigability, a vestige of print reading, and crisp editing of video and photographs hold sway with readers.

Marino, Jacobson, and Gutsche's eye-tracking study of digital longform users corroborates a suggestion by the American Press Institute (API) that a key method for engaging readers in digital longform is to "imagine stories unfold almost like movies" and to approach production like a film director by "directing the story to create a narrative arc."[53] Storyboards, formerly the building blocks of screenwriters and directors in cinema production, are now the bastion of mobile news producers. "A longform story," the API notes, "is no longer for the lone-wolf reporter."[54] Web-specific reporting and writing now take on entirely new implications for accepted notions of literary authorship, as the decline of the single byline has diminished in some cases, such as in legacy media production of digital longform, and been sustained in others, especially in independent start-up publishers.

New Production Models

The advent of the tablet is particularly well suited to literary reading's online renaissance. Digital design has adapted with an increase in imaginative integrative structures in response to this growing market. The movement toward immersive, virtually advertising-free online content of a literary nature has established journalism's prominence in the app economy. Digital literary journalism like that showcased on Epic and Byliner now circulates mainly in products designed for mobile devices, showcasing visuals and graphic animation in powerful new ways that have important implications for media convergence. Lee Gutkind has noted the rise of demand for nonfiction among editors in the publishing industry, a fact that has not escaped the attention of independent online start-ups such as Byliner and Atavist that have invested in high profile book publishing as a supplement to their digital revenue. He points out that the most prestigious and powerful literary book publishers, including HarperCollins, Random House, and Norton, are seeking titles in creative nonfiction more vigorously than in literary fiction and poetry. Gutkind also notes that creative nonfiction is the dominant form in journals such as the *New Yorker*, *Esquire*, and *Vanity Fair*, in addition to legacy outlets such as the *New York Times* and the *Wall Street Journal*.[55]

Print has made a comeback among slow journalism outlets like the French *XXI* and the British *Delayed Gratification*. Print looms large in the digital industry as a method of brand franchising with literary audiences in mind. *Grantland Quarterly* was an early entrant into the print literary journal market by way of its website run under the auspices of ESPN by Bill Simmons, who had a vested interest in revitalizing literary journalism for sports through contemporary and classical pieces, including works by Hunter S. Thompson. Ambitions of digital longform writers and editors alike eventually gravitated toward book publishing. Shane Bauer, author of an original 35,000-word manuscript that became his highly acclaimed "My Four Months as a Private Prison Guard," invested more time on a story than any other writer had in the history of *Mother Jones*, where it appeared.[56] Set in Winnfield, Louisiana, this story, which is listed on Longreads as one of the best of 2016, details the appalling treatment of both prisoners and guards in private correctional facilities along with the emotional transformation Bauer himself underwent in the process. Bauer's intention to develop the digital story into a book is part of a new wave of migration from born digital to print, including the Atavist's book publication of the best pieces from its platform of monthly e-shorts. From its inception, the Atavist earned critical acclaim, including eight Ellie nominations from 2011 to 2015. But its crowning achievement was its distinction as the first digital-only publisher to win a National Magazine Award for Best Feature Writing in 2015 for James Verini's "Love and Ruin." Verini's gripping tale prompted the creation of the anthology *Love and Ruin: Tales of Obsession, Danger, and Heartbreak from the Atavist Magazine*. The prestigious award and subsequent contract with publishing giant Norton is a telling sign of the new recognition of the literary stature of digital longform.

Often regarded as the exclusive domain of expensive prestige projects of large legacy news organizations such as *Sports Illustrated* and the *New York Times*, or considered the products of niche or boutique journalism outlets, digital longform has taken over mainstream digital media. Several new digital-only publications such as Narratively define themselves as platforms for literary journalism within the slow journalism movement, which has distinguished itself for radically innovative alternatives to the conventional online business model tethered to display advertising. Far from profaning the textual sacrosanct bond between journalist and reader, digital longform is now recognized among the world's most acclaimed literary journalism. Although a slew of imitations of "Snow Fall" have raised questions regarding the quality of the form—especially in light of such editorial blunders as Grantland's "Dr. V's Magical Putter"—several stellar works have won critical praise. "Cocainenomics," the product of WSJ Custom Studios and MEC Digital, for example, received the 2016 Webby for Best Branded Editorial Experience.

Platforms such as Byliner and Atavist still market brand-name literary authors, such as Jon Krakauer and Michael Sharer, thus adhering to traditional single contributor bylines. When Branch received the Pulitzer Prize for "Snow Fall," he was quick to insist that the work was produced by a large collaboration of graphic designers, computer engineers, photographers, videographers, and data visualization specialists.[57] The creative team behind the work pointed toward the increasingly collaborative nature of literary journalism online, suggesting a shift away from the assumption that fine narrative literature is necessarily the product of a single creative genius operating in isolation following their lone-wolf reporting.[58] This opens up exciting new possibilities for creative teams conjoining, as Branch recognized of the monumental achievement of "Snow Fall," textual narrative with visuals, graphics, and interactives. Michel Foucault's "What Is an Author?" and Roland Barthes's "The Death of the Author" help illuminate this shift toward the collaborative production of literary journalism, wedding written and visual aesthetics with computer engineering design. Literary journalism in the digital age is now more mobile, sharable, and open to discussion than ever, as "audiences show an increasing preference for online content," making the latest serious journalism either a combination of online and traditional or *only* online.[59] The socialization of literary journalistic production has become radically pluralized, much in the way that readership has through communities such as Longreads.

The pastiche of sources any author inherits—identified by Barthes, who deconstructs the romantic myth of the isolated literary artist as individual genius—points to the wealth of influences and data the writer must patch together. Like Barthes's concept of the author as the sum total of his or her intellectual inheritance, craftily rearranged in a unique literary expression, so too is the literary journalist in the digital age not only drawing from narrative and aesthetic precedent—whether reflecting or refracting it—but producing in a digital environment that requires teamwork and collaboration with data analysts and designers. "To give a text an author," writes Barthes, "is to impose a limit on the text, to furnish it with a final signified, to close the writing. When the author has been found, the text is 'explained'—victory to the critic."[60] It is telling indeed that the myth of single authorship has now yielded to Webby and ADDY awards going to teams rather than individuals. For better or worse, the internet has destabilized the professional identity of literary journalism, steering it closer to a model of film production, in which various collaborators including screenwriter and director receive recognition rather than a single isolated figure.

Notes

1 Bowden, "Black Hawk Down."
2 Eck, "Washington Post."
3 Mitchell, Stocking, and Matsa, "Long-Form Reading."
4 Mitchell, Stocking, and Matsa.
5 Boynton, "Notes."
6 Nelson and Webster, "Audience Currencies."
7 Conboy and Eldridge, "Morbid Symptoms," 117.

8. Hartsock, *Literary Journalism*, 28–29. My understanding of chronotope draws from Hartsock's application of Mikhail Bakhtin's original concept to literary journalism.
9. Enyedi, "*Into the Woods.*"
10. Puckett, *Narrative Theory*. For more on narrative theory in visual media, see García, "Storytelling Machine."
11. The leading voice against online reading, who argues the internet ecosystem is antithetical to linear print reading and has led to "the death of deep reading" and the cultural loss of "the literary mind" is Nicholas Carr (*Shallows*, 111–12).
12. Wolfe, acceptance speech.
13. Bowden, interview by Berning, September 24, 2009, quoted in Berning, "Narrative Journalism," 13; bracketed ellipses in the original.
14. Carr's assessment of hyperlinked reading as extraordinarily distracting to readers is well taken in light of Bowden's online features, which encourage readers to traverse his horizontal network of data, thus pulling them out of his narrative. More recent digital design, however, created to function more like self-contained apps, offers what I contend is a reading/viewing/listening environment arguably more immersive than print. This study therefore builds on the findings of Jacobson, Marino, and Gutsche, "Digital Animation"; Dowling and Vogan, "Can We 'Snowfall' This?"; Hiippala, "Multimodality"; Hernandez and Rue, *Principles of Multimedia Journalism*; Pincus, Wojcieszak, and Boomgarden, "Do Multimedia Matter?"
15. Tsukayama, "Year the Tablet Market"; Mims, "Why Tablets."
16. Dowling and Vogan, "Can We 'Snowfall' This?," 210.
17. Mims, "Why Tablets."
18. Bowden, *Three Battles*, xi.
19. Hartsock, *Literary Journalism*, 155.
20. Hartsock, 155.
21. Baym, *Personal Connections*, 72–74.
22. Mitchell, Stocking, and Matsa, "Long-Form Reading."
23. Ghiglione, "American Journalist," 461–62.
24. Jenkins and Kelley, *Reading*, 39.
25. Hartsock, *Literary Journalism*, 155.
26. Shapiro, Hiatt, and Hoyt, *Tales*, 218.
27. Ophir, Nass, and Wagner, "Cognitive Control," 15,583.
28. Ophir, Nass, and Wagner, 15,583.
29. Hiippala, "Multimodality," 421.
30. Smith and Pearson, "Contexts," 3.
31. Jenkins and Kelley, *Reading*, 39.
32. Hiippala, *Structure of Multimodal Documents*, 7.
33. Jacobson, Marino, and Gutsche, "Digital Animation," 530–31.
34. Lemke, "Multimedia Genres and Traversals."
35. Dowling and Vogan, "Can We 'Snowfall' This?," 220.
36. Davenport et al., "Greenland Is Melting Away."
37. Davenport et al.
38. Jacobson, Marino, and Gutsche, "Digital Animation," 533.
39. Jacobson, Marino, and Gutsche, 540.
40. Jacobson, Marino, and Gutsche, 540.
41. Hernandez and Rue, *Principles of Multimedia Journalism*, 154.
42. Hernandez and Rue, 155.
43. Hiippala, "Multimodality," 438.
44. Hiippala, 435.
45. Hiippala, 435.
46. Le Masurier, "What Is Slow Journalism?," 6.
47. Hiippala, *Structure of Multimodal Documents*, 204.
48. Dowling and Vogan, "Can We 'Snowfall' This?," 220.
49. Lassila-Merisalo, "Story First," 10.
50. Lehman, *Matter of Fact*, 36.
51. Sims, "Problem and Promise," 7.
52. Marino, Jacobson, and Gutsche, "Scrolling for Story."
53. Kovacs, "How to Engage Readers."

54 Kovacs.
55 Gutkind, "What Is Creative Nonfiction?"
56 Jeffery, "Why We Sent."
57 "Q. and A.: The Avalanche at Tunnel Creek."
58 Kovacs, "How to Engage Readers."
59 Bakker, "Mr. Gates Returns," 596.
60 Barthes, *Image, Music, Text*, 147.

Bibliography

Bakker, Piet. "Mr. Gates Returns: Curation, Community Management and Other New Roles for Journalists." *Journalism Studies* 15, no. 5 (2014): 596–606. https://doi.org/10.1080/1461670x.2014.901783.

Barthes, Roland. *Image, Music, Text*. Translated by Stephen Heath. New York: Hill and Wang, 1977.

Baym, Nancy K. *Personal Connections in the Digital Age*. 2nd ed. Cambridge: Polity Press, 2015.

Berning, Nora. "Narrative Journalism in the Age of the Internet: New Ways to Create Authenticity in Online Literary Reportages." *Textpraxis* 3, no. 2 (2011): 1–25.

Bowden, Mark. "Black Hawk Down: An American War Story." *Philadelphia Inquirer*, November 16–December 24, 1997. http://inquirer.philly.com/packages/somalia/sitemap.asp.

———. *Three Battles of Wanat and Other True Stories*. New York: Grove Atlantic, 2016.

Boynton, Robert S. "Notes toward a Supreme Nonfiction: Teaching Literary Reportage in the Twenty-First Century." *Literary Journalism Studies* 5, no. 2 (Fall 2013): 125–31.

Carr, Nicholas. *The Shallows: What the Internet Is Doing to Our Brains*. New York: W. W. Norton, 2011.

Conboy, Martin, and Scott A. Eldridge II. "Morbid Symptoms: Between a Dying and a Re-birth (Apologies to Gramsci)." In *The Future of Journalism: In an Age of Digital Media and Economic Uncertainty*, edited by Bob Franklin, 566–75. New York: Routledge, 2016.

Davenport, Coral, Josh Haner, Larry Buchanan, and Derek Watkins. "Greenland Is Melting Away." *New York Times*, October 27, 2015. www.nytimes.com/interactive/2015/10/27/world/greenland-is-melting-away.html.

Dowling, David, and Travis Vogan. "Can We 'Snowfall' This? Digital Longform and the Race for the Tablet Market." *Digital Journalism* 3, no. 2 (2015): 209–24. https://doi.org/10.1080/21670811.2014.930250.

Eck, Allison. "The Washington Post Crosses a Storytelling Frontier with 'A New Age of Walls.'" Nieman Storyboard, December 20, 2016. http://niemanstoryboard.org/stories/the-washington-post-crosses-a-storytelling-frontier-with-a-new-age-of-walls/.

Enyedi, Delia. "*Into the Woods*: The Promised Land of Narrative Hybridization." Review of *Into the Woods: How Stories Work and Why We Tell Them*, by John Yorke. *Ekphrasis: Images, Cinema, Theory, Media* 15, no. 1 (2016): 139–42.

García, Alberto N. "A Storytelling Machine: The Complexity and Revolution of Narrative Television." *Between* 6, no. 11 (2016): 1–25.

Ghiglione, Loren. "The American Journalist: Fiction versus Fact." *Proceedings of the American Antiquarian Society* 100 (1991): 445–63.

Gutkind, Lee. "What Is Creative Nonfiction?" *Creative Nonfiction*, 2015. www.creativenonfiction.org/online-reading/what-creative-nonfiction.

Hartsock, John. *Literary Journalism and the Aesthetics of Experience*. Amherst, MA: University of Massachusetts Press, 2016.

Hernandez, Richard Koci, and Jeremy Rue. *The Principles of Multimedia Journalism: Packaging Digital News*. New York: Routledge, 2015.

Hiippala, Tuomo. "The Multimodality of Digital Longform Journalism." *Digital Journalism* 5, no. 4 (2017): 420–42. https://doi.org/10.1080/21670811.2016.1169197.

———. *The Structure of Multimodal Documents: An Empirical Approach*. New York: Routledge, 2016.

Jacobson, Susan, Jacqueline Marino, and Robert E. Gutsche Jr. "The Digital Animation of Literary Journalism." *Journalism* 17, no. 4 (2016): 527–46. https://doi.org/10.1177/1464884914568079.

Jeffery, Clara. "Why We Sent a Reporter to Work as a Private Prison Guard." *Mother Jones*, July/August 2016. www.motherjones.com/politics/2016/06/cca-private-prisons-investigative-journalism-editors-note/.

Jenkins, Henry, and Wyn Kelley, eds. *Reading in a Participatory Culture: Remixing "Moby-Dick" in the English Classroom*. New York: Columbia University Press, 2013.

Kovacs, Kasia. "How to Engage Readers with Digital Longform Journalism." *American Press Institute*, December 1, 2016. www.americanpressinstitute.org/publications/reports/strategy-studies/engaging-long form-journalism/.

Lassila-Merisalo, Maria. "Story First—Publishing Narrative Long-Form Journalism in Digital Environments." *Journal of Magazine and New Media Research* 15, no. 2 (Summer 2014): 1–15.

Lehman, Daniel W. *Matter of Fact: Reading Nonfiction over the Edge*. Columbus, OH: Ohio State University Press, 1996.

Le Masurier, Megan. "What Is Slow Journalism?" *Journalism Practice* 9, no. 2 (2014): 138–52. https://doi.org/10.1080/17512786.2014.916471.

Lemke, Jay L. "Multimedia Genres and Traversals." *Folia Linguistica* 39, nos. 1–2 (2005): 45–56. https://doi.org/10.1515/flin.2005.39.1-2.45.

Marino, Jacqueline, Susan Jacobson, and Robert Gutsche Jr. "Scrolling for Story: How Millennials Interact with Long-Form Journalism on Mobile Devices." Donald W. Reynolds Journalism Institute, Missouri School of Journalism, University of Missouri, August 1, 2016. www.rjionline.org/stories/scrolling-for-story-how-millennials-interact-with-long-form-journalism-on-m.

Mims, Christopher. "Why Tablets Are the Future of Computing." *Wall Street Journal*, September 14, 2015. www.wsj.com/articles/why-tablets-are-the-future-of-computing-1442203331.

Mitchell, Amy, Galen Stocking, and Katerina Eva Matsa. "Long-Form Reading Shows Signs of Life in Our Mobile News World." Pew Research Center, May 5, 2016. www.journalism.org/2016/05/05/long-form-reading-shows-signs-of-life-in-our-mobile-news-world/.

Nelson, Jacob L., and James G. Webster. "Audience Currencies in the Age of Big Data." *International Journal on Media Management* 18, no. 1 (2016): 9–24. https://doi.org/10.1080/14241277.2016.1166430.

Ophir, Eyal, Clifford Nass, and Anthony D. Wagner. "Cognitive Control in Media Multitaskers." *Proceedings of the National Academy of Sciences* 106, no. 37 (2009), 15,583–87. https://doi.org/10.1073/pnas.0903620106.

Pincus, Hanna, Magdalena Wojcieszak, and Hajo Boomgarden. "Do Multimedia Matter? Cognitive and Affective Effects of Embedded Multimedia Journalism." *Journalism and Mass Communication Quarterly* 94, no. 3 (2016): 747–71. https://doi.org/10.1177/1077699016654679.

Puckett, Kent. *Narrative Theory: A Critical Introduction*. Cambridge: Cambridge University Press, 2016.

"Q. and A.: The Avalanche at Tunnel Creek." *New York Times*, December 21, 2012. www.nytimes.com/2012/12/22/sports/q-a-the-avalanche-at-tunnel-creek.html.

Shapiro, Michael, Anna Hiatt, and Michael Hoyt. *Tales from the Great Disruption: Insights and Lessons from Journalism's Technological Transformation*. New York: Big Roundtable Books, 2015.

Sims, Norman. "The Problem and Promise of Literary Journalism Studies" *Literary Journalism Studies* 1, no. 1 (Spring 2009): 7–16.

Smith, Anthony N., and Roberta Pearson. "The Contexts of Contemporary Screen Narratives: Medium, National, Institutional, and Technological Specificities." In *Storytelling in the Media Convergence Age: Exploring Screen Narratives*, edited by Roberta Pearson and Anthony N. Smith, 3–17. New York: Palgrave Macmillan, 2015.

Tsukayama, Hayley. "The Year the Tablet Market Grew Up." *Washington Post*, November 25, 2011.

Wolfe, Tom. Acceptance speech for the Medal for Distinguished Contribution to American Letters. National Book Foundation, 2010. www.nationalbook.org/amerletters_2010_wolfe.html#.W5l_GOhKi9I.

INDEX

12 Million Black Voices (1941) 468

Aare, Cecilia 389
A'Becket, John 87–88
abolitionism 34–36
abolitionist newspapers 29, 30–31, 36, 44, 45, 49, 400
Abraham Lincoln (Tarbell) 98
Abrahamson, David 3
Adams, Ansel 259
Adams, Tony 377–378, 381
Addams, Jane 105
Addison, Joseph 23
Adler, Renata 131–132
Adventures of Huckleberry Finn, The 271
advocacy journalism, ethics of 364–367
aesthetics of everyday experience 325–326, 333, 336, 339–340
Afghanistan, US War in 249–250
Africa, European colonial presence in 50–52
African American journalism 400–411, 411–412; advocacy and community building functions of 400–401, 411–412; Civil Rights era 403–404; Gates's theory of signifying 407–408; Harlem Renaissance and literary war journalism 242, 245; *see also* slave narratives
African American newspapers 44, 49, 51, 407; Democratic National Convention (1968) coverage 165–167; literary war journalism 242, 245
African Americans; Robert Park's reports of 374
African Canadian newspapers 44
Agee, James 138, 260, 278, 389–390, 467, 468
AIDS epidemic in Africa 328
"AIDS in the Heartland" (Banaszynski) 208–209
Alaimo, Stacy 491–492
Alexievich, Svetlana 457, 487

Algonquin Round Table 140
Ali, Muhammad 308
Allen, Everett 207
All in the Day's Work (Tarbell) 100
Allred, Jeff 3
alternative media; definition and overview of 183–185; literary journalism practice in 186–189, 191–192; local journalism reviews 189–191; post-World War II counterculture magazines 278–279
America Faces the Barricades (Spivak) 113–114, 116
American Chronicle (Baker) 97
American Jitters, The (1932) 278
American Journalism Review 185
American Literary Journalism, A Sourcebook of (Connery) 400
American Mercury magazine 293–294
American Museum magazine 276
American Press Institute (API) 537–538
American Society of News Editors (ASNE) 203–204, 205, 206–207, 208; Distinguished Writing Award 206–207
American Tragedy, An (1925) 71
America's Best Newspaper Writing (2001) 207
Among Schoolchildren (1989) 382
Anchorage Daily News, award-winning journalism by 215
Anderson, Chris 500
Anderson, Leon 379
Anderson, Sherwood 278
And Their Children after Them (1989) 339
anthropocentric journalism 489–491
antiwar protests, coverage of 165–177
Apocalypse Now (1979) 247
"Apostate, The" (1906) 93
Applegate, Edd 239
Arbus, Diane 470–471
Arce, Alberto 217–218

Aristotle, *Poetics* 338
Arlen, Michael J. 171, 202
Armies of the Night, The (Mailer) 220, 247
Around the World in Seventy-Two Days (1890) 388
art, Janet Flanner on 135–137, 140
Art of Fact, The (1997) 400, 456
"Art of Fiction" (1884) 274
Ashdown, Paul 456
Ashton, Susanna 46
ASNE (American Society of News Editors) 203–204, 205, 206–207
Associated Press 201–202, 387; award-winning investigative journalism 217–218; Manson Family murders coverage 229
"As Time Runs Out" (1993) 306
Atavist (publisher) 530, 538, 539
Atlanta Inquirer 407
Atlantic magazine; abolitionist stance 45; establishment of 277; Howell's editorial direction of 67, 274; Said's "A Native of Bornoo" in 50–53; Todd and Kramer write for 230
Atton, Chris 183
authenticity, in newspaper fiction 85–86
Autobiography (Steffens) 97
autoethnography; critiques of 379–381; emergence of 373–377; similarities between literary journalism and 373, 377–379; types of 377–378
award-winning journalism 206–208, 213–220; digital and collaborative 473, 538–539; women's 208

Baker, Ray Stannard 93, 95, 96, 97
Baker, Sir Samuel White 51
Bakhtin, Mikhail 326, 327, 333, 500
Bak, John 514, 515
Baldwin, James 319, 320
Baltimore Afro-American 242, 245
Baltimore Evening Sun 207–208
Baltimore Herald 290, 291
Banaszynski, Jacqui 207, 208–209
Bangs, Lester 436, 437, 438–440, 441, 442
Barbusse, Henri 112, 120, 121
Barnes, Djuna 457
Barnette, Kara 368–369
Barthes, Roland 539
Bauer, Shane 538
Beach, Sylvia 137
Beatles, the 439–440
Bell for Adano, A 246
Bennett, Bridget 273
Berkeley Barb 184, 186, 187
Bernard, Claude 112
Bernstein, Carl 214
Bertens, Hans 499
Best and the Brightest, The (1972) 269
Bibliography of Literary Journalism in America, A (1937) 264, 510
"Big Two-Hearted River" (1925) 133
Bintrim, Timothy 76

"Birth of an Industry, The" (1902) 95
Björk 445
"Black Hawk Down" (1997) 248–249, 339, 473, 529
Black Like Me (1961) 350
"Black Man in the Revolution of 1914–1918, The" (1919) 242
Black Panthers shooting deaths 190–191
Blais, Madeleine 208
Blix (1899) 73
Blonde (2000) 77
Blood Rites (1997) 262
Blumin, Stuart M. 63, 64
Bly, Nellie (née Elizabeth Jane Cochran) 94; *Around the World in Seventy-Two Days* 94, 388; "Ten Days in a Mad-House" (1887) 94, 345–346, 348, 349–351, 388, 389
Bochner, Arthur 376
Bock, Paula 328
Bodily Natures (2010) 491
Bogart, Leo 203–204
Bok, Edward 82
Bond, Julian 407
Boo, Katherine 215, 217
book history studies 315–316, 317–318; and literary journalism 318–319; and public sphere theory 320–321
Book of the Dead, The (1938) 420, 421–422, 424
book reviewing, literary journalism and 270–272, 274
"Bornoo, A Native of" 50–51
Boston Gazette 22
Boston News-Letter 18–19, 20
Botson Globe 205
Bottlemania (2008) 105
Boucharenc, Myriam 518, 520
Bourdieu, Pierre 115, 130, 131
Bourke-White, Margaret 468
Bowden, Mark 236; "Black Hawk Down" 248–249, 339, 473, 529; "The Desert One Debacle" 531; on digital publishing 531, 532
Bowman, William W. 263
Boyer, Brian 190–191
Boylorn, Robin 376
Boynton, Robert 248, 510, 511, 530
Bracken, Donagh 237
Branch, John 307, 539
Brand, Dana 64
"Breakable Rules for Literary Journalists" (Kramer) 484
Brentari, Carlo 490
Bright-Sided (2009) 261
"Broken-Down Van, The" (1892) 72
Brooker, William 22
Brown, Helen Gurley 277
Bruder, Jessica 92, 101–103, 104
Bryce, James (Viscount) 96
Buckley, Tom 168–169, 177
Buckner, John 70

"Buddha Boy" (2006) 504
Bunyan, John 94
Burroughs, William S. 164, 172, 173, 178, 326, 334

Caldwell, Erskine 468
Calhoun, John C. 35
Call of the Wild, The (1903) 76, 77
Campbell, Donna 74
Campbell, John 18–20, 22
Campbell, W. Joseph 289–290
Camp Jackson Affair 49
Camp, John 208
cancer 261, 262, 492
Cancer Journals, The (Lorde) 492
Canguilhem, Georges 490
Cannon, Jimmy 303
Capa, Robert 469
capitalism, critiques of 100, 104, 118
capital punishment; Fern on 36; Whitman on 29–30
Capote, Truman 71, 203, 390
Carbon Ideologies (2018) 485, 487, 488
Carnegie-Knight Initiative report 450
Carne y Arena (Flesh and Sand) 475
Carpenter, Theresa 208
Carroll, Fred 401–402, 403
Carson, Rachel 319, 487
Castleberry, Vivian 208
Cather, Willa 67, 68, 69, 70, 74–76, 132, 277
censorship; of leftist writers 278; World War I 239, 242
Century Magazine 277
Cerf, Bennett 131
Chautauquan (magazine) 96
"Cheyenne, Haunt of Misery and Crime" (1892) 70
Chicago 1968 Democratic National Convention *see* Democratic National Convention (1968)
Chicago Defender 165–167, 177
Chicago Globe 70
Chicago Journalism Review 185, 187, 190
Chicago School 373, 374, 375
Chicago Tribune 165
child labor 93, 100, 257, 259; and Spivak's "Letter" 113–115
Child, Lydia Maria 28–29, 30–32, 38
Children of the Poor, The (1892) 257
Choisy, Maryse 518
Christgau, Robert 435, 436, 437, 438
Christian Science Church 75
chronotopes 326–328, 329–330
Chuck, Collins 100
Circus magazine 437
Citizen (2014) 417, 425, 426–427
Civil Action, A (1995) 105
Civil Rights Movement 151, 403–407, 408
civil sphere theory 320
Civil War 237–238; documentary photography of 466

Clark, Roy Peter 205, 206, 207
Clark, Timothy 484
Clash (band) 438
climate change 487–488
Coal Mountain Elementary (2009) 417, 422
Cobb, Irvin S. 240
"Cocainenomics" 539
Code, Lorraine 360, 361, 365, 366, 368–369
Cohn, Nik 434–435, 438, 439
Coiner, Constance 120
Cold New World (1998) 354–356
collaborative literary journalism 539
Collier's magazine 244, 277
colonial era newspaper journalism 18–20
Color of a Great City, The (Dreiser) 71
Columbia Journalism Review 184, 187
Columbian Orator, The 35
"Coming of the Purple Better One, The" (1968) 173
Commentary magazine 278
Commercial Advertiser 97, 288, 289, 467
commercialization of journalism 289–290
Common Sense (1776) 276
Communities of Journalism (Nord) 315
competitions *see* award-winning journalism
Connery, Thomas B. 3, 18, 256, 400, 466, 510
Conover, Ted 351–353, 378, 518
"Consider the Lobster" (2006) 491
consumerism, music journalism and 439, 444–445
conventional newspaper journalism 201–202
Cookman, Claude 467
Corbett, Julia B. 489
Cordell, Ryan 520
Cornebise, Alfred 237
corruption, exposés on 93–94, 96–97, 98, 100, 105
Cosmopolitan magazine 277
Costello, Elvis 440
"Cost of Life, The" (2014) 392
counterculture press *see* alternative media
"Country Doctor" (1948) 469
"Couranteers" 18, 22, 23, 24, 25
Covington, Dennis 392
Cowley, Malcolm 112
"Cows and Horses Are Hungry" (1934) 116
Coyotes (1987) 351–353
Cramer, Richard Ben 307
Crane, Stephen 57, 67, 68, 69–70, 71–73, 93, 112, 201; New York City sketches 71–72, 238; on objectivity 329; Spanish-American War coverage 72–73, 238, 329; "When Man Falls" 387–388
Crawdaddy! (magazine) 437
Creative Nonfiction journal 219
CREEM magazine 437
crisis, journalism in times of 256
Crisis magazine 242
Critchfield, Richard 216, 362
Criterion magazine 274
critical reviews, literary journalism and 270–272, 274
critical thinking skills 455–456

criticism, performative *see* performative criticism
Cruise of the Snark, The (1911) 77
cubism 136
cultural capital, acquisition of 130–131, 136
cultural phenomenology 390–391
cultural relativity 362–364
"Curious Shifts of the Poor" (1899) 70–71

daily newspapers 200
Damrosch, David 516
Dana, Charles A. 289, 290–291
Darnton, Robert 317–318
Darrow, Clarence 98
Darwin, Charles 69, 92
Dash, Leon 346–347, 362
Davidson, Cathy 318
Davidson, Michael 418
Davidson, Sara 392
Davis, Richard Harding 112, 238–239, 240–241
Day, Dorothy 258, 263, 264
Day in the Bleachers, A 300–301
"Deal in Wheat, A" (1903) 73–74
Dear, Peter 325, 336
"Death of the American Dream, The" (Thompson) 177
Deegan, Mary Jo 375
Deford, Frank 305
Delamont, Sara 379–380
de la Peña, Nonny 474, 475, 476
DelConte, Matt 404
DeLillo, Don 77
Democracy and Social Ethics (1902) 105
Democratic National Convention (1968) 163–166; Enright's coverage for *Globe and Mail* 169; *Esquire* coverage of 172–174; Hardwick and Styron's coverage for *New York Review of Books* 169–170; Mailer's account of 175–176; New Journalists vs. daily reporters coverage 178; Schultz's counterculture commentary on 175; Thompson and 176–177
Dempsey, Jack 302
Dennett, Daniel 386
Dennie, Joseph 276
Derrida, Jacques 499–500, 501
Desmond, Matthew 105, 348
dialogue, as narrative technique 214, 216, 218–219
"Dialogue by Walter Whitman, A" 29–30
Dickens, Charles 30, 64, 201, 258
Dictionary of the English Language (Johnson) 17
Didion, Joan; Harrison's attack of 190; *Slouching Towards Bethlehem* 247, 390–391, 518; "Some Dreamers" 338
digital literary journalism 472–474; and long-form stories 532, 533–536; mobile devices and apps 531–532, 538; multimedia 529–532, 533–536; new production models 538–539; overview of 529–531; and reader engagement 530; risks of 511–512; video components 536–537
DiMaggio, Joe 303–304, 307

discursive prose, as literary journalism 294
Dispatches (1977) 236, 247–248, 329
"Displaced, The" (2015) 474, 475, 476
documentary film 472
documentary photography 259–260, 465, 466, 467; *see also* photojournalism
Don't Let Me Be Lonely (2004) 417, 425–426
Dos Passos, John 244–245, 467
Douglass, Frederick 28, 34, 38, 45
Dow, William 72, 261, 272, 357, 449, 511, 512, 513, 517
Dread Road, The (1991) 115
Dreiser Looks at Russia (1928) 71
Dreiser, Theodore 67, 68, 70–71, 73, 77, 118, 278
Dreyfus, Alfred 112
Driscoll, Jack 205
"Driving Mr. Albert" (2001) 326, 334, 339
Du Bois, W. E. B. 242, 405
Duenes, Steve 536
Duncan, David Ewing 492
Early Life of Abraham Lincoln, The (Tarbell) 98
Eason, David 91, 500–501
East Village Other (newspaper) 184, 187
ecocriticism; definitions of 482, 483, 484; and literary journalism 483–486; non-anthropocentric journalism and feminist theory 486–492
Ecocriticism Reader, The (1996) 482, 483
Ecological Thinking (2006) 360, 368
ecological thinking, literary journalistic ethics and 360–369; *see also* ecocriticism
Eddy, Mary Baker 75
Edelstein, Sari 96
Éditions du Sous-Sol (publisher) 513
editors; female 81–82, 208; letters to 21
education *see* liberal education and literary journalism
Ehrenreich, Barbara 260–262, 263, 264–265; *Nickel and Dimed* 104, 260–261, 348, 353
Einstein, Albert, "Driving Mr. Albert" 326, 334, 339
Eisenstein, Sergei 467
Eliot, T. S. 274
Ellis, Carolyn 376, 377, 380, 381
Elvis 438
Emerson, Ralph Waldo 45, 277
emotional engagement, literary studies and 456
English programs, enrollments in 449–450
Enright, Michael 169, 177
Enrique's Journey (2006) 348
entertaining literary essays 23–24
environmental advocacy *see* ecocriticism *ecological thinking, literary journalistic ethics and*
Epic of the Wheat, The 74
epistemology and journalistic ethics 360–364, 365, 366, 368
epistolary writing; familiar letters 20–21; manuscript newsletters 18–20
ESPN 307, 308, 538
Esquire, 1968 Democratic National Convention coverage 172–174

ethics; and advocacy 364–368; autoethnography 381; ecological approach to 360–369; ethical codes for journalists 360–361, 368, 467; photojournalism 467; transparency issues 381–382
ethnographic realism 348, 390
ethnography; definition and emergence of 373–374; and immersion 351; *see also* autoethnography
European colonialism in Africa 50–51
Evans, Walker 260, 467, 468
Evening Herald 291, 292
evening newspapers 291–292
Evening Sun 292
Everybody's Autobiography (1937) 133
Every Day We Live Is the Future (2017) 486
Evicted (2016) 105, 348
Executioner's Song, The (1979) 71
"Experiment in Luxury, An" (1894) 72
"Experiment in Misery, An" (1894) 72

Face of War, The (Gellhorn) 244
fact; emergence of, as concept 336–337; just-the-facts reporting 201–202
fact/fiction distinction; *American Mercury* magazine blurring of 293; and contemporary literary journalists 248; Couranteers, novels and "fictionality" 24–25; ecological thinking and truth claims 361; and historicity 331–333; and naturalist writers 67, 73, 76, 77, 112; and New Journalists 279
Factory Man (2014) 92, 101, 102, 103, 104
Fagin, Dan 105
Fairbanks, Eve 392–393
"fake news," in newspaper fiction 85–86
Falling Man (2007) 77
"familiar" letter 19, 20–21
family newspapers 36, 292
Family, The (1971) 228–229
"Fantaisie Printaniere" (1897) 74
Farm Security Administration (FSA) 467, 468
"'Fast Girl,' The" (1896) 74
Faulkner, William 138
Fear and Loathing in Las Vegas 247, 272
Fear and Loathing; On the Campaign Trail '72 227
feature writing 203, 207–210, 214–215; Pulitzer Prize awards in 207–208, 214–215
feminism 263–264; and ecocriticism 491–492
Fern, Fanny 28, 36–37
"Fetish of Being Outside, The" (1935) 120
fiction *see* fact/fiction distinction
Fiction and the American Literary Marketplace (1997) 319
Fiedler, Leslie 130
Fifteen Minutes Around New York (Foster) 60–61
Fifth Estate (newspaper) 184, 186
Figures in Black (1987) 402
Filler, Louis 93
film journalism 472
Finkel, David 217, 235, 247, 346
Fink, Sheri 92, 101, 102–103, 104
Finnegan, William 345, 353–356, 363

Fire Next Time, The (Baldwin) 319, 320
"Firestorm" (2011) 472, 536, 537
first-person narration; in advocacy journalism 366–367; in autoethnography 378; in literary journalism 385–387; and narrative theory 404–405; in literary music journalism 441; memoir and quest narrative 391–392; narrators as homodiegetic 388–389; twentieth century and self-conscious 389–391
Fishkin, Shelley Fisher 510
Fitzgerald, F. Scott 302
Fitzgerald, Sheryl 166–167
Five Days at Memorial (2013) 92, 101, 102–103, 104
Flanner, Janet 130, 132, 135–140
Flis, Leonora 499
Floating Off the Page (2002) 206
Fludernik, Monika 405
"follow-ups" and sequels 338–339
Ford, Edwin H. 264, 510
Forde, Kathy Roberts 218
Forked (2016) 104–105
Foster, Frances Smith 49
Foster, George C. 58–64
France; Janet Flanner reports from 135–136, 138; literary journalism in 509, 511, 513, 517–519
Frank Leslie's Illustrated Newspaper 466
Franklin, Benjamin 24, 275, 276
Franklin, James 21–22, 23, 24
Franklin, Jon 202; "Mrs. Kelly's Monster" 207–208
Frederick Douglass' Paper 35, 36
Fredman, Stephen 419
Free and Other Stories (1918) 70
Freedman, Richard 243
Freedom's Journal 44, 400
Freeman, Carrie Packwood 489–490, 491
Freeman, Joseph 111
Freneau, Philip 276
From Fact to Fiction (1985) 510
Frus, Phyllis 132, 500
"Frustrated 'Scoop,' A" 84, 85
Fuchs, Christian 184
"Full Circle, The" (Arbus) 471
Fuller, Margaret 28, 32–34, 38
Full Metal Jacket (1987) 247

Galaxy magazine 277
Gallagher, Catherine 24–25
Gallery of Women, A (1929) 71
Gallico, Paul 302
Gardner, Nathaniel 23
Garland, Phyllis 401
Gates, Bill, Sr. 100
Gates, Henry Louis, Jr. 402–403, 407–408, 410
Gauley Bridge disaster 420
Gazette of the United States 276
Geismar, Maxwell 110
Gellhorn, Martha 244, 246

gender stereotypes; and female newspaper fiction reporters 83–86; Fern's exploration of 36–38
General Magazine 275
Genet, Jean 164, 172, 173–174, 178
Gentleman's Magazine 275
George, Henry 92
"Getting Down to What Is Really Real" (2011) 502
Ghansah, Rachel Kaadzi 392
Ghiglione, Loren 206, 532
Gilded Age 92–93; *The New Gilded Age* (2000) 100
Giles, Bob 219
Gilman, Mildred 84
Gilmore, Hinton 81
Gitner, Seth 472
Glass, Loren 133
Globe and Mail 169
Glotfelty, Cheryll 482
Goffman, Alice 348
Golden Passport, The (2017) 104
Gold, Michael 113
Goldstein, Amy 105
"Gone Gitmo" (2007) 475
gonzo journalism 518; rock-writer 441–443; Thompson's "Kentucky Derby" 304
Good, Howard 257, 258, 260
Good Soldiers, The (2009) 235, 247
Grant, Jane 293
Grantland Quarterly 538
Great Depression era 110–111; documentary photography of 467–468; Le Sueur's reportages of 116–121; magazines, literary journalism in 278; Spivak's reportages of 113–115
Great Speckled Bird (newspaper) 188, 263
Greenberg, Susan 484
"Greenland Is Melting Away" (2015) 531, 535, 537
Griffin, John Howard 350
Griffin, Justine 392
Grimes, William 45–47
"Grooving in Chi" (1968) 172
Grub Street and the Ivory Tower (1998) 273
Guillermoprieto, Alma 217
Gutkind, Lee 219, 538

Habermas, Jürgen 320
Halberstam, David 269
Hall, David D. 318
Hamilton, James 184
Hamilton, John 22
Hano, Arnold 300–301, 308–309
Hardwick, Elizabeth 169–170, 178
Harlem Renaissance 242
Harper's Monthly magazine 95, 274, 277
Harris, John 437, 443–444
Harrison, Barbara Grizzuti 189–190
Harr, Jonathan 105, 338
Hart, Jack 202, 206
Hartsock, John; on advocacy journalism 71, 364; on the emergence of American literary journalism 68, 237, 386, 510; *History of American Literary Journalism* 68, 219, 400; on literary scholarship and journalism 272; on the loss of literary narrative in digital media 532; on Mencken and discursive essays 294; on the naturalist writers 68, 69; on subjectivity in literary journalism 400; on text selection for university courses 457
Harvard University, Nieman Foundation Program 219
Harvey, Thomas 326
Hayes-Brady, Clare 502
Haynes, Douglas 486–487
Hearst, William Randolph 238
Hekman, Susan 491
Hellmann, John 499, 500
Hemingway, Ernest 132, 133, 242, 243–244, 246, 248, 302, 390
Hempstead Inquirer 28
Hendrix, Jimi 188
Herbert, Christian 349
"Her Best Stuff" 85
Herbst, Josephine 120
Herman, David 329
Herr, Michael 236, 247–248, 329
Hersey, John, *Hiroshima* 228, 236, 246–247, 271, 338, 346
Higginson, Thomas Wentworth 32, 45
Hiippala, Tuomo 534, 536
"Hints for Fiction Writers" (*Life* magazine) 81
hip-hop music 445, 446
Hiroshima (1946) 228, 236, 246–247, 271; sequel to 338
Hirsch, Corey 308
Hirsch, Robert 471
History of American Literary Journalism, A (2000) 68, 219, 400
Hitchcock, Alfred 472
Holocaust (1975) 416, 418
Hoosier Holiday, A (1916) 71
Hopkinson, Francis 276
Horgan, Stephen H. 466
housing crisis 105
Howarth, William 91
"How Do You Like It Now" (1950) 390
Howell, Deborah 208–209
Howells, William Dean 67, 74, 271, 273, 274, 277
"How It Feels" (Barnes) 457
How I Wrote the Story (Scanlan) 205
How the Other Half Lives (1890) 93, 257, 258–259, 277; photography of 465, 466
Hoyt, Eleanor 87
Huckleberry Finn (1884) 277
Hudson, Berkeley 457–458
Hughes, Langston 38, 242; Spanish Civil War coverage 245–246
Hugo, Victor 331; *Les Misérables* 331–332
human-interest stories and the Penny Press 289
Humphries, David T. 132, 138

"Hunger in Los Angeles" (2012) 475
Hunter-Gault, Charlayne 403–404, 407, 408, 409, 410–411
Hurston, Zora Neale 242, 271
"hyperobject," Morton's concept of 488, 489

I Am Nujood, Age 10 and Divorced (Ali) 457
ideology, advocacy journalism and 263
Iggy Pop 440
illustrations, in counterculture publications 187
immersion, journalistic; and advocacy 257–258; in Banaszynski's "AIDS in the Heartland" 208; in Crane's poverty and wealth "experiments" 71; as crucial to literary journalism 164; described 217, 346–347, 484; in Ehrenreich's *Nickel and Dimed* 260–261; and ethnographic practices 351; in Guillermoprieto's coverage of Rio de Janeiro dance culture 217; in London's *The People of the Abyss* 76; of muckrakers Fink, Tarbell, and Bruder 101–102; in Nazario's *Los Angeles Times* reporting 214; race and racism in 349–350, 352; and second-order narrative 347; in university literary programs 457–458
immersion, virtual reality and 475
immigration; and climate change 487–488; Mexican, in Conover's *Coyotes* 351–353, 475; in Riis's *The Making of an American* 257
"In a Pig's Eye" (1968) 172–173
Iñárritu, Alejandro González 475, 476
In Cold Blood (1966) 71
"Individualism and the Jungle" (1932) 118
industrial system, critiques of 100
inequality, socioeconomic 72, 100–101
informed consent, in autoethnography 381
inoculation controversy 22–23
Insurgent Mexico (1914) 240
intellectual snobbery 130–131, 133–134, 137–138
"intellligences" 21, 22, 25
International Association for Literary Journalism Studies 213, 219, 453, 509
international literary journalism; American roots of 509–511; and digital media 511–512; French literary journalism 509, 511, 513, 517–519; global perspectives 514–516
"In the Case of Hannah Risser" 86
"In the Depths of a Coal Mine" (1894) 72, 77
"In the Ruins of the Future" (2001) 77
Into the Wild (1996) 391
"inverted pyramid" news model 201, 328
Investigative Reporters and Editors (IRE) 217
Irwin, Will 96, 240, 241
Isay, David 217, 472–473
Iser, Wolfgang 337, 338
Islam, Nicholas Said and 51, 52
Ivins, Molly 203
"Ivory-Billed Woodpecker" (2016) 498, 503–504
"I Was Marching" (1934) 118–121, 262

Jackson, Claiborne Fox 49
Jackson, Mattie 45, 48
Jaillant, Lise 131
James, Henry 274
Janesville (2017) 105
Jauss, Hans Robert 337
Jayaraman, Saru 104–105
jazz writers 435
Jeffrey, Alexander 320
"Jelly Roll" (1980) 118
Jenkins, Henry 532, 534
Jennie Baxter, Journalist 84, 85
"Joe Is Home Now" (Hersey) 246
"Joe Louis" (Talese) 303
John Reed Clubs 111
Johns, Adrian 318
Johnson, E. W. 199
Johnson, Lyndon B. 204, 261, 403
Johnson, Samuel 17, 275
Johnstone, John W. C. 263
Jordan, Elizabeth 82, 83, 84, 86
Jordan, Michael 307
journalism and journalist, in Johnson's *Dictionary* 17
journalism programs 213; enrollments in 449–450; exemplars 460–461
journalism reviews *see* local journalism reviews
Journalist and the Murderer, The (1990) 393
journalists; professional development for 205; sociological study of 263
Joyce, James 137–138, 139
"Judy's Service of Gold Plate" (1897) 74
Junger, Sebastian 236, 248, 249–250
Jungle, The (1906) 93, 100
Junod, Tom 308

Kadlec, David 422
Kandy-Kolored Tangerine-Flake Streamline Baby, The (Wolfe) 164
"Katrina and the Cat" (2007) 377
Kazin, Alfred 220
Keeble, Richard 4, 361, 515, 519
Kempton, Murray 303
Kent, Nick 440
Kent, Thomas 476
"Kentucky Derby, The" (1970) 176, 304
Kerner Commission 403
Kerrane, Kevin 400
Kerr, Steve 307
Kessel, Joseph 518
Kessler, Lauren 184
Keyser, Catherine 130, 132
Kidder, Tracy 382, 386
Kifner, John 167, 168
Kingdom of Fear (2003) 177
Kings, Queens and Pawns (1915) 240, 241
Kisch, Egon Erwin 112
knowledge production *see* epistemology and journalistic ethics

Kovach, Bill 362
Krakauer, Jon 391
Kramer, Jane 365
Kramer, Mark; on commonplace subjects in literary journalism 484; on conventional journalism and civic voice 202; on declining newspaper readership 219; on "mobile stance" of literary journalism 485–486; *Phoenix* rural life columns 227–228, 230; professorship and workshops 206, 230
Krugman, Paul 100
Kupfer, Joseph H. 333, 340

Ladies Home Journal 278
Laguerre, Andre 305
Lake, Thomas 307
Lange, Dorothea 467
Lardner, Ring 301
La Terre Promise (2010) 519
Latham, Sean 131, 138
Lauters, Amy 457
Lawrence, D. H. 64, 138
Leamnson, Robert 456
LEAP initiative; essential learning outcomes 450–453; and literary journalism 458–460, 461; survey results and method 453–458
LeBlanc, Adrian Nicole 217, 366–367, 375–376, 382, 518
Leddy, Tom 325–326
leftist publications 110, 111, 278; *New Masses* reception of "Women on the Breadlines" 117
Lemann, Nicholas 220, 512
Leonard, John 165, 178
Lerner, Kevin 187
Les Misérables 331–332
Le Sueur, Meridel; and advocacy journalism 263, 264–265; on being marginalized 122; *The Dread Road* 115–116; immersive journalism of 258; "I Was Marching" 118–121, 262; Lydia Maria Child, parallels between 38; and the subjective reporter 112; Whitman's influence on 117–118; "Women on the Breadlines" 116–118, 278
Letters from an American Farmer (1782) 387
Letters from New-York column 30–32, 38
Letters of the Republic, The (1990) 321
letters to editors 21
"Letter to the President, A" (Spivak) 113–115, 117
letter writing; familiar letters 20–21; manuscript newsletters 18–20
"Let Us Now Praise Famous Death Dwarves" 442
Let Us Now Praise Famous Men (1941) 138, 260, 278, 389–390, 468; sequel to 339
Levinas, Emmanuel 112
Lewis, Jerry Lee 441
Lewis, Oscar 73
libel, in *Masson vs. New Yorker* 218–219
liberal education and literary journalism 449; journalism programs, declining enrollments in 449–450; journalism programs, exemplars of 460–461; LEAP initiative 450–460, 461
Liberation News Service 184, 188–189, 192, 263
Libra (1988) 77
Liddick, Shane 217
Life (Grimes) 45–47
Life, "Hints for Fiction Writers" 81, 469–470
"Life in New York" (Whitman) 29
Life magazine 278
Life of Poetry, The (1949) 421
Life on the Mississippi (1883) 272
literacy, African American 402, 410
literacy, student performance in 451
literary criticism 137–138, 139, 270–272, 274; of Barbara West 139–140; *see also* performative criticism
literary journalism; American antecedents 289; as an American genre 509–511; characteristics of 57–58, 225, 386, 399–400; criticisms of 203, 214; definitions of 4, 17, 57, 199–200, 294, 509–510; fiction, relation to 329, 330; mainstreaming of 209; "mobile stance" of 485–486; New Journalism, relation to 183, 270; rhetorical elements of 57–58; rise of 237; techniques of 183, 214; terminology, British and American 270–272, 273
Literary Journalism (1995) 400
Literary Journalism and the Aesthetics of Experience (2016) 400
Literary Journalism in the Twentieth Century (Sims) 219
Literary Journalism on Trial (Forde) 218
literary journalism programs; conferences and workshops 219, 455–457; cross-disciplinary potential 460; international 519; and LEAP essential learning outcomes 455–457, 458–460; undergraduate and postgraduate 460–461
literary journalism studies 213, 219–220; anthologies and collections 510; comparative and multicultural approaches 514–518; conferences and workshops 219–220; and journalism as lower status 272; value of 451–453
Literary Journalism Studies (journal) 220
Literary Journalists, The (Sims) 58
literary muckraking; contemporary 92, 101–105; criticism of 94; definition and origins of 91, 94; demise of 277; and the emergence of magazines 95; exposés of corruption 96–97, 99–100; immersive 101–102; social democracy and 105; Tarbell and 98
literary music journalism; Cohn and rock and roll writing 434–435; gonzo style of writing 441–443; and other music writing forms 435–436; techniques of 436; technology and the future of 443–446
literary sports journalism 301–302; future of 308; Gary Smith for *Sports Illustrated* 305–307; and New Journalism 303–304; and personal narratives 307; and sports columnists 302–303; and *Sports Illustrated* magazine 304–305

literary techniques, newspaper journalism and 200–201
literary war journalism 236–237; African American 242, 245; American Civil War coverage 237–238; Iraq War, in Finkel's *The Good Soldiers* 235; journalistic integrity of 246; Mexican Civil War coverage 264; post-World War II coverage 246–249; sensationalism in 250; Spanish-American War coverage 238–239; Spanish Civil War coverage 242–243; World War I and Russian Revolution coverage 240–241, 264
Little Sandy Review 436
Livingstone, Dr. David 51
Living the Revolution (Stein) 164–165
local journalism reviews 184–185; literary journalism practice in 186–187, 191–192
London, City of 76
London, Jack 67, 68, 69–70, 76–77, 93
London Spy, The (1703) 387
Londres, Albert 518
longform journalism; award-winning 207–208, 214–215, 512; digital 529, 533–538
Long Island Patriot 28
Look (magazine) 278
Lorde, Audre 492
Los Angeles Free Press (newspaper) 184, 185
Los Angeles Times; Nazario's Pulitzer-caliber feature writing in 214
"Love and Ruin" (Verini) 538
Love, David 401
Lovelady, Steven 206
"Love-Making of Loo, The" 84, 85
"Loyalists Await Tortosa Assault" (1938) 243–244
Lubow, Arthur 471
Luce, Henry 304
Lukas, J. Anthony 167–168
Lutes, Jean Marie 349, 350–351
Lutz, Earle 238
Lyotard, Jean-François 499, 500

MacArthur Fellows Program 216–217
Macy, Beth 92, 101–102, 104
Madame Roland 96
Madigan, Mark 76
magazines; celebrated authors and literary journalism 274; countercultural 110, 111, 278–279; emergence of 95, 276–277; historical appearance of literary journalism in 275–276, 277, 293–295; leftist 110, 111, 278; literary journalism in 270–271; *McClure's*, rise of 98; music magazines 436–438; newspapers displaced by 204; photojournalism in 469–471
Maggie; A Girl of the Streets (1893) 71
Maguire, Miles 368, 449, 472
Maguire, Roberta S. 10, 44
Maharidge, Dale 339

Mailer, Norman 71, 164, 220, 247; on Arbus's work 471; Democratic National Convention account 175–176, 178
mainstreaming of literary journalism; in academic institutions 219–220; consequences of 220
mainstream journalism; decline of 220; literary journalism's reception by 213–214; literary journalism techniques incorporated by 215–216; *see also* alternative media
mainstream values; in *Life* magazine 469; rock and roll's rejection of 439
Making of Americans, The (1925) 133–134
Making of an American, The (1901) 257
Malcolm, Janet 218, 393
Mann, Thomas 138, 139
Manson Family murders, news coverage of 228–229
manuscript newsletters 18–20
Marble Index, The (music album) 440
Marcus, Greil 437, 440–441, 442
Marcus, Paul 112
Marino, Jacqueline 537
Markham, Lauren 487–488
Marland, Pippa 483, 491
Martin Eden (1909) 77
Martin, Marc 518
Martin, Trayvon 427
Mary Baker G. Eddy (1909) 75
masculine modernism 138; Flanner's criticism of Lawrence and Mann 138–139
"Masked Marauders" hoax 442–443
Massachusetts Journal 28
Masson v. New Yorker libel case 213, 218–219
Masterson, Kate 84, 85
Material Feminisms (2008) 491
Mauldin, Bill 187, 190
Mauriac, François 136
Mayborn Literary Nonfiction Conference 219
May Iverson's Career (1943) 85
Mazzini, Giuseppe 33
McCall's magazine 278
McCarthy, Mary 269
McClelland, Mac 498, 502, 503–504
McClure, H. H. 83
McClure's Magazine 72, 94–95, 98, 277, 288
McClure, S. S. 72, 73, 75, 94, 95, 98, 277
McDonald, Duff 104
McKenzie, Don 317–318
McMillian, John 184
McPhee, John 220
McQueen, Kate 455
McTeague (1899) 74
Meltzer, Richard 436, 437, 438, 441–442, 443
"Members of the Assembly, The" (1968) 173–174
Men and Monuments (1957) 137
Mencken, H. L. 71, 290–291, 292–295
"Men in the Storm, The" (1894) 69

Metropolitan Magazine, Reed's war reporting for 240, 264
Mexican immigration 351–353
Mexican Revolution, John Reed's coverage of 240, 264
"Mexico's Army and Ours" (1914) 77
Meyer, Steven 133
Miami and the Siege of Chicago (Mailer) 175–176
middlebrow readers *see* modernist style and middlebrow audiences
Middleton, Peter 130–131
migrant labor; in Conover's *Coyotes* 351–352; in Spivak's "Letter" 113–115
Minneapolis Teamsters Strike 118–120
minority groups; progressive journalism and 368; Western epistemologies and 360–361; writing about 362–363, 365
minority writers and literary journalism 279
Miraldi, Robert 387
"Miss Underhill's Lesson" 86
"Miss Upton's First 'Assignment'" 87–88
"Miss Van Dyke's Best Story" 85, 86
Mitchell, Elvis 279
Mitchell, Joseph 408
Mitchell, W. J. T. 465
Mitgang, Herbert 243
Modernism, Middlebrow and the Literary Canon (2016) 131
modernist style and middlebrow audiences 130–132; Dorothy Parker's performative criticism 140–143; Gertrude Stein's democratization of modernism 132–135; Janet Flanner's performative criticism 135–140
Modern Library (publisher) 131
Moehringer, J. R. 307
Monteath, Peter 112
Montgomery, Sy 491
Moran of the Lady Letty (1898) 73
[MORE] (newspaper) 185, 186, 187, 189–190
Morris, Richard 200–201
Morthland, John 444–445
Morton, Timothy 488, 489
Mosser, Jason 500
"Most American Terrorist, A" (Ghansah) 392
Mother Jones magazine 538
"Mr. Hunter's Grave" (1956) 408–410
"Mrs. Kelly's Monster" (Franklin) 207–208
Ms. Magazine 263, 279
muckrakers *see* literary muckraking
"Muck-Rake School, The" 91, 92
multimedia journalism 472–474, 529–530, 533–534
multitasking, attention loss and 533–534
Murphy, Priscilla Coit 319, 321–322
Murray, Donald 205, 206
Murray, Jim 303, 304
Musgrave, Philip 22
music journalism *see* literary music journalism

My City (1929) 71
"My Four Months as a Private Prison Guard" 538

Naked and the Dead, The (1948) 247
Napoleon Bonaparte (1895) 98
Narrating the Closet (2011) 377–378
narrative techniques and award-winning journalism 215–216
narrative voice, reflections on 226–229, 400; news voice 226; *see also* first-person narration; second-person narration
Nass, Clifford 533
National Anti-Slavery Standard 29, 30, 32
National Women's Political Caucus (NWPC) 264
"Native of Bornoo, A" 50–51
Native Son (1940) 71
naturalism; Campbell's "unruly naturalism" 74; emergence and development of 68, 77; Émile Zola, influence of 74, 112; influence on 1930s reportage 112; journalism and fiction, blurring of 73, 77; Norris's definition of 74; principles and techniques of 69
Nature of the Book, The (Johns) 318
Nazario, Sonia 214, 348
"Negro and the War Department, The" (Scott) 242
Nelson, Ashlee 263
Nelson, Paul 436–437
New Documents exhibition 471
New-England Courant 18, 21–22, 21–24; Benjamin Franklin contributes to 24; influence of *Spectator* essays on 23–24
Newfield, Jack 199
New Gilded Age, The (2000) 100
New Journalism 25; African-American newspapers and 166–167; Burroughs and Genet and 172–174; literary muckraking and 91; Mailer's and 175–176; nature of 165; overlap with daily journalism 177; overlap with literary journalism 183; "personalism" of 390; post–World War II 246–247; principles and techniques of 69, 163–164, 183; "real life" appeal of 336; social activism and 263–264; sportswriting and 303–304; as synonym for literary journalism 270; Talese and 303; Thompson and 176–177; Wolfe on the literary devices of 475
New Journalism, The (1973) 69, 199–200, 205, 213, 215, 220, 518; 1972 issue in *New York* magazine 229–230
New Masses (formerly *Masses*) 110, 112, 113, 115, 116, 121, 264; "Inside China" published in 278; Reed as contributor to 240, 264; reform as goal of 119–120; "Women on the Breadlines," reception of 117
New New Journalism, The (2005) 248, 511
"New" New Journalists 248–250, 279–280, 511
New Republic magazine 278
"newsletters" 18–20
Newspaper Days (Dreiser) 68

newspaper fiction 81–83; women's 83–85
newspaper industry, circulation and profitability of 203–204, 206, 209
Newspaper Readership Project 203–204
newspapers; African American and African Canadian 44; antislavery 29, 30–31, 36, 44, 45, 49, 400; colonial era 18–19; evening papers 291–292; family papers 36, 292; photography in 466–467; readership decline 203–204; readers' letters in 21, 23
newspaper syndicates 319
"Newspaper Woman's Romance, A" 84
News People, The (1976) 263
New Statesman, Chicago Democratic National Convention coverage 170–171
news voice 225–226
New York Aurora 29, 30
New York by Gas-Light (Foster) 59, 60, 62, 63
New York City sketches *see* street life sketches
New York Commercial Advertiser 467
New York Daily News, award-winning journalism by 215–216
New York Daily Times 58
New-York Daily Tribune 32–33, 34
New Yorker 131–132, 276; Chicago Democratic National Convention coverage 171; Flanner writes for 137–139, 140; founding of 278; Hunter-Gault as first black staffer at 403; Janet Flanner writes for 135–140; *Masson v. New Yorker* libel case 218–219
New Yorker magazine 511; H.L. Mencken's influence on 293–294
New York Herald 387
New York in Slices (Foster) 59, 60, 63, 64
New York Journal 289
New York Ledger 36, 38
New York Post 403, 404
New York Review of Books 169–170
New York Sun 290
New York Times 289; award-winning journalism 215, 473, 474; Chicago Democratic National Convention coverage 167–168; longform journalism in 208; Manson Family murders coverage 229; "Snow Fall" and digital media 472, 473–474, 529, 535–536, 537
New-York Tribune 58, 59
New York World 71, 72, 82, 94, 289
Nichols, Bill 472
Nichols, Charles H. 46
Nickel and Dimed (2001) 104, 260–261, 348, 353
Nico (band) 440
Nieman conference for literary journalism 219
Nietzsche, Friedrich 327
"Nigger Jeff" (Dreiser) 70
Nixon, Rob 484–485
"Noble School of Fiction, The" (1865) 274
Nomadland (2017) 92, 101, 103–104
Noonday Demon (2001) 392
No One Was Killed (Schultz) 175

Nord, David Paul 315
Norris, Frank 67, 68, 70, 73–74, 93
North American News Alliance (NANA) 243
North, Joseph 110, 111, 113, 114, 118, 119–120, 121, 240, 486
North Star (newspaper) 34, 35
"Notes on the New Journalism" (Arlen) 202
"Novel Démeublé, The" (1922) 76
novels 20–21, 24–25; Victorian-era 97–98
Nowak, Mark 416, 417, 422–424
Numapresse project 520
"Number Seventeen" (1903) 86
"Nurse Midwife" (1951) 470

Oates, Joyce Carol 77
objectifying subjects 86
Objectivism (poetry) 418
objectivity 69; and anthropocentrism 489–491; and conventional newspaper style 201–202, 225–226, 328–329; critiques about 400; and cultural relativity 362; as elusive 138; as ideal of early news style 387; James Agee on 138; literary journalism criticized for lack of 380; modernist writers questioning 132; and Morton's "hyperobject" 488, 489; and naturalist writers 69, 112; and photography 466–467, 469–470; Stein's goal of 133, 134; "strong objectivity" and ecological thinking 360–361, 362–364, 365–366; "unlearning" existing ideas about 454–455
Occupy Wall Street 100–101
Octopus, The (1901) 74
"Of Our Spiritual Strivings" (Du Bois) 406–407
Ohio State Journal 64
"Oh My God" (Sack) 172
"Oil War" (Tarbell) 95
Olive Branch (newspaper) 36
On Boxing (1987) 77
One Big Self (2003) 417, 424–425
One Man's Initiation—1917 (1920) 245
"One Way of Putting It" (Cather) 74–75
One with Others (2010) 417
online literary journalism *see* digital literary journalism
On the Run (2014) 348
"Open Boat, The" (1897) 73, 238, 272
Oregonian (newspaper) 206, 209
O'Reilly, Karen 373
organized crime, award-winning journalism on 217
Other America, The (1962) 261
"Our Adventures in Tampico" (1914) 77
Our Kids; The American Dream in Crisis (2015) 105
"Out in the Great Alone" (2013) 472
Overset (journalism review) 187

Paine, Thomas 276
Pamela (1740) 21
Paper (newspaper) 184, 187
Parker, Dorothy 130, 132

Park, Robert E. 373–374
Patchett, Ann 380
Paterniti, Michael 326, 334, 339
Pater, Walter 136–137
Pattee, Fred Lewis 91, 92
Patterson, Eugene "Gene" 204–205
"Paul's Case" (1905) 75–76
Pauly, John 3, 5, 6, 12, 44, 91, 289, 390
Pearson, Anthony 534
pedagogy and literary journalism: see liberal education and literary journalism 455
Penny Press 289
Pentagon Papers 204
People of the Abyss, The (1903) 76
performative criticism 130, 143–144; Dorothy Parker's 130, 140–143; Gertrude Stein's 132–135; Janet Flanner's 130, 135–140; Rebecca West's 139–140
"personalism," in New Journalism 390
Peters, John Durham 501
Pettegree, Andrew 19, 21
Pettit, Rhonda 140
Philadelphia Inquirer 249, 529; award-winning journalism by 215
Philips, Brian 472
Phillips, David Graham 277
Phoenix (newspaper), Kramer's rural life column in 227–228
photography; documentary 259–260, 465, 466, 467; Gertrude Stein and 133; in newspapers and magazines 466–471
photojournalism 467, 469–471
Picasso, Pablo 133, 135
"Pigs, Prague, Other Democrats" (Schultz) 175
Pilgrim's Progress, The (1678) 94
Pit, The (1903) 74, 93
Pitzer, Andrea 416
Pius IX, Pope 33
Pizer, Donald 73
Playboy magazine 278
Players' Tribune website 308
Plimpton, George 305
Plumed Serpent, The (1926) 138
Poe, Edgar Allan 274, 277
poetry and literary journalism; C. D. Wright 424–425; Charles Reznikoff 416, 418–420; Claudia Rankine 425–427; Mark Nowak 422–424; Muriel Rukeyser 420–422; overview of 416–417
Point Reyes Light (Synanon) 214
police brutality; against protesters 165–167, 168, 170–171, 172–173, 174–175, 190; Rankine's exploration of 426–427
political cartoons 187
"Politics Goes into Street" (Enright) 169
"Pollution Within, The" (2006) 492
Poovey, Mary 336–337
Port Folio magazine 276

postal services and postmasters 18–19, 95
postmodern theory and literary journalism 498–501
Poston, Ted 403–404, 405–406
Pou, Dr. Anna Maria 103
Poynter Institute 206
"Prejudice and Progress" (Poston) 403–404, 405–407
presidential campaign of 1972 263–264
Press Divided, A (2017) 237
prisons/prisoners 36, 38
Progress and Poverty (1879) 92–93
"Project Syria" (2014) 475
proletarian literature 111, 113
Proletarian Literature in the United States 111
ProPublica, award-winning journalism by 215–216
Providence Journal-Bulletin 205
Provincial Freeman 44
pseudonyms, comical use of 23, 24, 276
"Psycho Shopper" (1989) 279
public life and literary journalism 320–321
public service journalism, award-winning 214, 215, 216
Pudd'nhead Wilson (1894) 277
Pulitzer, Joseph 82, 238
Pulitzer Prize 207–208, 213–216; Hersey awarded 246; and narrative techniques 215–216; *New York Times* awarded 473
Putnam, Robert 105
Puzzled America (1935) 278

Quammen, David 485–486
Quinn, John 136
Quinn, Katrina 18
quotations *vs.* extended dialogue, use of 218–219

Rabinowitz, Paula 110, 472
race and racism in immersive journalism 349–350, 352
Race News (Carroll) 402
race/racism; in "A Most American Terrorist" 392; Rankine's exploration of 426–427; *see also* African American journalism; minority groups
racial segregation 402, 403, 406–407
Radway, Janice 130, 131, 318, 351
rail system; expansion of 95; worker strikes 93
Random Family (2003) 366–367, 375–376, 382
Rankine, Claudia 416, 417, 425–427
Raskin, Jonah 76, 77
reader engagement and digital media 530, 537–538
readership, declining 209–210
Reade, W. Winwood 51
Reading Narrative Journalism project 454
reading revolution, eighteenth century 17–18
Reading the Romance (Radway) 318
realism 58–59; in Foster's New York sketches 59–65; *vs.* naturalism 67; newspaper fiction and 82–83
reality TV 502–503
Real Property (1980) 392
Red Badge of Courage, The (1895) 72

Red Record (1895) 348
Reed, John 240, 264–265
Reed, Lou 442
Renaissance, The (1893) 136
reportage, 1930s; definition of 110, 111; fact and feeling, emphasis on 111–113, 120; naturalist and romantic influences on 112–113, 118; reform as goal of 112; Spivak's "A Letter to the President" 113–115; Whitman's influence on 117–118
Reporter at Armageddon, A (1918) 240, 241
reporters, female 81
Reportorial Writing (1972) 214
Revenants (2000) 417, 422
reviews *see* local journalism reviews
Revolution and the Word (Davidson) 318
Reynolds, Bill 6, 515
Reynolds, G. 50
Reznikoff, Charles 416, 418–420, 424
Rice, Grantland 302
Richardson, Brian 405
Richardson, Samuel 21
Ricoeur, Paul 332
Rigby, Kate 483
Riggio, Thomas P. 70
"Right to Work, The" (1903) 95
Riis, Jacob 93, 257–260, 262, 263, 264–265, 465; documentary photography of 465, 466, 467
Rinehart, Mary Roberts 240, 241
Risley, Ford 237
Robertson, Michael 67, 72, 73
Robertson, Nan 208
rock and roll writing 434–435, 436–437, 437–446
"Rock-Crit Blood 'n' Guts" (Meltzer) 442
Rockefeller, John D. 94, 99, 103
Rodríguez, Adolfo, execution of 239
Rodriguez, Alex 307
Roggenkamp, Karen 3
Roiland, Joshua 57–58, 499, 502, 511, 512
Rolling Nowhere (1984) 378
Rolling Stone magazine 437, 443
romanticism and 1930s reportage 117
Roosevelt, Franklin D.; Spivak's "Letter" to 113–115, 117
Roosevelt, Theodore 94, 277
Rosenbaum, Ron 449
Rosenberg, Léonce 135–136
Rosinante to the Road Again (1922) 245
Ross, Harold 131, 135, 278, 293, 294
Rossi, Pellegrino, assassination of 33–34
Ross, Lillian 390
Rotzler, Frederick (Captain) 70–71
Rowlandson, Mary White 386
Royte, Elizabeth 105
Ruffel, Lionel 517
Rukeyser, Muriel 416–417, 424
Runyon, Damon 302
rural life, Kramer's *Phoenix* column about 227–228, 230

Russian Revolution 240, 264
"Ruth Herrick's Assignment" 83
Ryan, Michael 368

Sachsman, David B. 237
Sack, John 164, 172–173, 178
Said, Nicholas 45, 50–53
Salvation on Sand Mountain (1995) 392
Samuels, David 510, 511
Sanctuary (1931) 138
Sanders, Ed 228–229
San Diego Magazine, award-winning journalism by 217
Sandoval, Marisol 184
San Francisco earthquake of 1904 77
Saslow, Eli 216
satirical writing 22, 24
Saunders, George 498, 502, 504
Saussy, Haun 513, 516, 517
Sayre, Nora 170–171, 178
Scanlan, Christopher "Chip" 205, 207
Scanlan's magazine 304
"Scenes" (Whitman) 30
scene-setting 215
Schmidt, Thomas R. 187
Schudson, Michael 3, 362
Schulman, Norma M. 209
Schultz, John 175, 178
Schwartz, Mark 191
scoop, getting a 84, 86
Scott, Emmett Jay 242
Scribner's magazine 95, 277, 466
Sea-Wolf, The (1904) 77
second-order narrative and immersion 345–356; Bly's "Ten Days in a Mad-House" 345–346; Conover's *Coyotes* 351–353; Ehrenreich's *Nickel and Dimed* 353; Finnegan's *Cold New World* 353–356
second-person narration; Lydia Maria Child's 31; Ted Poston's 404–407
segregation, racial 402, 403, 406–407
Seierstad, Åsne 362
sensationalism; in documentary photography 468; in newspaper fiction 82, 86; Steffens accuses "commercial journalists" of 290; in war journalism 238, 239, 250
sequels and "follow-ups" 338–339
Sex Pistols 440–441
"Shame of Minneapolis, The" (1903) 95
Shapiro, Michael 533
Sheehan, Paul V. 214
Sheehy, Gail 203
Shi, David E. 69
Shields, David 386
Shirky, Clay 200
Shklovsky, Viktor 335
"Shot That Saved Lives, The" (2009) 307
Shriver, Ernest 84
Shuman, Edwin 82

Shut Up Shut Down (2004) 417, 422–424
Sieber, Charles 491
Siegel, Barry 455, 460
Signifying Monkey, The (1988) 407
"Silence Dogood" pseudonym 24
"Silent Season, The" (1966) 303–304
Silent Spring (1962) 319, 321, 487
Simmons, Bill 538
Sims, Norman 3, 58, 219, 237, 256, 514, 515
Sinclair, Upton 93, 100
Sister Carrie (1900) 70, 73
sketches *see* street life sketches
Sketches by Boz (Dickens) 64
slave narratives 44, 410; Grimes's *Life* 45–48; Jackson's *Story* 45, 48–49; *A Narrative of the Most Remarkable Particulars in the Life of James Albert Ukawsaw Gronniosaw, an African Prince, as Related by Himself* 410; Said's "A Native of Bornoo" 45, 50–53
Slawski, Edward J. 263
Slouching Towards Bethlehem (1968) 247, 390–391
slow journalism 484, 512, 538–539
Slow Violence (2011) 484–485
Smart Set magazine 293, 294
Smedley, Agnes 38
Smiley, Jane 271
Smith, Gary 305–307
Smith, Red 303
Smith, Roberta 534
Smith, William Eugene 469–470
Smoking Typewriters (McMillian) 184
"Snow Fall" (2012) 472, 473, 539; digital longform after 535–537
Snyder, Louis 200–201
Sob Sister 85, 86
social Darwinism 92
social democracy 105
social inequality 72, 100–101
socialist publications 110, 111, 278; *New Masses* reception of "Women on the Breadlines" 117
social media 458, 529, 537
social reform writing; documentary photography and 259–260, 465, 466, 467; Ehrenreich and 257; environmental advocacy 264; and ideology 263; Jack London's 76–77; and journalistic ethics 364–368; literary muckraking 92–93; naturalists and 69; Riis's advocacy journalism 257–260
social responsibility, as learning outcome 457
Society of Professional Journalists (SPJ) 360
soldier reports 237, 239
Solomon, Andrew 392
"Some Dreamers" (1968) 338
Son of the Wolf (1900) 76
Sontag, Susan 471
Sorrentino, Paul 72, 73
Soul of a New Machine, The (1997) 385
Soul of an Octopus, The (2015) 491
Southern, Terry 164, 172, 178

Spanish-American War 238–239
Spanish Civil War 242–246
Spanish Earth, The (1937) 244
"Spanish Village" (1951) 470
Spectator magazine 23–24, 275
Spencer, Herbert 69
Spivak, Gayatri Chakravorty 516
Spivak, John L. 112, 113, 116, 121; "A Letter to the President" 113–115, 117
Sports Illustrated 304–305
sports journalism *see* literary sports journalism
Standard Oil, Tarbell's investigation of 92, 94, 95–96, 98–100, 102, 103, 105
Stark, Judy 205
"Statement; Philippa Allen" (Rukeyser) 421
Steel, Richard 23
Steffens, Lincoln 95, 96, 97, 228, 240; *Commercial Advertiser*, tenure at 288–289; and reportage 96
Steinbach, Alice 208
Steinbeck, John 278, 467
Stein, David Lewis 164–165, 174, 178
Stein, Gertrude; democratization of modernism 132–135; middlebrow readers, attempt to attract 131, 132; on objectivity 133
Steinem, Gloria 263–264
Steiner, Linda 362, 364, 368
"Stephen Crane's Own Story" (1897) 73, 238
Stephens, Mitchell 471–472
St. John de Crèvecoeur, J. Hector 387
St. Louis Globe-Democrat 70
St. Louis Republic 70
Stooges, The (band) 440
"Stories of Working Girls" 85
"Story of an Eyewitness, The" (1906) 77
"Story of a Typhoon, The" (1893) 76
Story of Mattie J. Jackson, The (1866) 45, 107
Stowe, Harriet Beecher 45, 277
St. Paul Pioneer Press 208–209
"Strange Necessity, The" (1928) 139
"Strawberries Under Ice" (1988) 485–486
street life sketches; and the emergence of photography 467; George G. Foster's 58, 59–64; Lydia Maria Child's 31–32; Stephen Crane's 72; Theodore Dreiser's 70–71; Walt Whitman's 29, 58–59; Willa Cather's 74–75
strikes/striking 93, 264; in "I Was Marching" 118–120, 121, 262
"strong objectivity" 362–364, 365–366
Styron, William 169
subjectivity, journalistic; in 1930s reportage 111, 112, 113; in African American journalism 400–401, 412; criticism about 203, 214; as defining trait of literary journalism 400; and first-person narration 385
subjects of literary journalism, Kramer on 484
"Suburb" (1934) 418
suffering, Le Sueur on 118
Sullivan, John Jeremiah 498, 501, 502–503

Sunpapers (newspaper) 292–293
"Sunshine Hotel" (1998) 472–473
"Supposedly Fun Thing I'll Never Do Again, A" (1996) 501–502
Supreme Court ruling in *Masson vs. New Yorker* 213, 218
"Survival" (Hersey) 246
Suskind, Ron 214
syndicated newspapers 319
Syrian Civil War 474, 475

Talese, Gay 303–304, 307, 366, 390, 489
Tales of the City Room 83
Talking Book trope 410
Tarbell, Ida M. 92, 94, 95–96, 97–100, 102, 103, 105
Tate, Greg 445–446
Tate murders, news coverage of 228–229
Tatler magazine 23–24, 275
Tebbel, John 276
technology, media; digital and multimedia journalism 458, 472–474, 529–530; impact on music writing 443–444; risks to literary journalism 511–512; and social segmentation 501
telegraph communication 201, 291, 387
television news, displacement of print journalism by 204
"Ten Days in a Mad-House" (1887) 345–346, 388
Ten Days That Shook the World (1919) 111, 240, 264
Testimony (1934) 416–417, 418, 424
Thank You for Your Service (2013) 346
Their Eyes Were Watching God (Hurston) 271
Thérenty, Marie-Ève 518, 519
third-person narration 404; issues with 366–367, 385, 388; and naturalist writers 69
"Third Winter, The" (1938) 246, 272
Thomas, Isaiah 315
Thompson, Hunter S. 178, 203, 391; "American Dream" and *Kingdom of Fear* 164, 176–177; *Fear and Loathing* 247, 272; "flashy" narrative voice 227; "Kentucky Derby" 304
Thompson, Wright 307, 308
Thomsen, Mads Rosendahl 516, 517, 519
Thoreau, Henry David 264–265
Three Gringos (1896) 239
Three Lives (1909) 131
Three Soldiers (1921) 245
Tichi, Cecelia 3
Tiger, The (2010) 491
Todd, Dick 230
Todd, Richard 385–386
Toklas, The Autobiography of Alice B. (1933) 134
Tolich, Martin 381
Tom's River (2013) 105
Toronto Star 174
Tosches, Nick 436, 437, 438, 441, 443
"Touch of Human Brotherhood, A" (1902) 70
"Traders' War, The" (Reed) 240
Tragic America (1932) 278

trans-corporeality, Alaimo's concept of 491–492
transparency, critiques about 381–382
Traveler at Forty, A (1913) 71
travel narratives 71
"Treason of the Senate, The" (1906) 277
Treasury of Great Reporting, A (1949) 200–201
Treglown, Jeremy 273
Trillin, Calvin 366
"Trip to Leverton, A" (1965) 403–404, 407, 408, 409, 410–411
Troll Garden, The (1905) 75
True Flag 36, 37
Truth & Beauty (2004) 380
truth claims 360–362, 363, 367; and first-person narration 385
Tullis, Jillian 381
Tulloch, John 515
Twain, Mark 271, 272, 277
Twelve Men (Dreiser) 71

Uexküll, Jakob von 490
Ulysses (1922) 137–138
umwelt, Uexküll's concept of 490–491
"Under a Cracked Sky" (2017) 475
undercover journalism 217
Underground Press Syndicate 184, 192
Underwood, Doug 3, 68
unemployment crisis 102, 104
university communication programs, enrollments in 449–450
university courses in literary journalism 213, 219, 455–457
Unrequited; Women and Romantic Obsession (2015) 392
urban life sketches *see* street life sketches

Vaillant, Alain 519
Vaillant, John 490–491
VALUE (assessment) 451, 453–460
Vandover and the Brute (1914) 74
Vanity Fair magazine 131
Van Vorst sisters-in-law 94, 96
Velleman, David J. 386
Verbeken, Pascal 519
verification 362, 368, 381
Verini, James 538
Vietnam War 172, 247–248, 263, 269
Village Voice magazine 279
Viral Texts project 520
virtual reality 474–476
visual journalism; contemporary photojournalism and digital media 471–474; Depression-era and 1960s photojournalism 467–471; emergence of photojournalism 466–467; overview of 465–466; Riis's *How the Other Half Lives* 465, 466, 467; virtual reality 474–476
Vogue magazine 278
Voice of the Fugitive 44
Vollmann, William T. 485, 487, 488

Walden (1854) 264
Wallace, Aurora 51
Wallace, David Foster 491, 498, 501–502
Wall Street Journal; award-winning journalism in 214; longform journalism in 208; middle column "A-hed" features 206
War (2010) 248, 249–250
war accounts 76–77
Ward, Ned 200–201, 387
war, in Ehrenreich's *Blood Rites* 262
war journalism *see* literary war journalism
Warner, Michael 321
Washington, Booker T. 374
Washington, George 51, 52, 275, 276
Washington Journalism Review 185
Washington Post; award-winning journalism in 213–214, 217; Eugene Patterson direction of 204–205; Katherine Boo writing for 215; longform journalism in 208, 209
"Watching Whales" (2009) 491
Watergate scandal 213–214
Wave magazine 73, 74, 76
Webster, Daniel 35–36
Webster, Noah 276
Weight of the World, The (1999) 115
Wells, Ida B. 348
Wenner, Jann 437
Weschler, Lawrence 364
West, Rebecca 139
Wharton, Edith 240
What a Book Can Do (2005) 319, 321
"What Do You Think" (1986) 307
What Journalism Could Be (Zelizer) 521
"When Man Falls" (1894) 387–388
Whitman, Walt 28–30, 38, 58–59, 113, 121, 201; influence on 1930s reportage 117–118
Williamson, Michael 339
Williams, Paul 437
Williams, Serena 426–427
Willingham, Daniel 456
Willis, Ellen 435–436
Wilson, Christopher 454–455
Wilson, Edmund 142, 278, 294, 364
Wineapple, Brenda 135, 136
Winship, Tom 205
With the Allies (1914) 240–241
Wolfe, Tom; on dialogue 216; on first-person narration 390; on Herr's *Dispatches* 247; on Hersey's *Hiroshima* 220; on literary journalism as a fringe genre 220; on literary techniques 163–164, 214, 215, 216, 303, 475; and the naturalists 69;

The New Journalism 199–200, 215, 229–230; on "real life" appeal of New Journalism 336; on Talese's "Joe Louis" (1962) 303
Woman Who Toils, The (1903) 94
"Women Are Hungry" (1934) 116
women in journalism; Fanny Fern 28, 36–37; feature writing by 208–209; female editors 81, 208; female newspaper fiction reporters 81–88; feminist 263–264; gender issues, Fern on 36–38; Lydia Maria Child 28–29, 30–32, 38; Margaret Fuller 28, 32–34, 38
"Women Know a Lot of Things" (Le Sueur) 116, 118
"Women on the Breadlines" (1932) 116–117, 118, 119, 278
Women's pages 203
"Wonderful Hawaii" (1911–12) 93
Woods, Tiger 308
Woodward, Bob 214
Woolhopter, Philip David 46
worker strikes 93, 264; in "I Was Marching" 118–120, 121, 262
working poverty; contemporary muckrakers expose 104–105; in *Nickel and Dimed* (2001) 104, 260–261, 348, 353; in *Nomadland* (2017) 101–102, 103–104
World War I reporting 240–242
Wright, C. D. 416, 417, 424–425, 427
"Wrinkling the Fabric of the Press" (1995) 209
writing coaches and workshops 205–206, 209, 219, 230
writing competitions 205, 206–207, 216; *see also* award-winning journalism
Wypijewski, JoAnn 366–367

Yagoda, Ben 400
Year That Defined American Journalism, The (2006) 289–290
yellow journalism 81, 239, 241, 289
Yellow Journalist, A (1905) 84
You Have Seen Their Faces (1937) 468
You Know Me Al (Lardner) 302
"you," use of; Lydia Maria Child's 31; Ted Poston's 404–407

Zalucky, Andrew J. 444
Zelizer, Barbie 363–364, 521
Zinky Boys (Alexievich) 457
Zola, Émile 69, 74, 112
Zucchino, David 215